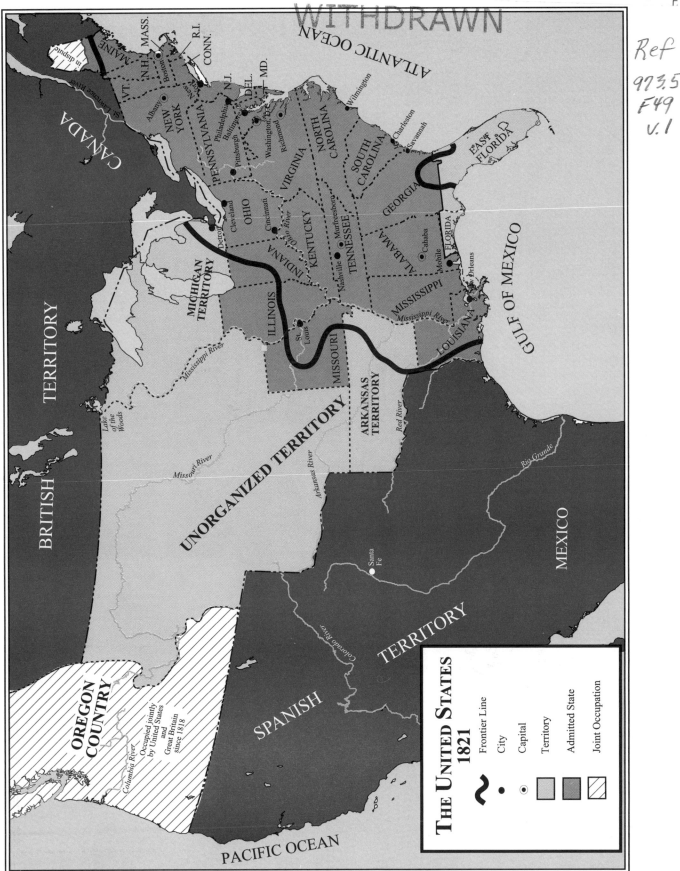

ATLANTIC OCEAN

CANADA

BRITISH TERRITORY

MAINE
in dispute
VT. N.H. MASS.
R.I.
CONN.
NEW YORK
Albany
Boston
PENNSYLVANIA
N.J.
DEL.
MD.
Philadelphia
Baltimore
Pittsburgh
Washington
Richmond
OHIO
Cleveland
Cincinnati
Detroit
INDIANA
VIRGINIA
NORTH CAROLINA
Wilmington
SOUTH CAROLINA
Charleston
Savannah
GEORGIA
EAST FLORIDA
KENTUCKY
Murfreesboro
Nashville
TENNESSEE
ALABAMA
Cahaba
FLORIDA
Mobile
Orleans
MISSISSIPPI
Mississippi River
LOUISIANA
GULF OF MEXICO

MICHIGAN TERRITORY

ILLINOIS
St. Louis
MISSOURI
Mississippi River
ARKANSAS TERRITORY
Red River

UNORGANIZED TERRITORY

Lake of the Woods
Missouri River
Arkansas River

Santa Fe

Rio Grande

MEXICO

Columbia River
Occupied jointly by United States and Great Britain since 1818

OREGON COUNTRY

SPANISH TERRITORY

Colorado River

PACIFIC OCEAN

THE UNITED STATES 1821

Frontier Line
City
Capital
Territory
Admitted State
Joint Occupation

ENCYCLOPEDIA
OF THE
UNITED STATES
IN THE
NINETEENTH
CENTURY

Editorial Board

ENCYCLOPEDIA
OF THE
UNITED STATES
IN THE
NINETEENTH
CENTURY

Paul Finkelman

Editor in Chief

VOLUME 1

Abolition and Antislavery–Government

CHARLES SCRIBNER'S SONS
An Imprint of The Gale Group
NEW YORK   DETROIT   SAN FRANCISCO
LONDON   BOSTON   WOODBRIDGE, CT

Charles Scribner's Sons
1633 Broadway
New York, New York 10019

Library of Congress Cataloging-in-Publication Data

Encyclopedia of the United States in the nineteenth century / Paul Finkelman, editor in chief.
    p. cm.
    Includes bibliographical references and index.
    ISBN 0-684-80500-6 (set : hardcover : alk. paper)—ISBN 0-684-80497-2 (vol. 1 : hardcover : alk. paper)—ISBN 0-684-80498-0 (vol. 2 : hardcover : alk. paper)—ISBN 0-684-80499-9 (vol. 3 : hardcover : alk. paper)
    1. United States—Civilization—19th century—Encyclopedias. I. Finkelman, Paul, 1949–

E169.1 .E626 2001
973.5—dc21   00-045811

This Encyclopedia is dedicated to

David H. Bennett
Ralph Ketcham
and
Otey M. Scruggs

who first introduced me to serious historical scholarship at Syracuse University. All three set an example of how fine teaching and scholarship go hand in hand.

Editorial and Production Staff

CONTENTS

List of Maps

PREFACE

The twentieth century has often been called the American century. But the nineteenth century, characterized by vast territorial expansion, great changes, and the national agony of civil war, was the most dramatic in American history—indeed, it was the century that made America.

In 1799 the United States hugged the eastern seaboard. Only three states—Vermont, Kentucky, and Tennessee—were not along the Atlantic coast. The American nation was hemmed in on all other sides. To the north a powerful British empire controlled not only Canada but also forts in the Great Lakes basin that Britain had promised to vacate at the end of the American Revolution. West of the Mississippi River the vast American continent was controlled by Spain, a declining but still powerful empire. Spain also controlled access to the great river port of New Orleans. In the south, Britain and Spain ruled Florida and parts of present-day Alabama and Mississippi. In the far northwest, the Russians held Alaska.

By 1899 the United States comprised forty-five states, stretching from the Atlantic to the Pacific, and covering the Gulf Coast. To the north Canada was a useful trading partner. The British flag still flew there, but Great Britain was, if not yet a close ally, no longer an enemy or a threat. The last remnants of the Spanish Empire in North America, Cuba and Puerto Rico, were firmly under control of the United States. American possessions included Alaska and islands scattered across the Pacific, including Hawaii.

In 1800 the United States contained 888,811 square miles; by 1900 it encompassed 3,022,387 square miles, including its possessions, Alaska and Hawaii. But population growth far outstripped physical growth. Between 1800 and 1900 the population grew from 5,297,000 to 75,944,575. Population density rose from 6.1 per square mile in 1800 to 25.6 per square mile in 1900.

Territorial and population growth was accompanied by rapid technological changes and huge economic expansion. In 1800 animal and wind power moved the nation on poor roads and oceans, with river traffic mostly limited to rafts floating downstream. By 1899 steam-powered trains and boats moved people and products across the nation. Waterpower and candles had been surpassed by oil, gas, and electricity to move machines and create light.

The great growth of the nation was not without cost. The century was marred by wars against one Indian nation after another, as the native peoples of America were forced from their traditional homelands onto reservations. Wars with Britain, Mexico, and Spain secured and expanded the nation's borders. Most important was the Civil War, which led to the end of slavery, a remaking of the constitutional order, and new forms of racial discrimination in the war's aftermath. Along with the revolution against Great Britain, it was one of the central events of American nationhood. The monetary cost was great; greater was the cost in human suffering, with more than 600,000 Americans killed and even more wounded or psychologically injured. As Abraham Lincoln noted in his Second Inaugural Address, it might be God's will that the war would "continue until all the wealth piled by the bondsman's two hundred and fifty years of unrequited toil shall be sunk, and until every drop of blood drawn by the lash shall be paid by another drawn by the sword."

Following the Civil War, the economy grew in ways unknown and unforeseen in the antebellum period. Huge settlements became great cities, such as New York and Chicago, while the seeds of other cities were planted and nurtured during the century. Immigrants flooded into America, creating the most diverse, complex, and fascinating conglomeration of people in history. In 1800 the United States was populated primarily by Protestants of British, German, and African ancestry. By 1899 Roman Catholics outnumbered any individual Protestant denomination, and Jews were common in some places, as well as Orthodox Christians from Greece, Russia, and various parts of the Austro-Hungarian Empire and the Ottoman Empire. Communities of Muslims, Buddhists, Hindus, and other non-Western religions found homes in America.

Thus, people, politics, war, economics, and technology shaped and created the United States in the nineteenth century. This encyclopedia is designed to capture and illuminate this extraordinary history.

The *Encyclopedia of the United States in the Nineteenth Century* is the third in a projected series of four reference works covering the history of the United States from first settlement of the New World to the end of the twentieth century. The series—which to date also includes the *Encyclopedia of the North American Colonies* (1993), edited by Jacob E. Cooke, and the *Encyclopedia of the United States in the Twentieth Century* (1995), edited by Stanley I. Kutler—provides comprehensive access to the events, trends, movements, technologies, inventions, cultural and social changes, and intellectual trends that have shaped America. Our goal in the present work is to provide an introduction to the central issues and questions of the nineteenth century. The bibliographies following each entry lead both students and specialists to the central literature surrounding each of the 599 entries in the Encyclopedia.

For students and librarians, we hope this encyclopedia will provide answers to major questions about the issues and ideas of the nineteenth century. A benchmark of our coverage is the National Standards for United States History, published by the National Center for History in the Schools. We provide multiple entries for every one of these standards. Students seeking information beyond their textbooks on any topic included in the standards will find a wealth of information in these volumes. For example, the standards touch on "the course and character of the Civil War and its effects on the American people." The synoptic outline in the back matter of Volume 3 shows that the set contains thirty-nine entries on sectionalism, slavery, the Civil War, and Reconstruction. But this does not cover the whole ground. Entries on law, such as "Fugitive Slave Laws," "Lynching," and the subentries of "Supreme Court" entitled "The Antebellum Court" and "The Court during the Civil War and Reconstruction," also provide valuable information on this period of U.S. history. So too do articles on political parties, nationalism, the franchise, foreign relations, and the military. Finally, a full understanding of the Civil War period would be served by essays on particular states, like Virginia or Tennessee, entries on social and cultural topics—such as painting, literature, and photography—and even the entry on the income tax, which was first imposed during the war.

The comprehensive index, used in conjunction with the synoptic outline, allows librarians, students, and scholars to find in the three volumes the full spectrum of American history in the nineteenth century. Particularly important is coverage of the diverse peoples of America. Thirteen entries on American Indians cover a range of issues that include internal tribal dynamics, Indian removal, wars and warfare, and the evolution of federal Indian policy. Entries covering nine geographical regions present a detailed picture of Indian life. Similarly, nineteen articles on immigration and ethnicity, along with twenty-six articles on African Americans and twelve on women, allow students to begin preliminary research on the shaping of America through the lens of those who have often been underrepresented, or hardly represented at all, in American history.

The Encyclopedia does not, however, ignore traditional methods and topics in American history. Ninety-four entries cover all aspects of separate essays on American politics, government, law, and public policy. Supplementing these are thirty-nine entries on the Civil War and sectionalism, twenty-four on foreign relations, ten on the military, and seventy-two on the economy and business. An entry appears for each of the fifty states, even those that were territories in the nineteenth century, as well as entries on regions, sectionalism, regionalism, urbanization, and the major cities of the century. Similarly, entries on literature, music, sciences, religion, and culture extend beyond both ethnic and political history to color the full spectrum of American life.

More than 480 pictures and maps supplement the text, illustrating both the changes in the nineteenth century and the changes in the technology of art. Pen-and-ink drawings, political cartoons, maps, etchings, and oil paintings were visual representations of America in the early part of the century. From the 1840s, photography began to alter the visual landscape of American culture. Photographs recorded the horror and devastation of the Civil War, the plight of immigrants, the poverty that accompanied urbanization, the natural wonders of the West, and the glorious new forms of architecture, beautiful bridges, and the magnificent World's Columbian Exposition of 1892–1893. In addition to photography, American painting and sculpture grew throughout the century, recording life in America. New printing methods further enhanced the way Americans represented themselves in pictures.

This Encyclopedia would not have been possible without the assistance of the scholars who contributed their time and expertise to write entries for the encyclopedia work. Without their cooperation and willingness to share their knowledge it would be impossible to create a reference tool like this one. My assistant at the University of Tulsa, Rita Langford, was invaluable to the management of this project. I owe a great debt to the editorial board—Fred Hoxie, Morton Keller, Eugene Leach, Glenda Riley, and Peter Wallenstein. They were superb advisers throughout the three years of this undertaking. They are all skilled historians and critics, and superb editors in their own right, as I learned when I wrote my own entries for these volumes. Editors at Scribners—Stephen Wagley, Timothy J. DeWerff, Deborah Gershenowitz, and Katherine Moreau—worked above and beyond the requirements of their jobs to develop and edit this Encyclopedia. They are all scholars, friends, and colleagues. Finally, special thanks for a very special publisher, Karen Day. Throughout the life of the project she encouraged and supported this Encyclopedia. Karen's enthusiasm is contagious and complements her leadership and creativity.

Paul Finkelman

CHRONOLOGY

1800   The U.S. population is 5.3 million, of whom 1 million are African American; approximately 75 percent of the U.S. labor force is engaged in agriculture. The federal government moves to Washington, D.C. The Harrison Land Act offers sale of lands in the public domain at two dollars per acre for 320-acre tracts; in May, Congress divides the original Northwest Territory, creating the Indiana Territory to the west, as a response to the swift migration of Americans to take up settlements under the Land Act. Gabriel Prosser plans a large-scale slave uprising in Virginia, but slave informants and torrential rains avert the rebellion. Southern farmers produce 73,000 bales of cotton.

1801   Thomas Jefferson is inaugurated as the third president of the United States. The first Barbary War, a four-year conflict between the United States and Tripoli, begins when President Jefferson refuses to pay increased demands for tribute to pirates. The Cane Ridge Revival in Bourbon County, Kentucky, draws thousands of participants and marks the beginning of the religious revivalist movement known as the Second Great Awakening.

1802   President Jefferson oversees acts of Congress establishing the Library of Congress and formally establishing the U.S. Military Academy at West Point, New York. Washington, D.C., is incorporated as a city. Nathaniel Bowditch publishes *The New American Practical Navigator.*

1803   Ohio is admitted as the seventeenth state in the Union (the first state carved out of the Northwest Territory). The United States takes possession of the Louisiana Territories (828,000 square miles), purchased for $15 million from France, doubling the area of the United States. *Marbury v. Madison* establishes the Supreme Court's power to declare acts of Congress unconstitutional.

1804   Ratification of the Twelfth Amendment institutes separate ballots for president and vice president. Meriwether Lewis and William Clark leave St. Louis in May on a federally funded expedition to explore the lands acquired in the Louisiana Purchase and find a water route to the Pacific Ocean. Alexander Hamilton is killed by Aaron Burr in a duel.

1805   The *Essex* decision by the British admiralty rules that neutral ships with enemy cargo aboard are liable to capture even if the cargo is being transshipped via U.S. ports; British warships and privateers begin patrolling the U.S. coast to seize American ships carrying French and Spanish goods; Britain increases impressment of U.S. sailors (alleging them deserters from the Royal Navy). Unitarianism, the theological "left wing" of Congregationalism, becomes the official religious position at Harvard College when the liberal Henry Ware is appointed to the Hollis Professorship of

Divinity. Thousands attend a Methodist camp meeting at Smyrna, Delaware. The Free Public School Society of New York is established.

1806   Congress passes the Non-Importation Act (effective in December 1807) prohibiting the importation from Britain of items that can be produced in the United States or imported from other countries. The Lewis and Clark expedition returns in September, having demonstrated the feasibility of traveling overland from the East to the Pacific Ocean. Zebulon Pike leads an expedition to the headwaters of the Arkansas and Red Rivers (sighting Pike's Peak in Colorado along the way) that lasts into 1807 and results in a report that stimulates expansion into Texas. Asher Benjamin's *American Builder's Companion* is published.

1807   The U.S.S. *Chesapeake* is sunk by British ships in American water. American trade with Britain is prohibited by the Embargo Act, which forbids U.S. ships to set sail for foreign ports. Former vice president Aaron Burr, who in 1806 was charged with conspiring to raise troops and build a personal empire from disputed Spanish territories in the West, is acquitted after a sensational trial; Supreme Court Justice John Marshall leads the decision that Burr's actions did not meet the strict constitutional definition for treason. Robert Fulton's *Clermont* inaugurates commercial steamboat navigation with a round trip on the Hudson River between New York and Albany.

1808   The population of slaves reaches 1 million. Congress formally abolishes the Atlantic slave trade. Jefferson increases the size of the U.S. Army to control smuggling into Canada. A massive internal improvements plan proposed by Secretary of the Treasury Albert Gallatin calls for $30 million in federal financing to construct a turnpike from present-day Maine to Georgia, an intercoastal waterway running roughly parallel to this turnpike, and a system of roads crossing the Appalachian Mountains at several key places; to make major improvements to the navigability of the major east-west river systems of the Appalachians; and to develop a system of canals linking these rivers to the Great Lakes. Congress grants a monopoly on trade throughout Minnesota to John Jacob Astor's American Fur Company. The Bible Society of Philadelphia, the first Bible society in the United States, is founded. Andover Seminary, America's first postgraduate theological school, opens to safeguard conservative Calvinist theology in response to Harvard's Unitarianism.

1809   James Madison is inaugurated as the fourth president of the United States. The Non-Intercourse Act bans trade with Great Britain and France; the economically disastrous Embargo Act is repealed. U.S. parochial school education is introduced with the founding by Elizabeth Ann Seton of a free Catholic elementary school in Baltimore.

1810   The U.S. population is 7.2 million. Western Florida declares independence and is annexed by the United States. The Supreme Court in *Fletcher v. Peck* invalidates a state law as unconstitutional for the first time. Dissident Presbyterians form the evangelical, prorevivalist Cumberland Presbyterian Church. The tradition of the American agricultural fair is initiated with the opening of the Berkshire Cattle Show in Pittsfield, Massachusetts.

1811   The first Bank of the United States (created by Congress in 1791) is allowed to expire. Congress meets secretly to make plans to annex Spanish East Florida. An uprising of more than four hundred slaves is put down in New Orleans; sixty-six blacks are killed. The Cumberland Road from

Maryland to Wheeling, Virginia, is started as part of the federal program to improve canals, roads, and bridges, but the rest of the 1808 Gallatin Plan is tabled. General William Henry Harrison defeats Shawnees in Indiana at the Battle of Tippecanoe. The fur baron John Jacob Astor and a group of settlers found the first white community in the Pacific Northwest, at Astoria, Oregon; another group of colonists settles at Cape Disappointment, Washington.

1812   In April, the United States burns Toronto and takes control of the Great Lakes at the Battle of York. At the urging of the president and a small number of "war hawks," but with all Federalists in opposition, the United States declares war ("Mr. Madison's War") on Great Britain (18 June). The first war bonds are issued, and the first interest-bearing Treasury notes are authorized. Louisiana is admitted as the eighteenth state in the Union (the first state created from the lands of the Louisiana Purchase).

1813   The American Indian chief Tecumseh is killed, leading to the fall of the Native American federation and the end of Indian support for the British in the war with the United States. Simeon North is awarded a U.S. government contract for twenty thousand pistols, to be made with interchangeable parts. The first ironclad ship is built by John Stevens, in Hoboken, New Jersey.

1814   The British capture Washington, D.C., burning the White House and the Capitol building and forcing President Madison to flee the city. New England Federalists opposed to the War of 1812 assemble at the Hartford Convention and reverse the party's earlier nationalist position by calling for states' rights and a weak central government. The Treaty of Ghent on 24 December ends the stalemated war between the United States and Great Britain, restoring prewar territorial conditions. Emma Hart Willard opens Middlebury Female Seminary in Vermont to offer young women classical and scientific studies at a collegiate level.

1815   Unaware that a peace treaty has ended the war of 1812, General Andrew Jackson's troops defeat British forces at the Battle of New Orleans and Jackson becomes a national hero. Stephen Decatur leads a successful expedition to end the Second Barbary War, a conflict between the United States and Algeria that began during the War of 1812 when the dey of Algiers plundered American commerce in the Mediterranean. The United States has a total of thirty miles of railroad track.

1816   The second Bank of the United States is chartered by Congress and creates a uniform national currency. Indiana (formerly part of Northwest Territory) is admitted as the nineteenth state in the Union. Congress passes a tariff bill that imposes a high import duty on foreign manufactures in order to give American industries a competitive advantage in the domestic market. The Supreme Court case *Martin v. Hunter's Lessee* establishes the Court's power to review the constitutionality of state civil court decisions. The American Colonization Society is established with the aim of returning free blacks to Africa. The African Methodist Episcopal Church (AME) is organized in Philadelphia. The American Bible Society is established.

1817   James Monroe is inaugurated as the fifth president of the United States. Mississippi is admitted as the twentieth state in the Union. The Rush-Bagot Agreement between the United States and Great Britain sets limits on naval power on the Great Lakes. The First Seminole War begins, with Seminole Indians battling American settlers along the border of Georgia and Spanish Florida. The New York Stock and Exchange Board (renamed the New York Stock Exchange in 1863) is created.

1818   Illinois (formerly part of the Northwest Territory) is admitted as the twenty-first state in the Union. The Convention of 1818 establishes the forty-ninth parallel as the northwest boundary between American and British territory from Lake of the Woods (on the Minnesota-Ontario border) to the Rocky Mountains. The U.S. flag is adopted, with thirteen red and white alternating stripes and a star for each state.

1819   Alabama is admitted as the twenty-second state in the Union. Spain cedes Florida to the United States as a result of the Adams-Onís Treaty. The Civilization Act formalizes federal policy to assimilate Indians into American society. The Supreme Court case of *Dartmouth College v. Woodward* establishes constitutional protection for corporations. Financial panic sets off an economic depression that lasts into 1822. The *Savannah*, sailing from Savannah, Georgia, to Liverpool, England, becomes the first steamship to cross the Atlantic. Jethro Wood patents a cast-iron plow that features replaceable parts at points of greatest wear.

1820   The U.S. population is 9.6 million; the U.S. Bureau of Census begins recording immigration statistics. The Missouri Compromise admits Maine (formerly a district of Massachusetts) to the Union as a nonslave state (the twenty-third state in the Union), balanced by agreement that Missouri will enter the Union (in 1821) as a state with no restrictions on slavery. The federal Land Act sets the price for public lands price at $1.25 per acre and the number of acres for purchase at eighty. Southern farmers produce 334,000 bales of cotton. The first African Americans from the United States slaves to be recolonized in Africa arrive in Liberia. Washington Irving's "Rip Van Winkle" introduces a new literary form, the short story.

1821   Missouri is admitted as the twenty-fourth state in the Union. Spain sells eastern Florida to the United States for $5 million. The Santa Fe Trail, blazed by William Becknell, opens the Southwest to trade. The African Methodist Episcopal Zion Church is organized in New York City. The first public high school in the United States is established by vote at a special town meeting in Boston.

1822   A slave insurrection led by Denmark Vesey in Charleston, South Carolina, involves nine thousand slaves and free blacks; an informer reveals the conspiracy and Vesey and thirty-four other blacks are hanged. Stephen Austin founds the first settlement of Americans in Texas ("the Old Three Hundred") with legal sanction of the Mexican government. The first section of the Erie Canal, stretching from Rochester to Albany, opens in New York State.

1823   President Monroe gives an address (the Monroe Doctrine) warning European powers to stay out of the Western Hemisphere, advising that colonization or interference by European governments in the internal affairs of North and South America would be considered an act of aggression against the United States. Clement Moore's Christmas poem "A Visit from St. Nicholas" appears anonymously in a Troy, New York, newspaper and becomes an overnight sensation that launches the American idea of "Santa Claus."

1824   No contender in the presidential election (among candidates Andrew Jackson, John Quincy Adams, William H. Crawford, and Henry Clay) gains a majority of the vote; the election is decided by the House of Representatives. Congress passes the Tariff Act to protect American industry from foreign competition. Thomas L. Kenney is appointed to head the newly created Bureau of Indian Affairs, an administrational entity within the U.S. War Department. The American Sunday School Union is formed. Russia relinquishes claims to territory in the Pacific Northwest.

1825   John Quincy Adams is inaugurated as the sixth president of the United States. Completion of the Erie Canal, 363 miles from the Hudson River to Lake Erie, gives farmers near the Great Lakes access to New York City. The first woman's labor organization is formed by women working in New York City's garment industry. The American Unitarian Association is founded in Boston as an institution separate from the Congregational Church.

1826   Founding fathers Thomas Jefferson and John Adams die on the same day, the fiftieth anniversary of the Declaration of Independence. Light sentencing for the murderers of a renegade Freemason who had threatened to reveal fraternity rituals creates an anti-Masonic backlash; the first national third party, the Anti-Masonic Party, is formed in Batavia, New York. The American Temperance Society is founded.

1827   The Supreme Court rules in *Martin v. Mott* that the president has sole authority for calling out the militia. John James Audubon publishes the first volume of his five-volume *Birds of North America*.

1828   Congress passes the Tariff Act, called by its southern opponents the "Tariff of Abominations." Construction of the first passenger railroad in America, from Baltimore to Ohio, begins. Noah Webster publishes his *American Dictionary of the English Language*.

1829   Andrew Jackson is inaugurated as the seventh president of the United States; an unruly crowd of celebrants mobs the White House at his reception. The postmaster general is elevated to cabinet rank. Congress authorizes construction of the first post office building, in Newport, Rhode Island. America's first true locomotive runs on the Delaware and Hudson Railroad.

1830   The U.S. population is 12.9 million. The Indian Removal Act gives the president authority to designate specific lands for the Five Civilized Tribes of the Southeast (Cherokee, Creek, Seminole, Choctaw, and Chickasaw), whom the federal government had been moving to lands west of the Mississippi beginning in the 1820s. Daniel Webster, defending the concept of the United States as one nation, and Robert Y. Hayne, defending the sovereignty of the individual states, square off in their famous debate over the nature of the Union. Southern farmers produce 732,000 bales of cotton. Joseph Smith Jr. publishes *The Book of Mormon* and forms the Mormon Church (the Church of Jesus Christ of Latter-day Saints) in western New York.

1831   In *Cherokee Nation v. Georgia* the Supreme Court rules that Cherokees cannot bring suit in federal court. Anti-Masons call the first national convention of a political party. Nat Turner leads a slave revolt in Southampton County, Virginia, that ends with fifty-five whites killed and twenty blacks executed. William Lloyd Garrison begins publishing his antislavery newspaper, *The Liberator*. The South Carolina Railroad begins the first regularly scheduled passenger service using an American-built engine. Cyrus Hall McCormick builds a horse-drawn grain reaper.

Mount Auburn Cemetery in Cambridge, Massachusetts, is the first burial ground designed as a rural landscaped park.

1832 In *Worcester v. Georgia* the Supreme Court rules that states have no legal authority over Indians or Indian lands. President Jackson vetoes the rechartering of the second Bank of the United States, leading to the creation of the Whig Party. The Democratic Party meets in Baltimore for its first national convention. Illinois militia kill most of a band of Sawk and Fox Indians who have migrated east under Chief Black Hawk, in fighting (called the Black Hawk War) meant to compel them to return to lands west of the Mississippi.

1833 President Jackson removes federal deposits from the Bank of the United States, effectively killing the bank. The Pendleton Act establishes a permanent federal Civil Service Commission. William Lloyd Garrison leads the formation of the American Anti-Slavery Society in Philadelphia. Benjamin Day founds the *New York Sun*, the first successful penny newspaper.

1834 The Indian Intercourse Act sets aside a region of the Great Plains as "Indian Territory." The Bureau of Indian Affairs (established in 1824) receives congressional authorization. Hiram A. and John A. Pitts of Maine invent a horse-powered threshing machine that beats the grain from the heads, separates the straw, and winnows the chaff. Nathan Currier opens a lithography business (later to become Currier and Ives, in 1857).

1835 A delusional house painter named Richard Lawrence unsuccessfully attempts to assassinate President Jackson. Indian resistance to removal initiates the Second Seminole War in Florida. Militia units made up of Anglos and Tejanos revolt against Mexican rule in Texas. Volume 1 of Alexis de Tocqueville's *Democracy in America* is published.

1836 Arkansas is admitted as the twenty-fifth state in the Union. Congress passes a "gag rule" prohibiting any antislavery bill or petition from being introduced, read, or discussed. Texas settlers asserting independence are defeated by the Mexican Army at the siege of the Alamo (23 February– 6 March), but gain success at the Battle of San Jacinto (21 April), and Sam Houston is installed as president of the Republic of Texas on 22 October. Samuel Colt begins manufacturing the Colt revolver, the famous "six shooter." Alonzo D. Phillips patents phosphorus matches. Hiram Moore and J. Haskall patent a "combine" that combines the principles of the reaper and the threshing machine.

1837 Martin Van Buren is inaugurated as the eighth president of the United States. Michigan (formerly part of the Northwest Territory) is admitted as the twenty-sixth state in the Union. Minnesota treaties with Dakotas and Ojibwas open the large delta between the St. Croix and Mississippi Rivers to white settlement. Financial panic sets off an economic depression that lasts into 1843. A mob in Alton, Illinois, kills the abolitionist newspaper editor Elijah Lovejoy. Mount Holyoke College for women is founded by Mary Lyon in Hadley, Massachusetts.

1838 The forced emigration known as the Trail of Tears begins in June and lasts until April 1839: the U.S. Army marches some fifteen thousand Cherokees from Georgia to Indian Territory (Oklahoma); about four thousand Indians die along the way. More than one hundred female antislavery societies are in existence. Ralph Waldo Emerson precipitates Unitarian controversy with an address to the graduating class of the Harvard Divinity School that rejects the Christian premise of Jesus Christ's divinity and ability to work miracles. An Illinois blacksmith named John Deere patents a steel plow that cuts through prairie sod.

1839   A conflict known as the Aroostook War begins between lumberjacks along the disputed border between Maine and New Brunswick, Canada. Congress enacts a law forbidding dueling. Fifty-three captive Africans seize control of the Spanish slave ship *Amistad* and try to return to Africa; the U.S. Navy seizes the *Amistad* off Long Island. Joseph Smith and his Mormon followers move to Nauvoo, Illinois. Charles Goodyear discovers a vulcanizing process that stabilizes rubber and makes it possible to use rubber products in virtually all spheres of life. Abner Doubleday establishes set rules for the game of baseball and lays out the nation's first baseball diamond, at Cooperstown, New York.

1840   The U.S. population is 17 million. Lucretia Mott and Elizabeth Cady Stanton are among eight women denied a seat and a vote at the World's Anti-Slavery Convention in London on account of their sex; they return to the United States agreeing to plan a women's protest meeting. President Van Buren sets a ten-hour workday for federal employees. Volume 2 of Alexis de Tocqueville's *Democracy in America* is published.

1841   William Henry Harrison is inaugurated as the ninth president of the United States; he dies a month after taking office and is replaced by his vice president, John Tyler. The Supreme Court rules that *Amistad* survivors are entitled to their freedom and returns them to Africa. Two Pennsylvania farmers, Moses and Samuel Pennock, patent a horse-drawn grain drill.

1842   The Webster-Ashburton Treaty settles the Maine boundary dispute with Britain and ends the Aroostook War. The Mount St. Helens volcano in Washington State erupts. Ether is used for the first time as an anesthetic, during a minor operation performed by a physician in Jefferson, Georgia. The Croton Aqueduct begins supplying water to New York City.

1843   President Santa Anna of Mexico informs the United States that U.S. annexation of Texas will be considered a declaration of war. Major westward migration of easterners hoping to settle in Oregon begins along the Oregon Trail. The millennialist William Miller gathers followers who await the imminent return of Jesus Christ to earth.

1844   James K. Polk wins the presidential election campaigning on the theme "Fifty-four forty or fight," promoting the idea of the United States' Manifest Destiny to be in possession of the entire west coast of North America. Samuel Morse sends the first telegraph message, over a line between Baltimore, Maryland, and Washington, D.C. The Mormon Church founder Joseph Smith and his brother Hyrum are killed by a mob that storms the jail where they are being held on charges stemming from ongoing conflicts between Mormons and their non-Mormon neighbors in Nauvoo, Illinois.

1845   Polk is inaugurated as the eleventh president of the United States. Florida is admitted as the twenty-seventh state in the Union. The Republic of Texas requests and is granted annexation to the United States in March; in December, Texas is admitted as the twenty-eighth state in the Union. Congress establishes a national presidential Election Day. The U.S. Naval Academy opens (as "the Naval School") in Annapolis, Maryland. *The*

Narrative of the Life of Frederick Douglass, an American Slave, Written by Himself is published.

1846   Taking advantage of disputes over border lines, the United States declares war on Mexico, initiating the first conflict driven by the American premise of Manifest Destiny. Iowa is admitted as the twenty-ninth state in the Union. The Oregon Treaty sets the forty-ninth parallel to the Pacific Coast as the boundary between British and American territory in the Far West. Mormons seek to escape persecution by departing Illinois for Utah under the leadership of Brigham Young. A crack in the Liberty Bell becomes too large to permit the bell to be rung.

1847   The U.S. Post Office begins issuing postage stamps. Cayuse Indians attack the Waiilatpu Mission run by Marcus and Narcissa Whitman in southern Washington, killing fourteen whites and setting off the Cayuse War (1848–1850). Frederick Douglass publishes the first issue of his newspaper, *The North Star*.

1848   The Mexican-American War ends with the Treaty of Guadalupe Hidalgo; Mexico cedes the Southwest, giving up one-half of its territory (Arizona, California, Colorado, Nevada, New Mexico, Utah, and Wyoming) and relinquishing any claim on Texas. Wisconsin (formerly part of Northwest Territory) is admitted as the thirtieth state in the Union. The Seneca Falls Convention organized by Mott and Stanton draws a crowd of three hundred that ratifies a platform demanding equal rights for women. The Free-Soil Party forms in response to sectional debate over extension of slavery following the territorial gains of the Mexican War. The California gold rush begins.

1849   Zachary Taylor is inaugurated as the twelfth president of the United States; he dies in July of coronary thrombosis and is replaced in office by his vice president, Millard Filmore. Minnesota becomes a territory. The Department of the Interior is created; the Bureau of Indian Affairs is transferred from the Department of War to the new Interior Department. Elizabeth Blackwell, the first woman doctor in the United States, graduates from Geneva Medical College.

1850   The U.S. population is 23.1 million. The Compromise of 1850 admits California as a nonslave state (the thirty-first state in the Union) and creates the Utah and New Mexico Territories. The Fugitive Slave Act empowers federal marshals to recover runaway slaves; the informal entity known as the Underground Railroad increases activity in behalf of fugitive slaves. The United States signs the Clayton-Bulwer Treaty stating that any canal in Central America would be a joint project with Great Britain. Jenny Lind arrives from Sweden for a concert tour sponsored by P. T. Barnum.

1851   Maine enacts a statute mandating statewide prohibition. The Young Men's Christian Association is organized in Boston. Isaac Singer patents the domestic sewing machine. Amelia Jenks Bloomer devises a women's outfit of a loose tunic worn over ankle-length baggy trousers known as "bloomers."

1852   Ohio enacts a law that sets a ten-hour workday for women and children under eighteen; in Massachusetts, a law is passed making twelve weeks per year of school attendance compulsory for children age eight to fourteen. The Wells Fargo Company forms as a general business agency serving the Far West, offering freight and letter delivery and banking services.

Uncle Tom's Cabin by Harriet Beecher Stowe (serialized in 1851) is published in book form and sells 300,000 copies in its first year.

1853   Franklin Pierce is inaugurated as the fourteenth president of the United States. The Gadsden Purchase of the Mesilla Valley (between the Rio Grande and the Colorado River) from Mexico for $10 million completes the outline of the contiguous United States. The invention of the steam elevator by Elisha Otis makes it possible to build apartment buildings taller than five or six stories.

1854   The Ostend Manifesto reveals U.S. convictions that it has a right to possess Cuba. The Kansas-Nebraska Act essentially repeals the Missouri Compromise and allows new territories on the Great Plains "popular sovereignty" in choosing whether to allow slavery. Henry David Thoreau's *Walden* is published.

1855   William Walker's filibustering expedition lands in Nicaragua. The Yakima War begins after Washington Indian tribes are forced onto reservations. The prepayment of postage stamps becomes mandatory, replacing the system of hand-marked postage due on receipt. Walt Whitman's *Leaves of Grass* is published.

1856   The U.S. Guano Islands Act encourages American fertilizer entrepreneurs to make claims on islands in the equatorial Pacific. Violent conflict between proslavery and Free-Soil forces in the Kansas Territory results in a regional civil war known as "bleeding Kansas." Gail Borden patents condensed milk; other instant foods are soon developed and popularized as well.

1857   James Buchanan is inaugurated as the fifteenth president of the United States. The Supreme Court decides in *Dred Scott v. Sandford* that blacks in the United States have "no rights that whites are bound to respect" and are therefore not entitled to citizenship and cannot sue in federal courts; the ruling also denies Congress the power to restrict slavery in federal territory by declaring the Missouri Compromise unconstitutional. Foreign coinage is no longer supported by law as legal tender. Financial panic sets off an economic depression.

1858   Minnesota is admitted as the thirty-second state in the Union. The Illinois Republican candidate Abraham Lincoln delivers his "House Divided" speech (in June) and debates his Democratic opponent Stephen A. Douglas (in October) in a Senate race that focuses on the slavery question; Lincoln's opposition to any extension of slavery into new states or territories garners him a reputation as an "antislavery extremist" in the South. Wells Fargo institutes the first regular cross-country passenger service. New York City commissioners sponsor a competition to design the new Central Park and choose the "Greensward Plan" by Frederick Law Olmsted and Calvert Vaux.

1859   Oregon is admitted as the thirty-third state in the Union. The militant abolitionist John Brown and twenty-one followers unsuccessfully raid the federal arsenal at Harpers Ferry, Virginia. A two-hundred-mile vein of silver that becomes known as the Comstock Lode is discovered in the eastern foothills of the Sierra Nevada. The Great Atlantic and Pacific Tea Company (A&P), the first modern chain store, is founded in New York City. Charles Darwin's *On the Origin of Species* is published.

1860   The U.S. population is 31.4 million. Southern secession begins with the departure of South Carolina from the Union (20 December) after the election of Abraham Lincoln as president. Southern farmers produce 4.5 million bales of cotton. William Walker is executed following a filibuster expedition attempt to land in Honduras. Wells Fargo establishes the Pony Express to compete with U.S. postal delivery and to establish the suitability of a northern route for the development of the transcontinental railroad.

1861   Lincoln is inaugurated as the sixteenth president of the United States. Kansas is admitted as a nonslave state, the thirty-fourth state in the Union. The Confederate States of America form a government (February) and adopt a constitution (March); on 12 April, Confederates fire on Federal troops at Fort Sumter (near Charleston, South Carolina), initiating the Civil War. The first American income tax is enacted. Congress enacts the Morrill Tariff, a heavily protectionist trade policy behind which emerging American industries can develop and expand their national markets. In October the telegraph spans the nation, making the Pony Express obsolete.

1862   The Battle of Glorieta in New Mexico establishes Union presence in the Southwest and confines the Confederate army to Texas. The United States formally extends diplomatic recognition to Haiti, the "Negro republic" that had gained its independence in 1804. The Militia Act authorizes Lincoln to enlist black troops for the Union Army. The Homestead Act provides 160 acres of lands in the public domain at no cost to those who will take out a claim and reside on and farm the land for five years. The Pacific Railroad Act gives companies generous loans and grants extensive tracts of land to complete a transcontinental railroad. Sioux Indians in Minnesota retaliate with bloodshed (known as the Sioux Uprising) over exploitative treaty terms. The Morrill Land-Grant College Act authorizes federal funding for the creation of state colleges for training in agriculture and the mechanical arts. The Department of Agriculture and the Office of the Commissioner of Internal Revenue are created.

1863   The Emancipation Proclamation granting freedom to slaves in rebelling states (issued by Lincoln in September 1862) takes effect on 1 January. The thirty-four westernmost counties of Virginia are reorganized as West Virginia and admitted to the Union as the thirty-fifth state. The Arizona Territory is separated from New Mexico. The National Banking Act creates a national banking system and begins the federal government's movement toward a monopoly over currency. Lincoln delivers the Gettysburg Address. California infantry kill 368 Shoshoni Indians in the Bear River Massacre. The U.S. Post Office begins free delivery in cities. New York City is wracked by violent antidraft riots. The Universalist Olympia Brown becomes the first woman in the United States to be ordained with full denominational authority.

1864   Nevada is admitted as the thirty-sixth state in the Union. The Sand Creek Massacre in southeastern Colorado, in which Colorado militia slaughter a peaceful village of Cheyennes and Arapahos, marks the beginning of confrontations between the United States and Plains Indians that lasts until the Wounded Knee Massacre in South Dakota in 1890. The National Convention of the Colored Men, held in Syracuse, New York, calls for granting black male suffrage.

1865   Robert E. Lee's surrender to Ulysses S. Grant at Appomattox on 9 April ends the Civil War; on 14 April, Lincoln is assassinated at Ford's Theater by the pro-Confederate actor John Wilkes Booth, and Lincoln's vice president, Andrew Johnson, is sworn in to replace him. The Reconstruction Proclamation grants amnesty to Confederates who took oath of allegiance. The Freedman's Bureau is established to assist blacks in making the transition from slavery to freedom. The Thirteenth Amendment abolishes black slavery. The Ku Klux Klan is founded as a social club, in Pulaski, Tennessee.

1866   The Civil Rights Act declares that all persons born in the United States are citizens, without regard to race, color, or previous condition of servitude. Various telegraph companies consolidate as Western Union, creating the first nationwide multiunit modern business enterprise. The first refrigerated railroad car is built. The Young Women's Christian Association is organized in Boston.

1867   Nebraska is admitted as the thirty-seventh state in the Union. Congress declares state governments reestablished under Johnson's Reconstruction program to be provisional and subjects them to control of military commanders; the Reconstruction Act also enfranchises black males; requires southerners to frame new state constitutions that establish equal civil and political rights; and orders southern states to comply with these terms and ratify the Fourteenth Amendment to be eligible for restoration to the Union. The United States purchases Alaska from Russia for $7.2 million.

1868   Congress brings impeachment proceedings against President Johnson, who is charged with having violated the Tenure of Office Act in March 1867 by removing Edwin Stanton as secretary of war; Johnson is acquitted. Ratification of the Fourteenth Amendment constitutionally defines citizens as all persons born or naturalized in the United States. After Georgia expels black members from its legislature, the state is placed under military rule. The world's first experimental elevated railway (propelled by steam) opens in lower Manhattan, setting the stage for urban rapid transit systems that operate on their own rights of way. Christopher Latham Shoals introduces the first practical typewriter.

1869   The Civil War hero Ulysses S. Grant is inaugurated as the eighteenth president of the United States. The Union Pacific Railroad links with the Central Pacific at Promontory Point, Utah, completing the first transcontinental railroad. The Wyoming Territory becomes the first major jurisdiction to extend voting rights to women. Elizabeth Cady Stanton and Susan B. Anthony form the National Woman Suffrage Association, which denounces the Fifteenth Amendment for denying the vote to women and calls for a constitutional amendment that will give women the vote; Lucy Stone and Julia Ward Howe form the American Woman Suffrage Association, which supports the Fifteenth Amendment as a step toward universal suffrage and works to persuade states to extend the ballot to women. Arabella Mansfield, the nation's first woman lawyer, is licensed by the Iowa bar. G. H. Hammond of Detroit makes the first long-distance shipment of refrigerated meats.

1870   The U.S. population is 39.8 million; the U.S. Census reveals that for the first time more laborers work for someone else than for themselves. The Fifteenth Amendment nationalizes black male suffrage. Georgia is readmitted to the Union after federal troops enforce restoration of expelled black members to the state's legislature. The Justice Department is established. A Ghost Dance ceremony begins among the Paviotso Indians in Nevada and spreads to tribes in California and Oregon.

1871   The Ku Klux Klan Act permits the president to declare martial law in order to enforce the Fourteenth and Fifteenth Amendments. Congress passes legislation prohibiting the United States from signing treaties with Indian tribes. A fire in Chicago leaves almost 100,000 people homeless. Race riots in Los Angeles result in the lynching of fifteen Chinese. The U.S. Weather Service is founded.

1872   The Post Office Department receives cabinet status. Congress approves creation of the first national park, Yellowstone. The Erie Canal has its peak year of tonnage. Sylvanus D. Lock develops a reaper called a binder, which binds stalks of grain into sheaves. A. Montgomery Ward publishes his first mail-order catalog.

1873   The Coinage Act eliminates the silver dollar and establishes the gold standard for U.S. currency. The Timber Culture Act enables a farmer to claim 160 acres provided he plants 40 acres of trees. Passage of the antipornography "Comstock Law" forbids the mailing of "lewd, lascivious, or obscene" material. The Supreme Court hears the *Slaughterhouse Cases*. Financial panic sets off an economic depression that lasts into 1879. Levi Strauss begins selling blue jeans in San Francisco.

1874   Hawaii signs a ten-year free-trade agreement with the United States to give it access to the U.S. sugar market. The Philadelphia Zoological Garden opens as the nation's first permanent urban animal menagerie. The Women's Christian Temperance Union is formed in Cleveland, Ohio.

1875   Congress passes the Civil Rights Act guaranteeing all citizens equal access to public accommodations and forbidding exclusion of blacks from jury duty. The American Theosophical Society forms in New York City. Mary Baker Eddy, the founder of the Christian Science Church, publishes *Science and Health,* outlining the church's doctrine.

1876   Rutherford B. Hayes is elected president despite Samuel Tilden's majority popular vote. Colorado is admitted as the thirty-eighth state in the Union. Three hundred troops under General George Custer are decimated by the Sioux chief Sitting Bull and his warriors at the Battle of Little Bighorn. The centennial anniversary of the Declaration of Independence is celebrated with a world's fair in Philadelphia. The independent inventors Alexander Graham Bell and Thomas A. Watson patent the telephone.

1877   Hayes is inaugurated as the nineteenth president of the United States. The Reconstruction era ends after Hayes removes Federal troops from the South as part of the compromise deal that sealed his disputed victory in the 1876 presidential election. The Desert Land Act allows a settler to claim 640 acres at $1.25 per acre provided he irrigates it within three years. The surrender of Chief Joseph after an unsuccessful retreat to Canada ends the Nez Percé War between the Idaho nation and the U.S. government. A worker uprising known as the Great Railroad Strike develops into the most violent and extensive labor action in U.S. history. Anti-Asian riots resulting from labor competition begin in San Francisco.

1878   State game departments are established by California and New Hampshire in response to overhunting of wildlife. A yellow fever epidemic in the South claims fourteen thousand lives. The American Bar Association is formed. The first elevated railroad in America begins operating, on Sixth Avenue in New York City. John Wesley Powell's influential *Report on the Lands of the Arid Region of the United States* is published. Washington A. Burpee begins selling seeds by mail order.

1879 The Public Lands Commission is created by Congress to codify federal statutes and make them consistent. A form of multifamily housing known as the dumbbell tenement, so called because of its shape, is introduced in New York City; the tenements are widely built through the end of the century but are notorious for their lack of light, air, and space. Frank W. Woolworth opens his first successful five-and-ten-cents store, in Lancaster, Pennsylvania.

1880 The U.S. population is 50.2 million. A treaty with China limits immigration of Chinese laborers. A pay-telephone service is established in New Haven, Connecticut.

1881 James A. Garfield is inaugurated as the twentieth president of the United States; he is shot by Charles J. Guiteau on July 2 and dies on 19 September; his vice president, Chester Alan Arthur, is sworn in to replace him. The Supreme Court upholds the constitutionality of the 1862 income tax in *Springer v. United States*. Clara Barton organizes the American Red Cross.

1882 The Chinese Exclusion Act suspending immigration of Chinese laborers becomes the first piece of U.S. legislation to restrict immigration based on nationality. The Standard Oil Company combines with a number of affiliated oil producers, refiners, and marketers to form a trust that gives it controlling interest in 90 percent of all oil produced in the United States. Edison Electric Company builds the first electric power plant, in New York City.

1883 The Supreme Court rules the Civil Rights Acts of 1866 and 1875 unconstitutional. The Pendleton Act establishes a permanent Civil Service Commission, replacing the spoils system. Construction of the Brooklyn Bridge is completed. Buffalo Bill Cody's Wild West Show holds its first performance.

1884 The Supreme Court in *Elk v. Wilkins* refuses to support the prerogative of an Indian to reside off the reservation and exercise the right to vote. Financial panic sets off an economic depression. Mark Twain's *The Adventures of Huckleberry Finn* is published.

1885 Grover Cleveland is inaugurated as the twenty-second president of the United States. The American Bell Company, which holds a monopoly on telephone patents, reorganizes as American Telephone and Telegraph. The first million-share day occurs in the stock market.

1886 The Haymarket Square riots in Chicago begin as a protest for an eight-hour workday and develop into violence that leaves seven killed and seventy injured. The American Federation of Labor holds its first annual convention, bringing together national trade unions with a combined membership of some 150,000. The Statue of Liberty, donated by France, is installed in New York Harbor.

1887 The Dawes General Allotment Act parcels out reservation acreage individually to Indians, ultimately enabling extensive white appropriation of Indian lands. Congress passes the Interstate Commerce Act to oversee interstate railroad operations via the Interstate Commerce Commission, the nation's first federal regulatory body. Thomas Edison introduces the phonograph. The Coca-Cola Company is formed by Asa G. Candler.

1888   The secret ballot is introduced as a voting reform in Massachusetts. The New York legislature passes a law designating the electric chair as the state's method for carrying out the death penalty. The first successful electric streetcar goes into service in Richmond, Virginia. George Eastman introduces the easy-to-use Kodak portable box camera, which captures images on rolls of film.

1889   Benjamin Harrison is inaugurated as the twenty-third president of the United States. As a result of the Omnibus Bill, Congress splits the Dakota Territory in two and admits to the Union: North and South Dakota, as the thirty-ninth and fortieth states; Montana, as the forty-first state; and Washington, as the forty-second state. The Sioux Act divides the Great Sioux Reservation into six smaller reserves and opens up surplus land to white settlement. The commissioner of agriculture is elevated to cabinet status. Jane Addams and Ellen Gates Starr found Hull-House in Chicago, setting off a nationwide settlement house movement. Some 2,200 people die in flooding after the collapse of a dam at Johnstown, Pennsylvania. The first female Presbyterian minister in the United States, Louisa Wolsey, is ordained by the Cumberland Presbyterian Church.

1890   The U.S. population is 62.9 million. Idaho is admitted as the forty-third state in the Union; Wyoming the forty-fourth. Sherman Antitrust Act prohibits trusts from engaging in monopolistic practices (but does not prohibit corporations from doing so). Congress passes legislation creating Yosemite National Park. The U.S. Army's attempt to suppress a Ghost Dance movement in South Dakota leads to the murder of Sitting Bull on 15 December and the massacre of some three hundred Lakota men, women, and children at Wounded Knee Creek fourteen days later. Formerly rival woman suffrage groups unite as the National American Woman Suffrage Association. William Kemmler is killed in the electric chair at Auburn Prison in New York, the first person to be executed by electrocution. The United Mine Workers of America is organized. Jacob Riis's photo essay *How the Other Half Lives* is published.

1891   The establishment of the Oklahoma Territory opens the region to white settlement. James Naismith invents basketball. Congress passes an International Copyright Act that protects American authors abroad and stops the flood of cheap English reprints into the U.S. market. The General Land Law Revision Act gives the president power to create forest preserves by proclamation.

1892   Kentucky is the last state to abandon voice voting for local and state elections. The People's (or Populist) Party, representing American farmers, holds a convention in Omaha and adopts a platform calling for the free coinage of silver, a lowering of the tariff, government ownership of railroads, telephones, and telegraphs, and a graduated income tax. A strike by iron and steel workers in Homestead, Pennsylvania, is brutally put down by state militia. Martial law is declared at the strikebound Coeur d'Alene silver mines in Idaho.

1893   Grover Cleveland is inaugurated as the twenty-fourth president of the United States. Colorado extends the ballot to women. Sugar planters in Hawaii plot a U.S. takeover to get around the heavy tariffs that have slowed sugar sales; U.S. Marines land in Hawaii ostensibly to protect American lives but aid the revolutionaries in overthrowing the monarchy of Queen Lili'uokalani and establishing a provisional government. Financial panic sets off an economic depression that lasts into 1897. The first successful U.S. automobile is produced by Charles and Frank Duryea. The World's Columbian Exposition in Chicago, which commemorates the four hundredth anniversary of the discovery of the New World, launches the City Beautiful Movement and the urban planning profession.

1894   When a national railroad strike ties up U.S. commerce, President Cleveland uses the Justice Department to break the walkout and punish Eugene V. Debs and the Pullman railroad union he led. An economic slump topples nearly six hundred banks. The Edison Kinetoscope has its first public showing in New York City.

1895   The Supreme Court declares the income tax unconstitutional. The Anti-Saloon League forms to undertake a systematic single-issue campaign for national prohibition. Black women's clubs federate as the National Association of Colored Women. The Ramakrishna Mission and Vedanta Society forms in New York City.

1896   Utah and Idaho extend the ballot to women. Utah is admitted to the Union (as the forty-fifth state) after the Mormon Church disavows polygamy. The Supreme Court accepts separate-but-equal arguments in *Plessy v. Ferguson*. In *United States v. Gettysburg Electric Railway Co.*, the first significant legal case concerning historic preservation, the Supreme Court rules that acquisition of the national battlefield at Gettysburg serves a valid public purpose. The U.S. Post Office institutes rural free delivery. Henry Ford's first automobiles appear on Detroit streets.

1897   William McKinley is inaugurated as the twenty-fifth president of the United States. The Library of Congress is moved from the Capitol to its own building. The subway, a European innovation, debuts in North America in the city of Boston. Thomas Edison patents a movie camera.

1898   The U.S.S. *Maine* sinks in Havana Harbor in February and United States declares war on Spain; the United States annexes the Hawaiian Islands in August; the Spanish-American War ends with the Treaty of Paris in December, which establishes the independence of Cuba and legalizes U.S. acquisition of Guam and Puerto Rico. In *United States v. Wong Kim Ark*, the Supreme Court concludes that everyone born in the United States is a citizen regardless of race. Manhattan, Brooklyn, Queens, Staten Island, and the Bronx are consolidated into one city under the charter of Greater New York.

1899   Secretary of State John Hay announces U.S. expectations of an "open-door policy" in Asia, affirming American interest in the territorial integrity of China and demanding the right to equal economic opportunity for U.S. business interests on the Asian mainland. Thorsten Veblen's *The Theory of the Leisure Class* is published.

1900   The U.S. population is 76 million; approximately 36 percent of the U.S. labor force is engaged in agriculture. The Boxer Rebellion, an antiforeign uprising in China, elicits a multinational (United States, Great Britain, Russia, Germany, France, Japan) relief expedition of five thousand troops. Ground is broken for the New York City subway system.

ENCYCLOPEDIA
OF THE
UNITED STATES
IN THE
NINETEENTH
CENTURY

A

ABOLITION AND ANTISLAVERY

ABOLITION AND ANTISLAVERY   Both reformers and historians have tended to use the word "antislavery" as a generic term to describe any proposal to limit, reform, or end slavery. By contrast, the word "abolition" describes proposals to end slavery altogether. The first plans for abolition, as the term was used between 1770 and 1830, focused on eliminating what reformers judged the worst feature of slavery, the African slave trade. These early abolitionists assumed that stopping all trade would be the first step toward complete abolition. Many shared this assumption that slavery would gradually be abolished, but few joined new abolitionists who, beginning in the 1830s and continuing until the 1865 passage of the Thirteenth Amendment, denounced gradual methods as ineffective and proclaimed immediate, unconditional emancipation the only way to end slavery.

Origins

In Britain's American colonies scattered criticisms of slavery were published as early as *An Exhortation and Caution to Friends Concerning Buying or Keeping of Negroes* (1693), by George Keith, a Quaker, and *The Selling of Joseph* (1700), by Samuel Sewall, a Puritan. An organized movement to end slavery in the United States, however, did not begin until the middle of the eighteenth century. Several leading Quakers voiced moral concerns about slavery and circulated antislavery tracts on both sides of the Atlantic. They were joined by Evangelicals whose contact with slaves had raised questions about the compatibility of slavery with Christian teachings.

America's political leaders encountered antislavery sentiment from two other sources: slaves who petitioned for the freedom they understood was the purpose of the revolutionary struggle, and records of the Somerset case of 1772. This landmark ruling declared the slave of a customs official free, because both owner and slave were temporarily residing in England, where the common and "natural" view of slavery was that it was so "odious, that nothing can be suffered to support it, but positive law."

Once the War for Independence was under way, slaves absorbed this heightened sense of personal liberty from the revolutionary atmosphere. Some petitioned colonial assemblies for their freedom, while many more took advantage of the struggle for independence to flee to whichever army had advertised liberty for slaves, usually in exchange for military service. Lord Dunmore's 1775 proclamation, for example, freeing slaves who bore arms for the British during the war, prodded colonials and their assemblies to likewise manumit slaves, on the condition that the blacks join the colonial military. As Gary Nash argues in *Race and Revolution* (1990), revolutionary leaders framed their freedom struggle as a natural right; thus some felt obliged to consider abolition of slavery as part of their program. If the war was being fought against tyranny, perhaps African slavery, and not just the slavery of being colonials, was incompatible with free, republican government.

This focus on freedom from tyranny made many aware that slaveholding by free citizens was incongruous. Still, after the Revolution religious arguments remained the more powerful weapons and Quakers continued to set the terms of debate. Only after John Wesley, the founder of Methodism, had read Anthony Benezet's *Some Historical Account of Guinea* (1771) did he pen the widely read *Thoughts on Slavery* (1774). Benezet and John Woolman pressed their antislavery agenda at religious meetings on both sides of the Atlantic, and by the 1780s the Society of Friends had eradicated slaveholding among members. American Quakers then refocused their antislavery concerns, forming manumission societies to promote abolition more broadly: for example, the Pennsylvania Abolition Society (1784), the New York Manumission Society (1785), the Providence (Rhode Island) Abolition Society (1789, also known as the Providence Society for Abolishing the Slave Trade), and the New Jersey Society for Promoting the Abolition of Slavery (1793). Maryland and Delaware activists also formed abolition societies and participated, as did activists in Virginia, in legislative debates about the best methods for phasing out slavery.

This legislative focus intensified in 1794, when representatives from several state groups met in Philadelphia to form the American Convention for Promoting the Abolition of Slavery and Improving the Condition of the African Race. They petitioned the U.S. Congress to control the slave trade and agreed to lobby in their respective state legislatures for antislavery laws. By 1804 all the northern states had passed legislation to end slavery, either immediately or in the next generation. An additional impetus for debating slavery came in 1793, when black Haitians were freed following a bloody insurrection begun in 1791 against their French governors. The event served as a continuing and dramatic object lesson about the dissemination of the precepts of liberty. Whether for moral, republican, or utilitarian reasons, Maryland and Virginia continued to debate various abolition schemes until, in 1808, the U.S. Congress banned all further importation of slaves. This move came in tandem with the British Parliament's similar ban on international slave trading, long considered the most repellent feature of modern slavery. English pressure on all Atlantic trading powers was effective in large part because British shipping dominated most sea routes and British military patrol vessels could take the lead in enforcement.

When this first, revolutionary wave of emancipations subsided, only a few groups continued to monitor antislavery progress. In New Jersey and New York legislation mandating immediate emancipation failed. There abolition groups eventually passed laws freeing slaves when they reached a specified, adult

Seal of the Society of the Abolition of Slavery in England. Originally designed in the 1780s, the design appeared on several medallions for the society made by Josiah Wedgwood. The image was later widely reproduced (here as an 1837 woodcut) and used by abolitionist organizations in the United States, notably the American Anti-Slavery Society. LIBRARY OF CONGRESS: BROADSIDE COLLECTION

birthday, but only if the slaves had been born after the legislation had been enacted. With these partial successes the first antislavery societies became moribund, although the Quakers Charles Osborn and Benjamin Lundy continued the antislavery fight by starting weekly newspapers. From Mount Pleasant, Ohio, Osborn edited the *Philanthropist* (1817–1818), and the peripatetic Lundy began his *Genius of Universal Emancipation* (1831–1835) in Ohio, later moving it to Tennessee and eventually to Maryland.

Osborn and Lundy were transitional figures, carrying on the revolutionary generation's concern that the process of emancipation continue in the southern slave states. Like more conservative reformers of his day, Lundy saw the colonization of free blacks in the West or in Haiti or West Africa as feasible and a step that would make slaveholders more amenable to emancipation. The less prominent Osborn opposed colonization, a stance shared by the abolitionists who organized in the 1830s. The more important western abolitionists during this interim period were David Barrow, a Baptist, and John Rankin, a Presbyterian. In 1807 Barrow published *Involuntary, Unmerited,*

Perpetual, Absolute, Hereditary Slavery, Examined.
Rankin's *Letters on American Slavery* appeared in
1823. Both attacked slavery for its opposition to natural law and to Christian scripture.

The New Abolitionism

New abolitionists rejected both colonization and
gradual emancipation as ineffective and often racist,
declaring their goal to be the immediate, unconditional end of slavery. Characterizing their strategy
for achieving this end as "moral suasion," reformers
adapted the new methods for evangelizing used by
the revivalist Charles Finney, employing antislavery
agents to work as missionaries pleading for converts.
Agents organized the converts into local antislavery
societies, the members of which pledged to spread the
gospel of immediatism and so serve as "auxiliaries"
to the national organization.

The best known of the new abolitionists was William Lloyd Garrison, who had learned his first lessons
in antislavery journalism in 1829, while assisting
Lundy. Garrison learned even more lessons from
James E. Forten, a wealthy black Philadelphian, who
explained to Garrison how most blacks rejected the
goals of the American Colonization Society, founded
in 1817 to sponsor the return of free blacks to Africa.
Forten helped Garrison document his tract *Thoughts
on African Colonization* (1832), which argued that
colonization, despite portrayals to the contrary, was
strengthening, not undermining, American racism.
Forten and other blacks provided the funds that enabled Garrison's newspaper, *The Liberator* (1831–
1865), to survive its first years. Philadelphia's black
leaders remained prominent in the movement, encouraging blacks in Boston, Providence, Newport,
and New Haven to circulate abolitionist tracts and
to collect funds for Garrison. A handful of converts
in New England, New York, and Pennsylvania
started small antislavery societies, several of which
collected funds for Garrison.

British support for American antislavery work
was substantial in this second period of reform, because reformers in Britain saw American antislavery
efforts as related to their own success in 1833 of pressing through Parliament the "First of August" bill,
which ended slavery in the island colonies. In 1833,
prior to the formation of the American Anti-Slavery
Society, Garrison toured Britain to collect moral and
financial support. Reformers used the British success
to try to shame patriotic Americans. In contrast to
those in Great Britain, abolitionists in the United
States did not easily build on the antislavery successes of the previous generation. The large slave
population in southern states continued to grow, from

less than one million at the time of the American
Revolution to four million in the 1860s, when U.S.
slavery was finally ended.

The success of British West Indian emancipation,
the frightening example of Haitian independence,
and support from American blacks and a few additional converts in New England led to the decision
by Garrison to form a new organization dedicated to
immediate abolition. In December 1833 Garrison
summoned converts to Philadelphia, where fifty-six
delegates founded the American Anti-Slavery Society. This group in turn helped organize several hundred local antislavery societies and sponsored the
publication and mass distribution of antislavery
tracts. Its members also recruited young missionary
agents, at one point dubbed "the Seventy," who
spoke at meetings from the Ohio Valley to Maine and
as far south as Philadelphia.

Those agents included the Ohioans John Rankin
and the young Theodore Dwight Weld, leader of a
contingent of students who withdrew from Lane
Theological Seminary in Cincinnati rather than submit to the school's ban on abolitionist talk and activities. Other notable agents during the 1830s included
Wendell Phillips, a Boston Brahmin; Abby Kelley, a
Massachusetts Quaker; James G. Birney of Alabama
and Kentucky; and Angelina E. and Sarah M.

William Lloyd Garrison (1804–1879). Garrison, an abolitionist, published the *Liberator* (1831–1865), in which he espoused views against slavery in the South. ARCHIVE PHO-
TOS

Grimké of Charleston, South Carolina. Because of their personal experience with plantation slavery, Birney and the Grimkés were in great demand as speakers. The Grimkés initially focused on women's gatherings, such as the conventions of abolitionist women held in 1836, 1837, and 1838 in New York and then Philadelphia. They wrote several powerful antislavery tracts, beginning with Angelina's *Appeal to the Christian Women of the South* (1836) and Sarah's *Epistle to the Clergy of the Southern States* (1836). When men began flocking to meetings led by the Grimkés, clergy response was harsh: in 1837 a group of Congregational ministers from Massachusetts published a formal condemnation of such antislavery meetings, singling out for special criticism the "promiscuous" (mixed) audiences at antislavery meetings and the impropriety of women publicly lecturing to men.

The new movement quickly attracted strong opposition across the North, where most colleges ruled that students could not discuss slavery, colonization, or emancipation. Where antislavery groups formed, as well as in slaveholding states, community leaders complained that pamphlets mailed to local elites were intended to undermine local authorities and, in the South, to instigate slave rebellions. This new abolitionist movement gained the greatest following in the sections of the Northeast that had experienced both evangelical revivals and economic prosperity—a growing middle class saw slavery not just at odds with religious beliefs, but slave labor as incompatible with the free labor system.

The American Anti-Slavery Society had begun its crusade by employing ministers as agents and holding as many meetings as possible in churches. Denominations and local congregations were generally cautious, however, and a series of anti-abolitionist riots between 1834 and 1837 persuaded most church leaders, even among the more egalitarian Baptists and Methodists, to avoid controversy by banning antislavery rallies and even announcements of such rallies from their meetinghouses. This violence backfired, however, when in 1837 a mob in Alton, Illinois, killed an abolitionist newspaper editor, Elijah Lovejoy. Blacks had died in earlier riots, but this first death of a white abolitionist shocked many Americans, who now realized that attacks on abolitionists could violate the civil rights of whites as well as blacks.

Also helpful in garnering sympathy for abolitionists was the gag rule adopted by the U.S. House of Representatives each year between 1836 and 1844. On the surface the rule was simply an attempt to manage the thousands of antislavery petitions being circulated by local antislavery auxiliaries and then submitted to Congress. The petitions variously asked Congress to ban interstate slave trading, slavery in the District of Columbia, and slavery in new territories, and accord diplomatic recognition to Haiti, areas over which petitioners assumed the federal Congress had jurisdiction. Most northerners still viewed the abolitionist agenda as radical, but Congressman John Quincy Adams's skillful maneuvering around the gag rule and the huge volume of antislavery petitions increasingly persuaded many that this proslavery restriction constituted a dangerous attack on citizens' First Amendment rights to free speech and to petition the government for a redress of grievances.

Encouraged by British emancipation, American reformers saw their cause as linked to antislavery efforts elsewhere. In 1840 more than fifty activists journeyed to London for the World Anti-Slavery Convention, called by the new British and Foreign Anti-Slavery Society. This group, formed with the blessing of elderly reformers such as Thomas Clarkson, mobilized a younger generation of reformers to monitor and aid both abolition and postemancipation reforms around the world, particularly in the United States. This group was especially interested in court cases, often involving international law, which determined the legal status of slaves being carried on the ships *Amistad* (1839–1841) and *Creole* (1841). Although not new, diplomatic disputes about slave trading and the publicity given the complicated legal maneuvers to free the "cargo" of these ships generated sympathy for both slaves and abolitionists.

Political Antislavery

Stymied in their efforts to convert church leaders, many abolitionist leaders concluded that James G. Birney was correct in an assertion he made as the title of a pamphlet: *The American Churches: The Bulwarks of American Slavery* (1836). Religious motives remained important, but many abolitionists abandoned attempts to work through the churches and instead pressed for change through political parties and legislation. This emphasis on political process coincided with a conflict among leaders of the American Anti-Slavery Society over the role of women within the organization. Lewis and Arthur Tappan, New York businessmen and early financial supporters of immediatism, led a faction that walked out of the organization's 1840 convention to form a second immediatist group, the American and Foreign Anti-Slavery Society, which did not advocate equality for women, as the older organization did. Members of this group favored a political strategy of using the ballot to end slavery and supported the new Liberty

Party in 1840 and 1844, when Birney stood as the party's candidate for president. By 1846 support for the party had faded, and most political abolitionists gave their votes to the new Free-Soil Party in 1848.

Free-Soilism, which sought to ban slavery from new western territories, was much more popular than any proposal for an immediate end to slavery. Seeing the Compromise of 1850, and particularly its provision of a new fugitive slave law, as proof that a southern elite, the "Slave Power," was encroaching on the rights of free, northern states, "Conscience Whigs" and "Free Democrats" joined other Free-Soilers who had already broken party ranks. With these party divisions the Liberty Party agenda of abolishing slavery through legislation disappeared from party politics. It was replaced by the more popular concern to ensure that western territories would be open for settlement by those not using slave labor.

"Free Soil, Free Speech, Free Labor, and Free Men" had been the motto of the third party convention of Free-Soilers in 1848. Support for this platform grew dramatically in the 1850s, not just because of the Fugitive Slave Act of 1850 and the dramatic and popular condemnation of it in Harriet Beecher Stowe's novel *Uncle Tom's Cabin* (1852), but also because of the violence precipitated in 1855 in Kansas by proslavery Missourians whose illegal votes elected a proslavery government for the new territory. "Bleeding Kansas," however, was seen as the responsibility of the U.S. Congress, which the previous year had opened the entire Kansas-Nebraska Territory, theoretically as far north as Canada, to slaveholding settlers.

Given this public agitation, party politics could not go on as usual, and the Whig Party was a first fatality. In 1854 opponents of the Kansas-Nebraska Act organized what quickly became known as the Republican Party, which was dedicated to stopping the spread of slavery into the western territories. In 1856 this party carried eleven northern states in the presidential election and sent numerous men to Congress and state offices. For those increasingly inclined to see the "Slave Power" in control of the federal government, the Supreme Court ruling in 1857 against Dred Scott's suit for freedom confirmed the need for this new party. As a candidate for the U.S. Senate, and later while running for president, Abraham Lincoln never attacked slavery in existing states, but he did insist that slavery be prohibited in the new western lands, a point that many southerners interpreted as a clear antislavery stance.

Ad Hoc Strategies

Convinced that a proslavery constitution made political efforts to end slavery futile, a small core of

radicals remained aloof from party politics, loyal to Garrison's "moral suasion" tactics. Among this band was a disproportionate number of women immediatists, who remained committed to working primarily through moral influence, not electoral politics. In the two decades prior to the Civil War, these stalwarts wrote, read, and circulated *The Liberator* and other antislavery tracts. Often led by black abolitionists, many worked on largely futile campaigns to integrate public transportation and schools. One notable success was an 1855 Massachusetts law that desegregated public schools, the result of an eleven-year campaign led by William C. Nell of Boston. Many of these same reformers served on the vigilance committees that provided aid to fugitive slaves passing through a given black community en route to freedom. Most also attended antislavery meetings and annual fairs, which in many communities functioned like integrated, antislavery churches. At such fairs leaders collected funds and mingled with the faithful, many of whom enjoyed the informal social time and the singing as much as the featured antislavery fare.

A few abolitionists, dubbed "ultras," were too extreme to sustain a formal organization. Making occasional appearances at antislavery fairs and meetings, these men provided critics with plenty of material to mock all abolitionists. The most extreme "ultra" was New Hampshire's Nathaniel P. Rogers, who in the interest of free speech, advocated "no organization," rejecting as tyrannical even the temporary use of officers to organize antislavery meetings. Unlike Rogers, "ultra" Henry C. Wright remained loyal to Garrison's organization, but his writings and lectures strayed far from antislavery to focus on pacifism or "non-resistance" as it applied to parent-child and spousal relations, a view that critics argued would undermine all social and political order.

Despite the organized efforts of moral and political abolitionists, colonization of free blacks outside the United States remained the program favored by most whites as the long-term solution to slavery and race relations. Colonization agents, never as controversial as antislavery agents, enjoyed broad, interregional support lasting into the 1860s. The American Colonization Society, and particularly state colonization societies, gained the endorsement of major religious denominations for their plans to resettle free blacks in Haiti or Liberia. Support for colonization, even if that support consisted of giving platform time to colonization agents at denomination meetings, kept church leaders free of any radical taint or major financial commitments, and at the same time allowed them to envision the repatriated blacks as the means of spreading Christianity to Africa.

Formed in 1843 by supporters of the *Amistad* captives, the American Missionary Association was another antislavery organization that continued support well into the twentieth century for colonies of former slaves in places as varied as Sierra Leone and Uganda. Particularly after the Fugitive Slave Act of 1850, some free blacks reconsidered colonization as providing a needed asylum. Martin Delany was the most prominent of these early black nationalists, and his report on an 1859 trip up the Niger River promoted colonization. Black hopes rose again on the eve of the Civil War, and as a result still another colonization plan was postponed indefinitely.

While not many black abolitionists joined Birney in becoming politically active, many of them became impatient with white organizations and their inattention to fugitive slaves. Frederick Douglass attended and spoke at both Liberty and Free-Soil Party meetings. But he too turned more frequently to separate "Negro Conventions," annual meetings held since the 1830s, as the best institution through which to organize against slavery and race prejudice. Black agents like Douglass garnered significant support, not just while in the northern United States, but also when touring England, Ireland, and Scotland. Among the more popular speakers were William and Ellen Craft, Henry "Box" Brown, and William Wells Brown. Each was skilled at depicting the horrors of slavery, and they all sold personal narratives and gathered funds to support further tours and publications, and sometimes to buy family members out of slavery.

More than most white reformers these black abolitionists bridged divisions among reformers. Both Douglass and Sojourner Truth, for example, attracted a wide variety of admirers, even after Douglass broke with the American Anti-Slavery Society in order to found his own newspaper. The diversity of topics in Douglass's weekly, begun with British funds as the *North Star* in 1847 and later renamed *Frederick Douglass' Paper*, reflected the varied strands of antislavery ideology as well as the range of tactics employed. Like Garrison in *The Liberator*, Douglass reported on court cases, incidents of slave abuse and racial discrimination, and the speeches and debates at meetings sponsored by the American Anti-Slavery Society and its local auxiliaries. He also followed the black convention movement closely, reporting on suggestions from within black communities on how to combat legal, educational, and economic discrimination. Further, Douglass covered any mention of slavery by party leaders, and he attended both Liberty and Free-Soil Party meetings, speaking in support of each party's stand against the extension of slavery.

Unlike the relatively short campaigns of British abolitionists, which began with attempts to ban slave trading and climaxed with Parliament abolishing West Indian slavery, the U.S. campaign against slavery had no central focus. Americans assumed that the Constitution left this issue to state governments and that the U.S. Congress could abolish slavery only in territories or in the federally administered District of Columbia. Leaders of the American Anti-Slavery Society continued to rail against all manifestations of the "Slave Power." Moderates like Douglass and the Tappans settled for nibbling away at slavery, through the courts in cases like *Amistad* and through legislative and party battles over the extension of slavery.

Slaves themselves argued with their feet, thousands running to free territory. These actions, together with his experiences fighting slaveholders in Kansas, convinced maverick John Brown that armed rebellion was the only path left open to freedom. Ironically, freedom came only after a period of sustained violence and with a great deal of help from runaway slaves, both as workers in the military camps and as members of fighting units.

The onset of civil war in 1861 unified antislavery factions. Differences about means of abolition were set aside as white and black abolitionists joined Frederick Douglass and William Lloyd Garrison in lobbying for immediate emancipation and the enlistment of free blacks in the Union army. Most Northerners accepted President Lincoln's pronouncement that the war was to preserve the union and initially resisted the idea of black regiments. Stymied in their political lobbying, abolitionists were more successful in organizing aid for thousands of former slaves who, as soon as war broke out, had fled to Union lines. Sponsored by church groups and freedman's aid societies, reformers moved to Washington, D.C.; New Orleans, Louisiana; and Port Royal, South Carolina, to be near the refugees and to provide material aid and basic schooling. These efforts continued and expanded after the war.

Midway through the war, Lincoln took two giant steps toward freedom for African Americans. Citing high casualties among Union troops, poor morale among potential white recruits, and the need to undermine the Southern slave workforce, in January 1863 Lincoln issued the Emancipation Proclamation, freeing slaves in Confederate states. He also announced the formation of black regiments. Despite the president's statement that these changes were strategic, designed to undercut the Confederate war effort, abolitionists embraced both as significant moves toward ending slavery. Skilled journalists and public speakers, Frederick Douglass, Mary Ann Shadd Cary, and other black abolitionists led recruiting drives and the subsequent fight to gain equal pay for black troops. All abolitionists hailed the passage in January 1865 of the Thirteenth Amendment as completing the legal process of abolition begun with the Emancipation Proclamation.

See also **Constitutional Amendments,** *subentry on* **Thirteenth, Fourteenth, and Fifteenth Amendments; Slavery.**

Bibliography

Bender, Thomas, ed. *The Antislavery Debate: Capitalism and Abolitionism as a Problem in Historical Interpretation.* Berkeley and Los Angeles: University of California Press, 1992.

Berlin, Ira, et al. *Slaves No More: Three Essays on Emancipation and the Civil War.* Cambridge, U.K.: Cambridge University Press, 1992.

Davis, David Brion. *The Problem of Slavery in the Age of Revolution, 1770–1823.* Ithaca, N.Y.: Cornell University Press, 1975.

———. *The Problem of Slavery in Western Culture.* Ithaca, N.Y.: Cornell University Press, 1966.

———. *Slavery and Human Progress.* New York: Oxford University Press, 1984.

Dumond, Dwight L. *Antislavery: The Crusade for Freedom in America.* Ann Arbor: University of Michigan Press, 1961.

Freehling, William W. *The Reintegration of American History: Slavery and the Civil War.* New York: Oxford University Press, 1994.

Lerner, Gerda. *The Grimke Sisters from South Carolina: Rebels against Slavery.* Boston: Houghton Mifflin, 1967.

Nash, Gary B. *Race and Revolution.* Madison, Wis.: Madison House, 1990.

Nash, Gary B., and Jean R. Soderlund. *Freedom by Degrees: Emancipation in Pennsylvania and Its Aftermath.* New York: Oxford University Press, 1991.

Ripley, C. Peter, ed. *The Black Abolitionist Papers.* 5 vols. Chapel Hill: University of North Carolina Press, 1985–1992.

Sewell, Richard H. *Ballots for Freedom: Antislavery Politics in the United States, 1837–1860.* New York: Oxford University Press, 1976.

Sterling, Dorothy. *Ahead of Her Time: Abby Kelley and the Politics of Antislavery.* New York: Norton, 1991.

Stewart, James B. *Holy Warriors: The Abolitionists and American Slavery.* Rev. ed. New York: Hill and Wang, 1997.

Yellin, Jean F., and John C. Van Horne, eds. *The Abolitionist Sisterhood: Women's Political Culture in Antebellum America.* Ithaca, N.Y.: Cornell University Press, 1994.

Zilversmit, Arthur. *The First Emancipation: The Abolition of Slavery in the North.* Chicago: University of Chicago Press, 1967.

DEBORAH VAN BROEKHOVEN

ABORTION.   See **Contraception and Abortion.**

ACADEMIC AND PROFESSIONAL SOCIETIES

Alexis de Tocqueville, a nineteenth-century French commentator, remarked in *Democracy in America* (1835) on the large number of voluntary associations in the United States. Among these were professional and intellectual organizations. Local and loosely organized at first, some developed into centralized national-state networks by the end of the century.

Professional Organizations

Local professional societies of doctors and lawyers in the early nineteenth century consisted of upper-class white male practitioners. Although organized for social purposes, these groups created opportunities for members to learn from each other. Medical societies did not, however, establish requirements for the practice of medicine, a process that was handled instead by regulatory bodies in some states. In the profession of law, courts certified some practitioners, and societies frequently centered on the sharing of law libraries.

During the 1820s and 1830s, when democracy expanded as a result of the end of property requirements for male suffrage and other changes, these professions became more open (many states dropped their medical certification requirements, for example) and less authoritative. Physicians faced competition not only from homeopaths, midwives, and sellers of "home remedies" but also from graduates of short-term medical schools, which proliferated at this time. In the legal field, many without any formal schooling set up practices, and courts relaxed their certification requirements.

In order to gain control over the qualification of practitioners and to improve medical education and standards, some physicians began to strengthen their local associations. They also organized state societies and in 1847 formed a national organization, the American Medical Association (AMA). State associations successfully lobbied for laws that gave them powers to certify and regulate practitioners. The national organization coordinated these efforts, established codes of conduct for the profession, and also set standards for medical schools. The AMA also sponsored conferences and published research and papers, first in the AMA *Transactions* (1848–1883) and then in the *Journal of the American Medical Association.* Women were excluded initially from these organizations, but in the 1870s they began to be admitted.

Not until the 1870s did lawyers begin to build their professional organization network. State bar associations pressed for state-level certification practices, ethical standards, and consistency and quality in legal practices. At the national level, the American Bar

Association was created in 1878. This organization and most of the state associations were limited to white males throughout the century.

Other professional organizations formed in the nineteenth century included the National Education Association (1857), the American Library Association (1876), and the American Society of Mechanical Engineers (1880).

Academic/Intellectual Organizations

Literary and other intellectually oriented societies originated in the eighteenth century. Those in larger cities, such as the American Philosophical Association (Philadelphia) and the American Academy of Arts and Letters (Boston), modeled themselves somewhat loosely on the British Royal Society and functioned in part as social clubs for leading gentlemen of their communities. They adopted formal practices, such as the reading of papers at society meetings. In their desire to advance knowledge and educate their fellow citizens in arts, sciences, and literature, literary societies sponsored lectures and organized libraries. Societies like these were replicated in smaller towns and cities as the nation expanded.

Intellectual societies that focused on specific interests, such as science, also formed; some developed into national academic organizations. Members of several science organizations and faculty from various eastern colleges organized the American Association for the Advancement of Science (AAAS) in 1847. Its middle- and upper-middle-class membership included amateurs, college teachers, government scientists, and researchers. African Americans were not allowed to be members, and white women were admitted on a very limited basis.

The AAAS held annual meetings where individuals socialized, gave papers, and presented the results of scientific experiments. From the start, the meetings were documented in a publication, the *Proceedings of the American Association for the Advancement of Science*, and, after 1901, in *Science*. Gradually the organization set limits on "amateur" participation by establishing approval processes for papers and by emphasizing connections with colleges and universities. Other associations based on science specialties developed, such as the American Chemical Society, founded in 1876. Several groups contributed to the formation of this organization including those attending a special celebration of Joseph Priestley's work held in 1874 as well as the members of the chemistry section of the AAAS.

Following the lead of the AAAS, Americans interested in the social sciences organized nationally as the American Social Science Association (ASSA) in 1865.

Although open to all, including women and African Americans, the ASSA drew a largely white upper-middle and middle-class membership composed of reformers, college teachers and administrators, lawyers, doctors, economists, businessmen, and government officials. These men and women used scientific methods to investigate social structures and processes and to address social, political, economic, and health issues. Members collected data, sponsored public lectures, held conferences at which papers were read and issues debated, and published articles, reports, and some of its proceedings in its organ, the *Journal of Social Science* (1869–1909).

In the context of increasing specialization and differing interests, the ASSA gave birth to separate associations, both professional and academic. In 1874 members interested more in practice than in theory formed the Conference of Charities and Correction, which eventually became a professional organization for social workers. The formation in 1884 of the American Historical Association was followed by that of the American Economic Association (1885). In 1890 the American Academy of Political and Social Science emerged from the Philadelphia Social Science Association, an ASSA chapter. These organizations continued ASSA practices—annual meetings, paper readings, and journal publication. They also developed close ties to colleges and universities and came to be increasingly dominated by faculty and others with vocational involvement in the evolving social science disciplines, though they were not entirely closed to others. Rather than lobby legislative bodies for credential requirements, the new professional organizations established symbiotic relationships with institutions of higher education to certify subject specializations through graduate programs and hiring and tenure practices. The growth of higher education during the last third of the nineteenth century strengthened these efforts.

Historians have advanced conflicting views on the purposes of professionalization and on the growth of professional and academic organizations. Interpretations range from seeing these societies as attempts to create professional monopolies to perceiving them as altruistic efforts to serve humankind. Universally acknowledged, however, is the considerable power that these institutions had gained by the end of the nineteenth century and the increasing influence that they would exert in the professions and the nation's intellectual life in the twentieth century.

See also **Clubs; Education,** *subentry on* **Graduate and Professional Education; Legal Profession; Libraries; Lyceums; Medicine; Professions; Sciences, Physical.**

Bibliography

Haber, Samuel. *The Quest for Authority and Honor in the American Professions, 1750–1900.* Chicago: University of Chicago Press, 1991.

Haskell, Thomas. *The Emergence of Professional Social Science: The American Social Science Association and the Nineteenth Century Crisis of Authority.* Urbana: University of Illinois Press, 1977.

Hatch, Nathan O., ed. *The Professions in American History.* Notre Dame, Ind.: University of Notre Dame Press, 1988.

Kohlstedt, Sally. *The Formation of the American Scientific Community: The American Association for the Advancement of Science, 1846–1860.* Urbana: University of Illinois Press, 1976.

KATHRYN WAGNILD FULLER

ADVENTISM.   See **Millennialism and Adventism.**

ADVERTISING   Advertising in the young republic was primarily local and of limited scale, confined to small type in newspapers and to word of mouth and circulars. Street criers provided news of the day, including commercial announcements. But with the rising industrial revolution and the growth of cities, advertising became an increasingly important economic factor during the nineteenth century, decried by some as unseemly but brash and innovative in ways that altered the marketing and distribution of goods—and ultimately people's lives—throughout the nation.

Early newspaper ads conveyed simple messages, most often aimed at retailers or their elite readers, often announcing the arrival of shipments from Europe. Alexander Hamilton (1755–1804) in 1803 noted in his *New York Evening Post* that "It is the advertiser who provides the paper for the subscriber" (Atwan, p. 14). By the 1830s, falling printing costs fueled the expansion of advertising. By 1832 the Hoe cylinder press could print two thousand impressions in a single hour, nearly twenty times more than earlier printers had been able to do. The resulting Penny Press greatly broadened the reading audience, and festered a growing use of advertising for popular commercial goods rather than for the narrower range of commercial interests.

Along with the burgeoning market, the style of advertising was affected by new promoters, forms of entertainment, and strategies of appeal. P. T. Barnum (1810–1891) blended advertising and promotion in a grand scale, becoming the "master of manipulative advertising" until his death, as Luc Sante has written in *Low Life: Lures and Snares of New York* (p. 59). Barnum promoted such entertainers as Jenny Lind (1820–1887), his American Museum, and later his circus by focusing on the exotic, the power of personality, or the attraction of spectacle. "There were no sharp boundaries between salesmanship and other forms of performance," observes historian Jackson Lears. A carnavalesque advertising tradition linked products to magical transformative possibilities. Barnum's success reflected the growing dominance of theaters and exhibitions in early ads, along with patent medicines.

Circulars and posters came into wide use during the century, as did chromolithographed trade cards, notably at the time of the Philadelphia Centennial Exposition in 1876. And word of mouth advertising by drummers or commercial travelers took on added importance with the rising impact of the railroad.

The national government engaged in what many regard as the first national advertising campaign during the Civil War in its attempt to sell war bonds. Posters helped to recruit volunteers, while Sanitary Fairs, photographic exhibits, and various propaganda campaigns promoted political perceptions. Local government had long paid for legal announcements, which provided significant revenue to early newspapers. Cheap postal rates facilitated the distribution of goods. In 1879 Congress created a special low postal rate for magazines, which helped in the distribution of advertisements to a national readership.

The industrial revolution facilitated novel products and types of demand, as well as changing the style of advertising. Newly created forms of distribution also showcased goods in novel ways. The department store, with its large store window, interior displays, and organization of goods, broke new ground in using goods in stylistic ensembles. Mass marketing to rural areas by newly created firms such as the one founded by Montgomery Ward (1843–1913) began in 1872, using mail-order catalogs to advertise their goods. Railroads, seeking customers for their own markets, sold the idea of emigrating to western states to thousands throughout Europe by the use of handbills. By the end of the century John Wanamaker (1838–1922), the head of the most prominent Philadelphia department store, epitomized the expansive nature of the new culture of promotion. He became chairman of the Republican Party and Postmaster General, organizing new techniques for advertising political candidates along the way.

Throughout the century, advertisers generally had a poor reputation in the minds of respectable Americans. The lack of ethical standards or government oversight allowed an endless array of dubious claims to go unchallenged. Patent medicines, according to

Advertisement for Payn's Sure-Rising Flour. Payn's competitors plummet off the table, while Payn's flour, doing a jig, remains on the table. Lithography by Ferdinand Mayer and Son, c. 1873. LIBRARY OF CONGRESS

some estimates, accounted for at least half the money spent by large budget advertisers as late as 1893. Criticism of advertising was heard from many pulpits and appeared in the pages of mainstream magazines. In 1850 Reverend Henry Ward Beecher (1813–1887) decried fraudulent ads as "incarnated lies." Yet in the final decades of the century, the growing effectiveness of ads and the impact of new technology and wealth achieved by success in advertising made the field more attractive to a burgeoning group of young men on the make.

Advertising increasingly took on the mantle of professionalism. George Rowell (1838–1908) opened an office in Boston in 1865 that sold newspaper space wholesale, and in 1869 he began to publish the *American Newspaper Directory*, which sought to offer accurate circulation estimates. Rowell later initialized the trade journal *Printer's Ink* in 1888. F. W. Ayer (1848–1923) opened an agency in 1869 in Philadelphia and developed an open contract system in which the agency represented the advertiser rather than the publisher. The Ayer firm hired the first full-time copywriter in 1892.

By the 1880s, new forms of packaging and the rise of national advertising through brand identification

altered marketing practices. Having nationally advertised goods shipped in packages from the factory rather than as bulk goods led to increased control and financial rewards for manufacturers, at the expense of middlemen. The National Biscuit Company's campaign for Uneeda Biscuit is the classic example.

New York and Chicago became the locus of power within the advertising industry. In 1883 Joseph Pulitzer's (1847–1911) *New York World* became the first newspaper to base ad rates on circulation figures. Magazines initially earned most of their revenue from subscriptions, but with the rising subsidy of advertising, lower cost helped expand their reach into millions of American homes. Posters also came into increasing prominence, advertising circuses, political campaigns, dime museums, and parades.

By the end of the century, what many believed to be scientific expertise as to the psychology of advertising became increasingly popular. Success was measured by whatever sold, with less deference to what were seen to be more antique moral values. The identification of personality through advertising was evident in the 1896 presidential campaign. In subsequent years, shoe manufacturer William Douglas's (1845–1924) face became so identified with ads for

Advertisement for Red Cloud Chewing Tobacco. American Indians appeared frequently in late-nineteenth-century advertisements, reflecting a popular image of the Indian as a staunch, traditional warrior. Advertisement, 1892. LIBRARY OF CONGRESS: PRINTS AND PHOTOGRAPHS DIVISION

his product that he ran for Governor of Massachusetts in 1904. The twentieth century saw the boundaries of hype and celebrity stretch beyond anyone's expectation. But there still is insufficient understanding of the breadth of the advertising industry's impact on American life and thought.

See also **Corporations and Big Business; Entrepreneurs; Merchandising; Newspapers and the Press.**

Bibliography

Garvey, Ellen Gruber. *The Adman in the Parlor: Magazines and the Gendering of Consumer Culture, 1880s to 1910s.* New York: Oxford University Press, 1996.

Laird, Pamela Walker. *Advertising Progress: American Business and the Rise of Consumer Marketing.* Baltimore: Johns Hopkins University Press, 1998.

Lears, T. J. Jackson. *Fables of Abundance: A Cultural History of Advertising in America.* New York: Basic Books, 1994.

Pope, Daniel. *The Making of Modern Advertising.* New York: Basic Books, 1983.

Spears, Timothy B. *100 Years on the Road: The Traveling Salesman in American Culture.* New Haven, Conn.: Yale University Press, 1995.

GREGORY BUSH

AFRICA, FOREIGN RELATIONS WITH

Official U.S. policies concerning Africa from the founding of the Republic through the nineteenth century were marked mainly by indifference, neglect, and fragmentation. Despite this relegation of Africa to backwater status in policymaking circles, important episodes held American attention, and numerous informal linkages involved Americans with Africans. The only African nation to awaken any continuing American interest was Liberia, established early in the century as a refuge for free African Americans.

As the century opened the United States experienced frequent encounters with the so-called Barbary pirates of North Africa. Sanctioned by the rulers of Algiers, Tunis, Tripoli, and Morocco, the Barbary pirates captured and held American sailors and ships for ransom. Soon after taking office in 1801, President Thomas Jefferson employed the U.S. Navy to maintain free commerce, which soon involved the nation in a war with Tripoli. This war ended in 1805 following the exploits of Americans such as Stephen Decatur, who, with a group of volunteers, burned the USS *Philadelphia*, which had been seized by the pirates after it had run aground outside Tripoli harbor. Naval actions during the War of 1812 helped extract favorable treaties from the Barbary rulers in 1815.

During the years before the Civil War, American merchants, especially from New England, engaged in African commerce. The war disrupted earlier trading patterns, and the availability of cheaper European goods shrank the American commercial presence in Africa later in the century. Nevertheless American colonization societies, missionaries, naval officers, adventurers, journalists, explorers, whalers, and mining engineers continued to maintain American interest in Africa.

The transatlantic slave trade and its legacy provided the most enduring links with Africa throughout the century. Although the eighteenth century was the chief era of the Atlantic slave trade, traffic in human beings continued well into the nineteenth century despite formal abolition of the trade by Congress in 1808. Beginning in the 1820s bitter disputes with Britain erupted over the rights to search American slavers, but the United States did attempt to relieve the impact of the trade by supporting Liberia as a West African settlement for freed slaves. This settlement movement was sponsored primarily by the American Colonization Society (ACS), founded by white Americans in 1817. The ACS was condemned by many African Americans as an instrument of slaveholding interests, although some prominent American blacks did favor the colonization movement. Among the most distinguished black proponents was the Reverend Alexander Crummell, who traveled to Liberia in 1853. Due in part to the half-hearted patronage of the United States, Liberia survived the European partition of the African continent. Liberia also suffered periodic conflicts between the African American settler communities on the coast and the indigenous African populations while the French and British were nibbling at its borders.

American trade with Africa was minimal in the second half of the century. Americans were periodically fascinated with the continent through the exploits of individuals such as Henry Morton Stanley, a naturalized American from Wales. As a reporter for the *New York Herald*, Stanley "found" the famous Scottish missionary and explorer David Livingston in East Africa in 1871 in one of the most dramatic news scoops of the century. Three years later Stanley led a long second expedition that mapped and made famous much of the Congo River basin. King Leopold II of Belgium employed Stanley's aid in a scheme to form a reputedly philanthropic organization to suppress the slave trade and promote legitimate commerce in the Congo region. Leopold also hired Henry S. Sanford, a former American ambassador to Belgium, to lobby in Washington to secure U.S. backing for the principle of free trade in the Congo. Early in 1884 Sanford's efforts led to American recognition of Leopold's International Association of the Congo as the paramount authority in the region, drawing the United States into the international dispute involving other European nations with claims in the Congo. Later that year the U.S. government sent Sanford and another delegate to the conference in Berlin that settled disputes and divided most of Africa between the European powers. The American delegates signed an agreement recognizing the authority of Leopold's International Association of the Congo in the region and guaranteeing an open door to trade. Although President Grover Cleveland, citing traditional American skepticism of entangling European connections, withdrew the agreement from the Senate ratification process, the United States continued to adhere to its terms. American commercial interests in the Congo, however limited, were therefore protected by international agreement. Throughout the century official diplomatic exchanges in Africa remained at the consular level, a reflection of the primacy of the commercial interests of the time.

Until the end of the century the United States was principally an observer as the European powers, especially Britain, France, and Germany, systematically expanded their colonial holdings in Africa. Washington pressed the colonial powers to keep the trading door open as increasing numbers of individual Americans engaged in activities in Africa. The American Board of Commissioners for Foreign Missions (ABCFM) first sent representatives to South Africa in 1835, and by the end of the century the ABCFM was one of the most important missionary groups on the continent. In addition to the substantial number of white American missionaries, a number of leading black churches, such as the African Methodist Episcopal (AME) Church, also sent representatives, especially to South and West Africa. Individuals such as the AME bishop Henry McNeal

Turner, who traveled to South Africa in the 1890s, led various movements to return black Americans to their homeland to convert and develop the continent. Through those contacts Africans became familiar with the black struggle in the United States and the work of prominent African American intellectuals, including W. E. B. Du Bois in the twentieth century. Another prominent visitor during this period was George Washington Williams, author of the first history of African Americans in the United States. In 1890 Williams traveled to Africa to study conditions in the Congo Free State and soon afterward published the widely discussed "Open Letter to King Leopold II," which condemned inhumane policies there. His reports helped initiate the campaign to end Leopold's personal rule.

In addition to missionaries and individuals pursuing their own activities, larger American capitalist enterprises gradually appeared in Africa and marked an important shift in American connections with the continent. In 1883 the Portuguese government granted Edward McMurdo, an American railroad developer, the concession to build a railroad from the Mozambique coast to the Transvaal frontier in South Africa. Following Portuguese breach of the contract in 1889, the United States pursued diplomatic and legal action until arbitration of the case in 1900 settled in favor of the American side. McMurdo represented a new sort of American commercial interest in Africa that foreshadowed the more extensive involvement of both private enterprise and the U.S. government in the affairs of Africa during the next century.

See also **Barbary War; Colonization, African American; Liberia; Slavery,** *subentry on* **African Slave Trade.**

Bibliography

Chester, Edward W. *Clash of Titans: Africa and U.S. Foreign Policy.* Maryknoll, N.Y.: Orbis, 1974.

Clendenen, Clarence C., Robert Collins, and Peter Duignan. *Americans in Africa, 1865–1900.* Stanford, Calif.: Hoover Institution on War, Revolution, and Peace, Stanford University, 1966.

Clendenen, Clarence C., and Peter Duignan. *Americans in Black Africa up to 1865.* Stanford, Calif.: Hoover Institution on War, Revolution, and Peace, Stanford University, 1964.

Duignan, Peter, and L. H. Gann. *The United States and Africa: A History.* Cambridge, U.K., and New York: Cambridge University Press, 1984.

Franklin, John Hope. *George Washington Williams: A Biography.* Chicago: University of Chicago Press, 1985.

Geiss, Imanuel. *The Pan-African Movement: A History of Pan-Africanism in America, Europe, and Africa.* Translated by Ann Keep. New York: Africana, 1974.

Redkey, Edwin S. *Black Exodus: Black Nationalist and Back-to-Africa Movements, 1890–1910.* New Haven, Conn.: Yale University Press, 1969.

Schraeder, Peter J. *United States Foreign Policy toward Africa: Incrementalism, Crisis, and Change.* Cambridge, U.K., and New York: Cambridge University Press, 1994.

THOMAS C. HOWARD

AFRICAN AMERICANS

[This entry includes an overview and four subentries on **Free Blacks before the Civil War, Blacks in the West, Blacks in the Military,** and **African American Religions.**]

OVERVIEW

Slavery and freedom form the backdrop for the history of African Americans in the nineteenth century. Before 1865 most black Americans were slaves working on southern plantations and farms to produce staple products for an Atlantic market. Rewards for their work went to their owners. The number of free blacks grew steadily up to the Civil War, though it never exceeded 10 percent of the total black population. Whether slave or free, African Americans in the pre–Civil War period identified with other blacks and looked to one another for support. When slavery ended in 1865, most of the formerly enslaved men and women remained in the South at similar work, as the region continued to produce staples while the North industrialized. Postwar efforts to provide the former slaves full citizenship rights did not last, and blacks remained without the means to reach the lowest rungs of America's economic and social ladders. By 1900 popular ideas of black inferiority supported white intentions to segregate and disfranchise African Americans and keep them economically dependent on whites. As earlier, black culture and community rested on an identity with other African Americans. Thus one of the telling points of nineteenth-century African American history is that life in slavery and freedom, at either end of the century, held many similarities.

Yet focusing solely on slavery, freedom, and the lack of improvement in blacks' living and working conditions conceals the enormous variety that existed among individual men and women of African descent in the nineteenth-century United States. Slave or free, urban or rural, northern or southern, old or young, accommodating or rebellious, African Americans did things differently over time and across space but also at the same time and in the same locales. Questions about how they became involved in and reacted to their varying situations defy simple answers. Thus a study of nineteenth-century black American history shows the complexity of African

American men and women and of the circumstances of their lives.

Slavery and Freedom: Formative Times

Over the country's early decades, slavery and freedom each became more firmly rooted. Slavery had existed on the North American mainland since early English settlement. By 1790 nearly 700,000 enslaved men and women, all of African descent, were a vital part of the American economy. The U.S. Constitution, in respecting rights to property above all, sanctioned slavery, and the racism that underlay the institution was evident in some of the early acts of Congress. One limited acquisition of citizenship to white immigrants, and another restricted militia participation to white men. Nor was slavery endangered following the Revolution, as historians once believed. From the areas farthest south, where slave-based agriculture was most economical, white elites took the plantation model and black slaves with them as they extended settlement westward. The Constitution allowed continuing importation of African slaves through 1807, showing America's willingness to allow staple-producing agriculture based on African and African American slave labor to recover following the Revolution and to extend into new areas of settlement.

In fact the beginning of the nineteenth century found the United States on the threshold of a commercial-agriculture boom, America's Cotton Kingdom. English textile mills manufactured cloth as fast as raw cotton could be grown. Invention and improvement of devices to remove the seed from cotton and experiments with new plants made cotton production feasible in the southern United States. Southern lands opened to settlement after 1814 encouraged whites to carve out new plantations. Between 1814 and the Civil War cotton drove the southern economy, and Louisiana experienced a sugar boom. Enslaved African Americans were the major workforce, and more were needed every year. Where would they come from?

Through 1807 the Atlantic trade helped meet the demand. Tens of thousands of enslaved Africans arrived over the final years of the legal trade, but after 1807 slave resources were limited to the population of African descent already in the country. The number of African Americans grew sufficiently through natural increase—more births than deaths—to meet much of the growing demand. Early in the century most lived in the Chesapeake area, yet the demand for slaves exploded in the new states to the southwest. A forced migration developed from the area of surplus to the area of shortage. Thus arose the domestic slave trade, the systematic buying, transporting, and selling of African American men, women, and children from the areas of tobacco and grain production in the Chesapeake and other parts of the Upper South to the new centers of cotton and sugar production in the Lower South. Altogether more than a million slaves were uprooted and sent south and west during the sixty years prior to the Civil War. The slave owners involved on either end of the trade had no interest in being kindly or paternalistic, as the romantic view of slavery once held. Profit ruled in the marketplace, and the trade broke marriages and separated parents from children. For the African Americans involved, it was the wrenching experience of a lifetime.

At the same time that slavery was becoming increasingly entrenched, so was freedom. Free Africans and African Americans had existed in the colonies as long as slaves, but not many—perhaps 30,000 in 1770, less than 5 percent of the black population. But the libertarian underpinnings of the American Revolution undermined slavery north of Maryland and brought a wave of manumission in the Upper South that increased the number of free blacks in the United States to nearly a quarter of a million by 1820. Indeed for a decade or more of the nineteenth century some free blacks viewed this trend, felt the revolutionary spirit issuing from Haiti in the Caribbean, and wondered if greater freedom and opportunity might be on the wind. It did not take long for most to find out that this was not the case.

Antebellum Slavery

Until the 1950s the accepted view of antebellum slavery was racist. The southern historian Ulrich B. Phillips, in *American Negro Slavery* (1918), used evidence from slave owners to support arguments for the benevolence of the institution; contentions that enslaved men and women were lazy, sensual, and loyal, with "a courteous acceptance of subordination" (p. 291); and ideas that "plantations were the best schools yet invented for the mass training of that sort of inert and backward people which the bulk of the American negroes represented" (p. 343). In 1956 Kenneth M. Stampp, in *The Peculiar Institution*, dashed the notion of harmonious race relations in slavery and generally condemned the institution for its brutality. Three years later Stanley Elkins, in *Slavery*, argued that the plantation's effect on enslaved African Americans was comparable to the effect of Nazi concentration camps on Jews: its "closed society" was so brutal that it rendered its subjects docile and childlike. In 1972 John W. Blassingame, in *The Slave Community*, turned to evidence from slaves as well as masters and found a range of personality types beyond the subdued and credulous and a strong black culture in the slave quarters. Later studies emphasize the variety and complexity of the slave experience.

Of course work was the basis for African Americans' existence in slavery, and the kind of work slaves did greatly affected their lives. Masters wanted as much productivity from slaves as humanly possible, and they had the law and a monopoly of force on their side. Slaves saw little point in laboring endlessly for someone else's gain, and they could assert their wills through malingering, breaking tools, damaging crops, setting fires, or running off. Thus a continuous if tacit struggle existed between master and slave to come up with standards of how much work was "enough." These standards varied according to such particulars as crop, crop prices, season, size of holdings, and individual personalities involved. Sugar was the most demanding crop, its harvest requiring six weeks of nearly constant work. Rice was next with

diking and digging to be done. Cotton demanded long hours at planting, chopping, and harvesttimes, and tobacco and grain involved steady but less-intense work. The type of crop dictated the organization of the workforce. Slaves growing rice tended to do so on a task system, each having specific duties to complete in a day, with time to themselves afterward. Other crops lent themselves to gang labor under close supervision. Larger holdings held the possibility for some, nearly always men, to become skilled craftsmen. Enslaved men and women often had enterprises of their own, working to produce food or something to sell. When export prices were low and food prices high, masters encouraged slaves to grow their own provisions.

Studies during the late twentieth century demolished the idea of slavery's benign nature. Making men, women, and children work beyond reasonable limits without personal gain required a level of force and brutality otherwise unknown in human dealings. Physical descriptions of slaves reveal the results,

Henry "Box" Brown. Brown, a slave from Richmond, Virginia, escaped in a 3' by 2.5' box to Philadelphia. He was shipped by a white friend, who was later jailed for similar efforts. Abolitionists used the box as a metaphor for the suffocation imposed on slaves by the institution of slavery. LIBRARY OF CONGRESS

which included scars, physical deformities, whip marks, cropped ears, and branding. The health of African American men, women, and children in slavery was poor for their day or any day. The American South was a difficult disease environment, persons of African descent had particular physiological problems, notions of hygiene were primitive, and slave diets lacked nutritional balance. What observers viewed as lazy or unmotivated slaves were ill or malnourished humans. Infants and children suffered most. In the 1850s half of all slave children died before they reached age five, a figure twice that for other Americans. Enslaved women were at a particular disadvantage. Contrary to popular thinking, women did a disproportionate amount of the field work because they had only domestic chores to take them away from the fields, whereas men had numerous out-of-field jobs. In addition women gave birth in difficult circumstances, reared children, cooked, and tended the household. Slave women in their late teens and early twenties also found themselves at the mercy of white men, a number of whom were sexual predators, their pious Christian pretensions notwithstanding.

In the slave quarters, beyond the master's gaze, existed a distinct African American culture, of which religion was an important part. The first half of the nineteenth century was a time of conversion of many slave men and women to Christianity. Around camp meetings and revivals in the century's first decades, masters and slaves accepted Christian teachings. The spread of evangelical Baptist, Methodist, and Presbyterian churches through the South before the Civil War brought additional conversions. Within broad bounds, African Americans framed their own Christianity, preserving concepts of a West African worldview and melding them with the views of American Christianity. Blacks' worship was fervent, their preaching emotional, their singing participatory and joyful. Other African elements were evident in the slaves' culture, especially kinship. Although a cyclical process of family formation, separation, and reconstruction dogged slaves through the years of the domestic slave trade, greatly extended families endured and served as building blocks of the African American community. Other aspects of culture in the slave quarters included music, dance, and folklore, all with strong African influences.

Of course, slaves were not alike. While slavery was a collective experience, it allowed for individual differences. Enslaved African American men and women had to work hard to eke out a satisfactory existence under difficult circumstances, and they found a variety of ways of doing so. To generalize about anything, from personal and group identity and individual personality types to ways of dealing with cruel overseers, is difficult.

Free African Americans

Across both North and South, whites perpetrated much ill on free African Americans. Northern state governments viewed blacks as inferior and carved out a legal status for them that made poverty a near certainty and humiliation a daily occurrence. Some northern states restricted black immigration, disfranchised blacks, curtailed legal protections, and permitted extralegal measures that relegated them to society's lowest level. Even white abolitionists were ambiguous about race. South of the Mason-Dixon Line, race lumped free blacks with slaves, adding further limits to their liberty.

Yet antebellum free blacks were far more than passive receptors of whites' bad deeds. Studies from the 1990s emphasize free blacks' own activities within the restraints of racism. Such activities included establishment of extended families and households; creation of an African American community, identity, and culture; and sustained efforts on the part of free blacks to win freedom for Americans of African descent still in slavery.

In such circumstances free blacks looked to one another for support and developed a strong sense of community. The basis of the free black community was households that included extended families, boarders, and friends. As the nineteenth century progressed, African American communal identity broadened with the proliferation of mutual aid societies, fraternal orders, schools, and churches. The black church in particular became central to African American culture. Free blacks formed their own institutions of worship, refusing mistreatment in white churches and desiring religious expression that re-

African-American Historical Composite (*opposite page*). Thirteen scenes pertaining to African American history are illustrated in this lithograph, created around 1897. Subjects include Christopher [*sic*] Attucks, a runaway slave killed in the Boston Massacre (*top center*); the abolitionist and civil rights activist Frederick Douglass (*top right*), the educator Booker T. Washington (*below Douglass*); the evolution and abolition of slavery in the United States (*left*); and symbols of African American progress after the Civil War (*right, below Washington*). These symbols include the Alabama Penny Savings Bank, Alabama's first black-owned bank; the Negro Exhibition in Nashville, Tennessee; and a table of statistics on African Americans, including the number of children in public schools, the number of mortgages owned by blacks, and other information. LIBRARY OF CONGRESS: PRINTS AND PHOTOGRAPHS DIVISION

AFRO-AMERICAN MONUMENT.

flected their culture. Increasingly black churches became places where African Americans attacked slavery, trained for leadership roles, and acquired education.

For a time issues surrounding colonization divided free blacks. Fed up with being denied the rights of citizenship, some African Americans early in the century looked to colonize blacks on a foreign shore, usually in Africa. In 1816 whites' efforts to rid the United States of a free black population they considered "troublesome" led to the formation of the American Colonization Society and brought money and organization to the colonization movement. The free blacks who settled on Africa's west coast under this society formed the Republic of Liberia in 1847, but as black enthusiasm over colonization waned after the 1820s, few African Americans made the Atlantic crossing. For most blacks born in the United States, Africa was part of their heritage, but America was their home.

By the 1830s and 1840s it was apparent that free African Americans were willing to stand together with others of their race to work toward ending slavery. If at the start of the century free blacks focused on personal uplift, by the 1820s many realized that their own liberty and opportunity were tied to those of their race who remained enslaved. The 1820 Missouri Compromise showed that the federal government was willing to allow slavery's expansion. White mob violence worsened, and American society in general was drawing clearer racial limits around full citizenship. In these circumstances free African Americans began to focus more on ending slavery.

African Americans and Slavery's End

Historians writing of the end of slavery in the United States once stressed the role of white abolitionists, sectionalism, and national political discord. Later studies recognize the role free blacks and slaves played in bringing the slavery issue to a head, turning the Civil War into a conflict to end slavery, and helping win the war.

Frustration and anger among free blacks boiled up around 1830 and brought action against slavery. The black Bostonian David Walker, in his 1829 *Appeal . . . to the Coloured Citizens of the World*, was unwavering about what slaves ought to do—"kill or be killed"—and about where free blacks stood: "Your full glory and happiness . . . shall never be fully consummated, but with the *entire emancipation of your enslaved brethren.*" At the same time the earliest black newspapers published calls for national meetings to address problems facing the African American community, and these meetings marked the start of a

trend among educated African Americans to focus their energies against slavery. Sometimes they did so with the assistance of whites and sometimes by themselves in writings and speeches. Frederick Douglass was one of the scores of escaped slaves who faced danger to spread awareness of slavery's evils. Through the 1840s black militancy heightened. In the 13 August 1841 edition of the *Liberator* the New Yorker David Ruggles exhorted slaves to "Strike for freedom or die slaves!" Similarly in 1843 Henry Highland Garnet, at a convention in Buffalo, New York, urged: "Strike for your lives and liberties. . . . Let every slave throughout the land do this, and the days of slavery are numbered."

Some slaves already had struck. Authorities foiled significant slave conspiracies around Richmond, Virginia, in 1800 and Charleston, South Carolina, in 1822, and no one stopped Nat Turner's band in Southampton County, Virginia, in 1831 until some sixty whites lay dead. But following Turner's uprising, white southerners tightened the restraints around slavery, so instead of revolting, as free blacks counseled, men and women in slavery struck out in individual attempts to escape. It remained for free blacks to help them once they were north of slavery's reach. The Underground Railroad involved bold flight without assistance until escapees were in the North. Slave owners believed northern abolitionists were more involved in an organized effort to steal their enslaved labor force and insisted on passage of the Fugitive Slave Act of 1850. As part of the Compromise of 1850, which involved California's admission as a free state and ending the slave trade in the District of Columbia, the Fugitive Slave Act made easier the apprehension of runaways and led to increased "vigilance" among northern free blacks. Vigilance sometimes extended to kidnapping and spiriting away alleged fugitives from the grasp of authorities.

Escape and vigilance were early activities in a struggle that escalated in the 1850s. Proslavery and antislavery forces shed blood in Kansas over slavery's extension after 1854. When the Supreme Court, in its 1857 *Dred Scott* decision, ruled that slaves were not citizens and that "a black man has no rights which a white man is bound to respect," more African Americans in and out of slavery considered desperate measures. Some thought anew of emigration, while others formed military groups to defend themselves or to participate in armed conflict. The white antislavery fighter John Brown received quiet support from black and white abolitionists in 1859 as he planned an assault on the federal arsenal at Harpers Ferry, Virginia, conceived as the first step toward a slave rebellion. Although Brown failed and was hanged, many white southerners viewed his raid as nearly the last straw. When Abraham Lincoln was elected president in 1860, southern states seceded and formed the Confederate States of America. The Confederates fired on Fort Sumter, a federal post off Charleston, South Carolina, in April 1861, leading Lincoln to call for volunteers to preserve the Union. Most African Americans, slave and free, had been awaiting such an occurrence.

The actions of slaves helped make the war one to end slavery. Soon after the outbreak slaves began fleeing and seeking refuge behind Union lines. Lincoln, who dared not irritate border state slave owners, was in a dilemma over these runaways. Congress eventually passed confiscation acts that freed fugitive slaves whom Confederates had used in the war effort. The farther south Federal forces reached, the more slaves sought freedom behind Federal lines. In the summer of 1862 Congress abolished slavery in U.S. territories and freed the fugitive slaves of Confederate masters. Lincoln issued the Emancipation Proclamation, directing that on 1 January 1863 "all persons held as slaves within any State, or designated part of the State, the people whereof shall be in rebellion against the United States, shall be then, thenceforward, and forever free." From that point no one doubted that a Union victory would end slavery.

The Union still had to win the long, bloody war, and African American soldiers were instrumental in that effort. Early prohibitions against black enlistment fell in the face of military necessity. In July 1862 Congress authorized Lincoln to enlist black troops, and by 1863 African Americans were pouring into the Union army. Black troops faced special difficulties, including lower rates of pay through much of the war. Black mortality rates were one-third higher than those of whites, the result of Confederate sentiments against taking black prisoners and duty at hard labor in difficult climates. By the war's end 186,000 black soldiers had fought for the Union, and 38,000 had died. The Thirteenth Amendment (1865) provided the constitutional guarantee of the freedom for which so many had fought and died.

Reconstruction

Reconstruction had two elements. One involved reestablishing social, economic, and political order in the defeated and devastated South and bringing southern states back into the Union. The other involved dealing with the four million African American men, women, and children freed by the war, a group largely illiterate, lacking property, and inexperienced in important aspects of life. A month before the war's end Congress created the Freedmen's Bureau to assist the former slaves, whose problems were indeed many.

Historical accounts of Reconstruction long focused on politics and reflected the racial views of the historians. Through the 1950s historians argued that the Radical Republicans in Congress forced black voting and officeholding on white southerners because the Radicals were intent on punishing the South and ensuring Republican ascendancy. In the 1960s the revisionists John Hope Franklin and Kenneth M. Stampp argued, from a belief in African American competence, that the Radicals acted out of an honest will to establish the basis for full African American citizenship. In 1988 Eric Foner suggested that Reconstruction was not radical enough because it failed to provide blacks with the basis for economic self-sufficiency.

Reuniting the North and South was difficult. Both Lincoln and his successor, Andrew Johnson, wanted easy terms, and Johnson permitted the southern states to form governments within months of the war's end. These all-white state governments, consisting of former Confederate officials and former slave owners, passed Black Codes designed to place the former slaves as close as possible to the subordinate, servile positions they held before the war. Such laws dictated binding labor contracts, denied freedpeople the right to bear arms, and in some states prohibited freedpeople's purchase of land. After Congress convened in December 1865, its Republican majority, over President Johnson's veto, passed a civil rights law that overturned the Black Codes and declared African Americans citizens. Congress placed the substance of that law in a proposed Fourteenth Amendment and required the former Confederate states to ratify the amendment prior to readmission to the Union. In 1867, after only Tennessee had been readmitted, Congress authorized black suffrage in the states of the defeated Confederacy (but not the rest of the nation). With the votes of black southerners the remaining states quickly ratified the Fourteenth Amendment and gained readmission. The Fifteenth Amendment (1870) solidified African Americans' right to vote.

Between 1870 and 1877 conservative white Democrats won control of the reconstructed states from the Republicans. In some states they did so merely by organizing their voting majorities, but in the Deep South, where more black voters lived, conservative whites used violence and intimidation to keep blacks from voting and used fraud in counting election returns. The Republican president Rutherford B. Hayes removed federal troops from the remaining southern states in 1877 as part of a deal that sealed his disputed election, and the South was thenceforth left alone to deal with its peculiar issues. The biggest issue was how to treat the large, mostly rural, poor, undereducated black population. Before the end of the century white southerners, unmolested by federal oversight, devised ways.

How could white southerners regain political control so rapidly? Foner asserted the answer had to do with issues outside the South. By the 1870s industrialism and class matters had replaced sectionalism in northern thinking. Wealthy leaders of northern industries, Republican in politics, held more affinity with southern planters and businesspeople than with poor workers. They were less concerned with the status and well-being of the former slaves and more likely to sit idly when conservative southerners resorted to violence to overthrow state governments, even Republican ones, that supported the rights of the lower classes. After 1877 northern whites became sufficiently involved in their own social and economic issues to leave the white South alone in its dealings with African Americans.

Through all of the political machinations, the former slaves struggled to make a living and to move ahead. With emancipation some left their rural homes and headed for one or another southern city. Unwelcome in business and residential districts, poor blacks came together in makeshift settlements on the cities' peripheries. These squatter colonies, where blacks lived without evident means of support, heightened white fears of the "black horde" and raised whites' desires to separate the races. The African Americans looked to the Freedmen's Bureau for such needs as food, medical care, clothing, and housing, then they searched for means to advance in a society in flux and lacking much of an economy. Ambitious former slaves sought education as the key to their rise, but they found schools inadequate, segregated, and unequal from the start.

In rural areas, where most of the formerly enslaved men, women, and children remained, white landowners, having failed with the Black Codes, turned to wage labor. The Freedmen's Bureau encouraged blacks to perform farm labor for wages, and this arrangement became the norm for southern African Americans by 1867. It was not something the former slaves cared for, however, since it meant paltry pay for daylong work in gangs as they had done in slavery. They wanted land—the proverbial forty acres and a mule—to establish their economic independence and improve life for their offspring.

But dirt-poor former slaves did not have money to buy land, and whites would not have sold them land anyway. Over the decade from 1868 to 1878 rural, southern African Americans opted for a system closer to land possession—farm tenancy, or sharecropping.

In this system a black family head negotiated with a landowner for a plot to live on and work, seed, tools, and a mule. In return the tenant pledged to the landowner a share of the crop at harvest, usually half. The tenant also arranged with the landowner or a nearby merchant for an advance of food, clothing, and other necessities on credit, which would be paid for, with interest, from proceeds of the sale of the crop. At harvest the landlord weighed the crop and took his share, then the tenant paid off the costs of his "furnish" with the remainder. In a good year, when market prices were high, tenants believed they could make enough on their remaining share to furnish their families through the next crop season and perhaps even save enough for the eventual renting or purchase of land. In practice this seldom happened. Landlords cheated on weights and prices, merchants' interest rates were usurious, and sharecroppers were powerless to do anything about injustice. State laws kept them from moving as long as they owed money and prescribed inheritance of debt. The result was a hopeless cycle of work, debt, and poverty that set the stage for southern black lives well into the twentieth century. By 1900 roughly three-quarters of all southern black farmers were tenants or sharecroppers.

In the face of massive northern indifference and lacking any basis for their own economic security, southern blacks were at the mercy of politically and economically powerful southern whites. This group of whites wanted to separate the races and ensure African Americans' absolute subordinance and servility by the century's end. Such was the basis for the Jim Crow era, which swept across the South in the 1890s and lasted for more than half a century.

Jim Crow

Legally sanctioned segregation and disfranchisement did not descend upon southern blacks immediately following the removal of federal troops in 1877. In *The Strange Career of Jim Crow* (1955), C. Vann Woodward pointed out forgotten alternatives of interracial coexistence and cooperation in the 1880s, blaming political frustrations of the Populist era of the early 1890s for the rush to disfranchisement and segregation after 1895. Joel Williamson, in *The Crucible of Race* (1984), credited psychological pressures on the part of southern white men. Economic depression rendered them unable to fulfill their accepted role of family protector, so they created a perceived threat, the "black rapist beast," from which they could protect others, especially white women. In either case the result was violence, intimidation, disfranchisement, and segregation, the hallmarks of the age, aimed at African Americans. The Supreme

Court's decision in *Plessy v. Ferguson* (1896), allowing separate public facilities as long as they were equal, was a sham. Virtually everything quickly became separate, but almost nothing was equal. In support, pseudoscientific racism accompanied white imperialism. White ministers, professors, politicians, and novelists portrayed blacks as lesser humans, dangerous to white civilization, incapable of self-government, and impossible to educate.

As the century neared its end, assumptions about race relations ran a circuitous path. Whites argued that because of their nature African Americans could not succeed as whites did. When blacks were successful, threatened whites reacted violently, rioting, burning, and lynching. Finding themselves in danger if they made any show of economic or social progress, enterprising African Americans stifled their ambition. Whites used the absence of black ambition and success to confirm their ideas about black inferiority.

Remarkably in such circumstances many African Americans clung to a faith in progress through hard work and thrift. Booker T. Washington, the builder of Tuskegee Institute in Alabama, championed these ideas. In 1895, giving an address in Atlanta, he encouraged fellow African Americans to accept second-class citizenship, work in manual labor, and rely on white goodwill. Consequently whites regarded Washington as a race leader. Others, like the Harvard-educated W. E. B. Du Bois, who advocated the highest education for race leaders and constant agitation for equal rights, were regarded as dangerous radicals. Blacks who failed to keep their "place" and follow the accommodationist doctrine faced terror, as evidenced by the 754 African Americans lynched in the first decade of the twentieth century.

Outside the South, African Americans fared only marginally better. Most northern blacks lived in cities. A small, urban black middle class continued to provide services for whites and others like themselves, though their access to skilled trades narrowed. By the century's end northern African Americans congregated in small urban neighborhoods, tiny predecessors of the larger ghettos that emerged with the dramatic northward migration of blacks in the twentieth century. Black women, who found work more easily, outnumbered men in these neighborhoods. By the 1890s African Americans in northern cities had to compete with the growing tide of European immigrants. Although the immigrants were no more educated or skilled than blacks, they had the advantage of race, so they advanced more rapidly.

America's black population a generation and more removed from slavery remained much as it was in 1800—at the very bottom of American society. With his finger on the pulse of American race relations, Du Bois in 1903 expressed the legacy of the nineteenth-century African American experience. "The problem of the twentieth century," he wrote in *The Souls of Black Folk*, "is the problem of the color-line."

See also **Constitutional Amendments**, *subentry on* **Thirteen, Fourteenth, and Fifteenth Amendments; Reconstruction; Slavery.**

Bibliography

Ayers, Edward L. *The Promise of the New South: Life after Reconstruction.* New York: Oxford University Press, 1992.

Berlin, Ira. *Slaves without Masters: The Free Negro in the Antebellum South.* New York: Pantheon, 1974.

Berlin, Ira, and Philip D. Morgan, eds. *Cultivation and Culture: Labor and the Shaping of Slave Life in the Americas.* Charlottesville: University Press of Virginia, 1993.

Blassingame, John W. *The Slave Community: Plantation Life in the Antebellum South.* New York: Oxford University Press, 1972.

Du Bois, W. E. B. *The Souls of Black Folk.* Edited by David W. Blight and Robert Gooding-Williams. Boston: Bedford Books, 1997. The original edition, *The Souls of Black Folks: Essays and Sketches,* was published in 1903.

Elkins, Stanley. *Slavery: A Problem in American Institutional and Intellectual Life.* 1959. 2d ed., Chicago: University of Chicago Press, 1968.

Foner, Eric. *Reconstruction: America's Unfinished Revolution, 1863–1877.* New York: Harper and Row, 1988.

Franklin, John Hope. *Reconstruction: After the Civil War.* Chicago: University of Chicago Press, 1961.

Franklin, John Hope, and Loren Schweninger. *Runaway Slaves: Rebels on the Plantation.* New York: Oxford University Press, 1999.

Hinks, Peter P. *To Awaken My Afflicted Brethren: David Walker and the Problem of Antebellum Slave Resistance.* University Park: Pennsylvania State University Press, 1997.

Horton, James Oliver, and Lois E. Horton. *In Hope of Liberty: Culture, Community, and Protest among Northern Free Blacks, 1700–1860.* New York: Oxford University Press, 1997.

Litwack, Leon F. *Been in the Storm So Long: The Aftermath of Slavery.* New York: Knopf, 1979.

———. *North of Slavery: The Negro in the Free States, 1790–1860.* Chicago: University of Chicago Press, 1961.

———. *Trouble in Mind: Black Southerners in the Age of Jim Crow.* New York: Knopf, 1998.

Phillips, Ulrich B. *American Negro Slavery: A Survey of the Supply, Employment, and Control of Negro Labor as Determined by the Plantation Regime.* New York: D. Appleton, 1918.

Stampp, Kenneth M. *The Era of Reconstruction, 1865–1877.* New York: Knopf, 1965.

———. *The Peculiar Institution: Slavery in the Antebellum South.* New York: Vintage, 1956.

Tadman, Michael. *Speculators and Slaves: Masters, Traders, and Slaves in the Old South.* Madison: University of Wisconsin Press, 1989.

Walker, David. *Appeal, in Four Articles; Together with a Preamble, to the Coloured Citizens of the World, but in Particular, and Very Expressly, to Those of the United States of America.*

Boston: D. Walker, 1829. The full text of the pamphlet is published in Herbert Aptheker, ed. *"One Continual Cry": David Walker's Appeal to the Colored Citizens of the World, 1829–1830: Its Setting and Its Meaning.* New York: Humanities Press, 1965.

Williamson, Joel. *The Crucible of Race: Black-White Relations in the American South since Emancipation.* New York: Oxford University Press, 1984.

Woodward, C. Vann. *The Strange Career of Jim Crow.* 1955. 3d rev. ed., New York: Oxford University Press, 1974.

DONALD R. WRIGHT

FREE BLACKS BEFORE THE CIVIL WAR

In 1860 more than 10 percent of the black population in the United States was free. Over half, 261,918, of the nation's 488,070 free blacks lived in the South. In an antebellum America that justified slavery on theories of black inferiority and dependency, free blacks often lived under stringent social and legal restrictions. Most endured severe legal disabilities and strong social and occupational discrimination. A small number lived in the few states where the law recognized a formal equality between blacks and whites. A few were even substantial slaveholders. The story of the antebellum free black population is multilayered, involving the quest for individual freedom, the effort to develop communities and institutions, and the larger struggle against castelike discrimination and slavery.

Origins

Free people of African descent had always lived in the American colonies. Some of the first Africans brought to the American colonies in the seventeenth century were treated like indentured servants and were freed after several years of service. Others purchased their freedom, were freed in wills, or seized freedom by running away. Nonetheless, it took the American Revolution to create a large, permanent class of free blacks. The libertarian sentiments unleashed by the Revolution played a large part in this development. A number of black men in the North had been freed in reward for their service with American forces during the Revolution. Responding to strong antislavery sentiments in the late eighteenth century, northern states began the process of legally abolishing slavery. Some states, including Pennsylvania, New York, and Rhode Island, passed gradual emancipation statutes, freeing people born after the enactment of the legislation. These individuals were usually required to serve as indentured servants, often into their twenties. In other states courts declared slavery incompatible with the equal rights provisions of their state constitutions. The most famous of these cases, *Commonwealth v. Jennison*, involving the slave Quock Walker, outlawed slavery in Massachusetts in 1783.

The discomfort with slavery that brought about emancipation in the North was felt to a lesser extent in the South, particularly the Upper South. Slavery was considerably stronger in the South than in the North, precluding general emancipation. Nonetheless, a considerable amount of private manumission occurred in the late eighteenth century. The ranks of free blacks in Maryland, Virginia, and North Carolina also increased because economic conditions in those states enabled some slaves to earn money and purchase their freedom. That region also had a strong demand for the labor of free blacks.

Progress and Retreat

The liberal post-Revolution sentiment that played such an important role in the expansion of the free black class rapidly yielded to harsher, less egalitarian sentiments in the nineteenth century. Southern states enacted legislation limiting private manumissions, and a number of western states passed laws restricting black settlement. In the nineteenth century a majority of states disfranchised black men, even though most states had allowed black men with property to vote immediately after the Revolution. As the nineteenth century progressed, southern states enacted increasingly restrictive measures designed to limit the basic civil rights of free blacks, including the rights to travel without a pass, to testify in court, to peacefully assemble, to own weapons, and to practice various professions, such as pharmacy and printing.

In the North the legal restrictions were considerably less severe, yet strong antiblack sentiment was evident, particularly in the cities, where the majority of blacks lived. A number of northern cities experienced vicious antiblack riots in the 1820s and 1830s. Racial attitudes also led to legal segregation of public schools and discrimination in public accommodations. Racism precluded most black workers from getting any but the most dangerous and menial jobs. Northern laws, unlike southern laws, recognized that free African Americans should enjoy basic civil rights, but political rights, such as voting and serving on juries, were frequently denied.

The Northern Experience— Community Adaptation and Struggle

In the cities of the North, free African Americans had sufficient freedom and large enough numbers to develop the community institutions that both sustained the African American culture that developed

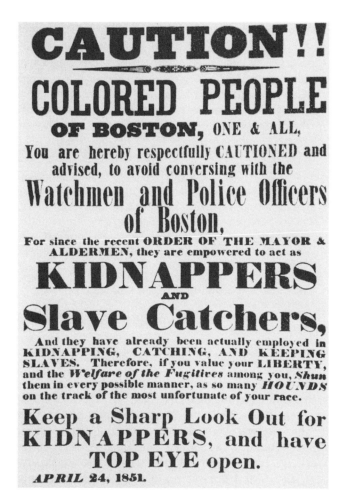

CAUTION!!

COLORED PEOPLE

OF BOSTON, ONE & ALL,

You are hereby respectfully CAUTIONED and advised, to avoid conversing with the

Watchmen and Police Officers of Boston,

For since the recent ORDER OF THE MAYOR & ALDERMEN, they are empowered to act as

KIDNAPPERS

AND

Slave Catchers,

And they have already been actually employed in KIDNAPPING, CATCHING, AND KEEPING SLAVES. Therefore, if you value your LIBERTY, and the *Welfare of the Fugitives* among you, *Shun* them in every possible manner, as so many *HOUNDS* on the track of the most unfortunate of your race.

Keep a Sharp Look Out for KIDNAPPERS, and have TOP EYE open.

APRIL 24, 1851.

Effects of the Fugitive Slave Law in the North. Handbill dated 24 April 1851, warning African Americans in Boston to beware of enforcement of the Fugitive Slave Law of 1850. Despite the passage of personal liberty acts in the North, free blacks, like fugitive slaves, could be seized by southerners. LIBRARY OF CONGRESS

during nearly two hundred years of northern slavery and functioned as vehicles for community betterment and protest. Churches emerged as the first of these institutions. Richard Allen founded the earliest denomination, the African Methodist Episcopal Church, in Philadelphia in 1787. Northern blacks established independent denominations soon after emancipation to escape the prevailing discrimination in white congregations. Black churches anchored schools, self-improvement organizations, temperance societies, and civil-rights groups.

Northern blacks almost constantly struggled against strong discrimination and prejudice in the antebellum era. Most opposed the efforts of the American Colonization Society to expatriate free blacks, who in turn provided important support to the abolitionist effort. Frederick Douglass, a former slave

from Maryland, gained international renown as a spokesman and writer for the abolitionist cause while living in New York and Massachusetts in the 1840s and 1850s. Sojourner Truth, a black woman, was a well-known antislavery orator in the decades before the Civil War. Other notable blacks, such as William Wells Brown, the Reverend Henry Highland Garnet, and William C. Nell, were prominent in national and international antislavery circles.

The American civil rights movement, which enjoyed national triumphs in the 1960s, originated in the protest movements of the free blacks in the antebellum North, dating from Paul Cuffe's successful protests against voter discrimination in Massachusetts in the 1780s. The movement continued throughout the North in the nineteenth century, particularly in reaction to new restrictions on suffrage, segregation in common schools and public accommodations, and bans on interracial marriages. Free blacks made their greatest gains in the struggles for political and civil rights in New England. They successfully reversed disfranchisement in Rhode Island in 1842. Massachusetts repealed the ban on interracial marriages in 1843 and passed legislation outlawing segregated schools in 1855.

Free blacks came close to achieving de jure equality in New England but made less progress elsewhere. Black men could not vote outside of New England and New York. John Mercer Langston, one of the few black attorneys in the nation, held public office in Ohio in the 1850s even though blacks could not vote in that state at the time. Blacks also held minor offices in Massachusetts and Rhode Island before the Civil War. Most northern states accorded blacks a wide array of civil rights other than political rights and passed personal liberty laws designed to protect free blacks from fugitive slave hunters. It should also be noted that most northern states allowed blacks to settle within their boundaries. Most states also made some provision for the education of black children in public schools.

The Southern Experience— Between Slavery and Freedom

Conditions were generally considerably grimmer in the South. Many southerners viewed the very existence of the free black population as a threat to the institution of slavery. Because white slaveholders justified slavery on the grounds of black inferiority, free blacks, with their ability to support themselves and their families, embarrassingly contradicted the prevailing ideology. More importantly slave owners feared free blacks as potential allies for and leaders of rebellious slaves, as indeed they were during such uprisings as the Denmark Vesey rebellion in 1822.

Because free blacks were an unwelcome presence in the antebellum South, they faced severe restrictions. Historians have characterized them as "inmates on parole" (Genovese, *Roll, Jordan Roll*, p. 399), or as Ira Berlin titled his 1975 book, "slaves without masters." They were denied the civil rights enjoyed by white Americans and northern blacks in the antebellum era. In some states blacks were not allowed to learn to read, to enter certain professions, or to own property. Unlike their northern counterparts, free blacks in the South had few enforceable legal rights and largely relied on the goodwill of whites in their communities for protection and survival. Excluding North Carolina and Tennessee, where free blacks could vote until the mid-1830s, they had no political rights in the antebellum South.

Among free blacks in the antebellum South, Louisiana's francophonic mulatto population, called *gens de couleur libre*, was an anomaly. In a pattern that resembled the multitiered racial classification systems in Latin America, the *gens de couleur libre* were treated as a third race by law and custom. They could testify against whites in the courts, and many were substantial slaveholders. Some even openly voted although it was illegal. South Carolina had a visible class of wealthy free mulattoes, some of whom owned slaves. Their rights and privileges, however, were less extensive than those of the *gens de couleur libre*.

Conclusion

Despite bleak circumstances, antebellum free blacks carved out a niche for themselves, their families, and their communities. Their limited success in securing civil rights in the North and their survival in the South were testaments to persistence and courage. Some, like the newspaper editor John Russwurm, the essayist William C. Nell, the actor Ira Aldridge, the businessman James Forten, and the lawyers Robert Morris and John Mercer Langston, achieved remarkable successes. Most lived humble lives, not slaves but not totally free.

See also **Abolition and Antislavery; African Americans; Civil Rights; Colonization, African American; Education,** *subentry on* **Education of African Americans; Emancipation; Newspapers, African American; Race and Racial Thinking; Race Laws; Segregation and Civil Rights; Segregation, Urban; Slavery,** *subentries on* **Slave Insurrections, Defense of Slavery.**

Bibliography

Berlin, Ira. *Slaves without Masters: The Free Negro in the Antebellum South.* New York: Pantheon, 1975.

Cottrol, Robert J. *The Afro-Yankees: Providence's Black Community in the Antebellum Era.* Westport, Conn.: Greenwood, 1982.

Curry, Leonard P. *The Free Black in Urban America, 1800–1850: The Shadow of the Dream.* Chicago: University of Chicago Press, 1981.

Finkelman, Paul. "Prelude to the Fourteenth Amendment: Black Legal Rights in the Antebellum North." *Rutgers Law Journal* 17 (spring and summer 1986): 415–482.

Genovese, Eugene D. *Roll, Jordan, Roll: The World the Slaves Made.* New York: Vintage, 1976.

Horton, James Oliver, and Lois E. Horton. *In Hope of Liberty: Culture, Community, and Protest among Northern Free Blacks, 1700–1860.* New York: Oxford University Press, 1997.

Johnson, Michael P., and James L. Roark. *Black Masters: A Free Family of Color in the Old South.* New York: Norton, 1984.

Litwack, Leon F. *North of Slavery: The Negro in the Free States, 1790–1860.* Chicago: University of Chicago Press, 1961.

ROBERT J. COTTROL

BLACKS IN THE WEST

While nineteenth-century African Americans usually are identified with living in the South, many settled in the western United States during this period. Blacks often met the same prejudicial attitudes in the West that had prompted them to leave the South, but they also found greater opportunities for economic and social gain in the West.

Slavery

Slavery flourished in some parts of the West, particularly in Texas and the Indian Territory. In 1860, over 180,000 African Americans were enslaved in Texas—30 percent of the state's population—and over 7,000 were enslaved in the Indian Territory—14 percent of the territory's population. Elsewhere, by 1860 slavery had been outlawed in every other state and territory in the region, with the exception of Utah. Nonetheless, significant tensions over slavery, especially during the 1850s in California, New Mexico, and Kansas, illustrate the pervasiveness of the institution during the mid–nineteenth century.

The African American experience in the West began with the travails of a single slave. York (d. 1833?), a black slave who accompanied the Lewis and Clark expedition (1804–1806), embodied the subsequent experiences of African Americans in the West. York's owner, Lieutenant William Clark (1770–1838), found him invaluable as a scout and hand on the expedition, especially when the party encountered Indians. The Native Americans, especially the Arikaras in present-day South Dakota, were enamored of York and negotiated with Meriwether Lewis (1774–1809) and Clark in part because of their belief that York was exotic. Upon the party's return to the East, York argued that he should be granted his freedom in exchange for his services on the trip, but Clark refused initially. Eventually, Clark freed York, whose emancipation was a precursor of attempts by slaves to use the free, western states as sources for liberty.

Like York, some enslaved African Americans were able to use the states of the West as springboards to freedom. In the 1850s several slaves in California argued successfully that because they were in a free state, they should be granted their freedom. The 1857 *Dred Scott* decision, however, ended this precedent until after the Civil War.

Fur Traders, Cowboys, and Buffalo Soldiers

Slaves made up a small fraction of the African Americans who experienced the West. Jim Beckwourth (1798–c. 1866), a black fur trader who assisted General Stephen Watts Kearny (1794–1848) during the California Bear Flag Rebellion, discovered a pass through the Sierra Nevada that shortened the land route to the Pacific Coast. Like Beckwourth, many free blacks sought greater economic opportunity in the West and migrated to California during the 1849 gold rush. By 1860, in spite of increasing racial prejudice, over four thousand African Americans lived in California, accounting for more than half the black population in the western states. For those not prospecting for gold, San Francisco became a hub of urban African American culture, with prominent black mutual benefit societies and the first African American newspaper in the West, *Mirror of the Times* (1856).

In the 1850s, many African American men began working in the cattle business. Some of these cowboys were born and raised in the Southwest, especially Texas, and remained there to work on ranches and cattle drives. After the Civil War, in order to escape persistent racism, blacks living in the Southeast moved to the West in search of jobs as cowhands. One such figure, Nat "Deadwood Dick" Love (1854–1921), was born a slave in Tennessee, settled in Texas following the Civil War, and became a highly regarded hand for cattle drives from Texas to the Upper West. Although black and Mexican American cowboys were underrepresented in twentieth-century movies about the West, both groups made up about 2 percent of the cowboy population.

Perhaps the best-known African Americans living in the West were black infantrymen and cavalrymen who, as part of the U.S. Army, fought in the Indian wars of the late nineteenth century. Deemed "buffalo soldiers" by their Indian enemies, the African American soldiers of the Ninth and Tenth Cavalries and Twenty-fourth and Twenty-fifth Infantries were organized in 1866 despite opposition by Lieutenant General William Sherman (1820–1891). Although they were poorly equipped and endured racism within the army, the buffalo soldiers took pride in their units and adopted the buffalo as their symbol. Led by white officers, the black regiments were instrumental in the wars against the Apaches in the 1870s and 1880s. In December 1890, the Ninth Cavalry played an important role at the Battle of Wounded Knee, South Dakota, in which the U.S. government effectively ended the Indian threat to white settlement of the West.

"Exodusters" and Late-Century Migrants

The prejudice and racism in the South and East that drove African American prospectors, fur traders, and cowboys to migrate west in the mid–nineteenth century prompted several thousand former slaves to do the same after the Civil War. Black tenant farmers living in the Deep South, disgruntled over broken government promises for free land in their home states, began moving to Kansas in the 1860s. These "exodusters" sought better social conditions and a more promising agricultural future in the little-populated state. By 1880, following Benjamin "Pap Moses" Singleton (1809–c. 1889) and Henry Adams (b. 1843), over twenty-five thousand transplanted black farmers had migrated to Kansas.

In 1878, after the African American political leader and migration proponent Edwin P. McCabe (b. 1850) moved to Kansas's best-known black settlement, Nicodemus, many white Kansans sought the prevention of black settlement in white towns. Avoiding another area of prejudice, black migrants found new hope in Oklahoma, where ten thousand African Americans used the Unsettled Lands Act of 1889 to claim parcels of newly opened, former Indian lands. Between 1890 and 1910, black migrants founded twenty-eight communities in Oklahoma, and the territory's black population increased by 53 percent. McCabe also moved to Oklahoma, where he founded Langston City, named after the African American leader and congressman from Virginia John Mercer Langston (1829–1897). McCabe's town quickly became populated, and he sparked the development of a vibrant, western black culture by creating Langston University and the *Langston City Herald*, one of the sixty African American, western newspapers that had begun publication by 1900.

Thus, after nearly a century of migrating westward, blacks finally had gained a foothold in the region. At the close of the nineteenth century, 765,000 African Americans lived in the West (specifically, the area bounded by the Pacific Ocean to the west and by the Missouri River, Oklahoma, and Texas to the east). Although much prejudice existed in the region, many blacks prospered from the economic and social opportunities they found in the West.

See also **African Americans,** *subentries on* **Overview, Free Blacks Before the Civil War, Blacks in the Military; Cowboys and Cowgirls; Gold Rushes and Silver Strikes; Indian Territory.**

Bibliography

Ambrose, Stephen E. *Undaunted Courage: Meriwether Lewis, Thomas Jefferson, and the Opening of the American West.* New York: Simon and Schuster, 1996.

Billington, Monroe Lee, and Roger D. Hardaway, eds. *African Americans on the Western Frontier.* Niwot: University Press of Colorado, 1998.

Katz, William Loren. *The Black West: A Documentary and Pictorial History of the African American Role in the Westward Expansion of the United States.* New York: Simon and Schuster, 1996.

Savage, W. Sherman. *Blacks in the West.* Westport, Conn.: Greenwood Press, 1976.

Taylor, Quintard. *In Search of the Racial Frontier: African Americans in the American West, 1528–1990.* New York: Norton, 1998.

KEVIN ROBERTS

BLACKS IN THE MILITARY

America's African American community waged a war against the military establishment to secure the right to fight for the United States. After the War of 1812, the states disbanded black militia companies. Louisiana was the last to do so in 1834. Yet African Americans continued to petition government for the right to train and fight. This guerrilla war of the antebellum period became a frontal attack on the United States Army during the Civil War, establishing the courage and ability of African Americans in combat. The U.S. Navy did not establish a color line during the century, and many black sailors fought during wartime with uncommon valor. Until the Civil War the pattern in the U.S. Army was one of black troops led by white officers. This was the army's way of telling African Americans that they must be led by, trained by, and disciplined by the dominant racial culture of the country. During and after the Civil War, a few blacks served as officers, but most black troops remained under white control.

During the War of 1812 some African Americans enrolled in state units, such as New York's two regiments of colored troops, but the war's black heroes fought with Oliver Hazard Perry (1785–1819) in the Battle of Lake Erie. Perry praised their bravery and declared that they were "insensible to danger." Another group of blacks fought with Andrew Jackson (1767–1845) at the Battle of New Orleans. Responding to Jackson's appeal "To the Free Colored Inhabitants of Louisiana," two battalions of black volunteers stood with Jackson's men behind the cotton bales to defeat British regulars.

The Civil War was the testing ground for the American military policy and the battle for the right to fight. Lincoln's call for volunteers spurred free blacks throughout the North to volunteer, but they were turned away. In spite of this slight, black volunteers formed companies, equipped themselves, and drilled, awaiting the call to service. Not hearing the call to battle from Washington or a statehouse, blacks began petitioning for the right to fight. Some field commanders accepted their service. General James H. Lane (1833–1907) formed two black regiments in Kansas. Benjamin Butler (1818–1893) had a regiment of free Louisiana blacks in his New Orleans command. Petitions and necessity resulted in Congress's 1862 repeal of the ban against black enlistment contained in the 1792 Militia Act. In 1863 numerous commanders formed black regiments, and in May the War Department formed the U.S. Bureau of Colored Troops to facilitate the formation of black regiments. By October fifty-eight regiments were ready for action, but many white military men doubted their efficiency in combat.

The fact that black soldiers could indeed endure combat with distinction was quickly evidenced. General Nathaniel P. Banks's (1816–1894) report on the Corp D'Afrique's performance at the Battle of Port Hudson made it clear that they were effective. The valor of the Fifty-fourth Massachusetts Infantry regiment at Fort Wagner in July 1863 received national praise.

Despite demonstrated performance in the face of the enemy, Congress had not provided blacks with equal pay. The Fifty-fourth and Fifty-fifth Massachusetts Infantry regiments refused all pay as a protest. Frederick Douglass (c. 1817–1895) and other African American leaders protested and lobbied President Lincoln for redress of this injustice. Finally in June 1864 Congress acted to provide equal pay for black and white soldiers.

In addition to unequal pay, black soldiers endured the lack of opportunity for promotion, and suffered from inferior weapons, equipment, and supplies; inadequate medical care, resulting in death from disease at a rate two and one-half times that of whites;

Company G, 9th U.S. Volunteer Infantry, 1899. Company G was among the large numbers of black soldiers that fought in the Spanish-American War, including the charge at San Juan Hill, for which Teddy Roosevelt's Rough Riders received credit. LIBRARY OF CONGRESS

and the knowledge that if captured they might be executed or sold into slavery. Further, most of their white officers made them dig, haul, feed, and slop rather than walk as equals with white soldiers. In addition military punishment was excessively harsh, abusive, and more frequently visited upon blacks than whites.

By October 1864 the U.S. Army had 140 black regiments. By the end of the war, 186,000 black men had served in 449 engagements, 39 of them major battles, and 17 soldiers and 4 sailors had been awarded the Congressional Medal of Honor. Black heroism under fire became a fact of military record.

The Reconstruction Congress pared black military strength down to six regiments in 1866, four of infantry and two of cavalry. This was further whittled down in 1869 to two of infantry, the Twenty-fourth and Twenty-fifth, and two of cavalry, the Ninth and

Tenth. These "buffalo soldiers" fought American Indians in the West from 1866 until 1890. In the nearly thirty years of campaigning against some of the greatest irregular warfare experts in the world, these black men fought in 2,704 engagements and were awarded sixteen Congressional Medals of Honor. Sergeant George Jordan was awarded a Medal of Honor for his May 1880 defense of Tularosa, New Mexico, with twenty-four soldiers of the Ninth Cavalry against Victorio's Apache band. Valor in closing with the enemy distinguished buffalo soldiers, and racism characterized far too many of the white settlements they defended, particularly in Texas.

Another aspect of the battle for the right to fight was the demand for access to leadership. Admission to West Point was a critical segment of the campaign. The first black won admission to the United States Military Academy at West Point in 1870. In 1877

Henry O. Flipper (1856–1940) was the first black to graduate, followed by John H. Alexander in 1887 and Charles Young (1864–1922) in 1889. Between 1866 and 1898 eight blacks won commissions as chaplains in the United States Army. Henry V. Plummer was a former slave and Civil War naval veteran who entered army service in 1884. Allen Allensworth also was a slave and navy veteran of the Civil War and entered army service two years later. Theophilus G. Steward won an army commission in 1891, George W. Prioleau in 1895, and William T. Anderson in 1897. As black chaplains they lived within a socially segregated military community. Plummer's experience in the Ninth Cavalry was one of social distance from white officers and their families, but officially very friendly relations in public. Allensworth was most successful forging educational programs that made a difference in soldiers' lives. Plummer was noted for success until he argued for social reforms, advocated temperance, and fought for the redress of grievances for himself and other black soldiers. The army reacted with a court-martial for conduct unbecoming an officer and gentleman and dismissal from the service in 1894.

War with Spain again brought military necessity and American racism into focus within the army. President McKinley's (1843–1901) war message sent all four black regiments to Florida for the invasion force and issued a call for volunteers, including regiments of "immunes," soldiers, assumed to be black, who possessed "immunity from diseases incident to tropical climates." These state regiments drew thousands of black volunteers, but the adjutant general instructed the governors not to commission any black officers. That set off a storm of protest resulting in the agreement to commission one hundred black second lieutenants for service only with the immune regiments. Service as officers in the immune regiments did not lead to permanent officer rank; regular army enlisted men who had been made commissioned officers in immune regiments had to return as enlisted men to the regular army or resign. Thus the army elite was still white.

The states responded and created black units of volunteers: the Third North Carolina, Third Alabama, Eighth Illinois, Twenty-third Kansas, and Sixth Virginia regiments; two companies from Indiana; the Ninth Ohio Battalion; and Company L, Sixth Massachusetts. (Texas blacks offered their services, but the governor turned them down.) These units remained stateside during the war, but their very formation and some of the racial hostility that followed clearly demonstrated the blatant racism within the country.

The racism that existed despite black willingness to fight was best demonstrated in the "Charge at San Juan Hill." The black buffalo soldiers of the Ninth and Tenth Cavalry led the charge, constituting 70 percent of the assault force, and took 63 percent of the casualties. But Colonel Theodore Roosevelt's Rough Riders passed through the dead and dying of the Ninth and Tenth and took credit for the victory. It was what white America expected and what the press pandered to. But as one white officer in the assault wrote, it was "the negros [that] saved that fight." Black heroism in the face of the enemy was again ignored by a public who wanted white heroes and an army that refused to recognize it.

The Spanish-American War also brought out the dark side of American attitudes toward African Americans in uniform. With the war against Spain over and an insurrection in the Philippines beginning, the army sent three of the four black regiments to the Philippines. The fourth traveled to Fort Logan near Denver, but the protests from white residents was so loud that the army replaced it with a white regiment. This foreshadowed the most disgraceful racial incident in army history. At Brownsville, Texas, in 1906 members of a battalion of the Twenty-fifth Infantry retaliated against a pattern of racist attacks with a shooting incident that left one dead and two white civilians wounded. In the investigation that followed, the army found that none of the men would testify against a fellow soldier. President Theodore Roosevelt, angered by this "conspiracy of silence," discharged the entire battalion. Roosevelt's action gave black troops a stigma that followed them in times of peace and into World War I.

The century closed with African Americans still waging their battle for the right to fight and be noticed by their nation. For Benjamin O. Davis (1880–1970), the Spanish-American War was the beginning of a career as an officer of volunteers, an enlisted man in the regular army, and ultimately a commissioned officer in the regular army and its first black general. The sacrifices of generations of black soldiers bore fruit in the next century.

See also **Army; Civil War,** *subentry on* **Black Soldiers; Navy; Race and Racial Thinking; Spanish-American War; War of 1812.**

Bibliography

Bolster, W. Jeffrey. *Black Jacks: African American Seamen in the Age of Sail.* Cambridge, Mass.: Harvard University Press, 1997.

Cornish, Dudley Taylor. *The Sable Arm: Black Troops in the Union Army, 1861–1865.* Lawrence: University of Kansas Press, 1987.

Fletcher, Marvin E. *America's First Black General: Benjamin*

O. Davis, Sr., 1880–1970. Lawrence: University of Kansas Press, 1989.

———. *The Black Soldier and Officer in the United States Army, 1891–1917*. Columbia: University of Missouri Press, 1974.

———. "The Black Volunteer in the Spanish-American War." *Military Affairs* 38 (April 1974): 48–53.

Leckie, William H. *The Buffalo Soldiers: A Narrative of the Negro Cavalry in the West*. Norman: University of Oklahoma Press, 1967.

Taylor, Quintard. *In Search of the Racial Frontier: African Americans in the American West, 1528–1990*. New York: Norton, 1998.

GORDON MORRIS BAKKEN

AFRICAN AMERICAN RELIGIONS

While the slave trade flourished, colonial authorities discouraged mission work among Africans. Many planters doubted that the Africans had souls worth saving. Slave conversions to Christianity intensified in the first half of the eighteenth century during a period of intense revivals known as the Great Awakening. Evangelicals believed in religious egalitarianism, and a scattering of independent black churches were founded in the South. Nevertheless, African religious traditions survived and were reinforced by the continued importation of African slaves, often after a time of "seasoning" in the West Indies. The end of the influx began after the American Revolution when the Continental Congress took up the matter of the closure of the external slave trade.

With the abolition on 1 January 1808 of the legal importation of slaves, the African American experience in the United States took on a more indigenous character. Blacks and whites found themselves in close proximity, and native-born blacks struggled to create a religious culture out of the shards of beliefs and traditions of West Africa and the gleanings white Christians were willing to leave them.

Slave Religion

When the nineteenth century began, nine out of ten African Americans lived in the South. Many thousands had been exposed to Christianity, but those who were church members or adherents probably accounted for not more than 10 percent of the total African American population. A number of independent black congregations existed, and they were generally Baptist, such as the First African Church of Savannah, founded in 1788 and led by Andrew Bryan. White evangelicals had yet to make a concerted effort to reach the more than 800,000 individuals counted as slaves.

In some places, such as among the Gullah peoples of the Sea Island district of South Carolina and in Louisiana, where Roman Catholicism and West Indian-derived practices of voodoo intermixed, religious syncretism was so strong as to violate orthodox Protestant sensibilities. In 1829 the Reverend William Capers appealed to plantation owners in South Carolina to allow him to go to their slaves. Supporters of plantation missions were motivated by the biblical mandate to share the gospel, but they also wanted to rid the slaves of their "heathen" ways and, as Capers argued, improve plantation efficiency on the premise that a Christian slave would be more obedient.

Nat Turner's insurrection in 1831 cast doubt on Capers's assertion, but gradually many in the white South were won over to the notion that lessons on salvation and lessons on duty were compatible. In addition many were convinced that the South had a divine mandate to convert and civilize the "children of Ham," as Africans were often called because of the proslavery interpretation of the story told in Genesis 9. When abolitionists chastised southerners for the sin of slavery, the apologists of "the peculiar institution" pointed to plantation missions as evidence of their fulfillment of the Christian duty to civilize and convert and of the legitimacy of their custodial rule over "the darker race."

Just how strongly, if at all, African American slaves internalized the religious model placed before them by whites is an important question. Was the Christian slave successfully indoctrinated with the notion that piety and obedience were inseparable? Or did Christianity as expressed in the secret or "hush arbor" meetings of slaves, in their prayers, and in their songs or spirituals offer a basis from which both individual psychological independence and organized resistance could spring forth? Frederick Douglass reported that he observed fellow slaves who scoffed at the religious pretensions of whites. Writing in his autobiography (1846), he personally found hypocrisy at the root of slaveholding Christianity, which he termed "bad, corrupt, and wicked." But he thought of the true Christianity of Christ as impartial and "good, pure, and holy." If we are to judge by the testimony of former slaves, many of whom eagerly sought to read the Bible for themselves once freedom came, they had successfully appropriated Christianity to give meaning to their lives and cope with the slaveholders' systematic efforts to deny their humanity. It is estimated that one in seven adult slaves belonged to an organized church, usually Baptist or Methodist, by the time of the Civil War, and many more had been exposed to the influence of Christianity.

The religious outlook of African American slaves

Bishops of the African Methodist Episcopal Church. Portraits include Richard Allen (1760–1831, *center*), a former slave who purchased his freedom in 1786 and established the first church for African Americans one year later in Philadelphia. He was a founder of the African Methodist Episcopal Church and served as its bishop from 1816 to 1831. LIBRARY OF CONGRESS: PRINTS AND PHOTOGRAPHS DIVISION

was a complex and highly creative adaptation of European Christianity and African traditional religion to their everyday needs. A few rejected Christianity altogether in favor of Islam or became skeptics. Others sought out the protection and power of the conjurer, but after a period of religious instruction and Christian baptism, many came to the conclusion that conjuring was the work of the devil. Although masters attempted to enforce discipline through Christianity, most slaves heard the sermons preached in the plantation chapels with a critical ear, sorted out the wheat from the chaff, and constructed a religious story in which they were the chosen of God. Although they might have, as the spirituals reflect, trouble and sorrow in this world, they could hope for the joys of heaven where "de' bottom rail become de' top rail."

Labeled as "other worldly" and "compensatory," this use of Christianity by slaves has been judged dysfunctional by historians, who argue that slavery should have been met with radical resistance. The opiate versus inspiration debate, as it is sometimes referred to, forces our view of the religious culture of African American slaves into arbitrary and limiting channels. By recognizing the multiple dimensions of the sacred cosmos operative in the slave quarters and hush arbors, we come close to understanding what African American slaves meant when they spoke of their beliefs as helping them "keep on keeping on." They testified that they had a home in glory land and

that no earthly master could close them out of God's house. Once they had been "killed dead" in the Spirit and were reborn, African American Christian slaves became participants in a community other than that which numbered them among the cattle and bales of cotton.

Developments in the North

Focusing too exclusively on the South runs the risk of missing important facets of the nineteenth-century African American religious experience. Prior to 1800 individual African American Christians of note lived in the North, among them Lemual Haynes, the first African American officially ordained to the Christian ministry and pastor of white congregations in New England; Phillis Wheatley, who wrote religious verse read in both America and Europe; and Jupiter Hammon, a slave on Long Island who counseled Christian endurance in the hope of heaven. But independent black churches did not appear in the North until after 1800.

African American Christians in the North kept the plight of their sisters and brothers in chains in their prayers, avidly supported temperance and education in large part to prove that African Americans could thrive in freedom, set up Underground Railroad stations, and assisted in the abolitionist cause. They organized voluntary associations to support educational endeavors, cared for widows and orphans, and served as focal points of black life in the northern city, where prejudice and discrimination were prevalent.

The northern religious landscape took on more definition with the formation of the first black denominations. Following the pattern of white Christians in the postrevolutionary era, black Christians organized themselves in collectives known as denominations. Sometimes the struggle for denominational independence was dramatic, as was the case with black Methodists in the Philadelphia area led by Richard Allen. A former slave and a convert to Christianity, Allen was convinced that the plain and simple gospel, as preached by the spiritual heirs of the English reformer John Wesley, was best suited to the unlettered black. But white authorities resisted when Allen and other Philadelphia black Methodists sought greater control over their own religious affairs. Armed with a decision from the Pennsylvania Supreme Court to the effect that Allen and his coadjutors had a legal right to church property and self-governance, the African Methodist Episcopal (AME) Church was organized in 1816. About six years later black Methodists in New York City likewise achieved denominational independence under the banner of the African Methodist Episcopal Zion Church.

As suggested by the label "Methodist," both groups replicated much of the white Methodist ritual, doctrine, and polity while seeking to liberate themselves from the prejudicial control of white Methodists. By the time of the Civil War the AME Church had about twenty thousand members and had planted new missions as far west as California. Urged on by the zealous efforts of Bishop Daniel A. Payne, the AME Church established its first institution of higher education, Wilberforce College, and its theological school, Payne Seminary, at Xenia, Ohio. The AME Zion Church numbered about five thousand and did not expand significantly beyond the Northeast until after the Civil War, when its representatives worked aggressively among the freedpeople. Eventually the denomination transferred its headquarters to North Carolina, where it established a church newspaper, publishing house, and Livingstone College in Salisbury. The AME Zion Church was the first black denomination to authorize women to occupy the pulpit, and Mary J. Small and Julia A. J. Foote were ordained in the late 1890s.

Separate black Baptist congregations appeared in northern cities in the early 1800s. Although blacks customarily worshiped with white Baptists, "the Negro pew" was tolerated, and eventually blacks sought to organize their own congregations. In 1805 Thomas Paul became the first pastor of the First African (or Joy Street) Baptist Church of Boston, and in 1808 he assisted in the organization of the Abyssinian Baptist Church in New York City. Independent black Baptist congregations eventually emerged in most northern cities, but the traditional Baptist emphasis on local autonomy retarded the development of translocal associations until the formation of the Providence Association in Ohio in 1834. The Union Association, also in Ohio, followed in 1836, then the Wood River Association in southwestern Illinois in 1839.

Sparked by an interest in developing missions in Africa, black Baptists gradually moved toward more national organizations. The American Baptist Missionary Convention became the first such cooperative arrangement in 1840. In the decades after the Civil War, black Baptists debated whether or not to continue partnerships with northern white Baptists in foreign missions and in the publication of religious literature. The nationalist or independent spirit finally triumphed with the formation of the first truly national organization, the National Baptist Convention, U.S.A., in 1895. The cooperationists formed the Lott Carey Foreign Mission Convention in 1897.

Because of Baptist disunity during most of the nineteenth century, the African Methodist story assumes center stage in accounts of the institutional history of African American religion. Better organized than the Baptists and fortunate to have denominational historians, such as Bishop Payne, the northern-based African Methodists dominate the documentary record. But statistics of denominational membership published by the U.S. Census Bureau reveal that black Baptists outnumbered black Methodists as the century drew to a close, largely due to expansion in the post–Civil War South. Although heavily recruited by agents of the northern-based denominations, black and white, former slaves elected to form new congregations, most of them Baptist, in which they could hear preachers familiar with the religious styles found in the antebellum plantation congregations.

The South after the Civil War

When slaves deserted their masters during the Civil War or became contraband as Union troops advanced on Southern soil, a new religious landscape began to emerge. Eager to read the Bible on their own and worship without white oversight, the freed slaves were convinced that their emancipation was tantamount to the deliverance of the children of Israel from the pharaoh of Egypt. African American Christians seized the moment and left the denominations of their former masters in large numbers. The Colored Methodist Episcopal Church, organized in 1870 in Jackson, Tennessee, consisted principally of former members of the Methodist Episcopal Church, South, who did not desire to join the northern-based African Methodists. As if by spontaneous combustion, black Baptist congregations appeared in great numbers throughout the South. These Baptist churches and their Methodist counterparts in the small towns and rural areas represented the core religious culture of African Americans in the South after the Civil War and World War I.

Heavily influenced by the folk practices of the "invisible institution" and often criticized for its demonstrative religious style, with emphasis on dramatic conversion experiences, emotional preaching, and "testifying," southern African American religion developed its own internal dynamic. African American churches in the North, with their educated ministers and more formal worship styles, developed differently. By the end of the nineteenth century two African American religious cultures existed—one northern and urban, the other mostly southern and rural.

Despite the cultural differences between northern and southern black religion, most observers agreed that the church was central to African American life as the twentieth century dawned. "The Negro church of today," W. E. B. Du Bois wrote in *The Souls of Black Folk* (1903), "is the social center of Negro life in the United States, and the most characteristic expression of the African character." "In proportion to their numbers," Booker T. Washington wrote in *The Negro in the South* (1907), "I question whether so large a proportion of any other race are members of some Christian Church as is true of the American Negro."

See also **Evangelicalism; Music,** *subentry on* **Spirituals and African American Music; Protestantism,** *subentries on* **Baptists, Methodists; Religion,** *subentry on* **Religion in Nineteenth-Century America; Slavery,** *subentry on* **Slave Life.**

Bibliography

Andrews, William L., ed. *Sisters of the Spirit: Three Black Women's Autobiographies of the Nineteenth Century.* Bloomington: Indiana University Press, 1986.

Johnson, Clifton H., ed. *God Struck Me Dead: Voices of Ex-Slaves.* Introduction by Albert J. Raboteau. Cleveland, Ohio: Pilgrim, 1993.

Montgomery, William E. *Under Their Own Vine and Fig Tree: The African-American Church in the South, 1865–1900.* Baton Rouge: Louisiana State University Press, 1994.

Newman, Richard. *Go Down Moses: A Celebration of the African-American Spiritual.* New York: Clarkson Potter, 1998.

Raboteau, Albert J. *Slave Religion: The "Invisible Institution" in the Antebellum South.* New York: Oxford University Press, 1978.

Sernett, Milton C. *Black Religion and American Evangelicalism: White Protestants, Plantation Missions, and the Flowering of Negro Christianity, 1787–1865.* Metuchen, N.J.: Scarecrow, 1975.

Washington, James Melvin. *Frustrated Fellowship: The Black Baptist Quest for Social Power.* Macon, Ga.: Mercer, 1986.

Williams, Walter L. *Black Americans and the Evangelization of Africa, 1877–1900.* Madison: University of Wisconsin Press, 1982.

MILTON C. SERNETT

AGRICULTURAL TECHNOLOGY   The technologies applied to the production of food and fiber in the United States in 1800 were virtually unchanged from those used by the colonists. Crops were cultivated using hand tools that were often homemade or of local design and manufacture. Historians L. W. Ellis and E. A. Rumely write that, "1850 marked the close of that period in American agriculture when the only farm implements and machinery, other than the wagon, cart, and cotton gin, were those which might be called the implements of hand production" (*Power and the Plow*, p. 276). The cotton gin, invented by Eli Whitney in 1793 and patented in 1794, was the technological catalyst for the creation of the cotton industry in the United States. The simple device, consisting of a rotating cylinder and a stationary comb, could be cranked by hand. Larger versions were driven by horse or water power. The cotton gin mechanized the labor-intensive process of removing seeds from raw upland cotton, making the production of such cotton economical.

There was remarkable growth in the use of animal power in agriculture in the last half of the nineteenth century. Over twenty-five million farm horses and mules were used to power agricultural production by 1900, more than four times the number used in 1850. Although steam power had been used in processing operations such as sugar milling in the 1820s, it was not until the 1870s that steam power came to the farm. The era of steam power was brief, and by the end of the nineteenth century, the American farmer received a glimpse of the true successor to the horse: the gasoline tractor.

During the nineteenth century, technological advancements impacted food and fiber production from seedbed preparation to harvest. Farmers benefited from plows and harrows of more effective design, made with better materials; the substitution of four-wheeled wagons for ox carts; and the application of horsepower to corn planting and cultivating, hay raking, reaping, and threshing. Prior to 1840, most efforts were directed toward improving crop culture through the use of improved implements. After 1840, the fundamental movement was in the direction of labor-saving devices and increased production through extension of areas under cultivation.

It was estimated that in 1830 one bushel of wheat could be harvested from the standing crop in a little over three hours at a cost of almost 18 cents. By 1896, harvesting one bushel took just ten minutes, at a cost of 3.5 cents. But the many measurable benefits from agricultural mechanization were not equal among all crops, producers, or regions. For instance, hand harvesting of cotton produced a higher quality product than the mechanical harvesting methods tried during the nineteenth century, and mechanized production proved more expensive than hand labor for peas, and especially for tobacco.

Tillage Machinery

Many farm machines were transformed during the nineteenth century—the plow serving as a prime example. In 1800 the typical plow was a cumbersome tool constructed of wood and drawn by an ox or team of oxen. The farmer was required to walk behind the plow to control the plowing process manually. By the end of the century the farmer could ride aboard a cast-iron or steel plow that performed at higher speeds and with less draft than ever before.

Improvement of plows occurred in two major ar-

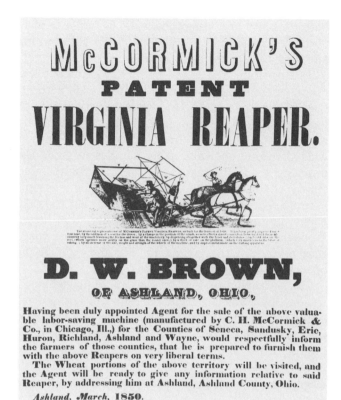

The McCormick Reaper. Cyrus McCormick patented his reaper in 1834, but it was not until the early 1850s that it was sold in quantity. LIBRARY OF CONGRESS

eas: design and materials. In 1788 Thomas Jefferson designed a moldboard plow using true mathematical principles. Prior to this innovation, plow design was strictly empirical. Charles Newbold patented a cast-iron plow in 1797. Many farmers, however, refused to use iron plows, believing they would poison the soil and encourage the growth of weeds. The real problem with Newbold's plow and those like it was its one-piece design. When one part wore out or broke, the entire plow had to be replaced. Jethro Wood patented in 1814 and 1819 an improved plow design, which featured several smaller castings bolted together, enabling replacement of a worn or broken part without having to replace the entire plow. This breakthrough was one of the first instances, if not the first, of the principle of standardization and interchangeability of parts in the manufacture of agricultural machinery.

By 1830 cast-iron plows were widely used. They could be pulled more easily and faster than wooden plows. They were not well suited, however, for use in prairie soils, which would stick to cast-iron mold-boards and prevent the plows from scouring. The steel plow industry began in 1837, when John Deere adapted a steel saw blade for use as a one-piece share and moldboard. Although twice as expensive as cast-iron plows, steel plows were found to be absolutely necessary for use in the "peculiar soil" of the West. As a result, by the late 1830s, plow making had become a factory industry. In 1838 a factory in Pittsburgh was manufacturing a hundred plows a day. By 1858 John Deere of Moline, Illinois, was producing more than 13,000 steel plows per year.

Another important tillage tool, the disk harrow, was introduced in about 1869, but did not attract much attention until the 1890s. The disk harrow had the ability to cut, then mix and/or bury stubble and crop residues, functions that were especially appreciated in the heavy clay soils of the corn belt. The use of pulverizers, such as harrows, cultivators, and clod crushers, helped to prepare seedbeds following plowing or disking. The Geddes Harrow was used for rough or uneven land. Its triangular shape permitted the harrow to maneuver around stumps and large rocks. On clear land, however, a two-horse, hinged harrow of rectangular design provided greater capacity and proved more economical. Both types of harrows used rigid teeth to penetrate and stir the soil. The spring tooth harrow was introduced in 1869. Clod crushers fashioned from hollow logs, fitted with wagon tongues, and pulled by horses were used in clayey soils to break down very hard clods.

Machinery for Planting and Cultivation

In 1840 corn was still dropped into the soil by hand and covered with a hoe. Wheat was sown by hand and incorporated into the soil with a harrow or steel-tooth cultivator. A patent for a two-row corn planter was issued in 1839. Grain drill-feeding mechanism patents were issued during 1840 and 1841. By 1850 drills were generally used in the wheat-growing regions of Pennsylvania and New York. A typical grain drill produced during this era sowed seven rows that were nine inches apart and three inches deep. Drawn by two horses, such a unit could plant ten to fifteen acres per day. Until 1860, a large portion of the grain grown in the Mississippi valley was still sown by hand.

Corn planters came rapidly into use in the 1850s. By 1860, much of the corn crop of the West was planted by one-row and two-row planters, hill planters, and drill planters. A two-row, two-horse planter could plant twelve to twenty acres per day and required two men to operate (one to drive and one to manage the lever that controlled the dropping of the seed). Hand planting was still necessary to remediate blown or washed out seeds and to fill in skips where horse-drawn planters jammed.

The horse-drawn cultivator was introduced in

about 1820. By 1840 the cultivator had largely supplanted the plow and hand hoe on Eastern farms for working between rows of corn. Early cultivators were designed to work between two crop rows. Straddle-row corn cultivators with steel teeth had appeared by 1860. A special implement for cotton cultivation was introduced in about 1840. Known as a "Mississippi scraper," it permitted shallow cultivation, shaving off earth, grass, and weeds without disturbing the growing cotton.

Machinery for Haying and Harvesting

The first machines for mowing or grass cutting were patented in the early 1820s. Horse-drawn rakes used for gathering hay were already in use at that time, but mowing had been limited to hand-tool applications. By 1860, mowers had taken on a remarkably modern appearance. The horse-drawn, ground-driven machines utilized cutter bars to shear grass in a swath five feet wide, as fast as the horses could advance.

Hay tedders were developed over the period from 1855 to 1870. These horse-drawn implements used iron or steel forks attached to a reel to spread and turn hay that had been cut by a mower and left to cure. Drying was more rapid and more uniform, and better quality hay was produced. The use of tedders permitted the farmer to cut a hay crop in the morning and remove it from the field the same day.

Dating from 1812, horse-drawn hay rakes, or horse rakes, resembled large combs ten feet wide with fifteen to eighteen teeth that were twenty inches in length. The units were dragged along the ground by a horse attached to the frame by ropes. The farmer walked behind the rake using handles to guide the implement, lift the teeth over rocks or stumps, and empty the accumulated hay. By 1820 new designs permitted horse rakes to be pivoted so that the rake could be emptied without stopping the horse. Wooden, walk-behind rakes gave way to steel rakes that permitted the farmer to ride and control the operation of the rake from a seat.

Horse-drawn hay loaders that could place hay on wagons for transport from the field did not achieve commercial success until 1890. Loose hay that had been accumulated and transported from the field using hay rakes and hay carriers was lifted into barn lofts by various types of hay elevators. In the West, large quantities of hay were stacked and stored outdoors. To facilitate the transport of hay over long distances, the hay press was developed in the early 1850s. It was claimed that some presses could reduce

Aultman-Taylor Threshing Machine, c. 1881. Established by Cornelius Aultman and Henry Taylor, the Aultman-Taylor Machinery Company of Mansfield, Ohio, built farm steam engines, threshers, and other machines. LIBRARY OF CONGRESS

hay to a "compactness nearly equal to that of solid wood."

The amount of wheat that a nineteenth-century farmer could produce was limited by the acreage that could be harvested in a timely manner. Once ripe, the crop was subject to relatively rapid deterioration if left standing in the field. The development of the reaper was critical to the widespread, commercial production of grain crops such as wheat. In 1833 Obed Hussey obtained a patent on a horse-drawn reaper. One year later, Cyrus McCormick patented his reaper.

The reaper was similar in construction to the mower but with the addition of a platform for holding grain as it fell from the cutter bar. In fact, early mowers and reapers were usually made interchangeable by designing the platform at the rear of the cutter bar to be easily removed and replaced. When a sufficient quantity of grain had collected on the platform, it was swept off and onto the ground in bundles using a hand rake. (Later reapers featured self-raking devices.) Hussey's machine required two horses, a driver, and a man to push off the grain. Five to seven men were required to remove the grain and bind it into sheaves as fast as it was cut to prevent it from being crushed by the horses and wheels of the machine on the succeeding round. The sheaves were then assembled into shocks. The crop, standing in shocks, was then loaded onto wagons for transport to a threshing machine. The light model reaper could cover twelve to fifteen acres per day while the heavy model had a capacity of fifteen to twenty acres per day.

Mechanisms to bind bundles with wire were added to reapers around 1850. Wire binders were not well received by farmers, who believed that the wire would be eaten by, and choke, livestock. Others believed that lightning would be attracted to that much steel in a field and burn up a crop tied by wire. Twine binders, perfected by 1879, succeeded wire binders.

Although the reaper was not yet established as a practical machine by 1840, McCormick was producing one thousand machines per year by 1851. Rising wheat prices caused a boom in agriculture from 1854 to 1857 and created an almost universal demand for reapers in the wheat-growing regions. Reaper sales totaled 60,000 units in 1880, then leapt to 250,000 in 1885.

Grain threshing was mechanized in the 1820s, though traditional methods involving treading by horses or cattle or the use of a flail were still widely used. One of the first mechanical threshing machines, the Groundhog, consisted of a box housing a spike cylinder through which grain passed. A one-horse treadmill powered the cylinder. Straw, grain, and chaff dropped to the ground beneath the machine. Straw was forked to one side and the chaff was separated from the grain by the wind.

A cylinder and concave machine was invented by Hiram and John Pitts in 1834. The unit, a threshing machine and fanning mill combined, threshed, separated the straw from the grain, and cleaned and delivered the grain for sacks or bags in one operation. The portable unit, usually powered by two horses, had a capacity of a hundred bushels of wheat per day. Threshers saved labor and worked more effectively than flailing, by reducing grain loss. Increased threshing capacity meant that grain could be marketed in the fall if the market was favorable.

The grain combine was invented by Hiram Moore and John Haskall in about 1836. It was described as a huge machine, drawn by sixteen or eighteen horses, that attacked the standing grain, severed the heads, threshed, cleaned, and sacked the seed ready for the mill. Although introduced in Michigan, the first successful application of the combine was made in California's San Jose Valley in 1854.

The first corn harvester was patented in the United States in 1850. Corn pickers were developed in the 1850s, but the first practical models were available in about 1895. The corn binder was patented in 1892.

A cotton-picking device was patented in 1850, and a stripper-type harvester was patented in 1871. Acceptance of mechanical cotton harvesting was very slow, due in part to the fact that cotton gins were not equipped to handle and clean machine-harvested cotton. Such cotton contained more leaves and trash than hand-harvested cotton. Cotton harvesting was not fully mechanized until well into the twentieth century.

Farm Power

Until the very end of the nineteenth century, horsepower was usually provided by horses. In addition to their use as draft animals to pull implements in the field, horses provided the power for stationary machines, such as threshers, circular saws, water pumps, and feed grinders. This was accomplished through the use of treadmills and sweeps. (For light tasks such as churning butter, dogs and sheep were employed to power treadmills.) A sweep harnessed the power produced by animals moving around a circular course. There was, however, a limit to the power that could be supplied by horses. For stationary operations, sweeps could usually accommodate no more than fourteen horses. In the field, a single driver could usually control no more than six draft horses. For those applications that required more power, steam was an attractive alternative.

In the United States, portable steam engines for farm use date from the 1849 introduction of "The Forty-Niner" by A. L. Archambault. In the 1850s there were several attempts to plow using steam power. The Illinois Central Railroad sought to promote the cause by offering a premium of $3,000 for the first successful steam plow. The Fawkes' steam plow was awarded the premium in 1859, but did not achieve commercial success. The first commercially viable steam traction engines were introduced in 1876. Portable steam engines gained popularity as power for stationary threshers during the late 1870s. By 1890, approximately three thousand steam traction engines and almost that many steam threshers were sold. By 1900 more than thirty firms were manufacturing five thousand large steam traction engines per year.

Steam traction engines were heavy, cumbersome machines that were limited to draft work and stationary belt work. Such engines were not suited to many of the field operations that occurred from planting through harvest. The true successor to the horse as a multipurpose power unit was the lighter, more maneuverable gasoline traction engine. These engines appeared, primarily in experimental form, starting in 1892. C. W. Hart and C. H. Parr conducted gas engine research from 1892 to 1896 while they were students at the University of Wisconsin. The Hart-Parr Company built its first traction engine in 1901 and is credited with the establishment of the tractor industry in the United States.

Machinery Sales and Distribution

As it developed during the nineteenth century, the distribution system for farm machinery consisted of manufacturers selling to wholesalers who sold to dealers or agents who sold to farmers. The wholesalers, or jobbers, built up personal, independent businesses that often represented a number of manufacturers at once. Dealers were expected to supply services for local customers, but jobbers were often poorly equipped to supply or deliver repair parts or advice on repair procedures. In the late 1890s, manufacturers began to establish sales and distribution networks to overcome the shortcomings of the jobbers. A difficult economy in that decade caused problems in the farm equipment industry. According to one trade magazine, margins were very small on all equipment, almost all large equipment sold to farmers had to be paid for over time, and collecting these payments took up much of the dealer's time, effort,

and money (profit). One bad crop rendered farmers unable to pay for their equipment.

The true impact of agricultural technology in the nineteenth century can be measured by the degree to which the vast majority of the American people were liberated from the toil of food and fiber production. In 1820, 97 percent of the U.S. population lived on farms and relied on hand labor for nearly every conceivable need. In that same census year nearly 72 percent of the U.S. labor force was engaged in agricultural pursuits. By 1900 the percentage of the labor force engaged in agricultural pursuits had fallen to less than 38 percent, a remarkable transformation.

See also **Agriculture; Cotton; Food; Steam Power; Work,** *subentry on* **Agricultural Labor.**

Bibliography

Bidwell, Percy W. and John I. Falconer. *History of Agriculture in the Northern United States, 1620–1860.* Baltimore: Lord Baltimore Press, 1925.

Currie, Barton W. *The Tractor and Its Influence upon the Agricultural Implement Industry.* Philadelphia: Curtis Publishing, 1916.

Ellis, L. W., and E. A. Rumely. *Power and the Plow.* Garden City, N.Y.: Doubleday, Page and Co., 1911.

Gras, Norman Scott Brien. *A History of Agriculture in Europe and America.* New York: F. S. Crofts, 1940.

Gray, Lewis Cecil (assisted by Esther Katherine Thompson). *History of Agriculture in the Southern United States to 1860.* Vol. 2. Washington, D.C.: Carnegie Institution of Washington, 1933.

Gray, Roy B. *The Agricultural Tractor: 1855–1950.* St. Joseph, Mich.: American Society of Agricultural Engineers, 1975.

Latta, W. C. *Outline History of Indiana Agriculture.* Lafayette, Ind.: Alpha Lambda chapter of Epsilon Sigma Phi in cooperation with Purdue University Agricultural Experiment Station, 1938.

McColly, H. F., and J. W. Martin. *Introduction to Agricultural Engineering.* New York: McGraw-Hill, 1955.

McCormick, Cyrus. *The Century of the Reaper.* Boston: Houghton Mifflin, 1931.

Mills, Robert K. *Implement and Tractor: Reflections on 100 Years of Farm Equipment.* Overland Park, Kans.: Intertec Publishing, 1986.

Schafer, Joseph. *The Social History of American Agriculture.* New York: Macmillan, 1936.

Thomas, John J. *Farm Implements and Farm Machinery and the Principles of Their Construction and Use.* New York: Orange Judd Co., 1879.

Thurston, Robert H. *A History of the Growth of the Steam-Engine.* New York: D. Appleton and Co., 1878. 4th ed. 1903.

U.S. Department of Agriculture. *The Yearbook of Agriculture 1960—Power to Produce.* Washington, D.C.: U.S. Department of Agriculture, 1960.

DANIEL R. ESS

AGRICULTURE   The rhythm of the seasons and the days governed agriculture during the nineteenth century. For men spring meant planting; summer, cultivating; and autumn, harvesting. Threshing, repair work, and land clearing were reserved for winter. Women customarily cooked for family and farmworkers, milked cows, and tended poultry. Despite routine activities for men, women, and children on farms, revolutionary changes in agriculture took place during the nineteenth century. Where markets existed, farmers specialized and produced crop surpluses for sale. In sparsely settled areas, commonly called the frontier, they practiced safety-first agriculture, that is, they attempted to meet the subsistence needs of their families before engaging in commercial production. They were never entirely self-sufficient. During the nineteenth century, farmers exploited the soil, often with new implements, and many moved west to acquire land from the public domain. Many farmers supported federal and state aid for the construction of canals and railroads to enable the efficient shipment of their produce to market. Improved transportation enabled farmers to specialize their crop- and livestock-raising practices for the market economy.

The South

In the South large-scale planters used slave labor to produce staple crops, such as cotton, tobacco, rice, and sugar, for sale at home and abroad. Cotton became the principal commercial crop in the South because it was well suited to the climate, the soil, and slavery, that is, an extensive and relatively cheap labor force. Most southern farmers, however, did not own slaves. One person could cultivate approximately ten acres, which produced about three bales of cotton per acre on the best land. Stable and profitable prices, together with demand by American and foreign textile manufacturers and the cotton gin, which enabled the easy separation of the fiber from the seeds, encouraged southerners to raise cotton. In 1800 southern farmers produced 73,000 bales of cotton, each weighing between 400 and 500 pounds. The rapid expansion of cotton farming across the South and increased foreign demand boosted production to 732,000 bales by 1830. In 1860 farmers raised cotton from Virginia to Texas, with production reaching 4.5 million bales (three-quarters of the world's cotton supply). Prior to the Civil War cotton was the major American export, making up 14 percent of the total exports by value in 1802 and 63 percent by value in 1860. Planters usually reinvested their profits in land and slaves in order to produce more cotton. Cotton production and slavery made the South the most rural section of the nation; by 1860, 84 percent of the labor force there was engaged in agriculture, compared with 40 percent in the United States as a whole. Plantation agriculture in the South drove small-scale farmers and tenants to less fertile lands, and perpetuated the institution of slavery because an extensive labor force was needed to raise cotton in the absence of labor-saving technology such as tractors and cotton pickers.

After the Civil War most large-scale landowners divided their plantations into small farms ranging from twenty to fifty acres and employed the freed African Americans to raise cotton or tobacco. Known as sharecroppers, these farmers were paid with a portion of the crop, usually half, by the landowners. Low prices, overproduction, and usurious credit, usually provided by a local merchant or the landowner, kept sharecroppers in poverty. In 1898 cotton farmers produced a record crop of 11.3 million bales; the price dropped below six cents per pound when farmers needed at least eight cents per pound to earn a profit. Southern farmers continued to produce cotton because it had an established market and there were no well-developed markets for other agricultural commodities. As a result, poverty and one-crop farming continued to characterize southern agriculture at the turn of the twentieth century. At that time more than one million farms (54 percent of the farms in the South) emphasized cotton production. They would continue to do so until New Deal agricultural policies and World War II changed the credit and labor system in the South.

The North

At the turn of the nineteenth century, small-scale family farms typified northern agriculture. A growing urban population and improved transportation by railroad and steamboat gave farmers access to markets and encouraged them to specialize and produce surpluses for commercial gain. In 1825 the opening of the Erie Canal gave farmers near the Great Lakes access to New York City, which soon became the major agricultural market in the United States. The extensive and large-scale production of grain and livestock west of the Appalachians forced farmers in the East to specialize in the production of high-value, noncompetitive commodities, such as milk, butter, cheese, and fruits, for sale at nearby urban markets. By the turn of the twentieth century, New England farmers had shifted from diversified farming to specialized production. Specialized production for the market economy forced farmers to become dependent on banks and middlemen who financed their purchases of seed and fertilizer and arranged transportation and sale of their produce. As commercial farmers they lost considerable freedom of action in

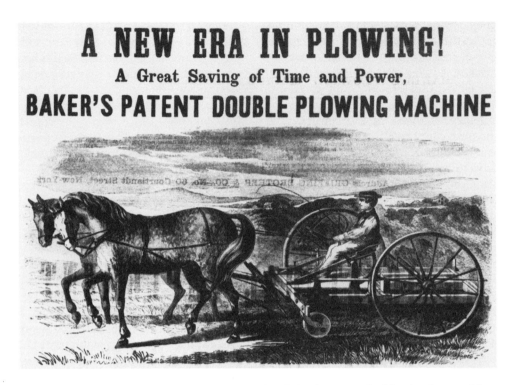

Advances in Plowing. Woodcut advertisement for Baker's patent double plowing machine, 1862. Prices for the plow ranged from $80 for the smallest machine, which cut two eleven-inch-wide furrows, to $115 for the largest machine, which cut three eleven-, thirteen-, or fifteen-inch-wide furrows at a time. LIBRARY OF CONGRESS: BROADSIDE COLLECTION

terms of decision making, cropping practices, and production.

The West

In the West ranchers first used the Great Plains for extensive cattle production. In 1867 Joseph G. McCoy organized the first cattle drive from Texas to the railhead at Abilene, Kansas; from there the livestock were shipped to slaughterhouses in Kansas City and Chicago. By the mid-1880s overgrazing of the range and severe winters, along with an increasing number of settlers, brought an end to the open-range cattle industry. The Homestead Act and the railroad companies made the Great Plains attractive to settlers, who either bought land from the railroads or from speculators or acquired it free from the federal government. By the turn of the twentieth century, much of the Great Plains had been settled by men and women who raised wheat and cattle and who fenced their lands with barbed wire (patented by Joseph F. Glidden, of DeKalb, Illinois, in 1874).

By the early 1870s California had become a major wheat- and cattle-producing state. Farmers took advantage of the moderate climate to raise oranges, lemons, and grapes; the transcontinental railroads and refrigerated cars transported the citrus crops to markets in the East. The construction of extensive irrigation systems during the 1870s and 1880s and the employment of cheap Chinese labor enabled large-scale farmers to produce fruits and vegetables at relatively low cost to offset high shipping expenses to distant markets. By 1882 Chinese workers made up more than 50 percent of the agricultural labor force in the state.

Technology

Agricultural technology changed dramatically during the nineteenth century. Farmers sought improved technology to make their work easier, faster, and more efficient as well as to reduce labor costs. Technological change moved American agriculture from the age of hand-powered tools to the age of steam-powered implements.

In 1800 farmers typically used a wooden moldboard plow with a wrought-iron share. By 1820 they had begun to adopt cast-iron plows. The prairie lands of the Midwest, however, proved unsuitable for these implements because they could not cut through the root system of the grasses and the heavy prairie soils clung to the moldboard. Between the 1820s and 1840s prairie farmers used a breaking plow to make the initial cut through the soil. It consisted of an iron mold-

Haymaking. Note the pitchfork, rake, and scythe, foreground, and horse-drawn thresher, background. Lithograph from *Prang's Aids for Object Teaching.*, published by L. Prang & Co., 1875. LIBRARY OF CONGRESS

board that often weighed 125 pounds and a fourteen-foot beam supported by two small wheels. The weight of the moldboard and beam helped keep the plow in the soil. Two or three yokes of oxen were needed to pull the breaking plow and turn about three acres per day.

In 1837 John Deere, a blacksmith in Grand Detour, Illinois, improved the moldboard plow for prairie soils. He made a plow with a highly polished wrought-iron moldboard and a steel share. This plow easily cut through and scoured tough prairie sod. Deere did not use steel to make the moldboard until the 1850s because the expense proved prohibitive. The steel moldboard was lighter and easier to handle than that of the prairie breakers and required less draft than cast-iron plows. His steel plow produced a whine as it turned the furrow and thus earned the nickname "singing plow."

At the turn of the nineteenth century, farmers sowed grain by hand or with broadcast seeders. The crop stand depended on the farmer's walking speed, his consistency turning the seeder's crank or bow, and wind conditions. Usually the seed scattered too thinly or thickly. In 1841 Moses and Samuel Pennock of Chester County, Pennsylvania, built a grain drill that dropped the seeds into the ground through tubes

set in a horse-drawn seed box. By 1850 farmers commonly used a grain drill to seed their grain crops at the rate of about fifteen acres per day. During the 1850s they also began to use a mechanical planter to seed their corn crop. In 1857 Martin Robbins, a Cincinnati inventor, developed a planter that automatically dropped the seed in evenly spaced rows. During the 1860s farmers quickly adopted the time-saving corn planter because it enabled them to seed twelve to twenty acres per day, about twenty times more than a farmer could plant with a hoe.

In 1800 farmers customarily used a sickle or cradle scythe, also known as a grain cradle, to harvest their grain. They could cut only about three-quarters of an acre per day with a sickle or about three acres per day with a cradle scythe. In 1831 Cyrus Hall McCormick built a horse-drawn reaper in Rockbridge County, Virginia. He did not patent this implement until 21 June 1834. In the meantime Obed Hussey, an Ohio inventor, patented a reaper on 31 December 1833. Although the cutting mechanisms differed on these implements, they were alike in that a blade cut the stalks, which then fell onto a platform. A worker raked the grain off and others bound it into sheaves. The reaper enabled farmers to harvest larger crops with fewer workers. By 1860 reapers had a self-raking device, and farmers commonly used this implement to harvest about twelve to fifteen acres per day. In 1872 Sylvanus D. Locke of Janesville, Wisconsin, developed a reaper called a binder, which automatically bound the stalks into sheaves with wire. The wire created a disposal problem for farmers, however, and in 1880 the Deering company replaced it with a binding mechanism using twine. By the mid-1890s farmers also used a mechanical binder to harvest the corn crop at the rate of about seven to nine acres per day.

In 1834 Hiram A. and John A. Pitts of Winthrop, Maine, invented a horse-powered threshing machine that beat the grain from the heads, separated the straw, and winnowed the chaff; they received a patent in 1837. By the 1850s grain farmers used machines to thresh five hundred bushels of wheat per day, far more than the seven bushels that they could thresh with a flail. Hiram Moore of Climax Prairie, Michigan, combined the principles of the reaper and threshing machine in an implement called a combine, which he and J. Haskall patented in 1836. By the late 1840s his combine could harvest twenty-five acres per day, but it required sixteen horses for draft and proved too expensive for the small-scale farmers of the Midwest. The combine was more suitable for the large farms in the West, where dry conditions made threshing easier. By 1886 combines pulled by as many as forty horses cut and threshed between twenty-five and thirty-five acres per day in the wheat fields of California.

During the late 1860s farmers used steam engines to power their threshing machines. These engines increased the speed and capability of threshing machines but were limited to operating other machines via a belt because they lacked traction. In 1873 the firm of Merritt and Kellogg of Battle Creek, Michigan, sold the first self-propelled steam engine. Gearing problems, however, prevented these early engines from pulling a plow. By the 1890s steam-traction engines easily plowed thirty-five to forty-five acres per day, far more than the five to seven acres per day possible with a two-bottom moldboard riding or sulky plow. Most farmers could not afford steam-traction engines or large threshing machines, and therefore hired itinerant workers to provide the equipment and conduct the work.

Agricultural Policy

The federal government played an important role in the expansion and improvement of agriculture during the nineteenth century by selling the public lands, disseminating information, and sponsoring experimentation. The Land Act of 1800, also known as the Harrison Frontier Land Act, enabled the sale of the public domain at two dollars per acre for 320-acre tracts. Most small-scale farmers could not afford so much land at this price, and the federal government reduced the minimum purchase to 160 acres in 1804, but few besides speculators could afford the $320.00 cost. In 1820 Congress reduced the price to $1.25 per acre and lowered the minimum purchase to 80 acres. The $100.00 purchase price still proved too expensive for most settlers. Consequently many settlers on the public lands remained squatters. In 1841 Congress passed the Preemption Act, which gave squatters the first right to buy the land on which they had settled as soon as the federal government had it surveyed and ready for sale at the price of $1.25 per acre for a maximum purchase of 160 acres.

Most settlers, however, demanded that the federal government provide free public lands for settlement in order to encourage expansion, strengthen the national economy, and prevent hoarding by speculators. Southerners opposed this policy because it would encourage westward expansion and eventually reduce southern power in Congress. After the South seceded, Congress passed the Homestead Act in 1862, which enabled any individual person or head of a household over twenty-one years of age, who was a citizen or who had filed for citizenship, to claim 160 acres of public land without cost, provided he or she lived on the land and improved it for five years. Otherwise, the land could be purchased for $1.25 per acre after six months. Settlers claimed only about 10 percent of the public domain under this law, and speculators gained considerable acreage under it by fraud. Still, the Homestead Act became one of the most important laws in American history, because it reflected the American commitment to small-scale family farms as the foundation of the economy and the desire for the rapid settlement of the public domain.

The Timber Culture Act (1873) enabled a farmer to claim 160 acres of public domain for free, provided he planted 40 acres of trees. The harsh environment of the Great Plains forced Congress to reduce the required tree planting to 10 acres in 1878. Farmers in Kansas, Nebraska, and the Dakota Territory primarily used this act to claim 9.7 million acres. Similarly the Desert Land Act (1877) allowed a settler to claim 640 acres of land for $1.25 per acre, provided he irrigated it within three years. In 1891 Congress reduced the irrigation requirement to 80 acres, but settlers claimed only 8.6 million acres because of environmental conditions and technical and financial difficulties that made meeting the terms of the law difficult.

On 15 May 1862 President Abraham Lincoln signed the bill authorizing the creation of the Department of Agriculture (USDA). This agency had the responsibility to acquire and disseminate useful agricultural information to farmers. On 1 July 1862 Isaac Newton became the first commissioner of agriculture. Under Newton the USDA emphasized research and education to help farmers become more productive and efficient and thereby improve their standard of living. During the 1880s the USDA expanded its responsibility by regulating the manufacture of oleomargarine and the importation of livestock. Thereafter the USDA continued to expand its regulatory powers to benefit consumers and farmers. On 9 February 1889 President Grover Cleveland signed the bill that elevated the position of commissioner to cabinet status and appointed Norman J. Colman as the first secretary of agriculture. Because this appointment came less than a month before

Cleveland left office, Jeremiah McLain Rusk essentially became the first full-time secretary of agriculture on 6 March 1889, appointed by Benjamin Harrison. By 1900 the USDA had become the center for scientific expertise in agriculture. It wielded considerable educational influence and regulatory authority, and it had become one of the largest and most powerful agencies in the federal government.

Also in 1862 Congress passed the Morrill Land-Grant College Act. This legislation authorized federal funding for the creation of state colleges for the teaching of agriculture and the mechanical arts. The Morrill Act authorized the federal government to give each state thirty thousand acres of public domain for each U.S. senator and representative, to be sold for the support of an agricultural college. The

The Centrality of Agriculture. This lithograph, created in 1875, reflects the feelings of the Granger movement, an organization composed mainly of Midwestern farmers, who were against the monopolistic practices of the railroads and grain elevators. The importance of the farmer in American society is clear, and the caption underneath the farmer—"I Feed You All!"—echoes the Granger movement's motto, "I Pay for All." Several smaller illustrations surround the farmer, including *(clockwise from left)* a lawyer, President Ulysses S. Grant, a military officer, a clergyman, a ship owner, a shopkeeper, a doctor, a broker ("I Fleece You All"), a trader, and a railroad owner. LIBRARY OF CONGRESS

states without public lands were issued scrip for the equivalent amount of land that they could sell to help support these colleges. Until the late 1880s, however, the land-grant colleges suffered from an inadequate knowledge base for teaching. Farmers criticized them as impractical.

On 2 March 1887 Congress attempted to solve the educational deficiencies of the agricultural colleges by passing the Hatch Act. This legislation authorized the creation of agricultural experiment stations in every state; federal funds would help support both pure and practical research at the stations. The agricultural experiment stations and the agricultural colleges were closely linked, often sharing the same campus. The research conducted at the experiment stations reached farmers through special training institutes, the classroom, and publications. On 30 August 1890 Congress approved the second Morrill Act, which prohibited racial discrimination at land-grant colleges. It also provided funds to black colleges for agricultural education and permitted the states to support separate land-grant colleges for African Americans. Seventeen states eventually established a land-grant college for blacks or provided funds to an existing African American college to support agricultural research and education.

Families

The farm family was both patriarchal and nuclear, and it served as the social, economic, and educational institution for most country people. It divided labor by gender; the men and boys were primarily responsible for field work and livestock, while the women and girls maintained the home and produced and preserved food for domestic consumption and sale. Society generally considered men farmers and women farmwives; that is, men made the decisions about the farm, such as buying land, equipment, and livestock. Women obeyed their husbands and took care of the home, children, garden, and poultry. Men produced for the market while women usually produced for family self-sufficiency. Often children began helping with farm chores as early as age five, and by twelve they were expected to do the work of an adult. Children helped reduce labor costs and increased productivity, which meant more money at harvest time and an improved standard of living. Families shared labor by helping neighbors in time of need with such tasks as plowing, harvesting, threshing, and barn building.

No matter the region of the country, farm women were essential to the expansion of American agriculture during the nineteenth century. Their lives were governed by the seasons and family needs. Where markets offered the opportunity for commercial sales, they produced vegetables, butter, and cheese. In the South they helped raise tobacco and cotton. Women also had responsibility for raising poultry and selling eggs, all of which contributed to the family income. In the grain-producing region women also had the responsibility for cooking meals for the harvest and threshing crews.

Agrarian Revolt

After the Civil War many farmers organized to solve common problems through collective action. They became part of a large movement to gain economic, social, and political change. On 4 December 1867 Oliver Hudson Kelley, a Minnesota farmer and a USDA employee, organized the National Grange of the Patrons of Husbandry, known as the Grange. Kelley intended for this organization to meet the social and educational needs of farmers and lessen rural isolation. Instead, the groups that emerged at the county and state levels began an active program of cooperative buying and selling to help reduce operating and living costs for farm families. In some states the Grange played a role in gaining railroad regulation, particularly concerning freight charges. The cooperative business ventures of the Grange proved difficult to maintain, and many organizations went bankrupt. By the mid-1870s the organization experienced a rapid decline in membership and influence.

During the late 1880s another organization, the Farmers' Alliance, became important across the South and the Great Plains, where farmers suffered economic hardship at the hands of the furnishing merchants, the lenders who provided goods, such as seed, fertilizers, food, and clothing, on credit, or the railroad companies, which charged exorbitant rates for their services. In North Carolina, Leonidas L. Polk, editor of the *Progressive Farmer*, became a leading supporter of the Alliance. Officially named the National Farmers' Alliance and Industrial Union in 1889, this organization resurrected the cooperative buying and selling practices of the Grange and attempted to convince Congress that the federal government should establish a subtreasury to loan negotiable certificates—that is, currency—on agricultural commodities for 80 percent of their value at 2 percent interest. A subtreasury operated by the federal government would revolutionize the credit system in the South by breaking the hold of the furnishing merchants over cotton and tobacco sharecroppers. The Alliance also advocated federal ownership of the railroads and expansion of the currency supply through unlimited coinage of silver. Like the Grange the Alliance was not a political party, and when Congress and state governments failed to meet the demands of the organization for economic reform, many members advocated the creation of a third party based on the principles of the Farmers' Alliance.

On 4 July 1892 the People's Party, or Populist Party, based on the economic goals of the Farmers' Alliance, became a major political force when it held a national convention and nominated James B. Weaver, the presidential nominee of the Greenback party in 1880, for the presidency. The People's Party, in part, advocated government ownership of the railroads, a subtreasury, and expansion of the currency supply. In 1896 the party nominated William Jennings Bryan, who also received the nomination of the Democratic Party for the presidency. Because of racial divisions, the People's Party could not break the loyalty of southern farmers to the Democratic Party, nor could it gain sufficient support nationwide to win enough offices at the state and national levels to achieve significant economic, social, and political change. After the presidential election of 1896, the People's Party collapsed.

A Century of Change

By 1900 American agriculture had undergone revolutionary change. In general most farmers had committed to a mix of subsistence and commercial agriculture by 1860, and they pursued economic gain by choice. The Civil War ended slavery as the preeminent agricultural labor institution in the South. High wartime prices encouraged northern farmers to adopt labor-saving technology that helped increase production. In areas well suited for commercial agriculture, rapid settlement and expansion of the population occurred. Free or relatively cheap lands and the completion of the transcontinental railroad system enabled the development of extensive one-crop and specialty agriculture in the Midwest, Great Plains, and Far West.

Between 1870 and 1900 American agriculture expanded rapidly. The number of farms increased from 2.7 to 5.7 million, acreage increased from 407.7 to 841.2 million, and the value of farm property rose from $9.4 to $20.4 billion. New technology and markets encouraged farmers to expand wheat production from 254 to 599 million bushels, and corn production rose from 1.1 to 2.7 billion bushels. Cotton production expanded from 4.4 million to 10.1 million bales. Cattle increased from 24 million to 68 million head, and the number of swine rose from 25 million to 63 million. Part of this expansion resulted from the settlement of the Great Plains, and another part from industrial and urban growth in the United States and Europe, which expanded markets. Improvements in railroads and steamship transportation brought agricultural produce to market quickly, efficiently, and cheaply.

Although many farmers turned to commercial production at the beginning of the twentieth century, others were locked in poverty on small-scale farms, particularly in the South. There inadequate credit, racism, and the absence of applied science and technology kept small-scale farms unproductive and unprofitable. Farmers in the Midwest and Great Plains often experienced financial hardship, but they had better access to land, credit, and markets. In the Far West large-scale wheat production on "bonanza" farms and specialty fruit and vegetable production became profitable forms of agriculture. Still, while new forms of technology helped improve production, surpluses decreased agricultural prices, which together with the growth of manufacturing and the creation of higher-paying jobs lured many men, women, and children from the farms.

By the turn of the twentieth century, American agriculture remained dynamic rather than progressive. It had changed rapidly during the course of the nineteenth century, but not all changes had been for the better. Although the interests of farmers remained too diverse to enable their long-term organization for economic reform, with the exception of the black and white sharecroppers in the South, most farmers experienced an improved standard of living through commercial production by 1900. Most farmers also had rejected agriculture as a way of life by the turn of the twentieth century and instead considered it a business based on commercial production and as an endeavor in which interest rates, foreign exchange rates, and market demands were as important as the weather in determining success or failure.

See also **Agricultural Technology; Cotton; Federal Land Policy; Populism; Ranching and Livestock Raising; Work,** *subentry on* **Agricultural Labor.**

Bibliography

Barron, Hal S. *Those Who Stayed Behind: Rural Society in Nineteenth-Century New England.* New York: Cambridge University Press, 1984.

Bogue, Allan G. *From Prairie to Corn Belt: Farming on the Illinois and Iowa Prairies in the Nineteenth Century.* Chicago: University of Chicago Press, 1963.

Danbom, David B. *Born in the Country: A History of Rural America.* Baltimore: Johns Hopkins University Press, 1995.

Danhof, Clarence H. *Change in Agriculture: The Northern United States, 1820–1870.* Cambridge, Mass.: Harvard University Press, 1969.

Daniel, Pete. *Breaking the Land: The Transformation of Cotton, Tobacco, and Rice Cultures Since 1880.* Urbana: University of Illinois Press, 1985.

Fite, Gilbert C. *Cotton Fields No More: Southern Agriculture, 1865–1980.* Lexington: University Press of Kentucky, 1984.

———. *The Farmers' Frontier, 1865–1900.* New York: Holt, Rinehart, and Winston, 1966.

Gates, Paul W. *The Farmer's Age: Agriculture, 1815–1860.* New York: Holt, Rinehart, and Winston, 1960.

Goodwyn, Lawrence. *The Populist Moment: A Short History of the Agrarian Revolt in America.* New York: Oxford University Press, 1978.

Hurt, R. Douglas. *American Agriculture: A Brief History.* Ames: Iowa State University Press, 1994.

Jensen, Joan M. *Loosening the Bonds: Mid-Atlantic Farm Women, 1750–1850.* New Haven, Conn.: Yale University Press, 1986.

Jordan, Terry G. *North American Cattle-Ranching Frontiers: Origins, Diffusion, and Differentiation.* Albuquerque: University of New Mexico Press, 1993.

McMath, Robert C., Jr. *American Populism: A Social History, 1877–1898.* New York: Hill and Wang, 1993.

Osgood, Ernest Staples. *The Day of the Cattleman.* Minneapolis: University of Minnesota Press, 1929.

Osterud, Nancy Grey. *Bonds of Community: The Lives of Farm Women in Nineteenth-Century New York.* Ithaca, N.Y.: Cornell University Press, 1991.

Shannon, Fred A. *The Farmer's Last Frontier: Agriculture, 1860–1897.* New York: Farrar and Rinehart, 1945.

Woodman, Harold D. *King Cotton and His Retainers: Financing and Marketing the Cotton Crop of the South, 1800–1925.* Lexington: University of Kentucky Press, 1968.

Woods, Thomas A. *Knights of the Plow: Oliver H. Kelley and the Origins of the Grange in Republican Ideology.* Ames: Iowa State University Press, 1991.

R. DOUGLAS HURT

ALABAMA   Alabama is a diverse land, comprising the Appalachian Mountains in the northeast, rich farming areas in the Tennessee Valley and southern Alabama, and a major outlet to the Gulf Coast in Mobile. In 1817 Congress created the Alabama Territory, and in 1819 Alabama became a state. At that time the land was largely populated by the Cherokee, Creek, Choctaw, and Chickasaw Indians. In the first decades of statehood, migrants came from established eastern states. Generally, those from Virginia, Georgia, and South Carolina settled in southern Alabama, bringing with them a sense of aristocratic hierarchy that fit plantation society. North Alabama was, again generally speaking, settled by small farmers from Tennessee and North Carolina who embraced more egalitarian values. Throughout the state's history the two sections often differed over political, economic, and social policies.

Politically, the common man ruled Alabama. The state's first constitution, written in 1819, provided for universal white male suffrage, and at no time did large planters constitute a majority of the legislature. In the late 1830s the Whig Party emerged in the state, but popular fear that it was the wealthy man's party convinced the majority of Alabamians to support the Democrats. In the mid-1850s the Whig Party collapsed and was temporarily replaced by the American Party, an anti-Catholic organization also known as the Know-Nothings. This party soon failed, and by 1857 the Democrats faced no opposition.

Long, hot summers and mild winters made Alabama an agrarian state. In 1860 Alabamians used slave labor to produce 23 percent of American-grown cotton. Even though large planters existed in the state, 82 percent of slave owners held fewer than twenty slaves. In the 1850s, Alabama became increasingly modernized with the growth of cities and a dramatic increase in railroads. During that decade, 610 of the state's 743 miles of railroad were laid.

These political and economic factors helped lead Alabama to secession. The economic changes caused social disruptions that created anxiety among the masses. In the late 1850s the state's politicians excited the people with visions of a northern conspiracy to abolish slavery. With the people already in a hypersensitive mood, the politicians' message was taken to heart. By 1861 many Alabamians had fallen under the spell of William L. Yancey, a magnetic speaker who preached secession as a liberating gospel. After the election of Abraham Lincoln, a convention met at the state capitol in Montgomery, and on 11 January 1861 the delegates voted sixty-one to thirty-nine to secede. On 4 February six Deep South states met in the city and established the Confederate States of America. Montgomery was made the first capital of the new nation.

Civil War and Reconstruction profoundly affected Alabama. Approximately ninety thousand to one hundred thousand Alabamians served the Confederacy. The state provided the South's first secretary of war, Leroy Pope Walker, and its chief of ordnance, Josiah Gorgas. An estimated twenty-seven hundred white and ten thousand black Alabamians joined the Union army. The only major conflict in the state was the Battle of Mobile Bay in 1864. However, Union raids in the latter part of the war demoralized the home front. When peace returned, presidential and congressional Reconstruction required Alabamians to ratify the Thirteenth and Fourteenth Amendments, enfranchise blacks, and disenfranchise certain whites who had contributed to the Confederate war effort. In 1874 these whites regained their political rights, and through the Democratic Party they resumed control of the state.

In postbellum politics, the Democrats retained supremacy. They faced their only significant challenge in the 1890s from the Jeffersonian Democrats, a

State House, Tuscaloosa, Alabama. Tuscaloosa was Alabama's state capital from 1826 to 1846. Engraving by S. Stiles & Co., New York, after *An Accurate Map of the State of Alabama and West Florida* by John LaTourette, 1837. LIBRARY OF CONGRESS

populist-oriented party that represented frustrated, poor farmers. Blacks continued to vote in the nineteenth century, although white intimidation sometimes corrupted the franchise. Economically, declining cotton prices and a lack of capital forced both white and black farmers to borrow money yearly that they could not repay, leading to a cycle of poverty that nearly enslaved them to their debtors. The growth of business opportunities in Alabama's mineral region, especially around the postwar town of Birmingham, caused the usual problems associated with rapid industrialization. Even more dramatic changes occurred socially. Although discriminated against, blacks were able to create their own communities with thriving churches, fraternal organizations, and schools—a shining example of which was Booker T. Washington's Tuskegee Institute.

At the end of the nineteenth century, Alabamians struggled with poverty, social dislocation, a racial caste system, and political corruption. Although these problems were addressed in the twentieth century, they continued to trouble Alabamians and perhaps always will.

See also **Confederate States of America; Reconstruction,** *subentry on* **In the South.**

Bibliography

Dorman, Lewy. *Party Politics in Alabama from 1850 through 1860*. 1935. Reprint, Tuscaloosa: University of Alabama Press, 1995.

Going, Allen J. *Bourbon Democracy in Alabama, 1874–1890*. 1951. Reprint, Tuscaloosa: University of Alabama Press, 1992.

Hackney, Sheldon. *Populism to Progressivism in Alabama*. Princeton, N.J.: Princeton University Press, 1969.

Mills, Gary B. "Slavery In Alabama." In *Dictionary of Afro-American Slavery*. Edited by Randall M. Miller and John David Smith. Westport, Conn.: Greenwood Press, 1988.

Rogers, William Warren, et al. *Alabama: The History of a Deep South State*. Tuscaloosa: University of Alabama Press, 1994.

Thornton, J. Mills III. *Politics and Power in a Slave Society: Alabama, 1800–1860*. Baton Rouge: Louisiana State University Press, 1978.

HENRY WALKER

ALASKA   In 1867 Alaska became the first noncontiguous U.S. possession. Discovered in 1741 by Vitus Bering, a Danish navigator commissioned by Peter the Great for Russia, the territory had been only lightly settled before the American purchase; the largest number of Russians ever in the colony at one time was 823. Having exhausted the territory's fur supply, and fearing its vulnerability to foreign attack, Russia sold the region to the United States for $7.2 million.

Though the United States had not previously expressed a desire for Alaska, Secretary of State William Seward thought the region would help facilitate American trade with the Orient and that it would prove useful as the U.S. Navy developed a presence in the Pacific. Despite some early criticism (those who opposed the purchase referred to Alaska as "Seward's Folly," "Icebergia," and "Walrussia"), the Senate quickly and decisively approved the purchase

Klondikers in Alaska. Klondikers climbing the "Golden Stair" and "Peterson's Trail," Chilcoot Pass, Alaska. Published by Keystone View Company, Meadville, Pennsylvania, c. 1898. LIBRARY OF CONGRESS

treaty by a vote of 37–2, and national editorial opinion was generally favorable.

Because there was no economic base to support settlement, Congress did not immediately provide civil government, though numerous scientific and U.S. Army teams undertook exploratory missions. A group of San Francisco investors secured a lucrative government lease for an annual harvest of fur seals on the Pribilof Islands in the Bering Sea, and prospectors began to examine the mineral potential of river valleys in the interior. Nevertheless, the territory was largely dormant for seventeen years, governed at first from Sitka by the U.S. Army, and later by the U.S. Navy. Several conflicts with the native people, mostly the result of insensitive administration of justice, were put down by the military force. Coverage of these incidents in the national press led to official criticism of the military government. The

discovery of major lode gold deposits at present-day Juneau in 1880 led Congress to pass the Organic Act of 1884, which appointed a civil governor, a federal district judge, and other officials. The act also directed the federal government to establish schools throughout the territory.

The canning of Pacific salmon began in Alaska in 1878 and by 1890 had become the dominant economic activity. However, because the industry was seasonal and brought its own labor force, the territory reaped little economic benefit.

In 1879 the California naturalist John Muir explored Glacier Bay in the Alexander Archipelago, where he discovered and named Muir Glacier. His rhapsodic celebration of the region's wilderness and natural environment, published in magazine articles and scientific journals, led to an embryonic tourist industry. Much to Muir's displeasure, however, the tourists came on excursion boats and did little but gawk at the shoreline.

Despite a program for setting up village grammar schools established by the government and missionary societies to acculturate the native people, the nonnative population of about five thousand had a minimal impact on the thirty thousand Indians, Aleuts, and Eskimos, most of whom continued to pursue their traditional customs, including subsistence hunting and gathering. Congressional legislation in 1891, authorizing homesteads for business purposes to aid the canning industry (authorization for residences came in 1898) and providing for the platting of townsites and the sale of town lots, failed to stimulate new settlement.

The 1896 discovery of the great Klondike gold deposits, just over the border with Canada, finally brought settlers to Alaska. This spectacular gold rush attracted forty thousand people to the Yukon (Canada) and Alaska; the towns of Dawson, Nome, and Fairbanks arose soon afterward. The "Trail of '98," over Chilkoot Pass near Skagway, brought Alaska into the twentieth century, leading to new towns, a permanent settler population, and sustained economic development.

See also **Alaska Purchase; American Indian Societies,** *subentry on* **Alaska; Gold Rushes and Silver Strikes.**

Bibliography

Gibson, James. *Imperial Russia in Frontier America: The Changing Geography of the Supply of Russian America, 1784–1867.* Oxford: Oxford University Press, 1976.

Hinckley, Ted C. *The Americanization of Alaska, 1867–1897.* Palo Alto, Calif.: Pacific, 1972.

Pierce, Richard A. *Russian America: A Biographical Dictionary.* Kingston, Ont.: Limestone, 1990.

Sherwood, Morgan. *The Exploration of Alaska, 1865–1900.* Fairbanks: University of Alaska Press, 1992.

STEVE HAYCOX

ALASKA PURCHASE   The Alaska Purchase (1867–1868) was the culmination of a long period of diplomatic negotiation and commercial rivalry between the United States and Russia. U.S. interest in the area known as Russian America (comprising present-day Alaska and extending southward along the Pacific Coast into northern California) dated back as early as the 1790s. Drawn by lucrative trading possibilities, which included the fur industry, whaling, and fishing, American merchants soon provided stiff competition to the handful of Russian businessmen and colonists in Alaska. In September 1821, Alexander I issued a *ukase* closing the north-west coast of the North American continent to all but Russian traders. This brought forth vehement opposition in the United States and was one of the factors that led to the issuance of the Monroe Doctrine in 1823 calling for no further European colonization in the New World. Diplomatic protests by Secretary of State John Quincy Adams led Russia to reconsider its action and in 1824 a treaty between the two nations restored the Americans' trading rights in the region.

After 1824, Americans steadily and successfully began to dominate the Alaskan economy. Tremendous growth in the whaling and ice industries more than made up for the shrinking fur resources. In 1846 the United States purchased the Oregon Territory (into which thousands of American settlers had already moved) from the British, and the Mexican cession of California after the Mexican War of 1846–1848 gave the United States nearly complete control of the Pacific Coast of North America. The growing American presence in the region, together with the recognition that Alaska was a monetary drain on the Russian treasury, moved the Russian government to begin tentative negotiations in 1854 for the sale of the territory to the United States. Though the sectional crisis and resulting Civil War in America postponed the negotiations, they were begun with new vigor in 1866 by U.S. Secretary of State William Seward, a committed market and territorial expansionist. In March 1867, Seward and Russian minister Eduard Stoeckl agreed that the United States would pay Russia $7.2 million for Alaska.

The treaty engendered heated debate in the Senate. Supporters argued that the purchase would aid U.S. commerce in the region, assist in opening greater U.S. trade with Asia, and help to fulfill America's manifest destiny to control the North American continent. Opponents charged that the Russian price was too high, that the territory was virtually worthless, and that America's action might provoke difficulties with British Canada. The chairman of the Senate Foreign Relations Committee, Charles Sumner, made an eloquent plea for the purchase, however, and the treaty was approved on 9 April 1867. A year later, the House of Representatives approved the $7.2 million appropriation.

Charges of bribes, kickbacks, and illegal lobbying were raised after the treaty had been approved. Although the ensuing investigations of the scandal turned up little concrete evidence to support the charges, the odium associated with the Alaska Purchase may have set back simultaneous U.S. efforts to purchase the Danish West Indies and Santo Domingo.

Bibliography

Holbo, Paul S. *Tarnished Expansion: The Alaska Scandal, the Press, and Congress, 1867–1871*. Knoxville: The University of Tennessee Press, 1983.

Jensen, Ronald J. *The Alaska Purchase and Russian-American Relations*. Seattle: University of Washington Press, 1975.

Kushner, Howard I. *Conflict on the Northwest Coast: The United States and the Pacific Northwest, 1790–1867*. Westport, Conn.: Greenwood Press, 1975.

MICHAEL L. KRENN

ALCOHOLIC BEVERAGES   The manufacture and use of alcoholic beverages changed dramatically in the United States during the nineteenth century. In 1800 most Americans drank large quantities of distilled spirits, usually whiskey. Although a few large-scale distillers existed, most producers were farmers who converted small quantities of surplus grain, customarily corn and rye, into preservable liquid assets that could be consumed, traded, or sold later. Aged only slightly, if at all, this colorless whiskey was often taken straight or mixed with water. Only the wealthy could afford to add sugar. Whiskey was drunk by men and women, adults and children, and all races and social classes, although adult white males consumed the greatest amount, perhaps as much as five-sixths of all the whiskey produced. In the early 1800s the typical American man drank a half-pint of whiskey per day.

Because of a national corn glut, which increased after settlement of the agriculturally lush Midwest in the early 1800s, whiskey was cheap. At five cents per fifth, it cost less than coffee, tea, milk, rum, or wine. From 1801 until the Civil War there was no federal tax on whiskey. In contrast duties were levied on imported wine and rum or American rum made from imported molasses. The high price of wine limited its market to the wealthy, and consequently it became associated with snobbery. Although Thomas Jefferson and others tried to establish vineyards, these efforts failed.

In 1800 Americans drank little beer, partly because American brewing techniques produced an unappetizing, bitter brew. In addition the small size of cities, the difficulty of transportation, and the lack of refrigeration burdened brewers. Many taverns did not even sell beer because demand was so slow that a tapped keg often went stale before it was empty. Some housewives made mildly alcoholic small beer, which kept only a few days.

After whiskey, the most important alcoholic beverage in the first third of the century was cider. Farmers in apple-growing areas routinely pressed large quantities of fruit. Cider fermented to about 10 percent alcohol, roughly double beer's potency, and was stored for use throughout the winter. Although city dwellers drank little, rural Americans took prodigious quantities. In some areas a majority of the alcohol that was consumed was in the form of cider. John Adams claimed that his good health came from drinking a tankard every morning. After the temperance movement took hold in the 1830s, many farmers abandoned cider, and some even cut down orchards.

Cider also had other uses. Some makers set hard cider outside on cold autumn nights to freeze the water in the beverage. In the morning the more potent portion was separated from the ice and poured off as applejack, which averaged about 20 percent alcohol. Cider was also distilled into brandy. In the South, where peaches grew better than apples, people drank fermented peach juice called peachy, or they distilled peachy into brandy.

Temperance and Mixed Drinks

During the 1830s and 1840s American drinking patterns underwent a dramatic change. The Second

Advertisement for Lager Beer. Polar bears distribute mugs of beer to sweating men and boys. A young polar bear is fed beer by an older bear, bottom right. Lithograph by A. Hoen and Co., Baltimore, Maryland, c. 1877. LIBRARY OF CONGRESS: PRINTS AND PHOTOGRAPHS DIVISION

Great Awakening, a series of evangelical Protestant revivals that swept across the country during the first third of the century, led to the temperance movement. A majority of participants in both the revivals and the antiliquor campaign were women. They attacked male drinking because of ties to prostitution, gambling, and wife beating and because husbands spent money on liquor rather than on family needs. Although rooted in religion and morals, the temperance movement also promoted abstinence to increase productivity and efficiency in an emerging industrial economy.

At first antiliquor forces mainly attacked hard liquor since Americans consumed so much whiskey, and temperance advocates merely urged restraint in use. Over time, however, antiliquor leaders found that promoting moderate drinking was difficult because virtually all topers proclaimed themselves moderate no matter how much they consumed. Opponents began to demand that drinkers abandon hard liquor altogether to avoid any temptation toward drunkenness. After temperance supporters were accused of seeking to deprive the poor of whiskey while the wealthy continued to drink wine, the antiliquor movement adopted teetotalism, a pledge to oppose alcohol in all forms.

By 1850 drinking patterns showed the effect of the temperance movement. While whiskey was still the dominant alcoholic beverage, its consumption had fallen by half or more. During the previous two decades about half the population, especially evangelical Protestants, had become abstainers. Whiskey lost its prestige, and many Americans now equated its use with moral degradation. Although earlier patterns of drinking raw whiskey straight or with water continued among the lower classes and especially in western frontier saloons, the emerging middle class, obsessed with respectability, was committed to abstinence. Teetotalism prevailed among evangelical Protestants who lived in rural areas, in small towns, and in middle-class neighborhoods in cities.

Meanwhile, wealthy drinkers began to consume mixed drinks. They invented the cocktail, which included whiskey, water, ice, sugar, and usually a bit of lemon, bitters, or other flavoring. Rich southerners combined whiskey, water, sugar, and fresh mint into mint juleps. Americans tried other kinds of distilled spirits. Wealthy women took fruit-flavored cordials, made by adding crushed fruit to brandy and allowing it to set a considerable time. Recipe books told women how to make cordials at home. The most prominent new mixed beverage was the martini, composed of imported gin and vermouth with crushed ice. The invention of ice-making equipment and carbonated water encouraged further experiments in mixed drinks.

By 1850 bartending had emerged as a specialized profession that required detailed knowledge of how to mix numerous drinks. Many guides were published, and they often included instructions on how to dilute or doctor beverages, how to use cheaper substitutes, or how to mislabel items to fetch a higher price. For example, whiskey, water, and food coloring could be sold as red burgundy wine, which was more expensive than watered whiskey. Bartenders also learned how to use chemicals, some poisonous, to put a head on stale beer.

Immigrants and Prohibition

By the middle of the century the large numbers of German immigrants had brought to the United States both an increased demand for beer and new brewing techniques. They made lager beer with a yeast that operated slowly on the brew during storage. Germans often drank beer on Sundays in suburban beer gardens, where families gathered to drink, eat, talk, and sing for the day. Temperance advocates keenly disliked these well-advertised, highly visible, and very popular establishments on the edges of most large American cities. Beer gardens promoted alcohol use, encouraged children to drink or to watch their parents drink, and did a brisk business on Sunday, which evangelicals believed should be a holy day of rest.

By the 1840s, after opponents of alcohol recognized that the call for voluntary abstinence through evangelical religion had no effect on heavy drinkers, the wealthy, the self-indulgent, or immigrants, they turned to local prohibition. Wet areas, however, supplied their dry neighbors, so antiliquor forces then demanded statewide bans. In 1851 Maine became the first state to outlaw alcohol, and several other states followed. All eventually repealed these early prohibition laws, but local and state prohibition remained an important political issue for the rest of the century.

In 1873–1874 women organized a nationwide crusade to close saloons. Out of this movement, which enjoyed considerable success in small towns dominated by evangelical Protestants, came the Woman's Christian Temperance Union (WCTU). This group became the largest women's organization in the country, with 150,000 members in the late nineteenth century. Under the dynamic leadership of Frances Willard, the WCTU lobbied to ban saloons, urged schools to teach abstinence, called for local and state prohibition, opposed politicians who rejected prohibition, and demanded the vote for women. While the

WCTU had ties to the evangelical movement, it also benefited from a widespread belief that women were society's moral guardians. The WCTU demanded an end to drinking in the name of respectability.

Beer and Moonshine

Despite opposition, beer consumption gradually rose. Most of the increase was among immigrants until the Civil War, when the federal government, desperate for revenue, imposed a high tax on distilled spirits. The high price of hard liquor caused popular consumption to shift from whiskey to beer. Many temperance advocates had always considered whiskey the greater evil, and pressure from antiliquor forces ensured that the spirits tax remained after the war.

By the 1880s beer had displaced whiskey as the most popular alcoholic beverage in the United States. Tax policies that favored beer and growing German immigration played roles, but the larger reason for the shift was the changing nature of the country. The United States now had numerous large cities, an industrial economy, and many recent European immigrants who came from cultures that accepted alcohol. Large cities supported vast breweries that, through economies of scale, turned out cheap beer. City residents entered saloons to drink a beer for five cents and to eat a free lunch. The largely immigrant working class spent its free time and discretionary income in saloons not only drinking beer but also seeking jobs, getting loans, organizing unions, and participating in politics.

Ever since the beginning of the industrial age, factory owners, who wanted to maintain rigid work discipline and who had expensive machinery that could be easily damaged, had opposed alcohol. Many capitalists, including John D. Rockefeller, supported both temperance and prohibition. A number not only banned alcohol at work but sought to prevent employees from imbibing off the job. In large cities, however, such control proved impossible, and many employers settled for keeping alcohol out of the workplace and encouraging beer over whiskey. One way to do this was to make sure that only beer was sold nearby. Many employers felt that allowing an employee to take a beer before work at a nearby saloon was a small price to pay to keep whiskey off the factory floor.

The most successful brewers made fortunes and quickly realized that they could make even more money by controlling sales as well as production. Brewers owned or controlled large numbers of urban saloons, and the profits from vertical integration enabled brewers in Milwaukee and St. Louis to dominate the industry. By 1900 industry consolidation produced nationally recognized and marketed brands of beer.

Throughout the century Americans had used alcohol-based patent medicines, but this industry exploded after the Civil War. Better advertising and sales techniques contributed to the acceleration, but so did the antiliquor movement. Because no labeling was required, users who took patent medicine did not always know what they were drinking. One alcohol-laden product, Lydia Pinkham's Elixir for Female Complaints, was widely favored by members of the WCTU.

An unforeseen consequence of the high tax on distilled liquor after the Civil War was the promotion of illicit spirits. Distilling technology was relatively simple and widely known throughout Appalachia, where many farmers continued to distill corn in violation of the tax law. Confederate veterans in particular took pride in defying the federal tax. Curiously, areas that supported moonshiners also tended to back prohibition. Moonshiners often preferred local prohibition because it meant that they did not have to compete with legitimate distillers. Prohibitionists believed that, while they could not stop drinking, they could at least humiliate consumers by forcing them to buy from unsavory and perhaps unsafe suppliers. Opponents of alcohol were determined to link drinking to a lack of respectability.

At the end of the nineteenth century more than half of Americans still lived on farms, but the rapidly growing cities, filled with factories and immigrants, were about to overtake rural America. During the century alcohol consumption had declined among the rural populace. These people no longer produced or consumed much cider, tended toward temperance and prohibition, and in the days before bottled beer were outside the beer distribution network. Urban immigrants primarily drank beer in politically influential saloons that wealthy, powerful brewers owned or controlled. Well-to-do urban sophisticates sampled a variety of mixed beverages and sometimes even drank wine, but whiskey remained the most prominent of the distilled spirits.

See also **Blue Laws; Brewing and Distilling; Patent Medicines; Reform, Social; Saloons and the Drinking Life; Temperance Movement; Working-Class Culture.**

Bibliography

Blocker, Jack S., Jr. *American Temperance Movements: Cycles of Reform.* Boston: Twayne, 1989.

Bordin, Ruth. *Frances Willard: A Biography.* Chapel Hill: University of North Carolina Press, 1986.

Edmunds, Lowell. *The Silver Bullet: The Martini in American Civilization.* Westport, Conn.: Greenwood, 1981.

Hooker, Richard J. *Food and Drink in America: A History.* Indianapolis, Ind.: Bobbs-Merrill, 1981.

Lanza, Joseph. *The Cocktail: The Influence of Spirits on the American Psyche.* New York: St. Martin's, 1995.

Miller, Wilbur R. *Revenuers and Moonshiners: Enforcing Federal Liquor Law in the Mountain South, 1865–1900.* Chapel Hill: University of North Carolina Press, 1991.

W. J. RORABAUGH

ALGER, HORATIO

ALGER, HORATIO   The best-known nineteenth-century American writer of fiction for boys, Horatio Alger Jr. (1832–1899) was born near Boston into an improvident Unitarian family. Alger was educated at Harvard College, from which he graduated in 1852, and at Harvard Divinity School, where he earned a diploma in 1860. Dismissed from the Unitarian pulpit in Brewster, Massachusetts, in 1866 for pederasty, he settled in New York and began to earn his living as a writer of juvenile fiction. His novel *Ragged Dick* was serialized in 1867 and established the formula he followed in more than one hundred subsequent stories about virtuous boys who rise from rags to respectability. Alger traveled to Europe in 1860–1861 and 1871 and to the American West in 1877, 1878, and 1890 to gather material for his fiction, although he hardly varied the basic plot of his novels. To compete with the dime novelists, Alger began to write increasingly sensational novels in the late 1870s. In failing health from heart disease, he retired to Natick, Massachusetts, in 1896 and anointed Edward Stratemeyer (1862–1930), later the creator of the Rover Boys series (1899–1926), as his literary heir. Alger died in Natick three years later, leaving a small estate. Shortly before his death, he estimated that 800,000 copies of his novels had been sold. A decade later approximately one million copies of Alger's books were being sold each year, with about seventeen million sold by the end of the 1920s, when they finally began to lapse from print.

See also **Dime Novels and Story Papers; Literature,** *subentry on* **Children's Literature.**

Bibliography

Nackenoff, Carol. *The Fictional Republic: Horatio Alger and American Political Discourse.* New York: Oxford University Press, 1994.

Scharnhorst, Gary, with Jack Bales. *The Lost Life of Horatio Alger Jr.* Bloomington: Indiana University Press, 1985.

GARY SCHARNHORST

AMERICAN COLONIZATION SOCIETY.
See **Colonization, African American**

AMERICAN INDIANS

[This entry includes an overview of American Indians and subentries on **American Indian Religions, American Indian Art, Law in Indian Communities, Wars and Warfare, Treaties and Treatymaking, U.S. Government Policies, Indian Removal,** and the **Image of the Indian.**]

OVERVIEW

In the eighteenth century the economic and military alliances that tribal communities forged with European colonial powers shaped American Indian life in every corner of North America. These alignments drew some tribes into formal alliances that produced episodes of warfare and military strife. Other Indians were pulled into an expanding population of Native American consumers, who exchanged furs and other indigenous goods for European-made clothes, weapons, and foodstuffs. During the colonial era tribes and non-Indians vied with one another for dominance and influence.

The victory of the American colonists over King George in 1783, the French exit from the Mississippi Valley in 1803, and the gradual contraction of the Spanish empire in the succeeding two decades spelled defeat for most eighteenth-century Indian alliances. Without potential European allies to call on for protection, tribal leaders were forced to turn to other native groups for assistance or to face these "Americans" alone. Tragically this lonely resistance was quickly overwhelmed. In the cruel arithmetic of the nineteenth century, the additions to the power and international prestige of the United States more than equaled the simultaneous subtractions from the influence and autonomy of the continent's native peoples.

During the nineteenth century the Native American population of the United States reached its lowest point in history. By 1800 the combination of European diseases, disruptions in food supplies, and forced removal from traditional homelands had reduced the Indian population from a precontact level of approximately 5 million to 600,000. Despite the losses suffered in the colonial era, many sections of the United States were largely Native American in population and character. In 1800 Indians were by far the majority population in the Southwest, across the trans-Mississippi West, in Florida and the interior Southeast, and across the Great Lakes. By century's end the non-Indian population of the country had grown from 5 million to 76 million and the native population had fallen to 250,000. Infectious diseases, endemic illnesses associated with poverty and poor sanitation, warfare, and forced migration made it virtually impossible to maintain steady communities. Only the Navajos in Arizona and New Mexico, who suffered periods of intense suffering but who were isolated from frequent contact with outsiders and were remarkably resilient in adapting to new technologies, saw their numbers increase over the course of the century.

For Native Americans, as for factory workers in Pittsburgh or railroad men in Chicago, the nineteenth century was a century of steel. Steel weapons decimated their game, killed their warriors, and destroyed their villages; steel rails penetrated and divided their homelands; and conditions as hard as steel separated them from the relative freedom and prosperity of earlier times. Despite this grim prospect, however, most Indian groups began the century hoping to maintain some measure of autonomy and political independence. Military discipline and a sharp eye at the trader's block had been the keys to Native American survival in the eighteenth century, and Indian people expected those skills to continue to serve them well in the decades to come. After all, despite Anthony Wayne's ambiguous victory in 1794 over the Ohio Indian confederacy at Fallen Timbers, the United States emerged from its war with Great Britain and the turbulent decade of the 1790s little more than a paper empire. Its standing army was small and poorly armed, its people were divided and self-absorbed, and it seemed unlikely to muster the strength to extend its influence across the vast territory that lay within its newly drawn national borders.

Events quickly shattered the Indians' hopes for an extension of their earlier status. First, in 1803 France unexpectedly decided to divest itself of the Louisiana Territory, and its war with England made the United States the only logical customer for the property. Cash and credit totaling $15 million transferred enough new territory to the United States to double the extent of its official boundaries. French military leaders and French traders no longer had an interest in supporting their Choctaw, Osage, Sauk, and Sioux allies. Barely a decade later Great Britain, which had sacked the U.S. capital and run roughshod over the American fleet during the War of 1812, decided a reliable English-speaking ally in North America was preferable to endless conflict. The armistice that concluded the War of 1812 secured the northern border of the United States and set in motion the demilitarization of the entire relationship between London and Washington, D.C. Leaders like Tecumseh, the Shawnee who perished in the war fighting alongside a retreating British regiment, or the Creek William Weatherford could no longer look to the British for weapons, ammunition, and encouragement. Finally,

Spain's withdrawal from Florida and the Rio Grande Valley in 1821 eliminated yet another source of support from Native Americans. Pensacola traders and Rio Grande missions would no longer help block the white American onslaught. To be sure, the opening of the Santa Fe Trail in 1821 demonstrated that Mexican merchants could be important allies of Indian people but no longer did a military force behind the local officials threaten or intimidate the United States.

By mid-century the resolution of the Oregon boundary dispute with Britain and the military defeat of Mexico had eliminated the remaining parties who might have been willing to help Indian communities maintain their independence in the face of expansion. At the same time the trading relationships that underlay the old alliances and brought Native Americans new fabrics, new weapons, and new tools declined in monetary value and overall economic significance. Furs and skins were less important in a manufacturing economy whose mills spewed out mountains of woolen goods and other ready-made clothes. Foodstuffs were mass-produced on commercial farms, and native handicrafts represented only a microscopic portion of the nation's output. In business as in warfare tribal groups had few customers and little access to suppliers from outside the United States.

Three major periods of conflict marked the lives of Indian people in the nineteenth century. The first took place east of the Mississippi in the two decades following the end of the War of 1812. During that period the American military secured its control of the Southeast and the Ohio Valley, and federal officials systematically expelled native groups from the region. This was the "era of removal," when Andrew Jackson fueled his populist support by insisting that no amount of progress in education or economic development could spare a tribe from forced dislocation. By the end of the 1830s Georgia's Cherokees had reestablished their national capital beyond the Arkansas River, while the Indiana Miamis, the Illinois Potawatomis, and the Wisconsin Winnebagos had moved westward across the Mississippi. Episodes of resistance, such as the Cherokees' valiant struggle in 1831 to stop removal in the U.S. Supreme Court and Black Hawk's attempted reentry into Illinois in 1832, were ridiculed by Jackson's supporters. All were defeated.

The second period of conflict took place between 1862 and 1877, when the same nationalist forces that brought victory to the North in the Civil War inspired a process of conquest in the Southwest and on the Great Plains that spelled the end of armed resistance and the advent of the reservation era. Diplo-

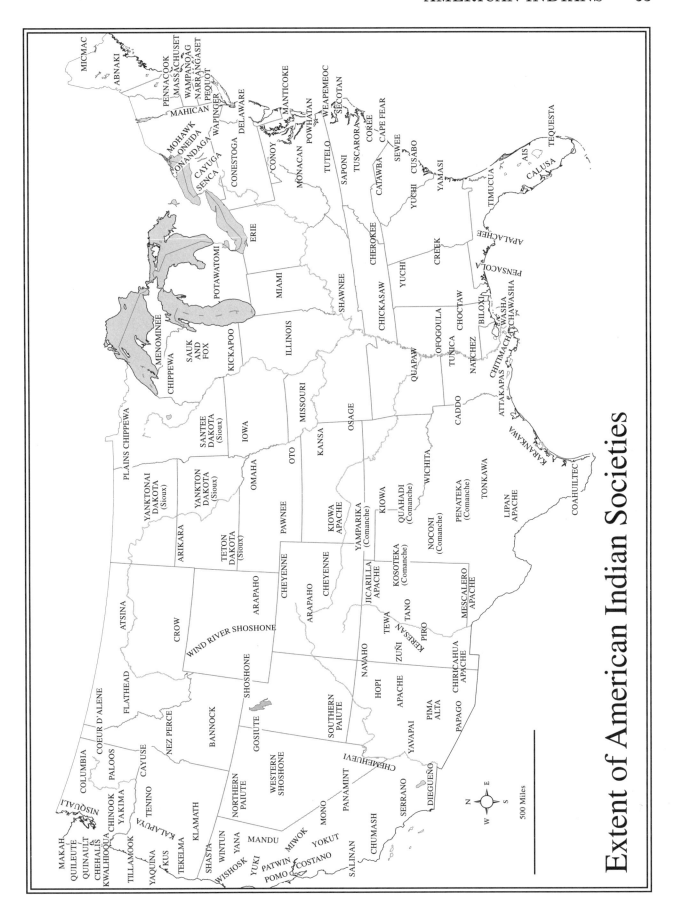

Extent of American Indian Societies

Two Generations of Sioux. Sitting Bull (c. 1831–1890; *left*) and his nephew One Bull. Copyright by Palmquist & Jurgens, 1884. LIBRARY OF CONGRESS: PRINTS AND PHOTOGRAPHS DIVISION

macy and military action secured a route for the transcontinental railroad, thereby dividing the great western buffalo herd and placing native communities within easy reach of a rapidly modernizing army. At the same time the political victory of the Republican free-soil ideology redefined a region that had once been called the "Great American Desert" as the new cradle of American democracy and economic prosperity. Dramatic military campaigns against the Santee Sioux in Minnesota, the Cheyennes in Colorado, the Navajos in Arizona, the Kiowas and Comanches in Indian Territory, and the Oglala Sioux and Cheyennes in the Dakotas and Montana punctuated this era of U.S. military conquest and economic growth.

During the third period, in the 1880s, political and military leaders in every region forced Indian communities to inhabit enclaves the white people called reservations. This policy was fueled by a humanitarian desire to concentrate Indian people into agricultural communities as well as by a ferocious demand for "unused" tribal lands. From the north woods of Michigan, Wisconsin, and Minnesota to the western prairies of the Dakotas, the arid regions of the Great

Basin, and the rangelands of the interior Northwest, Indian people found themselves with no choice but to live in new homelands with fixed borders and limited resources. Within the boundaries of these reservations, government-subsidized missionaries, schoolmasters, and policemen enforced a program designed to "civilize" and "uplift" native people.

Reservations did not always contain all the members of a single tribe. In Dakota Territory, for example, the Sioux were divided among eight separate agencies (Pine Ridge, Rosebud, Cheyenne River, Standing Rock, Crow Creek, Lower Brule, Yankton, and Santee). Other branches of the group lived in Minnesota and Montana. Agencies such as Wind River, Wyoming, and Warm Springs, Oregon, administered the affairs of two or more groups. Because Indian Office administrators believed all the Indians were evolving toward a common future as "civilized" Americans, they were not concerned that tribal traditions and leadership patterns would be disrupted by this practice.

Overt resistance to the government's policies was extremely dangerous. Bands who refused to join their kinsmen on the reservations were generally pursued by regular army units and returned by force. The most famous of these recalcitrant groups were the Apaches who followed Geronimo and the Sioux bands led by Crazy Horse and Sitting Bull. Geronimo surrendered in 1886 and the "hostile Sioux" stayed away from the Dakota agencies until 1877 when the military operations launched in the wake of the Seventh Cavalry's defeat at the Little Big Horn in 1876 caused Crazy Horse to surrender and Sitting Bull to retreat to Canada.

On the reservations themselves, tribal leaders tried to negotiate concessions from federal authorities, but often the most successful resistance leaders were religious figures who promised a millennial solution to the white onslaught. The most effective of these was Wovoka, a Paiute man from Mason Valley, Nevada, whose visionary teachings promised that all Indians who lived in peace, danced in celebration of the creator, and cooperated with non-Indians would be rewarded in heaven. His message of hope won adherents in reservation communities from California to Oklahoma, but the Ghost Dance gatherings on the western Sioux reserves frightened the authorities, setting off a chain of overreactions that led to the murder of Sitting Bull on 15 December 1890 and the tragic massacre at Wounded Knee fourteen days later. These events underscored how ruthlessly government authorities were prepared to act once they believed the reservation system was under assault.

Remarkably Native Americans in the nineteenth century developed an array of strategies to cope with and occasionally defeat the actions of the white American expansionists. Beginning in the East but spreading elsewhere during the century, Indian communities resisted the white onslaught by disappearing—retreating to tiny rural hamlets, intermarrying with other groups, or migrating across the border into Canada or Mexico. In addition American Indian leaders forced government officials to implement their policies with written treaties or laws. While frequently ignored in the nineteenth century, many of these documents were called back to life in the twentieth century as revived and educated tribes took their complaints to Congress and the courts. Even in defeat, obstinate opponents of white American nationalism, like the Cherokee chief John Ross, the Paiute author Sarah Winnemucca, the Navajo leader Manuelito, the Omaha writer Susette La Flesche, or the Sanpoil religious figure Skoalskin, left examples of resistance that inspired men and women who came after them to continue their fight.

See also **American Indian Societies; Education,** *subentry on* **Indian Schools; Expansion; Federal Land Policy; Indian Territory; Missions,** *subentry on* **North American Indians; Seminole War(s); Slavery,** *subentry on* **Indian Slaveholding.**

Bibliography

Hoxie, Frederick E., ed. *The Encyclopedia of North American Indians.* Boston: Houghton Mifflin, 1996.

Nabokov, Peter, ed. *Native American Testimony: A Chronicle of Indian-White Relations from Prophecy to the Present, 1492–1992.* New York: Viking, 1991.

Prucha, Francis Paul. *The Great Father: The United States Government and the American Indians.* Lincoln: University of Nebraska Press, 1984.

Trigger, Bruce G., and Wilcomb E. Washburn, eds. *The Cambridge History of the Native Peoples of the Americas.* Volume 1: *North America.* Cambridge, U.K., and New York: Cambridge University Press, 1996.

FREDERICK E. HOXIE

AMERICAN INDIAN RELIGIONS

By 1800 American Indian religious ideas and practices had undergone many changes because of the preceeding three hundred years of contact with invading Europeans and their descendents. Prior to meeting the newcomers, the tribal peoples had no codified, widely practiced, scriptural religion such as Christianity, Judiasm, or Islam. Rather, they had spiritual concepts and religious ceremonies that drew few distinctions between the spiritual and secular realms. Much of Indian society was intensely local and native religious practices reflected that. Villages celebrated successful hunting and mourned when men were lost in battle. Shamans conducted ceremonies, administered potions, and sang songs based on knowledge of local spiritual sites or available herbs. Even the horse-based plains peoples, who traveled frequently, had appointed places for conducting hunting ceremonies and the summer sun dance.

The colonizing Europeans failed to recognize or understand Indian religious practices. Rather, they sought large-scale conversion to Christianity and employed varied techniques to achieve that goal. The Spanish established missions from southern Florida all of the way west to northern California. In time some Pueblo groups in New Mexico adapted certain aspects of Catholicism. Elsewhere, French and English missionaries labored, usually in a less organized fashion. The results varied widely. Many tribal groups rejected or ignored the new religious teachings. Some added a few Christian practices to their existing ceremonies. Others accepted Christianity—or what they understood of it.

Those experiences led to a variety of tribal religious movements in the nineteenth century. Generally, these movements were responses to diseases

Navajo Shaman. He is seated with his priestly accoutrements. Photograph, John Hillers, c. 1872–1885. LIBRARY OF CONGRESS: PRINTS AND PHOTOGRAPHS DIVISION

brought by whites, alcohol abuse, loss of land, and collapsing economies. At other times the movements were local initiatives meant to bring fundamental changes in tribal life. In either case prophets came to the fore. The prophets usually experienced a coma or trance, during which spirits conducted them into the heavens, where they received instructions about new doctrines and ceremonies and how to redirect Indian life. As a result, the significant Indian religious movements of the century share many elements. Most called for a return to some traditional practices and reduced dependence on white trade goods. Some demanded a total rejection of non-Indian goods and even warfare against the whites, while others sought to incorporate new items as they strove to purify the village societies.

Anthropologists describe these movements as having elements of both religious and cultural revitalization. The first of the new religions began in the Northeast among the Senecas. In 1799 Handsome Lake, brother of the Seneca leader Cornplanter, appeared to have died. As the family prepared his corpse for burial, he awakened with news of his journey to the spirit world, where he had experienced visions and received a mission from the Creator. From then until his death in 1815, he taught what is known as the Code of Handsome Lake, and his ideas evolved into the Long House Religion. His code called for people to avoid alcohol, to take precautions when near those practicing witchcraft, to cease the use of "love medicines," and to have a positive attitude toward marriage and the family. He encouraged the Senecas to accept literacy, better housing, and agriculture from the whites—and to maintain peace with them.

As the Long House Religion developed, its influence spread to the other Iroquoian groups. The code prescribed that sacred rituals, including the men's chant, the great feather dance, the drum dance, and the sustenance dance, be carried out each winter. Handsome Lake's teachings incorporated elements of Christianity such as punishment of sinful behavior and warnings about the devil. He also predicted that spectacular natural disasters would herald the end of the world, a belief clearly reflecting millennial Christian ideas of the time. Seen during his life as a religious and cultural reformer, he influenced other prophets with his ideas, and the Long House Religion continued throughout the twentieth century.

Farther west another important prophet emerged among the Shawnee people in the Ohio Valley. In 1805 an alcoholic and unsuccessful shaman, Lalawethika (Noisemaker), fell into a coma. His family feared he had died, but a few hours later he regained consciousness. He reported visiting a place from

Hopi Snake Dance. The priest, with snake in mouth, performs a Hopi snake dance. Phoenix, Arizona, c. 1899. LIBRARY OF CONGRESS

which he could see both heaven and hell, where he received instructions for helping the Shawnees end their cultural decline. Announcing that he had a new name, Tenskwatawa (Open Door), he began to teach. First he denounced the white Americans as descendents of the Great Serpent, the Shawnee personification of evil. Those who cooperated with the white Americans he labeled as witches, and he led campaigns to have them burned to death. Then he introduced new ceremonies and urged his listeners to avoid white American foods, implements, and clothing. He promised those who accepted his teachings that their dead friends and relatives would return. Like Handsome Lake, he included ideas taken from Christianity. For example, he threatened those who rejected his teachings with an afterlife in a fiery hell.

To many Shawnees Tenskwatawa's preaching

came at just the right time. In June 1806 he learned of a coming solar eclipse and then predicted it to his followers. Using this as a sign of his spiritual power, he broadened his influence rapidly, and hundreds from other tribes flocked to his village, creating an immediate food shortage. In 1808 the prophet and his adherents moved to a new settlement in Indiana called Prophetstown.

At this point Tecumseh, Tenskwatawa's brother, began his effort to forge an antiwhite, multitribal alliance. Using the religious base Tenskwatawa had built, he traveled from tribe to tribe urging unity and a refusal to surrender more land to the expanding United States. His efforts ran head-on into growing frontier tensions, which led to war. In November 1811 General William Henry Harrison, who later became president, led troops to Prophetstown and defeated the Shawnees at the Battle of Tippecanoe. Tenskwatawa's promises that his ceremonies and prayers would protect the warriors from the whites' firearms failed. The loss at Tippecanoe brought many Ohio Valley Indians into the War of 1812 as allies of the British, and Tenskwatawa's religious movement almost collapsed.

A little more than three decades later, soon after the California gold rush of 1849, Indian peoples of the Pacific Northwest turned to spiritual means to retain their traditional way of life. Smohalla, a Wanapam shaman living near Walla Walla, Washington, experienced frequent visions as a young man and had a well-established following before the whites reached the area. He predicted the opening of the annual salmon run, succeeded in helping hunters locate game, directed those gathering roots to good locations, and forecasted natural phenomena such as eclipses and earthquakes. Smohalla claimed that the spirits gave him these skills, and he wielded considerable influence. A thorough traditionalist, Smohalla by 1850 argued against cooperation with the incoming white Americans. He raised public objections to ceding tribal land, to adopting white-style farming, and to abandoning Indian cultural practices. When his arguments persuaded only a few, he established a new village for his followers.

Responding to pressures from increased white settlement in the Northwest, the U.S. government sent Isaac Stevens, the territorial governor, to negotiate treaties for land and to establish Indian reservations in present-day Washington and Oregon. In 1855 he signed agreements with the larger tribes that pushed smaller groups onto reservations against their wishes or ignored them. Treaties negotiated with Stevens forced many Washington tribes onto reservations, often outside their traditional homelands. This brought armed resistance that culminated in the Yakima War of 1855–1856 and an 1858 conflict led by the Palouse and Spokane tribes. During these wars Smohalla urged neutrality and in doing so infuriated many other Indians. Following a dispute, his followers thought he had died. Returning to life after a visit to the spirit world, Smohalla proclaimed new teachings called the Washani, or Dancers, Creed, which mixed traditional practices with new ones to achieve a spiritual unity between the villagers and the natural world.

Smohalla taught his adherents not to work but to seek dreams and visions that would help them enjoy the fruits of nature. This emphasis on vision seeking earned his teachings the name Dreamer Religion. Unlike the Shawnee Tenskwatawa, Smohalla eschewed violence. If adherents to the Washani Creed dreamed enough, their ancestors would return to life, and they would achieve a balance between themselves and Mother Earth. Smohalla's teachings remained influential in the Northwest for decades after his death in 1895.

While the Dreamers had sought to keep the whites and Indians separated, another group emerged in the Northwest that called for doing just the opposite. In 1882 a Salish Indian named John Slocum slipped into a coma but soon revived and began sharing the revelations he had received while among the spirits. Slocum urged the tribes of the Northwest to quit smoking, drinking alcohol, and depending on tribal shamans. At first he attracted little attention, but a year later he sickened again. While his wife prayed for his recovery, she began to shake uncontrollably. Her experience led to the name Shaker, and by the 1890s they had organized the Indian Shaker Church. Its doctrines combined direct revelations from God through dreams with the Bible. The Shakers often "spoke in tongues" and resembled some charismatic white church groups. Originally exhibiting a thorough amalgamation of Indian and Christian religious ideas, the group split in 1927 because of differences over leadership and the use of the Bible in the services. Two organizations, the Indian Shaker Church and the Indian Full Gospel Church, emerged and continued to function as of the 1990s.

The Ghost Dance was another significant Indian religious movement of the nineteenth century. The first occurrence was in the late 1860s, when a Paiute Indian named Wodziwob fell into a trance and began preaching about his visions. While his ideas spread into the Northwest, this early movement faded quickly. The later and better-known Ghost Dance developed out of the teachings of another Paiute named Wovoka (Jack Wilson). During an 1889 solar eclipse he fell into a coma and awoke with new spiritual insights; he advocated avoiding violence, cooperating with the whites, and practicing a traditional round dance. He promised that the dancers would be blessed when they reached heaven. He also predicted droughts and claimed to enter the spirit world when in trances caused by the dancing. Some of his listeners later asserted that he promised that special Ghost Dance shirts would protect the dancers from being harmed by firearms.

A delegation of Lakota (Sioux) people visited him in 1889 then returned to their reservations and spread news of the religion. Wovoka's teachings offered hope for a better life, and soon many Indians left the reservations, gathering in the Dakota Badlands to dance and receive visions. They dreamed of long-dead friends, of the buffalo's return, and of the whites disappearing. Some Lakota shamans gave directions for preparing the Ghost Dance shirts that they claimed would provide invulnerability against the whites' weapons. As larger numbers of Indians participated in the new ceremonies, white officials became increasingly worried about violence, and James McLaughlin, the Indian agent at Standing Rock, was frightened by the rumors that circulated. Because Sitting Bull, a Hunkpapa Sioux shaman, supported the new dancing, McLaughlin ordered his arrest. Sitting Bull's followers, trying to protect him, resisted the Indian police sent to arrest him. In the melee that ensued, the police shot and killed Sitting Bull. News of the shooting spread quickly. At the Cheyenne River reservation the Lakota chief Big Foot led his band away to avoid violence and to continue the dancing, but the Seventh Cavalry pursued them. On 29 December 1890 at Wounded Knee, as the soldiers tried to disarm the Indians, a shot rang out, setting off a one-sided fight in which about two hundred Sioux and sixty soldiers were killed or wounded. This massacre ended the belief that the Ghost Dance shirts offered wearers any protection, and the movement receded almost as quickly as it had appeared.

As the century drew to a close, the Indians found themselves totally subjugated in their own homeland. They had tried military actions, trade and diplomacy, and even flight in dealing with the invading whites. Their religious initiatives demonstrated how central spiritual ideas and practices were in their tribal cultures. From Handsome Lake and the origins of the Long House Religion in 1799 through the Ghost Dance tragedy of 1890, tribal people used ceremonies and ideas obtained in traditional ways to help them face their vastly changed circumstances. New Indian religious teachings and formal groups developed because Indian dealings with the U.S. government and the pioneers brought only misery and disruption to their societies. Throughout the nineteenth century organized religious practices and groups spread far beyond individual tribes, and several attracted adherents throughout the twentieth century.

See also **Missions,** *subentry on* **Indian Responses to White Missionaries.**

Bibliography

DeMallie, Raymond J., Jr., and Douglas R. Parks, eds. *Sioux Indian Religion: Tradition and Innovation.* Norman: University of Oklahoma Press, 1987.

Dowd, Gregory Evans. *A Spirited Resistance: The North American Indian Struggle for Unity, 1745–1815.* Baltimore: Johns Hopkins University Press, 1992.

Edmunds, R. David. *The Shawnee Prophet.* Lincoln: University of Nebraska Press, 1983.

Miller, Christopher L. *Prophetic Worlds: Indians and Whites on the Columbia Plateau.* New Brunswick, N.J.: Rutgers University Press, 1985.

Ruby, Robert H., and John A. Brown. *Dreamer-Prophets of the Columbia Plateau.* Norman: University of Oklahoma Press, 1989.

Wallace, Anthony F. C. *The Death and Rebirth of the Seneca.* New York: Knopf, 1969.

ROGER L. NICHOLS

AMERICAN INDIAN ART

The nineteenth century was a period of great upheaval and change for Native Americans. Native culture, language, and religion came under increasing pressure from white missionaries and settlers. At the same time, manufactured trade goods became widely available and were incorporated into traditional art forms, creating a rich and vibrant framework for cultural expression.

Eastern Woodlands

By the time Meriwether Lewis (1774–1809) and William Clark (1770–1838) set out on their journey of discovery in 1804, most native peoples in the Eastern Woodlands had been in contact with Europeans for at least 150 years. During this time they had incorporated many new items, such as glass beads, wool cloth, and silk ribbon, into their traditional arts. In the nineteenth century native artists continued to invent ways of using these materials in greater quantity and with more expressive force. Such traditional arts as woodworking, birch-bark working, rush mat weaving, and porcupine quillwork continued much as they had for hundreds of years.

In the 1830s many eastern native groups were forced to relocate to reservations west of the Mississippi, where they shared design elements with local groups to create a new artistic style, characterized by abstract floral designs in bright contrasting colors, in both beadwork and silk ribbon appliqué. In the middle of the nineteenth century, native artists in the Great Lakes region began to produce elaborately beaded clothing and personal items. Beaded floral designs in basic colors were applied to a dark wool or velvet background. Large works were being woven on box looms to create colorful beaded sashes, garters, and large bandolier bags. By the last quarter of the nineteenth century, large quantities of native beadwork and basketry were being produced for the tourist market. This work is characterized by crowded design elements, bright colors, and the use of Victorian motifs.

Great Plains and Plateau

During the first half of the nineteenth century, native peoples of the Great Plains and Plateau regions utilized few European trade goods in their artwork. Decoration was added to clothing, leather containers, and personal items with porcupine quills, paint, and a few glass beads in predominantly white, blue, and red colors. Designs tended to be fairly similar across the region.

After 1850 Plains art began to incorporate more small glass beads in a wider range of colors. Designs usually were based on combinations of geometric units, similar to quillwork and painted designs. Some tribes, including the Lakotas, Arapahos, and Cheyennes, used long parallel rows of beadwork called "lazy stitch." Others, especially in the Plateau region, preferred to sew the beads in long, even lines following the contours of the design elements. Often the background was filled in with white or light blue beads. As more tribes were forced onto reservations, beadwork styles began to reflect specific cultural identities.

During the 1880s beadwork reached a peak, with moccasins, leggings, vests, and other articles of clothing being completely covered in beads. Many pieces were produced for sale to tourists, and new styles were introduced to meet the demand. Plains women began to use floral styles from the East and Midwest as well as pictorial images usually reserved for painted designs. During the last two decades of the nineteenth century, native women also began to incorporate the American flag into their beadwork. This design was especially popular among the Lakotas and the Plateau tribes. New objects, such as tea cozies, handbags, and wall pockets, were introduced to appeal to Victorian customers.

Southwest

The native arts of the Southwest were influenced heavily by almost 250 years of Spanish occupation.

Traditional arts among the Pueblos continued under Spanish rule. Wool and introduced dyes were used in traditional cotton weaving. Basketry and pottery production continued in form, decoration, and function much as they had for thousands of years. In 1848, as part of the Mexican cession of territory, the United States claimed New Mexico and Arizona, ending Spanish rule but not Spanish cultural influences. Sometime in the mid–nineteenth century, the Navajos learned silverworking from Mexican silversmiths. At first, bracelets, rings, and conchas were done in flat silver with little surface decoration. Later the Navajos incorporated turquoise stones and elaborately stamped designs.

The Navajos began to focus their economic activities on sheepherding and the production of large quantities of wool serapes and blankets. Soon these were in demand throughout the western United States as trade goods and for sale to tourists and collectors farther east. During the last decades of the nineteenth century, native artists began to use brighter commercial dyes and elaborate pictorial designs.

Pueblo people kept up centuries-long traditions of pottery production and cotton weaving. Each pueblo had its own style of pottery form and decoration, which often depended on available clays. At the end of the century tourism spurred new designs and forms made specifically for sale, such as the burnished black wares produced by Julian (1897–1943) and María Martínez (c. 1881–1980) of San Ildefonso pueblo in New Mexico.

Among the more nomadic peoples of the Southwest, basketry was a well-established art form. Traditional designs were woven into coiled baskets in black, brown, and red. Toward the end of the nineteenth century, the Apaches, Pimas, and Papagos began to produce large quantities of coiled basket trays, bowls, and large jars for trade to their neighbors and local white dealers. The Western Apaches became famous for the quality of their baskets, especially ollas, or large jars, which were often three to four feet high.

California

For the first half of the nineteenth century, California was under Spanish and Mexican control. The native inhabitants were forced onto large missionary estates and later onto plantations, where they were used as slave labor. The United States acquired California in 1848, and within a year thousands of whites were migrating there to join the gold rush. Throughout this very turbulent period traditional arts were a strong force for maintaining cultural identity and survival among the native Californians.

American Indian Baskets. Twelve woven Aleutian and Eskimo baskets are displayed. Photograph, c. 1899. LIBRARY OF CONGRESS

Basketry was one of the most prominent of these art forms. California basketry styles varied considerably between the northern and southern regions. The southern people preferred a coiled method of manufacture. In the central and northern areas the baskets usually were made with a twined and woven construction. Unique to this region was the addition of shells, glass beads, and small brightly colored feathers that were woven into the baskets. The Pomos especially were noted for their feather-decorated baskets. Designs were created using the natural colors of the feathers: red from the woodpecker, yellow from the flicker and goldfinch, and green from the male mallard duck. Feathers also were woven into colorful belts and made into elaborate headdresses. During the last two decades of the nineteenth century, California baskets became highly desirable and were sold to tourists at such popular resorts as Yosemite National Park.

Native peoples in California also were skilled at carving and shaping elk antler spoons and purses. The spoons were carved with elaborate geometric projections along the handle and were used for eating acorn soup. The purses were made from hollowed sections of elk antler decorated with incised lines and ridges. These purses were used for carrying dentalium shells and were symbols of wealth and status.

Northwest Coast

The Northwest Coast of North America was almost free of European settlement for the first half of the nineteenth century. However, Russian, French, Spanish, English, and American traders and explorers had sailed along the coast since the late eighteenth century. Native arts of the region were focused on ceremonial displays of wealth and status. Designs or "crests" usually were owned by a specific family lineage that reserved all rights to their use. These items were displayed ritually and often given away or destroyed in a large ceremonial feast called a *potlatch*, whose purpose was to demonstrate the wealth and prestige of a host's family.

The most prominent form of artistic expression throughout the Northwest Coast was wood sculpture. Many of the traditional designs date back a thousand years or more. A whole range of items were carved and decorated from wood, usually cedar or alder. These included large dugout canoes used for hunting whales, storage boxes, feast bowls, masks, totem poles, and speaker's staffs. Totem poles were usually erected as memorials to important lineage chiefs, or to mark special events, such as potlatches or the construction of new houses. These items were carved with animal and spirit totems as symbols of strength, power, and family allegiance. The introduction of European steel tools allowed for an increased production in wood carving and created more elaborate forms of decoration.

Another important art form of the area was weaving. Blankets and robes were woven by hand from mountain goat hair and domestic dog fur. Some of these robes, called Chilkat blankets, were woven with family crest designs in black against the natural off-white background. The introduction of European wool blankets in the middle of the nineteenth century gave rise to a new form of robe. These were decorated with mother-of-pearl buttons sewn in simple crest designs.

At the end of the nineteenth century, American anthropologists and museums began an intensive collecting campaign in the Northwest Coast area, and government officials and missionaries started to break up the traditional potlatch. These events, coupled with a series of devastating epidemics, served to severely undermine the traditional arts throughout this region.

Conclusion

Despite warfare, white encroachment, relocation, and disease, native peoples managed to continue traditional forms of artistic expression throughout the nineteenth century. As new materials became available through trade, they were incorporated into existing art forms. In some cases entirely new styles were developed to utilize these new materials. Native peoples met the increased economic pressure from European settlement by producing items for sale. The tourist market for Native American art helped both to feed struggling reservation families and to sustain cultural traditions. While some art forms are no longer practiced, many have flourished and continue to provide vehicles for the cultural identity and pride of Native American peoples into the twenty-first century.

See also **American Indian Societies.**

Bibliography

Dockstader, Frederick J. *Indian Art in America: The Arts and Crafts of the North American Indian.* New York: Promontory Press, 1974.

Hill, Tom, and Richard Hill, Sr., eds. *Creation's Journey: Native American Identity and Belief.* Washington, D.C.: Smithsonian Institution Press and the National Museum of the American Indian, 1994.

King, J. C. H. *First Peoples, First Contacts: Native Peoples of North America.* Cambridge, Mass.: Harvard University Press, 1999.

Maurer, Evan M. *The Native American Heritage: A Survey of North American Indian Art: The Art Institute of Chicago, July 16–October 30, 1977.* Chicago: the Institute, 1977.

Penney, David W., and George C. Longfish. *Native American Art.* New York: Hugh Lauter Levin Associates, 1994.

Phillips, Ruth B. *Trading Identities: The Souvenir in Native North American Art from the Northeast, 1700–1900.* Seattle: University of Washington Press, 1998.

STEPHEN COOK

LAW IN INDIAN COMMUNITIES

In 1800 hundreds of distinct Indian societies occupied what is now the continental United States. Social and political organization varied widely, from the loosely affiliated fishing communities of the Pacific Northwest to the nomadic hunting cultures of the Plains to the sedentary agricultural societies of the Southwest and the Southeast. The customary law of any given group was tailored to the needs of that society, making any generalizations about the law of Indian tribes difficult. Nonetheless, the laws of many Indian tribes shared several fundamental characteristics.

First, tribal law focused on the individual's responsibilities to the community rather than the individual's rights within the society. Tribal law did not distinguish between civil (private) and criminal (public) wrongs. As a result, tribal law also often did not distinguish between damages or restitution for private offenses and punishment for criminal conduct. Second, tribal law focused on dispute resolution designed to restore order and harmony within the society and reintegrate the wrongdoer within the community. Ostracism, public shaming, and various forms of compensation to the family of the victim were common remedies. Finally, retribution was employed in certain instances. The blood revenge of the Cherokee, for example, required the execution of the killer or a member of the killer's family, whether the death was deliberate or accidental, in order to free the spirit of the dead.

Whatever the specifics of the law within any given Indian society, the development, application, and implementation of that law were matters solely for the tribal community. In the early decades of the nineteenth century, the United States did not interfere with the internal law of the tribes, a situation that changed dramatically by the close of the century.

In the early 1830s, the U.S. Supreme Court considered for the first time the status of the Indian tribes within the American legal and political system. In the Cherokee cases, *Cherokee Nation v. Georgia* (1831) and *Worcester v. Georgia* (1832), Chief Justice John Marshall declared that Indian tribes were "domestic dependent nations," neither fully incorporated within the United States nor fully independent of it. The United States was authorized by the Constitution and the treaties to regulate trade and other external relations with the Indian nations, but the right of self-government, of regulating internal relations, belonged exclusively to the tribes themselves. The laws of the states could have no force within tribal territories, Marshall declared, and the federal government was obligated by treaty to protect the Cherokee Nation's right to govern itself.

Despite Marshall's holdings, individual states continued to assert their right to extend state law into Indian country. The state of Georgia, in a series of laws that precipitated the Cherokee cases, outlawed the Cherokee government, declared the Cherokee courts illegal, and required non-Cherokees to have a state permit to enter Cherokee country. Even after the Supreme Court declared these laws invalid, several states extended their criminal laws to tribal Indians, prosecuting and punishing Indian offenders in violation of federal law.

As a matter of federal law, nontribal jurisdiction over conduct within Indian country was limited to certain situations involving non-Indians. Under the authority of the Trade and Intercourse Act (1790, as amended in 1834) and the "bad men" provisions of many treaties, the United States tried and punished non-Indians who committed offenses against Indians within tribal territories. A more serious and far-reaching extension of American authority occurred in a line of Supreme Court cases—*United States v. McBratney* (1881) and *United States v. Draper* (1896)—holding that state courts had exclusive jurisdiction over Indian country crimes between non-Indians. With these exceptions, however, federal law protected the supremacy of tribal law within Indian territories for most of the nineteenth century.

In some instances, tribal law changed in response to contact with American law and culture. The Five Civilized Tribes of the Southeast acquired that designation because they accommodated many of the structural and substantive norms of American law within tribal law and society. The Cherokee Nation, traditionally the most adaptive of the tribes, began to enact written laws in 1808, outlawing blood revenge for accidental killings in 1810. The Nation created a judicial branch in 1820 and adopted its first constitution in 1827, modeling its tripartite form of government and its individual liberty guarantees on the U.S. Constitution. Others of the Five Tribes, such as the Creeks, also adopted written laws during the early to mid–nineteenth century (although the Creeks chose far less Anglo-American substance or structure than the Cherokees).

The success of the Cherokees and other tribes in building strong, central governments with laws often adopted from American models occurred against a backdrop of substantial change in federal Indian pol-

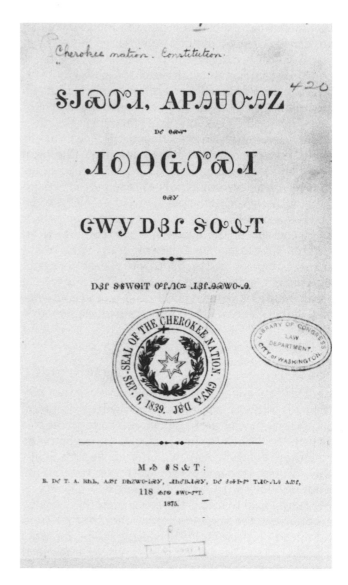

Cherokee Law. Title page, *Constitution and Laws of the Cherokee Nation,* published by the authority of the National Council of the Cherokee Nation, 1839. The page is written in Cherokee. LIBRARY OF CONGRESS: LAW LIBRARY RARE BOOK COLLECTION

icy. In the early years of the century, federal policy was oriented primarily toward keeping the peace and establishing federal primacy over the states in Indian affairs. Throughout the first three decades, however, sentiment for removal of the eastern tribes west of the Mississippi was growing. With the election of Andrew Jackson in 1828 and passage of the Removal Act in 1830, Indian removal became official governmental policy. In a generally accepted historical irony, the Cherokees' success in asserting a sovereignty that rivaled Georgia's contributed to the push for their removal from their homelands in the Southeast to the Indian Territory.

When it became apparent that an Indian territory to which all tribes could be induced or forced to remove would not be possible, the removal policy gave way to a federal policy of establishing Indian reservations. Although reservations were created throughout the nineteenth century, the reservation policy was at its peak from the Civil War until the late 1880s. Reservations were designed primarily to set limits between Indians and whites, provide the tribes with a substantial measure of separatism, and to school Native Americans in Anglo-American culture, religion, and economic ways.

Beginning in the 1870s, U.S. Indian policy began to change again. In 1871 Congress declared that no treaties would thereafter be concluded with Indian tribes. Although that statute changed little in actual practice, it nonetheless signaled a shift in federal perception of the Indian tribes, from separate sovereigns to internal groups. Policymakers began to agitate for an end to tribal separatism, pushing a doctrine of assimilation for Indian people that became official with passage of the General Allotment (or Dawes) Act in 1887. The central features of the act and the new federal policy were the allotment of tribal land in severalty to tribal members, the sale of the "surplus" lands to homesteaders, and the extension of citizenship to "civilized" Indians. This system of individualization was viewed as the cornerstone of bringing the Indians into a civilized, Christian, and agricultural way of life.

Assimilationists, perceiving Indian societies as essentially lawless, also urged Congress to enact federal laws for tribal Indians. In particular, the reformers focused on the need for federal law protecting personal and property rights and defining and punishing criminal conduct. They viewed tribal law as a "serious detriment" to the assimilation and civilization of the Indians. Preparing the Indians for full participation in the majority society required that native Americans both have the protection of American law and be held responsible under that law.

Implementing the assimilation policy, the Office of Indian Affairs (OIA), located in the Department of the Interior, pursued two strategies to control Indians' conduct and supplant tribal law. First, in 1879, the OIA established the Indian police under the control of the Indian agents. Second, in 1883, the OIA created the courts of Indian offenses to enforce an OIA-promulgated code of Indian offenses. Indian agents appointed judges from among tribal members. The code they enforced was aimed at suppressing Indian dances and the influence of medicine men, and promoting monogamous marriage and property rights. The code of Indian offenses was amended in 1892 to include any misdemeanors under state or territorial law, and to provide specifically that an Indian's failure "to adopt habits of industry, or to engage in civilized pursuits or employments" constituted a misdemeanor punishable by fines and imprisonment.

In establishing the Indian police and the courts of Indian offenses, the OIA acted without statutory authority from Congress. The OIA's actions were challenged in 1888 in a case involving an Umatilla woman who was jailed to await trial for adultery, which was not an offense under either the federal criminal code or Umatilla law. In *United States v. Clapox* (1888), the federal district court held that the courts of Indian offenses were a valid exercise of the OIA's administrative power, determining that the courts were not courts in fact, but "mere educational and disciplinary instrumentalities" that the federal government employed to "improve and elevate" the Indians.

Although the OIA had simply taken authority to regulate conduct on reservations under the code of Indian offenses, it had also been arguing since at least 1874 for federal prosecution of on-reservation crimes committed by Indians. The OIA found its test case in August 1881 when one Sioux leader, Crow Dog, killed another, Spotted Tail, on the Rosebud Reservation of the Brule Sioux. Crow Dog and Spotted Tail, both Brule warriors, were leaders of different philosophies for dealing with the might of the United States. Depending on the account, Crow Dog either laid in wait for and assassinated Spotted Tail, or killed him in self-defense. The day following the killing, the tribal council met and sent peacemakers to the families of both men. The family of Crow Dog promptly paid the family of Spotted Tail the agreed-upon compensation of $600 cash, eight horses, and one blanket. Under Brule law, the matter thus was quickly settled and tribal harmony restored.

Nonetheless, Crow Dog was immediately arrested and taken into federal custody to await trial. In 1882 he was tried in the federal territorial court, found guilty of murder, and sentenced to hang. Crow Dog appealed his conviction to the U.S. Supreme Court on the ground that the federal courts had no jurisdiction over crimes on Indian reservations. In 1883, in *Ex parte Crow Dog*, the Supreme Court ruled that nothing in the Sioux treaties granted authority to the federal government to prosecute crimes between Indians. Instead, the relations among tribal members were solely a matter for tribal law. Although the Court's decision is couched in racially offensive terms, it is a strong affirmation of Indian tribes' right to maintain "order and peace among their own members by the administration of their own laws and customs."

Crow Dog's case and the public outcry orchestrated by the OIA prompted Congress to quickly enact the Major Crimes Act (1885). The act extended federal criminal jurisdiction over seven major crimes, such as murder and rape, committed between Indians in Indian country. For the first time, Congress regulated the internal relations of the Indian tribes.

Shortly afer passage of the Major Crimes Act, a Klamath named Kagama killed another Klamath, and was prosecuted under the act. Kagama challenged the legality of the act in an appeal to the U.S. Supreme Court. In the 1886 case of *United States v. Kagama,* the Court acknowledged that Congress had no constitutional basis for the Major Crimes Act but ruled that the act was justified nonetheless by the weakness and dependency of the Indians and the corresponding power of the United States that was "necessary for their protection." The *Kagama* decision formed one of the core cases of the plenary power era of the Court's jurisprudence, allocating to Congress essentially unlimited authority to do with the Indian tribes whatever it wished.

And what of the Cherokee Nation whose legal challenges had opened the century with rulings supporting the right of tribes to be governed by their own laws? In 1896, in a case arising in the Cherokee country, *Talton v. Mayes,* the U.S. Supreme Court clarified that the U.S. Constitution did not govern the operations of tribal law and government. Questions of Cherokee law, the Court stated, are "solely matters within the jurisdiction of the courts of that nation." Nonetheless, the federal government pursued the same policy of allotment and assimilation for the Five Tribes as it did elsewhere in the country, in order to clear the way for Oklahoma statehood. Allotment of lands was forced on the Five Tribes in the 1890s, and in 1898 Congress enacted the Curtis Act, which unilaterally abolished all tribal courts in the Indian Territory.

A time of tremendous change in tribal law, the nineteenth century began with tribal law as the sole authority respecting Indians' conduct within their societies, but ended with a deliberate campaign to crush tribal customary law and replace it with federal administrative regulations and federal criminal law. By the close of the nineteenth century, in much of Indian country, tribal law was driven underground by the Office of Indian Affairs, Congress, and the Supreme Court. It is a testament to the perseverance of the Indian tribes that tribal law survived the allotment and assimilation years to eventually reemerge as a vital force in the twentieth century.

See also **American Indians,** *subentries on* **U.S. Government Policies, Indian Removal; American Indian Societies; Law,** *subentry on* **Federal Law.**

Bibliography

Harring, Sidney L. *Crow Dog's Case: American Indian Sovereignty, Tribal Law, and United States Law in the Nineteenth Century.* Cambridge, U.K.: Cambridge University Press, 1994.

Prucha, Francis Paul, ed. *Americanizing the American Indians: Writings by the "Friends of the Indian" 1880–1900.* Cambridge, Mass.: Harvard University Press, 1973.

Prucha, Francis Paul. *The Great Father: The United States Government and the American Indians.* Lincoln: University of Nebraska Press, 1984.

Strickland, Rennard. *Fire and the Spirits: Cherokee Law from Clan to Court.* Norman: University of Oklahoma Press, 1975.

Strickland, Rennard, ed. *Felix S. Cohen's Handbook of Federal Indian Law.* Charlottesville, Va.: Bobbs-Merrill, 1982.

JUDITH V. ROYSTER

WARS AND WARFARE

At the core of American Indian life lay a belief in an intimate relationship between the physical and metaphysical worlds. Indians acknowledged the endowed powers of animals and plants as a part of a system of clans or societies that included spiritual beings overseen by a Supreme Creator or Great Mystery. The acceptance of greater powers guided them to ask for supernatural assistance in battle and in surviving war. They prayed to clan totems of bears, wolves, eagles, and other powerful animals for strength, endurance, aim, speed, cunning, keen eyesight, invisibility, and prophecy. Ceremonies and rituals contributed the assistance of spiritual beings or powerful animals seen in visions or dreams to each warrior's own medicine for protection.

After the American colonists signed the Declaration of Independence in 1776, the new United States encountered many problems. Indian affairs consisted primarily of fighting the Indians and negotiating peace with them. Consequently, 371 treaties between the United States and Indian nations were forged between 1778 and 1871.

As the nineteenth century began, U.S. settlers made clear their interest in Indian lands and trade relations. The pressures of U.S. expansion led to Indian resettlement and eventually Indian removal. Following the Louisiana Purchase of 1803, the British claimed the Great Lakes region and struck an alliance with the Shawnee leader Tecumseh. Along with his brother Tenskwatawa, who was known as the Shawnee Prophet, Tecumseh rallied several Indian nations into a massive army along the Wabash

Indian Battles, 1801–1845

Arickara, 1823

Bad Axe, 1832
Wisconsin Heights, 1832
Pecatonica, 1832
Kellogg's Grove, 1832
Apple River Fort, 1832
Stillman's Defeat, 1832
Campbell's Island, 1814
Fort Dearborn, 1812
Fort Wayne, 1812
Fort Madison, 1812
Mississinewa, 1812
Fort Mason, 1813
Tippecanoe, 1811
Fort Harrison, 1812
Sink Hole, 1815

Talishatchee, 1813
Talladega, 1813
Enotachapco, 1814
Emuckfau, 1814
Horseshoe Bend, 1814
Calebee, 1814
Holy Ground, 1813
Autosse, 1813
Village Creek, 1841
Fort Sinqefield, 1813
Burnt Corn, 1813
Neches River, 1839
Fort Mims, 1813
Enconfino, 1818
Lake Pithlachoka, 1812
Plum Creek, 1840
Suwanee, 1818
Dunlawtown, 1836
Camp Izard, 1836
Fort Mellon, 1837
Withlacoochee, 1835
Wahoo Swamp, 1836
Dade's Massacre, 1835
Lake Okeechobee

River in Indiana, where they founded Prophetstown. In 1811, while Tecumseh traveled south to recruit more warriors, the governor of Indiana, William Henry Harrison, marched on Prophetstown. Contrary to his brother's wish to avoid engagement with the army, the Prophet allowed eager Indian warriors to attack at Tippecanoe Creek before dawn on 7 November. Harrison's troops suffered 37 dead and 150 wounded, but the Indians scattered. Tecumseh joined the British army in the War of 1812 and was killed at the Battle of the Thames in Canada in 1813. This pan-Indian resistance ended with Tecumseh's death. Also in 1813 Little Warrior led the Muscogee Creeks in a massacre of white Americans on the Raisin River in the Ohio Country.

In the South, Creek victories in Alabama at Burnt Corn Creek in July 1813 and at Fort Mims in August provoked U.S. Army action. After an encounter at the town of Tallassee, the Creeks besieged the fort at Talladega, but in November Andrew "Old Hickory" Jackson's militia rescued the fort and its occupants. However, Creek successes at Emuckfaw and Enotachopoco in January 1814 caused concern among whites. On 27 March, in the Battle of Horseshoe Bend on the Tallapoosa River, the Muscogee Creeks met their ultimate defeat at Jackson's hands, and the resulting treaty cost them twenty-three million acres of land. The Muscogee Creeks who escaped to northern Florida joined the Seminoles, whose bands included the Mikisuki Seminoles in southern Florida. In late 1816 the First Seminole War broke out in Florida, which was still under Spanish rule. Jackson emerged victorious over the Seminoles in early 1818.

As settlers increasingly pushed into the Ohio Country, wars with Indians became inevitable. The encroachment of settlers and miners seeking lead in southwestern Wisconsin spurred the Winnebago (Ho-Chunk) uprising of 1827 known as the Red Bird War. The U.S. government sent agents to negotiate with the Indians for their lands, but a Winnebago attack on a white family near Prairie du Chien, Wisconsin, forced Red Bird into a defensive position.

In 1804 the Sauk and Fox Indians relinquished their land in a treaty, but Ma-ka-ta-i-me-she-kiakiak, known as Black Hawk, refused to accept the treaty. The Jackson administration's Indian Removal Act of 1830 provoked outrage among the Sauks, Fox, Creeks, Seminoles, and other groups. In 1832 Black Hawk led Sauk and Fox warriors in three battles to regain their original homelands at Saukenuk, now Rock Island, Illinois. The Indians won the first two battles, Stillman's Run, Illinois, on 5 April

Indian Battles, 1846–1890

and the Battle of Wisconsin on 21 July. On 3 August a force of 1,300 U.S. soldiers confronted the famed Indian warrior at Bad Axe River in Wisconsin. The remaining small band of warriors was no match for the army, and soldiers clubbed, stabbed, and shot Indians in the resulting massacre. About two hundred Indians crossed the Mississippi River, where hostile Sioux scalped them or took them prisoner. Black Hawk escaped to a camp of Winnebagos, who turned him over to U.S. authorities for a reward of $100 and twenty horses.

The U.S. government negotiated treaties for removal of the Creeks, Choctaws, Chickasaws, and Cherokees, and then focused on the troublesome Seminoles in Florida. Between 1835 and 1842 diverse Seminole bands, which included Creek allies and escaped African American slaves, fought twelve U.S. generals in eight engagements. The Indians finally, in small bands, accepted removal to the West, but the leader Osceola resisted. After achieving several victories, he eventually caught pneumonia and surrendered in 1837. Coacochee, the last holdout, surrendered in 1841. The Seminole Wars cost the United States $15 to $20 million.

In the West the Republic of Texas in 1836 petitioned the United States for statehood. When Texas

War Dance. War dance of the Sauks and Foxes by Corbould, after a painting by P. Rindisbacher. Printed by C. Hullmandel, c. 1825–1834. LIBRARY OF CONGRESS

finally entered the Union in 1845, it brought conflicts with a new universe of tribes. Comanches and Kiowas ruled the southern plains, including much of Texas, as part of their raiding economy. All peoples who trespassed into their domain were subject to attacks.

Small-scale Indian wars broke out frequently in the Northwest. In 1847 a band of Cayuse Indians in Oregon killed Marcus Whitman; his wife, Narcissa Whitman; and twelve other white settlers and seized fifty men, women, and children as hostages. The clergyman Cornelius Gilliam, who had fought Indians in the East and believed in extermination, raised a militia of Oregonians to hunt the Cayuses. After two years of retreating, the Cayuse leaders surrendered, and they were executed. In 1855 and 1856 the Yakimas and their allies the Walla Wallas, Umatillas, and Cayuses attacked settlers in the Washington State area. In September 1858 Colonel George Wright met a united force of Coeur d'Alenes, Spokanes, and Palouses led by the Yakima chief Kamaiakan on the Spokane Plain and defeated them badly. The Indians also lost the Battle of Four Lakes the same week. In Oregon volunteer soldiers massacred twenty-three Indian women, children, and old men in the fall of 1855, and warriors from the Taklema and Tututni tribes raided the Rogue River valley, killing twenty-seven whites at one settlement.

The discovery of gold in California in 1848 and the subsequent inrush of whites in 1849 alarmed the entire Indian population. In 1850 the California Indian population numbered about 100,000, but thirty years later the population had declined to 16,000. Gold miners and Miwok and Yokut Indians fought the Mariposa War in California in 1850 and 1851. Chief Tenaya led the Miwok and Yokut Indians in attacks on miners in the Sierra Nevada foothills and in the San Joaquin Valley. After his trading post was burned, James D. Savage led the Mariposa Battalion in pursuit of the Indians, and hostilities declined. Throughout 1851 the Yumas and Mojaves skirmished with settlers in California and Arizona.

During the Civil War several western Indian nations fought for the Confederacy, while other Indians assisted the Union east of the Mississippi. From 1861 to 1863 Apaches raided U.S. and Mexican settlements along the Arizona-Mexico border. When blame for a raid on John Ward's ranch fell on Cochise (1810?–1874), a chief of the Chiricahua Apaches, Lieutenant George N. Bascom seized Cochise's relatives. Cochise was falsely accused of kidnapping a settler's child. But the famed leader escaped, slashing his way through the tent in which he was talking with Bascom. Cochise, leading the Chiricahua Apaches, took American prisoners of his own, whom he tortured and killed, and killed Mexicans along the But-

Custer's Last Charge. General George Custer's final engagement at the Battle of Little Bighorn, Montana, 25 June 1876. Lithograph by the Milwaukee Litho. & Engr. Co, 1876, after drawing by Feodor Fuchs. LIBRARY OF CONGRESS

terfield Route. The Mimbreno Apaches, led by Mangas Coloradas, Cochise's father-in-law, and the White Mountain Apaches, who were likely the band guilty of raiding Ward's ranch, joined in the hostilities. Bascom hung the Apache hostages, including Cochise's brother and two nephews. During the succeeding months of 1861 the hostile Apaches killed about 150 whites and Mexicans. The army captured Mangas Coloradas during peace talks near Pinos Altos on 17 January 1863. Mescalero Apaches continued attacks to the east, near El Paso. By the spring of 1863 the scout and Indian agent Kit Carson ended those confrontations, and the Mescalero Apaches moved onto the Bosque Redondo (Round Grove of Trees) reservation in New Mexico. However, Cochise continued his campaign until 1869.

In 1862 the Santee Indians, facing starvation, left their reservation and raided German farms for small livestock, leading to the Minnesota War, or Little Crow War. On 18 August the Santees began attacking, killing about four hundred whites. Subsequently Little Crow led two assaults on Fort Ridgely and sacked the village of New Ulm. At Birch Coulee, Little Crow attacked soldiers on burial detail, but the soldiers circled their wagons and resisted for thirty-one hours while waiting for a relief force. About seven hundred Santees struck Wood Lake on 23 September but were no match for the soldiers' artillery, and many of the defeated Santees scattered to the Dakota Territory and Canada. More than three hundred Santees were indicted for the attacks, but President Abraham Lincoln commuted the sentences of most. Nevertheless, thirty-eight Indians were hung on 26 December 1862 at Mankato, Minnesota.

The Kickapoos and some Potawatomis moved their camps into Mexico. In 1862 a Confederate battalion unsuccessfully engaged Kickapoos at Little Concho River, and some Texas Rangers experienced defeat at Dove Creek in 1865. Kickapoos in Kansas and Texas sought to join the bands in Mexico, but in 1873 Colonel Ranald Mackenzie and the Fourth Cavalry crossed the Rio Grande to bring all the Kickapoos to Indian Territory. While the warriors were away hunting, the soldiers captured more than three hundred Kickapoos. Although some warriors elected to remain in Mexico, most joined their families in Indian Territory.

The Shoshoni War broke out in 1863, when western Shoshonis began attacking settlements in Utah and Idaho. When Chief Bear Hunter attacked Mormon settlers, Colonel Patrick E. Connor led the Third California Infantry through more than 140 miles of snow to the Bear River in Utah. Although some soldiers suffered from severe frostbite, on 27 January 1863 Connor ordered an assault, during which Bear Hunter and 224 of his supporters died, ending the war. Also in 1863 the Navajos began a war with settlers in New Mexico and Arizona that lasted three years. After a defeat in 1864, 2,400 Navajos endured the Long Walk, three hundred miles to Bosque Redondo. About two hundred Navajos died along the way. By the end of 1864 two thousand more Navajos capitulated, raising the total to eight thousand, the largest tribal surrender of the Indian wars. The Manuelito Navajos surrendered in 1866.

The Third Cavalry, led by Colonel John M. Chivington, massacred roughly three hundred peaceful Cheyennes and Arapahos, led by Black Kettle, at Sand Creek in Colorado in 1864. Black Kettle's people responded but were defeated in 1868 by Colonel George Armstrong Custer's Seventh Cavalry at the Battle of the Washita in western Oklahoma.

On the northern Plains the Fort Laramie Treaty of 1851 provided a safe route for whites along the Oregon Trail. In a confrontation over a stolen cow in August 1854, Lieutenant John L. Grattan and his thirty soldiers died. Retaliating on 3 September 1855, General William S. Harney annihilated a Brule Lakota village at Blue Water. The Lakotas, Cheyennes, and Arapahos, led by Red Cloud, protested the newly built Bozeman Trail that crossed into Sioux territory in Wyoming and Montana. In December 1866 Crazy Horse and fifteen hundred warriors ambushed Captain William Fetterman and eighty men, and in August 1867 the Lakota attacked workforces. Although the U.S. Army declared victory at Hayfield and the Wagon Box in 1867, a second Fort Laramie Treaty signed in 1868 closed the trail.

On the central Plains the Cheyennes and Arapahos fought the Hancock campaign in 1867. In the Sheridan campaign on the southern Plains, the U.S. military overcame the Cheyennes, Arapahos, Kiowas, and Comanches during 1868 and 1869. In Montana, Major Eugene Baker attacked a winter camp of Piegan Indians on 29 January 1870, killing fifty-three women and children and provoking public criticism.

In the Pacific Northwest the northern Paiute groups, composed of Yakuskins and Walpapis, known as Snake Indians, confronted gold miners between 1866 and 1868. Colonel George Crook assumed command against the Indians in 1866 and in some forty skirmishes killed an estimated 330 Paiutes and took 225 prisoners.

The Modocs of northern California and Oregon waged war on local settlers during 1872 and 1873. In an effort to halt the rising expenses of fighting Indians, President Ulysses S. Grant initiated the "Peace Policy" of negotiating treaties and agreements with Indian nations. Alfred Meacham and the Reverend Eleasar Thomas, Grant's peace commissioners, requested a peace conference with the Modocs. At the talks, on 11 April 1873, the Modoc leader Kintpuash, or Captain Jack, drew a hidden revolver and shot Brigadier General Edward Canby. Finally defeated later that year at Dry Lake, California, Captain Jack and three of his warriors were hanged. The surviving fifty-one Modocs were transported to Indian Territory, but they were allowed to return to northern California in 1909. General Crook fought the Apaches and Yavapais in the Southwest in 1872 and 1873. During the Red River War, 1874–1875, involving the Comanches, Kiowas, and Cheyennes in Texas and Indian Territory, the Comanches and Kiowas attacked buffalo hunters at Adobe Wallas, Texas.

At the Battle of Rosebud in Montana in 1876, Crazy Horse led seven hundred Lakota and Cheyenne warriors against Crook's one thousand soldiers and forced them to withdraw. Colonel Custer pursued the Indians. In probably the most well-known incident of the Indian wars, on 25 June Custer and the Seventh Cavalry encountered the Indians at the Little Bighorn River and not a single soldier survived. Subsequently Cheyennes suffered serious defeats at War Bonnet in Nebraska in July 1876 and at the Battle of Dull Knife in Wyoming in September 1876. On 8 September Captain Nelson A. Miles defeated American Horse's Teto band at Slim Buttes, South Dakota. Miles was successful in January 1877 against Crazy Horse's band at the Battle of Wolf Mountain and in May against Lame Deer's Miniconjou Tetons in Montana. Crazy Horse surrendered in fall 1877, and more than one thousand, mostly Oglalas, joined him.

In May 1877 General Oliver Howard instructed the Nez Percé Indians to move to the Lapwai reservation in Idaho Territory. Chief Joseph was willing to comply, but Wahlitits and his friends killed four white men, spurring warfare. On 17 June the Nez Percés soundly defeated Captain David Perry at White Bird Canyon in Idaho. On the run, Chief Joseph escaped encounters at Clearwater Creek, Idaho, on 11 and 12 July; Big Hole, Montana, on 9 August; Camas Creek, Idaho, on 20 August; Cow Island, Montana, on 2 September; and Canyon Creek, Montana, on 13 September. At Bear Paw Mountain, Montana, Chief Joseph and his followers fought for five days. On 5 October 1877 Chief Joseph surrendered, stating, "I will fight no more, forever." He had led the Nez Percés on an estimated 1,700-mile retreat that ended only thirty miles from Canada and possible help from Sitting Bull and his Lakota band.

At Mill Creek, Colorado, on 29 September 1879, Ute warriors killed several people, forcing the army into action. The Ute leader Ouray quickly negotiated with the Peace Commission, and Secretary of the Interior Carl Schurz supported the peace effort. By 26 October 1879 the Ute War had ended without further bloodshed.

In 1871 about 150 western Apaches led by Chief Eskiminzin, desiring peace, moved to Camp Grant. On 30 April 1871 a vigilante mob of whites, Mexicans, and Papagos (now known as Tohono O'dam) mercenaries, driven by hatred for Apaches, slaughtered eighty-five Apaches near Camp Grant. A renewed Apache War instigated General Crook's Tonto Basin (Arizona) campaign, resulting in more than twenty clashes. Decisive battles at Salt River Canyon, Arizona, on 28 December 1871; Skull Cave, Arizona; and Turret Peak, Colorado, on 27 March 1873 broke the Apache and Yavapai resistance. However, Victorio continued to lead Membreno Apache raids until his death at the Battle of Tres Terrazas, or Three Peaks, in 1880. During the summer of 1881 the aged Apache leader Nana led warriors across more than a thousand miles, winning eight battles before escaping to Mexico. He finally surrendered in March 1884. The Apaches Juh; Nachise, Cochise's son; and Chato together led the Mescalero Apaches on raids until March 1884. Geronimo, who had fought with Cochise, led the Chiricahua Apaches in raids and clashes for several years before surrendering for the fourth and final time on 4 September 1886.

The Bannock War, involving the Bannocks, northern Paiutes, and some Cayuses and Umatillas, sprang from disagreements in 1878 over Indians digging camas roots, an activity guaranteed in a treaty signed the year before. On 8 July General Howard defeated the Indians, led by Buffalo Horn and Oyte, a Paiute medicine man. Following a second defeat at Umatilla Agency near Pendleton, Oregon, Oyte surrendered on 12 August 1878. In 1879 Idaho underwent the Sheepeater War involving the Sheepeater Indians and some Bannocks, and Colorado experienced the Ute War the same year.

The expansion of mining interests, railroads, ranching, and professional hunting across the trans-Mississippi West continually precipitated military clashes with Plains Indians. Sitting Bull of the Lakotas and 187 of his followers surrendered to officials at Fort Buford, North Dakota, in 1881. The final major confrontation in the West between the U.S. military and American Indians was the 1890 Wounded Knee massacre of about 300 Minnoconjou Lakotas led by Big Foot. The General Allotment Act of 1887, which distributed Indian lands among tribal members for farming, spawned the Crazy Snake resistance in 1901. Chitto Harjo of the Muscogee Creeks and ninety-four Snake Indians in Indian Territory led a patriotic movement of small skirmishes against local law enforcement.

During the nineteenth century numerous wars and foreign diseases devastated the Indian population in the United States, reducing it from up to ten million to 237,196 by 1900. Native Americans became known as "Vanishing Americans," left with destroyed cultures, lost languages, demographic catastrophes, and negative images.

See also **American Indian Societies; Army; Civilization; Civil War,** *subentries on* **The West, Indian Territory; Expansion; Federal Land Policy; Frontier; Homesteading; Indian Territory; Interpretations of the Nineteenth Century,** *subentry on* **Popular Interpretations of the Frontier West; Jacksonian Era; Manifest Destiny; Seminole Wars; Territorial Government; Trails to the West.**

Bibliography

Keenan, Jerry. *Encyclopedia of American Indian Wars 1492–1890.* New York: Norton, 1999.

McDermott, John D. *A Guide to the Indian Wars of the West.* Lincoln: University of Nebraska Press, 1998.

Paul, R. Eli, ed. *The Nebraska Indian Wars Reader, 1865–1877.* Lincoln: University of Nebraska Press, 1998.

Starkey, Armstrong. *European and Native American Warfare, 1675–1815.* Norman: University of Oklahoma Press, 1998.

DONALD L. FIXICO

TREATIES AND TREATYMAKING

In the case of *Cherokee Nation v. Georgia* (1831), Chief Justice John Marshall described the relationship between the United States and the American Indian tribes as "unlike that of any other two people in existence." This anomalous condition was a consequence of the U.S. decision in the late eighteenth century to use the diplomatic treaty as its primary means of conducting relations with the Indian tribes. Between 1778, when the United States signed its first Indian treaty, and 1871, when Congress ended the practice, the United States concluded over 370 treaties with the tribes. After 1871 many tribes negotiated agreements with the United States that courts have recognized as having the same legal status as Indian treaties.

Although the treaties defined almost every aspect of U.S.-Indian relations, two general concerns guided American negotiators in the late eighteenth century and the nineteenth century—national security and expansion. American leaders sought to establish peaceful relations with the tribes in order to protect the country's population and secure its borders. At the same time the U.S. government used the treaty to acquire Indian lands and expand the geographical boundaries of the United States. According to the scholar Robert M. Kvasnicka's count, 96 of the Indian treaties executed by the United States provided for the establishment or reestablishment of peace with a particular tribe, while 230 resulted in the American acquisition of land rights.

Native American leaders entered into negotiations with their own peoples' interests in mind. Some wanted to obtain economic and trade concessions, some wanted to provide for their own security, and some wanted to achieve a peaceful accommodation with the United States.

Development of the Treaty System

During the Revolutionary War the United States followed the British precedent of treatymaking and concluded neutrality agreements and military alliances with several tribes. For example, in 1778 the Delawares and the United States declared that "a perpetual peace and friendship" existed between them. After the war the United States negotiated a number of treaties that ended hostilities with Great Britain's native allies. In treaties at Fort Stanwix (1784), Fort McIntosh (1785), Fort Finney (1786), and Hopewell (1785–1786), the signatory Indian nations renounced hostile relations with the United States. The tribes who were parties to these agreements also accepted a form of protectorate status under the United States, surrendered large tracts of land, acquiesced to the establishment of specific borders, and agreed to refrain from conducting independent trade or diplomatic relations. On one hand, the treaty relationship created U.S. guardianship over Native Americans. On the other, by adopting the same diplomatic process that it used with foreign nations, the United States admitted that the Indian tribes retained important aspects of political sovereignty.

The U.S. decision to conduct Indian relations by treaty emerged from the language of the U.S. Constitution, which granted Congress the authority "to regulate commerce with foreign nations, and among the several States, and with the Indian tribes," and from precedents established during George Washington's first term as president. Washington's management of the negotiation and ratification of the treaties of Fort Harmar (1789) and New York (1790) established a process that the federal government followed until the abandonment of the treaty system ninety years later.

In a decision that reflected the U.S. perception of its relationship with Native Americans, Washington delegated the responsibility for negotiating Indian treaties to the secretary of war. Washington and Secretary of War Henry Knox also envisioned the treaty as a mechanism for preparing Native Americans for assimilation by the United States. In 1849, in the aftermath of the Mexican War, Congress transferred responsibility for Indian affairs to the newly created Department of the Interior, suggesting that the United States at that point viewed Native Americans as a domestic concern.

Federal commissioners, specially appointed by the president, conducted the actual negotiations of treaties. The commissioners and the tribe customarily negotiated at a site chosen by the tribe. The negotiations were solemn occasions marked by high ceremony, lengthy oratory, and the formal exchange of diplomatic gifts. When necessary, interpreters assisted in the communications between the parties and served as witnesses to the agreements. All treaties were written in English. Upon the completion of a treaty, the commissioners forwarded it to the president for consideration. If he found the treaty acceptable, the chief executive submitted it to the Senate for ratification. After ratification, the Senate returned the treaty to the president, who signed it and publicly proclaimed it to be in effect. President James Madison ended the practice of public proclamation in 1814. During the treaty era, the U.S. Senate ratified 367 of the federal-Indian agreements. Upon ratification, these treaties became, in the words of Article VI of the Constitution, "the supreme law of the land," immune from unilateral revision or alteration by disruptive state governments.

Convinced that acquiring lands by military conquest and coercion would continue to provoke conflict on the American frontier and expanding upon the spirit of the Northwest Ordinance (1787), which declared that Congress would observe "utmost good faith" toward the Indians, Knox and Washington concluded that the United States should deal honorably with Native Americans. Knox argued that Indians possessed, at the least, a right of occupancy in their lands and that the United States should pay to extinguish that right. The treaties signed pursuant to this new direction established firm boundaries between the tribes and the United States, prohibited white settlers and traders from entering the Indian country without a license from the federal government, and provided for the extradition and punishment of whites who committed crimes against natives in the Indian country.

At the same time that federal officials attempted to draw native leaders into legally regulated relationships, they also encouraged "civilization" programs to teach Indians how to live as American agrarians on private property. Federal funds supported missionaries and federal agents, who taught Indian men how to farm in the expectation that they would abandon their hunting grounds and settle on small farms. According to advocates for the program, the United States could then acquire the unused hunting grounds of Native Americans and distribute them to white yeoman farmers. Acculturated Indians would then assimilate into the white society engulfing them. The federal government used treaties to implement this scheme. Treaty provisions often prescribed, in addition to Christian missionaries and federal agents, teachers, livestock, farm tools, and other materials to encourage the Indian transition to agrarian life. The proponents of the civilization program, however, underestimated the rate of white American population growth, the insatiable voracity of whites for Indian land, the degree of native resistance to this radical cultural transformation, and the persistent white American resistance to Indian assimilation. U.S. land demands thus outpaced the timetables envisioned in treaties and native interest in acculturation. Though the assimilation element of the treaty policy was a general failure, the United States persisted in its civilization efforts throughout the nineteenth century.

Removal Treaties

American interest in the peaceful integration of Indians into white American society waned after the War of 1812. In that war the United States routed Tecumseh's pan-Indian confederacy in the Northwest and decimated the Redstick Creeks in the South. After the war, American commissioners negotiated twenty treaties with tribes that had allied themselves with Great Britain or demonstrated independent hostility toward the United States. The elimination of the Indian and British military threat east of the Mississippi destroyed the negotiating leverage of the Indians in that region, leaving Native Americans subject to U.S. demands.

The Louisiana Purchase (1803) had reignited in President Thomas Jefferson an idea that he had first broached in 1776—the removal of the eastern tribes to areas west of the Mississippi River. After the War of 1812, Andrew Jackson, John C. Calhoun, and a

Peace Conference, 25 May 1886. Geronimo *(seated, in bandana)* meets with George Crook *(second from right)* in the Sierra Madre Mountains. Crook wanted to negotiate with Geronimo about ending Apache raids on settlers and Apache settlement within San Carlos Reservation. LIBRARY OF CONGRESS: PRINTS AND PHOTOGRAPHS DIVISION

coterie of southern state officials embraced removal as a way to acquire Native American land and maintain separation between Indians and whites. Jefferson and Jackson suggested that removal would provide eastern Indians with the ability to acculturate at their own pace. In reality, federal officials were more concerned with expanding the nation and acceding to southern political demands. Congress passed the Removal Act of 1830, which authorized the president to initiate the removal process. By 1843 the United States had signed over 170 removal treaties with the eastern tribes and had moved them, sometimes at bayonet point, across the Mississippi.

When Indian leaders resisted federal removal overtures, U.S. treaty commissioners used unscrupulous negotiating tactics to obtain native signatures. For example, in the Treaty of New Echota (1835) the United States responded to the refusal of the official Cherokee government to consider a removal proposal by concluding a treaty with a small group of dissenters. Unprincipled federal methods like these were not limited to the removal period. U.S. commissioners often used deceit and duress to achieve their objectives during the treaty era. Time and again the United States promised a tribe that a request for a cession would be the last, but shortly thereafter federal officials would renege on their promises and come back asking for more land. For example, in the Treaty of Fort Laramie (1868), the United States granted the Sioux title in perpetuity to the Great Sioux Reserve, located between the Missouri River and the western boundary of the Dakota Territory. However, after the discovery of gold in the Black Hills in 1874, the United States initiated an effort to acquire the Black Hills from the Sioux. The Sioux's refusal to surrender its territory resulted in a series of violent conflicts marked by the decimation of General George Custer's three hundred troops at Little Bighorn (1876) by the Sioux chief Sitting Bull and his warriors and the U.S. Army's massacre of perhaps as many as 350 Sioux men, women, and children at Wounded Knee, South Dakota, in 1890.

The West

Despite the plans of removal proponents, the Mississippi River did not serve as an impenetrable wall of racial separation. Almost as soon as the eastern tribes had settled in the West, white settlers were encroaching upon them again. In addition, between 1845 and 1848 the United States acquired the lands of Texas, Oregon, California, and New Mexico and opened them up for settlement. As immigrating whites moved westward, they came into contact and conflict with hundreds of Indian peoples. By military con-

quest or negotiation, federal officials forced Indian groups to sign cession treaties and to relocate to reservations, protected enclaves designed to separate Indians from onrushing settlers. By the end of the nineteenth century, the United States had by treaty consigned all of the great tribes of the West to reservations.

The Civil War did not interrupt federal-Indian treatymaking. While the United States concluded agreements with the Cheyennes, Chippewas, Arapahos, Comanches, Kiowas, and Apaches, among others, the Confederate government followed the U.S. precedent of Indian relations and signed nine treaties of its own with tribes in the Indian territory and the southern Plains. After the war the federal government refused to renew relations with the Southern-allied tribes until they had surrendered new cessions and abolished slavery.

The End of the Treaty System

In 1862 Secretary of the Interior Caleb B. Smith urged Congress to abolish the treaty system, end the legal recognition of tribal governments, and deal with Indian individuals as wards of the federal government. In 1869 Ely S. Parker, the commissioner of Indian affairs, joined Smith's opposition to the treaty system, arguing that the treaties filled Indians with unrealistic dreams of nationalism. Parker, a Seneca Indian, suggested that Indians did not have governments capable of legally coercing individuals into abiding by their agreements. The United States violated treaties more often than did the Indians during the nineteenth century. Following the leads of Smith and Parker, the House of Representatives, also unhappy with its exclusion from the ratification process, promulgated legislation prohibiting the United States from signing treaties with the Indian tribes. The Senate ultimately adopted this view, and in 1871 President Ulysses S. Grant signed the bill into law. An agreement signed with the Nez Percé in 1868 was, consequently, the last formal Indian treaty ratified by the Senate. The legislation, however, reaffirmed the legality of existing treaties, and the United States continued to enter into contracts with Indian groups in the years after the repudiation of the treaty system. For example, the U.S. government and the tribes continued to negotiate over the size of reservations and the provision and amount of annuities. Federal officials referred to these negotiated settlements, which were approved by both houses of Congress, as "agreements."

In particular, the United States negotiated these agreements to reduce the size of the reservations established under earlier treaties. For example, Congress passed the Sioux Act of 1889, which divided the Great Sioux Reservation into six smaller reserves and opened up the surplus land to white settlement. At first the Sioux bands united in their refusal to accept the reduction of their territory, but General George Crook of the U.S. Army eventually persuaded the requisite three-quarters of the tribe to reduce Congress's will to a binding agreement.

The United States also used agreements to implement Congress's allotment and acquisition plan. Between 1890 and 1892, the congressional Jerome Commission cajoled and intimidated allotment and cession agreements out of the Sac and Fox, Iowas, Cheyennes, Arapahos, Comanches, Apaches, Kiowas, and Pawnees. In these agreements, tribal members usually received an individual allotment of 160 acres. After allotment, the tribes conveyed their surplus lands to the United States. All told, these agreements opened up over fifteen million acres of Indian land to white settlement. In 1893, after the United States acquired the Cherokee Outlet, over 100,000 people flooded into the land to set up homesteads. Between 1897 and 1902 the Dawes Commission also coerced allotment and cession agreements out of the Choctaws, Chickasaws, Creeks, Seminoles, and Cherokees. These agreements subsequently led to the political dissolution of the Indian Territory tribes.

A dangerous precedent for the viability of treaty obligations was the U.S. Supreme Court case of *Lone Wolf v. Hitchcock* (1903), which held that Congress could abrogate existing treaties without the consent of the Indian signatories so long as it exercised "perfect good faith towards the Indians," a determination that the Court left for Congress to decide. With Congress empowered to unilaterally construe and countermand its own promises, the hundreds of Indian tribes holding signed treaties with the United States were left in the twentieth century to the will and whim of American political winds.

See also **American Indians,** *subentries on* **Indian Removal, U.S. Government Policies; Civilization; Confederate States of America; Federal Land Policy; Indian Territory; Louisiana Purchase; Missions,** *subentry on* **North American Indians; War of 1812.**

Bibliography

Cohen, Felix S. *Felix S. Cohen's Handbook of Federal Indian Law. 1982 Edition.* Edited by Rennard Strickland. Charlottesville, Va.: Michie Bobbs-Merrill, 1982.

DeMallie, Raymond J. "American Indian Treaty Making: Motives and Meanings." *American Indian Journal* 3 (1977): 2–10.

Kvasnicka, Robert M. "United States Indian Treaties and Agreements." In *Handbook of North American Indians.* Edited by William C. Sturtevant. Volume 4: *History of Indian-White Relations,* edited by Wilcomb E. Washburn. Washington, D.C.: Smithsonian Institution, 1978–1988.

Prucha, Francis Paul. *American Indian Treaties: The History of a Political Anomaly.* Berkeley: University of California Press, 1994.

Wunder, John R. "No More Treaties: The Resolution of 1871 and the Alteration of Indian Rights to Their Homelands." In *Working the Range: Essays on the History of Western Land Management and the Environment.* Edited by John R. Wunder. Westport, Conn.: Greenwood, 1985.

TIM ALAN GARRISON

U.S. GOVERNMENT POLICIES

In the nineteenth century the U.S. government attempted to centralize its authority over American Indian peoples. Policymakers tried to civilize and assimilate Indians, control trade and intercultural contact, secure land cessions through treaties and violence, remove and concentrate Indians, and then reindividualize them by allotting reservations to speed Indian integration or disappearance. At the heart of this changing policy was a set of assumptions, based on Enlightenment ideas of social evolution, that human societies naturally evolved through a hierarchy of stages from savagism through barbarism to civilization. Each stage was defined by certain social and material characteristics, but subsistence activity was central to the progression—savage hunter-gatherers, barbarous nomadic herders, civilized settled agriculturalists. When combined with European legal theories linking proper land use with a people's right to claim and hold land, western-style row agriculture became the yardstick for measuring Indian progress and rights. Throughout the nineteenth century white Americans expressed the beliefs that Indians could be drawn through these stages rapidly, that Indians could and should be assimilated into white society as yeomen farmers and farm families, and, barring assimilation, that Indians would be overwhelmed and would disappear. This certainty in the unilinear progress of societies and the superiority of agrarian civilization unified nineteenth-century U.S. Indian policy actions.

Civilization and Trade

In the beginning U.S. Indian policy was disastrously disorganized. Under the Articles of Confederation individual states retained authority over Indians within their borders. Following ratification of the Constitution in 1789, President George Washington (1789–1797) and Secretary of War Henry Knox began fashioning a more centralized approach to Indian affairs. They attempted to negotiate rather than dictate treaties with tribes as separate nations, to purchase rather than seize Indian lands, to avoid warfare, and to implement a civilization policy with appointed agents working out of government factories (trading posts) who would regulate trade, distribute useful implements, and encourage Indians to settle down.

This civilization program expanded during the administration of President Thomas Jefferson (1801–1809), but Indian policy continued to contain contradictory goals. Jefferson signed a second Indian Trade and Intercourse Act in 1802 to expand the factory system and to encourage Indian sedentariness, agriculture, and rapid assimilation. He believed that teaching Indians to farm would speed them through the stages of social evolution and inculcate the values of an agrarian republic. At the same time Jefferson viewed the factory system as a way to foster Indian acquisitiveness and debt, whereby they would be forced to cede their "surplus" lands. He recognized that westward-moving Americans would not wait for Indian acculturation, nor would they tolerate Indian interference in their expansion.

Removal

After the purchase of the Louisiana Territory from France in 1803, Jefferson broached the subject of voluntary Indian removal to lands west of the Mississippi River but found few takers. Between 1803 and 1809 the government coerced land cession treaties from tribes throughout the Old Northwest and attempted to do so in the Southeast, precipitating armed resistance, including the emergence of the intertribal Shawnee Confederacy led by Tenskwatawa and Tecumseh. General William Henry Harrison's attempt to crush the confederacy by military force in 1811 became the opening salvo in the War of 1812 between the United States and Britain and the Indian allies of the British.

At the conclusion of this war that settled little else, the federal government asserted its authority in the Northeast and Old Northwest by removing Britain's Indian allies and constructing new forts and factories. An additional Indian civilization act, passed in 1819, signaled the government's desire to assimilate Indians as yeomen farmers, to control trade and liquor, and to protect Indians from rapacious white settlers. However, enforcement was lacking. Funds from the act went to Christian missionary societies willing to open schools and churches and staff factories. Federal supervision increased in 1824, when Thomas L. McKenney, superintendent of Indian trade (1816–1822), became the first commissioner of Indian affairs (1824–1830) and headed the newly cre-

ated Office of Indian Affairs within the War Department.

While McKenney championed the civilization program, he and his successors recognized that Indians were not abandoning their traditions and assimilating as rapidly as expected. Responding to growing conflicts between land-hungry frontiersmen and tribes in the Southeast, particularly between the state of Georgia and the Cherokee Nation, President James Monroe (1817–1825) reopened the issue of removing Indians to a permanent Indian Territory in the southern Plains west of the Mississippi River. In 1830 Congress approved a removal bill, and President Andrew Jackson's administration (1829–1837) aggressively negotiated new treaties with the Five Southern Tribes—the Cherokees, Choctaws, Chickasaws, Creeks, and Seminoles—many of whom, like the Cherokees, were living a "civilized" agrarian lifestyle.

Opponents of removal helped the Cherokees file suit with the Supreme Court to defend their lands and sovereignty from legal incursions by the state of Georgia. In *Cherokee Nation v. Georgia* (1831), Chief Justice John Marshall ruled that the Cherokees, as a foreign entity, could not bring suit in federal court, but he also legally defined tribes as "domestic dependent nations." Building on that decision, Marshall ruled in the landmark case *Worcester v. Georgia* (1832) that states had no legal authority over Indians or Indian lands. However, President Jackson refused to enforce the Court's decision. Georgia continued to harass the Cherokees, and Jackson pushed removal through coercive treaty renegotiations and military force. Between 1830 and 1842 the Southern Tribes either voluntarily relocated or were forcibly removed to Indian Territory (now Oklahoma). The Cherokee "Trail of Tears" and the Seminole War (1835–1842) became symbols of the brutality of removal and the resistance of Indian peoples.

Reservation

By 1840 the majority of eastern Indians had been removed to the trans-Mississippi West. But U.S. territorial acquisitions in the West in the wake of the Mexican War (1846–1848) and the transfer of the Office of Indian Affairs (soon renamed the Bureau of Indian Affairs) from the War Department to the Department of the Interior (1849) necessitated new policies for peacefully concentrating rather than removing Indian peoples. In the 1850s federal officials negotiated peace and land cession treaties with tribes to restrict them to small enclaves within their formerly extensive territories. Federal Indian agents were to protect and supervise Indians on these res-

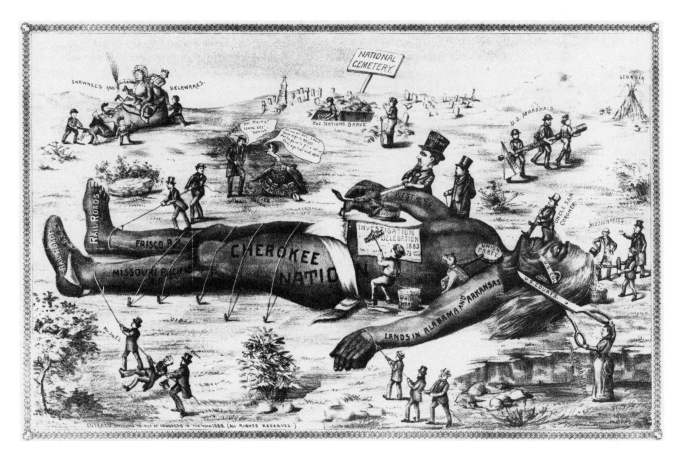

The Cherokee Nation. An 1886 cartoon showing the effects of U.S. policies on Cherokees residing in Indian Territory. Following the Indian Removal Act of 1830, Cherokees and other tribes from the southern and southeastern United States were forced to migrate to Indian Territory, in present-day Oklahoma. By the 1880s, the government had forced tribes to cede land to various white interests, such as the military, ranchers, and the railroad industry, among others shown in this caricature. At the bottom right, a judge, portrayed as the Bible's Delilah, cuts the Indian's hair with shears marked "U.S. Courts," and in so doing saps the Cherokee nation's last strength. LIBRARY OF CONGRESS

ervations, providing them with schools, agricultural implements, and instruction to encourage their self-sufficiency and assimilation. For their land cessions Indians received annuity payments in agricultural implements, livestock, and subsistence rations instead of cash or trade goods. Most treaties included continued hunting rights, but Indians leaving their reservations to follow seasonal rounds were subject to harassment by the U.S. Army, which established forts near reservations and along important transportation corridors. Designed to be temporary locations for holding Indians apart from American society while they learned to become part of that society, reservations became an enduring component of U.S. Indian policy and American Indian tribal identity.

During and immediately following the Civil War (1861–1865), the completion of the transcontinental railroad and expansion of white settlement in the West ignited new demands for Indian lands. U.S. Army and volunteer regiments, assigned to defend the West against the threat of Confederate activities, spent their time attacking off-reservation Indians. The Bear River (1863) and Sand Creek (1864) massacres and military campaigns against the Dakotas in Minnesota (1862) and the Navajos and Apaches in the Southwest (1862–1868) demonstrated a division in national opinion over the effectiveness of civilization programs versus force.

Concerned with the escalating violence, Congress created a joint committee in 1865 headed by Senator James R. Doolittle of Wisconsin. The Doolittle Committee investigated the conditions of Indian tribes and considered the debate over whether to keep the Indian Bureau in the Interior Department or transfer it back to the War Department. The committee reported that assimilation policies were ultimately more economical and just than warfare. Their report, released in 1867, led to the creation of a Peace Commission, set up to conduct new treaties with Plains tribes to guarantee them distinct reservations, protection from white encroachment, and instruction in farming and ranching. In the East reform-minded Christian groups mobilized to halt government corruption and to civilize Indians. Most influential among these groups was the Society of Friends, or Quakers, who encouraged President Ulysses S. Grant (1869–1877) to pursue peaceful assimilation.

Peace Policy and Reform

The Grant peace policy consisted of several initiatives. In 1869 Congress created the independent Board of Indian Commissioners, appointed by the president. Prominent individuals from various Christian and humanitarian organizations, the commissioners were charged with investigating reservation conditions and Indian Bureau operations. A second initiative was the apportionment of Indian agencies among various church groups that in turn nominated their own missionary agents and reservation employees. The purpose of both initiatives was to mitigate charges of graft and corruption leveled against the Indian Bureau while cutting federal costs. Unfortunately the good intentions of these missionary agents fell short of solving the "Indian problem." The lack of qualified and experienced individuals willing to live on remote reservations and the failure of those individuals to fully appreciate native cultures or the realities of western environments undermined their effectiveness. Indians continued to leave their reservations to hunt and to evade efforts to Christianize them, and agents were quick to call in the military to round up resisters. After 1877 church participation in the peace policy declined rapidly, and the Indian Bureau returned to using civilian or military agents.

One other aspect of the peace policy was the 1871 congressional prohibition on further U.S.-Indian treaties. Thereafter the government negotiated "agreements" with tribes, especially for land cessions. While the purpose of the ban was to diminish the status of Indians to federal wards, which it did in many people's minds, pragmatically the government continued to recognize existing treaties and therefore the legal status of tribes as "domestic dependent nations."

Between 1877 and 1887 living conditions for reservation Indians continued to deteriorate. The concentration of more Indians on ever-smaller reservations, decimation of the buffalo herds, inadequate supplies and agricultural instruction, suppression of native religions and customs, disease and death, uncontrolled settler trespass, military brutality, and the threat of further removals left tribes in disarray. Legally, the courts limited the rights of individual Indians, as in *Elk v. Wilkins* (1884), and affirmed

Congress's jurisdictional power over Indians and reservations, as in *United States v. Kagama* (1886). Philanthropic and humanitarian reform groups, like the Women's National Indian Association, the Indian Rights Association, the National Indian Defense Association, and the Lake Mohonk Conferences of Friends of the Indians, organized in the East to inform the public about the plight of Indians and to reshape an assimilative Indian policy.

Reformers and government officials saw education as a key element in transforming Indians. Reservation day schools were numerous but ineffective, and reformers began pushing for more off-reservation boarding schools to remove Indian children from their families, cultures, and lands for extended periods. In 1879 Captain Richard H. Pratt established Carlisle Indian School in Pennsylvania as a vocational training school. Using an "outing" system to place student apprentices in the local community, Carlisle quickly became the model for a series of off-reservation boarding schools and for Indian curricular education.

Allotment

A second approach to transforming Indians was to break up the reservation system itself. Reformers and politicians viewed communal Indian landholding as antithetical to the American ideal and pressed for the individualization of reservation lands. The General Allotment Act, or Dawes Severalty Act of 1887, introduced by the Massachusetts senator Henry L. Dawes, established a process for surveying Indian reservations and allotting heads of Indian families 160 acres and all others 80 acres. Title to these individual allotments would be held in trust for twenty-five years to prevent their sale. At that end of that period Indians would be given title to their allotments and become citizens. Surplus lands were opened to general entry, and sale proceeds were used for the benefit of the tribe. In 1891 Congress allowed allotments to be leased, and later acts made it easier to alienate the allotments of minors, students, the aged, and the sick. The alienation of Indian lands occurred rapidly as whites found ways around the law, and in 1898 the Curtis Act authorized the allotment of Indian Territory. Indian landholdings fell from 156 million acres in 1881 to 104 million acres in 1890 and to 78 million acres in 1900. By 1928, when allotment was suspended, Indians held only 33 million acres of allotted and reservation land, a 79 percent reduction. At the same time the government reduced agency budgets and distributions of rations. Indian farmers and ranchers, already struggling on environmentally marginal lands, foundered without adequate instruction or support. Unrest increased as allotment and other assimilation policies threatened tribal lands and identity. Resistance occurred most graphically in the spread of the Ghost Dance religion and the ensuing massacre of Lakota people at Wounded Knee in December 1890.

As the nineteenth century came to an end, the American Indian population reached its nadir. From an estimated two to five million at first contact with Europeans, only 237,000 Indians remained in 1900. Nineteenth-century U.S. Indian policy, intent on civilizing and integrating Indians as it reduced their lands to make way for white settlers, was only successful in the latter. Full of good intentions and a firm belief in the cultural superiority of their way of life, U.S. policymakers saw no alternatives. Nevertheless, American Indians tenaciously defied physical destruction and cultural submersion and found ways to subvert such policies through both active and passive resistance.

See also **American Indian Societies; Civil War,** *subentry* **on Indian Territory; Education,** *subentry on* **Indian Schools; Federal Land Policy; Indian Territory; Missions,** *subentry on* **North American Indians; Race and Racial Thinking.**

Bibliography

Adams, David Wallace. *Education for Extinction: American Indians and the Boarding School Experience, 1875–1928.* Lawrence: University Press of Kansas, 1995.

Berkhofer, Robert F., Jr. *Salvation and the Savage: An Analysis of Protestant Missions and American Indian Response, 1787–1862.* Lexington: University of Kentucky Press, 1965.

Dippie, Brian W. *The Vanishing American: White Attitudes and U.S. Indian Policy.* Middletown, Conn.: Wesleyan University Press, 1982.

Hagan, William T. *The Indian Rights Association: The Herbert Welsh Years, 1882–1904.* Tucson: University of Arizona Press, 1985.

Hoxie, Frederick E. *A Final Promise: The Campaign to Assimilate the Indians, 1880–1920.* Lincoln: University of Nebraska Press, 1984.

Keller, Robert H., Jr. *American Protestantism and United States Indian Policy, 1869–82.* Lincoln: University of Nebraska Press, 1983.

Prucha, Francis Paul. *The Great Father: The United States Government and the American Indians.* 2 vols. Lincoln: University of Nebraska Press, 1984. See also the abridged ed., 1986.

Satz, Ronald N. *American Indian Policy in the Jacksonian Era.* Lincoln: University of Nebraska Press, 1975.

Sheehan, Bernard W. *Seeds of Extinction: Jeffersonian Philanthropy and the American Indian.* New York: Norton, 1973.

Sturtevant, William C., ed. *Handbook of North American Indians.* Volume 4: *History of Indian-White Relations,* edited by Wilcomb E. Washburn. Washington, D.C.: Smithsonian Institution, 1988. See especially U.S. Indian policy chapters by Reginald Horsman, Francis Paul Prucha, and William T. Hagan.

Washburn, Wilcomb E. *The Indian in America.* New York: Harper and Row, 1975.

Weeks, Philip. *Farewell, My Nation: The American Indian and the United States, 1820–1890.* Arlington Heights, Ill.: Harlan Davidson, 1990.

DAVID RICH LEWIS

INDIAN REMOVAL

The policy of removal displaced American Indian peoples from productive lands adjacent to Euro-American settlements to underdeveloped areas that were isolated from population centers. By 1825 hopes for the assimilation of Indian peoples into Euro-American society through Christianization, agricultural occupations, and intermarriage had lost their vigor as numerous Indian peoples preferred to maintain their traditions, even after they had decided to convert and settle down. Consequently, policymakers turned to removal. Proponents of this strategy argued that it would protect the rapidly declining Indian population from the debilitating effects of frontier society while opening tribal resources to white settlers. Removal promised both segregation and assimilation by opening valuable lands for white exploitation without Indian contact while giving assimilationists more time to transform Indian peoples into Christian yeomen. In all, the U.S. government confiscated the land of over one hundred tribal groups, of which some received compensation but many did not. Following the negotiation of removal treaties, the army escorted tribes to reservations west of the Mississippi River. Whether voluntary or forced, removal inevitably affected tribal customs, material culture, and identity.

Organizing Removal

The idea of forced relocation had a long history. In 1803 Thomas Jefferson envisioned the Louisiana Territory as a potential home for Indians and suggested that their lands in the East could be traded for lands west of the Appalachians. After the War of 1812 the rapid expansion of Euro-American settlements westward made removal an attractive option. In 1825 federal authorities formed the Indian Territory, withdrawing a huge area from the public domain in Missouri and Arkansas westward to the 100th meridian for use as an Indian homeland. The southeastern tribes, the Cherokees, Choctaws, Chickasaws, Creeks, and Seminoles, relocated to Indian Territory in Oklahoma, are most closely associated with removal. The tribes' successful adoption of Euro-

American lifeways made a mockery of the logic of removal and added insult to their injurious treatment. Public sympathy for their plight created a wave of criticism of Andrew Jackson and provided the president's Whig enemies with political fuel. However, removal affected tribes throughout the United States until the 1880s. Dozens of tribes from the Old Northwest were displaced to Kansas, Nebraska, and Iowa, and in 1877 Chief Joseph's band of Nez Percé was forced to relocate from Oregon to the Colville reservation in Washington Territory.

Initially removal of Indian tribes from one designated place to another was somewhat haphazard. For some tribes, like the Delawares and the Shawnees, migration was a way of life, and neither group was living in its ancestral home in 1830. Removal of these tribes farther west of the Mississippi was voluntary and piecemeal, as different bands chose different locations in which to settle. Contributing to the disorganization, the government's primary objective was not the safe passage of the tribes to more secluded areas but the rapid extinguishment of Indian title to lands being settled by whites. Indian resistance, such as the Black Hawk War, added further difficulties. The United States did not recognize Black Hawk as a Sauk band leader, and Black Hawk stubbornly refused to leave his ancestral village of Saukenak in Illinois. In 1831 he briefly joined a band in Iowa led by Keokuk, but rumors of British aid and a falling-out with Keokuk emboldened Black Hawk to return to Illinois with about two thousand supporters. A costly military campaign in 1832 eventually ended Black Hawk's ambitions and forced him to move west, but Indian removal persisted as a controversial topic in American politics for several years thereafter.

In 1830 Congress passed the Removal Act, which attempted to standardize a routine for removing tribes. The U.S. government first negotiated for title to all tribal lands at a set rate of compensation. In the meantime the tribes sent emissaries west to scout out new lands. To gain the favor of the tribal leadership, the U.S. government often allowed individual Indians to retain the title to choice sections of land, which the Indians usually sold to speculators at a handsome profit upon removal. Inevitably monetary windfalls attracted traders, who extended high-interest credit to the tribes for everyday necessities as well as for worthless trinkets and alcohol. By the time the members of the tribe were ready to move, nearly all their money had been spent for subsistence.

Removal in the North

The Potawatomi Indians provide a good example of the way the removal system worked among the northern tribes. Land cessions were acquired mostly through bribes to lesser chiefs, or they were orchestrated by merchants who wished to see the Indians receive the highest possible price for their lands. In the case of one group of Potawatomis led by Menominee, however, the blatant use of removal as a way to satisfy white land hunger was especially poignant. Converts to Catholicism, Menominee and his followers were granted small tracts of land before official removal negotiations were started. Secretary of War Lewis Cass promised Menominee in writing that so long as he held title to his land he did not have to leave it, and the local Catholic missionary, who wished to convert the group into peaceable farmers and stockmen, gave him similar assurances. As the time for the Potawatomis' general removal approached, the government attempted to purchase these small tracts to make a clean sweep of all Indian title in the region, but Menominee steadfastly refused to sell his land. Cass instructed local agents to purchase Menominee's land by whatever means, and three co-owners of the Menominee tract were eventually bribed into selling the entire tract without Menominee's knowledge or approval. On 6 August 1836 U.S. troops arrived to escort Menominee's band to its new reserve in Kansas. The elderly chief was captured and removed at gunpoint. To make matters worse, the emigration party was poorly supplied, and the soldiers exposed the Indians to cholera. Forty-two Indians died in transit, and dozens of sick were left along the way to be removed later.

Removal in the South

In 1825 Georgia legislators took the creation of an Indian homeland in the West as their cue to remove the twenty thousand Cherokees living in the state. Resolutions by the Georgia legislature in 1826 and 1827 asserted that the federal government had not taken the Cherokee lands into the public domain in 1802, when the state ceded its western lands; thus the state was within its legal rights to confiscate them. Understanding that they were challenging federal prerogatives, the Georgians gambled that President-elect Andrew Jackson would not interfere with their plans. Cherokee resistance led to a series of Supreme Court decisions that redefined the relationship of American Indians to the federal government. In spite of Chief Justice John Marshall's opinion that the United States was bound both to respect the autonomy of Indian nations and to protect their interests as "Domestic Dependent Nations," President Jackson approved the negotiation of a removal treaty with the Cherokees and ordered military supervision to enforce it. Historians debate whether Jackson ad-

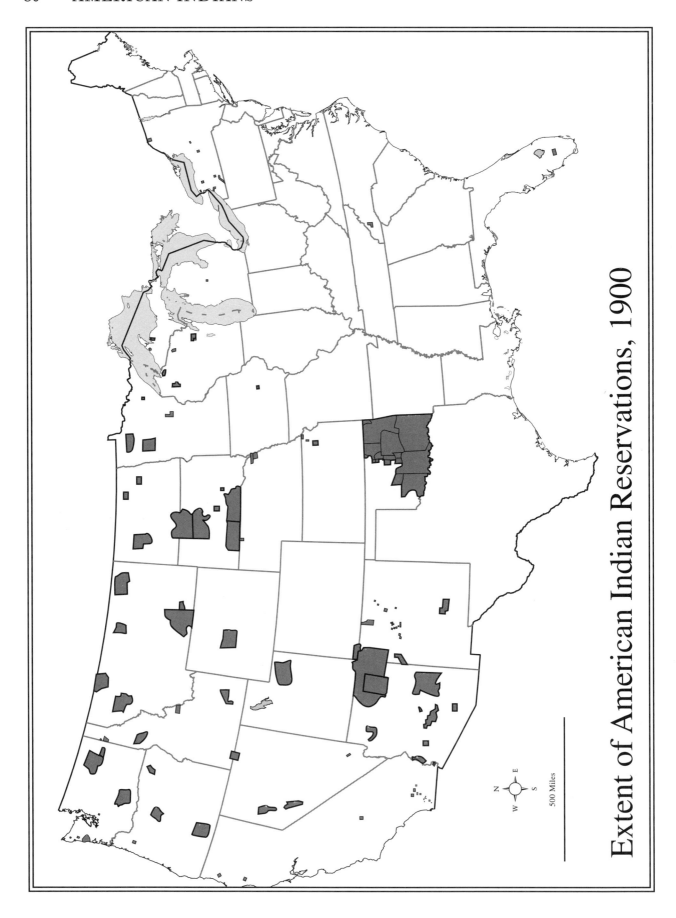

Extent of American Indian Reservations, 1900

500 Miles

vocated removal because he disliked Indians or whether he actually believed he did not have the power to protect them from land hunger in the East. In their new homes, Jackson wrote privately in 1829, "the General Government can exercise a paternal control over their interests and possibly perpetuate their race."

Jackson's paternalistic rationales meant little to those peoples forced to give up their homes in the South. Living as their white neighbors in brick homes with extensive crops and livestock cared for by African American slaves, some Indians had accumulated considerable material wealth. To them removal was simply a cover for white cupidity, and this view was bolstered as Indian landholders were evicted from their farms on flimsy legal pretenses. As in the Potawatomi removals, small factions of each of the tribes were either bribed or induced by promises of a better life to sign treaties of removal. The best known of these, the Treaty of New Echota (1835), disregarded the wishes of the Cherokees' principal chief, John Ross, and led to a division within the tribe that continued for decades. Shortly after the Cherokees' arrival in Indian Territory, Ross's allies murdered the signers of the New Echota treaty. In spite of numerous official delegations and petitions asking permission to stay in their homes, most of the Cherokees were rounded up for deportation in the early summer of 1838. The forced march of three different detachments of Cherokees in that summer resulted in the loss of at least four thousand people, and some estimates have suggested that eight thousand died either along the way or in the stockades before they began their migration west. With the removal of the Cherokees from Georgia, many other tribal groups gave up the fight. By 1840 some sixty thousand members of the Cherokee, Choctaw, Chickasaw, Creek, and Seminole tribes had been relocated to Indian Territory.

The losses in human life, material possessions, and tribal identity are impossible to estimate. Regardless of official expressions of concern and admiration for Indian peoples, removal revealed a callous disregard for Indian life and property that unfortunately characterized most official dealings with Native Americans during the nineteenth century.

See also **American Indians,** *subentries on* **Overview, Wars and Warfare, Treaties and Treatymaking, U.S. Government Policies; American Indian Societies; Federal Land Policy; Indian Territory; Missions,** *subentry on* **North American Indians; Race and Racial Thinking.**

Bibliography

Edmunds, David R. *The Potawatomis: Keepers of the Fire*. Norman: University of Oklahoma Press, 1978.

Mintz, Steven. *Native American Voices: A History and Anthology*. New York: Brandywine Press, 1995.

Perdue, Theda, and Michael D. Green, eds. *The Cherokee Removal: A Brief History with Documents*. Boston: Bedford Books of St. Martin's Press, 1995.

Prucha, Francis Paul. *The Great Father: The United States Government and the American Indians*. Lincoln: University of Nebraska Press, 1986.

BONNIE LYNN-SHEROW

THE IMAGE OF THE INDIAN

Images of American Indians typically have been divided into two categories, the noble and the ignoble savage. The Indian woman was either a princess or a drudge; the Indian man was an admirable or a fiendish warrior. These are venerable distinctions, entrenched in eighteenth-century European writings about New World natives and enshrined in American literature by James Fenimore Cooper's novel *The Last of the Mohicans* (1826). Progenitor of a host of Indian stories characterized by a critic in 1834 as "only the repetition of a sigh—melancholy and monotonous" (Dippie, *Catlin and His Contemporaries*, p. 17), Cooper's book personifies good and bad by tribe and individual, the noble Delawares, Uncas and his father, Chingachgook, and the evil Hurons, Magua and his "bloody-minded hellhounds." In addition Cooper describes how noble savages became ignoble in the first place: "Magua was born a chief and a warrior among the red Hurons of the lakes; he saw the suns of twenty summers make the snows of twenty winters run off in the streams, before he saw a paleface; and he was happy! Then his Canada fathers [the French] came into the woods and taught him to drink the firewater, and he became a rascal."

The starkness of the contrast between Uncas and Magua, between the noble and ignoble savage, obscures their common denominator: both were savages. The one was to be admired, of course, and his passing lamented; the other was to be deplored, his wickedness providing moral justification for his extermination. The fate of both was the same and wonderfully convenient. Noble and ignoble savages alike were destined to die off, freeing the land of its native population and making the process of colonization as benign as it was inevitable. This idea of the Vanishing American, a tradition steeped in romantic sentimentalism, gave the older European concepts a distinctive American twist. Because, the reasoning went, the universal law of human progress dictated that civilization displace savagery wherever the two met, the Indians, as America's savages, were doomed to disappear unless they could be civilized and thus saved.

Indian Remedy. The stereotype of American Indians as robustly healthy and long-lived was used by pharmaceutical companies to market their products. LIBRARY OF CONGRESS

In their uncontaminated wilderness state Indians certainly embodied savage vices, cruelty and ignorance foremost. But they also embodied savage virtues, such as stoicism, self-sufficiency, courage, independence, and even a rude poetry. If these were added to civilization's virtues—Christianity, education, the work ethic—Indian progress would be assured. An 1818 report by the House Committee on Indian Affairs outlined the process:

> Put into the hands of their children the primer and the hoe, and they will naturally, in time, take hold of the plow; and as their minds become enlightened and expand, the Bible will be their book, and they will grow up in habits of morality and industry, leave the chase to those of minds less cultured, and become useful members of society.

In short, old virtues would have to yield to new virtues. But as Magua demonstrated and experience proved, Indians, upon confronting civilization, surrendered their natural virtues and acquired only civilized vices. Whiskey summed up this transformation. The free-spirited, proud, self-sufficient hunter became the filthy, drunken, diseased, demoralized settlement Indian or the bloodthirsty savage who took to the warpath in futile resistance of the inevitable. The noble savage disappeared with the retreating wilderness. The corrupted savage, a phrase used by the Philadelphia artist George Catlin, a great admirer of the noble savage, was exterminated by his or her own vices or by the avenging sword. The Vanishing American encapsulated the fate of all savages, noble and ignoble alike.

Popular understanding of the Indian was buttressed by nineteenth-century scientific theories. At mid-century the theory of polygenesis, the multiple creation of human "types," provided a potentially potent, race-based explanation for permanent differences in capacity. This theory reinforced assumptions about the incompatibility of savagery and civilization and the inevitable death sentence for savage types. The Vanishing American found corroboration in science. But polygenesis clashed with religious orthodoxy, which, in stressing the kinship of all humanity, consistently rejected the notion that any group was destined for extinction.

Contexts for Indian Images

The imaginary Indian—noble, ignoble, vanishing—constituted a potent reality in the nineteenth century, because government policy was attuned to popular assumptions about Indian character and destiny. Indeed, these assumptions were constants in American thought and were set against a shifting backdrop of events. In 1800 the United States was a nation still hugging the Atlantic seaboard, bounded by Florida to the south and the Mississippi River to the west. By mid-century the United States was a transcontinental nation, and Indian Country, which once stretched from the Appalachians to the Mississippi, would survive only as reservations scattered across the Far West. This dynamic territorial expansion left established images of the Indian largely unaffected, even as U.S. policy accommodated new Indian realities. The government's commitment to Indian seclusion through removal, the dominant theme of policy prior to 1840, was no longer practical after mid-century. By the 1870s removal yielded to a policy of assimilation through allotment in severalty.

The idea of the Vanishing American had flourished as a corollary to national expansion, and artists doted on the theme. One popular motif showed civilization, often symbolized by a train, scattering savagery be-

"Civilized." The 1878 wood engraving reflects stereotypes of Indians as alcoholics and lazy—a view at odds with the healthy, robust Indian featured in the earlier illustration in this entry. From Beadle, *Western Wilds*. LIBRARY OF CONGRESS

fore its irresistible advance. Another placed Indians on a bluff gazing down with melancholic resignation on the world below, where civilized progress was represented by schools, churches, and a thriving, industrious population of white settlers. Dispossession had made the Indians outcasts in their own land. Assimilation mandated the Indians' disappearance through cultural absorption and, at its most literal, racial amalgamation. As for the dichotomous images of noble and ignoble savage, expansion rendered the former something of an eastern monopoly and the latter a western one.

The Indian wars that marked the westward advance of white settlers throughout the nineteenth century reinforced traditional stereotypes along regional lines. Westerners routinely denounced eastern philanthropists, humanitarians, and policymakers as sentimentalists. They blamed Cooper for Uncas and the tradition of the romanticized noble savage even as they accepted fully Magua and the bloody savage. Of course, sectional attitudes ranged across the board; no region or group was monolithic in its views.

The army, for example, included in its ranks outspoken Indian haters and sensitive students of Indian cultures. Similarly, individual westerners passionately championed Indian rights. Nevertheless, westerners collectively tended to disparage Indians, perceiving them as both encumbrance and threat. "Principles of peace and good will are fuel to the flames of red men's savagery," the *Weekly Democratic Statesman*—an Austin, Texas, paper—editorialized on 13 July 1876 after General George Custer's disaster on the Little Bighorn. Another Texas paper, the *Galveston Daily News* (18 July 1876), used poetry to make the same point:

> I want to be an Indian,
> A warrior of the plains;
> I want to wield a tomahawk,
> And scoop out people's brains.
>
> I want to build a camp-fire
> On a human-being's breast,
> And watch his writhing agony
> With a noble savage's zest.

Ambivalence and the Indian Image

Sectional considerations aside, ambivalence colored most nineteenth-century assessments of the Indian. After all, as the purest product of American nature, the Indian was essential to any definition of what it meant to be American. Advertisers latched onto this logic in the form of cigar-store Indians touting the virtues of tobacco, that New World gift to the Old. Patent-medicine companies utilized Indians to assert a link between aboriginal medicinal lore and whatever concoction they were hawking, be it Red Jacket or Old Sachem Bitters, Cherokee liniments, Tippecanoe cure-alls, or Kickapoo Indian remedies. The Indian was the guardian of nature's secrets and, in rudimentary form, the embodiment of America's potential. Two impulses collided in imagining the Indian, one celebrating civilized progress and Indian decline, the other commemorating the loss of the most American part of America in the process of taming a wilderness.

Thus, a visitor to Washington, D.C., in the early 1860s would have encountered a confusing array of Indian images. In the capitol rotunda, a relief of William Penn making peace with a group of friendly Indians contrasted with another of Daniel Boone overwhelming two fierce-looking warriors in hand-to-hand combat. Ferdinand Pettrich's sculptural tribute to the Vanishing American, *The Dying Tecumseh* (1856), was on display in the capitol, along with Horatio Greenough's 1837 *Rescue Group,* showing a towering pioneer in buckskins subduing a savage warrior about to tomahawk a woman and child. The U.S. Senate pediment featured an allegorical relief by Thomas Crawford, *Progress of Civilization* (modeled in 1854 and erected in 1863), depicting America surrounded by its white children who are crowding a band of Indians toward a yawning grave. In 1855 Crawford sculpted the figure *American Freedom* that graced the Capitol dome, her feathered headdress symbolizing a native love of liberty. Since 1854 America's one- and three-dollar gold pieces sported a befeathered Liberty, while from 1859 to 1909 an Indian in full headdress decorated the penny. The penny's lifetime spanned the conquest of the western tribes and the policy of Indian assimilation, suggesting the essential continuity in Indian imagery despite a century of change.

After the Civil War, with urban realities paramount in the rapidly industrializing United States, Indians might have been deemed irrelevant. But the conservative press found a correlation between the savages of the Plains and deserts and the savages who imperiled the established order—emancipated African Americans, immigrants, and anarchistic workers. Oddly, such identifications reached back to the founding myths of the nation. The Sons of Liberty had defied British authority in 1773 by holding their Boston Tea Party disguised as Mohawks. Fraternal organizations associated with political reform in the early Republic readily turned to Indian themes to establish their patriotic credentials. The Society of Red Men, formed during the War of 1812 as an expression of anti-British sentiment, evolved in the 1830s into the Improved Order of Red Men. Members delighted in Indian nomenclature, costume, and ritual even as they banned Indians from joining.

Ambiguity and ambivalence remained entrenched in Indian imagery as the nineteenth century came to an end. The negative image of the bloody savage had always qualified the regret occasioned by the noble savage's passing. Better the Indian disappear with nobility intact than degenerate into the kind of mindless brute who justified extermination. Better Uncas and Chingachgook leave the stage still heroes. When the frontier moment had passed, all Americans, with a certain sentimental regret, could look upon Indian peoples as worthy adversaries who had fought hard for their own way of life. Such notables as Sitting Bull and Geronimo made public appearances in touring shows and at fairs, where from the 1880s on Indian contingents were an expected part of the entertainment. The legendary Wild West showman, scout, and Indian fighter William F. "Buffalo Bill" Cody, beginning in 1885, employed Sioux to play themselves in the tableaux illustrating his heroic deeds, thereby crystallizing the image of the American Indian as a buffalo-hunting Plains warrior in feather warbonnet. It was the shortest of steps from Cody's celebration of the "winning of the West" to commemorations of the losers, who, once Indian wars were only a memory, poignantly symbolized the cost of progress. James Earle Fraser was inspired by the sculpture on display in Chicago in 1893 at the World's Columbian Exposition, where Buffalo Bill's Wild West was a sideshow. The next year Fraser modeled the prototype for his allegorical group *The End of the Trail* (1896). In 1913 Fraser designed one of the most popular American coins, the Indian head–buffalo nickel. That coin was the nineteenth century's legacy to the twentieth, fusing the noble savage with the Vanishing American to create a timeless Indian, symbolizing a past already receding into pure nostalgia.

See also **Frontier; Interpretations,** *subentry on* **Literary Interpretations; Race and Racial Thinking; West, The; Wild West Shows.**

Bibliography

Berkhofer, Robert F., Jr. *The White Man's Indian: Images of the American Indian from Columbus to the Present.* New York: Knopf, 1978.

Bieder, Robert E. *Science Encounters the Indian, 1820–1880: The Early Years of American Ethnology.* Norman: University of Oklahoma Press, 1986.

Bird, S. Elizabeth, ed. *Dressing in Feathers: The Construction of the Indian in American Popular Culture.* Boulder, Colo.: Westview Press, 1996.

Coward, John M. *The Newspaper Indian: Native American Identity in the Press, 1820–90.* Urbana: University of Illinois Press, 1999.

Deloria, Philip J. *Playing Indian.* New Haven, Conn.: Yale University Press, 1998.

Dippie, Brian W. *Catlin and His Contemporaries: The Politics of Patronage.* Lincoln: University of Nebraska Press, 1990.

———. "The Moving Finger Writes: Western Art and the Dynamics of Change." In *Discovered Lands, Invented Pasts: Transforming Visions of the American West,* edited by Jules David Prown et al. New Haven, Conn.: Yale University Press, 1992.

———. *The Vanishing American: White Attitudes and U.S. Indian Policy.* Middletown, Conn.: Wesleyan University Press, 1982. Reprint, Lawrence: University Press of Kansas, 1991.

Fryd, Vivien Green. *Art and Empire: The Politics of Ethnicity in the United States Capitol, 1815–1860.* New Haven, Conn.: Yale University Press, 1992.

Pearce, Roy Harvey. *The Savages of America: A Study of the Indian and the Idea of Civilization.* Baltimore: Johns Hopkins Press, 1953. Reprinted as *Savagism and Civilization: A Study of the Indian and the American Mind.* Baltimore: Johns Hopkins Press, 1965.

Slotkin, Richard. *The Fatal Environment: The Myth of the Frontier in the Age of Industrialization, 1800–1890.* New York: Atheneum, 1985.

Smith, Sherry L. *The View from Officers' Row: Army Perceptions of Western Indians.* Tucson: University of Arizona Press, 1990.

BRIAN W. DIPPIE

AMERICAN INDIAN SOCIETIES

[This entry includes nine subentries on American Indian Societies in various geographic regions:
New England
The Middle Atlantic Region
The Southeast
The Great Lakes
The Plains
California
The Northwest Plateau
The Southwest
Alaska]

NEW ENGLAND

According to a local history, the "last Abenaqui chief" died at Bellows Falls, Vermont, in 1856. The chief had canoed down the Connecticut River with Abenakis who went to fish and trade baskets every summer and, at his own request, was buried with his ancestors beside the falls. The other Abenakis returned north. Bellows Falls was once an important place in the Abenaki seasonal round, as evidenced by the petroglyphs on the rocks and the dying chief's desire to be buried there, but, as the account noted, their stay was temporary and no history existed of permanent Indian settlements in the area. The account is typical of references to American Indians in nineteenth-century New England town histories. Indians disappeared as towns grew. When they are mentioned, they are usually depicted as visitors on their way home or on their way to extinction.

The prevailing opinion held that only a few Indian "remnants" survived, and that they would soon be gone forever. Continuing pressures on Indian lands, cultures, and independence reinforced the impression of impending extinction. After 1820 the new state of Maine continued the assault on tribal lands that previously had been waged by Massachusetts. By midcentury most Penobscots were confined on a single island, and the Passamaquoddies were split between two small reservations. The state appointed agents to run the tribes' affairs and supervised the creation of new elective tribal governments. In 1869, after some New England Indians fought in the Union ranks during the Civil War, Massachusetts gave individual Indians citizenship and voting rights. Unfortunately this action also opened the way for unrestricted sale of their lands. In 1880 Rhode Island took away the Narragansets' tribal status and authorized the sale of their tribal lands at public auction.

As areas of New England became increasingly industrial and urban, many young Indian women left home to find work in textile mills in Lowell and Worcester, Massachusetts, or in Manchester, New Hampshire, and many men moved to Boston or New York City. A mobile Indian labor force developed. Indian men from coastal regions in southern New England continued to work in deep-sea whaling, and in the northern areas others found employment as seasonal laborers, loggers, trappers, and guides. Indian women crafted baskets and brooms, then peddled them door to door or sold them to tourists at summer resorts. Native people who experienced poverty and dislocation in the new economic climate were sometimes persecuted as paupers and vagrants.

During the nineteenth century many Indian people found it best to keep out of sight, both within and on the peripheries of New England communities. As Native Americans had long intermarried with their Yankee, African American, or French Canadian neighbors, many mixed families were able to conceal their Indian identity. Indians who worked in the same trades and walked the same paths as other New Englanders reinforced their belief in their own invisibility in the eyes of whites, who associated Indians with bygone days and exotic costumes and customs.

Some Indians defended their lands and rights. William Apess (1798–1839), a Pequot Indian who became a Methodist preacher and writer, confronted New Englanders with their past and present treatment of Indian peoples. In 1833 he spoke out on behalf of the Mashpees on Cape Cod, who openly defied the authority of the state of Massachusetts and won a measure of self-government in their community. His actions prefigured those of twentieth-century Native American leaders who defended tribal resources and the rights of Native Americans. But while national attention focused on removing tribes from the South and defeating those in the West, Indians in New England, a region of the country that ignored the presence of Native Americans and denied their existence, usually waged less dramatic struggles to preserve their ways and kinship-based communities.

See also **New England; Race and Racial Thinking.**

Bibliography
Apess, William. *On Our Own Ground: The Complete Writings of William Apess, a Pequot.* Edited by Barry O'Connell. Amherst: University of Massachusetts Press, 1992.

Calloway, Colin G., ed. *After King Philip's War: Presence and Persistence in Indian New England.* Hanover, N.H.: University Press of New England, 1997.

COLIN G. CALLOWAY

THE MIDDLE ATLANTIC REGION

By 1800 the Native American populations of the Middle Atlantic region had experienced two centuries of contact with Europeans and had been decimated by colonial and intertribal wars and epidemic disease. Large tribes had been splintered and the survivors had coalesced into new remnant groups. European settlers had pushed native peoples westward, and the colonial powers had reduced Indian political and territorial autonomy. The European presence had also significantly altered traditional native culture. Missionaries had converted some Native Americans to Christian practices, and the English, French, and Dutch had pulled Indians into the European mercantile and fur trade economy. These trade relationships and the trade goods themselves forced Indians to revise their cultural attitudes and to adopt more centralized governments to manage the new environment they confronted.

For most native groups across the East, the nineteenth century was marked by frequent land cessions and migrations to federally created reserves on the fringes of white settlement. After the United States defeated Great Britain and its Indian allies in the War of 1812, the tribes east of the Mississippi River lost forever their once substantial bargaining leverage with the U.S. government. As American settlers moved into tribal areas, the federal government responded to popular demands for native land cessions. Consequently, in the 1830s almost all of the eastern tribes sacrificed their remaining lands, signed removal treaties, and migrated to the West. By the end of the century the federal government had relocated most of the Middle Atlantic tribes to reservations in Wisconsin, Kansas, Oklahoma, or northern New York. Some groups were forced to move again and again to appease the onrushing settlers.

Portions of some tribes withstood the pressure for removal and remained on reservations carved out of their old tribal territories. For example, while a majority of the Oneidas were removed to Wisconsin and Ontario, about two hundred holdouts remained on about thirty-two acres of a domain that had once encompassed six million acres. Other small groups of Iroquois relocated to Wisconsin or Canada. A number of small native bands such as the Nanticokes in Delaware and Maryland remained in the East and were politically assimilated by the United States. In small enclaves in urban neighborhoods and rural outposts, these holdouts struggled to maintain their cultural identity, even as they endured impoverished economic circumstances and American cultural and demographic encirclement.

Individual Indians and native communities responded to the increasingly prevalent American influence in different ways. Some, encouraged by the civilization program of the United States, adopted Western agricultural techniques, embraced Anglo-American culture, and attempted to assimilate. Others joined prophetic revitalization movements, rejected Western culture, and continued to abide by their traditional mores and lifestyles. Many Iroquois, influenced by the visionary Handsome Lake, integrated their own traditional worldview with the religious doctrines proffered by Christian missionaries and developed a new syncretic faith called the Longhouse Religion. These alternative visions for the native future often provoked factionalism among the tribes over the issues of acculturation, economics, land cessions, and removal. In short, the nineteenth century was a period of challenge and transition for the native peoples of the Middle Atlantic.

See also **American Indians,** *subentries on* **American Indian Religions, Indian Removal; Federal Land Policy; Indian Territory; Missions,** *subentry on* **Indian Responses to White Missionaries; War of 1812.**

Bibliography

Brasser, T. J. "Mahican." In *Handbook of North American Indians.* Volume 15: *Northeast.* Edited by Bruce Trigger. Washington, D.C.: Smithsonian Institution Press, 1978.

Goddard, Ives. "Delaware." In *Handbook of North American Indians.* Volume 15: *Northeast.* Edited by Bruce Trigger. Washington, D.C.: Smithsonian Institution Press, 1978.

Tooker, Elisabeth. "Iroquois since 1820." In *Handbook of North American Indians.* Volume 15: *Northeast.* Edited by Bruce Trigger. Washington, D.C.: Smithsonian Institution Press, 1978.

Wallace, Anthony F. C. *The Death and Rebirth of the Seneca.* New York: Knopf, 1970.

TIM ALAN GARRISON

THE SOUTHEAST

The American Indians of the southeastern United States endured an onslaught of hardships in the nineteenth century. They struggled throughout, however, to maintain their tribal distinctiveness, preserve their political autonomy, and adapt to their changing circumstances.

In the 1790s the United States began providing farm implements, mechanical training, missionaries, and teachers to American Indians to prepare them for assimilation into white American society. So many of the Cherokees, Creeks, Choctaws, Chickasaws, and Seminoles were successful in conforming to the United States's wishes that they became known collectively as the Five Civilized Tribes. The pressure to acculturate, however, along with the continuing trespasses of white settlers onto Indian land, produced bitter tribal divisions. In some cases, competing visions for the future produced civil war. In 1811 the Shawnee leader Tecumseh (1768–1813) traveled among the Creeks and encouraged them to return to their traditional lifestyle, rise up in revolution, and expel the Americans from their lands. While about three-fourths of the "Red Stick" warriors from the upper Creek towns embraced Tecumseh's message, the official Creek leadership generally sought peaceful relations with the United States. In 1813 a group of Red Sticks attacked white settlers in western Tennessee; when the Creek government killed the Red Stick assailants, the two factions broke out into civil war. After the Red Sticks massacred several hundred Americans at Fort Mims, Andrew Jackson's (1767–1845) troops marched into Creek territory, annihilated the Red Stick forces at Horseshoe Bend (1814), and forced the Creeks to cede millions of acres to the United States.

During the 1820s, Georgia led the southern states in urging the federal government to remove the Indian tribes beyond the Mississippi River. In 1827 the Cherokee Nation responded by adopting a republican constitution and declaring itself independent of the United States. Over time, other southeastern tribes like the Choctaws (1834), the Chickasaws (1848), and the Creeks (around 1859 or 1860) adopted their own constitutional governments. Between 1828 and 1832, Georgia, Alabama, Tennessee, and Mississippi increased the removal pressure on the tribes by passing a series of draconian statutes outlawing tribal governments and extending state jurisdiction over individual Indians. In 1830 the U.S. Congress satisfied the southern states by passing the Indian Removal Act, which gave President Andrew Jackson the authority to negotiate removal treaties. Soon thereafter, the federal government began pressing the tribes to surrender their eastern homelands and relocate to the newly created Indian Territory in what is now Oklahoma.

The Cherokees, however, lobbied Congress and Jackson to reconsider their removal policy and brought suit to enjoin Georgia's extension legislation; these efforts produced two U.S. Supreme Court decisions. In *Cherokee Nation v. Georgia* (1831), the court held that the Cherokees comprised a "domestic dependent nation" rather than a foreign state, and

Seminole Mother and Child. The child is carried in traditional fashion, on the mother's back. Photograph, c. 1905. LIBRARY OF CONGRESS

therefore lacked standing to sue in the federal courts. In *Worcester v. Georgia* (1832), however, the court declared the Cherokee Nation was an autonomous state with legitimate title to its territory, and that Georgia's tactics of intimidation were unconstitutional. Jackson, however, refused to enforce this decision against the state. When the Cherokee government refused to sign a removal treaty, federal negotiators concluded an agreement at New Echota (1835) with a small group of dissident Cherokees. In 1838 the U.S. Army forcibly marched most of the Cherokees to the Indian Territory. Over a quarter of the tribe died on what became known as the Trail of Tears. Roughly one thousand Cherokees escaped removal, fled into the mountains of western North Carolina, and reemerged decades later as an independent tribe. The Choctaws (1830), Creeks (1832), and Chickasaws (1837) all signed removal treaties and emigrated to lands set aside for them in the Indian Territory.

The Seminoles, however, violently resisted the

United States's removal efforts. Animosities between the United States and the Seminoles began with the First Seminole War (1817–1818), when the Seminoles battled American settlers along the border of Georgia and Spanish Florida. In 1818, Andrew Jackson, then the commander of American troops on the Florida border, marched into Spanish territory, attacked the Seminoles, and seized the Spanish forts of Pensacola and St. Marks. Jackson also accused and executed two British traders for inciting Seminole attacks against American settlers. After hostilities ended, the United States acquired Florida from Spain; in 1823 the Seminoles signed a treaty ceding most of their land to the United States and retreated down the Florida peninsula. In 1832 the Seminole government signed a removal treaty at Payne's Landing. However, a large group of Seminoles, led by Osceola (c. 1804–1838), refused to move; and in 1835 the United States again marched into Seminole territory, starting the Second Seminole War. The Seminoles held off the American army in bitter guerrilla warfare for seven years. Finally, in 1842, most of the Seminoles surrendered and moved to Oklahoma. Still, a large group avoided capture and escaped into the Everglades—only in 1935 did the remaining Florida Seminoles come to terms with the United States.

Once they had been removed, the southeastern tribes quickly adapted to their new environment, reestablishing their governments and continuing to exert their independence from the United States. The Chickasaws, for example, had been forced to abolish their tribal government in the Treaty of Doaksville (1837) and had agreed to move to the Choctaw portion of the Indian Territory. The merger of the two tribes ignited nationalist feelings among the Chickasaws, and in 1856, after several years of negotiation, they formally separated from the Choctaws and reestablished themselves as a separate sovereign nation.

Divisions brought on by removal, however, continued to fester in the Indian Territory, and rival factions occasionally broke out into violent conflict. The American Civil War also divided the southeastern nations during the 1860s. In 1887 Congress passed the Dawes General Allotment Act, which divided tribal lands into individual allotments and opened up the remaining surplus for white settlers. In 1907 Congress merged the residents of the Indian Territory into the new state of Oklahoma and effectively abolished the sovereignty of the southeastern nations.

See also **Indian Territory; Jacksonian Era; Seminole War(s).**

Bibliography

Gibson, Arrell M. *The Chickasaws.* Norman: University of Oklahoma Press, 1971.

Green, Michael D. *The Politics of Indian Removal: Creek Government and Society in Crisis.* Lincoln: University of Nebraska Press, 1982.

McLoughlin, William G. *After the Trail of Tears: The Cherokees' Struggle for Sovereignty, 1839–1880.* Chapel Hill: University of North Carolina Press, 1993.

Perdue, Theda. *Slavery and the Evolution of Cherokee Society, 1540–1866.* Knoxville: University of Tennessee Press, 1979.

TIM ALAN GARRISON

THE GREAT LAKES

The Native American peoples of the Great Lakes suffered through white settler invasions, coerced land cessions, and forced relocations during the nineteenth century. Until 1800 the Great Lakes tribes played the United States, Great Britain, and (before 1763) France against each other in matters of trade, war, and diplomacy. At the outbreak of the War of 1812 many tribes allied with Tecumseh's nativist confederacy and Great Britain. The U.S. victory in that war, however, destroyed the Indian military threat east of the Mississippi, forced Great Britain to abandon the southern lakes area, and resulted in a dramatic loss of native land. By the late 1860s the Great Lakes tribes had ceded almost all of their lands and mineral rights to the United States.

Many of the tribes, including the Potawatomis, Ottawas, Winnebagos, Wyandots, and Kickapoos, signed removal treaties that relegated them to diminished territories in Kansas, Nebraska, and the Indian Territory. Often, as with the Winnebagos, the federal government used unscrupulous means to coerce Indian leaders into signing removal treaties. Despite their adaptation to commercial agriculture, removal expelled Great Lakes people from the eastern forests and provoked social disruption, moral despair, and tribal factionalism. To make matters worse, epidemic disease and poverty continued to disturb Indian populations after they arrived in the West.

Many Indians resisted U.S. removal demands. Some joined the revitalization movements of Wabokieshiek (Winnebago) in 1827 and Kenakuk (Kickapoo) in the 1820s and 1830s. Dynamic warriors such as Black Hawk (Sauk) in 1832 and Red Bird (Winnebago) in 1827 led unsuccessful military actions against the United States. Some Ojibwas, Ottawas, and Potawatomis moved into Canada to avoid removal. Still other small bands of Chippewas, Ottawas, Menominees, Potawatomis, and Winnebagos escaped federal agents, remained in the region in isolated enclaves, and took jobs with American lumber, mining, manufacturing, and farming interests.

The Indians of the Great Lakes also experienced dramatic cultural change during the nineteenth century. The United States subjected the Great Lakes tribes to an intensive civilization program and provided schools, missionaries, and training in farming and the mechanical arts. These acculturative pressures along with economic and environmental exigencies brought a decline in the importance of hunting and the fur trade for Great Lakes Indians. However, a large Métis class, the product of intermarriage between Indians and French, Scottish, and Irish fur traders, continued to be an important force in many native communities. Some of the Métis were assimilated into the major tribes; some formed their own separate communities in both the United States and Canada.

Reservations in the Great Lakes region were located largely in the northern areas of Michigan, Wisconsin, and Minnesota, far removed from the population centers of Detroit and Milwaukee. By the end of the nineteenth century many of the Great Lakes reservations had been divided up into individual allotments and the surplus sold to white settlers. Those tribes who were able to preserve their reservations faced poverty, continuing cultural degradation, and increasing marginalization by American society. Nevertheless, most Great Lakes Indians maintained their cultural identity and preserved many of their significant customs, mores, and institutions.

See also **American Indians**, *subentry on* **Indian Removal**; **Education**, *subentry on* **Indian Schools**.

Bibliography

Black Hawk. *Black Hawk (Ma-ka-tai-me-she-kia-kiak): An Autobiography.* Urbana: University of Illinois Press, 1955.

Lurie, Nancy Oestreich. "Winnebago." In *Handbook of North American Indians.* Volume 15: *Northeast.* Edited by Bruce Trigger. Washington, D.C.: Smithsonian Institution Press, 1978.

Stone, Lyle M., and Donald Chaput. "History of the Upper Great Lakes Area." In *Handbook of North American Indians.* Volume 15: *Northeast.* Edited by Bruce Trigger. Washington, D.C.: Smithsonian Institution Press, 1978.

TIM ALAN GARRISON

THE PLAINS

The Plains have been continuously inhabited from as early as 10,000 B.C. by successive waves of immigrant peoples coming from adjacent regions and speaking various languages who brought with them a variety of cultural and social practices. Never empty or abandoned, the region was periodically rich with flora and fauna, most notably buffalo, and further diversified by a range of microclimates. All the historic Indian peoples were already resident in the region at the opening of the nineteenth century and were

drawn increasingly into trade relationships with Euro-Americans. The resulting patterns of competition, cooperation, and conflict among these societies developed as they struggled for access to horses and trade goods, especially firearms. Some groups, for example, Assiniboines, Mandans, Hidatsas, Arikaras, Pawnees, Osages, Shoshones, and Comanches, acted as middlemen between antagonists, or distance groups, some of whom were in adjacent culture areas. Others competed directly for resources, triggering battles that made Plains Indian warriors famous for their tenacity in asserting and protecting their group's interests. By 1850, the Plains Indian way of life represented a combination of retained aspects of traditions carried forward from previous generations elsewhere and adaptations adopted to cope with the contingencies of their localities.

The diversity of societies inhabiting the Plains was reflected in the range of language families and constituent groups represented—Algonquians (Arapaho, Blackfoot, Cheyenne, Gros Ventre, Plains Cree, Saulteaux), Siouans (Assiniboine-Stoney, Crow, Dakota-Lakota, Hidatsa, Mandan), Chiwere (Iowa, Missouri, Oto, Winnebago), Dhegiha (Omaha, Osage, Ponca, Kansa, Quapaw), Caddoans (Arikara, Pawnee, Wichita), Numics (Comanche, Shoshone, Ute),

Oglala Sioux. White Hawk, an Oglala Sioux woman, posed for Alexander Gardner, who photographed her between 1870 and 1880. LIBRARY OF CONGRESS: PRINTS AND PHOTOGRAPHS DIVISION

Salish (Flathead), Penutian (Nez Percé), and Athapascans (Kiowa-Apache, Sarcee). To make matters more complicated, the U.S. removal policy of the 1830s and 1840s relocated portions of the Five Civilized Tribes (Cherokee, Chickasaw, Choctaw, Creeks, Seminoles) and Delawares, Shawnees, Sauk, and Mesquakie (Fox), among others, into lands of present-day Oklahoma and Kansas. These late arrivals were viewed as displaced eastern Indians and not considered traditional Plains Indian societies, but they interacted with the region's indigenous peoples. Trade languages and diplomatic practices fostered multilingualism and produced new interactions and, ultimately, still other new cultural practices.

The social structures of Plains Indians rested on a tension between individualism and cooperation as well as a struggle over the means whereby older generations exercised authority over youth. The environmental options and subsequent adaptations allowed several distinct institutional variations to emerge. Many groups pursued buffalo and other larger game year-round, supplemented by gathering. Others had a mixed economy of horticulture and seasonal hunting and gathering. The composition of camping bands living year-round in movable tepees compared to fortified villages of earth lodges with adjacent fields meant that social forms varied; sedentary groups stressed cooperation, while hunters relied to a greater extent on the process of individuals. In both adaptations, kinship prerogatives were crosscut by men's military and women's crafts sodalities (associations), which articulated distinctive values and maintained order while carrying out their responsibilities. Religio-political sanctions reached extensive elaboration among the Mandan, Hidatsa, Arapaho, Gros Ventre, and Blackfoot, who had sodalities that were age graded—one generation purchasing rites and obligations from their predecessors who were busy buying out the next generation. Among the Dhegiha and Chiwere Siouans, membership in clans tracing lineage through either mothers' or fathers' family was further organized into two larger groups, which were defined by specific roles and obligations that could only be performed for the one group by the other, for example, the burying of the dead, or source of marriage partners. Among the fully nomadic warriors and hunters, sodalities became social resources appointed to maintain social order, especially in communal hunting ventures and to organize labor necessary for tasks and rituals. Achieved status was the basic by-product of these associations, much of it affiliated with warfare and its resulting booty. These societies provided systematic social cohesion for the maintenance of a system of status, as well as a means for maintaining authority over the young.

In the last decades of the nineteenth century, reservation/reserve policies incorporated Plains Indians by imposing regulated changes on most pre-reservation social structures whose practices were either adapted to the new conditions or abandoned. While values that informed previous forms of social relations persisted within group governance and ceremonial contexts, the new reservation way of life pulled the next generations toward increased accommodation and assimilation into modern American society.

See also **American Indians,** *subentry on* **Indian Removal; Great Plains.**

Bibliography

Ewers, John. *Plains Indian History and Culture.* Norman: University of Oklahoma Press, 1997.

Haines, Francis. *The Plains Indians: Their Origins, Migrations, and Cultural Development.* New York: Crowell, 1976.

Hoig, Stan. *Tribal Wars of the Southern Plains.* Norman: University of Oklahoma Press, 1993.

DAVID REED MILLER

CALIFORNIA

Just prior to the arrival of permanent European colonization the California Indian population numbered approximately 320,000. Representing six language families, this was the most numerous and diverse of the Indian populations in what became the United States. A multitude of independent native villages characterized the nature of these peoples' political, economic, and social organization.

By 1800 the California Indian population had been seriously disrupted by the establishment of Spanish colonial institutions along much of the coast and adjacent interior. Beginning with the introduction of the first missions, as much as 20 percent of the population had succumbed to the debilitating effects of introduced diseases and the displacement of much of the coastal population in the forced labor centers of the Franciscan missionaries. The importation of stock animals transformed the natural environment and deprived nearby independent tribes of essential natural plant and game food resources that supported their hunting-gathering economy. Frequent military assaults further crippled Indian efforts to resist the newcomers.

Despite these disadvantages, tribespeople offered many forms of resistance. Thousands of mission Indians ran away, and at least eight thousand made their escapes permanent. Several Franciscan padres were assassinated because of the cruel punishments inflicted upon the Indians, who endured slavelike conditions in the missions. A kind of guerrilla warfare evolved, pitting such Indian leaders as Estanislao, Yozcolo, Pomponio, and others against the colonists. Scores of large-scale mission Indian revolts erupted both before and after 1800. The most spectacular revolt occurred in 1824 at the missions Santa Ynez, Santa Barbara, and La Purisima in Chumash Indian territory along the central coast.

In 1822, when California became a distant province of the newly independent Mexico, the missions' dependency upon unpaid Indian labor increased, and these mission estates were vulnerable to stock raiding by emboldened and aggressive interior groups of Indians. Prompted by the democratic ideals of the Enlightenment and the possibility of personal gain, Mexican authorities in the 1830s seized control of the considerable wealth of the missions and "freed" the Indians from church control. Few of the 220,000 surviving California Indians received lands or resources during this program of secularization. Thousands of former mission Indians were promptly enslaved by Mexican colonists.

A royal Russian fur trade monopoly established an outpost at Bodega Bay and built Fort Ross about fifteen miles north of Bodega Bay between 1809 and 1812. Signing a peace treaty in 1817 with local Kashaya Pomo Indians, the Russians challenged Mexican hegemony. During the 1820s and 1840s the interior of California was hotly contested. Wild horse herds supplied interior tribespeople with valuable trade animals that they promptly sold to American fur trappers. The Mexican colonists, who called themselves "Californios," with inept and corrupt leadership, were frequently defeated in their military forays into the California central valley and eventually could control only coastal territory. A devastating malaria plague swept through the interior valley in 1833, and a smallpox epidemic in 1837 killed thousands of Indians north of the San Francisco Bay.

A revolt in 1846 of largely illegal immigrants from the United States triggered the American takeover of Mexican California. The first U.S. military attack of the war for California was the slaughter of some three hundred nonhostile Maidu Indians by Captain John C. Frémont in June 1846, a brutal event that foreshadowed the shocking violence of the gold rush. The discovery of gold in January 1848 triggered one of the darkest episodes of Indian genocide in American history. Thousands of lawless adventurers, scouring every inch of the state for gold, organized militias to hunt and kill Indians, slaughtering approximately 100,000 Indian men, women, and children by 1850.

California entered the Union in 1850 as a free state, but the state legislature in 1850 and 1851 passed two laws that provided legal means for whites to take custody of Indian children and adults.

Stripped of their legal rights to testify in court or to seek legal protection of life and property, the California tribespeople were subjected to massive land thefts and violence, which overwhelmed the stunned tribesmen. The United States negotiated eighteen treaties with scattered tribes of Indians during the height of the gold rush. Fearing that promised treaty lands might contain gold, Congress refused to ratify the treaties in 1852. In 1854 a corrupt Indian reservation system established six reservations and Indian farms, but fewer than three thousand Indians were provided with these lands. Except for one, the reservations were abandoned in the 1860s.

In 1870 the staggering population decline of more than one hundred years of colonization and the gut-wrenching devastation during the gold rush triggered a religious revival called the Ghost Dance. Suffering severe malnutrition and saturated with diseases, desperate Indians were drawn to a religious movement that promised resurrection of the dead, the disappearance of the oppressors, and the return of peace and prosperity for California Indians. Embraced by central and northern California Indians, the Ghost Dance permanently transformed many religious beliefs and rituals into a religion promising survival for a people on the verge of annihilation. In the final years before the turn of the century, impoverished and chronically ill Indians survived through wage labor and sought to establish permanent communities with the aid of a few reform organizations.

In 1900 only seventeen thousand California Indians had survived to witness the dawn of the new century. As prophesied by the Ghost Dance, the California Indian world appeared to end that year. For the next hundred years Indian lives in California would be engineered by various Christian denominations and federal bureaucrats.

See also **California; Federal Land Policy; Gold Rushes and Silver Strikes; Mexican War; Mexico; Missions,** *subentry on* **North American Indians.**

Bibliography

Cook, Sherburne F. *The Conflict between the California Indian and White Civilization.* Berkeley: University of California Press, 1976.
———. *The Population of the California Indians, 1769–1970.* Berkeley: University of California Press, 1976.
Heizer, Robert F., and Alan F. Almquist. *The Other Californians: Prejudice and Discrimination under Spain, Mexico, and the United States to 1920.* Berkeley: University of California Press, 1971.
Sturtevant, William C., ed. *Handbook of North American Indians.* Volume 8: *California,* edited by Robert F. Heizer. Washington, D.C.: Smithsonian Institution Press, 1978.

EDWARD D. CASTILLO

THE NORTHWEST PLATEAU

As the nineteenth century dawned, the Plateau Indian world, ranging between the Cascade Mountains in the west and the Great Rocky Mountains in the east, was experiencing unsettling change. With the arrival of horses, guns, disease, and intertribal warfare, the most basic political, spiritual, and social structures in the region underwent radical mutation. Where before the basic sociopolitical unit had been the village, with authority resting with hereditary headmen, now larger bands formed for mutual defense under the authority of mounted warriors, and a strong alliance system between Plateau bands enabled them to resist incursions. And where spiritual life had been highly flexible and decentralized, prophets began emerging who joined in predicting that strangers would bring a new era. The arrival of the Lewis and Clark expedition (1806) and later of the Canadian explorer David Thompson (1807) lent credence to the prophecies. Then, in about 1820, a group of Catholic Iroquois Indians settled in the region, bringing with them trading contacts and some elements of Christianity. During the next two decades, both missionaries and fur traders would capitalize on the Plateau people's readiness for participation in Euro-American economic and religious life.

Incorporation of Christian elements into the prophet cult led Plateau Indians to invite missionaries to their homeland, attracting many Euro-American settlers during the 1830s and 1840s. By 1843, tension between the Indians and these newcomers led federal authorities to arbitrarily divide the Plateau Indians into tribes, designating head chiefs for each to serve as liaisons with the government. Despite these efforts, violence finally erupted in 1847 in the "Whitman Massacre," in which the Cayuse killed the missionary physician Marcus Whitman and destroyed the mission, setting off the Cayuse War (1848–1850).

Tense but peaceful relations followed until 1855, when Indian agents negotiated with Plateau Indians a series of treaties designed to clear a potential railroad right-of-way. Drawing on the complicity of appointed head chiefs, negotiators pressured the tribes to accept reservations that would free up the railroad route and potential ranching land. The extent to which traditional intergroup cooperation had been undermined was demonstrated shortly thereafter when the Yakima Indians went to war with the United States (1855–1856) and virtually none of their former allies assisted.

The suppression of Yakima resistance and the apparent docility of the other Plateau tribes encouraged white ranchers to encroach on the region's rich grass-

---

Plateau Ethnic Groups with Linguistic Affiliations

Kutenai Language Group

Kutenai

Lutuami Language Group

Klamath	Modoc

Salish Language Group

Coeur d'Alene	Okanagon
Colville	Pend d'Oreille
Flathead	Sanpoil
Kalispel	Shuswap
Lake	Sinkaietk (Southern Okanagon)
Lillooet	Spokan
Nespelim	Wenatchee
Ntlakyapamuk (Thompson)	

Sahaptin Language Group

Cayuse	Tenimo
Klickatat	Umatilla
Molala	Wallawalla
Nez Percé	Yakima

---

lands during the late 1850s, but the discovery of gold on the Nez Percé reservation in 1861 created a virtual invasion. In 1863 federal authorities pressed the various Nez Percé bands to negotiate an agreement for a new reservation only about one-tenth the size of the existing one. Seeking to protect their own band interests, headmen from villages within the new boundaries pressed relentlessly for the new treaty, while those whose lands were at risk resisted. The Nez Percé nation split into two parts: a protreaty group under Chief Lawyer and an antitreaty faction under Joseph (Tuekakas) and White Bird (Peopeo Kiskiok Hihih). Failing to recognize the split, when the protreaty headmen signed the treaty, government officials declared it binding on all Nez Percé bands.

A nativist prophet named Smohalla became especially influential in the uncertain atmosphere that followed. Launching what his followers called the Washani (Dancer's) Cult, Smohalla taught that dividing up the land and selling nature's bounty for money were sins and that Indians who signed treaties would lose everything. An ardent pacifist, Smohalla urged passive resistance, telling his followers to avoid relations with whites and look to their dreams for spiritual guidance.

Although he never joined the Washani Cult, Tuekakas's son and heir, Young Joseph (Heinmot Tooy-alakekt), found Smohalla's teaching compelling and often quoted the Plateau prophet in discussions with white officials as they tried to convince him to move his people onto the Nez Percé reservation. Joseph and his Wallamotkin Band of Nez Percés refused to relocate. Finally in spring of 1877 General Oliver Otis Howard ordered all nontreaty Indians to move onto reservations. As Joseph's band rounded up their horses and other possessions to make the move, several young men got into a conflict with some white ranchers and killed them. Fearing retaliation, Joseph and other nontreaty leaders fled the area, heading for sanctuary in Canada. In what would be called the Nez Percé War (1877), two U.S. Army forces attempted to contain the fleeing Indians, finally stopping them only a few miles from the international border. Joseph's people were herded onto the reservation while he and the other nontreaty leaders were deported to Kansas and Oklahoma and finally ended up on the Colville Reservation near Nespelem, Washington.

The Nez Percé War ended Plateau Indian resistance. Across the region, tribal leaders tried to maintain their reservation communities, but in the last quarter of the century the Dawes Act (1893) broke most reserves into individual homesteads. Lands declared "surplus"—almost 90 percent of reservation territory on the Plateau—were incorporated into the federal public domain. Because of the influence of missionaries and government agents, many Plateau people became Presbyterian or Roman Catholic farmers, ranchers, or agricultural laborers. Yet others continued secretly to follow Smohalla's teachings, looking to their dreams to find their way in the new century to come.

See also **American Indians; Missions,** *subentry on* **North American Indians; Washington State.**

Bibliography

Campbell, Sarah K. *Post-Columbian Cultural History in the Northern Columbia Plateau, A.D. 1500–1900.* New York: Garland, 1990.

Miller, Christopher L. *Prophetic Worlds: Indians and Whites on the Columbia Plateau.* New Brunswick, N.J.: Rutgers University Press, 1985.

Walker, Deward E., ed. *Plateau.* Volume 12 of *Handbook of North American Indians.* Edited by William C. Sturtevant et al. Washington, D.C.: Smithsonian Institution, 1998.

CHRISTOPHER L. MILLER

THE SOUTHWEST

In the nineteenth century, southwestern Native Americans shared a common thread of encounters with outsiders through successive Spanish, Mexican, and U.S. governments. At the end of the century these peoples resided on reservations in New Mexico and Arizona.

By 1800 the Pueblos and the Hopis had dealt with outsiders for 260 years. After the 1680 Pueblo Revolt, the Pueblos had reached an accord with the Spanish, and the U.S. government reconfirmed the Pueblos' Spanish-Mexican land grants in the 1848 Treaty of Guadalupe Hidalgo. Until 1913 the federal government recognized the Pueblos as different from other American Indians, thus they retained some citizens' rights.

The Athabaskan-speaking Navajos and Apaches also reached a painful accord with outsiders. During the 1860s the Dine (Navajo) bands, led by Barboncito, Manuelito, and others, offered strong resistance to U.S. military attacks on their homes, crops, and livestock, but starvation pushed more than 8,500 Navajos on a forced march to incarceration at the Bosque Redondo, a desolate reservation by the Pecos River in New Mexico. In 1868 the Navajos signed a treaty that established their reservation in Dinetah, their traditional homeland. For the Dine this era of "The Long Walk" marked a milestone. They returned, reestablished their sheep and goat herds, and formed the Navajo Nation.

For the Apaches, resolution of outsider pressure was less clear-cut. While most Navajos returned to Dinetah, the Apache bands never coalesced in one location. American military and bureaucratic measures collided with tenacious Apache resistance. In the late nineteenth century the Jicarilla and Mescalero Apaches settled on reservations on their traditional lands in New Mexico. In the 1870s, Western Apaches settled on the White Mountain (Fort Apache) and San Carlos reservations in Arizona. Two other bands, the Chiricahua and Warm Spring Apaches, struggled for independence and suffered severely. The Warm Spring Apaches, under the leadership of Victorio, fought in vain to retain homelands in southwestern New Mexico. The Chiricahua, whose famous leader Geronimo eluded U.S. forces until 1886, faced imprisonment in Florida and later at Fort Sill in the Indian Territory. Freed from prisoner of war (POW) status in 1913, some of the survivors returned to Mescalero, while others remained at Fort Sill. The famous Chiricahua sculptor, Allan Houser, was the first Chiricahua child born in freedom.

The Piman-speaking Tohono O'odham and Akimel O'odham, people of the Sonoran Desert, had met the Spanish in the 1690s, when Father Eusebio Francisco Kino established missions among them. In 1853 the Gadsden Purchase divided the Tohono O'odham homeland between the United States and Mexico, and the Tohono O'odham did not gain their U.S. reservation until 1916. The Gila River valley Akimels welcomed the Yuman Maricopas to their homeland in the early 1800s. During the California gold rush they sold food and animals to travelers, but during the late nineteenth and early twentieth centuries upstream American settlers diverted Akimel irrigation water to produce "the years of famine." Colorado River people, also known as Yuman, include the Mohave, Chemehuevi, Hualapai, and Havasupai. The Upland Yuman Yavapai settled on three reservations, including Fort McDowell, Arizona. The famous Yavapai Carlos Montezuma, an Indian activist and medical doctor who practiced in Chicago, returned to that reservation in the 1920s.

See also **Federal Land Policy; Gadsden Purchase; Indian Territory.**

Bibliography

Spicer, Edward Holland. *Cycles of Conquest.* Tucson: University of Arizona Press, 1962.

Sturtevant, William C., ed. *Handbook of North American Indians.* Volumes 9 and 10. Washington, D.C.: Smithsonian Institution, 1979, 1983.

Margaret Connell-Szasz

ALASKA

Four major aboriginal groups inhabited Alaska in the nineteenth century: Athabascan Indians, Pacific Northwest Coast Indians, Eskimos, and Aleuts. The latter are non-Indian. Because of Alaska's late entry into the United States by purchase in 1867, the status of Alaska natives differed from that of American Indians in the contiguous states. Generally the U.S. government had no treaties with the Alaskans, and they had no reservations or federally recognized tribes. Little remained of the old Russian colonial apparatus in Alaska within just a few years of its purchase by the United States. The Russians, who had been confined to the coast, never numbered more than 850 people in the colony.

The Russians had the greatest impact on the Aleuts, whose culture they effectively destroyed through brutalization and disease and whose numbers they reduced from about 20,000 to fewer than 2,000 by the mid-1800s. Adoption of the Russian Orthodox faith by Aleuts and the occurrence of Russian names demonstrate a significant Russification of Aleut culture. After 1867 the remaining Aleuts survived in isolation, affected only by the annual arrival of scores of New England whaling vessels in the Bering Sea and by the annual harvest of fur seals on the Pribilof Islands. Otherwise, the Aleuts were largely ignored. They lived on the far fringe of American territory and consciousness until their islands were invaded by the Japanese during World War II.

By contrast the Tlingit and Haida Indians of the southeast Alaska coast were well known to New England maritime traders in the early nineteenth century before the United States purchased Alaska and to the country's most famous anthropologists afterward. Inhabiting a land of abundant resources and manifesting highly organized social and economic structure, the Tlingits and Haidas successfully resisted Russian attempts to subjugate them. In fact, through intimidation, confrontation, and control of resources the Tlingits and Haidas maneuvered the Russians into heavy reliance on Indians for supplies. After the American purchase, federal government and Christian mission acculturation efforts met with significant success. In addition the canned salmon industry eroded the Indians' independence by exploiting their primary food staple. In the early twentieth century the Tlingits and Haidas organized a regional association that pursued their rights effectively.

The Russians had little impact on the coastal Eskimos of western Alaska. At mid-century whaling ships began to stop at some villages to trade for furs and to obtain temporary laborers, but the resulting shortage of seasonal hunters forced some villages into destitution. In 1891 Sheldon Jackson of the federal schools program imported four Siberian reindeer to alleviate the food shortage and to provide the Eskimos with an export resource. The following year, about one hundred reindeer were brought to Alaska. However, the endeavor failed because the sedentary Eskimos refused to embrace the nomadic life necessary for herding reindeer successfully.

Not until the Klondike gold rush after 1896 did the interior, riverine Athabascans experience frequent Western contact. Many Athabascans cut forest wood for fuel for steamboats on the Yukon River, and others worked as packers on the mountain trails to the gold fields. By the end of the century they and all other Alaska natives were undergoing rapid acculturation and accommodation.

See also **Alaska Purchase; Missions,** *subentry on* **Indian Responses to White Missionaries; Whaling.**

Bibliography

Hinckley, Ted C. "The Early Alaskan Ministry of S. Hall Young, 1878–1888." *Journal of Presbyterian History* 46 (1968): 175–196.

Kan, Sergei. *Symbolic Immortality: The Tlingit Potlatch in the Nineteenth Century.* Washington, D.C.: Smithsonian Institution Press, 1989.

Krause, Aurel. *The Tlingit Indians: Results of a Trip to the*

Chilkat Indians of Alaska. The men and boys wear native dancing costumes, c. 1895. LIBRARY OF CONGRESS

Northwest Coast of America and the Bering Straits. Translated by Erna Gunther. Seattle: University of Washington Press, 1972.

Langdon, Steve J. *The Native People of Alaska.* Anchorage, Alaska: Greatland Graphics, 1987.

Schneider, William. "Chief Sesui and Lieutenant Herron: A Story of Who Controls the Bacon." *Alaska History* 1 (1985–1986): 1–18.

Wyatt, Victoria. "Female Native Teachers in Southeast Alaska: Sarah Dickinson, Tillie Paul, and Frances Willard." In *Between Indian and White Worlds: The Cultural Broker,* edited by Margaret Connell Szasz. Norman: University of Oklahoma Press, 1994.

———. *Images from the Inside Passage: An Alaskan Portrait by Winter and Pond.* Seattle: University of Washington Press, 1989.

STEVE HAYCOX

AMUSEMENTS.   See **Recreation.**

ANTHROPOLOGY   The study of humankind originated during the Enlightenment. In the course of the eighteenth century continental scholars, such as Carolus Linnaeus, George-Louis Leclerc de Buffon, and Johann Blumenbach, developed classificatory schemes based on their own cultural chauvinism and ethnocentrism. These schemes would form the basis of American scholarship on human differences, and they fostered rigid, racial hierarchies that persisted through the twentieth century.

Paradoxically during the Enlightenment most scholars in America opposed rigid classificatory schemes. These people argued for the unity of humankind, believing it a self-evident principle that "all men are created equal." As a consequence such American thinkers as Samuel Stanhope Smith and Benjamin Rush attributed the state of "civilization" evident among human groups to environmental factors. The universalism of these American apostles of the Enlightenment was potent indeed, for it inspired the campaign to abolish slavery and the attempt to assimilate Native Americans into the general population.

Anthropology in the Early Republic

Between 1783 and 1833 a cultural reorientation occurred in the United States that revised scholarly beliefs regarding nature, the supernatural, and human nature. As a result of this new orientation, attempts on the part of whites to abolish black slavery in the South and to assimilate the Indians gave way to the idea that the United States was a white man's country. Thus, not surprisingly, from 1810 to 1859 scholars wrestled with the conflict between their original commitment to Enlightenment monogenism, the theory that humankind has a single origin, and the new proponents of the theory of polygenism, a belief in the separate origins of races. The group of polygenists whose work became known as the "American School of Ethnology," such as Samuel George Morton, Josiah Nott, the Briton George Gliddon, and Louis Agassiz, argued that measurements of cranial cavities and studies of material culture proved scientifically that nonwhites were inferior to whites. They turned their backs on the universalistic theory of humankind of the Enlightenment to rationalize a racism that excluded "savages" from the domain of "people." The polygenist position provided a rationalization for westward expansion, Manifest Destiny, Indian removal, slavery, and race discrimination.

Darwinism and Anthropology

Charles Darwin published *On the Origin of Species* in 1859. His theory of evolution profoundly affected both anthropometrists and ethnologists. During the antebellum period the pre-evolutionary anthropometrists measured the physical traits among whites and blacks to establish that a vast gulf separated whites and blacks and that blacks constituted a distinct species. Anthropometrists thereby provided the scientific basis for the South's proslavery argument. Darwin argued that the races originated from a common ancestor, but he did not rule out the possibility that through the process of natural selection nonwhites fell behind whites in their capacities for survival and progress. Since Darwin did not eliminate the possibility of white superiority, anthropometrists during the Civil War measured black and white soldiers and sailors to prove that blacks were inferior to whites. The U.S. Sanitary Commission and the Provost General's Bureau drew on these studies to justify differential treatment of black servicemen. After the war some white southern physicians continued to study the bodily forms of the races. Such studies revitalized the proslavery argument and strengthened the resolve of white southerners to resist any change in the status of freedpeople during Reconstruction. As the century came to a close, anthropometric studies proliferated. These studies sought to prove that blacks were facing impending extinction and to justify the extension of segregation laws across the South.

Elsewhere ethnologists, such as Edward B. Tylor, Lewis Henry Morgan, and John Lubbock, drew on Darwin's work to develop the theory of cultural evolution. Tylor, Morgan, and Lubbock argued that three distinct and discrete categories defined the

Lewis Henry Morgan (1818–1881). A foremost anthropologist and ethnologist, Morgan was influenced by Charles Darwin's work. LIBRARY OF CONGRESS: PRINTS AND PHOTOGRAPHS DIVISION

stages of cultural development, savagery, barbarism, and civilization. By assuming that their civilization was the most progressive and the standard by which other cultures could be judged, these Victorian ethnologists were extremely ethnocentric. Of the three men, Morgan was the most important figure in the American context. Morgan, who was interested in Native American kinship systems, disseminated his evolutionary views effectively as the president of the American Association for the Advancement of Science (AAAS), and he was influential in government circles. He had a profound influence on the preacademic pioneers of American anthropology, including Daniel Garrison Brinton, John Wesley Powell, and W. J. McGee.

Brinton was professor of American archaeology and linguistics at the University of Pennsylvania and sat on the board of the Pennsylvania Museum of Archaeology and Anthropology. He used Darwin's theories to demonstrate that blacks and Indians occupied a low rung on the evolutionary ladder. Powell, who established the U.S. Geological Survey (USGS), was a powerful figure in the AAAS, the Smithsonian Institution, the Bureau of American Ethnology (BAE), the National Academy of Sciences, and among decision makers in Washington, D.C. Although he believed the indigenous cultures of Native Americans should be overthrown, he prodded Congress to pass land reform legislation for Native Americans despite opposition from railroad and development interests. McGee, a glacial geologist at the USGS, went on to become chief ethnologist at the BAE. In 1904, at the Louisiana Purchase Exposition in St. Louis, McGee organized anthropology exhibits that justified American imperialism in the Pacific and Jim Crow in the South.

In short, Darwin's theory of natural selection was attractive for those scholars who thought that whites had a higher destiny than black and red "savages." White Americans of the late nineteenth century could, in essence, rationalize lynching, Jim Crow, disfranchisement, genocide, and other repressive measures by appealing to hereditarian theories that made the status quo seem inevitable.

The Influence of Franz Boas

As the nineteenth century came to a close, Franz "Uri" Boas, a German-born immigrant who had been trained in physics and who had gradually transferred his career to ethnology, gained prominence. Of Jewish birthright, Boas was affected adversely by anti-Semitism in both his native Germany and the United States. He was skeptical of the self-serving claims of cultural evolutionists and anthropometrists. Through his particularistic, empirical approach to the study of cultures, he demonstrated that the cultural evolutionists had confounded achievement with an aptitude for achievement. Thus Boas argued that Western civilization could be accounted for on the basis of historical events rather than the white race's purported mental faculty. Furthermore, Boas showed by pointing to the overlapping of the cranial cavities of whites and "savages" that the anthropometrists were wrong in assuming all whites were mentally superior to all savages.

Between 1899 and 1920 Boas, as professor of anthropology at Columbia University and head of that department, trained such distinguished anthropologists as Alfred L. Kroeber, Robert H. Lowie, Edward Sapir, and Alexander Goldenweiser. After 1920 his students included Melville J. Herskovits, Ruth Benedict, Margaret Mead, Ashley Montagu, and Otto Klineberg. Boas's impact on the composition of an-

thropology was so great that in the 1950s virtually all of the anthropologists in the country had been trained under Boas or one of his students. Indeed Boas almost single-handedly professionalized anthropology and ushered in modern conceptions of race and cultural relativism.

In the nineteenth century anthropology was transformed from a field that rationalized white Americans' innumerable crimes against humanity into a discipline that exposed the contradiction between ideals of racial equality and the fact of racial oppression.

See also **Biology; Civilization; Evolution; Race and Racial Thinking; Sciences, Physical; Slavery,** *subentry on* **Defense of Slavery.**

Bibliography

Baker, Lee D. *From Savage to Negro: Anthropology and the Construction of Race, 1896–1954.* Berkeley: University of California Press, 1998.

Degler, Carl N. *In Search of Human Nature: The Decline and Revival of Darwinism in American Social Thought.* New York: Oxford University Press, 1991.

Harris, Marvin. *The Rise of Anthropological Theory.* New York: Crowell, 1968.

Smedley, Audrey. *Race in North America: Origin and Evolution of a Worldview.* Boulder, Colo.: Westview, 1993.

Stanton, William Ragan. *The Leopard's Spots: Scientific Attitudes toward Race in America, 1815–59.* Chicago: University of Chicago Press, 1960.

Stocking, George W., Jr. *Race, Culture, and Evolution: Essays in the History of Anthropology.* New York: Free Press, 1968.

Williams, Vernon J., Jr. *Rethinking Race: Franz Boas and His Contemporaries.* Lexington: University Press of Kentucky, 1996.

VERNON J. WILLIAMS JR.

ANTI-CATHOLICISM   The sources of anti-Catholic sentiment in the nineteenth-century United States were deeply rooted, going back to the earliest colonial days. The Puritans were named for their commitment to purify the Church of England of its remaining Catholic elements, in doctrine and in ritual. Other Protestants also hated and feared Catholicism, in part because the mortal enemies of England and its colonies were Catholic Spain and then Catholic France, often in league with Irish Catholic rebels at home. In the period preceding the American Revolution, American colonists, the great majority of them Protestants, were infuriated by the Quebec Act, which gave virtually dictatorial powers to the royal governor and recognized the Roman Catholic Church as the official church of the Quebec colony.

In the American Protestant mind, Catholicism

was associated with religious persecution, owing to the reign of "Bloody Mary" Tudor in England (1553–1558), King Philip II's rule in Spain (1556–1598), and revocation by Louis XIV (1643–1715) of the Edict of Nantes in France. In addition to religious intolerance, Catholicism was associated by many Protestants and freethinkers with political despotism, especially on account of James II (1685–1688) and the events leading to the Glorious Revolution.

From the 1830s through the 1860s a major eruption of anti-Catholicism occurred in U.S. politics and culture. In part this was a reaction to the influx of Catholic immigrants, especially Irish Catholics, who began coming over in large numbers in the 1830s and whose numbers greatly swelled with the Irish potato famine of 1845–1849. Such immigrants were often perceived as drunken, violent, disease ridden, ignorant, poor, corrupt, and utterly unsuited by temperament and otherwise to take up their civic duties as American citizens.

To make matters worse, during the very period of

"**The Pope's New Hobby.**" The pope rides a harnessed American eagle, fueling anti-Catholic sentiments that Catholics would eventually control American politics. Wood engraving in *Harper's Weekly*, 23 May 1868. LIBRARY OF CONGRESS

the American Republic's commitment to greater democratization, the Vatican seemed to many to have formed an alliance with monarchical government everywhere. The structures of the Catholic Church were regarded as fundamentally undemocratic, the papacy was viewed as an absolute monarchy, and the ecclesiastical offices were considered a clerical aristocracy.

The rule of celibacy for Catholic clergy inspired lurid tales and febrile imaginings, typified by Maria Monk's *Awful Disclosures of the Hotel Dieu Nunnery of Montreal*, published in 1836 and given the widest dissemination. Lithographs depicting the mother superior of a convent strangling and burying a newborn infant were common, as were semipornographic themes. Catholic objections to the King James Version of the Bible further inflamed Protestant prejudices, as did Catholics' rejection of public schools and their insistence upon creating a system of parochial education. Protestant fears and hatreds led to the founding of anti-Catholic newspapers, such as the *American Union*, the *Boston Observer and Religious Intelligencer*, and the *Christian Watchman*, and anti-Catholic magazines, such as the *Home Missionary*, the *Christian Review*, and the *Presbyterian Quarterly Review*.

In 1830 a battle between the Roman Catholic bishop Francis Patrick Kenrick and the congregation of St. Mary's Cathedral in Philadelphia over control of finances and church property ended with the imposition of an interdict on that church, forbidding any priest to say Mass or to administer the Sacraments therein. This forced the congregation to give way to the bishop's authority. Taking up the issue for their own purposes, Protestants began to demand laws vesting control of property in the hands of lay congregation boards. In several states, they succeeded, especially in New York State, where the law placed the property rights in congregation boards elected by the general church membership.

Violent attacks on Catholics and Catholic institutions spread through eastern cities. In 1834 a mob burned the Ursaline convent in Charlestown, outside of Boston. In the following year attacks on Catholic churches became so commonplace in New England that armed guards were often stationed by parishioners to protect the buildings. In 1844 Philadelphia was convulsed by anti-Catholic rioting that lasted for days and led to several deaths and the destruction of much property. On the political front, a number of parties took up the cause of anti-Catholicism. The Anti-Masonic Party tended to be anti-Catholic, as did the infamous American or Know-Nothing Party, which won the governorships of Massachusetts and Connecticut in the 1850s. A subtler anti-Catholicism was promoted by the old Whig Party as well as by some members of the new Republican Party that replaced it.

By the end of the Civil War, in which many thousands of Catholics proved their fitness for citizenship by courageous service in the Union Army, the most violent and dangerous aspects of anti-Catholicism had passed from the scene. But a strong strain of distrust for those outside of the Protestant mainstream persisted and fed campaigns for immigration restriction in the United States, incited by groups as varied as the Ku Klux Klan and the American Protective Association, well into the middle of the twentieth century.

See also **Catholicism; Immigration and Immigrants,** *subentries on* **Anti-immigrant Sentiment, Ireland.**

Bibliography

Billington, Ray Allen. *The Protestant Crusade, 1800–1860: A Study of the Origins of American Nativism.* New York: Macmillan, 1938. Reprint, New York: Rinehart, 1952.
Shea, John Gilmary. *A History of the Catholic Church within the Limits of the United States.* 4 vols. New York: J. G. Shea, 1886–1892.

PATRICK M. O'NEIL

ANTI-MASONRY. See **Masons.**

ANTI-MORMONISM Anti-Mormonism (a militant opposition to the Church of Jesus Christ of Latter-day Saints and its members, nicknamed Mormons because of their belief in the *Book of Mormon*) forced members of the church to migrate west (ultimately to Utah), contributed to the assassination of the church's founder, Joseph Smith Jr. (1805–1844), and stimulated a number of federal statutes aimed at suppressing the church, ostensibly because of its doctrine of sanctioning and even encouraging polygamous marriage. The conflict, however, was typical of nineteenth-century America. An intolerant and xenophobic majority society long had sought to marginalize and even rid itself of a conspicuous—although native and indigenously developed—American ethnic minority.

Persecution followed Smith for several years prior to the publication of the *Book of Mormon* in 1830 because of his claims of having received biblical-style heavenly visions and revelations, including a prophetic and apostolic calling and priesthood. Smith explicitly proclaimed a "restoration" of original biblical Christianity, putting the status of other churches in question.

A plagiarized satire and attack on the *Book of Mormon* appeared in local newspapers at the time of its printing. After its publication in New York, Mormon proselytizing brought about rapid growth of the church and even greater opposition to it. Conversions of a substantial number of Campbellite Christians in Ohio (who were seeking a restoration of biblical Christianity) led to the publication of the first anti-Mormon book, Alexander Campbell's *Delusions* (1832). At the same time, what Mormons understood to be the "restoration of all things" led them to embrace a New Testament–style economic system, based in part upon Acts 2:44–47, that rejected private property. A congregational style of church governance in which women also had franchise (common consent, extending even to an open canon of scriptures) was combined with the concept of an unpaid lay clergy. Through such policies the Mormons became even more out of step with the values of mainstream white America.

The Mormons moved to Missouri, where they were repeatedly driven from lands they had settled. Their largely Yankee population threatened pro-slavery voters' power and interests. Their cooperative economic system and rapid acquisition of lands frightened their pro-slavery neighbors, who were already hostile to Mormon religious beliefs and their racially integrated congregations in other states. The extreme nature of the anti-Mormonism that sprang up among their neighbors was reflected in Missouri Governor L. W. Bogg's 1838 extermination order to the state militia: "The Mormons must be treated as enemies, and must be exterminated or driven from the state, if necessary for the public peace." All this occurred before polygamy was an issue.

The Mormons evacuated to Nauvoo, Illinois, where persecutions continued, culminating in the political arrest and murder while in jail of Joseph Smith on 27 June 1844. Before his assassination, Smith ran a third-party campaign for president of the United States, advocating, among other things, a cut in congressional salaries and the elimination of slavery by purchasing the slaves' freedom to avoid war. After Smith's death, most of the Latter-day Saints, led by Brigham Young (1801–1877), moved out of the United States and settled near Great Salt Lake in 1847. They had barely arrived, however, when the Mexican War brought this territory, later known as Utah, into the Union.

It was only after Mormons publicly embraced "celestial marriage," including polygamy, in 1852 that anti-Mormon groups gained national leverage by uniting with Whigs, Free-Soilers, and anti-slavery

Democrats. In 1856 the Republican Party platform called for the "abolition of the twin relics of barbarism: slavery and polygamy." Countless other accusations against the Mormons soon followed, such as theocratic despotism, rebellion against the government of the United States, and anti-Americanism. In 1857 President James Buchanan began the disastrous "Utah War" against the Mormons in what is now recognized as a Democratic Party attempt to co-opt a major part of the Republican platform prior to the 1860 presidential election. Starting in 1862, with the passage of the Morrill Act, the Republicans began to implement their anti-Mormon program, which would continue through the rest of the century.

As Reconstruction tapered off in the South, its legal mechanisms—test oaths, disenfranchisement, carpetbag government, and so forth—were transplanted west.

In the 1870s, the federal government began prosecuting polygamists and other Mormons throughout Utah and the surrounding territories. The Poland Act (1874) placed the Utah territorial judiciary directly under federal control and allowed all Utah cases to be taken directly to the Supreme Court. The *Reynolds v. United States* decision (1879) had deemed previously legal polygamous marriages an "act made criminal" in the territories. In the same way, the Edmunds Act (1882) created the new federal crime of "unlawful cohabitation" to expedite prosecutions of Mormons and increased penalties for polygamists. The Edmunds-Tucker Act (1887) abolished for all polygamy prosecutions the common law rule prohibiting wives from being forced to testify against husbands. The Supreme Court upheld these prosecutions in, among other cases, *Reynolds v. United States* (1879), *Cannon v. United States* (1886), and *Davis v. Beason* (1890).

In 1887 the United States, acting under the Morrill Act and the Edmunds-Tucker Act, successfully sued to revoke the charter of the Mormon Church and seize its properties. The Supreme Court of the United States upheld this result in *The Late Corporation of the Church of Jesus Christ of Latter-day Saints v. United States* (1890).

Between 1862 and 1893 Congress and the Supreme Court took away from the Mormons virtually all normal civil rights. Prominent among these were the right of Mormon men and women to vote (the Mormons had granted women the vote in 1870), to serve on juries, to be eligible for elective office, and to hold positions of public trust. Legal Mormon immigrants were denied naturalization as citizens. In the 1880s government demonization of the Mormons grew so extreme that in propaganda the Mormons were accused of instigating all the wars by Native Americans against the United States from the Rocky Mountains to the West from the 1850s onward.

Governmental anti-Mormonism declined dramatically after 1890, when the church prohibited the formation of new polygamous marriages in the United States. By that time, more than one thousand Mormons had been convicted under various federal laws banning polygamy and cohabitation. In 1894 Congress restored the church's charter, and in 1896 Utah was granted statehood, with a constitution requiring a strict separation of church and state. Shortly thereafter, property seized by the United States following the charter revocation was returned, but the church was left nearly bankrupt because of the enormous legal expenses and related debts.

See also **Mormonism; Polygamy, Mormon; Religion,** *subentry under* **Religion as a Political Issue; Utah.**

Bibliography

Allen, James B., and Glen M. Leonard. *The Story of the Latter-day Saints.* Salt Lake City: Deseret Book Company, 1976.

Arrington, Leonard J., and Davis Bitton. *The Mormon Experience: A History of the Latter-day Saints.* New York: Knopf, 1979.

Arrington, Leonard J., and John Haupt. "Intolerable Zion: The Image of Mormonism in Nineteenth Century American Literature." *The Western Humanities Review* 22, no. 3 (summer 1968): 243–260.

Bunker, Gary L., and Davis Bitton. *The Mormon Graphic Image, 1834–1914: Cartoons, Caricatures, and Illustrations.* Salt Lake City: University of Utah Press, 1983.

Davis, David Brion. "Some Themes of Counter-Subversion: An Analysis of Anti-Masonic, Anti-Catholic, and Anti-Mormon Literature." *Mississippi Valley Historical Review* 47, no. 2 (September 1960): 205–224.

Firmage, Edwin Brown, and Richard Collin Mangrum. *Zion in the Courts: A Legal History of the Church of Jesus Christ of Latter-day Saints, 1830–1900.* Urbana: University of Illinois Press, 1988.

Hansen, Klaus J. *Mormonism and the American Experience.* Chicago: University of Chicago Press, 1981.

Ludlow, Daniel, ed. *Encyclopedia of Mormonism: The History, Scripture, Doctrine, and Procedure of the Church of Jesus Christ of Latter-day Saints.* New York: Macmillan, 1992.

Thomasson, Gordon C. "The Manifesto Was a Victory." *Dialogue: A Journal of Mormon Thought* 6, no. 1 (spring 1971): 37–45.

GORDON C. THOMASSON

ANTI-SEMITISM   Although some works explain that the roots of anti-Semitism lie in economics, hatred of the city, and psychological abnormalities, absolutely no question exists that American anti-Semitism is based on Christian teachings brought to the New World by European immigrants. Manifestations of anti-Semitism in the United States, how-

Anti-Semitic Drawing. Caricature of a Jewish-American family. Published in *Judge*, 1898. Library of Congress: Prints and Photographs Division

ever, were modified from those in the Old World by American rhetoric, culture, and laws. Whereas in Europe reigning monarchs were affiliated with either the Protestant or Catholic churches, education included religious instruction, and established churches were the norm, none of these factors existed by law in the United States. The U.S. Constitution, written in 1787, requires no religious tests for government officeholders and establishes no official church. Individuals, including schoolteachers, government officials, and business leaders, often spoke of the United States as a Christian nation, yet the folkways and mores of the federal government and the general population stressed the equal opportunities available for all white men, regardless of their heritage.

Rhetoric and reality, however, did not always coincide. Many state governments required voters and officeholders to declare themselves Christians, and not until 1877, when New Hampshire lifted this requirement, were Jews allowed to hold office in all of the states.

On the other hand, economic opportunities in the nineteenth century were vast, and enterprising individuals could engage in any endeavors they chose. Economically it did not matter that many Christian Americans scorned and denounced Jews, questioned their honesty and reliability, and were incredulous that Jews did not accept the alleged truth of Chris-

tian thought, or avoided them socially. As a result, unlike in Europe, where occupational, residential, educational, and even marital restrictions curtailed opportunities for Jews, in the United States individual prejudices did not hamper their ability to earn a living or to expand the range of their activities.

To be sure, Jews were often likened to monsters, held responsible for the death of Jesus, and denounced for having hearts of stone. Individual Jews were occasionally beaten for no other reason save that they were Jewish, and during the Civil War many Americans in both the North and the South accused Jews of usury and disloyalty.

Of course, being blackballed from private clubs and discriminated against in housing, resorts, and employment offended Jews and they made different kinds of efforts to fight back. In 1906 the American Jewish Committee began as an agency to protect the rights of Jews wherever they were threatened; in 1913 B'nai B'rith inaugurated its Anti-Defamation League and during World War I the American Jewish Congress began to try to use its influence to obtain a Jewish state in Palestine. After World War II all three of these agencies, along with several other Jewish groups, made concerted efforts to change the laws in the various states and the federal government, to prevent discrimination in all public areas. It also went after private clubs by trying to get states to deny liquor licenses to clubs that discriminated on the basis of race or religion.

At the end of the nineteenth century the United States experienced an influx of close to one million east European Jews of modest economic means, and the established American Jews correctly predicted that this inundation would exacerbate existing anti-Semitism. As the number of immigrants increased, so did incidents of beatings and discrimination in housing, employment, social clubs, and the distribution of justice. Jews were beaten and taunted by Christians in both urban and rural areas. Policemen often arrested the victims while supporting the perpetrators of these crimes, and courts of law showed little tolerance for complaints from Jews.

Despite such prejudicial attitudes and behavior, most Jews in the United States thrived economically and socially and were able to conduct their daily lives in peace. They did not experience the pogroms and legal restrictions common in most European nations, and their response to the existing prejudice was, until the arrival of the east Europeans, to acculturate quickly and never behave inappropriately in public. The Jewish strategy regarding the new immigrants was to "Americanize" the foreigners so that they, too, would not act in a manner offensive to Christians. Unfortunately, just being Jewish offended members of the dominant culture.

See also **Immigration and Immigrants,** *subentry on* **Jewish Immigrants; Judaism; Race and Racial Thinking; Religion,** *subentry on* **Religion in Nineteenth-Century America.**

Bibliography

Diner, Hasia R. *A Time for Gathering: The Second Migration, 1820–1880.* Baltimore: Johns Hopkins University Press, 1992.

Dinnerstein, Leonard. *Antisemitism in America.* New York: Oxford University Press, 1994.

Dobkowski, Michael N. *The Tarnished Dream.* Westport, Conn.: Greenwood, 1979.

Higham, John. *Strangers in the Land.* New Brunswick, N.J.: Rutgers University Press, 1955.

Korn, Bertram Wallace. *American Jewry and the Civil War.* Philadelphia: Jewish Publication Society of America, 1951.

LEONARD DINNERSTEIN

ANTISLAVERY MOVEMENTS. See **Abolition and Antislavery.**

APPALACHIA   The Appalachian Mountains extend from eastern Canada through New England to the Deep South, and the Appalachian Trail runs from Maine to north Georgia. But the term "Appalachia" is sometimes rendered the "Southern Appalachians" and typically refers to the area along the southern half of the range, a region that is itself far from homogeneous. If understood in terms of coal, Appalachia can be said to extend from Pittsburgh, Pennsylvania, to Birmingham, Alabama. Yet coal, while of central importance to West Virginia and eastern Kentucky, is insignificant to western North Carolina, and it did not become a hallmark of the region until the late nineteenth century. What remained true through political conflict and economic transformation was that the region boasted North America's highest mountains east of the Rockies, chief among them Mount Mitchell in western North Carolina (6,684 ft.) and Clingmans Dome in eastern Tennessee (6,643 ft.).

For one hundred years after the American Revolution, Appalachia proved more an obstacle to Americans' quest for well-being than the bonanza it became once railroads brought its coal and timber within reach of exploitation. Such breaks as the Cumberland Gap enabled easterners to move west, usually motivated by the wish to get beyond the mountains rather than into them. Nonetheless, many people settled in the Appalachians, including English, Scots-Irish, and Germans who made their way into Pennsylvania in the eighteenth century and then, often after a period of servitude, south and west through Maryland and Virginia and—they or their children—on into the mountain regions of Kentucky, Tennessee, and North Carolina.

Diversity and Conflict: Appalachia, the South, and the Nation

The Appalachian region of the southern United States contrasts with much of the rest of the South, and the differences not only set Appalachia apart but also proved central to the history of the South, and the history of the nation, in the nineteenth century. The rest of the South was home to slaves and their owners—groups far less present in Appalachia—who grew the tobacco, cotton, and sugar for which the South was renowned. The differences could reflect free people's individual preference, or they might indicate variable opportunity to participate in commercial agriculture given the presence or absence of transportation by river or rail to market. Regardless, residents of eastern Tennessee habitually clashed with those of the state's western region, as did residents of eastern and western Virginia.

One great monument to the magnitude of those differences is the state of West Virginia, which became a separate state after Virginia seceded from the nation in 1861. Western Virginians had long argued with eastern Virginians over voting rights and legislative apportionment; slavery; and roads, schools, and the taxes that might fund them. Virginia's constitutional convention of 1829–1830 foreshadowed the future, as each group threatened to divide the state rather than lose the contest to control it. In the winter of 1860–1861, western Virginians largely voted against secession, as did their counterparts in the Appalachian portions of other states, including northern Georgia, northern Alabama, and eastern Tennessee.

West Virginia also stands as a monument to Union success and Confederate failure in the Civil War. Although Appalachian men served on both sides, tens of thousands of white soldiers from West Virginia, together with tens of thousands from eastern Tennessee, donned blue uniforms rather than gray ones, and they did much to determine the war's outcome. After the war, Appalachian voters in former Confederate states were far more likely to vote Republican than were their white counterparts from the plantation areas. Many eastern Tennesseans remained Republican stalwarts well into the twentieth century. As one said in 1922, "I vote the way I shot" (Noe and Wilson, eds., *The Civil War in Appalachia*, p. 20).

Industrialization: Social, Economic, and Environmental Transformation

By the 1880s a network of railroads snaked through much of Appalachia. As railroads continued to reach one area after another, they fostered the infiltration of outside capital and generated many thousands of new jobs by facilitating the extraction of the region's timber and coal. Appalachians moved into company coal towns and timber camps and went to work mining coal or cutting trees.

Migrants, white and black from the non-Appalachian South, moved into Appalachia in response to the new job opportunities, as did Slavs, Italians, and other immigrants from Europe. At the same time, northern Alabama's Birmingham, the Pittsburgh of the South, grew into a major center of iron and steel production.

A People Apart? Local Color and National Culture

At about the same time that the railroads made their way into the region and the coal and trees were pulled out, Appalachia was discovered, especially by outsiders, as a place to write about. Appalachian people appeared as the subjects of such works as *The Southern Mountaineers* (1906), by Samuel Tyndale

Wilson, and *Our Southern Highlanders* (1913), by Horace Kephart. *The Loyal Mountaineers of Tennessee* (1888), by Thomas William Humes, ascribes to Appalachians a distinctive and crucial role in the Civil War South. A title like "Appalachian America" (*Woman's Home Companion*, September 1896), by William Goodell Frost, makes the mountain South sound like a distinct variation on an American theme. Frost's "Our Contemporary Ancestors in the Southern Mountains" (*Atlantic Monthly*, March 1899) suggests cultural backwardness, and two stereotypes appear in "Moonshine Men" (*Southern Bivouac*, February 1887), by Young E. Allison, and "The Land of Feuds" (*Munsey's Magazine*, November 1903), by Hartley Davis and Clifford Smyth.

"A Strange Land and Peculiar People" (*Lippincott's Magazine*, October 1873), by Will Wallace Harney, appears to render the place and its residents anything but American—from an earlier time or from any time. More than a century later, in *Generations: An American Family* (1983), John Egerton brought a very different understanding of the region and its relation to the broader themes of American history when he selected an Appalachian family about whom to write on the basis that Appalachian southerners have been and continue to be the quintessential Americans.

See also **Alabama; Coal; Kentucky; North Carolina; Tennessee; Virginia; West Virginia.**

Bibliography

Dunn, Durwood. *Cades Cove: The Life and Death of a Southern Appalachian Community, 1818–1937.* Knoxville: University of Tennessee Press, 1988.

Lewis, Ronald L. *Transforming the Appalachian Countryside: Railroads, Deforestation, and Social Change in West Virginia, 1880–1920.* Chapel Hill: University of North Carolina Press, 1998.

Noe, Kenneth W., and Shannon H. Wilson, eds. *The Civil War in Appalachia: Collected Essays.* Knoxville: University of Tennessee Press, 1997.

Pudup, Mary Beth, Dwight B. Billings, and Altina L. Waller, eds. *Appalachia in the Making: The Mountain South in the Nineteenth Century.* Chapel Hill: University of North Carolina Press, 1995.

Shapiro, Henry D. *Appalachia on Our Mind: The Southern Mountains and Mountaineers in the American Consciousness, 1870–1920.* Chapel Hill: University of North Carolina Press, 1978.

PETER WALLENSTEIN

ARCHAEOLOGY   Nineteenth-century archaeology began with the discovery by explorers and traders of earthen mounds scattered across the United

States. As the frontier moved west in the 1780s, thousands of small circular burial mounds, earthworks, and effigy mounds were discovered along major rivers. In a new country with few ancient monuments, the presence of these landscape features prompted intense interest. Unbridled conjecture about the mounds' creators led to theories of a vanished, ancient race of Mound Builders whose potential origins included the Old World, the lost tribes of Israel, and Mexico. Notably, few if any considered that ancestors of contemporary Indian peoples might have erected the mounds.

The earliest mound explorations were carried out by military officers and explorers, such as Brigadier General Rufus Putnam (1738–1824) and the botanist William Bartram (1739–1823). Thomas Jefferson completed one of the first scientific investigations of a mound in the 1780s. Hypothesizing that a low mound near Monticello, his home in Virginia, was an Indian burial place, Jefferson excavated the mound and meticulously recorded the various strata of soil, noting several layers with human bones. His experimental approach and stratigraphic control anticipated modern archaeology by over a century. However, his efforts were little noticed by contemporaries and failed to influence American archaeology.

By the early 1800s the scientific literature teemed with theories of an ancient, noble, and highly civilized race of Mound Builders that had disappeared or been destroyed by "barbarous" American Indian peoples. These ideas prompted new investigations of the mounds and increased their destruction by curiosity seekers and others seeking profit from selling artifacts. Many mound sites were also leveled in preparation for settlements and during field clearing.

From 1800 to 1850, mounds and their artifacts were studied largely by antiquarians who belonged to organizations like the American Philosophical Society, which was founded in 1769, and the American Antiquarian Society, which was founded in 1812. The volume of research and publications on mounds and Indian sites increased rapidly. The Antiquarian Society published Caleb Atwater's popular and detailed essay *Description of the Antiquities Discovered in the State of Ohio and Other Western States* (1820), and the Smithsonian published Ephraim George Squier (1821–1888) and Edwin Hamilton Davis's (1811–1888) comprehensive *Ancient Monuments of the Mississippi Valley* (1847).

By mid-century, interest in archaeology ran high, and the debate over the mounds' builders became increasingly important in justifying the removal or destruction of Indian peoples on lands coveted by western settlers. Advances in European archaeology and natural history stimulated American archaeology; research expanded under government, university, and museum sponsorship; and universities began training scholars in archaeology. Influential works included Samuel Haven's essay *Archaeology of the United States* (1856), which examined current hypotheses and used contemporary research to discern the true origins of the mounds and Indian peoples; the research of Frederick Ward Putnam (1834–1915), curator of the Peabody Museum and professor of archaeology at Harvard; and William Henry Holmes's (1846–1933) detailed classifications of prehistoric ceramics and stone tools. Although questions about the Mound Builders and the antiquity of humans in the New World abounded, researchers focused on the description and classification of sites and artifacts in the absence of either stratigraphic or chronological controls.

Military expeditions into the Southwest in the 1840s and 1850s provided details about ruins of Pueblo cultures. Lieutenant James Simpson and Richard Kern described Chaco Canyon, including Pueblo Bonito; the U.S. Geological Survey surveyed and recorded many sites; Holmes and the photographer W. H. Jackson (1843–1942) documented Mesa Verde; and Adolph Bandelier (1840–1914) combined archaeological survey and documentation with careful ethnography among southwestern tribes. Government and private expeditions contributed manifold data about early Indian peoples of the western United States and provided new evidence of a direct link between early mound and pueblo builders and contemporary Indians.

Not all American archaeologists concentrated on North America. John L. Stephens and Frederick Catherwood, for example, brought Mayan archaeology to the world's attention, based on their excavations from 1839–1845. Peabody Museum archaeologists conducted the first excavations at the Classic Mayan center of Copan, Honduras, and Squier explored Inca ruins in Peru. This work greatly interested U.S. scholars, who increasingly accepted a link between the ancient and contemporary peoples of the Americas.

Cyrus Thomas's monograph *Report on the Mound Explorations of the Bureau of Ethnology* (1894) finally put to rest the Mound Builder controversy. Comparing mound artifacts with contemporary ones and using historical eyewitness accounts of Mound Builders at work, he demonstrated the continuity between Mound Builders and modern Indians, discrediting previous theories. Although the profession of archaeology was not firmly established until the next century, Thomas's work marked a transition from amateur reporting and speculation to organized scholarly research in U.S. archaeology.

Human remains and artifacts removed from Indian mounds and other sites during the nineteenth century engendered conflict between archaeologists and native peoples in the United States through the twentieth century. The 1990 Native American Grave Protection and Repatriation Act (NAGPRA) launched a dialogue regarding the appropriate treatment and eventual return of much of these materials to tribal groups.

See also **Anthropology; American Indians,** *subentries on* **Overview, American Indian Religion, American Indian Art; American Indian Societies.**

Bibliography

Christenson, Andrew L., ed. *Tracing Archaeology's Past: The Historiography of Archaeology.* Carbondale: Southern Illinois University Press, 1989.

Fagan, Brian. *Elusive Treasure: The Story of Early Archaeologists in the Americas.* New York: Scribners, 1977.

Silverberg, Robert. *Mound Builders of Ancient America: The Archaeology of a Myth.* Greenwich, Conn.: New York Graphic Society, 1968.

Stiebing, William H., Jr. *Uncovering the Past: A History of Archaeology.* Buffalo, N.Y.: Prometheus, 1993.

Willey, Gordon R., and Jeremy A. Sabloff. *A History of American Archaeology.* San Francisco: Freeman, 1980.

DONALD W. LINEBAUGH

ARCHITECTURE

[This entry includes two subentries, **Professional Architects and Their Work** and **Vernacular Architecture.**]

PROFESSIONAL ARCHITECTS AND THEIR WORK

Professional architects, people who earn their livelihood by designing buildings for others, were responsible for only a small fraction of the buildings erected in the United States during the nineteenth century. The great majority of buildings were designed or adapted from traditional designs by property owners or by men who were primarily carpenters or builders by trade. Some builders, like Samuel McIntire (1757–1811) of Salem, Massachusetts, achieved great subtlety and elegance in their work. Professional architects were sought for the most important and prestigious commissions, however. Professionals, along with semiprofessional "gentlemen amateurs," set the artistic and technical standards that carpenters and builders generally attempted to emulate.

Architectural Training and Education

Many notable buildings of the early Republic were designed by amateurs, gentlemen of privilege and learning like Thomas Jefferson (1743–1826) and Charles Bulfinch (1763–1844), for whom architecture was a noble avocation, though Bulfinch later became a full-time architect. Both Jefferson and Bulfinch had traveled abroad and had experienced European architecture firsthand, and Jefferson had accumulated a sizable architectural library, which he relied on greatly for inspiration. Few Americans had such opportunities for travel and education, however. Most of America's first professional architects were born and trained in Europe. Among these influential immigrants were J. F. Mangin in New York, Stephen Hallett and George Hadfield in Washington, D.C., James Gallier in New Orleans, John Haviland in Philadelphia, and most importantly Benjamin Latrobe (1764–1820). Latrobe brought to the United States a new level of engineering skill and design sophistication, which he passed on to his apprentices, including Robert Mills (1781–1855) and William Strickland (1788–1854). The latest architectural ideas were widely disseminated through architectural handbooks or pattern books, like Asher Benjamin's *The American Builder's Companion* (1806), that for the first time were being published in the United States and illustrated with American examples.

Formal architectural education was not available in the United States until after the Civil War. The Massachusetts Institute of Technology began offering academic instruction in architecture in 1865, followed soon after by Cornell University and the University of Illinois. By the end of the century eleven schools of architecture had been established, all of them east of the Mississippi River. The curricula typically emphasized construction and the sciences. Some aspiring architects, including Richard Morris Hunt, Henry Hobson Richardson, Charles McKim, and Louis Sullivan, chose instead the classical and artistic training offered at the prestigious École des Beaux-Arts in Paris. Yet the total number of American architects who had a professional academic education remained relatively small. The most common way of learning architecture in the United States, especially outside the larger cities, continued to be through a period of apprenticeship with an established architect or builder or, by the end of the century, through enrollment in extension or correspondence classes such as the architectural course offered by the International Correspondence Schools of Scranton, Pennsylvania, founded in 1891.

Illinois was the first state to regulate the practice of architecture through licensing in 1897. In 1900 the

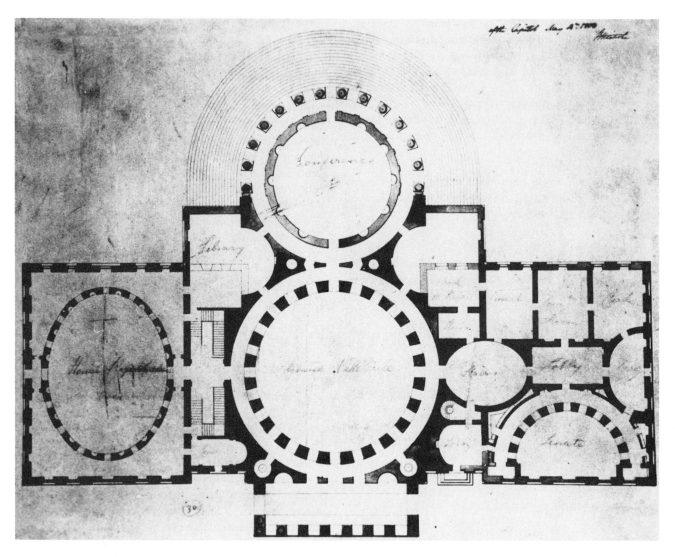

Floor Plan, U.S. Capitol. Given to H. B. Latrobe as the only existing drawing of the Capitol on 4 May 1803. Drawing by George Blagden, 1803. LIBRARY OF CONGRESS: ARCHITECT OF THE CAPITOL COLLECTION

American Institute of Architects required candidates for membership to have a degree from an approved school or to have passed a special examination.

Aspirations, Symbols, and Styles

Two conflicting currents drove the nineteenth-century debate about the proper nature of architecture in the United States. One was the heady search for a distinctly American style, an architecture derived from and expressing the unique circumstances of the new nation. The other was an enduring dependence on Europeans and on European traditions for inspiration and validation.

Fashionable architecture during the early Federal period was neoclassical, characterized by strongly geometric compositions, clarity of organization, and the knowledgeable use of ancient Greek and Roman orders. The relative simplicity and directness of American neoclassicism suited the nation's pragmatic temperament, while its rationalism fit the intellectual principles of the Enlightenment. The use of Greek and Roman precedents was quite natural for a society that often saw itself as the direct descendant of the republican phases of classical civilization.

American neoclassicism had several variants: the elegant, conservative Federal style developed by Bulfinch and McIntire in coastal New England; the more robust and daring civic buildings and churches of Latrobe and Mills in the Mid-Atlantic states; and the inventive, idealistic Roman revival of Jefferson in Virginia. Jefferson favored Roman forms not only for their nobility and beauty but also because they expressed visually the political analogy between the American Republic and republican Rome.

Trinity Church, New York City. Richard Upjohn began construction in 1841 and the building, at the western end of Wall Street, was dedicated in 1846. Upjohn was a leading American architect of the Gothic Revival style. Lithograph by John Forsyth and E. W. Mimee, c. 1847. LIBRARY OF CONGRESS

To Jefferson and his contemporaries, the task was not just to design buildings but also to help shape the nation's social institutions. Collectively they established neoclassicism as the architectural language for government buildings in the District of Columbia and many state capitals. Latrobe and Strickland made the temple front symbolic of solidity and dignity for banks. Mills created a new type of church with an auditorium at the center, designed so that large crowds could easily see and hear the preacher. Jefferson planned the curriculum and the campus for the University of Virginia at Charlottesville and designed the first buildings (1817–1826) around a concept of education that he called an "academical village." He laid out a grassy commons called the Lawn with a Pantheon-like building housing the library and other shared facilities at its head and student living quarters along the sides. Interspersed among the student rooms were ten pavilions, each housing a different academic discipline, with a lecture room below and accommodations for the professor above. The pavilions were all different, modeled after se-

lected classical buildings so they might serve as examples for architectural history lessons.

Greek architecture became more popular than Roman after the outbreak of war between Greece and Turkey in 1821. Americans generally supported Greece, which was fighting for independence and also was seen as the cradle of democracy. The Greek temple front and the Doric order, already admired for their beauty and practicality, took on ideological significance. In consequence, the Greek Revival was applied to every conceivable building type, from churches to banks, courthouses to city halls, mansions to modest farmhouses. The vision of a white-painted, classical America continued into the 1830s and 1840s. That image spread throughout the South, across New York, and into the burgeoning Midwest with the aid of a new generation of pattern books, such as Minard Lafever's *The Modern Builder's Guide* (1833). The vision was shared by local builders and professional architects migrating to developing areas, men like Francis Costigan (1810–1865), who moved from Baltimore to Madison, Indiana, about 1838. Because it transcended regional boundaries and social classes, Greek Revival has been called America's first truly national style.

Romantic sentiment was on the rise, however. By 1840 American taste in architecture had begun to shift from the refined, the balanced, and the classical to the picturesque, the rural, and the "natural." Alexander Jackson Davis (1803–1892) began his architectural career as a Greek Revivalist, but the country villas he created for wealthy clients were typically Italian or Gothic, like "Lyndhurst" in Tarrytown, New York (1838). Davis's Gothic and Italian villas were characteristically asymmetrical, irregularly massed, with verandas and terraces that tied them to the land and craggy rooflines that met the sky. The forms and the ideas they embodied were popularized by Andrew Jackson Downing (1815–1852), a horticulturalist and architectural theorist, in a series of books, of which *Cottage Residences* (1842) was the most popular. Downing believed a house should be strongly related to its landscape, which itself should be informal or natural. It should delight the imagination and have a distinct personality suited to its occupants.

Gothic styles became the favorite for churches in the 1840s under the influence of the ecclesiological movement. To the ecclesiologists, Gothic architecture connoted piety and moral authority because of its close association with medieval Christianity, whereas Greek and Roman styles had pagan implications. Historical accuracy was important. Gothic Revival churches generally were based on English precedents, as was Trinity Church in New York City (dedicated 1846) by Richard Upjohn (1802–1878). For the Roman Catholic St. Patrick's Cathedral in New York (begun 1858, dedicated 1879), James Renwick (1818–1895) drew eclectically from many sources, including the great European cathedrals.

An alternative medieval style, the Romanesque Revival, enjoyed a brief popularity alongside the Gothic during the 1840s. Romanesque, too, was considered appropriate for churches, and it was the choice for the Smithsonian Institution in Washington, D.C., designed by Renwick in 1846.

The romantic interest in the picturesque continued after the Civil War but with a dramatic difference. The increased mechanization of American agriculture and manufacturing after the war coupled with rapid population growth and urbanization to produce new wealth and an increased scale and complexity of building. With these came new levels of ostentation. The Gilded Age built brashly and boldly. Several fashions were popular, most importantly the Italianate, the French Second Empire, and the High Victorian Gothic. Less restrained than prewar styles, these were relatively ponderous, and they tended to get more ornate over time. The distinguished twentieth-century architecture critic Lewis Mumford, in *Sticks and Stones* (1924, 2d rev. ed.), dismissed them as representing "only the dispersion of taste and the collapse of judgment which marked the Gilded Age" (p. 105).

Some architects of the Gilded Age successfully broke the bounds of tradition. Frank Furness (1839–1912), Henry Hobson Richardson (1838–1886), and Louis Sullivan (1856–1924) developed distinctive languages that, while rooted in precedent, were exceptionally dynamic and powerful. Their works, though diverse, shared key characteristics that made them heroic to later generations of modernists. They were individualistic, sometimes exotic; the strength of expression came more from clarity of mass, form, and structure than from historical associations; the forms seemed fresh because of the directness with which functional requirements were accommodated; materials were used in ways that are true to their nature; and ornament was stylized and abstracted, made subordinate to the whole. Sullivan was influential also through his reformist writings, including *Kindergarten Chats* (1901, revised 1918) and *The Autobiography of an Idea* (1924).

Richardsonian Romanesque was widely imitated for commercial buildings in the 1880s, along with many other styles. The sidewalks of American commercial districts were being lined with an eclectic array of mixed-use buildings, typically two to four stories high, with glass-fronted shops in the first story and offices or living quarters above. The styles varied, but the basic organization did not. The result was a land-use pattern that became the image of the typical American Main Street, which prevailed in the central business districts of the nation's smaller towns and cities until the middle of the twentieth century.

By the late 1880s, however, some architects and social critics were becoming impatient with individualism, urban fragmentation, and visual anarchy. As an antidote they sought order, harmony, and a controlling discipline, qualities that were found once again in the classical tradition. The latest generation of architects returning from the École des Beaux-Arts had been trained in the architectural languages of antiquity and the Italian Renaissance. They also had learned the planning techniques needed to deal with the large size and programmatic complexity of modern building. Beaux-Arts principles were applied at the World's Columbian Exposition in Chicago in 1893 to great popular acclaim. The success of the fair revived the ideal of producing a national architectural style, established Beaux-Arts classicism as the language for the "American Renaissance," and generated widespread interest in large-scale urban planning.

Building Technology

The enormous changes taking place in architecture during the nineteenth century were accompanied by and to some extent were driven by the rapid development of new building materials and construction techniques.

Home building was revolutionized in the 1830s by the invention of the balloon frame, a structural system using lightweight, milled lumber fastened with nails. It soon replaced the older and more labor-intensive system of heavy timbers joined by mortises, tenons, and pegs. Other factory-made building components, such as window and door assemblies, were becoming available about the same time. Residential construction was suddenly simpler and cheaper.

For civic and commercial buildings, the most important developments were in the area of metal technology. In the late 1840s James Bogardus and Daniel Badger pioneered the factory production of building facades made of cast iron and glass. Sold through catalogs, cast iron facades usually were made to look like masonry but were quicker than masonry to erect and allowed larger windows. The repetitive nature of cast iron facades made them ideal for large warehouses and for the new department stores developed to facilitate retail sales. Cast iron elements were used in other types of buildings as well, including the enlargement of the U.S. Capitol, begun in 1851 and designed by Thomas U. Walter (1804–1887).

Increasing population density and rising land values at the centers of major cities made tall buildings inevitable. A height of five to six stories was the practical limit until after the Civil War, however. The invention by Elisha Otis of the safety elevator and the steam elevator in the 1850s and 1860s, along with improvements in indoor plumbing and artificial lighting, made greater heights possible. Still, masonry structural systems, traditional for tall buildings, could not efficiently go much above ten stories, and the maximum was sixteen stories. This cap was removed by the development of metal skeletal framing, a three-dimensional grid-work of columns, girders, and beams that supported the weight of the building without masonry.

The Home Insurance Building in Chicago (1883–1885) is usually regarded as the first true skyscraper to use a metal skeleton frame. The designer, William Le Baron Jenney (1832–1907), used masonry for the lower two stories but a frame of cast iron, wrought iron, and steel for the floors above. In later buildings the frame was made entirely of steel.

Jenney also employed and trained many of the architects who later wrestled with the aesthetic problems of skyscrapers and developed the style known as the "Chicago School" of architecture. Among them were Louis Sullivan, Daniel Burnham, William Holabird, and Martin Roche.

Women and Minorities

Women and minorities were involved with the design and construction of buildings in various ways during the nineteenth century but rarely in the capacity of professional architect. The profession was limited almost exclusively to white males. Catharine Beecher, although not an architect, designed in principle the modern "efficient" house, compactly and flexibly organized according to the needs of household management, in her best-selling book on domestic economy, *The American Woman's Home* (1869). Slaves in the antebellum South frequently served as builders and building artisans, and several free blacks were builder-designers. Margaret Hicks, who in 1878 was the first female graduate of the architecture school at Cornell University, designed tenement housing for the poor in New York City, and Sophia Hayden won the competition, entered by several women, for the design of the Women's Building at the World's Columbian Exposition. The well-known architect Julia Morgan was just beginning her prolific career at the end of the century. African Americans, too, were just entering the profession at the century's end. The pioneers were Robert R. Taylor (1868–1942) and John Anderson Lankford (1876–1946).

See also **Architecture,** *subentry on* **Vernacular Architecture; Cities and Urbanization; Civil Engineering,** *subentry on* **Building Technology; Parks and Landscape Architecture.**

Bibliography

Fitch, James Marston. *American Building.* Vol. 1, *The Historical Forces That Shaped It.* 2d ed. Boston: Houghton Mifflin, 1966.
Gifford, Don, ed. *The Literature of Architecture: The Evolution of Architectural Theory and Practice in Nineteenth-century America.* New York: Dutton, 1966.
Hamlin, Talbot. *Greek Revival Architecture in America.* London and New York: Oxford University Press, 1944.
Handlin, David P. *American Architecture.* London: Thames and Hudson, 1985.
Kostof, Spiro, ed. *The Architect: Chapters in the History of the Profession.* New York: Oxford University Press, 1977.
Mumford, Lewis. *Sticks and Stones: A Study of American Architecture and Civilization.* 2d rev. ed. New York: Dover, 1955. Originally published in 1924.
Pierson, William H., Jr. *American Buildings and Their Architects.* Vol. 1, *The Colonial and Neoclassical Styles.* Garden City, N.Y.: Doubleday, 1970–.
Roth, Leland M. *A Concise History of American Architecture.* New York: Harper and Row, 1979.
Stanton, Phoebe B. *The Gothic Revival & American Church Architecture: An Episode in Taste, 1840–1856.* Baltimore: Johns Hopkins University Press, 1968.
Weiss, Ellen. *An Annotated Bibliography on African-American Architects and Builders.* Philadelphia: Society of Architectural Historians, 1993.
Whiffen, Marcus, and Frederick Koeper. *American Architecture, 1607–1976.* Cambridge, Mass.: MIT Press, 1981.

ANDREW R. SEAGER

VERNACULAR ARCHITECTURE

A nascent field of scholarly pursuit, vernacular architecture is concerned with built form in the broadest meaning of the term, from the dawn of history to the present times. The use of the term dates back to the nineteenth century in reference to traditional rural buildings of the preindustrial era, but it was only in the last three decades of the twentieth century that the term became prevalent, coinciding with the scientific pursuit of material culture. Often used to denote that which is "native or originating in the place of its occurrence or use," its current usage in the field of architecture has come to mean local or popular building. It is the discipline that cares about ordinary, commonplace, everyday architecture and landscape. Vernacular architecture includes everything that is not consciously designed by or for the elite sector of a society, thereby excluding the high-style, formal monuments that represent the taste of those in power. This anonymous architecture, passed on from one generation to the next through the use of materials, tools, forms, and ornamentation, accounts for the vast majority of the built environment.

The field of vernacular architecture is object oriented: the buildings themselves are the physical evidence to be read as a text. This implies intimate firsthand knowledge of an object, hence field research. The documentation of buildings as artifacts constituted the first scholarly studies of vernacular architecture as far back as the 1890s, establishing a tradition that has continued into the twenty-first century. Norman Morrison Isham and Albert Brown are recognized for their pioneering 1895 study of Rhode Island's seventeenth- and eighteenth-century houses. In the twentieth century, object studies were complemented by socially oriented analysis that examined buildings and their changes over time through historical evidence.

While most of the published vernacular architecture studies have concentrated on rural domestic architecture of preindustrial America, studies of the late twentieth century show an increased interest in buildings constructed throughout the nineteenth and twentieth centuries. The scholarship in the field has also broadened beyond mapping and description to more rigorous analysis of artifacts, examined from a multidisciplinary perspective that includes not just art and architectural history and theory, but also anthropology, archaeology, sociology, cultural geography, folklore, and social history. This broadened view has helped scholars recognize that the vernacular is closely tied to a culture's economic system. The vernacular landscape is a visual metaphor of a period's social and aesthetic values. This culturally oriented approach includes queries of ethnicity and ethnic influence, addressing areas such as Native American environments and regional indigenous landscapes that have traditionally been neglected by architectural historians.

Native American Vernacular Architecture

Indigenous architecture is a product of the environment in which it is built and a direct expression of the fundamental needs of its inhabitants. The architecture of Native Americans is as varied as the landscape of the North American continent. The arid regions of the Southwest, the forests in the Northeast, the high plains and central prairies of the Midwest, and the frozen mountains of the North were all inhabited by Native Americans whose habitats were adapted to the physical environment and prevailing tribal lifestyle. The origin of all Indian dwellings is considered the primeval semisubterranean Siberian house, variations of which can be found across the North American continent. Among most Indian tribes, it was the women who were often the primary architects of their communities. They designed, fabricated, and constructed the dwellings, whether they were igloos, tepees, wigwams, long houses, or pueblos. Men obtained the building material (and did participate in the construction of pueblos). Building was a communal activity, and land was held in common by the tribe, not the individual. Land was allotted to women for cultivation. The code of hospitality prevalent among Native Americans and the practice of communal living ensured that food was shared.

The Indians of the Great Plains were nomadic, and the tepee was an efficient, comfortable, and simple form of shelter adapted to their migrant lives. Conical in shape, the tepee consisted of a light frame of wood made up of three or four main poles that was covered with buffalo hide. It could be erected or dismantled quickly. The tepee served as the dwelling for the extended family: a man, his first wife, her sisters (who often became wives if their husbands died), and their children. Regardless of status or rank, all members of the tribe lived in similar tepees; even the chief's tepee, though it might be larger, was not any more elaborate than the others. Kitchen tepees featured cut off bottoms for better ventilation, and the medicine tepee was the only one the Indians painted. As settlers moved westward, the buffalo became scarce and canvas purchased at trading posts re-

Tepees. Sioux chiefs before their tepees. Copyright by O. L. Wasson, 1905. LIBRARY OF CONGRESS

placed buffalo hides in tepee construction. It is possible that the lightweight design of the tepee influenced the American settlers when they later improvised constructions such as the balloon-frame and platform houses.

The Pueblo Indian was a farmer, so his home was in a fixed location, usually on a mesa or hill that could be defended. The oldest pueblo architecture is that of the Hopi in the Southwest. Prehistoric pueblo villages date back to 700 A.D. The Hopi village was divided into halves or *moieties* within which the clans were housed. Clans were determined by matrilineal descent—it was the women who owned the houses and the crops. Husbands were allowed to live in their wives' houses, but could be asked to leave, whereupon they would return to their mothers' homes. Wood was scarce in the semiarid climate, so the pueblos were built with stone (when available) or with adobe. The influence of the Pueblo Indians on Spanish missionaries resulted in what is known as the Spanish mission style of architecture. Although the Spaniards introduced premade sun-dried adobe brick, the architectural form of the pueblo remained constant. The house consisted of rooms with flat roofs that provided access to upper rooms. The flat terraced roofs also functioned as a communal viewing space during religious festivities.

Nineteenth-Century Vernacular Architecture

Prior to and throughout much of the nineteenth century the abundance of timber in the United States resulted in the proliferation of wooden structures, often shingle clad. Both public buildings, such as churches, and houses were timber framed and often shingle-clad. Building technology and construction methods were inherited from Europe and modified for use in America. In the early nineteenth century, when the architectural profession was still in its infancy, architectural pattern books provided practical guidelines to carpenters and builders throughout the eastern United States. One of the first of such books, Asher Benjamin's *The Country Builder's Assistant* (1797), was extremely popular and profoundly influenced the architecture of New England. The numerous handbooks of Benjamin and others served as both a pragmatic educational tool and an aesthetic template reflecting popular taste. By the 1830s the strong tradition in wood construction was further reinforced by the mass production of nails and machine-sawn wood, and later with the invention of the balloon frame, which became prevalent in the 1850s.

The second half of the nineteenth century witnessed the country's biggest building boom up until that time. As the American frontier was settled, every type of building from mansions to shanties was constructed. The balloon frame made possible efficient and economical rural houses that shared essential traits despite stylistic variations. With the expansive economy, pattern books and plan books proliferated to accommodate the building boom. Such books were scarce only during the Civil War, the 1870s depression, and the 1890s, with the disappearance of the frontier. The most influential author of these books, Andrew Jackson Downing (1815–1852), defined and codified the ideal domestic architecture to reflect the picturesque elements found in nature. Popular journals of etiquette also included aesthetic lessons and praised the picturesque. Vernacular buildings, especially rural farmhouses, often embodied practical wisdom, regardless of whether they embraced the picturesque. More often, the farmer had little use for sophisticated tastes in architecture and was more concerned with cost, simplicity, and flexibility of use. As with all vernacular architecture, the late-nineteenth-century farmhouse was shaped by economic, social, and environmental factors.

See also **American Indian Societies; Housing.**

Bibliography

Carter, Thomas R., and Bernard L. Herman. *Perspectives in Vernacular Architecture*. Vol. 3. Columbia: University of Missouri Press, 1989.

Fitch, James Marston. *American Building: The Environmental Forces that Shaped It*. 2d ed. New York: Oxford University Press, 1999.

Giedion, Sigfried. *Mechanization Takes Command: A Contribution to Anonymous History*. New York: Oxford University Press, 1948.

Glassie, Henry. *Pattern in the Material Folk Culture of the Eastern United States*. University of Pennsylvania Press, 1969.

Gowans, Alan. *Images of American Living: Four Centuries of Architecture and Furniture as Cultural Expression*. Philadelphia: Lippincott, 1964.

Jackson, John Brinckerhoff. *A Sense of Place, a Sense of Time*. New Haven, Conn.: Yale University Press, 1994.

Kimball, Fiske. *Domestic Architecture of the American Colonies and of the Early Republic*. New York: Dover, 1966. Reprint of original 1922 edition.

Marshall, Howard Wight. *American Folk Architecture: A Selected Bibliography*. Washington, D.C.: American Folklife Center, Library of Congress, 1981.

Rapoport, Amos. *House Form and Culture*. Englewood Cliffs, N.J.: Prentice Hall, 1969.

Stilgoe, John. *Common Landscapes of America 1580–1845*. New Haven, Conn.: Yale University Press, 1982.

Upton, Dell, and John Michael Vlach, eds. *Common Places: Readings in American Vernacular Architecture*. Athens: University of Georgia Press, 1986.

Wright, Gwendolyn. *Building the Dream: A Social History of Housing in America*. New York: Pantheon, 1981.

Mina Marefat

ARIZONA   The sixth-largest state, Arizona has an area of 113,956 square miles. Although much of Arizona is desert, the mountain range across the middle of the state receives enough rainfall to support the nation's largest ponderosa forest.

At the beginning of the nineteenth century Arizona, part of the *Provincias Internas* of Spain's northern frontier, was enjoying a period of relative peace. This ended with Mexico's war of independence. Attacks by Apaches and Navajos forced the ranchers, miners, and farmers of the region to seek protection in Tucson, the only community large enough to withstand the attacks.

Included in the Mexican Cession that concluded the war between Mexico and the United States in 1848, Arizona was initially part of the territory of New Mexico. After the California gold rush of 1849, the United States completed its acquisition of Arizona in 1853 with the Gadsden Purchase. Demand for reliable land transportation prompted surveys by the Army Corps of Topographical Engineers. By 1857 the U.S. government subsidized mail routes over the road built by the Mormon Battalion along the Gila Trail. Also during the 1850s steamboats began commercial service on the Colorado River. Transcontinental rail lines were completed along thirty-second and thirty-fifth parallels in the 18

In 1857 Charles D. Poston organized the Sc Exploring and Mining Company and reopened a doned Spanish mines near Tubac. Others quickly lowed. At about the same time placer mining str were discovered in Gila City, La Paz, and the Bra shaw Mountains. Mining development was a major factor in the creation in 1863 of a separate Arizona Territory with the capital, Prescott, near the shaw claims. The Civil War briefly interrupte ing activities, which remained slow for the ne decades because of Apache raids. However, n picked up in the 1870s with major strikes at Bis Clifton Morenci, Globe, Jerome, and Tombsto Mining of gold, silver, and copper became Arizona dominant industry.

The Spanish first introduced cattle ranching as an open-range longhorn operation, and white ranchers revived it in the late 1850s. Cattle ranching quickly spread across southern Arizona, but the largest ranch in the territory at 3,600 square miles was the Aztec Land and Cattle Company near Holbrook. In the 1870s ranchers in northeastern Arizona introduced sheep, which became an important industry, especially among the Navajo. Rustling and conflicts between cattle and sheep ranchers escalated into the Pleasant Valley War (1887–1892), the bloodiest nineteenth-century feud in the American West.

Agriculture grew in economic importance in the

1870s and 1880s. In 1876 Mormons established settlements along the Little Colorado River, and despite some clashes because of their practice of polygamy, they brought a stable farming element that made important contributions to peaceful growth. Farming also developed along the Salt River. Jack Swilling, recognizing the potential of the abandoned Hohokam canals, organized a canal company and began an irrigation system. With a reliable source of water, farmers planted crops of barley, alfalfa, and cotton across the valley.

By 1890 Arizona's population reached 88,243. Phoenix became the territorial capital in 1889, and in 1891 a convention there made a strong but unsuccessful appeal for statehood. Arizona contributed two companies of Rough Riders during the Spanish-American War, increasing the hopes of the territory's leaders for statehood. But Arizona remained a territory until 1912.

See also **American Indian Societies,** *subentry on* **The Southwest; Gadsden Purchase; Gold Rushes and Silver Strikes; Mexican Cession; Mining and Extraction; Ranching and Livestock Raising; West, The.**

Bibliography

Officer, James E. *Hispanic Arizona, 1536–1856.* Tucson: University of Arizona Press, 1987.

Sheridan, Thomas E. *Arizona: A History.* Tucson: University of Arizona Press, 1995.

Wagoner, Jay J. *Arizona Territory, 1863–1912: A Political History.* Tucson: University of Arizona Press, 1970.

Walker, Henry P., and Don Bufkin. *Historical Atlas of Arizona.* 2d ed. Norman: University of Oklahoma Press, 1986.

JAMES D. MCBRIDE

ARKANSAS   Arkansas is divided into two major geographic regions by a line that runs roughly from the northeastern corner to the southwestern corner of the state. To the southeast of that line are rich alluvial plains and river valley lands, particularly the Mississippi River delta, that provided the basis for plantation agriculture throughout the nineteenth century. To the northwest are uplands that were home to smaller commercial and subsistence farms.

The United States acquired Arkansas in the 1803 Louisiana Purchase. It originally was part of the District of Upper Louisiana and later of the Territory of Missouri. Arkansas Territory was created in 1819. A small number of Native Americans, including the Quapaw, Kadohadacho, Osage, and some Cherokee, lived in the territory, but beginning with the Osage Treaty of 1808, the tribes surrendered their land claims. White immigration began in the late eighteenth century, although rapid growth did not begin until statehood. Early communities developed along major rivers or along the Military Road, which followed an old Indian trail that crossed the state from the northeast to the southwest.

Arkansas became a state on 15 June 1836. Most settlers after statehood came from the slaveholding states to the east of Arkansas and introduced the dominant southern culture. Cultivation of cotton, the development of plantations, and the introduction of slavery occurred quickly where the newcomers had good land and access to national and international markets. Between 1850 and 1860 the state's cotton crop increased from 65,344 to 367,393 bales. The upland regions were left out of this early economic boom (although by 1860 all counties produced some cotton and had slaves), and upland farmers usually grew wheat and corn for local markets or subsistence.

Before the Civil War a vigorous two-party system sometimes existed, but generally Democrats controlled state and local governments. The Family, a group of men connected frequently by marriage or birth, dominated Democratic leadership in the antebellum years. Founded by Henry W. Conway, it included his first cousin Ambrose H. Sevier and his brothers James S. Conway, the first governor, and Elias N. Conway, the fifth governor. The state Democratic Party generally adopted states' rights, prosouthern, and pro-slavery positions. In the sectional crisis they sided with the South, despite Unionist opposition that prevented action before the surrender of Fort Sumter. That event changed sentiments. An ordinance of secession was adopted on 6 May 1861.

Its role in controlling Missouri made Arkansas strategically important during the Civil War. To deny Confederates the use of northern Arkansas, a Federal force entered the state and on 7–8 March 1862 effectively dispersed a Confederate army at the Battle of Pea Ridge. On 7 December 1862, at the Battle of Prairie Grove, Federals stopped a Confederate effort to regain the area. Despite secession, Unionist sympathy remained strong. While 60,000 white Arkansans fought for the Confederacy, 8,289 whites joined the Union Army, the largest number from any Confederate state except Tennessee. Federal troops occupied Little Rock on 10 September 1863 and organized a Unionist government in January 1864 under Isaac Murphy, but it was not recognized by Congress.

The Murphy government continued provisionally after the war. Under the congressional Reconstruction plan, Arkansas was readmitted in 1868 with a government headed by Powell Clayton, a Republican. Clayton's administration suppressed racial violence and implemented programs of railroad and edu-

cational development designed to boost the state's economy. The burden of financing such programs, antipathy to its position on race, and charges of corruption ultimately undermined the Republican government. The election of Elisha Baxter (a Republican) as governor in 1872, his removal of suffrage restrictions, and President Ulysses S. Grant's upholding of his administration against a challenge by Joseph Brooks in the so-called Brooks-Baxter War of 1874, paved the way for Democrats to return to power. In October 1874 voters elected Augustus H. Garland, a former Confederate congressman who later served in the U.S. Senate and as attorney general in the administration of Grover Cleveland, as the first Redeemer governor.

The Redeemer Democrats generally cut government programs, although they continued to back funding for railroad construction and other policies promising economic growth. Expanding railroads did spark some New South–type development. From 1880 to 1900 coal mining developed in western counties—production grew from 14,778 tons to nearly 2 million tons. Some small-scale manufacturing emerged; the majority of the firms engaged in processing timber and timber products. The value of manufactured goods increased from $6,756,159 to $45,197,731. Along with these economic changes came urban growth and significant social change.

Problems in agriculture blurred New South economic success, however. Declining cotton prices in the late nineteenth century created serious hardships, especially for small farmers. Rural poverty was pervasive. Tenant farms increased from 31 percent to 45 percent of all farms between 1880 and 1900. These problems made Arkansas a center of agrarian protest that spawned such local organizations as the Brothers of Freedom and the Agricultural Wheel. The near success of a biracial political coalition of farmers in the 1888 elections provoked a Democratic response of violence and ultimately black disfranchisement that ended the protest movement.

By 1900 the state had a population of 1,311,564. Arkansans had made modest gains in economic diversification and growth. New social trends were apparent. Economic and social problems, however, remained a check on rapid change.

See also **South,** *subentry on* **The New South after Reconstruction.**

Bibliography

Bolton, S. Charles. *Arkansas, 1800–1860: Remote and Restless.* Fayetteville: University of Arkansas Press, 1998.

Christ, Mark K., ed. *Rugged and Sublime: The Civil War in Arkansas.* Fayetteville: University of Arkansas Press, 1994.

Moneyhon, Carl H. *Arkansas and the New South, 1874–1929.* Fayetteville: University of Arkansas Press, 1997.

CARL H. MONEYHON

ARMY As the nineteenth century dawned, the new American nation was recovering from the threats of war with Great Britain and then with France. In 1792 the U.S. Congress passed the Uniform Militia Act, which recognized the primacy of the militias of the states in national defense. This weak act directed readiness standards but failed to provide federal support for these militias. At the beginning of the century the regular army of thirty-six hundred soldiers was posted mainly along the rivers and trails on the expanding frontier. One regiment of infantry and two troops of cavalry were in Georgia and Tennessee, while the remainder were mostly in small posts in the Northwest Territory. The major duties of the regular army during this period and for most of the century involved controlling the American Indians who confronted the swarms of settlers moving west into the wilderness. The army also carried out a broad range of civilizing duties, including exploring, surveying and mapping, guiding settlers, building roads and public facilities, and establishing the rudiments of law and order on the frontier.

A Republican Army

The Jeffersonian Republicans, who came into national office in 1801, rejected former President George Washington's recommendation for a small but strong professional army. For defense the government primarily relied upon citizens called to the colors. This policy remained a major feature of U.S. military affairs throughout the century, despite the poor performance of militias and volunteers in most campaigns. With the Military Peace Establishment Act of 1802, the Republican Congress reduced the regular army to three thousand soldiers. That act also established the U.S. Military Academy at West Point, New York, to "republicanize" the army as well as to provide a cadre of leaders with technical knowledge to build the infrastructure of the nation. Jefferson's secretary of war Henry Dearborn directed the army through clerks (later bureaus) of the general staff. The most senior general was designated commander of the army, but his authority was limited to certain field operations.

Though antimilitary by nature, Jefferson found the army useful in expanding the nation westward. In 1804 he dispatched Captain Meriwether Lewis and Lieutenant William Clark to explore the Louisiana Purchase and to establish the authority of the United States with Indian tribes encountered therein. The War Department established posts to control the Mississippi River and its tributaries and appointed army officers to govern the developing areas. Thus began another mission of long duration for the army, opening and governing the western territories.

In 1811 the frontier of the Northwest Territory erupted in warfare, as Tecumseh, the chief of the Shawnees, formed a confederacy to halt expansion of settlers into that territory. Tecumseh was supported by the British from within Canada and by British traders operating in the territory. Army commanders assigned to General William Henry Harrison, governor of Indiana Territory, the task of moving against the confederation, which was gathering in a village called Prophet's Town, along the Wabash River. The Fourth Infantry Regiment bolstered the militias General Harrison called up. On 7 November 1811 Harrison's encampment was attacked by Tecumseh's braves. Driving off the Indians, the soldiers counterattacked, routing the Indians and destroying the confederacy at the battle of Tippecanoe.

The War of 1812

U.S. troubles with Great Britain in the Northwest Territory and on the seas led to war in 1812. Urged on by "war hawks" in Congress, a poorly trained American force under the weak leadership of General William Hull moved to invade Canada. While organizing in Detroit, the Americans were surrounded by an inferior British-Canadian force and surrendered without firing a shot. This abject defeat revealed the "dry rot" in American military leadership, as old veterans of the American Revolution attempted to lead untrained young men against better trained and more disciplined British forces. Congress called for eighty thousand militia to join federal service, and the states assigned quotas and paid bonuses for volunteers. The ragged groups that assembled refused orders they disliked, and some stood on their constitutional rights to fight only for a short period and only within the United States. The lack of discipline caused a series of American defeats on land. Small U.S. victories at Chippewa and Lundy's Lane in July 1814 and the emergence of an officer of professional stature, General Winfield Scott, offset the defeats somewhat. The most significant American defeat of the war came in August 1814, as British forces, augmented by veterans of the Napoleonic Wars, invaded Maryland, driving a hastily assembled militia from the defenses at Bladensburg. The British then seized Washington, D.C., and burned the Capitol, the White House, and other public buildings.

Napoleon's return to the battlefields in Europe in 1814 and war weariness in Britain helped end the War of 1812 in December 1814. A peace treaty was signed in Ghent, Belgium. A postscript to that war came in January 1815, when General Andrew Jackson, with a mixed force of regulars, militia, and volunteers, decisively defeated a major British force at New Orleans. This victory ended foreign threats to American security for the remainder of the century and restored the faith of U.S. political leaders in the efficacy of the militia system, despite its poor overall record in the war. The Army Reorganization Act of 1821 reduced the strength of the regular army to six thousand even as it defined the purpose of the army as "preparation for a future war." Congress refused to enact the proposal of Secretary of War John Calhoun for a "cadre army" high in rank.

Army Support of National Expansion

The period between the end of the War of 1812 and the beginning of the Mexican War was one of tremendous growth in population and in the national economy accompanied by a great surge westward. It was also a period of significant development in the professionalism of the regular army. The U.S. Military Academy, under its enlightened superintendent, Major Sylvanus Thayer, produced military engineers who literally undergirded the nation with roads, railroads, bridges, and canals. The Rivers and Harbors Act of 1824 placed the Army Corps of Engineers in control of the nation's seaports and inland waterways. Infantry units moved west up the waterways of the Mississippi, establishing posts across the Great Plains. These posts brought security to the regions around them, and patrols of soldiers assisted the wagon trains of settlers crossing the Plains. Around these posts trading centers and ultimately cities grew. Army officers assigned to these posts acted for the federal government in enforcing trade regulations, codified by Congress in 1834 to protect the Indians in their dealings with traders, and adjudicated grievances between Indians and settlers.

Indian Removal

In 1830 Congress formalized a policy for removal of the eastern Indians to unpopulated areas in the West. The army, acting as the agent of the federal government, negotiated with the tribes and supervised their relocation. Most of the tribes moved peacefully to "Indian Country." The Cherokees and associated tribes initially resisted but were persuaded to take the "Trail of Tears" west beyond the Mississippi. Indian resistance to removal led the United States into a short confrontation, called the Black Hawk War,

with the Sauk and Fox Indians in Illinois in 1832. The Seminole Indians in Florida successfully resisted relocation, fighting guerrilla wars against army contingents in the swamps of central Florida from 1817 into the 1850s.

The Mexican War

The theme of the national election of 1844 was "Manifest Destiny," the belief that God had granted all of the central portion of the North American continent to the United States. The Democrat James Polk announced that he would "reannex" Texas. After Polk's election as president, Congress in 1845 voted to annex Texas, leading to war with Mexico. In March 1846 General Zachary Taylor moved his regular army units in Texas to a position near the Rio Grande. The Mexican forces, led by General Mariano Arista, drawn up south of the Rio Grande at Matamoros, were considered better trained and equipped than Taylor's army. However, the Americans had good junior leaders, graduates of the Military Academy, and the U.S. forces were in high spirits. The Mexicans made the first move, crossing the Rio

Winfield Scott (1786–1866). Portrait of the general in military uniform. Engraved from a daguerreotype by T. Doney. LIBRARY OF CONGRESS: PRINTS AND PHOTOGRAPHS DIVISION

Grande to meet Taylor at Palo Alto. Accurate U.S. artillery gunnery and strong U.S. leadership drove the Mexicans off the field and later across the river. The U.S. Congress then declared war and increased the strength of the regular army to fifteen thousand. President Polk called for fifty thousand volunteers to serve for periods of six months to one year. The volunteers were enthusiastic for adventure but were untrained and difficult to discipline.

Reinforced to a total of twelve thousand troops, Taylor's army drove into Mexico, taking Monterrey and Saltillo in aggressive individual and small-unit actions. Meanwhile General Winfield Scott, commander of the U.S. Army, under pressure from President Polk, organized an invasion of Mexico. With the cooperation of the U.S. Navy, the invasion planned to land at Veracruz then proceed across the country to capture the Mexican capital, Mexico City. The bulk of Taylor's troops moved to join Scott's forces at Tampico, while Taylor remained at Buena Vista with five thousand troops in defense. General Antonio López de Santa Anna, commander of Mexican forces, attacked Taylor's defenses at Buena Vista on 22 February 1847. Taylor's volunteers routed the Mexicans, and American artillery caused heavy casualties among the attackers.

Scott's forces moved to Veracruz in a well-coordinated amphibious operation. The U.S. Navy bombarded the city on 9 March 1847. The Americans seized Veracruz without difficulty, and the Mexicans withdrew to positions inland at Cerro Gordo. In a wide sweep, Scott's forces outflanked the Mexican defenses, and the Mexicans again retreated. Deep in Mexico, with a force reduced by the departure of many militia whose terms of service were ending, Scott abandoned his base of supplies and moved against Mexico City. In a classic campaign Scott repeatedly outflanked strong Mexican defenses. Driving in from the west, Scott's forces captured the city on 14 September 1847. Many junior officers, including Robert E. Lee and Ulysses S. Grant, fought with distinction, learning tactics they would use as senior officers in the Civil War. The fall of Mexico City ended the Mexican War, although the peace treaty granting Texas, California, and the Mexican territories between them to the United States was not concluded until 2 February 1848.

Pacifying the West

Policing the newly won areas in the Southwest expanded the scope of operations of the active army after the Mexican War. It was necessary and difficult to control the Plains Indians and the surging white population in the West, especially after the discovery of gold in California in 1848. War Department records for the 1850s show a total of 208 combats, most against the Apaches and Navajos in the Southwest and the Sioux and Cheyennes in the North. In the West the army, mostly cavalry units organized to combat the Indians, also pacified the Mormons in 1857 and stopped a civil war between free-state and slave-state activists in Kansas the next year. To accomplish these tasks in an increasingly hostile environment, the army was increased to sixteen thousand men on the active rolls. However, desertions were many, and the few troopers present for duty were spread thinly over the unsettled areas of the West.

The Civil War

When the Civil War began in 1861, the Confederacy actually had a greater number of men under arms than did the Union. The "rebels" also had better leadership and that high esprit of a people fighting for their unique identity. The Confederacy generally had the advantage of "interior lines" suited to defense, while the Union had to attack to restore national integrity. Otherwise the Union far outstripped the Confederacy in population, resources, industry, transport, and economic strength. After the Confederates seized Fort Sumter, South Carolina, on 14 April 1861, President Abraham Lincoln called on the states to provide seventy-five thousand militia. The capital itself was threatened by Confederate forces gathering across the Potomac River in northern Virginia, and with Congress in recess, Lincoln issued an executive order increasing the active strength of the army by twenty-two thousand men and called for an additional forty thousand volunteers.

As militia and volunteers gathered around Washington, D.C., the army headquarters was hard-pressed to control them, and training was desultory. General Scott, still the commanding general at seventy-five years of age, designed a grand strategy of blockading the Confederacy by sea and driving in Southern forces around their perimeter. Called the Anaconda Plan, Scott's proposal was rejected by Lincoln and Congress as being too slow to produce results. General Irvin McDowell, commander of the troops in the vicinity of Washington, was ordered to attack the rebels across the river. On 16 July 1861 McDowell's forces executed a wide turning movement around the west of the Confederates in the vicinity of Manassas, Virginia. Union forces rolled up the rebel positions and were near victory when Confederate reinforcements arrived by railroad from the west. The Confederates drove Union forces from the field on 21 July, and a disorganized mob of federal soldiers and onlookers, including some congressmen and their families, poured across the Potomac Bridge into Washington. It was a significant defeat for Union forces in their first major offensive. Following this loss, a reorganized Army of the Potomac under General George McClellan advanced on Richmond, only to suffer defeat in the summer of 1862 in heavy fighting on the Virginia Peninsula against the Army of Northern Virginia under General Lee. A subsequent Union advance by General John Pope suffered a similar defeat and withdrew. Lee then launched an invasion of the North, meeting McClellan's forces at Antietam, Maryland, in September 1862. Heavy fighting resulted in a draw, but Lee returned to Virginia uncontested.

In the West the Union armies were more successful, driving down the rivers with the support of the U.S. Navy. Under General Grant, Union forces drove Confederate forces from Kentucky and Tennessee in 1862. The Mississippi River was cleared of Confederate defenses with the Union seizure of Vicksburg, Mississippi, on 4 July 1863.

In the eastern theater a successful General Lee and his Army of Northern Virginia, having defeated a succession of Union commanders, again invaded the North, meeting Union forces at Gettysburg, Pennsylvania, in July 1863. Launching frontal attacks on Union defenses, Lee's forces suffered severe losses but again withdrew to Virginia. The strategic initiative now passed to the Union, whose growing military power greatly exceeded that of the Confederacy on each battlefield.

General Grant took command of all U.S. forces, more than one million strong, in March 1864. Launching total war against the Confederacy, Grant conceived of a giant pincer drive to encircle the rebel armies and force them to attritive battle. Charging his major subordinate in the West, General William T. Sherman, to cut through the heart of the Confederacy, Grant moved south against Lee's Army of Northern Virginia. Hard fighting on the road to Richmond used up Lee's forces, while Sherman drove from Atlanta to the sea and turned north. After breaking out of the Federal siege of Petersburg, Lee's forces were quickly trapped. General Lee surrendered the Army of Northern Virginia to General Grant on 9 April 1865. The remaining forces of the Confederacy surrendered shortly thereafter.

Reorganization, Reconstruction, Indian Fighting

After victory celebrations and parades, the Union armies disbanded. The volunteers went home, and the regular army, reduced in 1866 to forty-six thousand authorized soldiers, reorganized for peacekeeping duties. Brevet (temporary) ranks were canceled, and a small federal army, now strong in experience, turned

William Tecumseh Sherman (1820–1891). The Union general is most famous for his taking of Atlanta, Georgia. Photo taken c. 1861–1865. LIBRARY OF CONGRESS

to the difficult tasks of policing the defeated South and controlling the Plains Indians. Land grant colleges, growing out of the Morrill Act of 1862, required military training guided by army officers for all male students.

Executing the Reconstruction Acts of the Congress required that the army assume the responsibilities of occupying and governing the South, enfranchising and protecting the former slaves, and quelling the terrorism of the Ku Klux Klan. Pressed by Radical Republicans to purge the South of its evils and cursed by the white southerners for the excesses of the Freedman's Bureau, the army carried out this onerous duty with relative equanimity until the end of Reconstruction in 1877.

Most of the officers and soldiers of the postwar army opted for duty on the Great Plains, preferring to deal with hostile Indians rather than the recalcitrant South. Scattered through more than one hundred small posts and detachments, the "Indian fighting army" was at a considerable disadvantage versus the Indians. On the Plains the army encountered a nomadic Indian, a good fighter who was inured to hardship and austere living. Soldiers with black-powder muskets often faced Indians armed with repeating rifles, which they bought illegally from unscrupulous traders. Many of the soldiers were illiterate immigrants who had never before ridden a horse. They engaged Indians "born in the saddle" who were able to strike swiftly and fight while mounted. Records of the post–Civil War period reveal more than 950 army combats with the Indians, many of them Indian ambuscades and raids from which the Indians emerged victorious. Punitive campaigns by army task forces scattered but did not destroy Indian war bands; some campaigns, such as General George A. Custer's 1876 defeat at the Battle of the Little Bighorn, were blundering failures.

From this long and hazardous duty emerged army leaders, including Generals George Crook and Nelson Miles, who were good Indian fighters yet were sympathetic to the plight of oppressed Indians. The army ultimately accrued the advantages of industrialization, including organization and planning that led to effective campaigns, telegraph communications enabling coordination and convergence of widespread operations, and most of all the huge growth of population in the West from less than two million in 1866 to more than eight million by the end of the Indian wars in 1890.

The end of Reconstruction coincided with another unpopular army assignment, strikebreaking. A nationwide outburst of labor strikes in 1877 began with railroad workers, spread to the mines, and was joined by the unemployed in burgeoning cities. Governors called out militia units, which were ineffective. The militiamen occasionally joined the strikers. Directed to restore order, the regular army dispersed the strikers, combining restraint with the pressures of military formations. The army broke the strikes but took a black eye in terms of its image among the workers. In response to the strikes the federal government increased appropriations to help states strengthen their militias, which became the National Guard.

Military Education and Professionalism

The late nineteenth century has been called "the dark ages" of U.S. military history. The army, a constabulary force manning small posts in sparsely settled regions, was physically separated from the society it served. Reduced to twenty-five thousand men in 1874, the authorized military strength remained at that figure despite increasing and widespread commitments. In 1876, while Custer was fighting the Sioux, the Fifty-fourth Congress adjourned without passing a military appropriations act for the coming year. Not a single military man was paid for a year, until the next Congress passed the necessary appropriations. Without a foreign threat, the nation allowed its army to atrophy. Many military leaders turned their attentions to civil pursuits, and long absences from duty were common. At the dusty posts, duty was performed mostly in the morning. Officers only visited their commands, leaving the training and discipline of the troops to the sergeants.

This isolation prompted a surge of professionalism among army officers. General Sherman, commanding general of the army from 1869 to 1883, established and expanded a skein of schools and training programs to modernize the army. The Artillery School expanded, and the Engineering School, the Signal School, and the Army Medical School opened. Sherman's great contribution was founding the School for the Application of Infantry and Cavalry at Fort Leavenworth, directing it to study "the science and practice of war" (Millett and Maslowski, *For the Common Defense*, p. 256). Under his guidance the Military Service Institution, a professional society for the study of military affairs that published a bimonthly journal, was established.

During this period army officers traveled abroad to study the modernization of foreign armies. In 1875 Sherman appointed Emory Upton, a lieutenant colonel who had been a major general in the Civil War, to a commission to propose military reforms. Upton made a global trip to visit foreign armies and was particularly impressed with the German general staff and training system. On his return Upton wrote two books, *The Armies of Asia and Europe* (1878) and *The Military Policy of the United States* (1904). In the latter book Upton argued that a regular army, high in rank with a strong general staff, should prepare the United States for war during the time of peace. This strong cadre should expand in wartime, using "volunteers" led by regular army officers. The military leadership supported Upton's thesis, but it was roundly criticized in the press and by the politically powerful National Guard Association. Because it was highly critical of the nation's reliance upon the citizen soldier and because it would have been expensive to implement, Upton's program was never enacted.

The Spanish-American War

On 15 February 1898 the U.S. battleship *Maine* exploded in the harbor of Havana, Cuba, and the United States quickly declared war on Spain. The American people, aroused by newspaper stories of Spanish atrocities in Cuba, were ready for war, but the U.S. Army was not. The strong and modern U.S. Navy, already at sea, engaged the Spanish fleet deployed off Cuba and the Philippines. The regular army, increased to sixty-five thousand personnel, prepared for an invasion of Cuba, and regular units gathered near ports on the Gulf of Mexico.

While the army and navy frantically coordinated invasion plans, 200,000 enthusiastic but untrained volunteers joined the forces sweltering in the encampments. On 22 April 1898, Congress authorized the activation of ten volunteer regiments, the most famous of which was the 1st United States Volunteer Cavalry, popularly known as the "Rough Riders." Anxious to join the war against Spain, Theodore Roosevelt resigned his position as assistant secretary to the Navy and formed the regiment, whose numbers included cowboys that Roosevelt knew from the West, as well as businessmen and other men of wealth who were his friends. Gaining the rank of lieutenant colonel and the appointment as executive officer of the 1st Volunteer Cavalry regiment, Roosevelt persuaded Colonel Leonard Wood, a surgeon with long troop experience, to command the regiment. Using his political influence, Roosevelt secured transportation for the regiment to Cuba.

General William Shafter, an old, corpulent campaigner who had served in the Civil War, was designated to command the invasion, and his newly formed V Corps established headquarters at Tampa, Florida. On 31 May 1898 Shafter received orders to sail as soon as possible from Tampa, convoyed by the navy, and to invade Cuba in the vicinity of Santiago. Troops and cargo poured into Tampa on a single rail line. Loading programs were changed and interrupted as certain volunteer units fought their way onto ships ahead of schedule. With no supply accountability, soldiers lacked supporting weapons and equipment. Somehow the convoy got under way on 14 June, and V Corps combat units landed at Daiquiri and Siboney on 22 June.

The dismounted U.S. Cavalry, the first of three divisions to go ashore, landed unopposed and swiftly moved inland toward Santiago. After a short skirmish at Las Guásimas, the Spaniards withdrew to defenses in front of Santiago. Shafter moved his three divisions to El Pozo over narrow jungle trails. The thirteen thousand Spanish troops in the Santiago area, two thousand of whom were deployed in outpost positions along San Juan Ridge to the east of the city, were in good defenses with barbed-wire obstacles and were well armed with smokeless-powder Mauser rifles. The Americans were equipped with black-powder Springfields, whose smoke gave away their positions. Shafter attacked in two columns on 1 July. Under galling fire, the Americans advanced in bunches, losing unit integrity. Held up in the jungle for nearly a day in front of El Caney, the attack on the heights began late in the day. A few brave soldiers led groups of men through the barbed wire and up Kettle and San Juan Hills in rushes, including Theodore Roosevelt, who led the Rough Riders up Kettle Hill with enthusiasm and bravery. The hills were seized through high esprit and sheer courage but with heavy casualties.

Shafter's situation at Santiago was desperate. His combat strength was ebbing fast from Spanish fire, dysentery, and jungle fevers. Short on ammunition, food, and water, on 3 July he appealed to Washington to send reinforcements quickly. On that same day the Spanish squadron in the Bay of Santiago attempted to escape and was sunk by the U.S. squadron blockading the harbor. Acting with bravado, Shafter called upon the Spanish commander, General José Toral, to surrender. Toral's government could not reinforce him, and on 17 July he surrendered all Spanish troops in eastern Cuba. The United States then invaded Puerto Rico. Well-organized forces under General Miles, commander of the army, advanced toward San Juan with little resistance. On 12 August, Shafter and Miles received telegrams announcing that the United States and Spain had signed peace protocols.

The message regarding a peace treaty did not reach U.S. Army forces in the Philippines in time to stop the Battle of Manila, where Commodore George Dewey's Asiatic Squadron had defeated the Spanish squadron in Manila Bay in May 1898. General Wesley Merritt, commanding the VIII Corps, accepted the Spanish request for a mock battle in Manila before the surrender of their troops. Ignoring the Philippine insurgents who offered cooperation, the Americans advanced on the city's defenses on 13 August. Filipino guerrillas joined in the American attack. The Spanish quickly surrendered, and U.S. and Filipino groups jostled each other to take possession of parts of the city. Outlying Spanish garrisons at Cavite and Guam surrendered upon receiving word of the peace treaty.

An Army for Empire

When the twentieth century dawned, the U.S. Army had major forces outside the nation. In the Caribbean army units were engaged in humanitarian and occupation duties, in the Philippines army units were fighting Filipino guerrillas, and in Asia twenty-five hundred army troops under General Adna Chaffee were committed to the China Relief Expedition. In 1900 the active army included thousands of volunteers. Military groups and committees in Congress studied the poor performance of the army high command during the Spanish-American War. Major reorganizations in the twentieth century improved command and staff effectiveness and the army's preparedness for the demands of modern war.

See also **American Indians,** *subentries on* **Indian Removal, Wars and Warfare; Civil War,** *subentry on* **Battles and Combatants; Labor Movement,** *subentry on* **Unions and Strikes; Manifest Destiny; Mexican War; Military Academy, U.S.; Military Service; Military Technology; Militia, State; Reconstruction,** *subentry on* **In the South; Seminole War(s); Spanish-American War; War of 1812.**

Bibliography

Dupuy, R. Ernest. *The Compact History of the United States Army.* New York: Hawthorn, 1956.

Jamieson, Perry D. *Crossing the Deadly Ground: United States Army Tactics, 1865–1899.* Tuscaloosa: University of Alabama Press, 1994.

McCaffrey, James M. *Army of Manifest Destiny: The American Soldier in the Mexican War, 1846–1848.* New York: New York University Press, 1992.

Millett, Allan R., and Peter Maslowski. *For the Common Defense: A Military History of the United States of America.* New York: Free Press, 1984.

Prucha, Francis Paul. *The Sword of the Republic: The United States Army on the Frontier, 1783–1846.* Lincoln: University of Nebraska Press, 1969.

Utley, Robert M. *Frontier Regulars: The United States Army and the Indian, 1866–1891.* Lincoln: University of Nebraska Press, 1973.

———. *Frontiersmen in Blue: The United States Army and the Indian, 1848–1865.* Lincoln: University of Nebraska Press, 1967.

PAUL F. BRAIM

ASIA, FOREIGN RELATIONS WITH

Hundreds of years before the American Revolution, western Europeans envisioned the treasures and excitements that lay across the great ocean that Ferdinand Magellan had labeled "Pacific." After 1776 Americans set their sights not only on continental aggrandizement, or Manifest Destiny, but also on an empire on the Pacific that included access to the fabled markets of Asia. The U.S. flag followed settlement, as Americans streamed west and annexed vast stretches of North America through war and diplomacy. One of the motives of U.S. continental expansion to the west coast was to secure the fine ports and harbors, from present-day San Diego to Seattle, that would facilitate commercial and cultural expansion across the Pacific.

Armed with improved naval and maritime technology, the United States strove throughout the nineteenth century to become a Pacific power. In the antebellum era U.S. "scavenger diplomacy" in Asia followed in the British wake, especially in efforts to exploit the China market. After Britain secured its position in China in the Opium War (1839–1842), the United States demanded most-favored-nation trade status; with terms as favorable as those provided any other nation, it was granted in the 1844 Treaty of Wangxia. Britain continued to dominate the China trade, but the United States made inroads through its construction of clipper ships, graceful sailing craft that carried goods between the United States and its five treaty ports in China.

Antebellum politicians and poets offered romanticized visions of a future U.S. empire in Asia. While trade with China evolved steadily, hundreds of missionaries traveled across the Pacific to save "heathen" souls. Some missionaries displayed their earnest by learning Chinese, and they often acted as interpreters for Western traders and businesspeople.

The migration occurred on both sides of the Pacific, as, by 1868, more than 100,000 Chinese were in the United States. Although the nation encouraged immigration as essential to its agricultural and industrial expansion, Americans welcomed only European immigrants and not the exotic Chinese. While Chinese laborers built railroads and worked in mines, American nativists condemned their appearance, their food, and their lifestyle in the burgeoning Chinatowns. As the favored targets of American ethnocentrism, especially in California, Chinese were subjected to beatings, humiliation, and occasional murder. Congress, unable to resist the nativist impulse, passed the Chinese Exclusion Act in 1882, which suspended Chinese immigration and placed restrictions on Chinese already in the United States.

Japan was the next target for the expanding U.S. commercial empire. Reflecting on their own highly mobile society, Americans viewed the "open door," or free trade, as an inalienable right. Japan, however, remained largely closed to Westerners at mid-century. Japanese officials snubbed Commodore Matthew C. Perry when he arrived in 1853 but showed him more respect when he returned the next year equipped with a much larger fleet. Perry's opening evolved into a commercial agreement negotiated by the diplomat Townsend Harris in 1858 that opened five ports to U.S. traders.

Americans also demanded access to Korea, the "hermit kingdom" of Asia. The Korean Peninsula, which offered access to resource-rich Manchuria (northern China), had violently resisted Western intrusions for years. U.S. efforts to break into the hermit kingdom led in 1871 to a clash in which Americans killed more than two hundred Koreans in a shipboard battle on the Han River. In 1882, after persistent efforts, U.S. commodore Robert Shufeldt forced concessions, and the Koreans signed a treaty opening the peninsula to trade. Korea soon became an object of a power struggle between China and Japan that in 1894 erupted into a war, from which Japan emerged victorious.

Architects of the emerging American empire sought stepping stones in the form of harbors and outposts en route to China, Japan, and other Asian markets. In 1867 U.S. naval officers claimed the Midway Islands, named for their location halfway between California and Japan. Americans began to populate and dominate the Hawaiian Islands in the 1870s and in 1875 negotiated a trade reciprocity agreement ensuring profitable sugar production on the verdant volcanic atolls.

By 1890, however, indigenous forces led by a determined monarch, Queen Liliuokalani, sought to reassert control over the hegemonic Americans, who responded by fomenting a rebellion aided by the U.S. minister. The planters overthrew Queen Liliuokalani in 1893, but President Grover Cleveland rejected annexation, forcing the Americans to wait for a more propitious moment to solidify their control.

Even as Americans assumed control of Hawaii, architects of the emerging Asian empire coveted Samoa, a chain of islands strategically located 4,800 miles from San Francisco on trade routes to Australia and New Zealand. Germany and Great Britain, both of whom also sought control of the Polynesian isles, blocked U.S. efforts. Tensions had peaked by 1889, when a massive hurricane brought destruction to all concerned. Britain gradually withdrew, and in 1899 Washington and Berlin struck a deal that gave the United States control of Pago Pago, a favorable harbor and a perfect complement to Pearl Harbor on Oahu.

The partition of Samoa came amid the Spanish-American War and the climax of nineteenth-century U.S. expansion in Asia. During that war the United States captured the Philippines and annexed Hawaii, Guam, and Wake Island. Motivated by a quest for markets, religious zeal, intense nationalism (or "jingoism"), and the closing of the American continental frontier, the United States aggressively entered the age of imperialism.

The war with Spain stemmed from Madrid's maladministration of Cuba, located ninety miles from Florida and long claimed by expansionists as a natural extension of the continental Union. The United States quickly defeated Spain and seized Cuba and Puerto Rico, but Southeast Asia was the most significant theater of the war. When Commodore George Dewey opened fire on the Spanish squadron in Manila Bay, Americans scurried to their world maps to locate the Philippine archipelago. Like Cuba, the Philippines were a crudely administered Spanish colony involved in an indigenous revolt. The leader of the rebel forces, Emilio Aguinaldo, welcomed U.S. support in his bid to replace Spain with a native government.

Although Aguinaldo's forces took control of the massive island of Luzon, where Manila is located, and were fast spreading their authority across the entire archipelago, President William McKinley determined to secure the islands in the service of U.S. national interests. McKinley and his advisers sought a substantial outpost from which to compete for the markets of Asia and with which to establish the United States as a preeminent world power. Racism played a dominant role in American perceptions and in the brutal conduct of the subsequent war of subjugation. The Filipinos, Americans decided, were too dark-skinned and backward to govern themselves, so Washington would do it for them. The same attitude had long prevailed at home in relations with American Indians, African Americans, and other people of color. U.S. racial attitudes simply transcended the nation's borders during its emergence as a world power.

Not surprisingly the Filipino rebels made no distinction between Spanish and U.S. imperialism and refused to compromise in their goal of national independence. Hence war was inevitable. Fighting between U.S. forces and Filipino insurgents began on 4 February 1899. Two days later McKinley barely secured the necessary two-thirds (57 to 27) vote in the Senate to ratify a treaty negotiated in Paris ending the war with Spain. Under its terms the United States paid $20 million for possession of the Philippines.

To actually take possession, however, the United States fought its first bloody guerrilla war on Asian soil. Tens of thousands of Americans, particularly in the Northeast, opposed U.S. annexation diplomacy. The Anti-Imperialist League, founded in Boston in June 1898, failed to change the direction of U.S. policy, yet its members, many of them female, dissented outspokenly. Such prominent Americans as Jane Addams, Andrew Carnegie, and Mark Twain forcefully condemned the U.S. aggression in the Philippines as a violation of republican principles.

With U.S. forces ensconced in the cities and other strongholds, the Filipino rebels under Aguinaldo took to the countryside. U.S. officers and fighting men, thousands of whom had accumulated extensive experience in Indian fighting at home, proved adept at hunting down the guerrilla bands, and massacres and other atrocities occurred routinely.

The capture of Aguinaldo in March 1901 spelled defeat for the rebels, yet fighting continued in some places for years. Most of the resistance ended in 1902, by which time U.S. forces had killed 15,000 to 20,000 Filipinos and 200,000 other Filipinos had died from famine and disease. The Americans suffered some 4,200 dead and 2,800 wounded.

Annexation of the Philippines culminated nineteenth-century U.S. expansion into Asia and established the United States as a global power. Trade with China, Japan, and other Asian nations spiraled, though it remained only a fraction of overall U.S. commerce.

While Americans fought for their new empire in the Philippines, Chinese nationalism boiled over in opposition to U.S., western European, and Russian imperialism in Asia. The Boxer Rebellion (1900), an effort to repel foreigners from the Chinese capital of Beijing, gained the support of the Chinese government. The Boxers and their supporters attacked foreign embassies and wantonly murdered diplomats, Protestant and Catholic missionaries, and trade officials.

Without seeking congressional approval, McKinley, who is sometimes described as the first modern if not imperial president, dispatched five thousand U.S. troops to help an international force of some twenty thousand soldiers (from the western European powers, Russia, and Japan) put down the uprising. Both before and after the Boxer Rebellion, the U.S. secretary of state John Hay issued notes calling for an "open door" in Asia, that is, a policy of free trade rather than exclusive spheres. The foreign powers withdrew from Beijing in 1901 on the basis of the Open Door notes but not before exacting an indemnity of $333 million, which the declining Chinese government could not hope to pay.

The Open Door notes reflected U.S. success, at least for the time being, in establishing itself as a great power in Asia. Washington had expanded its trade and secured island possessions across the vast Pacific. An expanding navy and fortified bases in Guam, Pearl Harbor, and Subic Bay in the Philippines bolstered the new empire. However, U.S. possessions, especially the Philippine archipelago, stood vulnerable to Japan, another rising Asian power. Tokyo became increasingly resentful of Western intrusions in Asia and the overt racism that often accompanied it. When imperial Japan rejected the Open Door in the 1930s, another, bloodier war retained the empire that Americans had carved out across the Pacific during the nineteenth century.

See also **Chinese Exclusion Act; Cuba; Expansion; Hawaii; Immigration and Immigrants,** subentry on **Asia; Navy; Overseas Possessions; Spanish-American War.**

Bibliography

Cohen, Warren I, ed. *The Cambridge History of American Foreign Relations.* Vol. 2. *Empire for Opportunity, 1865–1913,* by Walter LaFeber. New York: Cambridge University Press, 1993.

Hunt, Michael H. *The Making of a Special Relationship: The United States and China to 1914.* New York: Columbia University Press, 1983.

Iriye, Akira. *Across the Pacific: An Inner History of American–East Asian Relations.* New York: Harcourt, Brace, and World, 1967.

Miller, Stuart Creighton. *"Benevolent Assimilation": The American Conquest of the Philippines, 1899–1903.* New Haven, Conn.: Yale University Press, 1982.

WALTER L. HIXSON

ASSASSINATIONS

Assassination is the premeditated murder of a political figure for reasons associated with the victim's prominence or political perspective or both. Four presidents elected in the nineteenth century were victims of such attacks. Since all but one of these incidents involved an individual acting alone, attention necessarily centers on the motives and mental states of the assailants. Of the three nineteenth-century assassins and the one would-be assassin, two were afflicted with severe mental disorders and two were political extremists. Yet the motives of all four have been attributed incorrectly to mental disorders.

The first attempt to assassinate an American president, in 1835, failed. Andrew Jackson's life was spared when his assailant's two pistols misfired. Three other presidents were not so fortunate. Abraham Lincoln was the first to be assassinated in 1865; James Garfield suffered the same fate in 1881; and so William McKinley in 1901.

President Jackson's would-be assassin was Richard Lawrence, an English-born house painter, who imagined that he was King Richard III of England. Lawrence tried to assassinate Jackson because he believed the president's opposition to the establishment of a national bank was part of a plot to deny the repayment of debts owed to him. Lawrence's delusional thinking, bizarre conduct, and long family history of mental illness convinced even the prosecutor, Francis Scott Key (best known as the composer of the National Anthem), that he could not be held criminally responsible for his actions. Lawrence was acquitted by reason of insanity and was confined in the Government Hospital for the Insane (later renamed St. Elizabeth's Hospital) in Washington, D.C., until his death in 1861.

When John Wilkes Booth shot and killed President Abraham Lincoln in 1865, an attempt was made to explain his actions as the work of a disordered mind. Commentators at the time, and historians since, have portrayed Booth, much like Lawrence, as a delusional, mentally disordered individual who killed the president to achieve the fame and notoriety

Assassination of President Lincoln. Depiction of John Wilkes Booth's assassination of President Lincoln at Ford's Theatre on 14 April 1865, while watching *Our American Cousin* from the presidential box. LIBRARY OF CONGRESS: PRINTS AND PHOTOGRAPHS DIVISION

that had eluded him in a failed career as an actor. The evidence, however, reveals a different story.

Throughout most of his administration Abraham Lincoln may have been the most controversial and unpopular president in American history. As commander in chief, presiding over the bloodiest war Americans have ever fought, Lincoln was hated throughout the South as a war criminal. He was also unpopular in parts of the North. Elected with a plurality of less than 40 percent of the popular vote nationally, but with well over 50 percent of the free-state vote, Lincoln had to battle strong antiwar sentiment outside the South. Without political support he could count on, Lincoln waged war by executive order, frequently without congressional consultation or approval. During his first year in office, he suspended the writ of habeas corpus so that activists who opposed the war and his policies could be arrested. His most unpopular decisions included conscription to replace casualties lost in a succession of disastrous Union military defeats and the exceedingly unpopular Emancipation Proclamation.

In contrast, John Wilkes Booth was probably the most widely acclaimed actor of his day. Theatrical reviews reveal that his fame knew no regional boundaries; he was as popular in the North as he was in the South. His withdrawal from the stage in 1864 was not due to throat problems and a failing career, as some

have suggested, but rather to his preoccupation with war-related activities on behalf of the Confederacy. Booth shot Lincoln as the president sat in Ford's Theatre on 14 April 1865, believing that three coconspirators would, the same evening, end the lives of those in line to succeed him: Vice President Andrew Johnson, Secretary of State William H. Seward, and the commander of the Union Army, General Ulysses S. Grant. But only Lincoln died. Had Booth's plan succeeded, he believed the result would have created political chaos in the war-weary North and revived the defeated Confederacy.

Charles J. Guiteau's motives were less rational, and less grounded in the political realities of the time, when he fired a bullet into the back of President James A. Garfield on 2 July 1881. Annoyed that the president had not recognized or rewarded his completely imaginary contributions to the president's successful campaign, Guiteau shot Garfield as he was about to board a train in Washington, D.C. Garfield lived another two and a half months before dying on 19 September. At his trial Guiteau insisted that his act was divinely inspired. "The Lord interjected the idea [of the assassination] into my brain and then let me work it out my own way," he explained. "That is the way the Lord does. He doesn't employ fools to do his work; I am sure of that; he gets the best brains he can find." Despite overwhelming evidence of mental

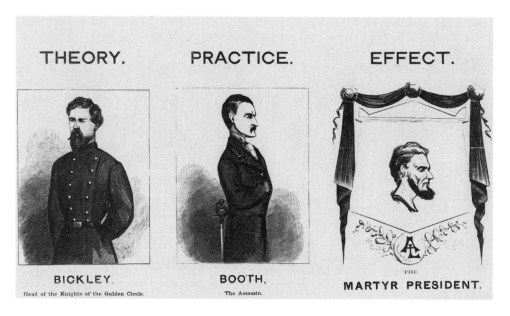

THEORY.   PRACTICE.   EFFECT.

BICKLEY.   BOOTH.   MARTYR PRESIDENT.

Head of the Knights of the Golden Circle.   The Assassin.

The Knights of the Golden Circle and the Lincoln Assassination. The Knights of the Golden Circle was a proslavery secret society. George W. L. Bickley, the head of the Knights of the Golden Circle, is at left. Booth is in the middle, holding a dagger behind his back. A portrait of Lincoln framed with black drapery and olive branches is at right. A three-part wood engraving, created in 1865. LIBRARY OF CONGRESS

impairment, including a long family history of mental illness, Guiteau was convicted and hanged. He died believing that his memory and remains would someday be honored by a grateful nation.

No such delusions afflicted Leon Czolgosz when he fired a bullet into William McKinley's stomach as the president stood greeting a line of well-wishers at the Pan-American Exposition in Buffalo, New York. The president died eight days later on 14 September 1901. An anarchist, Czolgosz believed, as did many in the socialist-labor movement of the era, that a revolution was necessary to eliminate the evils of industrial capitalism. He viewed the popular second-term president as a symbol of those evils. Before he was executed, Czolgosz's last words were "I killed the president because he was the enemy of the good people—the good working people. I am not sorry for my crime."

Bibliography

Clarke, James W. *American Assassins: The Darker Side of Politics.* Rev. ed. Princeton, N.J.: Princeton University Press, 1990.

———. *On Being Mad or Merely Angry: John W. Hinckley, Jr. and Other Dangerous People.* Princeton, N.J.: Princeton University Press, 1990.

JAMES W. CLARKE

ASTRONOMY   Around 1800, except for the work of the African American mathematician Ben-

jamin Banneker (1731–1806), very little activity in the United States could be called astronomy. By the end of the century, however, the United States was established as a major contributor to the field.

The work of astronomers naturally centered around telescopes and observatories, but at the beginning of the nineteenth century only a handful of telescopes and observatories existed in the United States. In 1825 President John Quincy Adams informed Congress that while Europe had more than one hundred observatories the United States had "not one." Despite this slight overstatement, Congress funded the organization that became the U.S. Naval Observatory (USNO), which soon developed into the preeminent authority in timekeeping and in the distribution of astronomical data required for accurate navigation and fundamental astronomy. Adams also supported the development of the Cincinnati Observatory in 1843 and the Harvard Observatory in 1844. By the end of the century the United States had at least thirty-five major observatories, both private and public.

The European tradition of amateur astronomy extended to the United States. Enthusiastic amateurs, rich and poor, bought or made telescopes and used them for noteworthy achievements. For example, in New York, Henry Draper (1837–1882) began making his own telescope mirrors around 1840, and Lewis M. Rutherford (1816–1892) set up an observatory in the rear of his garden in New York City in 1856.

On occasion, observatories were built to support civic pride. Gifts from wealthy Bostonians enabled the building of the Harvard Observatory after the appearance of a comet highlighted Boston's lack of a telescope. Pittsburgh businesspeople and amateur astronomers funded the Allegheny Observatory in 1858. Both of these observatories made a profit by accurately measuring the time and distributing that information via telegraph to railroads and other enterprises that depended on it to operate safely and efficiently.

During the nineteenth century more than thirty new observatories were affiliated with colleges and universities, and many vied to house the largest telescope and the most brilliant astronomers. Wealthy businessmen, whose goals were to immortalize their names, funded most observatories. In this respect James Lick (1796–1876) of California and Charles T. Yerkes (1837–1905) of Chicago established two of the most important observatories in the world late in the century, which opened in 1894 and 1897, respectively.

Telescope construction was of two basic types: refracting, which employs a glass lens at the forward end of the telescope, and reflecting, which employs a curved primary mirror at the rear end of the telescope. In either case larger diameter telescopes collect more light and give a brighter overall image. In 1800, due to the ease of its construction, the reflecting telescope was preferred in Europe, especially in England. No one had yet successfully built large refracting telescopes of adequate optical quality.

Alvan Clark (1804–1887), a self-taught New England lens maker, was unable to sell his early refracting lenses because the prevailing bias favored European lenses. Using his own lenses, Clark discovered a number of double stars, stars so close together in the sky that they appeared to the naked eye as a single star, and he communicated his findings to English astronomers, who were impressed enough to order his lenses. Clark's name spread throughout Europe, and he finally was recognized in the United States. In 1860, Clark founded the country's first telescope factory, in Cambridgeport, Massachusetts. Clark and his sons went on to make the finest refractors in the world, the largest of which, forty inches in diameter, belonged to the Yerkes Observatory. Almost every major American observatory subsequently purchased a Clark refractor. In 1879, for example, Clark installed his refractors at the University of Wisconsin's Washburn Observatory, as well as Van Vleck Observatory, at Wesleyan University in Middletown, Connecticut.

The heavy lenses in the giant refractors (the Clark forty-inch refractor primary lens contained two pieces of glass, whose combined weight totaled one thousand pounds) required enormous new mounts to aim these great telescopes. The American firm of Warner and Swasey met that challenge first and eventually dominated the development of mounts for large telescopes in the United States.

John William Draper (1811–1882), his son Henry Draper, William Cranch Bond (1789–1859), Rutherford, and Edward C. Pickering (1846–1919) were among those who adapted recent developments in photography to astronomy. Their accomplishments include the first telescopic photograph of any astronomical object, the Moon; the first photograph of a star, Vega; the first photograph of a double star, Alcor and Mizar; the first measurement of star positions on a photographic plate; and the first photograph of a nebula, the Great Orion Nebula. Their work, along with the labors of others, positioned the United States on a par with the leading European astronomers.

In the middle of the nineteenth century European astronomers discovered methods for analyzing the color of light from astronomical objects. The light was passed through a device such as a prism, which separated the white light into its spectrum of colors. In Munich in 1814 Joseph von Fraunhofer (1787–1826) discovered absorption lines in the spectrum of light from the sun, which led to the field of astrospectroscopy. American astrophotographers quickly developed the technique of photographing these stellar spectra, thus founding the field of astrospectrography. Given the intense light of the Sun and the very dim light of stars, they had many technical problems to overcome. In 1872 Henry Draper took the first photograph of the spectrum of a star, α Lyrae, and he spent most of the rest of his life improving methods of spectrography. Pickering perfected this work at Harvard Observatory and later compiled the *Draper Catalog* (first published in 1890), a spectrographic survey of stars in the northern hemisphere. The *Draper Catalog* became a primary resource for deductions on the nature of our galaxy and of the universe in the twentieth century.

During the nineteenth century observers discovered vast numbers of astronomical objects. As larger telescopes became available, more subtle observations were possible, but even with modest instruments alert astronomers achieved a great deal. In 1847, with her father's four-inch refractor, Maria Mitchell (1818–1889) launched her career as the first American woman astronomer by discovering a comet. Mitchell became the preeminent woman astronomer and the first woman member of the American Academy of Arts and Sciences.

Other important discoveries by Americans include Hyperion, the eighth satellite of Saturn, observed in

1848 by G. P. Bond (1825–1865); Deimos and Phobos, the two satellites of Mars, observed in 1877 by Asaph Hall (1829–1907), assisted by his wife Chloe Angeline Stickney (1830–1892); the time-varying spectra of certain stars, leading to the recognition of eclipsing binary stars in 1889 by A. C. Maury (1866–1952); and the fifth satellite of Jupiter, observed in 1892 by Edward Barnard (1857–1923).

Over the course of the nineteenth century astronomy experienced a transformation from discovery and cataloging to theoretical analysis. Astrophysics has its roots in spectrography, which opened the doors to understanding the chemical makeup of planets, stars, and nebulae. Combined with rapid advances in theoretical physics, this knowledge led to models of the life cycles of stars and eventually to cosmology. American astronomers, including Pickering, Rutherford, James Edward Keeler (1857–1900), and especially George Ellery Hale (1868–1938) led the emerging field of astrophysics.

Hale envisioned the observatory as a physics laboratory, and his leadership and strength of character changed the face of astronomy. He aspired to build the largest observatory in the world, and on three separate occasions he achieved his goal, each time building an observatory greater than before. In 1897 he constructed the Yerkes Observatory in Lake Geneva, Wisconsin. His twentieth-century projects, Mount Wilson Observatory and Palomar Mountain Observatory, brought the United States to a position of leadership in world astronomy.

See also **Museums,** *subentry on* **Science and Technology Museums; Photography.**

Bibliography

Asimov, Isaac. *Eyes on the Universe: A History of the Telescope.* Boston: Houghton Mifflin, 1975.

King, Henry C. *The History of the Telescope.* 1955. Reprint, New York: Dover, 1979.

Pannekoek, Anton. *A History of Astronomy.* 1961. Reprint, New York: Dover, 1989.

LOU COHEN

ASYLUMS   The idea of the asylum as a place of refuge for those deemed incapable of living in the community developed during the nineteenth century. Far from an isolated event, the establishment of this institutionally based framework for the care and control of those persons labeled as deviant and defective was tied to broader social and economic changes. In 1800 the community provided the focus of care for those undifferentiated individuals needing special attention. By 1900 institutional arrangements predominated, providing care in large custodial facilities designed specifically for individuals with discrete categories of difference. Opened in a blush of bourgeois optimism, the asylum alternative devolved into a warehousing system, whereby residents, usually called inmates to denote their similar status to penitentiary prisoners, were not cared for but controlled.

The Discovery of the Asylum

Nineteenth-century Americans developed institutional solutions to societal problems. These solutions were grounded in three interrelated social and economic phenomena that profoundly shaped American life from 1750 to 1850. First, the Enlightenment allowed Americans to view differences between individuals in a scientific rather than a theological or metaphysical framework. "Lunatics," for example, were no longer seen as random victims of God's wrath but as sufferers from organic disorders that could be pinpointed and potentially cured. Second, the market revolution fundamentally reoriented Americans, particularly those in the Northeast and Midwest, toward a capitalist market economy. This shift forced Americans into a changing conception of "the poor" from a small group at the bottom of society helped by local charity to a larger class that required separation into worthy and unworthy categories. The worthy poor could be improved by intervention, often at the state and not the local level. Frequently poverty and difference were conflated, as a person's worth began to be measured by his or her place in the capitalist economy. Finally, the Second Great Awakening of the 1820s and 1830s viewed benevolence as a high point of human existence. Middle-class notions of charity, often spurred by northern women, sparked an interest in the reformation of society. The idea of helping and protecting the infirm coexisted with notions of temperance and antislavery. These three trends—the Enlightenment, the market revolution, and the Second Great Awakening—produced a system for dealing with society's unfortunates that was full of contradictory impulses. The asylum was not a fully market-driven response to a burgeoning surplus population, a system of categorization based on scientific models, or a completely charitable impulse of Christian love. It ultimately failed to care for, cure, or control the varied populations hidden behind its walls.

The Asylum in Practice

The first institutions were small in scale and either local or private in character. Spurred by the forces mentioned above, Americans went on a building splurge from the 1810s to the 1870s that changed the way society dealt with the groups it labeled as "deviant, defective, and delinquent." States established large, congregate facilities, usually in rural areas, for discrete categories of individuals. The bucolic settings of these institutions were not random. The quiet parklike surroundings, away from the turmoil of growing urban areas, engendered tranquility and a therapeutic ambience. The increasing specialization of these asylums was similarly important. As cure was the expected outcome of asylum stays, it stood to reason that asylum directors, usually medical doctors, would accept only those individuals categorized with the infirmity they were trained to cure. Thus asylums increased not only in number but also in function. Facilities for the mentally ill, the blind, the feebleminded (or mentally retarded), and the deaf dotted the American landscape by the 1870s. This was particularly the case in the Northeast and Midwest, the two regions most affected by both the market revolution and the Second Great Awakening. The antebellum South, with its notions of a paternalistic, organic society, lagged behind in this endeavor. Southerners clung to the belief that families and local communities could, and should, handle these problems.

With the building of asylums came the establishment of professional organizations of asylum leaders, which both validated the asylum model and allowed for its continued growth. By the 1870s, the asylum, as demanded by Christian reformers such as Dorothea Dix and propounded by superintendents like Hervey Wilbur and Thomas Kirkbride, had become a beacon of hope as a major focus of the struggle to cure the ills of society and individuals.

The Enduring Asylum

By 1900 the asylum remained a major focus of reform, but the hope of its reformist forebears had been crushed. The quest for cure had been replaced by the desire to remove, often permanently, those deemed incapable of functioning "normally" within society. What went wrong? First, the asylum was never the wonderful panacea reformers envisioned. Governmental parsimony, inefficacious cure regimens, and administrative concerns for job security rather than patient interests plagued asylums from the beginning. These problems were exacerbated after the Civil War, as the reformist strand in American social and intellectual thought lost power. Asylums became afterthoughts, losers in the battle to industrialize America. A new, more scientific worldview also marginalized the concept of the curing asylum. Superintendents and professionals now viewed inmates as not only dangerous to themselves but also to future generations, as deviancy was thought to be inherit-

able. The type of inmate had also changed, reinforcing the trend toward control rather than cure. Increasingly, inmates were of immigrant origin and seen as blights on the landscape. In the South, newly opened public institutions were filled with ex-slaves, which tied in with notions of white superiority and the continued desire for control. In asylums for the deaf, oral language replaced manualism as leaders demanded a system of spoken English familiar to them. By breaking the bonds of benevolence from the asylum model, late-nineteenth-century professionals effectively set the stage for the twentieth-century institutional warehouse.

See also **Evangelicalism; Health and Disease; Hospitals; Market Revolution; Medicine; Mental Illness; Philosophy; Progress, Idea of; Psychology; Reform, Social; Religion; Revivalism; Sociology.**

Bibliography

Baynton, Douglas C. *Forbidden Signs: American Culture and the Campaign against Sign Language.* Chicago: University of Chicago Press, 1996.

Dain, Norman. *Disordered Minds: The First Century of Eastern State Hospital in Williamsburg, Va., 1766–1866.* Williamsburg, Va.: Colonial Williamsburg Foundation, 1971.

Deutsch, Albert. *The Mentally Ill in America: A History of Their Care and Treatment from Colonial Times.* Garden City, N.Y.: Doubleday, Doran and Company, 1937.

Dwyer, Ellen. *Homes for the Mad: Life inside Two Nineteenth-Century Asylums.* New Brunswick, N.J.: Rutgers University Press, 1987.

Gollaher, David. *Voice for the Mad: The Life of Dorothea Dix.* New York: Free Press, 1995.

Grob, Gerald N. *The Mad among Us: A History of the Care of America's Mentally Ill.* New York: Free Press, 1994.

———. *Mental Institutions in America: Social Policy to 1875.* New York: Free Press, 1972.

McCandless, Peter. *Moonlight, Magnolias, and Madness.* Chapel Hill: University of North Carolina Press, 1996.

Rothman, David J. *Conscience and Convenience: The Asylum and Its Alternatives in Progressive America.* Boston: Little, Brown, 1980.

———. *The Discovery of the Asylum: Social Order and Disorder in the New Republic.* Boston: Little, Brown, 1971.

Thielman, Samuel. "Southern Madness: The Shape of Mental Health Care in the Old South." In *Science and Medicine in the Old South,* edited by Ronald L. Numbers and Todd L. Savitt. Baton Rouge: Louisiana State University Press, 1989.

Tomes, Nancy. *The Art of Asylum-Keeping: Thomas Story Kirkbride and the Origins of American Psychiatry.* Philadelphia: University of Pennsylvania Press, 1994.

Trent, James W., Jr. *Inventing the Feeble-Mind: A History of Mental Retardation in the United States.* Berkeley: University of California Press, 1994.

Tyor, Peter L., and Leland V. Bell. *Caring for the Retarded in America: A History.* Westport, Conn.: Greenwood Press, 1984.

STEPHEN NOLL

B

BALLOONS Balloons, which first took flight just prior to the nineteenth century, generally consist of a large, airtight container holding lighter-than-air gas and have a suspended basket or gondola underneath. Military authorities quickly recognized the battlefield potential of balloons. The French used a tethered balloon for reconnaissance and observation against the Austrians during the Battle of Fleurus in 1794. During the American Civil War both sides attempted, with varying success, to use balloons for reconnaissance. Thaddeus Lowe, a scientist-showman from New England, convinced the federal army to employ three observation balloons and their supporting hydrogen gas generators during General George McClellan's ill-fated Peninsula campaign of 1862. In a subsequent demonstration of the possibilities offered by balloons, Union observers in balloons were given credit for spotting and reporting Robert E. Lee's opening movements of the Gettysburg campaign. Two later Southern efforts to employ reconnaissance balloons were thwarted by a lack of resources. Americans used balloons successfully during the Spanish-American War. By the end of the century, efforts to free balloons from the uncertainties of wind currents and weather were proceeding rapidly. When a suitable propulsion system was married to a more aerodynamic shape, spherical balloons gradually gave way to navigable airships, at least for military purposes.

For much of the nineteenth century, balloons found wider acceptance in Europe than in the United States. In the half-century after the introduction of balloons, more than eight hundred flights were made in England alone. Sport and recreation ballooning can be thought of as originating at this time. Authors like Edgar Allan Poe and Jules Verne popularized balloon exploits on both sides of the Atlantic. Poe described a three-day, transoceanic journey, for example. His story "The Balloon-Hoax" inspired Verne, who became something of a balloon fanatic. In turn, Verne's widely read stories helped inspire Gaspard-Félix Tournachon, a Parisian who eventually built a large, luxurious passenger balloon. This 210,000-cubic-foot giant with double-decker gondola, the largest balloon of its time, flew across Paris in 1853. Verne's fictionalized account of an intercontinental balloon flight, *Five Weeks in a Balloon* (1863), captured the public's imagination.

See also **Military Technology** *and illustration overleaf.*

Bibliography

Bailey, Ronald H. *Forward to Richmond: McClellan's Peninsular Campaign.* Volume 5 of *The Civil War,* edited by Thomas H. Flaherty. Alexandria, Va.: Time-Life, 1983–1987.

King, Lyndel. *The Balloon: A Bicentennial Exhibition.* Minneapolis: University Art Museum, University of Minnesota, 1983.

Kirschner, Edwin J. *Aerospace Balloons from Montgolfier to Space.* Fallbrook, Calif.: Aero, 1985.

MARK K. WELLS

BALTIMORE Baltimore was "North America's first boom town," in the words of one historian

Balloon at the World Columbian Exposition. A hot-air balloon heads toward the ferris wheel (*right*) at the World Columbian Exposition in Chicago, 1893. LIBRARY OF CONGRESS: PRINTS AND PHOTOGRAPHS DIVISION

(Larsen, *The Urban South*). Founded in 1729, late in the colonial period (and still an inconsequential hamlet of a handful of log houses in 1750), Baltimore received city status by state law in 1796, and by 1800 the city boasted 26,514 residents. The grain trade from upper and western Maryland fueled this growth, and the city quickly supplanted nearby Annapolis as the region's center of export, largely to Europe and the Caribbean. Its burgeoning status as a port city soon attracted a host of satellite industries, led by flour milling and shipbuilding. The design of the "Baltimore Clipper," a topsail schooner developed in the Chesapeake Bay area in the 1790s, quickly made the city one of the nation's shipbuilding giants. Baltimore's seaport status attracted an ethnically and racially diverse populace. Germans, French Acadians, and Jewish residents established enclaves, and the 1791 slave revolt on Saint Domingue brought French Caribbean émigrés, both black and white, attracted by Maryland's Catholic tradition.

At the turn of the nineteenth century Baltimore's traditional white leaders—merchants, professionals, and gentlemen—found their status challenged in the ensuing decades by a new elite composed of manufacturers and tradesmen (or mechanics). As the mercantile patriarchy gave way to a new industrial order in the years surrounding the panic of 1819, the city's political landscape saw great turmoil. The once Federalist, elitist hegemony of the city's leadership now fragmented as Republicans, espousing middle-class, democratic rhetoric, came to dominate the city's government.

Baltimore's economy suffered greatly during the War of 1812, as the British fleet blockaded the Chesapeake Bay and thus sealed off the city's export trade. However, it saw little of war until September 1814, when defenders at Fort McHenry repulsed a British attack. The failed invasion was immortalized in a poem written by a young Baltimore lawyer, Francis Scott Key, which achieved lasting fame as "The Star Spangled Banner," the national anthem since 1931.

Baltimore also became the center of African American life and culture for the upper Chesapeake. As the region moved its economic base from tobacco to grains, freed slaves made their way to Baltimore to begin new lives, while slavery in the city itself grew haltingly until 1810 and then declined steadily. The city's black population became overwhelmingly free. By 1860, with 25,680 free blacks and 2,218 slaves, Baltimore had the largest black population of any city in the United States. Unlike other urban black communities in the slave states, Baltimore's African Americans were largely poor and dark-skinned (without a mulatto elite) and largely unaffected by class and intraracial divisions.

In the 1840s and 1850s, a surge of immigration transformed Baltimore's demographics. By 1860 the city's 212,418 residents included 52,497 foreign-born, largely German and Irish. This immigration caused great labor unrest in Baltimore, giving strong enough impetus to the nativist Know-Nothing Party to carry the 1854 municipal elections. Labor competition in the 1850s only heightened the xenophobia as well as racist fears of the city's large free-black population, resulting in widespread violence and disorder that earned Baltimore a national reputation as a city of "plug-uglies," urban gangs consisting largely of nativists. The term has several disputed meanings, including the plug hats worn by urban working-class men, the member of a fire company that opened and closed the fire plug as water was needed to quell a fire, and a plug of tobacco. The fractured atmosphere spilled over into the secession crisis. A border city in a border state, Baltimore was the scene of the first true conflict of the Civil War as local residents attacked Federal troops passing through the city en route to Washington on 19 April 1861. The occupation of Federal troops bitterly divided the city throughout the war.

Baltimore's industrial preeminence in Maryland increased after the Civil War, so much so that by 1890 the city produced 82 percent of the state's total value of manufactured goods and products. Iron, copper, textile, and petroleum industries boomed. The city's physical size increased dramatically, sprawling into the surrounding county, and by the end of the century Baltimore's population had grown to 508,957, accounting for more than a third of the residents of the entire state. Although other former slave states passed racial proscriptions after the Civil War, Baltimore's influence temporarily forestalled such enactments in Maryland. Evinced in a wide array of social organizations, churches, libraries, hospitals, colleges and universities, and newspapers, the city's "middle temperament"—democratic and diverse—served as a bellwether for the entire upper Chesapeake Bay region for the duration of the nineteenth century.

See also **African Americans,** *subentry on* **Free Blacks before the Civil War; Cities and Urbanization; Maryland.**

Bibliography

Browne, Gary L. *Baltimore in the Nation, 1789–1861.* Chapel Hill: University of North Carolina Press, 1980.

Larsen, Lawrence H. *The Urban South: A History.* Lexington: University Press of Kentucky, 1989.

Olson, Sherry H. *Baltimore: The Building of an American City.* Baltimore: Johns Hopkins University Press, 1980.

Phillips, Christopher. *Freedom's Port: The African American Community of Baltimore, 1790–1860.* Urbana: University of Illinois Press, 1997.

CHRISTOPHER PHILLIPS

BANDS AND BAND CONCERTS   The nineteenth century witnessed the start, growth, and golden age of the American professional band. A broad spectrum of American society sought concerts for entertainment, rather than aesthetic enlightment. The audience varied according to venue, which ranged from city stages to upscale resorts.

The nation's oldest music group, the U.S. Marine Band, was founded in 1798 by an act of Congress signed by President John Adams. The Salem (Massachusetts) Brigade Band, consisting of five clarinets, two bassoons, one trumpet, and a bass drum, was established in 1806. Other early nineteenth-century bands included the Militia Band of Bethlehem (c. 1800?), Pennsylvania, and the Eleventh Regiment Band of New York, established in 1810. The instrumentation of these early bands consisted of assorted woodwind and brass instruments. Largely civilian groups associated with local militia groups, they presented concerts and participated in parades, military drills, and civic and patriotic ceremonies.

English bands were models for developing American bands, and pieces published by Boosey and Company and later by William Chappell for the British market entered the repertoires of American bands. Music by American composers, such as Alexander Reinagle's "Jefferson's March" (1805) and Samuel Holyoke's "Massachusetts March" (1807), began to appear in print and were performed by bands of oboes, clarinets, bassoons, and horns. Brass bands were very active in New England from the 1830s to the beginning of the Civil War. A leading example was the Providence Brass Band, organized in 1837 and in 1853 renamed and incorporated as the American Band of Providence, Rhode Island. This group gained fame when David Wallis Reeves, one of America's great bandmasters, became its leader in 1866.

The first American community band, the Allentown (Pennsylvania) Band, formed in 1828, and the nation's first completely professional band, the Independent Band of New York, organized in 1825. Among the latter's members were Thomas Dodworth and his sons Allen Dodworth and Harvey Dodworth, all conductors, composers, music publishers, and instrument dealers who introduced and implemented new concepts in instrumentation and performance. Eventually Thomas Dodworth changed the band's instrumentation to all brass, and in 1836 it became Dodworth's Band, which was the finest band in New York until Patrick Gilmore arrived on the scene in the 1870s. Other bands, including the Salem and Boston Brigade Bands, also changed to all brass instrumentation in the 1830s. Their repertoires consisted of arrangements of overtures by such composers as Esprit Auber, Luigi Carlo Cherubini, Antonio Rossini, and Giuseppe Verdi along with polkas, gallops, quadrilles, waltzes, and popular music.

In 1853 the talented French musician and supreme promoter-showman Antoine Jullien toured the United States, presenting dazzling and spectacular concerts. He became extremely popular, and his extravagant productions fired the imagination of Gilmore, a newly arrived Irish immigrant musician and cornet virtuoso who eventually became the father of the modern American concert band. Shortly after arriving in the United States, Gilmore accepted the position of leader of the Boston Brigade Band, which he quickly transformed into a professional ensemble. Renamed Gilmore's Band, it became America's first great concert wind band under his leadership. During the Civil War the Gilmore Band enlisted as a unit and served one year with the Twenty-fourth Massachusetts Volunteer Regiment. Returning to Boston, the band performed concerts as part of the home front effort to bolster morale for the remainder of the war.

Gilmore, the P. T. Barnum of American bandmasters, organized three gigantic musical events between 1864 and 1872. The first, in New Orleans, Louisiana, in honor of the inauguration of Governor Michael Hahn, featured a band of 500 musicians and a chorus of 5,000 schoolchildren in concert. The second, the National Peace Jubilee, was held in Boston in 1869. This time Gilmore doubled the number of his performers, creating a band of 1,000 and a chorus of 10,000 voices. The culmination of his series of extravaganzas was the 1872 World Peace Jubilee also held in Boston, featuring an orchestra of 1,000, a band of 2,000, and a chorus of 20,000. Gilmore invited several European bands to perform at the World Peace Jubilee, among them the Band of the Grenadier Guards, the Kaiser Franz Grenadier Regiment Band, the National Band of Dublin, and the Garde Républicaine Band. These visiting bands stimulated American bands to improve their performance standards, instrumentation, and repertoires.

In 1873 Gilmore became leader of the Twenty-second Regiment Band of New York, which he also

John Philip Sousa. The "March King" published more than 130 compositions, including "The Stars and Stripes Forever" (1896), the official march of the United States. LIBRARY OF CONGRESS

renamed Gilmore's Band. Making this the most celebrated one in the United States, Gilmore expanded the band's repertoire to include transcriptions of orchestra music by such composers as Beethoven, Mozart, and Wagner. An innovator in instrumentation, he shifted the emphasis from brass to the woodwinds, especially clarinets. In 1878 Gilmore's Band consisted of thirty-five woodwinds and twenty-seven brass. Gilmore was a prolific composer. He reputedly wrote "When Johnny Comes Marching Home" (1863), which was published under the pseudonym Louis Lambert. Gilmore died in St. Louis in 1892 while on tour with his band.

John Philip Sousa, the "March King," is generally considered the greatest bandmaster, and the Sousa years (1880–1925) were the golden age of the American professional band. During this time bands and band music became the nation's most popular form of entertainment. Sousa was appointed leader of the Marine Band in 1880, and by the time he resigned in 1892 to form his own professional band, he had molded it into one of the world's greatest bands. Sousa hired some of the finest white instrumentalists in the United States to play in his professional band. Believing his band should entertain and give the public what it wanted, he created programs that followed

Gilmore's format, inserting his own popular marches. The Sousa Band, the most popular and successful of the many professional bands touring the country and the world, performed in parks, resort areas, and concert venues.

Other important bandmasters of the era were Thomas Preston Brooke, Patrick Conway, Giuseppe Creatore, Mace Gay, Frederick Innes, Bohumir Kryl, Alessandro Liberati, Jean Missud, Arthur Pryor, and D. W. Reeves, whom Sousa called "the Father of Band Music in America." The American college and university band was also born in the nineteenth century. Notre Dame (1845), Luther College (1878), the University of California at Berkeley (1880), and Florida Agricultural and Mechanical College (1892) were among the first institutions to organize bands.

See also **Music,** *subentry on* **Folk Songs, Parlor Music, and Popular Music; Recreation.**

Bibliography

Bierley, Paul E. *John Philip Sousa, American Phenomenon.* Columbus, Ohio: Integrity Press, 1973.
———. *The Works of John Philip Sousa.* Columbus, Ohio: Integrity Press, 1984.
Fennell, Frederick. *Time and the Winds.* Kenosha, Wis.: G. Leblanc, 1954.
Goldman, Richard Franko. *The Concert Band.* New York: Rinehart and Company, 1946.
———. *The Wind Band, Its Literature and Technique.* Boston: Allyn and Bacon, 1961.
Rehrig, William H. *The Heritage Encyclopedia of Band Music.* Westerville, Ohio: Integrity Press, 1991–1996.
Schwartz, Harry W. *Bands of America.* Garden City, N.Y.: Doubleday, 1957.
Sousa, John Philip. *Marching Along.* Boston: Hale, Cushman and Flint, 1928.
———. *Through the Year with Sousa.* New York: Thomas Y. Crowell and Company, 1910.

FRANK L. BATTISTI

BANKING AND FINANCE

[This entry includes two subentries:
The Banking Industry
The Politics of Banking.]

THE BANKING INDUSTRY

Banks in the Early Republic

Banking rose from a relatively minor element of the American economy in 1800 to a significant industry by 1900. Early banks relied on states to provide them with a charter, which not only licensed them to issue banknotes but also, in some cases, conferred monopoly powers and specified obligations owed to the state government. Most banks started when a group of investors, usually local merchants or manufacturers, sought large pools of capital that were otherwise unavailable. Although the central reason for starting a bank was to make loans to the primary founders and stockholders, these officials were not seen as engaged in "insider lending," and the practice was viewed as completely legal. A bank lessened the risk to members of the community who invested in local businesses by offering interest on their deposits or return on their capital stock. The founders of a bank put up specie (silver and gold coin), which formed the capital base of the bank. Using that capital base, and subsequent deposits that came in from people wishing to save their money, the bank made loans and issued banknotes. Banknotes, while technically backed by the specie reserves of the chartered bank, circulated largely on the basis of the public's willingness to accept them. If a bank failed to redeem its notes in specie on demand, it gained a bad reputation and usually also violated its state charter, making it subject to closure by the legislature.

Banks traditionally kept less than 20 percent reserves of specie against their banknotes, the issuing of which constituted the bulk of their business. Often, however, reserves fell to well under 10 percent. The reserve ratio itself did not accurately measure or predict the health or solvency of a particular bank: some high-reserve-ratio banks were forced to keep large reserves on hand to reassure the public, while some banks with extremely low reserve ratios reflected the high level of public trust in them. A better indicator of the health of a bank was the value of its notes, which merchants and other banks could discount, or sell for less than the par (face) value of the note. A highly discounted note indicated that the bank issuing it was in trouble; nondiscounted notes were as "good as gold." During times of economic crisis, however, virtually no banks could redeem all their notes in specie, and they then suspended specie payments (that is, temporarily refused to pay out specie for their own banknotes). Suspension technically violated most banks' charters, but in depressions few legislators enforced such provisions. Lawmakers had to choose between allowing banks to violate their charters and eliminating all banks in a state, which some states did (for example, Arkansas and Wisconsin after the panic of 1837).

Beneath the system of note-issuing chartered banks lay a system of "private banks"—a confusing term given that chartered banks were themselves mostly privately owned. (Exceptions to private ownership existed, however, in the form of "state banks" owned and managed by state governments. Tennessee, Alabama, Ohio, North Carolina, and other states had such institutions.) The "private banks" generally took deposits and made loans but did not issue banknotes, although some railroad companies and "insurance companies" printed "money" in the form of notes. The Wisconsin Marine and Fire Insurance Company (1839–1854), for example, was specifically chartered as a "nonbank" insurance company; nevertheless, the company insisted that its notes (which it carefully avoided calling banknotes) be fully redeemable in gold. This, in turn, ensured that the company's money circulated widely, at one point as far away as Atlanta. Such long-distance exchanges are particularly impressive, considering that money of this kind had to be bundled up and shipped back to its place of origination for payment, a process that carried transportation charges.

The Antebellum Period

A third element of the banking industry, with state-chartered and private banks, was the first Bank of the United States (BUS), chartered by Congress in 1791 and expiring in 1811, and its successor, the second BUS (1816–1836). The first BUS was conceived by Secretary of the Treasury Alexander Hamilton as an institution that could assure the U.S. government of emergency or necessary credit. It had a large capitalization for the day ($10 million), and had branches in several states, all of which emitted uniform BUS notes. The second BUS, like the first, could print notes that were emitted from its branches across the nation; it had branches in many states (a practice called interstate branch banking), the only bank with such a privilege; and it had a capitalization that dwarfed that of any state-chartered bank. Private investors owned four-fifths of the stock of both banks of the United States, and much of that stock went into the hands of foreign investors. This situation opened the institutions to charges that they allowed foreign manipulation of the U.S. economy, claims that contributed to the willingness of Congress to allow the first BUS to expire without rechartering it.

In addition to the first and second Banks of the United States, by 1834 more than five hundred state-chartered banks (including several dozen branches), as well as perhaps thousands of private banks, conducted operations. Underneath that layer was one of unchartered private lenders in agricultural areas, known as "factors." Collectively the state-chartered banks, private bankers, and the BUS formed the antebellum American banking system.

In all cases banknotes emitted by a bank circulated almost entirely on trust, backed up by the record of the institution in redeeming its notes in gold and silver. Several banknote reporters, such as *Thompson's Bank Note and Commercial Reporter* and *Hunt's Merchants' Magazine*, took into account the cost of transportation in redeeming notes from distant regions, and every exchange agent or banker kept a copy of *Thompson's* or another banknote reporter handy. Such reporters also measured the depreciation of notes that had less than complete trust. A note with a discount of 0.5 percent could circulate, although at a disadvantage against notes emitted by other banks without a discount, but a discount of more than a few percentage points would signal the impending difficulty of the notes to circulate.

Neither the first nor second BUS competed directly with the state banks often or effectively. Their contribution to the money supply remained relatively small, and the national banknotes served more as a measuring stick for local currencies than as a regulatory device. After Congress chose not to recharter the first BUS in 1811, state-chartered banks began inflating their note issue, partly because of wartime pressures and partly because of the fact that even the modest restraining influence of the BUS no longer existed. Congress responded by chartering the second BUS in 1816. In 1818, under the president William Jones, the BUS extended a large amount of western loans, for which Jones was criticized. His replacement, Langdon Cheves of South Carolina, made an effort to tighten credit, which some historians saw as the cause of the panic of 1819.

Hostility to the bank over Cheves's actions led to attempts by states to exercise some control over the BUS by levying taxes on it as a business corporation. Further, critics argued that the charter of the BUS itself was unconstitutional, since there is no mention of a national bank in the U.S. Constitution. The state of Maryland's attempt to tax the BUS resulted in *McCulloch v. Maryland* (1819), in which the Supreme Court held that the charter of the BUS by the federal government was constitutional under the "necessary and proper" clause and that as a duly appointed arm of the federal government the BUS was immune from state taxation.

Although the second BUS gained a stellar reputation and won the approval of most state-chartered banks, the president of the BUS, Nicholas Biddle, antagonized the president of the United States, Andrew Jackson, by attempting to push through a recharter bill in 1832. There is little evidence—contrary to popular belief—that Jackson was opposed to either banks in general or a national bank in particular. Rather, he interpreted the recharter effort as a political attack. He vetoed the recharter bill and then, in 1833, pulled the deposits out of the BUS, effectively killing it. Jackson then placed the deposits

First Bank of the United States, Philadelphia. Chartered in 1791, the bank was housed in temporary quarters until a permanent structure, believed to be the first neoclassical building in the United States, was completed in 1795. Engraving by William Birch and Son, 1800. LIBRARY OF CONGRESS

into Democratic-controlled institutions, quickly labeled "pet banks."

The "bank war," as it was called, formed the basis for party divisions during much of the antebellum period; Whigs and, later, Republicans supported a national bank and Democrats opposed such an institution. Democrats had no commonly held view of banks: some favored a "hard money" standard consisting only of gold and silver, while others wanted state-controlled banks that could, as monopolies, issue notes. Most, however, wanted some sort of specie-backed currency. Their diverse positions made it all the more puzzling for their followers after the Civil War, when many Democrats called for circulation of "greenbacks"—paper money printed by the government to finance the war effort but not specifically backed by specie.

From 1836, when the BUS charter expired, until 1863 the United States operated entirely on the financial services provided by the state banks and the private banks. As the number of charter requests expanded, nearly doubling by 1850, the pressure on the chartering process increased to the point that many states passed general incorporation laws for banks, called "free banking laws." Under these laws a bank

had only to place a deposit of bonds with the secretary of state as a condition to open for business. The bonds represented security against default on its notes. Some states drafted their free banking laws poorly, specifically in regard to the wording of the value of the bonds, which had a par value that could differ dramatically from the market value (the value on the open market). Poorly designed laws encouraged some bankers to engage in unscrupulous activities, such as printing and redeeming notes at obscure branch locations ("where a wildcat wouldn't go"), or using the decline in market value of a bond from its par value to skip town with the deposits and forfeit the bonds. But where states crafted their laws to reflect market valuation of the bonds, the free banks proved quite stable. Free banking laws also fused with other general incorporation laws to end the close connection between a charter and a grant of monopoly power.

The Civil War and Afterward

Although the banking system remained solvent and stable until the Civil War, it was not capable of providing the credit needed to finance the Union military effort. The secretary of the Treasury, Salmon P. Chase, conceived of a new system of national banks to finance the war: the national banks would obtain charters by placing U.S. government bonds on deposit with the comptroller of the currency. Thus the system would raise revenue with each new bank chartered. National banks had tougher restrictions than the state-chartered banks—they could not have branches or hold real estate—but they had a substantial advantage in that the National Bank and Currency Acts of 1863–1864 placed a 10 percent tax on state banknotes. Virtually overnight the private notes disappeared and the national banknotes became the national currency. By 1870, with the destruction of the Southern banking system, national banks outnumbered state banks by a ratio of almost five to one. The national banking system was biased against the South in that few Southerners and virtually no freedmen could obtain charters. Quickly, however, the state governments recognized that they had a competitive advantage in issuing charters, and by 1890 state banks outnumbered national banks.

While the Civil War produced a new national banking system, it utterly destroyed the state banking systems in the Southern states, all of which had committed themselves (willingly or by force) to supporting the Confederacy. At the outbreak of the war, the Confederacy had confiscated the banks' specie for wartime uses; and subsequently the banks had extended loans to the Confederate government through bond purchases. When those Confederate bonds collapsed, the Southern banks lost much of their capitalization. The remainder of their capitalization disappeared with the Emancipation Proclamation, which overnight turned slaves, who had served as "property" collateral for loans to plantations, into people who had no property value. With millions of dollars in assets vanishing from Southern state balance sheets, the banks simply folded. The collapse of the Southern banking system removed some of the most successful branch banking examples then in existence and was made even worse by the passage of the National Bank and Currency Acts of 1863–1864, which biased the system in favor of unit banks in the national system. Over time the unit-bank bias—or, more properly, the inability of branching systems to penetrate many unit-bank states—contributed to the instability of the entire national system.

With the issue of banknotes confined to the national banks, many areas of the nation, particularly the South and West, suffered a shortage of money. More significant, though, was the fact that the national banking system could not expand or contract the money supply rapidly enough to offset upheavals in the economy, as in 1873, 1893, and 1907. Bankers and the public clamored for more elasticity in the money supply, which the national banks seemed incapable of providing. One reason currency supply appeared to be falling behind demand was that banks had increasingly begun to deal in demand deposits, later known as checks. With more of the financial transactions of the nation handled by checks, the pressure for an expanding money supply diminished slightly. National banknotes, which had risen from $276 million in 1866 to $352 million in 1882, reached a plateau, declined in the general deflation of the late 1800s, and did not again climb to their 1882 levels until after 1900. Nevertheless, the national banks could have issued still more notes; their issues never constituted more than 30 percent of the amount they were permitted between 1875 and 1900. Per capita currency in 1900 had fallen to 22 percent of the 1870 average.

The shortage of currency was blamed for falling price levels during the 1870s and 1880s, although subsequent research attributes the deflation to worldwide forces, and not to American banking policy in particular. Nevertheless, the solutions tended to be directed at either the banking system or the money supply, including the attempts to "monetize" silver (make silver coins official U.S. money) in the 1870s. Congress refused to monetize silver—in an act termed the "Crime of '73"—and quite possibly may have caused the panic of 1893; at the same time it sparked a new political movement by the Populists. Some in the Populist party urged the emission of greenbacks.

At the state level banking moved from a system in which the security and solvency of the bank relied on the individual owner and public perception of the bank to one in which professional, permanent government regulators examined and supervised the system. Prior to 1870 banks were founded by wealthy (usually) merchants, transport agents, or gold dealers who established themselves in business, amassed a personal fortune, and built an ostentatious physical institution that represented tangible capital. Those "symbols of safety" hinged extensively on the reputations of the individual and of the bank; but after about 1870 the appearance of state-level regulators began a shift away from industry-directed solvency to government-supervised stability. This consisted of, at first, "sunshine laws" requiring banks to make public their statements of conditions and open their books to government examiners. By 1900, however, the assumption changed from the view that an educated public would protect itself to one that required state governments—and, eventually, the federal government—to regulate banks in the "interest" of the public.

Professionalization and Banking Associations

The shift toward government regulation coincided with a broader professionalization of banking in which, as in other areas of American industry, the sector started to employ and promote professional managers. Traditionally the bank owner had hired a cashier, who took care of the books and supervised all but the most important loans. Even so, as late as 1900 all but the largest banks, such as National City Bank of New York, relied on the owner to play a role in the daily affairs of the institution.

Once the shift toward government regulation became apparent to bankers, they started to form associations to control and shape the inevitable legislation. The American Bankers Association, founded in 1875, provided a national body for uniting and presenting the positions of bankers. Bankers associations actively participated in the crafting of most bank regulation at the state level, and, more important, in the long-term drive for "bank reform" that began in earnest after the panic of 1893. Although J. P. Morgan, the preeminent banker of the day, formed a syndicate that successfully rescued the system during that crisis, bankers searched for changes that would prevent another depression. New York had developed a clearinghouse association that proved exceptionally effective at transmitting information—the key to preventing runs—and at "clearing" obligations among member banks. Founded in 1853, the New York Clearinghouse Association had many of the characteristics of a central bank, monitoring its members' soundness and liquidity and acting as a lender of last resort in times of emergency. The clearinghouse concept was introduced at several monetary conferences, beginning with the American Bankers Association conference at Baltimore in 1894, where it was agreed that the desired system would ensure stability, elasticity, and a lender of last resort.

Nevertheless, the most significant reform that could have improved the banking system—nationwide branch banking—could not penetrate the political lobby at the state level and was resisted by the unit bankers, who feared that branch systems would drive the unit banks out of business. Many states either prohibited branch banking in their constitutions or defeated attempts to introduce it at the legislative level. The bankers helped shape the legislation designed by a monetary committee headed by Senator Nelson W. Aldrich of Rhode Island, which eventually found its way into the plan advanced by Representative Carter Glass of Virginia, which in turn became the Federal Reserve System.

By 1900 the United States had 3,731 national banks and 8,696 state banks, with combined assets

J. P. Morgan. A towering figure in nineteenth-century finance, Morgan also supported numerous philanthropic ventures. LIBRARY OF CONGRESS

of over $800 billion. In addition to the commercial banks, individuals such as J. P. Morgan had led the way in separating banks that provided large-scale investment (investment banks) from firms that handled daily or short-term commercial paper. Investment banks tended to restructure companies that they loaned to or, in the worst cases, took over. They generally put into place a management system remarkably similar to the banks' own, and thus banks contributed to the ongoing professionalization of American industry. The investment banks were successful enough that some larger commercial banks began to form, or affiliate with, securities companies, but before 1900 the two types of banks remained separate in function and ownership and were distinct in the mind of the public. Thus, in the areas of demand deposits, investment banking, and commercial banking, the financial services sector played a critical role in the development and expansion of American industry—at times reflecting broader changes but just as often driving the transformation.

See also **Corporations and Big Business; Monetary Policy; Panics and Depressions.**

Bibliography

Doti, Lynne Pierson, and Larry Schweikart. *Banking in the American West: From the Gold Rush to Deregulation.* Norman: University of Oklahoma Press, 1991.

Friedman, Milton, and Anna J. Schwartz. *A Monetary History of the United States, 1867–1960.* Princeton, N.J.: Princeton University Press, 1963.

Hammond, Bray. *Banks and Politics in America, from the Revolution to the Civil War.* Rev. ed. Princeton, N.J.: Princeton University Press, 1985.

Klebaner, Benjamin J. *American Commercial Banking: A History.* Boston: Twayne, 1990.

Knox, John Jay. *A History of Banking in the United States.* Edited by Bradford Rhodes and Elmer H. Youngman. New York: B. Rhodes, 1903.

Redlich Fritz. *The Molding of American Banking: Men and Ideas.* 2 vols. New York: Johnson Reprint, 1968.

Rockoff, Hugh. *The Free Banking Era: A Reexamination.* New York: Arno, 1975.

Schweikart, Larry. *Banking in the American South from the Age of Jackson to Reconstruction.* Baton Rouge: Louisiana State University Press, 1987.

———. "U.S. Commercial Banking: A Historiographical Survey." *Business History Review* 65 (autumn 1991): 606–661.

Schweikart, Larry, ed. *Banking and Finance to 1913.* New York: Facts on File, 1990.

Timberlake, Richard H., Jr. *Origins of Central Banking in the United States.* Cambridge, Mass.: Harvard University Press, 1978.

Van Fenstermaker, J. *The Development of American Commercial Banking: 1782–1837.* Kent, Ohio: Kent State University Bureau of Economic and Business Research, 1965.

LARRY SCHWEIKART

THE POLITICS OF BANKING

Banking has been a political issue in the United States since the Continental Congress appointed Robert Morris to stabilize the government's finances. After the establishment in 1781 of the Articles of Confederation, Morris suggested creating a bank that would serve as a "national bank" (the Bank of North America, chartered 31 December 1781), to provide loans to the national government and provide a uniform money supply. The first secretary of the Treasury, Alexander Hamilton, understood the necessity of securing the new nation's credit, and to that end he recommended creation of a national bank, eventually approved, called the Bank of the United States. Founded on 25 February 1791, the Bank of the United States had as its chief mission the extension of loans to the government.

At the state and local level, banks intertwined with politics in a different way: state governments controlled the charter process by which an individual could form a bank, and states imposed a variety of restrictions on banking institutions, ranging from the life of the charter to penalties for failing to redeem their bank notes in gold or silver (called specie). Often, states sought to use banking institutions for purely political purposes, such as with the creation of state banks in Alabama, Arkansas, and Tennessee. Members of state legislatures expected and received regular loans from such banks, fanning the envy of other citizens (often, members of the political party out of power) and disgust about banking itself. The politicization of banking in several states (Arkansas and Wisconsin, for example) led to a reaction that ultimately prohibited banks entirely in those states. Other states, especially after reviewing the effects of the panic of 1837, prohibited banks in their constitutions. Such prohibitions only drove consumers to neighboring states' financial institutions.

Charters also often included monopoly rights, as was the case with the first and second Bank of the United States (1791–1811 and 1816–1836, respectively), which had unprecedented powers, including the privilege of establishing branches in several states ("interstate branch banking"). In addition, these national banks held the deposits of the United States. Although most historians agree that the destruction of the second Bank of the United States by President Andrew Jackson resulted from a political struggle with the probank forces, rather than from genuinely held beliefs on Jackson's part or from real abuses on the part of the Bank of the United States, he nevertheless succeeded in removing the federal deposits in 1833, effectively killing the bank.

From 1833 to 1863, the U.S. banking system operated without a national bank and without much debate over banking issues, despite somewhat regular invocations of the issue by the Whig Party. The economy operated well, and the state banks appeared more than capable of supplying necessary currency and loans, especially after the appearance in the 1840s of "free banks," which needed no charter, but put bonds on deposit with the secretary of state as security against default. Northern banks suffered during the panic of 1857, but there were no failures among southern banks, where intrastate branch banking was prevalent.

The onset of the Civil War brought substantial changes to the state-oriented system that had worked well for twenty years. Abraham Lincoln's secretary of the Treasury, Salmon P. Chase, a Democrat, looking primarily for a way to generate revenue to sustain the war effort, developed a concept of allowing Congress to charter a new series of national banks (completely unrelated to the original first and second Bank of the United States) that would purchase government bonds as their security. Thus, the federal government would have a broad and renewable market for its securities. To encourage entrepreneurs to seek national charters, the government added several inducements, including the right to issue national bank notes, which quickly took on monopoly status when the notes of private banks and state banks were driven out of the market through imposition of a 10 percent federal tax. There was little opposition to the National Bank and Currency Acts (1863–1864), largely because the Southern states had already left the Union and the Democratic legislators most likely to object to the acts muted their criticism due to the need to finance the war. Nevertheless, the postwar expansion of national banks, after a brief upward surge, started to decline relative to the chartering of state banks. The federal charters contained several disincentives, including prohibitions against branch banking and against holding real estate.

States, meanwhile, had gradually moved to regulate banks anew. New state regulation generally took the form of the creation of bank boards or bank commissions that examined and inspected banks on a regular basis. (That marked a change from the self-regulation of the bankers, who had used "symbols of safety," such as the bank building and the personal wealth of the banker, as the chief means of convincing the public that the bank was solvent.) To shape new bank regulation, bankers organized into bank associations that engaged in lobbying at state capitals. By the time the Federal Reserve System was created in 1913, the state banks had become far more numerous than the national banks, ultimately forcing the federal government to change its branch banking laws to attract large state systems with numerous branches.

Bibliography

Doti, Lynne Pierson, and Larry Schweikart. *Banking in the American West from the Gold Rush to Deregulation*. Norman: University of Oklahoma Press, 1991.

Hammond, Bray. *Banks and Politics in America from the Revolution to the Civil War*. Princeton, N.J.: Princeton University Press, 1957.

Redlich, Fritz. *The Molding of American Banking: Men and Ideas*. 2 vols. 1947. Reprint, New York: Johnson Reprint, 1968.

Sharp, James R. *The Jacksonians vs. the Banks: Politics in the States after the Panic of 1837*. New York: Columbia University Press, 1970.

White, Eugene. *The Regulation and Reform of the American Banking System, 1900–1929*. Princeton, N.J.: Princeton University Press, 1983.

LARRY SCHWEIKART

BARBARY WAR   The Barbary War was actually a series of maritime engagements fought from 1801 to 1805 and in 1815 between the United States and Algiers, Morocco, Tripoli, and Tunis. These Mediterranean states had prospered through piracy since the sixteenth century. European countries and, after the American Revolution, the United States paid tributes to protect their ships from depredations by the pirates of the Barbary States.

The Tripolitan War (1801–1805)

Early in 1801 the pasha of Tripoli determined that the treaty of 1796 with the United States was no longer workable and demanded an immediate payment of $225,000 plus another $25,000 annually. When the United States refused to pay, the pasha in retaliation declared war on 14 May 1801. President Thomas Jefferson sent a squadron under the command of Commodore Richard Dale to the Mediterranean. Dale's blockade persuaded Algiers and Tunis to abandon their plans for a war alliance with Tripoli and to renew their treaties with the United States. But the issues were far from resolved. A subsequent squadron under Commodore Richard V. Morris sent to bring Tripoli to terms failed to accomplish its mission conclusively.

Commodore Edward Preble, commanding a squadron that included the *Constitution*, which was affectionately called "Old Ironsides," and the *Philadelphia*, succeeded in blockading Tripoli from the autumn of 1803 until the summer of 1805. However, on 31 October 1803 the *Philadelphia* ran aground off the shores of Tripoli and was captured. The Tripolitans floated the *Philadelphia* and anchored it in their harbor. In February 1804 Stephen Decatur, a young naval officer, led an expedition into the harbor, where his sailors boarded and burned the vessel. For this feat Decatur earned the appreciation and applause of his country, a promotion, and a sword of honor from Congress. Commodore Samuel Barron, who succeeded Preble in 1804, relinquished command to Commodore John Rodgers during the summer of 1805.

The United States resorted to a coordinated land and sea attack to finally turn the tide. Captain William Eaton, previously the U.S. consul in Tunis and now the U.S. naval agent to the Barbary States, crossed the desert from Alexandria, Egypt, to Derna, Tripoli. On 27 April 1805 Eaton stormed Derna and on 13 May repulsed an attempt to recapture it. Fearing internal insurrection and further U.S. bombardments, the pasha hastily signed a peace treaty with the American plenipotentiary Tobias Lear on 4 June 1805. The United States paid $60,000 for prisoners taken by the Tripolitans, and in return the pasha agreed to forgo all tributes thereafter.

Over the next several years the United States continued to make regular payments to the other Barbary States. The embargo of 1807 slowed U.S. commerce in the Mediterranean, but when trade resumed in 1810 the pirates renewed their activities. In 1812 the dey of Algiers demanded more tribute, but because of the War of 1812, U.S. commerce had come to a virtual standstill.

The War with Algiers (1815)

After the War of 1812 Commodores William Bainbridge and Decatur were assigned in early 1815 to combat a resurgence of piracy in the Mediterranean. Decatur caught the Algerian fleet at sea and cut it off from port, threatening to destroy Algiers itself. On 30 June 1815 he convinced the dey of Algiers to avoid the demolition of his capital and the capture of the rest of his fleet by signing a treaty. The dey renounced all tributes, returned all U.S. prisoners, and paid restitution. This accomplished, Decatur then extracted similar treaties from the rulers of Tunis and Tripoli. An American squadron remained in the Mediterranean to guarantee the safety of U.S. shipping.

The treaties ended the Barbary States' attacks on U.S. ships, but the pirates continued to plague the ships of other countries until 1830. The "Marine Corps Hymn" memorializes the Barbary War in its beginning lines, "From the halls of Montezuma, to the shores of Tripoli."

See also **Africa, Foreign Relations with; Navy.**

Bibliography

Castor, Henry. *The Tripolitan War, 1801–1805: America Meets the Menace of the Barbary Pirates.* New York: Watts, 1971.

Chidsey, Donald Barr. *The Wars in Barbary: Arab Piracy and the Birth of the United States Navy.* New York: Crown, 1971.

Nash, Howard P., Jr. *The Forgotten Wars: The Role of the U.S. Navy in the Quasi War with France and the Barbary Wars, 1798–1805.* South Brunswick, N.J.: Barnes, 1968.

BARBARA HUGHETT

BARRIOS   The word "barrio" originated from both Spanish and Aztec history and designates a neighborhood where people share a common culture. Areas known as barrios developed during the settlement of far northern Mexico and continued after 1848, when that region became part of the United States. Into these urban spaces came immigrants from Mexico, individuals relocating from other parts of the United States, and migrant workers looking for a base in which to sojourn while working in the fields. The process of barrio formation occurred because people of Mexican origin preferred living among those with a similar heritage and because white society enforced de facto policies of segregation.

After the 1870s and 1880s the largest barrios existed in San Antonio, El Paso, Los Angeles, San Diego, Santa Barbara, and Tucson. Although these sections of towns were generally plagued by poverty, substandard housing, illness, crime, and neglect by city officials, they also helped preserve important elements of Mexican heritage such as family customs. Patriarchal tradition dictated that women conform to strict rules of modesty and care for the children. Catholicism retained its vigor among barrio residents, supported by white priests, lay leaders, and religious festivals. Self-help associations, patriotic societies, and literary groups flourished in the barrios.

While impoverishment and desperation certainly had a demoralizing effect on some barrio dwellers, these ethnic enclaves simultaneously served as buffers shielding residents from external problems. Barrios were places where Mexican lifestyles might reinforce one's identity, and centers where Mexican culture experienced gradual change with increased exposure to U.S. institutions.

See also **Immigration and Immigrants,** *subentry on* **Mexico and Latin America; Mexican Americans.**

Bibliography

Camarillo, Albert. *Chicanos in a Changing Society: From Mexican Pueblos to American Barrios in Santa Barbara and Southern California, 1848–1930.* Cambridge, Mass.: Harvard University Press, 1979.

Griswold del Castillo, Richard, and Arnoldo De León. *North to Aztlan: A History of Mexican Americans in the United States.* New York: Twayne, 1996.

ARNOLDO DE LEÓN

BASEBALL.   See **Sports,** subentry on **Baseball.**

BEAUTY.   See **Personal Appearance.**

BEAUTY CONTESTS   The first commercial beauty contest in the United States involving women's display of face and figure before judges was held by Phineas T. Barnum in his American Museum in 1854. When no contestants appeared, however, Barnum bowed to Victorian prudery and only required applicants to submit photographs for judging.

By the 1890s newspapers throughout the nation adopted the photographic beauty contest as a promotional device, especially after the circus entrepreneur Adam Forepaugh's photographic beauty contest in 1888 to crown a "Ten Thousand Dollar Beauty" drew eleven thousand applicants for the prize of ten thousand dollars.

May Day celebrations throughout the century frequently included crowning a queen, as did Twelfth Night parties and the tournaments that were popular early in the century, especially in the South. City festivals often held contests to select queens, especially after the New Orleans Mardi Gras, the festivals' esteemed progenitor, added a queen in 1871. The Philadelphia Centennial Exposition of 1876 held a beauty contest that drew two thousand applicants. By the 1880s beauty contests were staged to draw people to dime museums and carnival midways. So ubiquitous was the phenomenon that in 1898 the Elks Clubs of Akron, Canton, and Zanesville, Ohio, awarded a prize to the township sending the most attractive wagonload of women to their local carnival.

Both the World's Columbian Exposition of 1893 in Chicago and the Atlanta International Cotton Exposition of 1895 held "Congresses of Beauty." The first beach beauty contest was held at Rehoboth Beach, Delaware, in 1880, predating the Miss America pageant by forty years.

See also **Circuses; Country Fairs; Sexual Morality; Women,** *subentry on* **Woman as Image and Icon.**

Bibliography

Banner, Lois W. *American Beauty.* New York: Knopf, 1983.

LOIS W. BANNER

BIBLE AND BIBLE READING, THE

The Bible's influence on American culture in the nineteenth century is difficult to overestimate. Alternately invoked as a blueprint for institution building and a key to time's end, the Bible was the chief inspiration for a diverse legion of charismatic leaders whose religious movements survive to this day. Some, such as the Disciples of Christ founders Thomas and Alexander Campbell, helped make a fundamental principle of the Reformation into a popular slogan: No creed but the Bible. Others, such as the Mormon founder Joseph Smith, penned American sequels to biblical history in the familiar idiom of the King James version of the Bible. Scriptural language and imagery were the common currency of disparate Protestant groups, who often revered the King James Bible as an icon of Americanness—much to the cha-

grin of Catholics, who objected to its use in public schools, partly because the 1611 translation was almost never printed with the Apocrypha, which Catholics regarded as canonical.

Although the recurring conflicts between Protestants and Catholics demonstrated the Bible's limitations as a document of national unity, evangelical Protestant reformers were undeterred in their vision of the United States as a biblical nation. The American Bible Society, formed in 1816 by the consolidation of over one hundred local societies, distributed millions of Bibles throughout the nineteenth century in an effort to place the Scriptures in every American home. Evangelical reformers invoked biblical texts in every cause, most notably in the war to abolish slavery, even as southern Protestant theologians cited biblical passages to justify the "peculiar institution." Meanwhile, African Americans developed their own scriptural interpretations of American destiny, often contrasting the old Puritan image of an "American Israel" with the image of an "American Egypt" whose captives still longed for the freedom of the promised land.

Debates over biblical interpretation took on a different character after the Civil War as Americans began to encounter the results of academic biblical studies. A generation of antebellum scholars, including Andrews Norton, George Rapall Noyes, Edward Robinson, and Moses Stuart, had pioneered biblical studies in America, but during the 1870s, as contact between U.S. scholars and their German and British counterparts increased, American biblical studies developed rapidly on two fronts, soon known popularly as "higher" and "lower" criticism. Higher (or historical) critics tended to deny the divine authorship of Scripture and question the accuracy of certain biblical stories. The most celebrated of these critics, Charles Augustus Briggs, was suspended from the Presbyterian Church in 1893 but retained on the faculty of Union Theological Seminary (New York), which severed its Presbyterian ties in 1892. Historical criticism also influenced the authors of *The Woman's Bible* (1895), an early feminist Bible commentary whose chief contributor, Elizabeth Cady Stanton, insisted that the Scriptures "bear the impress of fallible man." At the same time, lower (or textual) critics made rapid progress in the reconstruction of the Bible's long-lost Greek and Hebrew originals and their accurate translation into English. The Revised Version (New Testament, 1881; Old Testament, 1885), a British-American translation and the first major new English Bible since 1611, was a transatlantic publishing sensation.

See also **Catholicism; Evangelicalism; Protestantism,**

subentry **Overview; Religion,** *subentry on* **Religion in Nineteenth-Century America.**

Bibliography

Barlow, Philip L. *Mormons and the Bible: The Place of the Latter-day Saints in American Religion.* New York: Oxford University Press, 1991.

Brown, Jerry Wayne. *The Rise of Biblical Criticism in America, 1800–1870: The New England Scholars.* Middletown, Conn.: Wesleyan University Press, 1969.

Gutjahr, Paul C. *An American Bible: A History of the Good Book in the United States, 1777–1880.* Stanford, Calif.: Stanford University Press, 1999.

Hatch, Nathan O., and Mark A. Noll, eds. *The Bible in America: Essays in Cultural History.* New York: Oxford University Press, 1982.

Thuesen, Peter J. *In Discordance with the Scriptures: American Protestant Battles over Translating the Bible.* New York: Oxford University Press, 1999.

Wosh, Peter J. *Spreading the Word: The Bible Business in Nineteenth-Century America.* Ithaca, N.Y.: Cornell University Press, 1994.

PETER J. THUESEN

BICYCLING Americans first demonstrated an enthusiasm for self-propelled wheeled transportation in the late 1860s with the introduction of the velocipede, a high, front wheel–driven machine. Difficult to ride, velocipedes nonetheless proved very popular in a number of American cities. True individualized transportation came with the low, rear wheel–driven safety bicycle in the mid-1880s. Immediately popular, the safety bicycle offered Americans a form of individual, long-distance transportation. Women especially found in the bicycle a new freedom of movement and of dress, as the bicycle helped legitimize and popularize bloomers. The safety bicycle also contributed to the widespread popularity of bicycle racing in the late nineteenth century.

Bicycles proved influential in a number of other areas. As more and more cyclists took to the roadways, they demanded better paved roads. Lobbying by such groups as the League of American Wheelmen led to smoother road surfaces, which were instrumental in the rapid adoption of the automobile. The bicycle industry also contributed to the nascent automobile industry by pioneering the use of steel-frame tubing, differential gearing, pneumatic tires, and new techniques of quantity production using special machine tools and electric resistance welding. The human quest for flight also benefited from lessons learned from bicycle manufacturing. Orville and Wilbur Wright designed and constructed their own brand of bicycles, which honed many of their engineering and mechanical skills, and they used parts

A Novelty Bicycle. After the bicycle was invented in the 1860s, manufacturers experimented with numerous variations, including Oldreive's New Tricycle (or the New Iron Horse), pictured above. These inventions were not always successful. LIBRARY OF CONGRESS

from their cycle shop, including bicycle chains, on their Kitty Hawk flyer. Their cycling experience also helped them conceptualize and understand the problems associated with controlling a machine in flight.

See also **Recreation; Sports,** *subentry on* **Sports and the Sporting Life; Transportation,** *subentry on* **Roads and Turnpikes.**

Bibliography

Crouch, Tom D. *The Bishop's Boys: A Life of Wilbur and Orville Wright.* New York: Norton, 1989.

Flink, James J. *The Automobile Age.* Cambridge, Mass.: MIT Press, 1988.

McGurn, James. *On Your Bicycle: An Illustrated History of Cycling.* New York: Facts on File, 1987.

JANET R. DALY BEDNAREK

BILL OF RIGHTS The Bill of Rights, ten amendments designed to limit the power of the national government, was added to the U.S. Constitution in 1791. The amendments concern four subjects. The First Amendment prohibits the government from infringing on basic civil liberties, such as the freedom of assembly, speech, and religion. The Fourth, Sixth, and Eighth Amendments guarantee fair trials and reasonable treatment of people accused of crimes and people convicted of them. The Third, Seventh, and parts of the Fifth protect private property. The Second and Tenth Amendments regulate the relations between the states and the national government.

The First Amendment begins with the phrase "Congress shall make no law." None of the other amendments so limits its jurisdictional scope. Early on, however, most Americans saw the Bill of Rights as restricting only the power of the national government. This was confirmed by Chief Justice John Marshall in *Barron v. Baltimore* (1833). A public works project in Baltimore Harbor had lowered the water level, making it impossible for ships to reach Barron's wharf, which became "of little or no value." Barron sued under the Fifth Amendment, alleging that his "private property [had been] taken for public use without just compensation." In rejecting Barron's suit, Chief Justice Marshall firmly held that "the fifth amendment must be understood as restraining the power of the general government, not as applicable to the States." A decade later, in *Permoli v. First Municipality of New Orleans* (1845), the Taney Court reaffirmed this concept, refusing to apply the religion clauses of the First Amendment to the states.

The Bill of Rights received little attention from the Supreme Court before the Civil War in part because Congress and the executive branch rarely attempted to contravene its restrictions on governmental power. The Sedition Act of 1798, passed to suppress criticism of President John Adams, was by twenty-first-century standards clearly an unconstitutional violation of the First Amendment. But a challenge to its validity never reached the Supreme Court. In 1801 President Thomas Jefferson pardoned all those convicted under that law, and a few years later Congress remitted all fines. Congress passed no similar regulation of the press or of speech until the Sedition Act of 1917, enacted during World War I. However, in the 1830s and 1840s Congress seemed to violate the right of petition guaranteed by the First Amendment when abolitionists flooded Congress with petitions to end slavery within federal jurisdictions. Rather than address these petitions, the House of Representatives adopted a "gag rule" that prevented even reading them. The struggle against the gag rule in the end benefited the opponents of slavery,

who used it as an illustration of slavery's threat to the liberty of all Americans, not just blacks.

Even though the Bill of Rights did not formally limit the actions of the states during this period, its ideology had a powerful impact throughout the nation. As states entered the Union before the Civil War they adopted the Bill of Rights. All states instituted jury trials, even Louisiana, where they had been absent under Spanish and French rule. Political expression was generally robust, especially in the North, although by the 1820s the South was suppressing criticism of slavery by whites or blacks. Throughout the nation, state and local governments prosecuted blasphemy and other forms of expression that offended traditional morality. But by the 1840s most states abolished formal ties to religious institutions and adopted rules that protected minority faiths. In New York, for example, the courts refused to force Roman Catholic priests to give testimony about what they heard in confessionals. However, some religious practitioners found less tolerance. Jews were fined in some places for refusing to serve as jurors on their Saturday Sabbath while members of the Church of Jesus Christ of the Latter-day Saints (the Mormons) were vigorously persecuted in a number of places, their leader, Joseph Smith, was murdered, and they were forced to move to a remote section of Utah to escape the religious intolerance of the age.

Ironically, the most significant antebellum Supreme Court case to implement the Bill of Rights was the proslavery decision in *Dred Scott v. Sandford* (1857). Chief Justice Roger B. Taney struck down the portion of the Missouri Compromise of 1820 that banned slavery in the western territories, asserting that freeing slaves in the territories violated the Fifth Amendment's prohibition on taking private property without "due process of law."

Abolitionists argued that the laws supporting slavery in the federal territories and the District of Columbia and the Fugitive Slave Law of 1850 violated the Fifth Amendment protection against deprivation of "life, liberty, or property." Abolitionists also argued that the Fugitive Slave Law violated the Sixth Amendment guarantee of a jury trial. These arguments had no success in the political and legal systems because southerners held a majority on the Supreme Court and, in alliance with northern Democrats, controlled the White House and Congress.

In the late 1850s, many Republicans, including Congressman John Bingham of Ohio, argued that the Bill of Rights did indeed restrain the states and that *Barron v. Baltimore* had been wrongly decided. The election of Abraham Lincoln and secession gave these men new political power. During and after the Civil War the Republicans repealed the Fugitive Slave

The Bill of Rights Infringed. Originally titled "Abolition Frowned Down," the 1839 cartoon satirizes the enforcement of a "gag rule" in the House of Representatives, an internal procedural rule that prohibited members of Congress from reading and discussing petitions presented to them by abolitionists to end slavery. John Quincy Adams, serving in the House after his presidential term had ended, opposed the ruling, which infringed on First Amendment rights. LIBRARY OF CONGRESS

Laws, abolished slavery in all Federal jurisdictions, and finally moved to end slavery in most of the Confederacy with the Confiscation Acts and the Emancipation Proclamation. Uncertain of the constitutionality of freeing slaves, the Republicans pushed through the Thirteenth Amendment (1865), which prohibits slavery throughout the nation, and the Fourteenth Amendment (1868), which specifically forbids anyone from making a claim for compensation for loss of any slaves during the war.

Beyond slavery, the Civil War affected the Bill of Rights in two other major ways. The Lincoln administration suspended habeas corpus in the border slave states, occasionally suppressed antiwar newspapers, and expelled the antiwar activist Clement Vallandigham from the United States. Compared to the suppression of dissent in the Confederacy, however, the Lincoln administration's control was mild in its violations of civil liberties. During the war the U.S. Army tried a few civilians, but it executed none. In *Ex Parte Milligan* (1866) the Supreme Court ruled that such military trials violated the Fifth and Sixth Amendments.

More importantly the Fourteenth Amendment, ratified in 1868, declared that no state could "make or enforce any law which shall abridge the privileges and immunities of citizens of the United States." Congressman John Bingham of Ohio, the primary author of the amendment, intended for this clause to make most of the provisions of the Bill of Rights applicable to the states. However, in *The Slaughterhouse Cases* (1873) the Supreme Court interpreted the privileges and immunities clause in the most narrow way conceivable, thus preventing the application of the Bill of Rights to the states. The Fourteenth Amendment also provided that no state could "deprive any person of life, liberty, or property, without due process of law." In *Hurtado v. California* (1884) the Court asserted that this clause did not make the Fifth Amendment's requirement of a grand jury indictment applicable to the states. In *Chicago, Burlington and Quincy Railroad v. Chicago* (1897) the Court ruled that the Fourteenth Amendment made the takings clause of the Fifth Amendment applicable to the states. This was the beginning of a series of Supreme Court decisions that used the Fourteenth Amendment's due process clause to apply the Bill of Rights to the states. Called "incorporation," these decisions determined that most of the liberties protected by the Bill of Rights from federal interference fall within the due process safeguard in the Fourteenth Amendment and are thus applicable to the states.

In the last quarter of the nineteenth century neither the Court nor Congress demonstrated much concern for the rights to freedom of expression or freedom of religion of people who advocated new or radical ideas. In a series of laws Congress effectively criminalized the doctrines of the Mormon Church. In *Reynolds v. United States* (1879) the Court upheld the conviction of a Mormon for polygamy, denying his argument that plural marriage was a religious doctrine protected by the free exercise clause of the First Amendment. In *Davis v. Beason* (1890) the Court upheld the conviction of a Mormon who advocated but did not practice polygamy, showing that neither the religion nor the speech clauses of the First Amendment were available for those whose beliefs offended the majority of Americans. Similarly the Comstock Act (1873) authorized the post office to suppress the interstate movement of "immoral" publications. Rather than using the law to suppress pornography, officials applied it most vigorously against medical books and tracts that discussed birth control and literature that offended conservatives, such as Walt Whitman's *Leaves of Grass* (1855) and Leo Tolstoy's "Kreutzer Sonata" (1891). The most famous victim of the law was Margaret Sanger, the founder of the modern birth control movement. In the last decades of the century the courts used injunctions to suppress labor radicals.

As the century ended the Bill of Rights was of little use to those who most needed its protection. Majority politics led state and national legislators to suppress vulnerable minorities. The Supreme Court, dominated by conservatives with little sympathy for minority rights, refused to use the Bill of Rights to overrule oppressive laws. Blacks in the South, despite the Fourteenth Amendment, were denied their rights to fair trials or a free press. The Mormon faith was attacked until the church abandoned one of its central tenets. Birth control advocates and avant-garde intellectuals faced federal prosecution for spreading their ideas, while injunctions silenced labor organizers, who were jailed if they dared protest. At the same time the Fourteenth Amendment, one of the greatest developments in the nineteenth-century Constitution, pointed toward a more democratic future in the next century.

See also **Civil Rights; Constitutional Amendments; Constitutional Law; Courts, State and Federal; Federal-State Relations; Liberty; Supreme Court.**

Bibliography
Curtis, Michael Kent. *No State Shall Abridge.* Durham, N.C.: Duke University Press, 1986.
Hyman, Harold M., and William M. Wiecek. *Equal Justice under Law: Constitutional Development, 1835–1875.* New York: Harper and Row, 1982.
Nye, Russell B. *Fettered Freedom: Civil Liberties and the Antislavery Controversy, 1830–1860.* East Lansing: Michigan State University Press, 1963.
Rabban, David M. *Free Speech in Its Forgotten Years.* New York: Cambridge University Press, 1997.

PAUL FINKELMAN

BIOLOGY   For much of the nineteenth century, biology did not exist as a separate scientific discipline in the United States. While the word had been coined (as "biologie") by both the Frenchman Jean-Baptiste Lamarck (1744–1829) and the German Gottfried Treviranus (1776–1837) at the beginning of the century, the discipline in its American context remained annexed to its antecedents—natural philosophy, natural theology, and natural history—until the 1870s. Nevertheless, American interest in what would later be known as biology was evident at the beginning of the century, in popular organizations and avocational pastimes, national expeditions of discovery, and public museums dedicated to the study of nature.

"Popular" Natural History in the Early United States

Natural history's popularity derived from its twin applications: natural theology and popular culture. Natural theology, developed prominently in the writings of the English cleric William Paley (1743–1805), held that God gave evidence of his beneficence and wisdom through design observable in nature. The marvelously intricate workings of the Venus's-flytrap were one of the many examples cited in support of the design argument. Using Paley's *Natural Theology* (1802) as well as other texts, natural history and natural philosophy courses in the nation's colleges taught Americans to discover God's perfection in nature. Natural history's other application to popular culture borrowed heavily from natural theology and offered catalogs, journals, study clubs, and exchange networks to Americans seeking to learn more about design and purpose in nature.

Natural history's appeal in the young United States was illustrated by Charles Willson Peale's (1741–1827) paleontological museum in Philadelphia and John Scudder's (d. 1821) American Museum in New York. These early-nineteenth-century institutions displayed nature's ordinary and extraordinary artifacts to throngs of curious and inquisitive Americans. More professional establishments emerged alongside these entrepreneurial ventures, such as Philadelphia's Academy of Natural Sciences (1812), the Albany Lyceum of Natural History (1823), and the Boston Society of Natural History (1830). Other institutions sent collectors to the American West in search of exotic plants and animals, especially following the Lewis and Clark expedition (1804–1806) and the U.S. Exploring Expedition (1838–1842). Specimens from the latter expedition became the foundation collection for the first federally supported museum, located originally in the National Gallery of the Patent Office, but later reorganized as the National Museum of Natural History of the Smithsonian Institution.

Natural history's popularity created opportunities for some naturalists operating as businessmen to collect specimens for sale. Henry A. Ward (1834–1906) operated Ward's Natural Science Establishment in Rochester, New York, where he developed a large and financially rewarding business supplying avocational naturalists, museums, natural historians, and colleges and universities with the accoutrements they needed. Later in the century Ward sold the bulk of his zoological materials to Marshall Field (1834–1906), who used them in 1893 to found what became Chicago's Field Museum of Natural History. Other collectors started journals, such as *The Museum, Natural Science Journal, The Nautilus,* and *The Oölogist,* in which they ran advertisements promising "we have the BEST at lowest prices" to eager consumers. Some of their customers were schools that needed specimens for museum collections, which were used to teach natural history courses.

Despite the vogue of natural history during the first half of the nineteenth century, the United States did not have a well-developed community of professional natural historians. Geologists working on surveys of the West, collectors gathering specimens in the fields, and museum curators organizing collections often needed other jobs to support themselves. Furthermore, most natural history work was done as an adjunct to other projects sponsored by the federal government (boundary surveys), railway companies (surveys for transcontinental railroads), and the military (U.S. Coast Survey).

"Scientific" Natural History Comes to U.S. Education

Institutional changes at mid-century led natural history in a new direction. In 1842 Harvard University hired Asa Gray (1810–1888) to become the institution's (and the nation's) first botanist not employed by a medical school. Soon, Gray's position was complemented by Louis Agassiz (1807–1873), who became the professor of zoology and geology in 1847, the first time that natural history was separated into distinct disciplines in the United States. Gray centered his activities within his herbarium, which eventually became Harvard's Gray Herbarium (1864), while Agassiz raised sufficient funds to build the famous Museum of Comparative Zoology in 1859. Harvard thus became the center for training a new generation of biologists, this country's first, marking the move of natural history from the extramural museum to the halls of academe. At the same time, Charles Darwin's (1809–1882) new ideas on speciation came across the Atlantic. Gray was Darwin's leading defender in the United States, while Agassiz argued against the natural evolution of species over time. Initially the controversies surrounding Darwin's new ideas focused on biological issues, not the religious arguments that emerged in the early twentieth century.

The Civil War interrupted the smooth development of American natural history. Indeed, it literally wreaked havoc on some of the older institutions, destroying, for example, South Carolina's Charleston Museum, one of the nation's oldest (1773). But the ending of the war also inspired many Americans to address glaring national cultural deficiencies in the rebuilding efforts that followed. One need was to reform and modernize the American educational system, long dependent on clerical instruction centered in the humanities but now in need of wholesale transformation. The immediate goal of many educators was to add a scientific curriculum, developed in Europe, to America's colleges and universities. First applied to medical education at Harvard in the 1870s, these reforms were best exemplified at Baltimore's new graduate university. From the time it opened in 1876, Johns Hopkins University offered a scientific curriculum, modeled on laboratories and research facilities in Europe. Characteristic of the changes, the new university elected not to build a museum.

This revised natural history came to be known by its practitioners as "scientific natural history." Recognizing the new direction, President D. C. Gilman (1831–1908) established a biology department at Johns Hopkins, the first academic unit with that designation in the United States. The department was headed by H. Newell Martin (1848–1896), a physiologist, and staffed by William Keith Brooks (1848–1908), a morphologist who was trained at Harvard by Agassiz. Thus the two main branches of natural history described by the English educational innovator Thomas H. Huxley (1825–1895), physiology and morphology, both were represented in the first American biology department.

Louis Agassiz. The zoologist and naturalist stands by a diagram of Radiates, one of the four classifications of animal life according to nineteenth-century taxonomy. Agassiz, who was Swiss-born, founded the Museum of Comparative Zoology at Harvard in 1859. LIBRARY OF CONGRESS

The kind of science practiced in the laboratory at Johns Hopkins was also new. Teaching and research were brought inside, within the new Biological Laboratory built and equipped for this purpose. The aim was not to expose students to new species in the field, but to new techniques in the laboratory. Physiological apparatuses filled one laboratory, while microscopes and microtomes filled the other. New questions were posed: it was no longer as important to name a new species as it was to investigate the genealogical relationships among species, a topic popularized by evolution theory, or to study the dynamic processes within organisms. Soon, the "Hopkins model" migrated to Harvard, then to Columbia, Pennsylvania, and throughout American higher education. Transfer of the model was aided by the training of new American biologists, including the four famous "Hopkins men," E. B. Wilson (1856–1939),

T. H. Morgan (1866–1945), Ross G. Harrison (1870–1959), and E. G. Conklin (1863–1952).

This new generation of American biologists made a significant mark on international science. Although they were the first to receive graduate training in a country with a meager scientific tradition, many of their studies were recognized as first-rate science by Europeans. The four Hopkins graduates were well regarded in Europe, especially through their summertime studies at the Stazione Zoologica in Naples and the Marine Biological Laboratory (1888) in Woods Hole, Massachusetts, specializing in embryology, heredity, cytology, and neuroanatomy. American biologists who studied the distribution patterns of plants and animals in the field, beginning at the new biology department at the University of Chicago, such as Frederic Clements (1874–1945) and Victor Shelford (1877–1968), helped to develop the new field of ecology at the turn of the century.

Thus, by the end of the nineteenth century, natural history in the United States was not just transformed into biology; the discipline of biology was given a completely new and different institutional character. It had shifted from the avocational and professional concerns of the naturalist located within museums, to the research-oriented professionalism of biologists located within university laboratories. This new tradition brought the discipline of biology into being, opening the way to the transformative discoveries and theories of the twentieth century.

See also **Education,** *subentry on* **Colleges and Universities; Evolution; Museums,** *subentry on* **Science and Technology Museums.**

Bibliography

Bruce, Robert V. *The Launching of Modern American Science, 1846–1876.* Ithaca, N.Y.: Cornell University Press, 1988.

Daniels, George H. *American Science in the Age of Jackson.* New York: Columbia University Press, 1968.

Greene, John C. *American Science in the Age of Jefferson.* Ames: Iowa State University Press, 1984.

Rainger, Ronald, Keith R. Benson, and Jane Maienschein, eds. *The American Development of Biology.* Philadelphia: University of Pennsylvania Press, 1988.

KEITH R. BENSON

BIRTH AND CHILDBEARING   At the beginning of the nineteenth century most women gave birth in their own homes with the help of women midwives from their communities. Family members, friends, and neighbors helped care for the family's other children during the new mother's several weeks of recovery, called "lying-in," after the birth. In the

South, African American slave midwives sometimes served as attendants for both blacks and whites. Neither doctors nor husbands were present at most births, which proceeded without much assistance and without instruments. Bacterial sources of infection remained undiscovered, and sterile techniques were nonexistent. Because cesarean sections were almost always fatal for the mother, they were rarely performed on women who were not already dead. Maternal death rates, while high by late-twentieth-century standards, were far lower than in the crowded cities of Europe. In New England (the only area for which detailed studies are available), more men than women died at the ages considered women's childbearing years, and on average women lived longer than men. Married women gave birth about every two years until they reached menopause. The hormones released while breast-feeding naturally spaced pregnancies.

By the century's end most middle- and upper-class women were attended by doctors during childbirth. However, recent immigrants from southern and eastern Europe and rural southern women, white and black, continued to use midwives from their own communities. Though most births still took place at home, charitable groups established lying-in hospitals for unmarried women who had no homes or families. Some hospitals were building new, private wings for middle-class women. Doctors received training by attending poor women at hospitals. Although in 1900 almost seventy-four hundred women practiced as physicians, only one thousand of twenty-six thousand medical students were women. Birth, once a women's event rarely seen by men, was firmly placed in the hands of male doctors. Increasingly doctors intervened during births, attempting to induce labor by inserting a balloon in the birth canal, routinely using forceps to hasten the birth, and making an episiotomy, a surgical cut in the mother's tissues to make more room for the baby's head to emerge. In 1860 the French biologist Louis Pasteur discovered streptococci, and by about 1885 an understanding of antisepsis made surgery safer. By the 1890s the cesarean section was fatal for the mother only 50 percent of the time. Chloroform and ether reduced the experience of pain but were used mostly at the end of labor, after the most painful period was over.

In spite of undeniable technological advances and greatly increased knowledge about the physiology of pregnancy and birth, it is questionable whether childbearing women were better off at the end of the century than at the beginning. Interventions led to increases in infection, pain, and the need for further interventions. Middle-class white families started to limit births after the Civil War. Contraceptive information was not readily available to poor and minority women, who continued to give birth as frequently as at the century's beginning. After passage of the Comstock Act in 1873, both information and contraceptive devices (including condoms) became illegal for all social groups. A period of mixed progress, the nineteenth century is noted primarily for the transition from midwives to doctors and for increased interventions in a basically natural event. How and why did this occur?

Transition from Midwives to Doctors

American midwives had no formal training in midwifery beyond their own experiences in giving birth and attending their neighbors' births. Unlike English midwives, they made no attempts to organize into a guild or to acquire licensure, and they wrote no books advocating their profession or opposing doctors' interventions. The overwhelming majority of births that midwives attended were successful because midwives did little except offer comfort by their presence. Although they occasionally converted a breech birth to the normal head-first position, midwives did not intervene often enough to cause widespread maternal infection. Most births need little or no assistance.

On those occasions when something went wrong during birth, midwives could do little. American midwives could not afford surgical instruments, which were also not part of midwifery tradition even though no laws forbade their use. In the eighteenth century midwives had to call a surgeon, usually a man with no formal education who sawed off limbs, pulled teeth, and perhaps cut hair, to dismember and deliver a dead baby. By the nineteenth century some midwives had the option of calling a physician who had received formal medical training, usually in Edinburgh or London but sometimes in one of the new American medical schools. Throughout most of the century medical education lasted only two years, the second year often a repeat of the first, and until midcentury it included no clinical training with actual patients. Nevertheless American families admired any claims to education. Doctors also had forceps, a lifesaving instrument originally developed in the seventeenth century. Consisting of two spoons that lock together around the baby's head, forceps, unlike most instruments, deliver a live baby.

Building on Americans' requests for education and their desires for upward social mobility, doctors by 1820 were campaigning against midwives as uneducated, lower-class, and too sympathetic with patients to make rational judgments. By 1830 no middle-class midwife worked in Boston, a circumstance that spread rapidly to other cities and towns. Some rural, white midwives still attended births at mid-century.

Middle-class families usually preferred an educated man of their own social class rather than a woman of a lower class. Doctors feared, however, that if women were allowed entry into medicine, women patients would prefer them. Medical schools excluded women until Elizabeth Blackwell gained entry to Geneva Medical College in upstate New York in 1847. Thereafter most women physicians served the poor and were excluded from the prestigious positions that determined the course of obstetrics.

The term "obstetrician," from the Latin "to stand before" the woman giving birth, was coined in 1828 to replace the earlier English term "man-midwife" or the French *accoucheur* (one who brings to bed). By the century's end most "obstetricians" were actually general practitioners. Specialists were few, and accreditation did not exist. The presence of semieducated doctors was not a demonstrable boon for women. As late as 1933 the New York Academy of Medicine found that immigrant midwives were safer than New York City's general practitioners. Sterile techniques were adopted slowly, and owing to the increased use of interventions, infection may have killed more women at the end of the century than at the beginning. By 1900 women's life expectancy was rebounding from a mid-century low, partly as a result of better nutrition and living standards and the rejection of constricting dress. But medicine was still as likely to harm as to help its patients.

The Women's Health Movement

In the 1830s and 1840s middle-class women banded together to educate themselves about their bodies with particular focus on pregnancy and birth. Ladies' Physiological Societies sponsored lectures and published books advocating diets, exercise, fresh air, and regular weekly baths to promote healthy and painless childbearing. White middle-class health educators extolled the American Indian woman as an example of painless birth in the state of nature, although most writers had no knowledge about Native American births. Women's life expectancy decreased, and difficulties in birth increased at mid-century. These developments reflected the successive waves of poor and malnourished immigrants who often developed rickets, a vitamin deficiency that constricts the pelvic bones, and middle-class women's penchant for lacing their preadolescent daughters into corsets that permanently deformed the internal organs.

Women continued to write and read books on birth throughout the century. Authors included the woman suffrage advocates Elizabeth Cady Stanton and Catharine Beecher along with many women doctors. However, throughout the century prenatal care usu-ally consisted of one visit at which touch was the only method used to check for massive obstructions or to measure the birth canal. Until 1850, when James White of Buffalo, New York, allowed his medical students to witness an Irish immigrant having her second illegitimate child, doctors were expected to conduct both prenatal care and the birth itself by touch alone, with the patient completely concealed.

The concept of antisepsis spread slowly, and epidemics of puerperal fever, a deadly infection that enters the mother through tissue tears during birth, broke out in European hospitals. American women fortunately escaped that fate, largely because most women gave birth at home, not because doctors were cleaner. The Boston physician Oliver Wendell Holmes, speaking in 1855 (before Pasteur's discovery that streptococci caused both surgical and birth infections), argued that "puerperal pestilence" was carried on doctors' hands. Many doctors rejected his theory, saying they were gentlemen and therefore their hands were clean. In spite of such resistance, by the century's end the hospitals founded for the poor had become sufficiently safe to attract some middle-class women expecting difficult births, and some institutions were building private wings.

New Technologies

Many new technologies emerged during the century and were often overused by eager doctors. In 1808 a German immigrant midwife introduced the application of ergot, a fungus that grows on rye, to increase the force of labor contractions. Other technologies included the labor analgesic chloroform, first used by James Simpson of Edinburgh in 1847, and ether, introduced by Walter Channing of Boston in 1848; the speculum, an ancient instrument not used in the United States until later in the century that enables a doctor to examine the birth canal visually; and antisepsis against bacteria beginning about 1885. Blood transfusions and antibiotics did not appear until the twentieth century.

Birth became firmly medicalized, setting the stage for its move to the hospital in the twentieth century. Subsequently Americans relied on high technology to a far greater extent than did people in other nations. During the nineteenth century gaps existed between rich and poor and white and black in maternal and infant mortality. These discrepancies became apparent with the first birth registrations in 1913 and persisted virtually undiminished throughout the twentieth century.

See also **Contraception and Abortion; Education,** *subentry on* **Graduate and Professional Education; Medicine; Midwives; Women.**

Bibliography

Donegan, Jane B. *Women and Men Midwives: Medicine, Morality, and Misogyny in Early America.* Westport, Conn.: Greenwood, 1978.

Leavitt, Judith Walzer. *Brought to Bed: Childbearing in America, 1750 to 1950.* New York: Oxford University Press, 1986.

Leavitt, Judith Walzer, ed. *Women and Health in America.* Madison: University of Wisconsin Press, 1984.

Wertz, Richard W., and Dorothy C. Wertz. *Lying-in: A History of Childbirth in America.* Expanded ed. New Haven, Conn.: Yale University Press, 1989.

DOROTHY C. WERTZ

BLEEDING KANSAS   "Bleeding Kansas" is the name generally given both to the warfare in 1856 between proslavery and Free-Soil forces in the Kansas Territory and, by extension, to the entire period of sectional strife in Kansas before the Civil War (1856–1861).

The Kansas-Nebraska Act (1854) opened the Nebraska Territory to land-hungry white settlers and allowed future inhabitants of the territories to determine for themselves whether they wished to include or exclude slavery. Although the Compromise of 1850 had called for such "popular sovereignty" in creating the Utah and New Mexico Territories, northerners overwhelmingly saw the Kansas-Nebraska Act as a betrayal of a sacred trust. It seemed an invitation to neighboring Missouri slaveholders to seize Kansas for the South.

Widespread outrage over the Kansas-Nebraska Act led to the rapid dissolution of old political allegiances in the North, and a new political party, the Republican Party, was born to protest it. As Senator William Seward of New York had predicted, a scramble to win Kansas ensued. Missourians responded when their firebrand former senator David R. Atchison warned that a free Kansas would threaten slavery in Missouri, Arkansas, Texas, and all the territories. Missourians soon founded the Kansas towns of Leavenworth and Atchison. Other southerners joined them in organizing companies of riflemen and secret societies dedicated to claiming Kansas for slavery. In Massachusetts, Congressman Eli Thayer and a textile manufacturer, Amos Lawrence, organized the New England Emigrant Aid Company, which helped build the free-state towns of Topeka and Lawrence. The Reverend Henry Ward Beecher sent Sharps rifles (called "Beecher's Bibles") to free-state colonists in the territory.

When the first territorial governor of Kansas called for the election of a legislature in March 1855, some four thousand to five thousand armed Missouri "border ruffians" crossed into Kansas and voted illegally. The resulting proslavery legislature threw out free-state representatives, enacted the Missouri slave code, and adopted criminal penalties for speaking out against slaveholding. President Franklin Pierce denounced as illegal a rival free-state legislature founded at Topeka in the fall of 1855. In 1857 free-staters boycotted a referendum on provisions of a proslavery constitution written at Lecompton, but President James Buchanan decided to submit it to Congress for approval, despite much greater support in Kansas for a free-state constitution written at Topeka. Buchanan's support for the Lecompton Constitution mocked the concept of popular sovereignty and deepened the growing split within the Democratic Party.

Isolated incidents of violence and the failure of the territorial government to prosecute proslavery wrongdoers soon sparked open war. On 21 May 1856 a proslavery federal posse of eight hundred, led by a Missouri sheriff bent on serving arrest warrants for treason, ran amok in Lawrence, destroying abolitionist printing presses, burning and shelling the Free State Hotel with cannon shot, and burning the home of the free-state leader, Charles Robinson. Three days later a small party led by John Brown silently butchered five men associated with the proslavery Law and Order Party in a midnight retaliatory act of terror on Pottawatomie Creek. On 2 June, Brown defeated a small force of Missourians at Black Jack. And on 30 August, Missouri irregulars routed Brown and burned the free-state town of Osawatomie. Although a new territorial governor, John W. Geary, the former mayor of San Francisco, obtained a truce before the November elections, violence resumed sporadically thereafter. On 19 May 1858 nine free-state men were massacred on the Marais des Cygne. Led chiefly by James Henry Lane, sometimes called the Liberator of Kansas, a free-state army won battles at Franklin, Fort Saunders, Hickory Point, and Slough Creek before fighting subsided in 1859.

Bleeding Kansas destroyed popular sovereignty, deepened distrust of the federal government in both the North and the South, breathed new life into the Republican Party, strengthened secessionist appeals, and foreshadowed the Civil War. In 1861, with most Southerners out of Congress, Kansas entered the Union as a free state.

See also **Kansas-Nebraska Act; Sectionalism.**

Bibliography

Rawley, James A. *Race and Politics: "Bleeding Kansas" and the Coming of the Civil War.* Philadelphia: Lippincott, 1969.

Stampp, Kenneth M. *America in 1857: A Nation on the Brink.* New York: Oxford University Press, 1990.

ROBERT MCGLONE

BLUE LAWS   Blue laws originated in seventeenth-century England when Puritans outlawed public activities and recreations, which they believed contravened God's command to keep the Sabbath holy. This same kind of legislation was passed regularly by state and local governments in the United States during the second half of the nineteenth century. As the century waned the official national culture of evangelical Protestantism reinforced the spirit of these blue laws.

The first wave of blue laws came with the Second Great Awakening (late 1820s–1830s) when citizens who had been swept up in the revival came to see politics in terms of moral perfection. The power of the government, they argued, could be used for moral reform as the United States became Christianized. Proponents argued that moral reform would liberate people from their sins. Prison reform, the public school movement, and the crusade against slavery shared the spirit of liberation. The more moralizing spirit of temperance and blue laws in the middle decades of the nineteenth century sprang from a similar hope of Christianizing and perfecting America.

Evangelical Protestants, touched by the Second Great Awakening, translated their convictions into political action to outlaw business and public amusements on Sunday. The Whigs were the Protestant party in the decades before the Civil War, and state and local parties often embraced moral reforms that would close shops, taverns, and theaters on the Sabbath, as well as prohibit delivery of the mail and various other forms of employment. One consequence, not altogether unintended, was that young working men were saved from "vice" on the day before the work week began, and the whole community was left with little else to focus on but its religious activities. Where Protestant majorities were dominant enough to enforce their type of Sabbatarianism, they did not do so from purely economic motives. They believed that abstaining from amusements and drinking, which the blue laws enforced, was sufficiently important to take precedence over using Sunday as a day of commerce.

The source of the blue laws was the cultural and political authority of established Protestantism. This in itself was quite significant because in the years after the Civil War, blue laws became one way to Americanize immigrants who otherwise did not seem to conform to the Anglo-Protestant norms of American life. Immigrant communities tended to treat Sunday as a day of feasting and recreation. Often it was the only day off for the immigrant workers who were building the great industrial cities of the late nineteenth century. Even as the evangelical impulse became institutionalized, blue laws became more im-portant for Republicans, who took up many of the Whig causes after the Civil War. They continued to insist that businesses remain closed on Sunday and tried to close or limit the business of taverns, restaurants, and theaters.

Even as America became more urbanized in the late nineteenth century, the role of blue laws became more, not less, significant. Such states as Missouri, Illinois, and New York, which combined large immigrant urban populations with native-born Protestant populations, found themselves debating laws to extend drinking hours and legalize mass entertainments, such as baseball. The blue laws had perhaps lost their evangelical fervor, but Protestant defenders continued to identify them with the preservation of the Sabbath in the American way of life. They sought to defend the "traditional" Sunday of attending church once or even twice, the Sunday of quiet family time in useful and instructive pursuits, such as Bible-reading and hymn-singing, and certainly undistracted by the secular pursuits of business and leisure, which many immigrants were determined to incorporate into the Sabbath. Many of these blue laws survived well into the twentieth century.

See also **Evangelicalism; Immigration and Immigrants,** *subentry on* **The Immigrant Experience; Protestantism; Recreation; Social Life.**

Bibliography

Johnson, Paul E. *A Shopkeeper's Millennium: Society and Revivals in Rochester, New York, 1815–1837.* New York: Hill and Wang, 1978.

Laband, David N., and Deborah Hendry Heinbuch. *Blue Laws: The History, Economics, and Politics of Sunday-Closing Laws.* Lexington, Mass.: Lexington Books, 1987.

McLoughlin, William Gerald. *Revivals, Awakenings, and Reform: An Essay on Religion and Social Change in America, 1607–1977.* Chicago: University of Chicago Press, 1978.

Schlereth, Thomas J. *Victorian America: Transformations in Everyday Life, 1876–1915.* New York: HarperCollins, 1991.

Silbey, Joel H. *The American Political Nation, 1838–1893.* Stanford, Calif.: Stanford University Press, 1991.

Walters, Ronald G. *American Reformers, 1815–1860.* New York: Hill and Wang, 1978.

IAN MYLCHREEST

BOOK PUBLISHING   Modern American book publishing emerged in the nineteenth century. In the colonial period, the term "publisher" was associated with printers who published newspapers and almanacs. Few printers *published* books in the sense of assuming the financial risk and coordinating the decisions of production and distribution. The colonial printer acted as publisher only for low-risk projects, including jobs contracted by governments or religious institutions; books sold by subscription (for which customers paid in advance of printing); or "steady sellers," such as almanacs that had a predictable annual demand. For the sale of most books, importing a few copies from England proved cheaper and safer for printer-booksellers than publishing their own editions.

Emergence of American Book Publishing

In the 1790s, the print trade diversified in Philadelphia and New York, America's largest cities. Some printers became embroiled in that decade's partisan warfare and moved decisively toward political publishing, focusing on newspapers and pamphlets. Others remained essentially job printers, taking work for customers. But other master printers turned to book publishing. Some printer-publishers, such as Mathew Carey (1760–1839) of Philadelphia, moved out of printing, concentrating their energies on publishing and contracting the printing work to other master printers—those who chose not to become book publishers. This new situation transformed the metropolitan print trade. In competing for publishers' contracts, the nonpublishing printers hired more apprentices, who eventually completed their contracts and glutted the ranks of journeymen printers. Perceiving the diminished opportunity to attain master status, some adventurous journeymen tried their hands at publishing instead. A larger number sought to organize *as* journeymen, asserting their rights to sufficient wages as master printers' low bids for publishing jobs threatened their livelihood.

Meanwhile, the new printer-publishers developed their own networks and sense of corporate identity. Book publishing required capital and markets. By selling shares in a prospective project to other booksellers who committed to take a certain number of copies, publishers could raise capital and insure a market for the publication. Mathew Carey offered such shares to printer-booksellers in other cities, creating the beginnings of a national book market. He also envisioned an annual literary fair, where booksellers from across the country would congregate to purchase each other's publications on the model of that in Leipzig, Germany. Although this brainchild survived less than five years, men like Carey were clearly thinking in terms of a publishing trade that would be distinct from printing. Over time, elaborate credit networks also developed among—and bound together—publishers and other agents in the book trade. Publishers circulated information about their books by publishing catalogs and broadside lists, advertising in newspapers, or binding their lists into the books themselves. Trade papers, which emerged around 1830 and proliferated at mid-century, became key sites in which publishers announced and advertised new and forthcoming works. These periodicals, which also included news of the trade, included *The Booksellers' Advertiser and Monthly Register of New Publications* (1834, 1836), *The Literary World* (1847–1853), and *American Publishers' Circular* (1855–1858), and culminated in the appearance of *Publishers Weekly* in 1872. Semiannual trade sales, auctions in the nation's publishing centers where booksellers came together to buy stock, provided another way for the trade to recognize itself as a distinct entity.

New technologies helped industrialize, consolidate, and nationalize book publishing. Robert Hoe's New York company developed and improved steam-powered cylinder presses, first demonstrated in England in 1814. By substituting machinery for muscle power, the new presses sped production and allowed even young women to perform presswork. Stereotyping (1811) and electrotyping (1841), processes in which pages of composed type were used to make molds from which metal printing plates were cast, came to replace printing directly from type and made new editions easy to publish. New typesetting machinery and other inventions further increased the capital required for large-scale book production. Harper and Brothers' New York headquarters, erected in 1855, testified to the new scale of publishing: two seven-story buildings housed the firm's operations, which covered every stage of bookmaking from receiving authors' manuscripts to making the stereotype plates to packing the finished books. The nation's burgeoning railroad system made distribution of books far easier than it had been a half-century before.

By the 1850s, the trade was concentrated in New York, Philadelphia, Boston, and to a lesser extent in Cincinnati. In addition to Harper and Brothers, the leading firms included New York's D. Appleton and Co. (which entered publishing in 1831) and Wiley and Putnam (begun as a bookshop in 1807, eventually G. P. Putnam's Sons); Philadelphia's J. B. Lippincott and Co. (1836) and the various successors to Carey's operation, notably Carey, Lea and Blanchard; and Boston's Little, Brown and Co. (1837) and Allen and Ticknor (1832), best known as Ticknor and Fields (1854–1868) and eventually absorbed into Houghton, Mifflin and Co. (1880). After mid-century, Chicago and San Francisco also became important regional print centers.

Publishers, Authors, and Copyright

The capitalization and industrialization of book publishing transformed author-publisher relations, particularly from the 1830s on. Earlier American authors had often acted as self-publishers, paying for the manufacture of their own work. Some authors of the 1830s and 1840s, including the poet Henry Wadsworth Longfellow and the historian William Hickling Prescott, retained ownership of their own stereotype plates, only leasing them to publishers and commanding a royalty higher than the common 10 percent. But most authors now participated in a process controlled by the publisher, who took the risks of manufacturing, paid the royalty, and owned the plates. By 1850, too, railroads enabled booksellers in the interior to buy directly from publishers. These changes freed authors from the commercial minutiae of publishing, but at the cost of control, as publishers encouraged writers to cater to their ideas of the public taste—for instance, pressing the author Nathaniel Hawthorne toward novels rather than short stories. The publishers represented themselves as gentlemen partners in the literary enterprise, who cultivated authors, their intellectual work, and an American literature. Wiley and Putnam published a "Library of American Books" series in the 1840s, and Ticknor and Fields helped create literary stars through its "Blue and Gold" editions of selected authors. Several book publishers' successful magazines, notably *Harper's Monthly*, *Harper's Weekly*, and *Scribner's Monthly*, also helped promote the firms' books through advertisements, reviews, and serialization.

In legal terms, publishers' relations with authors involved issues of copyright. The initial U.S. copyright act (1790) followed the English system, by which the author retained exclusive publication rights to his or her work for fourteen years; in 1831 the term was extended to twenty-eight years, with the possibility of a fourteen-year renewal. American copyright acts protected only native authors, however. Lacking an international copyright agreement, foreign works could be printed in the United States without payment or permission (and vice versa). American authors worried that publishers would reprint foreign works—which could be sold more cheaply, or at a greater discount to booksellers—rather than invest in American authors. English authors whose work was reprinted without royalty also suffered. A coalition of authors and publishers, led by George Palmer Putnam (1814–1872), pressed unsuccessfully for international copyright legislation in the 1840s and for an international copyright treaty in the 1850s.

Publishers themselves sought a system to regulate reprinting, in which they could undercut each other if unchecked (which occurred in the early 1840s). In their solution, which they called "courtesy of the trade," the exclusive right to republish a foreign work

Book Catalog. The April 1899 catalog for Charles Scribner's Sons, founded in 1846, with an illustration by Maxfield Parrish. © MAXFIELD PARRISH FAMILY TRUST/LICENSED BY ASAP, HOLDERNESS, NH AND VAGA, NY, NY. PHOTOGRAPH LICENSED THROUGH CORBIS.

belonged to the publisher who reprinted it first, or who purchased the right to do so from its author or original publisher. As a result many popular English writers were well compensated by their authorized American publishers. Courtesy of the trade functioned fairly successfully between 1845 and 1870, but after the Civil War new publishing firms challenged the older, exclusive arrangements between popular European authors and their American publishers. As these new firms practiced what the "gentlemen" publishers called "piracy," the movement for international copyright regained momentum. The establishment of the International Copyright Association in 1868 revived the discussion, and in 1878 Harper and Brothers proposed an international commission of authors and publishers to draft a treaty. Only in 1891, however, after authors and publishers had each formed a Copyright League, did Congress pass the International Copyright (Chace) Act. Copyright protection now extended to foreign-authored books that had been set, printed, and bound in the United States.

Forms of Specialized Book Publishing

Throughout the century, religious book publishing comprised a second network of print. In 1825 the New England Tract Society (founded in 1814) and several other regional tract societies merged to form the American Tract Society (ATS), the largest religious publisher in nineteenth-century America. Other religious publishers proliferated, including the American Sunday-School Union, the American Bible Society, and the Methodist Book Concern. Before 1830, the ATS and other tract societies pioneered many of the production technologies, such as stereotyping and steam-powered printing, that commercial publishers would exploit in subsequent decades. Their distribution methods differed, however: they endeavored to supply everyone—rich or poor, across the United States—with reading material. The ATS initially envisioned its role as that of a printer, taking advantage of economies of scale in production but selling its books to local societies, other benevolent associations, and individuals to distribute. But, as auxiliary societies failed to disseminate the materials nationwide, particularly in the West, the ATS developed its own highly centralized system of salaried book agents, or colporteurs.

By the 1860s, many commercial publishers specialized in particular genres or categories of books. Most prolific were the dime-novel firms, such as Beadle and Adams (founded in 1860), which printed full-length novels in multicolumned print with cheap orange or yellow paper covers. By the 1870s, dime-novel companies employed stables of writers to churn out exciting, formulaic fiction for ever-expanding series. Other publishers soon followed with cheap reprints in pocket sizes. Specialty publishers included John Wiley and Sons in scientific books, William Wood and Co. in medical books, the Orange Judd Publishing Company in farming and gardening books, Funk and Wagnalls in dictionaries, and Samuel French in plays. Schoolbooks were the province of A. S. Barnes and Co. in New York; G. and C. Merriam Company of Springfield, Massachusetts; and numerous textbook firms in Boston and Chicago. Several general publishers also became known in specialized areas, for instance Houghton Mifflin for its educational books (including the Riverside Series of literature).

Subscription publishing, an age-old sales method, revived after the Civil War. In the colonial period and the early republic, subscriptions had been an aspiring publisher's necessity in lieu of established credit networks or ready capital. Now they provided an alternative sales method for trade publishers to sell books (particularly special offerings, such as series of the works of a noted author) directly to readers. In addition, dozens of firms devoted exclusively to subscription publishing, such as A. S. Hale and Company, sprouted between 1865 and 1900, employing armies of book agents to canvass the nation with salesmen's "dummies," prospectuses for as-yet-unpublished volumes. If orders sufficed, production would commence. Subscription books were generally quartos or octavos (larger than trade publishers' typical products), often ornately embossed and gilded. Practical housekeeping books, anthologies, encyclopedias and dictionaries, biographies, histories, and especially family Bibles and other religious books were the subscription publishers' staples. Mark Twain (Samuel L. Clemens) published many of his works by subscription with the American Publishing Company of Hartford, capital of the subscription industry.

Technological innovations in the last decades of the century laid the foundations of much twentieth-century book publishing. Ottmar Mergenthaler's Linotype (first used in newspapers, 1886) inaugurated the successful mechanization of typesetting. Halftone photographic engraving (invented by Frederic Eugene Ives, 1878; perfected by 1886) allowed publishers to incorporate photographs onto the printed pages of books and magazines. As the century ended, the industrialization of publishing and the proliferation of cheap, commercially dictated books called forth a reaction. Inspired by William Morris's Kelmscott Press in England, some American printers reimagined their centuries-old craft as art. Daniel Berkeley Updike's Merrymount Press (1893) and Will Bradley's Wayside Press (1895) were among the first American fine letterpress firms, beginning an alternative tradition that flourished in the shadow of commercial book publishing through the twentieth century and into the twenty-first.

See also **Bible and Bible Reading, The; Communications; Dime Novels and Story Papers; Literacy and Reading Habits; Literature; Printing Technology.**

Bibliography

Charvat, William. *Literary Publishing in America, 1790–1850.* Philadelphia: University of Pennsylvania Press, 1959.

———. *The Profession of Authorship in America, 1800–1870.* Columbus: Ohio State University Press, 1968.

Lehmann-Haupt, Hellmut, in collaboration with Lawrence C. Wroth and Rollo G. Silver. *The Book in America: A History of the Making and Selling of Books in the United States.* 2d ed. New York: R. R. Bowker, 1951.

Moylan, Michele, and Lane Stiles, eds. *Reading Books: Essays on the Material Text and Literature in America.* Amherst: University of Massachusetts Press, 1996.

Nord, David Paul. "Systematic Benevolence: Religious Publishing and the Marketplace in Early Nineteenth-Century America." In *Communication and Change in American Re-*

ligious History. Edited by Leonard I. Sweet. Grand Rapids, Mich.: William B. Eerdmans, 1993.

Remer, Rosalind. Printers and Men of Capital: Philadelphia Book Publishers in the New Republic. Philadelphia: University of Pennsylvania Press, 1996.

Winship, Michael. American Literary Publishing in the Mid-Nineteenth Century: The Business of Ticknor and Fields. Cambridge, U.K.: Cambridge University Press, 1995.

Zboray, Ronald J. A Fictive People: Antebellum Economic Development and the American Reading Public. New York: Oxford University Press, 1993.

SCOTT E. CASPER

BOOMTOWNS   "Money was as plenty as dust, every individual considered himself wealthy, and a melancholy countenance was nowhere to be seen." Thus wrote that recent miner, now a newspaper editor, Samuel Clemens, about his new home, Virginia City, Nevada. "The 'flush times' were in magnificent flower!" (Twain, The Works of Mark Twain, p. 274).

Flush times, optimism, and confidence that wealth lay just around the corner created an economic explosion for a generation of mining towns and camps throughout the West. Mark Twain's Roughing It (1872) best captured the sense of those places and times. Mining produced an urban West from the days of the forty-niners, who rushed West in 1849, through the close of the era at Tonopah and Goldfield, Nevada, after the turn of the century. While mining camps were more numerous, they were smaller and tended to decline more rapidly. The towns had larger populations, wealthier and longer lasting mines, more permanent construction in brick and stone, and more diversified and specialized business communities. They also exhibited a greater attitude of confidence and success than did their smaller contemporaries.

Started on faith and built with confidence in a better tomorrow, these mining communities sometimes lasted only a season or two, others survived into the twentieth century. They all followed a cycle of birth, boom, stabilization, and decline. A very few, such as Lead, South Dakota; Helena, Montana; Aspen, Colorado; and Alta, Utah, managed to stave off terminal decline by continuing as mining centers, becoming a state capital, or reviving themselves through cultural activities and skiing. Many more, such as Tombstone, Arizona; Central City, Colorado; and Virginia City, Nevada, have survived in a reduced status as tourist destinations. A very few, such as Columbia and Bodie, California; and Virginia City, Montana, have become state parks.

Once mining gave these communities birth, the presence of the railroad nourished and sustained the larger, more prosperous towns and fewer camps. In the nineteenth century, the "iron horse" was the ultimate form of transportation. The town that did not gain railroad connections held little promise of a future. The completion of the transcontinental line in 1869 provided the beginning of a railroad building boom that lasted for two decades. The use of narrow gauge (three feet wide) track proved more adaptable in the mountains and helped promote mining and mining communities, particularly in Colorado.

In the fifty-five years following the 1849 gold rush, one mining rush after another touched various western states. Each of these produced boomtowns and lifestyles that intrigued, titillated, and fascinated eastern and European readers. These communities were well covered by journalists and photographers, who presented all sides of life found in them to their readers. Three towns against which any "true" mining town or camp came to be measured were Deadwood, South Dakota, and Tombstone, Arizona—with attention-grabbing names—and Leadville, Colorado, a certified bonanza district. It helped too that western sagas, unrelated to mining, occurred in these towns—the shooting of Wild Bill Hickok in Deadwood and Tombstone's gunfight between the Earps and Clantons at the O.K. Corral in October 1881. From Leadville came Horace Tabor, in many ways the epitome of the real, soon-to-be legendary, mining man of the boomtown West.

Contributions to legend aside, these communities also served a vital role in the settlement of the West. They were transmitters of eastern and European culture, fads and fashions, and a variety of developments to the larger region around them. Their schools, medical facilities, professional and business communities, and transportation networks were often the best available. Wherever possible and whenever needed, agricultural and industrial development started in or near them. Without question, these boomtowns helped open, promote, tame, and settle the West.

The people who resided in these communities came west for a variety of reasons. Some, perhaps most, never initially intended to stay once they had made their fortunes. Many of them, transitory folk, were willing to stampede off at a moment's notice should fortune beckon over the next mountain. Nevertheless, in their temporary boomtown homes they often strove to re-create the lives they had left behind. Contemporary tourists might have gawked at the unusual but, at the same time, would have found much to remind them of their hometowns.

In the end, boomtowns of the nineteenth century followed a life cycle that has been repeated in the twentieth century by many of their modern urban

Boomtown in Oklahoma Territory. Settled on land formerly belonging to the Cherokees, Guthrie, former capital of Oklahoma, was representative of towns that sprang up throughout the West as the United States rapidly expanded. Photograph c. 1893. NATIONAL ARCHIVES

western descendants and produced a heritage whose imprint is still widely felt in American culture.

See also **Gold Rushes and Silver Strikes; Mining and Extraction; Railroads; West, The.**

Bibliography

Mann, Ralph. *After the Gold Rush.* Stanford, Calif.: Stanford University Press, 1982.

Reps, John W. *Cities of the American West.* Princeton, N.J.: Princeton University Press, 1979.

Smith, Duane A. *Rocky Mountain Mining Camps: A History of Durango.* Rev. ed. Niwot: University of Colorado Press, 1992.

Twain, Mark. *Roughing It.* Volume 2 of *The Works of Mark Twain.* Berkeley: University of California Press, 1973.

DUANE A. SMITH

BOOSTERISM   The promotion of urban and regional growth lay at the heart of the phenomenon of boosterism, which gained wide popularity in the nineteenth century. Practiced by businesspeople who hoped to attract settlers and commerce to their towns or cities, boosterism aimed to create a positive image that sometimes exaggerated the true nature of a city's state of development. Boosters promoted the natural advantages of their localities, made extravagant claims about the cultural amenities available and the transportation possibilities of local waterways, boasted of superior and healthy climates, and touted their regions' natural resources, such as ore, timber, and other marketable commodities. The Omaha booster Nathan H. Parker, for example, published *The Kansas and Nebraska Handbook for 1857–1858,* in which he promoted Omaha's genteel and cultured lifestyle, which he claimed rivaled that of New York or New England towns of twice the size. With the success of canals and railroads in the 1830s, boosterism took on a new meaning as cities and towns across the United States vied to increase their growth and commerce by attracting first a canal and later a rail line. Boosting a community or region also became an important cement for a rising class of businesspeople and professionals in the nineteenth century. In the 1850s the Los Angeles promoter Phineas Banning organized local merchants to raise money to improve access and promote commerce through the construction of roads into the city. Banning's actions led to the construction of a series of roadways that allowed wagon trains to make the seventy-five-mile trip across the San Fernando Pass from Los Angeles to Fort Tejon in only nine days. As cities became more established, city building or boosting brought independent businesspeople together to create such organizations as chambers of commerce, which worked to ensure continued growth.

Boosterism spread westward with the land craze that began in the 1830s, and land speculators became boosters as they drew up and publicized plans for new cities in the West. Most of these cities never materialized, but a few booster dreams were realized with the growth of such great western cities as Chicago and St. Louis. The St. Louis promoter Logan U. Reavis, for example, believed somewhere in the world a final great city would emerge, and he argued that his Missouri town would be that city. On the other hand, the Chicago booster William B. Ogden believed that his city was naturally destined for greatness. Ogden arrived in Chicago in 1835, was elected mayor in 1837, and invested heavily in local real estate. Financial investment in new cities gave booster-businesspeople an added stake in their promoting urban growth. Ogden's actions on behalf of Chicago helped to make that city the gateway to the developing West. In the forty-five years after Ogden's arrival Chicago grew from a small city of just over three thousand residents to a large city with a population of more than half a million in 1880. Ogden's ardent boosterism also made him a rich man; his initial investment of $15,000 in Chicago real estate was worth $10 million in 1865.

The urban press was an important means of conveying the message of boosterism. An increase in the popularity of newspapers and journals in the nineteenth century, especially those inexpensive publications of the so-called penny press, made them the ideal venue for communicating booster dreams. Community newspapers were established with the express purpose of attracting settlers and business to new towns or cities, and they reached a circulation far beyond the city limits. In controlling the content of local publications, boosters ensured that negative information was suppressed, and readers learned only about the positive aspects of a city. Newspaper editors often became the most vocal advocates of city and regional growth, and the popularity of the booster press sometimes rewarded editors with elevated standing in the community or the region. One of the most widely known and respected urban boosters of the southern states was J. D. B. De Bow, who used his regional journal *De Bow's Review* to identify and promote the growth of railroads and industry in a number of southern cities, including Norfolk, Virginia, and his own home city of New Orleans.

See also **Advertising; Chicago; Cities and Urbanization; City and Regional Planning; Newspapers and the Press; St. Louis; World's Fairs.**

Bibliography

Boorstin, Daniel J. *The Americans: The National Experience.* New York: Vintage, 1965.

Cronon, William. *Nature's Metropolis: Chicago and the Great West.* New York: Norton, 1991.
Doyle, Don H. *New Men, New Cities, New South: Atlanta, Nashville, Charleston, Mobile, 1860–1910.* Chapel Hill: University of North Carolina Press, 1990.
Hamer, David. *New Towns in the New World: Images and Perceptions of the Nineteenth-Century Urban Frontier.* New York: Columbia University Press, 1990.

DIANE BARNES

BORDER STATES   The nineteenth-century conception of U.S. "border states" emerged with the abolition of slavery in the North. Border states originally consisted of the slave states bordering free areas. With the advent of the Civil War, this definition changed to include only those slave states that did not secede from the Union. Thus, by the 1860s, the border states consisted of Delaware, Maryland, Kentucky, Missouri, and West Virginia. The pro-Union area of east Tennessee, the Kansas Territory, and much of southern Indiana and southern Illinois were unified culturally with the border states, whose attitudes were pro-Union, proslavery, and antiblack. After the Civil War, the border region ameliorated the ongoing cultural and political conflicts between the North and the South, including issues like segregation. However, the border states were not a unified region; their peculiar geographic and cultural situations gave them a general but not specific unity.

From 1806 until his death, Henry Clay (1777–1852) of Kentucky was the leading politician representing the border states. He was the principal originator of the Missouri Compromise (1820), which admitted Missouri as a slave state and drew a line separating future slave and free states constructed out of the Louisiana Purchase. The border states especially influenced the national dialogue on the slavery question. Antislavery feeling typically was northern, but the first antislavery newspaper, Elihu Embree's (1782–1820) *Manumission Intelligencer,* began publication in 1819 in Jonesboro, Tennessee. Benjamin Lundy (1789–1839) moved his *Genius of Universal Emancipation* to Greenville, Tennessee, from 1822 to 1824 before finally moving that publication to Baltimore. There he hired William Lloyd Garrison (1805–1879), giving him his first antislavery writing position. Garrison would later lead the radical abolitionist movement through his Boston-based newspaper, *The Liberator.* Frederick Douglass (1817–1895), an escaped Maryland slave, became a prominent antislavery speaker. James G. Birney (1792–1857) of Kentucky served as the long-term secretary of the American Anti-Slavery Society, and Cassius Clay (1810–1903), Henry's cousin, was a southern abolitionist leader. There was also, of course, strong support for slavery in the area. The 1860 census showed 225,000 slaves in Kentucky, 115,000 in Missouri, and 90,000 in Maryland and the District of Columbia, but only 18,000 in what became West Virginia and less than 2,000 in Delaware.

In 1850 the nation was held together by a typical congressional compromise, proposed by the border states. Henry Clay, supported by others in the region, led the nation to admit California as a free state, while also strengthening the federal Fugitive Slave Law. The slave trade was abolished in the District of Columbia, but slavery was preserved there. In 1854 the Kansas-Nebraska Act abolished the Missouri Compromise line and allowed popular sovereignty in Kansas, which immediately became a battleground between free-state supporters and proponents of slavery. Eventually antislave elements prevailed and Kansas became more of a western than a border state. In 1857 the *Dred Scott v. Sandford* decision concerning the possible freedom of a Missouri slave declared the Missouri Compromise line to be unconstitutional and affirmed the ability of U.S. citizens to take their slaves into U.S. territories. At the end of the 1850s the abolitionist John Brown (1800–1859) raided the federal arsenal at Harpers Ferry, Virginia (now West Virginia), in an attempt to start a slave rebellion. He was hung for treason at Charles Town in December 1859.

The climactic presidential election of 1860 saw major involvement by the border states. John C. Breckinridge (1821–1875) of Kentucky was nominated by the southern Democrats. Both Abraham (1809–1865) and Mary Todd Lincoln (1818–1882) were originally from Kentucky and always maintained close ties to the border states. John Bell (1797–1869) of Tennessee was nominated by the Constitutional Union Party and carried Kentucky, Virginia, and Tennessee. Missouri went to Stephen Douglas (1813–1861), and both Maryland and Delaware went to Breckinridge.

Between December 1860 and February 1861, seven of the Deep South states seceded. Other slave areas were caught in a bind. The very definition of a border state was tested as each area declared its allegiance after the Fort Sumter conflict in April 1861. Arkansas, Tennessee, North Carolina, and Virginia seceded and became the Upper South. Missouri, Kentucky, Maryland, and Delaware did not secede and became the border states. West Virginia, with only 18,000 slaves as opposed to 472,000 in the rest of the state, was particularly divided. Fifty mountainous counties seceded from the Confederacy under the leadership of Francis Pierpont (1814–1899) and achieved statehood on 20 June 1863. East Tennessee

also tried to join the Union, but was occupied by Confederate forces. However, the east Tennessee Unionist Andrew Johnson (1808–1875) refused to leave Washington and became the military governor of Tennessee; he was elected vice president in 1864.

During the Civil War, most of the fighting occurred south of the border area. However, the border states did see many battles, including Wilson's Creek, Missouri, and Mill Springs, Richmond, Perryville, and Prestonsburg, Kentucky. Both Union and Confederate forces crossed the West Virginia panhandle and western Maryland several times, resulting in such major battles as Harpers Ferry, Antietam (the bloodiest single day of the war), and Monocacy.

After the Civil War, the country's political reconstruction did not affect the border states. Missouri, however, endured a decade-long guerrilla war before peace was restored. In every area, segregation became the way of life in public accommodations, schools, and social affairs. Economic reconstruction was particularly difficult in Kentucky, Missouri, and Maryland, due to the loss of numerous slaves. Diversity became the main economic theme. St. Louis and Baltimore emerged as key industrial centers before 1900 and attracted many immigrants from Europe and the South. The Du Pont company in Wilmington, Delaware, became one of the world's largest chemical producers. West Virginia was dominated by coal mining and the petroleum industry, while Kentucky saw coal, tobacco, and horses predominate.

Culturally, changes came in several areas. Two Baltimore railroad owners realigned American education: Johns Hopkins (1795–1873) willed money to establish his university (1876), which brought German-style graduate education to the United States and granted the nation's first Ph.D. degrees; George Peabody (1795–1869) established the Fund for the Advancement of Southern Education, which helped to upgrade public schools throughout the southern and border states. Also, St. Louis, Louisville, and Baltimore all had teams in the first major U.S. sports organization, the National League of Professional Base Ball Clubs. The St. Louis World's Fair earned international acclaim just after the turn of the century. By 1900 the border states were poised to join a new century while continuing their moderating position in the country.

See also **Abolition and Antislavery; Civil War; Compromise of 1850; Fugitive Slave Laws; Kansas-Nebraska Act; Missouri Compromise; Reconstruction; Sectionalism.**

Bibliography

Aron, Stephen. *How the West Was Lost: The Transformation of*

Kentucky from Daniel Boone to Henry Clay. Baltimore: Johns Hopkins University Press, 1996.

Baxter, Maurice G. *Henry Clay and the American System.* Lexington: University Press of Kentucky, 1995.

Douglass, Frederick. *The Life and Times of Frederick Douglass.* London: Christian Age Office, 1882. Grand Rapids, Mich.: Candace Press, 1996.

Munroe, John A. *History of Delaware.* Newark: University of Delaware Press, 1993.

Nagel, Paul C. *Missouri: A Bicentennial History.* Lawrence: University Press of Kansas, 1988.

Rice, Otis K. *West Virginia: A History.* Lexington: University Press of Kentucky, 1993.

FRED S. ROLATER

BOSSES, POLITICAL. See **Politics**, subentry on **Machines and Bosses**.

BOSTON

Boston entered the nineteenth century as the capital of Massachusetts and—with a population in 1800 of 24,937—the fourth largest urban center in the nation, behind New York, Philadelphia, and Baltimore. Boston was a mercantile seaport, more culturally and ethnically homogeneous than its major urban counterparts.

1800–1865

The seaport struggled to find new areas of trade to make up for its lack of a resource-rich hinterland. Boston merchants played a central role in opening the China trade and in the early nineteenth century came to dominate the trade. Sailing to the Pacific Northwest, the Boston traders exchanged trinkets, clothing, and copper for pelts, which they then sold in China for great profit. From China, they returned to Boston with tea and silk. In the 1830s Frederick Tudor developed the most innovative Boston-based trade route when he devised a method of shipping ice to Asia, making use of one of New England's few natural resources.

Boston's role, mainly as a shipper of other areas' goods, made sea trade an economically unpredictable undertaking, and the risks to sea trade during the wars between France and England in the early nineteenth century compounded the difficulty. In 1813 a group of Boston merchants, led by Francis Cabot Lowell, diversified their interests by investing in cotton textile manufacturing. Beginning with a factory in nearby Waltham, Lowell and his associates began the process of large-scale, power-driven manufacturing in America. Eventually, the mills of the "Boston Associates" would spring up across New England, with Boston as the command center.

In addition to economic change, Boston faced political change in the first forty years of the century. Boston was no longer the political center it had been in the revolutionary period. The diminution was in part the result of Boston's continued adherence to the Federalist Party, long after the party lost viability in other parts of the country, where Jeffersonian "democracy" had taken hold.

At the local level, the great change was the transformation of Boston from a town to a city in March 1822. Bostonians had long resisted attempts to change the town into a city, holding sacred the concept of the participatory democracy of the town meeting. But in a community that had a population of 43,298 in 1820, the town meeting had become unwieldy. Boston's second mayor, Josiah Quincy, known as the "Great Mayor," served from 1823 to 1828 and confirmed for Bostonians the benefits of city government. Quincy initiated a wide variety of projects to improve the city, particularly in sanitation and in the enlargement and improvement of the Faneuil Hall market area.

In the three decades before the Civil War, the Boston region became a major center for literary and reform activities. Ralph Waldo Emerson was the central figure in the literary and philosophical movement known as transcendentalism. Among his compatriots were Henry David Thoreau and Margaret Fuller, the period's leading woman intellectual. While transcendentalism was an American manifestation of romanticism, its specific values of optimism and belief in positive change greatly affected mid-century Boston and the nation. Transcendentalism nurtured, along with older Puritan reform traditions, a number of reform movements. Horace Mann, who sought to improve public education, had close ties to the transcendentalists. Mann's friend Dr. Samuel Gridley Howe developed innovative methods of educating blind children, and both men assisted Dorothea Dix in her valiant fight to improve conditions for the mentally ill and the imprisoned.

By the 1850s the abolitionist movement had overtaken all the reform efforts in Boston. African Americans had begun the abolitionist fight in the city, but it was William Lloyd Garrison and the publication of his newspaper, the *Liberator* (begun in 1831), that expanded the movement into a broader-based effort. Garrison developed a devoted band of supporters in Boston that included his close associate Wendell Phillips, women such as Maria Weston Chapman and Lydia Maria Child, and African Americans such as Lewis Hayden and Charles Remond. The efforts of Bostonians to resist the return of the fugitive slave

Beacon Hill, Boston. The Massachusetts State House, completed in 1798, is at right. Lithography by J. B. Smith, 1811–1812. LIBRARY OF CONGRESS

Anthony Burns in 1854 intensified northern opposition to the Fugitive Slave Act of 1850.

The stable, prosperous, and relatively homogeneous city underwent a major shock in the 1840s, with the massive influx of Irish immigrants. The peasantry in Ireland had faced increasing difficulty for several decades, but the potato rot, which first appeared in that country in 1845, created a disaster. Hundreds of thousands immigrated, many to Boston. The port's relative proximity to the British Isles, compared with other American ports, and the decision of the British government in 1841 to route mail to Canada through Boston, led to frequent sailings, particularly from Liverpool. Several of the major shipping companies seized the opportunity to carry Irish peasants in steerage at low costs. By 1855 the Irish-born made up 46,237 of Boston's 160,400 residents.

The city was ill prepared to deal with the newcomers. There were few jobs for unskilled workers in a city that had undergone little industrialization and was not a growing, dynamic commercial center. As early as 1834, when the first wave of Irish were appearing, an anti-Irish Catholic mob in nearby Charlestown set fire to the Ursuline Convent. Further violence occurred as the number of Irish increased dramatically. In the mid-1850s the nativist Know-Nothing Party swept the state elections.

The Civil War brought groups together. Massachusetts was one of the first states to heed President Abraham Lincoln's call for troops. Many Irish rallied to the Union cause. The African American community evoked admiration by sending 40 percent of its men of military age to fight for the Union, many in the famous Massachusetts Fifty-fourth Regiment. Their volunteering was all the more impressive in that for a good part of the war they received less pay than their white counterparts and were subject to death or enslavement if captured.

1865–1900

After the war Boston became a major industrial city. Industry had previously been located on fast-flowing rivers, which Boston lacked. The widespread adoption of steam power allowed Boston to industrialize on a large scale. Another factor in the city's industrialization was the realization that the city's vast Irish immigrant population could be put to work in factories. Beginning as early as the 1850s, factories employing hundreds of workers opened in Boston, making items such as ready-made clothes. The city went on to produce a wide array of industrial products, such as pianos, ships, sugar, candy, carpets, beer, iron, printed goods, and lithographs.

The industrialization of the late nineteenth century was a factor in the immigration of new groups to Boston. Jews had generally avoided Boston in the first half of the century, moving to more economically dynamic areas. In the late nineteenth century, as large numbers of eastern European Jews fled religious oppression and economic deprivation, many settled in Boston. During the 1880s and 1890s Boston's Jewish population increased from about five thousand to forty thousand.

Italians also arrived at this time. Like the Irish, the Italians were fleeing overcrowded lands, absentee landlords, and natural disasters, such as the vineyard disease of the 1870s. The Italian-born population increased from 1,277 in 1880 to 13,738 in 1900. Also, in the late 1800s, Canadians from the Maritime Provinces continued their migration to Boston, and a number of Poles and Lithuanians settled in the city. The African American community grew from 1,999 in 1850 to 11,591 in 1900.

The city, which needed large new areas of land to provide for this increase in population and industry, gained this area from landfill and annexation. Boston's acreage rose from one thousand in the 1830s to thirty thousand by the 1870s. Beginning in the early nineteenth century, Boston began one of the nation's most ambitious programs of landfill. Leveling the hills of the original Shawmut Peninsula, and later bringing in fill from suburban areas, Boston filled in many of the bays and inlets along its shoreline, including the 580 acres of the Back Bay. In the 1860s and 1870s, Boston gained new territory by annexing five towns and cities.

Boston led the nation's cities in per capita expenditures for public services during the late nineteenth century. Much of the funding went to new areas of the city for sewer, storm drain, and water services. Boston also developed, under the guidance of Frederick Law Olmsted, a linear greenbelt around the settled sections of the city, which tied together the older city and some of the newer annexed areas. The city also opened in 1895 one of the most magnificent public libraries in the world and in 1897 the first subway in the United States. Despite the benefits to smaller towns and cities of joining Boston, annexation essentially ended in 1874. Only one town would join Boston after that date. Outlying communities now looked to the state government rather than Boston to provide needed services. Beginning in 1889 the state government created metropolitan commissions to provide sewer, water, and park services for the metropolitan area.

One major reason for the loss of interest in annexation was alienation from what suburbanites perceived was the growing Irish domination of Boston.

For most of the last third of the century, a coalition of Yankee and Irish Democrats controlled the mayor's office. In 1884 the coalition elected the first Irish mayor, the highly respected Hugh O'Brien. The Irish made much greater inroads in the board of aldermen and city council, and a ward boss system began to take shape.

The Boston-Cambridge area increased its eminence in higher education in the late nineteenth century. The Massachusetts Institute of Technology was founded in 1861 in Boston and remained in the city until 1916. At Harvard University, located mainly in Cambridge but with some facilities in Boston, the educational reforms of President Charles W. Eliot (1869–1909), emphasizing the elective course system, research, and professional programs, enhanced Harvard's leadership role in American higher education.

Boston entered the twentieth century an ethnically and culturally heterogeneous city. It boasted a diversified economy based on industry, commerce, finance, and government services. The city's population was 560,892, the fifth largest in the nation, and it served as the center of a metropolitan area of more than 1 million people.

See also **Cities and Urbanization; Immigration and Immigrants,** *subentries on* **Ireland, Jewish Immigrants, Southern Europe, Canada; Massachusetts.**

Bibliography

DeMarco, William M. *Ethnics and Enclaves: Boston's Italian North End.* Ann Arbor, Mich.: UMI Research Press, 1981.

Handlin, Oscar. *Boston's Immigrants, 1790–1880: A Study in Acculturation.* Rev. and enl. ed. New York: Atheneum, 1972.

Horton, James Oliver, and Lois E. Horton. *Black Bostonians: Family Life and Community Struggle in the Antebellum North.* New York: Holmes and Meier, 1979.

Kennedy, Lawrence W. *Planning the City upon a Hill: Boston since 1630.* Amherst: University of Massachusetts Press, 1992.

O'Connor, Thomas H. *Bibles, Brahmins, and Bosses: A Short History of Boston.* Rev. ed. Boston: Trustees of the Public Library of the City of Boston, 1984.

Pease, Jane H., and William H. Pease. *Ladies, Women, and Wenches: Choice and Constraint in Antebellum Charleston and Boston.* Chapel Hill: University of North Carolina Press, 1990.

Sarna, Jonathan D., and Ellen Smith, eds. *The Jews of Boston: Essays on the Occasion of the Centenary (1895–1995) of the Combined Jewish Philanthropies of Greater Boston.* Boston: Combined Jewish Philanthropies of Greater Boston, 1995.

Warner, Sam Bass, Jr. *Streetcar Suburbs: The Process of Growth in Boston, 1870–1900.* 2d ed. Cambridge, Mass.: Harvard University Press, 1978.

THOMAS A. MCMULLIN

BREWING AND DISTILLING   The American brewing and distilling industries underwent profound changes during the nineteenth century. In 1800 the United States had only 5 million people, almost all of whom lived on farms, and the most populous city, Philadelphia, had seventy thousand people. At that time beer was rare. Small local markets, poor transportation, and lack of cold storage inhibited commercial brewing, although some housewives made mildly alcoholic weak beer for personal use. Roadside taverns seldom stocked beer because low sales meant that a tapped keg went stale before it could be emptied.

After 1840 the cities grew. Beer production soared as large numbers of German immigrants raised demand and introduced lager beer into the United States. During the Civil War heavy taxes on hard liquor favored beer, and Union army soldiers received beer in place of rum rations. By the 1880s beer outsold whiskey, and giant companies dominated the industry. Except for Coors, which was of Dutch origin, virtually all breweries were founded by German immigrants.

Producers included the Milwaukee companies Schlitz, Pabst, and Miller (originally Mueller) and the St. Louis company Anheuser-Busch. Breweries could not operate in hot weather, which gave Milwaukee an edge. During that city's cool summers, Milwaukee brewers shipped beer to hotter cities. Busch gained an advantage when it invented the refrigerated railway car. By 1900 Busch and the Milwaukee brewers were on their way to controlling the industry nationally. The powerful major brewers owned saloons that dominated big city politics, and until 1917 they effectively blocked Prohibition.

Distilling followed a different path. In 1800 New England rum was in sharp decline due to competition from cheap whiskey. In that year a few large-scale whiskey producers shared the market with thousands of small distillers. Although large companies had economies of scale, they did not dominate because they paid taxes that small producers evaded. The technology as well as the name "whiskey" came from Ireland, and on the frontier Scots-Irish farmers became famous for their efficient grain stills. Most distillers made whiskey by mixing corn and rye. Consequently production was concentrated in areas of surplus corn—first Kentucky, then Ohio, and finally Illinois.

During the first half of the century, distilling was a major industry, accounting for 10 percent of all manufacturers in the United States in 1810. Americans not only drank whiskey but also used it as medication, both internally and externally. Industrial alcohol was an important solvent in manufacturing. During the Civil War the federal government imposed high taxes on hard liquor. Because the excise taxes had to be paid during distillation, prior to aging and sale, only highly capitalized, large-scale distilleries survived financially. Unlike breweries, distilleries required few workers.

In 1875 the U.S. Treasury caught many distillers bribing government inspectors to underreport production on which taxes were due, and the subsequent Whiskey Ring scandal discredited the industry. In the 1880s the distillers combined to create the whiskey trust, an attempted monopoly, which further reduced the industry's reputation. Although the distillers were skilled at backroom politics, their low prestige gave them less influence than brewers, who developed greater public support, profits, and political ties.

See also **Alcoholic Beverages; Patent Medicines; Politics,** *subentry on* **Corruption and Scandals; Saloons and the Drinking Life; Temperance Movement; Trusts.**

Bibliography

Baron, Stanley. *Brewed in America: A History of Beer and Ale in the United States.* Boston: Little, Brown, 1962.

Carson, Gerald. *The Social History of Bourbon: An Unhurried Account of Our Star Spangled American Drink.* New York: Dodd, Mead, 1963.

Downard, William L. *Dictionary of the History of the American Brewing and Distilling Industries.* Westport, Conn.: Greenwood, 1980.

W. J. RORABAUGH

BRIDGES.   See **Civil Engineering,** subentry on **Bridges and Tunnels.**

BROOKLYN   In 1800 Brooklyn consisted of a small core directly across the East River from New York City (Manhattan Island) and scattered Dutch farming villages. Largely dependent on enslaved black labor, the Dutch farmers still lived and worked much as they had when Kings County was first formed in 1683. Change was rapid in the nineteenth century, however. In 1898 Brooklyn, a city of 800,000 people, was incorporated with four other boroughs into Greater New York. Though much of Brooklyn remained rural into the early twentieth century, the borough's destiny was shaped by the behemoth city across the East River.

Transportation Revolution

Transportation developments aided Brooklyn's initial growth. Spurred by the opening of the Erie Canal in 1825, manufactories along Brooklyn's waterfront produced paint, glass, and glue. Ancillary occupations included wheelwrights, coopers, and clerks. Freight terminals soon lined the southern shores all the way to Red Hook. Regular steam ferry service from New York City to Brooklyn Heights started in 1814, when developers championed the small city as a suburban refuge from New York. New streets were planned and graveled in the next few years, and Brooklyn Heights's population changed from Dutch farmers to Manhattan businesspeople and their families. The city was incorporated in 1816, and soon characteristic Federal and Greek Revival homes stretched southward across the county. Farther north the Dutch town of Bushwick was incorporated as Williamsburg in 1827, and by 1850 it had more than thirty thousand residents. Railroad construction propelled settlement of such neighborhoods as Bedford-Stuyvesant, Canarsie, and Flatlands, pushing their populations from a few hundred into the thousands. Two African American entrepreneurs, William Thomas and James Weeks, promoted Bedford-Stuyvesant, creating black neighborhoods known as Weeksville and Carrville.

Political institutions accompanied population growth. Established in 1834, the city of Brooklyn in 1839 developed a plan for a rectangular grid of streets crossed by diagonal avenues and broken regularly by parks. Gaslights were introduced in 1848 and fresh water in the 1850s. Kings County Hospital opened in 1831, and Green-Wood Cemetery was incorporated in 1838. In 1843 schools were reorganized under the Brooklyn Board of Education.

Beautifully constructed churches, including the Plymouth Church of the Pilgrims in Brooklyn Heights (1847); the Reformed Church of South Bushwick (1853); the Grace Protestant Church of Brooklyn (1840); and the historic Canarsie Plymouth Congregational Church (1877), founded by free blacks descended from local slaves, accentuated the family orientation of Brooklyn. The first Catholic church, St. James, was built in 1822, and the Roman Catholic diocese of Brooklyn was established in 1853.

Brooklyn kept pace with New York's cultural institutions. The Apprentices Library, the forerunner of the Brooklyn Museum, started operating in 1823, and the Brooklyn Academy of Music opened its doors in 1861. Brooklyn Collegiate and Polytechnic Institute first held classes in 1853, and two years later

The Brooklyn Bridge. Formally known as the Great East River Suspension Bridge, the bridge connects New York and Brooklyn, which were independent cities at the time of its construction. The bridge was completed in 1883. LIBRARY OF CONGRESS

Brooklyn's great nineteenth-century poet, Walt Whitman, published *Leaves of Grass*. In 1858 the National Association of Base Ball Players listed seventy-one teams from Brooklyn.

By 1860, with 279,122 residents, Brooklyn was the nation's third-largest city behind New York and Philadelphia. Immigration stimulated a transition from farm to neighborhood in the southern parts of Kings County. For example, Coney Island, once used largely for grazing animals, became a popular summer attraction by 1840, and when railroads connected the neighborhood with the rest of the city, it attracted a year-round population. By the end of the century Coney Island was an internationally known amusement and hotel area. Prospect Park was built in the late 1860s as a magnificent nexus of woods, meadows, and ponds in the center of Brooklyn.

Greater New York

The Brooklyn Bridge, completed in 1883, was the product of a dozen years of construction. Planned by the father-son engineering firm of John Roebling and Washington Roebling, the bridge is an engineering marvel of two massive stone towers and a crisscrossing network of steel cables. Spanning 1,595 feet, the bridge immediately brought a human rush into New York City in the mornings and back to Brooklyn in the evenings. A visible symbol of the interdependence of the two cities, the Brooklyn Bridge paved the way toward unification. As the city of Brooklyn grew and annexed smaller towns across the county, the political machinery exhausted its ability to issue bonds and could no longer support development. The New York Chamber of Commerce first proposed annexation of Brooklyn into New York City in 1887, but the issue remained controversial for the next few years. Backed by commercial interests in Manhattan and fueled by fears that Chicago might surpass New York as the nation's largest city, the state legislature in 1890 established the Greater New York Commission to study consolidation.

The old Anglo-Protestant community centered in Brooklyn Heights opposed annexation, contending that their city of homes and churches would be overwhelmed by the human evils, rich and poor, of New York City. Brooklyn developers getting rich from a frenzy of construction favored consolidation. Developers, worried that without consolidation transportation networks into New York would remain weak, noted that supplies of water from Long Island were limited while New York's reservoirs were filled and argued that Brooklyn's residential character had a limited tax base, furthering the potential for bankruptcy. A great debate over the city's future finally ended with the Charter of Greater New York, signed by Governor Frank Black on 5 May 1898. In 1900 Brooklyn had 1,166,582 inhabitants.

See also **Cities and Urbanization; City and Regional Planning; Civil Engineering,** *subentry on* **Bridges and Tunnels; New York City; New York State; Sports,** *subentry on* **Baseball.**

Bibliography

Burrows, Edwin G., and Mike Wallace. *Gotham: A History of New York City to 1898*. New York: Oxford University Press, 1999.

Manbeck, John B., ed. *The Neighborhoods of Brooklyn*. New Haven, Conn.: Yale University Press, 1998.

McCullough, David. *The Great Bridge*. New York: Simon and Schuster, 1972.

GRAHAM RUSSELL HODGES

BUFFALO, N.Y.   During the nineteenth century, Buffalo, New York, experienced profound changes in all areas of life. Industrial development propelled the region from the "age of homespun" to the modern age. In 1805 Buffalo was a small hamlet of some 250 people primarily engaged in marginal subsistence farming, and farm life dominated the settlement's Main Street. By 1904, the Bethlehem Steel plant in nearby Lackawanna was producing a million tons of steel, boasted six open-hearth furnaces, and employed six thousand workers.

Economic change formed the vortex of Buffalo's modernization, and the opening of the Erie Canal in 1825 transformed its economy. Situated at the juncture of Lake Erie and the canal, the city became the hub of transshipment for wheat and other agricultural products. The volume of grain moving through Buffalo increased dramatically with Joseph Dart's (1799–1879) development of the steam-powered grain elevator in 1842. In 1860 more than 4.5 million tons of freight were passing through the city, as it experienced rapid commercial growth based on shipping. Major figures in Buffalo's antebellum economic development included the financier Elbridge Gerry Spaulding (1809–1897), the ironmaster Sherman Jewett (1818–1897), and the founder of Wells, Fargo and Company, William G. Fargo (1818–1881).

After the Civil War, Buffalo witnessed heavy industrialization with the emergence of the steel, railroad, hydroelectric, and consumer products industries. Under the driving influence of a German immigrant, Jacob Schoellkopf (1819–1899), the new business sector of hydroelectric power emerged with the harnessing of the mighty Niagara River. Moreover, a consumer products sector was added. Emblematic of the emergence of corporations targeting a national consumer market, the Larkin Soap Company pioneered mass advertising and mail-order marketing techniques under the aegis of the firm's vice president, Elbert Hubbard (1856–1915).

Buffalo's economic transformation was accompanied by demographic, societal, and cultural changes. The population of the metropolitan area grew from 8,668 in 1830 to 433,686 in 1900, making it the eighth-largest U.S. city at the turn of the century. In the antebellum period, Irish and German immigrants came to Buffalo; after the war, they were joined by Poles and Italians. In 1855 the city's population was 60 percent foreign born, with 31,000 German and 8,000 Irish residents. Even after second-generation Irish and Germans are considered, Buffalo's population in 1890 was nearly 30 percent foreign born, with 19,448 Polish and 6,257 Italian residents.

These new population groups carved residential niches and created ethnic neighborhoods. The Irish huddled in shacks on the Lake Erie Flats or in cramped quarters of the First Ward on the South Side, enduring a marginal economic existence as manual laborers or domestic servants. Clinging to their Roman Catholic faith, they were encouraged by the appointment of John Timon (1797–1867) as the first bishop of the newly created diocese of Buffalo in 1849. The economic hardship of the Irish burst into unrest and violence in the Tow Path Revolt in 1849 as well as the "bread or work" movement in the late 1850s. The German migration, swelled by refugees fleeing the abortive 1848 revolutions in Europe, settled in the near East Side of Main Street close to employment opportunities in the stockyards and tanneries and foot traffic for their small shops. In the latter years of the nineteenth century, Polish immigrants moved into the developing East Side, while Italians settled on the West Side near an industrial strip along the Niagara River. With St. Stanislaus Roman Catholic Church as the heart of Polonia, the Polish community retained much its Old World cultural orientation, emphasizing church activities and extended-family values. Similarly, the Italian neighborhoods preserved much of the social and cultural patterns of Sicily.

Throughout the nineteenth century, Buffalo represented in microcosm many of the nation's fundamental trends. As the Pan-American Exposition opened in 1901, Buffalo's residents proudly reviewed the achievements of the past century and were optimistic about the future.

See also **Catholicism; Immigration and Immigrants; New York State; Transportation,** *subentries on* **Canals and Waterways, Railroads.**

Bibliography

Gerber, David A. *The Making of an American Pluralism: Buffalo, New York, 1825–60.* Urbana: University of Illinois Press, 1989.

Goldman, Mark. *High Hopes: The Rise and Decline of Buffalo, New York.* Albany: State University of New York Press, 1983.

Horton, John T., et al. *History of Northwestern New York: Erie, Niagara, Wyoming, Genesee, and Orleans Counties.* 3 vols. New York: Lewis Historical, 1947.

Yans-McLaughlin, Virginia. *Family and Community: Italian Immigrants in Buffalo, 1880–1930.* Ithaca, N.Y.: Cornell University Press, 1977.

WALTER SHARROW

BUREAUCRACY.   See **Government.**

BUSINESS.   See **Corporations and Big Business; Regulation of Business; Small Businesses.**

C

CABINET Although the Constitution does not provide for a cabinet, among the first actions that George Washington took as president was to name the heads of the new Departments of State, War, and the Treasury, and two officers whose agencies did not have cabinet status, the attorney general and the postmaster general. These secretarial posts, except for the postmaster general, came to be known as the cabinet. Very little expansion of the cabinet occurred in the nineteenth century. The postmaster general joined the cabinet in 1829; the Post Office Department received cabinet status in 1872. Two more cabinet departments were created, the Department of the Interior in 1849 and the Department of Agriculture in 1867. The attorney general's post was upgraded to full secretarial status in 1870. During the nineteenth century, presidents molded the cabinet to their own needs and successfully limited congressional attempts to wrest control of it from the executive branch.

The cabinet never developed into a policymaking body that would bind a president to particular courses of action. At most it became a forum where top administration personnel discussed policy, but always the president decided whether or not to heed that advice. John Quincy Adams once allowed a majority vote of his cabinet to overrule him, but most presidents did not give the cabinet such power. Andrew Jackson refused to convene his official cabinet, instead relying on a "kitchen cabinet" of trusted friends for advice. And Abraham Lincoln, who met with his cabinet frequently in hopes of unifying it behind his war policies, used the cabinet meeting to issue policy pronouncements to his secretaries, with the expectation that they would carry out his directives faithfully.

The cabinet's more important function was political. Presidents used secretarial appointment as a way to repay important constituencies for their electoral support, to represent and include rival and conflicting factions within the party in the administration, and to compensate for their own personal and political weaknesses. For instance, Lincoln, not a well-known or highly experienced politician when he became president, named men of great stature to his cabinet in order to build up his administration's reputation.

During much of the nineteenth century, Congress and the president clashed over who would control the cabinet. Advocates of the congressional position argued that the secretaries and department personnel were answerable to Congress because it created the position of secretary, created the departments, and confirmed secretarial nominations. Throughout the century, although Congress generally confirmed presidential nominees, presidential-congressional conflict erupted over who had the power and right to remove a sitting secretary from office.

The first removal clash occurred in 1833, during Andrew Jackson's presidency. Jackson, an ardent opponent of the second Bank of the United States, removed his secretary of the Treasury for refusing to carry out administration policies with regard to the bank. Congress subsequently censured the president for his action (the censure was lifted in 1836).

A more severe crisis occurred during Andrew John-

Cabinet Departments, 1789–1913

1789	1798	1829	1849	1862	1870	1889	1903	1913
State	State	State	State	State	State	State	State	State
Treasury	Treasury	Treasury	Treasury	Treasury	Treasury	Treasury	Treasury	Treasury
War	War	War	War	War	War	War	War	War
	Navy	Navy	Navy	Navy	Navy	Navy	Navy	Navy
Attorney General	Attorney General	Attorney General	Attorney General	Attorney General	Justice[a]	Justice	Justice	Justice
(Postmaster General)[b]	(Postmaster General)	Postmaster General	Postmaster General	Postmaster General	Postmaster General[c]	Postmaster General	Postmaster General	Postmaster General
			Interior	Interior	Interior	Interior	Interior	Interior
				(Agriculture)[d]	(Agriculture)	Agriculture	Agriculture	Agriculture
							Commerce and Labor	{Commerce {Labor

[a] The attorney general became head of the Justice Department when the department was created in 1870.

[b] Positions in parentheses are heads of departments but not members of the cabinet. The postmaster general was not added to the cabinet until 1829; the postmaster general was dropped from the cabinet in 1971, when the United States Postal Service replaced the United States Post Office.

[c] The Post Office became a cabinet department in 1872.

[d] The Department of Agriculture was created in 1862; the Secretary of Agriculture was added to the cabinet in 1889.

son's presidency. In 1867 Congress passed the Tenure of Office Act over the president's veto. That act stipulated that a president could not remove a cabinet secretary from office until Congress confirmed a successor. In effect, if Congress wanted to keep the current secretary in office, it could do so by refusing to confirm a successor.

Matters blew up when the secretary of war, Edwin Stanton, a holdover from the Lincoln administration, battled with Johnson over Reconstruction policy. Stanton favored a policy that gave greater protections to former slaves, while Johnson wanted to speed southern reentry into the Union with former Confederates able to hold office. Upon Stanton's refusal to carry out a presidential directive, Johnson tried to remove him from office but was blocked by the Tenure of Office Act. The removal attempt led to presidential-congressional conflict, which resulted in impeachment proceedings.

Although impeached, Johnson was not convicted and served out his term. The political fallout of the impeachment proceedings rendered Johnson ineffective throughout the remainder of his term, but Congress's failure to remove him from office had important implications for the presidential-congressional struggle over control of the cabinet. Congress effectively lost the battle in trying to control the composition of the cabinet. Presidents, who almost always got the secretaries they wanted, would now decide how long they would serve. In effect, cabinet secretaries now served at the pleasure of the president.

Although some sections of the Tenure of Office Act were repealed in 1869, it remained on the books until Congress fully repealed it in 1887; it did not reemerge as a factor in presidential control of the cabinet. Thus, by the end of the nineteenth century, the cabinet had emerged as a fixture in American politics, under the firm control of the president, but without independent policymaking power.

See also **Congress; Government; Presidency; Reconstruction,** *subentry on* **The Politics of Reconstruction.**

Bibliography

Cohen, Jeffrey E. *The Politics of the U.S. Cabinet: Representation in the Executive Branch, 1789–1984.* Pittsburgh: University of Pittsburgh Press, 1988.

Fenno, Richard F., Jr. *The President's Cabinet: An Analysis in the Period from Wilson to Eisenhower.* Cambridge, Mass.: Harvard University Press, 1959.

Fisher, Louis. *The Constitution between Friends: Congress, the President, and the Law.* New York: St. Martin's, 1978.

Horn, Stephen. *The Cabinet and Congress.* New York: Columbia University Press, 1960.

Hoxie, R. Gordon. "The Cabinet in the American Presidency, 1789–1984." *Presidential Studies Quarterly* 14 (1984): 209–231.

JEFFREY E. COHEN

CALIFORNIA   With the addition of the state of California to the Union in 1850, the nation gained twelve hundred miles of coastline, as well as the lowest point, Death Valley, and the highest peak, Mount Whitney, in the contiguous United States. It also gained a variety of fertile environments, which had supported a Native American population of about 310,000 at the time of first European contact in the sixteenth century. Evidence of material culture, while scarce, reveals that California Indians, who represented all the major linguistic groups in North America, had complex belief systems and organized tribal structures. They produced a variety of arts and crafts, which they traded throughout the region. In 1542 the Spaniard Juan Rodríguez Cabrillo explored the California coast. In 1702 the Jesuit missionary and cartographer Father Eusebio Kino explored the eastern border of the region, leading him to declare that California was not an island.

Spanish and Mexican California

Unaware of California's rich mineral resources, Spain did not settle this northern perimeter of the viceroyalty of New Spain for more than two hundred years. Only when confronted by the encroaching presence of Russians to the north and British to the east, did the visitor-general José de Gálvez organize a four-pronged plan of Spanish settlement. The vanguard, headed by Gaspár de Portolá and the Franciscan friar Junípero Serra, reached San Diego in 1769. The first presidio and mission were founded, forerunners of a chain of garrisons, towns, and missions established by Spain. The twenty-one Franciscan missions had the dual responsibilities of converting and acculturating the indigenous people.

Following Mexico's independence in 1821, California experienced reduced economic support and diminished political representation, causing political instability in the region. Mexico's secularization of the missions, implemented by Governor José Figueroa in 1833, resulted in the distribution of some land to the mission Indians, while the majority of the land was allocated to more than six hundred rancho grantees. The grantees, at least 10 percent of whom were women, expanded the cattle economy, trading hides and tallow with Yankee merchants. The profitable trade permitted frontier luxury for the rancheros and their families.

During the Mexican period the non-Indian population, numbering about seven thousand, included American and European traders and settlers. Members of the Bidwell-Bartleson and Workman-Rowland parties crossed harsh terrain to reach California in 1841. Their reports, as well as increased British and French diplomatic interest in California, led the United States to negotiate unsuccessfully for its purchase from Mexico. Colonel John C. Frémont, the son-in-law of Missouri senator Thomas Hart Benton, a strong supporter of U.S. expansion, was dispatched, beginning in 1843, on three expeditions to California.

When Frémont returned to California in 1846, American settlers, encouraged by the U.S. presence, arrested Commander Mariano Vallejo and at Sonoma declared themselves representatives of the "California Republic." Assured that war with Mexico had been declared, Commodore John Sloat, who had sailed with 250 marines aboard the flagship *Savannah*, raised the U.S. flag over Monterey on 7 July 1846. While resistance was minimal, southern Californios vanquished U.S. forces at the Battle of Dominguez Ranch. Before signing in 1847 the capitulation at Cahuenga, leading to U.S. acquisition of California, Californios claimed another victory on 5 December 1846 at San Pascual, where twenty-two Americans died.

The Thirty-first State

Four months before the final ratification in 1848 of the treaty ending the war with Mexico, James Marshall discovered gold while constructing a sawmill for John Sutter on the south fork of the American River. President James K. Polk's announcement of the discovery in December 1848 resulted in an international influx of gold seekers, which would be vividly described by such writers as Mark Twain and Bret Harte. While forty-niners panned for surface gold, the rich veins of ore were tapped by using the more capital intensive and ecologically destructive techniques of shaft and hydraulic mining. The three-quarters of a billion dollars in precious metals extracted financed additional mining ventures, commercial enterprises, and agricultural expansion. California's gold also enriched the federal treasury and significantly affected the world's financial markets.

Although few forty-niners made fortunes panning gold, new residents created towns, enriched shopkeepers, and made San Francisco a cosmopolitan center. The growing population soon overwhelmed the Californios, mostly located in rural southern California, and accelerated demands for statehood.

As part of the Compromise of 1850, California was admitted to the Union, without slavery, as the thirty-first state. Its population reached 92,597 that year. Ten years later census takers counted 379,994 residents, 72 percent of them male in a mining men's world. The leading sources of migration had been China, Ireland, New York, the German states, the United Kingdom, Missouri, Ohio, and Massachusetts.

Demands for better transportation and communication led to expansion of Wells, Fargo and Company; federal funding in 1857 of the Butterfield

Modesto, California. Modesto's town plan was laid out in the 1870s. The city was incorporated in 1884. Photograph of Tenth Street, c. 1870 to 1900. LIBRARY OF CONGRESS: PRINTS AND PHOTOGRAPHS DIVISION

Stage; and establishment in 1858 of the Pony Express, which was supplanted by the telegraph in 1861. The prospect for transcontinental transportation promised in the Pacific Railroad Act of 1862 was made feasible by the railroad engineer Theodore P. Judah and four entrepreneurs: Charles Crocker, Mark Hopkins, Collis P. Huntington, and Leland Stanford. Although they used the political system to personal and financial advantage, their rails populated California, bringing tourists, health seekers, and throngs of settlers, particularly during 1886 and 1887, when a rate war between the Southern Pacific and the Santa Fe Railroads resulted in a real estate boom in southern California.

Rails transformed California's commerce and agriculture, inspiring the novel *The Octopus* (1901), Frank Norris's indictment of the Southern Pacific. The railroad provided access to the fertile Central Valley as California shifted from cattle and sheepherding to the cultivation of wheat and deciduous crops, especially citrus. By the 1890s oranges and lemons thrived in southern California in a "citrus triangle" extending from Santa Paula to Redlands and southward through Orange County. In 1916, 95 percent of the nation's navel orange crop was shipped from that triangle.

Vineyards were first planted by the Franciscans at San Diego in 1771. In 1862 the state legislature sent Agoston Haraszthy, owner of Buena Vista Vineyard at Sonoma, to select 100,000 cuttings of 300 varieties of European wine grapes. As a result of the increased production, in 1897 there was insufficient cooperage in California to hold all the wine produced from Anaheim in the south to the Italian Swiss Colony in the north.

Agriculture relied on workers, including Chinese immigrants, but by 1867 "anti-coolie clubs" had grown strong. In 1871 a score of Chinese were massacred in Los Angeles, and in San Francisco, Denis Kearney organized anti-Chinese labor riots. In 1877 he joined in founding the Workingmen's Party of California, which for a time was a force in California politics helping to assure regulation of railroads and corporations and limit land monopolies; these same issues would be championed two decades later by the California Progressives. Kearney's party succeeded in making Chinese immigration a national issue, resulting in the passage of the federal Chinese Exclusion Act of 1882.

Toward the end of the century Los Angeles communities annually produced 1.4 million barrels of oil, fuel essential to the air and automotive travel that would shape California in the next century.

See also **American Indian Societies,** *subentry on* **California; Chinese Exclusion Act; Exploration and Ex-**

plorers; Gold Rushes and Silver Strikes; Los Angeles; Mexican Cession; Mexican War; San Francisco; Transportation, *subentry on* Railroads.

Bibliography

Bancroft, Hubert Howe. *History of California.* 7 vols. San Francisco: History Company, 1884–1890.

Cleland, Robert Glass. *The Cattle on a Thousand Hills: Southern California, 1850–1880.* San Marino, Calif.: Huntington Library, 1951.

Deverell, William. *Railroad Crossing: Californians and the Railroad, 1850–1910.* Berkeley: University of California Press, 1994.

Holliday, J. S. *The World Rushed In: The California Gold Rush Experience.* New York: Simon and Schuster, 1981.

Lavender, David. *California: A Bicentennial History.* New York: Norton, 1976.

Starr, Kevin. *Americans and the California Dream, 1850–1915.* New York: Oxford University Press, 1973.

GLORIA RICCI LOTHROP

CANADA At the onset of the nineteenth century, British North America was a far-flung and sparsely populated collection of colonies, provinces, charter lands held by the Hudson Bay Company (HBC), and territorial homelands of varied indigenous peoples. Governance and public issues were, not surprisingly, more fully developed on the eastern seaboard, along the St. Lawrence River, and on the shore of Lake Ontario. On the Atlantic coast Newfoundland was governed as a crown colony; Prince Edward Island, Nova Scotia, and New Brunswick were royal provinces with single elective assemblies; and Cape Breton Island was administered through an appointed council. Farther inland the governance of Upper and Lower Canada was effected by an elected lower assembly, an appointed upper assembly, and a legislative council in each colony. In the years before the War of 1812, internal political concerns concentrated on the developing English-French hostilities, the nature of English constitutional governance, the Loyalist presence, and the perennial debate over relations between aboriginal peoples and settler society and government. To the west lay Rupert's Island, the enormous drainage basin of the Hudson Bay, administered by the HBC in accordance with its 1670 charter granted by Charles II. Still farther west were the distant Pacific and Arctic coasts to which the British crown lay claim but in which no form of colonial governance had been established.

For British North Americans, the deteriorating state of relations between Napoleonic France and England at the beginning of the nineteenth century had immediate consequences. The restriction of trade and the increasing belligerency of the British Navy in the impressment of English seamen serving on American vessels added to a growing list of unresolved questions, including American commercial rights in the West Indies, uncertainty over the border separating New England from Nova Scotia, lingering animosity over the delayed withdrawal of British troops from the Ohio Valley, and growing tension in the interior between American settlers and indigenous peoples retaining pro-British sympathies. Congressional elections in 1810 returned a large group of southern and western expansionists led by Henry Clay, and these "war hawks" eventually pressed President James Madison, on 18 June 1812, to place the question of war before the Congress.

The subsequent War of 1812 was an indecisive conflict that settled little in terms of Anglo-American relations and ended in a stalemate reflected in the Treaty of Ghent of 1814. Although it failed to address the issues that gave rise to the war, the treaty set the stage for a series of international agreements from 1815 to 1822, which in turn clarified the terms for Anglo-American and then U.S.–British North American relations for the ensuing generation. The Rush-Bagot agreement of 1817 limited naval armament on Lake Champlain and the Great Lakes, and one year later the forty-ninth parallel was established as the boundary between American and British territory running from Lake of the Woods (on the present-day Ontario-Minnesota border) to the Rocky Mountains. Lost in the treaty and subsequent agreements, however, were British commitments to an aboriginal buffer state.

Pressures for Reform

Napoleon's defeat and the cessation of hostilities between Britain and the United States inaugurated a new era for British North America. One of the immediate changes was a shift in immigration patterns. Since the fall of New France and the end of the American Revolution, British North America had benefited from an essentially land-based migration of Loyalists. This all but ceased and was replaced by a seaborne movement of people from Britain and, to a lesser degree, from Europe. The economic depression following the Napoleonic war and the dislocation caused by expanding industrialization compelled many to set out for British North America with the hopeful expectation of a new start. As a consequence, between 1815 and 1850 nearly eight hundred thousand Britons arrived in British North America. The shift not only accelerated regional development but also gave emergent communities an increasingly British character. At the same time, these immigrants served to diversify colonial society. The wide cross-section of English, Scotch, and Irish arrivals did not subscribe to a single vision of social, religious, political, or economic relations. Indeed, some imported liberal or reform notions that eventually collided with the conservative outlook of the postwar governing elite and set the stage for the political battles of the ensuing thirty-five years.

The impetus for reform across British North America during the twenty years after 1820 was derived from a number of different sources. The general background to events was provided by the changing tenor of empire relations. Although the British Colonial Office eventually embraced a free-trade policy undercutting the rationale for colonies, it did so in fits and starts between 1815 and the mid-1840s. Further, the state of internal affairs in the British North American colonies was of only passing interest to both the imperial government and the Colonial Office. So long as nothing untoward occurred, there seemed to be little impetus to effect thoroughgoing change, especially as most of the calls for reform were aimed at colonial leaders, not at the empire per se. However, as reform agitation continued, the nature of governance in British North America was inevitably called into question. In failing to take account of the growing unrest, the imperial government tacitly supported an increasingly unpopular oligarchic system. And as reform pressures continued to mount, the issue concentrated on the question of how government would function if shaped by the democratic will of the colonists.

In Upper Canada (present-day Ontario) protest was framed by comparisons with the robust economic and political environment of Jacksonian America. Of particular note were grievances aimed at the so-called Family Compact, a tight collection of families who seemingly shared political spoils, patronage positions, bank and canal charters, land-grabbing schemes, and the belief that the Anglican Church deserved preeminent status within the community. In turn, the reformers espoused a set of beliefs aimed at eliminating privilege based on economic position, expanding credit for small businesses, and, most important, the creation of a political system wherein executive power was controlled by a broad electorate. French-English animosities and suspicions in Lower Canada (present-day Quebec) complicated similar grievances, in concert with localized concerns over the state of agriculture and commerce and the emerging presence of French Canadian nationalism. Specifically, the governing elite, identified as the Château Clique, was tied to the English-speaking minority, while the French Canadian majority controlled the elected House of Assembly. As a consequence, while the generalization was not always accurate, it was common practice to reduce most disputes to contests pitching the French Canadians against the English. Although similar reform tensions existed across British North America, only in Lower and Upper Canada would open rebellion actually erupt.

As events in Upper and Lower Canada followed their course, the state of affairs in the Maritimes and Newfoundland was decidedly less antagonistic. Lacking the cultural animosities found in Lower Canada and the influence of imported republican ideals from

Ottawa, Canada. Government buildings in Canada's capital city of Ottawa. The Parliament Building appears at center.

the United States, most communities along the eastern seaboard successfully directed calls for reform into the existing political system. Significantly, the governing oligarchies of the region were less obdurate, and in the case of Prince Edward Island, the primary grievance concerned absentee landlords, not the system of government. In New Brunswick the preeminent concern involved the control of crown reserves and regional timber. The resulting battles between competing lumber interests served to siphon off much of the energy that might have been directed at reform. Only Nova Scotia experienced calls for political reform similar to those found in Upper and Lower Canada, but such campaigns were arrayed against the backdrop of staunch British loyalty. Defenders of Nova Scotia's Council of Twelve, a local oligarchic collection of individuals linked by office holding, marriage, and patronage, were thus unable to cast reform advocates in the role of dangerous republicans. Led by the articulate newspaper editor Joseph Howe, Nova Scotia's reformers consistently demonstrated that reform need not adopt the mantle of extremism and revolution. For its part, Newfoundland had only emerged from its status as a fishing post with the appointment of Sir Thomas Cochrane as civil governor in 1825. Subsequent agitation for an elected assembly eventually produced enabling legislation in 1832, and one year later the assembly met for the first time. Cochrane was withdrawn in 1836 and election violence flared a year later as reformist tensions across British North America began to rise. It deserves to be noted, however, that reform agitation remained loyal to the notion of British constitutional governance while finding fault with local cabals and conservative governors bent on obstructing political reform.

Responses to Protest

Sparked in part by a financial panic in the United States, the Lower and then Upper Canada rebellions of late 1837 were feeble affairs that were quickly crushed. Reform leaders Louis Joseph Papineau of Lower Canada and William Lyon Mackenzie of Upper Canada fled to the United States almost as soon as hostilities erupted. Though the rebels were routed, the fact of rebellion finally alerted British officials to the necessity of paying closer attention to affairs in British North America, while at the same time demonstrating that reports from colonial administrators ought not to be taken at face value. Further, the economic dislocation caused by the financial panic, the presence of disaffected Irish nationalists in the United States, and the fact that a number of rebels fled across

the border served to strain Anglo-American relations in the late 1830s and early 1840s.

A number of events, including the burning by Canadian volunteers of the American ship *Caroline* on the United States side of the Niagara River in 1837, the eruption of the so-called Aroostook War between lumberjacks along the disputed border between Maine and New Brunswick in 1839, and the formation of American Hunter's Lodges bent on forwarding Irish independence, combined once again to raise the specter of open hostilities between the British and Americans. The British freeing of slaves on board the American vessel *Creole* after a slave revolt in 1841 nearly precipitated the outbreak of war, but negotiations between the American secretary of state Daniel Webster and Lord Ashburton produced the Webster-Ashburton Treaty of 1842, which defused the situation. The treaty reconfirmed the Canadian-American boundary from the Atlantic Ocean to the Rocky Mountains, extended it to the Pacific coast, provided for the policing of the international slave trade, and created the mechanism for extradition of criminals between Great Britain and its colonies and the United States.

The Colonial Office response to the rebellions was to name John Lambton, the first earl of Durham, to the post of governor general and commissioner to investigate public affairs in British North America. Although his term ended prematurely under allegations of overstepping his authority in exiling convicted rebels, Durham nonetheless completed a famous report recommending the concession of responsible government, the union of Upper and Lower Canada, and the separation of local and imperial jurisdictions. In effect, the report envisaged a regional assembly and government controlled by elected representatives possessing autonomy in local affairs and governing a single colony in which Upper and Lower Canada (popularly renamed Canada East and Canada West) had equal representation. With his recommendations, Durham effectively legitimized calls for political reform and undercut those who had labeled reformers disloyal revolutionaries. Assailed by Tories for allegedly rewarding rebellion with democratic reform, by French Canadians fundamentally opposed to the report's assimilationist rhetoric, and by the English-speaking business elite of Montreal who expected recommendations more to their advantage, Durham effectively set the stage for political debate in British North America for the ensuing decade and beyond.

Although the union of Upper and Lower Canada advocated by Durham was effected in late 1840, his recommendation favoring responsible government attracted criticism on both sides of the Atlantic. The

The Aroostook War. As a result of the failure of Great Britain and the United States to determine the boundary between New Brunswick and present-day Maine, lumberjacks from Maine and Canada fought a bloodless war from 1838 to 1839 over the border, which lay along the Aroostook River. LIBRARY OF CONGRESS: PRINTS AND PHOTOGRAPHS DIVISION

crux of opposition to responsible government was both philosophical and practical, for colonial status, by definition, precludes self-government. Furthermore, there existed the very sticky problem of determining how the queen's representative should respond in those instances when either his instructions from the Colonial Office or British legislation clashed with the assembly's advice in regard to local matters. Charting a course through such eventualities was a complicated business, but a coalition of Canadian reformers ably led by Robert Baldwin and Francis Hincks from Canada West, and Louis Lafontaine from Canada East, in concert with Charles P. Thomson, viscount Sydenham, governor from 1839 to 1841, and James Bruce, eighth earl of Elgin, whose governorship began in January 1847, eventually maneuvered through long-standing biases, loyalties, and fears to institute responsible government in the united province of Canada in the spring of 1848. Ironically enough, two months earlier in Nova Scotia, where no rebellion occurred, reformers led by Joseph Howe quietly achieved responsible government through persistent advocacy of British constitutional principles and unquestioned loyalty. By the mid-

1850s, all provinces and colonies in British North America, save British Columbia, had instituted responsible governments that were autonomous save for enactments concerning the disposal of public lands, trade, foreign affairs, and the form of the constitution.

Settlement in the West

Although far removed from international and domestic political hostilities during the first half century, the interior and Far West fur trade nonetheless mirrored the Anglo-American tensions and the degree to which British North America hung in the balance. Beginning with Alexander Mackenzie's arrival on the Pacific coast in July 1793 under the auspices of the Montreal-based North West Company, sustained efforts to establish routes, supply lines, and posts in the Far West assumed dramatic proportions. Aided by French Canadian voyageurs, Meriwether Lewis and William Clark replicated Mackenzie's effort in 1805 and tacitly declared that the competition to hold the Northwest had begun. Joined by the explorers Simon Fraser and David Thompson and entrepreneurs such as John Jacob Astor, the race to exploit the resources of the Northwest was soon under way. Ironically, while the HBC was successful in maintaining its fur trade monopoly, which had been established by royal grant from King Charles II in 1670, its failure to respond to the influx of American settlers into the Oregon Territory proved to be the company's undoing in the region. Under the pressure of an Anglo-American entente after the War of 1812 and the saber rattling of presidential candidate James Polk, who employed the slogan "Fifty-four Forty or Fight" in his successful campaign in 1844, the British compromised their claims to the entire Oregon Territory and accepted the forty-ninth parallel, across the Rocky Mountains to the Pacific Ocean and jogging around the southern tip of Vancouver Island, as the international border. Admittedly, few British North Americans were concerned about the implications of the loss sustained under the Oregon settlement of 1846, save to the extent that the Americans were pacified by the agreement.

Two years after the 1846 settlement, the British proclaimed Vancouver Island a colony as a partial response to mounting criticism of the HBC's administration and dilatory efforts to bring settlers to the West and the Far West. Within a decade company rule on both the island and mainland was completely undone in the wake of the Fraser gold rush of 1858. The influx of predominantly American miners was reminiscent of the process whereby squatters had effectively claimed the Oregon Territory for the United States, and it compelled the Colonial Office to forcefully demonstrate British sovereignty. This was effected by the institution of British colonial government on Vancouver Island and in the new mainland province of British Columbia. Through the operation of courts of law in the goldfields that were, in turn, eventually serviced by government-constructed roads, the Colonial Office effectively staked its claim to this Pacific outpost.

As was demonstrated by events on the coast during the 1840s and 1850s, the monopoly that the HBC had so jealously guarded was beginning to crumble. By the mid-1840s, independent traders had established themselves in the heart of HBC territory. One trader, Norman Kittson, did so just across the border in American territory at Pembina, south of HBC operations at Red River. The company's monopoly was eventually subjected to investigation in Britain, where in an atmosphere colored by free-trade rhetoric, the HBC was depicted as an anachronism. Cast in this light, the Red River trial of the Métis free-trader Pierre-Guillaume Sayer on 17 May 1849, wherein Sayer was charged with illegal trafficking in furs, marked the end of an era. Although found guilty of trading liquor for furs, Sayer was spared any pun-

ishment and when he emerged from the courthouse to announce the result, two hundred to three hundred armed Métis discharged their weapons in celebration, recognizing that the HBC monopoly had, in fact, been broken. Played out against the growing criticism of the HBC's behavior, the Sayer trial signaled a significant dilution of the company's ability to effectively govern the interior.

The British withdrawal from the Oregon Territory and the acceptance of responsible government were products of the so-called Little England movement of the post-1840 era, a sentiment that increasingly favored balanced domestic budgets and free trade in preference to colonial entanglements and military obligations in the far-flung corners of empire. Not only did the movement feed into the political aspirations of Canadian reformers seeking responsible government, it also forwarded the notion that, aside from India, the colonies had become an expensive nuisance. The subsequent British decision to repeal the protective Corn Laws in 1846 sent shock waves through British North America. Following close on the heels of this end to preference was the passage and final assent to the Rebellion Losses Bill (1849), which compensated a number of rebels who had suffered property losses during the hostilities of 1837 and 1838 and that was perceived by faithful Tories as amounting to a reward for treason. The response was a wave of rioting in which a mob set the parliament buildings afire. Feeling abandoned by Britain, some Montreal-based business leaders soon claimed that annexation by the United States was inevitable. Almost as soon as the Annexation Manifesto was drawn up and circulated for signatures in 1849, however, its backers distanced themselves from both the Rebellion Losses riots and the manifesto's extravagant claims.

In fact, while the Montreal merchants panicked, a new economic relationship between British North American provinces and the United States was coming to fruition. Indeed, since Britain had embraced free trade there was nothing, save political will, impeding a similar policy between the two North American neighbors. Championed by William Hamilton Merritt, Thomas Coltrin Keefer, and Israel DeWolf Andrews, British North America slowly realized an economic reorientation. All three envisioned a single marketplace geographically defined by Newfoundland, Lake Superior, the mouth of the Missouri, and the mouth of the Hudson River, wherein natural waterways, man-made canals, and railways would link to create an enormous infrastructure for the movement of goods and raw materials to the Atlantic seaboard. Active negotiations involving American, British, and British provincial governments began in earnest in 1847 and eventually produced the Reciprocity Treaty of 1854, which held until 17 March 1866, when it was abandoned amidst recriminations and reprisals for British behavior during the Civil War.

The relatively good relations flowing from the treaty lasted until the economic depression of 1857 gave rise to protectionist sentiments in the British provinces. As duties began to creep upward, it became increasingly clear that the treaty was imperiled. Before such sentiment upset the agreement, the American Civil War erupted. While British North Americans had long since staked their position against slavery through its abolition and their limited participation in antislavery activity, the American seizure of the British mail steamer *Trent* in 1861 threatened to spark an eruption of hostilities between the British, their colonies, and the Union forces. Although the crisis was defused, British North American empathy for the Union cause had been seriously undermined.

A number of incidents, including the seizure of the Southern raider *Chesapeake* by the United States Navy off the coast of Nova Scotia; the 1865 raid on St. Alban's, Vermont, by Confederate agents based in Canada; and British complicity in outfitting a number of Southern raiders, such as the *Alabama*, *Florida*, and *Shenandoah*, all served to embitter feelings on both sides of the border. So too did the activities of the Fenian Brotherhood, which launched a series of invasions into British territory from American soil in the name of Irish independence. Further, American annexationist rhetoric, encouraged in part by the U.S. secretary of state William H. Seward and Senator Charles Sumner, claimed it was merely a matter of time before Britain's colonial remnants assumed their place within the American republic. Thus, as the tide of the Civil War turned in favor of the North, negative attitudes toward Britain and its colonies began to harden, and by March 1864, both the Rush-Bagot Agreement for naval disarmament on the Great Lakes and the Reciprocity Agreement were terminated.

These strained international relations roughly coincided with a fragmentation of Canadian public life in the aftermath of union and responsible government. In effect, the political reforms of the 1840s set in motion a series of developments creating political deadlock in an assembly divided equally between Canada East and Canada West in the 1850s and 1860s. Split along political, linguistic, religious, and ethnic lines, public life degenerated into a never-ending series of coalitions and factions striving to control the balance of power. Emerging from this morass was a reconstituted Conservative Party led by the charismatic Kingston lawyer John A. Macdonald. In partnership with George Étienne Cartier, a self-confident and conservative legal practitioner from Montreal, he effectively reestablished the balance required to manage, if not always maintain control over, political life in the unified province. Arrayed against Macdonald and Cartier was a bumptious collection of agrarian reformers from Canada West who, led by the abolitionist newspaperman George Brown, espoused an unflinching democratic faith in concert with an abiding fear of French domination. These so-called Clear Grits found themselves in an uneasy and often antagonistic alliance with anticlerical French Canadian liberal nationalists led by the fiery lawyer A. A. Dorion. Given this volatile mixture, the Conservatives proved more successful at governance, although by the late 1850s even the artful manipulations of Macdonald and Cartier were having diminishing success. A solution of sorts, that of a wider union with the Maritime colonies, was once again broached and, by the early 1860s, most public figures in Canada West and East had begun exploring the possibilities of such an option.

Only the representatives from Canada West were enthusiastic supporters of a broader union, for neither French Canadians nor Maritimers thought the idea either timely or well-conceived. But the ever-present concern over American intentions, in concert with subtle but firm pressure from the Colonial Office in London, ensured that notions of a wider union were encouraged. Promises of railway construction, enlarged internal markets, and aspirations of nationhood were also offered up as inducements, although all these benefits would accrue almost entirely to Canadians. Thus, when the leading statesmen of all parties in the Province of Canada learned that the Maritime colonies were to meet to discuss union, they seized the opportunity to champion their broader national vision. Led by Macdonald, Brown, Cartier, and the former minister of finance Alexander Galt, the Canadians not only succeeded in forwarding their own agenda but at meetings in Charlottetown and Quebec City in 1864 they also hammered out the broad outlines of the union scheme of 1 July 1867. After a poorly handled transfer from the HBC, allowing the Louis Riel–led Métis of Red River to seize power and exact a set of concessions from the Canadian government, Manitoba joined the confederation in 1870. One year later British Columbia entered the union, in response to both Colonial Office pressure and the promise of a rail connection to Canada within a decade. Finally, in 1873 Prince Edward Island, which had withdrawn from union discussions when the scheme was first proposed, relented under the financial pressure of its localized railroad-building schemes and accepted the blandishments of union.

Not only was the Canadian confederation of 1867 a sharp rejoinder to American manifest destiny, it did nothing to settle the outstanding disputes between Britain, the United States, and the newly constituted Dominion. Relations were complicated by ongoing questions over the specific border between British and American possessions south of Vancouver Island, as well as the lingering question of reparations for the *Alabama* claims, the status of the Atlantic and inshore fisheries after the Reciprocity Treaty had been ended, and Canadian concerns over Fenian incursions. After a number of years of preliminary inquiries and discussions, it was finally announced on 9 February 1871 that an international joint commission to settle all Anglo-American differences would be established. British unease at possibly offending the Americans and a corresponding unwillingness of the Americans to seek creative solutions ensured that Canadian concerns would not carry much weight. As it turned out, the subsequent Treaty of Washington provided the means for Britain to express regret over its involvement in Southern depredations during the Civil War. The treaty established an international tribunal for settling the San Juan boundary, opened up the Canadian inshore fishery for ten years, plus two additional years for notice of termination, and opened the St. Lawrence River to American shipping in exchange for Canadian access to the distant Yukon, Porcupine, and Stikine Rivers in Alaska and free entry of fish and fish oil products from Canada into the United States. The treaty failed to mention, let alone provide compensation for, the Fenian raids into Canada.

The treaty also signaled a number of developments for both Canada and the United States. The agreement indicated that while American opinion maintained an expectation that the new Dominion would eventually be swallowed whole by the Republic, there was also an acceptance of Canada's existence, at least for the immediate future. For Canadians, the entire treaty process demonstrated that, in matters framed by the broader interests of the British and Americans, Canadian concerns would remain of minor importance and that while gains might be made by playing the British and Americans against each other, such tactics could not be overused for fear of antagonizing both nations. Essentially, the United States accepted the fact of Canada while, at the same time, Canadians awoke to the realization that their role in the world for the foreseeable future would be that of a lesser power.

In the quarter century after the Treaty of Washington, both Canada and the United States increasingly turned their attention toward western expansion. However, while the American West filled with land-hungry settlers, the Canadian prairies remained largely uninhabited, save for the indigenous peoples, the Métis, and a few hardy homesteaders. Yet in the hopeful expectation that settlers would come, the Canadian government finalized a series of treaties with the various aboriginal nations of the interior during the mid and late 1870s. Once the treaties were signed, however, federal authorities proved to be miserly and duplicitous in fulfilling their obligations, and by the 1880s, poverty, starvation, and hardship characterized much of aboriginal life on the Canadian prairies. At the same time, the Métis who had relocated farther west in the aftermath of the Red River troubles of 1869–1870 felt increasingly hemmed in and threatened by the slow trickle of settlers and the society they represented. Turning once again to Louis Riel to articulate their concerns to the federal government, the Métis soon found themselves in armed conflict with the North West Mounted Police and the Canadian militia. It was a contest that the Métis could not win, and when the dust finally settled, Riel was on trial for his life. Refusing to plead insanity, Riel was found guilty and sent to the gallows on 16 November 1885.

Although it played a critical role in delivering the Canadian militia to the northwest to aid in quelling the Métis uprising, the Canadian Pacific Railway failed to create sustained development in the prairie west until the final years of the century. In fact, as elements of the so-called national policy articulated by the Macdonald Conservatives in the federal election of 1878, the railway and a high tariff wall had achieved uneven results. While the tariff helped nurture Quebec and Ontario industrialists, it also served to increase the cost of living while it alienated the Maritimes and, by the late century, both rural and urban residents in the West. Consequently, as the standard of living in Canada dropped, an increasing number of residents opted for better opportunities south of the border. So while immigrants were arriving in Canada in increasing numbers after the mid-century, many continued on to settle eventually in the United States. During the ten years between 1881 and 1891, when the total Canadian population totaled slightly less than five million, over one million Canadians immigrated to the United States.

The departing tide would only be stemmed, however, in the early 1890s and the first fourteen years of the twentieth century. A rising surge of European immigrants arriving in North America, the disappearance of free or nearly free land in the American West, international markets buoyed by the South African and Klondike gold rushes, and a connected Canadian effort to attract agriculturalists, all served to people the Canadian prairies with homesteaders. By 1914, American immigrants to Canada had exceeded one million. So great was the influx from all sources that in the decade between 1901 and 1911 the overall Canadian population grew by an astounding 34 percent, distinguishing Canada as the fastest-growing country in the world.

In terms of Canadian-American relations, the nineteenth century drew to a close with the nations still disagreeing over international boundaries. Framed by discoveries of gold in the Yukon and Alaska, the question of the precise location of the boundary assumed increasing importance. Though defined by the Anglo-Russian treaty of 1825, the boundaries of Alaska had remained the source of debate throughout the century, and when diplomatic efforts to clarify the line failed, the decision to establish an international tribunal to settle the issue suggested that Canadian interests would once again be sacrificed to broader Anglo-American concerns. Indeed, the two Canadian jurists appointed to the tribunal were countered by three American representatives and the English lord chief justice Lord Alverstone, who took it upon himself to side with the American view of the boundary—a none-too-subtle effort at currying American favor at a time when Anglo-American relations were strained over access to, and control of, the Panama Canal. Thus, notwithstanding the weak Canadian case in terms of the Alaska boundary, the possibilities of a brokered understanding that accounted for the practical needs of Canadian riverborne access to the Yukon were dashed by broader interests less concerned with Canadian sensibilities.

Ultimately, Canada's history during the nineteenth century was arrayed against evolving Anglo-American relations in the postrevolutionary era. For British North Americans, this meant that much of the century was spent grappling with the philosophical and emotional substance of their connections to England while, in practical terms, interacting with the world from a North American perspective. Yet even this depiction fails to embrace the complexity of the situation for British North Americans, whose ties of birth, family, nation, and loyalty potentially included any number of European countries, the United States, and the more regional attachments maintained by various indigenous peoples north and west of the Great Lakes. Consequently, there was no single Canadian response to events as they developed throughout the century. Rather, one can discern a series of reactions situated along a sliding scale in which the maintenance of the colonial status quo was contrasted with possible annexation to the United States, with various forms of colonial unification and confederation situated at points in between. As the century wore on, the articulation of a British North American and then, after 1867, a Canadian position on this scale increasingly involved navigating a course between British and American policy in which Canadian interests were rarely of paramount concern.

See also **Foreign Relations; Foreign Trade and Tariffs,** *subentry on* **Trade and Tariffs; Fur Trade; Manifest Destiny; Oregon; War of 1812.**

Bibliography

Barnes, James J., and Patience P. Barnes, eds. *Private and Confidential: Letters from British Ministers in Washington to the Foreign Secretaries in London, 1844–1867.* Selinsgrove, Penn.: Susquehanna University Press, 1993.

Bothwell, Robert. *Canada and the United States: The Politics of Partnership.* New York: Twayne, 1992.

Brebner, John Bartlet. *North Atlantic Triangle: The Interplay of Canada, the United States and Great Britain.* New Haven, Conn.: Yale University Press, 1945.

Careless, J. M. S. *The Union of the Canadas: The Growth of Canadian Institutions, 1841–1857.* Toronto: McClelland and Stewart, 1967.

Creighton, Donald. *The Empire of the St. Lawrence.* Toronto: Macmillan, 1956.

Dickason, Olive Patricia. *Canada's First Nations: A History of Founding Peoples from Earliest Times.* Norman: University of Oklahoma Press, 1992.

Friesen, Gerald. *The Canadian Prairies: A History.* Lincoln: University of Nebraska Press, 1984.

Granatstein, J. L. *Yankee Go Home? Canadians and Anti-Americanism.* Toronto: Harper Collins, 1996.

Lipset, Seymour Martin. *Continental Divide: The Values and Institutions of the United States and Canada.* New York: Routledge, 1990.

Martin, Ged. *Britain and the Origins of Canadian Confederation, 1837–67.* Vancouver: University of British Columbia Press, 1995.

Martin, Ged, ed. *The Causes of Canadian Confederation.* Fredericton, N.B.: Acadiensis, 1990.

Mills, David. *The Idea of Loyalty in Upper Canada, 1784–1850.* Kingston, Ont., and Montreal: McGill-Queen's University Press, 1988.

Nicholson, Norman L. *The Boundaries of the Canadian Confederation.* Toronto: Macmillan of Canada, 1979.

Otter, A. A. den. *The Philosophy of Railways: The Transcontinental Railway Idea in British North America.* Toronto: University of Toronto Press, 1997.

Stacey, C. P. *Canada and the Age of Conflict: A History of Canadian External Policies.* Volume 1: 1867–1921. Toronto: Macmillan of Canada, 1977.

Stewart, Gordon T. *The Origins of Canadian Politics: A Comparative Approach.* Vancouver: University of British Columbia Press, 1986.

Thompson, John Herd, and Stephen J. Randall. *Canada and the United States: Ambivalent Allies.* Athens, Ga.: University of Georgia Press, 1994.

Wise, S. F., and Robert Craig Brown. *Canada Views the United*

States: Nineteenth-Century Political Attitudes. Seattle: University of Washington Press, 1967.

JONATHAN SWAINGER

CAPITAL PUNISHMENT

In the closing decade of the eighteenth century, the new American nation relied on the death penalty much as it had prior to the Revolution, when the colonial system of criminal justice preserved many prominent features of the system found in the mother country. Murder and other common-law felonies were normally punished by hanging. (In the seventeenth century blacks and Indians were sometimes punished by burning at the stake.) Appeals were rare, delays unusual. Slave codes in the southern states authorized the death penalty for many crimes that if committed by a white would have been punished less severely. Lynching of free blacks often obviated recourse to a capital trial and an official death sentence. Yet reform was in the air. In his essay of 1779 to the Virginia legislature, Thomas Jefferson (1743–1826) argued for proportioning the severity of a punishment to the gravity of the crime; this led him to oppose the death penalty for all crimes except murder and treason. "Cruel and sanguinary laws," he observed, "defeat their own purpose by engaging the benevolence of mankind to withhold prosecutions, to smother testimony, or to listen to it with bias. . . . " Others were bolder. Benjamin Rush (1745–1813), a distinguished Philadelphia physician and a signer of the Declaration of Independence, was the nation's leading opponent of the death penalty. "Capital punishments," he declared, "are the natural offspring of monarchical governments. . . . But the principles of republican governments speak a very different language" (Masur, *Rites of Execution*, p. 65). Thomas Paine (1737–1809), the radical pamphleteer, went further: "Sanguinary punishments . . . corrupt mankind" (Masur, p. 66). Nevertheless, by 1800 each of the sixteen state governments and the federal government enforced statutes that authorized a mandatory death penalty by hanging for any of several crimes. Xenophobic voices were occasionally heard defending the death penalty as necessary, given that the American population was "composed so largely of foreigners and Negroes."

Major Reforms

During the nineteenth century, several important developments transformed the status and administration of the laws affecting the death penalty. The first, pioneered by Pennsylvania in 1793, made the distinction between charges of first-degree and second-degree murder, with the death penalty confined to the former. By 1900 all but a few states had adopted this distinction.

Second, the mandatory death penalty was generally replaced by statutes that gave the jury the power to choose between a prison sentence and a death sentence. Tennessee pioneered this reform in 1833, and by the end of the century nearly two dozen states had followed suit.

Third, the types of crimes punishable by death were reduced. Felonies other than murder and crimes against property were increasingly likely to be punished by long-term imprisonment. Pennsylvania again led the way by eliminating the death penalty for robbery, burglary, and sodomy.

Fourth, executions were no longer festive public occasions frequently marred by debauchery. Once more, Pennsylvania (in 1834) took the lead, requiring hangings to be carried out "within the walls or yard of the jail" (Masur, p. 94).

Fifth, a new method of execution—the electric chair—was introduced in New York in 1890. It was soon adopted in many states on grounds of its superior efficiency, reliability, and humanity when compared with hanging.

Finally, by 1900 the nation's thirty-nine states included six that had abolished the death penalty even for murder: Michigan (1847), Rhode Island (1852), Wisconsin (1853), Maine (1876), Iowa (1878), and Colorado (1897).

Notable Abolitionists

At the end of the eighteenth century, Benjamin Rush was the nation's most influential opponent of the death penalty. His *Considerations on the Injustice and Impolicy of Punishing Murder by Death* (1792) was widely read and cited. Over the course of the next century, other prominent figures joined in the struggle against the death penalty.

First among these was Edward Livingston (1764–1836), a New York politician. Asked in 1821 by the Louisiana Assembly to draft a penal code, he used the occasion to attack capital punishment, stating, "The punishment of death should find no place in the code" (quoted in Mackey, *Voices against Death*, p. 15).

At least as influential as Rush and Livingston was Robert Rantoul Jr. (1805–1852), a leading Massachusetts politician. In his report on the death penalty to the state legislature in 1836, he voiced a novel objection not taken seriously until more than a century later: capital punishment is unconstitutional because it violates the Eighth Amendment prohibition against "cruel and unusual punishments."

Rantoul's counterpart in New York was John L. O'Sullivan (1813–1895). As chairman of a special committee of the state assembly to evaluate the death penalty, O'Sullivan submitted a book-length report and an abolition bill in 1841. The bill failed by a narrow margin, but the report was widely circulated and joined the writings of Rush, Livingston, and Rantoul as a standard source for abolitionist arguments.

Opposition to the death penalty was supported by a wide variety of prominent Americans. The poet John Greenleaf Whittier attacked executions in his poem "The Human Sacrifice" (1843). Charles Spear, a Boston Universalist minister, published his *Essays on the Punishment of Death* in 1844. He was probably the most widely read clerical opponent of the death penalty in his day. Walt Whitman (1819–1892), newspaper editor and poet, attacked the death penalty in his essay "A Dialogue" (1845), and Horace Greeley (1811–1872), the founder and nationally influential editor of the *New York Tribune*, also voiced his opposition to capital punishment. Elizabeth Cady Stanton (1815–1902), well known for her leadership of the women's movement, expressed her view in forceful language in a letter of 1868: "The gallows ... is the torture of my life. Every sentence and every execution I hear of, is a break in the current of my life and thought for days" (quoted in Mackey, p. 121).

Conclusion

Opposition to the death penalty during the nineteenth century was not (as it would be in the twentieth) focused on racial biases; little or nothing was typically argued about the death penalty, as administered, singling out black offenders or blacks as the murderers of white victims. Nor was abolition of the death penalty defended on the ground that capital punishment is meted out unfairly and that its maladministration is beyond repair. The great nineteenth-century voices against the death penalty—Spear, Rantoul, O'Sullivan, Livingston—focused their objections elsewhere: on the lack of any evidence to support the threat of death as a superior deterrent, the risk of executing the innocent, jury nullification, the sanctity of human life, and the New Testament doctrine of forgiveness and mercy,

Anti–death penalty political agitation reached its peak about mid-century. Many states could boast strong antigallows societies, and in 1844–1845 the American Society for the Abolition of Capital Punishment was organized, holding its first meetings in New York and Philadelphia. In several states (Ohio, Pennsylvania) abolition efforts nearly succeeded, but the fight against slavery, culminating in the Civil War, increasingly absorbed the attention and energies of reformers. By the latter third of the century, opposition to the death penalty had lost its political significance and was not to be revived until the Progressive Era of the early 1900s.

See also **Prisons and Punishment; Progressivism; Reform, Social.**

Bibliography

Mackey, Philip English, ed. *Voices against Death: American Opposition to Capital Punishment, 1787–1975.* New York: Burt Franklin, 1976.

Masur, Louis P. *Rites of Execution: Capital Punishment and the Transformation of American Culture, 1776–1865.* New York: Oxford University Press, 1989.

Vila, Bryan, and Cynthia Morris, eds. *Capital Punishment in the United States: A Documentary History.* Westport, Conn.: Greenwood, 1997.

HUGO ADAM BEDAU

CARIBBEAN BASIN.   See **Central America and the Caribbean; Cuba; Haiti.**

CARTOGRAPHY.   See **Geography and Cartography.**

CARTOONS, POLITICAL   During the early days of the Republic, the appearance of a political cartoon was a rare event. One expert counts only seventy-eight political caricatures issued before 1828, and they were sold individually as broadsides for a few pennies. Cartoons appeared in newspapers and magazines even less frequently. Cartoons were laboriously engraved on copper or cut into wood. The woodcut process was especially tedious, requiring the drawing to be made in reverse and fitted to exact measurements. Early cartoons usually dealt with general principles, and a drawing might even appear a second or third time, accompanied by a different caption.

Certainly the most famous of the early nineteenth-century cartoons was "The Gerrymander," drawn for the *Massachusetts Centinel* in 1812, which added to the lexicon a new word to describe strangely shaped electoral districts. For many years the drawing was attributed to Gilbert Stuart, but the actual artist was Elkanah Tisdale. The War of 1812 inspired two or three dozen amusing cartoons by William Charles, notable for his earthy humor. One of his best-known works shows King George sitting on a commode.

If political cartoons were ever to reach the public at large and gain mass appeal, a process was needed that would cut the cost of production. The answer was lithography, based on the principle that grease and water do not mix. Much simpler than engraving or woodcut, lithography was introduced in the United States by Bass Otis in the July 1819 issue of *Analectic Magazine,* and the first lithographed political cartoon was published in 1829.

The most famous lithography firm, Currier and Ives, founded in 1835, produced black-and-white political cartoons for all sides and then sold them to party headquarters at bulk rates, some in printings of 50,000 and 100,000. Several artists often worked on a single cartoon, taking the portraiture directly from daguerrotypes.

The cartoon humor was often based on puns, often on surnames, like those of Matthew Lyon, John Bell, and Thurlow Weed, that lent themselves to the device. Settings were frequently sporting events, such as a horse race or foot race, a boxing match, a game of brag (an early version of poker), or (by 1860) a baseball game.

Mid-century produced a flock of humor magazines with names like the *Brickbat* and *Diogenes hys Lanterne.* Most never celebrated a first birthday, largely because they were not very funny. Nevertheless they did feature one first-rate cartoonist, Frank Bellew.

Abraham Lincoln, with his elongated frame and homely features, was an especially good target for cartoonists. His severest critics, however, were the English artists associated with *Punch.* He had little to fear from Confederate cartoonists, the most skilled of whom was Adalbert J. Volck, a Baltimore dentist.

The century's greatest cartoonist, Thomas Nast, was born in Germany in 1840. He arrived in the United States at age six and at fifteen became a staff artist for *Frank Leslie's Illustrated Newspaper.* In 1862 he joined *Harper's Weekly,* the most important political voice in postbellum publishing, and for the next quarter-century his name was inextricably joined with that magazine. Nast's fame rests mainly on some fifty drawings he did in 1871 that were directed at William Marcy "Boss" Tweed and his Tammany ring, which controlled New York City. Some of Nast's centerfold cartoons, measuring fourteen inches by twenty inches, are unsurpassed for raw power, and his good-government fight with Tammany tripled the magazine's circulation. But Nast's cartoons were also anti-Catholic and fiercely loyal to the administration of President Ulysses S. Grant, even when it was rightly accused of corruption.

As Nast's popularity began to wane, another great cartoonist captured the fancy of the American public.

Slavery Emerges as the Primary Issue. Political cartoon portraying the alliances of the four presidential contenders of the 1860 presidential campaign. The candidates were *(from the upper left, clockwise)* John Breckenridge, Abraham Lincoln, John Bell, and Stephen A. Douglas. LIBRARY OF CONGRESS

Joseph Keppler, the son of a Viennese baker, had started a German-language weekly called *Puck* in 1876 and added an English edition the next year. If Nast's artistic weapon was the broadsword, Keppler's was the rapier. Keppler's cartoons often appeared in vivid color, with a touch of Viennese gaiety. His magazine introduced a recurring theme in each presidential contest, such as Winfield Scott Hancock as Samson in 1880 and Benjamin Harrison lost in grandpa's hat in 1888. It is hard to overestimate the political influence of *Puck* and its rival *Judge* during the century's last two decades. *Judge,* whose chief cartoonist was Bernard Gillam, was allied with Republicans and *Puck* with the Democrats.

The final great cartoon wars were fought in New York between Joseph Pulitzer's *New York World* and William Randolph Hearst's *New York Journal.* The *World* published a cartoon titled "The Royal Feast of Belshazzar Blaine and the Money Kings" across its front page on 31 October 1884, and some analysts contend it caused Blaine to lose the election in New York and hence the presidency. Hearst's cartoonist, Homer Davenport, made his considerable reputation attacking Mark Hanna, the Republican national chairman, and the trusts. The Pulitzer and Hearst cartoonists ended the century successfully promoting war with Spain.

See also **Communications; Lithography and Prints; Politics,** *subentry on* **Parties and the Press.**

Bibliography

Fischer, Roger. *Them Damned Pictures.* North Haven, Conn.: Shoe String, 1996.

Hess, Stephen, and Milton Kaplan. *The Ungentlemanly Art.* Rev. ed. New York: Macmillan, 1975.

Hess, Stephen, and Sandy Northrop. *Drawn and Quartered.* Montgomery, Ala.: Elliott and Clark, 1996.

Nevins, Allan, and Frank Weitenkampf. *A Century of Political Cartoons: Caricature in the United States from 1800 to 1900.* New York: Scribners, 1944.

STEPHEN HESS

CATHOLICISM   In the early years of the nineteenth century, Roman Catholicism occupied a very marginal position on the American religious landscape. In 1800 Catholics numbered only about forty-seven thousand and were concentrated in the border states of Maryland and Kentucky with growing communities in New York and Philadelphia. In 1789 the American clergy elected the American-born John Carroll to be the bishop of Baltimore. The first Catholic bishop in the United States, Carroll was the recognized leader of the Catholic Church in the country. He led the church into the nineteenth century with a vision that was greatly influenced by the spirit of republicanism that had swept across the American landscape during and after the American Revolution. For example, he supported the lay trustee system of church government, in which elected laymen worked with the clergy to govern the local parish community. American legal norms favored this type of church government, and Catholics were quick to adopt it. Though at times the trustee system created conflict between clergy and laity over the question of who was in charge of the parish, the system worked well in the vast majority of American Catholic parishes, which by 1820 numbered about 120.

In addition to favoring a republican style of government at the local parish level, Carroll wanted Catholicism in the United States to be free from foreign influence. Seeking to train a clergy that would be familiar with what he described as "the American way of life," Carroll in 1789 founded Georgetown Academy, later Georgetown University. In 1791 he helped found St. Mary's Seminary in Baltimore to prepare young men for the priesthood. Carroll was a strong supporter of religious freedom and separation of church and state, ideas enshrined in the First Amendment to the U.S. Constitution.

John Carroll died in 1815. Two years later the Frenchman Ambrose Maréchal was named archbishop of Baltimore and took the vacant position. Raised and educated during the ancien régime era in France, Maréchal's vision of Catholicism was entirely different from Carroll's. He brought with him a monarchical understanding of the church, in which the clergy ruled and the laity were left to pay, pray, and obey, and he strongly opposed any notion of democracy in the church. His hierarchical approach to Catholicism was quite common in Europe at the time and was brought to the United States by foreign-born clergy and immigrant lay Catholics. As immigration transformed the Catholic population, this European style of Catholicism became normative in the United States, but the desire to harmonize Catholicism with the democratic ethos of the country remained alive throughout the nineteenth century. The two differing understandings of Catholicism were another source of conflict between clergy and laity concerning power and authority in the parish community.

Conflicts occasionally led dissident parish communities to separate from the Roman Catholic Church. A major schism took place in 1904, when several Polish parishes joined together to form the Polish National Catholic Church. Though it never embraced more than 5 percent of the Polish American population, the creation of this schismatic church illustrated the intensity of the conflicts over authority

St. Lima's Convent. The Mother Superior is surrounded by students or postulants. Sisters engaged in teaching, hospital work, and social welfare. By the end of the century, the number of Catholics in America increased dramatically. Photography by Coovert. LIBRARY OF CONGRESS

that sometimes plagued nineteenth-century Catholicism.

Another major schism among Catholics emerged in the 1890s and involved Eastern-rite Catholics, who did not follow the Latin rite of worship services, which the majority of Catholics did follow. In addition Eastern-rite priests in Europe were allowed to marry, a practice the American bishops could not accept. American bishops' intransigence on marriage and on sharing power with the laity at the local parish level eventually led to a major exodus of Ukrainian Catholics from the Roman Catholic Church. By 1916 about 163 Eastern-rite parishes, with over 200,000 members, had joined the Russian Orthodox Church.

Immigration

The 1820s ushered in a period of mass immigration to the United States. The millions of Catholics who

immigrated so increased the numbers of the Catholic community that by the middle of the nineteenth century Roman Catholicism had already become one of the country's largest religious denominations. By the end of the century the number of Catholics had increased to an estimated twelve million, making them the largest religious denomination in the nation.

Though Catholic communities developed in the farming areas of the Midwest, the vast majority of immigrating Catholics settled in cities, where there were jobs. Catholics also concentrated heavily in the industrialized core, a region that stretched from Milwaukee to Boston and from St. Louis to Baltimore. Constituting an overwhelmingly blue-collar, urban community, Catholics were ethnically diverse. As many as twenty-eight different language groups claimed membership in the church. The Irish and Germans were the most numerous, but Polish and Italian immigrant Catholics were on the increase in the closing decades of the century and eventually challenged the hegemony of the Irish and Germans. French Canadians, Mexicans, Slovaks, Czechs, Lithuanians, and Ukrainians constituted the other sizable Catholic immigrant groups in the late nineteenth century.

The influx of large numbers of Irish and German Catholics in the years before the Civil War unleashed a backlash against immigrant Catholics. The opening salvo took place in the summer of 1834, when a mob attacked the Ursuline convent school in Charlestown, Massachusetts, ransacked the building, and burned it to the ground. This incident marked the beginning of a nativist Protestant crusade against Catholics that lasted into the 1850s. During this period more than a dozen Catholic churches were destroyed, convents were attacked, and priests were beaten and stoned. In Philadelphia in May and July 1844 riots tore apart Irish neighborhoods, and fires destroyed two Catholic churches and numerous homes. More than a dozen people died, and many more were injured. Only the intervention of the state militia restored order to the city.

In the 1850s the American, or Know-Nothing, Party, whose motto was "Americans must rule America," rose to political prominence. Antiforeign and anti-Catholic, party members took an oath that they would not vote for any foreigners, Roman Catholics in particular. By 1854 the Know-Nothing Party had over one million members and had put into office eight governors, more than one hundred congressmen, and the mayors of Boston, Chicago, and Philadelphia. The controversy over slavery soon split the party, and its decline was as rapid as its rise. Nonetheless, the Know-Nothings taught Catholics a hard lesson, that they were not welcome in the United States. As one Irish immigrant lamented, "The great majority of the American people are in heart and soul, anti-Catholic, but more especially anti-Irish; everything Irish is repugnant to them" (Miller, *Emigrants and Exiles*, p. 323).

As slavery and the Civil War took center stage in the 1860s, popular support for the crusade against foreigners and Catholics declined. In the late 1880s and the 1890s, however, a nativist movement surfaced once again. The American Protective Association, founded in 1887, spearheaded a crusade against foreigners and Catholics that never duplicated the intensity or popularity of the antebellum movement. The majority of Americans had grown tired of such bigotry. Nevertheless, repeated Protestant outcries against Catholics had left their imprint on the immigrant Catholic community.

A Catholic World

Victims of prejudice and discrimination, Catholics gathered together in their own cultural enclaves, where they created a world set apart from the rest of American society. The key institution of this Catholic world was the national parish. Traditionally, Catholic parishes were organized by territory. People worshiped in the neighborhood where they lived, and nationality had little to do with church membership. That was not the case in the immigrant neighborhoods of urban America. Immigrant Catholics wanted to worship in a church where services and sermons were in their native language and where they could continue the traditions and customs of the Old World. By the end of the century, when Catholicism had become an ethnically diverse denomination, city neighborhoods commonly had several Catholic churches, one for each major immigrant group. On any given Sunday in such neighborhoods Catholics would walk past one or more Catholic churches on their way to the church of their choice. In Chicago, for example, several different ethnic groups, including Irish, German, Bohemian, Polish, Slovak, Lithuanian, and Ukrainian Catholics, settled in the neighborhood west of the city's stockyards known as Back of the Yards. Each ethnic group had its own institutions, and chief among them was the church. In addition to offering religion to the people, ethnic churches fostered a strong sense of nationalism within each group. In doing so they cultivated a nationalist, sectarian mentality that set Catholics apart from the rest of society and created deep fissures within the Catholic community. Like separate planets, each ethnic group lived and worshiped within its own orbit, oblivious to what was going on in other ethnic communities. Intermarriage between ethnic groups was rare.

National parishes were more than places to worship. In the immigrant neighborhood they were the cement that bound the people together, enabling them to establish a community life. Prior to 1880 most parishes were primarily devotional or religious, but after 1880 they took on a myriad of functions. As organizations with explicit social, recreational, charitable, or educational goals appeared, the immigrant parish became the major cultural and social institution in the neighborhood. In addition to the church, parishes often included a school, a convent for the sisters who worked in the parish, a home for the parish clergy, a hall for social and recreational events, and possibly a high school or orphanage. With buildings for each of those purposes, a parish could occupy an entire city block.

An important entity, the parish, or parochial, school developed over the course of the nineteenth century, championed by Archbishop John Hughes of New York and Archbishop John Purcell of Cincinnati. Since support for parochial education was not unanimous among the clergy, considerable debate en-

"The Three Days of May 1844—Columbia Mourns Her Citizens Slain." Nativists, commemorated in this lithograph, fought Irish American Catholics in Kensington, Pennsylvania, 6–8 May 1844. Lithograph by Colon & Adriance, Philadelphia, 1844. LIBRARY OF CONGRESS

a number of Catholic colleges for men and women in the nineteenth century. Quite different from their Protestant or public counterparts, Catholic colleges were modeled on a European system that combined both secondary and collegiate education in seven-year institutions. Only in the twentieth century did these institutions clearly differentiate between secondary and collegiate education according to the American pattern.

Essential to the development of the parochial schools were the sisters who taught in them. The women religious of many orders became legendary for their dedicated work in Catholic education. Sisters were also involved in other apostolates in the nineteenth century, founding hospitals and orphanages and performing a variety of social welfare tasks. In the early part of the century many of these women immigrated from Ireland or Germany and were essential to the development and expansion of the immigrant church. In the 1820s fewer than four hundred sisters belonging to a handful of religious orders worked in the United States. As many as 152 congregations of women religious from central and eastern Europe founded convents in the United States between the Civil War and World War I. By 1900 the number of sisters in the United States had increased to 46,583, and they belonged to 170 different religious orders.

Diversity and Divisions

Ethnic diversity among Catholics created a great deal of conflict. In the early part of the century American-born Catholics wanted Irish newcomers to shed their Irish habits and become assimilated into the American way of life. Later on, the Germans accused the Irish of forcing them to assimilate too rapidly. The Polish did not get along with the Germans, and the Italians believed that the Irish discriminated against them. At the root of the conflict was the strong bond between religion and ethnicity. Each ethnic group closely identified its Catholic faith with its native culture, customs, and language. In a particularly prolonged culture war in the late 1880s, Germans concertedly resisted any attempts to weaken their attachment to their language and culture.

Though German Catholics were a sizable subculture within the American Catholic mosaic, bishops and clergy of Irish descent held most positions of authority. Many German Catholics believed that the Irish clergy discriminated against them and treated them as second-class citizens. The German clergy mounted the first phase of a campaign for equal rights in the church and equal representation in the church hierarchy in the mid-1880s, when they complained to Roman authorities about efforts on the

sued. Finally, in 1884 at the Third Baltimore Council, the bishops came out in support of parochial schooling and urged that all parishes build a school within two years. Though that did not happen, Catholic communities raised schools to equal importance with the church. One ardent advocate of the parochial school, Bishop Bernard McQuaid of Rochester, New York, stated that he "would rather see the schoolhouse without the church than the church without the schoolhouse" (Dolan, *The American Catholic Experience*, p. 272). Catholic high schools appeared toward the end of the century. As the number of schools increased, integrated school systems developed, with superintendents of schools and an emerging educational bureaucracy.

Throughout the nineteenth century there never was a total commitment to the parochial school, either on the part of the clergy or the people. A major reason for this was the high cost of education. As a result by 1900 only 37 percent of Catholic parishes were able to support a school. For this reason many Catholic children attended public schools, which became religiously neutral by the closing decades of the century.

The Catholic educational enterprise also included

part of Irish clergy and bishops to force German Catholics to Americanize. For German Catholics such attempts at Americanization would mean a loss of language, and "language saves faith" became their battle cry. In 1890 Peter Paul Cahensly, a German layman who had founded an emigrant aid society in Germany, St. Raphaelsverein, presented a memorial to the pope claiming that millions of immigrants were lost to the church in the United States because of a lack of pastoral care. To resolve the problem he recommended that each national group have its own parishes, schools, clergy, and bishops. In effect, he recommended that Catholicism in the United States be divided into separate language churches, each with its own hierarchy. Such an arrangement would encourage a spirit of nationalism that most Americans found unacceptable, and Cahensly's memorial sparked a furious uproar. The nationalist Germans favored it, while the American hierarchy opposed it. Pope Leo XIII finally decided against Cahensly's proposals.

The late 1880s and the 1890s were a turbulent time in American Catholic history. Along with the debates over parochial schools and the Americanization of foreign-born Catholics, the issue of the legitimacy of labor unions divided the church. Many clergy were suspicious of labor unions because of the secret initiation rituals some unions then practiced. Labor violence was also commonplace, making the clergy even more wary. The Knights of Labor was the major labor organization of the 1880s, and perhaps as many as two-thirds of its members were Catholic. In Canada the Catholic hierarchy had persuaded Vatican authorities to outlaw the union, and Canadian bishops wanted to extend the condemnation to the Knights of Labor in the United States. Several members of the church hierarchy intervened on behalf of the union, and in a letter to the pope, James Cardinal Gibbons of Baltimore defended the right of workers to organize. Pope Leo XIII accepted Gibbons's argument, and in 1888 he lifted the ban on the Knights. Gibbons's defense of labor and the pope's decision, perceived as a victory for labor, officially put the leadership of the church on the side of labor, the first step in forming a social gospel tradition among American Catholics.

Liberals and Conservatives

By the 1890s American Catholics were divided into two broad, opposing schools of thought. One group, labeled liberals, wanted Catholicism to be more American, more modern. They wanted the church to adapt to the age. Their opponents, described as conservatives, emphasized the unchanging nature of Ca-

tholicism. Change was anathema to them. Archbishop John Ireland of St. Paul, Minnesota, was the acknowledged leader of the liberals, and Archbishop Michael Corrigan of New York led the conservatives. The debate over parochial schools revealed the fault line that divided Catholics. Conservatives championed parochial schools and attacked any effort at compromise with the "godless" public schools. The liberals wanted to work out some type of compromise with the public schools whereby Catholic children would still be able to study religion in a school supported by public monies. The liberals also endorsed the separation of church and state. The conservatives gained the support of influential members of the pope's curia, who persuaded the pope to condemn American efforts to adopt the liberal ideas. In 1899 Pope Leo XIII issued a letter, *Testem Benevolentiae*, that spoke against "Americanism" and the liberal position that the church should adapt to the modern age.

The conservative victory over Americanism ended sustained efforts to fashion a theologically modern Catholicism. The American Catholic romance with modernity was over, and the twentieth century ushered in an era distinguished by the Romanization of Catholicism. The American church developed closer ties to the Vatican and its concepts. Rome became both the spiritual center and the intellectual center of American Catholicism.

See also **Anti-Catholicism; Religion,** *subentry on* **Religion in Nineteenth-Century America.**

Bibliography

Barry, Colman James. *The Catholic Church and German Americans*. Milwaukee, Wis.: Bruce, 1953.

Billington, Ray Allen. *The Protestant Crusade 1800–1860*. New York: Macmillan, 1938.

Carey, Patrick W. *People, Priests and Prelates: Ecclesiastical Democracy and the Tensions of Trusteeism*. Notre Dame, Ind.: University of Notre Dame Press, 1987.

Cross, Robert D. *The Emergence of Liberal Catholicism in America*. Cambridge, Mass.: Harvard University Press, 1958.

Dolan, Jay P. *The American Catholic Experience: A History from Colonial Times to the Present*. Garden City, N.Y.: Doubleday, 1985.

———. *The Immigrant Church: New York's Irish and German Catholics 1815–1865*. Baltimore: Johns Hopkins University Press, 1975.

Ellis, John Tracy. *The Life of James Cardinal Gibbons: Archbishop of Baltimore, 1834–1921*. 2 vols. Milwaukee, Wis.: Bruce, 1952.

Hennessey, James. *American Catholics: A History of the Roman Catholic Community in the United States*. New York: Oxford University Press, 1981.

McAvoy, Thomas Timothy. *The Americanist Heresy in Roman*

Catholicism, 1895–1900. Notre Dame, Ind.: University of Notre Dame Press, 1963.

Melville, Annabelle M. *John Carroll of Baltimore: Founder of the American Catholic Hierarchy.* New York: Scribner, 1955.

Miller, Kerby A. *Emigrants and Exiles: Ireland and the Irish Exodus to North America.* New York: Oxford University Press, 1985.

O'Connell, Marvin R. *John Ireland and the American Catholic Church.* St. Paul: Minnesota Historical Society Press, 1988.

Shanabruch, Charles. *Chicago's Catholics.* Notre Dame, Ind.: University of Notre Dame Press, 1981.

JAY P. DOLAN

CATHOLIC SCHOOLS. See **Education**, subentry on **Elementary and Secondary Schools**.

CATTLE DRIVES. See **Ranching and Livestock Raising**.

CEMETERIES AND BURIAL Two contrasting images reveal the changing relationship between the living and the dead in the United States during the course of the nineteenth century. On 24 September 1831 a field in Cambridge, Massachusetts, previously known to college students as "Sweet Auburn" for its invitation to dalliance, was consecrated to a new use as the nation's first memorial park. Mount Auburn Cemetery astonished Bostonians with its spacious and inviting grounds. Within less than a decade "rural cemeteries" were established in other cities, and by mid-century much of the nation had taken up the idea of placing their dead in what Blanche Linden-Ward describes as "landscapes of memory" (*Silent City on a Hill*, p. 2).

On 11 November 1863 a weary and ailing U.S. president made a brief address to a crowd that could barely hear his high-pitched voice. The occasion of Abraham Lincoln's Gettysburg Address was the dedication of the first national cemetery. Although burying fallen soldiers near the battlefield was practical, more important was the symbolism of national unity. The designation of a national cemetery emphasized the public rather than the private significance of a death in the line of duty. A nation shocked by the appalling loss of life now had a focal point and therefore a place to begin the long and painful process of healing. At the end of the Civil War fourteen such cemeteries had been established for both the Union and the Confederate dead. In the twentieth century the National Cemetery System provided gravesites for more than two million veterans in 114 sites on more than ten thousand acres of land.

Beauty, Conflict, Violence, and the Nineteenth-Century Cemetery

Mount Auburn and Gettysburg Cemeteries were memorials and also testimonials to salient features of the nineteenth-century experience. Most existing burial grounds were gloomy places, often neglected, seldom visited. Some grave markers did express hopeful sentiments about a better life on the other side of the grave, for example:

Here lies
In a state of perfect oblivion
John Adams
who died Sept 2 1811
Death has decomposed him
And at the great resurrection Christ
will recompose him

Nevertheless, the graveyard was a place to be avoided, with its grim reminders of human frailty and its pessimistic overtones. This attitude was challenged robustly by the generation that was coming into its own in the 1820s and 1830s. Although most of the leaders of cemetery reform were people of religious faith, they did not regard life as vain and death as punishment. Appreciation for the beauty of nature as well as artistic achievements experienced renewal. Life should be enjoyed and the beloved dead should be remembered within a peaceful environment. Furthermore a well-planned and maintained cemetery eliminated the health hazards that were generated by overcrowded and untended gravesites. In its nineteenth-century origins the memorial park offered an alternative conception of the relationship between the living and the dead. Sorrow would remain sorrow, but the dead would now be honored and the living comforted as optimism and romanticism made their marks on the nineteenth century.

Conflict and violence were also characteristics of the national experience, however, and their influence often followed people to the grave. The powerful weapons unleashed in the Civil War, for example, left many of the fallen with massive disfigurations that would have horrified family and friends. Embalming and cosmetic repair were used on an unprecedented scale as a humanitarian measure before bodies were transported home. Routine embalming and cosmetic alteration originated in the attempt to allow families to bury their dead without witnessing the unmitigated horrors of modern warfare.

Racial and ethnic conflict surged throughout a century of turbulent geographical expansion, tech-

Burial of the *Maine* Dead. The coffins of those who perished in the sinking of the *Maine* in Havana Harbor are draped with American flags. The incident resulted in widespread support for the Spanish-American War. Photograph, 1898. LIBRARY OF CONGRESS

nological advances, and increasing multiculturalism. Creativity and opportunity were shadowed by discrimination and violence, memorably expressed in 1942 by Stephen Vincent Benét's poem "American Names," which opens "I have fallen in love with American names" and closes "Bury my heart at Wounded Knee" (*Selected Works*, p. 367).

More telling than the frequent outbursts of lethal violence are the testimonies of segregated burial grounds. Much of this segregation was self-imposed, as people who had come to the United States from various other lands affirmed their group identities by establishing cemeteries for their compatriots and co-religionists only. With its rich history, New Orleans provides particularly clear examples of cemeteries established by people with a specific national origin and religion. Throughout the nation other cemeteries also declare the nineteenth-century people's desire to remain separate in death as well as life. Sometimes, however, people of a particular ethnic, racial, or religious background had no choice about segregated burial grounds—rather, they were excluded from the major established cemeteries. Furthermore, segregation by ethnicity or social class was common in general community cemeteries. W. L. Warner, in *The Living and the Dead* (1959), observes that social standing was scrupulously maintained in the cemeteries of the New England city he studied intensively. The wealthy, powerful, and connected kept their advantage even in death.

The spirit of equality did express itself with slowly gathering strength. By the end of the nineteenth century, for example, African American residents of Newport, Rhode Island, had established their right to control their own gravesites rather than be forced to conform to white practices that stripped them of their own cultural values. Later, Mormons on the frontier literally found common ground with the Navajo and Zuni people in establishing a cemetery that allowed each group to express its own beliefs and practices.

The epidemic diseases that claimed many lives during the nineteenth century also left a lasting mark on cemeteries. Across the nation cemeteries record many deaths from influenza and yellow fever in the 1840s and 1850s. In the 1870s victims of influenza and cholera filled many graveyards. Most poignant of all are the family plots everywhere that reveal the deaths of infants, young children, and all too often their mothers as well.

Nineteenth-century cemeteries left a complex message of hope, fatalism, and stark reality. They make a mute statement of the human condition that links present to past as perhaps nothing else can.

See also **Death and Dying; Health and Disease; Monuments and Memorials.**

Bibliography

Cunningham, Keith. "Navajo, Mormon, Zuni Graves: Navajo, Mormon, Zuni Ways." In *Cemeteries and Gravemarkers:*

Voices of American Culture. Edited by Richard E. Meyer. Ann Arbor, Mich.: UMI Research Press, 1989.

Kastenbaum, Robert. "Embalming." In *Encyclopedia of Death.* Edited by Robert Kastenbaum and Beatrice Kastenbaum. Phoenix, Ariz.: Oryx, 1989.

Linden-Ward, Blanche. *Silent City on a Hill: Landscapes of Memory and Boston's Mount Auburn Cemetery.* Columbus: Ohio State University Press, 1989.

Morris, Richard. *Sinners, Lovers, and Heroes: An Essay on Memorializing in Three American Cultures.* Albany: State University of New York Press, 1997.

Tashjian, Ann, and Dickran Tashjian. "The Afro-American Section of Newport, Rhode Island's Common Burying Ground." In *Cemeteries and Gravemarkers: Voices of American Culture.* Edited by Richard E. Meyer. Ann Arbor, Mich.: UMI Research Press, 1989.

Wallis, Charles L. *Stories on Stone.* New York: Oxford University Press, 1954.

Warner, W. Lloyd. *The Living and the Dead: A Study of the Symbolic Life of Americans.* New Haven, Conn.: Yale University Press, 1959.

ROBERT KASTENBAUM

CENTRAL AMERICA AND THE CARIBBEAN

Throughout the nineteenth century the United States maintained a very high degree of interest in Central America and the Caribbean. Strategic and economic concerns drove that interest, and by 1900 the United States was well on its way to becoming the dominant power in both areas. The growth of its power in Central America and the Caribbean often involved the United States in diplomatic conflicts with the nations of those regions as well as with extrahemispheric powers such as Great Britain.

Central America

U.S. relations with Central America got off to a very rocky start. When in 1821 the captaincy-general of Guatemala, which encompassed most of Central America as well as a portion of southern Mexico, declared its independence from Spain, the United States knew less about that region than any other in Latin America. After a short alliance with Mexico, the governments of Honduras, Guatemala, El Salvador, Costa Rica, and Nicaragua announced in 1823–1824 the formation of the United Province of Central America, which broke up in 1838. The United States was the first major power to grant recognition to the new government, but getting U.S. representatives to the area proved an almost insurmountable problem. No consistent travel or communications lines existed between the United States and Central America, and the first U.S. representatives seemed positively jinxed. The first two men sent to the post died en route. In 1826 John Williams became the first U.S. chargé d'affaires to arrive in Guatemala, but he left after six months. His successor never reached Central America. Three years passed before another appointment, and that person also failed to make it to his post. The next appointee died in transit. In 1833 Charles Dewitt arrived for a five-year stay. Aside from longevity, however, he accomplished nothing. His replacement died before leaving the United States.

It is hardly surprising, therefore, that U.S. policy toward Central America was, in these early years, hazy at best. Nevertheless, several issues concerned U.S. officials. First and foremost was the American interest in securing transit, both overland and by means of a canal, across the Central American isthmus. The protection and promotion of American trade was also a priority. A final issue was controlling the growing British influence in Central America. By the 1830s Great Britain had established British Honduras (now Belize), had set up a "protectorate" over the Miskito Indians living along the Atlantic coasts of Nicaragua and Honduras, and was dominating trade and commerce in the region. In contrast to the futility of American attempts at representation in Central America, one man, Frederick Chatfield, represented British interests there from 1833 to 1852.

Squier's maneuvers

By the late 1840s the tempo of American interest in Central America quickened appreciably. The spoils of the Mexican War and the annexation of the Oregon Territory had made the United States a nation stretching from the Atlantic to the Pacific. Suddenly, transit across the Central American isthmus was of critical importance, and the surge of travelers to the California gold rush of 1848–1849 magnified that significance. At precisely this time E. George Squier was appointed as the new U.S. representative to Central America. By then the Central American Confederation, comprising El Salvador, Honduras, and Nicaragua, had collapsed, so Squier represented U.S. interests in all five nations.

Squier faced a delicate situation. His primary directive from Washington was to secure a canal concession for the United States. This was not an easy task. The British were making aggressive moves of their own. In 1848 British troops had occupied San Juan del Norte, Nicaragua, using their "protectorate" over the Miskito Indians as an excuse. The town was a likely starting point for a canal. Undaunted, Squier in 1849 secured a contract between Nicaragua and a company owned by Cornelius Vanderbilt for the construction of a transit system across the country. He also secured a treaty vowing U.S. protection

The *Jessie H. Freeman*. Captain Lorenzo Baker's first steam-powered ship brought bananas from Jamaica to the United States in June 1870. COURTESY OF UNITED FRUIT COMPANY/LIBRARY OF CONGRESS

of any canal route through Nicaragua (the treaty was not ratified by the United States). Finally, he pressured a Honduran official to sign over rights to Tigre Island in the Gulf of Fonseca, where a canal would likely end.

Matters quickly turned nasty. The British, hearing about Squier's manuevers, seized Tigre Island. It was obvious that a confrontation was brewing, but cooler heads prevailed. In 1850 the United States and Great Britain signed the Clayton-Bulwer Treaty, which stated that any canal in Central America would be a joint project, that neither country would claim exclusive control over any such canal, that no fortifications would be constructed in regard to a canal, and that neither signatory would occupy any part of Central America. Both sides agreed to give up their claims on Tigre Island, which was returned to Honduran rule.

Forms of neocolonialism

The signing of the treaty, however, did not mean an end to U.S.-British confrontations. In 1854 an American representative was slightly injured during a riot in Greytown (formerly San Juan del Norte), Nicaragua, raising tensions anew. In retaliation an American warship bombarded the area, and though no one was killed in the attack, the British were angered. Further suspicions were raised when William Walker's filibustering expedition landed in Nicaragua in 1855. Walker was eventually expelled from the country, and in 1860, following an attempt to land in Honduras, he was caught and executed. The fact that

Walker's expedition was privately funded and violated U.S. law did nothing to alleviate the fears of the British that the United States intended to dominate Central America—and any canal built there.

These events also caused concern among the Central American nations. For years, many of the governments in that region had courted U.S. trade and influence in order to balance the tremendous power of the British, which threatened to reduce Central America to a condition of near colonialism. The attack on Greytown and the Walker expeditions suggested that one form of neocolonialism might be replaced with another.

As the concerns of Central American governments were growing, however, U.S. interest in the region diminished due to the outbreak of the Civil War and various diplomatic moves by the British. Great Britain, perhaps sensing that conflict with the United States over Central America was not in its best interest, removed its protectorate over the Miskito kingdom (which remained a self-governing area), and in 1862 resolved the uncertainty over Belize by making it an official British colony. Central America did not disappear from the thinking of American officials, however. President Abraham Lincoln, long intrigued by the notion of "resettling" the black population of the United States, began to consider Central America for this plan. Several proposals were discussed with the governments of the region, but U.S. officials were shocked to discover that such plans incensed the Central Americans, who wanted no part of America's "castaways." The entire episode served to heighten

William Walker (1824–1860). Arriving in Nicaragua in 1855, Walker and his recruits fought in the revolution. Walker eventually became commander in chief of the army, and in July 1856 he made himself president. His ascendency was short-lived; in 1860 after a court martial, Hondurans executed him before a firing squad. © BETTMANN/CORBIS

the suspicion that the United States, far from being Central America's savior, might become its biggest threat.

Growing ties

After the Civil War, U.S. policy toward Central America continued to center on securing a canal site and, as the nineteenth century wore on, protecting and encouraging trade with the region. Moving quickly on the canal issue, the United States in 1867 signed a treaty with Nicaragua for transit rights across that nation and made surveys elsewhere in Central America, including Panama. However, it did not move quickly enough. In 1878 the French entered the race for a canal by securing a concession in Panama. The French action, along with the growing de-

sire for overseas markets and territorial expansion during the late nineteenth century, drove the United States to take an increasingly aggressive stance. American presidents and other officials began calling for the abrogation of the Clayton-Bulwer Treaty and an exclusively U.S.-controlled canal in Central America.

U.S. economic penetration of Central America also developed rapidly during the last decades of the 1800s. In 1870 total U.S. trade with Central America was less than $1 million. By 1900 that figure had increased to nearly $15 million. The primary Central American exports to the United States were coffee and bananas. The banana industry, in particular, grew to enormous proportions, and in 1899 the United Fruit Company was formed. American investments poured into the region. In addition to banana and coffee lands, U.S. money flowed into mining, railroads (Minor C. Keith was the leading American figure), and port construction. Most Central American nations witnessed the establishment of enclave economies, with thousands of American entrepreneurs and workers carving out semi-independent systems within the five republics.

Though the United States tried to refrain from active involvement in the political problems of Central America, in the case of José Santos Zelaya, who rose to power in Nicaragua in 1893, involvement was unavoidable. Zelaya declared martial law in his nation, set higher taxes on banana exports, and began to press for incorporation of the Miskito region. In response the British reasserted their "special interest" in the Miskito, and the stage was set for a confrontation. U.S. officials, though equally angered by Zelaya's actions, ended up supporting his claims over the Miskito, believing that the British posed more of a threat than the Nicaraguan leader. The British, with problems of their own elsewhere in the world, quietly withdrew from the contest.

By 1900 the United States had made clear its position in Central America. The arduous journey of U.S. naval vessels around the tip of South America during the Spanish-American War had made clear the strategic necessity of a canal. A canal, should it be built, would be an American canal. The intrusion of European powers into the region would no longer be tolerated, and American trade and investment would be encouraged to replace existing European patterns. The United States was ready to become the dominant power in Central America.

The Caribbean

The United States faced a very different situation in the Caribbean during the nineteenth century. Aside from Haiti and Santo Domingo the region was completely in the grips of European colonialism. Direct and official contacts between the United States and the Caribbean were, therefore, somewhat limited. Nevertheless, the United States did have a great deal of interest in the area.

Colonialism and revolution

Prior to the 1840s U.S. interest in the Caribbean was primarily economic. By the 1810s, for example, approximately one-third of all U.S. exports went to that region. Trade was always uncertain, however. European wars and new regimes that brought with them new colonial rules and regulations complicated the picture. By the 1840s U.S. officials were reconsidering their policies toward the Caribbean. U.S. expansion into the Louisiana Purchase, the Florida cession, and the annexation of Texas brought new strategic and economic importance to the Caribbean.

Basic U.S. policy was simple: colonialism in the islands of the Caribbean, which had large black and mixed-race populations, was preferable to revolutions for independence. The "black revolt" of 1804 on the island of Hispaniola, divided between Haiti and Santo Domingo, convinced U.S. officials that peaceful and profitable colonialism was preferable to race rebellions. Even in the case of Cuba, which U.S. policymakers always believed was destined to fall under American control, no aid or support was forthcoming when revolt against Spanish rule began to brew in the 1810s and 1820s. A corollary to U.S. policy was that the situation in the Caribbean would remain as it was; no colonies would be transferred from one European power to another.

Despite this outlook, during the expansionistic fervor of the 1840s and 1850s, the United States became more aggressive in pursuing its plans for Cuba. Offers to purchase the island from Spain; the filibustering expeditions of Narciso López, which originated from U.S. territory; and the extraordinarily undiplomatic Ostend Manifesto in 1854 all indicated the increased desire of the United States to acquire the island. The manifesto—a document prepared by three U.S. diplomats in Europe—had gone so far as to suggest that if Spain refused to sell the island, the United States would be justified in taking it by force. All efforts failed. In the 1860s the American government vigorously expressed its dissatisfaction at the Spanish attempt to reestablish colonial control over Santo Domingo.

Strategic concerns

After the Civil War, U.S. interest in the Caribbean grew dramatically, and strategic concerns came to the fore. The growing demand for a stronger U.S. navy meant securing naval bases, and the Bay of Samaná in Santo Domingo (now the Dominican Republic) and Môle St.-Nicolas in Haiti were two of the most promising sites. In addition U.S. interest in a canal through Central America meant that the Caribbean passageway would have to be protected. The overseas economic expansion of the United States during the late nineteenth century also focused attention on the Caribbean. More and more, therefore, European colonialism, once seen as a bulwark of stability in the region, was viewed as an impediment or even a threat to the achievement of U.S. goals.

The end of slavery in the United States also had something to do with the new American outlook. With slave rebellion in the United States no longer a concern, American officials could more rationally discuss the end of European control over the islands of the Caribbean. With typical American confidence that the United States could guide and teach the inhabitants of those islands the basics of independence, the nation began to take a much more aggressive stance.

During the 1860s the United States tried to negotiate the purchase of the Virgin Islands from Denmark, and President Ulysses S. Grant took a special interest in acquiring Santo Domingo. Both efforts failed in Congress, where members held deep suspicions about how the negotiations were carried out, as well as concerns about incorporating a large number of nonwhites into American society. The United States also pushed vigorously for trade treaties with Haiti, Santo Domingo, Cuba, and the British West Indies. In 1898 the United States declared war on Spain, and in the ensuing conflict took control of the Spanish colonies of Cuba and Puerto Rico. Both retained a semicolonial status through the end of the nineteenth century.

By 1900 the United States was poised to turn the Caribbean into an "American lake." The occupations of Cuba and Puerto Rico were followed in the early twentieth century by Theodore Roosevelt's gunboat diplomacy; the Roosevelt Corollary, which established U.S. economic control over Santo Domingo; and, during the Woodrow Wilson administration, the military occupations of Haiti and Santo Domingo and the purchase of the Danish Virgin Islands. As in Central America, the United States moved its Caribbean policy during the nineteenth century from relative disinterest and lack of involvement to a position of near dominance. In both the Caribbean and Central America, such dominance raised suspicions and fears among many of the regions' people about U.S. intentions.

See also **Cuba; Filibusters; Haiti; Spanish-American War.**

Bibliography

Findling, John E. *Close Neighbors, Distant Friends: United States–Central American Relations.* New York: Greenwood, 1987.

LaFeber, Walter. *Inevitable Revolutions: The United States in Central America.* 2d ed. New York: Norton, 1993.

Langley, Lester D. *Struggle for the American Mediterranean: United States–European Rivalry in the Gulf-Caribbean, 1776–1904.* Athens, Ga.: University of Georgia Press, 1976.

Leonard, Thomas M. *Central America and the United States: The Search for Stability.* Athens, Ga.: University of Georgia Press, 1991.

Maingot, Anthony P. *The United States and the Caribbean: Challenges of an Asymmetrical Relationship.* Boulder, Colo.: Westview, 1994.

Schoonover, Thomas D. *The United States in Central America, 1860–1911: Episodes of Social Imperialism and Imperial Rivalry in the World System.* Durham, N.C.: Duke University Press, 1991.

Stansifer, Charles L. "United States–Central American Relations, 1824–1850." In *United States–Latin American Relations, 1800–1850: The Formative Generations,* edited by T. Ray Shurbutt. Tuscaloosa: University of Alabama Press, 1991.

Michael L. Krenn

CHAIN GANGS   In the late nineteenth century the chain gang became an important way of mobilizing labor to construct and maintain public roads. It was also designed to reduce the costs of feeding and housing convicts. Outside the South, such states or territories as New York, New Mexico, Michigan, and Montana had laws providing for convicts to work on the roads "secured by ball and chain" or "well chained and secured" (Steiner and Brown, *The North Carolina Chain Gang,* p. 17). Most of the eleven former Confederate states used convict labor on public roads by the mid-1880s, and the rest did so by the early twentieth century. As the language of the statutes suggests, convicts could be chained individually to a heavy ball, coffled together at their labors, or otherwise controlled.

Although authorized in most states, the chain gang developed a particularly strong association with the South. It emerged there after the end of slavery in 1865, and it later grew in tandem with the Good Roads movement, a turn-of-the-century campaign by town merchants and commercial farmers for improved transportation. During the first generation after the Civil War, southern states established the system's roots, and by the second generation it was in full flower.

Statute Labor, Road Duty, Corvée

In colonial times, through much of the nineteenth century, and even into the twentieth century, an ancient method persisted of securing labor on public roads in the United States. Widely used, it was variously known as "statute labor" or "road duty," and it resembled a French system, the corvée. A tax, paid in labor rather than cash, was levied on most men, who were called out a few days each year to work on the roads. Citizens sometimes challenged the system in the courts, citing the Thirteenth Amendment and other constitutional grounds, but only in Nevada (1874) and Virginia (1894) were such efforts successful. The U.S. Supreme Court upheld the system in a case from Florida, *Butler v. Perry* (1916). In most states, therefore, the system came to an end through legislation or declining local use.

As the traditional system faded in the late nineteenth and early twentieth centuries, the North and the South diverged. In the North, a cash tax and a free labor force, recruited through the offer of wages, replaced the corvée. In the South, the chain gang, recruited through the administration of the criminal justice system, replaced it. In the early stages of the transition, southern states used misdemeanor convicts. As reliance on the chain gang grew, those states added felony convicts who had formerly been subject to the convict lease. Most members of southern chain gangs were black men, whose unfree labor on the roads and cruel life in work camps escaped the Thirteenth Amendment's prohibition on slavery "except as a punishment for crime."

The Civil War left southern jurisdictions bereft of funds, in need of public works, and awash in freedmen who could be mobilized for work on the roads. In Georgia, the city of Milledgeville convicted Charles Harris, a freedman, of a misdemeanor in August 1865 and put him to work for fifteen days "wearing Ball and Chain and working on the streets" (Wallenstein, *From Slave South to New South,* p. 198). In Atlanta the next year, a Fulton County grand jury proposed that misdemeanor convicts be "organized in chain gangs and put to work on our public roads" (Wallenstein, p. 199).

The Georgia legislature authorized the chain gang in 1866 to deal with road maintenance and criminal punishment, and other states took a similar approach. The system sometimes encountered official opposition, however, as when a Freedmen's Bureau

The Wages of Crime. Chain gang at Richmond, Virginia. Sketch, W. S. Sheppard. LIBRARY OF CONGRESS

agent in Alabama directed that "the chain gang system of working convicts on the streets" in Selma be discontinued because, he said, it conflicted with the Civil Rights Act of 1866 (Fleming, *Civil War and Reconstruction in Alabama*, p. 393).

In the 1880s and 1890s, southern states moved more aggressively to adopt the chain gang as a significant way, even the preferred way, to secure labor for public roads. An 1887 law spurred development of the chain gang in North Carolina, as did an 1891 law in Georgia. Georgia took the final step into the world of the chain gang in 1908 when the legislature abolished the convict lease system and directed that felony convicts, like their misdemeanor counterparts, be placed in chain gangs working on the roads. Under a program adopted two years earlier, Virginia reassigned to work on the roads convicts who had been sentenced to the penitentiary.

Like the convict lease system, the chain gang rose and then fell in public favor and in the number of people caught up in its toils. In the South its high point came in the first third of the twentieth century. Late in its reign, Robert E. Burns published a book, *I Am a Fugitive from a Georgia Chain Gang!* (1932), that recounts in vivid fashion the realities of life in a peculiarly American gulag.

See also **Convict Leasing; Emancipation; Prisons and Punishment; South, The,** *subentry on* **The New South after Reconstruction; Transportation,** *subentry on* **Roads and Turnpikes.**

Bibliography

Fleming, Walter L. *Civil War and Reconstruction in Alabama.* New York: P. Smith, 1949.

Lichtenstein, Alex. *Twice the Work of Free Labor: The Political Economy of Convict Labor in the New South.* London: Verso, 1996.

Steiner, Jesse F., and Roy M. Brown. *The North Carolina Chain Gang: A Study of County Convict Road Work.* Chapel Hill: University of North Carolina Press, 1927. Reprint, Westport, Conn.: Negro Universities Press, 1970.

Wallenstein, Peter. *From Slave South to New South: Public Policy in Nineteenth-Century Georgia.* Chapel Hill: University of North Carolina Press, 1987.

PETER WALLENSTEIN

CHARACTER The question of character, defined by Noah Webster in his *American Dictionary of the English Language* (1843) as "the peculiar qualities, impressed by nature or habit on a person, which distinguish him from others," loomed large in the nineteenth-century United States. Orators proclaimed the nation's moral superiority over corrupt Europe, but the hyperbole masked uncertainty. As an agrarian social order gave way to a market economy and urban growth, it became difficult to know the background or situation of those one fleetingly encountered in the bustling city. In this impersonal social setting, to be perceived as a person of good character and to be able to discern those qualities in others were urgent necessities. Further, character became linked to social class. To achieve middle-class status, the young urban newcomer had to emulate the behavior associated with that class. Accordingly, a flood of advice books prescribed for young men and women the behavior that would assure their acceptance as persons of impeccable character. The antebellum moral-reform organizations, tract societies, and Sunday School associations, while seeking to uplift the poor, also assured their middle-class volunteers that, by associating with other like-minded persons, their characters would be strengthened and safeguarded from the city's temptations.

The issue of character also figured in antebellum politics. For Democrats the ideal was the "self-made man," the autonomous, self-reliant individual personified by the party's founder, Andrew Jackson. Government must grant citizens full liberty to pursue their ambitions and mold their characters in a wide-open, laissez-faire society. Although beginning from different premises, Ralph Waldo Emerson and the transcendentalists espoused a similar ideal of the autonomous, self-formed character. For Whigs, by contrast, good character meant morality, self-control, and social responsibility. For them character formation was a prime duty not only of parents and churches but of secular institutions as well. The public school system, argued Horace Mann, existed not merely to impart information but to mold the character of the young, on whom the nation's future depended.

Debates over character formation surfaced in antebellum religious discourse as well. For evangelical revivalists like Charles G. Finney, achieving a good character meant conversion or a dramatic surrendering of one's will to Christ. Religious liberals took a different view. In *Christian Nurture* (1847), Horace Bushnell rejected the conversion-crisis model in favor of a more gradual process by which the child, surrounded from the cradle by uplifting influences, would naturally and spontaneously absorb Christianity and acquire a good character.

Implicitly or explicitly, the antebellum discourse about character always had a gender component. In countless sermons, poems, funerary tributes, and prescriptive manuals, women's character was defined in terms of women's subordinate role in a male-dominated world. Women must cultivate moral sensibility and the gentler virtues to provide a tranquil, uplifting counterweight to the man-made hurly-burly of society at large.

By the 1850s deepening sectional tensions added a new dimension to the debates about character. Southern planters justified slavery by arguing that it enabled them to mold the character and moral sense of their simple, childlike charges. Northern abolitionists vehemently disagreed. For them slavery's worst aspect was its devastating effect both on the slaves' character, by undermining the sanctity of marriage, for example, and, even more insidiously, on the character of the slave owners and the northerners who acquiesced in the system. Uncle Tom and Simon Legree, created by Harriet Beecher Stowe in *Uncle Tom's Cabin* (1852), are unforgettable images of the slave, whose profound Christian faith transcends his debased condition, and the slave owner, whose character is utterly degraded by his absolute power over other human beings. When war came in 1861, Northern intellectuals like Thomas Wentworth Higginson, long worried about the decadence of the younger generation, welcomed the conflict for its bracing effect on the character of the young men fighting in a righteous cause. Robert Gould Shaw, a Boston Brahmin killed while leading his black troops in a doomed assault on Fort Wagner, became an exemplar of shining heroism to inspire the post–Civil War generation.

As industrialization accelerated at the end of the century, the concern with character urgently revived. Some drew upon social Darwinist survival of the fittest ideas to celebrate the autonomous self-made man, personified in the hard-driving captain of industry, but doubts arose. Would the traditional virtues of honesty, forthrightness, and piety be lost in the headlong rush to get money? Wall Street scandals and Gilded Age political corruption seemed to be eating away at the nation's moral fiber. Mark Twain's *The Adventures of Huckleberry Finn* (1884) is a novel of character formation, as adolescent Huck challenges the racism of his culture and remains loyal to the slave Jim. In cautionary novels, such as *The Rise of Silas Lapham* (1885), William Dean Howells portrays the corrupting effect of greed and social climbing on the character of his aggressive businesspeople and young professionals.

Feminist intellectuals, meanwhile, criticized the patriarchal order for inhibiting women's character development. In "The Solitude of Self," published in 1892 in the American Woman Suffrage Association's journal *Woman's Column*, Elizabeth Cady Stanton rejected the prevailing belief that women should be viewed solely in terms of their relationships to men. Every woman like every man, insisted Stanton, is an autonomous agent, responsible for her own moral destiny. Charlotte Perkins Gilman agreed. So long as women remained economically dependent upon men, Gilman wrote in *Women and Economics* (1898), their potential for full character development would remain unrealized.

Rising waves of immigration shaped the evolving debate over character as well. Some native-born Americans reacted xenophobically, deploring as a grave moral threat the onslaught of ignorant, shiftless, licentious immigrants from southern and eastern Europe. The settlement-house leader Jane Addams took a radically different view, however. In an 1892 lecture entitled "The Subjective Necessity for Social Settlements," she warned that the great threat to the character of educated, well-off, native-born young people was precisely their isolation from the teeming social life of the immigrant cities. Human contact across the boundaries of class and ethnicity through the settlement-house movement, Addams insisted, would improve the character of the middle-class volunteers at least as much as it would benefit the immigrants.

As Addams's essay suggests, the emphasis was on the social formation of character rather than self-reliance when the nineteenth century ended. But while the nature of the debate changed, the earnest preoccupation with character itself, so central in American thought throughout the century, remained as strong as ever.

See also **Civilization; Manliness; Victorianism.**

Bibliography

Blumin, Stuart M. *The Emergence of the Middle Class: Social Experience in the American City, 1760–1900.* Cambridge, U.K.: Cambridge University Press, 1989.

Fredrickson, George M. *The Inner Civil War: Northern Intellectuals and the Crisis of the Union.* New York: Harper and Row, 1965.

Halttunen, Karen. *Confidence Men and Painted Women: A Study of Middle-Class Culture in America, 1830–1870.* New Haven, Conn.: Yale University Press, 1982.

Hilkey, Judy. *Character Is Capital: Success Manuals and Manhood in Gilded Age America.* Chapel Hill: University of North Carolina Press, 1997.

Howe, Daniel Walker. *Making the American Self: Jonathan Edwards to Abraham Lincoln.* Cambridge, Mass.: Harvard University Press, 1997.

PAUL BOYER

CHARITY.   See **Welfare and Charity.**

CHARLESTON   In 1800 the population of Charleston, South Carolina, was composed of 10,104 African Americans and 8,820 whites. It was the fifth city in size in the country and on the eve of a boom fueled by high prices for rice, cotton, and slaves. Within a few years slavers would bring more than forty thousand blacks into Charleston. Meanwhile, efforts made by the city council to remedy the notorious unhealthiness of the city proved wanting. Between 1800 and 1860 the city experienced twenty-five yellow fever epidemics.

When the United States and Great Britain went to war in 1812, troops garrisoned the several fortifications in Charleston. Postwar booms in the export trade sputtered in the 1820s, but the city became the playground of the great low country planters, who enjoyed Charleston's annual social season. Their emphasis on family connections, sociability, and conspicuous leisure influenced the city's character. Indeed, William Gilmore Simms, the city's famous literary figure, was unhappy with the local attitude toward the intellectual life. Nevertheless, the city's physicians and naturalists made significant contributions to the life of the mind.

Rumors of servile unrest frequently rocked the city. In May 1822 a slave informed authorities of an impending insurrection. Hundreds of armed whites patrolled the streets and blacks were arrested and intensely questioned. Denmark Vesey, a prominent, free black artisan, was named the ringleader of the plot and incarcerated. Very quickly he and thirty-four of his supposed coconspirators went to their deaths by hanging; thirty-one others were banished. The alleged "plot" may be traced to an overreaction to remarks taken out of context during the interrogation of slaves; on the other hand it may have been the most elaborate slave conspiracy in American history.

During the 1832 contest for the South Carolina legislature, the Nullifier Party swept to victory in Charleston and across the state. Its members threatened secession over high protective tariffs imposed by the U.S. Congress and northern antislavery agitation. In November the legislature issued an ordinance declaring the tariff acts of 1828 and 1832 null and void. President Andrew Jackson condemned the ordinance as treason, and Congress passed the Force Act to compel South Carolina to collect the tariff duties at Charleston; seeking compromise, Jackson also signed into law a lower tariff bill. The state legislature then repealed the Ordinance of Nullification but nullified the Force Act. Secession had been averted, but only temporarily.

By the 1850s local businesspeople had made Charleston the manufacturing center of the state; however, the economy was soon in trouble again from competing railroads. Unemployment increased and prostitution flourished in the city of 40,522 whites and blacks. The most populous of the South Atlantic ports, Charleston was a major distribution center. The out-migration of slaves and the immigration of Irish and Germans transformed Charleston's labor force. The inequality in the distribution of wealth in the city was enormous by comparison to northern cities. A well-to-do, slaveholding, brown elite of approximately five hundred free mulattoes laced together by intermarriage lived among the free African American population of Charleston of more than three thousand. Rivaled in numbers only by those of New Orleans, Charleston's brown elite was an aristocracy of status, color, and wealth. They looked down on blacks, denied them admittance to their social clubs, and identified more closely with their white patrons than they did with black African Americans.

In October 1859 southerners and Charlestonians panicked following the attack by the antislavery fanatic John Brown on the federal arsenal at Harpers Ferry, Virginia. Reports of "incendiary attempts" in Charleston swept the city. The Charleston Vigilance Association was formed to monitor the activities of slaves, free blacks, and "traitorous" whites. Soon after the nomination of Abraham Lincoln for president by the national Republican Party, Charleston police began systematic door-to-door searches and interro-

gations of the free black community; poor free blacks unable to produce proof of their status were reenslaved and even the city's slave-owning mulatto aristocracy was terrorized. Hundreds of free blacks sold what they could, packed what they could carry, and fled Charleston. Some sold their property at huge losses and felt cheated by white persons who took advantage of their predicament.

Following the election of President Abraham Lincoln in 1860, delegates from across South Carolina convened in Charleston and adopted an ordinance of secession from the Union. Following the formation of the Confederacy, Southern leaders ordered that Fort Sumter, which guarded the harbor at Charleston and was occupied by Federal troops, be reduced by bombardment. Upon the surrender of the fort, President Lincoln called for 75,000 volunteers, and the Civil War had begun.

Determined to seize "the cradle of secession," Union forces by land and sea tried unsuccessfully three times to take Charleston. Union troops occupied the city only after Confederate forces evacuated in February 1865. For nearly two centuries Charleston had been the most important city in the region and Charlestonians primarily had controlled South Carolina. But during the war Charleston lost forever its vast influence.

Bird's Eye View of Charleston. Charleston was considered the cultural center of South Carolina and its largest city. Engraving from *The Progress of the Republic* by R. S. Fisher, 1856. LIBRARY OF CONGRESS

Bitterness and separation characterized black-white relations in postwar Charleston. Following enfranchisement, black males organized a local Republican Party, helped write a new state constitution, and assumed important roles in local and state politics. But in the gubernatorial election of 1876 violence rocked the city and state, and a counterrevolution soon reestablished white supremacy.

The economy of Charleston revived by the early 1880s. With a population of fifty thousand, it was the largest port city south of Baltimore and was South Carolina's rail and trade center. But compared to other urban centers of the New South, Charleston's economy remained anemic, due in part to a local lifestyle that emphasized conviviality over diligence and to several natural disasters during the late nineteenth century. Local business also was hurt by a new southwest-northeast rail axis and antiquated port facilities, which made the city a commercial backwater by 1900. Not until the mid–twentieth century was Charleston's economy revived by tourism and federal spending to create a massive military-industrial complex near the city.

See also **South Carolina.**

Bibliography

Fraser, Walter J., Jr. *Charleston! Charleston!: The History of a Southern City.* Columbia: University of South Carolina Press, 1989.

Rogers, George C., Jr. *Charleston in the Age of the Pinckneys.* Norman: University of Oklahoma Press, 1969.

Weir, Robert M. *Colonial South Carolina: A History.* Millwood, N.Y.: KTO, 1983.

WALTER J. FRASER JR.

CHAUTAUQUA.   See **Lyceums.**

CHEMICALS   For most of the nineteenth century, the United States lagged behind Great Britain and Germany in chemical expertise and production. While the British excelled in inorganic chemicals and the Germans in dyestuffs, Americans produced mainly organic chemicals. But U.S. producers made impressive advances in electrochemicals and sulfuric extraction after the Civil War, and began to move into inorganics, synthetic dyes, and new fine chemicals late in the century.

Between 1800 and 1850, most U.S. chemical production was comprised of explosives (especially black powder), fertilizers, and mineral acids, such as sulfuric acid and nitric acid. Production was centered in the East, from Maryland to Massachusetts, with Philadelphia the center of both chemical and pharmaceutical production. John Harrison (1773–1833), a former druggist, began making sulfuric acid in Philadelphia in 1792 and soon diversified into white lead and other colors. Charles Lennig, who introduced a new process for making sulfuric acid in the late 1820s, was the city's largest chemical producer by the 1850s, when he made alum, acid, alkali, and tin salts. Farr & Kunzi began to make fine chemicals in 1812.

Elsewhere, the Du Pont family of France set up their first black powder mills along the Brandywine River in 1802, and later in the century moved into explosives. In the 1820s, William T. Davidson (d. 1881) began making sulfuric acid in Baltimore, and the New York Chemical Manufacturing Company was formed to produce acids, alums, copperas, dyes and paints, and drugs. New England trailed the Mid-Atlantic with smaller and later manufactories.

The typical chemical firm in the early 1800s was family owned and operated and served local markets. The United States imported most of its chemical know-how, in the form of chemists and engineers, and investment capital from Germany, Great Britain, the Netherlands, and Switzerland before the Civil War. Eight American colleges offered chemical courses in 1800, and a few had laboratories. Benjamin Silliman (1779–1864) of Yale, a leading promoter of academic chemistry in the early century, launched the influential *American Journal of Science* in 1818. Several early chemical societies were born in this period, most notably the Columbian Chemical Society of Philadelphia (1811), which counted Thomas Jefferson among its original officers.

By mid-century, 170 U.S. chemical establishments produced output valued at $5 million and employed 1,400 workers, an average of just 8.2 workers per firm. Low tariffs made the United States an attractive market for British soda and bleaching powder made with the LeBlanc process, and discouraged domestic investment in those processes. But the expansion of the American railroad network and the rise of large petroleum and steel industries in the 1870s and 1880s spurred heavy domestic investment in sulfuric and inorganic acids.

But the United States continued to lag behind in dyestuffs, pharmaceuticals, and fine chemicals. Those produced on American shores typically were made by subsidiaries of European—especially German—firms. Thomas Holliday and Charles Holliday of England began producing synthetic dyestuffs in Brooklyn in 1864. A small number of U.S. dyemakers followed suit, but they were driven out by German imports after the U.S. duty on aniline dyes was lowered in

1883. The United States still relied heavily on synthetic dyestuff imports in 1899, when it produced only $1.3 million worth domestically.

During the 1880s and 1890s the United States made rapid advances in alkalis, with the rapid spread of the Solvay soda process, and in electrochemicals, thanks to the electrolytic cell and an abundance of inexpensive hydropower. By 1899, a total of 530 U.S. chemical producers employed 24,000 workers and manufactured product valued at $80 million ($35 million of value added by manufacturing), a sixteenfold increase since 1850. That year General Chemical Co., formed by the merger of twelve chemical producers with a combined capital of $14.1 million, became the largest American heavy chemical manufacturer, using a domestically developed process for making sulfuric acid.

The Dow Chemical Company, incorporated in 1897 to make bleaching powders, signaled the beginning of the end of Great Britain's long dominance of the U.S. bleach market. The application of scientific theory and cooperation among government, industry, and university researchers began to emerge at the end of the nineteenth century and became commonplace in the twentieth, when demand for chemicals and pharmaceuticals by new consumer industries catapulted those industries to world leadership.

Bibliography

Arora, Ashish, and Nathan Rosenberg. "Chemicals: A U.S. Success Story." In *Chemicals and Long-Term Economic Growth: Insights from the Chemical Industry.* Edited by Ashish Arora, Ralph Landau, and Nathan Rosenberg. New York: Wiley, 1998.

Haber, Ludwig F. *The Chemical Industry During the Nineteenth Century: A Study of the Economic Aspect of Applied Chemistry in Europe and North America.* Oxford: Clarendon Press, 1958.

Haynes, Williams. *American Chemical Industry: Background and Beginnings.* New York: Van Nostrand, 1954. Reprint, New York: Garland, 1983.

DAVID B. SICILIA

CHICAGO   Chicago's history in the nineteenth century in many respects exemplifies the history of the United States in that period. Moreover events in nineteenth-century Chicago contributed to the nation's rise from an infant republic to a world power. In eighty years Chicago grew from a fort with a few homes around it to a metropolis of more than one million people. From an economy based on goods transfer and commerce in agriculture-related products, the city evolved into one of the largest manufacturing capacities in the world, a factor in America's wealth and power. That changing and growing economy provided employment to European immigrants flocking to the United States, and immigration in turn produced problems in Chicago that many cities shared. Finally, Chicago's advances in architecture and building technology spread throughout the country, and its 1893 triumph, the World's Columbian Exposition, both showcased American inventiveness and influenced urban planning throughout the United States in ensuing decades.

Geography and Economics

Chicago would seem to bear out the saying that "geography is destiny." Other early Great Lakes settlements had better natural harbors, but few had an access to the Mississippi watershed that rivaled Chicago's. The opening of New York State's Erie Canal in 1825 greatly facilitated transportation into and settlement of the West. Twenty years later the Illinois and Michigan Canal connected Lake Michigan directly to the Mississippi, creating a continuous inland water route from New York to New Orleans with Chicago at the pivotal location. But Chicago did not depend solely on water transportation. One railroad ran into the city in 1850, four more in 1852, and ten by 1856. By 1860 young Chicago was the world's largest rail center. It was the primary destination for crops and livestock produced on midwestern farms and the place to go for goods from the East.

Rail and lake traffic also stimulated industrial development in Chicago. By the 1830s meatpacking and lumber milling existed along the river. Both industries grew rapidly. Timber from the upper Great Lakes fed the lumber mills, and in the 1860s Chicago slaughtered and packed one-third of all western livestock. The city became a natural meeting place for iron ore from the north, coal from Ohio and Pennsylvania, and limestone from Michigan. In 1847 Cyrus McCormick moved his reaper factory to Chicago, and other agricultural implements and metals industries soon followed. The city's railroad network provided some of the demand for iron and steel rails and railroad cars. By the 1870s Chicago produced more rails than any other U.S. city.

Every advance in transportation, commerce, or industry sparked a wave of real estate development. Chicago's original grid plan was easily extended as the city expanded. Shops and offices opened near the grain elevators, and warehouses opened along the river. Initially each railroad had its own terminal, with a surrounding circle of commerce and industry. To handle all the livestock, in the 1860s the packers collaboratively built the Union Stock Yards southwest of the city center, with pens for more than

Michigan Avenue, Chicago. The economic capital of the Midwest, Chicago was the terminal city of several railroad lines. Lake Michigan is pictured at left. Published by Jevne & Almim. LIBRARY OF CONGRESS

110,000 cattle, hogs, and sheep, along with places for people to eat and sleep. As the economy grew, shops and office blocks replaced private homes in the city's center. Fashionable residential neighborhoods developed on the south, west, and north sides, connected to the city center first by horse-drawn omnibuses, then by street railways. Still farther out the first suburbs, such as Evanston and Lake Forest, stretched along the rail lines. By 1880 Lake Shore Drive provided a picturesque carriageway as far north as Evanston. Within a few years cable cars, electric trolleys, and the electrification of the street railways had created a complex transportation network that formed a loop around the downtown business district and served Chicago and its outlying areas. Neighborhood and suburban retail and commercial districts developed around the transit stops. The city did not expand evenly in all directions, however. Because existing or proposed transportation extensions prompted real estate development, the city expanded in a starfish pattern, with transportation routes as the spines. Fewer good connections to the west in the latter part of the century gave Chicago its peculiar "cinched-waist" profile.

Population and Demographics

Chicago's economic growth and physical expansion required an influx of people, of course, and the city's population growth can only be called phenomenal. Chicago had perhaps fifty residents in 1830 but more than four thousand when it adopted its first charter seven years later. By 1850 almost thirty thousand people called Chicago home. The city grew tenfold, to almost 300,000 in the next twenty years. Each annexation that physically expanded the city automatically brought in the people who lived in the annexed area. The rate of increase slowed after 1870 but only because the numbers were so large. The city grew to more than 500,000 in 1880, almost 800,000 in 1890, and more than 1,000,000 at the turn of the century. By 1880 Chicago had surpassed much older cities in the East and its rapidly growing midwestern rivals to become the "Second City" of the United States.

Where had all these people come from? In the 1840s and 1850s many of them came from Ireland and Germany, and English, Scots, and Scandinavians, too, arrived in the century's middle years. They dug the canals and built the railroads. Some had skilled trades, and others worked in the packinghouses, in the lumber mills, in the warehouses, and on the docks. The Civil War limited immigration in the 1860s, but it soon rebounded, though with some changes. The Irish, Germans, and Scandinavians continued to come, but in the 1880s and 1890s increasing numbers of Italians, Poles, Czechs, and other eastern Europeans joined them. Russian Jews followed the earlier Jewish populations from Germany and Austria. Newcomers settled where others shared their language and religious practices, so the city became a patchwork of neighborhoods identified by national origin.

Not all of the newcomers were foreigners. Mechanized farm equipment altered agricultural production in the latter third of the nineteenth century, greatly increasing yields and reducing the number of farmers needed to produce the nation's food. Instead of raising grain or livestock, former farm workers came to Chicago and joined Europeans making reapers for McCormick and packing meat for Swift or Armour. This migration also included a hint of the "great migration" African Americans would make in the twentieth century. Although they were just under 2 percent of the population in 1900, blacks were a very visible minority on the near South Side.

Urban Problems

It is an American article of faith that growth is good and brings prosperity. Unplanned growth like nineteenth-century Chicago's is not cost-free, however. By mid-century increased traffic aggravated the poor drainage that had plagued the city's streets almost from the beginning. To address this problem, the city began a twenty-year project to raise the grade, forcing owners to elevate buildings while the city installed a new drainage system and paving. In the 1860s, when sewage and industrial growth threatened water quality, Chicago tunneled two miles into Lake Michigan to draw in clean water. Because rapid growth threatened to occupy every piece of land and leave the city with no open space, Chicago developed a ring of parks in the 1860s and 1870s.

The city served its middle and upper classes fairly well by the standards of the day. While Marshall Field and Philip Armour built $200,000 mansions on Prairie Avenue, however, the working classes crowded into small, poorly constructed frame houses, cottages, and shacks in districts with no paving or sewers. The great Chicago fire of 1871 left almost 100,000 people homeless, most of them working people. The city responded by limiting new construction in the city center to brick, but since working people found that too expensive, they crowded into older dwellings that had survived the fire. Dense blocks of flats, tenements, and apartment buildings were quickly built to house the homeless and the new immigrants.

Chicago's poor and working classes were probably better off than those of some other American cities, where the population was more dense and living conditions even worse. Still Chicago's poor could not escape polluted air and water; they lived in overcrowded or deteriorated dwellings; they worked long hours in unsafe conditions; and many struggled to learn the language and customs of their new country. Consequently in 1889 Jane Addams opened Hull-House, which she modeled on the settlement houses of London and New York, to assist Chicago's poor and to help them help themselves. Not surprisingly given living and working conditions in Chicago, the city was a center of late-nineteenth-century labor organizing. William "Big Bill" Haywood and Eugene V. Debs were both active in Chicago, and the city was the site of major strikes, including the strike that sparked the Haymarket Riot in 1886 and the Pullman strike of the 1890s. Neither settlement house workers and social reformers like Addams nor labor activists like Debs had much success in improving the lives of Chicago's poor and working classes in the nineteenth century, however.

Architecture and Urban Design

Chicago's accomplishments in nineteenth-century social issues may have been minimal, but the city's contributions to building technology, architecture, and urban design were considerable. Chicago was a leader from the very beginning. In the 1830s builders developed what was sometimes called "Chicago construction," substituting a balloon frame for the post-and-beam construction in use for centuries. Balloon-frame buildings could be erected more quickly and cheaply, needing only machine-made nails and milled lumber. Balloon-frame construction spread throughout the country, and it allowed Chicago to house its rapidly growing population. Forty years later Chicago builders pioneered and then perfected the use of iron and steel "skeleton" frames in masonry buildings to produce the nation's first skyscrapers. The great fire in 1871 encouraged iron and steel skeleton construction, for the thriving city needed to replace many buildings quickly with fire-resistant structures at the same time that rising land values in the central city made building taller an economic necessity. Chicago architects were as progressive as the building engineers and contractors, indeed challenging the latter with their designs. While the firms of Adler and Sullivan and Burnham and Root imprinted the landscape of the Loop, Frank Lloyd Wright pushed the boundaries of domestic architecture in the suburb of Oak Park.

Chicago's accomplishments in this area extended beyond individual buildings to the larger field of urban planning, and three projects in particular continued to educate planners one hundred years later. In 1869 the famed landscape architect Frederick Law Olmsted designed Riverside, a suburb just south of Oak Park. There Olmsted laid out curving roads that followed the gently rolling topography, unlike the rectangular lots on a grid typical of speculative subdivisions. Development controls limited what could be built on the generous lots, and parkland along the river was reserved from development. A dozen years later the industrialist George Pullman had a model town named for himself on the South Side for his factory and its employees. The town included a park, a hotel, shops, a school, and a variety of housing types at varying rents. Depression and labor strife cut short Pullman's life as an independent community, however.

Chicago's final design triumph of the nineteenth century was the 1893 World's Columbian Exposition, a world's fair to commemorate the discovery of the New World and to showcase U.S. accomplishments. The Chicago architect Daniel Burnham directed noted artists, architects, and landscape architects in producing an elegant neoclassical but also efficient and functional "White City" in Jackson Park that contrasted sharply with the dirty, crowded industrial city outside its gates. More than twenty-seven million people toured the fair, and in following years the exposition influenced efforts at civic improvement in cities across the United States.

Conclusion

Chicago gave the United States much more than a fair to remember, of course. The individuals named here are only a few of those associated with the city who made major contributions to some aspect of American life. Moreover the city itself contributed. By 1900 the United States was a world power on a par with England and Germany. U.S. industrial capacity was a critical factor in that rise, and Chicago had played a principal role.

See also **Architecture; Cities and Urbanization; City and Regional Planning; Fires and Firefighting; Illinois; Industrialization and the Market; Labor Movement,** *subentry on* **Unions and Strikes; Meatpacking; Midwest, The; Parks and Landscape Architecture; Settlement Houses; Transportation; World's Fairs.**

Bibliography

Cronon, William. *Nature's Metropolis: Chicago and the Great West.* New York: Norton, 1991.
Duis, Perry R. *Challenging Chicago: Coping with Everyday Life, 1837–1920.* Urbana: University of Illinois Press, 1998.
Ebner, Michael H. *Creating Chicago's North Shore: A Suburban History.* Chicago: University of Chicago Press, 1988.
Mayer, Harold M., and Richard C. Wade. *Chicago: Growth of a Metropolis.* Chicago: University of Chicago Press, 1969.
Miller, Donald. *City of the Century: The Epic of Chicago and the Making of America.* New York: Simon and Schuster, 1996.
Pierce, Bessie Louise. *A History of Chicago.* 3 vols. New York: Knopf, 1937–1957.

PATRICIA BURGESS

CHILDBIRTH.   See **Birth and Childbearing.**

CHILD LABOR.   See **Work,** subentry on **Child Labor.**

CHILDREN.   See **Life Cycle,** subentry on **Childhood and Adolescence.**

CHINATOWNS   Chinatowns are often seen as ethnic enclaves established because of the "clannish" ways of Chinese immigrants. But the formation of Chinatowns was not voluntary. At the height of Chinese immigration to America in the late nineteenth century, perceived economic competition with the white working class, the legacy of Orientalism (the historical perception of Chinese as being different or "other"), and nativism, expressed as "yellow peril" fears, gave rise to ethnic-specific local ordinances and state and federal legislation that sought to exclude Chinese from American citizenship and due process. Some of these laws, such as the Page Law of 1875, specifically targeted women, which, in turn, stymied early attempts of Chinese to enter the United States. Other legislation, since it also reflected anti-Asian violence, discouraged Chinese men from bringing their families to America.

Following the passage of the Chinese Exclusion Act of 1882 and subsequent related legislation, Chinese were driven out of small towns and the countryside. They sought refuge in the downtown districts of urban centers, first in the West Coast cities of San Francisco, Los Angeles, Portland, and Seattle, and then in New York, Philadelphia, Chicago, Boston, and Washington, D.C. The retreat into these growing Chinatowns was further hastened by the racially segmented labor market.

Victims of ethnic antagonism in the mines, factories, and fields, the majority of Chinese moved into self-employment as a strategy for economic survival. Within Chinatowns, they ran stores, restaurants, and laundries that served both Chinese and, to a lesser extent, non-Chinese. These low-capital ventures also burgeoned since most Chinese immigrants of this period lacked financial resources. Such economic enterprises were largely unconnected to the dominant economy, a situation that further reinforced the segregation of Chinatowns from mainstream life.

Unlike other ethnic-specific communities or ghettos, Chinatowns were unique for their almost complete absence of families. Because exclusion laws after

Mott Street, New York City. A *Harper's Weekly* illustrator depicts the city's Chinatown as a crowded and chaotic area. Printed in *Harper's Weekly,* 29 February 1896. LIBRARY OF CONGRESS

1882 kept most unmarried women and wives out of America, many Chinatowns were virtually "bachelor societies." Throughout the nineteenth century Chinese women never exceeded 7 percent of the total Chinese population. Chinese men also found it difficult to establish conjugal relations since miscegenation laws, which began taking form in 1850 and were struck down as unconstitutional only in 1948, made Chinese–Euro-American unions illegal. Cultural barriers also reduced the stream of Chinese women immigrants to the United States to a trickle. Confucian ideology dictated that women remain confined to the home, attend to their children and in-laws, and await the return of their spouses. Even though some women did not adhere to such prescriptive standards, most women were controlled by these patriarchal values. The prohibitive cost of emigration also prevented women from participating in the transpacific voyage.

Because of the nature of Chinatowns, male-dominated organizations emerged such as mutual-aid associations and secret societies associated with gang violence (popularly known as tongs). Such institutions, bound loosely by the umbrella association, the Chinese Consolidated Benevolent Association (or Chinese Six Companies), often oversaw and controlled economic and cultural activities and ethnic politics. With community life shaped by such organizations and the continual persistence of anti-Asian sentiments, Chinatowns served as sites that resisted acculturation into dominant society. Ironically cultural retention lent itself to the development of certain Chinatowns, such as that in San Francisco, as tourist centers. Beginning in the early 1900s Chinese and non-Chinese business interests intentionally reshaped these neighborhoods into "gilded ghettos" that projected an exotic, "Oriental" image, one that has lingered long after the early twentieth century.

See also **Chinese Exclusion Act; Immigration and Immigrants,** *subentry on* **Asia.**

Bibliography

Armentrout-Ma, Eve L. "Urban Chinese at the Sinetic Frontier: Social Organizations in United States' Chinatowns, 1849–1898." *Modern Asian Studies* 17, no. 1 (1983): 107–135.

Chinn, Thomas W., Him Mark Lai, and Phillip P. Choy, eds. *A History of the Chinese in California: A Syllabus.* San Francisco: Chinese Historical Society of America, 1969.

McClain, Charles J. *In Search of Equality: The Chinese Struggle against Discrimination in Nineteenth-Century America.* Berkeley: University of California Press, 1994.

Saxton, Alexander. *The Indispensable Enemy: Labor and the Anti-Chinese Movement in California.* Berkeley and Los Angeles: University of California Press, 1971.

Tchen, John Kuo Wei. "New York Chinese: The Nineteenth-Century Pre-Chinatown Settlement." In *Chinese America: History and Perspectives 1990,* 157–192. San Francisco: Chinese Historical Society of America, 1990.

Tong, Benson. *Unsubmissive Women: Chinese Prostitutes in Nineteenth-Century San Francisco.* Norman: University of Oklahoma Press, 1994.

BENSON TONG

CHINESE EXCLUSION ACT

The Chinese Exclusion Act was passed in 1882 in response to demands by westerners at a time when there were perhaps 125,000 Chinese in the United States. Anti-Chinese agitation emphasized both economic competition with whites and the supposed racial inferiority of Chinese.

An 1879 bill passed by Congress to limit Chinese immigration severely was vetoed by President Rutherford B. Hayes because of treaty obligations to China. A renegotiated treaty in 1880 countenanced the suspension of Chinese immigration. In 1882 Congress passed a bill suspending Chinese immigration for twenty years. President Chester A. Arthur vetoed it, indicating that he would sign a more limited suspension. Congress responded with a bill that Arthur did sign into law. It did not exclude all Chinese, but suspended the immigration of Chinese laborers for ten years. The law specifically allowed the entry of merchants and their families, scholars, students, and "travelers for pleasure." It was renewed for another

Race Discrimination: Who Is Next? The wider implications of the Chinese Exclusion Act are explicit in the fears of an Irish and a German immigrant. Wood engraving of a drawing by Thomas Nast. *Harper's Weekly,* 1882. LIBRARY OF CONGRESS

Chinese Immigration, 1850–1900

1851–1860	41,397
1861–1870	64,301
1871–1880	123,201
1881–1890	61,711
1891–1900	14,799

Source: U.S. Department of Justice, Immigration and Naturalization Service. *1996 Statistical Yearbook of the Immigration and Naturalization Service.* Washington, D.C.: Government Printing Office, 1997. Table 2, pp. 26–27.

Chinese Population, U.S. and California, 1860–1900

	United States	California
1860	n.a.	34,933
1870	63,199	42,277
1880	105,465	75,132
1890	107,488	72,472
1900	89,863	45,753

Source: U.S. Census data.

ten years in 1892, and made "permanent" in 1902. Total exclusion of Chinese immigrants was effected by the barring of "aliens ineligible to citizenship" in the Immigration Act of 1924.

Despite its limited impact, the Chinese Exclusion Act can be seen as the hinge on which American immigration policy turned. It was the first piece of effective immigration-restriction legislation ever enacted, and it can be said to have inaugurated an age of immigration restriction that lasted until 1943, when, as a gesture to a wartime ally, Congress repealed the fifteen statutes and parts of statutes that had restricted Chinese immigration.

See also **Immigration and Immigrants,** *subentry on* **Asia.**

Bibliography

Peffer, George Anthony. *If They Don't Bring Women Here: Regulating Chinese Female Immigration before Exclusion.* Urbana: University of Illinois Press, 1999.
Sandmeyer, Elmer C. *The Anti-Chinese Movement in California.* 1939. 2d ed., Urbana: University of Illinois Press, 1991.
Saxton, Alexander. *The Indispensable Enemy: Labor and the Anti-Chinese Movement in California.* Berkeley: University of California Press, 1971.

ROGER DANIELS

CHRISTIANITY. See **African Americans,** subentry on **African American Religions; Bible and Bible Reading, The; Catholicism; Protestantism.**

CHRISTIAN SCIENCE In 1879 Mary Baker Eddy (1821–1910) founded a religious healing movement called Christian Science. Eddy was raised in traditional New England Calvinist Protestantism and was educated at home. From childhood she was frail, nervous, and often ill, frequently so debilitated that she became a semi-invalid. She sought a cure among the many healing regimens then competing for legitimacy, including orthodox medicine, the water cure, and homeopathy. In 1862 Eddy encountered the teachings of Phineas Quimby, a renowned healer from Maine whose flamboyant mental treatment techniques were derived from mesmerism. From Quimby she took the notion of illness and disease as "false belief" and the concept of telepathic magnetism, which she later developed into the twin concepts of absent treatment for healing and malicious animal magnetism (MAM).

In Lynn, Massachusetts, in 1866 Eddy slipped and fell on some ice and was bedridden. She wrote later that on the third day she experienced an instantaneous healing of her injuries not by any material or psychic means but by the application of spiritual principles through prayer. While reading the story of Jesus's healing miracles, she suddenly grasped that reality was "wholly spiritual." Her discovery of this principle, she wrote, would be scientifically provable and could be taught to anyone who accepted its premises as true. Eddy published her metaphysical method in 1875 in *Science and Health with Key to the Scriptures.* She offered her services as a healer and taught the science to others, incorporating it as the Church of Christ, Scientist, in 1879.

By 1889 Eddy had taught Christian Science to six hundred students and had collected $100,000 in tuition from the short-lived Massachusetts Metaphysical College and private teaching. She then reorganized the church on the model of a highly centralized business corporation with a handpicked, all-male board of directors in control of the Mother Church in Boston. All local churches became subordinate branches of the Mother Church. In 1895 Eddy published the *Manual of the Mother Church,* which contained the rules of governance and practice for the rapidly growing organization.

Eddy made the great majority of her converts among middle- and upper-class women in cities and sizeable towns, women searching for a religious practice that addressed their spiritual needs, a healing method that offered intense individual attention, and remunerative and respectable careers as Christian Science practitioners. In the anxious spiritual ferment of New England in the second half of the nineteenth century, Christian Science and its positivist outlook answered all of these needs.

As described by the historian of religion Sydney Ahlstrom, Christian Science, like transcendentalism and universalism, is a harmonial religion, one of the many nineteenth-century responses to the struggle between science and religion, the natural and supernatural understandings of the nature of reality (*A Religious History of the American People,* 1972). These responses also included spiritualism and interest in Asian religions and in the occult. In addition to such new religious bodies as Christian Science and Theosophy, the reactions issued in more conservative movements split many of the existing Protestant churches.

See also **Protestantism; Religion,** *subentry on* **Religion in Nineteenth-Century America; Spiritualism.**

Mary Baker Eddy (1821–1910). A chronic semi-invalid, Eddy founded the Christian Science church. She published the influential work *Science and Health with Key to the Scriptures* in 1875. LIBRARY OF CONGRESS

Bibliography

Christian Science Publishing Society. *Christian Science: A Sourcebook of Contemporary Materials.* Boston: Christian Science Publishing Society, 1990.

Cunningham, Sarah Gardner. "A New Order: Augusta Emma Simmons Stetson and the Origins of Christian Science in New York City, 1886–1910." Ph.D. diss., Union Theological Seminary, 1994.

Gottschalk, Stephen. *The Emergence of Christian Science in American Religious Life.* Berkeley: University of California Press, 1973.

Knee, Stuart E. *Christian Science in the Age of Mary Baker Eddy.* Westport, Conn.: Greenwood, 1994.

Peel, Robert. *Mary Baker Eddy: The Years of Authority.* New York: Holt, Rinehart, and Winston, 1977.

———. *Mary Baker Eddy: The Years of Discovery.* New York: Holt, Rinehart, and Winston, 1966.

———. *Mary Baker Eddy: The Years of Trial.* New York: Holt, Rinehart, and Winston, 1971.

SARAH GARDNER CUNNINGHAM

CHRISTIAN SETTLEMENTS AND COMMUNITIES. See **Communitarian Movements and Groups.**

CINCINNATI   The entrepôt of the Ohio River valley, Cincinnati once seemed destined to become the largest city in the nation. First settled in 1788, its population ballooned to 24,831 in 1830 and 161,044 in 1860. By then Cincinnati was the nation's sixth largest city and third largest manufacturing center, and its many cultural institutions had earned it the title "Queen City of the West." The University of Cincinnati and Dr. Daniel Drake's Medical College, both founded in 1819, established the city as an educational center. Xavier University, a Jesuit institution founded in 1831; Lane Seminary, founded in 1829 and where Lyman Beecher clashed with the abolitionist student body in 1834; and Hebrew Union College, established in 1875 and the oldest rabbinical seminary in the United States and a center of reform Judaism, rounded out Cincinnati's educational institutions. Drake's Western Museum (1818, now the Museum of Natural History), the Music Hall (erected in 1878 to accommodate the May Festival, America's leading nineteenth-century musical event), the Cincinnati College of Music (1878), the Cincinnati Art Museum (1881), and the Cincinnati Symphony Orchestra (1895) added to the city's cultural infrastructure.

Situated on an elevated plain along the Ohio River, between the Great and Little Miami Rivers and opposite Kentucky's Licking River, Cincinnati owed its early growth to commerce. Hundreds of thousands of settlers provisioned themselves in Cincinnati. After 1815 steamboat traffic upstream and down opened new markets and stimulated the city's manufactures, including steamboat construction. The processing of agricultural products, from meatpacking, milling, and distilling to the utilization of by-products in candle production, soap making, and leather goods, resulted in the city's being nicknamed Porkopolis. The opening of the Miami and Erie Canal, which reached

to Dayton in 1828 and to Toledo and the Great Lakes in 1845, expanded dramatically the reach of Cincinnati's merchants and manufacturers. Cincinnati's growth began to slow in the 1850s, when railroads running east and west began to replace rivers flowing south as the primary means of commercial transportation. In the 1870s Cincinnati restored its traditional trade with the municipally financed Southern Railroad, but weak southern markets were no match for the eastern railroad capital of Chicago, which was now the gateway to the trans-Mississippi West.

The Ohio River also placed Cincinnati on the border between slavery and freedom. The economic opportunities and social mobility that made Cincinnati an exemplar of the free labor North were, paradoxically, dependent on markets in the slaveholding South. Ambitious artisans like William Procter, a soap maker, and James Gamble, a candle maker, the founders in 1837 of what is now a Fortune 500 firm, relied on northern farmers who sold hogs and purchased soap and candles. But manufacturers of furniture, machine tools (cotton gins, sugar mills, guns), shoes, and clothing needed plantation markets. Much of the city's population hailed from the South, but the Northwest Ordinance (1789) had made Ohio a free state from its inception. Transplanted New Englanders also made Cincinnati an outpost of Yankee enlightenment. The negrophobic Irish emigrants who poured into Cincinnati after 1840 feared competition from black labor, but German immigrants brought radical egalitarian ideals. Cincinnati thus became a microcosm of national tensions, as fugitive slaves and abolitionists shared its streets with slave catchers and visiting slaveholders. Infringements on civil liberties and free speech included the seizure of suspected fugitive slaves from the city's streets and the 1836 mobbing of the offices of James G. Birney's abolitionist journal, the *Philanthropist*, and the destruction of its press. When the Civil War erupted and Southern trade connections were severed, Cincinnatians rallied around free labor and the Union. By the war's end, the city had retooled and become a major center of Union war production.

By 1890, outpaced by Chicago and other Great Lakes cities, Cincinnati had slipped on the urban hierarchy to ninth in population and seventh in manufacturing. An effort in the 1870s to become the nation's most livable city failed to halt the slide, although its music festivals and residential suburbs won wide praise. In the 1880s civil disorder and the rise of a corrupt political machine, organized by George B. Cox and relying on his control of inner-city Democratic votes, tarnished the city's image. Yet the contest between the Cox machine and its reformist opponents in both parties would bring positive government to the city, restoring order and improving public services. By century's end, with a population of 325,902, the city was on its way to becoming serene Cincinnati, a provincial and puritanical backwater to its critics, an orderly and wisely conservative community to its boosters.

See also **Midwest, The; Ohio.**

Bibliography

Aaron, Daniel. *Cincinnati: Queen City of the West: 1819–1838.* Columbus: Ohio State University Press, 1992.

Miller, Zane L. *Boss Cox's Cincinnati: Urban Politics in the Progressive Era.* Chicago: University of Chicago Press, 1968.

Ross, Steven J. *Workers on the Edge: Work, Leisure, and Politics in Industrializing Cincinnati, 1788–1890.* New York: Columbia University Press, 1985.

JOHN D. FAIRFIELD

CIRCUSES At the turn of the nineteenth century, the American circus resembled other forms of popular entertainment; as with theater performances and museum exhibits, circuses took place indoors in cities along the eastern seaboard. By the beginning of the twentieth century, however, the American circus had evolved into a unique cultural form—a nomadic, three-ring, tented amusement that rumbled across the nation by rail.

The Early Circus

In colonial America, itinerant jugglers, clown prototypes, acrobats, and animal trainers performed in theaters and tavern yards and on street corners. John Bill Ricketts, an acrobatic English horseman, started the American circus when he placed these amusements together in a circular arena in Philadelphia in 1793. Staged inside a wooden building, the entertainment provided by Ricketts and his troupe dazzled President George Washington (1732–1799) and other elite audience members.

At the turn of the nineteenth century, Ricketts and his few competitors limited their performances to large cities; arena construction costs were high and showmen needed large audiences to meet expenses. These showmen traveled between cities by horseback or boat. Inspired by the itinerant animal menagerie business, the circus owner Joshua Purdy Brown (circa 1802–1834) pioneered the practice of traveling by wagon and showing under a canvas tent in 1825. Tent shows could perform cheaply and relatively easily in most communities, regardless of size. Tent

P. T. Barnum, Reformer

The Bridgeport, Connecticut, showman P. T. Barnum (1810–1891) was best known for his enormous, three-ring "Greatest Show on Earth" and for satisfying the American public's appetite for hoaxes and celebrity. However, Barnum was also an avid temperance reformer who wrote widely about morality and sobriety. A passage from Barnum's best-selling autobiography illustrates his sense of moral mission after joining the temperance movement in 1847:

I felt that I had now a duty to perform—to save others, as I had been saved, and on the very morning when I signed the pledge [of temperance], I obtained over twenty signatures in Bridgeport. I talked temperance to all whom I met, and very soon commenced lecturing upon the subject in the adjacent towns and villages. I spent the entire winter and spring of 1851–1852 in lecturing free, through my native State, always traveling at my own expense, and I was glad to know that I aroused many hundreds, perhaps thousands, to the importance of the temperance reform. (*Life of P. T. Barnum: Written by Himself*, p. 261)

shows also adopted the English circus parade to drum up business on "circus day."

New technologies helped the circus to grow. After Robert Fulton (1765–1815) invented the commercial steamboat in 1807, several circuses created sprawling river palaces. In the 1850s Gilbert R. "Doc" Spalding (1812–1880) and Charles J. Rogers (1817–1895) built the *Floating Palace*, a circus riverboat that held two thousand seats. Its shows also included theatrical productions like the temperance drama *Ten Nights in a Barroom* (1858). Circuses began to travel by rail in the 1830s. Early railroad shows were small, and travel was often slow because they had to contend with multiple railroad gauges. The full effect of rail travel in expanding the circus would not occur until after the Civil War.

In contrast to the elite audiences of early circuses, diverse crowds attended the tented circuses. In the South, African Americans sat in segregated areas of the big top. The circuses' itinerancy also fostered ill repute. Gamblers and confidence men followed these shows and some worked in tandem with show owners. Like minstrelsy and popular theater, the antebellum circus was primarily an adult male entertainment. Circuses were banned in Boston (among other places) because of their unsavory reputation and their displays of scantily clad female performers in an era

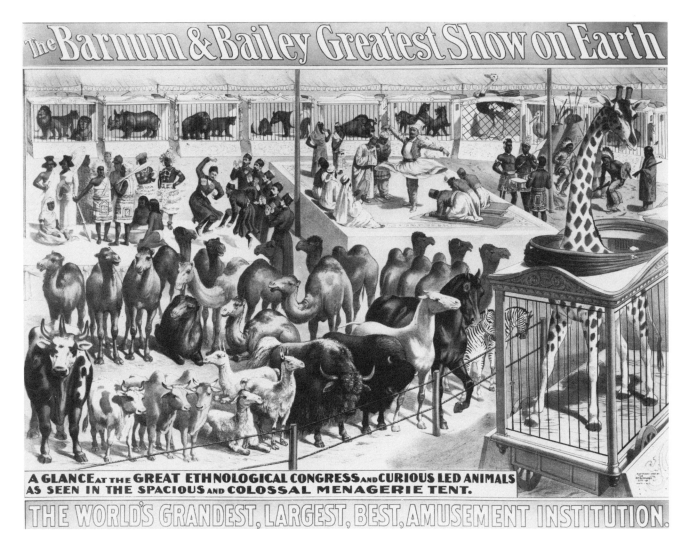

Family Entertainment. Unlike the disreputable antebellum circuses, P. T. Barnum's show was promoted as decent and educational. Poster, c. 1895. LIBRARY OF CONGRESS: PRINTS AND PHOTOGRAPHS DIVISION

when middle-class reformers exalted the place of "respectable" women in the private sphere.

The American circus frequently borrowed features from other amusements. In 1827, Brown added the first animal menagerie to a circus. Clowns sometimes worked as blackface minstrel performers and vice versa. Dan Rice (1823–1900), the most famous circus clown in American history, also worked in blackface during his long career. Clowns and blackface performers both used humor and physical antics to poke fun at society, while reinforcing racial stereotypes. In the small setting of the one-ring tented circus, the clown often spoke several languages, teased the ringmaster, and made political jokes.

Circuses also borrowed ideas from the museum business. Both contained animal menageries and "freak" shows. The author, politician, reformer, and future circus owner P. T. Barnum (1810–1891)

opened the American Museum (or Barnum's Museum; 1841–1868) in New York City; it was the most successful museum of its day. Barnum's display of a "happy family" of prey and predators became a classic circus act. He also employed "freak" players who later worked at the circus sideshows. William Henry Johnson (1841?–1926), an African American who performed silently as "Zip . . . What Is It?," represented Charles Darwin's (1809–1882) evolutionary missing link between man and ape. Charles Sherwood Stratton ("General Tom Thumb"; 1838–1883) joined Barnum at age four and played a military general midget who charmed audiences in the United States and Queen Victoria in England. Stratton's presentation was a model for subsequent midget circus "freaks." Barnum promoted his museum as an educational amusement, suitable for female audiences. Barnum's management of Swedish opera star Jenny

Lind during her first U.S. tour (1850–1851) demonstrated his resolve to attract respectable patrons. With great financial success, Barnum marketed the "Swedish Nightingale" as an "angelic" philanthropist. When Barnum entered the circus business in 1870, he successfully marketed his show as wholesome family entertainment and employed Pinkerton detectives to monitor the grounds.

Circuses after the Civil War

The Civil War disrupted circuses by making overland and water travel hazardous in war-torn areas. However, immediately after the war, the circus business grew rapidly, reflecting the country's industrial transformation. Within weeks of the completion of the transcontinental railroad, in 1869, Dan Castello's (1832?–1909) Circus and Menagerie made the first transcontinental train journey in circus history. In 1872, P. T. Barnum put his new circus on the rails, outfitting his show with specially designed flatcars that facilitated speedy loading and unloading of the cumbersome wagons. This innovation, coupled with a nationally standardized railroad gauge, enabled Barnum's circus train to triple in size over the next twenty years, from 1,200 feet to 3,600 feet.

Barnum and James A. Bailey (1847–1906), his partner, used the train to create a distinctive American circus, characterized by its enormous size. In contrast to the intimate one-ring European circus, the American railroad circus eventually featured three rings, two stages, and an outer racetrack, all in operation at once. Barnum and Bailey's canvas big top held ten thousand spectators. According to Barnum and Bailey show programs, their circus also contained a menagerie, sideshow, ethnological congress of exotic "strange and savage tribes," and spectacles re-creating contemporary foreign events. In this cacophonous milieu the talking clown, once an integral part of the show, fell silent. These huge shows also featured giant parades that contained a steam calliope—an American innovation signaling the parade's completion since 1872. Great crowds then followed the calliope to the show grounds.

The postwar railroad circus had an elaborate division of labor. Barnum and Bailey sometimes employed over one thousand people, including laborers, waiters, porters, laundry personnel, and performers. In contrast to the mid-nineteenth-century circuses, where alcohol was consumed freely (and even budgeted into weekly expense accounts), the large railroad shows of the late 1800s enforced strict codes of sobriety and conduct to meet the rigid railroad timetables. Like other powerful businessmen of the day, Barnum and Bailey (and other show owners) participated in merger mania as they bought competing circuses.

By the end of the nineteenth century, the sheer size of contemporary circuses made their presence a major community event. Almost one hundred circuses dotted the landscape, more than at any other time in U.S. history. The breadth and content of the railroad circus at the turn of the twentieth century reflected the nation's status as an emergent industrial world power.

See also **Minstrel Shows; Popular Culture; Recreation; Transportation,** *subentry on* **Railroads.**

Bibliography

Adams, Bluford. *E Pluribus Barnum: The Great Showman and the Making of U.S. Popular Culture.* Minneapolis: University of Minnesota Press, 1997.

Barnum, P. T. *Life of P. T. Barnum: Written by Himself.* Buffalo, N.Y.: Courier Company, 1888.

Dahlinger, Fred, Jr. "The Development of the Railroad Circus." Parts 1–4. *Bandwagon: The Journal of the Circus Historical Society, Inc.* 27 (November/December 1983); 28 (May/June 1984): 6–11, 16–27, 28–36, 29–36.

Harris, Neil. *Humbug: The Art of P. T. Barnum.* Boston: Little, Brown, 1973.

Saxon, A. H. *P. T. Barnum: The Legend and the Man.* New York: Columbia University Press, 1989.

Thayer, Stuart. *Traveling Showmen: The American Circus before the Civil War.* Morristown, N.J.: Astley and Ricketts, 1997.

JANET DAVIS

CITIES AND URBANIZATION

During the nineteenth century, as the United States extended its reach across much of North America, the nation also became increasingly urbanized. Cities became places of manufacturing and consumption, points of transportation for raw materials and finished goods, and social spaces both joined and fragmented by class, race, ethnicity, gender, and generation. For many historians the rapidity and scale of these changes was the most significant aspect of the nineteenth century, with the period from 1840 to 1900, in the words of David Schuyler, "arguably the most crucial" in producing a "new urban landscape." Yet the intense urbanization of the nineteenth century was more than simply a story of shifting land-use practices and territorial growth. It was also the story of millions of ordinary people who became enmeshed in a global industrial economy influencing all facets of urban life.

Migrants from the countryside and around the world made their way to American cities to better their social and economic conditions despite an increasing gap between rich and poor. Euro-American middle-class reformers and politicians constructed urban parks to provide moral "uplift" to the working class, only to be challenged by workers with alternative views about how those spaces should be used. Along with a vast transformation in work came new forms of sport and recreation, products of life in the city. Despite an increasing fragmentation of urban space, city people developed local attachments to neighborhood or city block. Despite the kinship provided by such enclaves, the increasing size of cities gave many young men and women opportunities to develop independence from parental supervision, community watchfulness, or other agents of social control. Symbolically, the city came to represent American "progress," especially in the West, where commentators drew sharp distinctions between "civilized" urban settlements and what they described as the surrounding wilderness. For others, especially moral reformers, cities became synonymous with danger, vice, and immorality.

The City as Geographical Space

As a general rule, American cities increased geographically and demographically through the course of the nineteenth century. As the U.S. Census reported, the number of areas classified as urban—generally those with a population of 2,500 or higher—increased dramatically, with the greatest growth in small- to medium-sized cities (see table). Yet, reflecting the uneven nature of industrialization, the scale of urbanization differed by particular city or region, shaped primarily by economic, political, and demographic factors.

Economic change was perhaps the most significant. New York, for example, became commercially dominant at the end of the War of 1812, and the completion of the Erie Canal opened up the region's hinterland during the 1830s. Chicago, with the construc-

tion of a canal and then rail lines during the 1840s and 1850s, attracted eastern capital, becoming the "gateway to the West," spawning the rise of other western regional cities. As a result of these shifts in economic position, New York and Chicago experienced rapid spatial growth in relatively short periods of time. Not all cities increased in size or with such rapidity. Jeffrey Adler described antebellum St. Louis as experiencing "prolonged stagnation and frequent crises," losing its initial regional clout with Chicago's ascent. In addition, many southern cities increased in size at a much slower pace than their northern counterparts, the result of increasingly northern domination of commercial trade and manufacturing, loss of the Civil War, and a degree of antiurban bias among some southern elites.

Incorporation of cities as independent entities, annexation of surrounding territory, and consolidation among formerly independent cities and towns became the most common means by which American cities increased in physical size. Each of these methods, however, was profoundly political. By incorporation, cities were able to create a degree of separation from state legislatures, permitting greater local control. By annexation, cities could expand beyond a historic core to embrace outlying areas. Often contentious, such methods permitted cities to increase territory, expand their tax base, and construct greater regional political influence, especially for those who controlled city government. Boston, for example, increased its size by incorporating outlying towns, such as Jamaica Plain, which became part of Boston proper in 1873. City promoters in Los Angeles, a city synonymous with the urban sprawl of the twentieth century, began the voracious process of acquiring territory in the nineteenth century. By annexation of the San Pedro harbor, for example, Los Angeles politicians and city boosters were able to increase the city's regional dominance as a major port.

Number of U.S. Places Characterized as Urban Territory by Size of Population, 1800–1900

	1800	1810	1820	1830	1840	1850	1860	1870	1880	1890	1900
1,000,000 or more	—	—	—	—	—	—	—	—	1	3	3
500,000–999,999	—	—	—	—	—	1	2	2	3	3	3
250,000–499,999	—	—	—	—	1	—	1	5	4	7	9
100,000–249,999	—	—	1	1	2	5	6	7	12	17	23
50,000–99,999	1	2	2	3	2	4	7	11	15	30	40
25,000–49,999	2	2	2	3	7	16	19	27	42	66	82
10,000–24,999	3	7	8	16	25	36	58	116	146	230	280
5,000–9,999	15	17	22	33	48	85	136	186	249	340	465
2,500–4,999	12	18	26	34	46	89	163	309	467	654	832

Source: *Historical Atlas of the United States, Colonial Times to 1970.* Volume 1. Washington, D.C.: Bureau of the Census, 1975. Series A 43–56, p. 11.

Twentieth Street, Birmingham, Alabama. The trolley car, horse-drawn carriages, and commercial establishments attest to Birmingham's recovery from the Civil War and position as an urban center. Photograph, 1890 to 1910. LIBRARY OF CONGRESS

Finally, consolidation of formerly independent towns under a wider city umbrella created grand-scale urban areas, the most famous example being the creation of Greater New York in 1898, with the consolidation of Manhattan, Brooklyn, Queens, Staten Island, and the Bronx. Described by Edwin Burrows and Mike Wallace as "a municipal counterpart of the giant corporations busily being born," the consolidation of New York at the end of the century was a fitting reminder of just how significant cities had become to the creation of a strong American industrial capitalist economy.

The development of urban infrastructure was equally political, especially the location of canals, railroads, and intraurban rail and trolley lines, as well as the emergence of basic city services. With the widening of the franchise during the Jacksonian period, (male) voters created a ward-based politics in many cities, producing intense class and ethnic competition for political control. However, by the end of the century, most cities had professional police and fire de-

partments, new public health boards, and public works programs to pave streets or create public transportation.

Boosterism, through which city promoters sought to attract new immigrants, private investment, and public funding for infrastructural improvements, became an especially important aspect of city development in the West. Eric H. Monkkonen notes that boosterism often glossed over local racial, ethnic, class, or religious conflict in order to promote an image that a particular city was a favorable space for public and private investment. As Jeffrey Adler has suggested of St. Louis, for example, while local boosters may have claimed that a city's "natural advantages" ensured its success, political decisions involving transportation and infrastructure were greater catalysts for city building.

During the century, migration from rural hinterlands and abroad gave human dimension to changing urban size. The population of New York, for example, increased from 60,000 in 1800 to 800,000 by 1860.

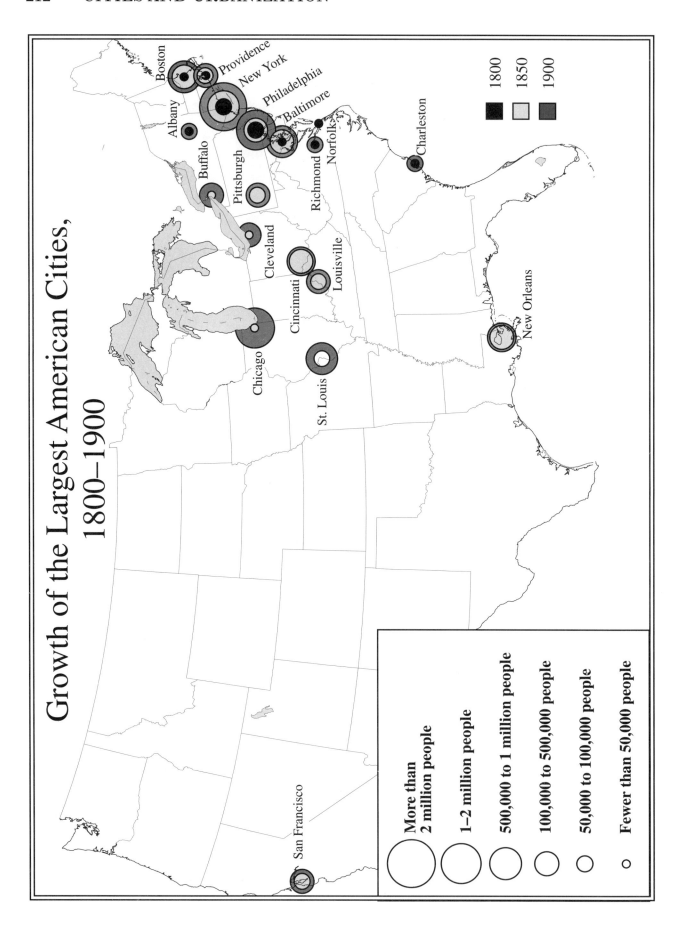

Growth of the Largest American Cities, 1800–1900

1800 1850 1900

Boston
Providence
New York
Philadelphia
Baltimore
Albany
Buffalo
Pittsburgh
Richmond
Norfolk
Charleston
Cleveland
Cincinnati
Louisville
Chicago
St. Louis
New Orleans
San Francisco

More than
2 million people

1–2 million people

500,000 to 1 million people

100,000 to 500,000 people

50,000 to 100,000 people

Fewer than 50,000 people

With consolidation at century's end, its population was more than 3.4 million, by far the largest in the United States. In the West, population increases were frequently quick and dramatic. San Francisco, initially the location of a Spanish colonial presidio, was a small Mexican administrative municipality on the eve of the U.S. conquest of California. Between the gold rushes of the late 1840s and 1850s and the Civil War, it became a major manufacturing and commercial center, with 342,000 people by 1900. Seattle, providing perhaps the most dramatic example of population growth, increased from 3,500 residents in 1880 to more than 80,000 by 1900 and to 237,000 by 1910.

While the rural hinterland initially provided the most significant source of population for most cities, by mid-century numbers of foreign-born men and women had increased measurably. New York's 18,000 foreign-born residents in 1830 made up only 9 percent of its total population. By 1845 there were 125,000 foreign born, making up 35 percent of the city's population. Nationally, the percentage of people residing in cities had increased from 8 percent of the population at the beginning of the nineteenth century to nearly 35 percent by 1900, the bulk of "city people" being immigrants or their children.

Changes in the internal geographies of cities were equally great. Boston, New York, Philadelphia, and Baltimore are good examples. In the eighteenth century, each of these cities was a political and commercial center, relatively small, and tied to a wider European colonial system. Located along rivers, favorable ports, or other trade routes, their spatial design meshed with colonial function. As "walking cities," there was a mixed use of space as artisan families lived where they worked, rich merchants occupied town homes nearby, and the city contained political, educational, and religious institutions. The rural fringe was within walking distance of the city center, with space for country homes and agriculture to feed the city's residents.

After independence, these same urban spaces became more specialized. By the mid–nineteenth century, banks, lawyers' offices, newspapers, hotels, and retail establishments concentrated along downtown streets in central business districts. In northern cities especially, manufacturing, which originally developed in outlying areas near sources of waterpower, raw materials, and transportation, was increasingly located within cities, frequently surrounded by working-class residential districts, while middle-class families began to relocate to the suburban fringe. By the 1880s multilayered urban industrial cities had replaced the mixed-use trading city of the early nineteenth century.

Urban space became a commodity itself, evident in the widespread adoption of the grid system to divide urban space, hastening the segmentation of the city. While the application of the grid was never uniform, developers of many towns in the West especially favored the practice, reflecting the importance of land speculation to design. Often including spatial patterns that were not feasible in more concentrated eastern towns, western towns, as the historian Carol O'Connor argues, featured "broad streets [that] tended to typify broad plans," thus symbolizing the centrality of urbanization to the U.S. conquest of the West.

The commodification of urban space had a strong impact on housing. For example, as greater numbers of immigrants made their way to cities, they were forced to seek housing in overcrowded and less expensive areas of cities as real estate speculators and industrial manufacturers obtained the more desirable land for themselves and for their business ventures. Upper- and middle-class residents who remained in cities occasionally carved out particular residential sections, working to limit commercial development in these neighborhoods. As Mona Domosh has suggested of Boston, such sections promoted the emerging "values and aspirations" of an urban bourgeoisie. As such, by the end of the century there were discernible concentrations of boardinghouses for young men and women, tenements for recent migrants, small working-class houses, and middle-class apartments or homes in distinct sections of U.S. cities.

New transportation technologies made much of this spatial change possible. Canals, steamboats, and railroads permitted greater links between cities and hinterland. One reason for Chicago's success in marketing lumber, cattle, and agricultural products was the construction of a canal (1848) and railroad lines (1850s). In the South, railroads also contributed to the emergence of such "inland cities" as Memphis, Tennessee, and Atlanta, Georgia. Within cities, horse-drawn omnibuses (introduced in New York in the 1820s) and electric street railways and trolleys, in service by the century's end, diversified the walking city, enabling the further separation of work from home as well as facilitating the creation of separate sections for commerce, housing, and manufacturing. For example, local businesses increasingly concentrated along transportation routes, especially at major intersections, hastening the development of commercial corridors. Such specialization of urban space may not have been as significant in outlying neighborhoods. Jamaica Plain in Boston, for example, contained working-class districts, suburban middle-class homes, light industry, and commercial thoroughfares throughout the century.

Changes resulting from the new transportation

technology were also profoundly political. Commercial elites used their influence with state and municipal governments to promote canal and railroad construction that would benefit their particular city, or themselves, exacerbating rivalries with nearby communities. State legislatures were especially important in granting charters to individual private investors for such municipal internal improvements. In cities as different as Philadelphia and Los Angeles, real estate developers constructed streetcar lines to entice middle-class residents to move to subdivisions on the urban fringe.

As these examples suggest, the transformation of urban geography was pronounced during the nineteenth century. Moreover, these changes were not part of the "organic" growth of cities but due to the interaction of economic, political, and demographic factors, resulting in increasing numbers of people who called cities home. Their stories are equally complex.

The City as Social and Cultural Space

Like the uneven transformation of urban geographies, the lives of men and women who lived in cities did not follow a uniform path; each city dweller's experience was shaped by class, race, ethnicity, gender, generation, region, and the degree of industrialization in a given area. As a result, any generalizations about the experience of urbanization are difficult, if not impossible, to make. The historian Gunther Barth argues that differences of race, ethnicity, and class did not preclude the development of an interdependent "city culture" that forged a "common urban identity" in most cities. Other scholars have suggested that urbanization was fragmenting, resulting in radically different experiences among groups and individuals and producing shifting, often conflicting, identities.

The fact of migration, whether from the countryside or from abroad, was common to most city residents in the nineteenth century. Its meaning, however, was another matter. In Lowell, Massachusetts, for example, young women left their homes in the countryside for wage work in textile mills. While they generally lived in company-owned boardinghouses, underwent near constant supervision, and worked at a new, quicker pace, many young women nevertheless

Boston Street Scene. Market Street and Court Street, Boston. Photograph, Clinton Johnson, c. 1895. LIBRARY OF CONGRESS

experienced a degree of independence in the mill towns that was impossible at home.

In the South the history of slavery had a profound impact on the racialization of urban space. During the antebellum period most urban African American slaves lived and worked under close supervision of their white owners. Free blacks, in contrast, commonly lived on the outskirts of cities in areas most whites found least desirable. Raleigh, North Carolina; Atlanta, Georgia; and Nashville, Tennessee; for example, all had free-black settlements surrounding the urban fringe. In other cases, while blacks and whites may have lived in the same section of town, they did not necessarily inhabit the same streets. The end of slavery only strengthened, and in some cases intensified, residential segregation. In addition, many African Americans favored segregated areas as a means to maintain a distance from white supervision so prominent in other parts of their lives. Creating black churches, schools, building and loan associations, and philanthropic societies aided in maintaining vibrant African American communities in the face of white racism. Migration from the countryside fueled the growth of such communities across the postbellum urban South. African American men and women made their way to southern cities seeking education, employment, and an escape from rural persecution after the Civil War. These emerging black urban communities and institutions proved critical to the emergence of African American political power and cultural identities. In Richmond, Virginia, for example, a "black city" emerged that, while not geographically fixed to a specific section of the city, was nevertheless linked by public ritual, churches, community organizations, schools, and businesses.

Urban immigrant communities provide another striking example of the complexity of the migration experience. While most migrants came to U.S. cities in search of work, they chose their destinations carefully. Immigrants often followed family or friends who had preceded them, resulting in a degree of ethnic clustering in many industrial cities that was as much the product of immigrant preference as the planning of factory owners or industrialists. In such enclaves, migrants could maintain ethnic and religious institutions, live with neighbors who spoke a familiar language, and receive support in times of economic trouble. Yet despite such ethnic solidarity, most immigrant communities were differentiated by social class, religion, family, and generation. While some embraced life in the United States, others saw themselves as sojourners, their aim being to raise money and then return to their native lands. The formation of such communities exemplifies how the migration experience produced a variety of city worlds,

which infused city spaces with layers of cultural meaning.

The formation of many ethnic enclaves in western cities had different historical roots. In Los Angeles, for example, Mexican Americans sustained communities around the historic plaza where mestizo inhabitants of the late eighteenth century had created the settlement. With U.S. conquest and the arrival of Euro-American "immigrants," the plaza area became an important social space for maintaining a Mexican American identity despite increasing economic dislocation caused by Euro-American real estate speculation and commercial influence in southern California. Euro-Americans, in contrast, created neighborhoods on the city's fringe, laying the groundwork for urban sprawl, a prominent feature of the next century.

Nineteenth-century industrialization produced new forms and understandings of social class, which exacerbated the increasing gap between wage workers and those who controlled the means of production. This shift became evident in the experience of city life. As some scholars have suggested, urbanization produced an American middle class. Increasingly defined by nonmanual male employment, segregated housing sustained by an ideology of domesticity, and specific leisure patterns, the new middle class was also born of the city. Notions of proper dress, particular table manners, and controlled public behavior reveal an emerging class consciousness among the middle class, which was both the result of and intensified by urbanization.

For workers, however, transformations in the experience of work and the working-class home were central to the development of a working-class consciousness. Cities provided the backdrop for the articulation of that consciousness as the settings of social protest, labor unrest, and working-class political organizations and through the organization of the household and distinct forms of popular culture. For example, early in the century an "artisanal republicanism" developed among New York's workingmen, culminating in the formation of workingmen's political parties. These parties articulated a class-based critique of early industrialization and the resulting transformation in work. Class consciousness also infused urban leisure. Saloons created the context for maintaining a male world of sociability amid industrial transformation and also provided spaces for political organizing and the maintenance of a discrete working-class worldview as an alternative to middle-class standards.

Struggles over the organization of urban social space exemplify the intense class conflict of nineteenth-century urban life. With the intensification of industrialization and waves of urban migration in the early nineteenth century, some middle-class men and women began to see the city as a "mission field." By visiting working-class families, attempting to influence the organization of their homes, promoting religious instruction in Sunday Schools, or distributing Bible tracts, reformers began to see the urban world as a dangerous place in need of their constant vigilance. Such efforts were especially important for middle-class women, who were able to take on such "public" roles despite an ideology of domesticity that otherwise worked to relegate them to the home.

But such middle-class notions of "proper" domestic organization often clashed with the realities of working-class life. For example, middle-class reformers often criticized working-class women's housekeeping, especially what they perceived as a lack of personal and familial privacy. But as Christine Stansell has shown with respect to New York, such privacy was often not possible, or necessarily desirable, for working-class women. Rather, urban working-class women created a culture of neighborliness, "the difference between survival and destruction," by sharing child care, mediating family quarrels, and creating households extending across the hall and into the street, notions of "home" that were quite different from middle-class standards. Working-class families constantly struggled with seasonal unemployment, harsh living and working conditions, and frequent mobility throughout the century. As S. J. Kleinberg has commented of working-class households in Pittsburgh, "the mills forged daily life as well as molten metal," suggesting the centrality of work to working-class lives, for both men and women. Women, for example, maintained the family economy by doing the cooking and housework for their own families but also by taking in boarders, doing laundry for a fee, or through supplemental piecework performed at home.

Nineteenth-century cities were also sites for intense conflict over the use of urban space. Public parks offer a good example. Beginning in 1858 with the construction of Central Park in New York, upper- and middle-class urban residents across the United States began to promote the park as a means to relieve the stress and ill effects of urban life, believing, as Stanley Schultz suggests, that this amelioration would offer "improvement of human nature." However, many workers had alternative conceptions of the function of the public park. While most middle-class men and women saw the park as a natural haven, many workers desired to use the park for recreation and play. The resulting class conflict became articulated in disputes over park use, suggesting the complex ways that urban social spaces came to embody the contradictory process of urbanization itself.

See also **Class, Social; Immigration and Immigrants,** *subentry on* **The Immigrant Experience; Industrialization and the Market; Transportation,** *subentries on* **Canals and Waterways, Urban and Interurban Transportation; Work,** *subentry on* **Middle-Class Occupations; Working-Class Culture.**

Bibliography

Adler, Jeffrey S. *Yankee Merchants and the Making of the Urban West: The Rise and Fall of Antebellum St. Louis.* Cambridge, U.K.: Cambridge University Press, 1991.

Barth, Gunther. *City People: The Rise of Modern City Culture in Nineteenth-Century America.* New York: Oxford University Press, 1980.

Blumin, Stuart M. *The Emergence of the Middle Class: Social Experience in the American City, 1760–1900.* Cambridge, U.K.: Cambridge University Press, 1989.

Bodnar, John. *The Transplanted: A History of Immigrants in Urban America.* Bloomington: Indiana University Press, 1985.

Boyer, Paul. *Urban Masses and Moral Order in America, 1820–1920.* Cambridge, Mass.: Harvard University Press, 1978.

Brown, Elsa Barkley, and Greg D. Kimball. "Mapping the Terrain on Black Richmond." In *The New African American Urban History.* Edited by Kenneth W. Goings and Raymond A. Mohl. Thousand Oaks, Calif.: Sage, 1996.

Burrows, Edwin G., and Mike Wallace. *Gotham: A History of New York City to 1898.* New York: Oxford University Press, 1999.

Domosh, Mona. *Invented Cities: The Creation of Landscape in Nineteenth-Century New York and Boston.* New Haven, Conn.: Yale University Press, 1996.

Kasson, John F. *Rudeness and Civility: Manners in Nineteenth-Century Urban America.* New York: Hill and Wang, 1990.

Kleinberg, S. J. *The Shadow of the Mills: Working-Class Families in Pittsburgh, 1870–1907.* Pittsburgh: University of Pittsburgh Press, 1989.

Larsen, Lawrence H. *The Urban South: A History.* Lexington: University Press of Kentucky, 1990.

Miller, Zane L., and Patricia M. Melvin. *The Urbanization of Modern America: A Brief History.* 2d ed. New York: Harcourt Brace Jovanovich, 1987.

Monkkonen, Eric H. *America Becomes Urban: The Development of U.S. Cities and Towns, 1780–1980.* Berkeley: University of California Press, 1988.

O'Connor, Carol A. "A Region of Cities." In *The Oxford History of the American West.* Edited by Clyde A. Milner II. New York: Oxford University Press, 1994.

Rabinowitz, Howard N. *Race, Ethnicity, and Urbanization: Selected Essays.* Columbia: University of Missouri Press, 1994.

Schultz, Stanley K. *Constructing Urban Culture: American Cities and City Planning, 1800–1820.* Philadelphia: Temple University Press, 1989.

Schuyler, David. *The New Urban Landscape: The Redefinition of City Form in Nineteenth-Century America.* Baltimore: Johns Hopkins University Press, 1986.

Stansell, Christine. *City of Women: Sex and Class in New York, 1789–1860.* Urbana: University of Illinois Press, 1987.

Wade, Richard C. *The Urban Frontier: The Rise of Western Cities, 1790–1830.* Cambridge, Mass.: Harvard University Press, 1959.

Warner, Sam Bass. *Streetcar Suburbs: The Process of Growth in Boston, 1870–1900*. Cambridge, Mass.: Harvard University Press, 1962.

Von Hoffman, Alexander. *Local Attachments: The Making of an American Urban Neighborhood, 1850 to 1920*. Baltimore: Johns Hopkins University Press, 1994.

DAVID A. REICHARD

CITY AND REGIONAL PLANNING

CITY AND REGIONAL PLANNING   Trends in city and regional planning in the United States during the nineteenth century were influenced by extraordinarily rapid urban development patterns. These rapid development patterns were chiefly the result of industrialization and other entrepreneurial activities. As the nation industrialized, most heavy industry was sited in urban centers. These centers served heavy industrial enterprises well because they were the transportation hubs and labor population bases of the nation. As commerce increased, American cities experienced severe adverse impacts, including unsanitary living conditions, overcrowded tenement housing, and social inequity. From this chaos, however, arose the idea that ultimately urban development must be planned rather than completely left to entrepreneurial devices.

Urbanization and Industrialization in the Nineteenth Century

More than any other form of transportation, railroads promoted the growth of cities. Between 1830 and 1840 approximately 5,000 miles of railroad track was constructed. As an anticompetitive measure, railroad companies often operated on separate track gauges. In addition, schedules were deliberately designed to conflict so passengers could not easily connect by using another company's service. In the middle of the nineteenth century, railroads began to adopt standard schedules, signaling, and equipment. By the 1860s rail systems no longer served small independent routes, and by 1886 all railroads ran on the standard gauge. A system of trunk lines fed by a large number of feeder lines became the norm. The demand for rail transportation increased immensely, and from 1881 through 1890 the nation built more than 70,000 miles of new track.

The majority of railroad traffic accommodated freight delivery to industrial urban centers. Freight was most often in the form of raw materials for factories—the basis of an industrial complex. Steel mills were the primary forces of the emerging industrial empire and typically were located in major cities to take advantage of both rail and water transportation. Other significant labor-intensive industrial ac-

Daniel H. Burnham (1846–1912). Burnham designed the Flatiron Building in New York City and was chief of construction for the World's Columbian Exposition in Chicago, which opened in 1893. LIBRARY OF CONGRESS

tivity, such as petroleum processing, cloth and garment manufacturing, and agricultural commodities processing, also were integral portions of the new industrial complex.

This industrial complex had an insatiable appetite for labor. Thus, new cities experienced a population surge. At the beginning of the nineteenth century, urban population increases resulted predominantly from migration from rural areas. However, toward the end of the century urban growth was primarily due to immigration from central, eastern, and southern Europe. By 1890, 80 percent of New York City's residents were either of foreign birth or the offspring of immigrants. In the same year immigrants and their children made up 75 percent of Chicago's population, 66 percent of Boston's, and 50 percent of Philadelphia's.

The sheer numbers of immigrants arriving in major cities created housing shortages. For economic reasons, the only housing opportunities for many city residents often were crowded tenement houses jammed together on unsuitably surveyed, narrow rectangular lots. New York City was the site of two attempts to plan tenement house design. In 1855 the first model tenement house was introduced, followed in 1879 by the "dumbbell" tenement design. The "dumbbell" featured an airshaft in the center of the structure, which was intended to allow light and circulation. However, the design also crowded twenty-four families into a lot only 25 feet by 100 feet. A miserable failure, the airshaft provided neither light nor air but filled with garbage and stench and allowed fires to spread upward. Ultimately the design was banned in the early twentieth century.

Health problems were numerous in tenement housing districts. Most tenement houses lacked adequate running water, ventilation, light, and sewage disposal. Sanitation usually involved a privy connected to individual drains. This decentralized sewage system burdened whole neighborhoods with a tremendous odor as well as waterborne diseases, such as cholera, diphtheria, and typhus.

Sanitation Advancement

Sanitation advancement was the first major initiative of planning in the nineteenth century. New York City (1842) and Boston (1850) were the first cities in the United States to provide centralized public water delivery. With cleaner water available, demand and consumption rose. The increase in potable water consumption promoted a higher volume of stagnant wastewater, so sewers were constructed as a necessary measure to protect public health. Edmund Chadwick developed the first modern sewer system in 1842. Chadwick learned from John Roe, a Holborn public works engineer, that moderate amounts of water flowing through a narrow passage produced enough force to carry away large amounts of debris. Chadwick thus applied Roe's discovery and created a self-cleansing sewer system consisting of small-radius pipes that transported both human waste and rainwater. The first engineered sewer systems in Boston and New York were ineffective, constructed in separate pieces without a unified plan. In some instances large sections of pipe carried low volumes of water and small sections of pipe carried large volumes of water; the systems also failed to take advantage of the natural slope of the land. Learning from these oversights, Chicago engineers in 1857 constructed a planned and integrated sewer system, for which many streets were raised so sewer lines could be constructed above muddy ground. By the 1890s planned sewer systems were installed in several major cities, such as Brooklyn, Providence, San Francisco, and Cincinnati.

Sanitary surveys became planning tools during this period. Government officials used surveys to record unhealthy conditions according to each individual structure or parcel, and the surveys were then applied to a comprehensive plan for remediation and abatement. Unhealthy conditions included inadequate wastewater removal, overcrowding, and the presence of infectious disease. The first use of a sanitary survey occurred in 1878 in Memphis. That city had succumbed to a severe yellow fever epidemic, and in response the U.S. Congress created the National Board of Health in 1879 to establish quarantine and other disease control procedures. The board extensively mapped existing health hazard conditions in order to produce a comprehensive and enduring improvement plan. Within a few years the use of the sanitary survey as a planning tool spread to other major cities in the United States and became the frontline defense against urban health threats.

Impacts on Intra-urban Transportation

Planning for intra-urban public transportation increased during the nineteenth century. Intra-urban public transportation began in the form of the horse-drawn omnibus in New York City during 1831. Further advances in public transit came a year later, when the omnibus was replaced by horse-drawn street railway cars. Improvements in speed and comfort continued, and in 1855 New York City initiated a sunken-track street railway. This virtually eliminated the trackless omnibus because the track could be built anywhere without hindering other forms of street transportation. In 1870 New York City pioneered the nation's first rapid transit system, in which trains were elevated above street level and pulled by a continuously moving cable. A year later steam locomotives replaced the cable, and by the end of the century rapid transit cars powered by electricity existed in most major cities in the Northeast and Midwest. Light-rail trolley cars became the primary mode of public transit for street-level transportation. In 1887 San Francisco put into service a light-rail surface transit system by adapting the continuously moving cable for the steep grades throughout the city. Boston initiated an underground transit system in 1897.

City Planning, Surveying, and Design

In 1806 the New York Common Council undertook development of a comprehensive plan of property subdivision and street networks in New York City, which at that time consisted only of Manhattan. The plan was a landmark undertaking because it applied to public and private landholdings alike. Foreseeing the likelihood that many property owners would object to the plan, the council created the New York

Improvement Commission, staffed by Gouverneur Morris, Simeon De Witt, and John Rutherford. By order of the New York Common Council, the commissioners' plan was "final and conclusive." The final plan, as presented in 1811, provided 100-foot-wide streets running north and south and intersecting 60-foot-wide streets (east-west) creating an extensive gridiron street network. The gridiron formed narrow rectangular lots that, as population rose, promoted the development of tenement housing for the poor as described above. The plan also lacked open space, public parks, and civic monuments. Despite these drawbacks, the plan was a successful intervention by municipal government in urban development for the good of the city as a whole.

George Pullman, the industrialist who created and manufactured the luxury Pullman passenger train car, hired the architect Solon Bemen to plan a community for the Pullman Company's workers. The community was located fifteen miles outside Chicago and housed eight thousand people. Housing in the community differed according to an employee's position within the company. Upper management resided in large, Queen Anne houses, while workers were placed in cottages, but all housing was equipped with water, gas, and indoor plumbing. The town's many amenities included a shopping arcade, a library, and a gymnasium. The city of Pullman's success, however, was short-lived due to ensuing labor unrest.

Civic Pride

Throughout the nineteenth century, civic pride was cultivated through monumental urban design. This began in the latter half of the eighteenth century, when the French architect Pierre Charles L'Enfant designed the new U.S. capital in Washington, D.C. The design superimposed wide boulevards radiating out from circular intersections on a street grid. Public buildings and monuments reflected the baroque era.

Civic pride was also the goal of Frederick Law Olmstead, who designed many urban parks. His most notable achievement was his design for Central Park in New York City in 1857. He pioneered integrating civic art with nature to create peaceful recreational environments in the midst of an urban morass. This technique was applied to Prospect Park in Brooklyn, the Capitol grounds in Washington, D.C., and the campus of Stanford University in Palo Alto, California.

At the end of the century Daniel Burnham pioneered the City Beautiful movement. The crux of the movement was to create an aesthetically pleasing urban environment through the use of monumental architecture, large parks, and wide boulevards. In 1893

Burnham designed the Columbian Exposition, which displayed this new concept, located on drained wetlands south of downtown Chicago in Jackson Park. The grounds contained the White City, which consisted of arranged classic buildings laid out in an aesthetic and orderly fashion. This paved the way for the Chicago Plan and other City Beautiful plans in the early twentieth century.

See also Cities and Urbanization; Housing; Transportation, subentry on Urban and Interurban Transportation.

Bibliography

Divine, Robert A., T. H. Breen, George M. Frederickson, and R. Hal Williams. America: Past and Present. Glenview, Ill.: Scott, Foresman, 1983.
Guttenberg, Albert. "Pathways in American Planning History: A Thematic Chronology." Chicago: American Planning Association, 1998. Available online from http://www.planning.org/info/1785.htm.
Hall, Peter. Cities of Tomorrow: An Intellectual History of Urban Planning and Design in the Twentieth Century. Oxford, U.K., and New York: Basil Blackwell, 1998.
Historic American Buildings Survey and the Historic American Engineering Record. Historic America: Buildings, Structures, and Sites. Washington, D.C.: Library of Congress, 1983.
Kreuckeberg, Donald. Introduction to Planning History in the United States. New Brunswick N.J.: Center for Urban Policy and Research, Rutgers University, 1983.
Kurian, George Thomas. Datapedia of the United States, 1790–2000: America Year by Year. Lanham, Md.: Bernan, 1994.
Pushkarev, Boris S., Jeffrey M. Zupan, and Robert S. Cumella. Urban Rail in America: An Exploration of Criteria for Fixed-Guideway Transit. Bloomington: Indiana University Press, 1982.
Schuyler, David. The New Urban Landscape: The Redefinition of City Form in Nineteenth-Century America. Baltimore: Johns Hopkins University Press, 1986.
U.S. Department of Commerce, Bureau of the Census. Historical Statistics of the United States, Colonial Times to 1970. Washington, D.C.: U.S. Government Printing Office, 1975.

BARRY BAIN

CIVIL ENGINEERING

[This entry includes three subentries on Building Technology, Bridges and Tunnels, and Sewage and Sanitation.]

BUILDING TECHNOLOGY

The nineteenth century witnessed a major transformation in building technology. This transformation was integrally related to both industrialization and urbanization. Not unique to the United States, these transitions nevertheless took different forms from those in Europe due to the abundance of natural resources and the scarcity of skilled labor in the United States. The three phenomena—advances in building technology, industrialization, and urbanization—affected each other in what was essentially a three-way symbiotic relationship. Consequently, by 1900 both individual structures and the built environment were fundamentally different from what they had been a century earlier.

Building Technology and Materials

In 1800 most structures were built much as they had been for centuries, using wooden posts and beams with mortise-and-tenon joints to frame the structure and exterior walls of wood siding or masonry. Few buildings were larger than 50 feet by 150 feet, and those that were had interior posts or load-bearing walls for additional support. Contemporary architectural fashion determined the "style" or exterior appearance of a building. No mechanical systems to speak of existed.

By the 1830s, however, major changes in construction with wood, masonry, and iron had begun. Traditional post-and-beam construction was slow and required skilled labor to form the joints properly, which was not feasible in a growing, mobile society. The wooden balloon frame met U.S. needs more effectively. Balloon-framed buildings replaced the heavy posts and beams with rows of smaller, lighter members. This distributed the building's weight over more supports, thus reducing the importance of any one of them. Since balloon frames had more connections and the thinner, lighter pieces were not suitable to mortise-and-tenon joining, nails joined the pieces of the frame to one another. Two industrial developments—mechanized lumber milling and machine-made nails—facilitated use of the balloon frame. Timber was plentiful in much of the United States, and balloon-frame buildings required fewer workers and less skill to assemble, so balloon framing quickly became the norm. It was especially suitable in rapidly growing communities and for houses, shops, and farm buildings.

Developments in masonry and iron construction paralleled those in wood. Although masonry construction dates from ancient times, the cost and skill required to erect masonry buildings had generally limited its use to very important structures, such as government buildings or churches. Timber trusses in masonry buildings advanced designs of vaults and domes, as in the Cathedral St. Louis (built in 1831–1834) in St. Louis, Missouri. Masonry was also used for industrial buildings. As more industries turned to mechanized production and the sizes and types of industrial machines increased, the need arose for bigger, sturdier industrial buildings. Multistory, masonry industrial buildings with increased floor areas required thicker walls with enough strength to support the combined weights of the building and the machinery it would contain.

The Chestnut Street Theater and the U.S. Naval Asylum built in Philadelphia in the 1820s introduced iron-framed construction to the United States. Major fires in New York City in the 1830s and 1840s prompted calls for fireproof buildings, which stimulated more iron-framed construction. The need for warehouse buildings that could support increasingly heavy loads further spurred demand. By the 1850s iron construction was the method of choice for large or tall buildings, and it was particularly well suited to New York's burgeoning commercial economy. In the 1860s, New York City's Wanamaker Department Store was the nation's largest iron building with more than 300,000 square feet of floor area. Over the course of several decades wrought iron substituted for cast iron because the former was stronger and could be produced by machines more easily and less expensively than the latter. Iron was not without problems, however. The heat from a major fire could weaken iron frames and cause buildings to fail even if the heat did not reach iron's melting point.

Covering the iron interior framing with bricks and using masonry exterior walls increased the fire resistance of buildings. During the 1870s and 1880s the combination was used often, and Chicago buildings in particular exhibited a high degree of both design and skill in iron and masonry combination buildings. The great Chicago fire of 1871 stimulated the use of combination construction there, for after the fire the city had to replace a large number of commercial buildings quickly and cheaply. The Chicago Opera House and the Chicago Auditorium Building, both built in the 1880s, were among the most notable examples of this type of construction. The sixteen-story Monadnock Building (1889–1891) in Chicago pushed the development further with its rows of bow windows.

The iron and masonry combination also allowed the development of the skyscraper. At mid-century the elevator freed building height from the limitations of stairs, but technology had not developed sufficiently to take advantage of the device. New York City's thriving financial district created pressures for ever larger buildings, and the narrow lots typical of Manhattan should have encouraged buildings to go higher. But New York architects and engineers hesitated to use iron construction in tall buildings. Consequently, Chicago is generally considered the birthplace of the skyscraper. There William Le Baron Jenney's Home Insurance Building (1884–1885) was the first to use an internal iron skeleton and curtain walls rather than load-bearing walls. Some of the load was still borne by masonry, but the Home Insurance Building clearly showed the benefits of skeleton framing as it provided more natural light and open space in the interior. The next logical development was to substitute steel, which was stronger and more fire resistant, for iron, allowing buildings such as the Rand McNally Building (1889–1890) in Chicago to eliminate masonry altogether. Structural steel framing proved an effective way to handle a variety of construction and design problems, so it quickly became the standard for big buildings in Chicago, New York, and elsewhere by the 1890s.

The last major nineteenth-century advance in building technology and materials involved concrete. That material was used only sporadically until a new concrete manufacturing process was patented in the 1870s. By the 1880s concrete was commonly used where its compressive strength was important, such as for footings and piers. However, solid concrete was not suitable for beams or floor slabs until the development of reinforced concrete, which added the tensile strength of iron or steel to the compressive strength of concrete. The museum on the Stanford University campus, which in 1892 was the first structure made completely of reinforced concrete, illustrated the advantages of reinforced concrete construction, but the technique's greatest impact occurred after the turn of the century.

Industrialization

The advances in building technology would not have occurred or spread so quickly had the United States not been a developing industrial nation. Industrialization created new demands on building technology and provided the means to meet them. For example, trains required strong bridges to support the weight of moving, loaded trains and large, unobstructed spaces for train station shed and platform areas. Over several decades different types of trusses, some wood, some iron and wood, and eventually some of steel, developed. Trusses and the broader concept of diagonal bracing found other applications in building technology. Moreover the railroad facilitated industrial development by carrying raw materials to the iron and steel factories while demanding more iron and steel for rails, cars, and train engines. As the number, size, and weight of trains increased, so did the demands on the structures associated with them. A train shed that was big enough when the Civil War began was inadequate ten years later. A factory pro-

ducing rails or engines in 1870 could not meet production demand in 1880, when one that could handle bigger, heavier furnaces or machines was needed. Architects and engineers thus continually pushed building technology to meet the demands of industrial production.

Of course, the iron foundries and steel mills that received raw materials by rail also produced the wrought iron and steel beams and girders used in skeleton construction, just as an earlier generation of sawmills had produced millions of two-by-fours for balloon-framed houses in the growing towns and cities. Plentiful reserves of timber, iron ore, coal, and other natural resources made industrialization possible in the United States, and the short supply of skilled labor made it necessary. Any development that would reduce the number of people or the level of skill required to do a job was preferred. The principles of standardization and mass production in industrial production had their parallels in building technology. Two workers could erect a balloon-frame house with lumber prepared elsewhere, whereas a house of post-and-beam construction required fifteen or twenty workers. Iron or steel framing girders, which had to be produced in a factory, were made in standardized sizes and then assembled into a building skeleton at the site. Although buildings were not interchangeable by type or use, their component parts were. Through the 1800s U.S. buildings increasingly were constructed using an "open" system process in which modules or segments of the structure were assembled in the factory and then joined together on the site to create the whole building. Such a process relied on large numbers of identical parts. Since the skill of the craftsperson was much less important in this type of construction, builders and those providing building materials became industry oriented rather than craft oriented. This system was particularly well suited to a nation where skilled workers were in short supply and where laborers working together on a single building site might speak several different languages. Overall, advances in building technology aided industrialization by allowing construction of bigger and stronger industrial buildings. At the same time building technology relied on industrialization to produce the standardized parts that were assembled into buildings.

Urbanization

Urbanization was the third phenomenon that both fed and was fed by industrialization and advances in building technology. By the 1830s steam power allowed factories to locate in cities, where the labor supply was. Trains brought raw materials from different places to a single industrial facility in the city. Steam power also encouraged concentration of all stages of production, spurring the demand for larger industrial buildings with stronger floors and increased roof spans. Balloon framing allowed quicker construction of more dwellings for the growing population. Iron framing produced the larger commercial and industrial buildings needed in the flourishing cities.

Building technology and industrialization greatly altered the urban landscape. In 1800 the tallest buildings in most cities were churches, and the largest most often were government buildings. By 1900 the tallest were office skyscrapers, and the largest were factories. In 1800, homes, shops, small manufactories, churches, and government buildings were jumbled together. No defined industrial, commercial, or residential districts existed, and one building might serve different purposes at different times. By 1900 industrial production required large factories close to the rail lines that brought raw materials and took away finished goods. Specialized warehouse districts sprouted up near freight stations and the commercial structures whose tenants they supplied. Whole neighborhoods of balloon-framed doubles and row houses or iron-framed apartment buildings and tenements sheltered the expanding industrial population. Streetcars and interurban rail lines, themselves technological and industrial advances, fostered the development of residential suburbs for middle- and upper-income families far from the dirt and noise of business and industry. The occasional epidemic or major fire in crowded industrial cities also spurred calls for building and housing codes for safer homes, factories, shops, and offices.

Each advance in industry or building technology stimulated further urbanization, which provided labor and placed new demands on technology. The result was a major transformation in building technology, industrial development, and the urban built environment by 1900.

See also **Architecture; Cities and Urbanization; Housing; Industrialization and the Market; Iron; Labor Force; Lumber and Timber Industry; Natural Resources; Population; Railroads; Steam Power; Steel and the Steel Industry; Suburbs; Transportation,** *subentry on* **Railroads.**

Bibliography

Condit, Carl W. *American Building: Materials and Techniques from the First Colonial Settlements to the Present.* Chicago: University of Chicago Press, 1968.

Fitch, James Marston. *American Building.* Volume 1: *The Historical Forces That Shaped It.* 2d ed. New York: Schocken, 1973.

Goldfield, David R., and Blaine A. Brownell. *Urban America: A History.* 2d ed. Boston: Houghton Mifflin, 1990.

Marcus, Alan I., and Howard P. Segal. *Technology in America: A Brief History.* San Diego, Calif.: Harcourt Brace Jovanovich, 1989.

Peters, Tom F. *Building the Nineteenth Century.* Cambridge, Mass.: MIT Press, 1996.

Relph, Edward. *The Modern Urban Landscape.* Baltimore: Johns Hopkins University Press, 1987.

PATRICIA BURGESS

BRIDGES AND TUNNELS

Civil engineers in the nineteenth century transformed their profession from a tradition of intuitive construction to a science of "rationalized" analysis and building. At the heart of this transformation were new training programs and widely available publications. In the first half of the nineteenth century, many of the American engineers who would develop important bridge and tunnel designs trained in Europe or in the new U.S. engineering programs at West Point (1802) and Rensselaer Polytechnic Institute (1835). Because formal education was expensive and limited, some gained practical knowledge by working on the major internal improvement projects of the era—the Erie Canal, the Pennsylvania Main Line, or the Baltimore and Ohio Railroad (B&O)—under the supervision of skilled engineers. Later in the century engineering schools created by the Morrill Act (1862) made professional training more readily available throughout the United States. Such publications as *Work on Bridge Building* (1847) by Squire Whipple (1804–1888) and *General Theory of Bridge Construction* (1851) by Herman Haupt (1817–1905), as well as such magazines as *Scientific American* and the *American Railroad Journal,* publicized patented solutions and analytical techniques to a wide engineering audience.

Bridges

Availability of new and improved structural materials revolutionized bridge construction in the nineteenth century. At the beginning of the 1800s, wood and stone were the only bridge-building materials. Over the century improvements in the production of cast and wrought iron led to their use for long spans. At mid-century structural steel was specified for some components in the initial plans for the St. Louis Bridge, while reinforced concrete ushered in a return to masonry at the end of the century.

But the major nineteenth-century engineering innovations in bridges related to form. Colonial bridges were basically of two forms: stone arches or wood

The Erection of the St. Louis Bridge. James Eads (1820–1887) used innovative concepts to construct the St. Louis Bridge. The ribs are shown completed and the roadways begun. The bridge was finished in 1874. LIBRARY OF CONGRESS

beams on pilings. The first required skilled labor, plentiful building stone, long construction time, and "falsework" scaffolding under the arch until it could support itself. The second called for large dimensional timber for pilings and multiple beams. Bridges of both forms blocked waterways, or altered their flows so drastically that the bridged streams became difficult if not impossible to navigate. Throughout the nineteenth century, engineers sought to resolve these problems with innovative bridge forms and new materials.

Stone arch bridges

Many nineteenth-century stone arch bridges spanned streams above the head of navigation. For example, stone arch bridges along the National Road in western Maryland and Pennsylvania carried wagon traffic over local streams. Stone arch aqueducts carried sections of the Erie Canal over the Mohawk and Genesee Rivers. The Aqueduct Bridge (New York, 1848) and Cabin John Bridge (Washington, D.C., 1864) brought fresh water to growing cities.

However the most pervasive use of stone arch construction appeared in the viaducts of the eastern railroads. The B&O Railroad completed the 80-foot span of Baltimore's Carrollton Viaduct in 1829 and immediately began to construct the Thomas Viaduct, an eight-span, granite bridge with an overall length of 612 feet. This marvel was eclipsed by the New York and Erie Railroad's Starrucca Viaduct (1848) of seventeen arches totaling 1,040 feet. In the frenzy of railroad enthusiasm at mid-century, railroads turned to less expensive construction in wood or wood and iron; but by the 1880s the Burlington Northern Railroad had built the twenty-eight-arch Great Stone Bridge in Minneapolis across the Mississippi River. Consolidated eastern railroads, such as the New York Central and the Pennsylvania, also were willing to pay more to build permanently in stone. The record holder of the era was the forty-eight-arch Rockville Bridge over the Susquehanna River with a total length of 3,830 feet.

Wood trestles and trusses

Colonial bridge builders also spanned streams with wood beam bridges on pilings. Like stone arch bridges, early wood structures required skilled labor and blocked waterways with their multiple pilings. But wood was more plentiful than stone and construction time was short. In the nineteenth century engineers developed two divergent forms of wood beam bridges. The first form, maintaining the simple beam and pile, became the trestle of the western railroad systems. The second, the rationalized wood truss, connected short wood members to create a large frame or truss that could carry loads and span distances like a huge beam, but with far less material.

The most famous colonial pile and beam bridges crossed the Charles River at Boston. These trestle form bridges had the advantage of quick and inexpensive construction, but they blocked the watercourse with their multiple piers. Yet the form was especially well adapted to locations that did not require passage underneath, for example, where early railroads crossed broad valleys and deep ravines. Used occasionally on the eastern rail lines in the early nineteenth century, the trestle reached its heyday in the mid–nineteenth century in the West. The race to complete the transcontinental railroad (and to garner federal funds based on the mileage of track laid) spurred the Central Pacific and Union Pacific Railroads to build line at a frantic pace. Trestles were ideally suited to the project. The Central Pacific's trestle across the American River (east of Sacramento) was 2,200 feet long, but only 6 feet above high water. The Union Pacific's Dale Creek Valley trestle (over 500 miles west of Omaha) was only 700 feet long, but an amazing 126 feet high. The longest wooden trestle, originally built in 1883, was the Southern Railway's twenty-one-mile crossing of Lake Pontchartrain, near New Orleans.

The development of the second form of wood beam bridge drew on the arched truss, which dated back to the Roman era. The first arched trusses were simple beams propped from underneath to increase span. Later builders propped these supports for even greater span, ultimately creating a wood arch of multiple props. Drawing inspiration from medieval roof trusses, colonial builders refined the propped design into two superimposed arcs of wood connected by a web of diagonal braces.

This new trussed-arch configuration had rigidity provided by the web of wood triangles and the economy of short members; but it also had difficult mortise and tenon connections and the need to jam the ends of the truss between abutments to restrict the horizontal thrusts of the arch. Timothy Palmer (1751–1821) built two trussed arch spans in New England in the late 1700s, but is best known for his 1805 Permanent Bridge over the Schuylkill River in Philadelphia, which had a center trussed arch span of 64 feet. Seven years later Lewis Wernwag (1769–1843) built the remarkable Colossus Bridge nearby with a trussed arch span of 340 feet.

The next step in wood bridge design was to use the truss as a beam, in other words, to let the truss rest on top of its supports. The earliest known example of this form is Theodore Burr's (1771–1822) Waterford, Connecticut, bridge (1804), which featured a wood arch inside a beam truss. The truss component spanned the waterway, while the interior arch reduced sag caused by the truss deflecting under loads. Burr patented his design, which was subsequently used for hundreds of bridges.

Burr's truss was soon improved by the architect Ithiel Town (1784–1844), who designed and patented a simple lattice truss in 1820. Town boasted that his truss could be "built by the mile and cut off by the yard." Its repetitive members made it much easier to fabricate and erect than trussed arches. Town's lattice truss also was reproduced by the hundreds.

Within a decade the final development in wood truss design had been created: a simple truss of vertical posts separating crossed diagonals into a series of panels. In 1829 the first Long truss carried the Baltimore-Washington Turnpike over a railroad line. Stephen Long (1784–1864), its designer, had calculated the forces and sized the members of the bridge to carry its anticipated loads efficiently. A promoter of the first rank, Long wrote booklets on constructing his trusses and distributed them around the country through his network of agents.

Burr, Town, and Long trusses dominated timber bridge construction in the first half of the nineteenth century. However, after 1840, other truss configurations and new materials relegated these early designs to the backroads of America. Today, these truss configurations, hidden under protective wood sheathing and roofed over with shingles, still stand as much-loved "covered" bridges.

Metal truss bridges

By the middle of the nineteenth century, American railroads had developed from small, independent lines running between cities into regional carriers of "through" traffic. The newer trains traveled longer distances at higher speeds and hauled heavier loads. While Burr, Town, and Long wood trusses had been adequate in the early years of railroading, by mid-century the railroads needed heavier, stiffer, longer bridges that could span the great rivers of America. Engineers met these needs by creating new trusses, using new materials, and by inventing new methods of connection.

Important new truss designs, such as those by William Howe (1803–1852), Thomas Pratt (1812–1875), and Squire Whipple, employed iron for some or all structural members. Howe's truss, patented in 1840, used turnbuckled iron rods for the vertical tension members; Pratt's truss, patented in 1844, used iron diagonal tension members. Soon the Pratt truss was being executed completely in iron. Whipple's 1840 bowstring truss used cast iron for the compression members, wrought iron for the tension members, and in later renditions included eyebars (iron members with machined holes at each end) connected by iron pins driven through the holes. The eyebar and pin connection became the hallmark of American metal bridge design.

Another hallmark of American bridges in the late nineteenth century related to their production. Such engineers and ironmakers as Wendel Bollman (1814–1884) not only designed and patented iron truss bridges; beginning in about 1860, they also formed companies that manufactured trusses and sold them through illustrated catalogs. The client supplied the needed measurements and picked a favorite design from the catalog. Then the bridge company produced the appropriately dimensioned iron truss parts, shipped them to the building site, and arranged for their erection by local laborers. The Berlin Iron Works, Phoenix Bridge Company, Keystone Bridge Company, and others fabricated thousands of railroad and highway bridges in the last decades of the nineteenth century.

But iron also presented problems: it was expensive and far from reliable. It has been estimated that as many as 25 percent of all metal bridges built in the United States between 1870 and 1890 failed. Some collapses were due to poor fabrication, others to design faults, still others to material flaws. Probably the most famous American bridge failure occurred on 29 December 1876, when a wrought-iron Howe truss collapsed under the Pacific Express at Ashtabula, Ohio. Ninety-two passengers died at the scene or within a few days. Leading newspapers denounced both the railroads and the engineering profession.

Public outcry over iron bridge failures led some railroads to return to stone arch construction, while others chose to build in steel. The first important steel truss spanned the Missouri River at Glasgow, Missouri, in 1879. Steel was soon the material of choice for a new form of bridge—the movable span.

By the late nineteenth century railroad engineers had bridged navigable rivers with new bridge forms and materials. In addition, river interests had adapted their operations to bigger boats and barge towing to compete with the railroads for freight carriage. River interests also demanded that bridges not obstruct navigable waterways. Movable spans allowed river traffic to pass through low-clearance railroad bridges by literally moving the bridges out of the way. Important nineteenth-century configurations for movable spans included swing or pivot bridges, drawbridges, and vertical lift bridges.

Several of these spans were first introduced in Chicago.

Suspension bridges

The suspension bridge captured the American public's imagination in the 1800s. Since suspension systems could span even greater horizontal distances than truss spans, they also allowed river traffic to pass unimpeded. But from the public's point of view it was a more dramatic form than the utilitarian truss. Suspension bridges had soaring towers, delicate cables, and a graceful sweep of deck.

The first American suspension bridge was built by James Finley (1762–1828) in 1801 over Jacob's Creek near Uniontown, Pennsylvania. In the next fifteen years Finley constructed about forty more bridges in the eastern United States. Finley's (and subsequent designers') main problem was to determine the appropriate length of the suspension chains and suspenders to keep the bridge deck level at a given height. Finley solved this problem empirically by hanging a scale model of the main chain at the appropriate height along a board fence, and then calculating the necessary suspender lengths to scale. The first wire suspension span, a footbridge that crossed the Schuylkill River (4.5 miles upstream from Philadelphia) in 1816, probably was designed using the same experimental approach.

Not until mid-century did American energies return to suspension spans. The two foremost American suspension bridge designers of the era, Charles Ellet Jr. (1810–1862) and John Roebling (1806–1869), had studied suspension spans in Europe, and had learned to analyze the structures mathematically so they could be designed to withstand the forces acting upon them. Both designers had learned that the catenary curve of the suspended wire cables carrying even loads behaved as an inverted arch. In a series of design competitions for new bridges at Fairmount (Pennsylvania), Wheeling (now in West Virginia), Cincinnati, St. Louis, and Niagara, Ellet and Roebling submitted proposals for suspension bridges. Ellet won the competitions for Fairmount, Wheeling, and the first Niagara Bridge; Roebling won at Cincinnati and the second Niagara Bridge. Ellet's Fairmount Bridge (1842, near the site of the first wire suspension bridge of 1816) spanned 357 feet using ten cables. The Wheeling Bridge (1849) spanned 1,010 feet with twelve cables (making it the longest span in the world). Roebling in the meantime built the Pittsburgh Suspension Aqueduct (1845, with seven short spans of 162 feet each carried by two cables) and the Smithfield Street Bridge (1846, eight spans of 188 feet each). Ellet began the suspension bridge at the Niagara Gorge (1850), but was fired by the proprietors who then hired Roebling to finish the work (1855). Roebling's Niagara Bridge spanned 821 feet on four cables and carried two decks: one for a railway above and another for vehicular traffic below.

The contract for the St. Louis Bridge finally was awarded in 1867 to James Eads (1820–1887), a river salvage businessman. Eads specified a steel arch bridge of three spans with their piers founded on bedrock below 100 feet of Mississippi River mud. He audaciously turned formal suspension analysis on its head and reinstituted an intuitive arch form. Eads also proposed using pneumatic caissons to excavate the bridge piers. The caissons (basically boxes open at the bottom, on top of which the bridge piers were built) rested on the riverbed and were filled with compressed air. As workmen in a caisson removed mud and workmen above raised the piers, the caisson sank further into the riverbed until it reached bedrock. Eads's crews still hold the depth record of 136 feet. Once the four piers were in place and work on the superstructure had begun, the new problem of maintaining free river navigation had to be solved. With yet another innovation, the iron and steel arches were erected by cantilevering the two halves from the masonry piers. Final connections of the two halves were made with adjustable closure tubes designed by Eads, and the bridge opened to traffic in 1874.

Two years after work began on the St. Louis Bridge, Roebling began construction on the Brooklyn Bridge. The plan for the largest suspension bridge in the world included two monumental stone towers and a bridge suspended from four cables of galvanized steel wire. Designed to span the East River entrance to New York City, the bridge was seen immediately as the gateway to America. Although Roebling died before work began on the bridge, the job was completed by his son Washington (1837–1926). The elder Roebling's design called for pneumatic caissons similar to those in use at St. Louis, and fraught with the same perils. In fact, the younger Roebling fell victim to "caisson disease" or decompression sickness in 1872 while directing digging and remained an invalid for the rest of his life. He continued supervising the bridge project with the help of his wife, Emily (d. 1903). Once the piers were complete, cable "spinning" commenced. This technique, developed during earlier projects at Wheeling and Niagara, involved sending loops of steel wire on a wheel across a rope strung between the Brooklyn and New York piers. Each of the four main cables of the bridge contained 5,434 wires. By 1878 the last wire had been run across and in 1881 the deck was complete. The bridge opened on 24 May 1883 and remained the preeminent example of suspension technology well into the twentieth century.

Tunnels

Like the bridges that spanned major rivers to connect regional railroads, or crossed streams to link local roads or rail lines, tunnels also reduced the effects of natural barriers by joining segments of canals or railroads, or by unifying urban transportation networks. In the mountains, tunnels shortened routes and diminished grades. Crossing waterways, they reduced conflicts over rights-of-way between land and water vehicles. In cities, they eased traffic congestion and accommodated utility lines.

Tunneling in America began in about 1818 with the construction of the Pattison Tunnel in Cheatham County, Tennessee. This tunnel diverted water from the Harpeth River to power the waterwheels of the Pattison Forge. Although later tunnels also served industry, especially mining, the major technical advances and greatest achievements in tunnel design relate to nineteenth-century transportation.

The first major transportation tunnel, the 729-foot Union Canal Tunnel (1827) at Lebanon, Pennsylvania, connected the Schuylkill and Susquehanna Rivers through the watershed ridge. But the Union and other canals soon were eclipsed by railroads that also needed to reduce grades and shorten routes. Three important railroad tunnel projects illustrate most of the technical advances in nineteenth-century tunnel design.

At the time of its completion in 1858, the Crozet Tunnel at Rockfish Gap, Virginia, was the longest (4,273 feet) railroad tunnel in the United States. The Crozet and three other single-track tunnels of the Blue Ridge Railroad first penetrated the slopes of the Appalachian Mountains to connect the seaports of the Atlantic Coast with the Ohio River basin. Although the Crozet Tunnel was the product of traditional manual labor with hand drills, pick axes, and black powder blasting through hard rock, its innovative engineer, Claude Crozet (1790–1864), designed the tunnel to drain water from the lower east end and to ventilate locomotive smoke from the higher west end. Crozet also designed a clearance car to find the narrow sections of the tunnel.

In 1876 the 4.75-mile, double-track Hoosac Tunnel in northwestern Massachusetts connected Boston to the markets of western New York by means of the Troy and Greenfield Railroad. During the tunnel's twenty-five years of construction, hard-rock tunneling evolved from the traditional hand methods that had been used for centuries to a mechanized process using compressed-air drills mounted on movable carriages to drill blastholes, and on nitroglycerin as a blasting agent detonated with an electric ignition system. These innovations increased the length of tunnel cleared per blasting operation by 40 percent; reduced the time needed to complete the operation; and, when coupled with the sinking of two auxiliary shafts (each of which provided two additional work faces and extra ventilation), permitted one thousand men in eight-hour shifts to work around the clock.

While the Crozet and Hoosac Tunnels bored through mountains of hard rock, the Hudson-Manhattan Railroad Tunnel (1908) passed under the 60-foot deep Hudson River to join the New Jersey and New York sections of the rail line. This mile-long, subaqueous tunnel was constructed over thirty years. Its builders adapted the principles of pneumatic caissons to keep the initial iron tunnel shell in place with compressed air until the permanent masonry liner was installed. Difficulties maintaining the tunnel shell with air pressure alone were corrected by using the shield system employed on the London Underground. Cast-iron rings replaced the masonry liner, and hydraulic rams attached to the rings forced the cutting edges of the shield forward into the river silt, which could then be removed through doors in the shield.

Street and highway tunnels rarely were built before the growth of automobile traffic in the twentieth century. However, an early example, the Washington Street Tunnel, passed under the Chicago River in 1870 and within a decade a highway tunnel penetrated the hills south of San Francisco.

Tunnels also brought water to cities. The Croton Aqueduct (1837) carried much-needed clean water forty miles from the Croton River to New York City, passing through sixteen tunnels between 160 and 1,263 feet long. Expansion of the system, called the New Croton Aqueduct (1893), included the construction of a thirty-mile water tunnel, which was then the longest and largest in the world. Chicago also built a tunnel to supply the city with fresh water. In 1867 the city completed a two-mile-long, brick-lined tunnel through the clay bed of Lake Michigan. At the lake end of the tunnel, a vertical shaft rose 60 feet to the lake surface where fresh water entered the shaft intake and passed through the tunnel to the pumping station in the city.

By the end of the nineteenth century, tunnels also were being used to relieve traffic congestion in Boston, where the first subway sections had opened in 1897. To accommodate the underground utilities already in place and to protect adjacent structures, engineers designed a shallow tunnel constructed by cut-and-cover operations; the trench was excavated, the tunnel structure of vertical and horizontal I-beams was installed, and the top was covered over to the original grade. Electricity solved the major problems associated with public safety below ground by powering ventilating fans and lights as well as the cars.

New York had been the scene of an early experimental subway (1870) built by Alfred Ely Beach (1826–1896). Beach and his men excavated in secrecy at night under Broadway, and in the process developed a primitive hydraulic excavating shield and cast-iron tunnel linings used later on other, larger tunneling projects. Although it was never more than a curiosity, Beach's subway opened to the public, and in one year provided four hundred thousand people with a round-trip ride in a passenger car. A large blower pushed the car forward and, when reversed, sucked the car back along the 312-foot subway. Although abandoned in 1874, Beach's tunnel and car were rediscovered early in the twentieth century when the main tunnels of the New York City subway system were constructed.

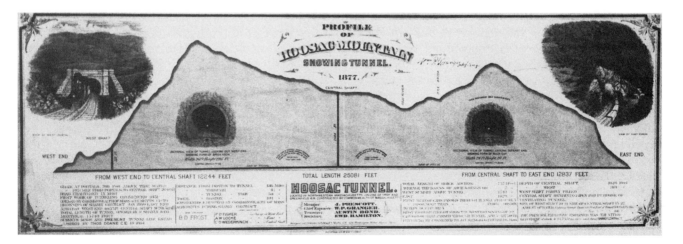

An Engineering Feat. The east and west ends of the tunnel that was drilled through Hoosac Mountain in Massachusetts. Lithograph, J. B. Richards Co., 1877. LIBRARY OF CONGRESS

See also **Civil Engineering**, *subentry on* **Building Technology; Internal Improvements; Transportation**, *subentries on* **Roads and Turnpikes, Canals and Waterways**, *and* **Railroads.**

Bibliography

American Wooden Bridges. New York: American Society of Civil Engineers, 1976.

Brown, David J. *Bridges: Three Thousand Years of Defying Nature.* New York: Macmillan, 1993.

Condit, Carl W. *American Building Art: The Nineteenth Century.* New York: Oxford University Press, 1960.

Finch, James Kip. *The Story of Engineering.* Garden City, N.Y.: Doubleday, 1960.

Jacobs, David, and Anthony E. Neville. *Bridges, Canals, and Tunnels.* New York: American Heritage, 1968.

Kirby, Richard Shelton, et al. *Engineering in History.* New York: Dover, 1990.

Kranakis, Eda. *Constructing a Bridge: An Exploration of Engineering Culture, Design, and Research in Nineteenth-Century France and America.* Cambridge, Mass.: MIT Press, 1997.

Lay, M. G. *Ways of the World: A History of the World's Roads and of the Vehicles That Used Them.* New Brunswick, N.J.: Rutgers University Press, 1992.

McKee, Brian J. *Historic American Covered Bridges.* New York: American Society of Civil Engineers and Oxford University Press, 1997.

Petroski, Henry. *Engineers of Dreams: Great Bridge Builders and the Spanning of America.* New York: Knopf, 1995.

———. *To Engineer Is Human: The Role of Failure in Successful Design.* New York: St. Martin's Press, 1985.

Plowden, David. *Bridges: The Spans of North America.* New York: Norton, 1984.

Schodek, Daniel L. *Landmarks in American Civil Engineering.* Cambridge, Mass.: MIT Press, 1987.

ELIZABETH BRAND MONROE

SEWAGE AND SANITATION

Water supply and waste disposal had a local focus during the first half of the nineteenth century. Potable water came from wells, rainwater cisterns, and nearby streams and ponds. Kitchen garbage and other household waste were thrown into the street or into vacant lots. Pigs rooted through wet garbage, and scavengers hauled away what remained along with the excrement left by horses and pigs. Human waste and most wastewater were disposed of in privy vaults and cesspools—holes in the ground, sometimes lined with brick, from which waste and wastewater leached into the surrounding soil. Gutters or open channels down the center of streets carried off rainwater. Only the largest cities constructed storm sewers.

Large cities also instituted periodic emptying of

"How to Dispose of Sewage." Poor sanitation practices plagued the nineteenth century. Wood engraving from *Harper's Weekly*, 15 January 1881. LIBRARY OF CONGRESS

privy vaults by contracting with scavengers. The "night soil" was dumped into nearby waterways or composted with sawdust and waste from streets, dairies, slaughterhouses, and fish markets. The compost was sold as fertilizer for farming, following what Lemuel Shattuck, the Massachusetts sanitary commissioner in 1850, thought was a "law of nature." Through the 1850s the cleanliness and public health of American cities largely depended on a huge recycling system. Growing cities gave farmers incentive to increase crop production and then turned wastes and manures into the agricultural fertilizers the farmers needed. New York City's waste, for example, was sold to farmers on Long Island, who in turn sold energy to New Yorkers in the form of food, fuel wood, and hay for the horses used in urban transportation. The western end of Long Island became known as one of the "gardens of America" (Wines, *Fertilizer in America*, p. 9).

So long as communities were small this was a satisfactory water supply and waste disposal system. But cities grew, and the system ultimately broke down. It became increasingly difficult to supply urban dwellers with sufficient quantities of good water for drinking, washing, fire fighting, industry, and flushing streets during epidemics. By the 1790s privies and cesspools in Philadelphia, America's largest city, already had saturated the surrounding earth and contaminated public and private wells. A series of devastating yellow fever epidemics persuaded city leaders to hire the English-born engineer and architect Benjamin Henry Latrobe to build a waterworks to pump potable water from the Schuylkill River. Subsequently New York, Boston, Detroit, and other cities constructed waterworks. By the time of the Civil War, America's 16 largest cities plus another 120 communities had waterworks. By 1880 the number reached almost 600, and by 1902 municipal indebtedness incurred, largely through the sale of bonds, to build water systems had reached $1.4 billion.

New water supplies made it possible for city residents to pipe fresh water into their homes. Between 1800 and the 1850s per capita water consumption increased from 2 to 3 gallons per day to 50 to 100 gallons per day. In 1855, only seven years after introducing water from the Cochituate Aqueduct, Boston supplied almost 18,000 households and 1,200 fire hydrants through over 110 miles of distribution pipes, and demand soon led the city to build a second reservoir. New York City built the famous Croton Aqueduct to meet its water needs; Wilmington, Delaware, an average American city, built three reservoirs between 1827 and 1877; and San Francisco contracted with the Spring Valley Water Company to supply its water from a nearby reservoir. Although many cities built or contracted for systems to supply potable water, "not one made, at the same time, suitable provisions for removing the water from the cities once it had been brought in and used" (Pursell, *The Machine in America*, p. 140).

As the modern American city evolved between 1860 and 1910, householders installed modern sinks and bathtubs. Worse was the adoption of the water closet, a British invention. By 1864 Boston had 14,000 water closets for its nearly 130,000 people. By 1880 roughly one-third of the nation's urban households had flush toilets. The water closet plus the dramatic increase in kitchen and other household wastewater overflowed privies and cesspools, making the existing waste disposal system intolerable. An 1880 Newport, Rhode Island, sewage plan report clearly stated the problem:

> There are in our town residents who having introduced water into their dwellings find no way of ridding themselves of it. Their cesspools . . . that formerly required cleaning about twice or three times in a season must be emptied as often as every ten days. The expense of removing the contents of the cesspool at one house last summer was $300. The amount in dollars we can appreciate, but the danger to health cannot be realized. (Tarr, *The Search for the Ultimate Sink*, p. 116)

The new technology of running water had resulted in the adoption of another new technology, the flush toilet, that, when combined with growing urban population densities, broke down the privy vault–cesspool waste disposal system and created a serious sanitary problem.

American cities looked to England and Europe for waste and sanitation solutions. They discovered that Hamburg, Germany, in 1843 had replaced privy vaults and cesspools with a comprehensively planned sewerage system that was combined with storm drainage and used wastewater as well as storm water to carry away the waste. At the heart of the system was the conventional "filth theory" of disease etiology that gases or miasmas emanating from decaying organic matter caused disease. A water-carriage system of waste disposal removed organic waste before it could begin to putrefy. The British sanitarian Sir Edwin Chadwick argued that human waste should be removed from the household in a sewerage system separated from storm runoff sewers. He believed that a combined system would not remove wastes quickly enough to prevent the release of disease-propagating miasmas and further argued that the sewage from a separate system could be recycled as fertilizer and make the system self-financing. London officials rejected Chadwick's arguments and adopted a combined sewerage system, basing their decision on the view that animal excrement made "rain falling upon the streets . . . as much polluted as sewage, and ought to be treated as such" (Tarr, *The Search for the Ultimate Sink*, p. 136). Based on the English and European experiences, Brooklyn and Chicago, the only American cities that built major sewerage systems before the Civil War, chose the combined system. Their decisions in turn established the basic sewerage model for other large American cities, with property owners abutting sewer mains and municipal bond issues footing the bills.

The new sewerage systems emptied waste into nearby waterways to be diluted and purified. City officials and sanitary engineers operated on the belief that flowing water cleansed itself of impurities, a notion associated with the filth theory of disease. Unfortunately no one knew how fast or how far water in rivers, lakes, and oceans had to move to accomplish purification. By the 1870s sanitary engineers were aware that waterways could become nuisances and even health hazards when overloaded with sewage, but the economic savings gained from depositing untreated sewage into waterways eclipsed any uncertainties about water self-purification. To be sure the separate sewerage system had its American champion in the sanitary engineer George E. Waring. After he introduced the system in Lenox, Massachusetts, in 1875–1876, he was selected to construct one in Memphis, Tennessee, which had experienced a series of yellow fever and cholera outbreaks in the early 1880s. Waring argued, as had Chadwick in London, that combined systems could harbor potentially lethal "sewer gases" and that the agricultural benefits of sewage recycling made the separate system cost-effective. Sanitarians and civil engineers debated the efficacy of the two systems for more than twenty years. The separate system was adopted only by smaller cities, generally those not requiring underground removal of rainwater.

Even as cities constructed their sewerage systems, however, it became clear that this new method of waste disposal caused pollution of community water supplies, much as overflowing privy vaults and cesspools had polluted groundwater in the beginning of the century. Moreover studies during the 1860s in bacteriology by the Frenchman Louis Pasteur and the German Robert Koch led to isolation of the typhoid bacillus and cholera vibrio in the early 1880s and a scientifically valid germ theory of disease. These findings confirmed causal connections between disease and water pollution made by sanitarians carrying out systematic studies of water quality in Massachusetts. Starting in 1884 Ellen Swallow Richards, instructor of sanitary chemistry at Massachusetts Institute of Technology (MIT), focused on analysis of food, water, and sewage for fledgling sanitary engineers, who later initiated experimental laboratories modeled after hers. Under the auspices of the Massachusetts State Board of Health, Richards and colleagues from MIT in 1887 established the Lawrence Experiment Station, where they undertook research on water purification and other sanitation problems that enabled cities to combat waterborne diseases. In 1889 MIT established the first American degree program in sanitary engineering.

By the end of the century urban water and waste disposal systems had assumed a technological momentum of their own. The filth theory of disease and the belief that running water purified itself had guided engineers to adopt combined waste and storm sewerage that deposited raw sewage in waterways. Faced with polluted water supplies, engineers favored filtration of drinking water instead of waste treatment because sewage plants were expensive and treatment technology difficult. Thanks to research in bacteriology and, in the 1890s, to chlorination, polluted water supplies could be made potable. Nevertheless, the massive systems lacked flexibility. Twentieth-century planners and engineers faced difficulties adjusting the systems to deal with new realities, such as ever-widening regional pollution and disposal of industrial waste.

See also **City and Regional Planning; Conservation; Health and Disease; Internal Improvements.**

Bibliography

Armstrong, Ellis L., ed. *History of Public Works in the United States, 1776–1976.* Chicago: American Public Works Association, 1976.

Cain, Louis P. *Sanitation Strategy for a Lakefront Metropolis: The Case of Chicago.* De Kalb: Northern Illinois University Press, 1978.

Elkind, Sarah S. *Bay Cities and Water Politics: The Battle for Resources in Boston and Oakland.* Lawrence: University Press of Kansas, 1998.

Galishoff, Stuart. *Safeguarding the Public Health: Newark, 1895–1918.* Westport, Conn.: Greenwood Press, 1975.

Hoffecker, Carol. *Water and Sewerage Works in Wilmington, Delaware, 1810–1910.* Essays in Public Works History no. 12. Chicago: Public Works Historical Society, 1981.

Melosi, Martin V. *The Sanitary City: Urban Infrastructure in America from Colonial Times to the Present.* Baltimore: Johns Hopkins University Press, 2000.

Pursell, Carroll. *The Machine in America: A Social History of Technology.* Baltimore: Johns Hopkins University Press, 1995.

Rosenkrantz, Barbara Gutmann. *Public Health and the State: Changing Views in Massachusetts, 1842–1936.* Cambridge, Mass.: Harvard University Press, 1972.

Tarr, Joel A. *The Search for the Ultimate Sink: Urban Pollution in Historical Perspective.* Akron, Ohio: University of Akron Press, 1996.

Wines, Richard A. *Fertilizer in America: From Waste Recycling to Resource Exploration.* Philadelphia: Temple University Press, 1985.

JAMES C. WILLIAMS

CIVILIZATION   Civilization was not a dominant concept for nineteenth-century Americans. Between 1857 and 1865, *Harper's Weekly* used the word eighty-four times, but only twice with specific regard to the United States. Each was an offhand reference in an article with another subject. Foreign and domestic commentators on American ways avoided the concept. The French observer Alexis de Tocqueville, who would have been familiar with French debates about civilization and culture, preferred to write about American "democracy" (1835). The novelist James Fenimore Cooper used almost the same term at almost the same time to describe *The American Democrat* (1838). Charles Dickens confined his mid-century U.S. travel observations to a mere *American Notes* (1842). The more acerbic overseas critics, such as the British writer Harriet Martineau, probably would not have agreed that "civilization" or any of its synonyms described Americans at all.

Yet distinctively American concepts like "Manifest Destiny" and images of "wilderness" giving way to a "garden" served much the same purpose as the European concept of civilization. Euro-Americans understood those terms as benign and progressive. To Native people losing the continent that had been theirs and the ways of life they had developed, and to enslaved Africans for whom America was a place of captivity and unrewarded lifelong labor, the American Republic's expanding continental empire was anything but benign.

American Distinctiveness

All agreed that Americans were distinctive, and most thought that republicanism was at the heart of their distinctiveness. In 1800 the United States was the only republic in the Western Hemisphere. The restoration of European monarchy by the Congress of Vienna (1815) left the United States virtually the only republic in a hostile world. At mid-century, Cambridge University still regarded American republicanism as so dangerous that it refused Harvard College's offer to establish a lectureship at Cambridge about the United States.

According to the historian William McLoughlin, American republican identity passed through two phases. Initially it rested on the premise that "enlightened" acceptance of American values could lead to membership in the American community, provided that a person was European or Native American. But by Andrew Jackson's presidency (1829–1837), this had yielded to a "romantic" belief that Americans formed a unique "race," which no non-Europeans and not even all Europeans could join. The Supreme Court's denial of legal standing to tribal Indians in *Cherokee Nation v. Georgia* (1831) and citizenship to all black people in *Dred Scott v. Sandford* (1857), anti-Catholic and anti-Semitic nativism, and the Chinese Exclusion Act of 1882 all rested on that assumption. This conception of American civilization made it appear to be simply and self-consciously a variant of European, and especially British, civilization, stripped of monarchy, economically and politically more egalitarian, and culturally cruder, but otherwise much the same.

A Neo-Europe

Despite the break with Britain, many white Americans certainly saw themselves in this way. One widespread example was in the design of buildings. The "Federal" style that was adopted in New York, Boston, and Philadelphia, especially for residences, was openly derived from the "Georgian" style of contemporary London, Bath, Bristol, and Edinburgh. The neoclassicism that followed expressed a perceived link to ancient Greece and Rome. Both were instances of the more general phenomenon that historian Richard Bushman has called America's "refinement." The wide avenues of Washington, D.C., bespoke an emulation of the imperial capitals of Europe, however incomplete were the American capital's public buildings. Joel Barlow's attempt at an American epic poem, *The Vision of Columbus* (1793), tried to celebrate its subject in the poetic manner of Milton, Virgil, and Homer.

More than a White Person's Country

But the nineteenth-century American Republic was more than a "neo-Europe." One feature that set it apart was its unashamed capitalist individualism. West of the Appalachian Mountains the nation adopted a grid plan for dividing the land that it was wresting from Native Americans. That plan marked the capitalization of rural land, providing as it did for surety of title and easy sale. In its full development, with the Homestead Act of 1862, the grid promised to free adult children from parental control by allowing both men and women to take up their own farms at very little cost. The grid plan exhibited no remnants of colonial-era neofeudalism. Viewed from the air, the irregularly divided east coast landscape still looks European. The midwestern landscape does not. Save for Washington, D.C., city plats likewise expressed capitalist values. No American church building erected after the Revolution enjoys the urban centrality and dominance of St. Paul's in London, Notre Dame in Paris, or the Stefansdom in Vienna.

American uniqueness involved more than republicanism and early capitalism. In 1853 the Republic's mainland boundaries reached their modern form. Within those boundaries dwelled a white population of more than 17 million who were American-born, along with more than 2 million immigrants from western Europe. They shared the space of America with 3,600,000 black people, 400,000 of whom were free. Although the 1850 census recorded no data on either tribal Indians or the Hispanic people of Texas, New Mexico, Arizona, and California, historians believe that these people also were numerous. Whatever the law said, these groups formed part of American civilization. Indians, African Americans, and conquered Hispanics were under severe pressure from the dominant group, but that pressure did not obliterate their cultures. African American and Euro-American evangelical Christianity already had diverged. As active participants in East Coast and southern cultural life, Africans and African Americans were laying the basis for the great flowering of black American music and art that came after slavery's end. West of the Mississippi, both Native Americans on what was left of the frontier and former Mexicans in conquered provinces were shaping powerful and uniquely American forms of expression.

The writers of the mid-century "American Renaissance" understood these facts. They cast aside provincialism, much as had the political thinkers who founded the Republic. For some writers, such as James Fenimore Cooper, Henry David Thoreau, and Ralph Waldo Emerson, the prime issue facing the young nation was the problematic contact of civilization with supposedly raw nature, a theme that the landscape painters of the Hudson River School also explored. For others, including Herman Melville and Harriet Beecher Stowe, the central drama of American development lay in the contact of different kinds of people within the Republic. Stowe was not the only writer who understood that gender as well as race, region, and class placed real limits on America's seemingly unlimited possibilities. Perhaps Walt Whitman saw the issue most clearly. The contrast between Joel Barlow's failed attempt at an American epic poem, *The Columbiad* (1807), and the successful innovations in both poetic form and poetic content that mark Whitman's *Song of Myself* (1855) reflects more than the superior ability of Whitman as a writer. Like Barlow, Whitman celebrated the American Republic. But Whitman understood that republicanism was only the beginning of what was unique about his people, even if he did not employ "civilization" as a term to describe their ways.

See also **Literature; Nationalism; Republicanism.**

Bibliography

Bushman, Richard. *The Refinement of America: Persons, Houses, Cities.* New York: Knopf, 1992.

Countryman, Edward. *Americans: A Collision of Histories.* New York: Hill and Wang, 1996.

Reynolds, David. *Walt Whitman's America: A Cultural Biography.* New York: Knopf, 1995.

Stuckey, Sterling. *Slave Culture: Nationalist Theory and the Foundations of Black America.* New York: Oxford University Press, 1987.

EDWARD COUNTRYMAN

CIVIL RIGHTS   Before the Civil War the concept of civil rights in the United States was ambiguous. In the Anglo-American political and legal tradition, civil rights were those rights human beings

Frederick Douglass (1817/1818?–1895). In his later life, the famous abolitionist became an activist for the civil rights of African Americans. LIBRARY OF CONGRESS

secured by forming societies and giving up the natural rights they had held in a state of nature. As such, civil rights could be defined narrowly as merely the right to do things permitted by law. However, most English people and Americans concluded that all free societies guaranteed some basic civil liberties.

These civil liberties were defined loosely in proclamations like the Magna Carta (1215), legislative enactments like the Declaration of Rights (English Bill of Rights) of 1689, various British statutes, and the procedural rules of the common law. Many of the American colonies had specified rights in legal codes. After the Declaration of Independence, American states customarily included bills of rights in their constitutions. The U.S. Constitution, written in 1787, faced a good deal of opposition because it lacked a bill of rights. Congress in 1789 proposed ten amendments, known as the Bill of Rights, that were ratified in 1791.

Prior to the Civil War the federal Bill of Rights was interpreted as securing liberty against only the national government. Because most legislation and court adjudication was conducted at the state level, Americans related civil rights more to state than federal governance. State constitutions protected citizens from being deprived of life, liberty, or property without due process of law; specified particular procedural rights in trials; guaranteed the right to assemble and petition the government for redress of grievances; and protected freedom of speech, the press, and religion. However, except for property rights, the courts did not aggressively protect civil liberties against infringing government action.

Discrimination in the civil rights of different groups was common. For example, the legal identity of married women was merged into that of their husbands. Married women could not sue in their own names to enforce contracts, and any money they earned or property they acquired belonged to their husbands. These old common-law rules were not perceived as violations of women's civil rights and remained in force until passage of the Married Women's Property and Married Women's Earnings Acts from the 1840s through the 1880s. In addition, most antebellum states also discriminated against African Americans. Some states did not allow blacks to testify against white people in court. No state permitted women to vote, and few enfranchised African Americans. Consequently neither group could serve on juries, which were selected from voting rolls. The Pacific Coast states applied the same rules against Chinese immigrants, who were also banned from purchasing land. Half the states allowed slavery despite constitutional provisions that no person could be deprived of liberty without due process of law. Those states interpreted laws against inciting slave resistance as limiting the rights of visitors or residents to criticize slavery. Southerners even called upon northern states to outlaw abolitionist societies.

Moreover, protection of nonproperty civil rights was often weak. Mormons, for example, were driven from New York, Illinois, and Missouri, and they finally fled to the wastes of Utah. While other aspects of their behavior contributed to their unpopularity, Mormon religious beliefs played a key role, and they had little legal recourse to defend their freedom of conscience. The government restricted freedom of speech and freedom of the press to promote Victorian ideas of morality.

Article IV of the U.S. Constitution specifies that "the citizens of each State shall be entitled to all privileges and immunities of citizens in the several States." The federal court decision in *Corfield v. Coryell* (1823), attempting to interpret this confusing clause, named a broad range of rights that states could not deny to citizens of another state. Some analysts argued that Article IV prevented states from depriving their own citizens of fundamental rights, but others insisted that it only guaranteed visitors from other states equal rights with a state's own cit-

izens. Most agreed that the article empowered courts to strike down inconsistent legislation or other government action but did not give Congress any power to protect those rights. In an instance that became a cause célèbre in the North, southern states violated Article IV by forbidding African American sailors from northern states from freely leaving their ships. When Massachusetts sent a lawyer to South Carolina to file a suit against one of these laws, he was forced to flee the state. There was nothing Congress could do.

Indeed, Congress passed laws in support of slavery that violated the Bill of Rights. The Fugitive Slave Act of 1850 required judges and commissioners to return accused runaways to the South without allowing them to present any evidence of their freedom. The Supreme Court overturned state laws protecting free black northerners from such legalized kidnapping.

The federal government restricted the civil liberties of white Americans during the Civil War. President Abraham Lincoln and Congress suspended the privilege of the writ of habeas corpus all over the country, subjecting people to temporary detention without trial. Strict rules limited expressions of support for the Confederacy in the occupied parts of the South, and Southerners were subjected to military trials until their states were restored to normal relations in the Union. The Supreme Court restrained these extensions of power somewhat but backed away from a direct challenge. The Confederate government was even more aggressive in suppressing dissent among Southern whites who opposed Confederate policies.

The abolition of slavery after the Civil War forced the federal government to define and protect civil rights through constitutional amendments and legislation. To protect African Americans and other racial minorities, Congress passed the Civil Rights Act of 1866, which required states to guarantee all persons the same rights that white people had—to make and enforce contracts, to sue, to give evidence, and to acquire and dispose of property and to guarantee all persons equal benefit of laws protecting personal security and property. The law also made all persons subject to the same criminal laws and punishments.

The Fourteenth Amendment, ratified in 1868, forbid states to abridge the rights of U.S. citizens; deprive any person of life, liberty, or property without due process of law; and deny any person equal protection of the laws. In 1875 Congress passed another Civil Rights Act that guaranteed all persons equal access to public institutions, schools, and public and private accommodations and transportation facilities regardless of race.

In the last decades of the nineteenth century the

Supreme Court interpreted the Fourteenth Amendment narrowly, limiting Congress's ability to protect civil rights and freeing the states to discriminate between races. In the *Civil Rights Cases* (1883) the Court ruled the Civil Rights Act of 1875 unconstitutional, holding that the Fourteenth Amendment banned only state discriminatory action, not that of private individuals. In *Plessy v. Ferguson* (1896) the Court ruled that state laws requiring racial segregation did not violate the Fourteenth Amendment. The Supreme Court also indicated in *Hurtado v. California* (1884) that the Fourteenth Amendment did not apply the federal Bill of Rights against the states, a position confirmed early in the twentieth century in *Twining v. New Jersey* (1908).

The Supreme Court, however, restricted state controls on private property, such as railroad rates, and limited the ability of states to regulate working conditions, hours, and wages, finding that such rules violate the freedom of workers and employers to enter contracts freely. Thus, with the exception of the Civil War era, property rights were protected more effectively than other civil rights throughout the nineteenth century.

See also **Bill of Rights; Constitutional Amendments,** *subentry on* **Thirteenth, Fourteenth, and Fifteenth Amendments; Constitutional Law; Courts, State and Federal; Emancipation; Fugitive Slave Laws; Law; Race Laws; Reconstruction,** *subentry on* **The South; Segregation,** *subentry on* **Segregation and Civil Rights; Slavery,** *subentry on* **Law of Slavery; States' Rights; Supreme Court; Voters and Voting; Women,** *subentry on* **Women's Rights.**

Bibliography

Benedict, Michael Les. "Victorian Moralism and Civil Liberty in the Nineteenth-Century United States." In *The Constitution, Law, and American Life.* Edited by Donald G. Nieman. Athens, Ga.: University of Georgia Press, 1992.

Hyman, Harold M., and William M. Wiecek. *Equal Justice under Law: Constitutional Development, 1835–1875.* New York: Harper and Row, 1982.

Nelson, William E. *The Fourteenth Amendment: From Political Principle to Judicial Doctrine.* Cambridge, Mass.: Harvard University Press, 1988.

Nieman, Donald G. *Promises to Keep: African-Americans and the Constitutional Order, 1776 to the Present.* New York: Oxford University Press, 1991.

Nye, Russel B. *Fettered Freedom: Civil Liberties and the Slavery Controversy, 1830–1860.* East Lansing: Michigan State College Press, 1949.

MICHAEL LES BENEDICT

CIVIL SERVICE REFORM   Civil service reform began in the mid–nineteenth century in response to two developments, the growing need for skilled administrators to carry on the increasingly complex functions of government and revulsion at the failure of earlier, less formal systems to provide sufficiently honest and qualified public employees. It replaced the so-called "spoils system," which filled government administrative positions through patronage, giving out public jobs as a reward for support in elections. The patronage system had been perfected by the followers of Andrew Jackson. One of Jackson's allies, New York senator William Marcy, gave the system its name in an 1832 speech when he observed, "To the victor belong the spoils of the enemy."

By the late nineteenth century the federal and state governments had assumed increasingly complex tasks. They administered agricultural research programs, factory inspection laws, educational institutions, statistical bureaus, and public health programs. Even many traditional government activities, such as the military, were more technically complex. In the Jacksonian era the spoils system seemed a democratic means to avoid elite bureaucratic control of civil offices. Reformers had defended the rotation of administrative officeholders as refreshing, although those who experienced rotation could be quite depressed, as described in the introduction to Nathaniel Hawthorne's *Scarlet Letter* (1850).

Support for the spoils system ebbed during the Civil War, when demands on the government grew astronomically. In the 1870s the American Social Science Association and the American Bar Association lobbied intensely for a civil service to foster more honest and efficient conduct in governmental affairs. In 1871 Congress established the short-lived U.S. Civil Service Commission, charged with designing a screening procedure for federal job applicants. Reformers continued to press for a permanent system through the 1870s, and agitation intensified in reaction to the corruption of the Ulysses S. Grant administration. Without legislative authorization, President Rutherford B. Hayes launched a voluntary civil service procedure. In 1881 two events accelerated the movement. Reformers in 1881 founded the National Civil Service Reform League, which gathered widespread support when President James Garfield was assassinated by a deranged office seeker.

In 1883 Congress passed the Pendleton Act, establishing the permanent Civil Service Commission. Middle-class reformers, such as the mugwumps in the Republican Party, made the expansion and protection of civil service a hallmark of their efforts to control political corruption and gain a place in public management for people like themselves. Young political leaders and academics in both parties, such as

CIVIL SERVICE REFORM.
OFFICE-SEEKER. "St. Jackson, can't you save us? Can't *you* give us something?"

Opposition to Civil Service Reform. Seekers of civil service jobs appeal to a statue of Andrew Jackson for a return to the spoils system that marked his tenure as president. Civil service reformers sought to eliminate government jobs based on political patronage and to offer them to the most qualified candidates, regardless of political party. Wood engraving of a drawing by Thomas Nast. *Harper's Weekly,* 1877. LIBRARY OF CONGRESS: PRINTS AND PHOTOGRAPHS DIVISION

Theodore Roosevelt and Woodrow Wilson, campaigned together for civil service reform. Since the Pendleton Act gave the president authority to expand the U.S. Civil Service at will and thereby protect current officeholders, each chief executive added positions to the system at the end of his term. In the short run this process protected his own appointees, but in the long run it expanded permanently the scope of civil service and the numbers it employed.

In 1887 Wilson, the future president who was then a political science professor at Bryn Mawr College, published a seminal article, "The Study of Administration," in *Political Science Quarterly.* Arguing that the nation focused exclusively on political innovation and failed to develop a science of administration, he urged elected officials to establish policy and position expert administrators to implement it. Since most public services were carried out by local and state governments, Wilson and other reformers concentrated on change at those levels. In 1894 they created the National Municipal League to fight for nonpartisan civil service in urban government.

The civil service movement was fueled by growing demands on government and the persistent problem of corruption. In addition the rise of professions controlled by the college-educated middle class spurred reform efforts. By the 1880s a host of specialized fields of study and work had emerged. These professionals called on the government to license them and give them control over the qualifications for related government jobs. Training for the professionals was entrusted to the universities. Professional societies, such as the American Public Health Association, proliferated and developed direct links to government. American civil service reformers faced the difficult dilemma of balancing democratic inclusiveness with calls for professional expertise that bordered on elitism. However, institutions of higher education multiplied, establishing a skilled public service in the United States without the exclusive entry process found in European bureaucracies. Rather than copy the English model and create a cadre of public servant generalists trained at a few elite institutions, the United States developed a civil service linked to specialized study in numerous public and private universities.

See also **Academic and Professional Societies; Diplomatic Corps; Government; Jacksonian Era; Politics,** *subentry on* **Corruption and Scandals; Reform, Political.**

Bibliography

Bledstein, Burton J. *The Culture of Professionalism: The Middle Class and the Development of Higher Education in America.* New York: Norton, 1976.

Hoogenboom, Ari. *Outlawing the Spoils: A History of the Civil Service Reform Movement 1865–1883.* Urbana: University of Illinois Press, 1961.

Jacoby, Henry. *The Bureaucratization of the World.* Translated from German by Eveline L. Kanes. Berkeley: University of California Press, 1973.

Rabin, Jack, and James S. Bowman, eds. *Politics and Administration: Woodrow Wilson and American Public Administration.* New York: Dekker, 1984.

Skowronek, Stephen. *Building a New American State: The Expansion of National Administrative Capacities, 1877–1920.* New York: Cambridge University Press, 1982.

Stillman, Richard J., II. *Preface to Public Administration: A Search for Themes and Direction.* New York: St. Martin's, 1991.

EDWARD C. LORENZ

CIVIL WAR

[This entry includes ten subentries:
**Causes of the Civil War
Battles and Combatants
Black Soldiers
Women on the Front
The Home Front in the North
The Home Front in the South
The West
Indian Territory
Consequences of the Civil War
Remembering the Civil War.**]

CAUSES OF THE CIVIL WAR

The Civil War's immediate cause was the chain reaction of events that began with Abraham Lincoln's election to the presidency in November 1860: the secession of seven states, the formation of a Confederate government, the North's refusal to countenance secession, the firing on Fort Sumter, and the departure of four more states after Lincoln called for seventy-five thousand volunteers to suppress the insurrection. The war's deeper cause, however, was more than thirty years of mounting sectional antagonism over slavery, during the last fifteen of which political strife reached fever pitch.

A clash in 1819–1820 over whether Congress would require Missouri to undertake gradual emancipation as a condition of its admission to the Union prefigured the conflict ahead. The crisis ended in compromise, but not before belligerent southerners had threatened secession. Sectional acrimony was renewed in the early 1830s with the launching in the north of a radical abolitionist movement that demanded immediate, uncompensated emancipation and advocated civil and political equality for African Americans. Widely reviled as unrealistic and fanatical, the movement converted only a relatively small number of free-state residents, many of them voteless blacks and women. Nevertheless, unrelenting abolitionist agitation prevented northerners from ignoring the contradiction between their democratic ideals and the stark reality of slavery. This helps explain the slow but steady growth of the more moderate type of antislavery exemplified by Lincoln, who spurned abolitionism but found slavery morally objectionable and wanted to prevent its expansion in hopes of putting it "in the course of ultimate extinction" (quoted in Basler, vol. 2, p. 461). Northerners also became increasingly resentful of the southern political elite—called "Slave Power"—whose highhanded and bullying tactics many northerners came to see as endangering republican government.

Slavery, already a central fact of southern life, became even more deeply entrenched during the three antebellum decades. Despite the ending of the overseas slave trade in 1808, the slave population multiplied rapidly: from 1.2 million in 1810 to nearly 4 million in 1860. Only a minority of southern white families owned slaves (25 percent in 1860), but nonslaveholders tenaciously supported the system as the only way to control the "barbaric" blacks. The South reacted vehemently to abolitionism, fearing that it would provoke bloody insurrections like Nat Turner's 1831 revolt in Virginia. Furthermore, southerners, always sensitive about their honor, were profoundly offended by abolitionist charges that slaveholders were un-Christian "man-stealers" and "traffickers in human flesh." In the 1830s southern whites largely abandoned the "necessary evil" justification of slavery and were proclaiming it to be a "positive good."

Bent on preserving slavery at all costs, southerners demanded that the North suppress the abolitionists, silenced critics at home, and created a political culture that encouraged politicians to outdo one another in proslavery militancy. As northern criticism escalated, so did southern defensiveness. Knowing they were out of step with the liberalism ascendant elsewhere in the Western world but bound to slavery by racism and economic self-interest, southerners felt increasingly beleaguered, developing by the 1850s what historian David Potter calls "the psychology of a garrison under siege" (*The Impending Crisis*, p. 475).

Slavery Politicized

Chastened by the Missouri crisis, mainstream politicians strove to banish the slavery issue from national politics. But intensifying sectional consciousness prevented its permanent exclusion. In 1844–1845, a heated contest erupted over Texas's annexation as a slave state. The ensuing war with Mexico (1846–1848) then thrust slavery to the very center of the national political stage. The critical event came on 8 August 1846, when Pennsylvania Congressman David Wilmot proposed barring slavery from any Mexican land the United States might acquire. The House passed the Wilmot Proviso, with all but four northerners voting "aye" and all but two southerners "nay." It never became law, since the Senate repeatedly rejected it. But it raised the fundamental question that bedeviled the country from then until secession: Should slavery be allowed to enter new areas or be forever confined to the fifteen existing slave states?

Southerners adamantly resisted any limitation on more slave territory, because it might lead to a time when there would be enough free states to abolish slavery by constitutional amendment. Some southerners, moreover, considered slavery's geographic expansion essential to its continued profitability. Some also feared that if the institution were hemmed in, the South would be overwhelmed—"Africanized," as they put it—by the burgeoning slave population. Finally, southerners found the Wilmot Proviso unbearably insulting, because it stigmatized their peculiar institution and would deny slaveholders equal rights in the territories. Seeing a vital point of honor at stake, many who did not expect slavery to take root in the West nonetheless condemned any legal restriction on it.

Northerners' determination to halt slavery's expansion also had several causes. Believing that the Constitution made slavery untouchable in the states, northerners had to turn to the territories as the main outlet for their antislavery impulses. Furthermore, the free labor ideology so popular in the North conceived the West as the place where the common man could achieve economic independence and upward mobility—but only if it was spared slavery's retrograde socioeconomic effects. Racism also played a part: many northerners wanted to reserve the territories exclusively for whites by barring all blacks, slave and free.

The Wilmot Proviso provoked not only political uproar but also fervent constitutional debate. Northern Whigs claimed that the Constitution empowered Congress to outlaw slavery in the territories; so did the Free-Soil Party (created in 1848 by dissident Whigs and Democrats) and subsequently the Republican Party. At the opposite extreme, numerous southerners embraced South Carolina Senator John C. Calhoun's argument that the territories were the "common property" of all the states and thus citizens of the southern states had the right to take slaves there without hindrance. Seeking middle ground on which to unite their party, northern Democrats advocated "popular sovereignty," under which Congress would let each territory's residents, acting through their territorial legislature, decide slavery's status. The hope—ultimately dashed by events—was that removing the locus of decision from Washington, D.C., to the far-distant West would eliminate the issue from national politics.

The Tumultuous 1850s

By 1850, controversy over slavery's fate in the Mexican Cession—an area of more than 500,000 square miles that Mexico surrendered at war's end—had reached crisis proportions. Southerners talked openly of dissolving the Union if the Wilmot Proviso was applied to the Cession or if the portion of it comprising California became a free state. After prolonged wrangling, Congress patched together the Compromise of 1850. It admitted California as the sixteenth free state, abolished the slave trade in the nation's capital, enacted a strict fugitive slave law, and settled a festering dispute over the Texas–New Mexico boundary in New Mexico's favor, with the federal government, in return, assuming the former Republic of Texas's public debt. Most important, slavery's fate in the rest of the Mexican Cession—the huge New Mexico and Utah territories—was to be decided by popular sovereignty. To gain bisectional support, however, the legislation left it ambiguous whether local residents could bar slavery forthwith, as northern

Democrats believed, or had to wait until the territory qualified for statehood, the position southerners espoused, because it would give slavery time to gain a firm foothold.

The Compromise of 1850 temporarily reduced sectional discord. Still, tensions persisted. The new fugitive slave law troubled northern consciences, and occasional rescues of runaways seized under the law outraged southerners. Harriet Beecher Stowe's powerful antislavery novel *Uncle Tom's Cabin*, published in 1851–1852, bred additional animosities. Then, in 1854, the Kansas-Nebraska Act renewed the struggle with unprecedented fury. Sponsored by Illinois Democratic Senator Stephen A. Douglas, it provided territorial government for the unorganized portion of the Louisiana Purchase, a vast area that Congress divided into Nebraska and Kansas territories. Slavery had been barred there by the Missouri Compromise, but powerful southern senators forced Douglas to include a provision repealing the prohibition and replacing it with the same ambiguous popular sovereignty language applied to New Mexico and Utah in 1850. This provoked impassioned northern opposition, which, in turn, heightened southern ardor for the bill. The Senate approved it, by a comfortable margin of thirty-seven to fourteen, but it met fierce resistance in the House, where many of the ninety-two northern Democrats deemed it suicidal to back a measure that so many of their constituents abhorred, especially with northern Whigs and Free Soilers in full cry against it. After a lengthy deadlock, the bill's proponents mustered just enough votes to enact it. Northern Democrats split down the middle (forty-four to forty-four), evidence of how party unity was succumbing to sectional pressures.

The political landscape was transformed following the Kansas-Nebraska Act. The Democrats, who in 1852 had elected Franklin Pierce as president in a landslide, carrying twenty-seven of thirty-one states, paid a steep price for it in the North, losing sixty-seven of their ninety-two northern House seats and control of all but two free-state legislatures. The Whig Party, increasingly viewed by the electorate as unresponsive, and with its northern and southern wings hopelessly estranged, had disappeared by 1856. Most significant, the Kansas imbroglio gave birth to the Republican Party, a coalition of antislavery former Whigs, Free Soilers, and Democratic opponents of the Kansas-Nebraska Act, which was committed to restoring the prohibition on slavery in Kansas and Nebraska and blocking its spread elsewhere in the national domain. Simultaneously, the Know-Nothing (American) Party burst on the scene in reaction against an unprecedented wave of immigration. (Nearly three million newcomers, many of them Irish

and German Catholics, arrived between 1845 and 1854.) Exploiting nativist fears, the party scored impressive victories in 1854 and 1855, in both North and South. Many Know-Nothing leaders hoped to shunt the slavery question aside and unite northerners and southerners around shared hostility to immigrants, particularly Catholics. This appealed to both Whiggish southerners cut adrift by their party's demise and conservative northern former Whigs concerned more about the Union than slavery. Most northern Know-Nothing voters, however, proved to be more fearful of slavery's expansion than of immigrants. Thus, when the party's 1856 national convention refused to endorse a territorial ban on slavery, much of its free-state support shifted to the Republicans.

The vitriolic 1856 presidential race, pitting the Democrat James Buchanan against the Republican John C. Frémont and Know-Nothing (and former president) Millard Fillmore, was punctuated by southern threats to secede if Frémont won. In Kansas, a no-holds-barred struggle between free soilers and proslavery forces—virtually a civil war in miniature—intensified sectional enmity, as did South Carolina Representative Preston Brooks's caning of vociferously antislavery Massachusetts Senator Charles Sumner. The Republicans' forceful advocacy of "free soil, free labor, free men" and their trenchant critique of the South's slavery-induced backwardness resonated strongly in the North. Frémont carried eleven of sixteen free states, a striking achievement for a party barely two years old. Buchanan emerged victorious, however, taking the other five free states and fourteen of fifteen slave states (Fillmore won Maryland). The Democrats also rebounded in northern House races, increasing their seats from twenty-five to fifty-three. Still, the party's northern base had eroded badly. If sectional conflict persisted, Republicans might well prevail in 1860—an ominous possibility, since countless southerners swore they would not live under a Republican president.

Developments during the next two years bolstered the Republicans at the northern Democrats' expense. In the *Dred Scott v. Sandford* decision (1857), a southern-dominated Supreme Court ruled that Congress could not outlaw slavery in the territories. The decision, which Republicans attributed to a Slave Power conspiracy, caused widespread northern indignation, while it reinforced southern determination not to yield on the territories. It also hurt northern Democrats by casting doubt on popular sovereignty's constitutionality. In 1858, they were further discredited when southern Democrats, backed by President Buchanan, tried to force Kansas's admission as a slave state under the Lecompton constitution, which had been approved in a fraudulent election against the wishes of a great majority of Kansas's population. The attempt failed, but it convinced many wavering free-state voters that the Democracy was captive to the Slave Power and only the Republicans stood for northern rights. These events, together with an economic depression that began in 1857, cost the party twenty-one northern House seats and allowed Republicans to make other important gains, many in former Democratic bastions like Pennsylvania.

The Final Crisis: Election, Secession, War

As the critical year 1860 opened, Democratic prospects of retaining the presidency were bleak. Even if the party carried every slave state, it still had to win thirty-two electoral votes in the North, a daunting task, given its declining fortunes there. Its chances fell to nil when it could agree on neither a candidate nor a platform. Douglas, the only Democrat who might have captured the requisite free-state electoral votes, was anathema to southern Democrats because he had helped lead the fight against Kansas's admission as a slave state. Their demand that the party renounce popular sovereignty in favor of federal legislation protecting slavery throughout the territories was equally anathema to Douglas and his partisans, since that would be fatal in the North. Two successive national conventions failed to break the impasse, many slave-state delegates bolting in protest both times. After the second walkout, northern Democrats proceeded to nominate Douglas on a popular sovereignty platform, while their erstwhile southern brethren chose Vice President John C. Breckinridge of Kentucky and endorsed a territorial slave code. The dissolution of the last *national* political party portended the dissolution of the Union six months later.

Meanwhile, a united Republican Party had nominated Lincoln, whose debates with Douglas in 1858 had brought him national attention. A moderate, he seemed best able to carry Pennsylvania, Indiana, and Illinois, critical states that Frémont had lost. While still emphasizing opposition to the extension of slavery and the domineering Slave Power, Republicans augmented their appeal by endorsing a higher tariff, free western homesteads, and federal aid for a transcontinental railroad. A fourth candidate, Senator John Bell from Tennessee, ran on the Constitutional Union ticket, which had been cobbled together by Union-loving conservatives in both sections but drew its support mostly from the Upper South.

The campaign unfolded in an extremely volatile atmosphere. Southerners, aghast over John Brown's antislavery raid on Harpers Ferry, Virginia (now West Virginia), in October 1859, and filled with fore-

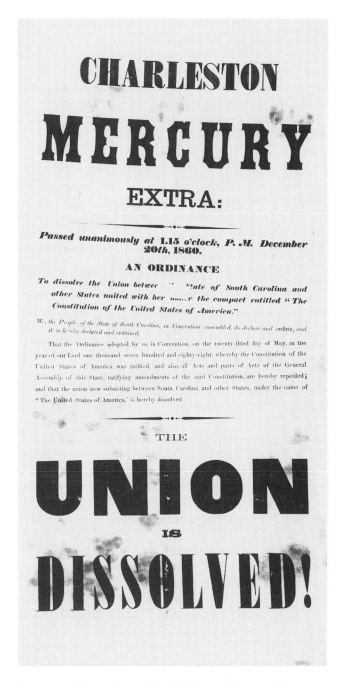

Secession. Poster from the *Charleston Mercury Extra* announcing that an ordinance to dissolve the Union was passed unanimously in South Carolina on 20 December 1860. LIBRARY OF CONGRESS: RARE BOOK STERN COLLECTION VOL. 1 NO. 7A

boding at the thought of a "Black Republican" president, vowed to secede should Lincoln triumph. Republicans dismissed these threats as mere bluster meant to intimidate northern voters. In the end, Lincoln received 55 percent of the North's popular vote and 180 of its 183 electoral votes—twenty-eight more than needed for victory. (Not on the ballot in most slave states, he took 39 percent of the popular vote nationwide.) Secessionist "fire-eaters" moved swiftly to dissolve the Union. South Carolina seceded on December 20, as did the other six Deep South states by February 1—more than a month before the new president's inauguration.

Why did Lincoln's election trigger the Deep South's secession? Southerners everywhere, their feelings rubbed raw by three decades of northern criticism, took the Republican victory as a shocking affront to their honor and also a potentially mortal threat to their social system. But most border states and Upper South leaders, recalling Lincoln's pledges not to interfere with slavery in the states, argued that secession was a last resort, to be undertaken only if he committed an overtly aggressive act. In the Deep South, however, where the percentage of slaves was much higher and the siege mentality more intense than elsewhere, the dominant elements rejected delay. They envisioned a Republican administration inspiring slave uprisings, encouraging John Brown–style raids, using federal patronage to erect a southern antislavery party, and otherwise undermining their whole system of racial subordination and control. Characteristic was a prominent South Carolina clergyman's warning that if the South submitted to Lincoln's election, "abolition preachers will be at hand to consummate the marriage of your daughters to black husbands" (McPherson, *The Battle Cry of Freedom*, p. 243). Such doomsday scenarios lent the drive for immediate independence—a kind of preemptive strike—special urgency from South Carolina to Texas.

Meanwhile, Congress struggled to find a Union-saving compromise. Attention centered on six constitutional amendments proposed by Kentucky Senator John J. Crittenden that would establish slavery in all territories below 36°30′ north latitude "now held, or hereafter acquired," forbid any future amendment abolishing it in the states, and furnish the South other safeguards. Northern Democrats and border state and Upper South congressmen embraced Crittenden's plan, but Republican opposition ensured its defeat. The Republicans' anticompromise stance reflected their conviction that secessionists were imperiling majority rule by trying to overturn the results of a democratic election, that they were traitors with whom it was wrong to make deals, and that granting them concessions under threat would lead to demands for further concessions—for example, acquisition of slaveholding Cuba—as a condition of continued loyalty. Ardent nationalists who venerated the Union and were fed up with constant threats to it, Republicans were determined to face down the Slave Power once and for all. Urging his party to

"stand firm" against slavery expansion, President-elect Lincoln wrote: "The tug has to come, & better now, than at any time hereafter" (quoted in Basler, vol. 4, p. 150).

It is unlikely that the Crittenden compromise would have been sufficient to entice the seceded states back into the Union. Given all the accumulated mistrust and fear, the only thing that might have appeased them was ironclad northern pledges to stop condemning slavery. As Howell Cobb of Georgia, an architect of the Compromise of 1850 who had turned secessionist, declared, "It is not the Constitution and laws that need amendment, but the hearts of the northern people." That, Cobb added, was "an impossibility" (Barney, *The Road to Secession*, p. 191). There was the rub: the North could no more abandon its belief in the superiority of a free-labor society than the South could abandon its commitment to slavery and the society based on it. The conflict had become irresolvable. All that remained was to transfer it from the political to the military arena. This the fledgling Confederacy did on 12 April 1861 when it opened fire on Fort Sumter in Charleston harbor, pummeling it into submission—but also sounding, albeit unknowingly, the death knell of both slavery and the 620,000 Americans whose lives the Civil War would claim.

See also **Abolition and Antislavery; Kansas-Nebraska Act; Slavery, Overview,** *and subentries on* **Slave Insurrections** *and* **Defense of Slavery; South, The,** *subentry on* **The South before the Civil War.**

Bibliography

Anbinder, Tyler Gregory. *Nativism and Slavery: The Northern Know Nothings and the Politics of the 1850's.* New York: Oxford University Press, 1992.

Barney, William L. *The Road to Secession: A New Perspective on the Old South.* New York: Praeger, 1972.

Basler, Roy, ed. *The Collected Works of Abraham Lincoln.* 9 vols. New Brunswick, N.J.: Rutgers University Press, 1953–1955.

Channing, Steven A. *Crisis of Fear: Secession in South Carolina.* New York: Simon and Schuster, 1970.

Cooper William J., Jr. *The South and the Politics of Slavery, 1828–1856.* Baton Rouge: Louisiana State University Press, 1978.

Crofts, Daniel W. *Reluctant Confederates: Upper South Unionists in the Secession Crisis.* Chapel Hill: University of North Carolina Press, 1989.

Fehrenbacher, Don E. *The Dred Scott Case: Its Significance in American Law and Politics.* New York: Oxford University Press, 1981.

Finkelman, Paul. *An Imperfect Union: Slavery, Federalism, and Comity.* Chapel Hill: University of North Carolina Press, 1981.

Foner, Eric. *Free Soil, Free Labor, Free Men: The Ideology of the Republican Party Before the Civil War.* New York: Oxford University Press, 1970.

Freehling, William W. *The Road to Disunion.* Vol. 1, *Secessionists at Bay, 1776–1854.* New York: Oxford University Press, 1990.

Gienapp, William E. *The Origins of the Republican Party, 1852–1856.* New York: Oxford University Press, 1987.

Holt, Michael F. *The Rise and Fall of the American Whig Party: Jacksonian Politics and the Onset of the Civil War.* New York: Oxford University Press, 1999.

Johannsen, Robert W. *Stephen A. Douglas.* New York: Oxford University Press, 1973.

McPherson, James M. *The Battle Cry of Freedom: The Civil War Era.* New York: Oxford University Press, 1988.

Nevins, Allan. *The Emergence of Lincoln.* 2 vols. New York: Scribners, 1950.

———. *The Ordeal of Union.* 2 vols. New York: Scribners, 1947.

Potter, David M. *The Impending Crisis, 1848–1861.* Completed and edited by Don E. Fehrenbacher. New York: Harper and Row, 1976.

Reid, Brian Holden. *The Origins of the American Civil War.* New York: Longman, 1996.

Stampp, Kenneth M. *America in 1857: A Nation on the Brink.* New York: Oxford University Press, 1990.

———. *And the War Came: The North and the Secession Crisis, 1860–1861.* Baton Rouge: Louisiana State University Press, 1950.

J. RONALD SPENCER

BATTLES AND COMBATANTS

Following the election of 1860, seven states in the Deep South, fearing the impact of the triumph of the Republican presidential candidate Abraham Lincoln upon the future of slavery and southern political interests, seceded from the Union (December 1860–February 1861) and formed the Confederate States of America with Jefferson Davis as president. Eight other slaveholding states decided to wait and see what the new administration in Washington would do. Anticipating the possibility of armed confrontation, especially in its efforts to gain control of federal installations, the Confederates began raising an army. When Lincoln refused to abandon additional coastal fortifications, the Confederates, under the command of Pierre G. T. Beauregard, attacked Fort Sumter, located off Charleston, South Carolina, on 12 April to head off a resupply effort. Immediately afterward, as Lincoln called for volunteers and mobilized state militia units to subdue an insurrection, four more states joined the Confederacy. Civil war had begun.

Clearly the Union held material advantages over the Confederacy that, if properly utilized, would go far to tilt the balance in its favor. Factories, foundries, and armories were far more numerous in the North. For every factory worker in the South, the North had a factory. Northern farms outproduced their Southern counterparts when it came to foodstuffs, and the Confederate rail network was far inferior to its Northern counterpart. Although the Union had more than three times the white population of the Confederacy (some 20 million to 6 million), neither side could count on the full support of all its people. The 3.5 million black slaves in the Confederacy freed up a far larger percentage of its adult white male population for military service than could the Union. However, it remained uncertain whether the slaves would remain in place should Union armies appear.

Superior numbers and resources by themselves rarely guarantee victory in war, and this was certainly the case between 1861 and 1865. The vast territorial expanse of the Confederacy offered a daunting challenge to an invading army, as did the tactical advantages that accrued to defending forces. Moreover, for the Union to declare victory, it would have to conquer the Confederacy. Should the Confederates manage to hang on long enough, war weariness might force the Union to abandon its struggle to reunify the nation. If the Confederates achieved several significant successes in the field, European nations, notably France and Great Britain, might well contemplate mediation or even intervention in support of Southern independence.

Between 1861 and 1864 the Union failed to develop an overall approach to waging war. Even Winfield Scott's so-called Anaconda Plan, which featured the use of a blockade and a drive to regain the Mississippi Valley, was designed for a limited conflict, expecting that once these objectives were achieved the Union armies would wait while the combination of resurgent unionism and dwindling supplies brought the Confederates to their senses. Whatever the merits of Scott's plan, a combination of political pressures and military necessity rendered the region between Washington, D.C., and Richmond, Virginia, a major battleground. Generals on both sides realized the symbolic as well as real gains that would accrue to the side that captured the enemy capital, so thrusts and feints followed by pitched battles became the order of the day in the East. Except for a short period between March and July 1862, no one general was in charge of Union operations in the region between the Appalachian Mountains and the Mississippi River until October 1863, and it proved virtually impossible to coordinate the movements of field armies under such conditions.

The Confederacy confronted obstacles to military victory. It had to disperse its limited resources to defend territory lest Yankee invaders uproot plantation-based slavery and occupy the very homes many Confederate soldiers were pledged to defend. Efforts by the government in Richmond to mobilize its resources through conscription (starting in April 1862) and impressment of slaves for use on military projects encountered resistance from those people who characterized such acts as smacking of tyranny. Measures to offer some deferments to large slaveholders sparked cries from nonslaveholders and small slaveholders that this was a rich man's war and a poor man's fight.

The Opening Campaigns

With the decisions of Virginia, North Carolina, Tennessee, and Arkansas to join the Confederacy, Davis's military prospects brightened. Their addition augmented Confederate manpower and resources considerably. Just as important was the military talent acquired by the Confederates from these new member states, notably Robert E. Lee, Thomas J. "Stonewall" Jackson, and Joseph E. Johnston. Union authorities moved quickly and forcefully to make sure that Maryland and Missouri did not add to the growing number of defections. Both sides kept a wary eye on Kentucky, which attempted to maintain its neutral status as Unionist and secessionist forces struggled for control. The Confederacy's decision to transfer its capital from Montgomery, Alabama, to Richmond, Virginia, a mere hundred miles south of Washington, D.C., prompted both sides to mobilize armies there in anticipation of a clash in northern Virginia. Finally, in July a Union army of some thirty-five thousand men under the command of Irvin McDowell ventured forth as newspaper headlines cheered them "On to Richmond!" They encountered Confederate defenders posted along Bull Run Creek, south and west of Centreville, Virginia, on 18 July. Three days later McDowell launched a major attack. Beauregard, reinforced by a contingent of Confederates under Johnston, who had eluded Union forces in the Shenandoah Valley and traveled by rail to Manassas Junction, checked the Yankee advance, and a Confederate counterattack that afternoon won the day. The rout of McDowell's army in front of hundreds of spectators who had come to witness the destruction of the rebel army proved highly embarrassing to the Lincoln administration, although the Confederates were so disorganized by their own victory that they failed to mount a serious pursuit.

The Union defeat at First Manassas (Bull Run) overshadowed triumphs elsewhere by Federal forces throughout the second half of 1861. A series of victories in western Virginia secured the foundation of what would eventually become West Virginia, and despite a setback at Wilson's Creek (10 August),

Union forces tightened their hold on Missouri. In September a precipitous Confederate thrust into Kentucky helped tilt that state against secession. A timely countermove by a then-obscure brigadier general, Ulysses S. Grant, seized Paducah at the confluence of the Tennessee and Ohio Rivers, placing the Yankees in an ideal position to exploit those waterways in an advance into the Confederate heartland by both land and water. Union amphibious operations against the Confederate coast established a major lodgement along South Carolina's Sea Islands in November.

Even in Virginia, Union prospects brightened in the aftermath of defeat. Lincoln replaced McDowell with George B. McClellan. Long known as a military man of great promise, McClellan brought to his new position a commitment to discipline, organization, and drill as well as an ability to inspire the soldiers of the newly christened Army of the Potomac. Chastened by what had happened at First Manassas, Lincoln let McClellan have his way, and impressed by the general's confidence and ability, Lincoln named him to replace Scott as general in chief when the old war horse stepped down in November 1861. After failing to exploit whatever opportunity they had gained at Manassas, the Confederates sat and waited to see what the new idol of the North would do.

It was not in Virginia, however, that Union armies scored several successes as 1862 began. While McClellan waited for the right opportunity to move, other generals advanced. A Yankee triumph at Mill Springs, Kentucky (19 January), opened the winter offensive. The following month Grant, aided by a river flotilla under the command of Andrew H. Foote, captured Forts Henry and Donelson, located along the banks of the Tennessee and Cumberland Rivers respectively, just south of the Kentucky-Tennessee border. The capitulation of the Confederate garrison at Fort Donelson on 16 February in response to Grant's demand for its "unconditional and immediate surrender" proved the largest single force captured to that date by any American army (some fifteen thousand men) and made Grant a national hero. Thus pierced, the Confederate defensive perimeter in Kentucky and much of Tennessee gave way, and Nashville fell to the advancing Federals. An effort to turn back the Yankees at Shiloh, Tennessee (6–7 April), resulted in the bloodiest single battle in American history to that date, but Grant's army survived a Confederate surprise attack and drove back the rebels with the assistance of reinforcements. By the beginning of June the Federal offensive had captured the crucial rail junction of Corinth, Mississippi (30 May), and Memphis, Tennessee (6 June). Another Union combined arms operation, featuring a naval contingent commanded by David G. Farragut, took New Orleans on 25 April. Union operations along the south Atlantic coast made inroads along the Carolinas, establishing additional bases for blockading operations.

Meanwhile McClellan, after much prodding and increasing impatience at his failure to attack Johnston in northern Virginia, transported his army to the banks of the James River preparatory to an advance against the Confederate capital of Richmond. Lincoln stripped him of the responsibilities of general in chief. The outnumbered Confederates skillfully held him in check for nearly a month at Yorktown, then gave way in May before the overwhelming Union buildup. Within a week the rebels abandoned Norfolk, in the process sacrificing the ironclad *Virginia* (previously known as the *Merrimack*), which only two months before (8–9 March) had threatened to make a shambles of the Union wooden warships guarding the mouth of the James. The *Virginia* was battled to a draw in an encounter with the Union ironclad gunboat *Monitor*, which mounted a revolving turret, the first clash of ironclad vessels. In an effort to divert forces earmarked for McClellan, the Confederate general Stonewall Jackson moved northward through the Shenandoah Valley, skillfully pinning down a far larger number of Union troops. While an attempt to head off McClellan at Seven Pines (31 May–1 June) proved abortive, it marked the appointment of Robert E. Lee to command the Army of Northern Virginia in place of the wounded Johnston. Within four weeks Lee launched a major counterattack that drove McClellan's army away from the outskirts of Richmond and revived sagging Confederate morale. When McClellan refused to renew the offensive, the new general in chief, Henry W. Halleck, directed him to transfer his army from the banks of the James to central Virginia and link up with a second army under John Pope in anticipation of an overland offensive that would threaten Richmond while shielding Washington.

Not content to rest on his laurels, Lee decided to hit Pope before the two Union armies united and dealt the Yankees a major blow at the Battle of Second Manassas (28–30 August). He then invaded Maryland in hopes of stirring up support for the Confederacy in the border states and to gain another battlefield triumph that might dampen Union morale and enhance the prospects for European recognition and possibly intervention. However, McClellan rallied the disorganized Federals and marched out to confront the Confederates. After the two sides battled each other to a standstill along Antietam Creek on 17 September in the bloodiest single day of combat during the entire conflict, Lee decided to return to Virginia. Lincoln seized upon the result to issue his preliminary Emancipation Proclamation, which promised to recognize as free all slaves held in Confederate-controlled areas on 1 January 1863. McClellan's failure to bring his opponent to battle over the next eight weeks eventually cost him his command in November 1862. Confederate efforts to take the offensive in Tennessee and Kentucky in September and October also fell short of success.

Gettysburg, Vicksburg, and Chattanooga

Three Union thrusts at the end of 1862 brought more bloodshed and little else. In Virginia, Ambrose Burnside's effort to turn Lee's flank gave way to the futile frontal assaults at Fredericksburg (13 December). Grant and his lieutenant, William T. Sherman, failed to capture Vicksburg, Mississippi, the major point along the Mississippi River still in rebel hands. The Union Army of the Cumberland under William S. Rosecrans wrestled Braxton Bragg's Confederate Army of Tennessee to a draw at Stones River, Tennessee (31 December 1862–2 January 1863). Union military fortunes did not improve immediately the following spring. While Grant struggled with ways to cross the Mississippi and strike Vicksburg and Rosecrans refitted his command, in Virginia haughty Joe Hooker, who replaced Burnside in January, was outfoxed and humiliated by Lee at Chancellorsville during the first week of May. The victory proved costly because it claimed Stonewall Jackson's life. Even as the armies in Virginia licked their wounds, word came that Grant, in a rather daring campaign that took full advantage of Union naval superiority on western waters, had crossed the Mississippi and was advancing inland against the Confederate forces in Mississippi with the goal of capturing Vicksburg. This time Grant was not to be denied. Instructing his men to live off the land, he fought and won five battles against a divided and confused enemy before laying siege to Vicksburg itself.

Rejecting requests to go west to counter Grant, Lee instead proposed a second invasion across the Potomac, this time with Pennsylvania as the destination. Although he argued that this move would take the war out of Virginia and damage Union morale, Lee may also have hoped that he would bring the foe to a decisive battle. In the campaign that followed, Confederate leadership fell short of previous performance, while the Army of the Potomac, led by George G. Meade, proved equal to the challenge when Lee attacked at Gettysburg (1–3 July). Repeated Confederate assaults bent but did not break the Union lines, and a final charge against the Yankee center on 3 July proved disastrous. Total losses for both sides for the three days of fighting exceeded fifty thousand killed, wounded, and missing. Holding off a half-hearted pursuit, Lee made his way back into Virginia by mid-July. Grant claimed Vicksburg and its garrison of some thirty thousand men on 4 July.

Throughout the rest of the summer and the fall the contending armies in Virginia maneuvered and marched but did not meet in a major battle. Portions of each army were sent westward in support of operations in Tennessee and Georgia. In June, Rosecrans finally commenced an advance against Bragg in Tennessee, driving the Confederates from the state without a major battle and seizing the critical rail junction of Chattanooga (9 September). To the north Burnside occupied Knoxville (2 September). Reinforced by two of Lee's divisions, Bragg struck back, defeating Rosecrans along Chickamauga Creek in northwest Georgia (19–20 September) and laying siege to the Federals at Chattanooga. Eventually he detached a column to threaten Burnside. In response, two corps from the Army of the Potomac moved by rail toward Chattanooga, as did elements of Grant's Army of the Tennessee. In October, Lincoln named Grant head of Union operations between the Appalachian Mountains and the Mississippi, and George H. Thomas replaced Rosecrans. Making his way to Chattanooga, Grant approved a plan to restore the Army of the Cumberland's supply line, united the arriving reinforcements, and on 23–25 November drove Bragg away. Several days later Burnside fended off an attack on Knoxville, securing Tennessee for the Union.

Waging Modern War

By the end of 1863 generals and soldiers alike had ample opportunity to learn the lessons offered by the battlefield. Rifled muskets and minié balls had helped to make infantry fire far more deadly than in Napoleonic times and had upset the traditional combined arms assaults of infantry, cavalry, and artillery. Mounted horsemen no longer charged across open fields, sabers in hand, ready to slice into defending infantry. Instead they usually fought dismounted and gathered information about the composition of enemy forces and their movements through reconnaissance. Pitched cavalry battles were the exception rather than the rule. Only one such engagement, on 3 July east of Gettysburg, was part of a larger battle plan. Artillery proved useful in pre-assault bombardments but not decisively so. Cannons were somewhat more valuable as defensive weapons, especially at

Devil's Den: A Fallen Confederate Soldier. Gettysburg, Pennsylvania, was in the main eastern theater of the Civil War. Photograph, Alexander Gardner, June–July 1863. LIBRARY OF CONGRESS

Gettysburg, Pennsylvania. The dedication of the Gettysburg battlefield took place in November 1863 when Abraham Lincoln gave his Gettysburg Address at the Soldiers' National Cemetery. LIBRARY OF CONGRESS

close range, although without supporting infantry artillerists and guns they were vulnerable to capture by determined attackers.

The infantry shouldered the burden of success or failure on the battlefield. Much has been made of how the extended effective range of the rifled musket over the flintlock muzzleloader rendered traditional tactics obsolete, but a combination of circumstances militated against such a dramatic transformation. On most battlefields a combination of woods, fields, and undulating terrain reduced the effective field of fire, and officers often ordered their men not to open fire until attackers were well within range. Attacks were deadly because of the increased accuracy of fire due to the combination of rifled barrels and bullets and the increase in rate of fire offered by the advent of the percussion cap. Defenders also were more adept at using cover, although entrenching did not become a daily habit until 1864. Although breech-loading rifles and multiple-round magazines were introduced rather gradually and sporadically, units armed with such weapons, especially cavalrymen with carbines, were even more difficult to dislodge.

Generals were slow to realize the impact of these changes on battlefield tactics, in part because every once in a while an old-fashioned frontal assault succeeded. For example, during the assault on Missionary Ridge east of Chattanooga on 25 November 1863,

due to a combination of circumstances what appeared to onlookers to be a nearly impregnable defensive position crumbled in the face of determined Union attackers. Defenders at Antietam, Fredericksburg, and Gettysburg took advantage of natural features in the terrain to shield themselves against enemy fire, and field fortifications were the exception rather than the rule. That changed in 1864 along with the pattern of a major battle followed by weeks of relative quiet. Instead of generals looking to manage a campaign toward achieving a single decisive battle, battlefield engagements were woven into the larger pattern of a campaign, following the models offered by Stonewall Jackson in the Shenandoah Valley and Grant at Vicksburg.

The nature of the armies also changed during the twelve months after Gettysburg and Vicksburg. Early in the war Lincoln had called for volunteers to serve two-year then three-year terms of service. Companies formed early in the war drew their personnel from the same communities, and a majority of regiments hailed from the same region of a state. The advent of conscription in 1863 and the expiration of enlistments had a major impact on the Union army. Draftees and conscripts were not bound by notions of community toward their fellow soldiers, impairing one source of unit cohesion. In May 1863 several fine regiments dissolved when the terms of two-year men

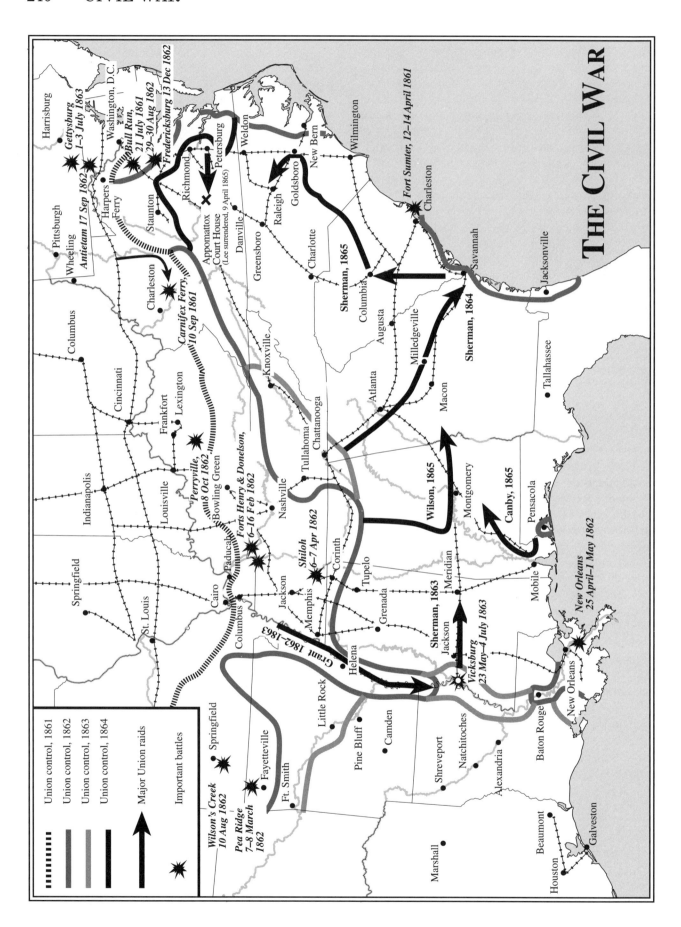

THE CIVIL WAR

Harrisburg

Gettysburg
1–3 July 1863

Washington, D.C.

Bull Run,
21 July 1861
29–30 Aug 1862

Fredericksburg 13 Dec 1862

Pittsburgh

Wheeling

Antietam 17 Sep 1862

Harpers Ferry

Staunton

Richmond

Petersburg

Appomattox Court House
(Lee surrendered, 9 April 1865)

Danville

Weldon

New Bern

Wilmington

Fort Sumter, 12–14 April 1861

Charleston

Charleston

Columbus

Carnifex Ferry,
10 Sep 1861

Greensboro

Raleigh

Goldsboro

Charlotte

Sherman, 1865

Columbia

Augusta

Savannah

Jacksonville

Cincinnati

Frankfort

Lexington

Knoxville

Milledgeville

Sherman, 1864

Tallahassee

Indianapolis

Perryville,
8 Oct 1862

Bowling Green

Forts Henry & Donelson,
6–16 Feb 1862

Nashville

Tullahoma

Chattanooga

Atlanta

Macon

Springfield

Louisville

Paducah

Shiloh
6–7 Apr 1862

Corinth

Tupelo

Wilson, 1865

Montgomery

Canby, 1865

Pensacola

St. Louis

Cairo

Columbus

Jackson

Memphis

Grenada

Meridian

Sherman, 1863

Mobile

New Orleans
25 April–1 May 1862

Grant, 1862–1863

Helena

Jackson

Vicksburg
23 May–4 July 1863

Little Rock

Pine Bluff

Camden

Shreveport

Natchitoches

Alexandria

Baton Rouge

New Orleans

Fayetteville

Ft. Smith

Marshall

Houston

Beaumont

Galveston

Union control, 1861
Union control, 1862
Union control, 1863
Union control, 1864

Major Union raids

Important battles

Wilson's Creek
10 Aug 1862

Springfield

Pea Ridge
7–8 March
1862

ended. Far more serious was what the Union army confronted in the spring of 1864, when the terms of the men who signed up for three years in the spring of 1861 expired. Approximately half of those men reenlisted in response to a combination of financial incentives, furloughs, and a desire to see things through to the end. Those soldiers who did not reenlist posed a problem during the spring campaigns, for many who were close to going home wanted to make sure that they did not make the journey in a wooden box and were thus loathe to expose themselves to fire. In such circumstances the enlistment of black soldiers, which commenced in earnest in 1863 following the issuance of the Emancipation Proclamation, bolstered Union numbers. As garrison troops, blacks were often deployed in the West, or they served on the front line, especially during the Petersburg campaign.

1864: Year of Decision

For all of the campaigns and battles that took place during the first two years of conflict, both sides knew that what happened in 1864 would be decisive. If the Confederacy could fend off Union offensives throughout the spring and summer, war-weary Northern voters might decide that it was time for a change and not reelect Lincoln. The president sought to achieve victory by naming Grant as general in chief with the rank of lieutenant general. Grant went east and established a satisfactory working relationship with the president, in part because he accepted the constraints placed upon him by political necessity, including the retention in independent commands of generals who owed their commissions to their political clout. Such appointments were counterproductive, for the failures of three of these generals, Benjamin F. Butler and Franz Sigel in Virginia and Nathaniel Banks in Louisiana, thwarted Grant's plans and added to the growing sense of frustration in the Northern electorate as the optimism of the spring gave way to the stalemate of the summer.

Grant brought order and system to Union strategic planning by calling for coordinated drives against key targets in the belief that under the pressure of simultaneous attacks the Confederates would give way somewhere. In Virginia he would supervise Meade's Army of the Potomac against Lee, while columns under Sigel in the Shenandoah and Butler along the James River were to threaten supply sources and Richmond, promising to cut off the Old Dominion from the Confederate heartland. Sherman would take Grant's place in the West and drive toward Atlanta, Georgia, which was defended by Joseph E. Johnston's Army of Tennessee. Grant's hopes for an operation

to take Mobile, Alabama, and use that city as the base of operations into the Confederate interior were dashed when Banks pursued an ill-fated thrust up the Red River in Louisiana.

What followed was not according to plan. Sigel met disaster at New Market (15 May), and Butler failed to endanger Richmond or its railroads. Freed from concerns about the security of his supply lines or Richmond, Lee concentrated on contesting Grant's efforts to push southward. In nearly two weeks of continuous and costly combat below the Rapidan and Rappahannock Rivers, neither general achieved decisive success in the Wilderness (5–7 May) or at Spotsylvania (8–19 May). Nevertheless, Grant, unlike his predecessors, refused to pull back and instead forced Lee to counter repeated marches against the rebel right. As June began, Grant, having pressed Lee to the outskirts of Richmond, sought to smash through the Confederate line at Cold Harbor, but the assault on 3 June turned into a bloody disaster. Its failure did not deter the Union commander, who decided to swing to his left once more, cross the James River, and attack Petersburg, a railroad junction due south of Richmond. Subordinates bungled the assault itself, however, and the opposing armies settled down to siege operations.

In an effort to break Grant's siege, Lee dispatched Jubal Early to strike northward through the Shenandoah Valley toward Washington. Grant shifted forces by water to reinforce the Union capital's defenses just in time, but during the next three weeks Early remained an irritating presence. A column from his command set fire to Chambersburg, Pennsylvania, after its citizens failed to meet the Confederates' demand for money (30 July). On the same day Grant failed to exploit the opportunity offered by the explosion of a mine under the Confederate lines near Petersburg. Such embarrassments underlined the stalemate in the East, leaving Northern voters unhappy with the Lincoln administration's prosecution of the war.

In Georgia, Sherman and Johnston played a cautious game of Confederate withdrawals and deliberate Union advances punctuated by an occasional battle. However, Davis grew impatient with Johnston's refusal to stand and offer battle, and as Union forces approached Atlanta he decided to replace Johnston with John Bell Hood. Living up to his reputation as a fighting general, Hood launched three attacks in a span of nine days (20–28 July), but he failed to turn back Sherman. The following siege was shorter, for Sherman severed Atlanta's rail links one at a time. At the end of August he swept around the Confederate left. When Hood followed, Sherman shifted back, and on 2 September, Union forces entered Atlanta. Coming on the heels of a Union naval triumph at Mobile Bay (5 August) and succeeded by Philip H. Sheridan's series of victories in the Shenandoah Valley in September and October, the fall of Atlanta restored the morale of voters in the North. Lincoln claimed victory in the fall presidential contest. Whatever hopes the Confederacy had of wearing down the Yankees had dissipated.

The Closing Campaigns

Frustrated by his inability to bring Hood to bay and aware of the vulnerability of his supply line, Sherman proposed that, after detaching sufficient force to keep an eye on the Confederates, he take the remainder of his command on a march into the interior of Georgia to destroy Confederate resources. He also hoped to intimidate Confederate civilians in an effort to erode the ability and the will of the Confederates to persist in their struggle for independence. A week after Lincoln's reelection, Sherman commenced his march through Georgia, and a month later he arrived at the outskirts of Savannah, which the Confederates evacuated on 20 December. Much was made of the activities and behavior of Sherman's men during this march, although that destruction paled in contrast with what came in South Carolina the following February. These exaggerated reports suggested the effectiveness of the march as psychological warfare. At the same time Hood moved north into Tennessee but failed to intercept withdrawing Union columns before launching a series of futile frontal assaults at Franklin, Tennessee (30 November). Dragging his bloodied and exhausted men north to Nashville, Hood was unable to do much more than watch as George H. Thomas organized his command and awaited a break in the weather. Thomas smashed into what remained of the Army of Tennessee on 15–16 December in a battle that effectively ended major Confederate operations between the Appalachians and the Mississippi River.

As the final year of the war opened, Grant looked to close out Confederate resistance in the Carolinas and Virginia. A Union amphibious assault took Fort Fisher, North Carolina, on 15–16 January, and five weeks later the federals entered Wilmington, closing off the last major Confederate port east of the Mississippi. Sherman advanced northward into South Carolina, occupying Columbia (17 February). That same day the Confederates evacuated Charleston. Johnston unsuccessfully attempted to check the Yankee advance at Bentonville, North Carolina (19–23 March).

Grant kept Lee pinned in place at Richmond and Petersburg, aware that with the arrival of spring and dry roads the Confederate commander might well seek to shake his grip. Lee did not disappoint him, but his effort to force Grant to contract his lines by striking close to the Union supply hub at City Point, Virginia, failed when the Yankees repulsed his attack

A Counsel of War. Ulysses S. Grant sits among his officers prior to the surrender of Confederate forces at Appomattox, Virginia, 1865. LIBRARY OF CONGRESS

on Fort Stedman (25 March). Four days later Grant commenced an operation to sever Lee's remaining supply links and contain any subsequent withdrawal. When Sheridan overran the Confederate defenders at Five Forks (1 April), Grant followed with an assault on Petersburg (2 April), compelling Lee to abandon Richmond and Petersburg (2–3 April). The Army of Virginia struggled westward in an attempt to unite with Johnston in North Carolina, but a vigorous Union pursuit blocked that effort, then hammered Lee's rear guard at Sayler's Creek (6 April). The next evening Grant called upon Lee to surrender. On 9 April, at Appomattox Court House, Lee, his dwindling army surrounded by Yankees, acceded to the inevitable and accepted the generous terms tendered by Grant.

Although the capitulation of the Army of Northern Virginia signaled to most observers that the war was substantially over, several Confederate armies remained in the field. John Wilkes Booth, a Confederate sympathizer and actor, assassinated Lincoln on 14 April, contributing to concerns that the war might simply be entering a new stage marked by guerrilla operations. Moved by such concerns, Sherman offered Johnston exceedingly lenient terms transcending his rightful exercise of military authority when the two men met at Durham Station, North Carolina, on 18 April. Authorities in Washington rejected the proposed agreement, and on 26 April, the same day Booth was cornered and killed, Johnston surrendered on the same terms Grant offered to Lee at Appomattox. On 10 May the new president, Andrew Johnson, declared that armed resistance was "virtually" at an end. That day Union cavalry caught up with and captured the fugitive Confederate president. Other surrenders followed, and President Johnson formally declared the insurrection at an end the following year.

See also **Army; Confederate States of America; Foreign Relations,** *subentry on* **The Civil War; Military Service; Military Technology; Militia, State; Naval Technology; Navy.**

Bibliography

Beringer, Richard E., Herman Hattaway, Archer Jones, and William N. Still Jr. *Why the South Lost the Civil War.* Athens, Ga.: University of Georgia Press, 1986.

Boritt, Gabor S., ed. *Why the Confederacy Lost.* New York: Oxford University Press, 1992.

Catton, Bruce. *The Centennial History of the Civil War.* 3 vols. Garden City, N.Y.: Doubleday, 1961–1965.

———. *Grant Moves South.* Boston: Little, Brown, 1960.

———. *Grant Takes Command.* Boston: Little, Brown, 1969.

Foote, Shelby. *The Civil War: A Narrative.* 3 vols. New York: Random House, 1958–1974.

Gallagher, Gary W. *The Confederate War.* Cambridge, Mass.: Harvard University Press, 1997.

Grimsley, Mark. *The Hard Hand of War: Union Military Policy toward Southern Civilians, 1861–1865.* Cambridge, U.K., and New York: Cambridge University Press, 1995.

Hattaway, Herman, and Archer Jones. *How the North Won: A Military History of the Civil War.* Urbana: University of Illinois Press, 1983.

McPherson, James M. *Battle Cry of Freedom: The Civil War Era.* New York: Oxford University Press, 1988.

———. *For Cause and Comrades.* New York: Oxford University Press, 1997.

McPherson, James M., and William J. Cooper Jr., eds. *Writing the Civil War: The Quest to Understand.* Columbia: University of South Carolina Press, 1998.

Parish, Peter J. *The American Civil War.* New York: Holmes and Meier, 1975.

Reed, Rowena. *Combined Operations in the Civil War.* Annapolis, Md.: Naval Institute Press, 1978.

Simpson, Brooks D. *America's Civil War.* Wheeling, Ill.: Harlan Davidson, 1996.

Thomas, Emory M. *Robert E. Lee: A Biography.* New York: Norton, 1995.

Williams, T. Harry. *Lincoln and His Generals.* New York: Knopf, 1952.

Woodworth, Steven E. *Davis and Lee at War.* Lawrence: University Press of Kansas, 1995.

———. *Jefferson Davis and His Generals.* Lawrence: University Press of Kansas, 1990.

BROOKS D. SIMPSON

BLACK SOLDIERS

The Union and the Confederacy grappled over the issue of what role, if any, African Americans were to play during the war. Both anticipated the employment of blacks as laborers, but the decision to employ them as soldiers was complex and was reached slowly. During 1861 and 1862 Tennessee and Louisiana were the first to enroll companies of free blacks, on a temporary basis, and other Confederate states seriously considered it. Several blacks fought unofficially throughout the war, but not until March 1865 did the Confederate Congress approve black enrollment as Confederate States Colored Troops. It planned recruitment campaigns for Alabama, Florida, Mississippi, South Carolina, and Virginia, where several African Confederates drilled before crowds in Richmond. Although a handful saw combat, these desperate measures came too late.

Northerners generally opposed using black soldiers, but in view of declining white enlistments, the unpopularity of conscription, and continued rebel resistance, Congress authorized black federal employment under the Second Confiscation and Militia Act of 17 July 1862. This allowed President Abraham Lincoln to receive them into military service, yet he

Black Union Soldiers. Black regiments made a courageous contribution to the war effort. More than 200,000 black men served as soldiers and sailors, some earning the Congressional Medal of Honor. Drawing by Thomas Nast. *Harper's Weekly,* 14 March 1863. LIBRARY OF CONGRESS: PRINTS AND PHOTOGRAPHS DIVISION

did not formally accept black soldiers until after the issuance of his Emancipation Proclamation.

Blacks served unofficially long before federal authorization. The volunteer Black Brigade of Cincinnati served for three weeks during 1862, in response to a threatened attack against the city. After the Union army took control of New Orleans, three black regiments were organized there as the First, Second, and Third Louisiana Native Guards (later the Seventy-third, Seventy-fourth, and Seventy-fifth U.S. Colored Infantry) by the fall of 1862. The First South Carolina Infantry was officially organized in January 1863, but three of its companies were involved in military maneuvers as early as October 1862 and eventually became the Thirty-third U.S. Colored Infantry. Recruiters mustered the First Kansas Colored Infantry (later the Seventy-ninth U.S. Colored Infantry) into service in January 1863, but it had become the first black regiment in combat when it drove off a Confederate force at the battle of Island Mound, Missouri, on 27 October 1862. The North's first black regiment, the Fifty-fourth Massachusetts Volunteer Infantry, was organized during the period January–May 1863.

States organized the first black regiments, and some, including the Twenty-ninth Connecticut Volunteer Infantry, the Sixth and Seventh Louisiana In-

fantries, the Fifth Massachusetts Cavalry, and the Fifty-fourth and Fifty-fifth Massachusetts Volunteer Infantries, retained their state designations. Federalized units bore a variety of designations: Chasseurs d'Africa, Corps d'Afrique, U.S. Colored Heavy Artillery (USCHA), U.S. Colored Cavalry (USCC), U.S. Colored Infantry, U.S. Colored Troops, U.S. Colored Volunteers. The Bureau of Colored Troops formally designated black regiments as U.S. Colored Troops (USCT).

Northern black leaders such as Frederick Douglass successfully recruited black regiments. Although blacks eagerly embraced the role of citizen-soldier, the typical black soldier's first allegiance was to the nation, not his state. Many patriotically took up arms for racial revenge, freedom, and equal rights even though America had long denied their rights. To become a soldier meant citizenship and validation of black manhood; it offered social and civic identity. With rifles in hand and authorization to destroy white Confederates portrayed as traitors, blacks sought a nation without slavery.

Blacks' military service was fraught with danger on the South's killing fields. They risked brutal reprisals, including execution, enslavement, or ill treatment. Confederates massacred 262 black soldiers at Fort Pillow, Tennessee, in April 1864. Three months later rebels murdered several surrendering blacks after the Battle of the Crater in Petersburg, Virginia. The Lincoln administration enacted a retaliation order but rarely implemented it. Although they had little chance for promotion as commissioned officers, nearly ninety blacks were appointed officers. Among the highest-ranking officers were Major Martin Delany of the 104th and 110th USCT, Major Francis E. Dumas of the 74th USCT, and Lieutenant Colonel Alexander T. Augusta, surgeon for the 7th USCT. White commanders of black regiments often encountered prejudice, ostracism, or even violent wrath from other commanders. The Confederacy announced a policy of treating these white officers as criminals subject to execution "for inciting servile insurrections." Colonel Robert Gould Shaw, killed during a failed assault on Fort Wagner, South Carolina, in 1863, was buried under a pile of his fallen soldiers of the Fifty-fourth Massachusetts.

Black troops were often used as menial laborers or garrison troops because most whites did not believe they would make competent soldiers. Pay discrimination was another problem. White privates received $13 a month with $3 deducted for clothing; blacks received $10 a month, less a $3 clothing deduction. They and their white officers protested this discrimination; some units refused to accept discriminatory pay, and a few mutinied. In June 1864 and finally in March 1865, Congress enacted equal pay for all soldiers. Some black regiments had not been paid for the previous two years.

Black soldiers fought heroically in many battles, including Port Hudson, Louisiana (May 1863); Milliken's Bend, Louisiana (June 1863); Olustee, Florida (February 1864); the Petersburg campaign (June 1864–April 1865); Nashville, Tennessee (December 1864); and Appomattox, Virginia (April 1865). Twenty-two received the Congressional Medal of Honor, thirteen were awarded medals for gallantry at the Battle of New Market Heights (Chaffin's Farm), Virginia (September 1864), and two black sailors received medals for their service. Among the first Union regiments to enter the Confederate capital of Richmond were the 5th Massachusetts Cavalry and the 22th, 36th, 38th, and 118th U.S. Colored Troops, all part of the 25th Corps. This organization, created in December 1864, was the largest single concentration of African American troops in the history of the American military; its thirty-three regiments totaled fourteen thousand soldiers.

By war's end over 200,000 free blacks and slaves had served as soldiers (including 30,000 sailors)—10 percent of all Union troops—in 175 regiments (145 infantry, 22 artillery, 7 cavalry, 1 engineer). Nearly 93,000 enlisted from the South. Of 68,000 black casualties, 37,700 were listed as having died: 290 as prisoners of war, 3,000 in battle, and the remainder from sickness, or from wounds received in action, or were listed as missing (and presumed dead). Blacks participated in 449 engagements, including 250 skirmishes and 39 battles. The National Park Service has developed an electronic database of 235,000 names of U.S. Colored Troops and their white officers. African American soldiers had far more at stake in the war's outcome than any other group. Their military participation, one of the war's great turning points, symbolized a new birth of freedom in the United States.

See also **African Americans**, *subentry on* **Blacks in the Military; Confederate States of America.**

Bibliography

Berlin, Ira, Joseph Reidy, and Leslie S. Rowland, eds. *Freedom: A Documentary History of Emancipation 1861–1867. Selected from the Holdings of the National Archives of the United States.* Series 2: *The Black Military Experience.* New York: Cambridge University Press, 1982.

Burchard, Peter. *One Gallant Rush: Robert Gould Shaw and His Brave Black Regiment.* New York: St. Martin's, 1965.

Cornish, Dudley Taylor. *The Sable Arm: Negro Troops in the Union Army, 1861–1865.* New York: Norton, 1966.

Glatthaar, Joseph T. *Forged in Battle: The Civil War Alliance of Black Soldiers and White Officers.* New York: Free Press, 1990.

Regimental Flag of the 22d Regiment, U.S. Colored Troops. The motto at the top of the image, "Sic semper tyrannis," is the motto of the state of Virginia, "Thus ever to tyrants." Colored and created by David Bustill Bowser and published between 1863 and 1870. LIBRARY OF CONGRESS

Hollandsworth, James G., Jr. *The Louisiana Native Guards: The Black Military Experience During the Civil War.* Baton Rouge: Louisiana State University Press, 1995.

Jordan, Ervin L., Jr. *Black Confederates and Afro-Yankees in Civil War Virginia.* Charlottesville: University Press of Virginia, 1995.

McPherson, James M. *The Negro's Civil War: How American Negroes Felt and Acted During the War for the Union.* Urbana: University of Illinois Press, 1982.

Quarles, Benjamin. *The Negro in the Civil War.* Boston: Little, Brown, 1953.

Redkey, Edwin, ed. *A Grand Army of Black Men: Letters from African American Soldiers in the Union Army, 1861–1865.* New York: Cambridge University Press, 1993.

Williams, George Washington. *A History of the Negro Troops in the War of the Rebellion 1861–1865.* New York: Harper, 1888.

ERVIN L. JORDAN JR.

WOMEN ON THE FRONT

After the firing on Fort Sumter in 1861, most American women strongly identified with and supported either the Union or the Confederate side in the Civil War, but their involvement in the conflict was usually less direct than that of men. A priority of almost all slave women was to do whatever they could to advance the cause of emancipation. Women's activities were important to the war effort of both sides and to the destruction of slavery. Women themselves were affected by the war. Some began to think and to act in new ways. Whether or not these changes were significant or long lasting is a matter of debate among historians.

Support Work

From the beginning of the war, women contributed their time and labor to provide supplies for Union and Confederate soldiers. Working in thousands of local aid societies, they sewed clothing and blankets, knitted socks, and gathered food and medical supplies. Some women raised money for soldiers' aid by organizing fairs and entertainments. The largest fund-raising fairs, held in Northern cities, raised over $4 million. The efforts of women's aid societies in the Union were increasingly controlled and coordinated by the Sanitary Commission. In the Confederacy women's relief work was primarily done early in the war, before shortages of supplies and disruptions of wartime brought it to an end. Volunteer work allowed women to show their patriotism and perform essential services without challenging traditional notions about gender roles.

Some of women's work was less traditional. When women went to work as army nurses, providing medical care for sick and wounded men, they were doing something that was unconventional for women and controversial. Public opinion questioned the propriety of such work for "ladies." Most army surgeons initially objected to women nurses, saying that they were untrained for and unsuited to the task. But the need for their services outweighed the objections. By 1863, after many women nurses had demonstrated their competence, resentment against them lessened.

Women who took up medical care were drawn from all ranks of society and included many slaves and free blacks as well as whites. Some worked as volunteers; others were paid. A few women, such as Phoebe Pember of the Chimborazo army hospital in Richmond, Virginia, were administrators. Some, like Annie Wittenmyer of Iowa, who developed special-diet kitchens, brought much-needed reforms to military hospitals. Although most women worked in general hospitals far from the fighting, some women, like the Union nurses Clara Barton and Mary Ann Bickerdyke, preferred to work close to the battlefields.

Some adventurous women found opportunities during the war to be spies, couriers, scouts, and smugglers. Among those who spied for the Confederates were Rose O'Neal Greenhow, a popular Washington, D.C., woman who knew influential politicians, and Belle Boyd, who provided information to General Thomas "Stonewall" Jackson during the

Clara Barton (1821–1912). Barton tirelessly nursed soldiers on the battlefronts, such as at Antietam and Fredericksburg, risking her life to help the wounded and dying. She founded the American Red Cross in 1882. LIBRARY OF CONGRESS

Shenandoah Valley campaign. Elizabeth Van Lew, regarded by her Richmond neighbors as a harmless eccentric, was an effective Union spy who helped Federal prisoners escape and supplied information to General Ulysses S. Grant during the latter part of the war. Slave women surreptitiously aided Union soldiers in the South. Many white women tried to smuggle contraband goods into the Confederacy and carried mail and messages across the lines. Those who faced the gravest dangers were slave women and their children who fled from masters to make their way to freedom within Union lines.

An estimated 400 women disguised themselves as men and enlisted in Union and Confederate armies. Some were discovered and discharged; others served for years without being detected. The most famous case was Sarah Edmonds, who served as Private Franklin Thompson in the Second Michigan Infantry and revealed her wartime identity many years later in order to claim a soldier's pension.

New Responsibilities

Perhaps the most important contribution women made during the war years was keeping their families fed and clothed and keeping their societies going. Maintaining the role of provider was enormously difficult, since massive numbers of men were serving in the military, approximately 620,000 men died, and much of the South was devastated by warfare and economic chaos. Many women in the South became refugees. In Indian Territory, women and their dependents suffered and often fled from their homes because of guerrilla warfare, looting and pillaging by raiders, and violent conflict between rival pro-Union and pro-Confederate Indians.

In both the North and the South women took over unaccustomed tasks. Some managed farms and plantations and tried to direct and discipline slaves. Economic necessity drove many women to take paying jobs. Many became teachers, and others found clerical jobs in government offices, a new type of employment for women. Hundreds of women worked in the Treasury, War, and Post Office Departments of the Union and the Confederacy. Thousands of women made clothing and tents for the military, while others held dangerous jobs in munitions factories, where some died in explosions and fires.

Women and the War

The actions of women, in addition to being supportive of their societies and families, had a large impact on important developments of the war years. Slave women, for example, helped destroy the institution of slavery and shape the meaning of freedom when they defied the commands of masters or mistresses and refused to work as before. Many escaped to Union lines and insisted on remaining there despite the hostility and, at times, abusive treatment they faced in contraband camps.

Many white women in the South by 1864 and 1865 were disenchanted with the Confederate cause and no longer willing to give the war effort priority over their own needs. Poor women, whose circumstances were desperate, joined in bread riots and encouraged their men to leave the army. Some elite Southern women pursued pleasure and gaiety, rejecting calls for further sacrifice. Several historians see these developments as contributing to a general loss of will among Confederates to continue the war.

The long-term effects of the war were different for various groups of women. Northern middle-class women gained the most. The expanded roles of wartime continued in their postwar world, giving them broader public and professional opportunities. After the war Southern white women largely returned to traditional roles in a conservative society. Black women made important but limited gains. Few achieved full autonomy and freedom in the nineteenth century. The lives of Native American women in Indian Territory became more precarious and impoverished because of the Civil War. Unlike black women, they could not view their difficulties in a context of hope for the future.

See also **Women,** *subentries on* **Woman as Image and Icon, Women's Labor.**

Bibliography

Campbell, Edward D. C., Jr., and Kym S. Rice, eds. *A Woman's War: Southern Women, Civil War, and the Confederate Legacy.* Richmond and Charlottesville: Museum of the Confederacy and University Press of Virginia, 1996.

Faust, Drew Gilpin. *Mothers of Invention: Women of the Slaveholding South in the American Civil War.* Chapel Hill: University of North Carolina Press, 1996.

Leonard, Elizabeth D. *Yankee Women: Gender Battles in the Civil War.* New York: Norton, 1994.

Massey, Mary Elizabeth. *Bonnet Brigades.* New York: Knopf, 1966. Reprinted as *Women in the Civil War.* Lincoln: University of Nebraska Press, 1994.

Rable, George C. *Civil Wars: Women and the Crisis of Southern Nationalism.* Urbana: University of Illinois Press, 1989.

SHARON HANNUM SEAGER

THE HOME FRONT IN THE NORTH

Between Abraham Lincoln's election in 1860 and the fall of Fort Sumter the following April, Americans in both the North and the South slowly came to realize that civil war was upon them. But patriotic pundits in both regions insisted that it would be only a matter of weeks before their enemy was vanquished. Northerners were particularly confident that the upstart Confederacy would soon prove no match for the Union's superior economic and military might. Of course the American Civil War actually lasted four years and cost over 600,000 military deaths. In the process the North went through several distinct stages of development as the Union learned how to fight such an enormous conflict on the battlefield while supporting the war effort at home.

Emergency Mobilization

After the fall of Fort Sumter, Northerners overwhelmingly rejected all talk of conciliation and compromise, and enthusiastic patriotism ruled the day. Towns and cities across the North answered President Lincoln's initial call for volunteers with a series of makeshift responses. Volunteers rushed to join local companies and regiments, anxious to share in the glory before the Confederacy collapsed. Quartermasters depleted existing stores of military matériel and turned to private suppliers. Northern women formed thousands of Soldiers' Aid Societies to sew clothing, roll bandages, and otherwise support the volunteers. Whole towns turned out to watch the first recruits leave for the war.

For most Northerners the war was fought at a safe distance. Eventually photographs of bloated corpses, published lists of fallen soldiers, and the grim reality of crowded military hospitals tarnished the luster of any martial displays. For those living in the border states, the line between battlefield and home front was less clear. Only days after Fort Sumter's fall a mob attacked Massachusetts troops passing through Baltimore on their way to Washington. Soon Union troops occupied the strategically vital city, and vocal secessionists faced incarceration. Elsewhere in the Northern border states, the Union army used its military might to solidify political control. Confederate invasions brought the war to otherwise quiet Northern communities in Kentucky, Maryland, and southern Pennsylvania, and for much of the conflict, Missourians suffered through a bloody guerrilla war. Nonetheless, for most Northerners the battlefield remained a distant abstraction.

An Organized War

By the end of the summer of 1861, the initial frenzy had given way to a more organized structure, with most Northerners weaving war-related activities into their daily routines. Once the torrent of volunteers slowed to a trickle, local, state, and federal governments began experimenting with inducements to meet the rising demands. Volunteers earned bounties provided by governments at all levels, sometimes supplemented with private funds. Many communities made special provisions for the families of volunteers, thus easing the worries of many soldiers. In 1862 Congress approved the drafting of state militias. The Enrollment Act (1863) established a Federal conscription apparatus that required military-age men to enroll for drafts to be determined by state and local quotas. Still, recruitment depended on local efforts and monetary inducements. The Federal drafts yielded only about 46,000 conscripts who served and another 118,000 paid substitutes. But the threat of a draft energized local recruiting efforts, enabling the more populous Union to maintain superior numbers in the field.

By the winter of 1861 the Union had settled into a mixed system of private contracting and limited Federal manufacturing to supply its huge army. The demands on heavy industry were fairly modest, and the bulk of expenditures were for uniforms, tents, food, animals, and the like. At first this military supply system suffered from inefficiency and corruption, prompting angry attacks on "shoddy" merchandise and claims that a handful of entrepreneurs were getting rich off the nation's despair. But soon the quartermaster general had solved the worst problems, and Union war contracting proceeded with remarkable efficiency. By the close of 1862 the Northern economy boomed. The employment rate was high, but the overheated economy created inflation. Thus, despite the general prosperity, many workers experienced declining real wages, a situation that helped to trigger numerous labor disputes.

Thousands of women and men developed a web of voluntary societies to provide the troops with comfort and supplies both at home and in the field. Many of these were small-scale local efforts dominated by female volunteers following paths established by antebellum reform groups. Other institutions, most notably the U.S. Sanitary Commission and the U.S. Christian Commission, were national bodies with hundreds of local auxiliaries. Fund-raising fairs for branches of the Sanitary Commission soon dotted the calendar.

Politics and Wartime Legislation

With Southern Democrats out of Congress, Republicans had unanticipated political strength in Washington. The war provided the ideal justification for a series of bills expanding the federal role in economic affairs. The Legal Tender Act (February 1862) authorized the Treasury to issue notes, known as greenbacks, that were not backed by specie. The following year the National Banking Act established a new national system of banks. Congress also enacted a protective tariff in 1861 and a limited federal income tax near the end of the war. In the meantime Congress enacted other pieces of the 1860 Republican platform, including the Homestead Act (1862), providing for the distribution of western lands; the Pacific Railroad Bill (1862); and the Morrill Act (1862).

The most controversial wartime initiative was not a piece of legislation but Lincoln's Emancipation Proclamation. Presented as a war measure in the fall of 1862, the official proclamation on 1 January 1863 asserted the freedom of all slaves in Confederate hands. Thus Lincoln turned the Union army into an army of liberation while leaving slave owners and their slaves in Union territory at least temporarily unaffected. Maryland waited until the summer of 1864 to abolish slavery, and Delaware, with only 2,000 slaves, refused all attempts at wartime emancipation. The Thirteenth Amendment, abolishing slavery, did not pass both houses of Congress until early 1865, and even then Delaware, New Jersey, and Kentucky initially refused to ratify it.

White abolitionists and African Americans celebrated the Emancipation Proclamation and rallied to the Union cause with new vigor. Others, wanting no part of a war for emancipation, objected to the expanded war aims. Despite the controversy, the Emancipation Proclamation helped open the door to the use of black volunteers in the Union army. As black regiments assembled and went off to war, African American communities formed their own societies to encourage enlistment and support the men in uniform. Clearly the presence of black troops had an impact on the attitudes of many whites both at home and on the battlefield, but other whites continued to resist any notion of racial equality.

By the close of 1862 the North's patriotic consensus had begun to fragment under the weight of military frustrations and controversial Republican legislation. The Democrats divided between War Democrats, who supported the war but decried the Republican legislation, and antiwar Copperheads. The Emancipation Proclamation gave the Democrats a crucial rallying point, and in the 1862 elections they enjoyed substantial gains, particularly in Democratic strongholds in the Midwest. Over the next two years Copperhead dissent grew more vocal, with Clement Vallandigham of Ohio serving as a fiery spokesman until his arrest and exile in mid-1863. In the meantime partisans on both sides organized to distribute political pamphlets.

While political leaders debated constitutional issues ranging from the suspension of the writ of habeas corpus to the National Banking Act, the rank and file took to the streets to protest the draft and emancipation. The worst wartime home-front violence occurred in New York City in July 1863. A largely Irish mob rioted against the Federal draft but quickly turned on black homes and institutions. Other violent episodes across the North revealed the intertwined tensions surrounding race, class, and ethnicity ignited by the draft but on occasion provoked by labor conflicts.

Peace and Beyond

As the election of 1864 approached, Lincoln fully expected to lose to the Democratic challenger, General George McClellan. General Ulysses S. Grant's tremendous losses in northern Virginia that spring seemed almost more than a democracy could endure, and by fall the Army of the Potomac had stalled outside of Petersburg, Virginia. Fortunately for the president, Atlanta fell to General William T. Sherman's army only two months before Election Day, providing a surge of enthusiasm that helped bring a Republican victory and buying Grant and Sherman the time they needed to bring the war to a close. The following April the Confederacy crumbled, producing a series of wild celebrations across the North. But the festivities did not last long. Less than a week after Confederate general Robert E. Lee's surrender, news of Lincoln's assassination threw the North into weeks of public mourning.

Lincoln's death dramatized the transition from the military conflict to the political battles to come. The war of course left the South radically transformed, but what of the North? The war had both direct and indirect effects on the Northern economy. Certainly many individual businesses profited from war contracts, but few sectors of the economy experienced long-term shifts because of those demands. Several pieces of wartime legislation—particularly those concerned with banking, greenbacks, tariffs and taxation, and western lands—had a lasting effect on the federal government's role in the economy, suggesting the importance of the Republican ascendancy as much as the effect of the war itself. The public and private institutions created to support the war effort contributed to the nineteenth century's larger pattern of bureaucratization and centralization, but such effects were consistently offset by the persistent power of localism and tradition. Certainly the greatest impact was felt by those men who fought and by those at home who lost loved ones. African Americans and white women earned some recognition for their contributions to the war effort, but this public approval was certainly not translated into civic equality in the decades to come. The war did expand the presence of women in some professions, most notably nursing, and the volunteer experiences of some women helped shape their postwar activism.

See also **Abolition and Antislavery; Emancipation; Military Service.**

Bibliography

Clinton, Catherine, and Nina Silber, eds. *Divided Houses: Gender and the Civil War.* New York: Oxford University Press, 1992.

Engerman, Stanley, and J. Matthew Gallman. "The Civil War Economy: A Modern View." In *On the Road to Total War: The American Civil War and the German Wars of Unification, 1861–1871,* edited by Stig Förster and Jörg Nagler. New York: Cambridge University Press, 1997.

Gallman, J. Matthew. *The North Fights the Civil War: The Home Front.* Chicago: Ivan Dee, 1994.

Paludan, Phillip Shaw. *"A People's Contest": The Union and the Civil War, 1861–1865.* New York: Harper and Row, 1988.

Vinovskis, Maris, ed. *Toward a Social History of the American Civil War: Exploratory Essays.* New York: Cambridge University Press, 1990.

J. MATTHEW GALLMAN

THE HOME FRONT IN THE SOUTH

Tales of military drama dominate Civil War historiography. Only recently have historians shifted their perspectives away from the battlefield toward the effects of the Civil War on society. For the South the twin themes of localism and class dominate the narrative of the war years. Early in the Confederacy white social unity generally prevailed, but as the war continued many white Southerners came to feel that their society had fundamentally failed them. In the midst of wartime dislocation, the contrast between the lifestyles of the planter-lawyer "aristocrats" and the common folks reveals the divisions in white Confederate society.

After the war an older South Carolinian planter precisely defined his relationship to the wider world: "I go first for Greenville, then for Greenville District, then for the up-country, then for South Carolina, then for the South, then for the United States, and after that I don't go for anything" (DeForest, *A Union Officer in the Reconstruction,* p. 177). First and foremost Southerners understood the unfolding drama through the lenses of their own local societies. However, the local societies and communities varied enormously. The aggregate of communities that formed the Confederacy was far from a monolith. The social geography of the antebellum South provides the essential backdrop to the developments of the war years.

Southern Society on the Eve of War

The Confederacy was overwhelmingly rural, with only one city of more than fifty thousand. About half (54.4 percent) of all farms were between twenty and one hundred acres, and less than 1 percent had a thousand or more acres. Smallholders controlled the fate of the South, as their labor would win or lose the war.

The South's situation was complicated by slavery. Overall the Confederacy had a free-to-slave ratio of 3 to 2, but that deviated significantly among the eleven states. Free blacks, few in number, were concentrated in Virginia and North Carolina. Less than 30 percent of all free families in the South held slaves, and "planter" and "slaveholder" were hardly synonyms. Of the 306,300 slaveholders, 45 percent held fewer than five slaves, and 85 percent held fewer than twenty slaves, the number generally considered enough to be a planter. Moreover, as with the size of farms, great deviations in slaveholding existed among the Confederate states and within each state. Alabama (17.9 percent), Mississippi (18.6 percent), and especially South Carolina (19.9 percent) had the largest share of slaveholders with more than twenty slaves.

The Depredations of War

Bare statistics cannot do justice to the chaos inflicted upon the Southern people by the war. Citizens of the Confederacy suffered from the physical effects of being in a battle zone, the mass migration of refugees away from the front lines, and the deprivations of bushwhackers, Union raids, and Confederate foraging details. The population was subject to the burdens of impressment, conscription, and taxes levied at national, state, and county levels. Not surprisingly, some Southerners found their loyalty to the Confederacy challenged, a tendency that at best produced noncooperation and at worst desertion, outright obstruction, and armed insurrection. Significant numbers of whites in Virginia and Tennessee fought for the United States and against the Confederacy.

Almost from the outset of the war the South suffered from shortages in every category of goods, and prices escalated wildly. Especially serious was the lack of foodstuffs, clothing, footwear, and medicines. These shortages were the product of various factors, including the Union blockade, the cessation of trade with the North, the military nature of the Southern economy, the South's rudimentary transportation

War Transforms a Town. A deserted street in Chattanooga, Tennessee, during the Civil War attests to the deprivations that supporters of the Confederacy endured. LIBRARY OF CONGRESS

system, the overmobilization of Southern white manpower, the desertion of slave labor and the consequent fall in civilian production, the wearing out of irreplaceable tools and implements, impressment for the military, and a growing reluctance to plant at all lest the crop be impressed by the Confederacy or destroyed by the Union. The prices of all goods increased dramatically when they were available at all. Coffee and sugar all but disappeared from the Confederacy within a year of the outbreak of war. The lack of salt was a particular problem as it restricted the ability to cure meat. In May 1861 a sack of salt cost sixty-five cents. By October it cost seven dollars, an almost elevenfold increase in five months. According to Eugene M. Lerner's figures the general price index of the Confederacy rose by only 27 percent in that period.

Desertion

Deprivation had serious repercussions for both the military and civilian populations of the Confederacy, demonstrating the intimate connection between home front and battlefronts. One of the harshest ironies was that soldiers who had gone to war to protect their kinsfolk quickly realized they could best fulfill that obligation by returning home. Thousands of ordinary citizens wrote to politicians and military leaders begging them to release their menfolk from service. When their entreaties went unanswered, many implored their menfolk to desert.

Approximately one in eight Confederate soldiers deserted, compared with the Union rate of one in ten.

More significant is the rate of capture and return. Of Union deserters, 40 percent were returned to the colors. Only 20 percent of Confederate deserters suffered a similar fate because the Southern civilian population was more likely to shelter those who were simply returning home to fulfill the obligations to their families that the authorities had neglected. Furthermore the patterns of desertion reinforce the notion that soldiers fought for their communities more than for the Confederacy. As the armies of the Confederacy retreated from state to state at the end of the war, desertion rates of soldiers from the abandoned states rose dramatically.

Government Actions

What the Confederacy provided for its citizens was wholly negative. It demanded their lives and goods and gave little in return. Impressment in particular drove a mighty wedge through Southern society, causing sharp class divisions and disloyalty to the Confederacy. Farmers stopped producing above a subsistence level or hoarded what surplus they did produce. By the end of the war the official prices for impressed goods were less than a third of the market prices. The furious railing of newspapers against "speculators" and "extortioners" did nothing for those forced to starve for want of food or those who forbore from planting because their crops would be seized.

The Confederate government took no significant measures to alleviate the distress of its citizens. It continued to call for greater sacrifices from people who had reached the limits of their endurance, fomenting disaffection, disloyalty, desertion, and defeatism. Many ordinary Southerners despaired and wished for the end of the war regardless of the consequences to their homeland. In contrast to the inaction of the national government, state and local authorities were much more successful in helping the needy and protecting the citizenry from the demands of Confederate officials. Peter Wallenstein's study of Georgia's Civil War finances illustrates that, as the Confederate government assumed the burden of military expenditure, the state treasury poured money into civilian welfare relief. By 1864 just over half of the state's expenditures went into relief efforts. While such efforts were never enough, they were tangible proof to the people that something could be done and that the Confederacy was not doing it.

What the Confederacy did do appeared to be heavily biased in favor of those already well off. Common people felt that the burdens of the war, financial as well as physical, fell disproportionately on their shoulders. Although the wife of the rich man was just as likely to be left a widow and his children orphans if he served, men of wealth and influence had opportunities to evade service that were not available to lesser men. They could purchase substitutes who were conscripted in their places or secure exempted employment for themselves and their sons. Similarly, although the proportion of total revenue raised in the Confederacy by taxation was relatively low, when combined with the burdens of impressment and rampant inflation, taxes bore down most heavily on those least able to pay. Government measures hit the poor hardest of all, as the loss of a family's sole horse was infinitely worse than the loss of one horse to a planter with ten such animals and field hands besides. Even more damaging to the image of the Confederate government was the furor raised over the infamous Twenty Negro Law. Passed in October 1862 to combat the very real fears of a slave insurrection in the aftermath of the first Emancipation Proclamation, this act permitted the exemption from military service of one white man for every twenty or more slaves on a plantation. Although it only affected a small number of Southerners, it quickly became a powerful symbol to the common people that they were fighting the war on behalf of the planters.

Wartime Social Changes

A class schism developed in the Confederacy as a result of the war. Common Southerners felt that the government was ignoring their plight and exploiting them to defend an institution from which they were purposefully excluded: slavery. The poor were reduced to a subsistence level, while the rich had to forgo ice cream and wear calico dresses. The greatest burden of the war fell upon Southern women, and they personify the ultimate failure of paternalism that characterized Confederate society. No group was more ardently partisan for the Confederacy, but no group was more abjectly war weary. The trend in civilian morale was steadily downward as women had to fend for themselves and their families unaided, worry or grieve for their menfolk, and in unprecedented numbers seek employment. No other group was asked to give up so much, and no other group offered as much to the Southern cause as did women. But Confederate authorities never adequately addressed their needs.

White Southern women, more than any other group, had been socialized in the doctrines of paternalism. Inherent in that creed was a promise of reciprocal obligation that led them to expect that their sacrifices would be rewarded and their needs met. Failure to fulfill this divinely ordained responsibility contributed to the belief that God was punishing the South for its sins. Many Southerners attributed the defeat of the Confederacy to a divine judgment on its lack of concern for its people.

A revolution cannot be sustained on the field of battle alone. It needs to carry with it the hearts and minds of all of its participants. The Confederacy proved incapable of winning either the military or the civilian war. The most telling example of this, bread riots conducted mainly by disgruntled women, shook Southern cities in 1863. Beginning in late 1862 in Greenville, Alabama, they spread into Georgia, South Carolina, North Carolina, Virginia, and even Texas through the subsequent months.

African Americans during the War

The story of free blacks in the Civil War is complicated, particularly because free African Americans fought on and aided both sides in the conflict. Their loyalties often depended upon their positions within the local society, but their participation was sometimes coerced. Before the Civil War free blacks were a small minority often allowed some leeway by a white society unafraid of their privileges. During the war, however, they came under great scrutiny. The majority concentrated on survival, and indeed black independent farmers and artisans persevered despite white opposition during the hostilities.

Some Southern states disallowed antebellum free blacks from military service altogether. While early in the war some permitted "colored men" to muster into local or state militia units, no Southern state allowed African Americans to serve as regular soldiers.

Some light-skinned free blacks became "honorary white men," enlisted, and fought for the Confederacy. Free blacks in cities like New Orleans, Mobile, Savannah, Richmond, and Charleston served in fire companies and were impressed into labor battalions, as were slaves, to dig ditches and such. Families of free blacks were not eligible for even the meager aid furnished to whites by state and local governments.

The war changed the nature of race relations, and even slavery changed during the war. As white men left with the army, the racial balance of power shifted dramatically in rural areas and on plantations. Fear of slave insurrections pervaded white Confederate society. In many areas slaves negotiated more freedom and autonomy for themselves and their families as the war progressed. African Americans understood, perhaps better than whites, that the success of the Confederacy meant the perpetuation of slavery.

Although the war was hard on the African American families whose men were forced into Confederate service, it also benefited them by increasing their autonomy. Freedom for slaves did not await the Emancipation Proclamation but started to take hold with the initiation of the Civil War. Especially in more remote rural areas, as institutional control and close personal supervision of slaves lessened, slave families attained greater personal freedom. While masters were away at war slaves took advantage of the situation, expanding their own garden spots and traditional spaces around their cabins. Black women spent more time with their own families and in their own homes. Parental authority, especially that of the father, increased when the white boss was away at the front.

The extent of the changed nature of race relations and slavery is evident in one of the last desperate acts of the Confederate Congress, which provided for the arming of slaves as Confederate soldiers. Whether a consequence of actions taken by the Confederacy, the Union, or the slaves themselves, the Civil War ended slavery and that was the greatest change in Southern society. More than anything else, this development encapsulates the profound effect of the war on the Southern home front.

See also **African Americans,** *subentry on* **Blacks in the Military; Emancipation; Slavery; South, The,** *subentry on* **The South before the Civil War.**

Bibliography

Burton, Orville Vernon. *In My Father's House Are Many Mansions: Family and Community in Edgefield, South Carolina.* Chapel Hill: University of North Carolina Press, 1985.

De Forest, John William. *A Union Officer in the Reconstruction.* Edited by James H. Croushore and David M. Potter. New Haven, Conn.: Yale University Press, 1948.

Lerner, Eugene M. "Money, Prices, and Wages in the Confederacy, 1861–1865." In *The Economic Impact of the American Civil War.* 2d ed. Edited by Ralph Andreano. Cambridge, Mass.: Schenkman, 1967.

Rable, George C. *Civil Wars: Women and the Crisis of Southern Nationalism.* Urbana: University of Illinois Press, 1989.

Ramsdell, Charles W. *Behind the Lines in the Southern Confederacy.* Baton Rouge: University of Louisiana Press, 1977.

Vinovskis, Maris A. "Have Social Historians Lost the Civil War? Some Preliminary Demographic Speculations." *Journal of American History* 76 (June 1989): 34–58.

Wallenstein, Peter. *From Slave South to New South: Public Policy in Nineteenth-Century Georgia.* Chapel Hill: University of North Carolina Press, 1987.

ORVILLE VERNON BURTON
IAN BINNINGTON

THE WEST

The Civil War affected the West in different ways. People in large sections of the region viewed the war from afar, and it had little impact on their daily lives.

Military Activity

Those near the Kansas-Missouri border lived in constant fear of raids by William Quantrill and his pro-Confederate Missouri bushwhackers. These raids reached their height in 1863, when Quantrill's forces struck Lawrence, Kansas, and left 150 men dead and many more wounded.

While minor skirmishes took place in other parts of the West, the most notable military engagements occurred at Glorieta Pass in New Mexico and at Westport, Missouri. The Confederate general Henry Hopkins Sibley moved north along the Rio Grande in March 1862, intending to capture gold supplies in Colorado with which to purchase military equipment on the international market. His movement was stopped at Glorieta Pass, just east of Santa Fe, by a small Union force commanded by General Edward Canby that was augmented by volunteer units from the New Mexico and Colorado Territories. The battle has sometimes been referred to as the "Gettysburg of the West," because it ended Confederate ambitions to extend to the Pacific Ocean.

In 1864 General Sterling Price invaded Missouri with twelve thousand Confederate troops, hoping to increase his strength with volunteers from pro-Southern counties in the northeastern part of the state and to make a last-ditch effort to detach Missouri from the Union. Met by General Samuel Curtis and a Union force of volunteers from Kansas and Colorado at Westport, just south of Kansas City, the Confederates encountered defeat in late October. For the next several weeks Union troops pursued the demoralized Confederates into Indian Territory. Desertions finally reduced Price's force to three thousand men, most of whom returned to their homes rather than continue fighting.

Attitudes toward the War

While the West was overwhelmingly pro-Union during the entire war, pockets of Southern sympathy did exist, and some western men returned to the South to fight for the Confederate cause. Arizona consisted of only a few small American settlements at the time but was awarded a delegate in the Confederate Congress because of its empathy for the South. Other areas of Southern sympathy were southern California, Montana, and Idaho. Indeed, Unionists in the latter two territories claimed that a large portion of the Confederate army defeated at Pea Ridge, Arkansas, in 1862 fled to Montana and Idaho, where the men engaged in mining the recently discovered gold fields. Men from southern California who fought for the Confederacy and returned to the West Coast at the end of the war were welcomed back and often given financial assistance to reestablish themselves.

Both the Mormons of Utah and the Mexican population in New Mexico remained aloof from the conflict. The Mormons were wary of the Republican Party because of its criticism of polygamy, and they feared Republican interference in their religious affairs. Aware of this attitude, President Abraham Lincoln appointed Brigham Young to the territorial governorship and adopted a hands-off policy to keep the territory peaceful. In New Mexico the Mexican population regarded the war as an affair that did not concern them, and they were apprehensive about the future of peonage should Republicans retain control of the federal government. As the Mexicans expected, the U.S. government informed territorial officials in 1866 that the Thirteenth Amendment abolished peonage as well as black slavery.

The West continued to attract immigrants from the eastern states during the war. An unknown number of them were draft dodgers and deserters from the North because the federal government did not enforce the draft laws in the territories. One westerner branded Julesburg, Colorado, as a city of "bounty jumpers, secesh, deserters [and] people fleeing the draft" (Berwanger, *The West and Reconstruction,* 1981). Most individuals who went west during wartime, even if they were not avoiding military service, opposed the Union war effort. Republican appointees to territorial offices worried that the new influx might make the West a Democratic enclave, but their fears were lessened by the inflow of large numbers of Republicans in the postwar years.

Indian-White Relations

The removal of regular army troops from western forts to eastern battlefields allowed a number of American Indian conflicts to escalate into bloody conflagrations. Relations between the Sioux and whites in Minnesota had been strained ever since the creation of the territory in 1849, and the rapid increase in the white population during the 1850s escalated tension. By 1862 the Indians, who were starving from lack of promised federal support, saw the frequent changes in military personnel at the forts. Taking advantage of the situation, they attacked New Ulm in August 1862 and within a week killed more than seven hundred settlers. Led by Henry Hastings Sibley (no relation to the Confederate general mentioned above), Minnesota militia tracked down the Sioux and by October had taken some fifteen hundred prisoners. General John Pope, who had recently arrived from his disastrous defeat at the Second Battle of Bull Run (Second Manassas) to take command of military forces in the Minnesota area, favored executing three hundred of the prisoners. Lincoln's intervention stayed such action, yet thirty-eight Sioux prisoners were hanged shortly after Christmas in 1862. Small outbreaks occurred for another year.

Increasing immigration along the front range of the Rocky Mountains became a major concern for the Cheyennes, Arapahos, and other tribes who followed the buffalo in their yearly migrations on the Plains. By 1864 these tribes were attacking wagon trains and stage routes and creating major concern about the safety of white settlements in Colorado. Talks between Indians and white leaders in Colorado seemed to be making progress when Colonel J. M. Chivington and undisciplined troops of the First Colorado Volunteers attacked and killed some two hundred warriors and five hundred women and children at their Sand Creek encampment in southeastern Colorado. The massacre caused such an outcry in the East that Congress investigated the matter, condemned Chivington, and forced the resignation of Colorado's territorial governor. This did not satisfy the territory's various Indians tribes, who retaliated in January 1865 against Julesberg, Colorado, killing eighteen soldiers and civilians. For the next year they continued to raid military and civilian settlements between the Arkansas and Platte Rivers.

See also **American Indians,** *subentry on* **Wars and Warfare; Kansas; Minnesota; Missouri; West, The.**

Bibliography

Berwanger, Eugene H. *The Frontier against Slavery: Western Anti-Negro Prejudice and the Slavery Extension Controversy.* Urbana: University of Illinois Press, 1967.

———. *The West and Reconstruction*. Urbana: University of Illinois Press, 1981.

Castel, Albert. *Civil War Kansas: Reaping the Whirlwind*. Lawrence: University Press of Kansas, 1997.

Josephy, Alvin M., Jr. *The Civil War in the American West*. New York: Knopf, 1991.

McGinnis, Ralph Y., and Calvin N. Smith, eds. *Abraham Lincoln and the Western Territories*. Chicago: Nelson-Hall, 1993.

Roske, Ralph J. *Everyman's Eden: A History of California*. New York: Macmillan, 1968.

EUGENE H. BERWANGER

INDIAN TERRITORY

In 1861 Native Americans living in the Indian Territory (now Oklahoma) were swept into the American Civil War. In the 1830s the southern states had successfully urged the federal government to remove the Cherokees, Creeks, Choctaws, Chickasaws, and Seminoles (also known as the Five Civilized Tribes) from their southeastern homelands to the Indian Territory. Nevertheless, within months after the firing on Fort Sumter, all of these tribes signed treaties of alliance with the Confederate States of America. Several exigencies pushed the southeastern Indians to the Confederate side. First, the Indian Territory was situated between the Confederate states of Arkansas and Texas, so an alliance with the Union might have prompted retaliation by the South. Second, the United States had recently antagonized the southeastern tribal governments by renouncing treaty promises and annuity obligations. Third, some native leaders feared that Republican leaders intended to open tribal lands to white settlers. Finally, many southeastern Indians shared a common culture and economic interests with Southern whites. In particular, a number of wealthy territory Indians owned slaves.

In negotiating agreements with the tribes Confederate officials guaranteed the territorial title and the right of self-determination of each tribe and offered financial support and representation in the Confederate government. In exchange tribal leaders promised to support Southern interests and engage in hostilities against the Union. Hundreds of Indians, many of whom were conscripted into the conflict by their tribal governments, fought on the side of the Confederacy. Some leaders, like Stand Watie (Cherokee) and Tandy Walker (Choctaw), organized separate Confederate Indian companies.

The Choctaws and Chickasaws were generally unified in their support of the Confederacy. The Cherokees, however, were bitterly divided by the war. In October 1861 the Cherokee government signed a treaty with the Confederacy even though John Ross, their principal chief, argued for neutrality. Ross's kinsmen responded by enlisting in the U.S. Army. In 1862 Union forces invaded the Indian Territory, captured Ross, and forced him into exile. In Ross's absence, Stand Watie claimed the office of principal chief, forcing those who opposed the Confederate alliance into hiding. Alliance with the Confederacy also splintered the Creek government. In November 1861 Opothle Yohola, a prominent Creek leader, led several thousand Creek and Seminole dissenters out of the Indian Territory into Union-controlled Kansas. They were pursued and attacked by a group of Confederate-allied Cherokees, Choctaws, and Chickasaws.

The Civil War brought terrible economic and social disruption to the Indian Territory. The Union and Confederate armies, guerrillas aligned with each side, and opportunistic looters swarmed over the territory during the war. The conflict caused food shortages in the territory, forced thousands of Indians into exile in Kansas, and shut down native schools, courts, and legislatures. To make matters worse, when the war ended the United States severely punished the southeastern tribes for their Confederate alliance, forcing the tribes to cede tribal territory and issue railroad rights-of-way. These rail passages soon opened the Indian Territory to non-Indian settlers and eventually undermined the national sovereignty of the Five Civilized Tribes.

See also **American Indians,** *subentry on* **Indian Removal; American Indian Societies,** *subentry on* **The Southeast; Indian Territory; Reconstruction,** *subentry on* **The West; Slavery,** *subentry on* **Indian Slaveholding.**

Bibliography

McLoughlin, William G. *After the Trail of Tears: The Cherokees' Struggle for Sovereignty, 1839–1880*. Chapel Hill: University of North Carolina Press, 1993.

Prucha, Francis Paul. *The Great Father: The United States Government and the American Indians*. Lincoln: University of Nebraska Press, 1984.

TIM ALAN GARRISON

CONSEQUENCES OF THE CIVIL WAR

Northern victory in the Civil War shaped subsequent American political and economic development in the United States in several major ways. Union armies abolished slavery and eliminated secession as a political possibility. Relations between state and society were fundamentally altered as the federal government became an active supporter of national expansion and development.

Secession, Sectionalism, and National Unity

First and most immediately, Northern victory settled the constitutional issue of whether or not a state could secede from the Union. In the decades following the Revolutionary War, two very different regional political economies had emerged in the North and the South. Their developmental trajectories were destined to follow different paths, regardless of whether or not the Civil War was fought or which side won. Given the increasing and unavoidable hostility between the rapidly expanding free-labor economy of the North and the plantation slavery in the South, the South was certain to have tested, at some point or another, the bonds that tied the region to an increasingly dominant and threatening North.

The right of secession had been debated for decades, but neither the Constitution nor the records of the Philadelphia convention were of much use in answering the question. Moreover, had the U.S. Supreme Court had an occasion to condemn secession before South Carolina left the Union in December 1860, the seceding states almost certainly would have ignored the Court. Later ratifying the new political reality forged by Union armies, the Supreme Court played but a minor role in settling what may have been the most important single constitutional issue ever raised in American history.

Slavery, Race, and Emancipation

The war began as a Northern effort to suppress Southern secession but became a crusade against slavery. The Emancipation Proclamation declared free all slaves in all Confederate territory unoccupied by Union armies as of 1 January 1863. This presidential order freed most slaves in the South when Confederate armies surrendered in April 1865, but in loyal border states and territory conquered by the Union early in the war, many blacks remained in bondage. In these areas, the institution was abolished by the adoption of the Thirteenth Amendment in December 1865, which prohibited slavery throughout the United States. These measures granted freedmen the right of free movement and freedom of contract but little else. The enrollment of Southern black men in the Union military and their subsequent allegiance to the Republican Party identified freedmen as the only large faction in Southern politics loyal to the Union. The Fifteenth Amendment, supporting the role of freedmen as the Republican arm of Reconstruction, gave them the right to vote.

In the decades following the Compromise of 1877, however, southern white Democrats denied voting rights to most blacks by adopting literacy tests, poll taxes, and other suffrage qualifications that more or less effectively discriminated on the basis of race. The disenfranchisement of southern blacks followed decades of white vigilante activity in many parts of the region. Beginning with the transformation of

Carpetbaggers and Scalawags. Tensions ran high during Reconstruction, prompting this warning that lynchings would be enforced by the Ku Klux Klan. *Independent Monitor*, Tuscaloosa, Alabama, 1 September 1868. LIBRARY OF CONGRESS

the Ku Klux Klan from a social fraternity into a terrorist organization in the early years of Reconstruction, southern whites threatened, assaulted, and frequently murdered blacks in a campaign for racial supremacy in politics, society, and economic relations. Between 1865 and World War I, thousands of southern blacks were lynched by white mobs while state and local officials stood aside.

By the turn of the century the most enduring influence of emancipation was its impact on the organization of labor on the southern cotton plantation. There the shift from the gang labor system to sharecropping and tenant farming imposed many changes on planter-merchant relations, the location of farm homes, and patterns of field cultivation. Much of the promise of emancipation in the southern society and politics had vanished. In the twentieth century the right to mobility would be exercised by countless black southerners as they abandoned their native region for the North.

State and Society

Emancipation and the suppression of southern separatism alike depended upon the refounding of the American state on a new social base. This refounding, the second major impact of the Civil War on American development, shifted the federal government from the dominating influence of southern planters, who used the Democratic Party as their political vehicle, to a northern orientation under the umbrella of the Republican Party coalition.

In the 1850s, as the population of northern and western free states rapidly rose and their electorates turned hostile to slavery, the southern commitment to the Union became increasingly tentative and fragile, even though the Democratic Party retained control over most of the branches of the national government. Replacement of the Democrats by the insurgent Republicans, accelerated by southern secession, replanted American nationalism and federal authority upon a much more vibrant and increasingly robust northern political economy. Thus refounded, the American state fought the Civil War to a successful conclusion and then plotted a much more activist course of economic development, one systematically favoring northern industrial expansion and western settlement.

One of the first fruits of this refounding was the Morrill Land Grant Act of 1862, which was similar to a bill that President James Buchanan had vetoed three years earlier. Over the next several decades, the act subsidized the establishment of agricultural and mechanical schools throughout the nation, ranging from New York's Cornell University to Texas A&M and the University of California. Before the end of the century, research as well as instruction at those institutions, by then at least one in every state, had contributed to increased agricultural production and the training of countless engineers.

Economic Development

A composite of several loosely related policies, the enactment of the Republican economic developmental program was the third great impact of the Civil War. Most importantly the suppression of southern separatism liberated market forces on a national scale by allowing a Republican-appointed Supreme Court to use both the commerce clause and the new Fourteenth Amendment to strike down state and federal regulatory measures. Under the auspices of judicial protection and enabled by the consolidation of the railroad network, the emergence of a free national market promoted the rise of the modern business enterprise in transportation, industry, and commerce by allowing the market exploitation of economies of scale in production. This intensive development of the Northeast and Great Lakes littoral was matched by the expansion of homestead agriculture into the western plains and mountain territories. Tied together by complementary markets for industrial goods and foodstuffs, the two regions were also united by a heavy flow of capital from the East to the West as wealthy investors on the East Coast invested in farm mortgages, banks, and mining ventures in the newly opened regions.

The immense debt that funded the Northern war effort during the Civil War stimulated the emergence of capital markets in New York City in the postwar decades. As the Federal Treasury engaged in refunding programs to stabilize and refinance Union bonds, the Federal government came into close, continuous contact with private bankers and commercial houses in New York. The creation of the national bank system, itself a product of Union war mobilization, and this convergence of purpose and policy were the major reasons for the resumption of the gold standard by the United States in 1879. In turn the gold standard reinforced the growing integration of the London and New York financial markets in such a way as to promote investment in the transportation and urban infrastructure that underpinned northern industrial expansion.

One of the first and most enduring developmental consequences of the Civil War was the passage and implementation of a heavily protectionist trade policy behind which emerging American industries could develop and expand their national markets. The Morrill Tariff was enacted in March 1861, after the

Lower South had seceded from the Union but before Abraham Lincoln was inaugurated. Subsequent revisions sometimes lowered particular duties but the protectionist design of American trade policy remained in place for the next half century. After the war, in fact, tariff revenue became the primary support for pension payments to Union veterans, sponsored by the Grand Army of the Republic and their allies in the Republican Party.

In this and other ways, the political coalition supporting tariff protection was expanded beyond industry to encompass much wider portions of northern and western society. Thus the Civil War enabled northern Republicans to craft a developmental program standing, like a tripod, upon three legs: the expansion of a national market of almost continental breadth, the implementation of a conservative monetary regime that promoted the elaboration of a national financial system with strong international ties, and the institution of a protectionist policy that redistributed wealth from southern agriculture to northern industry by heavily tilting the terms of interregional and international trade in favor of the latter.

To say that all of these were consequences of the Civil War is not to imply that they would not have occurred, in some form or another, had the war not have been fought. However, the Civil War was directly responsible for some of the major features of subsequent American development. For example, without the war and a huge federal debt to refinance, the Federal Treasury would not have developed a close working relationship with northern financiers. The war also created the hundreds of thousands of Union veterans who later became politically mobilized in the Grand Army of the Republic.

These elements facilitated the much more fundamental occupation of the American state by northern Republicans during and after the Civil War, a development that southerners apprehended would occur sooner or later whether or not their region seceded from the Union. In a more direct way the Civil War was responsible for the abolition of slavery, but here, too, the conflict may have only hastened a transformation that was already in the wings. While slavery appeared robust and healthy in the Deep South, the institution was in decline in the border states.

Union Victory and the Twentieth Century

Union victory in the war reinforced and accelerated northern and western development along an industrializing path. While some observers discerned the emergence of a New South in the decades following Reconstruction, the region remained heavily dependent on a plantation economy in which cotton still reigned as king. Aside from industrializing enclaves in parts of Virginia, the Carolinas, and Alabama, the South was, by far, the most impoverished, worst educated, and least urbanized section of the United States. The war thus embedded and reinforced a pattern of uneven regional development in the United States. For more than a century to come, this pattern shaped American society and the national party system and even now survives in some of the emblems and alignments of contemporary politics.

See also **Banking and Finance; Constitutional Amendments,** *subentry on* **Thirteenth, Fourteenth, and Fifteenth Amendments; Currency Policy; Democratic Party; Emancipation; Federal-State Relations,** *subentry on* **1861–1900; Foreign Trade and Tariffs; Interstate Commerce; Ku Klux Klan; Lynching; Market Revolution; Monetary Policy; Race and Racial Thinking; Reconstruction; Republican Party; Segregation,** *subentry on* **Segregation and Civil Rights; South, The,** *subentry on* **The New South after Reconstruction; Stock Markets; Taxation and Public Finance.**

Bibliography

Bensel, Richard Franklin. *Yankee Leviathan: The Origins of Central State Authority in America, 1859–1877.* New York: Cambridge University Press, 1990.

Foner, Eric. *Reconstruction: America's Unfinished Revolution, 1863–1877.* New York: Harper and Row, 1988.

Kirkland, Edward C. *Industry Comes of Age: Business, Labor, and Public Policy, 1860–1897.* New York: Holt, Rinehart, and Winston, 1961.

Woodward, C. Vann. *Origins of the New South, 1877–1913.* Baton Rouge: Louisiana State University Press, 1951.

RICHARD FRANKLIN BENSEL

REMEMBERING THE CIVIL WAR

In the three and a half decades following Appomattox, memories of the Civil War touched all aspects of late-nineteenth-century American culture, Northern and Southern. In literature, the Civil War was an important theme in a host of novels, most notably Stephen Crane's *The Red Badge of Courage* (1895) and Ambrose Bierce's realistic *Tales of Soldiers and Civilians* (1891). Between 1884 and 1887 *Century Magazine* commissioned and published a series of recollections of famous generals from both sides. Never had memory possessed such a commercial value as the highly successful "Battles and Leaders of the Civil War," which was reissued in book form in 1887–1888. Civil War memory became a creature of the mass market. Ulysses S. Grant's best-selling *Personal Memoirs* (1885–1886) and Jefferson Davis's two-volume *Rise and Fall of the Confederate Government* (1881) quickly assumed places on parlor tables across the nation along with the recollections of other noted generals and leaders. Countless tales of camp and battle appeared in general circulation magazines and newspapers, among them George Lemon's *National Tribune,* which reached the thousands of veterans who were America's first Civil War buffs. Published photographs from the Civil War, particularly the work of Mathew Brady and Alexander Gardner, offered the public enduring and haunting images of that conflict.

In politics, beginning with the 1866 congressional elections and continuing intermittently well into the 1890s, Republicans preserved memories of Civil War divisions by associating both the Democrats and the South with rebellion and disloyalty in order to garner votes. In conducting "bloody shirt" campaigns, Republicans waved blood-soaked shirts in the air to symbolize Northern lives lost in the war, an effective practice since even in 1890 one of every ten eligible voters was a Civil War veteran.

Monuments

In architecture, countless communities, state organizations, private groups, and the federal government played a role in creating and preserving the public's memory of the war by building monuments. By the mid-1870s dozens of monuments commemorating the service of the common soldiers and sailors appeared in towns and cities across the North. Usually placed in town squares or in city parks, the typical memorial featured a realistic bronze or stone statue of a lone anonymous soldier. During the 1890s and early 1900s, equestrian statues were erected in Washington to Generals Grant, William T. Sherman, Philip Sheridan, George G. Meade and other prominent heroes, and scores of cities from San Francisco to New York built statues of Abraham Lincoln to honor the martyred president's memory. In addition, there were entire buildings, such as Harvard University's Memorial Hall, dedicated in 1874, and the Memorial Hall of New Orleans (also known as the Confederate Museum), built in 1891, whose purposes were to honor fallen soldiers.

Formed in the decade immediately following Appomattox, ladies memorial associations sponsored most of the early Confederate monuments, usually obelisks placed in Confederate cemeteries, which these same women's organizations also created. By the late 1890s the United Confederate Veterans (UCV), which attracted the largest number of veterans, and the United Daughters of the Confederacy (UDC), founded in 1894, had assumed responsibility for the construction of monuments featuring a lone Confederate soldier with his musket at parade rest, "guarding" county courthouses or city squares. Scores of others memorialized Robert E. Lee, Thomas "Stonewall" Jackson, J. E. B. Stuart, and Jefferson Davis.

Holidays

Veterans groups, such as the Grand Army of the Republic (GAR), the largest and most influential organization of Union veterans, and the UCV also encouraged the commemoration of special holidays and sponsored rituals to ensure that Americans remembered the war dead. The GAR influenced Congress to turn Memorial Day (30 May) into a national holiday beginning in 1889.

In the South, where former Confederates largely shunned Memorial Day and the Fourth of July, a new holiday celebrated the sacrifice of the common soldiers who had died for a just and noble cause. Emerging from several independent origins, Confederate Memorial Day was almost universally observed in the Deep South on 26 April, the anniversary of Joseph E. Johnston's surrender, while towns in the Carolinas chose 10 May, the anniversary of Stonewall Jackson's death, and Virginia societies selected days ranging from 10 May to mid-June. The UDC served as an umbrella organization for memorial groups and shaped public memory in the South, convincing various state legislatures to declare Robert E. Lee's birthday (19 January) and Jefferson Davis's birthday (3 June) as special holidays of the "lost cause."

Battlegrounds and Cemeteries

The most visible reminders of the Civil War were the sacred places and hallowed grounds where the battles were decided and the war dead were laid to rest. In the 1890s Congress started acquiring Civil War battlefields as permanent war memorials and established national military parks at Chickamauga and Chattanooga, Shiloh, Gettysburg, and Antietam. Congress also allowed states and veterans organizations to erect memorials and markers in these parks honoring their individual regiments, both Confederate and Union. At Gettysburg alone, state and veterans organizations dedicated nearly four hundred monuments. In contrast only a handful of Civil War memorials commemorated the service of African Americans. Prominently, on 31 May 1897 the Boston Brahmins dedicated a monument across from the statehouse in Boston to the memory of Colonel Robert Gould Shaw and the fallen black volunteers of the Fifty-fourth Massachusetts Infantry.

Congress in 1866 authorized an extensive system of permanent military cemeteries for the Union war dead and made it a federal crime to vandalize a national cemetery, such as the one at Arlington, the site of Robert E. Lee's former plantation in northern Virginia. On these sites, too, state governments and private groups erected suitable memorials marking the service of a particular regiment, state, or individual. In 1900 a Washington, D.C., chapter of the UCV persuaded Congress to reinter the remains of 128 Confederate soldiers in a special Confederate burial section at Arlington, and the UDC received permission to place a memorial there a few years later.

Parades and Pensions

As if Americans required further reminders of the war, veterans organizations sponsored war lectures and dramas, furnished relic rooms or museums, and published war narratives. The GAR, the UCV, and the UDC and its Northern counterpart, each wanting to implant its version of the war, lobbied state legislatures to mandate "correct" Civil War history in schools and textbooks. Americans of all ages witnessed such symbolic acts as military parades, cross of honor ceremonies, reunions, national encampments, and "campfires," where mock-ups of wartime camps, drilling exhibitions, group singing, theatrical presentations, and sham battles were staged by Civil War veterans who wore uniforms, slept in tents, and reenacted the "real" war.

The federal and state governments provided generous pensions. Between 1890 and 1907 pension payments totaled more than $1 billion. By 1900 the bloody shirt had given way to blue-gray reunions and even talk of federal pensions, never enacted, for indigent and disabled former Confederates, to whom state legislators awarded pensions and artificial limbs. Needy veterans in both regions could find medical care, comfort, and companionship in state-sponsored soldiers' homes. By 1870 the federally funded National Homes for Disabled Volunteer Soldiers (NHDVS), based in Washington, D.C., had branches in Maine, Ohio, Wisconsin, and Virginia, and state-sponsored soldiers' homes opened in a dozen other states. By 1901 nine states had Confederate soldiers' homes, where the most tangible reminders of the war were dressed in uniforms and exhibited as combatants against public amnesia.

See also **Cemeteries and Burial; Holidays; Monuments and Memorials; National Parks; Sculpture.**

Bibliography

Foster, Gaines M. *Ghosts of the Confederacy: Defeat, the Lost Cause, and the Emergence of the New South, 1865 to 1913.* New York: Oxford University Press, 1987.

Kelly, Patrick J. *Creating a National Home: Building the Veterans' Welfare State, 1860–1900.* Cambridge, Mass.: Harvard University Press, 1997.

McConnell, Stuart. *Glorious Contentment: The Grand Army of the Republic, 1865–1900.* Chapel Hill: University of North Carolina Press, 1992.

Panhorst, Michael Wilson. "Lest We Forget: Monuments and Memorial Sculpture in National Military Parks of Civil War Battlefields, 1861–1917." Ph.D. diss., University of Delaware, 1988.

Piehler, G. Kurt. *Remembering War the American Way.* Washington, D.C.: Smithsonian Institution Press, 1995.

Rehberger, Dean. "The Mystic Chords of Memory: Nationalism, Historical Novels, and the American Civil War." Ph.D. diss., University of Utah, 1992.

Rosenburg, R. B. *Living Monuments: Confederate Soldiers' Homes in the New South.* Chapel Hill: University of North Carolina Press, 1993.

R. B. Rosenburg

CLASS, SOCIAL   To consider class as a social category in nineteenth-century America from the perspective of historical scholarship in the late twentieth century is to grapple with two periods of uncertainty and controversy over the meaning of "class." Americans of the early nineteenth century encountered one another across lines of wealth, power, and status that many today would see as "class" divisions, but they were just beginning to develop a language to describe opposing economic interests. In the late eighteenth and early nineteenth centuries, public discussion of social distinction in America still often invoked older terms such as "rank," "order," or "estate" to refer to social divisions. These terms carried the "republican" implication that oppositions between social orders developed not from opposed economic interests but from subversions of the political system whereby corrupt ambitions upset the balance of interests achieved within a constitutional government. What is more, many Americans throughout the nineteenth century subscribed to the creed of "American exceptionalism" that saw American social development as a departure from the traditional ranks as well as from the emerging industrial classes of European societies. By the late nineteenth century, fierce industrial class conflicts, among other social changes, weakened their faith in American exceptionalism. Americans of diverse social backgrounds increasingly viewed their society as one divided by socioeconomic class interests.

Over the course of the twentieth century, historians devised many approaches to the study of how nineteenth-century Americans came to affiliate themselves with specific classes. In the process they raised important questions about how to define class as a category of historical explanation and interpre-

The Orphanage as a Safe Haven. Three poor, fatherless children were taken from their mother by the "humane society." Their mother, characterized as being "in a beastly state of intoxication," was committed to a workhouse and the children were committed to an orphan asylum. Photograph, c. 1890. LIBRARY OF CONGRESS

tation. Early-twentieth-century Progressive historians assumed that the American constitution and the Jacksonian political battles that reshaped American politics in the nineteenth century expressed class divisions. In the mid–twentieth century, a generation of "consensus" historians rejected class divisions as important features in American social life in favor of "status," religion, and ethnicity. "New" social historians of the 1970s and 1980s returned economic class divisions to the center of nineteenth-century history but relocated class identity in such arenas as leisure, religion, culture, community, and politics as well as work. More recently, historians who embrace post-structuralist methods see class divisions deriving from cultural and political rhetorics rather than material interests. In this view, class distinctions continuously shift as they intersect with equally potent categories of identity such as gender, ethnicity, and race. To summarize the range and development of class distinctions in the nineteenth century is also

necessarily to grapple with the contested meanings of "class" as a dimension of multiple nineteenth-century identities.

Working-Class and Middle-Class Formation in Antebellum America

The emergence of divisive class distinctions within early nineteenth-century America has been most closely studied from the perspective of artisans—journeymen craft workers—who were increasingly frustrated in the economic and political expectations they associated with American freedom. They had regarded the American Revolution's legacy as a promise of independence, citizenship, and equality available to apprentice and journeyman workers as well as to the masters of their trades. Journeymen saw themselves as working together with their masters to provide quality goods to their customers and to increase the prosperity of their society. They expected that their labor would eventually yield economic independence and political voice. However, as commerce expanded and new markets for cheaper ready-made goods opened up outside the craftsmen's customary local commercial networks, master craftsmen and their employees developed divergent interpretations of republican independence.

Some former master craftsmen became manufacturing employers increasingly distant from the labor, daily life, and beliefs of their employees. Eager to take advantage of enlarged markets for ready-made goods—many of which, in such industries as shoes and clothing, went to clothe southern slaves—they organized higher volume production by subdividing tasks in crafts that apprentices and journeymen had previously learned as whole units. A once common culture of craft skills dissolved as employers used the competition of former journeymen and new urban migrants from the countryside to depress wages, and demanded longer and longer hours from workers. They began to define republican independence in the pious terms of evangelical Protestantism rather than of common skills.

Displaced journeymen who had become permanent wage earners responded to these developments with their own visions of republican independence. Combining in emerging manufacturing centers like New York and Philadelphia to combat falling wages and lengthening hours of work, these workmen based their demands for better working conditions on their participation in a republican government. The 1820s saw the flowering of the Workingmen's Parties throughout the Northeast as the vehicles of wage earners' republican sympathies. Some "Workies" demanded a complete redistribution of property, the solution proposed in New York City machinist and Workingmen's leader Thomas Skidmore's 1829 tract *The Rights of Man to Property!* Most Workingmen's activists proposed more modest changes, such as the abolition of corporate charters through which government facilitated the growing power of capital; free public education to ensure a broadly enlightened citizenry; and the provision of homesteads in the West for urban and rural wage laborers. Nor was this political perspective confined to urban artisans. In rural areas like upstate New York, tenants engaged in antirent campaigns with rhetoric that emphasized the egalitarianism and independence they associated with the republican legacy.

In an era of mass parties appealing to an expanding electorate, the small, special-purpose Workingmen's Parties were soon overwhelmed. The Jacksonian Democrats incorporated some of their demands, along with those of rural antirent activists, while blunting others. But the journeymen's republican ideals lived on in the trade union movement. General Trades Unions (GTUs) and their national counterpart, the National Trades Union (NTU), founded in 1834, created a network of meetings, lyceums, libraries, and newspapers. Through this network, journeymen came to see their labor as a form of property entailing inherent rights. Their collective efforts to protect these rights provoked further refinements of middle-class republicanism, which increasingly emphasized individualism as the heart of republican independence.

Though conflicts between journeymen and employers led to some of the earliest expressions of class division in nineteenth-century America, neither side invoked a vision of completely opposed social classes. Journeymen confined their complaints to "unmanly" or "tyrant" employers who had betrayed a republican legacy that workers had once shared with master craftsmen. Nor did their collective defense of their "property" in labor unite them to all wage laborers. They sought to maintain a political and economic independence based on the culture of craft skills in which they had been trained. Accordingly their organizing efforts excluded those whom they saw as having no reasonable expectation of such independence. Many white males who worked as day laborers in the country's emerging transportation network and as operatives in the growing textile industry fell into this category. With Irish immigrants filling many such jobs, both skills and ethnicity marked their differences from journeymen. Even among skilled craftsmen ethnicity limited class solidarity as specific crafts became associated with particular immigrant groups. But the greatest barriers to inclusion in the culture of artisanal "independence" were distinctions of race and gender.

Nineteenth-century journeymen who asserted their republican independence did so in terms that defined the freedom and dignity of white laborers against the dependence and subservience of black slaves. From early in the century white workers rejected labels like "servant" as evoking a lowly and degraded state associated with black slaves; they preferred "help" or "hired man" or "hired woman." By mid-century some journeymen activists adopted the notion of "white slavery" to describe the degraded conditions of wage labor. For some, the connection between permanent wage work and slavery led them in the direction of antislavery and abolition. But even abolitionist labor activists such as George Henry Evans emphasized that the significance of the comparison lay in differentiating the status of free white workers from the degradation associated both with slavery and with the African Americans who endured it. At pains to differentiate themselves from black slaves even as they invoked the comparison, northern white workers—particularly those attracted to the Republican Party by the 1850s—rallied around "free white labor" as an economic and political self-definition. Under this banner they entered the Civil War more opposed to black slaves than to chattel slavery. After Emancipation, race remained a deeply ingrained fault line in constructions of American working-class consciousness.

When antebellum labor activists spoke of "white slavery," they identified it not with their own status but with that of women and children engaged in sweated labor. In so doing, they reflected a patriarchal domestic hierarchy that also shaped the formation of working-class identities. Though they might pity female "white slaves" who labored in factories or at "outwork" in their homes, journeyman activists did not include such women in their defense of "independence." The cultural and political legacy of republicanism offered no promise of independence to women, who were regarded as dependents within households and a polity headed by men. Thus, though organizations like the GTUs and the NTU complained that female laborers threatened their independence by working for lower wages, they did not offer to help women secure the conditions that journeymen craftsmen demanded.

Besides being excluded from the networks of assistance that defined an emerging antebellum working class, working women found that their efforts to secure aid also brought them up against the gendered character of middle-class identity. By the 1820s, middle-class wives from both merchant and artisan backgrounds drew on evangelical religion to craft new social roles as moral guides for their families and communities. They organized tract societies, missionary societies, and maternal associations to protect their children's morals and to extend their pious concerns to the homes of the poor and unchurched. Eventually these efforts crystallized into a middle-class cult of domesticity that emphasized the role of mothers in shaping the moral character and individual aspiration on which middle-class identity increasingly depended. As they crafted this domestic ideal through public crusades and charity, evangelical women demanded that those receiving aid adhere to their standards of temperance and moral character. Poor working women who could not or would not were often turned away.

As such cases suggest, by mid-century class distinction developed as much through cultural debates as through changing economic relations. Nor did cultural distinctions divide classes neatly into camps opposing bourgeois evangelical purity to proletarian bravado. Many journeymen artisans shared their former masters' evangelical faith, and chastised them for failing to attend to Christian teachings that sanctified labor and condemned greed. In short, class distinctions emerged in fights within shared cultural arenas at the same time that these emerging class divisions reshaped those arenas and their boundaries. Evangelical religion was only one such arena; even more visible were the rituals of urban street life and amusements of the mid-to-late nineteenth century.

Street Life, Popular Performance, and Class Distinction

Social distinctions within daily life shifted significantly over the course of the nineteenth century. At the beginning of the century, aristocratic standards of decorum and expectations of deference still competed with republican ideals of egalitarian treatment in encounters between the well-heeled and the "lower orders." European travelers and merchant elites who expected their refinement and gentility to set them apart from those they regarded as rustic or plebeian were surprised to find people they regarded as subordinates affecting their own refinements and demanding due respect in public. Institutions for public edification and entertainment steered a middle course between these hierarchical and egalitarian cultural impulses. Charles Willson Peale tried to make his Philadelphia collection of artworks and natural history artifacts into a museum to educate and uplift patrons to a common level of republican reason. Unable to win federal funding, however, Peale's program of cultural uplift fell prey to popular tastes when he unwillingly transformed his lecture hall into an entertainment stage to attract paying customers. The diversity of cultural styles assembled through this marketing made for an increasingly class-inflected and divisive cultural life, especially in the theater.

By the 1830s theaters offered diverse fare—programs usually featuring a several-act melodrama or Shakespearean drama interspersed with variety acts and musical novelties, and followed by a short comedy sketch or farce. These evening-long affairs appealed to a broad audience whose developing class differences were reflected in their spatial segregation. In the "boxes" sat elites aiming to display their finery and refinement. The highest tier of balcony seats, "the gallery," was the resort of young laborers and journeymen who demonstrated their pleasure and displeasure with cheers, jeers, and missiles. African American patrons were segregated here as well, or in a special section of the "third tier" otherwise reserved for prostitutes and their patrons. In the "pit" sat the "middle classes": respectable artisans, clerks, storekeepers, and their families.

But the theater could not long contain such distinctions. Elites began deserting their boxes for more exclusive theatrical venues decried as aristocratic by republican "gallery gods." Many felt that the breaking point came with the May 1849 riot outside one of these upper-class retreats, New York City's Astor Place Opera House. Offended by the erection of the opera house well north of the theater and retail district where classes previously met, the crowd that attacked the new institution was further incensed by the appearance there of the English actor William Charles Macready in the role of Macbeth. Macready maintained an intense rivalry with the reputedly more "democratic" American favorite, Edwin Forrest. Many of the rioters injured and killed by militiamen were young craftsmen. According to Lawrence Levine, a newspaper reporter commented a few days later that the riot left behind "a feeling that there is now in our country . . . what every good patriot has hitherto considered it his duty to deny—*a high class and a low class*" (Levine, *Highbrow/Lowbrow*, p. 66).

A cultural opposition of high and low characterized public amusements through the rest of the century as entertainments and audiences split into distinct genres and venues. The character sketches and farces of mid-nineteenth-century theater were collected into popular amusements that addressed the complex social distinctions defining working-class identity. Blackface minstrelsy was one of the first popular theatrical genres to take up these themes. Blackface performers borrowed animal tales through which African American slaves had masked their criticisms of white masters in order to comment on the growing class divisions that white working-class audiences experienced. But they also depicted their caricatures as buffoons in order to maintain racist divisions that sustained white working-class pride.

These cultural constructions of race persisted in popular culture even after the Civil War, though former minstrel performers increasingly focused on caricaturing the European ethnic groups who generated rivalries within working-class communities. In the 1870s Edward Harrigan and "Tony Hart" (Anthony Cannon) turned ethnic caricature into full-length musicals popular across ethnic lines, though they stressed the preeminence of Irish American themes in working-class popular culture. In the 1880s, variety shows took up these themes in programs consisting of disconnected character sketches interspersed with class-inflected songs of performers like Antonio "Tony" Pastor, who emphasized pride in manual labor and moral indignation at accumulations of great wealth in an increasingly corporate industrial order. Performers and audiences favored styles of swaggering masculinity and exuberant feminine display that departed from emerging middle-class norms of domesticity, emphasizing again the importance of gender to the definition of class identities.

Meanwhile, the separation of theatrical "high" culture into its own domain, confined to upper-class audiences, continued. By the late nineteenth century, urban elites were actively building new institutions to develop "high" cultural canons in theater, music, and art. Some of these institutions—from opera houses to metropolitan symphony halls to art museums—were the projects of arriviste elites newly formed with the manufacturing and retail profits of America's post–Civil War industrial economy. Whether new or old money was organized to fund cultural enclaves, the focus on cultural acquisition and display displaced older aristocratic commitments to philanthropic moral leadership. Even the self-made philanthropist Andrew Carnegie focused on such cultural charities as his well-known libraries, and emphasized the role of the wealthy as conservators of culture and art in his *Gospel of Wealth*. Some observers interpreted upper-class cultural institutions and the fashions required to attend them less sympathetically. In his *Theory of the Leisure Class* (1899), the economist Thorstein Veblen coined the term "conspicuous consumption" to refer to these activities, arguing that they retarded social progress by inspiring emulation among lower classes, thereby distracting them from more productive pursuits.

Middle-class identity in the mid– to late nineteenth century had its own cultural character, as seen in the domestic culture of sentiment and the etiquette manual. Defining correct deportment in the domestic interiors where middle-class character was modeled, these cultural forms also expressed anxious uncertainties about identity itself that characterized middle-class consciousness. Made up largely of rural transplants and aspiring craftsmen who found themselves in increasingly anonymous social milieux, urban middle classes crafted a culture of sincerity predicated on the fear of appearing to be insincere.

The "Social Question" and Some Late Nineteenth-Century Answers

From the 1870s to the end of the nineteenth century, class divisions assumed a larger place in American public discourse and political conflict. The rise of large corporations and the accelerating application of mechanization to organize and control labor evoked increasingly militant protests from industrial workers, punctuated by such events as the railroad strike of 1877; the eight-hour movement of 1886, which culminated in the Haymarket riot in Chicago; the Homestead strike of 1892; and the Pullman strike of 1894. These events raised doubts as to American exceptionalism among both participants and observers, and focused attention on what became known as the "social question": the centrality of class conflict in economic and social life.

The decline of working-class republicanism was one of the most important consequences of these new conditions. It had its final and most widespread institutional expression in the Noble and Holy Order of the Knights of Labor in 1869. Consisting of local and state assemblies that reached the peak of their power in the 1880s, the Knights both drew on the legacy of republicanism and extended its boundaries. Their appeal, like those of working-class republicans before them, was to the dignity of "producers," emphasizing temperance, self-improvement, and an eight-hour working day, and attacking corrupting combinations of wealth. Unlike the journeymen republicans of the 1830s and 1840s, however, the Knights extended this appeal to unskilled workers, women, and even African Americans. Crushed in the antilabor climate after Haymarket, which associated them with the anarchists blamed for violence in Chicago, the Knights were the apotheosis of producerist republicanism. However, their vision of worker dignity and solidarity persisted through a popular culture of dime novels with worker heroes.

Along with urban industrial protest there was a reassertion of class divisions in the countryside. The Grange, the Farmers' Alliance, and later the Populists protested the threat posed by corporate economic interests to their members as independent producers, and refashioned republican themes into cooperative ideals.

The labor movement after the Knights transformed working-class republicanism. The American Federation of Labor (AFL) gained prominence in the 1890s. Under the leadership of an immigrant cigar-maker, Samuel Gompers, the AFL maintained the republican ethic of "manly dignity," but associated it with the skills of a relative elite of well-paid craftsmen who sought to force employer compliance with their standards through the strike and the boycott. This trade-unionist approach to industrial class relations accepted, as the Knights and previous labor "republicans" had not, the permanence and inevitability of class conflict, and sought to increase the strength of working-class solidarity within that conflict. But it also shrank the boundaries of that solidarity, representing skilled, predominantly northern European and native born male workers against the competition of women, African Americans, and "new immigrants" from southern and eastern Europe. In the early twentieth century the AFL formed strategic accommodations with employers designed to protect skilled workers' high wages, and moved away from any possible alliance with low-skilled workers or protesting farmers.

Such accommodation brought the AFL into conflict with socialists, who drew on indigenous utopian socialism and European Marxism. Articulated most popularly by a former railroad worker, Eugene V. Debs, American socialism also drew on republican ideals of the dignity of labor. But rather than look back to a lost artisanal culture, socialists looked forward to the political and social triumph of workers in a socialist state.

Despite divergent strategies for addressing class conflict, trade unionists and socialists recognized a common class enemy in America's corporate industrial elite. But they also shared some terms of social distinction with that elite, which turned increasingly to Darwinian science and its evolutionary narratives to legitimate its leadership and wealth. Though disputed by social scientists, the idea of "the survival of the fittest" helped to justify American elites' seeming lack of interest in the plight of poor workers. Darwinian ideas were popular among union leaders and socialists as well, particularly for the way they embedded in "nature" and "science" distinctions between native white workers, on the one hand, and African American as well as "new" immigrant workers, on the other. AFL unionists and socialists deployed such divisions to explain their antipathy to nonwhites who might otherwise seem to be candidates for class solidarity. They also borrowed from the primitive "vigor" that Darwinian language associated with the "lower" classes and races to celebrate their own robust masculinity.

These images also proved attractive to a "new" middle class of managers and reformers, for whom proletarian ruggedness began to seem an invigorating antidote to the piety and sentimentality of their own nineteenth-century class culture. Venturing to "know" and describe the working class to broader audiences by donning their garb and experiencing the rigors of their daily lives, middle-class investigators traced the uncertain lines of their own turn-of-the-century class position. A new identity as Progressive activists attempting to answer the social question through "social" work and mediation grew out of the effort to reconcile Darwinian class divisions with older traditions of evangelical uplift and activism. These middle-class reformers were also motivated by new popular cultural forms like vaudeville and film, where audiences who had fractured along class lines in the mid–nineteenth century met each other again in the early twentieth. Presented with new images of ethnic self-assertion, feminine display, and class division as the stuff of a common culture, they began to redraw the cultural contours of social class through the mass entertainments as well as the economic relations of a new century.

See also **Consumerism and Consumption; Dime Novels and Story Papers; Domestic Life; Home; Industrialization and the Market; Industry (The Work Ethic); Labor Movement,** *subentry on* **Unions and Strikes; Lyceums; Manners; Minstrel Shows; Philanthropy; Popular Culture; Recreation; Theater; Vaudeville and Burlesque; Wealth; Work,** *subentries on* **Artisans and Craftsworkers; The Workshop; Working-Class Culture.**

Bibliography

Arneson, Eric, Julie Greene, and Bruce Laurie, eds. *Labor Histories: Class, Politics and the Working Class Experience.* Urbana: University of Illinois Press, 1998.

Blumin, Stuart M. *The Emergence of the Middle Class: Social Experience in the American City, 1760–1900.* Cambridge, U.K., and New York: Cambridge University Press, 1989.

Burke, Martin J. *The Conundrum of Class: Public Discourse on the Social Order in America.* Chicago: University of Chicago Press, 1995.

Denning, Michael. *Mechanic Accents: Dime Novels and Working Class Culture in America.* London and New York: Verso, 1987.

Fink, Leon. *Workingmen's Democracy: The Knights of Labor and American Politics.* Urbana: University of Illinois Press, 1983.

Gutman, Herbert G. *Work, Culture, and Society in Industrializing America: Essays in American Working-Class and Social History.* New York: Knopf, 1976.

Hall, John R., ed. *Reworking Class.* Ithaca, N.Y.: Cornell University Press, 1997.

Halttunen, Karen. *Confidence Men and Painted Women: A Study of Middle-Class Culture in America, 1830–1870*. New Haven, Conn.: Yale University Press, 1982.

Jaher, Frederick C. *The Urban Establishment: Upper Strata in Boston, New York, Charleston, Chicago, and Los Angeles*. Urbana: University of Illinois Press, 1982.

Johnson, Paul E. *A Shopkeeper's Millennium: Society and Revivals in Rochester, New York, 1815–1837*. New York: Hill and Wang, 1978.

Kasson, John F. *Rudeness and Civility: Manners in Nineteenth-Century Urban America*. New York: Hill and Wang, 1990.

Lazerow, Jama. *Religion and the Working Class in Antebellum America*. Washington, D.C.: Smithsonian Institution Press, 1995.

Levine, Lawrence W. *Highbrow/Lowbrow: The Emergence of Cultural Hierarchy in America*. Cambridge, Mass.: Harvard University Press, 1988.

Lott, Eric. *Love and Theft: Blackface Minstrelsy and the American Working Class*. New York: Oxford University Press, 1993.

Montgomery, David. *The Fall of the House of Labor: The Workplace, the State, and American Labor Activism, 1865–1925*. Cambridge, U.K., and New York: Cambridge University Press, 1987.

Moody, J. Carroll, and Alice Kessler-Harris, eds. *Perspectives on American Labor History: The Problems of Synthesis*. Dekalb: Northern Illinois University Press, 1989.

Peiss, Kathy. *Cheap Amusements: Working Women and Leisure in Turn-of-the-Century New York City, 1880–1920*. Philadelphia: Temple University Press, 1986.

Pittenger, Mark. "A World of Difference: Constructing the 'Underclass' in Progressive America." *American Quarterly* 49 (1997): 26–65.

Roediger, David R. *The Wages of Whiteness: Race and the Making of the American Working Class*. London and New York: Verso, 1991.

Ryan, Mary P. *Cradle of the Middle Class: The Family in Oneida County, New York, 1790–1865*. Cambridge, U.K., and New York: Cambridge University Press, 1981.

Stansell, Christine. *City of Women: Sex and Class in New York, 1789–1860*. New York: Knopf, 1986.

Sutton, William R. *Journeymen for Jesus: Evangelical Artisans Confront Capitalism in Jacksonian Baltimore*. University Park: Pennsylvania State University Press, 1998.

Wilentz, Sean. *Chants Democratic: New York City and the Rise of the American Working Class, 1788–1850*. New York: Oxford University Press, 1984.

KATHRYN J. OBERDECK

CLOTHING

What people wore in the nineteenth-century United States reflects that era's aesthetic tastes and attitudes toward modesty, gender roles, and individualism versus uniformity. Clothing suggests an individual's economic class, ethnicity, occupation, and regional affiliation. Clothing historians study the styles of the elite trendsetters and the attire of ordinary people, such as telephone operators and plantation workers, using photographs, portraits, fashion magazines, diaries, and surviving clothing and textiles. Each of these sources must be evaluated carefully. For example, a fashion plate in *Godey's Lady's Book* is an important but idealized image for middle- and upper-class consumption.

Clothing was an integral part of the watershed events of that time. National territorial expansion led to regional garment variations based on different climatic and working conditions. The Civil War caused severe shortages in consumer goods and the money with which to buy them. The plantation system fostered a complex system of domestic clothing manufacture. The Industrial Revolution eventually brought women into the workplace, and it reinforced slavery with the northern textile mills' increased demand for southern cotton. Factory-made clothing, in turn, supported a mass consumer market, and workplace abuses led to the labor union movement. Reformers addressed not only child labor but the idea of fashion itself, such as the health hazards of tight clothing for a pregnant woman or a growing child and the obstacles posed by a hoopskirt on a woman playing tennis.

Despite some ethnic, class, and regional differences, clothing styles for men and women followed certain conventions. The less affluent imitated the current styles with cheaper fabric and decoration. Gender differentiation in clothing increased, however. Men's clothing became plainer and more standardized as the century progressed, but women's clothing remained decorative to reflect the family's economic status. Regardless of class, women's skirts rarely rose above the ankle, and tight corsets and voluminous petticoats inhibited physical movement. Sometimes, however, changes in men's and women's styles complemented each other. The waists on men's and women's clothes tended to get lower and slimmer at the same time, requiring both sexes to wear corseting for some styles. In general nineteenth-century women's clothing required padding and corsetry to shape the body into the desired silhouette. Men's clothing moved away from this trend early in the century as tailors learned to shape wool to fit the client, not the other way around. Working-class people adopted looser clothing for ease of movement.

In the beginning of the century clothing was more formal, and people held expectations about which clothing should be worn at which hour or on which occasion, including etiquette about wearing black mourning clothes for funerals, visitations, and extended bereavement periods. These strictures gradually relaxed as the century progressed.

Clothing historians continually debate what nineteenth-century clothing signified. Many claim that corseting, high necklines, and long skirts intentionally hid the body's sexuality, while others contend that undergarments like the bustle were sexually provocative because they suggested large hips. Women's historians point out the physical harm and confinement inflicted on women and argue that, as the century progressed and women began to rally for the vote and other rights, the corsets got tighter. Still others say that the rise of the capitalist class and bourgeois society necessitated that sexuality be restricted to procreation only, and in such an environment pornography and prostitution flourished to fulfill repressed sexual desires.

Rejecting the above notions, which they believe are based on common myths about Victorian prudishness, many historians point out that men's suits in the twentieth century, a sexually permissive era, were as concealing as their nineteenth-century counterparts. Others argue that women were willing to sacrifice some physical discomfort to look their best and that they tightened their corsets so they could transcend their matronly roles. The progression of women from the private to the public sphere did not have a parallel linear progression in fashion changes to accommodate those new roles. For example, skirts did not get progressively shorter. Also some suffragettes continued to wear conventional clothing to avoid accusations of blurring gender distinctions.

Men's Clothing

Men's fashion opened the nineteenth century with remnants of the eighteenth—highly ornamental coats, tight knee breeches, and stockings. Then British tailors, from whom American men's fashion took its cue, adopted scientific tailoring methods made possible by the tape measure and woolen fabric. The result was higher precision in fit and cut and garments that fit the body more loosely and casually. While wigs were sometimes worn by older men or those in such professions as law and the ministry, wigs were gradually shed for natural, short hairstyles.

The essential pieces of a middle-class man's daytime wardrobe were a coat, pants, waistcoat, shirt, collar, and tie. The 1800s began with the cutaway coat with tails for both day and evening. By mid-century the frock coat, mid-thigh to knee length with straight front edges, replaced the cutaway as typical daytime wear. Variations on a short, informal jacket, or "paletot," appeared in the 1830s and in the 1860s became part of the three-piece lounge suit, the precursor to the twentieth-century three-piece suit. Pants evolved into tight-fitting calf- or ankle-length pantaloons. By 1820 the longer but still tight trouser was replacing the pantaloon for daytime wear. During the latter part of the century, these pants became looser and added cuffs and a front crease. The waist-

coat, or vest, could be showy in color or silky texture, as could the cravat, which became a shaped necktie by the 1860s. Shirts were fine linen or cotton and by mid-century had detachable collars. Footwear included boots for everyday and square-toed pumps for more formal occasions. By mid-century alternatives to the ubiquitous top hat, such as the bowler or straw boater, had developed.

Women's Clothing

American women of the early 1800s enthusiastically copied the Empire style inspired by the French Revolution. It was at this time, not later in the century as might be expected, that women rejected corseting in favor of flowing, high-waisted dresses made of sheer cotton muslin. Undergarments consisted of a soft camisole slip and flesh-colored leggings. Women wore caps or turbans that were softly constructed, though they still wore bonnets also. Women's shoes were similar to ballet slippers—flimsy with no soles—and thus discouraged physical activity. By the 1820s the waistline dropped, and the narrow bodice construction with pleats folding into a V-shaped waistline required extensive corseting. Leg-of-mutton sleeves became popular, skirts widened, and stiffer fabric, like taffeta, produced a more modest appearance. During the 1830s skirts grew even wider, requiring several petticoats. High-necked bodices had collars that expanded over the shoulders to look like capes, and fabric designs ranged from small-patterned chintz to plaid taffeta. This is the style most often associated with nineteenth-century dress.

During the 1850s and 1860s the Victorian domed skirt reached its heyday. It was supported by a hooped cage called a "caged crinoline" and by numerous petticoats. By the 1860s the roundness was thrust backward, and padded bustles with flat fronts were fashionable. Newly invented aniline dyes introduced brilliant blues, greens, and purples. In the 1870s a narrower silhouette came into vogue, reviving long stays to maintain the sleek look of a long bodice, and skirt fabric was drawn back into flounces to replace the bustle. This style eventually became so tight that women's magazines complained that women had difficulty sitting and kneeling.

In the late 1880s and the 1890s women's clothing began the slow process of reform. Fabrics used had already become lighter weight, but women still negotiated countless yards of fabric during even the lightest physical activity. Bustles were abandoned in favor of the simple gored A-line skirt. The U.S. magazine illustrator Charles Dana Gibson popularized separates, usually a white blouse and dark skirt, as the "Gibson Girl" look, which became the favorite apparel of office women around the country. Clothing was still heavily boned to achieve a small waist, and blouse sleeves were voluminous. Although in 1851 Amelia Jenks Bloomer devised a women's outfit of a loose tunic worn over ankle-length baggy trousers, known as "bloomers," everyday clothing remained heavily corseted at the end of the century, and skirt lengths were still close to the floor.

Shoes began as soft slippers and evolved into sturdier but uncomfortably narrow pumps with square or pointed toes or high-buttoned boots. Hats, considered essential outdoor attire for modesty and protection from the elements, followed the silhouette of the current dress, so that a domed skirt called for a wide-brimmed hat. The sizes of bonnet brims and crowns fluctuated, as did the closeness of a bonnet to the wearer's face. By the century's end women were wearing smaller hats made of straw or felt that were heavily decorated and perched on top of the head.

In mid-century doctors warned women that tightly

The Bloomer Costume. Created by Amelia Bloomer, loose trousers were worn under a tunic and donned by women participating in physical activity. Lithograph by Currier and Ives, 1851. LIBRARY OF CONGRESS: PRINTS AND PHOTOGRAPHS DIVISION

laced corsets could cause problems with pregnancies and advised pregnant women to loosen their corsets or go without. However, few dress styles could be adapted accordingly, so pregnant women remained housebound, or confined, and either wrapped themselves in a cape if forced to go out or ventured out after dark. When a style like the tea dress, which had a loose waist secured by ties, became available in the 1870s and 1880s, pregnant women adopted it as maternity wear because its loose fit did not require a corset.

Underwear

Men's undergarments included knee-length drawers made of muslin, jersey, or wool with a drawstring at the waist. During the decades of the tiny waist, men sometimes wore corseting.

For most of the century women's underwear consisted of a one-piece camisole, a petticoat attached to a simple bodice. The breasts were enhanced by padding or, during the last half of the century, early versions of the twentieth-century bra. By the 1820s women were wearing muslin or flannel drawers consisting of two separate legs open in the crotch that were attached to a waistband. Originally they were ankle-length and showed below the skirt. Petticoats, corsets, hoops, and bustles varied intermittently.

Horsehair crinolines and hoops reduced the number of petticoats needed. The hoop was a collapsible series of wood, metal, or whalebone tiers connected by tape to a waistband. Hoops were an attempt to address the annoyance of voluminous petticoats getting caught in women's legs, but they presented their own problems, such as causing falls or catching fire before the woman noticed. Factory workers were at particular risk for getting them caught in machinery. Corseting was made of whalebone, which was flexible and could be shaped when heated. The corset body was cotton or muslin, with the whalebones inserted in casing, and it had metal eyelets for lacing. Corsets varied in length to fit the current style. A documented 1880s style had twenty separate pieces and sixteen whalebones on each side. Because corsets were drawn tightly to "train" the female body into slenderness, health activists, feminists, and dress reformers alike attacked them by the end of the century.

Children's Clothing

Early in the nineteenth century U.S. children's clothing styles reflected Jean-Jacques Rousseau's romantic beliefs about the innocence of youth. Gender difference was blurred for as long as possible, and boys and girls wore white dresses until they could walk.

The Tyranny of the Corset. The ideal figure type for late-nineteenth-century fashions was the hourglass figure, which could be achieved only by wearing a corset. LIBRARY OF CONGRESS

Toddlers of both sexes wore skirted outfits. Around the age of five or six, boys got their first knicker-bockers (knee-length pants) and girls lengthened their skirts. Boys wore a long-trousered, short-jacketed suit that was somewhat looser than the adult version, and small girls wore simple dresses but covered their legs with pantaloons.

By the 1850s these gains were lost to the Victorian belief that children were miniature adults. Children's clothing imitated their parents' styles, which meant intricately constructed suits and dresses at the expense of freedom of movement. Sporting garments appeared in the 1860s for boys and in the 1890s for girls. In the 1890s children's clothing was folded into the politics of child labor reform, and children wore light, durable, loose clothing of soft, breathable fabrics. Adolescents, however, wore clothes much like those of adults without an interim teenage market.

Many Americans did not wear the middle-class wardrobes described above. The lower classes sewed less expensive versions, and others, spurning the idea of fashion, dressed in comfortable clothes, especially for leisure activities. Some religious and immigrant groups retained their distinctive garb as a symbol of their desire to remain separate from the general culture; others were eager to assimilate and therefore adopted the prevailing styles. The Amish, for example, retained their handmade, distinctively colored clothing, hats, and bonnets, while the Chinese gradually replaced their native clothing with Western styles, because their distinctive garb (and hairstyles) had subjected them to much ridicule and discrimination. And everyone was affected by the difficulty of obtaining fabrics and other manufactured goods and the general shortage of money during the Civil War.

Native Americans

American Indian dress varied widely according to tribal custom, region, and climate. Settlers forced native peoples who converted to Christianity and moved into their communities to adopt European standards of modesty in clothing. However, European Americans learned tanning from the native peoples and made good use of such Indian clothing as moccasins and deerskin suits for the rough frontier life. Meriwether Lewis and William Clark found that Indians were interested in trading their furs for European-style clothing and had, in fact, begun wearing knickers, vests, calico or flannel shirts, and hats.

African Americans

As early as the eighteenth century some southern legislatures enacted dress codes for enslaved African Americans. Whites were concerned that slaves with finery would desire more of the same and would steal or rebel to get it. Slaves' clothing, often hand-me-downs from the plantation owner's family, reflected the owner's economic and social status. In some instances the women of plantation households made clothes for each slave, two or three sets annually, from "Negro cloth," a coarse, itchy fabric that was actually prescribed in such states as South Carolina and was used as a means to maintain the social hierarchy on plantations.

On many plantations slaves were in charge of clothing production, from cotton picking to carding, weaving, clothing design, and production. They preferred bright colors and combinations reminiscent of African styles and often dyed their own cloth accordingly. For everyday plantation work blacks and whites sometimes wore a similar style, but the whites' clothing was made from better cloth and was more elegantly designed. Women's dresses were long with a simple, loosely constructed, long-sleeved bodice attached to a gathered skirt. Women covered their heads with a turban or sunbonnet. Black men with such jobs as coachman or house servant might have a frock coat, white shirt, and top hat, while field

"The Way It Is Done." Instructions for closing women's skirts, c. 1899. LIBRARY OF CONGRESS

hands wore a shirt and trousers and sometimes a waistcoat. Slave children typically wore long shirts for everyday. Some slave women attended church in hoops and petticoats. Female house servants' clothes often reflected the current shape, including a low waist and full skirt or a bustlelike gathering. African American slaves had "Sunday best" clothing for church purchased with the proceeds from cash crops grown on small plots of land loaned to them by the plantation owner.

Free blacks in the urban North often dressed in the style of northern whites of the same class. Like whites, they spent some of their disposable income on manufactured clothing. They displayed their finery publicly on Sunday strolls and during parades advocating the abolition of slavery.

Occupational Clothing

During the Civil War soldiers usually had uniforms, though not always. Postbellum businessmen wore suits to work, where they took off their coats and rolled up their sleeves but did not loosen their neckties. Office women late in the century wore the two-piece Gibson Girl look. Women textile workers copied current styles in cheaper fabrics or bought ready-made clothing. The work clothes of both genders were frequently covered with aprons.

Frontier work clothing for men and women was similar to that described for plantation workers. Only prostitutes wore hoops or extensive corseting. Some men adopted the western style with cowboy boots and fringed buckskin jackets. Philadelphia's Stetson Hat enterprise and California's Levi Strauss Company developed during mid-century to provide cowboy hats and denim jeans to western miners and farmers. Dry-goods merchant Levi Strauss had moved to San Francisco in mid-century to open a branch of his brothers' New York City business. On 20 May 1873 he began selling blue jeans, made from a denim fabric manufactured in a New Hampshire mill and with a patented metal riveting process that kept the pants' pockets from ripping. While denim pants had been workwear for many years, the rivets made them "jeans," and Strauss held the patent on the riveting process until 1908. "Levis" eventually became a worldwide U.S. cultural trademark.

Reformers

Nineteenth-century U.S. dress reformers included children's advocates, doctors, feminists, and the aesthetes. They had varying agendas but shared enough common concerns to persuade the public by the end of the century that some changes were in order for the twentieth century. For health, feminist, or aesthetic reasons, dress reformers shared a disgust for tight corseting and hoops. The aesthetes loathed the fabric colors and imposed a standardized style.

In the 1850s, after the Seneca Falls suffrage convention, the American feminist and abolitionist Amelia Bloomer and her friend Elizabeth Cady Stanton designed an outfit for women that allowed them more freedom of movement for public and leisure activities. The short overdress partially covered knee- or ankle-length bloomers. Although received negatively and satirized in the press by both genders, this outfit by the end of the century saw wear in bicycling and other leisure activities. In England, William Morris and the pre-Raphaelite movement called for more beautiful clothing—flowing, uncorseted, in soft colors, without the ugly lumps of bustles. This aesthetic movement was enthusiastically adopted in the United States by "rational" dress reform movements and such utopian communities as New Harmony, Indiana.

Dandies were nineteenth-century urban British males preoccupied with self-presentation. They daily spent hours searching for the ultimate cravat, grooming their skin, and finding the best tailor. Many contemporaries denounced these individuals as morally decadent, while others lauded their healthy opposition to the standardized style of the majority of men. Dandyism, which included such Romantic artists as Lord Byron, was prevalent in New York City's Lower Broadway and Greenwich Village. The press chided free African Americans for their devotion to this kind of "stylin'" at their parades and other festivities.

Manufacturing and Mass Consumption

The Industrial Revolution brought to the United States a consumer culture and a revolution in the provision of clothing to all levels of society. Before the 1850s clothes for the upper classes were handmade by dressmakers and tailors. Working-class people wore hand-me-downs, or the women sewed for themselves and their families, performing the tasks of spinning, weaving, dyeing, and stitching. Women also bartered or sold handmade clothing. Northern textile mills attracted "mill girls," who left their rural homes to work in the factories and spent some of their wages on ready-to-wear clothing.

In 1851 Isaac Singer patented the domestic sewing machine. Ellen Curtis Demorest, a milliner, in the 1860s cofounded with her husband, William, a New York City company that made paper patterns in graded, standardized sizes based on designs in the popular American fashion magazine *Godey's Lady's Book*. From 1860 to 1869 her company published a competing pattern magazine, *Mme. Demorest's Mirror of Fashions*, and established a nationwide distribution system with door-to-door saleswomen. In 1863 Ebenezer Butterick of Massachusetts began making paper patterns for menswear. Outwork, in which workers took pieces home to complete for low wages, began in the nineteenth century. From this practice developed the sweatshop and child labor problems that prompted the twentieth-century clothing worker unionization movement.

Commonwealth v. Hunt (1842) is considered a landmark case for the right of workers to organize. A court had convicted the Journeymen Bootmakers' Society of common law "criminal conspiracy" after the group attempted to organize bootmakers to improve wages and restrict hiring to society members. Chief Justice Lemuel Shaw of the Massachusetts Supreme Judicial Court overturned this decision, stating that such workers' organizations can be used for such "proper purposes" as raising "intellectual, moral, and social condition." This case was an important precedent for textile and clothing workers in the decades ahead.

See also **Industrialization and the Market; Personal Appearance; Textiles; Victorianism.**

Bibliography

Ewing, Elizabeth. *Dress and Undress: A History of Women's Underwear*. New York: Drama Book Specialists, 1978.

Foster, Helen Bradley. *New Raiments of Self: African American Clothing in the Antebellum South*. New York: Berg, 1997.

Genovese, Eugene. *Roll, Jordan, Roll: The World the Slaves Made*. New York: Pantheon, 1974.

Hall, Lee. *Common Threads: A Parade of American Clothing*. Boston: Little, Brown, 1992.

Hill, Margot Hamilton, and Peter A. Bucknell. *The Evolution of Fashion: Pattern and Cut from 1066 to 1930*. New York: Reinhold, 1968.

Kidwell, Claudia Brush, and Valerie Steele, eds. *Men and Women: Dressing the Part*. Washington, D.C.: Smithsonian Institution Press, 1989.

Severa, Joan L. *Dressed for the Photographer: Ordinary Americans and Fashion, 1840–1900*. Kent, Ohio: Kent State University Press, 1995.

Steele, Valerie. *Fashion and Eroticism: Ideals of Feminine Beauty from the Victorian Era to the Jazz Age*. New York: Oxford University Press, 1985.

White, Shane, and Graham White. *Stylin': African American Expressive Culture from Its Beginnings to the Zoot Suit*. Ithaca, N.Y.: Cornell University Press, 1998.

Wilson, Elizabeth. *Adorned in Dreams: Fashion and Modernity*. Berkeley: University of California Press, 1987.

Worrell, Estelle Ansley. *Children's Costume in America, 1607–1910*. New York: Scribners, 1980.

BARBARA M. JONES

CLUBS

[This entry includes subentries on **Fraternal Societies and Clubs, Women's Clubs and Associations,** and **Religious Clubs and Associations.**]

FRATERNAL SOCIETIES AND CLUBS

It is a cliché that the United States always has been a nation of joiners. Indeed, Sinclair Lewis (1885–1951) satirized Americans' propensity to join and "boost" in *Babbitt* in 1922. However, the cliché holds much truth. Throughout the nineteenth century and into the late 1950s, America was a nation of joiners, particularly of fraternal (and sororal) organizations, for they offered individuals something the body politic could not or would not offer.

Beginning with the Freemasons in the late 1700s, white Americans formed and joined an amazingly wide variety of organizations. After the Masons—and often based on their format—groups blossomed throughout America. White men, and later white women, joined, among thousands of other organizations, the Odd Fellows, the Elks, and the Independent Order of Foresters. For African Americans, the roots of fraternalism run almost as deep. They are found in Philadelphia, where the Reverend Richard Allen (1760–1831) began much the same joining trend among black Americans in the late 1700s, when he founded the Free African Society, the first African American benevolent society, in 1787. More than thirty years later he presided over the founding of the American Society of Free Persons of Color. In the North and especially in the South after the Civil War, more blacks joined fraternal societies in proportion to their numbers than whites. After 1865 African Americans often joined "separate-but-equal" versions of white fraternal organizations, such as the Knights of Pythias and the Good Templars; they also formed many fraternal societies of their own, such as the Grand Fountain United Order of True Reformers in Richmond, Virginia, which eventually became the largest black fraternal order in America, and the Brown Society in Charleston, South Carolina, a fraternal organization for freedmen.

Fraternal societies generally are separated into two groups—secret societies and mutual benefit societies—although this distinction was weak in the nineteenth century (Schmidt, *Fraternal Organizations*, p. 4). Secret societies derived their appeal from rituals, oaths, passwords, and handshakes known only to members. This insistence on secret lore sometimes hurt societies, most notably the Masons during the militantly democratic and evangelical Jacksonian era, as prejudice against them and paranoia about their "secret intentions" spread, especially in the Northeast.

The mutual benefit societies offered insurance, burial benefits, and charity to their members and the community. During hard times, members could count on their fellows' support, often both financial and psychological. Benefit societies that developed a full array of benevolent services often became associated with or themselves became full-fledged businesses, selling insurance, making and selling the regalia worn by the order, establishing stores, and publishing newspapers. By doing so, they further integrated themselves into the local community while bringing more money into their coffers to be used for charitable purposes.

Nineteenth-century fraternal societies grew steadily because they appealed to the increasing numbers of people in a mobile and turbulent America who lacked connections to local communities or suffered forms of disfranchisement. Immigration and emancipation brought millions of restless and rootless newcomers into American society. Fraternal orders often offered immigrants a place and a chance to interact in their native tongue and to meet more established members of their ethnic communities. These fraternal organizations also offered, and in many cases stressed, opportunities to learn the prerequisites of citizenship, a first and important step to becoming Americans. In light of their being kept out of the body politic, especially in the South, blacks relied on their organizations chiefly for social cohesion and socioeconomic betterment. Women's auxiliaries of fraternal societies, while more often than not subsumed by and subservient to the main men's groups, offered the same benefits to women. Membership in these auxiliaries and in the new women's clubs that emerged toward the end of the century gave women a sense of control and confidence few could gain in the home or workplace. Indeed, for a great many of those who joined fraternal and sororal organizations, the opportunities to rise within the society, gain respect, and hold positions of importance were cherished because they were denied so often outside the group.

It was prestige, most of all, that joiners craved. The first white fraternal societies grew out of a need or desire for political power and social stability. The white middle and lower-middle classes, blacks, immigrants, and women who generally were kept out of serious political participation sought in these societies the prestige and participation denied them by the society at large. Since their inception, most fraternal societies have featured systems of "degrees," hierarchical tiers of rank and responsibility that members ascend over time by attending faithfully to the rules and rituals of the order. These systems, combined with the sometimes grandiose titles the nineteenth-century societies conferred on their members, the distinctive uniforms or regalia, and the chances to participate in public events, such as parades, and to speak from the platform at meetings and other quasi-

Knights of Pithias. Connecticut brigade of the Knights of Pithias, Washington, D.C., 1894. LIBRARY OF CONGRESS

public events, gave members a "chance to be somebody." Finally, and perhaps most importantly, these societies offered "fictive kinship networks" that were of tremendous value to their members, extending their resources in communities often hostile to their needs and desires.

The importance of fraternal societies can be seen in the numbers of men and women who joined them. While historical membership statistics are not definitive, one writer estimated that by 1920, nearly half of the U.S. population belonged to some sort of fraternal organization. Historians have paid little attention to this significant social and cultural phenomenon. Fraternalism in its heyday—the late-nineteenth and early-twentieth centuries—is a subject ripe for more scholarly exploration.

See also **Masons.**

Bibliography

Brown, Elsa Barkley. "Uncle Ned's Children: Negotiating Community in Postemancipation Richmond, Virginia." Ph.D. diss., Kent State University, 1994.

Fahey, David M. *The Black Lodge in White America: "True Reformer" Browne and His Economic Strategy.* Lanham, Md.: University Press of America, 1994.

Greenwood, Janette Thomas. *Bittersweet Legacy: The Black and White "Better Classes" in Charlotte, 1850–1910.* Chapel Hill: University of North Carolina Press, 1994.

Schmidt, Alvin J. *Fraternal Organizations.* Westport, Conn.: Greenwood Press, 1980.

Treadway, Sandra Gioia. *Women of Mark: A History of the Woman's Club of Richmond, Virginia, 1894–1994.* Richmond: Library of Virginia, 1995.

JAMES D. WATKINSON

WOMEN'S CLUBS AND ASSOCIATIONS

In the nineteenth century most people believed a woman's place was in the home, yet a great many American women defied convention by joining voluntary associations to engage in activities unrelated to domestic life. Unwelcome in men's groups, women formed separate associations. Oftentimes they used women's societies to assert a collective voice for change on public issues. In the antebellum era, the Protestant Church propelled women members to engage in charitable or benevolent work and missionary activity via moral reform and ladies aid societies and temperance organizations. At regular meetings members prayed, read uplifting texts together, raised money for good works, and founded such institutions as Sunday Schools, orphanages, trade schools, and homes for the friendless, including "fallen women" or unwed mothers. Some groups bravely took on more volatile issues, including reform of prostitutes, abolition of slavery, or enfranchisement for women.

The Civil War occasioned patriotic work for women in new organizations, such as the U.S. Sanitary Commission in the Union and ladies aid societies among Confederate women. Such clubs plainly secularized the voluntary activity to revolve around fund-raising and sewing for the soldiers. Once the war ended women formed new clubs devoted to a broad range of interests.

The late nineteenth century saw an explosion of clubs that attracted middle-class, middle-aged, Protestant women in cities and towns throughout the nation. Boston's New England Woman's Club and New York's Sorosis, both founded in 1868, pioneered in the literary club movement, inviting members to present papers to their peers on historical and fictional topics and addressing contemporary issues. Dozens of similar groups formed in the late nineteenth century, including the Chicago Woman's Club, the Civic Club of Philadelphia, the Century Club of San Francisco, and the Rhode Island Woman's Club of Providence. Dozens of clubs united into the General Federation of Women's Clubs in 1890. The Association of Collegiate Alumnae, founded in 1882, linked clusters of college-educated women to press for educational reform. The Woman's Christian Temperance Union, founded in 1873, campaigned against the abuse of alcohol and also agitated for health education, divorce, and dress reform. The American Woman Suffrage Association and the National Woman Suffrage Association, both founded in 1868, merged in 1890 into the National American Woman Suffrage Association and led the struggle to win the vote for women.

Women of color, unwelcome in almost all white-dominated organizations, formed networks of their own. The National Association of Colored Women (later the National Association of Colored Women's Clubs) formed in 1896 from a merger of the National Federation of Afro-American Women and the Colored Women's League.

The fraternal orders popular with men of the late nineteenth century developed women's auxiliaries, such as the Ladies of the Maccabees, Job's Daughters, Order of the Eastern Star, Order of the King's Daughters, and Daughters of Norway. A wave of patriotic groups developed late in the century, including the Daughters of the American Revolution (1890)

and the United Daughters of the Confederacy (1894). Religious groups did not disappear but rather evolved into larger structures to do good works at home and abroad. Examples of these are Women's American Baptist Foreign Mission Society, National Council of Catholic Women, and Women's Relief Societies of the Church of the Latter-day Saints. In 1893 the World's Columbian Exposition in Chicago ignited several special-interest groups to form in the 1890s, including the National Federation of Music Clubs, National Council of Jewish Women, and National Congress of Mothers (later National Congress of Parents and Teachers).

Few celebrities sprang from women's organizations, although the suffragist Susan B. Anthony and the temperance advocate Frances Willard were household names in their lifetimes. Nevertheless, several women leaders inspired organization members to engage in a broad platform of reform. Among the leaders were Elise Massey Selden of Memphis, Jane Cunningham Croly of New York City, Phoebe Hearst of San Francisco, Annie Laws in Ohio, May Wright Sewall in Indianapolis, Fanny Purdy Palmer in Providence, Mary Gibson in Los Angeles, Sarah Platt Decker in Colorado, Julia Ward Howe and Josephine St. Pierre Ruffin in Boston, and Ida Wells-Barnett, Bertha Honoré Palmer, and Ellen Henrotin in Chicago. These women led regional organizations that taught members to research, write, think, and offer public presentations; to collect, budget, and spend dues and donations; to organize committees and investigate social problems; and to lobby legislators, write press releases, and raise public awareness on municipal reforms. Clubwomen grew in numbers, skills, and commitment, and they became effective at bringing about change in their communities. Without the vote, they managed to establish public libraries, parks, playgrounds, beautification programs, public school improvements, and social welfare programs.

Public criticism against women's activism in the public arena never abated. In 1868 *Harper's Magazine* printed a cartoon belittling club members as masculine for engaging in activity outside the home. As late as 1907 the former U.S. president Grover Cleveland used the *Ladies Home Journal* to criticize clubwomen for neglecting their homes and children. Nevertheless women's organizations attracted millions of members in the nineteenth century and in the early twentieth century.

See also **Academic and Professional Societies; Clubs,** *subentry on* **Religious Clubs and Organizations; Gender,** *subentry on* **Interpretations of Gender; Magazines, Women's; Temperance Movement; Voters and Voting,**

subentry on **The Women's Vote; Women,** *subentry on*
Women's Rights.

Bibliography

Blair, Karen J. *The Clubwoman as Feminist: True Womanhood Redefined, 1868–1914.* New York: Holmes and Meier, 1980.

Gere, Anne Ruggles. *Intimate Practices: Literacy and Cultural Work in U.S. Women's Clubs, 1880–1920.* Urbana: University of Illinois Press, 1997.

Scott, Anne Firor. *Natural Allies: Women's Associations in American History.* Urbana: University of Illinois Press, 1991.

KAREN J. BLAIR

RELIGIOUS CLUBS AND ORGANIZATIONS

In his study of antebellum American life, Alexis de Tocqueville suggested that the separation between church and state and the propensity for joining associations were particularly American. The combination of these two factors brought about a distinctly American system of religious associations in the nineteenth century.

The formal separation between church and state, which was complete by 1833, led some Americans to predict the downfall of organized religion. Instead, religion and religious institutions remained central to American public life as pluralism and voluntary organizations replaced state-sanctioned religion. A series of revivals that swept through the nation between 1800 and 1840, collectively known as the Second Great Awakening, inspired increased religious enthusiasm and promoted a belief in the perfection of self and society.

Beginning in the first decades of the nineteenth century, large numbers of Americans joined religious, social, and charitable associations within their respective congregations; these were probably the most common religious organizations to which Americans belonged. There were two categories of voluntary associations within congregations. One was based on faith and devotion, and included Protestant prayer groups and Catholic rosary societies. The second type encompassed charitable and missionary societies, which were organized in a wide variety of Protestant and Catholic churches. Christians were not alone in their social welfare efforts; in 1819, for example, Rebecca Gratz founded the Female Hebrew Benevolent Society to aid poor Jewish women and children.

As charity and missionary societies spread, some united together into cross-denominational national organizations, such as the American Bible Society (1816) and the American Sunday School Union (1824). Most national organizations were not affiliated with a single congregation or denomination but brought together members from a range of mainstream Protestant churches. The belief that ordinary people had a moral and religious responsibility to transform society encouraged Americans to organize tract societies, maternal associations, Sunday schools, and missionary societies. These groups, sometimes referred to collectively as the Benevolent Empire, shaped American religious and political culture during the antebellum period. Women predominated in voluntary religious organizations, just as they did in church membership. Religious groups afforded women opportunities for activity outside the home and a chance to improve society.

Growing up alongside organizations with roots in congregations were reform societies that promoted temperance, moral reform, and abolitionism. Groups such as the American Temperance Society (1826), the American Anti-Slavery Society (1833), and the New York Female Moral Reform Society (1834) did not emerge from specific congregations but took their inspiration from shared Protestant beliefs.

The growth of religiously inspired organizations slowed during the 1840s and 1850s, but large numbers of Americans continued to join religious groups. According to one study, a third of New York's adult population belonged to religious associations in 1860. The Young Men's Christian Association (YMCA), which was founded in England in 1844, took root in the United States in the 1850s and worked to provide a moral and religious environment for young men in cities. Alongside many secular fraternal societies, groups like the Jewish B'nai B'rith (1843) and later the Catholic Knights of Columbus (1882) organized on the basis of religious identity or church membership.

In the post–Civil War period, church-based and religiously inspired voluntary organizations burgeoned across the country. The Woman's Christian Temperance Union, the activities of followers of the Social Gospel movement, and especially African American church groups illustrate this vitality. Churches became the institutional center of African American life and members formed a wide array of organizations, including missionary groups, education societies, prayer societies such as Bible Bands, and mutual benefit societies such as the Sisters of Charity.

See also **African Americans,** *subentry on* **African American Religions; Catholicism; Protestantism; Religion.**

Bibliography

Boylan, Anne M. *Sunday School: The Formation of an American Institution, 1790–1880.* New Haven, Conn.: Yale University Press, 1988.

Higginbotham, Evelyn Brooks. *Righteous Discontent: The Women's Movement in the Black Baptist Church, 1880–1920.* Cambridge, Mass.: Harvard University Press, 1993.

MAUREEN A. McCARTHY

COAL   Coal was a familiar fuel to the European colonists who settled North America. Depletion of the forests had prompted Britons to substitute coal for wood by the end of the seventeenth century. The lack of wood was not a concern in the American colonies, however, where a vast and seemingly endless virgin forest retarded the development of alternative fuels well into the nineteenth century.

Chronology of Industry Development

The only commercial coal field in colonial America was located near Richmond, Virginia, where as early as the 1740s mines were hoisting coal for the Tidewater settlements along the James River. Between 1790 and 1830 Richmond coal production expanded until it dominated the intercoastal trade that served the principal Atlantic cities as far north as Boston. By the 1830s, however, Richmond coal was unable to

Working in the Coal Mine. Elk Mountain Coal Mines, Pennsylvania. Shipment of coal from western Pennsylvania depended on the Pennsylvania Railroad. Photograph, William Henry Jackson, c. 1892. LIBRARY OF CONGRESS

compete with eastern Pennsylvania anthracite, which was of a higher quality and was located nearer to the Atlantic markets. Anthracite, much harder than bituminous coal and more difficult to ignite, produced such an intense heat that a special grate had to be developed before it could be utilized commercially. Even after these problems were resolved, the lack of adequate transportation stifled the growth of anthracite well into the 1820s, when the first canal was built into these fields.

Development of the new nation's bituminous coal fields also stagnated until the markets and a transportation infrastructure were established. The George's Creek region of western Maryland produced bituminous coal that was used locally in the 1790s and by the 1830s floated coal down the Potomac River in specially designed coal "arks." Production in the western Maryland field expanded with the arrival of the Baltimore and Ohio Railroad in Cumberland, Maryland, in 1842 and the Chesapeake and Ohio Canal in 1850, two carriers that hauled large quantities of George's Creek coal to the Tidewater. For a number of years this field provided a major portion of the bituminous coal sold east of the Appalachians.

Mining in western Pennsylvania originally centered in Pittsburgh but gradually spread upstream along the Monongahela River and downstream along the Ohio River. The lack of adequate transportation for Ohio Valley coal to the eastern markets vigorously stimulated the local brick, glass, and iron industries of the upper Ohio during the early nineteenth century. Although the Pennsylvania Mainline Canal reached Pittsburgh in 1834, not much coal made its way eastward over the mountains via this route. Some of the region's coal followed a northern path through the Erie Canal network, but substantial shipments to the eastern markets did not begin until the Pennsylvania Railroad reached western Pennsylvania in 1854. Meanwhile bituminous coal found a growing market firing the boilers of Ohio and Mississippi River steamboats and in the homes and industries of the towns and cities that sprang up along these major interior waterways.

In Ohio mining began first along the Ohio River across from Wheeling, Virginia (now West Virginia), and expanded with the state's canal system in the 1830s. But Ohio's big coal boom did not come until the 1850s, when the railroads penetrated the state's interior. Hocking Valley coal, for example, moved along an all-rail route to Chicago by 1860. Further railroad development after the Civil War opened more direct routes to the Great Lakes and led to a still greater expansion of the coal industry.

In West Virginia, which became a state in 1863,

the mining industry developed somewhat later. The mountains were a major barrier to profitable large-scale mining. Construction of the Baltimore and Ohio Railroad across the northern part of the state during the 1850s initiated commercial mining in that section, but the state's southern fields were not opened until the Chesapeake and Ohio Railroad was completed from Norfolk, Virginia, to Huntington, West Virginia, by way of the New and Kanawha Rivers in 1873. Coal had been used extensively during the antebellum era as fuel for the saltworks furnaces along the Kanawha River, but the market remained primarily local until the end of the century. The Central Appalachian coal fields boomed at the turn of the twentieth century as the Norfolk and Western Railroad penetrated the western sections of Virginia and West Virginia and branch lines of the Louisville and Nashville Railroad reached into eastern Kentucky and northern Tennessee. Railroads did not reach the northern Alabama coal fields until after the Civil War, when the growth of the Birmingham iron industry provided a ready market.

The Midwest fields in Indiana, Illinois, western Kentucky, Missouri, and Iowa developed at different times during the nineteenth century. Small amounts of coal were being shipped down the Ohio and Mississippi Rivers prior to the War of 1812, but it was not until the 1840s, when steamboats plying the interior waterways replaced wood with coal, did a significant market exist. Real growth in Midwest production, however, awaited the expanding railroad network in the 1850s for mining to be profitable beyond the riverbanks.

In the Far West the Mormon leader Brigham Young initially resisted the development of Utah coal because he feared a disintegration of civil society similar to that which had accompanied the gold and silver booms. The need for iron products, however, soon overcame his reservations, and by the 1850s Utah coal was smelting the state's iron. Coal mining flourished in Colorado, Wyoming, and northern New Mexico after the railroad opened the region during the 1870s, but the coal seams of Montana and Washington were not tapped until the 1890s. The vast distance of the Far West fields from major markets was a serious competitive disadvantage that was not overcome until the end of the nineteenth century.

Expansion and Organization

The antebellum coal industry expanded tenfold in the two decades prior to the Civil War, from 2.5 million tons in 1840 to 20 million tons by 1860. Even though coal was mined in more than twenty states, Pennsylvania, Ohio, Illinois, Virginia, and Maryland produced about 90 percent of all the coal mined in the United States. Pennsylvania alone supplied nearly half the national tonnage. In addition to its abundant coal resources, Pennsylvania was strategically located between the urban Atlantic markets to the east, the interior markets of the Ohio and Mississippi Valleys, and the Great Lakes cities to the northwest. Internal improvements undertaken by Pennsylvania, such as canals, river improvements, and particularly completion of the Pennsylvania Railroad in 1854, linked the state's eastern and western markets and greatly facilitated the expansion of the industry. Only Virginia enjoyed similar resources and geographical advantages, but its general assembly, divided by geography and political sectionalism, failed to undertake the internal improvements required to develop the state's western coal resources.

Historically Americans have assumed that the exploitation of natural resources should be limited only by the dictates of the marketplace, and this conviction resulted in serious problems for the coal industry. Corporation managers increasingly came to believe that access to such a critical resource as coal should not be entrusted to vagaries of the free market. Naturally many Americans found corporate control of such a vital resource unacceptable and, therefore, opposed such efforts. Moreover rapid, unrestrained development encouraged too many operators to enter the business, which intensified competition and generated a wasteful boom-bust cycle in the coal markets, a problem that plagued the industry through the twentieth century. Efforts to bring an orderly balance to the supply and demand for coal resulted in two major developments that restructured the industry: the organization of large, vertically integrated corporations and the emergence of railroads as the dominant owners of coal lands. The eastern Pennsylvania anthracite industry was the first to undergo this transition and provides what some scholars regard as the prototype for the modern corporate organization.

The anthracite fields were organized into three economic regions, each served by a single transportation company. The northern region, the Wyoming, shipped its coal along the Delaware and Hudson Canal to New York City and northern ports. The eastern region, the Lehigh, shipped its coal to Philadelphia and later to canals terminating in New York City via a canal of the Lehigh Coal and Navigation Company. The southern field, the Schuylkill, was linked to Philadelphia by a canal built by the Schuylkill Navigation Company. The carriers serving the northern and eastern fields were granted commercial development rights over the coal lands, and these districts were under firm corporate control by 1830. In the Schuylkill district, however, the Schuylkill Navigation Company was granted only the rights of a carrying company and not those of a landowning or mining company as was the case in the neighboring districts. In the early decades, therefore, Schuylkill County offered great opportunities for small entrepreneurs, who encountered three types of landowners: local land speculators, local elites who themselves invested in and helped to build the industry during its early years, and powerful absentee investors who formed large land companies and leased small blocks to independent mine operators. The landowners first established a legal separation of subsurface and surface rights and then implemented a royalty system based on a minimal annual tonnage or cash payment by the lessee. The typical lease was for a short period of time, usually between five and fifteen years, and for relatively small blocks of land. Improvements were made to the property at the expense of the lessee, and as deeper seams were worked and the technology of mining became more complex with the use of steam-powered breakers, pumps, and large ventilation fans, the cost of opening new mines rose accordingly. The leasing system enabled small operators with little capital to enter the industry, but the royalty system forced operators to produce coal even in the times of no demand or excess supply in the markets. Producing coal even when the market was glutted ensured that coal prices would be chronically depressed even as costs rose.

No system of mining coal could be less economical than to fit out a number of separate operations upon small leases, and to rationalize this system the Philadelphia and Reading Railroad expanded during the early 1870s beyond its tracks and into the mining business. Through the use of railroad pools and vertical integration, the Reading succeeded in gaining complete control over the coal industry in Schuylkill County.

Although bituminous coal was more widely distributed than anthracite, railroads that carried soft coal also were compelled to defend their freight traffic by acquiring large holdings of coal lands along their rights-of-way and leasing them to independent operators. These railroads were never able to control the bituminous industry to the degree that the Reading controlled anthracite, but their roles as lease owners and coal carriers gave them powerful influence in the industry.

Labor

America's rise as a leading industrial power is measured by the dramatic expansion of the railroads, the emergence of gigantic iron and steel industries, and the explosion in coal production that fueled both industries. The Industrial Revolution also spawned a social transformation marked in the coal industry by a rapid growth in the number of coal miners. In 1840 the census counted 6,811 mine workers. Their numbers grew to 36,500 by 1860, doubled during the Civil War decade, surpassed 127,000 in 1900, and reached a peak of more than 650,000 in 1920. The earliest southern miners were slaves, but local farmers generally supplied what little seasonal labor was needed in the earliest northern mines. As the demand for coal escalated, so did the demand for skilled miners, most of whom immigrated to the United States from Britain. At least half of the American mine workers in 1870 were born outside the United States, and as late as 1880 one-third of the miners of Ohio and Illinois were Britons. Of course, the British were not one people. The Irish, Welsh, Scots, and English all regarded themselves as distinctly separate nationalities. Historic national conflicts were further aggravated by class conflicts. The English, Welsh, and Scots dominated the skilled mining and managerial positions, while the far more numerous Irish disproportionately worked as manual laborers. By the end of the century much of this tension had been reduced by the elevation of the Irish within the craft and by the unity among all established miners against the incoming waves of new immigrants from southern and eastern Europe, whom they perceived as a threat to their security.

In the nineteenth century skilled miners were craftsmen who owned their own tools, hired and paid their own "helpers," individually contracted their services to coal operators, and usually were paid according to the tonnage they produced. They were, in fact, petty subcontractors largely free from direct company supervision. Skilled miners, not the companies, controlled the work process and assumed responsibility for regulating production to meet market demand and to keep prices high.

By the 1870s, however, changes in the organization of the industry were already altering the traditional system that had prevailed for centuries. Management's efforts to gain control over the production process by reorganizing labor around machinery required the investment of more capital, and operations became larger and more mechanized. A new professional class of managers emerged as the coal industry underwent this transition from cottage industry to modern corporate organization.

Industrial restructuring challenged the miners' traditional independence and control of the craft. Between 1860 and 1890 they organized numerous unions to protect themselves from the growing power of the corporations. The influence of these unions was limited, however, because their power was local and regional rather than national and because of the internal fragmentation between skilled craftsmen and laborers. Finally a national union was organized in 1890, when delegates from the nation's coal fields met in Columbus, Ohio, to establish the United Mine Workers of America (UMWA). The union's proclaimed mission, as stated in its constitution, to organize "all those who work in and about the mines," demonstrates that the miners no longer perceived themselves as independent craftsmen but as industrial workers who sought collective solidarity to protect their interests from the arbitrary power of modern industrial capitalism. By the end of the nineteenth century the coal industry had undergone a radical restructuring that set its course for the next century.

See also **Disasters; Immigration and Immigrants,** *subentry on* **Great Britain; Internal Improvements; Iron; Labor Movement,** *subentry on* **Unions and Strikes; Mining and Extraction; Natural Resources; Pennsylvania; Railroads; Steam Power; Steel and the Steel Industry; Transportation,** *subentries on* **Canals and Waterways, Railroads; Virginia.**

Bibliography

Berthoff, Rowland. *British Immigrants in Industrial America, 1790–1950.* Cambridge, Mass.: Harvard University Press, 1953.

Eavenson, Howard N. *The First Century and a Quarter of American Coal Industry.* Pittsburgh, Pa.: privately printed by Baltimore Weekly Press, 1942.

Harvey, Katherine A. *The Best-Dressed Miners: Life and Labor in the Maryland Coal Region, 1835–1910.* Ithaca, N.Y.: Cornell University Press, 1969.

Jones, William D. *Wales in America: Scranton and the Welsh, 1860–1920.* Cardiff: University of Wales Press, 1993.

Lewis, Ronald L. *Coal, Iron, and Slaves: Industrial Slavery in Maryland and Virginia, 1715–1865.* Westport, Conn.: Greenwood, 1979.

Long, Priscilla. *Where the Sun Never Shines: A History of America's Bloody Coal Industry.* New York: Paragon, 1989.

Roy, Andrew. *A History of the Coal Miners of the United States: From the Development of the Mines to the Close of the Anthracite Strike of 1902, including a Brief Sketch of Early British Miners.* Columbus, Ohio: J. L. Trauger, 1907.

Wallace, Anthony F. C. *St. Clair: A Nineteenth-century Coal Town's Experience with a Disaster-prone Industry.* New York: Knopf, 1987.

RONALD L. LEWIS

COINS. See **Money and Coins.**

COLONIZATION, AFRICAN AMERICAN

The first former slaves to return to Africa from the United States, who came to be known as colonizers, were the nearly three thousand black loyalists who evacuated New York City with the British navy in May 1783. As a reward for their wartime service, 1,336 men, together with their families, received from Britain certificates of manumission and settled at Birchtown, Nova Scotia. But the cold, bleak land proved inhospitable, and faced with starvation, the colonists planned a mass exodus to West Africa. In February 1792 a fleet of fifteen British ships ferried 1,196 black Tories from Halifax to the new city of Freetown, Sierra Leone.

Influenced in part by this mass emigration, Virginia governor Thomas Jefferson advanced a detailed plan for emancipation and deportation in 1783 when it appeared that Virginia might call a state constitutional convention. Included in Jefferson's model constitution was a clause to liberate all children (on reaching adulthood) born of slave parents after 1800. Because Jefferson could not envision large numbers of free blacks living in harmony beside their former masters, the plan also required the immediate colonization of those emancipated (which would have resulted in the forced separation of parents and children). The constitutional convention never materialized, but the draft appeared in 1785 as an appendix to Jefferson's *Notes on the State of Virginia*.

Two decades later, then-president Jefferson had the opportunity to put his plan into action. In the wake of Gabriel's rebellion, a slave conspiracy in Virginia, several influential voices, most notably that of state legislator George Tucker, publicly advocated colonizing Virginia's entire slave population on the "western side" of the Mississippi River. In the hope of avoiding future servile rebellions, the state assembly in 1802 urged Governor James Monroe to correspond with the president about obtaining land near Sierra Leone to which slave rebels and "such negroes as may be emancipated" by their owners could resettle. Once more, the plan came to nothing. British officials wanted no further American bondmen, and Jefferson concluded that liberating slave rebels in the land of their ancestors might actually inspire future rebellions.

The idea of colonization resurfaced in Virginia in 1816 when a young Federalist, Charles Fenton Mercer, stumbled on a published record of the abortive 1802 debates. Armed with this information, in December 1816 Mercer helped found the American Society for Colonizing the Free People of Color in the United States. For a brief time, the American Colonization Society, or ACS, as it was more commonly known, attracted moderate abolitionists and free blacks by promoting the voluntary removal of former slaves to western Africa. The Supreme Court justice Bushrod Washington served as its first president, while House Speaker Henry Clay and society founder Representative Mercer ran the board of managers, the governing body of the society. In January 1819, at the request of the society, Congress allocated $100,000 to facilitate removal and pay the salary of a colonial agent in Africa; using but three hundred dollars of these funds, society employee Eli Ayres purchased most of Liberia at gunpoint in 1821.

Because many northern freedpeople had for several decades considered the possibility of following the black loyalists to Africa, several influential African Americans, including Paul Cuffe, a successful merchant with commercial ties to Africa, initially made overtures to northern philanthropists connected with the ACS. In the South former slaves who concluded that they would never be allowed to prosper in a country that guaranteed equality only to whites often proved willing to accept the society's as-

Joseph Jenkins Roberts (1809–1876). Roberts, first appointed governor of Liberia, West Africa, by the American Colonization Society in 1842, was inaugurated as Liberia's first president in July 1847. LIBRARY OF CONGRESS

sistance in starting anew in a foreign land; even the staunch abolitionist Denmark Vesey briefly considered the option of emigration in 1818. But once it became clear that no African Americans would be allowed to hold leadership posts in the society, the free black community began to separate from the organization. Most of the society's leaders were petty slaveholders who resorted to crudely racist arguments to justify the removal of free blacks, and because the organization hoped that all freedpersons could be prodded into leaving the United States, society spokesmen stubbornly refused to condemn the segregation emerging in the North.

Philadelphia's rapidly growing free community took the lead in denouncing the society. On 15 January 1817, just days after the organization was founded, the Reverend Richard Allen arranged a meeting of more than a thousand blacks at his Bethel Church to condemn colonization schemes and announce his people's determination to remain in the land of their birth. *Freedom's Journal,* the first national black newspaper in the United States, was initially an anticolonization publication; the *Journal* lost its readership shortly after its editor, John B. Russwurm, altered his stance and began to write prosociety editorials. Ensuing black newspapers and pamphlets, including David Walker's 1829 *Appeal to the Colored Citizens of the World,* proved consistently hostile to any plan for emigration directed by a white-run organization. In 1832 William Lloyd Garrison denounced the society in the lengthy treatise *Thoughts on African Colonization.*

Despite these objections, the society was never the planter-run organization Garrison and the northern black community depicted it to be, and modern assertions that proslavery theorists backed the ACS in hopes of removing dangerous free blacks are largely without foundation. Proslavery politicians in Virginia, such as John Tyler and Abel P. Upshur, hoped to use the organization to rid the border South of free blacks, who served as dangerous models of liberty for yet-enslaved African Americans. But despite the racist tone of their rhetoric, most white colonizationists privately held progressive views of black abilities. Society spokesmen suggested that southern economic weakness was not the result of alleged African American incompetence, but rather that the institution of slavery deprived blacks of both the incentives and education that made northern workers so productive. Because many border-state colonizers boldly advocated the elimination of the entire African American labor force, bond and free, in the name of regional prosperity, planter-politicians like Robert Turnbull of South Carolina bitterly castigated the organization as an "Abolition Society."

In response to Lower South demands, President Andrew Jackson ended federal aid to the society in 1830, after which the organization ceased to be a viable part of the broad antislavery movement. In 1832 Maryland's legislature seceded from the parent body and incorporated a state society. The following year William Jay and James G. Birney followed Garrison's lead, formally abandoning the organization. In an unsuccessful effort to regain its northern support, the ACS tried to appease the American Anti-Slavery Society by firing five southern board members. The ACS formally continued to exist until 1899, but by the time the Thirteenth Amendment freed approximately four million blacks, only 11,213 free blacks and former slaves migrated to Liberia under society auspices.

Even as support for the white-run ACS dissipated in the black community, interest in departing the United States continued to run high in the urban North. With each new political assault on the rights of black Americans, influential black leaders concluded that they would have to abandon the land of their birth to find true liberty. In the wake of the Fugitive Slave Act of 1850, which empowered federal marshals to recover runaways, Martin Delaney called for a major convention to meet in Cleveland, Ohio, to discuss emigration to Haiti or Central America. The call precipitated a spirited debate in the northern black community and angry denunciations from antiemigrationists like Frederick Douglass. The 1854 Cleveland convention failed to win many converts, but the *Dred Scott* decision of 1857 reinforced the idea, as the writer Frances Ellen Watkins put it, that the federal government was "the arch traitor to liberty." By refusing the right of citizenship to American-born blacks while denying Congress the authority to ban enslaved labor in the western territories, Chief Justice Roger B. Taney scared many former slaves into believing that unfree labor would soon return to the northern states. Many sailed for Africa or followed Delaney to Canada.

With the outbreak of the Civil War, President Abraham Lincoln and the Republican Party formally endorsed colonization as an answer to slavery and the growing number of black refugees; the Preliminary Emancipation Proclamation of September 1862 recommended colonization for all freed people. But late in the year Attorney General Edward Bates, ignoring Taney's Supreme Court, announced that "men of color, if born in the United States, are citizens," the first federal admission of black citizenship. The decision to recruit black soldiers forced Lincoln to reject colonization. The final Emancipation Proclamation of January 1863 did not mention black emigration. As blacks participated in Emancipation Day celebra-

tions, any considerations of a mass return to Africa momentarily vanished. Black emigration to Liberia dropped from a high of 783 persons in 1853 to 73 people by 1873.

Not surprisingly, the reemergence of colonization coincided with the administration of Woodrow Wilson, the most aggressively antiblack president of the twentieth century. In 1914 Marcus Garvey, a native of Jamaica, launched the Universal Negro Improvement Association. Like Martin Delaney before him, Garvey regarded emigration not merely as an escape from American injustice and violence but as a method of rebuilding Africa's "noble past." His newspaper, the *Negro World*, editorialized that racism was so much a part of Western civilization that any appeals to the conscience of America were futile. But just as Delaney had failed to win the support of Frederick Douglass and other free black leaders, Garvey's proposed Empire of Africa was denounced by W. E. B. Du Bois and the National Association for the Advancement of Colored People as "bombastic and impracticable." Garvey's "Negro Zionism" collapsed in 1923 when he was imprisoned for mail fraud. Pardoned but ordered deported as an undesirable alien, Garvey died in London in 1940.

See also **Abolition and Antislavery; African Americans,** *subentry on* **Free Blacks before the Civil War; Liberia; Race and Racial Thinking; Segregation,** *subentry on* **Segregation and Civil Rights.**

Bibliography

Egerton, Douglas R. "Averting a Crisis: The Proslavery Critique of the American Colonization Society." *Civil War History* 43 (1997): 142–156.

———. *Charles Fenton Mercer and the Trial of National Conservatism.* Jackson: University Press of Mississippi, 1989.

Horton, James Oliver, and Lois E. Horton. *In Hope of Liberty: Culture, Community, and Protest among Northern Free Blacks, 1700–1860.* New York: Oxford University Press, 1997.

Staudenraus, P. J. *The African Colonization Movement, 1816–1865.* New York: Columbia University Press, 1961.

Thomas, Lamont D. *Rise to Be a People: A Biography of Paul Cuffe.* Urbana: University of Illinois Press, 1986.

Tyler-McGraw, Marie. *At the Falls: Richmond, Virginia, and Its People.* Chapel Hill: University of North Carolina Press, 1994.

DOUGLAS R. EGERTON

COLORADO   The approximately 104,000 square miles that became Colorado Territory in 1861 were partly acquired from France as a portion of the Louisiana Purchase in 1803, partly wrested as war spoils from Mexico in 1848, and partly purchased from

Texas in 1850. Before 1858 a handful of Hispanic farmers and herders in the South and scattered trappers and traders, including the fort builder William Bent and the mountain man Christopher (Kit) Carson, settled in the area. But most Americans shunned it, heeding explorers Zebulon Pike and Stephen Long, who warned of its harshness and aridity. With dry plains in the east, even drier plateaus and deserts in the west, and rugged mountains in between, most thought it a land best left to the native tribes, principally the Cheyennes and Arapahos in the northeast, the Comanches and the Kiowas in the southeast, and the Utes in the mountains and the west.

Gold discoveries in 1858 triggered the 1859 gold rush that lured perhaps as many as 100,000 people to the area. Most, finding little gold, quickly returned home. Those that remained, in piedmont supply centers such as Denver, founded in 1858, and in mountain mining towns such as Central City, put pressure on the native tribes to give up their hunting grounds. In 1861 the Treaty of Fort Wise took away most of the land of the Cheyennes and Arapahos. In 1864 U.S. Army troops led by Colonel John Chivington massacred more than 150 Cheyennes and Arapahos, many of them women and children, at Sand Creek. Eventually only the Utes retained tribal land, in southwestern Colorado.

William Gilpin, the territory's first governor, raised Colorado troops who helped save New Mexico for the Union at the Battle of Glorieta in 1862. His successor, John Evans, promoted railroads, including the Denver Pacific, which in 1870 connected Denver with the Union Pacific in southern Wyoming to provide a crucial link to the rest of the nation. Inside Colorado, William Jackson Palmer's Denver and Rio Grande Railway tied eastern cities such as Colorado Springs, which Palmer founded in 1871, and Pueblo to remote places such as Durango in the southwest.

Gold initially created Colorado, and although ranching, agriculture, coal and base-metal mining, petroleum production, manufacturing, and health care gradually grew in importance, gold and silver continued to fuel the economy. Leadville silver made Horace Tabor a millionaire and stoked the boom of the 1880s. Victor and Cripple Creek gold helped dispel the depression of the mid-1890s and gave Winfield Scott Stratton a fortune. Others made money in more mundane ways. John K. Mullen milled wheat. John Wesley Iliff ranched. Charles Boettcher sold hardware. Adolph Coors brewed beer. Neither these homespun moguls, nor the eastern and foreign capitalists who controlled many of Colorado's mines, ranches, and railroads, were much loved by workers and farmers, who, in usually futile efforts to gain a greater share of the wealth, organized granges and joined unions such as the Knights of Labor and the Western Federation of Miners.

Colorado became a state in 1876, with Denver as its capital. For the next sixteen years Republicans dominated the state's politics. The most notable, Henry Moore Teller, served as the nation's secretary of the interior from 1882 to 1885 and was a U.S. senator for more than three decades. Falling silver prices led to depression in the early 1890s and caused Teller to abandon the Republicans. Tabor lost his fortune and Leadville's glory faded. The decline also prompted the 1892 election of Davis Waite, a Populist, as governor. Many of his plans, including a scheme to have Colorado mint its own silver dollars in Mexico, came to nothing, but his support of woman suffrage bore fruit in 1893 when Colorado became the nation's second state to give women equal voting rights.

Colorado's population grew from 39,864 in 1870 to 539,700 in 1900. At the turn of the century almost half the population lived in cities. Denver's 133,859 residents made it by far the largest city. Most inhabitants were Caucasians born in the United States; fewer than 2 percent were African Americans. Seventeen percent were of foreign birth, many having come from Germany, England, Sweden, Ireland, Canada, and Italy.

As Coloradans entered the new century they looked back on four amazing decades. In fewer than fifty years trails had given way to more than forty-five hundred miles of railroad. In 1859 Denverites boasted of their first wheat crop: two stalks yielding 148 grains. In 1900 the state had nearly twenty-five thousand individual farms. In 1859 William Byers founded the region's first newspaper, the *Rocky Mountain News*. By 1900 there were scores of weeklies and dailies. Not surprisingly, when old-timers such as Byers died, their families inscribed "Pioneer" on their tombstones, proud of the part they played in transforming a wilderness into a state.

See also **Denver; Gold Rushes and Silver Strikes; West, The.**

Bibliography

Abbott, Carl, et al. *Colorado: A History of the Centennial State*. Niwot: University of Colorado Press, 1994.

Ubbelohoe, Carl, et al. *A Colorado History*. Boulder, Colo.: Pruett Publishing, 1945.

Wynar, Bohdan S., ed. *Colorado Bibliography*. Littleton, Colo.: Libraries Unlimited, 1980. Lists more than nine thousand items.

STEPHEN J. LEONARD

COMMUNICATIONS

The nineteenth century saw dramatic changes in the speed and form of communications in the United States. At the beginning of the century, it took twenty-five days for news to travel by post from the eastern seaboard of the new republic to its western borders. By the end of the century, news could be transmitted almost instantaneously across the entire continent through the newly developed media of telegraph, telephone, and wireless.

The Postal Service

The primary form of communications available to Americans in 1800 was the postal service. In that year, Postmaster General Joseph Habersham oversaw a postal system consisting of approximately nine hundred post offices connected by more than twenty thousand miles of postal roads that stretched as far west as Vincennes, Indiana, and as far south as Natchez, Mississippi. Mail was carried from city to city by postal coaches, often operated by private contractors who also carried passengers and freight. Letters and other mailed items had to be picked up at the local post office, because home delivery service did not exist until mid-century. Postage was normally paid by the recipient; stamps were not introduced until the 1840s.

Although the Post Office had initially generated a surplus, rapid expansion into the developing areas of the West and South began to create deficits by the 1820s. The introduction of the railroads in the early 1830s greatly increased the speed of mail delivery. Amos Kendall, the postmaster general under President Andrew Jackson, reorganized the Post Office in 1836 to improve its efficiency and initiated the use of the railroads for the delivery of mail.

The Telegraph

Communications entered a new era in May 1844, when Samuel F. B. Morse sent the first telegraph message over a line between Baltimore, Maryland, and Washington, D.C. The invention made possible instantaneous electrical communication over vast distances. With the telegraph, according to one contemporary observer, "Time and space are now annihilated!" (Mabee, *American Leonardo*, p. 206). Almost every aspect of American life was affected by this new technology.

The telegraph's ability to transcend temporal and spatial limitations made it an important factor in the settlement and governing of the vast expanses of the American West. The use of the telegraph to transmit news of the Mexican War generated interest in the new medium among the general public, and newspapers and the Associated Press quickly came to rely on the telegraph for news reports. The telegraph played an important role in the rise of industrial capitalism, as businessmen began to use it for commercial transactions and stock quotations. By 1850 it was possible to send a ten-word telegram from New York to New Orleans for two dollars and fifty cents.

Although some pundits predicted that widespread use of the telegraph would lead to the demise of the mails, in actuality the postal service continued to expand in the mid-nineteenth century, due in large part to reductions in postal rates during the 1850s. In 1851 the letter rate was reduced to as little as three cents for some destinations. Postal rates were also reduced on newspapers and periodicals in the early 1850s, and it became possible to mail books for the first time during this era. The Post Office's ability to distribute newspapers and other printed material in a fast and economical way played an important role in the political and intellectual life of the American public in the nineteenth century. The reduction in rates for books and newspapers brought about a great increase in newspaper circulation and contributed to the rising popularity of dime novels. Abolitionists used the mails to send antislavery literature to the South prior to the Civil War. This postal campaign led to riots in some southern cities, as mobs burned mail coming from the North that was believed to contain "incendiary" material. The adoption of lower postal rates also meant the gradual abandonment of the principle that the Post Office should be self-supporting, and acceptance of the notion that the Post Office should submit a request for operating funds to Congress annually.

One of the major problems faced by the early railroads was trying to operate by "sun time" in the era before the establishment of standard time zones. Each town would set its clocks according to the position of the sun in the sky; thus, high noon occurred twelve minutes earlier in New York than in Washington, D.C. This led to great confusion in establishing train schedules and contributed to the high incidence of railroad accidents. During the 1850s, to alleviate this problem, the railroads first began to employ telegraph operators to synchronize train movements by signaling train arrival times from one station to the next. The practice of placing a telegrapher in every railroad depot not only enabled trains to run safely and efficiently, but also made it possible for many small communities to have telegraph service where it would not otherwise be economically feasible.

In 1856 Hiram Sibley consolidated a number of telegraph companies into the Western Union, creating the first telecommunications "common carrier." As the name suggests, one of the primary goals of the new company was expansion into the new markets of the West. Sibley proposed a transcontinental telegraph line, to run through Omaha and Salt Lake City to San Francisco. He took his idea to Congress and obtained government backing for the scheme. Congress passed the Pacific Telegraph Act on 16 June 1860, granting a stipend of $40,000 annually for ten years for the purpose of building such a line.

The Pony Express

The annexation of additional territory at the end of the Mexican War in 1848 made it necessary for the Post Office to offer transcontinental mail service. In 1857 mail could be sent to California every two weeks by means of a steamship that carried mail from Atlantic seaports to the Isthmus of Panama, where it was carried overland to the Pacific coast by railroad and then onward by ship to California. Since this was a lengthy and expensive process, attempts were made to develop an overland mail route to the West Coast. A private company, the Pony Express, was formed by William H. Russell, Alexander Majors, and William B. Waddell in 1860 to offer a land route to California through Nebraska and Wyoming. Beginning in April 1860, relay teams of Pony Express riders carried mail from St. Joseph, Missouri, to Sacramento, California, in about ten days.

The Pony Express was in operation for only about eighteen months. It was made obsolete by the completion of the Transcontinental Telegraph in October 1861, when the lines from the West met the lines from the East in Salt Lake City, Utah. One of the most important pieces of news carried by the Pony Express during its short existence was a report of the bombardment of Fort Sumter in April 1861, which heralded the beginning of hostilities in the Civil War.

Communications and the Civil War

The telegraph saw its first military use during the Civil War with the formation of the Military Telegraph Corps of the Union army in 1861. Military telegraphers accompanied the armies as they marched, stringing wires and keeping the commanders in constant communication with the War Department in Washington, D.C. The deployment of this communications network gave the Union army a significant strategic advantage over the Confederates.

During the war, postal services continued to be provided in the North by the Post Office, under the direction of Postmaster General Montgomery Blair. In the South, U.S. post offices, which had been closed after secession, were reopened under the direction of John H. Reagan, who was named postmaster general of the Confederate States of America in 1861. With the abandonment of the less profitable southern routes, the northern postal service flourished during the Civil War. It routinely generated a surplus, and it began to offer several new services for the first time. Free home delivery in cities with populations of more than fifty thousand was first offered in 1863, and postal money-order service began in 1864. A standard postal rate of three cents for delivery of a half-ounce letter anywhere in the United States was established in 1863. In the South, however, Reagan's postal service was continually beset by a lack of funds and was forced to gradually close its post offices. By 1865 the postal service in the Confederacy was almost nonexistent. After the Civil War the postal service was gradually rebuilt in the South, and its westward expansion continued. The use of railroad sorting cars to sort mail while en route to its destination, first initiated by the Union during the Civil War, greatly increased the speed and efficiency of mail delivery.

By 1866 the Western Union Company monopolized the telegraph business in the United States. Capitalized at $40 million, it owned more than 100,000 miles of telegraph lines, which connected every major town in the United States and controlled the flow of messages to Europe over the newly completed submarine cable. Responding to allegations that the telegraph company manipulated the flow of news and charged exorbitant rates for personal messages, John A. J. Creswell, postmaster general under President Ulysses Grant, held congressional hearings in the 1870s to determine whether the telegraph system should be placed under the control of the postal administration, as was commonly done in Europe. Although attempts to create a postal telegraph system were unsuccessful, a measure of government oversight was obtained in 1887 when the Interstate Commerce Commission was chartered to regulate and monitor the rates charged by the railroads and the telegraph companies.

The Telephone

The next major change in communications technology came with the development of the telephone by Alexander Graham Bell in 1876. The invention quickly grew in popularity after it was exhibited at the Centennial Exhibition in Philadelphia in June 1876, and the Bell Telephone Company was formed to market the invention the following year. Western Union at first attempted to enter the newly developing telephone market but agreed to leave the telephone business to the Bell company in 1879 after a series of legal disputes. The telephone quickly replaced the telegraph as the primary means of sending personal messages over short distances. Long-distance telephony, however, was not perfected until the twentieth century, so the telegraph continued to be the primary means of sending long-distance messages until after 1900.

The telephone was particularly popular in rural areas, where it helped overcome the isolation of rural living. Independent telephone companies and rural cooperatives sprang up to provide telephone service to rural residents after the original Bell patent expired in 1893. In 1900 the number of telephones per capita in Iowa actually exceeded the number in New York City. In the entire United States at that time there were 1.4 million telephones in service, or one for every sixty inhabitants.

Another factor in overcoming the isolation of rural life was the establishment of rural free delivery by the U.S. Postal Service in the 1890s. First proposed by Postmaster General John Wanamaker in 1891, and widely supported by the Grange movement and the Populists, rural free delivery was inaugurated on a limited basis in 1896 and became universal in the early years of the twentieth century. By 1901 the United States had more than 79,000 post offices.

Women and Communications

Both the telegraph and the telephone created new employment opportunities for women. Women worked as telegraph operators from the 1840s onward, and by 1900 they constituted 13 percent of the 55,852 telegraph operators reported in the census. Some women occupied senior technical and managerial positions. After the development of the telephone switchboard in 1878, males were first employed as telephone operators. They were quickly replaced by women, however, and by 1900, 80 percent of the 19,195 telephone operators in the United States were female.

Wireless

By 1900 the experimental use of wireless, or radio, was just beginning to usher in the next phase of communications technology. The development of communications technology not only played a major role in the industrialization of the United States in the nineteenth century but also led to a change in the way people perceived the passage of time. While George Washington lamented the fact that it took six to nine months to deliver a letter to his friend the Marquis de Lafayette in Paris in 1779, Guglielmo Marconi's instantaneous transmission of radio messages across the Atlantic in 1901 heralded the onset of the modern information age and the fast-paced life of the global village.

See also **Inventors and Inventions; Pony Express; Post Office; Telegraph.**

Bibliography

Andrews, J. Cutler. "The Southern Telegraph Company, 1861–1865: A Chapter in the History of Wartime Communication." *Journal of Southern History* 30 (1964): 319–344.

Andrews, Melodie. " 'What the Girls Can Do': The Debate over the Employment of Women in the Early American Telegraph Industry." *Essays in Economic and Business History* 8 (1990): 109–120.

Brooks, John. *Telephone: The First Hundred Years.* New York: Harper and Row, 1976.

Fuller, Wayne E. *The American Mail: Enlarger of the Common Life.* Chicago: University of Chicago Press, 1972.

Gabler, Edwin. *The American Telegrapher: A Social History 1860–1900.* New Brunswick, N.J.: Rutgers University Press, 1988.

Jepsen, Thomas C. "The Telegraph Comes to Colorado: A New Technology and Its Consequences." *Essays and Monographs in Colorado History* 7 (1987): 1–25.

———. "Women Telegraph Operators on the Western Frontier." *Journal of the West* (April 1996): 72–80.

John, Richard R. *Spreading the News: The American Postal System from Franklin to Morse.* Cambridge, Mass.: Harvard University Press, 1995.

Mabee, Carleton. *American Leonardo: A Life of Samuel F. B. Morse.* New York: Knopf, 1943.

Norwood, Stephen H. *Labor's Flaming Youth: Telephone Operators and Worker Militancy, 1878–1923.* Urbana and Chicago: University of Illinois Press, 1990.

Thompson, Robert L. *Wiring a Continent: The History of the Telegraph Industry in the United States, 1832–1866.* New York: Arno, 1972.

THOMAS C. JEPSEN

COMMUNITARIAN MOVEMENTS AND GROUPS

Individualism and the search for private economic advancement have often been seen as primary forces in American history. From early colonial days to the present, however, cooperative impulses and the quest for community have also motivated many Americans. Beginning with the early American Pilgrims and Puritans, who sought freedom to develop their own distinctive cooperative forms of life in the New World, a host of diverse religious, ethnic, and social reform groups have attempted to create ideal societies in America. While immigrant groups brought with them varied communal traditions, many native-born Americans developed new and more satisfying communal patterns of their own.

Among the most colorful and controversial of these experiments were those in which property was held in common. Variously and rather confusingly described by terms such as "utopian communities," "communitarian socialism," "communes," "intentional communities," "utopian socialism," "communistic societies," and "cults," such groups have fascinated scholars and the general public alike. Throughout the nineteenth century hundreds of communitarian experiments sought to develop forces of cohesion in the rapidly changing environment of nascent capitalist America. Many of these communities were religiously motivated groups preparing for the millennium, the veritable "kingdom of heaven on earth," while others were motivated by secular ideologies and aspirations for social progress.

Religious Communitarian Experiments before the Civil War

Like the earlier and less explicitly communitarian Pilgrims and Puritans, the first fully communitarian experiments of European origin in America had millennial religious roots, often hearkening back to the passage in Acts 2:44–45, which describes the early Christians as having "all things common." The best known and most influential of these religious movements in nineteenth-century America was the group popularly known as the Shakers. Originating in a small revivalistic English group whose leader Ann Lee and seven followers immigrated to America in 1774, the Shakers by the 1830s had attracted some four thousand members to more than sixty communal "families" in locations from Maine to Indiana. Controversial in the nineteenth century for charismatic religious services in which they sang, shouted, and shook with emotion, their requirements of celibacy and close-knit communal living, and their veneration of Ann Lee as the second embodiment of Christ's spirit in human history, the Shakers have survived for more than two hundred years, although at the turn of the twenty-first century only one small community remained in rural Maine. In the nineteenth century, Shaker success inspired both religious and secular reformers, ranging from the Oneida Community leader John Humphrey Noyes to the socialist ideologue Friedrich Engels. Today, they are best remembered for the influential role they gave women,

The Shaker Mode of Worship. A community near Lebanon, New York, c. 1830. Stipple and line engraving, drawn from life. LIBRARY OF CONGRESS

the simplicity of their furniture, textiles, and other products, and their songs, such as "Simple Gifts."

Many religious groups of Germanic and northern European origin also established colorful and long-lived communitarian experiments in America. Among these was the Harmonist movement, founded by the patriarchal George Rapp, who led more than one thousand of his German Pietist followers to America in 1804. Rapp eventually established three flourishing Harmonist communities at a succession of locations from Harmony, Pennsylvania, to New Harmony, Indiana, to Economy (now Ambridge), Pennsylvania. The last of these communities, at Economy, survived until 1905. Equally complex and economically successful were the Inspirationists, another Pietist group that eventually set up seven closely knit villages at Amana, Iowa, where they maintained communal living from 1855 to 1932. Their descendants produce the well-known Amana refrigerators and other products. At Zoar, Ohio, some three hundred religious Separatists founded a thriving community that survived from 1819 until 1898. Followers of the charismatic Wilhelm Keil founded a successful colony at Bethel, Missouri, in 1844, and then migrated west to Oregon in 1855, founding the Aurora colony, which survived until 1883. And the controversial Swedish Pietist leader Eric Jansson founded a Swedish immigrant community at Bishop Hill on the Illinois prairie in 1846 that maintained its communal principles until 1861.

Most successful of all the Germanic immigrant communitarians to come to America were the Hutterian Brethren, an Anabaptist group whose founder, Jacob Hutter, was martyred in 1536. After fleeing persecution and reestablishing themselves at various locations from Bohemia to Russia, four hundred Russian Hutterites migrated to America in 1847 and founded three colonies there. At the end of the twentieth century more than forty thousand Hutterites lived in some four hundred communities in the western United States and Canada. Although closely related to the Amish, who eschew the use of modern technology, the Hutterites have enthusiastically adopted modern technologies ranging from fax machines to the latest farm machinery.

Among the religious movements native to America that have engaged in significant communal experimentation, the largest and most successful is the Church of Jesus Christ of Latter-day Saints, better known as the Mormons. In 1831, less than a year after the church's official founding, the Mormon prophet Joseph Smith stressed communal values in his first United Order movement, utilizing a set of rules for living that has become known as the Law of Consecration and Stewardship. The movement at-

Robert Dale Owen (1801–1877). Owen, a social reformer and member of the New Harmony, Indiana, experiment and the Nashoba, Tennessee, community, also worked for emancipation of the slaves. With Frances Wright he became involved with the group the "Free Enquirers" who were against organized religion. LIBRARY OF CONGRESS: PRINTS AND PHOTOGRAPHS DIVISION

tempted to reduce economic disparities within the group while retaining individual dwellings and entrepreneurial responsibility. More far-reaching and fully communitarian was the second United Order movement begun under Brigham Young's leadership and flourishing in the 1870s and 1880s at locations such as Orderville, Utah, where for a time private property was abolished and all activities were supervised by the community as a whole. Such efforts were intensified expressions of the larger cooperative focus of nineteenth-century Mormons as they settled the arid Great Basin region of the American West. Mormons emphasized commitment to their distinctive theology, strong in-group loyalty, and unorthodox social practices, including polygamous marriage.

A far smaller and even more unorthodox American religious movement, led by John Humphrey Noyes, founded the Oneida Community in central New York State in 1848. Oneida Community members, who shared a common perfectionist religious commitment and numbered more than two hundred adults at the group's peak, considered themselves married to the group. They exchanged heterosexual partners frequently within the community, rejecting exclusive romantic attachments as antithetical to community order. Oneidans lived together in one large communal Mansion House, ate together, worked together, practiced communal childrearing, and shared all but the most basic property in common. Their system of complex marriage at Oneida lasted from 1848 until 1879, when it was given up due to a combination of internal dissatisfaction and external pressure. In 1881 the group also officially gave up its communistic system of economic organization, reorganized as a joint-stock corporation, and went on to become a successful business, best known for its silverware.

Secular Communitarian Experiments before the Civil War

During the pre–Civil War years, two secular waves of communitarian excitement swept through America. The first of these was inspired by the idealistic Welsh industrialist Robert Owen, who made his fortune operating model textile mills in New Lanark, Scotland. Owen, who addressed the U.S. House of Representatives and the president of the United States as part of a well-publicized visit in 1825, sought to build the utopian prototype for a "new moral world" in his community at New Harmony, Indiana, where he purchased the Harmonist land and buildings. During the two years of New Harmony's existence, from 1825 to 1827, it attracted a diverse collection of more than eight hundred idealists, reformers, and progressive educators convinced that rational individualism could create a new and more harmonious society.

Outside New Harmony itself, a total of twenty-eight Owenite and Owenite-influenced communities were founded, most of them in the United States and the British Isles, during the 1820s and 1840s. The most controversial of these diverse communities was at Nashoba, Tennessee, where the feminist social reformer Frances Wright scandalized society by countenancing not only free love but interracial sex. The last community influenced by the Owenites, Josiah Warren's individualistic Modern Times settlement on Long Island, New York, closed in 1863. Although internal and external problems caused New Harmony and most of the other Owenite communities to shut down after only a few years, Owen's reform ideas remained influential in working-class circles throughout the nineteenth century, both in Britain and in America.

During the depression years of the 1840s and after, a second wave of secular communitarian experimentation swept through the United States. It was inspired by the ideas of the eccentric French social theorist Charles Fourier, as mediated through the writings of his American disciple Albert Brisbane. Fourier was convinced that the cure for the evils of competitive capitalism was the creation of elaborately planned cooperative communities or "phalanxes," which he envisioned eventually spreading throughout the world. American Fourierists established more than two dozen miniature phalanxes in the United States, the longest lived of which was the North American Phalanx at Red Bank, New Jersey (1843–1855). The most famous of the communities that became associated with Fourierism was Brook Farm (1841–1847), where George Ripley and a spirited group of Transcendentalist ministers, reformers, and writers created an excellent school and campus-like environment satirized by Nathaniel Hawthorne in his novel *The Blithdale Romance* (1852). Despite the short life spans of most Fourierist communities, the larger Fourierist movement in more than two dozen cities promoted a variety of innovations, including provisions for mutual life insurance, changes in the U.S. banking and currency system, and a movement among workers to found cooperative economic enterprises.

The longest lived of the secular communitarian groups, the French Icarians, sought for fifty years beginning in 1848 to create a model society in America based on the ideals that the French political radical Étienne Cabet had expressed in his utopian novel *Voyage en Icarie* (1839). The Icarians established seven communities in Texas, Missouri, Illinois, Iowa, and California, the last of which, at Corning, Iowa, dissolved in 1898.

Communitarian Experimentation after the Civil War

Perhaps the greatest misconception about American communitarianism is that it largely disappeared following the Civil War. In fact, as the historian Robert Fogarty has shown, between 1860 and 1914 more than one hundred new communitarian experiments began in the United States, while many older groups also remained active. The focus of post–Civil War communal experimentation increasingly shifted with the population, away from New England–settled areas in New York State and the Midwest toward the West and South. The types of experimentation also changed, with increasing activity by secular communitarians committed to labor and socialist politics and by new religious and ethnic groups.

Rapidly growing California was a focal point for many new communities, especially those inspired by American socialist critiques of capitalism. Californian groups as diverse as the Theosophical Society's Point Loma (1897–1942) and the radical socialist Kaweah Co-operative Commonwealth (1885–1892) were strongly influenced by Edward Bellamy, whose best-selling utopian novel *Looking Backward* (1888) also inspired numerous Nationalist clubs and utopian experiments in other parts of the country. Other notable nineteenth-century California groups with socialist inspiration included Winters Island (1893–1898) and Altruria (1894–1895).

The Puget Sound area of Washington State also attracted numerous freethinkers, religious and political radicals, and commune builders shortly before and after the turn of the twentieth century. One of the most successful colonies founded was Home (1896–1921), a community distinguished by cooperative living, the publication of several influential anarchist newspapers, and toleration of personal eccentricities. Other Puget Sound communities that developed their own cooperative enterprises and radical newspapers included Equality (1897–1907), Burley (1898–1913), and Freeland, on Whidbey Island (1899–1913).

New communal groups were also forming in the South. Ruskin (1894–1899), founded by the influential socialist newspaper editor J. A. Wayland on land near Nashville, Tennessee, had a brief and turbulent history, inspiring three other short-lived colonies in Georgia and Minnesota. Among the most successful of the secular communitarian efforts were groups founded on the ideas of the American economist Henry George, who advocated an unorthodox single tax on the value of unimproved land as a panacea for the ills and injustices of a capitalist economy. The best-known and most enduring of the twelve single-tax colonies—where residents legally held their land communally but rented and lived on separate lots—throughout the nation was the Fairhope Community, founded by Ernest Gaston near Mobile, Alabama, in 1895, which survived into the twenty-first century.

Numerous religious groups also founded communal groups in late-nineteenth-century America. Some of these were influenced by Christian "social gospel" concerns to meet the needs of those left behind by capitalist society. Notable among such groups was the Christian Commonwealth near Columbus, Georgia (1896–1900), the Straight Edge Industrial Settlement in the New York City area, which was active for several decades after its founding in 1899, and the Salvation Army farm colonies in California, Colorado, and Ohio. Evangelical Protestantism furnished the principles that underlay the controversial Shiloh community, founded by Frank W. Sandford in rural Maine in 1893, where harsh discipline, disease, and legal problems contributed to the disintegration of the communal settlement by the early 1920s, and the Women's Commonwealth group in Belton, Texas (1879–1898), where a group of celibate and feminist-oriented "sanctified sisters" ran a successful hotel before moving to Washington, D.C., where the last sister died in 1983.

Other noteworthy religious communal ventures were the nearly one hundred Jewish farm colonies founded in twenty-seven states between the 1880s and 1940s, inspired by some of the same impulses that gave rise to Zionism and the kibbutz movement; Roman Catholic monasticism, influenced by the nineteenth-century revival of monasticism in Europe and the search for identity by Catholic immigrants to America; and various theosophical and spiritualist communal experiments, precursors of twentieth-century New Age communitarian efforts. Among a number of hard-to-categorize groups, one of the most colorful was Cyrus R. Teed's Koreshan Unity, which established a celibate, ecologically oriented community at Estero, Florida, in 1894, attracting more than two hundred members during its heyday prior to Teed's death in 1908.

Common Concerns of Communitarianism

What elements do such disparate communitarian movements have in common? Whether religious or secular in inspiration, nineteenth-century communitarian groups were convinced that excessive individualism and selfishness were threatening America. They believed that unrestrained capitalism should be replaced by cooperative communities in which the good of the individual was subordinated to the larger welfare of the group, and they sometimes experimented with alternative family and sex role patterns as part of their larger religious and communal efforts. The most successful communitarian groups, in terms of longevity, were those in which strong leadership and deep commitment to a religious or quasi-religious ideology provided foci for cohesion and discipline. Such groups typically viewed themselves as models that the larger society would learn from and eventually imitate.

See also **Liberalism; Millennialism and Adventism; Mormonism; Progressivism; Radicalism; Reform, Idea of; Reform, Social; Religion,** *subentry on* **Religion in Nineteenth-Century America; Social Gospel; Transcendentalism.**

Bibliography

Alyea, Paul E., and Blanche R. Alyea, *Fairhope, 1894–1954: The Story of a Single-Tax Colony.* Birmingham: University of Alabama Press, 1956.

Andrews, Edward Deming. *The People Called Shakers: A*

Search for the Perfect Society. New enl. ed. New York: Dover, 1963.

Arndt, Karl J. R. *George Rapp's Harmony Society, 1785–1847.* Rev. ed. Rutherford, N.J.: Fairleigh Dickinson University Press, 1972.

Arrington, Leonard J., Feramoz Y. Fox, and Dean L. May. *Building the City of God: Community and Cooperation among the Mormons.* 2d ed. Urbana: University of Illinois Press, 1992.

Barkun, Michael J. "Communal Societies as Cyclical Phenomena." *Communal Societies* 4 (1984): 35–48.

Barthel, Diane L. *Amana: From Pietist Sect to American Community.* Lincoln: University of Nebraska Press, 1984.

Bestor, Arthur E. *Backwoods Utopias: The Sectarian and Owenite Phases of Communitarian Socialism in America, 1663–1829.* 2d enl. ed. Philadelphia: University of Pennsylvania Press, 1970.

Brewer, Priscilla J. *Shaker Communities, Shaker Lives.* Hanover, N.H.: University Press of New England, 1986.

Carden, Maren Lockwood. *Oneida: Utopian Community to Modern Corporation.* Baltimore: Johns Hopkins University Press, 1969.

Fogarty, Robert S. *All Things New: American Communes and Utopian Movements, 1860–1914.* Chicago: University of Chicago Press, 1990.

Foster, Lawrence. *Religion and Sexuality: The Shakers, the Mormons, and the Oneida Community.* Urbana: University of Illinois Press, 1984.

Guarneri, Carl. *The Utopian Alternative: Fourierism in Nineteenth-Century America.* Ithaca, N.Y.: Cornell University Press, 1991.

Harrison, J. F. C. *Quest for the New Moral World: Robert Owen and the Owenites in Britain and America.* New York: Scribners, 1969.

Hayden, Dolores. *Seven American Utopias: The Architecture of Communitarian Socialism, 1790–1975.* Cambridge, Mass.: MIT Press, 1976.

Hinds, William Alfred. *American Communities and Co-operative Colonies.* Chicago: Kerr, 1908.

Hine, Robert V. *California's Utopian Colonies.* New Haven, Conn.: Yale University Press, 1966.

Hostetler, John A. *Hutterite Society.* Baltimore: Johns Hopkins University Press, 1974.

Kanter, Rosabeth. *Commitment and Community: Communes and Utopias in Sociological Perspective.* Cambridge, Mass.: Harvard University Press, 1972.

LeWarne, Charles. *Utopias on Puget Sound.* Seattle: University of Washington Press, 1975.

Miller, Timothy. *The Quest for Utopia in Twentieth-Century America. Volume 1: 1900–1960.* Syracuse, N.Y.: Syracuse University Press, 1998.

Nordhoff, Charles. *The Communistic Societies of the United States.* New York: Harper, 1875.

Noyes, John Humphrey. *History of American Socialisms.* Philadelphia: Lippincott, 1870.

Parker, Robert Allerton. *A Yankee Saint: John Humphrey Noyes and the Oneida Community.* New York: Putnam, 1935.

Pitzer, Donald E., ed. *America's Communal Utopias.* Chapel Hill: University of North Carolina Press, 1997.

Spann, Edward K. *Brotherly Tomorrows: Movements for a Cooperative Society in America, 1820–1920.* New York: Columbia University Press, 1989.

Stein, Stephen J. *The Shaker Experience in America: A History of the United Society of Believers.* New Haven, Conn.: Yale University Press, 1992.

Sutton, Robert P. *Les Icariens: The Utopian Dream in Europe and America.* Urbana: University of Illinois Press, 1994.

Swift, Lindsay. *Brook Farm: Its Members, Scholars, and Visitors.* New York: Macmillan, 1900.

Wagner, Jon. "Success in Intentional Communities: The Problem of Evolution." *Communal Societies* 5 (1985): 89–100.

LAWRENCE FOSTER

COMPROMISE OF 1850   The Compromise of 1850 consisted of a series of statutes passed separately in the early fall of 1850 that: (1) provided a new mechanism for the return of runaway slaves under the Fugitive Slave Law of 1850, (2) created New Mexico and Utah Territories with no ban on slavery, (3) admitted California as a free state, (4) excluded the slave trade from Washington, D.C., (5) settled the Texas–New Mexico boundary in favor of New Mexico, and (6) provided for federal assumption of the debts accumulated by Texas when it was an independent republic. While temporarily reducing tensions over slavery, the compromise did little to solve the nation's seemingly intractable sectional conflict.

The compromise must be considered in the context of the annexation of Texas in 1845, the U.S. victory in the Mexican War (1846–1848), ongoing southern dissatisfaction with the enforcement of the Fugitive Slave Law of 1793, and the rise of strong antislavery sentiment in the North.

After the Mexican War the United States acquired vast territories that later became the states of California, Arizona, New Mexico, Utah, Nevada, and part of Colorado. During the war Congressman David Wilmot of Pennsylvania proposed what is known as the Wilmot Proviso, which would have prohibited slavery in any territories acquired as a result of the war. In 1847 the proviso easily passed the House of Representatives but failed in the Senate, where the South held a temporary majority and where a few northerners always willingly supported the South. By 1850, however, the issue of slavery in the new territories had precipitated a crisis. The nation had an equal number of slave and free states, fifteen of each, but California, with a huge population attracted by the gold rush, was demanding immediate statehood. Northern opponents of the spread of slavery were also demanding that the essence of the Wilmot Proviso be applied to the rest of the new territories. Meanwhile, a number of southern states had called for a convention to consider secession or disunion.

In January 1850, an aging Henry Clay proposed the compromise. Slave owners would gain access to the new territories, while the North would gain a majority in the Senate through the immediate admission

Architects of the Compromise of 1850. A commemoration of the efforts of legislators who engineered the Compromise of 1850, including Senators Henry Clay *(seated, center)*, Daniel Webster *(right, with hand on compromise)*, and John Calhoun *(left, with hand on compromise)*. Calhoun's inclusion is particularly interesting, as he opposed the compromise and died prior to its passage. Also shown are General Winfield Scott *(far left, seated)* and President Millard Fillmore *(holding a shield)*. Engraving, 1852. LIBRARY OF CONGRESS: PRINTS AND PHOTOGRAPHS DIVISION

of California as a free state. The bill would ban the slave trade in the nation's capital, which many northerners found especially outrageous. At the same time, a new fugitive slave law would empower newly created federal commissioners to call on federal marshals or the military, to help southerners gain custody of runaway slaves. Texas taxpayers as well as a small number of northerners who held Republic of Texas bonds would benefit from the federal assumption of the debt, and the eastern boundary of New Mexico would be settled in favor of that new territory, where slavery would be allowed.

The Senate debated the bill for nearly six months. The moderates like Clay, Thomas Hart Benton of Missouri, Sam Houston of Texas, Stephen A. Douglas of Illinois, and Daniel Webster of Massachusetts delivered impressive speeches in favor of the compromise. The hard-core opponents Jefferson Davis of

Mississippi, John C. Calhoun of South Carolina, and James M. Mason of Virginia argued that it was too favorable to the North. Some younger northerners, like William H. Seward of New York, Salmon P. Chase of Ohio, and Hannibal Hamlin of Maine refused to make any more concessions to the endless demands of the South for more protection for slavery and more slave territories and states.

Calling his proposal an "omnibus bill," Clay expected northerners to support it to gain California statehood and southerners to back it to obtain a stronger fugitive slave law with federal enforcement. Clay's strategy backfired when many northerners voted against the bill because of the fugitive slave provisions and the opening of Utah and New Mexico to slavery. In addition numerous southerners voted against it because making California a free state would, they believed, give the North a permanent majority in the Senate to match its existing House majority. In July, to Clay's shock, the bill failed. In August and September, Senator Douglas, a brilliant young politician, pushed the compromise through Congress by forging fragile majorities for each component of the bill. President Millard Fillmore, a northerner who had few scruples about slavery, signed each as it reached his desk.

The Fugitive Slave Law proved the most controversial aspect to the compromise and in the end undid the handiwork of Clay, Webster, and Douglas. The law imposed draconian penalties on anyone who helped a fugitive slave escape or who resisted the capture and return of a runaway slave. Under it the status of a seized black was determined by a federal commissioner, generally a patronage appointee, who was paid ten dollars if he found in favor of a claimant but five dollars if he held for the alleged slave. No state or federal writ of habeas corpus could free a black arrested under the law, and the alleged slave could not testify at his or her own hearing. Fines of one thousand dollars, a huge sum at the time, and jail sentences of up to six months awaited anyone who helped an arrested black escape. The law never worked well, and relatively few runaways were returned. A small number of highly publicized rescues in Boston, Syracuse, Oberlin, and Milwaukee and failed rescues in Boston and elsewhere gave southerners the false impression of a vast northern conspiracy to interfere with their rights.

The attempt to settle the issue of slavery in the territories through the Utah and New Mexico territories was also a failure. In 1854, the issue reemerged to remain on the national agenda until the Civil War.

In the short run the Compromise of 1850 staved off the total collapse of the Union for another decade, but in the end it was a monumental failure. The careers and reputations of some northerners, including Webster, were destroyed because they supported the compromise. On the other hand, sectional opponents of the compromise, including Davis and Chase, thrived. As the historian David Potter noted in *The Impending Crisis*, the series of laws was hardly a "compromise" and might be more accurately known as the "armistice of 1850."

See also **Fugitive Slave Laws; Mexican War; New Mexico; Slavery; Supreme Court,** *subentry on* **The Antebellum Court; Texas; Utah.**

Bibliography

Freehling, William W. *The Road to Disunion.* Vol. 1: *Secessionists at Bay, 1776–1854.* New York: Oxford University Press, 1991.

Hamilton, Holman. *Prologue to Conflict: The Crisis and Compromise of 1850.* Lexington: University of Kentucky Press, 1964.

Potter, David M. *The Impending Crisis, 1848–1861.* New York: Harper and Row, 1976.

PAUL FINKELMAN

CONFEDERATE STATES OF AMERICA

The Confederate States of America came into existence on 4 February 1861, when delegates from the six Deep South states that had departed the federal Union by that date (South Carolina, Mississippi, Florida, Georgia, Alabama, and Louisiana) assembled in Montgomery, Alabama, to form a southern confederacy. Within days Texas also joined the Montgomery proceedings. The rebel delegates moved anxiously to expedite the process of nation building, which they essentially completed in less than two months. During this time the Montgomery convention accomplished a great deal. The delegates wrote a provisional constitution and assigned themselves the dual functions of both a provisional congress and a constituent assembly charged with framing a permanent constitution. They also elected a president, Jefferson Davis of Mississippi, from a pool of prominent aspirants that included the Alabama fire-eater William L. Yancey and the Georgia triumvirate of Howell Cobb, Robert Toombs, and Alexander H. Stephens, who was chosen vice president. Further, by mid-March the fledgling Confederate government had confirmed several cabinet posts, provided for the circulation of its own currency, authorized the recruitment of an army, adopted a legal code composed of all U.S. laws except those deemed hostile to slavery, and finalized a constitution for the Confederate republic.

In drafting a permanent constitution for their new nation, the founders of the Confederate republic borrowed heavily from the U.S. Constitution. The Montgomery government took up the business of constitution making in the first two weeks of March 1861. During this span the Provisional Congress conducted affairs of state by day and assembled as a constitutional convention in the evenings. Two factions emerged in convention. One of these, led by Stephens, looked to fashion a virtual replica of the U.S. Constitution with a few key proslavery measures added. The other more radical faction, led by the fire-eating South Carolinian Robert Barnwell Rhett, advocated a more extreme states' rights compact grounded in the theories of state sovereignty articulated by John C. Calhoun a generation earlier. Due in part to the moderating influence of Cobb, the convention's president, the final instrument was largely patterned after the U.S. Constitution, although it contained significant concessions to the Rhett faction. The preamble, for example, enshrined states' rights and certified the sovereign character of the constituent states. Likewise it omitted the general welfare clause of the U.S. Constitution, which had been construed to augment the power of the central government during the antebellum period. On the other hand the fire-eaters were disappointed that the new constitution remained silent on the issue of nullification and that it created a "permanent federal government," thereby implying rather hypocritically that the states did not possess a right of secession.

The Confederate constitution incorporated verbatim large segments of the U.S. Constitution, including its first twelve amendments. Nevertheless, the Confederate document departed substantially from its predecessor in regard to the relationships among government branches and the relationship between the central government and the states. The constitution vested all legislative power in the bicameral Confederate Congress, which was practically identical to the U.S. version. However, in enumerating the powers of Congress, the Confederate charter expressly forbade the national legislature from enacting protective tariffs or funding internal improvements. Naturally the constitution also protected the South's peculiar institution, prohibiting Congress

from passing any "law denying or impairing the right of property in negro slaves" (Article I, section 9). Through these provisions the constitution addressed the three cardinal points on which Southern states' rightists believed the antebellum U.S. government had overstepped its bounds.

In creating an executive branch, the Confederate constitution made only slight modifications to Article II of the U.S. Constitution, but these changes were significant. At once the Confederate constitution provided for a chief executive with more power than his U.S. counterpart while imposing novel limits on presidential tenure. For example, the Confederate president had line-item veto power and discretionary authority to dismiss civil officers yet was limited to a single six-year term.

The Confederate constitution outlined a national judicial structure that mirrored precisely the federal judiciary of the United States. It vested all judicial power in a supreme court and in other inferior national courts created by the Congress. However, the Confederate judiciary operated much differently in practice. The Confederate Congress did establish a system of federal district courts, but these "lower" courts functioned as the only extant arm of the national judiciary. The Confederate supreme court never came into being because the Congress purposely neglected to pass enabling legislation to create

"Secession Exploded." An anti-Confederate cartoon portrays a fantasy of the Union's assault against the seccessionist movement. Printed, 1861. LIBRARY OF CONGRESS: PRINTS AND PHOTOGRAPHS DIVISION

Jefferson Davis (1808–1889). The president of the Confederate States of America, Davis was a graduate of West Point. LIBRARY OF CONGRESS

that tribunal. Sensitive to potential federal inroads upon state prerogatives, Confederate lawmakers worried that a supreme court might become a vehicle for consolidation. Southern states' rightists pointed to the example of the U.S. Supreme Court under the chief justice John Marshall, whose judicial nationalism expanded the scope of central power at the expense of local authorities, particularly in exercising federal appellate jurisdiction over state court rulings. To preempt such judicial usurpation in their own republic, Confederate legislators chose to ignore their constitution and declined to erect a national high court.

The Confederate constitution was no revolutionary instrument. It was a conservative document, designed by its framers to perpetuate the world of the Old South, including slavery and a racial hierarchy based on white supremacy. As vice president, Stephens affirmed in March 1861 that slavery formed the "cornerstone" of the Southern nation, which was founded "upon the great truth that the negro is not equal to the white man; that slavery, subordination to the superior race, is his natural and moral condition" (Durden, pp. 7, 8). Such a social order, assumed the Confederate framers, was best safeguarded in a republic anchored upon the principles of states' rights. In this case, however, states' rights proved to be the cure that killed. Political decentralization greatly hampered the Confederate war effort and provided the basis for the crippling opposition to President Davis's wartime administration. In this sense the Confederate constitution sowed the seeds of destruction for the nation it intended to bring to life.

The Provisional Congress that wrote the constitution remained operative until February 1862. A unicameral assembly, the Provisional Congress was not an elective body. Rather, the delegates were the appointees of the secession conventions of their respective states. From the outset the radical fire-eaters, whose militant Southern nationalism inspired the initial formation of the Confederacy, were shunted aside by more moderate statesmen who took the reins of government. After April 1861 congressional membership swelled with the addition of representatives from the four Upper South states (Virginia, North Carolina, Tennessee, and Arkansas) that seceded following the bombardment of Fort Sumter. Extralegal secessionist councils in the Unionist border states of Kentucky and Missouri also sent delegates to the Confederate Congress, which explains why the national flag displayed thirteen stars when only eleven states seceded. In July 1861, Richmond, Virginia, superseded Montgomery as the capital of the Confederacy.

The nature of congressional legislation was determined by the course of the war. Unlike future congresses, the Provisional Congress cooperated fairly well with President Davis, endorsing most of his emergency war measures. After Abraham Lincoln called for U.S. volunteers to suppress the Southern rebellion in April 1861, the Confederate government faced the urgent tasks of raising an army, mobilizing the home front for war, and funding military operations. To these ends President Davis requested and the Provisional Congress approved a program of three-year enlistments, the suspension of habeas corpus, and various war appropriations.

The Provisional Congress created six executive departments: State, Treasury, War, Navy, Justice, and Post Office. These mimicked the cabinet structure of the old Union except in two instances. First, the Confederacy omitted a department of the interior. Second, it enlarged the office of attorney general by creating a Department of Justice under his direction, a step the U.S. government would not emulate until 1870. Chronic turnover of department heads gave Davis's cabinet far less stability than Lincoln's. In all, fourteen secretaries and three ad interim appointees held cabinet posts during the life of the Confederacy. Personality clashes with Davis led to some cabinet resignations, while other officers left to accept military commissions or alternate political appointments or to escape unrelenting congressional criticism. Only the navy secretary Stephen R. Mallory and postmaster general John H. Reagan held their assignments for the duration of the war. Judah P. Benjamin, who was Davis's ablest and most influential cabinet adviser, also served for the entirety of the war, but he juggled three different portfolios, those of attorney general, secretary of war, and secretary of state.

Cabinet issues strained relations between the executive and legislative branches throughout the war. The Provisional Congress strenuously objected to two of Davis's original selections, though it eventually confirmed all the president's nominations. As opposition to Davis's administration mounted during the war, the president's congressional detractors consistently blasted the cabinet as incompetent, thereby taking a sideswipe at Davis himself. Beginning as early as winter 1861 the Confederate Congress repeatedly called on Davis to restructure his cabinet. He angrily refused, asserting executive privilege of appointment while aggressively defending his bureau chiefs against congressional charges.

Despite congressional opinions to the contrary, the Confederate cabinet was not inept. Although only a few of Davis's secretaries, like Benjamin, possessed extraordinary talent, most executed their duties adequately. Congress simply demanded miracles from the executive personnel, who never had sufficient resources at their disposal to fulfill legislative expectations. Davis chose his department heads carefully if not always wisely. He sought men of accomplished ability, though of course his decisions reflected political considerations. Before nominating a candidate Davis conferred with influential state leaders, and he made selections that he hoped would mollify all major political factions. Likewise Davis was determined to represent the broadest possible array of states in his cabinet. These practices, while politically savvy, did not always ensure the placement of the best person for each job. Nevertheless Davis maintained good relations with his department heads, meeting with them regularly and giving them an active role in formulating policy.

In November 1861, as the incumbency of the Provisional Congress neared expiration, the Confederate republic held elections to its First (regular) Congress. Little actual campaigning or electioneering accompanied the first elections, which involved few substantive issues. In this election candidates with strong secessionist credentials or who were outspoken antebellum Southern rights advocates enjoyed only minimal advantage over other candidates. Delegates

to the First Congress took their seats in February 1862 and remained until December of the following year. Meanwhile, in summer 1863 the Confederacy held elections to its Second Congress, which assembled in May 1864 and continued until March 1865. A bicameral body consisting of a Senate and a House of Representatives, the regular Confederate Congress differed little from its U.S. counterpart. In fact about one-third of the 267 men who served in either chamber of the regular Congress had previous U.S. congressional experience, and one, John Tyler, had been president of the United States.

Relations between President Davis and the Congress, shaky from the start, deteriorated as the war progressed. The First Congress did enact most war measures initiated by Davis and his cabinet, but it did so grudgingly, with vociferous criticism, and only because the legislators had no better plans to offer. Much to the infuriation of Davis, even when the Congress ultimately approved administration policies, stubborn opposition invariably delayed or weakened legislation on such vital matters as conscription, impressment, revenue, and military governance. For example, the First Congress discussed but failed to renew the suspension of habeas corpus. Hoping to keep taxes low, Congress hesitated in passing income-tax legislation and a tax-in-kind on agriculture until spring 1863. In the meantime, for revenue the Treasury had to rely almost solely on bond issues, which proved insufficient. As the tide of the war turned increasingly against the South, congressional hostility toward the executive mounted. In 1862 the Confederacy suffered staggering defeats at Shiloh, New Orleans, Antietam, and Corinth, Mississippi. At the same time the South's "King Cotton diplomacy" failed to secure foreign recognition of the Confederate nation. By early 1863 the Congress made it clear that it had lost faith in Davis's conduct of the war, as evidenced by its openly combative posture toward the administration and by several needless and spiteful investigations into executive departments.

The Second Congress showed even more antagonism toward the president and his advisers, although it conducted legislative business more decisively than its predecessor. Despite some but not overwhelming dissension, the Second Congress passed rigid conscription legislation, and it finally reenacted the suspension of habeas corpus in cases of desertion or treason. These actions, however, scarcely signaled approbation for Davis's war policies. Rather, they merely reflected the desperation of the times, for by 1864 and 1865 Confederate military fortunes were sinking fast. In a final act of desperation the Congress approved the limited emancipation of black slaves and their induction into the military. Favoring the use of slaves in any way that might aid the Confederate war effort, President Davis was an early proponent of enlisting black troops. But the issue was hotly contested, as it entailed a virtual recantation of the racial doctrines, not to mention the legal and constitutional structures governing the Southern republic. The idea that slaves could be trusted to perform competent and loyal armed service and deserved liberty in exchange did great damage to the assumptions that blacks were innately inferior, unable to function in free society, and suited only to servitude. As Cobb flatly declared, "If slaves will make good soldiers our whole idea of slavery is wrong" (Durden, p. 184). Nevertheless in March 1865 Congress did authorize black enlistments, but the measure came too late to save the Confederacy.

To be sure, Davis had an important cadre of supporters in the Confederate Congress. The speaker of the House of Representatives, Thomas S. Bocock of Virginia, and the senators Benjamin H. Hill of Georgia and Robert W. Barnwell of South Carolina consistently backed administration war measures and urged fellow legislators to cooperate with the president for the sake of national solidarity. Davis, however, had more adversaries than friends in Congress. Among his more venomous critics were the senators Louis T. Wigfall of Texas, Robert M. T. Hunter of Virginia, and Yancey of Alabama. These states' rights extremists obstructed all administration attempts to prosecute the war more vigorously, blasting energetic federal initiatives as catalysts of centralized despotism. The politics of personality also accounted for much of the vitriolic opposition to the Davis government. For example, the leading oppositionist in the Confederate House was the Tennessee congressman Henry S. Foote, whose anti-Davis harangues were motivated by personal spite. Foote and Davis had been bitter rivals in Mississippi state politics before the war. Because of a similar personal enmity, Davis was the target of scathing criticism from his own vice president, Stephens, who probably did more to sabotage the administration than any other individual.

To a large degree the extraordinary extent of political infighting within the Confederacy stemmed from its lack of a two-party political structure. The Confederate founders had deliberately eschewed dual-party politics, hoping to cultivate a one-party system in which partisanship would not dilute patriotism for the cause of Southern independence. Ironically, the lack of party structure produced the opposite result, allowing the debilitating effects of vindictive personal politics to spread unchecked. In the Union government President Lincoln effectively used the Republican Party to channel Federal authority, to unite the state administrations behind Federal war aims, and to enforce party discipline, thereby minimizing the impact of personal political jealousies. With no party apparatus at his disposal, President Davis was unable to contain internecine political divisions, to bind Confederate leaders to a unified political purpose, or to compel state compliance with federal war directives.

Indeed the most devastating opposition to the Davis administration came from the states. Obstructionist governors, such as the infamous Joseph E. Brown of Georgia and Zebulon B. Vance of North Carolina, undermined the Confederate war effort by resisting federal military policies at every turn. Brown, for instance, railed against conscription laws that placed Georgians in Confederate rather than state service. Likewise he deprived Confederate authorities of the use of Georgia militia, decrying the federalization of state troops as a usurpation of gubernatorial prerogatives. While he claimed powers of impressment, the right to commandeer private property for public use in wartime, Brown fought Confederate impressment endeavors as a transgression against state sovereignty. On more than one occasion Brown told the people of his state that they had less to fear from the Union army than from their own tyrannical government in Richmond. Vance took a similarly defiant stance. He refused, for example, to allocate his state's resources to provision any but North Carolina troops. When General Robert E. Lee finally surrendered his tattered, hungry, and ill-equipped Confederate army in April 1865, Vance bragged that he still had huge surpluses of food and supplies idling in state storehouses.

Such incidents highlighted the Achilles' heel of the Confederate experiment: the incongruity between the commitment to states' rights and the wartime need for strong central controls. Virulent state particularism exposed the fallacy of Confederate national unity and rendered authorities in Richmond unable to truly nationalize the Southern war effort. Thus the unwillingness of the South to surmount its states' rights mentality in order to function as a nation played no small role in the demise of the Confederate republic, whose epitaph might well have read, "Died of States' Rights."

See also **African Americans,** *subentry on* **Blacks in the Military; Border States; Civil War; Foreign Relations,** *subentry on* **The Civil War; Race and Racial Thinking; Reconstruction; Richmond; Sectionalism; Slavery,** *subentry on* **Defense of Slavery; South, The; States' Rights.**

Bibliography

Beringer, Richard E., Herman Hattaway, Archer Jones, and William N. Still Jr. *Why the South Lost the Civil War.* Athens, Ga.: University of Georgia Press, 1986.

Davis, William C. *A Government of Our Own: The Making of the Confederacy.* New York: Free Press, 1994.

———. *Jefferson Davis: The Man and His Hour.* New York: HarperCollins, 1991.

DeRosa, Marshall L. *The Confederate Constitution of 1861: An Inquiry into American Constitutionalism.* Columbia: University of Missouri Press, 1991.

Durden, Robert F. *The Gray and the Black: The Confederate Debate on Emancipation.* Baton Rouge: Louisiana State University Press, 1972.

Eaton, Clement. *Jefferson Davis.* New York: Free Press, 1977.

Faust, Drew Gilpin. *The Creation of Confederate Nationalism: Ideology and Identity in the Civil War South.* Baton Rouge: Louisiana State University Press, 1988.

Lee, Charles Robert. *The Confederate Constitution.* Chapel Hill: University of North Carolina Press, 1963.

McKitrick, Eric L. "Party Politics and the Union and Confederate Efforts." In *The American Party Systems: Stages of Political Development.* 2d ed. Edited by William Nisbet Chambers and Walter Dean Burnham. New York: Oxford University Press, 1975.

Owsley, Frank Lawrence. *State Rights in the Confederacy.* Chicago: University of Chicago Press, 1925.

Rable, George C. *The Confederate Republic: A Revolution against Politics.* Chapel Hill: University of North Carolina Press, 1994.

Schott, Thomas E. *Alexander H. Stephens of Georgia: A Biography.* Baton Rouge: Louisiana State University Press, 1987.

Yearns, W. Buck. *The Confederate Congress.* Athens, Ga.: University of Georgia Press, 1960.

ERIC TSCHESCHLOK

CONGRESS   Throughout the nineteenth century Congress was regarded as the most important and influential branch of the national government. Closer to the people than the presidency, the House and Senate addressed the economic and political issues that shaped the nation's development. Lawmakers usually aimed at promoting the growth of the economy rather than regulating business or labor or adopting social welfare, civil rights, or environmental policies.

The Structure of Congress

The nineteenth century opened with the inauguration of Thomas Jefferson as the third president in March 1801. The Senate had begun meeting in the basement of the Capitol a few months earlier, and the House convened in its larger chamber upstairs. The Senate soon moved to the second floor, where it met until 1859, when it shifted to the room in the North Wing.

Congress did not meet year-round. The oppressive heat and humidity of Washington before air-conditioning ruled out summer sessions except at times of national crisis. The Constitution specified that lawmakers assemble in December of the year following their election, unless a special session was called. Thus senators and representatives chosen in a November election for terms beginning the next 4 March might wait more than a year before taking the oath of office. When the session began, both houses heard the president's annual message read by clerks rather than delivered in person. Jefferson started that custom in 1801. In odd-numbered years the legislators remained in session until they decided to adjourn, usually at the end of the spring. When a session began in an even-numbered year, Congress had to adjourn by the following 4 March. The short session that met after the congressional elections or a presidential contest often consisted of defeated legislators who were "lame ducks," the label by which these sessions were known. The rhythms of congressional sessions became an accustomed part of Washington life that House and Senate leaders took into account in planning their strategies.

The sizes of both houses expanded over the course of the century. In 1801 the House had 106 members and the Senate had 32. By 1840 the Senate had 52 members and 90 members by 1900. The House rose to 242 members in 1840, stood at 332 by 1880, and reached 391 in 1900. For most of the century lawmakers had no staff and no offices, their work was part-time, and their pay was relatively modest. At the outset of the century members received $6 per day during attendance at sessions. That figure rose to $8 per day in 1818 after an attempt to set an annual salary of $1,500 had engendered hostile public reaction a year earlier. In 1856 the annual pay was $3,000, and it rose to $5,000 in 1866. An effort to make it $7,500 in 1873 became known as the "salary grab" and was rescinded. The pay stayed at $5,000 for the rest of the century.

Although the presence of senior members became more customary by the end of the century, a high turnover of representatives and senators was the rule for most of the nineteenth century. Voters believed that men should be sent to Washington for a limited time and then returned to their constituencies. Thus, newcomers were usually a majority in the Congresses that met before 1877, and serving more than three terms in the House was unusual. While popular opinion often expressed disdain for Congress, little sense that it was removed from the people existed before the Gilded Age. Running for the House did not require large sums of money, and frequent rotation made it easier for political novices to go to Washington.

The deliberations of Congress were followed closely in the partisan press of the nineteenth century. To know what lawmakers did during the first two decades, citizens had to rely on press accounts. In 1813 Congress commenced publishing journals of its proceedings. Eleven years later a private firm produced

The House of Representatives. The House of Representatives in session with spectators observing. Drawing by Sachse, 1866. LIBRARY OF CONGRESS: PRINTS AND PHOTOGRAPHS DIVISION

the *Register of Debates*, which was replaced by the weekly *Congressional Globe* in 1833. The *Globe* became a daily publication in 1865 and was succeeded in 1873 by the *Congressional Record*. Traditions of revising speeches to remove embarrassing remarks, inserting extraneous materials, and using the *Record* to produce political documents were well established by 1900. The privilege of "franking" or mailing out documents at government expense was also an entrenched perquisite of congressional incumbents.

The House of Representatives

As the branch of Congress closest to the American people, the House of Representatives enjoyed a prestige in the nineteenth century that it later relinquished. The salient features in the evolution of the House were the flowering of the committee system, the impact of partisan politics, and the appearance of strong Speakers at the beginning and end of the century.

The most important of the many House committees was Ways and Means, which supervised issues of taxation and appropriations and for a time acted as an oversight panel for the executive departments. In

1816 Speaker Henry Clay used standing committees to supervise the executive branch. The number of standing committees grew between 1816 and 1840, when it reached thirty-three. Over the course of the century the House adapted the committee system to meet changing national needs. In 1865 the duties of the Ways and Means panel were divided among three committees, Appropriations, Banking and Currency, and Ways and Means, to deal with finance and taxation. The House Rules Committee, set up in 1880, provided a mechanism for bringing legislation to the floor in an orderly manner.

During the Civil War the House employed select committees to assert its influence on issues relating to slavery and Reconstruction. The Joint Committee on the Conduct of the War became notorious for its difficult relationship with President Abraham Lincoln. In the struggle with President Andrew Johnson over Reconstruction, the Joint Committee on Reconstruction authored the Fourteenth Amendment to the Constitution.

The power of House committees mounted during the last three decades of the century as members' length of service increased. Powerful committee

Impeachment. The House of Representatives managers of the impreachment proceedings and trial of President Andrew Johnson. Standing, from left to right, are James Falconer Wilson, Iowa; George Sewel Boutwell, Massachusetts; John Alexander Logan, Illinois. Seated, from left to right, are Benjamin Franklin Butler, Massachusetts; Thaddeus Stevens, Pennsylvania; Thomas Williams, Pennsylvania; John Armor Bingham, Ohio. Bingham was the author of the Fourteenth Amendment, and Logan and Butler served as generals during the Civil War. Photograph by Matthew Brady, 1868. LIBRARY OF CONGRESS

chairs gained national attention. James Bryce in 1888 called the House "not so much a legislative assembly as a huge panel from which committees are selected" (*American Commonwealth*, vol. 1, p. 159). Seniority became the route to a committee chairmanship and the power that accompanied it. The head of the Ways and Means Committee could attach his name to tariff legislation, as did Roger Q. Mills of Texas in 1888, William McKinley of Ohio in 1890, and Nelson Dingley of Maine in 1897.

A second force shaping the character of the House of Representatives was the development of the party system and the issues that engaged the partisan organizations. In the first decade of the century the Jeffersonian Republicans overshadowed the fading remnants of the Federalist Party. By 1812 the Federalists had ebbed, and differences among the Republicans set the stage for the emergence of the "War Hawks" and the origins of the war with Great Britain. Following the end of the fighting in 1815, partisan issues

receded, although lawmakers dealt with such concerns as banking, tariffs, and slavery in the Missouri Compromise of 1820. The House played a decisive role in settling the presidential election of 1824, when that contest was not resolved in the electoral college. John Quincy Adams won the White House over Andrew Jackson when Clay threw his support to Adams.

The election of Jackson to the presidency in 1828 led in turn to the emergence of the second party system, with Democrats and Whigs contesting for control of the House. During the 1830s the slavery issue agitated House deliberations. A wave of petitions attacking bondage led lawmakers to institute a rule that put such documents on the table, effectively stifling them without further action. The controversial "gag rule" intensified sectional passions without interrupting the tide of petitions. During the 1840s and 1850s, the House grappled with sectional questions, argued first between Democrats and Whigs and after the 1854 election between Democrats and Republicans, and a series of bitterly contested Speakership elections.

From 1860 to 1874 the Republicans controlled the House and enacted a program of economic nationalism, war against the Confederacy, and Reconstruction of the South. Thaddeus Stevens, James G. Blaine, and Roscoe Conkling became national figures during this period. In 1874, as a result of the economic hard times following the panic of 1873, the Democrats regained control of the House and dominated its proceedings for the next two decades. Another economic downturn in 1893 paved the way for a Republican resurgence in 1894, when the Democrats lost 113 seats, the largest transfer of seats from one party to another through the twentieth century. By the end of the nineteenth century the Republicans controlled the House with a substantial Democratic presence from the "Solid South," which invariably sent members of the Democratic party to Washington and was thus "solid" for the Democrats.

The Speaker of the House did not attain genuine and enduring influence over the deliberations of the body until the last decade of the century. Clay, who held the post from 1811 to 1820 with brief interruptions and then again from 1823 to 1825, achieved national fame as an orator and a forger of legislative compromises. But he did not shape the rules of the House to broaden the powers of his office.

With the rise of Democratic and Republican rivalry after the Civil War, Speakers gained authority. Blaine, Speaker from 1869 to 1875, achieved a national reputation as a forceful and effective leader of the House Republicans. Samuel J. Randall of Pennsylvania (1876–1881) and John G. Carlisle of Kentucky (1883–1889) were equally prominent Democratic Speakers during their party's dominance of the House.

The key innovator in the evolution of the Speakership was Thomas B. Reed of Maine (1889–1891 and 1895–1899). Reed faced the problem of the "disappearing quorum," a Democratic tactic to frustrate Republican action. Although physically present in the chamber when quorum calls occurred, Democrats refused to answer to their names. With only a slim majority, the Republicans could not achieve the quorum necessary to conduct business. Although Reed supported this stalling device when his party was in the minority, he decided to change the rules when he became Speaker in 1889. On 29 January 1890 he instructed the House clerk to count Democrats present in the chamber as in their seats for the purposes of a quorum. Over the protests of the Democrats, the Republicans sustained Reed. The Speaker also proposed rules that limited dilatory motions, made the Committee of the Whole subject to a quorum of one hundred members, and facilitated action on legislation that key committees sponsored. These rules were adopted on 14 February 1890.

Although what Reed did was extended by Joseph G. Cannon (1903–1911) and modified during the twentieth century, Reed's changes enabled the House to conduct its business in an orderly manner during the turbulent 1890s and beyond. The modern outlines of the Speakership date from Reed's creative tenure.

By 1900 the House was a reasonably efficient legislative body. Seniority was a major determinant of institutional power; lengthy tenure for members, especially from the South, was more common; and committee roles were more decisive. Meanwhile the Senate became the more celebrated and controversial house of the Congress.

The Evolution of the Senate

At the beginning of the nineteenth century the Senate was not the preeminent branch of Congress, and its members were not public figures. Much greater fame attached to House members. As time passed the Senate's six-year term became attractive, and the prestige of the upper house rose. At the beginning of the century the Senate had few standing committees and relied heavily on select committees chosen by all the members. After 1816 standing committees were more common. Many Senate traditions emerged during the nineteenth century. The filibuster tactic frequently delayed legislation in the mid-century years, though its success in frustrating action was rare.

During the two decades after 1809 the Senate exerted its influence more directly over presidential nominations, cabinet appointments, and foreign policy issues. The Senate also became the focus of major debates when important national debates arose. The most famous occurred in 1830, when Daniel Webster of Massachusetts and Robert Y. Hayne of South Carolina debated the doctrine of nullification. Generations of school children later memorized Webster's stirring defense of nationalism.

As slavery assumed a large place in the conduct of government in the 1840s and 1850s, the Senate dealt with the question or reflected its passions. Debate over the Compromise of 1850 featured oratory by Clay, Webster, and John C. Calhoun, and the sectional crisis ultimately was postponed through the leadership of Stephen A. Douglas. In a sensational episode of sectionalism, Representative Preston S. Brooks of South Carolina assaulted Charles Sumner of Massachusetts on the Senate floor in 1855.

The Senate's power increased during the Civil War and Reconstruction, and Senate Republican leaders often pressed President Lincoln regarding racial policy and the treatment of the defeated South. After Johnson succeeded Lincoln in 1865, Senate Republicans increased their opposition to the president's lenient policy toward the South. The dispute between Johnson and the Republicans culminated in the president's impeachment in 1868. The resulting Senate trial, which was not repeated for more than 130 years, narrowly acquitted Johnson. Nonetheless, the war and its aftermath dramatically increased senatorial power relative to that of the White House.

The Dominance of the Senate

For the last three decades of the century the Senate was in many respects the most powerful arm of the national government. Individual lawmakers, in control of the electoral machinery in their states, insisted the president honor their requests for federal appointments. Senators deferred to each other through the custom of "senatorial courtesy." Soon the more dominant Republican senators, such as Conkling and Oliver Morton of Indiana, treated the White House as an instrument of their patronage desires. The same attitude spilled over into policy questions. John Sherman of Ohio, an influential senator, believed that in the Republic the executive branch should be subordinated to the legislature.

As the nation industrialized during the Gilded Age, business interests played an ever larger part in the selection of senators. Influence and sometimes outright bribery swayed state legislatures to select the candidate that a railroad, steel industry, or mining interest favored. Wealthy businesspeople could virtually purchase a seat in a small state such as Nevada. By the 1890s popular critics described the Senate as a millionaires' club, and some reformers talked of electing senators through the vote of the people in each state. Congress approved a constitutional amendment for the direct election of senators in the early twentieth century.

The balance of power between the Senate and the White House clearly lay with the Senate in the 1870s, but a slow but perceptible change took place from 1877 to 1901. President Rutherford B. Hayes (1877–1881) challenged Conkling's right to dictate appointments to lucrative patronage positions at the customhouse in New York City. Despite Conkling's opposition, the Senate confirmed Hayes's selections. President James A. Garfield confronted Conkling in 1881, and the senator was again defeated. In the decade that followed reforms in the civil service laws and patronage procedures gave the chief executive more control over who served in key positions in government.

Within the Senate a more disciplined form of conducting business emerged. The Republican Steering Committee, formed in 1880, evolved into the Committee on Committees and played a large role in selecting committee members. Nelson Aldrich of Rhode Island, William Boyd Allison of Iowa, Orville H. Platt of Connecticut, and John Coit Spooner of Wisconsin, known as "the Four," shaped the agenda of national legislation when Republicans were the dominant party in the upper house. Arthur Pue Gorman of Maryland was an important Democratic leader.

While presidents gradually gained authority, the process did not follow a straight line. During Grover Cleveland's second term (1893–1897) Senate Republicans frustrated Cleveland's hopes for tariff reform when they rewrote the bill that became the protectionist Wilson-Gorman Tariff of 1894. The president let the bill become law without his signature.

During the presidency of McKinley (1897–1901) the relationship changed. The president appointed senators to the commission to negotiate a treaty with Spain following the Spanish-American War in 1898, smoothing the way for narrow Senate approval of the Treaty of Paris in February 1899. McKinley's adroit leadership involved senators in policy deliberations over foreign affairs in Cuba and the Philippines without ceding any real presidential discretion. The Senate remained a force to be reckoned with in legislative matters, but the initiative lay more with the White House as the twentieth century opened.

Congress in Perspective

During the first half of the nineteenth century Congress stood at the center of American political life. In a slower-paced agrarian society, the rhythms of legislation matched the currents of economic and business affairs. As the nation grew and industrialized, the need for central direction and faster decisions moved power toward the presidency. In institutional terms, however, Congress in the nineteenth century established the broad patterns that shaped its future. The committee system, seniority, and the authority of the Speaker of the House and the Senate leadership directed the manner in which laws were made and the nation was governed. To a large extent Congress remained a nineteenth century institution for much of the twentieth century.

See also **Civil Service Reform; Civil War,** *subentry on* **Consequences of the Civil War; Compromise of 1850; Government; Jacksonian Era; Jeffersonian Era; Law; Missouri Compromise; Orators and Oratory; Politics; Presidency; Reform, Political; Sectionalism.**

Bibliography

Bacon, Donald C., Roger H. Davidson, and Morton Keller, eds. *The Encyclopedia of the United States Congress.* 4 vols. New York: Simon and Schuster, 1995.

Benedict, Michael Les. *A Compromise of Principle: Congressional Republicans and Reconstruction, 1863–1869.* New York: Norton, 1974.

Bogue, Allan G. *The Congressman's Civil War.* New York: Cambridge University Press, 1989.

Bryce, James. *The American Commonwealth.* 2 vols. New York: Macmillan, 1910.

Cunningham, Noble E., Jr. *The Process of Government under Jefferson.* Princeton, N.J.: Princeton University Press, 1978.

Galloway, George B., and Sidney Wise. *History of the House of Representatives.* 2d ed. New York: Crowell, 1976.

Keller, Morton. *Affairs of State: Public Life in Late Nineteenth Century America.* Cambridge, Mass.: Harvard University Press, 1977.

Morgan, H. Wayne. *From Hayes to McKinley: National Party Politics, 1877–1896.* Syracuse, N.Y.: Syracuse University Press, 1969.

Rothman, David J. *Politics and Power: The United States Senate, 1869–1901.* Cambridge, Mass.: Harvard University Press, 1966.

Silbey, Joel H. *The Shrine of Party: Congressional Voting Behavior, 1841–1852.* Pittsburgh, Pa.: University of Pittsburgh Press, 1967.

Thompson, Margaret Susan. *The "Spider Web": Congress and Lobbying in the Age of Grant.* Ithaca, N.Y.: Cornell University Press, 1985.

Young, James Sterling. *The Washington Community, 1800–1828.* New York: Columbia University Press, 1966.

LEWIS L. GOULD

CONNECTICUT   The Pequot War, the first war between Native Americans and white settlers, decimated Connecticut's native population in 1636 and 1637 and opened the way for European colonization of southwestern New England. Indian influences long persisted, however, including the name Quinatucquet, or Quonehtacut, by which the Pequots had referred to the "long tidal river" that flowed through the region. The two main towns, New Haven, at the mouth of the Connecticut River, and Hartford, at that river's fall line, shared honors as the capital of the colony and then of the state from the 1660s to the 1870s, when Hartford became the sole seat of state government.

Between the 1790s and the 1890s Connecticut underwent various transformations. Whalers and clipper ships once sailed from New London and other port towns in Connecticut. Such activities faded by the end of the nineteenth century, though shipbuilding persisted at Mystic and elsewhere. From the first waterpowered textile factory in the 1790s through later manufacturing powered by steam and then electricity, Connecticut was one of the nation's most industrialized states. Its population grew slowly from the 1790s to the 1840s, but immigration, industrialization, and urbanization subsequently led to a more rapid population increase. Originally overwhelmingly British in ethnicity, Connecticut absorbed large numbers of Irish, Germans, Italians, and other immigrants from Europe. Late in the nineteenth century it had a larger percentage of foreign-born and Catholic residents than any other state.

As in social and economic patterns, various changes in politics and policies marked Connecticut's course through the nineteenth century. In 1784, Connecticut legislated a gradual end to slavery, a policy that the other northern states also implemented. Leading the nation on another front, Connecticut established the country's first school for deaf children in Hartford in 1817. Sharing with the other states of southern New England, Massachusetts and Rhode Island, a bitter distaste for the War of 1812, Connecticut hosted the Hartford Convention at the Old Statehouse in 1814–1815 to express many residents' anger and frustrations. Soon after that war ended a coalition called the Toleration Party broke the Federalist hold on state politics. The state adopted a new constitution in 1818 that disestablished the Congregationalist Church, which had been the established church of the state, though freedom of worship at other churches had been permitted. (This was also the case in Massachusetts, where the church-state connection was not dissolved until 1834.)

A generation later, in 1845, the state abolished property requirements for voting, though the system of legislative apportionment remained a divisive issue for the rest of the century as rural areas fought to retain their overrepresentation. When the Republican Party emerged across the North after 1854, the Connecticut newspaperman Gideon Welles (1802–1878) helped organize the party in Connecticut and established the *Hartford Evening Press* to promote it. Welles ran unsuccessfully as the Republican gubernatorial candidate in 1856, and when the party came to national power he served as secretary of the navy throughout the administrations of Abraham Lincoln and Andrew Johnson.

The biographies of various Connecticut natives embody much of the cultural and economic history of the nineteenth-century United States. John Brown, the abolitionist associated with Bleeding Kansas and Harpers Ferry, was born in Torrington in 1800. Henry Ward Beecher, the preacher and reformer, and his sister Harriet Beecher Stowe, author of *Uncle Tom's Cabin* (1852), were born in Litchfield. P. T. Barnum, the quintessential American showman and a founder of the Barnum and Bailey Circus, was born in Bethel. Seth Thomas, a native of Wolcott, guided clock making from a craft to an industry during the first half of the century, and J. P. Morgan, who was born in Hartford, became one of the nation's leading bankers and financiers. Among those who resided for a time in Connecticut, Eli Whitney died in New Haven after a lifetime associated with the cotton gin, interchangeable parts, and the manufacture of guns, and Mark Twain lived in Hartford in the 1870s and 1880s, when he wrote *The Adventures of Tom Sawyer* (1876) and *A Connecticut Yankee in King Arthur's Court* (1889). During the nineteenth century, manufacturing, insurance, banking, and agriculture, including the only substantial tobacco farming in the North, brought great prosperity to this small but increasingly wealthy state.

See also **American Indians**, *subentry on* **Wars and Warfare; Education**, *subentry on* **Education of the Blind and Deaf; New England; Protestantism**, *subentry on* **Congregationalists; Republican Party; Textiles; Voters and Voting**, *subentry on* **White Male Franchise; War of 1812; Whaling.**

Bibliography

Niven, John. *Connecticut for the Union: The Role of the State in the Civil War.* New Haven, Conn.: Yale University Press, 1965.
Robertson, James Oliver, and Janet C. Robertson. *All Our Yesterdays: A Century of Family Life in an American Small Town.* New York: HarperCollins, 1993.
Roth, David M. *Connecticut: A Bicentennial History.* New York: Norton, 1979.

BARBARA HUGHETT

CONSCRIPTION.   See **Military Service.**

CONSERVATION   Attitudes toward land and resource use experienced a profound transformation during the nineteenth century. Early in the century, the prevailing viewpoint was that natural resources ought to be exploited as quickly as possible. By the end of the century, however, Americans came to appreciate that supplies of wildlife, timber, water, and other resources were finite, and they clamored for state and federal initiatives to conserve the remaining stock for future generations.

Early Attitudes

At the beginning of the nineteenth century, two basic assumptions guided most Americans' interactions with the land. Citizens of the young republic tended to view the New World as an inexhaustible storehouse of commodities waiting to be gathered up and sold at a profit. At the same time, they firmly believed they had a God-given mission to exploit this natural bounty as quickly as possible, while carrying the torch of civilization to the untamed, evil, and threatening wilderness they saw all around them.

Native Americans presented both an obstacle to this dream of conquest as well as alternative ways of viewing and interacting with the natural world. Before European contact, Native Americans tended to be highly mobile in order to take full advantage of seasonal changes in plant and game availability. In addition, they shared an animistic conception of nature (in which even inanimate objects were endowed with consciousness) and felt little inclination to organize large-scale exchange networks (through which natural resources might have been stored up in large quantities and turned to profit). These and other factors limited their impact on the landscape.

The Origins of Conservation Thinking

The emergence of romanticism provided a fresh perspective from which Euro-Americans might gain an appreciation of nature. The movement began at the end of the eighteenth century, among a handful of urban intellectuals, and slowly spread throughout the literate public at large. Among its chief tenets was an emotional, aesthetic, and spiritual attraction to nature. In the 1840s Ralph Waldo Emerson (1803–1882) and Henry David Thoreau (1817–1862) developed a particularly American strain of romanticism known as transcendentalism, which portrayed interaction with wild nature as a means to enlightenment, healing, and self-renewal. The success of the best-selling nature writer John Muir (1838–1914), an ardent disciple of the transcendentalists, was a sign of just how widely these ideas had become diffused through American culture by the end of the nineteenth century. So too was the creation of the first national parks from western lands in the public domain, beginning with Yellowstone in 1872 and Yosemite in 1890. These and other early national parks invariably contained prime examples of the sublime, monumental scenery that romantics so relished.

During the latter part of the nineteenth century, Americans also recognized for the first time that there were limits to nature's bounty. Local shortages of game and timber, soil exhaustion, and signs of overgrazing had long been commonplace throughout the more settled portions of the United States. Yet for much of the nineteenth century, the myth of inexhaustibility and the continuing availability of new land in the West prevented most people from coming to terms with the idea that they might be permanently depleting the nation's natural resources. Continued industrialization, the growth of markets and transportation networks, and accelerating rates of westward expansion placed increasing burdens on resource stockpiles, while forcing Americans to reconsider their ideas about the superabundance of nature. In the 1870s and 1880s, the rapid decline of the bison and the extinction of the passenger pigeon—both victims of intensive commercial hunting—provided convincing evidence that humans could profoundly affect the natural world. Following the 1890 census, a federal official noted that there was no longer a discernible frontier line separating the settled and unsettled portions of the United States. As the nineteenth century came to a close, many Americans lamented the implications of the end of the frontier.

The Conservation Movement

Concerns about the decline of wildlife led to the first organized conservation movement in the United States. Beginning in the 1870s and 1880s, sportsmen joined with humanitarians and nature lovers to call for the protection of game and nongame species. Working through such organizations as the Boone and Crockett Club and state Audubon Societies, wildlife conservationists lobbied for protective legislation, initiated education campaigns, and created the first wildlife refuges. In 1885 they also succeeded in establishing a federal agency, eventually known as the Bureau of the Biological Survey, to serve as a center for wildlife research and advocacy.

Widely circulated predictions of a nationwide "timber famine" fueled a second strain of American conservation. Few seemed to take notice when the diplomat and scholar George Perkins Marsh (1801–1882) first warned about the threat of wide-scale deforestation in his classic book, *Man and Nature* (1864). Not until 1891 did Congress pass an act authorizing the president to set aside forest reserves in the public domain. Among the most vocal agitators for expanding this system was Gifford Pinchot (1865–1946), a Yale- and European-trained forester who became head of the Agriculture Department's Division of Forestry in 1898. Pinchot argued that

John Muir (1838–1914). The naturalist and explorer Muir and Robert Underwood Johnson first promoted the idea of Yosemite National Park in 1889. LIBRARY OF CONGRESS

with efficient management practices, national forests could be harvested to provide a continual source of timber in perpetuity. With the ascendancy of Theodore Roosevelt to the presidency, Pinchot's idea found a willing ear. Roosevelt quickly tripled the size of the national forests, from 46 million to 151 million acres, and in 1905 appointed Pinchot as the first head of the newly created U.S. Forest Service.

Water conservation represented a third area of intense activity at the end of the nineteenth century. In the arid regions of the West, allowing fresh water to flow into the ocean was increasingly viewed as wasteful. Irrigation enthusiasts envisioned an extensive system of dams and canals to capture this water, encourage western settlement, and make the desert bloom. In the East, predominant concerns were controlling periodic flooding and creating vast, river-based transportation networks, such as the proposed waterway from the Gulf of Mexico to the Great Lakes. Both ideas soon found expression in federal agencies: the Bureau of Reclamation, established in 1902 to build and maintain irrigation works in the West, and the Army Corps of Engineers, which became increasingly active in managing eastern waterways. Not until the mid–twentieth century did environmentalists begin to recognize the tremendous environmental havoc these water projects can wreak.

By the end of the nineteenth century, the idea of natural resource conservation had become increasingly accepted. Though resistance remained significant, Americans gradually began to recognize that the wasteful practices of previous centuries could not continue in an age of growing populations, expanding economies, and ever-more-powerful technologies. Reflecting this shift in thinking, a series of state and federal agencies sought to manage efficiently the extraction of resources on some public lands (i.e., conservation) and to protect the landscape from development on others (i.e., preservation). Conservation practices made only limited inroads on private land, however, where short-term thinking continued to predominate.

See also **Federal Land Policy; Geography and Ecology; National Parks; Natural Resources.**

Bibliography

Clary, David A. *Timber and the Forest Service.* Lawrence: University Press of Kansas, 1986.
Cronon, William. *Changes in the Land: Indians, Colonists, and the Ecology of New England.* New York: Hill and Wang, 1983.
Dunlap, Thomas. *Saving America's Wildlife.* Princeton, N.J.: Princeton University Press, 1988.
Hays, Samuel P. *Conservation and the Gospel of Efficiency: The Progressive Conservation Movement, 1890–1920.* Cambridge, Mass.: Harvard University Press, 1959.
Nash, Roderick. *Wilderness and the American Mind.* 3d ed. New Haven, Conn.: Yale University Press, 1982.
Pisani, Donald J. *Water, Land, and Law in the West: The Limits of Public Policy, 1850–1920.* Lawrence: University Press of Kansas, 1996.
Shallat, Todd. *Structures in the Stream: Water, Science, and the Rise of the U.S. Army Corps of Engineers.* Austin: University of Texas Press, 1994.

MARK V. BARROW JR.

CONSTITUTIONAL AMENDMENTS

[This entry includes three subentries: **Amending the Constitution**; the **Twelfth Amendment**; and the **Thirteenth, Fourteenth, and Fifteenth Amendments.**]

AMENDING THE CONSTITUTION

Article V of the U.S. Constitution specifies the process for formally changing the supreme law of the land. There are two ways to propose amendments and two ways for proposed amendments to be ratified, or added to the Constitution. Amendments may be proposed by the U.S. Congress, with a two-thirds vote of approval from both the House and the Senate, or by a national convention called by Congress in response to petitions from two-thirds of the state legislatures. Proposed amendments then must be ratified by three-quarters of the states. In the legislation proposing the amendment, Congress must specify whether the amendment will be ratified by state legislatures or by special conventions called in the states. All of the nineteenth-century amendments to the Constitution were ratified by state legislatures.

The Constitution does not grant the president a formal role in proposing or ratifying amendments. However, the president may ask that an amendment be introduced in Congress, as well as publicly campaign for or against the ratification of an amendment. In the nineteenth century, Presidents James Buchanan (1791–1868) and Abraham Lincoln (1809–1865) displayed their support of amendments by signing them.

The process of amending the Constitution begins when a member of the House or Senate introduces an amendment in his or her chamber. Developing an accurate count of these introductions is difficult because many proposals are variations on a single theme. Historians estimate that more than eighteen hundred proposals were introduced from 1789 through the end of the Fiftieth Congress in 1889. Many of the proposed constitutional changes were spurred by major economic or political crises.

Several familiar ideas appear on the list of proposed amendments introduced in Congress during the nineteenth century. An amendment to prohibit the distribution and sale of alcoholic beverages first was introduced in the Senate in 1876. Woman suffrage first was introduced in 1878. Other topics included abolishing the electoral college, criminalizing dueling, and developing a uniform national law on divorce. In 1875, at the request of President Ulysses S. Grant (1822–1885), an amendment prohibiting polygamy was introduced.

Many nineteenth-century proposals were created to address the antebellum constitutional crisis. More than two hundred constitutional changes were introduced in the second session of the Thirty-sixth Congress (December 1860 to March 1861), leading the historian Herman Ames (1865–1935) to call it "the session of amendments" (p. 194). Among the proposed amendments was the Crittenden Compromise, a series of six proposals authored by Senator John J. Crittenden (1787–1863) of Kentucky to avert the Civil War. Crittenden's amendments included reenacting the Missouri Compromise of 1820; paying reparations to the owners of fugitive slaves that were not returned from the North; and protecting slavery in the District of Columbia. The Crittenden Compromise was defeated in the Senate in March 1861.

Congress proposed six amendments to the states in the nineteenth century. Four amendments subsequently were ratified by three-fourths of the state legislatures. One of the proposed amendments that was not ratified is called the "titles of nobility" amendment. Also known as the "missing" or "phantom" Thirteenth Amendment, it was proposed by Congress on 1 May 1810. This amendment, which garnered almost unanimous support in the House and Senate, would have strengthened the restrictions on titles of nobility found in Article I, section 9 of the Constitution. The proposal was included in an 1815 printing of the Constitution and was copied by a number of other publishers even though it was not ratified by the required number of states. Historians suggest that the amendment, introduced by the Republican senator Philip Reed (1760–1829) of Maryland, was motivated by fears that Napoleon's nephew (the son of Jérôme Bonaparte and his American wife, Elizabeth Patterson) might try to claim an American throne. The Federalists were forced to support the amendment to avoid the appearance of coveting English titles.

The other proposed amendment that was not ratified is known as the Corwin amendment. It was named for the Republican representative Thomas Corwin (1794–1865) of Ohio and was an attempt to avert the Civil War by protecting slavery in the states from congressional action. Approved by the House on 1 March 1861 and by the Senate two days later, the Corwin amendment was signed by the Democratic president James Buchanan before he left office. The new Republican president, Abraham Lincoln, expressed support for the amendment in his inaugural address. The amendment was ratified by three northern states—Ohio, Maryland, and Illinois—before supporters realized in early 1862 that it was not enough to keep the South in the Union.

Legal scholars continue to disagree about the status of the unratified nineteenth-century amendments. Neither proposal included a time limit, although the Corwin amendment may have been voided by the Thirteenth Amendment, ratified after the Civil War.

See also **Government**.

Bibliography

Ames, Herman Vandenburg. *The Proposed Amendments to the Constitution of the United States during the First Century of Its History.* Reprint, New York: B. Franklin, 1970. A detailed examination of the amendment process and classification of introduced, proposed, and ratified amendments.

Bernstein, Richard B., with Jerome Agel. *Amending America: If We Love the Constitution So Much, Why Do We Keep Trying to Change It?* New York: Times Books, 1993. Analyzes the process, politics, and history of amending the U.S. Constitution.

Earle, W. H. "The Phantom Amendment and the Duchess of Baltimore." *American History Illustrated* 22 (November 1987): 32–39. Assesses the politics surrounding the introduction of the "titles of nobility" amendment.

Lee, R. Alton. "The Corwin Amendment in the Secession Crisis." *Ohio Historical Quarterly* 70 (1961):1–26. Examines the development of the Corwin amendment as an attempt to avert the Civil War.

Silversmith, Jol A. "The 'Missing Thirteenth Amendment': Constitutional Nonsense and Titles of Nobility." *Southern California Interdisciplinary Law Journal* 8 (1999):577–611. Details and debunks the conspiracy theories surrounding the history of the "titles of nobility" amendment.

JOHN DAVID RAUSCH JR.

TWELFTH AMENDMENT

Article II, section 1, clause 1 of the Constitution vests the executive power of the United States in the president. Clause 2 establishes the indirect form of presidential election that we know as the electoral college. Clause 3, which describes the electors' voting process, became the subject of the Twelfth Amendment.

Under clause 3, electors voted for two candidates for president, and the person receiving the greatest number of electoral votes was declared elected so long as that candidate had a majority. In the event of a tie or lack of a majority, the House of Representatives would "immediately choose by ballot" the president. In a House tiebreaker, each state delegation had one vote. In either event, electoral majority or House vote, the candidate with the second-highest total became vice president.

Because of George Washington's popularity, the system worked as designed in the first two national elections. By the election of 1796 the emergence of partisanship in the form of political parties suggested the deficiency in the founders' plan. In order to assure that their two candidates, John Adams and Thomas Pinckney, would not finish in a tie, some Federalist electors threw away their second votes. While they succeeded in electing Adams, their strategy assured that the second place went to the Democratic-Republican Thomas Jefferson. The nation's two highest executives represented opposing parties, satisfying neither.

The election of 1800 spelled the end of the old system. When the electors' votes were counted in February 1801, it was apparent that each Democratic-Republican elector had voted for both Jefferson and Aaron Burr. That result threw the choice to the House of Representatives, which chose Jefferson on the thirty-sixth ballot.

The outcomes of the 1796 and 1800 elections confirmed the inadequacy of the original plan. From 1797 through 1802 members introduced resolutions in Congress proposing amendments to clause 3. In 1803, led by New York's George Clinton, the Senate developed the comprehensive resolution that became the Twelfth Amendment, which passed the Senate 22 to 10. On 9 December 1803 it passed the House by the exact constitutionally mandated two-thirds majority, 84 to 42. The Speaker's vote was decisive.

With the enthusiastic national backing of the Democratic-Republicans, the measure went to the states, which approved it. The amendment changed the electoral process in three ways. First, electors must cast separate votes for president and vice president. Second, in an election that goes into the House of Representatives, the House chooses from among the top three electoral vote-getters rather than the top five as in the original clause. Finally, the amendment clarifies that vice presidential candidates must be constitutionally eligible to hold the office of president, correcting an oversight in the original version of Article II.

Although Massachusetts, Connecticut, and Delaware rejected the amendment, ten states ratified it within months, and the secretary of state declared the Twelfth Amendment in force on 25 September 1804, in time for that year's presidential election.

See also **Elections,** *subentry on* **Presidential Elections; Politics,** *subentry on* **The First Party System.**

Bibliography

Ames, Herman V. *The Proposed Amendments to the Constitution of the United States during the First Century of Its History.* Washington, D.C.: U.S. Government Printing Office, 1897.

Magruder, Frank Abbott, and Guy Shirk Claire. *The Constitution.* New York: McGraw-Hill, 1933.

Sisson, Dan. *The American Revolution of 1800.* New York: Knopf, 1974.

DAVID JAMISON

THIRTEENTH, FOURTEENTH, AND FIFTEENTH AMENDMENTS

The three great Reconstruction amendments were the product of partisan politics, the immediate exigencies of the Civil War, and a larger and long-standing debate over what American citizenship meant and to whom it might be extended.

The 13th Amendment

Abraham Lincoln's Emancipation Proclamation of January 1863 has been attacked as legally dubious because it purported to free people in areas beyond the Union's control. But at the very least it stimulated national debate about the formal end of slavery in America, and changed the very nature of the Civil War, confirming it as a clash of social orders as much as one of armies. By December 1863, as part of his war strategy but looking toward the war's end and the end of slavery, Lincoln put forward his "Ten Percent Plan." Aimed at bringing Confederate states back into the Union, Lincoln's plan would offer pardons to Confederates (except the highest government officials) who would swear loyalty to the Union and pledge to acknowledge slavery's end. If 10 percent of the state's prewar voters swore such an oath, they could seek readmission for their state into the Union, but only under a new state constitution that prohibited slavery. If the Lincoln plan's emphasis on the ending of slavery was the germ of the Thirteenth Amendment, its limitations inspired the Fourteenth and Fifteenth Amendments. For while the proposed new state constitutions must ban slavery, the Lincoln plan did not require that they guarantee civil rights for former slaves. Abolitionist Wendell Phillips argued that the plan "frees the slave and ignores the Negro," and radicals of Lincoln's own political party developed plans for guarantees of political and civil rights for the freedmen.

In December 1863, as Lincoln was presenting his Ten Percent Plan, with its emphasis on state consti-

The Fifteenth Amendment. The passage of the Fifteenth Amendment, which prohibited racial discrimination in voting, was a momentous occasion. Lithograph, Thomas Kelly, 1870. LIBRARY OF CONGRESS: PRINTS AND PHOTOGRAPHS DIVISION

tutions as the legal documents to end the institution, radical Republicans in the Thirty-eighth Congress were attempting other approaches. While amending the Constitution seemed the clearest method, several legislators claimed that Congress had the inherent power to abolish slavery by statute. Representative Owen Lovejoy of Illinois introduced such a bill on 14 December 1863, and other measures followed. Some congressmen claimed that the state of war gave Congress the authority for abolition by U.S. statute. However, mainstream political thinking rejected the war power argument and conceded that the difficult process of constitutional amendment was the only sound path to accomplishing the goal.

The first two versions of abolition amendments were offered on the same day as Lovejoy's bill, one by Representative James Ashley of Ohio, the other by James Wilson of Iowa. Senators John Henderson of Missouri and the veteran abolitionist Charles Sumner of Massachusetts offered proposed constitu-

tional amendments in 1864, and soon all factions of the Republican Party agreed on the necessity of an abolition amendment. An ample majority in the Senate assured that Republicans there could muster the necessary two-thirds vote to move an amendment forward. The Senate originally considered a version proposed by Sumner that began "All persons are equal before the law, so that no person can hold another as slave." The Senate Judiciary Committee, which drafted the final language, was not ready for so radical a notion as full equality before the law. The version it presented was that which was finally adopted, a direct statement that "Neither slavery nor involuntary servitude . . . shall exist within the United States." When the abolition amendment came to a vote in the Senate, on 8 April 1864, every one of the thirty-six Republicans present (joined by two Democrats) voted for it. The amendment passed the Senate 38 to 6.

Because the Republicans did not have the two-thirds majority in the House of Representatives required by the Constitution, some Democrats would have to be convinced if the Senate's proposal were to be adopted. The Democratic Party was divided. War Democrats remained antislavery, but some conservatives and some "Peace Democrats," even in the North, either argued the unwisdom of amendments in general or, at the extreme, defended the institution of slavery. Some based their antiamendment arguments on the proposition that if freed, blacks must necessarily become citizens and voters. The fear of black political participation, which would inform the debate over the Fourteenth and Fifteenth Amendments, was already afoot. There was firm enough opposition that the amendment could not pass in the 1864 session. In fact, Representative Ashley changed his "yea" to a "nay," allowing him to have been on the prevailing side of the vote and thus move for reconsideration at the next session of Congress.

The election of 1864 was a victory for the Republican Party, and the second session of the Thirty-eighth Congress had a stronger Republican majority. Moreover, President Lincoln not only urged his own party to hold firm, but strongly lobbied Democrats to support the reconsidered amendment or at least not vote against it. In a vote taken 31 January 1865, eleven Democrat "nays" of 1864 had now changed to "yeas," while seven others were absent. The result was just sufficient: by 119 to 56 (two votes more than were needed) the abolition amendment passed the House.

The amendment was ratified by the states within the year. Of the three Reconstruction amendments, the Thirteenth is the one that is not merely a restriction on the states, but also limits individuals, prohibiting them from owning slaves. The amendment also gives Congress direct power to "enforce this article by appropriate legislation." The Supreme Court in 1882 interpreted the amendment as applying to all forms of slavery, "of white men as well as that of black men; and also to serfdom, vassalage, villanage, peonage, and every other form of compulsory labor" (*Railroad Tax Cases* [1882]). Later Supreme Court decisions interpreted the amendment as forbidding individual acts that amount to reducing people to slavery, and as rendering unconstitutional laws that would have made a sharecropper's leaving his contract a criminal offense (*Hodges v. U.S.* [1906] and *U.S. v. Reynolds* [1914]).

The Fourteenth Amendment

The passage of the Thirteenth Amendment removed the slave condition, but did not clarify the civil or political status of the freedmen. Indeed, without some clarification, the former slaves could have been seen as wards of the federal government. The nation's political leaders struggled with what the political condition of the former slaves should be, and they did so against the background of debate about the nature of Reconstruction. As the parties argued in late 1865 and 1866, reports reached the North of violence and intimidation against former slaves. In addition, most of the newly reconstituted Southern legislatures passed "Black Codes," severely restricting the political and civil rights of the freedmen and reducing them to a status as close to slavery as possible. The Republicans at first tried national legislation, like the Freedmen's Bureau Bill, but its renewal was vetoed by President Andrew Johnson. Johnson, bent on rapid reconstituting of the Union, declared Reconstruction over in December 1865, when the last of the postwar loyalist governments was seated in the South, and vetoed the historic Civil Rights Bill of 1866. This veto galvanized the Republican Party. Moderates joined Radical Republicans to muster the constitutional majority to repass the bill over Johnson's veto, the first time in American history such an event had happened.

Key party leaders now concluded that an aggressive national plan of Reconstruction would have to be led by Congress. Debate centered on a constitutional amendment, one that could put into the nation's highest legal authority the Republicans' understanding of what the new society that had emerged from the Civil War should be. The forum for debate was the Joint Congressional Committee on Reconstruction, formed in 1866 to evaluate whether, and how, the former Confederate states should be represented in Congress. Debate about this issue was not limited to Congress but was a nationwide topic. In fact, the first draft of what would become the amendment was authored not by a member of Congress but by Robert Dale Owen, a reformer and former chairman of the American Freedman's Inquiry Commission. The Owen plan, presented in April 1866 to members of the Joint Committee, included a requirement that the states guarantee black male suffrage by 1876, a specific guarantee of "the civil rights of persons," and spelled out in detail how the former Confederate states could reenter the Union. Although eventually discarded, Owen's proposal stimulated the committee to consider how to provide an assurance of protection of civil rights for blacks. The form that assurance finally took was authored by Representative John A. Bingham of Ohio. In 1865 Bingham had already offered a Constitutional Amendment to enlarge the power of the national government over civil rights. Now, as a member of the Joint Committee, he worked tirelessly, through complex committee maneuvers, and onto the floor of the House, to insert what became Section 1 of the Fourteenth Amendment, the comprehensive guarantee of equal rights. Bingham's firm belief was that the Constitution had been designed to secure equal justice for all, but had failed. It was necessary to amend it to restore the intent of the founders and to provide a means for the United States to secure equal justice through equal rights.

From April through June 1866, Congress debated the amendment proposed by the Joint Committee. Section 1, the Bingham proposal, included two provisions that would hold particular significance for twentieth-century jurisprudence. Clause 1 of Section 1 clarified that all persons born or naturalized in the United States are both citizens of the United States and of the state of their residence, affirming that there was such a thing as U.S. citizenship (some had argued national citizenship arose only from state citizenship). But most importantly, Section 1 contains the three great guarantees of what that citizenship means. It forbids the states from making or enforcing laws that abridge the "privileges or immunities" of U.S. citizens; from depriving any person of life, liberty, or property without due process of law; and from denying anyone the equal protection of the laws. These three powerful guarantees have emerged as the most important characteristics of what political and civil rights mean, taking their place with the Bill of Rights guarantees as limitations on government for the protection of its citizens.

Contemporaries did not even consider Section 1 as the most important; they were preoccupied with Sections 2 and 3. Section 2 repealed the three-fifths enumeration regarding slaves in the original Constitution (Article I, Section 2). Section 3, which disqualifies former Confederates from holding public office, except by special dispensation of the Congress, was critical to the politics of the time. Its targets were those who before the war had held public offices and thus had sworn to uphold and defend the Constitution of the United States, but had then joined the Confederacy. Such persons, having been disloyal, should be disqualified from federal or state elective or appointive office, the argument went. While such radicals as Thaddeus Stevens argued strongly for this clause ("Give us section three or give us nothing"), by 1868, the year of the final ratification of the amendment, President Andrew Johnson had pardoned most former Confederate officials, rendering Clause 3 moot for most purposes.

Section 4 of the Fourteenth Amendment had political motivation as well. The Union had incurred an estimated $1 billion debt in fighting the Civil War, and the Confederate government had large domestic and foreign debts as well. Republicans feared that reconstituted Southern representations would either try to repudiate the massive national debt, or to impose the Confederate debt on the national government. Clause 4 forbids both and expressly states that the debts or claims of the Confederacy are outlawed (to prevent the individual Southern states from assuming them).

Section 5, which gave the Congress power to pass legislation to enforce the other sections of the amendment, would see new life in the late twentieth century. But in the nineteenth century, still-strong notions of states' rights limited its impact. The Supreme Court held in 1883 that Congress was authorized under this section to adopt only corrective legislation to put right what a state may have erred in by legislation or action depriving a citizen of rights. Congress could not, the Court held, use this section to create general national legislation for the welfare of American citizens (*Civil Rights Cases* 109 U.S. 3 [1883]).

These five sections went to the states for ratification in 1866. They were the subject of intense debate in the state legislatures and became the key issue of the congressional elections of 1866. Congressional leaders argued that as part of earning the right to again be represented in Congress, Southern states must ratify the amendment. President Johnson vigorously opposed this idea and urged repudiation of Radical Reconstruction. Johnson won in the short term; no Southern state except Tennessee ratified. Frustrated by this setback, and with the amendment still out for ratification, Congress passed the Reconstruction Act of 1867, dividing the South into military districts, unseating the immediate postwar Southern state governments, and putting into law its suggestion that ratification of the Fourteenth Amendment would be a precondition to readmission. Radical Reconstruction had begun and would last for ten years.

Under Radical Reconstruction, black males in the South were given the vote, and new southern Republican governments emerged. As these newly constituted governments ratified the Fourteenth Amendment, it inched closer to the required majority. Finally, in July 1868, shortly after the impeachment trial of Andrew Johnson, Congress, by concurrent resolution, declared that the Fourteenth Amendment had been adopted by the requisite thirty states.

The Fifteenth Amendment

Radical, or Congressional, Reconstruction allowed the most ardent advocates of rights for the freedmen to push forward a program for their political participation. However, even the most aggressive Congressional Reconstructionists realized that the national legislature could not continue indefinitely to control Southern politics. When the day came for the end of Reconstruction, there needed to be a strong guarantee of voting rights for blacks in the South, which had been enforced in the short term by Freedmen's Bureaus or military occupiers. The only sure long-term protection for preventing erosion of black suffrage was a constitutional amendment.

The Joint Committee on Reconstruction had discussed making voting protection a separate clause of the Fourteenth Amendment. However, in 1866 there was not a strong enough support for direct suffrage protection. Instead, Amendment 14, Clause 2, included the provision that states that might deny voting rights to qualified electors could lose congressional representation in proportion to their denial. This punitive provision might be helpful but was still not an affirmative guarantee of voting rights.

Shortly after the presidential election of 1868, Washington, D.C., newspaper reporters received a tip from a "Radical Senator" that a suffrage amendment would soon be introduced. In January and February 1869 separate proposals were put forward in the House and Senate. Even though the Republicans retained a strong majority in this Congress, complicated debates, numerous proposed amendments, and arcane parliamentary maneuvers followed. While virtually every Republican agreed that black male suffrage in the South was desirable, moderates questioned whether the federal government should, or even legally could, control suffrage in the states that had fought as part of the Union.

Radical Republican George Boutwell of Massachusetts introduced the first version of a proposed amendment on 11 January 1869 and remained as floor manager during the subsequent debates. His proposal stated in plain terms that voting rights should not be denied by any state on the basis of the voter's "race, color, or previous condition of servitude." Boutwell's original motion is virtually the same as that which was finally adopted, although several vigorous debates preceded ratification. The most serious objection, and one that forecast what history ultimately proved, was that a guarantee based solely on color could be circumvented by Southern states bent on denying the franchise to the freedmen through such devices as literacy requirements or property qualifications. Ohio's Samuel Shellabarger therefore put forward a proposal for universal male suffrage, which was supported by his entire state delegation. It proposed that the states not be able to deny any citizen resident in the state the right to vote, except for women, minors, insane persons, criminals, or rebels against the Union. Other con-

gressmen, the ultranationalist faction, argued that voting qualifications should be taken from the states entirely and that the federal government should be the definer and guarantor of citizenship and suffrage.

Meanwhile, the Senate, in debate managed for the Republicans by Nevada's William Stewart, added other complications. Concerned about further violence and intimidation not only of voters but of successful black office-seekers in the South, Stewart's Senate draft added to the suffrage provision a guarantee of the right to hold office if elected. Further, Senator Henry Wilson of Massachusetts proposed that the amendment ban discrimination based not only on race, but also on nativity, creed, and, most importantly, property or education.

Several extensive rounds of debate and two conference committees later, the Fortieth Congress finally retreated to the simplest course, a slightly reworded version of Boutwell's original proposal, forbidding states to deny or abridge the right to vote "on account of race, color, or previous condition of servitude." The political considerations implied by universal suffrage were too sensitive for a broader guarantee, while the office-holding issue, it was believed, would be resolved as a natural result of voting rights.

Radicals and nationalists realized that they had achieved the best compromise that they could, and the suffrage amendment was passed by the House 144 to 44 on 25 February 1869 and the next day by the Senate by a vote of 39 to 13. It was ratified by the twenty-ninth state (achieving the required three-fourths majority) and declared in force on 30 March 1870.

The Reconstruction amendments were a product of political considerations, sectional rivalries, and complex legal theory. At the least, they set the course for the rebuilding of a divided nation. More importantly, they placed in the nation's highest governing document vital assurances: that no form of slavery or involuntary servitude would exist in the United States; that citizens would be secure against state interference in the rights of property and person, in their privileges and immunities as citizens, and in enjoying the equal protection of the laws; and that racial discrimination in voting is forbidden.

See also **Abolition and Antislavery; Civil Rights; Race Laws; Reconstruction.**

Bibliography

Flack, Horace Edgar. *The Adoption of the Fourteenth Amendment.* Gloucester, Mass.: Peter Smith, 1965.

Foner, Eric. *Reconstruction: America's Unfinished Revolution, 1863–1877.* New York: Harper and Row, 1988.

Foner, Eric, and Olivia Mahoney. *America's Reconstruction: People and Politics after the Civil War.* New York: HarperPerennial, 1995.

Franklin, John Hope. *Reconstruction after the Civil War.* Chicago: University of Chicago Press, 1994.

James, Joseph B. *The Framing of the Fourteenth Amendment.* Urbana: University of Illinois Press, 1956.

Maltz, Earl M. *Civil Rights, the Constitution, and Congress, 1863–1869.* Lawrence: University of Kansas Press, 1990.

Mathews, John Mabry. *Legislative and Judicial History of the Fifteenth Amendment.* Baltimore: The Johns Hopkins Press, 1909.

McKitrick, Eric L. *Andrew Johnson and Reconstruction.* Chicago: University of Chicago Press, 1960.

Meyer, Howard N. *The Amendment that Refused to Die.* Radnor, Pa.: Chilton Book Co., 1973.

Riddleberger, Patrick W. *1866: The Critical Year Revisited.* Carbondale and Edwardsville: Southern Illinois University Press, 1979.

Ten Broeck, Jacobus. *Equal Under Law.* Toronto, Ont.: Collier Books, 1965.

DAVID JAMISON

CONSTITUTIONAL LAW

[This entry includes two subentries on constitutional law before and after the Civil War.]

BEFORE THE CIVIL WAR

From the implementation of the Constitution in 1789 until 1801, the Supreme Court was a relatively weak institution and constitutional law was very uncertain. The most significant Supreme Court decision in this period, *Chisolm v. Georgia* (1793), led to the Eleventh Amendment, overturning the Court's interpretation of the Constitution. Most constitutional law was debated or "made" not by the Supreme Court but by Congress.

The debate in 1790–1791 over the creation of the First Bank of the United States was largely about the constitutional powers of the national government, rather than about the policy of having a bank. In early 1801, when Thomas Jefferson entered the presidency and John Marshall became chief justice, the locus of constitutional debate shifted. For the next six decades all three branches of government would participate in the debate over the meaning and interpretation of the Constitution.

In contrast to the modern era, the business of the Court and the nature of constitutional law rarely involved questions of individual rights. The Bill of Rights did not apply to the states, and from 1801 until 1861 Congress rarely interfered with individual liberty. Rather, constitutional law centered on the powers of Congress, the executive, and the states in the economic, political, and diplomatic arenas. The Supreme Court settled disputes between states and citizens of different states, as well as between Congress and the states. The great exception to these general rules was slavery, which required its own kind of constitutional law and interpretation, and eventually damaged the Court and drove the nation to its greatest constitutional crisis: the Civil War.

Constitutional Law in the Supreme Court

In *Marbury v. Madison* (1803), the Marshall Court asserted its power to interpret the Constitution and to rule on the legitimacy of laws passed by Congress. The Court would not use this power again until 1857, when it struck down part of the Missouri Compromise in *Dred Scott v. Sandford.* Nevertheless, the power of the Court to overrule Congress or the executive branch was clearly established. In *United States v. Hudson and Goodwin* (1812) the Court strengthened this position by holding that the executive branch could not initiate prosecutions under common law.

In a series of decisions including *Fletcher v. Peck* (1810) and *Trustees of Dartmouth College v. Woodward* (1819), the Marshall Court struck down state laws that violated the Constitution. In these cases the Court asserted the power of the national Constitution, as an independent force, over the states.

More significant were decisions overturning state laws that directly interfered with acts of Congress or the national government. In these cases the Court asserted enormous power for Congress and for the Constitution through the "supremacy clause" of Article VI, paragraph 2, which declares that the "Constitution, and the Laws of the United States which shall be made in Pursuance thereof; and all Treaties made, or which shall be made, under the Authority of the United States, shall be the supreme Law of the Land." Two strongly nationalist decisions, in *Martin v. Hunter's Lessee* (1816) and *McCulloch v. Maryland* (1819), led to almost hysterical responses by states' rights Jeffersonians, but in the end they further established the supremacy of both the Constitution and the Supreme Court. In *Martin v. Hunter's Lessee* the Court reversed a Virginia decision and a statute on the ground that it violated U.S. treaty obligations. The case also established the constitutionality of the Supreme Court's reviewing state court decisions. In an earlier phase of this case the Virginia Court of Appeals had boldly declared that "the appellate power of the Supreme Court of the United States does not extend to this court." In *Martin* the Supreme Court flatly and overwhelmingly rejected this contention. Justice Joseph Story asserted in the unanimous opinion: "If there were no revising authority to control these jarring and discordant judgments, and harmonize them into uniformity, the laws, the treaties, and the constitution of the United States would be different in different states, and might, perhaps, never have precisely the same construction, obligation, or efficacy, in any two states. The public mischiefs that would attend such a state of things would be truly deplorable."

In *McCulloch v. Maryland* Chief Justice Marshall, in what is generally conceded to be his greatest opinion, asserted sweeping powers for the Congress and the government of the United States. Maryland had challenged the authority of the United States to establish a national bank. Marshall found the bank constitutional in all its provisions because under the "necessary and proper" clause of Article I, Section 8, of the Constitution, Congress has power to pass laws that benefit the nation as a whole. Marshall wrote: "It is the government of all; its powers are delegated by all; it represents all, and acts for all." He declared, "We must never forget that it is a constitution we are expounding," a flexible instrument sufficient to the "exigencies of the nation." "Let the end be legitimate," Marshall declared in one of his most oft-quoted passages, "let it be within the scope of the constitution, and all means which are appropriate, which are plainly adapted to that end, which are not prohibited, but consist with the letter and spirit of the constitution, are constitutional." Less controversial, though in the same nationalist spirit, was *Gibbons v. Ogden* (1824). Here Marshall struck down New York's steamboat monopoly on the ground that it violated the commerce clause of Article I, Section 8, which securely vested power over interstate commerce in the Congress.

Over the next forty years the Court elaborated on the doctrines set out in the Marshall Court's first two and a half decades. Under Chief Justice Roger B. Taney the Court was somewhat more deferential to the states. In *Charles River Bridge Co. v. Warren Bridge Co.* (1837), the Court refused to broaden its contract clause doctrine, as set out in *Dartmouth College,* and instead indicated that corporate charters should be construed narrowly, in favor of the public where necessary. Similarly, in *Mayor of New York v. Miln* (1837), *The License Cases* (1847), and *Cooley v. Board of Wardens of Port of Philadelphia* (1852) the Court developed the doctrine of inherent police power of the states to allow for local regulation of immigrants, liquor and some other goods, and even international ports.

When dealing with cases that touched on slavery

and race, the court was inconsistent in its doctrine but entirely consistent in its outcomes: to protect slavery. Thus, in *Groves v. Slaughter* (1841) the Court refused to enforce a Mississippi constitutional provision that interfered with the interstate slave trade. On the other hand, in *Mayor of New York v. Miln* (1837) members of the Court indicated that the right of New York to regulate foreign immigrants was the same as the right of the southern states to regulate the influx of free blacks. In *Prigg v. Commonwealth of Pennsylvania* (1842) the Court flatly rejected the right of a free state to protect its citizens from kidnapping, and in effect said that states could not determine the status of people within their own boundaries. The majority held that although Congress had plenary power to regulate the return of fugitive slaves, individual masters were free to ignore the federal law and capture alleged runaways without resorting to due process. And in *Strader v. Graham* (1851) the Court said that Kentucky had the right to decide whether slaves who had been allowed to travel and work in free states were still slaves.

Finally, in *Dred Scott v. Sandford* (1857) the Court declared that Congress lacked any power to regulate slavery in the federal territories, despite apparently clear language in the Constitution giving Congress the power to make "all needful Rules and Regulations respecting the Territory" of the United States. These and other slavery-related cases had one thing in common: slavery as an institution always prevailed. Dred Scott made the Court and its power a political issue in all state and national elections from 1857 until the election of Lincoln in 1860. The decision cost the court some prestige—it was as Chief Justice Charles Evans Hughes would later say, a "self-inflicted wound." During the Civil War, however, the Court gradually regained some of its visibility and by the end of the war was able to challenge the political branches in overturning the court-martial of a civilian in *Ex parte Milligan* (1866).

Congress and Constitutional Theory

The Supreme Court was not the only arbiter of the Constitution or the only party involved in the development of constitutional law. Members of Congress debated the meaning of the Constitution as they determined public policy. In 1791 James Madison argued against the establishment of the Bank of the United States on constitutional rather than policy grounds. Senators and congressmen offered public explications of the Constitution while debating federal subsidies for internal improvements, the rechartering of the Bank of the United States, the Missouri Compromise, the Seminole War, the legitimacy of the war with Mexico, the Compromise of 1850, and the Kansas-Nebraska Act. In 1830 the nullification crisis led to a dramatic debate between Daniel Webster of Massachusetts and Robert Hayne of South Carolina over the right of a state to nullify a federal law. Without the votes to impeach him, the Senate censured President Andrew Jackson, after first debating the constitutionality of such a measure. Similarly, the House censured President John Tyler. In the 1830s and early 1840s, Congressman John Quincy Adams railed in the House of Representatives against gag rules that denied constituents the right to petition Congress on the issue of slavery. During the Civil War, members of Congress debated the constitutionality of the war itself, and of many of Lincoln's policies.

The Congress, the branch of government closest to the people, mirrored popular notions of constitutional law. Abolitionists used their First Amendment rights to petition Congress to attack slavery. They also debated among themselves, with northern politicians, and with southerners, the constitutionality of slavery. Ironically, the most vocal abolitionists, the Garrisonians, agreed with the most extreme southerners, and with the Supreme Court, that the Constitution protected slavery.

Presidents as Constitutional Interpreters

Even more than Congress, presidents consulted the Constitution, and their own constitutional oracles, when deciding how to act. In 1791 George Washington asked his cabinet members for formal opinions on the constitutional issues before signing the bill creating the Bank of the United States. Thomas Jefferson agonized over the purchase of Louisiana from France, fearful that it could not be legally done without a constitutional amendment. More afraid of not acting, he ultimately overcame his constitutional scruples. In 1816 James Madison reversed his constitutional theories and declared that he no longer believed the Constitution prohibited the chartering of a national bank, and when Congress passed such a law, he signed it. In asking Congress to create a new bank, Madison declared he was "waiving the question of the Constitutional authority of the Legislature to establish an incorporated bank as being precluded in my judgment by repeated recognitions under varied circumstances of the validity of such an institution in acts of the legislative, executive, and judicial branches of the Government, accompanied by indications, in different modes, of a concurrence of the general will of the nation." Madison had been embarrassed by the lack of a central financial institution while trying to run the country during the War

of 1812, and he now had concluded that a national bank was "necessary and proper" for implementing the powers of Congress. The fact that members of Madison's own party were not investors in banks may have helped smooth the passage of the bill in Congress. However, Madison did not believe the Constitution allowed the national government to fund internal improvements, despite his belief that this would be good policy. He repeatedly asked for a constitutional amendment to allow that funding. When none was forthcoming, in 1817 he vetoed a popular improvements bill that he personally liked, purely on constitutional grounds.

Andrew Jackson's veto of the recharter of the Second Bank of the United States (1832) also rested on constitutional grounds, although here the circumstances were quite different. In *McCulloch v. Maryland* the Supreme Court had upheld the constitutionality of the bank. Jackson hated the bank, and his constitutional arguments seemed a smokescreen for his policy and personal opposition to that institution. The fact that Jackson chose to use constitutional arguments rather than simply explain the veto on policy grounds illustrates the extent to which politicians, and the nation, took constitutional arguments seriously. Jackson also ignored the Supreme Court's rulings in *Worcester v. Georgia* (1832) and pushed Indian removal in the face of a Court saying that such actions violated the Constitution.

The reaction to *Dred Scott v. Sandford* (1857) indicates yet another way in which constitutional arguments became part of the political debate in antebellum America. The Republican Party was organized in 1854 on a platform of ending the spread of slavery into the territories. In *Dred Scott*, Chief Justice Taney essentially held that the fundamental organizing doctrine of the Republican Party violated the Constitution. Republicans did not accept this. In the 1858 Senate race in Illinois, Abraham Lincoln debated Senator Stephen A. Douglas on the authority of Taney's decision in *Dred Scott*. Lincoln argued that the decision went beyond Taney's power, and thus could be ignored. As president he would do just this.

Constitutional Law and the Civil War

Although the root cause of the Civil War was slavery, the immediate spark focused on constitutional issues. Before the outbreak of the war, Congress proposed a constitutional amendment—what would have been the Thirteenth—to protect slavery forever, as a way of defusing the crisis. Meanwhile, the southern states asserted they had a right to leave the nation, and in a sense withdraw from the constitutional arrangement. Lincoln, in his first inaugural address, argued that he had taken "an oath registered in heaven" to "preserve, protect, and defend" the Constitution. After the South's attack on Fort Sumter, he called for troops to preserve the Union and to defend the Constitution. Based on his reading of the Constitution, Lincoln refused to move against slavery, despite his hatred of the institution. When he finally did act, it was as a war measure, under his powers as commander in chief of the army. However, his nagging constitutional doubts led him, and other Republicans, to secure the Emancipation Proclamation with a constitutional amendment. After Lincoln's death his Republican allies furthered the goal of liberty and equality with two more amendments, the Fourteenth and Fifteenth, designed to remake American constitutional law.

See also **Fugitive Slave Laws; Law; Slavery,** *subentry on* **Law of Slavery; Supreme Court,** *subentries on* **The Marshall Court, The Antebellum Court, Slavery.**

Bibliography

Hyman, Harold M., and William M. Wiecek. *Equal Justice Under Law.* New York: Harper and Row, 1982.

Newmyer, R. Kent. *Supreme Court Justice Joseph Story: Statesman of the Old Republic.* Chapel Hill: University of North Carolina Press, 1985.

Urofsky, Melvin I., and Paul Finkelman. *A March of Liberty: A Constitutional History of the United States.* 2d ed. New York: Oxford University Press, 2001.

PAUL FINKELMAN

AFTER THE CIVIL WAR

Constitutional law in the late nineteenth century was shaped by the sweeping social and economic changes that transformed American life following the Civil War. Adoption of the Fourteenth Amendment, intended primarily to safeguard the status of newly freed blacks, altered the balance of power between the federal government and the states. Moreover, industrialization and the emergence of large-scale corporate enterprise gradually eclipsed an older United States based on agriculture and small producers. Corporate power rekindled deep-seated fears of monopoly. This new economic order touched every aspect of American life, benefiting many but disadvantaging others and exacerbating sectional tensions. The fundamental issue in the late nineteenth century was how the nation should respond to these rapid and often bewildering changes. Yet the states continued to exercise primary regulatory authority over economic activity. In addition, prevailing constitutional thought, as exemplified by the prominent treatise writer Thomas M. Cooley, stressed the sanctity of

private property, limitations on the scope of legitimate government, and hostility to class legislation.

Civil Rights

Reluctant to abandon the traditional federal system, the Supreme Court initially construed the Fourteenth Amendment narrowly. In the *Slaughterhouse Cases* (1873), for instance, the justices virtually eliminated the privileges and immunities clause as a guarantee of individual rights and pointedly refused to serve as "a perpetual censor upon all legislation of the States" (83 U.S. 78). Thereafter the Supreme Court curtailed congressional authority to protect the civil rights of racial minorities. In the *Civil Rights Cases* (1883) the justices ruled that the Fourteenth Amendment reached only state action that abridged civil rights. Accordingly Congress could not regulate the conduct of private individuals in order to curb racial discrimination.

By the 1890s southern states began to enact laws mandating racial segregation in various areas of social life, including education and travel. The Supreme Court in *Plessy v. Ferguson* (1896) upheld a Louisiana statute requiring that railroad passengers be assigned to cars on the basis of race. The justices implicitly determined that the equal protection clause was satisfied by providing separate but equal facilities. In so doing the Court seemingly placed its seal of approval on racial segregation in the South. Justice John M. Harlan dissented, asserting, "Our Constitution is color-blind, and neither knows nor tolerates classes among citizens" (163 U.S. 559). The justices, moreover, did not even insist that the public facilities available to blacks be equal to those of whites. Thus, in *Cumming v. Richmond County Board of Education* (1899) the Court declined to intervene when a local school board provided a high school education for white students but not blacks.

The justices, however, proved willing to give limited support to equal rights. In *Strauder v. West Virginia* (1880) they declared that a state law restricting jury service to whites violated the equal protection clause. The Court also proscribed discriminatory enforcement of ostensibly impartial laws. In *Yick Wo v. Hopkins* (1886) the justices struck down unequal administration of a permit system that effectively excluded Chinese from operating laundries.

Economic Issues

Although the Supreme Court displayed little consistent interest in safeguarding civil rights under the Fourteenth Amendment, the justices continued their historic role of protecting property rights and facilitating development of a national market. They gradually utilized the due process clause as a vehicle to review state laws regulating business activity and to vindicate economic liberty. State courts had been groping toward a substantive interpretation of due process throughout the nineteenth century. Drawing upon this jurisprudence, the Supreme Court gradually took the position that the due process clause placed substantive as well as procedural restraints on state legislative authority. Substantive due process rested on the notion that government could not arbitrarily restrict certain fundamental but unwritten liberties. Foremost among these were economic liberties, such as the right to pursue lawful trades and contractual freedom. Stephen J. Field became the leading champion of this view on the Court. Under substantive due process, courts scrutinized both the purpose behind governmental regulation and the means employed to accomplish the stated goal. They did not accept legislative exercise of police power at face value.

The first application of substantive due process by the Supreme Court came in the area of state-imposed railroad rates. Railroads were the most visible symbol of the new industrial age, and in the 1870s a number of states enacted so-called Granger laws to control the prices charged by carriers. This set the stage for a prolonged controversy over the extent to which government could limit the use of private property for economic value. In *Munn v. Illinois* (1877) the justices sustained state authority to control railroad rates on the ground that certain businesses had traditionally been "affected" with a public interest. However, the Supreme Court soon backed away from this deferential position and looked more skeptically at state regulatory power. In *Chicago, Milwaukee, and St. Paul Railway Company v. Minnesota* (1890), a landmark case in the evolution of substantive due process, the Court concluded that the reasonableness of state-fixed rates was a judicial question. Further, the justices cautioned that the state could not impose confiscatory charges that in effect deprived railroads of property without due process. Eventually, in *Smyth v. Ames* (1898), the Court ruled that a regulated utility or railroad was entitled to a fair return on the value of its assets. Although railroads remained subject to governmental regulation, the upshot of the *Smyth* rule was to place constitutional limits on the rate-making power of regulatory bodies. In reaching these decisions the justices were mindful of the importance of investment capital as a vehicle for economic growth and the penchant of legislators to use the rate-making process as a means to redistribute wealth.

At the same time the Supreme Court utilized substantive due process to protect freedom of contract.

For example, in *Allgeyer v. Louisiana* (1897) the justices struck down a state law that prohibited persons from obtaining insurance from a company not authorized to do business in the state. The Court in *Allgeyer* defined liberty, as protected by the Fourteenth Amendment, to encompass the right to pursue economic opportunity and to make contracts. This judicial solicitude for contractual freedom was not surprising. Contracts were at the heart of the market economy, and nineteenth-century Americans placed a high value on voluntary private arrangements. To be sure the liberty of contract doctrine placed at risk legislative efforts to regulate the terms and conditions of employment. But in *Holden v. Hardy* (1898) the justices concluded that a state could limit the hours of work in underground mines in light of unhealthy working conditions. Not until the early twentieth century would the Supreme Court apply the liberty of contract doctrine to invalidate workplace regulations.

Private Property

The justices also invoked other sections of the Constitution to protect the rights of property owners. In a line of decisions emanating from *Gelpcke v. City of Dubuque* (1864), the Supreme Court relied on the contract clause to check attempts by state and local governments to repudiate their financial obligations. The Court heard numerous municipal bond cases and ruled that default constituted an impairment of contract. In so doing the justices both safeguarded the position of bondholders, many of whom were not residents of the defaulting jurisdictions, and encouraged capital investments. Notwithstanding the municipal bond cases, the Supreme Court diluted the protection of the contract clause in the decades after the Civil War. For example, in *Stone v. Mississippi* (1880) the justices determined that a state could not bargain away its power over public health and morals, and hence contracts were subject to the police power.

In addition the Supreme Court enlarged the protection of private property under the takings clause of the Fifth Amendment. The justices in *Pumpelly v. Green Bay Company* (1871) held that a physical invasion caused by government action, such as flooding, that destroyed the utility of land constituted a compensable taking of property. Even more important, in *Chicago, Burlington and Quincy Railroad Company v. Chicago* (1897) the Court ruled that payment of compensation for private property taken for public use was an essential element of due process as guaranteed by the Fourteenth Amendment. Consequently the just compensation principle became in effect the first provision of the Bill of Rights to be applied to the states.

Concern for private property likewise informed the Supreme Court's construction of congressional taxing power. In *Pollock v. Farmers' Loan and Trust Company* (1895) the Court held that the income tax of 1894 was a direct tax that under the Constitution had to be apportioned among the states according to population. Striking down the income tax, the Court viewed the direct tax clause as a vehicle to safeguard both private property and state autonomy by curtailing federal taxing authority.

Constitutional law in the late nineteenth century stressed liberty, especially economic freedoms, rather than equality. It bears emphasis that state courts were similarly preoccupied with property rights during this era. Moreover judges, both state and federal, generally reflected the dominant economic and social attitudes of the age.

See also **Civil Rights; Constitutional Amendments; Courts, State and Federal; Federal-State Relations,** *subentry on* **1861–1900; Judicial Review; Law,** *subentries on* **Federal Law, State Law; Liberty; Race Laws; Regulation of Business; Segregation,** *subentry on* **Segregation and Civil Rights; Supreme Court; Taxation and Public Finance.**

Bibliography

Benedict, Michael Les. "Laissez-faire and Liberty: A Re-Evaluation of the Meaning and Origins of Laissez-faire Constitutionalism." *Law and History Review* 3 (1985): 293–331.

Cortner, Richard C. *The Iron Horse and the Constitution: The Railroads and the Transformation of the Fourteenth Amendment.* Westport, Conn.: Greenwood, 1993.

Ely, James W., Jr. *The Chief Justiceship of Melville W. Fuller, 1888–1910.* Columbia: University of South Carolina Press, 1995.

Hovenkamp, Herbert. *Enterprise and American Law, 1836–1937.* Cambridge, Mass.: Harvard University Press, 1991.

Keller, Morton. *Affairs of State: Public Life in Late Nineteenth Century America.* Cambridge, Mass.: Harvard University Press, 1977.

Kens, Paul. *Justice Stephen Field: Shaping Liberty from the Gold Rush to the Gilded Age.* Lawrence: University Press of Kansas, 1997.

JAMES W. ELY JR.

CONSTRUCTION. See **Civil Engineering,** subentry on **Building Technology.**

CONSUMERISM AND CONSUMPTION

A national consumer culture first emerged in the United States late in the nineteenth century. But the origins of a consumer society stretch back for at least a century before that. In the 1780s Thomas Jefferson had dreamed of a virtuous republic composed of self-sufficient yeoman farmers, untainted by the squalor associated with manufacturing. Consumption, in Jefferson's utopia, would revolve around the basic requirements of subsistence, all of which could be found in the land's bounty. His was a powerful vision, and its ideological influence was long-lasting. But it was not an accurate description of how most people lived in the new United States. Jefferson himself was one of the nation's most conspicuous consumers, going deep into debt to fill his home, Monticello, with expensive goods from around the world.

On small farms in Massachusetts, in elegant Philadelphia row houses, and on sprawling Virginia plantations, Americans at the end of the eighteenth century bought, bartered, and used a range of goods that they did not or could not produce themselves, including tea, china tableware, spices, calico, satins, clocks, Dutch ovens, and sugar. Even on the edges of the Appalachian frontier, peddlers and general storekeepers kept households supplied with whiskey, needles, hoes, and a myriad of other items.

Many of these goods came from or through Great Britain. All told, Britain's exports to North America and the West Indies expanded by more than 2,300 percent over the course of the eighteenth century. By the early 1800s North America and the West Indies bought more than half of Britain's exports, the overwhelming majority of which were manufactures, especially textiles and metalwares.

Antebellum Consumption

In the first decades of the nineteenth century most commercial connections within the United States were local. New England peddlers, for example, hawked Bibles, almanacs, and hymnals to individual farmhouses in rural Vermont as well as to regional merchants. Plantation owners in eastern Georgia traveled to Savannah to buy buckwheat, crackers, lard, and tea, using credit on their future cotton sales.

During a nine-month period at the beginning of the nineteenth century sixty-six different customers were noted in the ledger of one general store in Louisville, Kentucky. Most patrons were white men, but several women and African American slaves shopped there as well. In almost twelve hundred transactions, an average of about eighteen per customer or two visits each a month, these people bought thread, shoes, hats, chamber pots, spectacles, and other goods and paid for their purchases with cash, store credit, skins, and wood.

The inhabitants of early-nineteenth-century cities

had more choice in goods and outlets than those who lived in rural areas. Hundreds of stores filled urban streets, offering an assortment of groceries, dry goods, glassware, medicines, and even paint. Buoyed by rapid population growth and increased commerce, specialty shops also appeared in U.S. cities beginning in the 1820s. These outlets initially focused on broad categories of merchandise, such as groceries and hardware, but by 1850 urban consumers could find stores dedicated to narrow lines of goods, such as books, carpeting, tea and coffee, china, cutlery, and hats.

Nearly all stores were small, measuring a few hundred square feet in size. Many were operated informally from the owners' homes without elaborate displays or extensive advertising. Specie was frequently in short supply during the first half of the nineteenth century, and like their counterparts in the country large numbers of city dwellers paid for their purchases with other goods or on credit.

This localized consumer economy did not necessarily translate into widespread material affluence or comfort. In the 1830s, for example, most farm families lived in three- or four-room houses without basements or flooring, save for the bare earth. On average these households probably spent less than $200 (about $3,100 in late-twentieth-century dollars) a year for all expenses except housing. Rural families in the 1830s spent about 40 percent of their non-housing budgets on food. More than half of this went for cereals, flour, and cured meat and fish. Most of the remainder was spent on salt, spices, sugars, and beverages. In the city as well as in the country most Americans had bland and monotonous diets. Root vegetables (especially potatoes), meat, bread, and dried pulses (beans, peas, and lentils) made up the bulk of calories consumed. Men ate about fifteen pounds of food a week, and women ate about twelve or thirteen pounds. They washed it down not with water, which was often unsafe, but with large quantities of tea, coffee, hot chocolate, beer, wine, and spirits.

Before 1850 the majority of Americans could count the number of durable manufactured items they owned on the fingers of two hands. Some of these items, such as a Wedgwood vase, a grandfather clock, or silver spoons, occupied a special place in household inventories, prized symbols of gentility or, for those on the frontier, of people and places once close by and now distant. Recounting her family's move to Lowell, Massachusetts, in the antebellum period, one middle-class woman remembered

familiar articles [that] journeyed with us: the brass-headed shovel and tongs, that it had been my especial task to keep bright . . . the two china mugs, with their eighteenth-century lady and gentleman figures, curiosities brought from over the sea. . . . Inanimate objects do gather into themselves something of the character of those who live among them, through association . . . They are family treasures, because they are part of the family life, full of memories and inspirations (Larcom, *A New England Girlhood*, pp. 149–150).

The Emergence of a Consumer Society

During the middle and late nineteenth century the United States gradually developed a national market. Borne along by the dramatic expansion of the telegraph and railroad after the Civil War, people, livestock, and goods crisscrossed the continent faster, cheaper, and more reliably than had been possible previously. In 1830 it took three weeks to move calico or imported earthenware from New York to Chicago. In 1860 it took only three days, and by 1880 people and goods could make the journey in less than twenty-four hours.

This "transportation revolution," as historians have called it, knit together an economy of unprecedented scale. Previously scattered and localized transactions gave way to frequent commercial connections that spanned regions, industries, and the nation. By the 1880s even settlers in the remote Dakota Territory no longer produced most of their major food crops. Instead growing numbers of farmers concentrated on wheat or cattle for sale to eastern markets. For the rest of their foodstuffs, such as flour, bottled pickles, salt, spices, fruit, and some vegetables, these men and women increasingly relied on distant canners and other manufacturers.

The development of an integrated national market helped fuel mass production. In 1869 more than half of the goods produced in the United States were agricultural and about a third were manufactures. Thirty years later the ratio had flip-flopped: 33 percent of all commodities produced were agricultural and 53 percent were manufactures. The remaining 14 percent came from mining and construction.

To find work in these growing sectors, people poured into cities, where they adopted new patterns of consumption. Most fresh vegetables came from a street cart or a grocery shop rather than the family plot. New shoes, which rural households often purchased only when a peddler with appropriate sizes appeared, were available to urban families in an assortment of sizes and styles all year round.

Industrialization brought economic growth and rising incomes. From 1869 through 1900 real per capita income rose by 2.1 percent a year. Although the late nineteenth century was punctuated by several significant depressions beginning in 1873, 1884, and 1893, the long-term trend was strongly upward. This was the most significant and sustained expansion that the U.S. economy had thus far experienced, and its effects stretched far. One of the most visible results of the new prosperity was the mass production of countless new consumer goods, including canned soups, ready-made shirts, packaged meat, soft drinks, and watches. Some of the same improvements that created new things helped make established products, such as revolvers, clocks, corsets, gloves, and locks, better, cheaper, and more easily obtainable.

Late-nineteenth-century households encountered many of these goods in new forms and outlets. For most of the century, rural and urban customers purchased staples such as vinegar, soap, and soda crackers from local stores, where clerks poured, weighed, and scooped these bulk items into desired quantities, often advising customers on quality. After about 1880, however, fast-growing companies such as Heinz, Procter and Gamble, and the National Biscuit Company (Nabisco) began to brand and package a wide range of products for national distribution. Along with the American Tobacco Company, Singer Sewing Machine Company, Kellogg's, Eastman Kodak, and Pillsbury, these manufacturers used their brands and the marketing initiatives that supported them to build direct relationships with end users and create large markets for their offerings.

As the scale and scope of national distribution expanded, households relied less on the local retailer's assessment of a particular product. Instead consumers came to know and trust goods by the way new brands were advertised. Heinz's baked beans were "pure food for the table," and Coca-Cola, invented in 1886, was promoted as a "Delightful, Palatable, Healthful Beverage." Ads claimed that Singer sewing machines had helped bring the "women of the world into one universal kinship and sisterhood." Many of these branded products were sold through established distribution channels, such as urban specialty shops, country merchants, and "drummers," or traveling salesmen.

By the end of the century several important new outlets had emerged, including chain stores, department stores, and mail-order houses. A. Montgomery Ward published his first mail-order catalog in 1872. His venture was a huge success, and by the 1890s his catalog totaled more than one thousand pages, had a circulation of 730,000, and elicited an average of two and a half orders per catalog. The arrival of the Montgomery Ward catalog, one customer remembered, "was like having Christmas come three or four times a year." Spurred on by Ward's accomplishment

and the advent of rural free delivery in 1896, other retailers such as Sears, Roebuck also began offering goods by mail. By the end of the century almost twelve hundred mail-order concerns were competing for more than 6 million customers. For households, especially those in remote locations, mail-order catalogs were a vital link to an expanding world of goods.

One of the first and most important chain stores was the Great Atlantic and Pacific Tea Company (A&P), which began in 1859 as a small store selling hides and feathers in New York City. Within a few years the founder, George Francis Gilman, decided to specialize in tea. He and his partner, George Huntington Hartford, opened new stores and gradually broadened their lines to include groceries. By the end of the century the chain had nearly two hundred stores in twenty-eight states. Others quickly followed in A&P's wake. The Jones Brothers Tea Company, which later became Grand Union, began operations in 1872; F. W. Woolworth opened his first "five and ten cent store" in Lancaster, Pennsylvania, in 1879; and in 1882 the Great Western Tea Company of Cincinnati (later the Kroger Company) opened its doors. These chains gradually homogenized the U.S. grocery market, exposing millions of Americans to a growing and roughly similar array of goods.

Mail-order houses and chain stores relied on centralized buying and management, high inventory turnover, and modern accounting systems. These practices made possible lower unit costs than those faced by most local merchants. Chain stores passed on some savings to customers by offering national brands and private label goods at fixed prices below those of independent retailers.

The mid-century emergence of department stores also shaped urban consumers' wants and needs. By the end of the century most major cities and many smaller ones boasted at least one of these "palaces of desire." New York had A. T. Stewart's, R. H. Macy, and Lord & Taylor; Philadelphia had John Wanamaker; Boston was home to Jordan Marsh and Filene's; and Chicago was home to Marshall Field, the Fair, and Carson-Pirie. Department stores were very busy places that were far grander in scale than urban specialty shops or rural general stores. At the end of the century Marshall Field employed more than seven thousand people to staff its State Street store in Chicago, which included more than half a million square feet of selling space on twelve stories, each opening onto a great atrium with an enormous skylight. A vast assortment of merchandise, from women's furs to children's tricycles to South African diamonds, was displayed. As many as fifty thousand people a day crowded into Field's great store. By 1900 daily transactions numbered in the tens of thousands, and annual sales topped $17 million. With their dazzling window displays, elaborate lighting, and numerous rooms filled with goods, Marshall Field and other emporiums were magnets for residents and tourists alike. Most of the merchandising and advertising was aimed at women, who made up the majority of customers. Shoppers at department stores found themselves in a "fairyland," noted one contemporary observer, a scene of "splendor and of beauty."

In department stores, specialty shops, and open-air markets, urban women bought the food, clothing, and furnishings that were no longer produced at home. Consumption had become a vital component of the work of the household, and women assumed major responsibility for it, crafting new and significant public roles for themselves. This social shift happened more slowly in remote areas, where men continued to make up the majority of customers at general stores well into the twentieth century. By 1920 retailers, advertising executives, sociologists, and family members accepted women's position as households' chief purchasers of consumer goods.

As the twentieth century began most Americans had access to a substantially higher standard of living than that of their ancestors in 1800. Families still spent the bulk of their incomes, an average of about 70 percent, on food, shelter, and clothing, but they had more and often better choices in these expenditures than earlier generations had enjoyed. In 1890, for example, each urban American ate an average of a pound of fresh beef a week and drank more than a quart of milk.

The things that most Americans once considered luxuries, such as a bed frame and springs or a clock, had become indispensable to all but the very poor. Pianos and mirrors, scarcely dreamed of on the early-nineteenth-century frontier, found their way into the parlors of urban and rural middle-class homes. Working-class families in 1900, those with annual incomes below $600, often had carpets and curtains. Although vacations remained the province of wealthy households, working- and middle-class families spent small sums on an occasional trip to an amusement park or five-cent movie theater.

The consumer society ushered in during the late nineteenth century was a far cry from that of the late-twentieth-century United States. In 1900 only one in four families had running water, less than one in five had an icebox, and only one in six had a flush toilet. No televisions, day care centers, health clubs, birth control pills, video stores, or fast-food outlets were available. The majority of households did not rely heavily on installment credit to fund their purchases. Despite these differences, U.S. consumerism at the end of the nineteenth century looked forward rather than backward. The industrialization, urbanization, economic growth, mass production, and distribution that accelerated after 1870 greatly expanded Americans' sense of material possibility. These forces created consumers operating in a mass market, where once only customers interacted in local economies through personal connections. As a modern consumer society took firm hold at the beginning of the twentieth century, the values of an older, preindustrial culture that emphasized spiritual as well as material improvement began to weaken. In their stead arose a culture organized around the production and acquisition of goods and services, focused on self-fulfillment through economic prosperity.

See also **Advertising; Domestic Life; Gilded Age; Merchandising; Transportation; Wealth; Women.**

Bibliography

Atherton, Lewis E. *The Frontier Merchant in Mid-America.* Columbia: University of Missouri Press, 1971.

Boorstin, Daniel J. *The Americans: The Democratic Experience.* New York: Random House, 1973.

———. "A. Montgomery Ward's Mail-Order Business." *Chicago History* 2 (1973): 142–152.

Brady, Dorothy S. "Consumption and the Style of Life." In *American Economic Growth: An Economist's History of the United States.* Edited by Lance E. Davis et al. New York: Harper and Row, 1972.

Breen, T. H. "An Empire of Goods: The Anglicization of Colonial America, 1690–1776." *Journal of British Studies* 25 (1986): 467–499.

Cohen, Lizabeth A. "Embellishing a Life of Labor: An Interpretation of the Material Culture of American Working-class Homes, 1885–1915." In *Material Culture Studies in America.* Edited by Thomas J. Schlereth. Nashville, Tenn.: American Association for State and Local History, 1982.

Gallman, Robert E. "Commodity Output, 1839–1899." *Trends in the American Economy in the Nineteenth Century.* Report of the National Bureau of Economic Research. Princeton, N.J.: Princeton University Press, 1960.

Hendrickson, Robert. *The Grand Emporiums: The Illustrated History of America's Great Department Stores.* New York: Stein and Day, 1979.

Horowitz, Daniel. *The Morality of Spending: Attitudes toward the Consumer Society in America, 1875–1940.* Baltimore: Johns Hopkins University Press, 1985.

Jaffee, David. "Peddlers of Progress and the Transformation of the Rural North, 1760–1860." *Journal of American History* 78 (1991): 511–535.

Larcom, Lucy. *A New England Girlhood Outlined from Memory.* New York: Houghton, Mifflin, 1889.

Leach, William. *Land of Desire: Merchants, Power, and the Rise of a New American Culture.* New York: Pantheon, 1993.

Lears, Jackson. *Fables of Abundance: A Cultural History of Advertising in America.* New York: Basic, 1994.

Perkins, Elizabeth A. "The Consumer Frontier: Household Consumption in Early Kentucky." *Journal of American History* 78 (1991): 486–510.

Potter, David Morris. *People of Plenty: Economic Abundance and the American Character*. Chicago: University of Chicago Press, 1954.

Shammas, Carole. "Consumer Behavior in Colonial America." *Social Science History* 6 (1982): 67–86.

Strasser, Susan. *Satisfaction Guaranteed: The Making of the American Mass Market*. New York: Pantheon, 1989.

Tedlow, Richard S. *New and Improved: The Story of Mass Marketing in America*. New York: Basic, 1990.

Twyman, Robert W. *History of Marshall Field and Company, 1852–1906*. New York: Arno, 1954.

NANCY F. KOEHN

CONTRACEPTION AND ABORTION

Birthrates plummeted over the course of the nineteenth century. As Americans gradually embraced industrialization, they began to limit family size—a change that reflected a white middle-class yearning for havens away from the workplace; the gradual elimination, particularly in cities, of unpaid household labor in favor of a paid labor force apart from home; and the sentimentalization of domestic life, childhood, and marriage. These interrelated trends appeared first within a developing professional class of American-born whites, for whom the cost of living was relatively high and children's labor less essential to economic survival. The decline was dramatic: in 1800 white families boasted an average of 7.04 children; by 1900 that number dropped to 3.56. Because industrializing societies typically experience a demographic transition in which both fertility and mortality decline, these changes were hardly unique. Of greater interest is the fact that American men and women managed to control fertility in the face of governmental attempts to shore up declining birth rates by regulating information about and access to contraception and abortion.

By mid-century, men and women were turning increasingly to contraception and abortion as a way to limit family size. In the 1830s amidst a growing tide of self-help literature, including home medical guides and health books, Massachusetts physician Charles Knowlton (1800–1850) published the first book on contraception written expressly for an American audience. Increasingly, medical science supplemented and sought to displace traditional sources of information about such matters, including mothers and grandmothers, midwives, and nonlicensed "physicians." Itinerant lecturers, some of them allied with the antebellum women's rights movement, taught basic anatomy and contraception techniques. Before 1873 contraceptives and abortifacients were openly advertised in tabloid newspapers, penny presses, almanacs, and catalogs. Supplies could be secured by mail or requested from physicians and druggists; chemical or herbal mixtures could be concocted from products commonly found in pantries. The same market economy that led many Americans to consider limiting the size of their families increasingly supplied the means for doing so.

Victorian men and women typically did not practice contraception to avoid childbearing altogether; rather they tried to postpone the start of a family, to extend the number of years between births, or to limit the number of children born during the course of a marriage. But while information about contraceptive techniques and supplies was widely available, methods were imperfect and often as dangerous as childbirth, which became relatively safe only in the twentieth century. Common forms of contraception included coitus interruptus (withdrawal), abstinence (completely refraining from intercourse), avoiding sexual activity during a woman's fertile period, and the use of condoms, douching, sponges, and suppositories. Unfortunately, medical misinformation limited the effectiveness of such strategies. Many nineteenth-century physicians believed, for example, that women ovulated during menstruation and advised couples to undertake sexual relations between the eighth and twelfth day of the cycle, when conception was in fact most likely. The female ovulation cycle was not charted accurately until the 1920s and not fully understood in medical circles for another decade.

Condoms had been available and used since ancient times. Early condoms were made of animal skins and membranes. In 1837 Charles Goodyear (1800–1860) discovered a way to vulcanize rubber, allowing man-made, mass-produced condoms. But because these devices were relatively expensive, couples more often used douching, sponges, and suppositories. Douching, which cleared the vagina of sperm, could be done with water, which sometimes pushed the sperm toward the uterus and increased chances of conception, or with chemical and herbal spermicides, which could be toxic or caustic. Sponges blocked the cervical opening; suppositories and pessaries were designed to melt and form a spermicidal barrier across the cervix.

Victorian Americans of all social classes used abortion as a contraceptive method and saw contraception and abortion as equally acceptable ways to control fertility. As a consequence the number of abortions rose significantly after 1840; at mid-century fertile women probably aborted as many as one out of every five or six pregnancies. Private decisions against pregnancy contributed significantly to the century-long decline in fertility. As with contraceptives, abortifacients were advertised in newspapers and could be purchased from physicians, pharmacists, midwives, or quacks. Recipe books often contained abortifacient "receipts"; medical guides described in considerable detail abortion methods, including herbs and chemicals known to induce abortion.

Chemical abortions, however, often put women at great risk. As with chemical contraception, many abortifacients were harsh or poisonous; some permanently damaged the uterus, cervix, or fallopian tubes. Women also appealed to doctors or midwives for instrumental abortions; but in the hands of poorly trained practitioners and charlatans, intervention could be catastrophic. Trained physicians and midwives knew that rupturing the amniotic sac, introducing an irritant into the uterus, scraping uterine walls, or dilating the cervix might induce early labor. But surgical blunders, such as uterine perforation, and infection often accompanied such procedures, maiming or killing the patient.

In the early national era, the majority of the population probably did not consider abortion to be politically divisive or immoral, so long as it occurred prior to the detection of fetal movement in the fourth or fifth month of pregnancy, a phenomenon known as "quickening." The first state laws regulating abortion embraced the old English practice (abandoned after 1803 in Britain) of allowing pregnancy to be terminated until quickening. In *Commonwealth v. Bangs* (1812), the Supreme Judicial Court of Massachusetts, and subsequently other state courts, formally endorsed the idea that as long as abortion occurred before animation, it was both lawful and morally defensible. Before modern times, neither a woman nor her doctor could be certain of conception until she felt movement; if pregnancy ended, women noted simply that it had "slipped away" or that menstruation had been "restored." States therefore charged abortionists with misdemeanors only if it could be proved that they had known a fetus was animated. Only if women died were practitioners and accomplices charged with a felony (homicide).

By the 1840s, however, access to contraception and abortion had diminished appreciably. In 1821 Connecticut moved to severely punish doctors, midwives, and quacks who "maliciously" administered poisons to induce labor; nine years later, the state expanded the law to include herbal and surgical abortions. Other states followed suit. Even so, Anglo-American women did not enjoy bodily freedom before 1840. Childbirth, abortion, and some contraceptive practices carried serious risk of disability or death. But custom rather than law governed maternity, particularly before quickening. State legislators intervened, generally on the ground that governments had

an interest in controlling quackery and protecting the health and welfare of citizens. Lawmakers initially were less concerned about public morality than about the evils inherent in pell-mell expansion of contraceptive and abortifacient markets. An 1828 New York law code, and then the law codes of many other states, included what we now call a therapeutic exception, allowing abortion even after quickening to save the mother's life.

After mid-century, public interest in maternity and fertility, as well as arguments about the immorality of decisions to avoid or terminate pregnancies, steadily mounted. State lawmakers knew that white middle-class women were exerting control over family size. Particularly after the Civil War, many Americans believed that impoverished, uneducated immigrant women would inundate the nation's cities with thousands of Catholic, Jewish, or Russian Orthodox children and pollute or destroy traditional Protestant white American culture. After 1847 the American Medical Association (AMA) led crusades for increased superintendence of fertility and maternity, as did Roman Catholics and a number of conservative Protestant sects. While the AMA typically had in mind exerting professional control over unlicensed "irregulars," including competent, experienced midwives, religious leaders emphasized the immorality of what came to be called birth control, a term invented by political activist and lobbyist Margaret Sanger (1899–1966), probably in 1914.

Antiabortion and anticontraception campaigns also mirrored social anxiety about gender norms as middle-class white women demanded access to the public realm and to the professions, all of which seemed to threaten traditional middle-class home life. More and more, critics of the New Woman depicted birth control as immoral, unwomanly, and unpatriotic. In 1868, for example, just as the Fourteenth Amendment made its way through Congress, Horatio Robinson Storer (1830–1922) and Franklin Fiske Heard (1825–1889) published an influential tract entitled *Criminal Abortion: Its Nature, Its Evidence, and Its Law*. They noted that state law codes seemed "almost wholly to ignore foetal life, to refuse its protection, . . . and . . . to extend the very crime they were framed to prevent." They recommended that abortion at any stage of pregnancy be made a felony and that penalties extend both to women and to abortion providers. By century's end, virtually every state regulated or outlawed abortion and contraception. Lawmakers had asserted a public interest in maternity and affirmed the medical profession's control over obstetrics and societal reproduction.

The Comstock Law (1873), named for Anthony Comstock (1844–1915), a zealous moral crusader and agent for the New York Committee for the Suppression of Vice, made it illegal to sell, make, or possess "obscene" materials in the District of Columbia and federal territories. The law also prohibited mail trafficking throughout the nation in "any article" for the prevention of pregnancy or for "causing unlawful abortion." Deemed obscene were publications about human anatomy, contraception, venereal disease, natural childbirth, abortion, "free love," and substances or devices of potential use in preventing conception, including many ordinary herbs. In 1868 Comstock's New York had adopted a similar statute, and by 1880 twenty-five states had also done so. Connecticut aggressively prohibited not only the distribution of contraceptives but also their use, even in the marital bedroom. Into the 1890s female physicians sometimes joined the crusade, perhaps to distinguish themselves from "irregular" midwives.

Near century's end, women's demands for effective, legal, and safe contraception grew more insistent. A new birth control movement coalesced around the concept of voluntary motherhood. Margaret Sanger and other movement leaders viewed involuntary motherhood as the taproot of woman's oppression. Often they disapproved of "artificial" methods of family limitation; instead, they promoted abstinence and women's sovereign right to avoid pregnancy by refusing to have sexual relations. Many activists sentimentalized female maternalism in order to create a zone of feminine authority around the supposedly innate maternal instinct, thereby consolidating women's control over fertility. A significant number flirted with eugenicism. Only after long decades of struggle did feminists and birth control advocates, who sometimes occupied different political camps, begin to make headway. Much Comstock-era legislation remained on the books into the 1960s, when the U.S. Supreme Court began to dismantle it.

See also **Birth and Childbearing; Domestic Life; Midwives; Women.**

Bibliography

Brodie, Janet Farrell. *Contraception and Abortion in Nineteenth-Century America*. Ithaca, N.Y.: Cornell University Press, 1994.

Chesler, Ellen. *Woman of Valor: Margaret Sanger and the Birth Control Movement in America*. New York: Simon and Schuster, 1992.

Gordon, Linda. *Woman's Body, Woman's Right: A Social History of Birth Control in America*. New York: Grossman Publishers, 1976.

Grossberg, Michael. *Governing the Hearth: Law and the Family in Nineteenth-Century America*. Chapel Hill: University of North Carolina Press, 1985.

Mohr, James C. *Abortion in America: The Origins and Evolu-*

tion of National Policy, 1800–1900. New York: Oxford University Press, 1978.

Reagan, Leslie J. *When Abortion Was a Crime: Women, Medicine, and Law in the United States, 1867–1973*. Berkeley: University of California Press, 1997.

Reed, James W. *From Private Vice to Public Virtue: The Birth Control Movement and American Society Since 1830*. New York: Basic Books, 1978.

Smith, Daniel Scott. "Family Limitation, Sexual Control, and Domestic Feminism in Victorian America." In *A Heritage of Her Own: Toward a New Social History of American Women*. Edited by Nancy F. Cott and Elizabeth H. Pleck. New York: Simon and Schuster, 1979.

DEBRA VILES
SANDRA F. VANBURKLEO

CONVICT LEASING   The generic term "convict leasing" refers to a variety of legal contracts that, despite considerable diversity in the details of their provisions, shared several common features. Most notably they were devices by which states divested themselves of their responsibility to monitor and maintain their convict populations, transferring those obligations to private corporations in exchange for a sum that was usually established by statute. Some lessees made direct use of the convicts' labor; others were little more than labor agents who sublet the prisoners. The practice was nearly universal in the American South for half a century after the Civil War. Most southern states did not have penitentiaries in that era, and those that did, like Texas and Arkansas, used them to house prisoners who would be more of a burden than a benefit to the lessees.

Leasing was primarily important as a category of forced labor rather than as a system of private prison management. Lessees set up camps throughout the rural South in piney woods, in plantation fields, adjacent to coal mines, and along railroad rights-of-way. Prisoners endured conditions that ranged from serious hardship to extreme privation, and death rates in several areas, such as in Mississippi in the late 1880s, exceeded 10 percent annually. After death rates, the most striking statistics about convicts in the leasing states are the rates of escape. Indeed thousands of fugitives lived in southern towns, cities, and farms. Official records from Texas, for example, reveal that more than three thousand prisoners escaped from work camps there between 1876 and 1899.

Convict leasing arose in the aftermath of the Civil War, when the region's landowners expected a labor shortage and the South's ravaged infrastructure was in desperate need of reconstruction. To this volatile mix of economic conditions was added the catalyst of race, as the demise of slavery summoned fears of rootless black multitudes streaming across the southern landscape. Meanwhile, state treasuries were exhausted, and convict populations were growing. Within two years after Appomattox, every southern state except Virginia had established the system of convict leasing, sometimes officially, sometimes not.

As a race-based form of forced labor in the nineteenth-century South, convict leasing had a superficial resemblance to slavery. However, leasing lacked the elements of dishonor, permanence, and natal alienation (being cut off from ancestors and descendants) that, according to Orlando Patterson (1982), are among slavery's defining characteristics. Convicts, in short, did not undergo civil death. But if their legal and social status was far better than that of slaves, the material conditions in which they had to labor were often worse, as lessees had many incentives to cut costs by failing to provide adequately for their convicts' maintenance.

Opposition to convict leasing commenced almost immediately upon the practice's inception and persisted for decades. Most notable of the contemporary expressions of dismay and anger was a forceful speech delivered by the Louisiana novelist George Washington Cable in Louisville, Kentucky, on 26 September 1883 and published in an expanded version the following February in *Century* magazine. Cable combined eloquent humanitarian rhetoric with appeals to regional honor and hard-hitting factual reporting in such an effective way that his article became the rhetorical norm for the hundreds of denunciations that followed. But contrary to Cable's hope and prediction, his article had no impact on southern prison policy. In fact, another forty-five years passed before the last convict walked out of the Alabama coal mines at the expiration of the last leasing contract in May 1928.

The impact of convict leasing on the South's economic development has been the subject of some debate. Alex Lichtenstein argues that leasing was the key to postbellum southern modernization. Gavin Wright and others, however, maintain that the number of convicts who were leased, the productivity of convict forced labor, and the cost differential between convict and free labor were too small to have made leasing a significant factor in economic development.

Leasing came to an end in a variety of ways in different states. A violent rebellion by free miners helped destroy the system in Tennessee, for example, while in Louisiana abolition was part of a package of moralism, racism, and political retribution against lessees. During the two decades before World War I, rising lease prices everywhere approached the wage rates of free labor and contributed to the demise of the system.

See also Civil War, *subentry on* Consequences of the Civil War; Labor Force; Prisons and Punishment; Reconstruction, *subentry on* The South; South, The, *subentry on* The New South after Reconstruction.

Bibliography

Ayers, Edward L. *Vengeance and Justice: Crime and Punishment in the Nineteenth Century American South.* New York: Oxford University Press, 1984. Chapter 7 provides the best brief survey of convict leasing.

Cable, George W. *The Silent South, together with the Freedman's Case in Equity and the Convict Lease System.* New York: Scribners, 1885.

Lichtenstein, Alex. *Twice the Work of Free Labor: The Political Economy of Convict Labor in the New South.* New York: Verso, 1996. A deeply researched study that focuses on Georgia and puts forward the strong claim for leasing's impact on southern economic development.

Mancini, Matthew J. *One Dies, Get Another: Convict Leasing in the American South, 1866–1928.* Columbia: University of South Carolina Press, 1996.

Patterson, Orlando. *Slavery and Social Death.* Cambridge, Mass.: Harvard University Press, 1982.

Wright, Gavin. "Convict Labor after Emancipation: Old South or New South?" *Georgia Historical Quarterly* 81 (1997): 452–464. Balanced assessment of the secondary literature and of leasing's economic importance.

MATTHEW J. MANCINI

COOKING.   See **Food.**

CORPORATIONS AND BIG BUSINESS

When the nineteenth century dawned, corporations were virtually nonexistent, and all business enterprises were relatively small. By the end of the century large corporations dominated many industries in the United States. Two factors in particular contributed to this development. State and federal laws and judicial decisions created a legal atmosphere that favored incorporation, while technological developments and organizational innovations in transportation, communications, and manufacturing made large business enterprises possible as well as profitable.

Rise of the Corporation

At the turn of the century business enterprises in the United States operated on a small scale, and the dominant figures in American commerce were merchant capitalists. These individuals usually owned one or more ships and made all of the decisions in their businesses, though many were assisted by family members or worked in conjunction with a partner or partners. Most manufacturing concerns were operated by

Henry Clay Frick (1849–1919). Coke and steel manufacturer and capitalist, Frick was a partner with Andrew Carnegie in the steel business. He is best known for his strong position against labor in the Homestead Strike of 1892. *Magazine of Western History,* 1892. LIBRARY OF CONGRESS: PRINTS AND PHOTOGRAPHS DIVISION

an artisan, who was assisted by one or two apprentices or by family members. The textile and shoe industries relied on the putting-out system, whereby self-employed, home-based workers drew their materials from and delivered finished goods to a central warehouse. The largest industrial concerns, iron foundries and shipyards, rarely employed more than fifty workers.

Between 1815 and 1840 this situation changed dramatically for two major reasons. In the 1820s the Industrial Revolution gradually spread from England to New England, where the increased use of machinery and economies of scale gave rise to the factory system. At first confined to the manufacture of textiles and shoes, this system by 1840 had almost completely supplanted the artisanal and putting-out systems. Because an unusual amount of capital was required to build and operate factories, by the 1820s corporations had begun to replace individuals and limited partnerships as the primary mechanism of business ownership. In part these developments grew out of legal changes that made incorporation more attractive. States changed their incorporation laws so

that the simple payment of a fee, rather than a special act of the state legislature, sufficed to create a corporation. State court decisions, such as *Vose v. Grant* (Massachusetts, 1818) and *Spear v. Grant* (Massachusetts, 1819), established the precept of limited liability, which protected stockholders from financial ruin if a business enterprise failed. The Supreme Court's ruling in *Trustees of Dartmouth College v. Woodward* (1819) guaranteed the inviolability of a corporation's charter.

Between 1840 and 1860 the corporation became the preferred method by which to finance and organize a business. American merchant capitalists, whose shipping interests were being outpaced by government-subsidized British firms, were attracted by the limited-liability benefits of corporate investment and the substantial profits that factories produced, and many shifted their capital from trade to manufacturing. Beginning in 1848 European investors, fearful of the rising threat of political revolution on their own continent, began seeking investment opportunities in the United States. The efforts by American bankers and shipping agents to accommodate these investors led ultimately to the creation of Wall Street, the capital market centered in New York City through which stocks and bonds could easily be bought and sold. This development made it possible for investors to buy stock in a company that they had no intention of running, thus greatly increasing the amount of capital available to corporations. The growing scale and scope of business activity resulting from major developments in transportation, communications, distribution, and production demanded large amounts of capital, which could best be raised by a corporation.

Transportation

The first modern big business enterprises in the United States were railroads. The invention of iron rails, flanged wheels, and steam locomotives in the first half of the century allowed railroads to replace rivers, canals, and roads as the dominant mode of long-distance transportation. Unlike steamship lines, canal companies, and turnpike operators, railroad companies constructed and maintained rights-of-way and operated the equipment that used them. Huge amounts of capital were required to purchase and maintain the necessary land and equipment, and the corporation proved the best vehicle for raising such funds.

By 1860 several major rail systems connected eastern industry with western and southern agriculture. These systems employed thousands of workers in hundreds of different locations doing dozens of different jobs. This activity had to be coordinated so that passengers and products could be transported safely and profitably from one point in the system to another. Clearly the old ways of entrepreneurial behavior, whereby the owner-manager made all business decisions on an off-the-cuff basis, were no longer satisfactory. Instead railroad companies developed large managerial staffs composed of professionally trained employees, most of whom worked for a salary, owned little or no interest in the company, and made a career out of their specialty. These staffs developed and implemented complex administrative procedures for managing on a minute-by-minute basis the movement of passenger and freight trains. They also supervised the ancillary activities of finance, purchasing, locomotive and car repair, engineering and construction, rail maintenance, and communications necessary to keep the trains running. In addition they devised sophisticated methods of financial, capital, and cost accounting to keep track of income and expenses.

By the 1880s these methods and procedures were fully developed and universally applied throughout the railroad industry.

Once the solutions to internal operating problems had been found, the railroads moved to reduce competition and increase profits by creating a national rail network. Following the failure of informal freight-forwarding agreements in the 1860s and formal freight cartels in the 1870s, railroad companies attempted to create self-sustaining transcontinental systems. Although no one railroad ever managed to run from sea to shining sea, the effort to do so resulted in the creation of increasingly larger railroad systems. By 1893 twenty-six companies each operated over one thousand miles of track and had a capitalization of more than $100 million. The Atchison, Topeka, and Santa Fe Railway, which connected Chicago to California, included over nine thousand miles of track, approximately three times the distance from New York to San Francisco. The Pennsylvania Rail-

"The American Juggernaut." The plight of labor is characterized in the words of the artist: "everything noble, patriotic, and progressive is crushed beneath the remorseless tread of that mammoth monster of corruption, cruelty and fraud, the vampire of capital." Drawing by Matt Morgan. *Frank Leslie's Budget of Fun,* 1873. LIBRARY OF CONGRESS

road, which connected New York to Chicago and St. Louis, was capitalized at almost $850 million. In their capital, size, and sophistication of operations, railroads were the biggest businesses of the nineteenth century.

Communications

The growth of railroads was aided immensely by the telegraph, which was invented in 1844. Building their lines along railroad rights-of-way, telegraph companies handled most of the communications between railroad stations. Early on, telegraph companies were faced with the problem of coordinating through traffic over the lines, and in 1857 telegraph companies organized themselves into six regionally managed pools. In 1866 these pools were consolidated into one company, Western Union. The first nationwide multi-unit modern business enterprise in the United States, Western Union operated more than twenty-five thousand miles of line connecting more than three thousand different stations. To coordinate its operations, the company adopted many of the management and organizational techniques used by the railroads. Central and regional staffs composed of professionally trained career managers supervised traffic, repair and maintenance, purchasing, and accounting functions.

A similar pattern occurred in the telephone industry. Following the invention of the telephone in 1876, telephone service was quickly monopolized by the American Bell Company, which acquired all the patent rights. Although these patents expired in the 1890s, American Bell continued to dominate the industry because it owned the nation's only long-lines network. Reorganized in 1885 as American Telephone and Telegraph, the company managed its operations by using many of the same basic procedures and structures that prevailed in the railroad and telegraph industries.

Production

The rise of mass production during the late nineteenth century resulted partly from major developments in transportation and communications and partly from the development of new technologies. The invention in the mid-1830s of new mining equipment and techniques greatly increased the supply of anthracite coal, which made possible the use of steam for driving machinery in every industry. The introduction shortly after the Civil War of the Bessemer process, which produced steel on an unprecedented scale, led to the phenomenal rise of the steel industry. The appearance in the late 1860s of superheated steam distillation contributed significantly to major production increases in the refining and distilling of petroleum. The develop-

ment in the 1880s of continuous-process technology, whereby a series of integrated machines processed raw materials into finished products in a matter of hours, contributed to astronomical increases in the production of a diverse group of items, such as cigarettes, matches, soap, photographic negatives, flour, and canned goods.

As manufacturing companies grew, they organized themselves along lines similar to the railroads. Corporations were formed to raise the capital necessary to build huge factories and equip them with state-of-the-art machinery. Professional managers operated departments, each of which employed hundreds if not thousands of workers, dedicated to purchasing, manufacturing, repair, shipping, sales, and accounting. General managers and their staffs made sure that the various departments worked together in harmony, thus guaranteeing the steady flow of finished products from plant to public. In this endeavor they were greatly aided by the railroads, which speedily delivered raw materials and finished goods, and modern communications, which eliminated delay in placing, processing, and delivering orders.

Consolidation

The evolution of transportation, communications, and production led to the development of a number of manufacturing concerns in any given industry, all competing fiercely with one another. During the 1870s major corporations in most industries attempted to reduce competition and increase profits by forming a horizontal combination, so called because all of the companies taking part in the endeavor produced the same product. At first these entities took the form of trade associations, in which most if not all of an industry's manufacturing enterprises formed a cartel to set prices and limit production. Typically these cartels succeeded in curbing competition only to have one or more members revert to the old practices of cutting prices and raising production. To overcome this problem, in the 1880s competitors began forming trusts, whereby a number of competing companies exchanged their stock for trust certificates, thereby granting the trustees, who were always the most important figures in the industry, legal control over the participating firms. Only about a dozen trusts formed, and by far the largest and most profitable was Standard Oil. That trust organized in 1882, when Standard Oil Company, the country's largest petroleum refiner, combined with a number of affiliated oil producers, refiners, and marketers. At its peak the trust owned fourteen companies outright and a majority of the shares in at least two dozen others, an arrangement that gave it controlling interest over 90 percent of all oil produced in the United States.

Because the effects of trusts were so visible to the general public, who perceived the curtailment of competition negatively, Congress attempted to restrict the rise of big business via the Sherman Antitrust Act of 1890. Ironically, this act aided the growth of big business. Although it prohibited trusts from engaging in monopolistic practices, it did not prohibit corporations from doing so. After 1889, when New Jersey became the first of many states to permit a company to buy stock in its competitors without a special act of the state legislature, trusts took the form of holding companies, which differed from trusts mostly in terms of legal niceties. The Standard Oil Trust led the way by incorporating as Standard Oil Company of New Jersey in 1889, and over the next fifteen years smaller competitors in other industries merged into over one hundred giant corporations. Many of them, such as American Can, Continental Tobacco, General Chemical, International Harvester, National Biscuit, Union Bag and Paper, and U.S. Steel, controlled between 40 and 90 percent of their industry's market share.

Although horizontal combinations were the most visible big businesses of the nineteenth century, in most cases the more profitable ones were the vertical combinations. Generally speaking, these enterprises came into being when a manufacturing company experienced difficulty in obtaining raw materials or marketing its products and solved the problem by acquiring a controlling interest in suppliers, shippers, or distributors. One of the first and most important vertical combinations was Carnegie Steel. Formed in 1872 as J. Edgar Thomson Steel Works, the company worked assiduously to undersell its competitors by controlling costs. To this end the company purchased coalfields and iron ore deposits, thereby reducing the cost of raw materials, as well as ships and railroads to haul coal and ore to the mills, thereby reducing shipping costs. It also replaced independent manufacturing agents, who sold the company's products as well as the products of its competitors, with a force of salaried salespeople working out of branch offices, thereby reducing marketing costs. As a result Carnegie Steel became the nineteenth century's most important producer of steel with assets valued in 1901 at almost $500 million.

In some cases a vertical combination was absolutely necessary to bring a particular product to market because standard shipping or marketing facilities were inadequate for the task. In order to get the general public to buy beef that had been slaughtered and dressed days earlier in a distant city rather than local meat that was freshly butchered and more expensive,

Swift and Company built the first refrigerated railcars and warehouses and developed a national sales organization. Early manufacturers of electrical machinery and equipment, such as General Electric and Westinghouse Electric, established their own marketing operations because independent agents lacked the technological know-how to sell and service prospective customers.

Economic and Societal Effects

By the end of the nineteenth century giant corporations ruled the U.S. economy. Over one-third of all manufactured goods produced in the United States was made by 1 percent of U.S. manufacturers, a handful of railroads controlled interregional ground transportation, and two companies operated the nation's long-distance communications. Even retailing, the last refuge of the entrepreneur of modest means, was being taken over by the giant corporation. In 1900 Sears, Roebuck and Company, the nation's foremost mail-order house, did $100 million in sales, while chain stores such as F. W. Woolworth and the Great Atlantic and Pacific Tea Company (A&P) opened dozens of outlets across the country in direct competition with "mom and pop" stores.

The economic changes resulting from the rise of big business were generally beneficial to consumers and investors. Giant corporations contributed to substantial economic growth by developing new goods and services, often as a result of technological innovation that was beyond the capabilities of small enterprises to finance and exploit. These corporations also created a number of modern business practices, such as integrated operations, cost accounting, and mass production. The higher efficiency rates and lower operating costs that resulted from these practices led to lower prices for goods and services.

The social changes resulting from the rise of big business are harder to categorize. On the one hand giant corporations created millions of jobs for unskilled and propertyless workers, many of whom were immigrants, thereby enabling them to support their families. The managerial revolution, which big business brought about, created dozens of new specialties and middle-management positions. By thus allowing intelligent, educated people of average means to improve their lot, both socially and economically at an unprecedented rate, this revolution increased the numbers of the middle class and made it more prosperous and important in U.S. society than ever before.

On the other hand many Americans felt uneasy about the rise of giant corporations and their increasing influence over people's lives. Workers had virtually no bargaining power with their employers and were extremely vulnerable to economic downturns, which left them unemployed at a moment's notice. Similarly they were forced to accept the dangerous working conditions, long hours, and often low pay offered by large enterprises. Big business placed tremendous economic power in the hands of a few tycoons, who used their power and wealth to influence the political process. State legislators, judges, and U.S. senators wound up on the payroll of many corporations, and graft and corruption in politics became the rule. As a result many Americans feared that giant corporations, in their never-ending drive to monopolize their markets, would one day seek to restrict the ability of common people to get ahead and curtail individual freedoms. These fears were particularly strong among farmers, laborers, and owners of small businesses, who generally failed to share in the economic bonanza. The result was political unrest and the rise of the Socialist Labor Party in the 1870s and the Anti-Monopoly Party and the People's, or Populist, Party in the 1880s. Although these parties differed in many respects, each sought federal government regulation of railroads and large corporations.

Big business also created a class of fabulously rich people. By 1900, 1 percent of the population controlled approximately 75 percent of the wealth, while millions lived in poverty. Many tycoons contributed generously to charities and philanthropic organizations, including Andrew Carnegie, who gave away over $300 million of his own money. However, many more flaunted their wealth and justified their way of life by citing the tenets of social Darwinism, which glorified "survival of the fittest" and blamed poor people for their own misery.

Although Progressivism did not come to fruition during the nineteenth century, the abuses of giant corporations and the excesses of the wealthy led to the rise of that movement, which began during the 1890s. Because most Americans saw that big business was, in many respects, a good thing, the Progressive movement sought to regulate rather than destroy giant corporations. By 1920, as a result of the leadership of Presidents Theodore Roosevelt and Woodrow Wilson, the role of the federal government as a regulator of big business was firmly established.

Scholars continually debate the positive and negative effects of the changes wrought by giant corporations during the nineteenth century, but all agree that these enterprises laid the foundation for the twentieth-century economy of the United States. Many of the late twentieth century's leading corporations in transportation, communications, manufacturing, and distribution got their starts during the

nineteenth century. Many long-lasting revolutionary changes in management, production, and marketing, including mass production, rapid transportation, and near-instantaneous communications, were first developed and implemented by big business in the nineteenth century.

See also **Banking and Finance,** *subentry on* **The Banking Industry; Communications; Consumerism and Consumption; Entrepreneurs; Industrialization and the Market; Investment and Capital Formation; Petroleum; Railroads; Regulation of Business; Steel and the Steel Industry; Stock Markets; Trusts; Work,** *subentry on* **Factory Labor.**

Bibliography

Chandler, Alfred D., Jr. *Scale and Scope: The Dynamics of Industrial Capitalism.* Cambridge, Mass.: Belknap, 1990.
———. *The Visible Hand: The Managerial Revolution in American Business.* Cambridge, Mass.: Belknap, 1977.
Lamoreaux, Naomi R. *The Great Merger Movement in American Business, 1895–1904.* Cambridge, U.K.: Cambridge University Press, 1985.
Porter, Glenn. *The Rise of Big Business, 1860–1910.* New York: Crowell, 1973.
Porter, Glenn, and Harold C. Livesay. *Merchants and Manufacturers: Studies in the Changing Structure of Nineteenth-Century Marketing.* Baltimore: Johns Hopkins Press, 1971.
Temin, Peter. *Iron and Steel in Nineteenth-Century America: An Economic Inquiry.* Cambridge, Mass.: MIT Press, 1964.
Trachtenberg, Alan. *The Incorporation of America: Culture and Society in the Gilded Age.* New York: Hill and Wang, 1982.
Ward, James A. *Railroads and the Character of America, 1820–1887.* Knoxville: University of Tennessee Press, 1986.
Zunz, Olivier. *Making America Corporate, 1870–1920.* Chicago: University of Chicago Press, 1990.

CHARLES W. CAREY JR.

COSMETICS.   See **Personal Appearance.**

COTTON   No plant exerted a greater influence on the development of the United States during the nineteenth century than did cotton. It played an important role in keeping the antebellum South agrarian and in the industrialization of the North, particularly New England. Because its cultivation was both labor intensive and extremely lucrative, cotton also helped maintain the slave plantation as the hallmark of southern society. Overconfidence in the importance of cotton to the manufacturing sectors of Great Britain and France helped induce the South to secede from the Union, thus causing the Civil War. Southerners' hopes that the manufacture of cotton goods offered the best means of recovering from the economic devastation and profound social change brought about by the war resulted in the construction of cotton mills across the South. Expectations of gain also occasioned the spread of cotton cultivation into marginal lands and the rise of such debilitating socioeconomic institutions as tenant farming and sharecropping, developments that helped make the South an economic and cultural backwater until well into the twentieth century.

Cotton comes from a shrublike plant that grows about five feet tall under cultivation. Cotton fibers grow inside the small green seedpods known as bolls, which appear after the plant's creamy white flowers turn deep pink and drop off. Once the bolls ripen and burst open, the fibers are ready to be harvested. During the nineteenth century this was done manually. Although cotton can grow in a number of climatological conditions, it thrives in the fertile black soil and humid subtropical climate of the Lower South.

Origins and Development

Prior to the end of the eighteenth century, cotton production in the United States was largely confined to the coastal areas of South Carolina and Georgia, where Sea Island cotton flourished. This long-staple variety produced fine, lustrous fibers up to two inches long that were highly prized in the manufacture of fine fabrics and yarns. Equally important was the fact that the seeds from this variety could be removed easily from the fibers. Unfortunately for most southern planters, the short root system of Sea Island cotton did not permit it to grow very well in the drier interior regions of the South, where only short-staple cotton, which has a much longer root, thrived. This variety produced fibers less than an inch long, which were so difficult to separate by hand from the sticky seeds that it took one full day of manual labor to clean one pound of short-staple cotton. This problem was solved in 1793, when Eli Whitney, a recent Yale graduate sojourning in Georgia, perfected the cotton gin (from the word "engine"). The gin is a boxlike device that separates seeds from fibers by means of a wire-studded revolving cylinder, thus making it possible to clean fifty pounds of cotton per day.

In the decade after Whitney's invention, cotton production in the South increased significantly. In 1790 the United States produced about 2 million pounds of cotton, or about four thousand bales, yearly. By 1800 that figure had risen to over 18 million pounds, or approximately thirty-six thousand bales. Over the next twenty years the cultivation of short-staple cotton spread through the Old Southwest, especially the Black Belt region of Alabama

"The First Cotton Gin." The cotton gin revolutionized cotton manufacture by maximizing production. Drawing by William L. Sheppard. *Harper's Weekly,* 18 December 1869. Library of Congress

Cotton Production. African American laborers operate a cotton gin at a factory in Dahomey, Mississippi, in the 1890s. Several foremen oversee their work. LIBRARY OF CONGRESS

and Mississippi. This region received its name from its rich, dark soil, although the designation would also have been appropriate because of the large numbers of African American slaves who were employed in working that soil. By 1820 the South annually produced about half a million bales. After 1820 cotton cultivation also spread into Louisiana, eastern Texas, southern Arkansas, and western Tennessee. As in Alabama and Mississippi, cotton became the dominant cash crop. The use of cotton in the western South was aided greatly by the relocation of hundreds of thousands of slaves from the Upper South states of Kentucky and Virginia, where widespread cotton cultivation never caught on. By 1850 cotton production had risen to 3 million bales and by 1860 to 5 million or about two-thirds of all the cotton raised in the world. During the 1850s approximately two-thirds of the income from U.S. exports came from the sale of cotton.

The lion's share of southern cotton was exported to England, but a sizable amount also found its way to the cotton textile mills of the North. Cotton mill districts sprang up in New York, New Jersey, and Pennsylvania, but the increased availability of cotton had the greatest effect on the New England economy. Following the American Revolution, New En-

gland farmers began leaving their farms in hopes of acquiring land elsewhere that was more productive than the rocky, played-out soil they left behind. Meanwhile, New England merchant capitalists, whose prosperous commercial dealings during the colonial era suffered as a result of increased English competition after the Revolutionary War and the trade embargoes engendered by the Napoleonic Wars, sought better places to invest their money than in mercantile activity. The needs of both groups were answered, at least in part, by the development of the factory system. This system centered on the manufacture of textiles, an industry that had begun in Massachusetts 150 years earlier and had progressed steadily ever since, although in the early nineteenth century it remained essentially a cottage industry. By offering beleaguered farmers decent employment closer to home and merchant capitalists a surer investment than overseas trade, the factory system, coupled with the ready availability of southern cotton, contributed to the establishment of the textile industry as the region's most important economic sector.

The first modern factory in the United States was Samuel Slater's spinning mill, built in 1790 in Pawtucket, Rhode Island. This mill was the basic model for the development of the Rhode Island system, which predominated along the small rivers and streams of that state and central and southeastern Massachusetts. These mills tended to be small enterprises that relied on the labor of entire local families, including small children, and usually performed only one step in the manufacturing process, such as spinning or weaving. Often they were undercapitalized, and many were forced into insolvency as a result.

After the War of 1812, the Rhode Island system gave way slowly to the Lowell or Waltham system, named after the Massachusetts mill towns where it first appeared. This system featured large-scale, heavily capitalized operations that performed every textile manufacturing process but produced only one type of cloth, such as broadcloth, cheesecloth, corduroy, damask, gingham, denim, muslin, or Osnaburg (a type of coarse linen). The success of the Waltham system led to the rise of cotton mill towns along the larger rivers of northern New England, especially the Merrimack in Massachusetts and New Hampshire and the Saco in Maine. Prior to the 1840s these larger mills relied primarily on the labor of young, unmarried women, who were recruited from the region's declining rural areas and housed on company property. After 1840 mill operatives were drawn increasingly from the ranks of newly arrived European immigrants, a transition that also occasioned the return of entire families to the mills.

Regardless of the system by which a mill was organized, in almost every case water power drove its machinery. Wherever possible, mills were situated next to a waterfall to take advantage of the cascading water's tremendous force. The mill's waterwheel provided power via an ingenious arrangement of drive shafts, pulleys, and belts to its many specialized pieces of equipment. Pickers and lappers cleaned and flattened the raw cotton, carding machines separated and laid parallel the flattened fibers, drawing frames combined the fibers into one strand, roving frames stretched and twisted the strand, spinning frames combined the strand with others to make yarn, looms or knitting machines wove the yarn into fabric, and a variety of other machines bleached, dyed, finished, printed, and packaged the fabric into bolts of cloth for sale primarily to consumers in the United States.

Between 1820 and 1860, while cotton mills gained preeminence in the New England economy, cotton plantations became the dominant socioeconomic feature of the South. The largest of these plantations, which cultivated thousands of acres of cotton and employed a hundred or more slaves, were essentially self-sufficient units that made almost all of their clothing and raised most of their food. On many plantations, skilled slaves worked as blacksmiths, carpenters, and coopers, as well as in a number of other trades and were often hired out to neighboring farms. The proliferation throughout the Lower South of these plantations inhibited the growth of cities and towns, which in turn retarded the development of banking and transportation in the region. Consequently many yeoman farmers were forced to turn to the cotton planters when they needed to borrow money or to market their crops.

Even the South's nonfarm commercial sector revolved around the needs of the planters. In the absence of a sophisticated banking system, factors sold the planters' cotton crops and advanced them money when prices were depressed or yields were low. Slave traders furnished the planters with slaves to pick, gin, and bale the cotton when times were good and took them away as payment for a nagging debt or as settlement of a deceased planter's affairs. Steamboats, in many locales the only dependable means of long-distance transportation, plied southern rivers with bales of cotton stacked fore and aft, starboard and port. Most southern foundries produced implements for cotton cultivation, and most southern mills manufactured cotton goods. The centrality of cotton to the economy of the Lower South, which became known as the Cotton Kingdom, led inevitably to the political ascendancy of the wealthy planter class. By the middle of the nineteenth century the interests of this class, which included no more than a tenth of all white southerners, had become synonymous with the interests of the South.

Cotton and the Civil War

During the 1850s one of those interests, namely slavery, encountered increasingly vigorous opposition throughout the rest of the United States. In response, southern leaders began to contemplate secession, in large part because of their overconfidence in the importance of southern cotton to the world economy. They were greatly encouraged in this regard by the English, whose factories turned out over half of the world's manufactured cotton goods. Recognizing that almost 80 percent of the cotton used in English factories originated in the southern United States, English capitalists in the 1850s tried to increase India's capacity to serve as an alternative source for machinable cotton. When laments over the failure of this initiative filled English newspapers and magazines, southern planters became convinced that "cotton is king," as David King, a southern author, put it in 1855.

Because southern cotton also fueled the textile industries in France, Germany, Russia, Italy, and Spain, southerners convinced themselves that the nations of Europe, particularly Great Britain and France, would unhesitatingly lend their support to the South in the event of an American civil war in order to ensure their access to southern cotton. Moreover, southern leaders contended that New England industrialists would not support a war that threatened to cut off their own supply of cotton, thus greatly undermining the Union's ability to prosecute a war against the South for longer than a year. These notions, which evidently were accepted almost universally by white southerners, played a major role in inducing their leaders to refuse to compromise on the question of slavery in the late 1850s and then to secede from the Union in 1860–1861.

In the early stages of the Civil War, King Cotton diplomacy defined the Confederacy's foreign policy and led Southerners to commit a fatal strategic error. During the first year of the war the Union blockade of Southern ports was largely ineffective, and a large amount of cotton could have been slipped through to Europe, where it could have been exchanged for much-needed war matériel. According to one estimate, in 1861 the South could have exported enough cotton to equip an army of 150,000 men. Instead cotton planters and factors, with the full support of every segment of white Southern society, imposed a cotton embargo on themselves in an effort to coerce Great Britain and France into supporting its cause by cutting off the supply of cotton. Unfortunately for the Confederacy, the embargo had the opposite effect. It engendered resentment rather than sympathy in the capitals of Europe and created the impression that the Union blockade was much more effective than it really was. By the time Southern leaders realized that King Cotton diplomacy would not work, the Union blockade had tightened up, and the South could no longer finance the war with cotton.

Cotton and the Postwar South

The South's dependence on cotton continued after the Civil War, although for different reasons than before. The abolition of slavery brought about the demise of the large plantation, but instead of hiring gangs of laborers to work the fields, most large landowners leased land to newly emancipated blacks under various arrangements. Tenant farmers rented a cabin and acreage but provided their own tools and provisions, although these were frequently obtained from a furnishing merchant at exorbitant rates of interest. Sharecroppers provided only their own labor; the landlord furnished them with everything else they needed to farm and keep house in return for a sizable share of the crops come harvest time. In both cases landlords required their lessees to raise cotton,

largely because of the exceptionally high price cotton fetched after the war. When cotton prices returned to prewar levels in the 1870s, many tenant farmers and sharecroppers found themselves going further into debt with each passing year, while the landlords and furnishing merchants became wealthy.

The deaths of over 250,000 Southern men during the war and the passage of fence laws, which prevented livestock from trampling valuable cotton fields, made it virtually impossible for many white families of modest means to sustain themselves via subsistence farming as they had in the past. Only by raising cotton on their marginal land were these families able to survive. When cotton prices fell, a number of these families lost their farms and were forced into tenancy or sharecropping, a fate similar to that of blacks. By the end of the nineteenth century approximately 70 percent of all southern farmers were either tenant farmers or sharecroppers.

Around 1880 southern bankers and merchants began championing the cotton mill campaign, a program of industrialization designed to emulate that of the victorious Yankees that espoused the construction of cotton mills in close proximity to the fields. This campaign took off following the 1881 International Cotton Exposition in Atlanta, Georgia, after which practically every southern community of any size erected a cotton mill. These mills provided badly needed employment to dispossessed whites, including women and children, but often under conditions that enriched the mill owners while offering workers little more than a bare subsistence. Moreover, although prominent southerners usually served as presidents of the mills in their localities, the bulk of the stock was generally owned by northern capitalists, who dictated the terms under which the mills were run and drew off the profits for the benefit of the North. This development ensured that the South would remain a quasi-colonial appendage of the North until after World War II.

See also **Agriculture; Foreign Relations,** *subentry on* **The Civil War; Foreign Trade and Tariffs,** *subentry on* **Trade and Tariffs; Industrialization and the Market; Plantation, The; Reconstruction,** *subentry on* **The South; Slavery,** *subentry on* **Slave Life; South, The; Work,** *subentry on* **Agricultural Labor.**

Bibliography

Andrews, Mildred Gwin. *The Men and the Mills: A History of the Southern Textile Industry.* Macon, Ga.: Mercer, 1987.

Appleton, Nathan, and Samuel Batchelder. *The Early Development of the American Cotton Textile Industry.* 1858–1863. Reprint, New York: Harper and Row, 1969.

Burton, Anthony. *The Rise and Fall of King Cotton.* London: A. Deutsch, 1984.

Cohn, David L. *The Life and Times of King Cotton*. New York: Oxford University Press, 1956.

Dodge, Bertha S. *Cotton: The Plant That Would Be King*. Austin: University of Texas Press, 1984.

Owsley, Frank Lawrence. *King Cotton Diplomacy: Foreign Relations of the Confederate States of America*. 1931. Reprint, 1959. Chicago: University of Chicago Press.

Woodman, Harold D. *King Cotton and His Retainers: Financing and Marketing the Cotton Crop of the South, 1800–1925*. Lexington: University of Kentucky Press, 1968.

Wright, Gavin. *The Political Economy of the Cotton South: Households, Markets, and Wealth in the Nineteenth Century*. New York: Norton, 1978.

CHARLES W. CAREY JR.

COUNTRY FAIRS   The fairs that flourished in nineteenth-century America were first inspired by festive sheep shearings—imitations of English shows that started in 1778. George Washington Parke Custis held several shearings, beginning in 1803, on his farm at Arlington, Virginia. The Chesapeake region hosted more in the next few years, and Robert R. Livingston held shearings on his estate near Albany, New York. Livingston's guests in 1810 included Elkanah Watson, an Albany businessman and gentleman farmer with a farm in Berkshire County, Massachusetts. Watson was impressed by Livingston's "sumptuous hospitality" and by the sale of sheep for prices of up to one thousand dollars each. After exhibiting his own sheep and organizing the 1810 Berkshire Cattle Show, Watson founded the Berkshire Agricultural Society in 1811. The society's events, soon called fairs (an old term for trade shows), were devoted to celebrating farming in general. They triggered an enthusiasm for fairs that continued through the nineteenth and twentieth centuries.

Berkshire County's fairs began with private meetings of the society, followed by parades to churches for prayers, sermons, and sometimes poems on the moral beauties of farming. Society members then judged animals, farm produce, and domestic handicrafts while spectators enjoyed a plowing contest, made their own judgments of the exhibits, and were instructed—members hoped—by the examples of progressive husbandry on display. After winning exhibitors, usually society members, received their cash premiums, the fairs concluded with a dinner and dance. All of these events were designed to enlighten and entertain the whole community. But, as with the earlier sheep shearings, the success of the Berkshire fairs depended on the support of local gentry: they joined the society, provided most of the exhibits, won most of the premiums, did the official judging, and contributed all of the money.

Other New England agricultural societies soon adopted the "Berkshire plan" for organizing fairs. Thanks in large part to state funding, these county fairs grew quickly in number and popularity. In 1816 the Massachusetts legislature appropriated two hundred dollars for Berkshire's 1817 fair. In 1819 the Massachusetts, New York, and New Hampshire legislatures provided money for fairs to all of their county agricultural societies. When many state legislatures, like New York's, retreated from funding between 1825 and 1841, the number of fairs dropped precipitously. However, by 1858 state funding had reappeared and the country had more than nine hundred county and state agricultural societies, most of which conducted fairs. This growth continued well into the early twentieth century, especially in the Northeast and Midwest. Outside of those regions, only Kentucky held many fairs, with twenty-one in 1858. Its Lexington fair, begun in 1816, was long a "major social event in which Bluegrass farmers paraded their families and blooded stock with equal pride" (Clark, *Agrarian Kentucky*, p. 39).

As with the Berkshire fair, most nineteenth-century fairs served counties. These could be small events, like the Caledonia County, Vermont, fair, which attracted fifteen hundred spectators in 1838, or big events, as was the Worcester County, Massachusetts, fair, which in 1841 had thirty thousand attendees and offered two dances, oratory by Daniel Webster, plowing contests, and other treats.

The people who formed small and large fair audiences have been described in very different ways. Early and mid-nineteenth century Maine fairs attracted "rural people whose lives were narrowed by isolation" (Day, *History of Maine Agriculture*, p. 245) and who welcomed the ideas, competitions, and social pleasures that fairs offered. Urban fairs drew largely urban audiences that had some nostalgic interest in farming and more appetite for entertainment than for agricultural instruction. Descriptions of fair audiences suggest that nineteenth-century American crowds were varied, as were the fairs' locations and their sponsoring organizations' relations with the communities from which audiences were drawn.

In 1841 big county fairs like Worcester's began to face competition from state fairs. New York State's first fair, in 1838, was a failure, but its second, in 1841, attracted about half as many people as the Worcester show and grew steadily after that. Other state fairs proliferated between 1849 and 1861, when Michigan's and Oregon's fairs started. In the mid-nineteenth century only the Great Fair of St. Louis rivaled the state fairs in popularity. Begun in 1856 by the St. Louis Agricultural and Mechanical Association, the fair drew hundreds of thousands in the

Bucolic Festival. Fairgrounds of the Chartiers Valley Agricultural Association, Cannonsburgh, Pennsylvania. Lithograph by Pennsylvania Atlas, 1876. LIBRARY OF CONGRESS

1860s and even more a decade later. It was probably the most beautiful American fair. Landscape architecture, then becoming a popular art, influenced its arrangements of lawns, trees, fountains, and aesthetically ambitious buildings. The Great Fair also awarded exceptionally generous premiums: ten thousand dollars in its first year and more in subsequent years for hams, crops, beers, machines that made bricks, and other categories. Norman Colman, the editor of *Colman's Rural World* (1865–1911), wrote that farmers who wanted to keep up with their craft's development needed to attend, even though the fair was not exclusively agricultural. The St. Louis fair finally died after its sponsoring society went bankrupt in 1894. By then other midwestern fairs were suffering too. Chicago's World's Columbian Exposition of 1893 inspired some fairs to stop for that year and others regretted they did not. Happily, the death of St. Louis's fair opened the door for the creation of Missouri's state fair.

Critics of early-twentieth-century fairs, notably the agricultural educator Kenyon Butterfield, looked back on the nineteenth century, especially 1850 to 1870, as a golden age. However, the fairs from this period had serious problems, most of which involved maintaining a balance between serious efforts to improve agricultural practices and providing entertainment that would attract crowds. The fairs' mix of instruction and fun had changed by the 1840s, when horse races became essential parts of most fairs. Farm journals from the 1850s reported that fairs in both the East and the Midwest had essentially become horse races with a few agricultural sideshows. Some reporters were especially disturbed by the new enthusiasm for female equestrianism; the *Boston Cultivator* opined that "one of the fair contestants" in a race at Maine's 1858 state fair would "blush for shame" if she knew what "thousands of rude men" had seen as she galloped past them. After two women were seriously injured when they fell from horses at the Minnesota state fair, the *Minneapolis Journal* pointed out that racing in sidesaddles was absurdly dangerous. The source of the racing problem, in its various forms, was fair organizers' need for more income than they were getting from state governments. The fairs of the "golden age" were developing permanent facilities instead of rotating among multiple temporary sites. Real estate and buildings demanded money and generated debts that had to be serviced.

Other problems in the 1850s included amateur judging by agricultural society members, who often were businessmen and professionals with little farming experience. After the Civil War they were replaced by experts from agricultural colleges and then by a host of the colleges' extension agents in the early twentieth century. The Civil War was a bigger problem: it interrupted fairs, sometimes turning state fairgrounds into military training bases. Wartime interruption was uneven in the North and complete in the South, where fairs received little state financial aid and had never spread and flourished as they had in the North. Southern fairs began again during Reconstruction, when Republicans briefly controlled southern state governments.

Particular groups organized their own fairs in the late nineteenth century. Creeks and Cherokees began the Indian International Fair in Muskogee, now in Oklahoma, in 1874. The Kiowa, Cheyenne, Arapaho, and Comanche nations joined the fair a year later. It survived into the 1890s, when southern fairs were becoming segregated and African Americans were starting to hold their own fairs. Booker T. Washington's Farmers' Institutes, begun in 1897, inspired additional African American agricultural shows. The Order of the Patrons of Husbandry, or the Grange, started the Great Grangers' Picnic Exhibition of Williams Grove, Pennsylvania, in 1873. In 1889 the Texas Grangers created their own state fair, which excluded the horse races and liquor they thought had corrupted the state fair. Grangers, like the 4-H leaders and agricultural college extension agents who assumed much of the responsibility for fairs in the next century, hoped to achieve a balance between instruction and fun, which was what the founders of the early-nineteenth-century fairs also had meant to offer. By the end of the century fairs had changed since Elkanah Watson's day, but their basic purposes remained much the same.

See also **Agriculture; Social Life,** *subentry on* **Rural Social Life; World's Fairs.**

Bibliography

Alter, Judy. *Meet Me at the Fair: Country, State, and World's Fairs and Expositions.* New York: Franklin Watts, 1997.

Butterfield, Kenyon L. "Farmers' Social Organizations." In *Cyclopedia of American Agriculture.* Edited by Liberty Hyde Bailey. Volume 4. New York: Macmillan, 1909.

Clark, Thomas D. *Agrarian Kentucky.* Lexington: University Press of Kentucky, 1977.

Day, Clarence Albert. *A History of Maine Agriculture, 1604–1860.* Orono: University of Maine Press, 1954.

Marti, Donald B. *Historical Directory of American Agricultural Fairs.* New York: Greenwood, 1986.

Neely, Wayne Caldwell. *The Agricultural Fair.* New York: Columbia University Press, 1935.

Watson, Elkanah. *History of Agricultural Societies on the Modern Berkshire System, from . . . 1807, to . . . 1820.* Albany, N.Y.: D. Steele, 1820.

DONALD B. MARTI

COURTS, STATE AND FEDERAL   One cannot speak of an American judicial system, since no one system developed during the nineteenth century or exists today. Instead, Americans must refer to a complex judicial structure growing out of a federal division of power between national and state governments. During the 1800s the two sets of courts and jurisdictions flourished and formed a web of courts, legal rules, and laws. Each state (and territory before it became a state) established and maintained its own system of courts; at the same time the federal government had its system of courts. Both operated side by side, with jurisdiction over the same populations. To make this arrangement even more complex, a hierarchy of courts existed (and exists) within each jurisdiction. These horizontal and vertical layers of courts struggled to respond to the increasingly complex industrial, economic, and social environments of the nineteenth century. Their successes and failures have only recently piqued the interest of legal historians. Scholars have just begun to explore and interpret this institutional history, especially of the federal courts.

State Courts

With the American Revolution, the British colonies south of Canada transformed themselves into states; part of that transformation was the change of the colonial courts into state courts. Local courts have always held a special place in the hearts of Americans because they are just that—local. Territories that became states through the process set forth in the Northwest Ordinance of 1787 provided for territorial courts, which became state courts upon the territories' admission to the Union. Americans expected government to provide forums of order and conflict resolution, and the colonies, territories, and states met that social need.

Quieting noisy neighbors, disciplining petty criminals, and overseeing the condition of roads and bridges continued to be responsibilities of the local justice of the peace from the late eighteenth century into and throughout the nineteenth century. Justice of the peace courts, often the most local courts, along with county government (often called courts in the South and Midwest), provided the lowest level of judicial oversight and a forum for conflict resolution in overwhelmingly rural America. States granted large cities like Philadelphia and New York the power to establish their own municipal courts (also called police courts or city magistrates' courts) to provide forums of order for the states' growing urban populations.

Above these local courts were the state district courts (called supreme courts in New York State be-

The Seat of Justice. Courthouse, Jefferson Street between Fifth and Sixth, Louisville, Kentucky. Woodcut by German and Bros., c. 1840s. LIBRARY OF CONGRESS

cause they were the highest state courts within a county and called circuit courts in places like Kentucky). District courts were the primary trial courts for serious criminal prosecutions and civil disputes; some states, such as Texas, established separate criminal and civil district courts. These courts also could act as courts of equity or chancery, meaning that the court occasionally sat not to administer common law but to work justice between the parties. Some states, such as New York and Ohio, provided separate equity court systems early in the century; these systems gradually disappeared as states devolved equity jurisdiction to the state district courts. However, North and South Carolina maintained separate equity courts until after the Civil War.

Each state's constitution provided the specifics about the jurisdiction of the district courts, but generally their jurisdiction was either general or limited. Most state district courts possessed general jurisdiction; they could decide a variety of criminal and civil cases unless a state statute or the state constitution deprived them of a specific jurisdiction. Courts of limited jurisdiction possessed jurisdiction over one aspect of law or a particular type of case, such as small claims, probate, and family issues. These latter courts performed important services for their communities, attracted a heavy workload, and handled millions of dollars of property in some cases, such as probate. Courts of limited jurisdiction did not have limited importance.

Most cases were first tried in district courts. At the trial witnesses were called and the facts of the dispute were aired. A jury drawn from the locality sat in judgment of the crime or to settle the civil dispute, or a judge without a jury (if the parties agreed) decided the outcome of the case. The defendant and plaintiff received judgment; then, in a criminal case, a sentence was handed down, or, in a civil case, a judge or jury decided on damages. With the completion of the trial, the great bulk of litigation in the nineteenth century (as today) ended at the district level. Decisions by the district courts were reviewable, however, and could be overturned by the state appellate system. Occasionally some states provided that decisions by courts of limited jurisdiction were reviewable by district courts of general jurisdiction and then, if an issue of law still existed, could be appealed.

Because trials are good theater, court days drew people to the county seat or to the city. Court days provided the locality with both a legal and a social experience as people served on juries and saw the court and judge at work. It is not surprising, then, that Americans developed an attachment to their local courts and expected most issues to be resolved through them.

At the beginning of the nineteenth century, most appeals went directly from the district courts to the state's highest court. But as caseloads grew and the complexity of issues increased, states established intermediate appellate courts. These courts might have statewide jurisdiction to decide criminal and civil appeals, as in Virginia, or appellate jurisdiction by subject matter, with one appeals court for civil and another for criminal matters, as in Alabama. Pennsylvania established one appellate court for appeals from local government and, later, from administrative agencies and a second appeals court for all other cases. Regardless of jurisdiction, states intended these intermediate courts to handle the bulk of the appellate cases, thereby freeing the state's highest court to decide the most important cases relating to law and justice, cases important not just to the parties directly involved.

Capping the pyramidal structure of the state court system was the state's highest court. Called supreme courts in most states, these courts formed the tribunal of last resort for a state. New York and Maryland called their highest court the Court of Appeals; Massachusetts and Maine called the highest state court the Supreme Judicial Court. In 1891 a further variation in Texas established two courts of last resort: the Supreme Court for civil cases and the Court of Criminal Appeals for criminal cases.

State supreme courts interpreted the growing number of statutes and led the way in adapting law to the enormously changing world of the nineteenth century. Tort law, the law of civil wrongs covering injuries to persons not associated by contract, developed and flourished as the market economy of the era expanded. In an age when machines injured thousands of people a year, judges of the state supreme courts crafted legal rules that distributed the social cost of such accidents while maintaining a favorable business climate.

Among the most important and prominent members of the state bench in the antebellum nineteenth century were Chancellor James Kent of the New York Court of Chancery, Judge Lemuel Shaw of the Massachusetts Supreme Judicial Court, Charles Doe of the New Hampshire Supreme Court, and Thomas Ruffin of the North Carolina Supreme Court. Chancellor Kent proved to be a transitional figure in the American judiciary, committed to maintaining stability in contract and property law by protecting the "vested rights" of property owners at a time when the culture was shifting to favoring risk-takers in those areas. Lemuel Shaw is perhaps best known for his decision eliminating the stigma of criminality from labor unions in *Commonwealth v. Hunt* (1842) and for crafting the tort "fellow servant" rule in *Far-*

well v. The Boston and Worcester Railroad Company (1842). Judge Doe was recognized as a reformer of state procedure by retaining old forms of procedure while using new, judge-made amendments to overcome the technical rules burdening justice throughout the era. In *State v. Mann* (1829) and other cases Justice Ruffin articulated and developed a proslavery jurisprudence that jurists throughout the South followed.

All of these many courts reinforced the norms and responded to the needs and prejudices of the locality. When an issue regarding the state of the law arose in a case, the state provided an appellate court and a court of last resort to clarify and standardize the law both for the legal profession and for the consumers of nineteenth-century law, plain people and business people.

Federal Courts

Authority for the federal courts stems from Article III of the U.S. Constitution, which states: "The judicial Power of the United States, shall be vested in one supreme Court, and in such inferior courts as the Congress may from time to time ordain and establish." This constitutional mandate was fleshed out in the First Congress. The Judiciary Act of 1789 provided for one federal district court with one judge for each state: one district court for each of eleven states; two district courts for Virginia to cover its Kentucky territories; and two district courts for Massachusetts to cover its Maine counties. Under this statute Congress also established three circuit courts of three judges—two supreme court justices and the federal district judge. Capping off the federal judiciary, the 1789 Judiciary Act set the number of justices on the U.S. Supreme Court at six: five associate justices and one chief justice. Although amended and expanded throughout the nineteenth century to take account of new states and the large caseloads of the growing cities, the Judiciary Act of 1789 proved to be the foundation upon which Congress built the federal judiciary.

Unlike the state district courts, which exercised general jurisdiction, federal district courts had jurisdiction only over cases or issues specified by acts of Congress or in Article III, section 2: "all Cases, in Law and Equity, arising under this Constitution, the Laws of the United States, and Treaties made, or which shall be made, under their Authority." Not only were the federal courts bound to enforce the laws of the United States, but the federal Constitution became the "Law of the Land" under Article VI, and "the Judges in every State shall be bound thereby." While this "supremacy clause" proved controversial during the crisis of the Union in the 1850s, the outcome of the Civil War ended discussion over which court system was superior to the other. With the expanding economy the jurisdiction of the federal courts increased during the nineteenth century to include all issues involving federal rights. Following the Civil War, Congress expanded the federal courts' jurisdiction to include commerce issues, civil rights, some criminal law, and taxation.

To some degree the state and federal courts competed for business and litigants, especially since businesses often went "forum shopping" to find the more sympathetic court. Although under section 34 of the Judiciary Act of 1789 the federal district courts were to follow the rules of the states, the Supreme Court opened the door for the federal courts to develop their own common law of commerce in *Swift v. Tyson* (1842). While the Supreme Court hoped to create a single national, federal commercial common law on issues such as tort, contract, and negligence, instead the state and federal courts continued to develop their own bodies of commercial law. In 1938 the Supreme Court ended this confusion and overturned *Swift* in *Erie Railroad Company v. Tompkins*.

A review of the major case laws and decisions of the U.S. Supreme Court over the course of the nineteenth century is beyond the scope of this essay. Yet a few of the Supreme Court's most important decisions of the nineteenth century deserve mention: *Marbury v. Madison* (1803); *Dred Scott v. John F. A. Sandford* (1857); *Texas v. White* (1869); and *Plessy v. Ferguson* (1896). In *Marbury*, in a tour de force of judicial reasoning and political acumen, Chief Justice John Marshall, speaking for a unanimous Court, navigated the case's political shoals while assuming and asserting the Supreme Court's most important power—judicial review. With the power of judicial review, the Supreme Court became a fully formed third branch of the federal government and not simply a high court of law. With judicial review the Supreme Court defends its own powers from encroachment while policing individuals, the states, and the other branches of the federal government, at the same time protecting and interpreting the Constitution.

Legal and constitutional scholars hail *Marbury* as one of the most important decisions rendered by the Supreme Court and consider *Dred Scott* as perhaps its worst decision. Responding to a freedom suit from Missouri, all nine justices wrote opinions in the case, with Chief Justice Roger B. Taney's decision being the "Opinion of the Court"; two justices dissented from his opinion. Taney ruled that Congress had exceeded its powers when it passed the Missouri Compromise of 1820, limiting the expansion of slavery into the western territories. Taney further held that blacks had no rights that whites need respect. In an act of failed judicial statesmanship, Taney hoped to remove slavery from politics and thus cool the politics of the 1850s. Instead, *Dred Scott* became a major point of dispute in the growing sectional crisis.

Texas v. White (1869) raised the question of whether Confederate Texas was a state within the meaning of the Constitution. Speaking for a divided Court, 5–3, Chief Justice Salmon P. Chase held that Confederate Texas had been a group of illegal insurrectionists and that debts incurred by them could not be recovered. For Chase the Constitution created "an indestructible Union, composed of indestructible States." This decision, combined with the Fourteenth Amendment (1868), signaled a shift in American federalism.

Plessy v. Ferguson (1896) generated almost no notice when decided, but it became notorious in the twentieth century because of its judicial approval of the "equal but separate" rule in public accommodations. Justice Henry Billings Brown, in an 8–1 decision, upheld Louisiana's rule of separate railroad cars for blacks and whites. Justice John Marshall Harlan dissented, arguing that the Constitution was colorblind and that such segregation of the races was unconstitutional.

In the post–Civil War era, the federal judiciary (and to a lesser degree the state judiciaries) crafted decisions that aided the development of industrial America. Led by new justices sensitive to the needs of the burgeoning economy, such as Samuel Blatchford, David J. Brewer, Melville W. Fuller, and Rufus W. Peckham, the Supreme Court limited state and federal regulation of business, especially railroads, while fostering an economic and legal atmosphere conducive to investment. For example, in 1894, over the objections of the business community, Congress passed a popular income tax. For a divided Court, 5–4, Chief Justice Fuller declared the income tax to be a direct tax in violation of the Constitution in *Pollock v. Farmers Loan and Trust Company* (1895). The federal judiciary also aided businesses by limiting union activities through their injunction power to stop strikes and by interpreting labor unions as restraints of trade in violation of the Sherman Antitrust Act of 1890.

Another key way that the state and federal courts assisted the economic development of the country was through property law, especially in the West. Colorado led the way in 1876 with a statutory change to eminent domain law, which allowed private corporations to take private property for both public and private purposes. Copied widely by other western states in the late nineteenth century, this legal change helped natural resource development companies, such as the mining and logging industries, claim land needed for their operations.

Federal courts decided cases dealing with major policy issues, and the federal district courts brought the federal government into every congressional district. While the great bulk of litigation in the nineteenth century occurred at the state level, the business of the federal courts grew because of the greater role the federal government played in the lives of Americans. This growth of federal courts, together with the multiple layers of state courts, responded to the increasing industrial, economic, social, and legal complexity of the nineteenth century. Thus the state and federal courts formed a complex web of courts, legal rules, and laws to assist Americans in a rapidly changing environment.

See also **Federal-State Relations; Judicial Review; Supreme Court.**

Bibliography

Bakken, Larry A. *Justice in the Wilderness: A Study of Frontier Courts in Canada and the United States, 1670–1870.* Littleton, Colo.: Fred B. Rothman, 1986.

Ely, James W., Jr. *The Guardian of Every Other Right: A Constitutional History of Property Rights.* 2d ed. New York: Oxford University Press, 1998.

Hall, Kermit L., and Eric W. Rise. *From Local Courts to National Tribunals: The Federal District Courts of Florida, 1821–1990.* Brooklyn, N.Y.: Carlson, 1991.

Hurst, James Willard. *Law and Economic Growth: The Legal History of the Lumber Industry in Wisconsin, 1836–1915.* Cambridge, Mass.: Harvard University Press, 1964.

Karsten, Peter. *Heart versus Head: Judge-Made Law in Nineteenth-Century America.* Chapel Hill: University of North Carolina Press, 1997.

Levy, Leonard W. *The Law of the Commonwealth and Chief Justice Shaw.* Cambridge, Mass.: Harvard University Press, 1957.

Meador, Daniel John. *American Courts.* St. Paul, Minn.: West, 1991.

Morris, Jeffrey B. *Federal Justice in the Second Circuit: A History of the United States Courts in New York, Connecticut, and Vermont, 1787–1987.* New York: Second Circuit Historical Committee, 1987.

Reid, John Phillip. *Chief Justice: The World of Charles Doe.* Cambridge, Mass.: Harvard University Press, 1967.

Surrency, Erwin C. *History of the Federal Courts.* New York: Oceana, 1987.

Tachau, Mary K. Bonsteel. *Federal Courts in the Early Republic: Kentucky, 1789–1816.* Princeton, N.J.: Princeton University Press, 1978.

Wunder, John R. *Inferior Courts, Superior Justice: A History of the Justices of the Peace of the Northwest Frontier, 1853–1889.* Westport, Conn.: Greenwood, 1979.

THOMAS C. MACKEY

COURTSHIP. See **Marriage.**

COWBOYS AND COWGIRLS The meaning of the term "cowboy" changed several times during the nineteenth century. At first it described a cattle rustler, but by the end of the century it referred to the idealized hero of dime novels. In practice, though, a cowboy was someone who herded cattle or worked on a cattle ranch.

An early use of the word "cow-boy" dates to the 1830s in Texas, where it connoted lawlessness and illiteracy and referred to drifters who stole Mexican cattle. By the Civil War, however, the word no longer was associated with a thief but was used instead to describe someone who worked on a cattle ranch. A cowboy did not own land, rarely owned cattle, and usually claimed only his horse, saddle, and gear as his.

The cowboy's role originated with the vaqueros, who developed methods of herding cattle on ranches and missions in Mexico and Texas. Americans adopted these practices as they moved into the southwestern grasslands, and soon the methods spread to the northern Great Plains and the southern United States.

Historians estimate that between one-fourth and one-third of all nineteenth-century cowboys were either Mexican or African American. African Americans first became cowboys during their servitude to southern slaveholders, and many more took up cowboy work after emancipation, when blacks migrated to Kansas and the cattle ranges of the West.

A few blacks and whites, as well as Mexican vaqueros, worked on small ranches in Texas between 1830 and 1860, when longhorn cattle roamed about the brush country of South Texas. In the late 1860s, however, merchants and cattlemen began employing cowboys to corral and drive these cattle north from Texas to railheads in Missouri and Kansas. The ensuing golden age of the cattle drives in the 1870s and 1880s increased the number of cowboys and established the cowboy as part of western folklore. Though many of the new cowboys were white, 25 percent of the cattle-drive cowboys were black, and 12 percent were Mexican. These men put in long hours in tough circumstances; they worked in brush vegetation and dust, during droughts and river flooding, and, at times, with stampeding cattle spooked by thunderstorms or wild animals. As real and fictional accounts reached the East, the cowboy emerged as the first non-Union, non-Confederate hero of western settlement after the Civil War.

The role of the cowboy changed as settlement and

Myths of the Cowboy and Cowgirl

The popular American image of cowboys and cowgirls originated in the late nineteenth century, even as cowboys herded the last longhorns north on the great cattle drives of the 1880s. Pulp novels (cheap penny dreadfuls and dime novels) and Western shows created an idealized image of cowboys and cowgirls as kind, rugged individualists with courage and honor that epitomized the frontier spirit. Mythological cowboys always carried six-shooters, were ready and willing to finish a fight, and were perfect shots.

Fiction writers like Prentiss Ingraham and Ned Buntline created and elevated the cowboy myth with their portrayals of real men like William "Buffalo Bill" Cody and Buck Taylor, the "King of the Cowboys." The pulp novels, which featured stylized violence, lots of action, and a basic story of good prevailing over evil, gave urban readers an escape from their daily lives as they shared adventures in the West.

Cody organized a Western show depicting frontier life and cowboy and cowgirl characters that traveled across the United States and Europe. Buffalo Bill Cody's Wild West Show, first performed in 1883, featured former cowboys, American Indians, and individuals skilled in shooting and horsemanship. The show starred the trick rider and roper Buck Taylor, one of the cowboys from Cody's ranch, and the gun-toting cowgirl Annie Oakley. A champion sharpshooter, Oakley joined the show in 1885 and was the most popular attraction until she left the show in 1902. Cody crafted a cowgirl image for Oakley, a Midwestern native, by creating a fictive Western past.

Stories about Oakley, the outlaw Belle Starr, and Calamity Jane, the woman who dressed, drank, and cursed like a cowboy, helped create the first concrete images of women as cowgirls in the public mind. In reality women rarely performed cattle herding or ranching duties. Like Buffalo Bill and Buck Taylor, cowgirls were glamorized in pulp novels, Western exhibitions, and shows. In the twentieth century women's participation in rodeos and appearances as movie heroines expanded the myth of the cowgirl.

---

the erection of barbed-wire fences closed the open range in the 1880s. Cowboys no longer herded cattle or hunted for strays except during the annual roundup, when newborn cattle were gathered and branded. Instead, cowboys became workers employed by cattlemen to check and mend fences, mow hay, or give medical treatments to the herds on large ranches. During this period the cowboy also became known as a cowpuncher or cowpoke for literally prodding and poking cattle with a pole through chutes and cattle pens. His folklore image remained, though, and took on a life of its own (see sidebar, "Myths of the Cowboy and Cowgirl").

Clothing and Tools

Much of the cowboy's clothing and equipment came directly from the vaquero, and all of it was inherently practical for his trade. He wore a felt cowboy hat, evolved from the Mexican sombrero, with a wide brim and a high crown to keep off the sun and rain. He also used it folded over as a pillow and as a cup to scoop up water for drinking. A bandanna worn around his neck could be lifted over his mouth and nose to protect his face from dust and debris. Leather chaps, from chaparajos, covered the fronts and sides of his legs, protecting them from mesquite brush, thorns, and cacti. High-heeled boots afforded the means to rest his feet in stirrups or to give surer footing when handling steers.

The western saddle, based on Mexican and Spanish predecessors, had a deep seat, a horn to anchor a lasso, stirrups, and two cinches to keep it on a blanket placed on the horse's back. Vaqueros braided their own intricate leather ropes called *las reatas;* white cowboys made or purchased hemp ropes for their lariats. A saddlebag and bedroll completed the cowboy's working outfit.

Though the mythical cowboy never went anywhere without his Colt revolver or six-shooter, real-life cowboys rarely wore them. The historian Richard Slatta writes that many cowboys strapped on a gun for appearances in photographs, but on trail drives and roundups they usually left their six-shooters in the chuck wagon.

Pay and Treatment

A cowboy had a long and difficult job. On a cattle drive his workday might last twenty hours. He earned $25 to $40 a month, while cooks, trail bosses, and ranch foremen earned $50 to $100. Cattle drivers were not paid until they reached a cow town market. Their propensity to celebrate in the saloon after several months on the trail earned cowboys a stereotypically negative image among merchants and citizens

Chuck Wagon Stop. The heyday of the cowboy was in the 1870s and 1880s; grueling hours involving rough work earned him a hero's reputation. LIBRARY OF CONGRESS

of these western towns. Cowboys often were unemployed during the winter because ranches kept only a couple of men to perform odd tasks.

As whites came to dominate the cattle industry, African Americans and Mexicans became victims of extensive racism and discrimination. According to Slatta, vaqueros earned only one-third to one-half the wages of white cowboys, despite their reputation as superior ropers and horsemen. Few became ranch foremen or trail bosses.

Blacks suffered social stigmatism as much as or more than Mexicans, but they fared better economically. African American cowboys received salaries and raises comparable to those for white cowboys. Cattlemen sometimes rewarded a longtime black cowboy with the job of cook when he no longer could ride effectively, but that was the highest position he could reach. The horse wrangler, the lowest-level job on a cattle drive or roundup, was often black.

Cowgirls

Women were largely absent from the cattle-ranching world. Though the public widely believed that cowgirls worked and played alongside cowboys on the range, in reality women rarely appeared in cattle drive or ranch crews. Where women did participate, they either helped in a small family ranching operation or, more often, were the widowed owners of ranches or herds of cattle. The term "cowgirl" was first used to describe second-generation ranch women who demonstrated their cowboy skills at the Cheyenne Frontier Days rodeo in 1897.

See also **Ranching and Livestock Raising; Texas; West, The.**

Bibliography

Durham, Philip, and Everett L. Jones. *The Negro Cowboys.* New York: Dodd, Mead, 1965. Reprint, Lincoln: University of Nebraska Press, 1983.

Frantz, Joe B., and Julian Ernest Choate Jr. *The American Cowboy: The Myth and the Reality.* Norman: University of Oklahoma Press, 1955.

Roach, Joyce Gibson. *The Cowgirls.* 2d ed. Denton: North Texas State University Press, 1990.

Rollins, Philip Ashton. *The Cowboy: An Unconventional History of Civilization on the Old-Time Cattle Range.* Rev. ed. New York: Scribners, 1936. Reprint, Albuquerque: University of New Mexico Press, 1979. Originally published in 1922.

Slatta, Richard W. *The Cowboy Encyclopedia.* Santa Barbara, Calif.: ABC-CLIO, 1994.

CAMERON L. SAFFELL

CREOLES   In North America the term "Creole" was commonly used in the region colonized by the

French and Spanish, colonial Louisiana and the Floridas. Though the terminology was brought to the Gulf of Mexico region by the French and Spanish, it had a broader usage throughout the Americas. Creole originally derived from the Portuguese word "Crioulo," which referred to a slave born in the New World. After an undetermined period, however, Creole came to include people of European extraction born in the New World. In Louisiana and the Floridas the term meant anyone of African or European ancestry born in the region. The records of the Church of the Immaculate Conception in Mobile, Alabama, chronicle the funeral, 24 May 1745, of Robert Talon, "the first creole of the colony." Funeral and baptismal records in the region's Catholic churches and legal documentation make it clear that in the eighteenth century Creole indicated place of birth. A person was, for example, a European, an African, or a Creole, a native of this place.

After France and Spain ceded Louisiana and the Floridas to the United States, the term "Creole" took on another meaning. The original inhabitants of the Gulf region, those Catholic people of French, Spanish, and African heritage who spoke French, Spanish, or Creole, recognized that they were culturally different from the Anglo-Americans who poured into the area during the first decades of the nineteenth century. People who traced their roots back to the French and Spanish colonial period proudly distinguished themselves from those of Anglo-American ancestry. Creoles, whether black, white, racially mixed, slave, or free, were knit together in webs of kinship and fictive kinship, religion, and language. Few travelers to the region failed to note the antagonism between the Creoles and the Anglo-Americans. Each thought the other inferior.

As the nineteenth century progressed, the term "Creole" was redefined. For one thing, some racially mixed free Creoles of color, who recognized their African heritage but took great pride in their French ancestry, distinguished themselves not only from Anglo-Americans but also from enslaved and free blacks who were neither racially mixed nor of French ancestry. Also, by the later decades of the nineteenth century, Louisiana white Creoles, accepting the norms prescribed by scientific racism, redefined Creole to mean anyone of French ancestry who was white. The writer George Washington Cable and the historian Charles Barthelemy Rousseve, a Creole of color, disdained this newer version of Creole, which denied the past. In the twentieth century in Louisiana, Creole returned to the eighteenth-century usage, indicating anyone or anything of Louisiana origin, for example, "Creole tomatoes" or "Creole cattle."

See also **Alabama; Florida; Language; Louisiana; Miscegenation; Mississippi; New Orleans; Population; Race and Racial Thinking.**

Bibliography

Brasseaux, Carl A., Keith P. Fontenot, and Claude F. Oubre. *Creoles of Color in the Bayou Country.* Jackson: University Press of Mississippi, 1994.

Dormon, James H., ed. *Creoles of Color of the Gulf South.* Knoxville: University of Tennessee Press, 1996.

Hall, Gwendolyn Midlo. *Africans in Colonial Louisiana.* Baton Rouge: Louisiana State University Press, 1992.

Hirsch, Arnold R., and Joseph Logsdon, eds. *Creole New Orleans: Race and Americanization.* Baton Rouge: Louisiana State University Press, 1992.

VIRGINIA MEACHAM GOULD

CRIME

[This entry includes an overview and a subentry on **Sensational Crimes.**]

OVERVIEW

Nineteenth-century Americans had good reason to express persistent fears about crime and lawlessness. Though often exaggerated and romanticized, as in the images conjured up by such terms the "Wild West," there is no question that violence was endemic to American society and that a high crime rate prevailed for much of the century. Continental expansion, urbanization, disintegration of traditional communities, dislocations in the aftermath of the Civil War, and unprecedented mobility created a climate conducive to criminal activity. With laissez-faire and social Darwinism dominating the intellectual milieu, government was ill-equipped to combat crime. And yet, by the end of the century, professional law enforcement and a modern criminal justice system began to emerge as crime rates waned.

The breakdown of traditional sources of authority gave rise to criminality as the nineteenth century dawned. The new republic had been quick to shed the remnants of British royal authority, including the king's writs, vice admiralty courts, and other criminal justice procedures. As Americans rapidly moved westward, community authority, traditionally expressed through church and close family ties, began to weaken. While most communities remained peaceful, rollicking frontier towns and transient communities emerged. Young men—armed, mobile, and frequently drunk—clashed in every variety of brawl, shoot-out, riot, and disorder. A substantial minority of Americans adopted violent and criminal means to

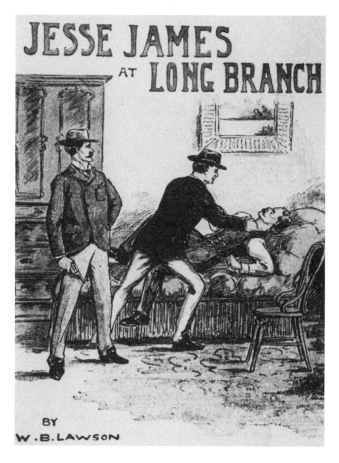

The Allure of the Crime Novel. Crime literature became popular with the public as the increase in violence gave rise to full-time police and detectives. *Log Cabin Library*, 16 March 1898. LIBRARY OF CONGRESS

pursue their own ends in an individualistic and fluid frontier society. Periodic economic collapses, such as the panics of 1819 and 1837, increased the ranks of the rootless unemployed for whom crime often became an option.

Expansion of the American republic became increasingly violent and essentially criminal. President Andrew Jackson (1829–1837), himself a brawler in his youth and a survivor of numerous duels and military campaigns, orchestrated a draconian policy—the Indian Removal Act of 1930—of seizing aboriginal lands. His successors, imbued with the self-serving justification of "Manifest Destiny," ultimately provoked a war with Mexico that had territorial aggrandizement as the clear goal.

The most violent institution in antebellum America, however, was African and African American slavery. Though not illegal until 1863, and then only partially so, a slave system based purely on racial hierarchy nonetheless clearly constituted the greatest crime of the nineteenth century. Not merely forced,

unpaid labor, but rape, whipping, torture, and even murder were endemic to the institution. Even though the importation of African slaves ended in 1808, southerners desperate to ensure a cheap labor source continued to illegally import slaves into the country until 1862. They also kidnapped free blacks and forced them into slavery. In 1850 Congress passed a new fugitive slave law that provided stiff fines and imprisonment for those who aided runaway slaves. Ironically, the number of runaways actually increased as abolitionists continued actively to aid them, openly violating the fugitive slave laws by utilizing the Underground Railroad.

Victory in the Mexican War (1846–1848) opened vast new expanses of land that proved impossible to police and which exacerbated the issue of slavery in a deeply divided nation. Following passage of the Kansas-Nebraska Act in 1854, pro- and antislavery forces flooded into the Kansas territory to battle over whether the new state would allow slavery. Proslavery Missourians rode across the border to clash with northern antislave forces, including the fanatical John Brown. "Bleeding Kansas" ensued, calling attention to lawlessness on the frontier as well as the nation's inability to resolve the slavery issue through political compromise.

The subsequent Civil War (1861–1865), bringing an end to slavery, was the most violent event of the century, as more than 600,000 Americans perished in the carnage. The conflict left much of the nation, and many veterans, hardened to violence.

Well before the Civil War, urban disorders, riots, bank and train robberies, and shootings spurred fear and a desire for social control on the part of the middle and upper classes. Crime statistics for the period are unreliable, but there appear to have been sporadic waves of criminal activity. City police forces and reforms in the administration of criminal justice emerged to combat crime. Full-time, night-and-day policing was an innovation of the nineteenth century. Beginning in the 1840s and 1850s, cities such as Baltimore, Boston, Chicago, Cincinnati, New Orleans, and Philadelphia established police forces. Over time they armed themselves with pistols and became powerful agents of law enforcement and social control.

Although police did bring some order to cities, the forces were highly politicized, with the rank and file dependent on politicians for their jobs. Payoffs, corruption, and favoritism were rife. Police lacked professional training, accountability, and supervision. Many drank on the job. They subjected suspects to a variety of violent "third degree" interrogations and tortures. Police rarely attacked the middle or upper classes, but had their way with the poor, the downtrodden, minorities, and immigrants.

Indeed, the American legal system clearly favored propertied elites, safeguarding the wealthy and powerful while subordinating the poor, laborers, women, and minorities. While corporate and financial crimes went largely unpunished, immigrants, radicals, and vagrants received inordinate attention and punishment under the law. African Americans fared the worst, even after abolition, continuing to be the targets of forced labor, violence, rape, and murder, mostly in the South. Assaults on African Americans grew more prevalent as the century progressed; some of the most severe violence and the highest recorded rate of lynchings occurred in the thirty years prior to World War I. However, during Reconstruction southern blacks also suffered violence at the hands of the Ku Klux Klan and other white terrorists. Vigilantism was not unique to the South, however. In the antebellum North and throughout the century in the West, vigilante groups, often composed of elites and the middle classes, frequently opted to maintain "order" by taking the law into their own hands.

Business elites and much of the middle class displayed hostility to organized labor during the industrial era, often viewing its agitations as not only radical but also criminal. When laborers went on strike in their quest for higher wages, better working conditions, or an eight-hour day, owners and managers frequently employed strikebreakers, thus prompting some of the most notorious class conflicts of the century. The Pinkerton Detective Agency, founded by Allan Pinkerton, a Civil War intelligence officer, embraced Christian virtue as well as the business ethos characteristic of the Gilded Age. Hostile to labor, Pinkertons served as strikebreakers, most famously during the strike at the Carnegie Steel Company Plant at Homestead, Pennsylvania, in 1892. Seven strikers and three Pinkertons died and scores were injured in the bloody clash. Private detectives played a particularly significant role in providing security for railroads, which spread their tentacles across the nation at a rapid pace, well ahead of the protective arm of local law enforcement.

Detectives such as the Pinkertons seem to have been both despised and revered by segments of public opinion. They acted not only as strikebreakers but also as spies, private soldiers, and agents provocateurs. Much of the public saw detectives as a source of order and stability in rapidly changing times. Others saw them as cynical agents of wealth, power, and repression. Public fascination with detectives gave rise to a new genre of literature, beginning with Edgar Allan Poe's stories in the 1840s. By the late 1880s an Englishman, Sir Arthur Conan Doyle, provided millions of readers with the most famous detective hero of all time, Sherlock Holmes.

Holmes's keen intellect was a reflection in the popular culture of the efforts by police and detectives in the late nineteenth century to employ more sophisticated methods to track down criminals. As a result of the extreme mobility of American society, famous nineteenth-century outlaws such as the James and Younger gangs and Butch Cassidy and the Sundance Kid had long eluded authorities, especially on the frontier. Not only these famous criminals, but also a wide variety of rustlers, thieves, swindlers, murderers, bigamists, and counterfeiters were able to commit their crimes and move on to the next community before the not-so-long arm of the law could bring them to justice.

An innovation pioneered by a Paris police consultant, Alphonse Bertillion, advanced efforts to identify and locate criminal offenders. Using the Bertillion method, U.S. law enforcement authorities began to record height, weight, and scars or other distinguishing characteristics in order to track down criminals. By the end of the century, photography, in the form of "rogue's galleries" of criminal suspects in public buildings across the country, added a new dimension to fighting crime. Fingerprinting soon followed.

By the latter part of the century, authorities had begun to reject crude applications of social Darwinism, which held that most criminals were badly evolved primitives who could be identified through such physical characteristics as low eyebrows, illshaped craniums, and small brains. Such theories, associated with the Italian psychiatrist Cesare Lombroso, were typical of highly racialized nineteenth-century pseudoscience. The nation's innovative penitentiary system, once considered advanced by foreign visitors such as Alexis de Tocqueville, had sharply deteriorated by the late nineteenth century. Although prison conditions varied widely among states, most penitentiaries were horrific, full of violence, disease, and forced labor.

Studies suggest that crime levels dropped by the turn of the century, although precise explanations for the lower rates are elusive. At the same time, reforms such as indeterminate sentencing, probation, parole, plea bargaining, and juvenile courts had begun to emerge across the country. Though the death penalty remained in force, the public turned against the once popular spectacle of the public hanging. Mob scenes at public hangings became unsettling to the middle class early in the nineteenth century, and gave way to the more "civilized" technological innovations such as the "electrical chair," introduced in New York in 1888.

At the end of a century marked by violence and dislocation, Americans had begun to establish the framework of a more rational, though still inequitable, system of modern criminal justice.

See also **American Indians,** *subentry on* **Indian Removal; Assasinations; Capital Punishment; Lynching; Manifest Destiny; Outlaws; Police; Prisons and Punishment; Race and Racial Thinking; Slavery; Sociology; Vigilantes; Violence.**

Bibliography

Friedman, Lawrence M. *Crime and Punishment in American History.* New York: Basic Books, 1993.

Walker, Samuel. *Popular Justice: A History of American Criminal Justice.* 2d ed. New York: Oxford University Press, 1998.

WALTER L. HIXSON

SENSATIONAL CRIMES

Myriad sensational crimes riveted the American public during the nineteenth century. Some of the most notorious crimes involved politicians, public figures, and labor–management struggles. Violence directed against African Americans and certain immigrant groups, such as the Chinese, was seemingly so routine for much of the century as to have excited little public interest. The crimes that most captivated public attention were those involving women as victims or perpetrators.

Some of the most shocking crimes of the nineteenth century involved the murder or assassination of political figures. If the assassination of William McKinley in 1901 is included, three presidents fell to assassins' bullets during the century (the other two were Abraham Lincoln in 1865 and James Garfield in 1881). Earlier, in 1805, former vice president Aaron Burr shot to death Alexander Hamilton, one of the nation's founding fathers and architect of the nation's financial system, in a duel in Weehawken, New Jersey—the same site where Hamilton's son had been gunned down in another affair of honor. Partly on the basis of the notorious Hamilton-Burr affair, dueling became more disreputable than honorable as the century progressed, though it lingered for decades in the antebellum South.

Sensational violence between labor and management claimed national attention during the Gilded Age. The 1886 Haymarket Square riot in Chicago and the 1892 Homestead steel strike in Pennsylvania were two of the more notorious incidents. Violent labor–management strife rumbled in the West as well, with the Western Federation of Miners demanding better pay and working conditions for miners. Riots erupted in the Coeur d'Alene district of Idaho in the 1890s. Simmering resentments underlay the spectacular bombing murder of former Idaho governor Frank Steunenberg in Caldwell, Idaho, in 1905. The bomber was captured and convicted, but three top officials of the miners' union, including the flamboyant, one-eyed William "Wild Bill" Haywood, narrowly escaped conviction for conspiring to commit the murder after Clarence Darrow, the preeminent defense attorney of the era, mounted a successful defense.

An increasingly literate public found crimes involving women, especially those which were violent or sexual, far more mesmerizing than labor strife. Women were not part of the Victorian justice system, only objects of its administration. There were few women lawyers and hardly any female judges or jurors before the twentieth century. Women committed far fewer crimes than men—less than 10 percent of the total—and most of these were uniquely "female" crimes such as prostitution. On the other hand, women quite often were the targets of crime; they were beaten, raped, and abused daily across the country. The law sanctioned patriarchal authority and often exonerated men from violent crimes against women, including rape and murder. On countless occasions men successfully employed the "she-had-it-coming" defense for beating or killing wives who resisted patriarchal domination.

The most sensational cases involved women who defied conventional sexual morality. Although denied citizenship and political rights, women in Victorian society were viewed as morally superior to men, whose aggressive, amoral instincts they were charged with tempering. Hence the "cult of true womanhood" confined women to a nurturing role in the domestic sphere. By mid-century, as urban-industrial growth began to sever traditional bonds of community, many women lived a lifestyle that defied society's norms. When a woman challenged the dominant mores, and met with a violent end, the public could not get enough of the story. Sensational crimes such as these illustrate the tensions over changing gender roles in Victorian society.

One of the most famous cases concerned Helen Jewett, a New York City prostitute murdered by one of her clients in 1836. The attractive, twenty-three-year-old Jewett had been bludgeoned with a hatchet and left smoldering in her burning bed. For years after the murder, a stream of narratives emphasized that, owing to her moral corruption, the violent end had been an inevitable fate for the beautiful but "fallen" Helen. Popular accounts suggested that by tempting and seducing men, rather than fulfilling woman's assigned role to temper destructive male urges, she had gotten what she deserved. The New

York court agreed, taking only fifteen minutes to exonerate the young man, Richard Robinson, who obviously had murdered the "disreputable" young woman.

Similar narratives emerged five years later with the mysterious disappearance and death in 1841 of Mary Cecilia Rogers. Known as the "Beautiful Cigar Girl," the twenty-one-year-old Mary worked in a tobacco shop and lived in a boardinghouse in a male-dominated district of New York. The discovery of her nude body floating in the Hudson River inspired sensational news accounts and reams of narratives, including an Edgar Allan Poe story. Mary, who had defied Victorian mores by being sexually active, apparently had died after being beaten and raped, or possibly as a result of a botched abortion. In any case, public fascination with her death reflected the powerful appeal of narratives of sex, death, and independent womanhood in the modern city.

By the 1890s, the advent of "yellow journalism," by which big city newspapers overplayed stories in competition for readership, placed even greater emphasis on sensational crime. A sensational murder and subsequent criminal trial could sell more newspapers than anything except a war. When such cases arose, newspapers battled to mount the most intense coverage and to uncover "scoops." The combination of changing gender mores and yellow journalism produced the most explosive national crime story of the era, and still one of the most sensational in American history, the case of Lizzie Borden.

On a hot August day in 1892, Andrew Borden, a prominent businessman, and his wife, Abby, were found brutally murdered in separate rooms of their home near the downtown textile mills that had transformed Fall River, Massachusetts, into a modern industrial city. Police and citizenry at first assumed that a deranged madman, or at minimum an immigrant, must have committed the crime, but evidence soon pointed to the younger of Andrew Borden's two daughters, Lizbeth Andrew Borden; she and the family maid were the only persons at home at the time of the murders. Lizzie denied the crime, but implicated herself in inquest testimony and by burning in the kitchen stove a dress that she may have worn while committing the murders. The murder weapon, a hatchet, was later found in the basement.

The allegation of female parricide—with a hatchet, no less—immediately made the case a national obsession. Although the evidence against Lizzie was substantial, the public rallied behind her, refusing to believe that a churchgoing young woman from a prominent family could have committed such a crime. In fact, Lizzie and her sister, both "spinsters" who were still living under their father's roof into their thirties, had grown bitterly resentful over Andrew's alleged favoritism of their stepmother and her family. Wealthy, yet notoriously parsimonious, Andrew Borden had been ungenerous with his daughters and, particularly galling to Lizzie, steadfastly refused to move away from the crowded mill district and into a new home in the residential district of the city. Volatile and unstable, Lizzie first tried to poison her father and stepmother and, failing that, apparently bludgeoned them to death in order to gain her inheritance.

Lizzie's defense, mounted by a former governor of Massachusetts, George D. Robinson, argued that a woman could not possibly have committed such a fiendish crime. To have acknowledged Lizzie's guilt would have been to shatter Victorian convictions of female piety and passionlessness. Such a verdict would have done violence to the prevailing myth that the home represented a separate sphere, a sanctuary from the harsh realities of the world, a place where the moral superiority of women held sway. In reality, as this case demonstrated, the Victorian home could also be a place of repression and violence. What made the Borden case so compelling was that a woman rather than a man had perpetrated the incident of domestic violence, and in horrifying fashion.

The leading citizens of Fall River, however, did not want to acknowledge that their thriving commercial city had nurtured a woman who could rain more than thirty blows (fewer than the "forty whacks" of the popular ditty) on the heads of her elderly parents. The three-judge panel in Massachusetts assiduously excluded evidence of Lizzie's guilt, such as her incriminating statements at the inquest and the testimony of a druggist that she had tried to purchase deadly prussic acid the day before the murders. Taking their cue from the lead judge, who stopped just short of charging the jury to return with a "not guilty" verdict, the all-male panel took less than an hour to exonerate Miss Borden. Though Lizzie Borden exploited popular anxieties to get away with murder, she lived as a pariah in her own community until her death in 1927.

See also **Dueling; Labor Movement,** *subentry on* **Unions and Strikes; Law,** *subentry on* **Women and the Law; Violence.**

Bibliography

Cohen, Patricia Cline. *The Murder of Helen Jewett: The Life and Death of a Prostitute in Nineteenth-Century New York.* New York: Knopf, 1998.

Halttunen, Karen. *Murder Most Foul: The Killer and the American Gothic Imagination.* Cambridge, Mass.: Harvard University Press, 1998.

Hixson, Walter. *Crimes of the Century: Four Cases of Sensa-*

tional Murder and Injustice in American History. Akron, Ohio: University of Akron Press, 2000.

Lukas, J. Anthony. *Big Trouble: Murder in a Small Western Town Sets off a Struggle for the Soul of America.* New York: Simon and Schuster, 1997.

Srebnick, Amy Gilman. *The Mysterious Death of Mary Rogers: Sex and Culture in Nineteenth-Century New York.* New York: Oxford University Press, 1995.

WALTER L. HIXSON

CUBA   U.S. policy toward Cuba during the nineteenth century was governed principally by economic and strategic interests. For most of the century, U.S. relations with Cuba were determined by the whims of the island's colonial rulers, the Spanish. By the mid-to-late nineteenth century, however, the United States had begun to play a leading role in Cuba's economy; this financial interest quickly translated into American political and cultural influence in Cuban society. The occupation of Cuba during the Spanish-American War in 1898 was merely the final step in America's domination of the island.

American Interests

As was the case in most of Latin America and the Caribbean in the early nineteenth century, U.S. in-

terests were primarily economic. American trade with Cuba fluctuated wildly during the early years of the century, primarily because of colonial Spain's hot-and-cold attitude toward the economic penetration of Cuba's economy by foreign merchants. In the 1790s, for example, Spain had thrown open the doors of Cuban trade to all nations. By 1800 the United States was exporting over $8 million worth of goods to the island, primarily lumber, foodstuffs, and slaves. In return Cuba sent nearly forty thousand tons of sugar to the United States. In 1801 Spain unexpectedly clamped down on foreign trade with Cuba; intercourse between the island and the United States was slashed dramatically. Yet a few years later, when Spain and France went to war against Great Britain, necessity forced the relaxation of trade restrictions, and trade between the United States and Cuba again flourished. When revolts in St. Domingue cut that colony's sugar exports to the United States, Cuban sugar quickly filled the void.

By the 1820s American traders and merchants were beginning to replace their Spanish counterparts in Cuba, and by the 1850s the United States had replaced Spain as Cuba's most important trading partner. Spain could only reply with tariffs and taxes that, while making trade more expensive and a bit more troublesome, did absolutely nothing to slow the growth of the American economic presence on the is-

Hotel del Telegrafo, Havana, Cuba. A substantial American community had settled in Cuba for economic reasons by the 1850s. Photograph, C. D. Fredricks y Daries, c. 1860. LIBRARY OF CONGRESS

land. By the 1850s what might be called an enclave economy had developed, with hundreds of Americans living and trading in Cuba. Investors from the United States moved into the banking and shipping industries, sugar mills and sugar plantations, coffee, mining, and railroads.

The tremendous American economic presence in Cuba influenced U.S. attitudes toward the political situation on the island. The United States proclaimed its support for an end to colonialism in Latin America and the Caribbean, and with the Monroe Doctrine in 1823, seemed to align itself with the independence movements that broke out in those regions in the 1810s and 1820s. Nevertheless, U.S. policy toward Cuba was consistent: Spanish colonial rule was preferable to Cuban independence. There were several reasons for this stance. First, many U.S. policymakers feared that a rebellion in Cuba, with its large slave and mixed-race population, could lead to "another Haiti," where slaves had risen up, and killed and overthrown their white masters in 1804. Second, a weak Spain was certainly preferable to a strong Britain or France in charge of Cuba, which might happen if Spain were forced to retreat. That preference led to the "no transfer" policy of the United States, which declared that New World colonies could not be transferred from one power to another. Finally, for U.S. policymakers the tenuous Spanish hold on Cuba was the best of both worlds. The United States reaped huge economic benefits while the Spanish incurred the costs of keeping a colony.

Annexation and Rebellion

While opposing independence for Cuba, however, U.S. policymakers were not averse to annexing the island. John Quincy Adams's dictum of 1823—in which he argued that Cuba was like an apple that, falling from the "tree" of Spain, would naturally gravitate toward the United States—summed up the feelings of many. During the height of Manifest Destiny in the 1840s and 1850s, the waning influence of Spain in Cuba and strong pressures from proslavery forces in the South, who saw Cuba as a perfect field for slavery's expansion, combined to create a more aggressive U.S. policy. In 1848 President James Polk offered $100 million to Spain for the island; by 1854 the offer had risen to $130 million. Also in 1854 the Ostend Manifesto, secretly written by a group of American diplomats in Europe, was leaked. The manifesto declared that the United State wished to purchase Cuba, and if refused, it had every right to take the island. Indeed, some unofficial efforts at conquest were launched. Narciso López, one of the most famous of the filibusters, attempted several attacks on Cuba during the late 1840s and early 1850s. López's expeditions, financed by southern interests, were failures; he was caught and executed during his third invasion of Cuba in 1851.

The Civil War in the United States ended talk of Cuban annexation. Legalized slavery in Cuba was one main impediment, as was the increasing concern about assimilating the racially and religiously different Cuba into American society. Events inside Cuba continued to concern U.S. policymakers. In 1868 the Ten Years' War began, as Cuban rebels fought against their Spanish colonial masters. American policy remained what it had always been: support for the Spanish coupled with demands for protection of American property and citizens. In 1873 an American-owned ship, the *Virginius*, which was leased by the Cuban rebels, was seized by Spanish officials, who executed fifty-three people, including the captain, members of the crew, and passengers; even this affair was eventually smoothed over. The war was horribly destructive, but that very destruction proved a gold mine for U.S. investors, who poured money into the devastated Cuban economy after the struggle ended in 1878. By 1890 the United States had invested $50 million in the island, and total trade with Cuba neared the $70 million mark. Baseball began to replace bullfights, Protestant missionaries began to gain converts among the Catholic population, and schools based on the American system began to spring up. At the same time tens of thousands of Cubans settled in the United States, giving rise to a vocal and sometimes effective pressure group that called for U.S. support for Cuban independence.

In 1895 a new and more destructive rebellion broke out in Cuba. President Grover Cleveland and his successor, William McKinley, were faced with a dilemma. Both were appalled by the destruction and brutality of the war, but neither wanted to intervene directly. Fears of war with Spain, uncertainty about British and French reactions, and grave suspicions about the Cuban rebels' reliability and capacity for self-government gave the United States pause. McKinley was pressured by advisers such as Theodore Roosevelt and Henry Cabot Lodge, who were convinced that Spain was incapable of putting down the rebellion. Public opinion was in favor of U.S. support for the rebels, and Congress declared war on Spain in April 1898.

During the Spanish-American War, Cuba was occupied by U.S. military forces. For the remainder of the nineteenth century, the island remained under military rule while U.S. policymakers decided what to do with it. Eventually Cuba was placed in a peculiar status, neither completely independent nor quite a colony, as a result of the Platt Amendment of 1901.

See also **Central America and the Caribbean; Filibusters; Haiti; Spanish-American War.**

Bibliography

Foner, Philip S. *A History of Cuba and Its Relations with the United States.* 2 vols. New York: International, 1962–1965.

Langley, Lester D. *The Cuban Policy of the United States: A Brief History.* New York: Wiley, 1968.

Mazarr, Michael J. *Semper Fidel: America and Cuba, 1776–1988.* Baltimore: Nautical and Aviation Publishing Company of America, 1988.

Pérez, Louis A. *Cuba and the United States: Ties of Singular Intimacy.* Athens: Ga.: University of Georgia Press, 1990.

MICHAEL L. KRENN

CULTURAL MOVEMENTS.   See Lyceums.

CURRENCY.   See **Monetary Policy; Money and Coins.**

CURRENCY POLICY

Three currency issues dominated the nineteenth century: whether the United States should have a central bank; greenbacks; and bimetallism. A central bank was abandoned in 1832, followed by greenbacks in 1879. Bimetallism effectively was dropped by Congress in 1853, defeated in the presidential election of 1896, and legally abolished in 1900.

The first two Banks of the United States (1791–1811 and 1816–1836) sought to establish a national currency by substituting their own notes for those issued by state banks. Nicholas Biddle (1786–1844), who eventually headed the Second Bank of the United States, had a clear idea of central banking, including the concept of the lender of last resort, at a time when the Bank of England was less advanced in its thinking. But Andrew Jackson's (1767–1845) war on the bank ended this development. Although Jackson's refusal to renew the bank's charter allegedly was done for the sake of the yeoman farmer, the president's actions actually profited financial and industrial interests, particularly those in New York. Business wanted cheaper credit, free of central bank restrictions. State banks sought to eliminate a powerful competitor. Prominent among these were the state banks of New York. The elimination of the Bank of the United States removed one of the few obstacles to New York's position as the financial capital of the nation. Once the federal government revenues were removed from the Bank of the United States, the customs receipts of the Port of New York, the largest port in the nation, no longer went to Philadelphia but were deposited in New York state banks. No central bank existed in the United States until the creation of the Federal Reserve system in 1913.

Many state banks issued their own notes. Initially, these commercial banks were granted charters from the state, which made them susceptible to political manipulation. In 1838 New York enacted a Free Banking Law, which allowed anyone who met certain conditions to establish a bank and issue notes. Counterfeits and notes of broken banks corrupted the circulation of currency, swindling the poor and the trusting. Only trained bankers' clerks could distinguish the good from the bad. Banknotes were discounted according to distance and the stability of the issuer. Banknote reporters and counterfeit detectors, published at weekly or monthly intervals, gave the rate of discount of nonlocal notes and described counterfeit bills.

Federal coins were not abundant; the most common denominations were the copper cent, the silver half-dollar, and (after 1834) the gold half eagle (5 dollars). Foreign coins filled the gap. The copper currency was made up of British halfpence and imitations of it. The silver currency was composed of Spanish-American 8 reals, 2 reals, reals, and medios (legal tender as a dollar, 25 cents, 12½ cents, and 6¼ cents in federal currency). The gold coinage was composed of Brazilian joes (6,400-reis pieces) and Spanish-American doubloons.

Through the 1830s, gold was overvalued in terms of silver, which meant that it did not circulate. Then in 1834 the weight and fineness of the gold coinage was reduced, allowing gold to circulate instead of silver; what actually happened was that banknotes, allegedly backed by gold, circulated. The California gold discoveries drove the value of gold down further and made silver scarce. In 1853 the weight of the silver coinage was reduced so that it was a fiduciary coinage; from that point on the United States had a de facto gold monometallist standard. In 1857 the legal tender status of the foreign coins was revoked, and the coins were redeemed. Spanish-American silver coins continued to circulate in the eastern United States up to the late 1870s. In the West, Spanish-American silver circulated as late as 1900.

The Civil War drastically altered the currency of the United States. The federal government issued irredeemable greenbacks to help pay for the Union war effort. Gold vanished from circulation, followed by silver. Local merchants filled the gap with one-cent tokens. In the darkest days of the war even copper disappeared, and merchants issued paper scrip. Postage stamps were used instead of coins. The federal government issued paper fractional currency, and also introduced new denominations. The three-cent coin, which had been issued in silver and was hoarded, was now issued in nickel. A nickel five-cent piece served in lieu of the hoarded silver half-dime. A copper two-cent piece was introduced as well. Political opposition from debtors who wanted the greenback currency to continue, represented in the National or Greenback Party, delayed specie resumption until 1879. At the same time, settlers in the Pacific West refused to accept greenbacks at par, and treated them as foreign exchange. Gold coins circulated there from 1861 through 1879.

The Confederacy financed its war with the printing press. Confederate notes had blue security printing on the back: "bluebacks" as opposed to the Union "greenbacks." By the end of the war, even Confederate troops insisted on being paid in greenbacks.

In 1865 the federal government taxed state banknotes out of existence. The banks entered the national bank system and issued national banknotes in exchange for purchases of federal bonds.

In 1873 the silver dollar was omitted from the coinage law; it had circulated only rarely before the Civil War. A trade dollar, heavier than the standard silver dollar, was introduced for trade in the Far East; this caused chaos when a collapse in silver prices led trade dollars to leak into U.S. circulation. In 1859 huge silver deposits (the Comstock Lode) were discovered in Nevada. The mining states of the Mountain West (Arizona, Colorado, Idaho, Montana, Nevada, New Mexico, Utah, and Wyoming) demanded that the United States operate a bimetallic system. In 1878 the Bland-Allison Act required the U.S. Mint to buy two million dollars worth of silver a month. But by the early 1890s the silver price had collapsed. The silver interests made silver the issue of the 1896 presidential election. William Jennings Bryan (1860–1925), the Democratic candidate, demanded that mankind not be "crucified on a cross of gold." Bryan lost the election, and in 1900 the United States adopted the Gold Standard Act.

There was much regional variation in currency circulation. Cut money—Spanish-American silver dollars cut into pieces to provide small change—was used along the frontier. Gold rushes in Appalachia led to the creation of private mints by Templeton Reid and the Bechtlers, and of the first federal branch mints at Charlotte, North Carolina, and Dahlonega, Georgia. In California the gold rush led to extensive private minting through 1855, until the San Francisco Mint went into full production. Branch mints were set up in other mining regions, including Carson City, Nevada, in 1870 and Denver, Colorado, in 1906. The Far West remained reluctant to use paper and base-metal coins until World War I.

The country's erratic nineteenth-century currency history fostered economic instability. Only in 1900 did the United States establish a stable currency backed by gold; only in 1913 did it establish a central bank. Britain, France, and Germany had established central banking systems long before.

See also **Banking and Finance,** *subentry on* **The Banking Industry; Gold Rushes and Silver Strikes; Monetary Policy; Money and Coins.**

Bibliography

Breen, Walter. *Walter Breen's Complete Encyclopedia of U.S. and Colonial Coins.* Garden City, N.Y.: Doubleday, 1988.

Carothers, Neil. *Fractional Money: A History of the Small Coins and Fractional Paper Currency of the United States.* New York: John Wiley and Sons, 1930.

Hammond, Bray. *Banks and Politics in America, from the Revolution to the Civil War.* Princeton, N.J.: Princeton University Press, 1957.

Kleeberg, John M. "The Silver Dollar and International Trade: A Study in Failure." In *America's Silver Dollars,* edited by John M. Kleeberg. New York: American Numismatic Society, 1995.

JOHN M. KLEEBERG

CURRIER AND IVES. See **Lithography and Prints.**

D

DANCE AND BALLET The *Encyclopaedia Americana* for 1857 characterizes dancing as both an "elegant amusement" and an "elegant spectacle." The two terms concisely capture the nineteenth-century concept of dancing as a formal social practice of white middle- and upper-class Americans and as a theatrical event for audiences. Although the encyclopedia's discussion of dance in theater focuses on European ballet, American theatrical dance actually encompassed a broader spectrum of performance. The encyclopedia does not recognize the dancing of African Americans, but twentieth-century historians worked to correct this omission.

Most recorded information about the art concerns ballroom dancing. Nineteenth-century etiquette books describe in detail the requirements for a successful ball, yet innumerable publications, most written by Protestant clergy of all denominations, denounced balls and parlor dancing. Gender issues proved the most difficult to resolve for those who opposed dancing. Opponents viewed the new "round dances" as dangerous to female purity. In these dances couples, typically in a closed position, traveled around the room as a duo. Dance opponents declared that such face-to-face proximity of male and female tempted them to sexual immorality. Nonetheless the waltz, the prime example of a round dance, was popular by the 1840s and sustained its appeal throughout the century. Other popular couple dances included the gallop, polka, mazurka, schottische, and *varsouvienne*. Traditional square dances and contra dances, which consisted of group figures, remained in social repertoires and were less morally suspect because partners typically danced side by side.

Dance instruction manuals provided directions for both square and round dances, but post–Civil War dance masters observed that round dances were more easily learned. By 1885 the New York dance master Allen Dodworth declared that a "complete revolution" had taken place and lamented the decline in manners and in the importance of dance lessons.

General dance histories contain some evidence that black people followed the white custom of participating in dancing assemblies and elaborate balls, but such information is brief. One institution, the Quadroon Ball, prominent in the early decades of the nineteenth century in New Orleans, limited attendees to white males and females of color. Given the Louisiana prohibition against marriage between whites and persons of color, the Quadroon Ball served as an opportunity for young women of mixed race to find white men who would keep them in a semirespectable lifestyle.

Surviving information about folk and national dances comes mainly from the oral tradition and is difficult to verify. Certainly the masses of immigrants crossing the Atlantic brought their ethnic dance and music to the United States. Histories of black dance contain incomplete and sometimes biased descriptions of slaves dancing on plantations and in segregated sections of cities like New Orleans. From these roots came the African steps, rhythms, and styling that spread irresistibly into the white world of the twentieth century as tap dance, the cakewalk, the Charleston, and the lindy hop.

By the mid-1850s African Americans entered the theatrical arena of blackface minstrels. This uniquely American genre received its impetus in 1828, when

Thomas D. Wright turned his imitation of an old black slave into a stage performance. Subsequently minstrel troupes of white men in blackface sang, danced, and told jokes to wide popular acclaim during the antebellum decades.

After the Civil War black and white touring minstrel troupes, including blacks in blackface, developed, and minstrel shows faced new competition from musical theater and vaudeville. The enormously successful production in 1866 of *The Black Crook*, a mix of burlesque, ballet, and spectacle, helped launch a musical theater genre that included both African Americans and European Americans. Unlike the male minstrel shows, musical theater and burlesque from the beginning depended on scantily clad women as a staple element. Perhaps the most famous troupe, Lydia Thompson's British Blondes, toured the United States in 1868 and performed successfully for the next twenty years.

Vaudeville, known first as "variety" in the 1850s, developed from the concert saloons and honky-tonks, whose "waiter-girls" sang, danced, and hostessed for male audiences. Later saloons featured olios with "ballet" by a corps of six or more young women who presented a range of terpsichorean exhibitions. Other venues for dance acts included circuses, carnivals, and medicine shows.

Ballet

Ballet flourished at the French court by the late sixteenth century but did not become firmly established in the United States until the second third of the twentieth century. Dancing schools in Philadelphia taught ballet by the 1830s, but the United States had no enduring schools or companies in the nineteenth century. For the most part Americans experienced ballet through the performances of foreign stars who toured the country intermittently throughout the century. The most acclaimed of these, Fanny Elssler, star of the European Romantic Ballet, toured from 1840 to 1842. Notable American performers included Augusta Maywood (1825–1876), who established her career in Europe, and Mary Ann Lee (c. 1823–?), who studied in Paris but returned to the United States in 1846 to stage *Giselle*. George Washington Smith (c. 1820–1899), America's first *premier danseur* and Lee's partner in the production, built a long and varied career. The absence of permanent companies meant that the names of individuals dominated the American stage. Histories do not detail any American choreographers, though Smith left a notebook of his work. *The Black Crook*, the most popular performance piece in post–Civil War America, featured Italian ballerinas in a production combining dance, music, drama, and spectacle. Variety and extravaganza appealed to American audiences of the Gilded Age.

See also **Manners; Minstrel Shows; Music,** *subentry on* **Orchestral Music; Sexual Morality; Social Life; Theater; Vaudeville and Burlesque.**

Bibliography

Barker, Barbara. *Ballet or Ballyhoo*. New York: Dance Horizons, 1984.

Emery, Lynne Fauley. *Black Dance: From 1619 to Today*. 2d rev. ed. Princeton, N.J.: Princeton Book Company, 1988.

Maynard, Olga. *The American Ballet*. Philadelphia: Macrae Smith, 1959.

Toll, Robert C. *Blacking Up: The Minstrel Show in Nineteenth-Century America*. New York: Oxford University Press, 1974.

Wagner, Ann. *Adversaries of Dance: From the Puritans to the Present*. Urbana: University of Illinois Press, 1997.

Zellars, Parker R. "The Cradle of Variety: The Concert Saloon." *Educational Theatre Journal* 20, no. 4 (December 1968): 578–585.

ANN WAGNER

DEATH AND DYING   George Washington died only a few weeks earlier, and his name was given to a slapdash city in a swamp that was to be the capital of a new nation. "I die hard, but I am not afraid to go. Tis well," were reportedly his last words. Now the United States, ready or not, entered a century in which the conditions of both life and death would be transformed. The agrarian nation of 5.3 million people living within the compass of 891,364 square miles would become an industrial power populated by more than 76 million people who claimed almost 3 million square miles from coast to coast. Youth was very much in evidence. More than half the free white males were under the age of sixteen, and a similar pattern existed for the white women and enslaved African Americans who were not so carefully counted.

How People Died

How did death present itself to life in the nineteenth century? The basic facts are clear, although the statistical reporting suffers from gaps and inadequacies. The specific numbers reported here are based on the more reliable information compiled at the end of the century and therefore underestimate the risks to life encountered during most of the preceding years.

Life was shorter as well as harder for people held in slavery, and emancipation did not erase this difference. By the end of the nineteenth century black men and women still had life expectancies about sixteen years shorter than their white counterparts.

Death ended many lives just at their beginnings. About one of every four African American newborns failed to survive the first year of life, twice the rate experienced among whites. Again, this figure underestimates the actual mortality rate because it represents positive changes that took place throughout the century. Large families were common throughout the century, and few escaped visitations from death. The risks of childbearing remained high, and consequently life expectancies for women remained low. Some deaths occurred from infections soon after delivery, and other deaths were hastened by the cumulative effects of repeated difficult births. Fear of a difficult and possibly fatal pregnancy often led to anxiety about sexual intercourse.

Contagious and infectious diseases were the leading causes of death throughout the century. Epidemics of cholera, smallpox, and yellow fever were among the scourges that appeared repeatedly, sometimes in particular regions, sometimes throughout the nation. Diphtheria among young children and pneumonia among the frail or aged were almost always fatal. Enlightened public health measures started to reduce this toll only late in the century, and physicians had few effective remedies once a disease had taken hold. This was the era in which many people experienced a life-or-death crisis for which families could offer only prayer. Tuberculosis became a threat as the potential for contagion increased with the growth of population centers. Families who helplessly watched loved ones die with this stressful and emaciating condition transmitted a heightened fear of the dying process to succeeding generations. Native populations were especially vulnerable to diseases brought to them unintentionally by people of European origin. Smallpox was a particularly lethal invader.

Wars with England in 1812 and Mexico in 1846–1848 could not prepare the young nation for the enormous death toll of the Civil War. An estimated 620,000 men were killed, more than all other U.S. wars combined through the next century. The South was especially hard hit, with the death of nearly one in five males of military age. The Civil War did more than leave many families in mourning and economic jeopardy. It also introduced the gun culture that took root in the turbulent years of Reconstruction and the pioneer days of the "wild West." The fact that through the twentieth century the United States consistently had the highest homicide rate in the world has been linked to the war-initiated love affair with the gun.

War apart, most deaths occurred at home. For much of the century hospitals were feared by many people as places to die, and it was years before hospitals proved effective in saving endangered lives. Funerals were mostly the responsibilities of families and churches, with professional undertakers becoming more active in the second half of the century.

How Death Was Experienced and Interpreted

Perhaps the most influential perspective on life and death in the nineteenth-century United States is the one articulated by the historian David E. Stannard in 1977. He described an emerging

> attitude toward death and dying that was characterized by self-indulgence, sentimentalization, and ostentation—a world rapidly diversifying and compartmentalizing its social and economic spheres . . . in which religion was becoming more and more the chief business of ministers and women. . . . The child of the Puritan was told to "think how it will be on a deathbed" . . . and to imagine what his well-deserved torments in Hell would be like. (*The Puritan Way of Death*, p. 173)

By contrast, the nineteenth-century child's attention was guided away from the physicality of dying to the image of death "as a peaceful and beautiful deliverance" (p. 174). The great age of sentimentality had dawned with emphasis on a new life after death. The rise of Romanticism also led in some quarters to a remake of death, especially as the young victims of tuberculosis entered poetry and fiction as embodiments of "almost unearthly lustre" (p. 174), dying in radiant beauty.

Broad interpretations of this kind, though useful, can obscure the actual experiences of the everyday

The Death of President William Henry Harrison. Elected to office in 1840, Harrison (1773–1841) did not live long enough to make a significant mark on the presidency. A month after his inauguration, Harrison died from pneumonia on 4 April 1841. CURRIER & IVES LITHOGRAPH, 1841. LIBRARY OF CONGRESS.

people whose lives were tragically altered by the death of a loved one. The desperate quest for understanding and meaning most frequently occurred within the depths of individual grief rather than religious oratory or literary invention. For example, in this 1842 diary entry Mary White tries to puzzle out God's purpose:

> First he took my dear little Norman & laid me upon a bed of suffering for many months. He then sent whooping cough into my family . . . & now he has come & smitten down our healthiest & one of our loveliest ones. Oh that he would teach me the meaning of all this & help me so to profit by it that he will not need to send upon me a heavier chastisement (Rosenblatt, *Bitter, Bitter Tears*, p. 61).

The Appalachian neighbors who silently joined a family in the deathwatch, the hard-pressed immigrants in city tenements who provided what comfort they could to their dying children, and the enslaved people who saw in death a release from oppression are among the many whose experiences cannot be understood by generalizations.

See also **Birth and Childbearing; Cemeteries and Burial; Health and Disease; Hospitals; Violence.**

Bibliography

Bellesiler, Michael A. "The Origins of Gun Culture in the United States, 1780–1865." *Journal of American History* 83 (1998): 425–455.

Crissman, James K. *Death and Dying in Central Appalachia.* Urbana: University of Illinois Press, 1994.

Kastenbaum, Robert. *The Psychology of Death.* 3d ed. New York: Springer, 2000.

Rosenblatt, Paul C. *Bitter, Bitter Tears.* Minneapolis: University of Minnesota Press, 1983.

Stannard, David E. *The Puritan Way of Death.* New York: Oxford University Press, 1977.

Taeuber, Cynthia M., ed. *Statistical Handbook on Women in America.* 2d ed. Phoenix, Ariz.: Oryx, 1996.

ROBERT KASTENBAUM

DELAWARE   Political, economic, and geographic contrasts characterized nineteenth-century Delaware despite its small size. Wilmington and northern New Castle County were oriented to Philadelphia and the North, while the rest of the state had a more southern outlook.

Regional variations shaped Delaware's economy. Early turnpikes and railroads served only the northern part of the state. The Chesapeake and Delaware Canal, completed in 1829, linked those two bays, but also became an unofficial dividing line between northern and southern Delaware. Only in 1859 did the railroad reach Seaford, in Sussex County, alleviating lower Delaware's traditional isolation.

Most of Delaware is flat, with rolling hills in the north. Early in the century, farmers in northern and central Delaware grew cash crops of wheat and corn, while large quantities of timber were cut from southern Delaware forests. Huge commercial peach orchards worked their way down the state beginning in the 1830s, transforming Delaware's agriculture and making it the nation's first major peach-producing state. An incurable disease affecting the peaches followed the orchards, however, and the industry was declining by 1900. Truck crops for urban markets replaced dying orchards.

Except for shipbuilding along southern Delaware waterways, industry was concentrated in and around Wilmington. The Brandywine River, north of Wilmington, powered early industry as other types of factories joined successful flour mills established earlier.

Industrialization, beginning in the 1840s, spurred rapid growth in Wilmington, Delaware's only city. Its products included iron ships, railroad cars, and leather among the most important. Wilmington, however, was too close to Philadelphia to grow into a major commercial center or port.

Sectional differences and an independent conservatism shaped politics. The first party system of Federalists and Democratic-Republicans functioned until the mid-1820s, much longer than elsewhere. Whigs then replaced Federalists as the majority party that controlled Kent and Sussex Counties, while the Democrats carried New Castle County.

Mid-century tensions and the Civil War changed the party structure once again. The Republican Party, strongest in Wilmington and northern Delaware, became the new minority party, while the Democrats, now strong elsewhere in the state, emerged as the majority party. This alignment lasted until the 1890s, when the Republicans became the majority party.

Delaware's population of 112,216 in 1860 included 1,798 slaves and 19,829 free blacks. The Civil War intensified Delaware's traditional dual orientation. Although slavery was dying through voluntary manumission, Delaware could not bring itself to abolish it. Many residents sympathized with the South and supported the right to secede peacefully, but Delaware remained in the Union. Many fought in the Union army, but a few fought for and aided the Confederacy. Thousands of captured Confederates were held at Fort Delaware, a military prison. Slavery in Delaware finally ended with the adoption of the Thirteenth Amendment to the U.S. Constitution in 1865.

Corruption characterized late-nineteenth-century Delaware politics at all levels. Democrats used tax laws to minimize black voting. Republican use of the system in the 1890s transformed it into the majority party.

Throughout the century, Delaware held conservative social positions. Law and custom kept blacks segregated. Expenditures for public education, social welfare, and criminal justice were low.

As 1900 approached, Wilmington and its environs were ready for new challenges, while southern Delaware greeted the twentieth century with reluctance. As always, Delaware was pulled in two directions.

Bibliography

Hancock, Harold Bell. *Delaware during the Civil War: A Political History.* Wilmington: Historical Society of Delaware, 1961.

Hoffecker, Carol E. *Wilmington, Delaware: Portrait of an Industrial City, 1830–1910.* Charlottesville: University Press of Virginia for the Eleutherian Mills-Hagley Foundation, 1974.

Munroe, John A. *History of Delaware.* 3d ed. Newark: University of Delaware Press, 1993.

CONSTANCE J. COOPER

DEMOCRATIC PARTY   The most enduring American political institution of the nineteenth century was the Democratic Party. Thomas Jefferson (1743–1826) was inaugurated as president on 4 March 1801 under the banner of the Democratic-Republicans. The origins of that organization reached back into the 1790s, and the efforts of Jefferson and James Madison (1751–1836) to defeat the economic policies of Alexander Hamilton (1755–1804). The resulting political warfare with the Federalists produced the First American Party System. In its early days, the Democratic-Republican Party stood for state rights, limited government, and a small military establishment. It was strongest in the South, and had the least support in New England. Southern slave owners and farmers, workers and independent artisans, and small farmers in the North formed the base of Jefferson's support.

For the next twenty-five years, the Democratic-Republicans dominated national politics. After eight years of Jefferson, Madison held the presidency from 1809 to 1817, followed by James Monroe (1758–1831) from 1817 to 1825. The Federalists gradually disappeared by 1816, and the Democratic-Republicans survived the factionalism and difficulties of the War of 1812. Jefferson's purchase of Louisiana in 1803 assured the nation's territorial expansion. After the end of the war, as the South and West grew, the United States entered a period of political peace that became known as the Era of Good Feelings.

The Emergence of Jacksonian Democracy

Although white male voters identified themselves as Democratic-Republicans, there was not yet a political party in the modern sense of the term. Presidential candidates were chosen in congressional caucuses where partisan affiliation was not a major consideration. Changes began to take place during the 1820s, as the tranquillity of the Monroe administration faded before new issues and emerging leaders. The most dangerous controversy involved the question of slavery that came to the fore in 1819 and 1820. Northerners in Congress endeavored to ban human bondage from new states in the West when Missouri sought admission to the Union. Although the Missouri Compromise of 1820 temporarily settled the problem, sectionalism became an important force in party organization. The state rights' doctrine of the Democratic-Republicans gave its candidates a natural appeal to those who wanted to preserve the rights of southern states to keep slaves.

More important still were the presidential ambitions of Andrew Jackson (1767–1845). In 1824 the popular western hero of the Battle of New Orleans lost to John Quincy Adams (1767–1848) in an election that was settled by the House of Representatives. Jackson denounced what he claimed was a "corrupt bargain" that made Adams president and Henry Clay (1777–1852) the next secretary of state. Jackson's supporters vowed to exact their revenge in the 1828 presidential contest.

One of the Jacksonian leaders, Martin Van Buren (1782–1862) of New York, began organizing a political base for his candidate in 1826 and 1827. Repudiating the caucus system and drawing on campaigning techniques developed by the Anti-Masonic Party, Van Buren used rallies, speeches, newspapers, and songs to rouse popular enthusiasm for Jackson. Local and state nominating conventions became a way of pledging men to vote for Jackson. The Democratic-Republicans, sometimes abbreviated to Democrats, put forward Jackson as the champion of the common man in contrast to the aristocratic Adams.

Van Buren's strategy paid off in 1828 when Jackson defeated Adams's bid for reelection by a decisive margin. Voter turnout was high, and Van Buren's approach to politics laid the foundation for the Democratic Party in the Jacksonian era. The opposition called themselves National Republicans. In office, Jackson extended the Jeffersonian legacy of small government, low taxes, and opposition to concentrated economic power. The president's main target became the Second Bank of the United States, which he destroyed as a national institution by vetoing its charter renewal and then withdrawing all federal deposits from the bank. Jackson wielded executive power to keep the national government in check, but he also made it clear that he would act vigorously to stymie efforts by South Carolina to nullify federal tariff legislation and threaten the Union from 1831 to 1832.

Jackson won reelection in 1832 over Henry Clay as the candidate of the National Republicans, who soon began calling themselves Whigs to prove their dislike of Jackson's monarchical style. During the campaign, the Democrats dropped all vestiges of the caucus system and held a nominating convention to select their presidential and vice presidential candidates. The opposition followed the same procedure. By the mid-1830s the Second American Party System was taking shape. The Democrats were the stronger of the two parties, with a solid base among southern slave planters, farmers across the country, and immigrants in the East's growing cities. The ethnocultural foundation of the party lay among Catholics, Presbyterians, and religious denominations that dissented from the more established Protestant churches. Irish immigrants would be an important element among Democrats after the 1840s.

After two controversial terms, Jackson gave way to his vice president, Martin Van Buren, in 1836. The Whigs put four candidates into the field against the Democrats; William Henry Harrison (1773–1841) was the best known. Van Buren won the presidency, but soon faced serious political difficulties as a party leader. The outbreak of the panic of 1837 and the hard times that followed demoralized the Democrats as the 1840 election neared. The Whigs borrowed some of the Democratic campaign techniques and improved on them in a campaign that featured a strongly emotional appeal for William Henry Harrison as the hero of the Battle of Tippecanoe in 1811. Harrison and his running mate, John Tyler (1790–1862), routed the unpopular Van Buren.

The Slavery Issue

The Whig triumph was brief. Harrison died one month after his inauguration and Tyler proved to be a disappointment to the Whigs. As the administration dissolved into bickering, the Democrats looked to the 1844 elections to regain national power. The issue of admitting Texas as a slave state produced divisions between northern and southern Whigs that worked to the advantage of the Democrats. Most Democrats favored the admission of Texas and territorial expansion. The party selected James K. Polk

(1795–1849) of Tennessee, a "dark horse" candidate, as its nominee, and he defeated Henry Clay and the Whigs. At the national convention, the Democrats reaffirmed the rule, adopted in 1832, that a candidate had to win two-thirds of the delegates to be nominated. The rule meant that a candidate could not be chosen without the consent of the South.

Polk pushed for war with Mexico and westward expansion. He was a vigorous chief executive in the mold of Andrew Jackson. The Mexican War (1846–1848) brought territorial gains, but it heightened differences over the future of slavery in the West among Democrats. The proposed Wilmot Proviso, which would have barred slavery from any areas acquired from Mexico, proved a major source of discord. Polk retired after a single term, and the Democratic Party grappled with the slavery question in picking its nominee in 1848. Lewis Cass (1782–1866) of Michigan advocated popular sovereignty, a method by which residents of a territory would decide when and if their potential state would be slave or free. Cass won the nomination, but lost the election to the Whig candidate, Zachary Taylor (1784–1850). The Free-Soil Party and its candidate, Martin Van Buren, took votes away from Democrats in the North.

The brief Taylor presidency and the Millard Fillmore (1800–1874) administration that followed when Taylor died in 1850 produced the Compromise of 1850, which sought to settle the issue of slavery in the territories. With sectional issues on hold temporarily, the Democrats turned in 1852 to a compromise candidate, Franklin Pierce (1804–1869) of New Hampshire. Pierce outpolled the Whig candidate, Winfield Scott (1786–1866), decisively and the Whig Party disappeared soon after the election.

Pierce was a weak and irresolute president, and Democratic political fortunes suffered. In 1854 Stephen A. Douglas (1813–1861), a Democratic senator from Illinois, pushed through the Kansas-Nebraska Act, which gave popular sovereignty on slavery in the West. Outraged northerners, fearing the expansion of slavery, defected to the American or Know-Nothing Party to some degree, but moved in even larger numbers to a new political party, the Republicans. Many northern Democrats experienced this change in electoral allegiance. Increasingly, the Democrats were seen as a pro-slavery party in the South and a pro-southern party in the North. Democratic doctrine denounced Republicans as pro-black, and claimed that political and social equality for African Americans was a goal of the new party.

The election of James Buchanan (1791–1868) in 1856 over the first Republican presidential candidate, John C. Frémont (1813–1890), represented a last victory for the old Democratic Party. It was clear that if the Republicans continued to grow at their current rate they would be the dominant party in the North by 1860. Buchanan came to the White House with distinguished credentials as a cabinet officer and lawmaker, but he was a very disappointing president. He endorsed the Supreme Court's *Dred Scott* decision (1857), which said slavery was legal in all U.S. territories, and Buchanan appeased the pro-slavery, pro-southern wing of his party in the struggle over the fate of Kansas as a future free or slave state. Meanwhile, the Republicans made steady gains in the North as the slavery issue became more polarized. It seemed unlikely that the Democrats could win the 1860 presidential election against the united Republicans and their ascendancy in the North. The South was unwilling to accept any northern Democrat opposed to the expansion of slavery. Northern Democrats, such as Douglas, knew that such a position would doom their chances against the Republicans. The two factions were irreconcilable.

The Civil War Decline

The events of the 1860 election proved disastrous for the Democrats. They put two tickets into the race against Abraham Lincoln (1809–1865) and the Republicans. Stephen A. Douglas represented the northern wing of the party, which was loyal to the Union. John C. Breckinridge (1821–1875) led the southern Democrats, who believed in slavery and planned to secede if Lincoln won. Although the anti-Lincoln candidates gained more popular votes, the Republican candidate had a secure majority in the electoral vote.

Democrats found it difficult to find a viable political posture during the Civil War. To the extent that they endorsed Lincoln and his war aims, they called into question the reason for their own existence. When they criticized the conduct of the conflict or talked about the need for a negotiated end to the fighting, they allowed the Republicans to label them as treasonous. The Copperheads in the North, who favored a negotiated settlement with the South, became indelibly associated with the Democrats. Despite these problems, the residual strength of the party in the North was impressive. In the 1864 campaign, the Democrats nominated George B. McClellan (1826–1885) who had led the Union armies in 1862. Even with patriotic appeals and the mistakes of the Democrats, Lincoln won reelection with only 55 percent of the popular vote.

The end of the war in 1865 and the death of Lincoln put a former Democrat, Andrew Johnson (1808–1875), in the White House. When the southern states were once again part of the Union, the Democrats seemed likely to benefit politically. White southerners

Stephen A. Douglas. One of the most prominent Democrats of his generation, Douglas (1813–1861) is remembered for his debates with Abraham Lincoln during Douglas's successful 1858 senatorial campaign in Illinois. ARCHIVE PHOTOS

were unwilling to accept the Republicans as a legitimate part of the political scene in the region, especially when the Republicans relied on the votes of former slaves as a major part of their coalition. The Democrats had every reason to favor the prompt readmission of the South and a lenient policy on the issues of Reconstruction. More and more the Democratic Party was identified with an antiblack racial posture that looked to the maintenance of white supremacy.

The imbedded electoral power of the Democrats was clear in the presidential election of 1868. The Republicans nominated the military hero of the Civil War, Ulysses S. Grant (1822–1885), and the Democrats named the former governor of New York, Horatio Seymour (1810–1886). Seymour's running mate was Francis Preston Blair Jr. (1821–1875) of Missouri, a staunch opponent of Radical Reconstruction. Even with the popularity of Grant and the advantages that the Republicans enjoyed in terms of organization, Seymour still garnered more than 47 per-

Clement L. Vallandigham. A congressman from Dayton, Ohio, Vallandigham (1820–1871) was a leader of the "Copperhead" faction of the Democratic Party. The Copperheads called for "peace at any price" and fought vehemently against every measure that came to Congress in favor of continuing the war. LIBRARY OF CONGRESS

cent of the popular ballots. The Democrats stressed the race issue in the campaign, and identified themselves even more strongly with white supremacy as a basic ideological position. While they were unable to overcome Grant's lead in the North, the Democrats were beginning to reestablish their base in the South as Reconstruction waned.

Any hopes for a Democratic rebound during the next presidential election in 1872 proved illusory. The prospects for the Democrats seemed more promising as the year began because of a developing split between pro-Grant Republicans and those reformers in the party who called themselves Liberal Republicans. If the Democrats and the Liberal Republicans could unite, their coalition could defeat Grant's reelection bid. In the end, however, the Liberal Republicans selected the New York *Tribune* editor Horace Greeley

(1811–1872) as their nominee. The Democrats had little choice but to accept Greeley, lest they split the anti-Grant vote. Neither the Liberal Republicans nor the Democrats were enthusiastic about Greeley, and the campaign turned into a rout for Grant. The Democratic Party had reached one of its low points of the nineteenth century.

The onset of the panic of 1873 and the economic distress that followed produced a dramatic improvement in the electoral fortunes of the Democrats during the 1870s. In 1874 the Democrats regained control of the House of Representatives for the first time in eighteen years and seemed poised to be a competitive force in the 1876 presidential election. The election of Samuel J. Tilden (1814–1886) as governor of New York meant that the Democrats could hope to carry that state for the presidency. The scandals of the Grant administration, the return of the South to full political power, and popular unhappiness with the programs of the Republicans led to a more even balance between the two major parties. For the next quarter of a century, American politics would see an electoral stalemate between the Republicans and the Democrats. This equilibrium between the two parties has been characterized as the Third American Party System.

Stalemate in the Gilded Age

In the 1876 election the Democrats chose Tilden as their running mate against the Republican nominee, Rutherford B. Hayes (1822–1893). The campaign produced a very close race, and on election night it seemed as if Tilden had been elected. He had 184 electoral votes, just one short of the number needed for the presidency. Hayes trailed with 165 electoral votes. Twenty electoral votes—from South Carolina, Florida, Louisiana, and Oregon—remained in dispute, and were claimed by both parties. The election of 1876 had to be settled by an electoral commission and a political bargain; the result was the election of Hayes and the defeat of Tilden. Nonetheless, the 1876 election demonstrated that the Democrats could compete on even terms with the Republicans. With the solidly Democratic South behind them, the Democracy (as it was known then) had about 137 electoral votes (from the states of the former Confederacy, plus Kentucky and Missouri) toward a majority. If it could add New York and a midwestern state, such as Indiana, the party would have a winning coalition.

The Democrats came close to victory again in 1880 when they selected Winfield Scott Hancock (1824–1886), a Civil War general, to oppose the Republican nominee, James A. Garfield (1831–1881). Hancock

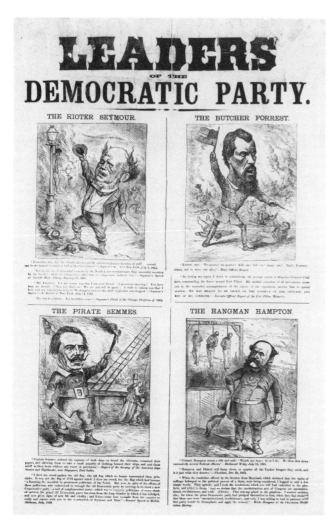

LEADERS OF THE DEMOCRATIC PARTY.

THE RIOTER SEYMOUR.   THE BUTCHER FORREST.

THE PIRATE SEMMES.   THE HANGMAN HAMPTON.

The Post–Civil War Democratic Party. Caricature (1868) by Thomas Nast of four leaders of the Democratic Party, who are portrayed as criminals. Three were former Confederate officers and the other, a New York governor, was commonly thought responsible for the 1863 New York draft riots. LIBRARY OF CONGRESS: RARE BOOKS AND SPECIAL COLLECTIONS DIVISION

would defuse the issues relating to Democratic attitudes toward the war, and was acceptable to the South because he had advocated a lenient Reconstruction policy. The popular vote was very close, with only 39,213 votes separating Hancock and Garfield. In the electoral college, Garfield won with 214 votes to 155 for Hancock. The South had become the bedrock of the Democratic Party.

Twenty-four years out of power ended in 1884, when the Democrats regained the White House behind the presidential candidacy of Grover Cleveland (1837–1908) of New York. The mayor of Buffalo in 1881, Cleveland was elected governor of New York in 1882. His ability to carry that state's electoral votes made him a national contender for the nomination. As a fresh face untainted with the battles of the past, Cleveland appealed to Democrats and to Republicans alienated with the candidacy of James G. Blaine (1830–1893) as their party's nominee. The campaign that ensued was one of the most bitter in American history. Cleveland's romantic entanglement with a woman named Maria Halpin and the illegitimate child for whom he took responsibility added an element of scandal to the race. Cleveland withstood the incident and went on to defeat Blaine narrowly in the popular vote and in the electoral tally. Happy Democrats celebrated their return to Washington.

In the late nineteenth century, the Democrats had assembled a powerful, if fractious, voting coalition. White Democrats in the South ensured that the region would provide a bloc of electoral votes for the party every four years. In the North, the Democrats appealed to Roman Catholics, who disliked the evangelical Protestantism of many Republicans. Americans who thought of themselves as consumers admired the Democratic belief in a low tariff on imported goods and modest taxation. The party also endorsed laissez-faire economic policies and emphasized states' rights and localism. The Republicans were the party of national authority and positive government; the Democrats upheld older traditions of a limited, nonintrusive state.

The Cleveland Era and Beyond

Cleveland's first term produced modest legislative accomplishments. The president alienated many party members by his civil service appointments at a time when patronage was a key element in the political system. Cleveland was more popular than his party, and his reelection in 1888 seemed likely. In 1887 the president made a lower tariff the sole theme of his annual message, and the issue became the dominant question in the 1888 presidential race. To oppose Cleveland the Republicans selected Benjamin Harrison (1833–1901) of Indiana, a Civil War general and the grandson of President William Henry Harrison. The younger Harrison ran on a platform that emphasized tariff protection, fair elections in the South, and an activist government.

At a time when incumbent presidents did not campaign for reelection, Cleveland played a passive role. In his campaign advisers and in his approach to the election, he muted the low-tariff themes of his annual message and did not emphasize the issue in the fall. Cleveland won a majority of the popular vote, in part because of the overwhelming Democratic strength in the South. But Harrison triumphed in the electoral

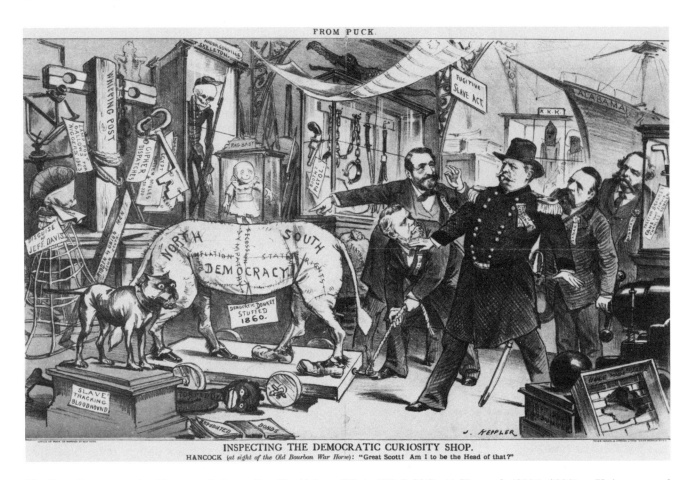

FROM PUCK.

INSPECTING THE DEMOCRATIC CURIOSITY SHOP.
HANCOCK (at sight of the Old Bourbon War Horse): "Great Scott! Am I to be the Head of that?"

The Post-Reconstruction Democratic Party. Presidential candidate Winfield Scott Hancock (1824–1886), a Union general and Civil War hero, is shown bewildered as he realizes the legacy of the party. His 1880 campaign lacked a substantial focus. Lithograph, 1880, J. F. Keppler. LIBRARY OF CONGRESS: PRINTS AND PHOTOGRAPHS DIVISION

tally. The Republicans also won control of both houses of Congress.

The Democratic eclipse was brief. The Republicans enacted an activist program of tariff protection and antitrust legislation and sought to pass a bill to ensure fair elections in the South. The Democrats rallied against the new Force Act that would have protected African American voting rights, and they also asserted that the higher tariffs had raised prices on consumer goods. In the Midwest, Republican laws to restrict sectarian schools and require the teaching of English alienated Catholic and Lutheran voters. The Democrats were the beneficiaries of these political mistakes. In the 1890 election, the Democrats regained control of the House of Representatives.

Two years later Cleveland defeated Harrison for the White House by the largest popular vote margin in twenty years. The Democrats kept control of the House and regained a majority in the Senate. It looked as if the Democrats had reestablished the preeminence that they had enjoyed earlier in the cen-

tury. Some observers forecast hard times ahead for the Republicans.

But the Democrats were an uneasy coalition. In the South and West, where the farm economy was suffering from low prices and a burden of debt, many Democrats, mindful of the challenge of the farm-based People's Party, wanted policies to inflate the currency through the coinage of silver into money on an equal basis with gold. Democrats in the Northeast regarded the gold standard as essential. These differences were papered over in 1892, but could resurface in a crisis.

Then the economic skies darkened. The panic of 1893 set off a four-year depression that defied the efforts of Cleveland and his administration to offset its effects. The president offered the familiar answer of limited government and patience with the business cycle. His only substantive answer was to call for the repeal of the Sherman Silver Purchase Act, which the Republicans had passed in 1890 to provide a small subsidy to silver miners. Cleveland charged that the bill had undermined business confidence. He called Congress into special session in August 1893 to repeal the measure.

The resulting battle split the Democrats, as southern and western lawmakers sought to stave off the gold standard. Cleveland wielded patronage and other weapons ruthlessly to achieve his goal. He got his way, but the party was fractured. The president's harsh policies during the Pullman Strike of 1894 and his general antilabor approach alienated many within the party. By the election of 1894, the Democrats were demoralized and disunited.

The Republicans won a sweeping victory in that election. The Democrats lost more than 110 House seats, in the largest transfer of power in congressional history. In many parts of the country the Democrats became an enfeebled minority. Only in the South, where whites used electoral machinery to fend off the Populists, did the Democrats retain a stronghold. The Republicans had become the majority party and would remain so well into the twentieth century. Cleveland had become a hated, repudiated leader in the Democratic ranks.

In the election of 1896, the Democrats turned away from the policies of Cleveland and abandoned the gold standard. They nominated a political newcomer, William Jennings Bryan (1860–1925) of Nebraska, who made an impassioned speech on behalf of free silver at the Democratic National Convention. The "cross of gold" speech transformed Bryan into a national figure and won him the nomination. He also received the nomination of the People's Party. Bryan conducted a vigorous campaign. He crisscrossed the nation, pressing the case for silver. But after an initial wave of enthusiasm, his candidacy faltered before the well-financed and well-organized appeal of the Republicans and their standard-bearer, William McKinley (1843–1901). Bryan was defeated soundly in the fall balloting as McKinley got 271 electoral votes to 176 for Bryan. The stalemated politics of the Gilded Age had ended, and the Republicans had emerged as the dominant force.

Bryan made another try at the White House four years later. The victories of the Spanish-American War of 1898 had made imperialism a key issue, and Bryan attempted to make the contest a referendum on overseas expansion. That did not work, and he returned to free silver along with an emphasis on the evils of business consolidation. The result was the same, with McKinley gaining an even more decisive triumph in the popular vote and the electoral total. At the end of the nineteenth century, the Democratic Party was in a subordinate status with little prospect of regaining national power in the immediate future. Republicans joked that the Democratic Party was like alcohol. It killed everything that was alive and preserved everything that was dead.

The Democrats did, however, have latent strengths that would enable the party to prosper in the twentieth century. Their base in the South meant that Democrats would be a power in Congress, where seniority gave power to lawmakers with safe seats. While the Democrats were still the party of small government, localism, and state rights, there had begun to be signs under William Jennings Bryan of a readiness to use the power of government to address concentrations of economic wealth and to deal with social injustice. Similarly, in industrial states in the Northeast and Middle West, Democrats began to use state regulatory power to engage issues of child labor, working conditions, and corporate misdeeds in what became in time the party's urban liberal wing. Any Democrat embarking on such a course would have to be careful of alienating the South, ever sensitive to the idea that a powerful government might attack segregation. Nonetheless, the possibility of becoming a party devoted to the interests of the small entrepreneur, the worker, and the consumer was one that many Democrats would be tempted to explore during the first decade of the new century to come.

When they talked of the Democratic Party in 1900, men spoke of the Jeffersonian-Jacksonian tradition and all that it represented. Americans distrustful of the government, wealth, and consolidated power had found a powerful instrument in the Democratic Party. At its best it represented virtues of rural life, proximity to the people, and the native wisdom of common Americans. In its less attractive elements, the Democrats' creed stood for racial injustice, the supremacy of white Americans, and negativism as to the role of government. Having survived the challenges of the Federalists, Whigs, and Republicans to remain one of the two major parties in the United States, the Democrats had become an indispensable part of the functioning of partisan politics and the operation of government. In that sense, the Democratic Party had become an integral part of American culture.

See also **Elections,** *subentry on* **Presidential Elections; Jacksonian Era; Jeffersonian Era; Politics; Republican Party; Whig Party.**

Bibliography

Baker, Jean H. *Affairs of Party: The Political Culture of Northern Democrats in the Mid-Nineteenth Century.* Bronx, N.Y.: Fordham University Press, 1998.

Blodgett, Geoffrey. *The Gentle Reformers: Massachusetts Democrats in the Cleveland Era.* Cambridge, Mass.: Harvard University Press, 1966.

Cole, Donald B. *Martin Van Buren and the American Political System*. Princeton, N.J.: Princeton University Press, 1984.

Holt, Michael F. *The Political Crisis of the 1850s*. New York: Wiley, 1978.

Kleppner, Paul. *The Third Electoral System, 1853–1892: Parties, Voters, and Political Cultures*. Chapel Hill: University of North Carolina Press, 1979.

McCormick, Richard P. *The Second American Party System: Party Formation in the Jacksonian Era*. Chapel Hill: University of North Carolina Press, 1966.

McGerr, Michael E. *The Decline of Popular Politics: The American North, 1865–1928*. New York: Oxford University Press, 1986.

Morgan, H. Wayne. *From Hayes to McKinley: National Party Politics, 1877–1896*. Syracuse, N.Y.: Syracuse University Press, 1969.

Rutland, Robert A. *The Democrats: From Jefferson to Carter*. Baton Rouge: Louisiana State University Press, 1979.

Silbey, Joel H. *The American Political Nation, 1838–1893*. Stanford, Calif.: Stanford University Press, 1991.

———. *A Respectable Minority: The Democratic Party in the Civil War Era, 1860–1868*. New York: Norton, 1977.

Welch, Richard E. *The Presidencies of Grover Cleveland*. Lawrence: University Press of Kansas, 1988.

Williams, R. Hal. *The Democratic Party and California Politics, 1880–1896*. Stanford, Calif.: Stanford University Press, 1973.

LEWIS L. GOULD

DEMOGRAPHY   See Population.

DENVER

Denver was founded in late 1858 by speculators anxious to capitalize on small placer gold discoveries made near the confluence of the South Platte River and Cherry Creek at the base of the Rocky Mountains. Mountain mines siphoned away gold seekers in 1859, but Denver survived as a transportation and supply center.

Beset by problems, including the lack of railroads, the Civil War, and occasionally hostile Cheyenne and Arapaho Indians, whose land the newcomers had occupied, the town grew by only ten persons during the 1860s to an 1870 population of 4,759. By mid-1870 rail lines linked it to the rest of the nation, and by 1890 it was tapping Colorado's riches through an internal rail network of more than forty-two hundred miles. High, sunny, and dry, Denver became the capital of Colorado and the county seat of Arapahoe County. The city profited from its government workers, its smelters and railroad shops, and its reputation as a healthy place where tuberculosis sufferers could recuperate.

Denver's 1890 population of 106,713 made it the twenty-sixth largest city in the United States and the largest in the Rocky Mountain West. Although native-born white Americans dominated, 24 percent of its residents were foreign-born, and 3 percent were African Americans. Its poor people lived mainly in the central sections and in such northern industrial suburbs as Globeville. Many of the wealthy congregated on Capitol Hill, east of the central business district. The middle class, beneficiaries of an extensive street rail network, spread out, some into such suburbs as Highlands, Montclair, and South Denver. In the 1890s rich and poor saw the city slide into depression caused by a crash in Colorado's silver mining. But by 1900 Denver, with a population of 133,859, was regaining its optimism.

See also **Colorado; Gold Rushes and Silver Strikes.**

Bibliography

Dorsett, Lyle W., and Michael McCarthy. *The Queen City: A History of Denver*. Boulder, Colo.: Pruett, 1986.

Leonard, Stephen J., and Thomas J. Noel. *Denver: Mining Camp to Metropolis*. Niwot: University Press of Colorado, 1990.

Smiley, Jerome C. *History of Denver, with Outlines of the Earlier History of the Rocky Mountain Country*. Denver, Colo.: Denver Times, 1901.

STEPHEN J. LEONARD

DEPRESSIONS   See Panics and Depressions.

DETROIT

Already a hundred years old as the nineteenth century dawned, Detroit (straits, in French) is situated on the river of the same name that connects Lake Erie with Lake St. Clair and then Lake Huron farther north. Founded by the French as a frontier outpost in their vast inland empire, Detroit was still just a trading post surrounded by a small farming community when the United States finally took it over from the British in 1796.

The opening of the Erie Canal in New York in 1825 was just one factor encouraging population migration to the Michigan territory by the 1830s, and Detroit grew rapidly, first as an outfitting site for settlers and then as a regional commercial center. Detroit-based steamers soon plied the waters of Lake Erie, and by the early 1850s the city was the eastern terminus of the Michigan Central Railroad that ran west to Chicago. The city continued to attract New Englanders and New Yorkers, but it also became home to Irish and German immigrants. By 1860 Detroit's 45,619 inhabitants, 47 percent of whom were foreign-born, made it the nineteenth largest city in the country, and to its commercial importance was added an industrial one: the processing of Great Lakes raw materials, mainly copper smelting and lumber milling.

The city grew out from and along the river predominantly in the classic grid pattern, leaving behind only remnants of a territorial official's "cobweb" plan, inspired by Pierre L'Enfant's design for Washington, D.C. Railroad tracks and warehouses crowded the riverfront, and a central business district formed around and north of the intersection of Jefferson and Woodward Avenues in the heart of the city. Over the second half of the century, a patchwork of mostly residential neighborhoods arrayed in an arc beyond the central business district, displaying fairly strong ethnic identities at the block level within a broader pattern of Irish concentration on the city's west side and Polish and German concentration on the east side. The influx of eastern Europeans toward the end of the century did not dislodge the Germans as the largest immigrant group in Detroit, whose population of 285,704 in 1900 was still one-third foreign-born. African Americans made up only 1.4 percent of the city's population, a lower percentage than in Cleveland, New York, Chicago, or Boston, but their presence had led to Detroit's most serious social disturbance of the century, the race riot of 1863.

Even as a commercial city and processing center, Detroit had begun to develop manufacturing, especially such iron products as steam engines, stoves, and furnaces. Toward the end of the century it also became a leading producer of railroad cars and wheels; indeed, in the early 1880s the city's Peninsular Car Works was the largest factory of its kind in the country. While pharmaceutical preparations grew in importance, foundries and machine shops still turned out Detroit's leading products in 1900. By then, Ransom Olds and Henry Ford were embarking on the work that would soon transform Detroit, the nation's thirteenth largest city but heretofore less dynamic than other Great Lakes cities such as Chicago, Buffalo, and Cleveland, into the automobile production capital of the world.

See also **Michigan.**

Bibliography

Oestreicher, Richard J. *Solidarity and Fragmentation: Working People and Class Consciousness in Detroit, 1875–1900.* Urbana: University of Illinois Press, 1986.
Schneider, John C. *Detroit and the Problem of Order, 1830–1880: A Geography of Crime, Riot, and Policing.* Lincoln: University of Nebraska Press, 1980.
Zunz, Olivier. *The Changing Face of Inequality: Urbanization, Industrial Development, and Immigrants in Detroit, 1880–1920.* Chicago: University of Chicago Press, 1982.

JOHN C. SCHNEIDER

DIET See **Food.**

DIME NOVELS AND STORY PAPERS

The nineteenth century witnessed a change in American attitudes toward fiction, a trend largely propelled by story papers and dime novels. These genres generated a cornucopia of fiction written to entertain in a manner that promoted quick consumption rather than prolonged reflection, and they utilized publication patterns and formats that encouraged frequent purchases and ready discards rather than thoughtful selection and careful preservation. A combination of external factors fueled their success. The gradual spread of literacy created a wider and more varied readership; technological improvements allowed more rapid and cost-effective printing; postal legislation provided favorable rates for newspapers and periodicals; the absence of an international copyright law permitted piracy of European fiction; and a nationwide distribution system via newsdealers helped to reach a diverse audience. Although the two genres differed in format and, to some extent, in era and readership, their development and content were often closely entwined, and their success resulted in mass-produced fiction for a mass audience.

Story Papers

Family story papers, descendants of literary newspapers, emerged in the 1840s and reached their zenith of popularity during the next three decades. Designed to look like newspapers (to capitalize on favorable postal rates), these papers of eight to sixteen pages carried serialized fiction, short stories, poetry, and essays, often with a dramatic front-page illustration. Chief among them was Robert Bonner's *New York Ledger,* which during the 1850s attained a circulation of 400,000 due in part to Bonner's successful use of extensive advertising, a technique other publishers soon imitated. Although they pirated European works, Bonner and his competitors frequently featured fiction by popular American authors, including Mrs. E. D. E. N. Southworth, Timothy Shay Arthur, and Sylvanus Cobb Jr. The constantly expanding market for stories made it possible for the first time for a significant number of authors to earn their livelihood through writing. In the 1870s the *Ledger's* popularity was eclipsed by Street and Smith's *New York Weekly* and challenged by a host of others, including the *Saturday Evening Post* and George Munro's *Fireside Companion;* like the *Weekly* and *Companion* many of these papers were issued by firms that also were, or soon would be, engaged in publishing dime novels. During the next few decades family story papers declined, and boys' story papers such as *Golden Days* and Street and Smith's *Good News*, intended for adolescent males, flourished briefly.

Fiction in the family story papers encompassed a variety of genres aimed at both male and female readers. Such fare included sensational romances, such as those pseudonymously penned by Louisa May Alcott; working-girl romances and success stories in the vein of Horatio Alger's rags-to-respectability tales; frontier stories and Westerns featuring fictional heroes or apotheosized versions of historical figures, like Ned Buntline's accounts of Buffalo Bill (which soon led to popular stage productions and Wild West shows); and urban dramas or detective stories (including Harlan Halsey's Old Sleuth, the first recurring series detective, who debuted in *Fireside Companion* in 1872). Since some publishers produced both story papers and dime novels, they sometimes recycled material, reissuing serials as paperbound books or featuring promising story characters in dime novel series. Stories that proved popular might later appear in inexpensive clothbound books. Boys' story papers also featured (and recycled) many types of fiction, including war adventures, urban success stories, science fiction, travel and hunting stories, detective fiction, and Westerns. Several authors who began their careers writing for boys' papers went on to create popular twentieth-century boys' books and series, among them Edward Stratemeyer (creator of Tom Swift, the Hardy Boys, and others), Harrie Irving Hancock, and James Otis Kaler.

Dime Novels

In June 1860 Erastus and Irwin Beadle published Beadle's Dime Novel number 1, *Malaeska: The Indian Wife of the White Hunter*, by Ann Stephens. Although inexpensive paperbound fiction had been available since the 1840s, the Beadles' success established the genre—a series of paper-covered, somewhat sensational novels published in a uniform format on a regular schedule and sold for ten cents. The first dime novels were small booklets of 64 to 128 pages; in the 1870s and after, the standard format was a 16-page quarto or 32-page octavo with lurid black-and-white cover illustrations. Like story papers, dime novels originally targeted an adult audience, albeit primarily male. Part of the Beadles' early success may be attributed to the Civil War market, for their books were a convenient size to carry, and the firm shipped thousands of dime novels to Union soldiers. As with story papers, the audience gradually changed. In 1877 the "nickel weeklies" (also considered dime novels), geared toward adolescent males,

Reading for the Masses. The epitome of popular fiction, *Beadle's Dime Novels*, begun by the Beadle brothers in 1860, was only one of twenty-five popular fiction series eventually published by Erastus Flavel Beadle and Robert Adams. LIBRARY OF CONGRESS: RARE BOOK AND SPECIAL COLLECTIONS DIVISION

appeared. By 1896, when Street and Smith began to issue Tip Top Library, the first successful series to utilize color illustrations on the cover, the audience consisted primarily of adolescents.

The earliest dime novels were predominantly Westerns and American historical adventures influenced by James Fenimore Cooper and Sir Walter Scott. Their plots blended frontier fights with romance and were filled with captures, escapes, and grand reunions. Often they starred disguised heroes who fused the earthiness of Cooper's Leatherstocking character with more genteel manners. The best-known dime novel protagonist was undoubtedly Edward Ellis's Seth Jones, the title character in Beadle's Dime Novel number 8 (1860), which ultimately sold about half a million copies. These stories often reflected the era's changing attitudes toward the wilderness and civilization, glorifying and mythologizing the open frontier, masculine adventure, and rugged individualism. As the dime novels' format evolved, so did the nature of the heroes: Edward L. Wheeler's Deadwood Dick, who first appeared in Beadle's Half-Dime Library in 1877, popularized the virtuous outlaw and the device of a recurring protagonist. The second wave of dime novel heroes, emerging in the 1880s, again reflected population shifts and topical cultural concerns. Urban detectives such as Old Sleuth and Nick Carter (the latter subsequently resurfacing in pulp magazines, radio dramas, and twentieth-century espionage fiction) often grappled with crimes paralleling those in current headlines. Like the Westerns, these stories played heavily on the detective's skill with disguises and his physical prowess. By the 1890s more boyish heroes prevailed. A few, like those in Upton Sinclair's pseudonymous *Army and Navy Weekly* stories (1897), were soldiers. More common were entrepreneurs and school and sports heroes such as Gilbert Patten's Frank Merriwell, who first appeared in Tip Top Library in 1896.

By 1915 the era of story papers and dime novels had ended, thanks to changing postal regulations; competition from magazines, pulps, and movies; and, perhaps, an audience seeking more sophisticated fare. In their time they helped to promote fiction for a mass audience. Subsequently they influenced such popular literary genres as detective fiction, Westerns, and science fiction.

See also **Alger, Horatio; Book Publishing; Literacy and Reading Habits; Literature,** *subentry on* **Fiction.**

Bibliography

Brown, Bill, ed. *Reading the West: An Anthology of Dime Westerns.* Boston: Bedford, 1997.

Cox, J. Randolph. "The Heyday of the Dime Novel." *Wilson Library Bulletin* 55 (1980): 262–266.

Johannsen, Albert. *The House of Beadle and Adams and Its Dime and Nickel Novels: The Story of a Vanished Literature.* 3 vols. Norman: University of Oklahoma Press, 1950–1962.

Noel, Mary. *Villains Galore: The Heyday of the Popular Story Weekly.* New York: Macmillan, 1954.

Sullivan, Larry E., and Lydia Cushman Schurman, eds. *Pioneers, Passionate Ladies, and Private Eyes: Dime Novels, Series Books, and Paperbacks.* New York: Haworth, 1996.

DEIDRE A. JOHNSON

DIPLOMATIC CORPS Throughout most of the nineteenth century, the U.S. diplomatic corps was characterized by a lack of professionalism and relatively unsuccessful attempts at reform. Unlike the massive diplomatic bureaucracy of the late twentieth century, the nineteenth-century Department of State was understaffed, underfunded, and viewed with suspicion by many citizens and government officials. Only in the 1850s, and again in the 1880s and 1890s, were serious efforts undertaken to professionalize the nation's diplomatic corps. These were met with limited success.

Diplomacy before the Civil War

In 1800 the Department of State employed a grand total of ten people. Twenty years later the number had increased to fifteen full-time employees, most of whom were secretaries and messengers. The position of assistant secretary of state and the geographical bureaus and divisions did not exist. The work of the department was left to the secretary of state and a handful of clerks. Not only was the department terribly understaffed, but at least in the early 1800s, it was also responsible for myriad duties completely unrelated to the nation's foreign policy, including issuing patents, handling copyright matters, and publishing the census figures.

Abroad, the United States was represented by only a handful of men. In 1800 the United States had permanent diplomatic representatives in just six nations—France, the Netherlands, Prussia, Great Britain, Spain, and Portugal. These few representatives were not ambassadors but ministers resident, envoys extraordinary, and ministers plenipotentiary. Not until 1893 was the first U.S. ambassador appointed. Since Congress passed no laws designating specific diplomatic offices, the United States was represented in other countries by a bewildering variety of titleholders, including chargés d'affaires, special ministers, and commissioners plenipotentiary. These early U.S. diplomatic missions were tiny affairs. A few of the most significant posts had a head of mission, a secretary, perhaps a few clerks, and, until they were abolished in 1856, an occasional attaché.

Like their colleagues in Washington, D.C., these foreign representatives were overworked. In addition to managing the day-to-day business of diplomacy, in many posts the head of mission had to serve as consul, dealing with commercial issues and handling complaints by U.S. citizens. Recognizing the burden this imposed on the missions, the U.S. government in the early nineteenth century began appointing more consuls to handle strictly commercial affairs. Indeed, as America's foreign trade blossomed, the number of consuls began to dwarf the number of U.S. diplomats. By 1830 U.S. diplomats were resident in only eighteen nations, whereas more than 150 consular officers served in 141 posts.

Diplomatic Personnel

It is not surprising that the U.S. diplomatic corps was a mixed bag. The pay was relatively low; diplomats received no training; the job had no requirements, such as language skills; and until the very late nineteenth century, no examinations for entrance into the diplomatic service existed. Few of the men who entered the service were looking for a career; considering their qualifications, this was perhaps fortunate. Most found their way into diplomatic work not because of their professional abilities or any pressing necessity for their services, but through the time-honored practice of patronage. Ministers and other heads of mission were likely to be discredited politicians seeking a respite from their troubles at home, longtime party supporters being repaid for their years of faithful service, or well-heeled contributors looking for a pleasant overseas stay. Secretaries, a necessary adjunct to the overworked heads of mission, also were often relatives or political patrons. Nearly two-fifths of the secretaries came from the same state as the head of mission, and in the early 1800s about one-fifth of them were relatives of the head of mission.

Attachés were perhaps the worst of the lot. No legal statutes provided for their appointment, but in an effort to alleviate the manpower shortages at various missions, U.S. presidents during the early 1800s allowed heads of mission to name, at their discretion, any number of unpaid attachés. Like secretaries, attachés were often relatives of the head of mission or the sons or nephews of political supporters who viewed the experience as an opportunity for a socially valuable overseas romp. Others were scholars, on leave from their institutions, who were more interested in conducting research than in helping to conduct the nation's diplomacy. Some were businessmen looking for foreign contacts.

Relying on patronage to fill the diplomatic ranks had another deleterious effect. Since officeholders (and, in the first half of the nineteenth century, political parties themselves) came and went, so, too, did the individuals they had appointed to various offices. For example, between 1800 and 1850 seventeen men served as head of the U.S. mission to France, seventeen served in Great Britain, and fourteen served in Spain. Of course, numerous changes in heads of mission have always been common when a new administration comes to power. The difference in the early 1800s, however, was that when the head of mission left, he took his staff with him, and no bureaucracy of trained professionals was ready to fill the void. Thus the next minister was free to bring in his flock of relatives and patrons. Since patronage ruled, hiring and promotion based on merit were unheard of.

It should be noted, however, that between 1800 and the Civil War some U.S. diplomatic representatives were sterling. Albert Gallatin and Richard Rush served as envoys extraordinary and ministers plenipotentiary to France; Charles Pinckney served in Spain; and four future presidents—James Monroe, John Quincy Adams, Martin Van Buren, and James Buchanan—served in Great Britain. These were the exceptions, however. As the list of representatives to Great Britain indicates, most looked upon their service as simply another step in their political careers.

Efforts at Reform

The sad state of America's diplomatic corps was the result of several factors. First of all, most U.S. citizens and many political leaders exhibited a general lack of interest in foreign affairs. Sectional differences, economic development, and continental expansion kept most Americans' minds focused on domestic matters. Political battles concerning diplomatic appointments and pay for those appointees between presidents and Congress also exacerbated the problems.

However, complaints about the performance of the diplomatic service and criticisms of the crass patronage that dominated the system increased, and as the United States more aggressively pushed into the international arena, efforts were undertaken to reform the diplomatic corps. Laws adopted in 1853, 1866, and 1874, intended to help the overworked secretary of state, established the offices of first, second, and third assistant secretaries of state. In 1856 a congressional act specified the titles and salaries, on a sliding scale, depending on the nation, of U.S. heads of missions. An important first step in promoting a more professional diplomatic corps, the act also provided for set salaries for secretaries and the appointment of additional secretaries to various posts, abolished the position of attaché, and fixed the salaries for consuls. Due to President Franklin Pierce's objections to any infringements on his powers of appointment, however, the bill merely permitted the president to make the specific appointments to the various nations enumerated in the act.

An overlooked section of the 1856 act gave the president the power to create regulations for the Department of State that he believed would best serve the public interest. In 1895 President Grover Cleveland, taking advantage of this clause, issued an order that future vacancies in higher positions in the consular service should be filled by individuals who passed an examination. Because individuals were appointed before the examination and only a tiny percentage failed to pass it, Cleveland's order was a very small change. Yet it was a significant one, as it set the stage for further professionalization of the diplomatic and consular services during the first quarter of the twentieth century and culminated in the Rogers Act of 1924, which established the basis for a fully professional foreign service.

By 1900 the U.S. diplomatic corps was just beginning to find its bureaucratic niche. Still a small department (just over two hundred employees by the time of World War I), it had struggled through years of overwork, understaffing, public and governmental apathy, inefficiency, debilitating excesses of patronage, and spotty efforts at reform. During the late nineteenth and early twentieth centuries, however, the Department of State began to professionalize in response to the needs of a nation and government developing significant relations with the rest of the world.

See also **Civil Service Reform; Foreign Relations.**

Bibliography

Etzold, Thomas H. *The Conduct of American Foreign Relations: The Other Side of Diplomacy.* New York: New Viewpoints, 1977.

Ilchman, Warren Frederick. *Professional Diplomacy in the United States, 1779–1939.* Chicago: University of Chicago Press, 1961.

Stuart, Graham H. *American Diplomatic and Consular Practice.* 2d ed. New York: Appleton-Century-Crofts, 1952.

Werking, Richard H. *The Master Architects: Building the United States Foreign Service, 1890–1913.* Lexington: University Press of Kentucky, 1977.

MICHAEL L. KRENN

DISASTERS Viewed from the twenty-first century, the natural and technological disasters of the nineteenth century—epidemics, transportation accidents, and catastrophic disturbances in weather and climate—may seem similar in form to such contemporary problems as computer viruses, spacecraft explosions, and global warming, but they are nonetheless different in their scope, their causes, and the ways in which society recovered from them. Understanding the causes and effects of these disasters, all associated with large loss of life or property, provides insight into the hopes and fears of nineteenth-century Americans as well as the changing dangers and risks of their everyday lives.

Disasters as Social Constructions

Often perceived as beyond human control, most disasters have a complex etiology. They occur at the intersection of natural or technological circumstances and a mode of human social organization. For instance, prolonged drought, heavy rains, severe thunderstorms, earthquakes, and hurricanes can be catastrophic, but these events do not become disasters until they interact with human society. Hurricanes have always swept the eastern seaboard of the United States, but they became increasingly disastrous as the Southeast grew more populous. Outside of that region, hurricanes remained largely outside the popular consciousness and even went without formal names until the twentieth century. Likewise, during the nineteenth century, new technologies, such as railroads and steamboats, created new risks to people and property. These technologies promised to make travel and commercial transport more rapid, and they heralded a new era of economic and social life. However, the degree to which these technologies affected society deleteriously was determined by their everyday use and the broader social practices surrounding them. For instance, steam boiler explosions were a common occurrence in the nineteenth century, but it was not until steamboats became a standard form of transportation that such explosions became disasters, occurring on vessels crowded with travelers or holiday revelers.

Based on real events, disasters are also social constructions whose impact and value are determined by social, economic, political, and cultural factors. The forces that transformed the Great Chicago Fire into an icon of nineteenth-century disaster all but erased popular memories of the blaze known as the Peshtigo Fire, which swept the lumber regions of northern Wisconsin on the same evening in 1871. In human terms, the death toll at Peshtigo—over one thousand people died—outweighed that of Chicago. Even in scope of damage, Peshtigo was more severe, with over twenty-four hundred square miles burned. However, in the language and memory of America's expansionist capitalist culture, the Chicago fire was a more significant event. Chicago symbolized the expansion and promise of American capitalism in the nineteenth century. The destruction of the city by fire threatened the future of that dream and of the nation. As Chicago rebuilt itself, it cast itself as a phoenix rising from the ashes, symbolizing the triumph of the nascent capitalist order over nature itself. Chicago's battle against and triumph over disaster captured the nation's imagination, revealing that disaster is not only about what actually happened, but also about how society construes the event.

Fire may well have been the most feared and common disaster in nineteenth-century America. Countless American cities burned in the years prior to the Civil War; fires in the nation's principal cities destroyed nearly $200 million in property before the 1860s. Sweeping conflagrations continued to erupt through the last three decades of the nineteenth century and into the early twentieth century. Portland,

Maine, burned in 1866, Chicago in 1871, Boston in 1872, and Baltimore in 1904. Although the causes of disastrous fires grew more complex over the course of the century, each conflagration remained the product of society interacting with nature. For instance, during the summer of 1871 it was a severe drought that initially created the conditions for fire in the upper Midwest. The forests surrounding Peshtigo, Wisconsin, became tinderboxes, and in Chicago—with its five hundred miles of wood sidewalks and thousands of wood dwellings—the risk of fire grew tremendously. In fact, during this period, the city's fire department grew fatigued from battling hundreds of small fires. Then disaster struck. As a line of thunderstorms, with hundreds of lightning strikes, ignited hundreds of square miles of Wisconsin forest, a cow in Chicago reputedly tipped over a lantern, setting a blaze that high winds whipped into a conflagration. Had the timberlands of upper Wisconsin been unpopulated, few would have known of the sweeping damage. Similarly, had Chicago not been weakened by drought, its fire might have not have become so devastasting. In both instances, nature and human social organization conspired to produce cataclysm.

Catastrophic floods and disease also affected the United States during the nineteenth century. Disease was particularly troublesome in the marshy lowlands along rivers and coastlines and in expanding urban centers without well-developed health and sanitation infrastructures. Outbreaks of disease could even affect the history and culture of a city or region, especially in the American South. For instance, Memphis, Tennessee, located on the banks of the Mississippi River, suffered greatly at the hands of disease from the 1820s through the century. After the city experienced tremendous population growth following the Civil War, it became subject to a series of severe epidemics. In 1873 alone, yellow fever, cholera, and smallpox struck, claiming over two thousand lives. In 1878 and 1879, yellow fever returned; over twenty thousand cases were reported and approximately six thousand people died. The disease so disrupted the town that most of its population fled, leaving the city virtually abandoned. The state of Tennessee even repealed the city's charter until the 1880s.

Of course, disease did not threaten just the American South. Many diseases, such as cholera, were in fact global contagions, spread by the heightened scope and intensity of economic connections and population migrations throughout the world. Indeed, before 1812 cholera does not appear to have extended beyond Asia, but it spread rapidly in the nineteenth century, with three especially virulent outbreaks in the United States in 1832, 1849, and 1866. Other diseases were also pandemic throughout North America

during the century, as repeated outbreaks of yellow fever, smallpox, and typhus attest. The spread of disease was aided by an improving transportation network, with rivers, railroads, and roads serving as conduits. Over eight thousand people died from yellow fever in New Orleans during 1853, and in 1854, approximately 2 percent of Chicago's population died of cholera. And much of the eastern seaboard and the South faced recurring epidemics of influenza and smallpox in the decade following the Civil War. In Chicago, tuberculosis caused as many as four thousand deaths per year in the 1890s. Rapid population growth, poor sanitation, and a population weakened by migration, hunger, or other social and economic stresses made Americans susceptible to such disasters, which only began to diminish as public health programs developed and urban sanitation systems improved following the Civil War.

By contrast, natural phenomena such as hurricanes and earthquakes remained largely outside the public's awareness unless they affected great numbers of people. Hurricanes did regularly sweep the eastern seaboard, killing people and destroying property. For instance, the South Carolina coast experienced such storms at regular intervals in every decade of the nineteenth century. The 1880s were especially difficult for Charleston, which experienced one of its worst hurricanes of the century—over twenty-one people died and nearly every home in the city was damaged—and one of the most severe earthquakes ever to hit the United States. Possibly the largest quake ever to strike the eastern United States, it caused as much destruction to Charleston as devastating fires had in 1838 and 1861. Earthquakes in populated areas, however, were the exception in the nineteenth century, before the American population had moved west to a region more prone to such disasters. Even when earthquakes did occur, like so many other disasters they only entered the historical record when they affected large numbers of whites. For instance, a devastating earthquake measuring an estimated 8.0 on the Richter scale occurred in New Madrid, Missouri, in 1811, but because it affected few European settlers, the event barely registered in the national consciousness. The Pacific coast of North America also suffered frequent tremors, but the area lacked a large population of European descent and the quakes were therefore not written very deeply into the consciousness of nineteenth-century Americans.

Although floods and tornadoes affected relatively few Americans until late in the century, disasters involving these phenomena became increasingly common. As the population began to move west more rapidly and as more Americans settled into flood-

The Johnstown, Pennsylvania, Flood. A natural disaster wreaks havoc on the warehouse of an iron works and railroad car. Langill and Darling, 1889. LIBRARY OF CONGRESS

plains, the possibility of a cyclical natural event becoming a disaster increased dramatically. In Johnstown, Pennsylvania, flooding occurred with great regularity, and residents became accustomed to wading through knee-deep water on downtown streets following heavy spring and fall rains. However, a variety of circumstances set off by social forces conspired to create a disastrous flood in 1889. Rapid population growth sent more of the town sprawling along the Conemaugh river, and deforestation along the river's banks allowed greater amounts of water to run off more rapidly. Meanwhile, shoddy workmanship on an old dam high above the city—built by wealthy Pittsburgh industrialists to create an exclusive social club that would allow its members to take a "cure" in the Alleghenies—set the stage for devastating flooding. In the wake of unusually heavy rains, the dam burst, and Johnstown was virtually destroyed. Similarly, tornadoes were a frequent occurrence across the American Midwest and Southeast but only became a cause of disaster as the population in those regions expanded. By the 1880s, tornadoes

had become a common enough occurrence in populated regions that the insurance industry considered offering separate policies to protect against tornado damage to homes.

Recovery and Rebuilding

Before the twentieth century, victims of disaster could not turn to a powerful federal government to subsidize relief and rebuilding. Stricken populations had to rely on the largess of their fellow Americans from across the nation. After the Johnstown Flood, for instance, hundreds of thousands of dollars poured into the city from individuals, municipal governments, and state governments across the nation, and even from abroad. More often than not, local governments and private charities organized and administered disaster relief to cities such as Johnstown or Chicago. The disaster relief arms of private relief organizations and charities such as the Red Cross became prominent only in the twentieth century. Nor could disaster victims turn to private insurance to help them recover after events such as floods and tornadoes because insurance for these types of events was not commonly available during the nineteenth century. Even in the case of fire, relief from insurance policies was not a certainty. Policies rarely covered a property's full value, and the fire insurance industry remained highly unstable into the twentieth century. Not only did paying claims after conflagrations leave many insurers bankrupt, but insurance coverage in general was not very reliable. In fact, over eight hundred fire insurance companies failed in the thirty years after the Civil War.

Reactions to disasters—from newspaper coverage to the actual dispensation of aid—reflected ethnic and class biases deeply buried in nineteenth-century American life. Through the voluminous print coverage following disasters, Americans sought to understand catastrophes and their causes in terms familiar to themselves. Immediately following disastrous events, the popular press produced huge numbers of sensational stories for ready audiences. These stories used language that mirrored broader economic, political, ethnic, and religious beliefs held by Americans, especially middle-class readers of newspapers and popular books. The stories and images transformed immigrant, working-class, and poor victims of disaster into pernicious threats to restoring order after the event. For instance, images produced shortly after the Johnstown Flood depicted Hungarians as "hooknosed" thieves, stealing jewelry from victims and threatening the restoration of order in the town. Although Hungarians accounted for less than 2 percent of Johnstown's population, such images reflected widespread attitudes about the continued influx of new immigrants to the United States. Immediately following other disasters, too, press reportage took on the patina of whatever intolerance was popular in the particular locale or region in which the disaster occurred. Even the provision of relief and recovery from disaster often broke down along ethnic and class lines, as Americans attempted to reassemble their fragmented social order and broken power structures. In Chicago, following the 1871 fire, the local government determined eligibility for relief with the aid of the local elite and the middle class. The General Relief Committee offered relief to those most "worthy," distinctions based upon class, ethnicity, and gender. Skilled workers, churchgoing middle-class residents, and men were far more likely to receive aid than unskilled workers, women, or recent immigrants. Taken together, efforts to restore order after disasters reflected the deep divisions and inequalities of class, race, gender, and ethnicity that saturated American life.

Technological Disasters

As industrialization created a new social order and landscape during the nineteenth century, new types of disasters began to appear. Tied to the technologies of transportation and industry that were transforming America, such technological failures became an increasing part of America's daily experience. As the scale of industry rose and as the number of workers in sweatshops, mills, factories, and mines increased, devastating industrial disasters became more likely. Perhaps most clearly represented in the nineteenth century through accidents on steamboats and railroads, technological disasters reflected the nation's growing reliance on mass transportation, with all of its inherent dangers.

Steamboat disasters illustrate the complex ways in which new technologies generated danger even as they created new opportunities. The steamboats described so eloquently by Mark Twain in his *Life on the Mississippi* became a reality on the lower Mississippi in the second decade of the nineteenth century. New Orleans, which had approximately twenty steamboat arrivals in 1814, had over twelve hundred arrivals every year by the 1830s. Through the 1870s, it and other cities along the Mississippi and Ohio River systems benefited from the economic and commercial dominance of steamboats. Steamboats also became common modes of transportation and luxury, outfitted as ornate hotels with rich decor, fabulous food, large service staffs, and entertainment. With the rise of steamboats as a commercial force came a new type of disaster heretofore not experienced in American society. Over four thousand Americans died in the first half of the nineteenth century from accidents on steamboats—ships whose average life spanned less than five years. The causes included unsafe construction, boiler explosions, navigational errors, changing river channels, and underwater snags. And, even though safety on these boats was of great popular concern, captains and crews frequently increased the risks associated with steamboat travel by engaging in dangerous races, on which passengers sometimes laid bets. After the 1850s, steamboat disasters began to decrease as a result of government regulations on steam boilers and racing. These disasters did not, however, lessen significantly until the railroad supplanted the steamboat as a mode of commercial and passenger transportation—once again altering the location and possibilities for disaster in American society.

Over the course of the nineteenth century, through their confrontations with the environment and more intensive use of technology, Americans became sus-

Boston Fire. The rubble left behind by fires and explosions in Boston, 1897. LIBRARY OF CONGRESS

ceptible to large-scale disasters for the first time. Especially in the last years of the nineteenth century, population expansion, technological change, and urbanization helped to create a landscape in which disasters became increasingly real to Americans. The geographical possibilities of disaster expanded as the population spread across the Midwest and into the West and South. In these new regions, regularly subject to flooding, tornadoes, hurricanes, and earthquakes, new settlement created a potentiality for crisis, and these possibilities were transformed into realities more and more often. The events of 1900 and 1906, to some degree, heralded the future; in 1900 a hurricane all but obliterated Galveston, Texas, and in 1906 an earthquake and fire destroyed San Francisco. Interestingly, about this same time, some old dangers, such as the threat of conflagration, began to diminish in a wave of strict building laws and more effective firefighting. Epidemics also became less threatening to most Americans during the twentieth century as sanitation improved. Ironically, even as Americans addressed the root causes of certain disasters, they created conditions that encouraged others. Moreover, to the degree that large-scale disasters plagued Americans during the nineteenth century,

these were not random events, but consequences of the world that Americans had constructed for themselves.

See also **Fires and Firefighting; Health and Disease; Steam Power; Travel, Technology of.**

Bibliography

Bloom, Khaled J. *The Mississippi Valley's Great Yellow Fever Epidemic of 1878.* Baton Rouge: Louisiana State University Press, 1993.

Howland, S. A. *Steamboat Disasters and Railroad Accidents in the United States: To Which Are Appended Accounts of Recent Shipwrecks, Fires at Sea, Thrilling Incidents, etc.* Worcester, Mass.: Warren Lazell, 1846.

McCullough, David G. *The Johnstown Flood: The Incredible Story behind One of the Most Devastating "Natural" Disasters America Has Ever Known.* New York: Simon and Schuster, 1968.

Smith, Carl. *Urban Disorder and the Shape of Belief: The Great Chicago Fire, the Haymarket Bomb, and the Model Town of Pullman.* Chicago: University of Chicago Press, 1995.

Steinberg Ted. *Acts of God: The Unnatural History of Natural Disasters.* New York: Oxford University Press, 2000.

MARK TEBEAU

DISEASE   See **Health and Disease.**

DISTRICT OF COLUMBIA   See **Washington, D.C.**

DIVORCE AND DESERTION   The nineteenth century witnessed a significant increase in numbers and availability of divorce in the United States. Native Americans had long practiced divorce, but divorce among whites first appeared in 1639, when a Massachusetts judge granted the first decree in the American colonies. By the mid-1800s every state except South Carolina offered some form of divorce to its white citizens.

Rationales for Divorce

The Anglo-American concept of divorce arrived with the Puritans, who viewed marriage as a civil contract rather than a religious sacrament. To void a marriage contract, one party had to demonstrate to the satisfaction of a court or a legislature the fault of the other party in causing a breach in the agreement. It was to a woman's advantage to be the plaintiff. If a wife could show that her husband caused the marital breakdown, she would not have to forfeit the financial support he had pledged at the time of their wedding. If a wife was at fault, however, she lost all claim to her former husband's earnings and estate.

The American Revolution (1776–1783) added a new twist to white ideas regarding divorce. Public ideals concerning liberty and happiness seemed to apply to individuals. The author of the Declaration of Independence, Thomas Jefferson, argued that divorce provided "liberty" and cured "domestic quarrels" and that it restored women to "their natural right of equality" (Dewey, "Thomas Jefferson's Notes on Divorce," pp. 216–219). In the 1800s divorce-seekers increasingly used such terms in their petitions as "tyranny," "misrule," "injustice," and "happiness of the individual."

Growth of Divorce and Desertion

The years between 1800 and the early 1850s constituted a growth period for the institution of divorce. Although most white men and women believed in marriage as a lifetime agreement, they recognized the necessity of ending some dysfunctional marriages through divorce. Because each colony had handled marriage and divorce, each state had the right to regulate the marital status of its citizens, including formulating its own divorce policies.

Some states offered divorce through the courts, others through legislatures, and a few followed a dual system in which either body could grant divorces. Each state also established its own list of grounds. Throughout the 1800s New York remained the most conservative state, allowing divorce only in cases of adultery. Other states gradually expanded grounds to include desertion, nonsupport, bigamy, impotence, and the catch-all category of cruelty, or "indignities" as it was commonly known.

In the Northeast—the former New England and middle colonies—two important trends emerged. One was a move to end legislative divorce. Legislators complained that they were overwhelmed with divorce cases that kept them from dealing with other important matters. Pennsylvania's 1838 constitution banned legislative divorce, and an 1849 law did so in Connecticut.

The second pattern was a steady expansion of each state's list of grounds based on the growing belief that divorce was a citizen's right in a democratic nation. Some states even added an omnibus clause, under which a divorce-seeker only had to prove to the court's satisfaction some evidence of marital breakdown. Of the northeastern states, Connecticut had the most comprehensive slate of provisions. In 1843 legislators added habitual intemperance and intolerable cruelty to an already generous list. In 1849 they appended life imprisonment, committing an infamous crime, and any act of "misconduct" that destroyed the "happiness" of the other spouse (Blake, *The Road to Reno*, pp. 60–61).

In the South similar trends developed but more slowly. North Carolina prohibited legislative divorce in 1835, Georgia in 1849, and Virginia in 1850. Southern states also expanded grounds for divorce. During the early 1800s Virginia accepted as causes adultery, physical abuse, and abandonment. In 1841 the general assembly adopted impotency, idiocy, and any cause for which marriage is "annulled by ecclesiastical law" (*Acts of the General Assembly of Virginia, 1840–1841*, Richmond, Va.: Division of Purchase and Printing, 1841, p. 79). In 1850 legislators added confinement in a penitentiary, conviction of an infamous offense prior to marriage, pregnancy of the wife at the time of the marriage by a person other than the husband, and the wife working as a prostitute prior to the marriage without the knowledge of the husband.

As the rapidly expanding population of the American Republic migrated across the Appalachian Mountains, divorce took on added flexibility. Iowa Territory, established in 1838, specified impotence and adultery as reasons for divorce. In 1842–1843 Iowa's Revised Statutes listed eight grounds, and in 1845 an amendment added an omnibus clause. In a particularly western innovation, territories and states handled the glut of divorce requests by divorcing more than one couple at a time. In 1825 Illinois parted two couples in one bill of divorcement. In 1842 the Iowa territorial legislature reportedly divorced eighteen couples at once.

Scores of other men and women chose not to pursue legal divorces. Instead, they deserted their mates. Newspaper notices regarding "runaway" spouses show that many people simply left their marriages behind them. In addition police "wanted" posters indicate that desertion was not limited to men; a significant number of women also disappeared. The very nature of desertion makes its occurrence difficult to assess. Although desertions only entered the formal record when cited in divorce petitions, other evidence suggests that the phenomenon was widespread. Moreover statistics collected late in the century revealed that desertion was the most common ground employed by divorce-seekers.

Opposition and Support

A large number of Americans opposed divorce. Ministers spoke against divorce from their pulpits, newspaper publishers editorialized against it, and numerous men and women shunned a relative or former friend who had divorced. Divorce was especially hard on women, who had been economically dependent on husbands, often lost custody of their children, and frequently experienced friends and neighbors turning against them. Some divorced women retreated into the homes of their parents or siblings, while others left for another vicinity.

Divorce also had its supporters. The utopian reformer Robert Dale Owen, who in 1825 founded the community of New Harmony, Indiana, spoke on behalf of divorce. Owen chose 4 July 1826, Independence Day, to declare that no one should be forced to remain in a distressing marriage. Two years later the free-love advocate Frances Wright revealed that marriage and thus divorce did not exist within her utopian community Nashoba, Tennessee. Wright hoped that this radical approach would maintain women's independence and rights.

Later the woman's rights advocate Elizabeth Cady Stanton added her voice to the escalating debate. Stanton and other woman's rights leaders, such as Jane Swisshelm and Ernestine Rose, believed that divorce provided an escape route that was as important to mistreated wives as the Underground Railroad was to black slaves. In 1860 Stanton publicly ridiculed the idea of indissolvable marriages and mocked the crusading editor Horace Greeley, who opposed divorce.

Unshaken by Stanton's words, Greeley continued his antidivorce campaign in the pages of the *New York Tribune*. Also in 1860 Greeley attacked Indiana's lenient statutes and sloppy procedures, branding the Hoosier State a place where people could "get unmarried nearly at pleasure" (*New York Tribune*, 18 December 1860). Greeley also claimed that divorce-seekers from such strict states as New York went to Indiana to obtain easy divorces.

This practice, called migratory divorce, caused a major problem for many states. According to the Constitution of the United States, each state had to give "full faith and credit" to the laws and judicial proceedings of any other. Theoretically a person's home state had to accept a divorce granted elsewhere. A number of inconclusive test cases appeared in state courts. In South Carolina the courts flatly refused to recognize divorces granted in other states.

In the meantime the practice of migratory divorce grew. After Indiana shed the "divorce mill" label by tightening its laws, other western states gained national prominence. During the 1870s and 1880s Utah had a reputation as a divorce mill. By the late 1880s and early 1890s attention shifted to Sioux Falls, South Dakota; Fargo, North Dakota; and Guthrie, Oklahoma Territory. Under public pressure, these jurisdictions revised their liberal codes and thus stepped out of the public limelight.

Not surprisingly the divorce mill scandal alarmed

Divorces in the United States, 1887–1906

	Total Divorces		Women's Divorces		Men's Divorces	
Adultery	153,759	16.3%	62,869	10.0%	90,890	28.7%
Cruelty	206,225	21.8%	173,047	27.5%	33,178	10.5%
Desertion	367,502	38.9%	211,219	33.6%	156,283	49.4%
Drunkenness	36,516	3.9%	33,080	5.3%	3,436	1.1%
Neglect to provide	34,670	3.7%	34,664	5.5%	6	*

(U.S. Department of Commerce and Labor, *Marriage and Divorce, 1867–1906*, pp. 11–13, 22–24)

* less than .1%

many Americans. White couples, especially of the lower classes, divorced in record numbers, and after the Civil War both Native American and African American petitioners appeared in courts seeking "legal" divorces. If divorce-seekers were thwarted in their own states, they temporarily migrated to other, more permissive states, usually located in the West.

On 28 July 1879, Greeley proclaimed in the *New York Tribune* that "truly the land needs a reform." Supporters of the National Divorce Reform League, headed by Samuel W. Dike, a Congregational minister from Vermont, agreed with Greeley. Organized in 1881, the league hoped to halt migratory divorce and to convince individual states to adopt a national uniform divorce code.

Both goals proved elusive. In 1900 the problem of migratory divorce remained unresolved by state or federal courts. In addition states demonstrated little willingness to hammer out a uniform divorce policy. Rather, statistics indicated that the U.S. divorce rate was one divorce to every fourteen or fifteen marriages. Women obtained about two-thirds of these divorces, and desertion remained the most popular ground. Apparently the Victorian emphasis on romance, hearts, and flowers did not always lead to lasting relationships.

See also **Domestic Life; Gender,** *subentry on* **Gender and the Law; Marriage; Sexual Morality; Women,** *subentry on* **Women's Rights.**

Bibliography

Blake, Nelson Manfred. *The Road to Reno: A History of Divorce in the United States.* New York: Macmillan, 1962.

Degler, Carl N. *At Odds: Women and the Family in America from the Revolution to the Present.* New York: Oxford University Press, 1980.

Dewey, Frank L. "Thomas Jefferson's Notes on Divorce." *William and Mary Quarterly,* 3d ser., 39 (1982): 216–223.

Grossberg, Michael. *Governing the Hearth: Law and the Family in Nineteenth-Century America.* Chapel Hill: University of North Carolina Press, 1985.

Lystra, Karen. *Searching the Heart: Women, Men, and Romantic Love in Nineteenth-Century America.* New York: Oxford University Press, 1989.

Mintz, Steven. *A Prison of Expectations: The Family in Victorian Culture.* New York: New York University Press, 1983.

O'Neill, William L. *Divorce in the Progressive Era.* New Haven, Conn.: Yale University Press, 1967.

Phillips, Roderick. *Putting Asunder: A History of Divorce in Western Society.* Cambridge, U.K.: Cambridge University Press, 1988.

Riley, Glenda. *Divorce: An American Tradition.* New York: Oxford University Press, 1991.

U.S. Department of Commerce and Labor, Bureau of the Census. *Marriage and Divorce, 1867–1906.* Reprint ed. Volume 1. Westport, Conn.: Greenwood, 1978.

GLENDA RILEY

DOMESTIC LIFE Domestic life changed more rapidly in the nineteenth century than in any previous one-hundred-year interval. American women, for example, began the century cooking over open hearths, and most ended it cooking on stoves. During the course of the century tens of thousands of women began using a machine to sew, lightening the labor of making clothes for themselves and their daughters. Their husbands and sons were probably already wearing ready-made clothing. Moreover, at the World's Columbian Exposition in Chicago in 1893 a display featured a number of appliances that became familiar parts of American households over the next several decades, such as electric pans and irons. Whether or not these technological changes genuinely eased the lives of housewives is subject to debate. Some have argued, for example, that standards of cleanliness rose with improved technology and created more work for women. Incontestably the extent of the change in the material underpinnings of domestic life can only be called dazzling. In addition to dramatic changes in material culture, family size decreased, as did household size, and the patterns of household authority altered significantly.

The Home and the Market

Fundamental to an understanding of the transformation in domestic life is a grasp of the evolving relationship between the home and the market. As the nineteenth century began American homes were virtually self-sufficient units in which household members produced much or most of what they consumed. By the century's end the situation had changed almost entirely, that is, people purchased most of what they consumed. Especially in middle- and upper-class homes, women bought a variety of products, such as soap, baking powder, and canned goods, that became available over the course of the century. Indeed the triumph of nationally advertised brand names was inevitable as new modes of transportation moved goods around the country.

Predictably people living in villages or on small farms who lacked access to good transportation were unlikely to become intertwined with the market. Steamboats, canals, railroads, and increasing urbanization stimulated many changes in domestic life during the nineteenth century. Starting early in the century, improved transportation led to regional specialization in cash crops or in market-driven manufactures. Regional specialization in turn meant that over the decades fewer people lived on subsistence farms or engaged in a barter economy. Instead, many of the men and some of the women found market-oriented employment, bringing home money with which to make purchases. People with money and improved transportation constituted powerful incentives to capitalists to develop goods to meet the inchoate demand. For example, by the 1890s housewives in the East could serve canned fruit that came to their tables from California.

New goods, many designed for domestic consumption, curtailed the traditional functions performed in the home. The locus of spinning, brewing, soap production, and intensive clothing manufacture metamorphosed into the locus of meal preparation and "housework" but very little else in the way of production. The socialization of children remained a constant role of the home. Not surprisingly, the physical shape of the home changed accordingly as the need for space dedicated to production shrank. Moreover, the reduced average number of people living in a household reshaped the character of domestic space.

Household Composition

In 1800 the average white married woman gave birth to 7.04 children; in 1900 she gave birth to 3.56 children. Each decade throughout the century saw a decline in family size. Non-Anglo families became smaller, too, although not at the same rate as Anglo families.

As family sizes decreased, so did household sizes, including both kin and non-kin residents. In 1800 tens of thousands of households, even in northern states, included domestic slaves. In 1800 bonded servitude, while less onerous than slavery, also limited the freedom of many people. In that institution a man or woman servant was under a contract of indenture for a specified period of time, usually somewhere between four and seven years. During the term of the contract he or she was neither paid nor free to leave. Like slavery, indentured servitude perished during the nineteenth century. Other non-kin household members in 1800 might include apprentices, if the family had a master craftsperson, or a large staff of servants. In addition, by the century's end young people of both genders were much likelier to be living alone or in small groups of the same gender.

The ethnic composition of American households was more complicated. When slavery was legal, the presence of one or more domestic slaves made many households ethnically diverse. By the time slavery ended mass immigration was bringing to American shores Irish Catholics and other groups culturally different from the Protestant Anglo majority. Many young immigrant women worked as domestic servants. Therefore, throughout the century a substantial portion of American households developed superordinate-subordinate social relationships characterized by great cultural distances and status differentials between mistresses and servants or slaves.

The shrinking size of the household and the loss of many household functions combined to increase the value of privacy. "A room of one's own" was not possible when households contained eight or ten children, an abundance of servants if the family was middle class, and possibly a sprinkling of apprentices. In *Oldtown Folks* (1869) Harriet Beecher Stowe vividly depicted early-nineteenth-century domestic life and its lack of privacy. Drawing on memories of her own girlhood in New England, where she was born in 1811, Stowe described a household in a small farming community. The orphaned narrator's grandparents raise him. Grandmother Badger is a formidable woman, a highly competent housewife, a reader, and a deep thinker about the finer points of theology. Most memorable is Grandmother Badger presiding over a huge kitchen into which wander an astonishing variety of people. Folks seeking shelter from bad weather, looking for gossip, or transacting business encounter the kitchen's welcoming embrace. They find a huge hearth, a crackling fire, and a convivial assemblage of other folks, including Native Americans, African Americans, and the Anglo oldtowners. Although Stowe could be patronizing about people of color, she described a remarkably open and flexible domestic environment that was virtually inconceivable by the century's end.

Domestic Authority and Domestic Values

Father was the preponderant moral and legal authority in 1800. In one of the most dramatic changes in the culture during the century, mother replaced him as the moral authority, and his legal authority diminished.

A number of scholars have grappled with explanations for this transition. It seems key that American culture, influenced by the powerful currents of romanticism, exalted the woman-centered emotional realm as never before. Feminist scholars have used the term "sentimental power" to characterize the resulting veneration of home and mother. Indeed home and mother were deemed so sacred that they were almost coequal with the cross as symbols of Christian redemption in the writings of the important Protestant theologian Horace Bushnell. In *The Empire of the Mother over the Character and Destiny of the Race* (1863), Henry Clarke Wright, another widely read male author, urged men to yield to a mother's influence in the domestic domain. To grant this much moral authority to women was unprecedented.

Anomalously the legal system treated women woefully. They had no control over property, even that

A Nineteenth-Century Kitchen. At the end of the century, progress is indicated by the indoor plumbing, but coal stoves were still a common feature. Illustration from *Harper's New Monthly Magazine,* October 1896, p. 725. LIBRARY OF CONGRESS: PRINTS AND PHOTOGRAPHS DIVISION

in their own names, and they lost custody of their children in the unlikely event of a divorce. That dissonance between an exalted ideal and the relatively powerless reality—along with the growing market economy's need to become unfettered by archaic laws—encouraged reforms that slowly gave married women some control over their own property. Between the late 1830s and the 1860s the states began to enact favorable property legislation. Reforms in divorce laws that resolved custody issues in favor of the mother did not take place until the end of the century or later.

Women deployed their new sentimental power in many ways both within and outside the home. Politically they launched a number of reforms that humanized American society in the name of their motherhood. As they used their sentimental power within the home, the birthrate dropped dramatically. Enjoined to revere their wives, husbands evidently acquiesced to requests for less-frequent marital sex to limit the family size. Women also employed their new moral authority in attempts to control male drinking behavior.

Scholars have used the term "companionate marriage" to characterize the newly democratic form of family life that emerged. Based less on patriarchal authority and more on affection, it featured intensified emotional bonds between parents and children—especially between mothers and children—and between husbands and wives. Nevertheless, scholars studying intrafamily decision making have found that fathers continued to exercise a disproportionate share of clout in large questions, such as whether or not to move west. Mothers' influence did not translate into across-the-board power. The home was contested terrain, where all residents contended for a voice and presumably loved one another. In the nineteenth century women did not become fully equal partners within the home, but they could draw on new sources of strength to advance their interests.

Among the most valuable sources documenting the new prestige for home and mother are the so-called "domestic novels" that flourished between 1830 and 1870. During those decades women writers, the greatest of whom was Stowe, wrote widely circulated and much-loved novels featuring highly competent and morally authoritative housewives, a "type" that was appearing in American letters for the first time.

The Home as a Center of Activities

In the nineteenth century people, especially men, worked less at home and more in offices and factories than previously. But everybody, men, women, and children, sought recreation in home-based activities, such as quilting bees, parlor games, musical evenings, and reading aloud. Holidays offered particularly gratifying opportunities for special food and ritualized activities. In the absence of the distractions afforded by movies, video arcades, organized sports leagues, and motor vehicles, home commanded both the time and the allegiance of its residents, even young people, when it came to having fun.

Home also was an important venue for the display of female prowess in cooking, sewing, and fancy needlework. As the range of home-centered production activities dwindled, middle-class women devoted considerable creative energy to the work that remained, investing it with more ornamental and ceremonial value. In earlier centuries elite women had spent time plying their needles to create beautiful pieces of embroidery and crewelwork, for example. Non-elite women had relatively less time for such aesthetic pursuits because they had to devote more time to practical necessities. During the nineteenth century countless women had time to spend on their beautiful handiwork.

One of the most important home activities always has been the socialization of children. However, during the nineteenth century the nature of childhood socialization changed in a number of ways. First, neither boys nor girls received much apprenticeship training for adult employment at home. Schools and workplaces took over such training for boys. For girls the sheer number of productive tasks to master dwindled, consequently the amount of information to impart concomitantly dwindled. Second, with family size shrinking, individual children commanded more intense attention from their mothers. Investing relatively more time per child, morally authoritative mothers were expected to inculcate patriotic values as well as religious ones.

Variations on a Theme

No American archetype of home or domestic life existed. Domestic life exhibited profound differences based on whether families lived on farms or in cities. On farms domestic life changed less and retained more production activities than in the cities. Class also played a huge role in determining how much time a woman devoted to the aesthetic, the extent of new technology in any given household, how many servants if any the family employed, the family's diet, and the amount of recreation time.

Certain households maintained comfortable and comforting domestic environments only through the heroic efforts of women, and maybe not even then. Slaves who did not live in the big house, for example, occupied cramped, primitive quarters that women brightened as best they could. Slave women made patchwork quilts for their own families, no doubt piecing together the necessary time in their overburdened lives as painstakingly as they pieced the quilts. Women living in the raw, new settlements of westward expansion made homes in sod houses, in leantos, and sometimes in covered wagons. Stories tell of women's despair when they first saw such homes, yet they almost invariably coped. Women immigrants were pioneers who often inhabited noisome tenements in big cities, where they made enormous adjustments to unfamiliar domestic settings.

Some households lacked a woman's touch. New settlements dedicated to mining rather than farming, as in California during the gold rush, contained few women and few homes recognizable in the East. This situation was usually temporary, though. More lasting was the dislocation among certain groups of immigrants with disproportionately male compositions, sometimes by their own choice of who immigrated and sometimes as a result of U.S. immigration policy. In these cases the immigrants, who could not form households based on the nuclear family, frequently lived in boardinghouses, occasionally for many years.

Domestic life showed powerful regional differences, among them southern households during slavery and California mining camps during the gold rush. In harvest season on midwestern farms a housewife and her daughters cooked for their own kin and for the temporary crew, all breaking bread together.

Even though production departed from the home, enough activities remained and the prestige of home was sufficiently high that in the nineteenth century the home was far more than the "haven" of the twentieth century. Home was a bulwark of the culture and a battering ram for benevolent social purposes in the hands of its votaries. In consequence domestic life had the quality of a secular sacrament. Many housewives, along with hard work and circumscribed lives, drew strength from this.

See also **Birth and Childbearing; Class, Social; Divorce and Desertion; Food; Gender; Home; Housing; Mar-**

riage; **Republican Motherhood; Transportation; Women; Work.**

Bibliography

Boydston, Jeanne. *Home and Work: Housework, Wages, and the Ideology of Labor in the Early Republic.* New York: Oxford University Press, 1990.

Clark, Christopher. *The Roots of Rural Capitalism: Western Massachusetts, 1780–1860.* Ithaca, N.Y.: Cornell University Press, 1990.

Cott, Nancy F. *The Bonds of Womanhood: "Woman's Sphere" in New England, 1780–1835.* New Haven, Conn.: Yale University Press, 1977.

Cowan, Ruth Schwartz. *More Work for Mother: The Ironies of Household Technology from the Open Hearth to the Microwave.* New York: Basic Books, 1983.

Dudden, Faye E. *Serving Women: Household Service in Nineteenth-Century America.* Middletown, Conn.: Wesleyan University Press, 1983.

Fox-Genovese, Elizabeth. *Within the Plantation Household: Black and White Women of the Old South.* Chapel Hill: University of North Carolina Press, 1988.

Grossberg, Michael. *Governing the Hearth: Law and the Family in Nineteenth-Century America.* Chapel Hill: University of North Carolina Press, 1985.

Hansen, Karen V. *A Very Social Time: Crafting Community in Antebellum New England.* Berkeley: University of California Press, 1994.

Kelley, Mary. *Private Woman, Public Stage: Literary Domesticity in Nineteenth-Century America.* New York: Oxford University Press, 1984.

McCurry, Stephanie. *Masters of Small Worlds: Yeoman Households, Gender Relations, and the Political Culture of the Antebellum South Carolina Low Country.* New York: Oxford University Press, 1995.

Matthews, Glenna. *"Just a Housewife": The Rise and Fall of Domesticity in America.* New York: Oxford University Press, 1987.

Osterud, Nancy Grey. *Bonds of Community: The Lives of Farm Women in Nineteenth-Century New York.* Ithaca, N.Y.: Cornell University Press, 1991.

Reinier, Jacqueline S. *From Virtue to Character: American Childhood, 1775–1850.* New York: Twayne, 1996.

Stevenson, Brenda E. *Life in Black and White: Family and Community in the Slave South.* New York: Oxford University Press, 1996.

Strasser, Susan. *Never Done: A History of American Housework.* New York: Pantheon, 1982.

GLENNA MATTHEWS

DRESS   See **Clothing; Personal Appearance.**

DUELING   A duel is a prearranged formal combat between two persons to settle a point of honor. Although dueling existed in America during the colonial period, its acceptance and popularity can be traced to its prevalence among European officers during the Revolutionary War.

The practice of dueling was more widespread in the South than in the North, but antidueling organizations lobbied for legislation in both regions. Their efforts were successful in the North, but southern gentlemen considered the preservation of reputation and honor more important than any legal or physical consequences. Duels occurred primarily in areas of the cotton culture. A man did not duel beneath his social class, and plantation owners and families from cities like New Orleans, Charleston, and Savannah sent their sons to dueling academies to learn the "sport." For many young southern males, participation in a duel was a rite of passage.

Although dueling was primarily a southern institution, the most famous duel in the United States occurred in Weehawken, New Jersey, on 11 July 1804 between two political opponents, Alexander Hamilton, the first secretary of the Treasury, and Aaron Burr, vice president under Thomas Jefferson. Hamilton, an opponent of dueling, was wounded and died the next day in New York.

In 1838 the former South Carolina governor John Lyde Wilson published *The Code of Honor* to serve as a "recipe" for dueling. All matters relating to the duel were to be conducted using this code, including the duties of both of the duelists and their seconds before and after the challenge and on the dueling grounds. Although dueling nearly disappeared following the Civil War, there is evidence that Wilson's code was used as late as 1877.

See also **Manliness; Manners; South, The; Violence.**

Bibliography

Williams, Jack K. *Dueling in the Old South.* College Station: Texas A&M University Press, 1980.

Wyatt-Brown, Bertram. *Southern Honor.* New York: Oxford University Press, 1982.

FRANK T. WHEELER

E

ECONOMIC REGULATION Throughout the nineteenth century, state governments were the primary locus of economic regulation. State legislators relied on police power as the constitutional basis for efforts to protect public health, safety, and morals. Regulations limited the use of private property and the conduct of business enterprises; for example, lawmakers imposed safety requirements, mandated licenses for certain occupations, and imposed rudimentary land-use controls. Even before the Civil War, state legislatures experimented with regulatory commissions to supervise such complex businesses as railroads and banking. Yet antebellum regulations were generally modest in scope and designed to address specific problems. These measurements made little systematic attempt to redistribute wealth, and their enforcement was lax.

By the last quarter of the nineteenth century, states increasingly enacted more ambitious regulations to ameliorate the harsh consequences of industrialization. They began to regulate workplace safety and limit the hours of work in hazardous occupations. Growing state regulation of railroads was especially controversial. It raised fundamental questions about the authority of the states to control prices and the extent to which they could regulate interstate commerce. Although inclined to leave most regulatory activity to the states, Congress in 1887 created the Interstate Commerce Commission to oversee interstate railroad operations. This first major exercise of federal regulatory authority provided a model for the national regulatory bodies that emerged in the twentieth century.

The states exercised broad regulatory authority, but they could not interfere with interstate commerce or infringe on constitutionally protected property rights. The Supreme Court early established the principle that the commerce clause, by its own force, limited state power to obstruct interstate commerce. In other words, the commerce clause created a national market for goods. Nonetheless, in *Cooley v. Board of Wardens of Port of Philadelphia* (1852), the Court recognized that the states retained concurrent authority to regulate local aspects of commerce unless Congress exerted its paramount power. At the same time the Supreme Court upheld federal authority over commerce when federal and state laws conflicted.

Another restraint on state economic regulation was the emergence of the doctrine of substantive due process. During the antebellum era state courts started to view the due process requirement as preventing legislative interference with certain basic rights of individuals to acquire and use property. The Fourteenth Amendment, adopted in 1868, declared that no state should "deprive any person of life, liberty, or property, without due process of law." This provision opened the door for more expansive federal court review of state economic regulations. Under substantive due process, both state and federal judges assessed state economic regulations against a reasonableness standard. In fact, courts sustained most challenged statutes as valid exercises of police power to safeguard the public. Still, courts tended to hold that some types of regulations violated due process guarantees: (1) laws denying regulated industries, such as railroads, a reasonable return on investment; (2) laws abridging the freedom of contract; and (3) class legislation benefiting one segment of society at the expense of others. Due process review of economic regulations was well established by the end of the nineteenth century. This judicial trend reflected a society that placed a high value on economic liberty.

See also **Interstate Commerce; Property; Regulation of Business; States' Rights.**

Bibliography

Ely, James W., Jr. *The Guardian of Every Other Right: A Constitutional History of Property Rights.* 2d ed. New York: Oxford University Press, 1998.

Hall, Kermit L. *The Magic Mirror: Law in American History.* New York: Oxford University Press, 1989.

JAMES W. ELY JR.

ECONOMIC THEORY Nineteenth-century American economic thought, nearly to the end of the century, patterned itself on European and especially British doctrine. Theoretical originality was so scarce among Americans prior to John Bates Clark and Thorstein Veblen that standard histories of the subject rarely mention any American thinker before them. But the tone and style of U.S. economic discourse—optimistic, nontheoretical, often grounded in theological principles—are distinctively American despite considerable variation across regions and among individual writers. Historians have an undeniable interest in understanding how that discourse was brought to bear on such issues as protectionism, slavery, and the government's role in building up the nation's infrastructure.

The intellectual authority of Adam Smith's *An Inquiry into the Nature and Causes of the Wealth of Nations* (1776) was almost as powerful in the young American nation as it was in Britain. Smith offered a vision of continuous economic progress that would prove well attuned to the hopes and expectations of Americans in the nineteenth century. Building on earlier models of society and economy, he laid down the basic theoretical structure of the market system, in which capital accumulation and division of labor were the keys to economic growth. The role of government was seen as strictly limited, in contrast to the earlier doctrines of mercantilism. Although Smith advocated free trade in principle and generally in practice, he did allow exceptions for retaliatory tariffs.

The "classical economics" that descended from Smith's work took a more pessimistic turn with the publication of T. R. Malthus's *An Essay on the Principle of Population* in 1798 and David Ricardo's *Principles of Political Economy and Taxation* in 1817. In later years American economic writers found much to criticize in the "Ricardo-Malthus school of political economy," as they sometimes dubbed it. Malthus posited a tendency for human numbers to increase faster than the means of subsistence, with population held in check by famine, disease, war, infanticide, prostitution, and abstention from marriage. According to Malthus any general rise in wage rates could be expected to trigger a population increase that would, in the long run, pull wages back down to the subsistence level. The theory of rent worked out by Malthus and Ricardo suggested a long-term pattern of income distribution favoring landlords at the expense of workers and capitalists. Ricardo postulated an eventual "stationary state" in which any further growth of population or economic output would cease.

Toward an American Economics

The views of American economists differed from those of the classical economists. In the United States land was not as scarce a resource as it was held to be in classical economic doctrine; the tripartite class division—workers, capitalists, and landlords—did not apply in a nation where farmers generally owned and worked their own land; and the prospect of a gradual winding down of the growth impulse seemed absurd in the fast-growing American economy. Thus, not surprisingly, many American economic writers and commentators defined their own positions by contrast with those of Malthus and Ricardo. Seldom, however, did they offer anything substantive or systematic in place of classical doctrine.

Significantly, in the nineteenth-century United States college-level economics or "political economy" formed part of the moral philosophy curriculum and was generally studied in a senior-year lecture course for a single term. The lecturer was often the president of the college, who in turn was frequently a Protestant clergyman. The most widely used text for two decades after its publication in 1821 in an American edition, J. B. Say's *Treatise on Political Economy* (*Traité d'économie politique*, 1803), was praised by Thomas Jefferson and heavily influenced by Smith's *Wealth of Nations*. It was rapidly supplanted, however, by the Reverend Francis Wayland's *Elements of Political Economy*, first published in 1837. President of Brown University for many years, a Baptist clergyman, and author of a hugely popular text on moral philosophy, Wayland (1796–1865) understood political economy to be the branch of moral philosophy pertaining to the God-given laws of wealth creation

Thorstein Veblen (1857–1929). The economist and social theorist Thorstein Veblen's best-known work, *The Theory of the Leisure Class* (1899), drew mixed reactions: his peers were critical; the literary community lauded it. His indictment of the business class was further developed in later books. Portrait, 1920. PRINTED WITH PERMISSION OF ROLF LANG

and distribution. All of the standard economic doctrines on topics from international trade to the necessity of individual exertion he attributed to the will of the Creator. Typical of the American ideology regarding social welfare provision was Wayland's firm opposition to poor laws because of their tendency to undermine industry and frugality.

A persistent theme of American economic thought for much of the nineteenth century was the need to promote domestic industry by various means, including the protective tariff. Rooted in the ideas of Alexander Hamilton, this doctrine came to be known as the "American system." In politics, Henry Clay of Kentucky became the foremost spokesperson for the American system during the 1820s and 1830s, advocating protective tariffs as one part of a larger program of national economic development. The program included a strong, if not paternalistic, role for the federal government in funding, with tariff revenues, a variety of internal improvements, such as the building of roads and canals. Daniel Raymond (1786–1849), in *Thoughts on Political Economy* (1820), considered the first systematic American treatise on economics, argued that tariffs were a proper tool for stimulating idle labor and enhancing a nation's productive capacity. Henry C. Carey (1793–1879), a more influential economist and the son of another notable protectionist, Matthew Carey, supported tariff protection as a means of encouraging closer "associations" among domestic producers and consumers, both of whom would reap real benefits in the form of lowered costs of production and transportation. Another member of the "Pennsylvania school" of protectionism was Friedrich List (1789–1846), a German immigrant to the United States, whose *Outlines of American Political Economy* (1827) made the infant-industry, nationalistic case for protection in opposition to the cosmopolitan free-trade position of the classical economists.

The works of nineteenth-century American economists often exhibit a barely suppressed chauvinism with regard to British ideas and institutions. Amasa Walker (1799–1875), considered the outstanding American economist of the Civil War era, provides a case in point. His *The Science of Wealth* (1866) was popular on both sides of the Atlantic. As was still typical at that time, his economic text devoted a separate chapter to the subject of population, but it was violently anti-Malthusian, deriding the "glut, famine, and death theories of Malthus" and offering in their place the usual optimistic American line on the subject. As Walker saw it the British "philosophy of population" was "perverted," and furthermore, the poverty observed in England was the simple result of "oppressive institutions" and "the relics of feudalism."

The institution of slavery was frequently the subject of American economic analysis before the Civil War. One defense of the slave-labor system pointed to the reproductive prudence believed to be exercised by southern white laborers fearful of a possible fall to the economic rank associated with slaves. Because no such fear restrained free laborers in the North, they tended to multiply with such rapidity as to depress industrial wage rates to a bare subsistence. A prime economic argument against slavery was that coerced labor was unmotivated, inefficient, and thus inferior to free labor. The "euthanasia" of slavery was predicted by some on classical economic grounds: as slave populations grew more dense in the slaveholding states, the value of slaves would fall so low that their owners would have little choice but to free them.

Professionalization and Reform

The most widely read American economic writer of the century was Henry George (1839–1897), whose *Progress and Poverty* (1879) made Ricardian rent theory the basis of a trenchant attack on the unearned wealth reaped by landowners in the form of rents. The remedy proposed by George, a tax on any rise in land values, launched the "single tax" movement, so called because according to George this one tax could replace all other sources of government revenue. Although not a Marxian, George struck the most radical note of any prominent American economist of his time. (It deserves to be noted that Marxism, for a host of cultural and historical reasons, never gained much of a foothold in nineteenth-century American economics.)

Toward the end of the century American economics took its first decisive steps toward professionalization. Because graduate economics training was unavailable in either the United States or Britain as late as 1870, young American economists studied at a number of German universities. There they encountered a historical orientation to economics and a strongly reformist view of the uses of economics. The German academic economists under whom they studied were, as a rule, far more willing to embrace government action to achieve societal change than were most American academics. Thus, mainly young, German-trained economists, who had a heightened appreciation for the ethical, historical, and political dimensions of economics and a positive view of the state's role in social amelioration, founded the American Economic Association (AEA) in 1885. Within a few years, however, the AEA shed its reformist outlook to become a more ideologically neutral organization.

John Bates Clark (1847–1938) and Thorstein Veblen (1857–1929) are considered the preeminent American economists of the last decade of the nineteenth century. Clark studied in Germany, and his early work reflected a Christian Socialist point of view. But his *Distribution of Wealth* (1899) took a different direction, arguing that under competitive conditions what an individual earned in the marketplace was based on what he produced or his "marginal product." The analysis behind this conclusion—welcomed by defenders of the existing distribution of wealth—was more technically proficient than perhaps anything previously seen in the United States. Veblen, once a student of Clark's, founded a new school of economics called institutionalism. Equally critical of Marxian economics and of conventional economic theory, Veblen faulted conventional economics for being too abstract, too mechanical. Economics, Veblen argued, should concern itself with the study of institutions, and because institutions were ever changing, economics should be an evolutionary science. His best-known work, *The Theory of the Leisure Class* (1899), was a biting, satirical attack on American business culture.

See also **Liberalism; Market Revolution; Reform, Social.**

Bibliography

Barber, William J., ed. *Economists and Higher Learning in the Nineteenth Century.* New Brunswick, N.J.: Transaction, 1993.

Coats, A. W. "The American Economic Association and the Economics Profession." *Journal of Economic Literature* 23 (1985): 1697–1727.

Conkin, Paul K. *Prophets of Prosperity: America's First Political Economists.* Bloomington: Indiana University Press, 1980.

Dorfman, Joseph. *The Economic Mind in American Civilization.* New York: Viking, 1946–1959.

O'Connor, Michael J. L. *Origins of Academic Economics in the United States.* New York: Garland, 1974.

Spiegel, Henry William. *The Rise of American Economic Thought.* Philadelphia: Chilton, 1960.

Staley, Charles E. *A History of Economic Thought: From Aristotle to Arrow.* Cambridge, Mass.: Basil Blackwell, 1989.

GEOFFREY GILBERT

EDUCATION

[This entry includes nine subentries:
Elementary and Secondary Schools
Public Policy toward Education
School Segregation
Colleges and Universities
Graduate and Professional Education
Education of Girls and Women
Education of African Americans
Indian Schools
Education of the Blind and Deaf.]

ELEMENTARY AND SECONDARY SCHOOLS

The American faith in the power of formal education to diffuse knowledge, enhance personal mobility, and promote social stability owes much to the nineteenth century. Between the decades following the American Revolution and the turn of the twentieth century, the nation built an increasingly comprehensive system of public schools, especially outside of the South; southern states also made notable educational strides after the Civil War. Private schools created by Roman

Catholics, Lutherans, and a handful of smaller religious groups provided an alternative to the public system. But the public schools came to enroll the great majority of school-age children, especially below high school, which remained out of reach for many working-class, southern, rural, and black families in 1900.

The Origins of Public Schools

The creation of a single system of public education marked a decisive change in the organization and delivery of formal schooling. In 1800 the United States was already one of the most literate nations in the world, an achievement reached through a variety of means. The Protestant emphasis on the importance of reading, especially the Bible, for religious instruction was crucial, and literacy was enhanced by the expansion of a market society, inexpensive newspapers, a more reliable postal service, and the widespread belief in the North that intelligence and virtue were the foundation of republican citizenship. Education was seen increasingly in the nineteenth century as the cure for poverty, crime, and family distress, a legacy that proved enduring.

While only one of many sources of education in the early 1800s, schools were growing in influence. Many schools existed, but there was as yet no school system. In the northern countryside, district schools, supported by public taxes, private donations, and occasionally tuition, were fairly prevalent. They enrolled boys and girls alike and taught the elementary branches of knowledge in ungraded classrooms for a few short terms each year. District schools first appeared in the rural North by the middle of the eighteenth century. Massachusetts, the nation's leader in school innovations, made the district the legal basis for education outside of the cities in 1789. District schools were often called common or public schools in the antebellum period, and the local control of schools became a hallowed political ideal.

Instead of district schools, urban areas in the early 1800s had an array of competing institutions that served different social classes. Some private academies mixed social groups, but the very poor could not afford the tuition, however low. Academies were privately controlled and occasionally incorporated by the state, which sometimes provided land grants or cash to the individuals or groups that sponsored them. Some were boarding schools, but most were day schools; some were single sex, others coeducational. Typically, academies offered a variety of elementary and advanced subjects, depending on market demand. They were found in many villages, towns, and cities, North and South, and often enrolled a broad range of middle-class children and youth. When located in the countryside, academies often provided students access to more advanced studies not easily taught in one-room district schools.

The education of the urban poor varied considerably from that of more privileged groups. Rising in number and engendering fear among the native middle and upper classes, poor children often attended charity schools, an English innovation supported by Protestant voluntary organizations. For example, the Free School Society of New York City, an interdenominational Protestant group, was formed in 1805 to educate the children of the unchurched poor; it received tax monies to help increase the number of charity schools, which grew dramatically by the 1820s. Voluntary associations also opened charity schools for the poor in Baltimore, Detroit, Charleston, and other large towns and cities. These schools— relatively inexpensive and emphasizing Christian morals and basic literacy—operated in church halls and basements, rented rooms, and other makeshift facilities. While there was a stigma associated with "free" education, charity schools tried to attract a wider range of social classes in the 1840s and 1850s and served as the basis for mass public education. Reformers worked diligently to undermine private schools by improving instruction in the elementary classes and by creating high schools that were academically respectable.

By the 1820s, therefore, many different kinds of schools functioned in rural and urban America, all of which contributed to the moral and intellectual training of the young. Reliable statistics on school enrollments and attendance are scarce, but Carl Kaestle and Maris Vinovskis, as well as other scholars, have shown that elementary enrollments were rising before the 1830s. Enrollment increases thus preceded the famous campaigns for free public schools led by Horace Mann of Massachusetts and his counterparts in other states. Statistics on private academies remained fairly unreliable in the 1850s, but these schools numbered in the thousands, joined by a fledgling parochial system of Catholic and Lutheran education. While the church-based schools, especially those of the Catholics, proved controversial, many academies and female seminaries disappeared as more citizens sent their children to the public system, especially outside the South.

The great dream of antebellum reformers by the 1830s was the creation of a universal public system. They envisioned a fully tax-supported system of schools open in theory to all children, who would study common academic subjects and receive uniform moral training. This was achieved to the greatest degree in the North before the Civil War but was

"**The Night School.**" A New York City classroom filled with the urban poor. Although this classroom appears to be age-graded, the teaching method is still based upon recitation from textbooks. From *Harper's Magazine*, 1873. LIBRARY OF CONGRESS: PRINTS AND PHOTOGRAPHS DIVISION

largely unrealized in the South, where a dual system of education based on racial segregation became the norm after Reconstruction in the 1870s. Northern schools were sometimes integrated, but segregated classrooms and schools were hardly unknown. In the antebellum South illiteracy rates for poor whites were high and for black slaves approached 95 percent. The former had some access to formal education in "old field" schools on the plantation, and blacks had some clandestine schools in the slave quarters taught by sympathetic whites or literate slaves. As in the North, urban free blacks sometimes ran their own African schools and Sunday schools or otherwise taught each other. The stigma associated with the concept of free schools remained powerful in the South. Poor whites often refused to send their children to such institutions, a view shared by their social betters, and elite white children on plantations had tutors or were sent away to boarding schools or academies. The idea of universal public education continued to arouse fears of social-class mixing and racial integration after the Civil War.

Country Schools versus City Schools

Most American children lived in rural areas before the Civil War; the common district schools of the North numbered in the many thousands by midcentury and shared much in common. Foreign visitors wondered how this was possible, since the states and the federal government supported the diffusion of learning but played a relatively small role in the establishment or maintenance of schools. The Northwest Ordinances of 1785 and 1787 reserved some land in the Midwest for public schools, but education remained a matter of local control and provision. While European nations created powerful, centralized ministries of education, the U.S. Bureau of Education, created in 1867, was politically weak. It dutifully gathered and disseminated educational statistics and printed bulletins and reports, but it lacked the authority to influence curricula and implement reforms. District schools, however, were the product of general community consent and remained subject to local government control, depending almost exclusively on local taxes. Schools—often one-room classrooms— were among the first buildings constructed in new agricultural communities as New Englanders moved west to Ohio, Nebraska, or California.

Throughout the nation, country schools shared common practices. They taught a basic curriculum and broad Christian values. The curriculum remained rudimentary: reading, writing, and arithmetic. By the 1830s the course of study expanded somewhat to include geography, grammar, and history as part of a basic education for all white children. These subjects taught pupils something of the wider world in which they lived as well as the grandeur of the nation's past. The genius of the institutions created by the founding fathers and the nation's fertile soils and superior natural resources all were extolled in school textbooks.

Schools taught secular subjects in an atmosphere that honored the word of God, inscribed in scripture, and tried to inculcate the ideals of hard work, delayed gratification, personal application, and respect for authority. Morning classes often began with the Lord's Prayer and a daily reading from the King James version of the Bible, reflecting majority Protestant consent. Educators and community leaders often praised the schools for their role in teaching moral values, Christian ethics, and the fundamental subjects. The religious tone of the schools, however, offended some strongly sectarian Protestants, who were unwilling to water down their theology, and Catholics, whose population grew dramatically as immigration swelled in the 1840s.

Teaching methods in the largely ungraded rural schools of the United States did not vary considerably. The guiding educational belief was that the mind was a muscle containing separate faculties and that the cultivation of the memory was learning's Holy Grail. Followers of European child-centered theorists such as Johann Pestalozzi and Friedrich Fröebel gained some following, but the idea of mental discipline through hard work in basic subjects proved hardy. In rural schools, where class sizes ranged from a handful to a few dozen, young children of all ages often sat with a sprinkling of older youth. Teachers typically emphasized the importance of memorization. Children learned by heart rules on grammar and punctuation, the names and dates of battles and important events, the names of mountain ranges and capitals, and procedures to convert English pounds to American dollars. This knowledge came from textbooks, the source of authority and the key instructional tool of the century. Maps, globes, and blackboards became more common in some districts by mid-century, but they did not alter the basic approach to instruction.

In countless classrooms the daily experiences were familiar. Standing near his or her desk, each child recited from memory material learned from a textbook, while classmates (at least in theory) sat quietly preparing for their turn. A few books, such as Noah Webster's *Blue-Backed Speller*, Lindley Murray's grammar books, William H. McGuffey's readers, and Joseph B. Ray's arithmetic series, became bestsellers, offering moral lessons and academic fare si-

multaneously. *McGuffey's Readers* were even published in German-language editions to help lure immigrants into the public school fold. Students parsed the epigrams of Benjamin Franklin on frugality and industry, read stories in which good triumphed over evil, and determined how to calculate compound interest on their savings. Since few parents could afford many books, children brought to the classroom whatever was at hand, often hand-me-downs from older siblings or relatives. One did not "graduate" from a country school but instead progressed at one's own pace through books, if they were available, of ever greater difficulty in a particular subject.

These ungraded country schools were usually modest buildings constructed of wood or other local materials and were a familiar sight in the northern countryside. Reformers throughout the century criticized them, contrasting them to the city schools, which were undergoing greater transformation and improvement. Cities often had greater wealth, a higher tax base, and a larger concentration of pupils of a similar age, which led reformers to see great possibilities for educational innovation. By the 1840s urban educators initiated notable reforms, especially in the primary schools. They established age-graded classrooms; assigned standardized textbooks; hired women, who were considered more adept at teaching younger children and demanded less pay, to teach in the lower grades; and built a rudimentary school bureaucracy with a superintendent at the top. Urban classrooms were also textbook oriented, and the appeal of didactic teaching methods had not dissipated. Urban classrooms, however, reflected the commercial and increasingly industrial rhythms of the city. Educators thus emphasized punctuality, published elaborate rules and regulations for students and staff, and desired greater efficiency in the system, sometimes taking railroads and factories as their models. Late in the century Denver's superintendent of schools boasted that, by looking at his watch, he could tell the number of the page on which each teacher was hearing pupil recitations.

High Schools

After the Civil War the spread of literacy among former slaves, poor whites, and immigrants was the pride of the nation's educators. Schools alone were not responsible for the achievement, since literacy was advanced at home, in church and Sunday school, and through self-help. Yet the emphasis on attendance at public schools remained a prominent civic goal. To boost enrollment or simply because of political pressures, foreign languages such as German were sometimes taught in rural or urban schools and occasionally served as the language of instruction. This, too, helped popularize the system and undermined the appeal of private schools. Many newspaper editors, ministers, and politicians continued to maintain that intelligence and virtue were the wellsprings of the Republic, nourished by the public schools.

Older pupils and precocious younger ones occasionally studied more advanced subjects in rural schools or in private academies in the early 1800s, but towns and cities built the first public secondary schools in the 1820s. These secondary schools followed the demise of most of New England's Latin grammar schools, where since the colonial period boys had traditionally prepared for college. Public high schools were another example of the advantages of the city, according to many educational reformers. At a special town meeting Boston voted to establish America's first public high school, which opened in 1821. Reflecting the timeless association of higher education with men, Boston's English High was restricted to boys, and other urban high schools on the eastern seaboard followed suit. But the typical public high school was coeducational, like the small country schools. Indeed, women were often the majority of secondary pupils, which proved decisive in shaping the curriculum, since girls were not admitted to college. High schools were found almost exclusively in towns and cities before the Civil War, though district schools consolidated and offered advanced subjects more regularly in northern villages after the 1840s.

Like the elementary and grammar grades below them, high schools taught an English, or modern, curriculum. A few specialized in preparing boys for college, but since few boys and almost no girls were college bound before the Civil War, the curriculum was an extension of the lower grades, offering higher mathematics and algebra, English, geography, history, and chemistry. Latin, the language of the learned, was often taught, but so were modern languages such as German, French, and Spanish. Admission to high school required passing an often rigorous entrance examination. These examinations were written, demonstrating the rising influence of writing in a world where oral communication was still prized, especially in the South. Questions covered arithmetic, grammar, spelling, history, and geography; they tested the scholar's capacity to memorize names, dates, rules, procedures, and the countless facts crammed into grammar school textbooks. Thus the tests were sometimes referred to locally as the Olympic Games.

Textbooks dominated instruction in high schools, and daily recitations and performance on written tests commonly determined promotion and class rank. A few wealthy high schools had science laboratories, rock collections, and other expensive teaching aids, but the typical secondary school relied on textbooks, the foundation of the course of study and of pedagogy. With a more graduated, sequenced curriculum, urban systems could offer rigorous studies in the advanced subjects. Most secondary school pupils came from a broad range of middle-class families, with few working-class children or immigrants present at mid-century. The poor were already in the workforce or otherwise helping their families, while the very rich continued to patronize academies, which grew more exclusive in the North after the 1880s as the less expensive ones lost their clientele to the public system. For a variety of reasons, including the need to work, high school pupils usually dropped out by the end of the tenth grade, even late in the century. Perhaps a quarter of entering scholars graduated, and most who received a diploma were women.

Many of the male secondary teachers were highly paid college graduates. The women teachers, who were paid less, were often, by late in the century, high school or normal school graduates. Teachers kept careful tallies on classroom performance and recitations and duly recorded a pupil's grades, attendance, and deportment on report cards. Overall, the course of study was academic, not vocational. Students nevertheless saw practical value in what they studied. Many of the women students became elementary school teachers. For boys, attending high school provided the knowledge, skills, and credentials to compete for white-collar jobs, which were expanding with the rise of commerce and industry. They often became clerks and bookkeepers, while other male alumni studied for the professions and enrolled in college.

Schools at the Century's End

By the late nineteenth century elementary and secondary school enrollments, especially in the North, had grown impressively, and private academies dramatically declined in number. The schools created by Catholics, Lutherans, and smaller Protestant groups continued to offer an alternative to public education, but the latter's extension to all parts of the nation was obvious by 1900. The South lagged behind the North in the length of school terms and accessibility of high schools, and its middle and upper classes favored private schools more than their northern counterparts. The South had more children per capita to educate, a weaker tax base, and a more dispersed population, but it nevertheless invested large amounts of money in schools after the Civil War. Pressure to create schools came from several sources:

through the federal government during the Republican-led Reconstruction; through the missionary zeal of northern philanthropists; and through the legendary efforts of blacks to rise up from slavery to freedom, in part through access to schools. Black control over segregated schools, churches, and other institutions was an important legacy of the Reconstruction era.

Despite the occasional existence of a racially integrated system, as in New Orleans briefly after the Civil War, a dual system of public education arose fairly quickly in the 1870s. This pattern was solidified by Jim Crow laws, custom, and violent opposition to integration from whites as the century came to a close. The South had nevertheless built the foundations of public education by the turn of the century, when southern progressives led new campaigns for school investment and improvement, especially for whites. Famous African Americans, such as Booker T. Washington and W. E. B. Du Bois, offered alternative visions of the purposes of formal education for black citizens, from the narrowly vocational to the highly academic.

In 1800 the United States was a highly literate nation, especially among its free white population. A great variety of schools dotted the countryside and expanding cities. No one could have predicted that elementary and secondary education a century later would largely emanate from a single system of public schools that were free, tax-supported, and ostensibly open to everyone, though strictly segregated racially in the South. Late in the century reformers placed new curricular demands upon the schools, calling for the addition of kindergartens, summer vacation schools, manual-training courses, and more vocationally oriented high schools. Various progressives denounced the reliance upon textbooks and the emphasis on rote memorization, and schools continued to struggle with issues of access for the working poor, black citizens, and new waves of immigrants.

The U.S. commissioner of education reported in 1900 that great strides toward popular education had been made during the nineteenth century. The statistics on common schools revealed that in 1870, 57 percent of all pupils between the ages of five and eighteen were enrolled in school; by 1900 the figure was 72 percent. Days spent in school dramatically increased, and other factors indicated change. Public school property was worth $130 million in 1870; by 1900 it was valued at over $500 million. Approximately one high school per day had been built since 1890, and nearly a quarter of a million public schoolhouses existed in the nation at the turn of the century. The principle of tax-supported free schools had become a reality for millions of children and an increasing number of adolescents.

See also **Education,** *subentries on* **Education of African Americans, Education of Girls and Women, Indian Schools, Public Policy toward Education, School Segregation; Literacy and Reading Habits.**

Bibliography

Anderson, James D. *The Education of Blacks in the South, 1860–1935.* Chapel Hill: University of North Carolina Press, 1988.

Blumin, Stuart M. *The Emergence of the Middle Class: Social Experience in the American City, 1760–1900.* Cambridge, U.K.: Cambridge University Press, 1989.

Brown, Richard D. *Knowledge Is Power: The Diffusion of Information in Early America, 1700–1865.* New York: Oxford University Press, 1989.

Cremin, Lawrence A. *American Education: The National Experience, 1783–1876.* New York: Harper and Row, 1980.

Elson, Ruth Miller. *Guardians of Tradition: American Schoolbooks of the Nineteenth Century.* Lincoln: University of Nebraska Press, 1964.

Howe, Daniel Walker. *The Political Culture of the American Whigs.* Chicago: University of Chicago Press, 1979.

Kaestle, Carl F. *Pillars of the Republic: Common Schools and American Society, 1780–1860.* New York: Hill and Wang, 1983.

Kaestle, Carl F., and Maris A. Vinovskis. *Education and Social Change in Nineteenth-Century Massachusetts.* Cambridge, U.K.: Cambridge University Press, 1980.

Katz, Michael B. *The Irony of Early School Reform: Educational Innovation in Mid-Nineteenth Century Massachusetts.* Cambridge, Mass.: Harvard University Press, 1968.

Labaree, David F. *The Making of an American High School: The Credentials Market and Central High School of Philadelphia, 1838–1939.* New Haven, Conn.: Yale University Press, 1988.

Reese, William J. *The Origins of the American High School.* New Haven, Conn.: Yale University Press, 1995.

Schultz, Stanley K. *The Culture Factory: Boston Public Schools, 1789–1860.* New York: Oxford University Press, 1973.

Sizer, Theodore R., ed. *The Age of the Academies.* New York: Bureau of Publications, Teachers College, Columbia University, 1964.

Tyack, David B. *The One Best System: A History of American Urban Education.* Cambridge, Mass.: Harvard University Press, 1974.

WILLIAM J. REESE

PUBLIC POLICY TOWARD EDUCATION

In the nineteenth century "educational policy" developed primarily out of translocal networks of voluntary associations. In the early nineteenth century economic and social forces overwhelmed older small town and village routines that largely controlled the shaping and application of social priorities. In response, these ubiquitous communities, attracted by the growth but worried about unpredictable threats to their autonomy, developed a distinctively democratic ideology of local control, one that endured and changed throughout the century.

This ideology reached a strategic apogee under the presidency of Andrew Jackson (1767–1845) and his historically significant veto of the second Bank of the United States in 1832. Jackson's efforts to ground decision making in local communities or in the states found ideological resistance in the nationally oriented Whig Party and from statesmen like Henry Clay (1777–1852) and Daniel Webster (1782–1852). In educational as well as in economic matters, such Whig leaders as Horace Mann (1796–1859) and Henry Barnard (1811–1900) put their hopes in larger organizations, which they felt should standardize resources and stabilize school policies. The first tax-supported common school system began in Massachusetts in 1837, providing a statewide model of public schooling for the nation.

It should be noted, however, that American policy-making did not move directly or linearly from local autonomy to centralized policy institutions. Even the Whigs harbored fears of overly centralized (potentially tyrannical) organizations and in 1837 granted the first state superintendent of schools, Horace Mann, no statutory power to coerce any town to specific implementations of the free-school law. Mann's enduring importance to policymaking lay not in institution building but in his annual reports (1837–1848). These documents contained a powerful and still persuasive argument about the mutually reinforcing values of democracy and education. His primary means of enforcing this new translocal policy was rhetoric. Showcasing particular towns as models and reporting the statistically documented underperformance of others made public shaming a strategic, though indirect, device of public policy. By the 1850s, compulsory attendance laws began to be passed in the states, but their implementation was often underfunded and relied on local initiatives. Emergent bureaucratic arrangements did not immediately or automatically take over policy implementation.

More important to a culture strategically dependent on oratory, Mann's antebellum career made a lasting contribution to the forceful voluntary culture of the nineteenth century. Among many others, Horace Mann contributed substantively to conceptions of policy that were considered at once orderly yet individualized. Formal policies, particularly those debated in voluntary associations, quickly appeared dangerously undemocratic if they led to changes that were not informal and benign, reliant on customary routines that many wished to view as natural.

Through many organizational networks, this brand of voluntarism nevertheless affected policy priorities with great efficiency and power, not readily acknowledged by twentieth-century institutional assumptions. This nineteenth-century culture modeled itself on many evangelical strategies, tried and proven over the previous century but which now espoused a consciously nondenominational mentality.

Even after the Civil War and the rise of powerful corporate organizations, echoes of the early-nineteenth-century debate between local and national organizations endured and affected policymaking. The 1862 Morrill Land Grant Act, for example, represented the most important national policy concerning education since the Northwest Ordinance (1787). That late-eighteenth-century act extended earlier policies of colonial tax support (which never was meant to cover all costs), of moral instruction (since Protestant culture provided common ground to the many denominations), and of voluntarism (since parents determined whether children attended formal schools). The ordinance intended to accommodate many geographic and cultural terrains while providing the basic legal precedent for financing the nation's public schools.

Like the precedent-setting ordinance, Morrill's national land grant policy to higher education proposed to affect each state in ways that reflected its indigenous traditions. The money from the national government flowed through the states for them to implement. Consequently, some states like New York invested in particular schools of Cornell University without mandating that the whole institution become public. Others separated their revenue. Massachusetts, for example, created an agricultural college in the western portion of the state (now the public University of Massachusetts at Amherst) and technical training at a new private school, which became the Massachusetts Institute of Technology. In the more western state of Wisconsin, the Land Grant Act translated into a single public institution, the University of Wisconsin at Madison. The second Morrill Land Grant Act, of 1890, similarly provided revenue to new states that had not been a part of the United States in 1862. The second Morrill Act deferred to the Jim Crow tradition of "separate but equal" social and educational facilities, but in the process created important, strategic black colleges with federal funding. This expenditure advanced the short-lived precedent set by the Freedman's Bureau (1865–1872), which provided federal funds to educate newly emancipated slaves after the Civil War.

In the nineteenth century the real national engines of social shaping were not the state organizations or even the data-collecting U.S. Bureau of Education

(1867) but the national voluntary associations, most notably the American Institute of Instruction (1830–1918). The voluntary networks guaranteed two things: a seemingly democratic accessibility to a range of educational voices (though no woman could speak her own mind until after the Civil War) and audiences (though no blacks participated at any point in its history) and a forum for airing differences with an eye to reaching a harmonious consensus on priorities. They worked within legal and institutional frameworks that they helped create and implement before the emergence of formal bureaucracies in the last quarter of the nineteenth century. Like Horace Mann's own reliance on public discourse, these associations—national, regional, and local—assumed that their members would be unified in their beliefs and orientations but would vary their policies according to their circumstances. Even with the rise of formal bureaucracies, the voluntary culture did not go out of existence, and its historical role in the policy enterprise remained highly elastic in concept and practice throughout the nineteenth and into the twentieth century.

In the early years of the nineteenth century, states continued the colonial policy of strategic support to education, which assumed that tuition and resources would come from parents and other contributors. The antebellum notion of a public policy made no distinction between "public" and "private." In the second quarter of the century, however, states began to reduce their direct outlays to educational institutions, especially to colleges within their boundaries. The proposal of a national university, advanced by several presidents from George Washington to John Quincy Adams, is a case in point. No locale or state could initiate such an institution alone. However desirable in theory, such a university raised knotty questions of political control and intellectual indoctrination. For a new country, expecting to break with European traditions, a national university also seemed to imply that national policy would at times not be the accumulated pattern of voluntary, local, and state initiatives but rather would become a design formulated by oligarchic or elitist groups. Fears of centralization made Congress hesitant to endorse a national research facility like the Smithsonian Institution (1846) or the Bureau of Education, which remained a highly circumspect agency until much later in its history.

Near the end of the century two episodes plotted the possibilities of new institutions and policies. The first was a national piece of legislation, the Hatch Act (1887), advanced by a former Confederate officer, Missouri Congressman William Henry Hatch. The successful bill provided federal money for an experi-

mental station in each state to encourage agricultural industry. The law gave new life to scientific practice outside universities. The Hatch Act seemed to legitimate limited federal initiatives in quasi-educational areas where states appeared reluctant to go, the forerunner of a major Progressive principle of federal government activism.

The second portending policy event arose from the first important activist initiative of the National Education Association (founded 1857). The association had created a Committee of Ten in 1892 to blueprint a model curriculum for secondary education in the United States. The Report of the Committee of Ten (1894) presented not one but four curricular programs, heavily biased by its committee members, who served selective institutions of higher learning. Its chair, Charles W. Eliot (1834–1926), president of Harvard University, sought to use his position and the resources of the national association to buttress a potent argument about university-trained expertise. Eliot advanced a notion of educational privilege in a democracy, a policy that expected sound initiatives for a newly industrial nation from an increasingly distinct private sector and educated social class. His strained effort to connect a new elitism with older notions of democracy found a wide audience, whose voices often obscured how changed this late-nineteenth-century notion of democracy was from its earlier nineteenth-century precedents. Although he was operating within an older voluntary culture, Eliot forecast its replacement in a new culture of professionalism.

See also **Education,** *subentries on* **Colleges and Universities, Elementary and Secondary Schools.**

Bibliography

Cremin, Lawrence. *American Education: The National Experience, 1783–1876.* New York: Harper and Row, 1980.

Hall, Peter Dobkin. *The Organization of American Culture, 1700–1900: Private Institutions, Elites, and the Origins of American Nationality.* New York: New York University Press, 1982.

Hawkins, Hugh. *Between Harvard and America: The Educational Leadership of Charles W. Eliot.* New York: Oxford University Press, 1972.

Katz, Michael B. *Class, Bureaucracy and Schools: The Illusion of Educational Change in America.* New York: Praeger, 1971.

Mattingly, Paul H. *The Classless Profession: American Schoolmen in the Nineteenth Century.* New York: New York University Press, 1975.

Mattingly, Paul H., and Edward W. Stevens, Jr., eds. " . . . Schools and the Means of Education Shall Forever Be Encouraged": A History of Education in the Old Northwest, 1787–1880.* Athens: Ohio University Libraries, 1987.

Tyack, David B. *The One Best System: A History of American

Urban Education. Cambridge, Mass.: Harvard University Press, 1974.

PAUL H. MATTINGLY

SCHOOL SEGREGATION

The nineteenth century is rightly regarded as the high-water mark of segregated education in the United States. School segregation existed throughout the nation at that time, either by force of law or custom. Before 1865 in all of the South and much of the North it took the form of virtually complete exclusion of nonwhites from public education, with no state support of separate educational institutions. After the Civil War, however, segregation in education was transformed into a system of separate and unequal public schooling for whites and nonwhites that was enshrined in both law and custom.

Although some northern white schools admitted African Americans before 1820, most states either excluded them altogether or established racially segregated schools for them. The means employed to exclude African Americans from the public schools varied only slightly from state to state. In the New England states, such as Massachusetts, some local school committees assigned African American children to separate schools regardless of the district in which they lived. While the Massachusetts legislature banned this practice in 1854, other New England states and New York State continued to permit it. Pennsylvania and Ohio required district school superintendents to establish racially segregated schools whenever twenty or more African American students were present in a community. At first many newer states, such as Indiana, Illinois, and Michigan, excluded African Americans completely from tax-supported public education but consented to segregated schools by 1860. In the South laws prohibiting the teaching of slaves and a general hostility toward public education forced that region's quarter of a million free blacks to rely on their own resources to acquire an education. Louisiana's Creole population preferred to send children to Europe for schooling.

Through convention appeals, court suits, editorial campaigns, political lobbying, and in some states voting, African Americans maintained a constant agitation against segregated schools in the 1840s and 1850s. In Boston, Benjamin Roberts challenged the legality of the Boston Primary School Committee's power to enforce segregation. A white primary school refused to admit his daughter Sara, even though it and five other such schools were closer to her home than the all-black school she attended. Charles Sumner, who would later become an antislavery leader in the U.S. Senate, took the case of the five-year-old plaintiff. The subsequent court decision, *Roberts v. City of Boston* (1849), resulted in an initial setback to supporters of desegregated schooling and established the controversial legal precedent of separate but equal in American law. It took five years of subsequent action by African Americans and their supporters to persuade the Massachusetts legislature to overturn the *Roberts* decision and pass a law prohibiting racial or religious distinctions in the admission of students to Massachusetts public schools.

After the Civil War many northern states, such as Indiana, either modified or repealed their earlier laws mandating segregated schools and placed that decision in the hands of local communities. In the post–Civil War South custom made separate schools a feature of the newly created public education system almost from the very beginning, with the notable exception of New Orleans, Louisiana. After the Civil War, California's African American community challenged school segregation in that state. Eventually the case reached the California Supreme Court, which ruled in *Ward v. Flood* (1874) that although African Americans had the right to an education, they had no right to receive it in an integrated school. African American children could attend schools for whites, but only in communities where no segregated facilities were available.

After the U.S. Supreme Court in 1883 declared the

6680. The Colored School, Charleston, S. C U. S. A.

The Colored School, Charleston, South Carolina. An example of separate and unequal schooling in the post–Civil War South, where segregation became law in most states by the mid-1880s. LIBRARY OF CONGRESS

Civil Rights Acts of 1866 and 1875 unconstitutional, however, the impetus to enshrine segregated education in law throughout the South and other regions of the United States accelerated. By 1885 most southern states had laws requiring segregated schools. In 1896 the U.S. Supreme Court upheld the legality of segregation in *Plessy v. Ferguson,* which made separate but equal the law of the land. Three years later the Court affirmed the constitutionality of racial segregation in schools in *Cummins v. Richmond County Board of Education* (1899).

In the West anti-Asian sentiment led to the racial segregation of Asian American students in states such as California as early as 1854. In line with how African Americans were treated, a separate school for Chinese children was established in San Francisco in that year. This school operated as an evening school until 1871, when it was closed by an order of the city's school superintendent, forcing the Chinese community to rely on private tutors for their children's education. Thirteen years later the Chinese parents of Mamie Tape challenged the denial of their daughter's right to a public school education. In response the city opened a new segregated school for Chinese American students in 1885.

The initial experience of Japanese students with segregated education was quite different from that of the Chinese. Many of the earliest Japanese students were young men on Japanese government scholarships, and they attended some of the most prestigious universities in the eastern United States. Poorer Japanese students, who ranged in age from fifteen to twenty-five, immigrated to the Pacific Coast, and by 1905 their growing numbers led San Francisco's school board to order all Japanese and Korean students to attend that city's segregated Chinese school. President Theodore Roosevelt directly intervened. In 1908 the Gentleman's Agreement reversed the decision, and in exchange the Japanese government stopped issuing passports to Japanese laborers.

In reality separate but equal in education for African American and Chinese American students was a fiction. Segregation afforded African American and Chinese American children an inferior educational environment in poorly constructed, indifferently maintained, and ill-equipped buildings. Segregated schools also encountered difficulties in securing competent teachers because of gross inequities in teachers' salaries and per-pupil expenditures. The obvious inferiority of segregated schools took on special significance as a symbol of inferior social status. Moreover, segregation in education, far from being a burden to the states and communities that practiced it, was a convenient means of economizing at the expense of African American and other nonwhite children.

Segregation in education continued into the twentieth century. The U.S. Supreme Court's decision in *Berea College v. Kentucky* (1908) extended the legality of segregation to private schooling. Nineteen years later, in *Gong Lum v. Rice* (1927), the Court consolidated its previous findings on school segregation and reinforced the practice. That decision suggested that the entire question was no longer open to debate, thereby giving the force of law to states' efforts to segregate all nonwhite children in public schools. San Francisco and several other California communities maintained segregated public schools for Chinese children into the 1930s. Existing laws compelled African American children to attend segregated schools throughout the South until the Supreme Court's *Brown v. Board of Education of Topeka* (1954) decision.

See also **Civil Rights; Segregation and Civil Rights; Segregation, Urban.**

Bibliography

Chan, Sucheng. *Asian Americans: An Interpretive History.* Boston: Twayne, 1991.

Daniels, Roger. *Asian America: Chinese and Japanese in the United States since 1850.* Seattle: University of Washington Press, 1988.

Harlan, Louis R. *Separate and Unequal: Public School Campaigns and Racism in the Southern Seaboard States, 1901–1915.* New York: Atheneum, 1968.

Kluger, Richard. *Simple Justice: The History of* Brown v. Board of Education *and Black America's Struggle for Equality.* New York: Knopf, 1976.

Litwack, Leon F. *North of Slavery: The Negro in the Free States, 1790–1860.* Chicago: University of Chicago Press, 1961.

Wollenberg, Charles. *All Deliberate Speed: Segregation and Exclusion in California Schools, 1855–1975.* Berkeley: University of California Press, 1976.

Woodson, Carter Godwin. *The Education of the Negro prior to 1861.* New York: Arno, 1968.

MONROE H. LITTLE JR.

COLLEGES AND UNIVERSITIES

American higher education expanded rapidly in the nineteenth century, growing from a relatively small collection of institutions dating from the colonial period to a national system of colleges and universities serving a variety of purposes. The century witnessed the transformation of many American colleges from small, parochial academies to complex and cosmopolitan institutions. Using funds from the sale of lands granted by Congress, the states established nonsectarian institutions to serve the public good. It was a period of growth and change, marked by a number of important developments. Dramatic curricular changes were instituted at leading institutions, and new groups, particularly white women, gained access to higher education. By the end of the century momentous changes were under way, even if some colleges and universities changed little outwardly. These developments set the stage for the emergence of the contemporary higher education system.

Origins

At the close of the revolutionary period only nine institutions of higher learning existed in the United States. These colleges—today's Harvard, William and Mary, Yale, Princeton, Columbia, Rutgers, Pennsylvania, Brown, and Dartmouth—were each affiliated with a Protestant religious denomination and a particular colony. They were entirely male, white institutions, offering a curriculum based largely on classical languages, history, biblical study, and rudiments of mathematics and science. Their mission was the training of clergy and of social elites through the preservation of Western intellectual tradition. By and large, the cultural orientation of these institutions was quite conservative. To be admitted required training in Latin and Greek, literature, history, and related subjects, which excluded the vast majority of the nation's population. Students also were expected to be pious and to observe religious conventions, even if they occasionally rebelled against such strictures. Less than one in a thousand colonial Americans attended these institutions, and fewer graduated.

Signs of change were evident after the Revolution, however. Starting slowly in the closing years of the eighteenth century and accelerating with the beginning of the Second Great Awakening in the 1820s, a wave of college foundings swept the country, continuing to the end of the century. Initially, most new colleges were established by religious groups seeking to advance the cause of a particular denomination as the country's population proceeded westward. State-sponsored institutions were established in Georgia, Ohio, the Carolinas, Virginia, and elsewhere. Enthusiasm for new colleges was abetted by local boosterism, as towns and villages in the expanding western states vied to find sources of distinction to promote growth and economic development. Altogether, almost three hundred new institutions were started by 1860, most with meager endowments and few students. With sometimes fierce competition between institutions for resources and clientele, nearly one in seven failed. But the pace of foundings did not abate. By the Civil War some 250 colleges dotted the countryside, and at the century's end they numbered more than a thousand. The very presence of such a large number of institutions gave American higher education a democratic flavor quite unlike that of other countries. The clergyman and educator Absolom Peters was justified when he declared in 1851, "Our country is to be a land of colleges."

The Age of the College

The colleges founded during the first half of the century were typically "old-time colleges," small institutions, usually with a denominational affiliation (formal or informal) and in most other respects not unlike earlier colonial institutions. Academic standards were often suspect, and in many cases these institutions featured a secondary school, usually called the preparatory department, that was larger than the college itself. This ensured a ready supply of students, particularly in areas of the country with few high schools or academies. Instruction in these institutions consisted primarily of recitation and review of classical languages, literature, and scripture. Discipline was often harsh, with administrators and faculty alike assuming responsibility for each student's moral development as well as for his academic success.

Students occasionally rebelled against college discipline and played elaborate pranks on their elders. But they also accepted responsibility for their education and organized student societies to discuss literature or debate politics. Many no doubt viewed such activities as essential to their future as educated members of society. The principal occupational goal for most students was the ministry, although many found careers in law, education, and business. Collegiate education was hardly required for these professions, but even though there was little in the curriculum of the old-time college that prepared young men for them directly, it did provide socialization, moral training, and academic preparation that was useful in the rapidly emerging urban, capitalistic society of the nineteenth century.

Colleges were chartered by the states but typically were not controlled by them. The Dartmouth College case, argued before the U.S. Supreme Court in 1819 by Daniel Webster, established the independence of private colleges from state interference. Even institutions established by state legislatures and supported with annual appropriations exercised considerable independence in this period.

But for most institutions political intrigue was hardly the most pressing problem. College finances were often precarious, especially as competition led institutions to reduce or even eliminate tuition

College Men on the "Yale Fence." A strong supporter of the standard classical education, which focused on the Greek and Latin languages, history, and biblical studies, Yale, in common with other well-established colleges, was a bastion of the elite. Photograph, 1870. © BETTMANN/CORBIS

charges to attract students. Administrators—usually presidents—were continually seeking contributions from potential benefactors and were not above petitioning state and local governments for support. Even Dartmouth eventually offered to exchange representation on its governing board for a state appropriation. Financial schemes, such as the sale of "perpetual scholarships," provided immediate relief but created long-term problems as colleges struggled with large numbers of nonpaying students. Having students work to reduce costs or raise money also proved problematic. As a result, faculty members often accepted pay cuts and bills went unpaid. Genteel poverty became a characteristic of collegiate life.

Almost from the beginning there was agitation for curricular change. Revolutionary leaders such as Benjamin Rush and Thomas Jefferson saw higher education as relevant to the development of republican virtues and to scientific advancement. Other would-be reformers called for a greater emphasis on modern languages and history and less on classics. Jefferson's 1818 plan for the University of Virginia featured eight separate schools for students to choose from, including mathematics, natural philosophy (or science), medicine, and law. Other institutions allowed students to substitute French or German, mathematics, or other courses for some of the classical curriculum. But such innovations were limited and often viewed as weakening the traditional course of study.

In 1828 the faculty of Yale issued a strong statement of support for the standard classical curriculum, a document that continued to be influential for decades. Describing the aim of college education as cultivating mental discipline, the Yale Report defended the existing course of study as "best calculated to teach the art of fixing the attention, directing the train of thought, [and] analyzing a subject . . . for investigation." For most Americans at the time, classical subjects remained the defining quality of collegiate education. Despite a new emphasis on science and mathematics at institutions such as Union College and Ohio University, and Francis Wayland's similar but ill-fated reforms at Brown, the debate over curricular offerings would wait until after the Civil War to be resolved.

Some changes were unavoidable, however. As the number of colleges increased, students changed also. Enrollment in U.S. colleges climbed from fewer than fifteen hundred at the start of the century to more than thirty thousand (including medical and technical students) by the time of the Civil War. Greater numbers of students from modest backgrounds enrolled, especially in the newly founded colleges. Inspired by religious fervor, many were drawn to the ministry and to the numerous denominational colleges opening their doors during this period. Tuition was low, and scholarships were often made available for especially needy candidates.

Institutions for women also were opened, although most were called "seminaries" or "academies" in the first half of the century. Oberlin College admitted women in 1837, and Elmira College, founded in 1854, was the first indisputably collegiate institution established for women. A small number of midwestern colleges practiced coeducation by the 1850s. The abolitionist movement encouraged African Americans to attend college and small numbers did. Here, too, Oberlin was a leader, along with Bowdoin College in Maine. Some institutions were established for blacks, most notably Lincoln University in Pennsylvania and Wilberforce University in Ohio (both after 1853). Even with these changes, however, American colleges and universities remained bastions of white male dominance throughout the first half of the nineteenth century.

The Rise of the University

Following the Civil War the pace of change picked up dramatically as institutions began to evolve in new ways. Debates on the curriculum produced new reforms, and the student body became considerably more diverse. After a wartime hiatus enrollments continued to rise even more rapidly than during the antebellum period. A new wave of institutions appeared, spearheaded by land-grant universities, normal schools (or teachers colleges), and women's colleges. And as the number of institutions increased, their purposes became differentiated in new ways.

One source of growth was federal largess. The government had set aside public lands to sell for the support of higher education with the Northwest Ordinance of 1787, and these funds aided a number of antebellum colleges. The Morrill Act of 1862 provided even more land for the creation of institutions "to teach such branches of learning as are related to agriculture and the mechanic arts." This led to the founding or expansion of state universities in dozens of states. The Second Morrill Act in 1890 guaranteed regular appropriations to these institutions, helping them to expand further. These measures laid the foundation for the great state universities of the midwestern and western states and also assisted institutions elsewhere.

At the same time the states also began to establish normal schools for teacher preparation, as expanding public school systems required thousands of new teachers each year. Scores of these institutions appeared, especially in the Midwest, and by 1900 their enrollments had grown twentyfold to nearly eighty thousand. Most were little more than glorified high schools, but many such institutions would evolve into state colleges and universities in years to come. In certain cities municipal colleges and normal schools

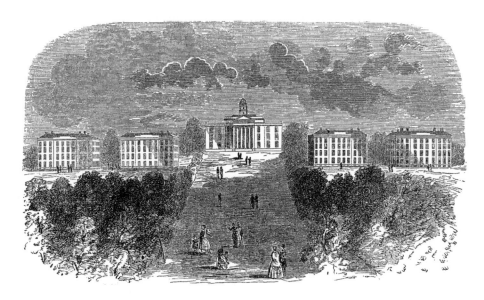

University of Wisconsin. Founded in 1848, the University of Wisconsin soon established departments of law, medicine, and liberal arts. © CORBIS

were established, providing advanced instruction to a nonresidential student body. New York's City College, established in 1847, was among the first such institutions, and Louisville, Kentucky; Cincinnati, Ohio; and Toledo, Ohio, followed suit in the latter half of the century. Others appeared later, along with a variety of private and church-sponsored institutions for city residents. As public interest in higher education increased, different types of institutions competed to meet the demand.

The latter nineteenth century was also a time of heightened interest in curricular reform, and in graduate education. A new generation of university leaders, epitomized by Harvard's Charles Williams Eliot, advocated liberalization of the undergraduate curricula. Eliot introduced the elective system in the 1870s, allowing students to choose courses based on their interests. This was emblematic of a new outlook on education, one placing individual choice and inquiry at the center of learning. As the University of Tennessee president Charles W. Dabney said in 1896, "That community is most highly educated in which each individual has attained the maximum of his possibilities in the direction of his peculiar talents and opportunities." Despite the bitter debate such views engendered, by the end of the century the elective principle was becoming firmly established in colleges and universities across the country.

Graduate education became another new feature of collegiate life. Following the example of German universities, some institutions proposed to make research a prominent aspect of university life, a departure from the old-time college preoccupation with drills and discipline. There was also renewed interest in science. Harvard and Yale had established "scientific" schools and graduate programs prior to 1850, and in 1861 Yale awarded the first Ph.D. degree in the United States. But the founding of Johns Hopkins University in 1876 as an institution devoted primarily to research and graduate training set an example for others to emulate. Other leading institutions soon established graduate programs, including the state universities in Michigan, Wisconsin, and California. Wealthy benefactors established such new research-oriented schools as Cornell University in Syracuse, New York; Clark University in Worcester, Massachusetts; the University of Chicago; and Stanford University in California. Although limited in number, these institutions wielded great influence. Even if there were only a few thousand students involved in graduate study by the end of the century, these developments would eventually transform the face of American higher education.

With changes such as these, a generation of forward-looking university presidents ushered in the new age in American higher education, at least in the larger, better-endowed institutions. Andrew D. White at Cornell, Daniel Gilman at Johns Hopkins, Frederick A. P. Barnard at Columbia, William Rainey Harper at Chicago, David Starr Jordan at Stanford, James Angell at the University of Michigan, and Charles Kendall Adams at Wisconsin, along with Harvard's Eliot, became captains of an emerging academic industry. Faculty members were valued assets, particularly if they were well-known scholars, and they increasingly moved from one institution to another to advance their careers. Institutional loyalties were weakened further as national scholarly organizations, defined by the pubescent academic disciplines, claimed faculty attention. At smaller colleges and church-affiliated institutions, on the other hand, these changes exerted considerably less influence. In these settings the practices of the old-time college, with its emphasis on teaching and moral development, often remained inviolate. But reform at the major research institutions would affect even the most isolated colleges in the years to come.

Growth and Diversity

The wide range of institutions reflected a period of rising demand for higher education. This was partly a consequence of the spread of high schools and rapidly rising secondary school attendance. It also may have been spurred by curricular reforms, which made collegiate study more attractive. College enrollments expanded by more than 400 percent between 1870 and 1900, to more than a quarter million, including students in medical, normal, and law schools. This pace was more than twice the rate of population growth. Even though only about 4 percent of those of college age were enrolled in 1900, higher education was becoming a mass institution.

With rapid growth the student body became more diverse. The largest new group was white women, who outnumbered men among high school graduates by almost two to one in 1890. New institutions were founded for them, many—such as Radcliffe, Barnard, and Pembroke—affiliated with elite men's institutions. Other women's colleges were founded by wealthy benefactors, including Vassar, Smith, and Wellesley. These may have been among the best-known such institutions, but dozens more were established in the East and the South, many with church affiliations. Coeducation was more commonplace in the Midwest and West, where women attended the normal schools, state universities, and even new research institutions, such as Chicago and Stanford. This was a source of controversy in some circles, as certain medical figures wondered whether

Wilberforce University. Founded in 1856 in Xenia, Ohio, Wilberforce was the first institution of higher learning owned and operated by African Americans in the United States. LIBRARY OF CONGRESS: PRINTS AND PHOTOGRAPHS DIVISION

too much study was harmful to women's health, especially in mostly male institutions. But such concerns had little effect on women's interest in higher education, and by 1900 they numbered about a third of all liberal arts students, and some had begun to enter medical and law schools. This represented a challenge to the traditionally male culture of colleges and universities.

African Americans were the other significant new group in American higher education. Following the Civil War the federal government and northern philanthropic groups established schools for freedmen, including colleges and universities. Led by the Freedmen's Bureau, the American Freedman's Aid Union, and a host of church-affiliated educational agencies, reformers founded some two hundred institutions of higher education for African Americans in the South. Plagued by financial difficulties and the lack of an educational infrastructure for southern blacks, the majority of these did not survive, and only a few offered collegiate-level instruction. Among the most successful were Howard University in Washington, D.C.; Fisk University in Nashville, Tennessee; and Morehouse College in Atlanta, Georgia.

After Reconstruction, northern philanthropic organizations, led by the Peabody and Slater Funds, supported industrial and agricultural training institutions for African Americans. The most influential of these was Booker T. Washington's Tuskegee Insti-

tute in Alabama. In 1893 Washington delivered an important speech at the Atlanta Exposition, calling upon blacks to eschew calls for social equality and to focus on technical training rather than collegiate studies. This "Atlanta Compromise" was fiercely debated by other black educational leaders, particularly W. E. B. Du Bois. But Washington's vision was influential and, following the 1890 Second Morrill Act, land-grant institutions were established throughout the South to provide blacks with agricultural and mechanical studies, along with teacher training. Only a few African Americans attended white institutions, virtually all of them in the North. At the end of the century higher education for blacks was almost entirely separate and generally not equivalent to that received by whites.

With the arrival of so many new students, and all of the other changes in this period, college life evolved in new directions. Some traditions of the old-time college remained, including perennial problems of student drinking and pranksterism, along with such laudable pursuits as literary societies and debating clubs. But a new array of extracurricular activities appeared to occupy students' time and to foster institutional loyalties. The most important of these was athletics. The first organized intercollegiate football game was held in 1869 between Rutgers and Princeton. By the 1880s such contests had become elaborate public events, generating enthusiasm among students and alumni alike. Greek-letter fraternities had existed since the 1830s but became especially popular in the postbellum period, often displacing other types of student organizations (such as literary societies). The appearance of coeducation at many institutions made romantic liaisons possible, although dancing and dating would not become features of college life until the twentieth century. As the faculty became more interested in research and professional scholarship, and less interested in student affairs, students became somewhat more autonomous. Relations between college professors and students, even if marked by less conflict than in the past, had become more distant by century's end.

A Century of Transformation

Over the course of the nineteenth century the nation's system of higher education grew from a relative handful of small colleges to nearly a thousand institutions of all shapes and sizes. Serving an ever-wider range of purposes, it became differentiated in ways that became familiar in the twentieth century. Well-endowed private institutions, along with certain flagship state universities, became committed to research and scholarship, while smaller, more traditional colleges clung to the classical curriculum and familiar mores of the old-time college. There was a growing interest in graduate and professional education, especially in the larger institutions and in urban areas. But popular demand for such programs would not blossom until the twentieth century. The nation's colleges and universities had changed a great deal since the start of the century and stood poised for still greater changes in the decades to come.

Collegiate life came to embrace a wider segment of the American population, even though it still only touched a small fraction of the nation's youth in 1900. White women gained access to higher education faster than African Americans and other groups, although they remained excluded from many institutions and never equaled more than half the number of men enrolled across the country. Blacks were relegated to segregated, underfinanced, and academically inferior institutions, yet they pressed ahead with ambitions for social advancement. Despite these fissures, higher education at the end of the nineteenth century held out the promise of individual improvement and a better society. As the frontier closed in the American West, duly noted by the Wisconsin historian Frederick Jackson Turner, American colleges and universities offered a new frontier for the nation to contemplate: a frontier of knowledge, inquiry, and progress. It was a vision that has proven to be enduring.

See also **Military Academy, U.S.; Naval Academy, U.S.; Philanthropy; Women.**

Bibliography

Allmendinger, David F. *Paupers and Scholars: The Transformation of Student Life in Nineteenth-Century New England*. New York: St. Martin's, 1975.

Anderson, James D. *The Education of Blacks in the South, 1860–1935*. Chapel Hill: University of North Carolina Press, 1988.

Brown, David K. *Degrees of Control: A Sociology of Educational Expansion and Occupational Credentialism*. New York: Teachers College Press, 1995.

Burke, Colin B. *American Collegiate Populations: A Test of the Traditional View*. New York: New York University Press, 1982.

Herbst, Jurgen. *And Sadly Teach: Teacher Education and Professionalization in American Culture*. Madison: University of Wisconsin Press, 1989.

Jarausch, Konrad H., ed. *The Transformation of Higher Learning, 1860–1930: Expansion, Diversification, Social Opening, and Professionalization in England, Germany, Russia, and the United States*. Chicago: University of Chicago Press, 1983.

Potts, David. "'College Enthusiasm!' as a Public Response, 1800–1860." *Harvard Educational Review* 47, no. 1 (1977): 28–42.

Rudolph, Frederick. *Curriculum: A History of the Undergraduate Course of Study since 1636*. San Francisco: Jossey-Bass, 1977.

Rury, John, and Glenn Harper. "The Trouble with Coeducation: Mann and Women at Antioch, 1853–1860." *History of Education Quarterly* 26, no. 4 (1986): 481–502.

Solomon, Barbara M. *In the Company of Educated Women: A History of Women and Higher Education in America*. New Haven, Conn.: Yale University Press, 1985.

Veysey, Lawrence. *The Emergence of the American University*. Chicago: University of Chicago Press, 1965.

Whitehead, John S., and Jurgen Herbst. "How to Think about the Dartmouth College Case." *History of Education Quarterly* 26, no. 3 (1986): 333–350.

JOHN L. RURY

GRADUATE AND PROFESSIONAL EDUCATION

From the United States's inception, education has been heralded as a solution to the problems of a republican society demanding an educated citizenry. For most of the nineteenth century, educational initiatives in America focused on elementary and secondary education, primarily in the development of common schools. Professional education, particularly in law and medicine, however, consisted mostly of apprenticeships to fellow professionals, rather than advanced learning and study in an institutional setting.

At the beginning of the nineteenth century, legal training usually took place in a lawyer's office, with the lawyer "reading" the law. Young law clerks copied forms and pleadings, did other forms of secretarial work, and when not busy, read the books a lawyer might have on his shelves, including Blackstone's *Commentaries*. There were a few chairs in law at some colleges—most notably at the College of William and Mary, Columbia, Yale, Harvard, and after 1825, the University of Virginia—where interested students might take classes from the law professors, but they would then go on to clerking for an attorney. There were also a few proprietary law schools, most notably the Litchfield Law School in Connecticut, founded by Judge Tapping Reeve in 1784.

A handful of Americans were devoted to developing institutions of higher education in the late eighteenth century. In 1788 the prominent physician Benjamin Rush called for the creation of a "Federal University" for the young republic, and each of the first six presidents asked the Congress to establish a National University. In an address to Congress in 1796, George Washington argued that in order to bind all citizens together in one union the United States desperately needed a national institution of study and learning.

Despite the republican dream for such an institution, the plans remained neglected. However, throughout the century states developed public normal schools, colleges, and universities, while private philanthropy, often tied to churches, local boosterism, or both, created colleges throughout the nation. In 1819, for example, Thomas Jefferson realized his long-cherished dream of a state university for Virginia, an accomplishment that he would regard as one of the greatest achievements of his life. Educators in the states and territories west of the Appalachians also viewed education as a key element in expanding democracy to the undisciplined frontier. Institutions such as Transylvania University (founded in 1780) in Kentucky provided a solid post-secondary education under the direction of Horace Holley (president, 1818–1827). For the most part these institutions and other antebellum American colleges did not provide extensive post-secondary training in formal research. Instead they focused on disciplining young minds and emphasized rote memorization for learning.

In the years before the Civil War, however, a growing chorus of Americans criticized the basic college curriculum and argued for a more serious dedication to professional research and study. By the 1840s, for example, young scientists found advanced training in such institutions as Harvard's Lawrence Scientific School and the Yale Scientific School. Renamed the Sheffield Scientific School in 1864, Yale's school became the first Ph.D.-granting institution in the United States when it awarded its first advanced degrees in 1861. Before 1861, various proprietary law schools opened and closed, including the Lumpkin School of Law, which evolved into the University of Georgia Law School after the Civil War. By the 1850s there were thriving law schools at Harvard, Columbia, New York University, the University of Pennsylvania, and Cumberland (in Tennessee).

Between 1865 and 1900, higher education in the United States changed radically. First, the federal government committed more support to higher education by assisting the states in establishing institutions for advanced study. The Morrill Act (1862) provided states with a land grant of 30,000 acres per member of Congress to promote the establishment of state universities. The Hatch Act (1887) expanded agricultural experiment stations in the states and furthered the development of agricultural colleges and departments. Although state legislatures did not uniformly use the money to establish public institutions, federal support provided key assistance for the expansion of higher education.

Second, the importation of the German model of university research provided Americans with a key example for advanced scholarship. A generation of young intellectuals trained in the German vision of high scholarship returned to the United States eager to improve the nation's educational institutions. The late nineteenth century represented the great boom years for American higher education. The major modern universities that took shape in the years following the Civil War included Cornell University (1865), the University of California, Berkeley (1868), and Clark University (1887). The Johns Hopkins University (1876) became the most important of these newly established universities. Under the direction of Daniel Coit Gilman, Hopkins established itself as the leading institution for advanced study in the United States in a wide range of fields, setting the standard in establishing the criteria for Ph.D. study.

In the latter part of the century, business also played a significant role in the establishment and growth of American universities. John D. Rockefeller (who founded the University of Chicago in 1892–1893) and Leland Stanford (founder of Stanford University in 1891), for example, both established institutions of higher education to preserve their own legacies of philanthropic support for professional training. In *The Higher Learning in America* (1918), economist Thorstein Veblen lamented the role that the "captains of erudition" played in the establishment of professional scholarship in the late nineteenth-century United States. Mocking the "business-like presumption . . . that learning is a merchantable commodity" (Veblen, p. 221), Veblen attacked the mechanistic and formulaic assumption in American higher education that there should be some monetary profit from learning and study.

Moreover, the institutions of higher learning in the United States did not provide for the education of all the nation's citizens. For most of the nineteenth century, white men benefited far more than women or minorities from the growth of graduate and professional education. The pressure for university expansion and the demand of women for institutional recognition, however, pushed many universities into coeducation in the last third of the nineteenth century. Stanford (1885), Cornell (1865), and the University of Chicago (1890) all opened as coeducational institutions. The University of Wisconsin began training women as normal school teachers when enrollment dropped during the Civil War, and the University of Michigan began coeducation in 1870 when the state legislature forced them to do so rather than build a new school. In addition, a growing number of women's colleges—Vassar in the 1860s, Wellesley and Smith in the 1870s, Bryn Mawr and Barnard in the 1880s—offered women advanced study and research in the sciences and humanities. Under the direction of M. Cary Thomas, Bryn Mawr College became in 1885 the first women's institution in the country to offer Ph.D. degrees for women, establishing itself as a leading center for women's professional education in the twentieth century.

Segregation forced most African Americans to seek advanced training abroad. Yet, important institutional expansion in the late nineteenth century provided the foundation for later developments in historically black colleges. Excluded from virtually all institutions of higher learning in the United States, African Americans developed their own universities and colleges in the years following emancipation. Fisk University (1867), Howard University (1867), and the Tuskegee Institute (1881) each offered advanced instruction to African Americans and, by the twentieth century, became the major training facilities for African American doctors and lawyers.

After the Civil War, legal education expanded, and increasingly law firms in larger cities sought out graduates of university-affiliated law schools. Between 1870 and 1895 Dean Christopher Columbus Langdell, at Harvard, developed the case method of teaching, in which law students learned how to find the reasoning behind a decision, rather than memorizing treatises, statutes, and forms. In 1881 the American Bar Association urged that all lawyers attend three years of law school before clerking with an attorney. During this period new law schools were opening throughout the country, including a number to train former slaves, most notably at Howard University in Washington, D.C. Howard also accepted women law students, including many who were white. The new land grant universities, like Michigan, Cornell, and Wisconsin, also built law schools. By 1900 there were nearly 100 law schools in the country, some affiliated with colleges and universities and others freestanding.

The patterns of university development established in the late nineteenth century continued into the twentieth century. In fact, the Ph.D. degree and professional training in fields such as law and medicine became the characteristic factor of participation in American intellectual and business life. The unique American educational emphases that arose in the late nineteenth century on scholarship, advanced training, and a business purpose would become key characteristics of the modern American university.

See also **Academic and Professional Societies; Education,** *subentry on* **Colleges and Universities; Legal Profession; Medicine.**

Bibliography

Bledstein, Burton. *The Culture of Professionalism: The Middle Class and the Development of Higher Education in America.* New York: Norton, 1976.

Cremin, Lawrence. *American Education: The National Experience, 1783–1876.* New York: Harper and Row, 1980.

Cremin, Lawrence. *American Education: The Metropolitan Experience, 1876–1980.* New York: Harper and Row, 1988.

Hofstadter, Richard, and Wilson Smith, eds. *American Higher Education: A Documentary History.* Chicago: University of Chicago Press, 1961.

Kimball, Bruce A. *The "True Professional Ideal" in America: A History.* Cambridge, Mass.: Blackwell, 1992.

Oleson, Alexandra, and Sanborn Brown. *The Pursuit of Knowledge in the Early American Republic: American Scientific and Learned Societies from Colonial Times to the Civil War.* Baltimore: Johns Hopkins University Press, 1976.

Oleson, Alexandra, and John Voss. *The Organization of Knowledge in Modern America, 1860–1920.* Baltimore: Johns Hopkins University Press, 1979.

Rothblatt, Sheldon, and Björn Wittrock, eds. *The European and American University since 1800: Historical and Sociological Essays.* Cambridge, U.K.: Cambridge University Press, 1993.

Veblen, Thorstein. *The Higher Learning in America: A Memorandum on the Conduct of Universities by Business Men.* New York: Huebsch, 1918.

Veysey, Lawrence. *The Emergence of the American University.* Chicago: University of Chicago Press, 1965.

EDWARD RAFFERTY

EDUCATION OF GIRLS AND WOMEN

A nineteenth-century American female was first a daughter, frequently a sister, traditionally a wife, and usually a mother. Ultimately a woman's family status provided the rationale, basis, and framework for the nature, condition, and content of her education. In the country's early years, when it was forging a national identity as a republic, Benjamin Franklin, in his translation of Enlightenment ideas into American terms, abandoned the Christian view of a female as a lesser creation, impulsive and emotional. He replaced it with an image of a rational being in pursuit of happiness, which, coupled with his thoughts on natural law and biological determinism, produced a new approach to female education. A woman should be educated to use her rational powers in the development of those qualities that insure happiness in marriage and reproduction, which were her natural destiny.

Formulating a "Suitable Education" for the "True Woman"

Franklin's design brought together marriage, the pursuit of happiness, and education, the last of which he left for the educational theorists to elaborate. In 1787 Benjamin Rush, a doctor at the Pennsylvania Hospital, declared in an address at the Ladies Academy in Philadelphia that female education "should be accommodated to the state of society, manners and government of the country in which it is conducted." To "our ladies" Rush assigned a "suitable education" for the instruction of "their sons" (Woody, *A History of Women's Education in the United States*, vol. 1, pp. 302–303).

Slight attention was given to the education of females before the late eighteenth century. Viewed as intellectually inferior to men, women were regarded as inappropriate subjects for education. Girls who learned to read, write, and figure did so in their own families or with older neighbor women in "dame schools" in an extension of mother's teaching.

In the early nineteenth century secondary schooling for girls appeared on the margins of the increased opportunities for boys and the academies created for boys' education. Girls from coeducational elementary level district schools of the middle and northeastern regions of the country, when admitted to academies for boys, were often treated as a distinct population, physically separated, and taught at different hours or in the off-season, summer. Other schools and academies opened to educate girls exclusively. Many were ephemeral, lasting long enough to meet the teacher's need for money and according to his or her ability to recruit students. Most, in contradiction to the emergent ideology of functional education at the beginning of the century, provided "accomplishments" to adorn the daughters of the wealthy through a characteristic curriculum of French, English, drawing, and embroidery.

In addition to the family role, class position was a factor in the development of education for women. From the political, religious, economic, and social changes of the revolutionary period, nineteenth-century women inherited their own ideology called "the appropriate sphere of women." The eighteenth-century portrait of a rural woman as co-laborer with her husband in farm and commercial enterprises gave way when fragmented societal functions dictated a new division of work. This was particularly true for women who in large numbers identified with the middle and upper classes of American society and from whose ranks emerged the constituents and proponents of advanced education for women.

Among the norms of femininity accessible to women between 1820 and 1860 was the "cult of true womanhood." Urbane men of the upper and middle classes along the Atlantic Coast and their counterparts in the older rural parts of the nation were well served by helping to perpetuate this ideology, which called for women's compliance with the assumption that their domestic role was at the center of meaningful living. The "true woman" was after all domestic, pious, pure, and submissive. To rally women to this point of view, male clergy and educators, such as John Abbott, Horace Bushnell, and Horace Mann, and female social counselors and commentators, such as Sarah Josepha Hale, Almira Hart Phelps, and Lydia Sigourney, flooded the literary market in the 1820s and 1830s with literature of domestic reform.

The first women educators were born in the 1790s and were raised under the influences of cultural forces whose manifestations would be demonstrably apparent in their educational designs. They embraced an educational philosophy that met the needs of the female as decreed by the political mandate of republicanism and the economic exigencies of a division of labor. Their schools recognized women's mental capacities and their special destinies. Women needed the best education as wives and mothers, the first and most important guardians in the instruction of the rising generation.

The assignment of women to teach educational rudiments and moral principles to the young led naturally to the emergence of the early-nineteenth-century woman teacher. The clarion call for the preparation of future wives and mothers resulted in a qualified contingent, some of whom delayed marriage and sought employment as teachers for the nation's expanding youthful population. Motherhood, involvement with children in the formative years, found expression in an extension of the home—the classroom. Significantly the pioneers in the education of women were the leaders of the female seminary movement, which at its height from 1830 to 1860 corresponded chronologically with the cult of true womanhood. The period's three most notable female educators, Emma Willard, Catharine Beecher, and Mary Lyon, exemplified the personal qualities of their generation and the rationale to educate women.

Emma Hart Willard (1787–1870) grew up on a Connecticut farm. With her father's encouragement, she disregarded the accepted view of women as intellectually inferior. Willard's district school and academy instruction were complemented by independent study and family discussions on politics, philosophy, literature, and religion. Even after returning to her former educational settings as a teacher, Willard continued her studies. She married, but her husband's financial reverses prompted her to resume her teaching career. In 1814 she opened Middlebury Female Seminary in Vermont, where her goal was to offer young women classical and scientific studies on the collegiate order. In 1819 New York State legislators refused her request for financial assistance for another seminary. Undaunted, in 1821 she founded the Troy Female Seminary without state aid. She developed an advanced course of study and innovative teaching methods and authored textbooks and examinations in her specialties of history, mathematics, and natural and physical sciences that gained national and international recognition. She trained teachers for the rapidly expanding western United States and contributed to the development of the common school movement.

Catharine Beecher (1800–1878), born on Long Island, was the eldest of thirteen children and the favorite of her father, Lyman Beecher, a Presbyterian minister famous for his defense of the evangelical faith. In her mother's "select" school and under her tutelage, Beecher acquired the knowledge and skills of household management. For a brief time she attended Miss Pierce's School in Litchfield, Connecticut. Upon the death of her fiancé, she permanently ruled out marriage and decided on a life of benevolent service and teaching.

In 1823 Beecher opened a school that was incorporated in 1827 as the Hartford Female Seminary, where she stressed the arts of teaching and domestic science. In 1831 she left for Cincinnati, where, in 1833, she founded the Western Female Institute with the mission to prepare and place teachers from the East in the expanding settlements of the West. Through writing and lecturing rather than teaching, Beecher advocated domestic education and teacher placement. Her educational reform sprang from an indignant sense of disparity between women's idealized role and their actual conditions. Inadequate air

and exercise, torturous conventions of dress, and irrelevant studies were crippling women physically, mentally, and emotionally. Her goals were to end these travesties, and to enable the development of women of energy and benevolence who would then joyfully accept as a sacred vocation the opportunity to shape the immortal minds placed in their care. Beecher viewed woman, with her peculiar domestic obligation, as a savior of society. She incorporated this philosophy into a domestic ideology of household hints, recipes, and psychology. Her 1841 best-seller, *A Treatise on Domestic Economy*, enjoyed fifteen yearly printings and established her as a national authority on the psychological state and physical well being of the American home.

Mary Lyon (1797–1849), born in the western Massachusetts hill town of Buckland, was the sixth of eight children of farmers descended from the area's first settlers. She learned a farmwoman's demanding crafts from her mother and the educational rudiments in the district schools. At seventeen she began teaching summer schools and boarded with local families. At age twenty she enrolled at Sanderson Academy, where she excelled in its advanced subjects. Alternating with district school teaching, she attended Byfield Female Seminary, where she formed a lifelong friendship with its preceptor Zilpah Polly Grant Banister. At Byfield and at Sanderson, where she returned to teach, Lyon experienced the deep religious interest of New England's Great Awakening, and she professed her faith.

For ten years Lyon taught under Grant at the Adams Female Academy and at Ipswich Female Seminary. A stimulating instructor, Lyon continued her education with individual college professors, primarily in the sciences, while she earned a reputation for adeptly preparing teachers. When health problems required Grant to take routine absences for long periods of time, Lyon led the Ipswich School. In 1834 she embarked on a mission to educate young adult women in the common walks of life, women like herself of moderate means, to prepare them to lead useful lives as wives, mothers, and teachers—those stations open to them. In 1837 she opened the Mount Holyoke Female Seminary. Founded and sustained by the Christian public, the seminary charged low board and tuition, domestic work was performed by its "family," and teachers labored for modest salaries. High standards distinguished Mount Holyoke from its inception. Admission required a minimal age of sixteen and demonstration of competency by examination in English, geography, history, arithmetic, and philosophy. The three-year curriculum was notable for its close similarity to the English and scientific courses of men's colleges. Lyon, whose fervor for re-

Traditional Skills Taught in the Classroom. Women students in a cooking class at Virginia's Hampton Institute, established in 1868 by General Samuel Chapman Armstrong. Lieutenant-Colonel of the Ninth United States Colored Troops Regiment during the Civil War, Armstrong became an agent of the Freedman's Bureau after the war to help former slaves in their transition from slavery to free life. Photograph, 1899–1900. LIBRARY OF CONGRESS

vivals and missionary activity gained an unsurpassed reputation for the institution, provided a strong religious character, which interested and enlisted the support of the clergy. The seminary supplied many of the nation's most sought-after teachers, several of whom, in the missionary role, founded schools in the United States and abroad that were based on the Holyoke plan, Lyon's legacy to the advancement of higher education for women.

Advanced Education for Women in America

The female seminary was the first effort to provide advanced education beyond a rudimentary level for American women, and it dominated from 1830 to 1860. A developing nation built upon the democratic ideal looked to the family as the basic unit of society upon which to depend for order. An educated American woman's role was to assist her husband in the supervision and management of home and property and to guide the education of their children. Increasingly the American man was away from home, engaged in the economic life that supported his family

and in the political environment that sustained his country. It was thought that a woman, with delegated responsibilities formerly held by a man, needed an education similar to his. The seminaries interpreted this responsibility in a wide variety of curricular programs that ranged from a modest advancement in the basics with an emphasis upon ornamental "female" accomplishments to an emulation of men's colleges with an education that approached that of the classical curriculum. They prepared women for roles as wives and mothers and in subsequent manifestations as teachers and missionaries. The female seminaries did not qualify as degree-granting institutions. Some, including Mount Holyoke, progressed to that point later in the century. Many emphasized teacher training and evolved into normal schools.

Prior to 1860 many small denominational colleges became coeducational, following the pattern of Oberlin, founded in 1833. Oberlin maintained that women's high calling was as mothers of the race. Within that sphere, future generations were ensured devoted and undistracted mother care. Coeducation at Oberlin reinforced the traditional subordination of women to men in social roles. Oberlin leaders demanded the right to educate women, for they believed that women were endowed with intelligence equal to that of men. Permitted "all the instructive privileges" (Circular, Oberlin Collegiate Institute, 8 March 1834, Box 17, Robert S. Fletcher Papers, Oberlin College Archives, Oberlin, Ohio) of the institution, women were offered an opportunity to equip themselves more completely as the peers of their brothers and husbands in knowledge, thought, and action. An 1836 questionnaire asked forty-six women about their future goals, and twenty-nine declared for missionary work or teaching. "Laboring more efficiently in the vineyard of Christ" may have camouflaged the earnest hope that typified those too modest to state marriage as a goal (Biographies of Woman Students, 1836, Oberlin College Archives, Oberlin, Ohio).

The Morrill Act of 1862 created land-grant colleges and universities, to which women were admitted on the same terms as men. Coeducation was the rule in the western states and in the new universities of the East, such as Cornell, which admitted women in 1872.

In the last half of the nineteenth century, following the female seminary movement, many institutions of higher education for women were created. Controversy surrounded the education of women. They needed to prove that they were intellectually, physically, and emotionally capable of meeting the demands of higher education. The foundings of Vassar in 1861, Wellesley in 1870, and Smith in 1871 were the first attempts to provide a collegiate education for women similar to that for men, distinguished by the classical curriculum and its award for completion, the baccalaureate degree.

When efforts to secure admission of women to Harvard and other centers of learning failed, advocates created an institutional format called the coordinate college. Affiliated with a college or university for men, it was a division for the education of women. In 1879 Harvard formed the Society for Collegiate Instruction of Women, called the "Harvard Annex." Named Radcliffe College in 1893, it was joined by other coordinate colleges, including Barnard at Columbia in 1889, Sophie Newcomb at Tulane in 1887, and Pembroke at Brown in 1891.

Between 1870 and 1890 the number of institutions of higher education in the United States almost doubled, increasing from 582 to 1,082. The percentage of those institutions that were for men only decreased from 59 percent to 37 percent, but the percentage of those for women only increased from 12 percent to 43 percent. In 1870, eleven thousand women attended institutions for advanced education; eight thousand were in normal schools and female seminaries, and three thousand were in degree-granting institutions.

In the second half of the nineteenth century public high schools became co-educational and graduated more girls than boys. Secondary schoolteachers required advanced education, and most were men who held degrees. Educated women without degrees taught in elementary schools. Increasing numbers of women sought degrees in single-sex, coeducational, and coordinate colleges to equip themselves for teaching in high schools. Educational opportunities for women had grown, but the roles toward which these experiences led remained essentially the same—wife, mother, teacher.

See also **Clubs,** *subentry on* **Women's Clubs and Associations; Domestic Life; Gender; Law,** *subentry on* **Women and the Law; Literature,** *subentry on* **Women's Literature; Magazines, Women's; Marriage; Republican Motherhood; Woman's Rights; Women; Women in the Professions.**

Bibliography

Conway, Jill K. "Perspectives on the History of Women's Education in the United States." *History of Education Quarterly* 14 (spring 1974): 1–12.

Cott, Nancy F. *The Bonds of Womanhood: "Woman's Sphere" in New England, 1780–1835.* New Haven, Conn.: Yale University Press, 1977.

James, Edward T., ed. *Notable American Women, 1607–1950.* 3 vols. Cambridge, Mass.: Harvard University Press, Belknap Press, 1971.

Newcomer, Mabel. *A Century of Higher Education for American Women.* New York: Harper, 1959.

Melder, Keith E. *Beginnings of Sisterhood: The American Woman's Rights Movement, 1800–1850.* New York: Schocken, 1977.

Welter, Barbara. "The Cult of True Womanhood: 1820–1860." In *The American Family in Social-Historical Perspective.* Edited by Michael Gordon. New York: St. Martin's, 1978.

Woody, Thomas. *A History of Women's Education in the United States.* 2 vols. New York: Science Press, 1929.

GLADYS HADDAD

EDUCATION OF AFRICAN AMERICANS

Blacks in the nineteenth century, whether free blacks in the North or South, enslaved, or freedmen, made gains in education, but struggled to achieve better schooling. After the Civil War, African Americans challenged discrimination and considered education their highest priority for social betterment.

Antebellum Education

Before the Civil War, the proportion of educated blacks was dismal because of oppressive laws against the schooling of African Americans. In 1850 only 4.7 percent of the 84,639 black children in slave states attended school. Of the 2,435,722 white children in slave states, 39.7 percent went to school. A decade later, the number of black children in slave states had risen to 94,116, but the number attending school had dropped to only 3.2 percent. On the other hand, the number of slave state white children rose to 3,155,576 with 43.9 percent enrolled in school. Black codes enacted during the 1820s and 1830s in the slave states outlawed the education of slaves. Though Georgia and South Carolina had enacted the first such laws in the mid-eighteenth century, the Nat Turner Rebellion in Virginia in 1831 sparked a new wave of harsh behavior controls that sought to prevent learned slaves, such as Turner, from instigating future slave revolts. In spite of these laws some slaves were educated. Whether taught by fellow slaves in their quarters or by sympathetic slaveowners and their families, an estimated 10 percent of enslaved African Americans were literate. Because of their routine contact with whites, those bondspeople who worked as domestic servants were the most likely slaves to be educated.

Free blacks fared only slightly better, but some were highly educated. In 1850 there were 70,475 black children residing in free states. Of these 31.3 percent went to school, compared with 64.9 percent of the 4,757,708 white children in these same states. By 1860 the number of black children in free states increased to 83,724, with 34.9 percent attending school. The number of free state white children rose to 6,365,185 of which 66.8 percent were in school. The 250,000 free blacks who resided in the North during the 1850s faced obstacles to receiving an education despite the public school tradition in the Northeast. In 1855 Massachusetts changed this trend when it became the first state to integrate its public schools, and other New England states followed suit. In 1833 the opening of Oberlin College in Ohio, the first college to admit women and blacks, was a boon to the ranks of educated, black professionals in both the North and the South.

Oberlin College, Harvard University, and several other private institutions in the North became important education centers for free blacks living in the United States. The South's 260,000 free blacks, most of whom were rural laborers and tenant farmers, had few literate members among their ranks. Nonetheless, a significant free black, educated elite, some of whom were slaveowners themselves, received a first-rate education. John Mercer Langston (1829–1897), who was born free, the son of a white plantation owner and an emancipated slave, was one of the first black graduates of Oberlin College, and he became a leading figure in the struggle for educational equality for African Americans. Blanche K. Bruce (1841–1898) and Hiram Revels (1822–1901), both senators from Mississippi during Reconstruction, were mulattoes who received private tutoring as children. Like many children of white owners and slave mothers, Revels was sent to college and graduated from Knox College in Illinois.

Postwar Education

Though a handful of northern and southern free blacks and even fewer slaves earned an education before the Civil War, strides toward universal education were not made until the 1860s and 1870s. The largest influence in the development of an education system for African Americans was the creation of the Freedman's Bureau in 1865. Under the direction of its commissioner, Oliver O. Howard (1830–1909), the Bureau began an ambitious program of black education. By 1869, the Freedman's Bureau had opened 3,000 schools and was supervising 150,000 African American students. Half of its 3,300 teachers were black, and most of the other half were northern women who volunteered their services to the agency. That the fledgling, underfunded agency had been able to open such a large number of schools in less than five years after the Civil War ended was a result of a campaign by African Americans to raise money for education. Although they were the most economically disfranchised group in American society, blacks by 1870 had raised more than $1 million toward the construction of new schools and the hiring of trained teachers.

This campaign and the efforts of Commissioner Howard resulted in limited success toward the goal of education for all African Americans. By 1877, more than 600,000 black children were attending school in the South, and the last decades of the century saw remarkable strides in black literacy rates. Whereas at the end of the Civil War black illiteracy rates were approximately 85 percent, by 1880 they had declined to 73 percent, and by 1900 to 50 percent. The absence of public schools in the South—no state legislature had created a public school system at mid-century—limited the progress toward universal education, but the relative educational success of African Americans in spite of the South's socioeconomic circumstances was important in the

Booker T. Washington (1856–1915). Foremost African American educator and leader at the end of the century, Washington was a protégé of General Samuel Chapman Armstrong, founder of the Hampton Institute, from which Washington graduated in 1875. As a young man he became the first principal of the Tuskegee Institute in Alabama, which he built and continued to oversee throughout his career. Photograph, 1906. LIBRARY OF CONGRESS

subsequent battles waged by black leaders against the continued unequal educational opportunities for African Americans.

The most important institutions for producing black leaders were black colleges. The American Missionary Association founded seven colleges for African Americans between 1866 and 1870, the most notable being Fisk University (1866) in Nashville and Atlanta University (1872). The Freedman's Bureau supplemented the AMA's goal of producing black teachers, ministers, and other professionals by founding Howard University (1866) in Washington, D.C., and northern philanthropists, led by Robert Curtis Ogden (1836–1913), donated money to new black schools, such as the Hampton Institute (1877) in Virginia.

New Directions in Black Education

In spite of these strides and significant philanthropic support from the North, black leaders by the 1880s held different opinions regarding the future of black education. Booker T. Washington (1856–1915), a graduate of the Hampton Institute, was a proponent of practical, or "industrial," education for blacks. Washington argued that this type of training would most quickly create a black workforce that could achieve economic independence from the farm tenancy system that had supplanted slavery in the postwar South. To that end, in 1881 he founded and became principal of Tuskegee Institute, a black college in Alabama modeled after Hampton's vocational curriculum. Other black leaders, most notably W. E. B. Du Bois (1868–1963), criticized Washington's position and called for classical education at black schools. Du Bois, who was educated in liberal arts at Fisk, believed that industrial training would result in only low-paying jobs for blacks and make permanent their oppressed position in society.

Thus after less than a half-century of access to a discriminatory educational system, at the turn of the century African Americans were still challenging the remnants of antebellum racial attitudes and the new racism that limited black educational success after the war helped to foment.

See also **African Americans,** *subentries on* **Overview, Free Blacks before the Civil War; Race and Racial Thinking; Race Laws; Segregation,** *subentry on* **Segregation and Civil Rights.**

Bibliography

Anderson, James D. *The Education of Blacks in the South, 1860–1935.* Chapel Hill: University of North Carolina Press, 1988.

Blassingame, John W. *The Slave Community: Plantation Life in the Antebellum South.* New York: Oxford University Press, 1972.

Litwack, Leon F. *Been in the Storm So Long: The Aftermath of Slavery.* New York: Knopf, 1979.

Morris, Robert C. *Reading, 'Riting and Reconstruction: The Education of Freedmen in the South, 1861–1870.* Chicago: University of Chicago Press, 1981.

U.S. Bureau of the Census. *The Seventh Census of the United States: 1850.* Washington, D.C.: Robert Armstrong, 1853.

———. *Statistics of the United States in 1860.* Washington, D.C.: Government Printing Office, 1864.

KEVIN ROBERTS

INDIAN SCHOOLS

Since the late 1500s, non-Indians have attempted to educate American Indians and to assimilate them into Euro-American society as an alternative to extermination. During the seventeenth and eighteenth centuries, North American colonists largely were unsuccessful in these campaigns. The U.S. government's Indian Civilization Fund Act of 1819 subsidized religious groups to provide Indian education. These efforts had limited impact. Although there were a few converts to Christianity and "white ways," most Indians were not interested in the type of education Americans had to offer.

After the Civil War, the push to assimilate Indians into U.S. society accelerated. Although many "reformers" meant well and were hopeful that education and acculturation could prevent the extinction of Indians, they still believed that Indians were inferior to whites. They argued that education would rid the tribes of their superstitions, savagery, and general ignorance of civilization; this could be accomplished by taking Indian children from their homes and educating them at off-reservation boarding schools. These youngsters then would serve as examples for their families to follow. The reformers' tactics were authoritarian and contained little room for native input.

Government Boarding Schools

During the late nineteenth century, the harsh methods used to educate Indians to the ways of white society were epitomized by the Army captain Richard Henry Pratt (1840–1924). In 1879 Congress allowed Pratt to use army barracks in Pennsylvania, where he founded the Carlisle Indian Industrial School. At Carlisle and other boarding schools, such as Hampton (Virginia), Chilocco (Oklahoma), Genoa (Nebraska), Keams Canyon (Arizona), and Rainy Mountain (Oklahoma), students suffered many difficulties, including homesickness and disease. Taught by white teachers and missionaries who assumed they knew what was best for Indian children, yet knowing nothing about Indian culture, they forced children to wear "civilized" clothing, relinquish their religious and ceremonial paraphernalia, cut their hair, perform manual labor, and cease speaking their native languages. The children also were told repeatedly that Indians were inferior beings. By 1900 the government maintained at least 20,000 students enrolled in 148 boarding schools and 225 day schools that were located closer to the tribes.

Despite the federal government's lofty goals, its Indian boarding schools were poorly funded and administered. The Meriam Report, issued in 1928, revealed that the children at the boarding schools faced health problems, poor living conditions, inadequate diets, and extreme punishments. In addition, the report disclosed that teachers largely were untrained and that school curriculums did not pertain to students' needs or account for differences between tribes. The report's conclusion was that, despite the educators' relentless efforts at changing American Indians' values, students and their families clung tenaciously to their Indian identities and cultures.

Tribal Schools

Indian tribes also established their own boarding and day schools to control their youths' education. The

Acculturation by Education. A female pupil of the Government School at Carlisle for American Indians visits her home at the Pine Ridge Reservation. The juxtaposition of western dress of the student versus the native costume of her relatives indicates white society's intent that students educate their families by example. *Frank Leslie's Illustrated Newspaper,* 15 March 1884. LIBRARY OF CONGRESS: PRINTS AND PHOTOGRAPHS DIVISION

Cherokee Male and Female Seminaries, for example, were established in the 1850s by the Cherokee Nation in Indian Territory. The elaborately built seminaries provided quality education through the first decade of the 1900s, including a rigorous curriculum patterned after those of Mount Holyoke Seminary and Yale. They were different from federal boarding schools in that parents voluntarily sent their children to the schools, many of the teachers were seminary alumnae, and the health care was as good as in white schools. The majority of Cherokees enrolled were acculturated mixed bloods, many of whom graduated and became politicians, physicians, educators, attorneys, and social workers. Other tribes that established their own boarding schools included the Choctaws, Chickasaws, Creeks, Quapaws, Osages, and Shawnees.

Impact of Education on Tribes

American Indians were affected profoundly by their children's experiences at the government boarding schools. The results of the combination of loss of tribal culture, family separation, and being told by white teachers that Indians were savage and uncivilized included depression, insecurity, and confusion. Some students committed suicide and others suffered loneliness. Ironically, after some Indian children were educated, they were not accepted into white society, nor could they fit into their tribe's society when they returned. Often, the jobs students were trained for at school were not available on their reservations. Many students absorbed much of what was taught to them at the schools, brought that knowledge home to their families, and, in effect, became agents of cultural change among their people.

While most Indian students resisted assimilation, some adopted the ways of white society and became successful according to white standards. Some children adapted well to the school environments by forming cliques that provided emotional support. They also were able to keep up with tribal ways, spoke their tribal language in secret, and often had fond memories of their school days while at the same time retaining their cultural identities as American Indians.

See also **American Indians,** *subentry on* **U.S. Government Policies; Missions,** *subentries on* **North American Indians, Indian Responses to White Missionaries.**

Bibliography

Adams, David Wallace. *Education for Extinction: American Indians and the Boarding School Experience, 1875–1928.* Lawrence: University Press of Kansas, 1995.

Coleman, Michael C. *American Indian Children at School, 1850–1930.* Jackson: University Press of Mississippi, 1993.

Ellis, Clyde. *To Change Them Forever: Indian Education at the Rainy Mountain Boarding School, 1893–1920.* Norman: University of Oklahoma Press, 1996.

Lomawaima, K. Tsianina. *They Called it Prairie Light: The Story of Chilocco Indian School.* Lincoln: University of Nebraska Press, 1994.

Mihesuah, Devon A. *Cultivating the Rosebuds: The Education of Women at the Cherokee Female Seminary, 1851–1909.* Urbana: University of Illinois Press, 1993.

Szasz, Margaret C. *Indian Education in the American Colonies, 1607–1783.* Albuquerque: University of New Mexico Press, 1988.

DEVON A. MIHESUAH

EDUCATION OF THE BLIND AND DEAF

Until the nineteenth century, the United States had no formal institutions for schooling either blind or deaf people, although private, informal teaching had taken place, particularly among elite families. Then new teaching techniques were adopted, and centralized schools were established for blind and deaf students. By the end of the century, most states supported a school for each group or, in some cases, a school that housed both types of students. Institutions dedicated to teaching blind and deaf people originated in western Europe, were transplanted to New England, and then spread to New York, Pennsylvania, and eventually across the nation. The southern states did not begin to address the educational needs of black blind and deaf residents until after the Civil War, and then schools were segregated by race.

Blind Education

The reformer Samuel Gridley Howe (1801–1876) took the lead in educating blind people in the United States. After traveling to Europe in 1831 to explore the approaches being undertaken there, he founded the New England Asylum for the Blind (later the Perkins School for the Blind) in Boston in 1832. Similar schools for the blind were later established elsewhere across the nation, and students were taught the skills to become musicians, teach at other schools, and follow trades, in particular broom making. For example, one graduate of a Philadelphia school for the blind helped establish a similar institution in Macon, Georgia, in 1852. Blind students learned to read and write using the system of "raised print" developed by Louis Braille (1809–1852) in France.

The programs at nineteenth-century schools for the blind reflected the students' determination that they could overcome whatever difficulties accompanied their impairments. The schools reflected, too, a broader social consensus that all people should be trained for self-sufficiency and that public funds should facilitate access to these schools. The schools were not fully public, especially in the early years. Students' families typically covered some costs themselves if they were able to, but public funds supplemented private funds, and students themselves generated money for the school through the sale of crafts or grew and processed food that fed the school population.

Deaf Education

The first successful U.S. school for deaf children, later named the American School for the Deaf, was established in 1817 in Hartford, Connecticut, by a hearing New Englander, Thomas Hopkins Gallaudet (1787–1851), and a deaf Frenchman, Laurent Clerc (1785–1869). Clerc brought to the new school both French sign language and a pedagogical model of deaf education based on sign language. At the school, French sign language began to combine with the "home sign" systems the students had developed to communicate with their nonsigning family and friends. American Sign Language emerged from this blending process.

At Gallaudet's schools, deaf children who had been isolated from other deaf people came together and formed a community. Beyond creating a distinct language, the students adopted group values that sometimes were at odds with those of the hearing community. This language and culture spread from New England to other parts of the country as new schools, formed elsewhere, often hired graduates of the Hartford school as the first teachers.

Before the establishment of formal schools for the deaf, some elite deaf people were taught in groups by private educators. Martha's Vineyard, Massachusetts, had such a large percentage of genetically deaf people that its hearing residents also often communicated by sign language. When deaf people from such groups attended formal schools, they shared their group's methods of communication. Thus, as in Hartford, the country's institutions for the deaf helped combine a variety of already-existing deaf languages and cultures into a new and increasingly national experience.

Culture and Conflict

Tensions often characterized relations between deaf students and their hearing teachers or the wider community. Much of this friction centered around whether to teach deaf students to communicate using sign language, an oral method, or some combination of the two systems. Although manualism (the use of sign language) was the dominant pedagogical method at antebellum schools for the deaf, an oralist approach was favored later in the century. Thomas Hopkins Gallaudet's son, Edward Miner Gallaudet (1837–1917), was the leading post–Civil War proponent of signing or, more precisely, of a combined system with an emphasis on sign language. Alexander Graham Bell (1847–1922) emerged as a champion of oralism.

Centralized schools allowed students to see their deafness as other than a handicap. In the students' eyes, their deafness was not a disability as long as sign language was used widely. Even though antebellum schools fostered this attitude, the hearing teachers and administrators often did not understand the students' perspective. Instead, they believed deaf people needed paternalistic guidance and protection. During the late nineteenth century, increasing numbers of teachers prohibited the use of sign language and instead trained students to speak and to read lips. But the debate about communication methods had little to do either with pedagogy or with the wants and needs of deaf people.

During the antebellum period, Americans typically worried that deaf people were separated from the Christian community by their inability to hear the word of God. Teachers of the deaf felt that manualism remedied this separation from religion. Using sign language, the reformers could teach Christian principles to deaf people. By the end of the nineteenth century, reformers were less interested in deaf people's isolation from Christianity. Instead, the post–Civil War emphasis on nationalism led reformers to fear the deaf community's separation from the larger English-speaking community. Only through the use of speech could the deaf prove they were part of the nation and not a threat to its unity.

As creationists, early-nineteenth-century Americans believed that God created pristine beings who continually fell from perfection. Because many Americans thought that early humans had used gestures rather than speech to communicate, sign language was deemed closer to God than spoken language. In the late nineteenth century, evolutionary theory swept the United States. Humans were seen as continuously improving, with each generation superior to the previous. The ability to speak was now the evolutionary marker between humans and beasts. According to oralists, therefore, the use of sign language doomed the deaf to a subhuman status. Only speech could restore them to their humanity.

Gender and economics also played into the conflict. Before the Civil War, most teachers of deaf people were men, who used sign language and taught students old enough to care for themselves. After the war, the teaching force became increasingly female. The shift to oralism encouraged this trend. Speech training required a lower teacher-student ratio. To avoid higher educational expenses, women were hired because they could not demand the high salaries men received. In addition, oral education was thought to be effective only for very young children, for whom men were seen as inappropriate caretakers. Moreover, oralist day schools cost less to run than signing-based residential schools.

Hearing manualists understood that the deaf were different from the hearing in both language and culture, but, because of their paternalistic attitudes, they could not accept deaf people in positions of authority. Oralists claimed they advocated equality for deaf people, but they would not allow sign language because it represented a difference between hearing and deaf people. Neither manualists nor oralists could accept both equality and difference.

Special Cases

Representing special challenges, and therefore special triumphs, were Laura Bridgman (1829–1889), born in New Hampshire, and Helen Keller (1880–1968), born in Alabama. Though each had been born seeing and hearing, each lost both abilities as a result of acute illness when still barely a toddler. Each demonstrated what could be accomplished once having broken through the barriers with the assistance of a gifted teacher. Samuel Gridley Howe taught Laura Bridgman at the Perkins School, and Helen Keller's

Single and Double Hand Alphabet, June 1864. Signing was developed in eighteenth-century France. Thomas Hopkins Gallaudet (1787–1851), an American, and Laurent Clerc of the Institut Royal des Sourds-Muets in Paris began teaching deaf Americans the alphabet in 1817. This language fell out of favor during the late nineteenth century since it was seen to promote the separateness of the deaf community from the American public. LIBRARY OF CONGRESS

first teacher, Anne Sullivan, who had only limited sight herself, was trained there.

Congress funded Gallaudet College, named in honor of Thomas Hopkins Gallaudet, in 1864, and Edward Miner Gallaudet served as its president for many years. Thus there emerged, beyond primary and secondary schooling, an institution of higher education for deaf Americans; beyond state responsibility, support from the federal government; and, beyond what emerged for blind Americans, an institution that could provide national leadership as well as academic training for an emerging national deaf community.

See also **Welfare and Charity.**

Bibliography

Baynton, Douglas C. *Forbidden Signs: American Culture and the Campaign Against Sign Language.* Chicago: University of Chicago Press, 1996.

Buchanan, Robert M. *Illusions of Equality: Deaf Americans in School and Factory, 1850–1950.* Washington, D.C.: Gallaudet University Press, 1999.

Farrell, Gabriel. *The Story of Blindness.* Cambridge, Mass.: Harvard University Press, 1956.

Gannon, Jack R. *Deaf Heritage: A Narrative History of Deaf America.* Edited by Jane Butler and Laura-Jean Gilbert. Silver Spring, Md.: National Association of the Deaf, 1981.

Groce, Nora Ellen. *Everyone Here Spoke Sign Language: Hereditary Deafness on Martha's Vineyard.* Cambridge, Mass.: Harvard University Press, 1985.

Koestler, Frances A. *The Unseen Minority: A Social History of Blindness in the United States.* New York: McKay, 1976.

Valentine, Phyllis Klein. "American Asylum for the Deaf: A First Experiment in Education, 1817–1880." Ph.D. diss., University of Connecticut, 1993.

Van Cleve, John Vickrey, and Barry A. Crouch. *A Place of Their Own: Creating the Deaf Community in America.* Washington, D.C.: Gallaudet University Press, 1989.

Wallenstein, Peter. "Laissez Faire and the Lunatic Asylum: State Welfare Institutions in Georgia—The First Half Century, 1830s–1880s." In *Before the New Deal: Social Welfare in the South, 1830–1930.* Edited by Elna C. Green. Athens: University of Georgia Press, 1999.

HANNAH JOYNER
PETER WALLENSTEIN

ELECTIONS

[This entry includes two subentries, **Campaigns and Elections** and **Presidential Elections.**]

CAMPAIGNS AND ELECTIONS

Political parties in the nineteenth century were conceived of as armies—as disciplined, hierarchical fighting organizations whose mission it was to defeat a clearly identified opponent. If defeated themselves, they knew how to retreat, regroup, and fight again another day. If they won, then the victory was sweet. In an era when many if not most political leaders had experience as militia officers and perhaps had engaged in actual combat, structuring parties along a militaristic chain of command seemed logical enough. The very language of politics bespoke combat, as this composite of frequently used words and phrases makes clear:

> From the opening gun, the standard bearer, marching alongside the other warhorses fielded by the party, rallied the rank and file. Precinct captains, having drilled their troops for a rigorous campaign, aligned their phalanxes shoulder to shoulder to mobilize votes for the Old Guard. Top strategists plotted moves while their newspaper allies opened fire with their heaviest artillery. Meanwhile the Mugwumps warned that the palace troops sought to plunder the treasury; their strategy was to crusade against the myrmidons of corruption. Even a man on horseback could not have saved the lost cause with his jingoism. But party headquarters changed tactics and emptied its war chest to buy mercenaries, ordering the troops to regroup. Finally the veterans closed ranks, rallied around their standard, overwhelmed the last ditch of the enemy camp, and divided the spoils of victory.

Party Organization

To fight a political battle, the party had to develop a chain of command. The heads of the state and national tickets normally were the acknowledged leaders. After the election, leadership reverted to the state and county committees, or sometimes to state "bosses," with little power held by the national chairman. County committees sent delegates to the state convention, where state nominees were selected. In turn the county committees were based on local conventions—mass meetings that were open to any self-identified partisan.

In the 1790s Thomas Jefferson and Alexander Hamilton created their supporting parties by working outward from the national capital, as did the Whigs in the 1830s. But major third parties typically emerged from the state level, including the Anti-Masons, Republicans, Know-Nothings, and Populists. By 1800 the Republicans had a well-developed system for recruiting troops throughout the country, and a correspondence system for state and local party leaders to keep in touch. As Boston Federalist Fisher Ames complained in a 1799 essay, "The jacobins have at last made their own discipline perfect; they are trained, officered, regimented and formed to subordination in a manner that our own militia have never yet equaled" (*Works*, p. 101). The Federalists began to imitate their opponents' tactics, but were always too aristocratic to appreciate the value of a grassroots movement.

The Jeffersonian Republican caucus in Congress chose presidential candidates for the party, while the Federalists invented (in 1812) the much more flexible system of a national convention. Unlike the caucus, the convention represented voters in every district, and the delegates were chosen specifically for the task of selecting candidates. By the 1830s the standard had been established that participation in the convention identified the person with the party and required him to support the chosen nominees. It was possible to bolt a convention before candidates were selected, as did the southern Democrats in 1860 and Theodore Roosevelt's supporters in 1912.

New York Democrats were perennially split into "hard" and "soft" factions, and the state's Whigs sometimes split as well. Typically both factions claimed their ticket was the one true legitimate party ticket. William Jennings Bryan perfected the technique of multiple appeals in 1896, running simultaneously as a regular Democrat, a Silver Republican, and a regular Populist. Voters of all parties could vote for him without crossing their personal party loyalty. Most states soon thereafter banned the practice of running on different tickets—one man, one party, one platform became the usual rule (except in New York, where third, fourth, and fifth parties flourished after the 1830s).

Mobilizing Voters

The basic campaign strategy was the maximum mobilization of potential votes. To find new supporters, politicians systematically canvassed their communities, talking up the state and national issues of the day and seeing which themes drew the best responses. In a large, complex, pluralistic nation, the politicians discovered that citizens were especially loyal to their own ethno-religious groups. These groups had distinctive moral perspectives and political needs. The Whigs and Republicans were especially effective in winning support among African Americans and among pietistic and evangelical denominations. The Democrats on the other hand did much better with Catholics and other high church (liturgical) groups, as well as with libertarians who wanted minimal government and whites who demanded that African Americans not be granted political or social equality.

As the parties developed distinctive positions on issues such as the modernization of the economy and westward expansion, voters found themselves attracted to one or the other of them. The Whigs and Republicans aggressively supported modernizing the economy, supporting banks, railroads, factories, and tariffs, and promising a rich home market in the cities for farm products. The Whigs always opposed expansion, as did the Republicans until 1898. The Democrats, meanwhile, talked of agrarian virtues, westward expansion, white supremacy, and how well rural life comported with Jeffersonian values.

By the late nineteenth century the parties in the Midwest combined to turn out over 90 percent of the eligible electorate in entire states, reaching over 95 percent in 1896 in Illinois, Indiana, Iowa, Michigan, and Ohio. Some counties passed the 100 percent mark, not because of fraud but because the parties tracked down people whom the census had missed. Fraud did take place in municipal elections in large cities, where the ward-heelers could expect tangible rewards. Apart from some Reconstruction episodes in the South, there was little fraud in presidential elections because the local workers were not in line for presidential rewards. The best way to build enthusiasm was to show enthusiasm. The parties used rallies, parades, banners, buttons, and insignia to display partisanship and promote the theme that with so much strength, victory was inevitable. The side that lost tended to ascribe defeat to factors out of their control, such as bad weather or treachery.

Communicating the Message

The parties created an internal communications system designed to keep in close touch with the voter. They set up volunteer organizations in every county, city, township, or precinct, charged with visiting every potential supporter, especially in the critical last days before the election. These workers comprised the activists who attended conventions and ultimately selected the candidates. Their intensive face-to-face networking provided excellent information—the leaders immediately found out what the rank and file liked and disliked.

The second communications system was a national network of partisan newspapers. Nearly all weekly and daily papers were party organs until the early twentieth century. Thanks to the invention of high-speed presses for city papers (1835), and free postage for rural sheets (1794), newspapers proliferated. In 1850 the census counted 1,630 party newspapers (with a circulation of about one per voter), and only eighty-three "independent" papers. The party line was behind every line of news copy, not to mention the authoritative editorials that exposed the stupidity of the enemy and the triumphs of the party in every issue. Editors were senior party leaders and often were rewarded with lucrative postmasterships. Top publishers, such as Horace Greeley, Whitelaw

Membership Certificate of Wide-Awake Club. The marching club endorsed Abraham Lincoln and Hannibal Hamlin for the presidential election of 1860. LIBRARY OF CONGRESS: PRINTS AND PHOTOGRAPHS DIVISION

Reid, Schuyler Colfax, Warren Harding, and James Cox ran on the national tickets.

After 1900, William Randolph Hearst, Joseph Pulitzer, and other big-city politician-publishers discovered that they could make far more profit through advertising, charging rates based on the size of their readerships. By becoming nonpartisan they expanded their base to include the opposition party and the fast-growing number of consumers who read the ads but were less and less interested in politics. Political news declined after 1900, apparently because citizens became more apathetic, in part transferring their partisan loyalties to the new professional sports teams that attracted larger and larger audiences.

Campaigns and Crusades

Campaigns were financed internally for most of the nineteenth century. Aspirants for office volunteered their services as speakers; wealthy leaders contributed cash; patronage appointees not only worked for the party but were expected to donate 2 to 5 percent of their salaries. The problem with the system was the winner's curse: in a close election, campaign managers promised the same lucrative jobs over and over again. If they lost, it made no difference; if they won,

they faced an impossible task, guaranteed to alienate supporters. Abraham Lincoln, for example, was a leading western supporter of Zachary Taylor in 1848, and wanted in return to be named commissioner of the Land Office. Instead he was offered a job in Oregon, which, while paying well, would have terminated his career in Illinois. Lincoln declined, and temporarily dropped out of politics. After civil service reform ratcheted into place late in the century, new revenue sources were needed. Mark Hanna found the solution in 1896, as he systematically billed corporations for their share of campaign costs.

At times party campaigns turned into passionate crusades. A body of intensely moralistic politicians would come to believe that the opposition, ensconced in power, was thoroughly corrupt and had plans to destroy the American republican experiment. Americans were profoundly committed to the principle that their system of politics and government could not be allowed to perish from the earth, and crusades roused their emotional intensity. The American Revolution itself had drawn strength from this attitude, as did Jefferson's followers in 1800. Andrew Jackson in 1828 led a crusade against the "corrupt bargain" that had denied him the White House in 1824; his next crusade targeted the Bank of the United States in 1832. Republicans crusaded against slavery in 1856, while Greeley rang corruption charges against President Ulysses S. Grant in 1872. And in 1896 William Jennings Bryan identified the gold and monied interests as responsible for depression, poverty, and plutocracy. Throughout the century crusaders became the targets of counteroffensives, identifying these individuals as extremists. Thus Adams was attacked as a monarchist, Jefferson as an atheist, Jackson as a murderer, radical Republican John Charles Frémont as a disunionist, and Bryan as an anarchist.

Defining the Electorate

In comparison with the other political systems of the world, the United States stood for democracy. Every government officeholder was elected, or chosen by elected officials. After 1848 many states revised their constitutions so that judges were elected to fixed terms and had to campaign before the voters like other officeholders. Election days were staggered, so there was little respite from constant campaigning. As the politicians discovered more and more potential blocs of voters, they worked to abolish the traditional property standards for suffrage. The principles of republicanism seemed to require that everyone be eligible, and indeed actually vote. Several states allowed immigrants to vote before they took out citizenship papers; elsewhere the parties facilitated the naturalization process. By mid-century, practically every adult white male was a potential voter—or indeed, an actual voter, as turnout nationwide reached 81 percent in 1860. America stood in stark contrast with Europe, where the middle classes, peasants, and industrial workers had to mobilize to demand voting rights. Late in the century Americans did create farmer and labor movements, but most were nonpartisan, and those that fielded candidates rarely lasted more than an election or two.

Black suffrage and woman suffrage were key issues of the 1860s and 1870s. Both reforms occasioned enough resistance to force Americans to rethink their notions of universal suffrage. By the early twentieth century, as turnout fell in the face of black disfranchisement and stiff registration hurdles facing new immigrants, the Progressives decided that a smaller, more select electorate would better defend the principles of republicanism. Once blacks and immigrants had been limited, the saloon defeated, and most ethnics Americanized during World War I, then it became possible to grant women the right to vote. The nineteenth century thus created democracy in practice, rallied the people to it, and proved that a government of the people, by the people, and for the people could survive and flourish.

See also **Politics; Voters and Voting.**

Bibliography

Dinkin, Robert J. *Campaigning in America: A History of Election Practices.* Westport, Conn.: Greenwood, 1989.

Formisano, Ronald P. *The Transformation of Political Culture: Massachusetts Parties, 1790s–1840s.* New York: Oxford University Press, 1983.

Gienapp, William E. *The Origins of the Republican Party, 1852–1856.* New York: Oxford University Press, 1987.

Jensen, Richard. *The Winning of the Midwest: Social and Political Conflict, 1888–1896.* Chicago: University of Chicago Press, 1971.

Kleppner, Paul. *The Third Electoral System, 1853–1892: Parties, Voters, and Political Cultures.* Chapel Hill: University of North Carolina Press, 1979.

McCormick, Richard P. *The Second American Party System: Party Formation in the Jacksonian Era.* Chapel Hill: University of North Carolina Press, 1966.

Schlesinger, Arthur M., Jr., ed. *History of American Presidential Elections, 1789–1968.* 4 vols. New York: Chelsea House, 1971.

Silbey, Joel H. *The American Political Nation, 1838–1893.* Stanford, Calif.: Stanford University Press, 1991.

RICHARD JENSEN

PRESIDENTIAL ELECTIONS

In the nineteenth century presidential elections helped shape the course of national politics in decisive ways. The process of electing the chief executive remained as the framers of the Constitution had specified it, with the exception of the Twelfth Amendment (1804), which was designed to correct a flaw in the operation of the electoral college. The college consisted of the electors from each state; their number was the same as the state's senators and representatives in Congress. Each elector was to vote for two candidates. To become president a candidate had to receive a majority of all the electors' votes. The candidate with the second-highest number of votes was elected vice president. In the elections of 1789 and 1792, George Washington was elected unanimously. By 1796 political parties had formed, and John Adams, a Federalist, won a narrow victory over his Democratic-Republican rival, Thomas Jefferson.

The Election of 1800

In 1800 Jefferson and his running mate, Aaron Burr, won decisively over Adams on the Federalist ticket. Because each Democratic-Republican elector cast his two votes for Jefferson and for Burr, there was a tie that put the contest into the House of Representatives. After thirty-six ballots, Jefferson was chosen. This controversy produced the Twelfth Amendment, which made the electoral college's votes for president and for vice president separate processes.

What made the 1800 presidential election so important was not this procedural tangle, bitter as it was at the time. When Thomas Jefferson took the oath of office on 4 March 1801, it demonstrated that a transfer of power from one political party to another could occur without violence or civil discontent. John Adams and his followers did not contest the result or question the legitimacy of Jefferson's election. In that sense the election of 1800 may have been the most important in the nation's history.

Three other presidential elections—1828, 1860, and 1896—produced changes in how the nation conducted its political affairs. A fourth contest, in 1876, led to the only disputed election result in American history. Together these elections demonstrate the evolution of the nation's politics during the course of the nineteenth century.

The Election of 1828

The contest between President John Quincy Adams and Andrew Jackson produced important changes in the way that Americans chose their national leader. Three significant developments came together in this contest to transform the conduct of presidential elections. The manner of waging campaigns was changed; a presidential candidate ran on his personality and national popularity, as well as his program; and a two-party system received a large impetus.

The transformation in campaign style occurred because of a more involved and active white male electorate. No longer did state legislatures (except in Delaware and South Carolina) choose presidential electors. The voters now made the selection, and they expected the candidates to court their support. The Jacksonian forces responded to this new situation with newspapers that proclaimed the message of their candidate across the country in a focused and disciplined manner. The rudiments of a national campaign organization also appeared with a network of committees that sent information to voters. State conventions endorsed Jackson, and rallies, parades, and marches provided political entertainment.

The personal appeal of Andrew Jackson was another central element in the 1828 contest. Jackson's heroic military record, particularly his success at the Battle of New Orleans in 1815, made him nationally known, and his appearance at the celebration of the thirteenth anniversary of the battle in January 1828 got his campaign off to a tumultuous start. Jackson's nickname, "Old Hickory," led to production of an abundance of trees, canes, brooms, and poles that conveyed the message of his resolute toughness. Its

emphasis on personality and popularity made the 1828 election one of the dirtiest in American history, as each party threw mud at the other's candidates. Jackson's opponents attacked his wife and questioned whether Andrew and Rachel Jackson were legally married. In the process the presidential election was being turned into a form of mass entertainment.

To finance and manage a national appeal, the political party became an indispensable organizational weapon. Although the 1828 election did not see the well-defined Democratic and Whig alignments that characterized the 1830s and 1840s, the outlines of the party system were evident by the time Jackson swept to a decisive victory over John Quincy Adams. From that point on, presidential elections placed greater emphasis on selling the candidates, merchandising their personalities, and entertaining the voters as they considered the choices for leadership of the country.

The Election of 1860

The importance of Abraham Lincoln's victory in the presidential election of 1860 lies in the brutal and protracted Civil War that followed. The contest revealed the extent to which the normal processes of national politics had broken down over the slavery question and the sectional bitterness that it spawned. Where the other decisive presidential elections of the nineteenth century showed the ability of the political system to manage change peacefully, the 1860 contest demonstrated the limits of democracy in the face of irreconcilable differences among the American people.

The election had four major parties and their candidates in the field: the Constitutional Union Party's John Bell of Tennessee; the Northern Democratic Party's Stephen A. Douglas; the Southern Democrats' John C. Breckinridge; and the Republican Party's Abraham Lincoln. It was clear that the election would be decided in the North, since neither Lincoln nor Douglas could expect any electoral votes from the South. Lincoln stayed home, avoided campaigning, and made no speeches. Douglas campaigned actively throughout the North. The Republicans poured their energies into organization, including such innovations as marching societies known as the Wide-Awakes. The martial spirit that infused the election would dominate campaign styles for a generation.

Lincoln won a decisive victory with 180 electoral votes, but his popular vote total of less than 40 percent meant that he was a minority president. In the North, however, he was the clear choice of the voters; even if the votes of his rivals had been added together,

Presidential Race, 1860. Lincoln and Douglas sprint toward the U.S. Capitol, with Lincoln in the lead. The rail and maul that Lincoln holds is a reference to his political persona as a rail-splitter. LIBRARY OF CONGRESS: PRINTS AND PHOTOGRAPHS DIVISION

he still would have attained his electoral college triumph.

The important aspect of the 1860 election was that the losers in the South did not accept the legitimacy of Lincoln's victory. They believed that the inauguration of a Republican president foreshadowed the end of slavery and the culture of the South as they had known it. Accordingly, in the wake of Lincoln's triumph, southern states began to adopt ordinances of secession from the Union. By Lincoln's inauguration on 4 March 1861, sectional tensions had reached such a height that hostilities had become inevitable. By April 1861 the North and South were at war. The election of 1860 stands as a testament to the inability of a democratic society to accommodate fundamental disagreements about the nature of society, the rights of all human beings within the nation, and the proper role of government in the settlement of disputes between major sections of the country.

The Election of 1876 and the Compromise of 1877

After the bloody Civil War ended, the nation embarked on the painful process of sectional reconcili-

ation and social change in the South, known as Reconstruction. For a dozen years after 1865, the North endeavored to establish the rights of the freed slaves to take part in the political life of the South on a basis approaching equality with whites. That campaign encountered a number of obstacles: southern resistance, including the violence of the Ku Klux Klan; growing northern indifference to the fate of blacks; and competing issues of industrialism and westward expansion. By the mid-1870s the Democratic Party had regained control of the House of Representatives, and the Republicans were clearly tired of their commitment to a multiracial South.

In the 1876 presidential election these crosscurrents produced a disputed result and a sectional bargain to end Reconstruction. On Election Night the Democratic candidate, Samuel J. Tilden, was within one electoral vote of the 185 needed to win. His Republican rival, Rutherford B. Hayes, had 165 electoral votes, and three states were undecided. In the weeks that followed, Congress found itself confronted with contested returns from those states—Florida, Louisiana, and South Carolina—with no clear way to resolve the impasse. A stalemate ensued as Con-

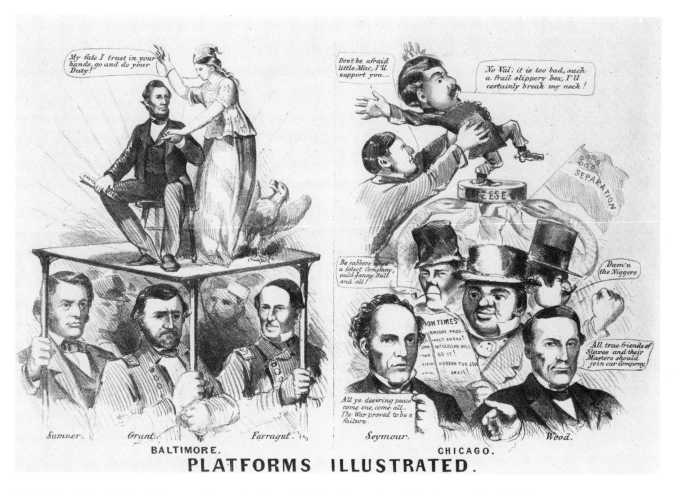

PLATFORMS ILLUSTRATED.

A Pro-Republican Political Cartoon. The contentious 1864 elections mirrored the issues of the Civil War and the splits within the Democratic Party. Lincoln's success was not assured; by November, however, he had won a solid majority. Published by Prang & Company, 1864. LIBRARY OF CONGRESS: PRINTS AND PHOTOGRAPHS DIVISION

gress tried to decide how to deal with the controversy and produce an acceptable tally of the electoral votes. The prospect of violence and unrest loomed.

Elaborate negotiations led to the creation of an electoral commission composed of three Republican and two Democratic senators, two Republican and three Democratic representatives, and two Republican and two Democratic Supreme Court justices (who chose a fifth justice). The commission voted 8–7 along party lines to give all the disputed electoral votes to Hayes. But what became known as the Compromise of 1877 had broader dimensions. Behind the scenes northern and southern economic interests brokered a deal. In return for an implicit Republican agreement not to extend Reconstruction and to let the white South determine its own destiny, southern Democrats accepted the election of Hayes. The losers in the compromise were black Americans, who saw their political fate returned to the hands of their former masters. The 1877 result produced a peaceful in-

auguration and electoral continuity at the price of avoiding the racial issue at the heart of Reconstruction.

The Election of 1896

The last notable nineteenth-century presidential election came in 1896, when William Jennings Bryan, the candidate of the Democratic and Populist parties, ran against William McKinley, the Republican nominee. The election occurred during one of the most turbulent decades in the nation's history. The economic downturn known as the panic of 1893 resulted in massive unemployment and a high degree of social discord. The administration of Grover Cleveland, a Democrat, became the focus for protests against the severity of the depression. The president, convinced of the rightness of his views on the gold standard and limited government, gave very little comfort to Americans who felt the weight of the hard times. In the congressional elections of 1894, discontent with the Democrats produced sweeping Republican gains in the House of Representatives. The Democrats and the agrarian third party, the Populists, were less successful with the unhappy voters. The election of 1894 realigned the American electorate and began a sustained period of Republican dominance.

All three major parties looked to 1896 as the election that would decide the nation's political and economic future. The Republicans selected their most popular figure, William McKinley. A Civil War hero and a midwesterner identified with the protective tariff, he had the greatest appeal to the mainstream of his party. He expected to run on the issues of Democratic failures and the tariff. To the surprise of the

Republicans, the Democrats repudiated Cleveland and nominated William Jennings Bryan, who ran on the inflationary platform of free silver. The Populists also selected Bryan to lead their farmer-based campaign.

Bryan aroused an initial surge of enthusiasm, helped by his decision to campaign personally across the country—his oratorical skills attracted enthusiastic audiences. McKinley and the Republicans had raised a large campaign fund from corporations and expended it on merchandising their appeal through newspapers and pamphlets. McKinley also made an effective "front-porch campaign" from his home in Canton, Ohio. In its use of advertising techniques, the Republican campaign looked forward to the practices of the twentieth century. Bryan's whistle-stop

The Presidential Campaign of 1868. Democratic Party racism and the reaction to Reconstruction were prevalent in this election, in which a strong Democratic Party was beset by weak candidates. The Democratic Party eventually chose Horatio Seymour, who was unenthusiastic about his nomination, after other candidates bowed out. LIBRARY OF CONGRESS: PRINTS AND PHOTOGRAPHS DIVISION

campaign became standard for future candidates, by train and later by airplane.

McKinley won a decisive electoral and popular vote victory in the election, and thus confirmed the Republicans as the majority party. The patterns that the election established—a Republican North and Midwest against a Democratic South—endured for decades. By the end of the nineteenth century, presidential elections had largely assumed the form that they would retain for the next century, in terms of how they were waged and the issues at stake.

Despite the convulsions of the 1860 and 1876 elections and their aftermaths, presidential elections in the nineteenth century developed into an accepted national means of selecting a leader for the country through a process that commanded broad popular support. To that important result the presidential elections of 1800, 1828, and 1896 made significant contributions in terms of political stability and the growth of national power.

See also **Constitutional Amendments,** *subentry on* **Twelfth Amendment; Politics,** *subentries on* **Party Organization and Operations, Parties and the Press; Presidency.**

Bibliography

Banning, Lance. *The Jeffersonian Persuasion: Evolution of a Party Ideology.* Ithaca, N.Y.: Cornell University Press, 1978.

Levy, Leonard, and Louis Fisher, eds. *Encyclopedia of the American Presidency.* Vol. 2. New York: Simon and Schuster, 1994.

Luthin, Reinhard. *The First Lincoln Campaign.* Cambridge, Mass.: Harvard University Press, 1944.

Polakoff, Keith Ian. *The Politics of Inertia: The Election of 1876 and the End of Reconstruction.* Baton Rouge: Louisiana State University Press, 1973.

Remini, Robert V. *The Election of Andrew Jackson.* Philadelphia: Lippincott, 1963.

Schlesinger, Arthur M., Jr., ed. *Running for President: The Candidates and Their Images, 1789–1896.* New York: Simon and Schuster, 1994.

Williams, R. Hal. *Years of Decision: American Politics in the 1890s.* New York: Wiley, 1978.

Woodward, C. Vann. *Reunion and Reaction: The Compromise of 1877 and the End of Reconstruction.* Boston: Little, Brown, 1951.

LEWIS L. GOULD

ELECTRICITY   At the outset of the nineteenth century, Alessandro Volta discovered a simple primary battery that encouraged experimentation with both the properties and possible applications of electricity. In 1808 Humphry Davy of the Royal Institution of London discovered that a bright arc of light was produced when electricity jumped between two carbon electrodes. A decade later the Danish scientist Hans Christian Ørsted observed that a magnetic field surrounded a wire carrying electricity, and the French mathematics professor André-Marie Ampère introduced the theory of electrodynamic interaction of magnets and electric currents. These discoveries led the English inventor William Sturgeon to produce the first electromagnet, which the American physicist Joseph Henry soon improved. During the 1830s the English scientist Michael Faraday invented the first electromagnetic generator.

Electricity's magical qualities caught the American imagination. Inventors and entrepreneurs drew on the work of the early electrical pioneers and created an electrical industry by intermingling science, technology, and entrepreneurship. In 1844, for example, Samuel F. B. Morse used electromagnetism as the basis for the telegraph, the first successful commercial application of electricity. Its success spurred others to consider voice communication, and within twenty years, on 14 February 1876, both Elisha Gray of Western Electric and the independent inventors Alexander Graham Bell and Thomas A. Watson applied for patents on the telephone. Soon a crisscross of telephone lines blanketed the skyscapes of growing American cities.

The first practical method of electrical illumination came shortly after the telephone. The Belgian inventor and engineer Zénobe Théophile Gramme, following the work of Faraday, built a practical continuous-current generator in 1871. Seven years later, building on Davy's early electric arc, the Ohio inventor Charles F. Brush introduced a practicable arc lighting system. The success of arcs in lighting streets and other large outdoor spaces quickly spawned another successful system developed by two Philadelphia high school teachers, Elihu Thomson and Edwin J. Houston. In 1879 San Francisco's California Electric Light Company became the first central arc-lighting station in the country. Within a year New York City, Philadelphia, Detroit, Chicago, and most other American cities had either Brush or Thompson-Houston arc-lighting systems.

Unfortunately, the intensity of arc lamps—in the thousands of candlepower—made them unfeasible for indoor lighting, for which ten to twenty candlepower was desirable. Thomas A. Edison, perhaps America's most famous inventor-entrepreneur, took on this problem in 1878, focusing on incandescent lighting. Within a decade he patented a practicable incandescent lamp and, more importantly, an electric lighting system of lamps, house wiring, metering devices, transmission cables, and a powerhouse. His Pearl Street generating station went on line in New

Thomas Alva Edison (1847–1931). Edison did not invent the incandescent lamp, but rather made its production inexpensive. In 1882 his Pearl Street power plant in New York City demonstrated the feasibility of electricity on a practical scale. LIBRARY OF CONGRESS

York City in 1882 and within two years was lighting 11,279 lamps in five hundred homes. Since Edison manufactured his own lamps, his triumph was commercial as well as technical. By 1885 he had a virtual monopoly in incandescent lighting, but he was not without competitors.

Edison's system was based on low-voltage direct-current (dc) electrical transmission. This worked well in densely populated urban areas, but transmission became economically impracticable beyond the radius of a mile or so because the amount of copper wire required for low-voltage dc transmission increased as the square of the distance. A competitive system emerged during the 1880s with the development of transformers that could raise and lower the voltage of alternating current (ac). The electrical engineer and inventor William Stanley assisted the entrepreneur George Westinghouse in developing ac power. Nikola Tesla, an electrical engineer who immigrated from Yugoslavia and for a time worked for Westinghouse, invented the induction motor and polyphase ac system that eventually bested dc systems.

During the 1890s engineers in California used polyphase power to pioneer long-distance high-voltage electrical transmission and hydroelectricity in order to harness the energy of Sierra Nevada rivers for coastal cities, such as Los Angeles and San Francisco. Meanwhile electric street railways, the nation's largest users of electricity, continued to rely on dc power. The inventor-entrepreneur Frank J. Sprague successfully introduced electric streetcars or trolleys in Richmond, Virginia, in 1887, and they literally reshaped American cities during the last decade of the century. Trolley entrepreneurs, often in collusion with real estate speculators, created "streetcar suburbs," linking city dwellers with arcadia and beginning what a century later would be called urban sprawl.

As the nineteenth century neared its end, Joseph Wetzler probably echoed the sentiments of most Americans when he wrote in *Scribner's* magazine: "Electricity is destined to be one of the most powerful factors entering our social condition. It must bring forth changes in the social order which are even now hardly realized" ("The Electric Railway of Today," *Scribner's*, April 1890, p. 443). In 1899 a writer for *Cassier's* magazine proclaimed that electricity was the "spirit of the nineteenth century" (R. B. Owens, "Electricity as a Factor in Modern Development," *Cassier's*, June 1899, p. 212).

See also **Inventors and Inventions; Telegraph; Transportation,** *subentry on* **Urban and Interurban Transportation.**

Bibliography

Friedel, Robert, and Paul Israel. *Edison's Electric Light: Biography of an Invention.* New Brunswick, N.J.: Rutgers University Press, 1986.

Hughes, Thomas P. *Networks of Power: Electrification in Western Society, 1880–1930.* Baltimore: Johns Hopkins University Press, 1983.

Israel, Paul. *Edison: A Life of Invention.* New York: Wiley, 1998.

Nye, David E. *Electrifying America: Social Meanings of a New Technology, 1880–1940.* Cambridge, Mass.: MIT Press, 1990.

Passer, Harold. *The Electrical Manufacturers, 1875–1900.* Cambridge, Mass.: Harvard University Press, 1953.

Rose, Mark H. *Cities of Light and Heat: Domesticating Gas and Electricity in Urban America.* University Park: Pennsylvania State University Press, 1995.

Sharlin, Harold I. *The Making of the Electrical Age: From the Telegraph to Automation.* London: Abelard-Schuman, 1964.

Williams, James C. *Energy and the Making of Modern California.* Akron, Ohio: University of Akron Press, 1997.

JAMES WILLIAMS

EMANCIPATION   The term "emancipation" connotes the end of slavery, brought about through public authority, as distinguished from manumission, or voluntary actions taken by private individuals to relinquish claims of ownership and recognize the freedom of individual people they had owned. The American Revolution induced a first emancipation, in which, between 1780 and 1830, slavery came to an end or virtual end in every state north of the Mason-Dixon line. The Civil War produced a second emancipation, in which slavery was abolished throughout the South. The process of achieving emancipation in each region requires some description. So does the aftermath.

Whether manumission brought freedom to small numbers of individuals or emancipation ended slavery in an entire state or region, the fact that someone was no longer a slave did not in itself specify what rights, opportunities, and obligations he or she would take on. The first emancipation foreshadowed the second, for in neither period did emancipation lead immediately to full citizenship and equal opportunity. The end of slavery began a process that, over time, led to a fuller definition of legal and economic freedom, so that freedom for blacks converged with freedom for whites. Whether black freedom ever flourished to the point that it and white freedom became identical was another matter.

Joseph Henry Lumpkin (1799–1867), chief justice of the Georgia Supreme Court in the 1850s, placed the narrowest possible construction on black freedom when he wrote in *Bryan v. Walton* (1853) that liberty for black Georgians "signifies nothing but exemption from involuntary service." Because "to become a citizen of the body politic, capable of contracting, of marrying, of voting, requires something more than the mere act" of manumission, Lumpkin continued, "the status of the African in Georgia, whether bond or free, is such that he has no civil, social or political rights or capacity, whatever, except such as are bestowed on him by Statute." Emancipation brought no more than "freedom from the dominion of the master, and the limited liberty of locomotion" (Wallenstein, *From Slave South to New South*, p. 94).

Emancipation and Its Aftermath in the North, 1750s–1830s

At the middle of the eighteenth century, there could have seemed no prospect that Great Britain's northern colonies would soon abolish slavery. During the next eighty years, emancipation nonetheless came to the region. By the 1750s, many Quakers in Pennsylvania and elsewhere perceived slavery as a sin and an abomination, and slave trading and slave ownership became ethically problematic, no longer taken for granted. Soon the American Revolution brought new concerns and new possibilities.

The American Revolution enabled the newly independent states to act in ways that were impossible while they remained colonies. Moreover, the rhetoric of revolution, couched as it was in terms of liberty and slavery, led more white northerners to oppose the slave trade and slavery, and religious concerns over slavery began to animate Baptists, Methodists, and other denominations. Economic competition, too, supplied an important incentive, and slave owners were too few to prevent significant changes in policy. In 1780 the Pennsylvania legislature set a precedent by adopting a public law of gradual emancipation.

That same year, the state of Massachusetts adopted a constitution that began with the declaration that "all men are created free and equal." Quok Walker, Elizabeth Freeman (1742–1829), and other Massachusetts slaves soon sued their masters and won their freedom, and the census of 1790 enumerated no slaves in the entire state. The rapid crumbling of slavery in Massachusetts applied, too, to its Maine District, and the institution vanished from Vermont and New Hampshire as well. At about the same time, the Northwest Ordinance of 1787 banned slavery from the territories north of the Ohio River.

By 1804, the states between Pennsylvania and northern New England—Rhode Island and Connecticut in 1784, New York in 1799, and New Jersey in 1804—adopted gradual emancipation measures similar to Pennsylvania's. Many people continued in slavery, but the children of slaves were scheduled to obtain their freedom at some age between eighteen and twenty-eight, depending on their gender and the state. By 1830 slavery had virtually vanished from every state north of Kentucky, Maryland, and Delaware.

Emancipation transformed the structure of opportunity and the matrix of race relations in the North, yet nowhere could black freedom be assumed to be the equivalent of white freedom. Massachusetts fostered as egalitarian a racial environment as could be found anywhere in the nation, yet even that state continued to ban interracial marriage until 1843 and to segregate schools until the 1850s. In many northern states, black residents encountered racial restrictions in voting and education, as well as private discrimination in housing and employment.

The South: Paths Taken and Not Taken, 1750s–1830s

In the 1750s, at just about the time Quakers in Pennsylvania adopted an antislavery stance, Georgia abandoned just such a stance and embraced slavery.

Georgia rapidly came to resemble its older neighbor, South Carolina, where slavery had flourished for many years. A generation later these two colonies had changed only in that they had grown more populous and that they were the southernmost states in a new nation. At the Constitutional Convention in Philadelphia in 1787, both insisted that they be allowed to buy more slaves on the international market. Soon, however, those two states joined the others in ending slave imports, not because their ferocious commitment to slavery had in any way diminished, but because they could grow enough slaves for their needs or buy enough in the domestic market, and because they saw the purchase of new African slaves as unnecessarily dangerous.

The Upper South ended slave purchases on the international market a generation sooner than did the Deep South. In fact, Virginia, home to more slaves than most of the other states combined in the late eighteenth century, softened its commitment to slavery as well as to the slave trade. The new state of Virginia enacted a law in 1778 to end all imports of new slaves, even from other states, except in cases of an out-of-state owner moving with his human property into the state. In 1782 the legislature passed a law facilitating slave owners' grants of freedom to able-bodied adult slaves, and the population of free black Virginians rapidly grew from perhaps 2,500 in 1780 to more than 20,000 in 1800 and more than 30,000 in 1810.

These acts of manumission freed thousands of slaves, but the state never passed a gradual emancipation measure of the sort that northern states did. Indeed, in 1806 the legislature stipulated that, in the future, newly freed slaves would have to leave the state within a year or forfeit their freedom. Slavery remained the dominant feature of the social, economic, and political landscape in Virginia. The total number of slaves in Virginia continued to rise, even as Virginia slave owners shipped off many tens of thousands of slaves to the new cotton regions of the Deep South.

A remote possibility of a more general emancipation in Virginia occurred in the 1770s and again in the 1830s. In November 1775 Lord Dunmore (1732–1809), colonial governor of Virginia, issued a proclamation offering freedom to male slaves and indentured servants who would help him put down the rebellion against British authority. Some slaves answered Lord Dunmore's call, and some of these did gain their freedom, as did others who fought in the rebel military as substitutes for their owners, but the numbers were small. Another crisis hit Virginia authorities in August 1831, as an insurrection by Nat Turner (1800–1831) and other black Virginians took place in Southampton County. The lower house of the state legislature debated a gradual emancipation measure in early 1832. It was narrowly defeated there, though, and could never have passed the upper chamber.

Antislavery and Abolition: Politics and War, North and South, 1830s–1860s

In 1831, the same year as Nat Turner's uprising in Virginia, William Lloyd Garrison (1805–1879) of Massachusetts began publishing *The Liberator*, committed to abolition and racial equality. Free blacks in Baltimore and points north had converted Garrison to his new commitment, and radicals, black and white alike, prodded the North through the years ahead. Abolition never secured mainstream northern support, however, until the middle of the Civil War.

Though northerners had acted to end slavery in their own states, most displayed no commitment to ending it in the South. In fact, such action was neither their concern, as they saw it, nor within their power. What did concern them, and was within their power, they hoped, was containment—to keep slavery from spreading into new territory and from increasing its power in national politics. Although abolition (ending slavery) did not animate most northerners, an antislavery orientation (a containment policy) increasingly did. This became clear after 1854, when a new political party burst on the scene in the North in the aftermath of the Kansas-Nebraska Act of that year. Committed to antislavery, the new Republicans ran a candidate in the presidential election of 1856. They gathered substantial support in the North but lost the election. They ran another candidate, Abraham Lincoln, in 1860 and won.

The 1860 Republican platform, explicit in its disavowal of abolition, was just as adamant in its commitment to antislavery. Southern leaders were unconvinced by the distinction, distrusted a national administration in Republican hands, and sought guarantees for slavery. States in the Deep South did not wait for Lincoln's inauguration to secede, and some Upper South states waited for only a short time after Lincoln moved into the White House. Several Border South states—Delaware, Maryland, Kentucky, and Missouri, all with populations less than 20 percent slave—stayed in the Union.

President Lincoln called for troops to put down the rebellion, and war began. The Confederate States of America had far fewer men, far less industry, and far less of many other resources than did what was left of the United States of America. Yet the Confederacy fought to a stalemate through 1863. Meantime, Congress enacted an antislavery policy for the territories,

Emancipation. Abraham Lincoln's portrait is featured in the center of this 1865 engraving by Thomas Nast commemorating the emancipation of the slaves. Scenes of the slaves' oppressive past dominate the left-hand side of the picture, while the middle depicts scenes of redemption and family reunions. Promising views of the future are featured at right. LIBRARY OF CONGRESS: PRINTS AND PHOTOGRAPHS DIVISION

preventing the expansion of slavery there, and an abolition policy for the District of Columbia, bringing slavery to an end there. Frederick Douglass and other proponents of an abolition policy eventually found Lincoln convinced that only by embracing abolition and recruiting black soldiers could the Union win.

The time had come for national emancipation, if it could be secured. Yet, like most Republicans, Lincoln viewed federal authority with regard to abolition as limited to national territories—the District of Columbia and the trans-Mississippi West—unless as a war measure. In September 1862, Lincoln issued a Preliminary Emancipation Proclamation that stated his intent, as commander in chief, to declare slavery abolished in any part of any state still in rebellion at the end of the year. On 1 January 1863, his Emancipation Proclamation did as he had promised. Perhaps an emancipation policy would enable the Union to win the war, and a Union victory might bring a general emancipation.

Approximately 200,000 black troops participated in the war on the Union side. Some were combat soldiers. Others did combat support work—construction, transport, preparing meals—and thus released white men for combat, much as was the case in the Confederacy. Free black soldiers from the North, together with men who escaped slavery in the South and donned blue uniforms, combined with the Union's other resources, human and material, to tip the outcome and bring a Union victory.

In 1864, meanwhile, Lincoln ran for reelection on a platform committed to a constitutional amendment that would achieve abolition everywhere in the United States. He won again. By April 1865, when the Confederacy crumbled, slavery had died almost everywhere, though not in Kentucky, and Congress had approved the Thirteenth Amendment and sent it to the states. Ratification of the amendment in December 1865, abolishing slavery throughout the nation, signified a transformation in law and racial policy in the United States. From 1776 to 1865, America moved from a condition of nationwide slavery to abolition and a nationalization of freedom.

After Slavery: The Meanings of Emancipation in the U.S. South

After emancipation, Chief Justice Lumpkin's words from 1853 continued to bear on developments throughout the South. Black southerners were all free now, to be sure, or at least they were no longer slaves. But the process of converting former slaves into voting citizens with equal rights had only begun, and at the end of 1865 there was little reason to assume that the process would go appreciably farther than it already had. Yet the process did continue to unfold. The Civil Rights Act of 1866 declared all African Americans to be citizens. The Fourteenth Amendment, approved in 1866 and ratified in 1868, secured that status. In 1867 Congress enfranchised black men in ten southern states, and in 1870 the Fifteenth Amendment eliminated race as the basis for denying anyone the right to vote.

Georgia can stand as a proxy for the transformation in status of black southerners through the 1860s. Until early 1865 Georgia law recognized "citizens," "slaves," and "free persons of color." By late 1865 the slave category had gone, but former slaves, not yet citizens, had simply moved into the other black category. By early 1866 Georgia law introduced the category "persons of color," which accommodated abolition by recognizing not only that the two black categories had become one but that even former "free persons of color" had far more rights after slavery ended than had been true before. The Civil Rights Act of 1866 led to a change in nomenclature to "citizen," and soon black men acquired political rights and became voting citizens.

What were called at the time "civil rights"—the rights to make contracts, own property, and testify in court—came first to former slaves in the aftermath of emancipation. Political rights came next, with voting and office holding. White southerners tended to put up the most resistance to what they often termed "social equality," whether that meant biracial schools or interracial marriages. Changes in these areas made the least headway, both because black southerners placed less of a premium on them and because white northerners expressed a commitment only to civil and political rights.

Change across the 1860s came at a dizzying pace. Yet much of that change did not endure. By far the most unambiguous evidence of a rollback in the revolution was the disfranchisement that, by 1908, had virtually eliminated black men from the electorate almost everywhere in the former Confederacy. African Americans were no longer slaves, yet black freedom, having come closer in 1870 than ever before to approximating white freedom, had diverged from it again. Convergence could not be assumed. At the end of the nineteenth century, emancipation remained extremely incomplete.

See also **Abolition and Antislavery; African Americans,** *subentries on* **Overview, Free Blacks before the Civil War; Civil War,** *subentries on* **Black Soldiers, Consequences of the Civil War; Reconstruction,** *subentries on* **In the South; Segregation and Civil Rights; Slavery,** *subentry on* **Overview; Voters and Voting,** *subentry on* **Black Voters after the Civil War.**

Bibliography

Berlin, Ira, et al. *Slaves No More: Three Essays on Emancipation and the Civil War.* Cambridge, U.K.: Cambridge University Press, 1992.

Blight, David W. *Frederick Douglass' Civil War: Keeping Faith in Jubilee.* Baton Rouge: Louisiana State University Press, 1989.

Cohen, William. *At Freedom's Edge: Black Mobility and the Southern White Quest for Racial Control, 1861–1915.* Baton Rouge: Louisiana State University Press, 1991.

Cox, LaWanda. *Lincoln and Black Freedom: A Study in Presidential Leadership.* Columbia: University of South Carolina Press, 1981.

Foner, Eric. *Reconstruction: America's Unfinished Revolution, 1863–1877.* New York: Harper and Row, 1988.

———. *The Story of American Freedom.* New York: Norton, 1998.

Hodges, Graham Russell. *Root and Branch: African Americans in New York and East Jersey, 1613–1863.* Chapel Hill: University of North Carolina Press, 1999.

Horton, James Oliver, and Lois E. Horton. *In Hope of Liberty: Culture, Community, and Protest among Northern Free Blacks, 1700–1860.* New York: Oxford University Press, 1997.

Litwack, Leon F. *Been in the Storm So Long: The Aftermath of Slavery.* New York: Knopf, 1979.

Melish, Joanne Pope. *Disowning Slavery: Gradual Emancipation and "Race" in New England, 1780–1860.* Ithaca, N.Y.: Cornell University Press, 1998.

Trefousse, Hans L. *Lincoln's Decision for Emancipation.* Philadelphia: Lippincott, 1975.

Wallenstein, Peter. *From Slave South to New South: Public Policy in Nineteenth-Century Georgia.* Chapel Hill: University of North Carolina Press, 1987.

Zilversmit, Arthur. *The First Emancipation: The Abolition of Slavery in the North.* Chicago: University of Chicago Press, 1967.

PETER WALLENSTEIN

ENGLISH IMMIGRANTS.   See **Immigration and Immigrants,** subentry on **Great Britain.**

ENTREPRENEURS

The nineteenth-century U.S. economy was dominated by risk-taking businesspeople known as entrepreneurs. Prior to 1840 merchant capitalists, who engaged primarily in commerce, dominated the entrepreneurial ranks. Between 1840 and 1870 railroad entrepreneurs gained ascendancy. After 1870 industrial entrepreneurs, who focused on manufacturing, became most important.

In all three periods entrepreneurs came from a variety of backgrounds. Although there were many "self-made men," numerous others built business empires by drawing upon the wealth and business expertise of close relatives. As in every era, entrepreneurs in the nineteenth century experienced varied degrees of success. Some became fabulously wealthy, but a large number succumbed to competition and lost everything they had. Some entrepreneurs were "robber barons" who bilked unsuspecting investors and bribed judges and legislators, yet most succeeded because they offered consumers better goods and services or a lower price than their competitors. Moreover, a number of nineteenth-century entrepreneurs engaged in philanthropic work and, as a group, probably donated more than a billion dollars to charity.

Merchant Capitalists

Before the Industrial Revolution took root in the United States in the 1830s, many goods purchased by Americans were manufactured or produced overseas. Merchant capitalists imported these goods from Europe and the Orient in their own ships, stored them in their own warehouses, and then distributed them to shopkeepers within their trading area, usually a city and its environs. They also purchased agricultural products such as cotton and grain from small producers and exported them by the shipload to foreign buyers. Most merchants operated out of New York, Philadelphia, or Boston and usually employed only their relatives and a handful of sailors and warehousemen. Larger ventures usually took the form of a limited partnership involving two or more mercantile firms.

Incessant warfare and revolution in Europe, piracy in the western Mediterranean, and the inscrutability of the Orient made merchant capitalism a risky business. British government subsidies for British merchants, whose steamships often outperformed Yankee clipper ships, made it increasingly unprofitable after 1830. By 1850 most American merchant capitalists had ceased operations and become railroad or industrial entrepreneurs.

Two of the most successful merchant capitalists were Thomas H. Perkins and John Jacob Astor. In 1785 Perkins, who was twenty-one years old, joined his family's mercantile firm, which traded primarily between Boston and present-day Haiti. In the late 1780s he made his first voyage to the Orient, and in 1792 he formed a partnership with his brother James that specialized in the China trade. Three years later the brothers began trading with French contacts as well. Following James's death in 1822, Thomas ran the firm alone until 1838, shortly before he went blind. In 1830 he combined his interests in China with another firm to make Perkins and Company, creating the largest American mercantile house in that region.

In the late 1780s Astor began selling fur coats and hats in a shop in New York City. Following a treaty in 1794 that opened up much of British North America to U.S. entrepreneurs, he began buying furs directly from the Indians. By 1800 his American Fur Company dominated the North American fur trade. That year Astor entered the China trade, exporting furs and importing tea, silk, chinaware, and spices. His domination of the fur trade ended during the War of 1812, when the British expelled his firm from its trading posts in and around Astoria, Oregon. However, the company remained profitable until he sold it in 1834. After the War of 1812 Astor began investing in New York City real estate, and at the time of his death in 1848 he was probably the wealthiest man in the United States.

Railroad Entrepreneurs

After 1840 the rapid development of railroads offered entrepreneurs exceptional opportunities for making a profit. However, the large sums required to build and operate a railroad precluded any one individual from being its sole owner. Therefore the most successful railroad entrepreneurs concentrated on selling stock and making mergers, leaving day-to-day operations to professional managers. Although the profits to be made were enormous, so were the risks. During the nineteenth century a substantial number of U.S. railroads declared bankruptcy; between 1884 and 1896 more than four hundred railroads went bankrupt. Bankruptcies usually occurred either because builders ran out of money before their railroads were completed or because a competing line offered better rates, faster service, or both. In some cases investors in the bankrupt company sold out to a more solvent competitor, but in others they lost everything they had.

Two of the most successful railroad entrepreneurs were John Murray Forbes and Jay Gould. In 1828 the fifteen-year-old Forbes went to work for his uncle, Thomas Perkins, who taught him the mercantile trade. Two years later Forbes was successfully representing Perkins's interests in China while making a small fortune for himself. In 1846 he led the group of investors that purchased the Michigan Central Railroad and completed its tracks from Detroit to Buffalo. Thirteen years later he put together several small midwestern railroads to create the Chicago, Burlington, and Quincy Railroad. At the century's end the Burlington Route stretched from the Great Lakes to the Rocky Mountains and was one of the Midwest's most important and profitable lines.

Having worked for several years as a railroad surveyor, Gould in 1863 became general manager of a small railroad in New York at the age of twenty-seven. After acquiring and rebuilding another small railroad in Vermont, he and his partners in 1868 gained control of the Erie Railroad and tried unsuccessfully to take away the business of the New York Central, at the time one of the most important east-west lines. After leaving the Erie, Gould made a fortune by gaining control of and then selling the Union Pacific Railroad. He then tried unsuccessfully to build a transcontinental system around the Missouri Pacific Railroad, although he came closer to accomplishing this feat than any other railroad entrepreneur of his day.

Industrial Entrepreneurs

After the Civil War major changes in technology, transportation, and communications made possible the rise of "big business" or large-scale manufacturing. Like railroading, industrial entrepreneurship required the ability to attract large amounts of capital. It also required the ability to survive cutthroat competition, which usually meant finding ways to spend less on raw materials, production costs, and marketing and shipping charges. Those who could do these things created industrial empires; those who could not either saw their organization become part of someone else's empire or went out of business entirely.

The century's foremost industrial entrepreneurs were Andrew Carnegie and John D. Rockefeller. After immigrating to the United States in 1848, Carnegie worked his way up through the management ranks of the Pennsylvania Railroad, after which he served briefly as general manager of a bridge manufacturer. By 1872 he had attracted enough capital to open his first steel mill. Carnegie held down production costs by introducing the Bessemer method of steelmaking into the United States and by making use of cost accounting techniques that the railroads had pioneered. Consequently he sold quality steel at considerably lower prices than any of his competitors. In the 1890s the Carnegie Steel Company became the first in the industry to practice vertical in-

tegration, acquiring the necessary sources of raw materials and the means to transport and distribute finished goods. By purchasing iron and coal deposits, lake-going ore ships, and railroads, and by abandoning independent marketing agents in favor of his own dedicated sales organization, Carnegie maintained his company's competitive edge and dominated the U.S. steel industry.

The career of John D. Rockefeller was even more spectacular. After succeeding in the farm commodities business, in 1863 he built an oil refinery in Cleveland, near the oil fields of western Pennsylvania. Over the next ten years he aggressively took business away from his competitors, then bought them out when they failed. He also began vertically integrating his Standard Oil Company by buying or building barrel factories, pipelines, terminal facilities, and tank railcars, and creating a national marketing division, thus controlling every step in the production and distribution of refined oil. In 1882 Rockefeller combined these enterprises with those of eight associates to form the Standard Oil Trust, a consortium of more than forty companies that controlled more than 90 percent of the nation's refined oil. In 1899, when the government sought to break up this trust because of its monopolistic practices, Rockefeller created Standard Oil of New Jersey, the nation's largest holding company, thus perpetuating his undisputed control of the oil industry.

Self-Made Men

Most nineteenth-century Americans, entrepreneurs included, regarded entrepreneurs as self-made men, implying that they had accrued their fortunes solely through their own ingenuity and hard work. This image was popularized in the novels of Horatio Alger, almost all of which tell the "rags to riches" stories of young men who overcome their humble origins to achieve wealth and respectability. Certainly this depiction fit a number of entrepreneurs. Astor, the son of a German butcher, began as a flute maker. Carnegie, a Scottish weaver's son, once worked as a common laborer in a cotton mill. Gould, the son of a poor hill farmer, once worked as a surveyor. Rockefeller, whose father was an itinerant patent-medicine salesman, entered business as an assistant bookkeeper.

However, many if not most of the century's entrepreneurs either inherited money or benefited in some way from a family business connection. The Perkins-Forbes connection offers one example of how this phenomenon played itself out over several generations. Before going into business for himself, Perkins learned the mercantile trade from his mother and brothers, and he received his early financing from the family business. When his brother-in-law's business failed, Perkins took his fifteen-year-old nephew, John Murray Forbes, under his wing, giving him the tutelage and opportunity he needed to become successful. Forbes did the same for his son, William Hathaway Forbes. The younger Forbes joined his father's railroad enterprises immediately after the Civil War, acquired sufficient experience and capital, and in 1879 began investing heavily in Alexander Graham Bell's telephone patents. That year Forbes became president of National Bell Telephone Company. During his eight-year term the company successfully defended its patents in court and established Western Electric Manufacturing Company as the sole maker of telephone equipment until the patents expired. Western Electric continued to be the dominant producer afterward. Although self-made men received the lion's share of the publicity, the majority of entrepreneurs succeeded in business largely because their families provided them with a head start relative to "Ragged Dick," a fictional character made popular by Alger.

Would-be entrepreneurs who lacked a family connection were usually forced to borrow money from impersonal financial institutions. This situation prevented many Ragged Dicks from getting ahead for two reasons. First, by 1850 banks and other lenders relied heavily on mercantile agencies to vouch for the creditworthiness of prospective borrowers. The most prominent of these agencies was the Mercantile Agency, founded in New York City in 1841 and known after 1859 as R. G. Dunn and Company. These agencies regularly discriminated in their reports against Irish, Jewish, and black people in particular, and in general against anyone who could not be categorized as a white Anglo-Saxon Protestant. Such discrimination made it extremely difficult to obtain the necessary capital to enter business or to secure a loan to see a business through an economic downturn. Second, the volatility of the U.S. economy during the nineteenth century made it all too easy for a fledgling business to overextend itself. With a major economic panic occurring approximately every twenty years, the businessperson who could not call upon a family connection for a quick loan was frequently forced to declare bankruptcy.

Robber Barons

Another myth that persists about nineteenth-century entrepreneurs is that they were arrogant, immoral monopolists hell-bent on enriching themselves at the expense of the general public. Certainly some entrepreneurs fit this description, including Gould, an unscrupulous stock manipulator who once allied

Jay Gould (1836–1892). One of the most famous financiers of the Gilded Age, Gould worked his way to success from a blacksmith's forge to director of Union Pacific Railroad, to owner of Western Union Telegraph. Photograph taken between 1865 and 1892. LIBRARY OF CONGRESS

himself with the notorious "Boss" Tweed in an elaborate scheme to "buy" the New York state legislature. However, the robber baron, like the self-made man, was largely a product of the imagination. Although many if not most entrepreneurs were ruthless opportunists who engaged in cutthroat competition in hopes of cornering the market, in almost every case the victors won because they offered the general public better goods and services, cheaper prices, or both. Rockefeller's sharp business practices drove many a lesser man out of the petroleum business, but he succeeded primarily because he cut consumer prices on oil products by about one-third.

Most successful entrepreneurs engaged in philanthropic endeavors, thus returning a significant portion of their profits to society at large. During their lifetimes Rockefeller donated more than $500 million and Carnegie over $300 million to a number of institutions and foundations, many of which bear their names. In addition to other donations, Astor gave enough money to create what became the core of the

New York Public Library, and Perkins was the major benefactor of the New England Asylum for the Blind.

Entrepreneurs transformed the U.S. economy. Their tireless efforts to reduce costs, introduce new methods of production and management, and develop new products laid the socioeconomic foundation for twentieth-century America. In the process some of them became wealthy, many more perpetuated the fortunes of their families, and an untold number lost what little fortune they possessed.

See also **Corporations and Big Business; Trusts.**

Bibliography

Folsom, Burton W., Jr. *Entrepreneurs vs. the State: The Myth of the Robber Barons.* Reston, Va.: Young America's Foundation, 1991.

Haeger, John Denis. *John Jacob Astor: Business and Finance in the Early Republic.* Detroit, Mich.: Wayne State University Press, 1991.

Hawke, David Freeman. *John D.: The Founding Father of the Rockefellers.* New York: Harper and Row, 1980.

Klein, Maury. *The Life and Legend of Jay Gould.* Baltimore: Johns Hopkins University Press, 1986.

Larson, John Lauritz. *Bonds of Enterprise: John Murray Forbes and Western Development in America's Railway Age.* Cambridge, Mass.: Harvard University Press, 1984.

Mackay, James. *Little Boss: A Life of Andrew Carnegie.* Edinburgh, Scotland: Mainstream, 1997.

Pier, Arthur Stanwood. *Forbes: Telephone Pioneer.* New York: Dodd, Mead, 1953.

Pusateri, C. Joseph. *A History of American Business.* Arlington Heights, Ill.: Harlan Davidson, 1984.

Seaburg, Carl, and Stanley Paterson. *Merchant Prince of Boston: Colonel T. H. Perkins, 1764–1854.* Cambridge, Mass.: Harvard University Press, 1971.

Seligman, Ben B. *The Potentates: Business and Businessmen in American History.* New York: Dial, 1971.

Sobel, Robert. *The Entrepreneurs: Explorations within the American Business Tradition.* New York: Weybright and Talley, 1974.

CHARLES W. CAREY JR.

ENTREPRENEURS, WOMEN   American female entrepreneurs of the nineteenth century ranged from street peddlers to capitalist innovators who risked their fortunes in expanding industries. Most nineteenth-century businesswomen in the United States, however, were involved in very small, home-based enterprises, providing such necessities of life as food, clothing, or shelter to their local communities. Although a few exceptional women throughout the century challenged gender stereotypes by entering male-dominated fields, such as finance, female-run ventures tended to be clustered within a limited number of trades that were either dominated by women (like dressmaking, millinery, and prostitution) or which employed women workers (as when actresses became the managers of theater companies, or female writers and editors entered publishing). However, women sometimes gained entry into a wider variety of fields, such as plumbing, by participating in family-run businesses and pursuing these endeavors due to the absence, illness, or demise of male relatives. In the Far West, seizing the opportunity, some women entrepreneurs made their fortunes as ranchers and land speculators.

Although female entrepreneurs often faced prejudices based on sexual stereotypes, as well as significant legal challenges, and while most encountered problems raising capital and securing credit, they also found ingenious ways to circumvent these difficulties and forge ahead with business careers. Whether they were elite entrepreneurial leaders, active contributors to family enterprises, or minicapitalists struggling to use a small business as a means of self-employment, women made a significant contribution to the burgeoning economy of the United States and formed a vital link in local business networks.

Notable Women Entrepreneurs

In comparison with the names of such prominent businessmen as John Jacob Astor, Cornelius Vanderbilt, and Andrew Carnegie, those of nineteenth-century female entrepreneurs remain relatively obscure. Several of the best-known include Lydia Pinkham, whose motherly image created confidence in her line of patent medicines; the legendary Mary Ellen ("Mammy") Pleasant, an African American boardinghouse keeper who made a fortune in San Francisco during the gold rush era; Miriam Leslie, the partner and wife of Frank Leslie, who legally changed *her* name to "Frank" after his death in 1880 in order to rescue their failing publishing empire; and financier-speculator Harriet ("Hetty") Green, known as the "witch of Wall Street," who built up an estate worth tens of millions of dollars.

Lists of remarkable nineteenth-century businesswomen often add Rebecca Lukens, an iron manufacturer in Pennsylvania's Brandywine Valley from 1825 to 1854; Margaret Haughery, the widowed Irish immigrant who worked her way from rags to riches in mid-century New Orleans by inventing packaged crackers; Ellen ("Madame") Demorest, a manufacturer of paper patterns for dressmaking and publisher of a fashion magazine (both in partnership with her husband) in the years after the Civil War; and Eliza Nicholson, who rescued the New Orleans *Picayune* from bankruptcy in 1876. Other women who made important contributions to nineteenth-century business concerns have been largely hidden from history by male relatives, as in the cases of Margaret Getchell LaForge, a cousin of R. H. Macy and supervisor of his famous department store in the 1860s, and Nettie McCormick, the wife of Cyrus McCormick, who helped build their agricultural machinery firm into an international concern. In addition, many exceptional female entrepreneurs, though once eminent within their communities, remain virtually unknown outside of local histories and women's biographical dictionaries.

Entrepreneurship, by definition, suggests risk-taking, innovation, and an ability to seize opportunities created by shifts in the marketplace. Since most nineteenth-century American businesswomen left neither business records nor personal papers, the ability of historians to judge their entrepreneurial abilities remains limited. Yet it is possible to ascribe

Hetty Green (1834–1916). Having inherited a fortune, Hetty Green was a prime mover on the New York Stock Exchange. She invested in railroad, government, and municipal bonds as well as real estate. LIBRARY OF CONGRESS: PRINTS AND PHOTOGRAPHS DIVISION

specific innovations to distinguished female entrepreneurs. For instance, recognizing growing opportunities in the clerical field, Mary Foot Seymour directed a stenographic business, four branches of a clerical school, an employment bureau, and a journal for businesswomen in Gilded Age New York. In southern California, ranch owner Harriet Williams Russell Strong introduced new crops and patented original designs for the construction of irrigation dams during the same period.

Microentrepreneurs

The exploits of the vast majority of nineteenth-century businesswomen, however, were never recorded by historians; indeed, they were not considered particularly remarkable in their own times and neighborhoods. Whether single, married, or widowed, these businesswomen often operated out of the front rooms of modest dwelling places and included artisans, shopkeepers, and small manufacturers, as well as keepers of boardinghouses and refreshment saloons. Millinery and dressmaking shops, dry and fancy goods stores, groceries and laundries were among the businesses commonly favored by women, while products manufactured by female-run enterprises tended to be clothing, trimmings, accessories, and cosmetics. Opportunities for remunerative female self-employment during the century included midwifery, nursing, and abortion services, as well as freelance journalism, the lecture circuit, adult education courses, music classes, and the establishment of private schools. Whatever their trades, in a period when most wage-work available to women offered options that were severely restricted and poorly paid, female capitalists made a significant contribution through their cash incomes to their own survival and the welfare of their families.

Much of the basic research on nineteenth-century businesswomen has yet to be done. Thus, it is almost impossible to assess the impact of the class, ethnic, racial, and regional differences that existed among female entrepreneurs throughout the century, or to describe changes in the trades, status, and success rates of businesswomen over time. However, in contrast to previous assumptions that only rare women were active in the marketplace during the nineteenth century, current research reveals that merely scratching the surface of nineteenth-century history exposes numerous ways in which women were involved in business projects. Focusing on a single historical episode—for instance, the assassination of President Abraham Lincoln—illustrates the significance of women "behind the scenes." The theater troop performing that night was owned and managed by a woman, Laura Keene, and a female boardinghouse keeper, Mary Surratt, was later convicted of helping plot the assassination. At the time, Mary Todd Lincoln's closest female companion and confidante was her dressmaker, Elizabeth Keckley, a former slave who had previously used the proceeds of her business to purchase her own freedom. As this example suggests, famous women entrepreneurs represent simply the tip of the iceberg of a broad participation by ordinary women in the business economy of the nineteenth-century United States.

See also **Clothing; Entrepreneurs; Magazines, Women's; Newspapers and the Press; Small Businesses; Women in the Professions.**

Bibliography

Bird, Caroline. *Enterprising Women.* New York: Norton, 1976.

Gamber, Wendy. *The Female Economy: The Millinery and Dressmaking Trades, 1860–1930.* Urbana: University of Illinois Press, 1997.

Kwolek-Folland, Angel. *Incorporating Women: A History of Women and Business in the United States.* Boston, Mass.: Twayne, 1998.

Walker, Juliet E. K. "Entrepreneurs in Antebellum America." In *Black Women in America: An Historical Encyclopedia.* Edited by Darlene Clark Hine. Volume 1. Brooklyn, N.Y.: Carlson, 1993.

SUSAN INGALLS LEWIS

ENVIRONMENT. See **Geography and Ecology.**

EPIDEMICS. See **Health and Disease.**

ERA OF GOOD FEELING   At the time of the American Revolution, American political theorists held that factions or parties should be avoided in the best interests of the Republic. Washington's presidency would camouflage the emergence of political parties, but once he had left the stage, substantial policy differences broke out into partisan warfare. The meaning of the Constitution and the intended role of the federal government were the central issues. Was government, as the Federalist Party claimed, a Hamiltonian, nation-building instrument, or was it, as the Republican Party envisioned, a Jeffersonian, democratizing instrument? Should the federal government lead the nation, or did that risk creating a new consolidated tyranny? Woven into all this argument was a fundamental disagreement over whether America's future was best secured by an alliance with France, or by cooperating with Britain. These issues created fierce partisan warfare during the presidencies of Washington's immediate successors, John Adams and Thomas Jefferson (1797–1809).

The succeeding "Era of Good Feeling" stood in enormous contrast with the angry years at the turn of the nineteenth century. The partisanship of the earlier time seemingly disappeared during the period that roughly corresponded with James Monroe's presidency (1817–1825). The War of 1812 had, almost accidentally, wiped out the issues that divided the Republicans and Federalists. In the wake of the war, Republicans softened their ideological opposition to any action that strengthened the federal government. When the first Bank of the United States went out of existence in 1811, Republicans welcomed its demise. But the war taught them that the United States needed some kind of central bank if it were to survive as a nation. They overcame their fears of the moneyed power, and rechartered the Bank of the United States in 1816.

The war had also demonstrated that spending on infrastructure was absolutely vital. Opposed to federal government spending on an extensive military, Republicans had preferred to rely on local militia. They saw naval spending leading them down the path that Britain had taken to national glory but also to moral ruin during the eighteenth century. After the war, however, many Republicans saw that the United States needed roads and other infrastructure to be financed by the federal government. Finally, they backed a tariff to protect many of the industries that had sprung up during the war years, but that could not survive once trade with Britain resumed. In spite of their original ideology, the Republicans in the 1810s embraced popular nationalist policies.

The Federalist Party had already had much of their policy taken from them, but they delivered the final death blow to themselves.

See also **Federalist Party; Politics,** *subentry on* **Party Organization and Operations; Republican Party; War of 1812.**

Bibliography

Dangerfield, George. *The Era of Good Feelings.* New York: Harcourt and Brace, 1952.

Remini, Robert Vincent. *The Era of Good Feelings and the Age of Jackson, 1816–1841.* Arlington Heights, Ill.: AHM, 1979.

IAN MYLCHREEST

ETIQUETTE. See **Manners.**

EUROPE, FOREIGN RELATIONS WITH

The relations between the United States and Europe during the nineteenth century fall into three well-defined periods. From 1800 to 1815 the new nation dealt with the effects of the British struggle with Napoleonic France. During the half-century from 1815 to 1865 the main foreign policy issues with Europe involved Anglo-American relations over the boundaries between the expanding United States and British control north of what became the Canadian border. From 1865 to 1914, American-European relations were the sum of individual U.S. foreign policy interactions with each of the major European powers.

The Napoleonic Years

During the first fifteen years of the nineteenth century the Napoleonic Wars between France and Great Britain presented the administrations of Thomas Jefferson and James Madison with a continual series of issues arising from British and French efforts to erode American neutrality. The tensions between Britain and the United States over such questions as the impressment of American merchant sailors into the royal navy and British infringements on American sovereignty culminated in the War of 1812.

Although the fighting did not go as well as Americans had anticipated, the peace settlement expressed in the Treaty of Ghent of December 1814, as well as Andrew Jackson's victory at the Battle of New Orleans, ended the first phase of foreign relations with Europe on a high note for the United States. The young nation turned westward to occupy the continental West. The sheltering presence of the royal navy ensured that further European threats would not disturb the movement toward the frontier. The Monroe Doctrine (1823), which asserted U.S. supremacy in the Western Hemisphere, depended on British maritime power to deter European incursions.

Problems of Expansion

From the early 1820s to the eve of the Civil War the primary issues were those between Britain and the United States over the boundary lines that separated Canada and British possessions in the Pacific Northwest from the expanding American nation to the south. The Webster-Ashburton Treaty of 1842 brought to an end five years of tension between the two countries over the Maine–New Brunswick boundary. In 1846 London and Washington resolved the question of the Oregon boundary in the Northwest. Four years later, the two nations signed the Clayton-Bulwer Treaty that pledged not to fortify a canal across Central America and to maintain the neutrality of the waterway.

Foreign affairs with Europe did not play a large role in American diplomacy until the Civil War. The possibility of British recognition of the Confederacy helped the United States settle quickly such episodes as the Trent Affair, in which two Confederate envoys en route to London were seized from the British vessel *Trent*. Despite further tensions during the war arising from Confederate raiders built in British shipyards, the two countries deferred their differences until the fighting had ended. French intervention in Mexico in 1863, which led to the installing of Archduke Maximilian as emperor of Mexico, heightened concern about a European presence at the southern border of the United States.

The Anglo-American Relationship, 1865–1914

The U.S. relationship with Great Britain moved from a degree of confrontation and controversy during the late nineteenth century to a growing warmth and sense of international kinship by 1914. After the Civil War tensions arose over the claims involving the damage that the Confederate raider *Alabama* had inflicted on Union shipping. Astute negotiations by Secretary of State Hamilton Fish settled the matter during the 1870s. In the 1880s and early 1890s disputes with Canada erupted over fishing rights in the Bering Sea and the Atlantic, but these, too, yielded to negotiations. In 1895 the United States objected to the British presence in South America during the border dispute between Venezuela and British Guiana (Guyana). President Grover Cleveland's assertion of the Monroe Doctrine in 1895 sparked war talk briefly, but the crisis eased.

The Spanish-American War contributed to a rapid improvement in Anglo-American relations before World War I. Of the European powers, Britain was the most friendly to the American cause in the war, resulting in a sense of transatlantic solidarity. Soon Washington and London addressed such issues as the Canadian boundary with Alaska and a revision of the Clayton-Bulwer Treaty. During the presidency of Theodore Roosevelt, the Hay-Pauncefote Treaty (1901) smoothed the way for the Panama Canal. The amicable settlement of the Canadian boundary case in 1903 further solidified the new friendship. By 1914 much of the traditional animosity between the United States and Great Britain had eased.

France and Germany

The United States made clear its objections to the presence of Maximilian and the French army in Mexico, but the end of that French adventure in 1866–1867 resolved the problem. Direct relations turned on trade issues and efforts to deal with the tariff barriers that protectionist forces created in both France and the United States. Negotiations over most-favored-nation status occupied the time of diplomats in both countries. In 1898 the French mediated an armistice between the United States and Spain. The French ambassador Jules Jusserand cultivated friendly relations with Presidents Theodore Roosevelt, William Howard Taft, and Woodrow Wilson.

Relations with Germany moved in an opposite direction from those with Great Britain and France. Many in the United States admired the achievement of German unification in 1871. In the 1880s trade disputes and quarrels over Samoa kindled U.S. suspicions regarding German intentions, and during the Spanish-American War, German warships in the Philippines were an irritant to U.S. naval forces. The administrations of William McKinley and Theodore Roosevelt expressed growing apprehension about the presence of Germany in the Caribbean.

During the first decade of the twentieth century a sense of potential discord lay below the surface of German-American relations. When Germany and Britain tried to collect debts owed by the government of Venezuela in 1902, resentment over the role of the Germans characterized American public opinion. Theodore Roosevelt used the occasion to wield naval power to underline his administration's opposition to European intrusion in the Western Hemisphere. The belligerent rhetoric and erratic policies of Kaiser William II aroused further suspicions about Germany's goals in the Americas. By 1914 U.S. policymakers eyed Berlin with distrust, a sentiment that would shape neutrality policy after 1914.

The War with Spain

The most dramatic U.S. interaction with a European country began in 1895, when a rebellion in Cuba inflamed American anger over the role of Spain as a colonial power. The Grover Cleveland administration allowed Madrid to attempt to subdue the Cuban insurgents, which alienated the Americans who sympathized with the uprising. By the time President William McKinley took office in March 1897, a variety of motives—economic, humanitarian, strategic, and political—had built a consensus that Spain had to leave Cuba.

The new president's policy was to persuade Spain to settle the Cuban war through negotiations with the rebels and an eventual withdrawal from the island. Spain, however, viewed Cuba as an integral part of its nation, and a peaceful departure was impossible for domestic reasons. The growing sense of confrontation in 1897 and 1898 culminated in the explosion of the U.S.S. *Maine* in Havana harbor on 15 February 1898. The crisis escalated, and by April it was evident that the two nations were on a course for war unless one or the other backed off its negotiating position. That did not happen. The United States insisted on Spain's withdrawal and Cuba's independence, two demands that Spain would not accept. War broke out in April 1898.

On the eve of the Spanish-American War other European powers tried to mediate the issues, but British opposition to coercing the United States doomed the effort. While the war was going on Britain supported the U.S. cause, while the rest of Europe quietly endorsed Spain without taking any specific actions. France became an intermediary between Washington and Madrid in arranging an armistice in 1898. Following that process, which took place largely in Washington, Paris was then chosen to be the site of official peace talks leading to a treaty. Germany sent warships to observe in the Philippines, an additional irritant to Commodore George Dewey, the American commander. The White House recognized that Berlin might become an influential force in the islands if the Americans departed. As far as the Europeans were concerned, this war raised the United States to the status of an equal participant in world affairs after 1899.

A Greater Involvement with Europe

In the decade and a half that followed, Washington moved slowly and cautiously toward a greater involvement with the major European nations. The strong U.S. currents of isolation and national disdain for overseas commitments precluded any alliances or overt intervention. Nonetheless, during the Theodore Roosevelt administration the United States mediated the Russo-Japanese War in talks that resulted in the Treaty of Portsmouth in 1905. A year later Roosevelt took an active part in managing from Washington the Algeciras Conference over the future of Morocco to defuse an international crisis in Europe. The United States also sent representatives to the Hague conferences on disarmament and international peace in 1899 and 1907.

By the time World War I broke out in August 1914 the United States had moved from its earlier aloofness toward Europe. Americans were reasonably well informed about European affairs in their newspapers, and the presence of sizable numbers of immigrants from southern and eastern Europe and important voting blocs of German Americans and Irish Americans ensured that many U.S. citizens had at least an emotional interest in what took place in Europe. But if someone had forecast in the spring of 1914 that substantial numbers of U.S. troops would be fighting in France in a European war within four years, that person would have been viewed as deluded or insane. Nonetheless, during the latter part of the nineteenth century the United States had become enmeshed in international relationships, giving Americans a larger political, economic, and diplomatic stake in the war's outcome than they realized. In 1901 President McKinley, in his last public address, said "the period of exclusiveness is past" (Gould, *The Presidency of McKinley*, p. 251). Thirteen years later the wisdom of his remark became apparent as the United States assumed the difficult role of being a neutral power in the midst of a European war. Within three more years, the United States was also a direct force in European affairs.

See also **Canada; Central America and the Caribbean; Confederate States of America; Cuba; Foreign Relations; Foreign Trade and Tariffs; Great Britain, Foreign Relations with; Louisiana Purchase; Mexico; Overseas Possessions; Spanish-American War.**

Bibliography

Campbell, Charles S. *The Transformation of American Foreign Relations, 1865–1900.* New York: Harper and Row, 1976.

Clarfield, Gerald. *United States Diplomatic History: From Revolution to Empire.* Vol. 1. Englewood Cliffs, N.J.: Prentice Hall, 1992.

Gould, Lewis L. *The Presidency of Theodore Roosevelt.* Lawrence: University Press of Kansas, 1991.

———. *The Presidency of William McKinley.* Lawrence: University Press of Kansas, 1980.

May, Ernest R. *Imperial Democracy: The Emergence of America as a Great Power.* New York: Harcourt, Brace, and World, 1961.

Offner, John L. *An Unwanted War: The Diplomacy of the United States and Spain over Cuba, 1895–1898.* Chapel Hill: University of North Carolina Press, 1992.

LEWIS L. GOULD

EVANGELICALISM   The term "evangelicalism" derives from the early Christian word "evangel," which refers to announcing the good news or gospel. This news, as Christians understand it, is that human beings are saved despite their sinfulness by the redemptive work of God in Jesus Christ. Personal acceptance of the good news is a precondition for the enjoyment of salvation. If one accepts the evangel, one is converted to Christ and blessed with eternal life with God. Thus an evangelist is one who pronounces the good news so that all persons can hear it, accept it, and be saved from eternal damnation.

In nineteenth-century America, evangelical preaching—an almost exclusively Protestant activity—was considered the primary obligation of ordained persons. Since the time of Martin Luther (1483–1546), Protestants had emphasized evangelical preaching from scripture, which they regarded as the sole authoritative source for God's saving word. Protestants downplayed the Roman Catholic emphasis on using the church's sacraments, doctrine, and rituals to convey God's saving acts to the faithful. Preaching was connected to the Great Commission enunciated by Jesus at the end of the Gospel of Matthew, "Go therefore and make disciples of all nations." Individuals had to hear the Word of God before they could be saved; therefore the Word needed to be preached.

One historical interpretation of the command to preach linked it to a belief that all persons are predestined by God to either salvation or damnation. Preaching helps people discern whether they are saved or not, but it does not bring about salvation. By the beginning of the nineteenth century, with the Second Great Awakening, many clergy and laity had accepted the differing Arminian view that individuals have some freedom to choose whether to accept the Word. Most earlier Protestants had rejected any element of free will in Christian theology.

Revivalism

Although evangelicalism often occurred in churches through formal preaching, it was most commonly expressed in the nineteenth century through revivals. These popular events were conducted by itinerant revivalists, many of whom were not ordained clergy. Revival meetings attracted church people from many denominations as well as unchurched persons. Revivalists revived a dormant faith or instilled a new belief in the possibility of salvation.

During the Second Great Awakening, evangelical revivalism had its earliest and most dramatic expression on the western frontier. The movement's occasionally undisciplined and emotional manifestations subsequently were curbed by revivalists in the East. Upstate New York saw evangelical revivalism sweep across it so often that the region came to be known as the "burned-over" district. The Methodists, with their emphasis on "heart" religion and their reliance on the circuit-rider system, became the chief denomination to carry evangelicalism into the American heartland. The Baptists were only slightly less forceful in bearing the evangelical message across the South and Midwest. A number of new Protestant denominations came into being directly as a result of the evangelical revivalism of the early nineteenth century. These included the Disciples of Christ, or Campbellites. The older, more established Congregationalists, Presbyterians, and Episcopalians grew more slowly during the evangelical era, in part because they were not as attuned to the revivalistic style that had become familiar to so many Protestant Americans.

Evangelicalism was frequently linked with millennialism, a belief that Jesus would return to reign for one thousand years before the world ended. Effective preaching and the conversions it produced would, in the opinion of many, help to bring on the millennium, or would at least be a sign of its coming. Some held that evangelicalism would help to bring about a morally reformed society that would begin to approximate the coming Kingdom of God (postmillennialism). Others, mostly a minority at the time, believed only individuals could be saved and that the reform of society was irrelevant (premillennialism). Theological descendents of the premillennialists formed the core of twentieth-century fundamentalism.

In most forms of revivalism, evangelicalism took the form of a preacher leading individuals to believe in their own sinfulness, feel sorrow for their state, be willing to repent, believe that they could be saved from sin by accepting the Word of God with the assistance of the Holy Spirit, and accept that they had been saved. This cycle of conversion is sometimes summarized as conviction, repentance, and reformation.

Perfectionism and Social Reform

Saved individuals, it was assumed, would lead a morally reformed life (sanctification). Some evangelicals, such as Charles Finney (1792–1875), believed the reformed life could approach moral perfection. A morally perfect individual would then, according to the logic of what came to be known as perfectionism, seek to perfect the society around him or her. From this belief sprang many of the reform movements in antebellum America, especially those associated with postmillennialism. Most of these movements were carried forward by voluntary agencies rather than by government action. They embraced a host of causes, including temperance, pacifism, prison reform, care of the insane, public education, and curtailing prostitution and dueling. Women played a particularly important role in many of these movements. Their experience in organizing and leading reform groups contributed to the emergence of the woman's rights movement later in the century.

One of the most important antebellum reforms was the antislavery, or abolitionist, movement. Believing that they had been freed from sin, many converted persons felt justified in passing moral judgment upon unjust social institutions such as slavery. Abolitionists like Sarah Grimké (1792–1873), Angelina Grimké (1805–1879), and Theodore Weld (1803–

Charles Finney (1792–1875). A revivalist, Finney converted to evangelical Christianity as an adult. He was a charismatic speaker who converted entire communities and reached an even wider public through his published lectures and sermons. © BETTMANN/CORBIS

1895) believed that through religious conversion they had become subject only to the Word of God. Therefore, they owed no ultimate allegiance to human beings and their political and social institutions. This gave them the evangelical freedom to denounce legally sanctioned practices such as slavery and the denial of woman's rights. This ultraism, as they called it, sometimes even extended to denouncing the power structure in established churches.

The missionary movements of the nineteenth century also owed their impetus to evangelicalism. Missions were sent not only to convert persons in foreign countries, but to tend to the unchurched on American soil, such as the American Indians and settlers on the ever-expanding western frontier. Related to the missionary movement was the rise of interest in Sunday School as a disseminator of key Christian ideas to young people.

Evangelicalism also contributed to a number of experimental moral communities whose members sought to live perfected, moral lives outside the boundaries of everyday society. These groups included the Shakers and the Oneida Community. The latter practiced a form of plural marriage and a communism of goods based on their founder John Humphrey Noyes's (1811–1886) belief that this was what moral perfection demanded.

After the Civil War, evangelicalism lost much of its social impetus; it became more focused on individual salvation and less concerned with reforming the whole society. Many clergy believed that the North's victory had sanctified American institutions and practices. Furthermore, many postwar revivalists believed that saved individuals (who were assumed to be ambitious, diligent workers) could not help but become materially successful in America's growing industrial society.

Representative of the more individualistic thrust of post–Civil War evangelicalism was Dwight L. Moody (1837–1899). He carried the evangelical message into the urban centers of an increasingly industrialized nation, utilizing many of the promotional techniques that would come to characterize revivalism in the twentieth century. Although most evangelical preachers in the latter half of the nineteenth century emphasized the salvation of individual souls, some were attracted by the social dimension of what became the Social Gospel movement. Like Walter Rauschenbusch (1861–1918) they recognized that social influences had a profound effect on an individual's ability to respond to God's purpose in history. Members of the Social Gospel movement contended that evangelical preachers must address the social and institutional setting of human life if they wish to speak credibly to the religious needs of individuals.

The Struggle with Modernism

By the end of the nineteenth century, evangelicalism had come under suspicion among some Protestants for being too emotional and too contrary to the modernist, scientific tenor of the times. In the view of many, it reflected a style of piety that could not meet the emerging challenges of Darwinism, the critical examination of the Bible as a human document, the discovery of other world religions, the rise of the scientific analysis of religion, and the emerging science of psychology. During this period evangelicalism began to be associated primarily with areas of the South and Midwest; the intellectual centers of the Northeast and upper Midwest (particularly Chicago) turned toward a more rational, liberal form of religious belief and practice.

Evangelicalism did not die at the turn of the century. Although it largely disappeared from the schol-

arly work focused on mainstream religion, it reemerged in the 1970s as fundamentalism. In this more vivid form, evangelicalism moved from its earlier, premillennial stance to one of postmillennialism and once again asserted claims on the moral life of the nation and its individuals.

See also **Millennialism and Adventism; Protestantism; Reform, Social; Revivalism; Social Gospel.**

Bibliography

Ahlstrom, Sydney E. "The Golden Age of Democratic Evangelicalism." In *A Religious History of the American People*. Garden City, N.Y.: Image, 1975.

Bruce, Dickson D. *And They All Sang Hallelujah: Plain-Folk Camp-Meeting Religion, 1800–1845*. Knoxville: University of Tennessee Press, 1974.

Cross, Whitney R. *The Burned-Over District: The Social and Intellectual History of Enthusiastic Religion in Western New York, 1800–1850*. New York: Octagon, 1981.

Essig, James D. *The Bonds of Wickedness: American Evangelicals against Slavery, 1770–1808*. Philadelphia: Temple University Press, 1982.

Holloway, Mark. *Heavens on Earth: Utopian Communities in America, 1680–1880*. 2d ed., rev. New York: Dover, 1966.

McLoughlin, William G., ed. *The American Evangelicals, 1800–1900: An Anthology*. New York: Harper and Row, 1968.

Smith, Timothy L. *Revivalism and Social Reform: American Protestantism on the Eve of the Civil War*. Baltimore: Johns Hopkins University Press, 1980.

FRANK G. KIRKPATRICK

EVOLUTION   Before Charles Darwin's *On the Origin of Species by Means of Natural Selection* appeared in 1859, a few Americans were already familiar with the theories of evolution in Erasmus Darwin's *Zoonomia, or the Laws of Organic Life* (1794–1796), Jean-Baptiste de Lamarck's *Philosophie zoologique* (1809), Robert Chambers's *Vestiges of the Natural History of Creation* (1844), and Herbert Spencer's *Social Statics* (1851). Although seriously flawed by later scientific standards, each theory assumed that existing life had developed from primitive organisms in response to changing conditions over a long period of time.

Theories of Evolution

Lamarck, the most important of the pre-Darwinian biologists, argued that traits acquired during the lifetime of an individual organism are passed to future generations. A popular if mistaken example was the process whereby the short-necked ancestors of giraffes allegedly developed elongated necks by feeding from trees over successive generations, a process termed "use inheritance." Although Lamarck was later ridiculed for ideas even more alien to modern science, for example, that individuals can cause changes in their bodily structure, American biologists continued to give credence to use inheritance into the twentieth century.

The English philosopher Herbert Spencer influenced several generations of Americans. Indebted to contemporary physics and to Lamarckianism, Spencer pictured evolution as a redistribution of matter and motion whereby objects in nature, including living organisms, achieve equilibrium with their environment. In *Social Statics* he argued that evolution in nature transforms simple (homogeneous) forms into complex (heterogeneous) ones. Under industrialism, the division of labor creates societies of free, independent individuals who naturally develop concern for one another or altruism. A champion of the "let alone" doctrine of laissez-faire, Spencer opposed government programs to remedy social problems. With *First Principles* (1862) he launched a multivolume "synthetic philosophy," surveying all knowledge from the perspective of his version of evolution. In *The Principles of Biology* (1864–1867) he substituted the phrase "survival of the fittest" for Darwin's "natural selection," thus assuring readers that evolution was progressive.

In 1872 Edward L. Youmans, Spencer's leading American disciple, founded *Popular Science Monthly* to propagate the Englishman's theories. The industrialist Andrew Carnegie joined more than a hundred other influential businessmen and intellectuals at a dinner to honor Spencer in New York in 1882, and in 1885 members of the New York elite organized the Brooklyn Ethical Association to further spread Spencer's teaching. By this time a younger generation of academics and reformers was criticizing the Spencerians for advocating social conflict that resulted in victory for the strongest, a charge Spencer himself vigorously denied. In reality "social Spencerianism," although sometimes blind to the ills of industrialism, expressed an overly sanguine view that struggle and suffering were destined soon to disappear. Eighteenth-century optimists hoped death could be abolished. One critic wrote that the Spencerians "appear to think that, if we will all be quiet and refrain from ill-omened words, it may be hushed up" (Bannister, *Social Darwinism*, p. 46).

Whereas earlier evolutionists believed that existing species were unchanging, Darwin proposed that species develop constantly through a process of "natural selection" in a "struggle for existence." Individuals vary within all species, and some individuals prove better able than others to adapt to existing conditions. Better-adapted individuals tend to leave more offspring. Through changes in conditions and splits within the population of a species, a new species may emerge. In *The Descent of Man, and Selection in Relation to Sex* (1871) Darwin extended this theory to human development.

Darwin rarely used the term "evolution," instead terming the theory "descent with modification," implying that natural selection proceeds with neither purpose nor direction. Within a decade, however, popular usage wed the theory to a faith in progress, first in the use of the term "evolution," which implied a progressive unfolding of preexisting forms as in embryology, and second in adopting the phrase "survival of the fittest," which Darwin included in later editions of *The Origin of Species*. Although natural selection remained the heart of Darwinian theory, the association of the theory with prevailing values allowed many Americans to accept evolution without endorsing natural selection.

Scientific and Religious Responses

American scientists and clergymen were divided in their responses to *The Origin of Species*. Leading anti-Darwinians included Louis Agassiz, a Harvard geologist, and Charles Hodge of the Princeton Theological Seminary, who attacked Darwin's book in *What Is Darwinism?* (1874). The *Catholic World* pronounced Darwin's theory an "absurdity," a view most Catholics echoed through the end of the century. Darwin's chief American defender was the Harvard botanist Asa Gray. In turn Gray gained support from the Congregationalist clergyman George F. Wright, who argued that natural selection was consistent with Calvinism. Wright prompted Gray to collect his pro-Darwinian essays in *Darwiniana* (1876).

Although colored by theology, much of the opposition to Darwinism was grounded in the science of the time. Physicists argued that the earth was not sufficiently old to have allowed enough changes to create so many species. Biologists, believing that no "leaps" occur in nature, reasoned that minor variations in organisms would cancel out one another. To this latter charge Darwin and his defenders had no ready reply, being unaware of the genetic theory of mutations first advanced in 1869 by the obscure Austrian monk Gregor Mendel and later developed by the Dutch biologist Hugo de Vries.

Darwin's theory of natural selection was also criticized on the grounds that it violated prevailing conceptions of scientific method, first in suggesting that science advances through wide-ranging hypotheses not immediately verifiable through observable data, and second in substituting a probabilistic conception of natural law, whereby nature produces multiple variations for selection, much as a roll of dice, for a mechanistic one, wherein cause and effect are directly related. It was not until the early twentieth century that biological science finally overcame these barriers, producing the "modern synthesis" in evolutionary biology.

Then and later controversies about Darwinian evolution were portrayed in military terms. In 1896 Andrew D. White, a former president of Cornell, published *History of the Warfare of Science with Theology*, but the metaphor is misleading. The debate over Darwinism was one within rather than between the scientific and religious communities. Prior to 1859 Protestants of various denominations had reached an accommodation with "science" as understood by most geologists, physicists, and biologists. These included even the Old School Presbyterians and other Calvinist predecessors of twentieth-century Protestant fundamentalism. Science consisted primarily of observation and classification, and hypotheses were viewed as "dangerous speculation." Although anti-Darwinian undercurrents existed within Christian America before 1900, the opposition that surfaced during the "monkey trial" of John Thomas Scopes in Dayton, Tennessee, in 1925 and continued through that century among supporters of

Asa Gray (1810–1888). Charles Darwin wrote the botanist Gray, the Fisher Professor of Natural History at Harvard, with his first account of his theory of evolution on 5 September 1857. LIBRARY OF CONGRESS

creation science was a product of the twentieth century, not a legacy of the nineteenth.

Beginning in the mid-1870s a compromise over Darwinism gradually emerged. Prominent clergymen embraced evolution as the unfolding of God's original plan while effectively ignoring natural selection. These "Christian evolutionists" included Henry Ward Beecher, the nation's best-known minister, and the editor of the popular religious magazine *Outlook*, Lyman Abbott, who made his peace with Darwin in *The Theology of an Evolutionist* (1897). Since Christian evolutionists assumed that technicalities are best left to scientific experts, these writers effectively conceded cultural authority to a rising group of rival professionals, weakening both the clergy and religion.

Social Evolutionism

In the 1870s growing acceptance of evolution spawned social theories based on evolution and occasionally on Darwinism. Charles Brace, a charity worker who had earlier used Darwin to defend racial equality, argued in *The Dangerous Classes of New York* (1872) that natural selection in human society produces virtue and temperance because "vicious and sensual and drunken" individuals fail to leave as many offspring as "the more self-controlled and virtuous" (p. 44). In *The Outlines of Cosmic Philosophy* (1874) John Fiske, a popular lecturer, invoked Darwin and evolution to argue for the inevitability of progress, the end of warfare, and a world federation of nations. Opponents of government interference in economic and social affairs appealed to nature and natural law, often citing the authority of Darwin.

Among these laissez-faire or classical liberals, the best-known was the Yale professor William Graham Sumner, an Episcopalian minister turned economist. In the early 1880s Sumner assigned his students Herbert Spencer's *Study of Sociology* (1873), a choice that almost cost him his job because the Yale administration viewed Spencer as irreligious. Influenced by the population theories of the English economist Thomas R. Malthus, whose work had also influenced Darwin's theory of selection through struggle, Sumner told audiences on several occasions that the only alternative to the survival of the fittest is "the survival of the unfittest." Following Malthus, Sumner drew a sharp distinction between the collective struggle against nature and a more benign "competition for life" that governed relations among human beings. Sumner's turn of phrase brought immediate criticism from the *New York Times* and other publications, revealing that evolution was becoming a two-edged sword. Although Sumner henceforth avoided references to evolution and did not read Darwin until near the end of his career, his rhetoric earned him a reputation as his generation's leading social Darwinist.

By the 1880s college-trained Americans were contemplating new readings of evolution, and evolutionism was stimulating innovation in the young social sciences. In seminal essays in *Popular Science Monthly* in 1878 Charles Sanders Peirce provided the earliest formulation of pragmatism, a philosophy later elaborated by William James and John Dewey. Bearing the imprint of evolutionism, pragmatism viewed ideas as instruments by which humans adapt to changing circumstances, their truth being measured by successful adaptation. In *The Common Law* (1881) and many subsequent court decisions, the jurist Oliver Wendell Holmes Jr. argued that the law and the Constitution should be reinterpreted in light of changing circumstances. Lester Frank Ward invoked Darwin in *Dynamic Sociology* (1883), arguing for government action guided by social scientists to remedy social ills. Richard T. Ely and other founders of the American Economic Association (1885) insisted that new conditions require new economic theories. Emphasizing experience over abstract theorizing, these intellectuals argued for the importance of emotion, volition, and even religious faith in human affairs.

During the 1880s appeals to evolution and Darwinism became the stock-in-trade of reformers, who proposed that improved education and environmental change could fix social problems. Laurence Gronlund combined Karl Marx and Spencer in *The Cooperative Commonwealth* (1884) to describe the coming of socialism. In *Looking Backward* (1888), a fictional account of an ideal American society in the year 2000, the best-selling novelist Edward Bellamy launched a tradition of evolutionary utopianism that later reached its apogee in Charlotte Perkins Gilman's *Herland* (1915). During the Progressive Era evolutionist arguments bolstered social reforms that ranged from trust-busting to measures for the alleviation of poverty.

Neo-Darwinism and Social Darwinism

In the 1890s debates over evolution took a new turn with the development of neo-Darwinism, a rigidly selectionist, hereditarian revision of Darwin's theory rooted in the work of the Austrian biologist August Weismann. Although neo-Lamarckians countered with arguments based on use inheritance, social planners questioned the optimistic faith that improvements in education and environment alone would cure social problems. Imperialists employed Darwinism in support of overseas expansion; eugenicists urged incarceration or sterilization of the unfit; ra-

cialists justified segregation and Jim Crow laws; and prohibitionists called for the elimination of alcohol. Like socialist evolutionists and other reform Darwinists, as they were later termed, neo-Darwinist social engineers typically argued that intervention was necessary to avoid the consequences of a Darwinian struggle of all against all.

In reaction to these arguments, all forms of social Darwinism came under increasing attack. The pejorative term "social Darwinism" first surfaced about 1880 among European socialists, who charged that Spencer and other laissez-faire theorists endorsed a brutal struggle for existence and survival of the fittest among human beings. The epithet drew its power from a long-standing ambivalence toward certain implications of Darwin's theory, for example, that evolution guarantees progress and that natural selection involves bloody conflict or, more simply, that nature dictates destiny. Subsequently the label "social Darwinist" was applied to anyone who argued that biology determines social and psychological characteristics among humans as well as physical attributes, whether to justify eugenicist, imperialist, racist, or sexist policies.

Applied to laissez-faire liberals the label is misleading because Darwin had little or no influence on Spencer or even Sumner. "I have never seen any distinctly Darwinian principle appealed to in the discussion of 'social Darwinism,' " wrote Lester Ward (Degler, *In Search of Human Nature*, p. 12). No friend of laissez-faire, Ward added that it was thus "wholly inappropriate" to apply the label to political economists. Those who continue to employ the term nonetheless argue that it expresses Darwin's debt to the economist Malthus and to the entire capitalist ethos. Applied to eugenicists, the phrase justly stigmatizes the racist and sexist side of some turn-of-the-century reform ideas. On balance, however, its negative connotations obscure the emancipating and progressive nature of evolutionism, a theory Dewey later termed the nineteenth century's "greatest dissolvent . . . of old questions, the greatest precipitant of new methods, new intentions, new problems" (*The Influence of Darwin on Philosophy*, p. 19).

See also **Biology; Philosophy; Pragmatism; Radicalism; Reform, Social.**

Bibliography

Bannister, Robert C. *Social Darwinism: Science and Myth in Anglo-American Social Thought.* Philadelphia: Temple University Press, 1979.

Bowler, Peter J. *Evolution: The History of an Idea.* Berkeley: University of California Press, 1984.

Darwin, Charles. *The Origin of Species: A Variorum Text.* Edited by Morse Peckham. Philadelphia: University of Pennsylvania Press, 1959.

Degler, Carl N. *In Search of Human Nature: The Decline and Revival of Darwinism in American Social Thought.* New York: Oxford University Press, 1991.

Dewey, John. *The Influence of Darwin on Philosophy and Other Essays in Contemporary Thought.* New York: Holt, 1910.

Hawkins, Mike. *Social Darwinism in European and American Thought, 1860–1945.* Cambridge, U.K., and New York: Cambridge University Press, 1997.

Hofstadter, Richard. *Social Darwinism in American Thought, 1860–1915.* Philadelphia: University of Pennsylvania Press, 1944. Rev. ed., Boston: Beacon Press, 1955.

Moore, James R. *The Post-Darwinian Controversies.* Cambridge, U.K., and New York: Cambridge University Press, 1979.

Pittenger, Mark. *American Socialists and Evolutionary Thought, 1870–1920.* Madison: University of Wisconsin Press, 1993.

Roberts, Jon H. *Darwinism and the Divine in America: Protestant Intellectuals and Organic Evolution, 1859–1900.* Madison: University of Wisconsin Press, 1988.

Russett, Cynthia Eagle. *Darwin in America: The Intellectual Response, 1865–1912.* San Francisco, Calif.: W. H. Freeman, 1976.

ROBERT C. BANNISTER

EXERCISE. See **Health Consciousness and Fitness.**

EXPANSION   Territorial expansion was one of the most significant features of life in the United States during the nineteenth century. In the one hundred years following Thomas Jefferson's election to the presidency, the nation's area quadrupled. When the nineteenth century began, the U.S. borders were the Mississippi River on the west, Florida on the south, and Canada on the north. A century later the nation reached from the Atlantic to the Pacific between the Rio Grande and the modern border with Canada, plus Alaska, Hawaii, Cuba, Puerto Rico, the Philippines, and a number of other Pacific islands. This growth had dramatic consequences for the nation and its people. It nearly destroyed many of North America's indigenous peoples, lured millions of Europeans to America, shaped U.S. economic growth, and brought the nation into bitter conflict both with foreign powers and within itself.

Spanning the Continent

Nineteenth-century U.S. expansion began with the Louisiana Purchase. When the century opened few Americans gave much thought to Louisiana, an ill-defined area extending west from the Mississippi River to the crest of the Rocky Mountains and north from Texas to the Canadian border. With millions of acres beyond the Appalachians yet to settle, few Americans yearned for more land. Louisiana did include the Mississippi River, however, and many Americans were eager to control that waterway. Without access to the Mississippi western farmers would be cut off from world markets, and Jefferson's agrarian republic would be smothered in its cradle. Louisiana was Spanish territory, acquired from France under the treaty ending the French and Indian War (1754–1763), and Americans believed Spain was not strong enough to stop U.S. travel on the river or U.S. expansion into Louisiana. So before 1800 American officials showed little interest in the region.

In 1800, however, France regained Louisiana. This reacquisition greatly concerned the United States because France might soon block American access to the Mississippi River and beyond. The fate of the Republic, it seemed, hung in the balance. Thus in 1803 Congress authorized the president to open negotiations with France concerning American navigation of the Mississippi and, perhaps, the sale of New Orleans to the United States. By then renewed fighting in Europe demanded French attention and resources, and the French were anxious to divest themselves of their vast American holdings. As a result, when Jefferson's envoys in Paris were offered all of Louisiana at the bargain price of $15 million, they quickly accepted despite the fact that they had no authority to do so. The action was popular, and within a few months Congress ratified the treaty and appropriated the money. In October 1803 the Louisiana Territory became part of the United States.

With the Mississippi secure, American attention turned toward East and West Florida, two weak and sparsely inhabited Spanish colonies. West Florida, lying between the Mississippi River and the eventual state of Florida, attracted settlers and land speculators from the United States. Americans were drawn by its agricultural potential and its strategic position astride several rivers that drain into the Gulf of Mexico. East Florida, the region that became the state of Florida, had more strategic than economic value to the United States. It had long been a haven for slaves fleeing Georgia and South Carolina and was becoming a base from which Creek and Seminole Indians staged raids against Americans. Jefferson had hoped to acquire part or all of the Floridas from France along with New Orleans, but the French were unwilling to claim that the colonies were part of Louisiana and sell them to the United States. The United States was reluctant to move decisively against the Floridas by itself because England might come to the

Floridas' defense in order to protect its own profitable trade with Latin America. Instead, the Americans bided their time and took the Floridas in pieces.

Beginning in 1804 American officials claimed that West Florida was part of the land transferred to the United States by the Louisiana Purchase. They did not act on this claim, though, until Napoleon's seizure of the Spanish throne (1808) and a rebellion by American settlers in the colony (1810) raised questions about the exact status of West Florida. President James Madison restated America's claim to West Florida in 1811. The following year half of the colony was included in the new state of Louisiana, while the other half was added to the Mississippi Territory. The arrival of American troops in 1813 completed this stealth conquest, and with war still raging in Europe neither Spain nor England could resist.

East Florida was a bit messier. With the Napoleonic Wars and the War of 1812 behind them, Spain and the United States opened negotiations to define the bounds of the Louisiana Purchase and to resolve their conflicting claims to the Floridas. The negotiations did not go well, however, and by 1817 they were deadlocked. Early in 1818 Andrew Jackson, commanding the American army's Southern Division, concentrated Spanish minds when he invaded East Florida to punish the Seminole Indians, whom the United States accused of raiding American settlers in Georgia. Jackson went far beyond his orders and spent more time pursuing the Spanish than he did the Seminoles. By June 1818 he had defeated the Spanish, appointed an American governor for East Florida, and returned to American territory. When the Monroe administration refused to censure Jackson, Spain made the best of a bad situation. In 1819 the Adams-Onís Treaty formally ceded the Floridas to the United States in return for the settlement of American claims against Spain amounting to $5 million.

The Adams-Onís Treaty also spurred American expansion into the Pacific Northwest by finally settling the border between Louisiana and the Spanish colony of Alta California. Since buying Louisiana from France, the United States had gradually advanced the claim that its territory extended beyond the Rockies to the Pacific Ocean through what Spain claimed was part of California and Britain claimed was part of British North America. Extending Louisiana to the Pacific would give the United States control of the Columbia River, access to a safe harbor in Puget Sound, and perhaps an important advantage over British Canada in the lucrative fur trade with China. Both Britain and Spain challenged the American claims, but after 1815 the Monroe administra-

tion set out to negotiate its way to the Pacific. The Adams-Onís Treaty removed the Spanish claim, and by the time that pact was signed Anglo-American negotiators had already agreed (1818) that Britain and the United States would jointly occupy the Pacific Northwest for ten years, though neither would enjoy sovereignty there. In 1827 this Joint Occupancy Agreement was renewed and made open-ended. Finally in 1846 Britain and the United States agreed to divide the territory along the forty-ninth parallel, and the region south of that line officially became U.S. territory.

Formal acquisition of the Oregon Country was just one aspect of the increasing U.S. interest in territorial expansion between 1825 and 1850. The second quarter of the nineteenth century saw a growing conviction among white Americans that territorial expansion was part of God's plan for them and for the American continent. This belief, eventually labeled Manifest Destiny, was a blend of ethnic, religious, and political chauvinism plus a healthy dose of economic self-interest. God, claimed white Americans, wanted them to "rescue" North America from any nonwhite, non-Protestant, nonrepublican peoples. Britons, Russians, Hispanics, and Native Americans all fell into one or more of these categories and thus had to make way for American expansion. Conveniently for white Americans, their destiny was most clearly manifest in those parts of the continent where they stood to make a profit.

During the 1820s and 1830s Americans established trading connections with the new Mexican Republic, especially with California and Santa Fe. Americans also moved in growing numbers to the potential cotton-growing lands of the Mexican state of Texas-Coahuila and played a major role in precipitating the 1836 revolution, by which half of that state became the Republic of Texas. By the early 1840s American farmers ruined by the panic of 1837 were migrating west along the Oregon Trail to settle the rich Willamette Valley of the Oregon Country. In 1844 the desire for expansion into all of these areas was strong enough to elect James K. Polk to the White House on a platform calling for the immediate acquisition of Oregon, Texas, and California.

Oregon became U.S. territory through the 1846 treaty with Britain. Texas, still an independent republic, was annexed to the United States in 1845, triggering a war in which Mexico yielded to the United States California and most of the American Southwest. Mexico had never accepted Texas independence and continued to dispute its southern and western borders when Texas entered the United States. In 1846 American troops patrolling the dis-

Emigrant Train, California. Strawberry Valley in California's Sierra Nevada Mountains was once a prosperous mining area, experiencing both the influx of those seeking gold and other opportunities and the departure of those who elected to move on. Such migration was common in the expanding West. Photographer unknown, 1866. LIBRARY OF CONGRESS

puted southern border clashed with Mexican troops, precipitating war. In eighteen months of war the United States defeated Mexico, capturing Mexico City in September 1847 and occupying both Santa Fe and California. The Treaty of Guadalupe Hidalgo was signed in early 1848, and under its provisions the United States gained almost all land from Texas to California. Five years later the Gadsden Purchase slightly altered the border between Mexico and the New Mexico Territory and completed the acquisition of the forty-eight contiguous states of the Union.

Beyond Adjacent Territory

In fifty years the nation had spanned the continent and tripled in size, but with barely a pause it continued to expand beyond its contiguous territory. In the late 1850s the United States laid claim to several uninhabited islands in the South Pacific in order to mine their guano deposits for fertilizer. A decade later, in 1867, the United States also occupied Midway Atoll, which an American expedition had discovered in 1859. The most important mid-century acquisition, though, was Alaska. Russia decided in 1866 to sell its distant and not very profitable Alaskan possessions before the United States or Britain simply seized them. The United States quickly accepted the Russian offer and purchased Alaska early in 1867. For the next thirty years Americans concentrated on consolidating their hold over the lands they had already taken, especially those occupied by the Plains Indians.

At the end of the century, however, economics and geopolitics motivated a flurry of American expansion. By the 1890s the United States, Britain, Germany, and others were competing to become the world's leading industrial power. Economists and politicians, steeped in social Darwinism, believed that only the fittest nation would survive this competition. To ensure success the United States needed continued access to the raw materials that fueled modern industry and to customers for its industrial products. No longer was it enough just to dominate North America. Global success depended on global markets, and secure access to those markets depended on a nation's ability to project force. As Albert Beveridge told the Senate in 1899: "Most future wars will be conflicts for commerce. The power that rules the Pacific, therefore, is the power that rules the world."

Americans already had a foothold in the Pacific. Since early in the nineteenth century U.S. missionaries and businesspeople had been active in the Hawaiian Islands, and by the last quarter of the century they dominated the islands' economy, especially the sugar industry. To strengthen their positions, the sugar barons worked to reduce the power of Hawaii's native monarchy and in 1893 led a rebellion they hoped would lead to the annexation of Hawaii by the United States. It led, instead, to the Republic of Hawaii, which was established in 1894. Annexation had to wait until 1898, when the United States needed a Pacific base for its navy during its war with the Spanish Empire.

The Spanish-American War broke out in the spring of 1898 over the issue of Spanish "tyranny" in Cuba. It quickly spread to other remnants of the Spanish Empire, as the United States seized the opportunity to burnish its democratic credentials while gaining an advantage over its global business rivals. By the end of the year the United States had captured Cuba, Puerto Rico, Guam, and the Philippines, the last of which Senator Beveridge called "a self-supporting, dividend-paying fleet." For good measure the Americans also took Wake Island and joined Germany and Britain in partitioning Samoa (1899).

Consequences of Expansion

The consequences of American expansion during the nineteenth century were multiple and mixed. For Native American inhabitants of the lands conquered or annexed by the United States the consequences were often disastrous. Indians were considered a lesser race who had to be elevated to the status of whites. If Indians died of disease or starvation through ill-conceived assimilation strategies, that was the cost of progress. Those who survived had few rights that the United States and its citizens were willing to recognize or protect. Though the government sometimes recognized native property rights and negotiated purchases with tribal leaders, it rarely prevented individual settlers from ignoring native claims and squatting on Indian land. Moreover Native Americans were not granted legal rights to protect their land themselves. As noncitizens they could neither sue their enemies nor vote for their friends, and armed defense of their homelands was suicidal.

The situation for Hispanics was almost as bad. While French residents of Louisiana and British residents of Oregon were generally well treated, Hispanics in Texas, California, and New Mexico often lost their property or their positions in society under American rule. In California, for example, the Treaty of Guadalupe Hidalgo stipulated that the United States would recognize legitimate Mexican or Spanish land grants, but the process established for proving such claims was so complex and so biased that most Hispanic residents lost their land to the Anglos and their lawyers. Hispanics were also subject to discriminatory taxes and, eventually, to segregated schools and restricted political rights.

Even U.S. citizens both gained and lost as a result of nineteenth-century expansion. As a benefit expansion brought the United States legal title to millions of acres of land and the wealth they contained. Numerous American fortunes began with the gold, copper, and timber resources acquired through expansion. Land was also a powerful lure to new settlers, drawing millions of European immigrants to the United States. Immigrants in turn provided labor for farms, ranches, and mines in the new territory and customers for the goods and services of American factories and railroads. At a time when the world's wealth flowed from farms, mines, and factories, territorial expansion made America rich.

But American expansion came with a price. Almost every acre of new land was purchased with hatred and blood because expansion frequently led to or resulted from a war. Louisiana and Oregon passed quietly from European powers to the United States, but years of bitter fighting to conquer their native inhabitants followed. The war that gained California killed more than twelve thousand American soldiers and precipitated decades of Mexican resentment toward the United States. Winning Cuba, Puerto Rico, and the Philippines from Spain cost more than five thousand American lives, and more servicemen were lost subduing the Filipino independence movement. The greatest cost, however, may have been the 600,000 Americans killed in the Civil War. Antebellum expansion amplified the debate over slavery. Every time the nation added to its territory, advocates and opponents of slavery argued over the institution's expansion into that new territory. This repetition of the debate no doubt contributed to the fears and passions that triggered the Civil War.

See also **Alaska Purchase; American Indians,** *subentry on* **U.S. Government Policies; California; Cuba; Europe, Foreign Relations with; Federal Land Policy; Florida; Gadsden Purchase; Hawaii; Louisiana Purchase; Manifest Destiny; Mexican Cession; Mexican War; Northwest Territory; Oregon; Overseas Possessions; Spanish-American War; Texas; Trails to the West.**

Bibliography

Jackson, Donald. *Thomas Jefferson and the Stony Mountains: Exploring the West from Monticello.* Urbana: University of Illinois Press, 1981.

LaFeber, Walter. *The New Empire: An Interpretation of American Expansion, 1860–1898.* Ithaca, N.Y.: Cornell University Press, 1963.

Limerick, Patricia Nelson. *The Legacy of Conquest: The Unbroken Past of the American West.* New York: Norton, 1987.

Merk, Frederick. *Manifest Destiny and Mission in American History: A Reinterpretation.* New York: Knopf, 1963.

Milner, Clyde A., II, Carol A. O'Conner, and Martha A. Sandweiss, eds. *The Oxford History of the American West.* New York: Oxford University Press, 1994.

Pletcher, David M. *The Diplomacy of Annexation: Texas, Oregon, and the Mexican War.* Columbia: University of Missouri Press, 1973.

Traxel, David. *1898: The Birth of the American Century.* New York: Knopf, 1998.

Weeks, William Earl. *John Quincy Adams and American Global Empire.* Lexington: University Press of Kentucky, 1992.

White, Richard. *"It's Your Misfortune and None of My Own": A History of the American West.* Norman: University of Oklahoma Press, 1991.

DANIEL B. THORP

EXPLORATION AND EXPLORERS

The motivation for exploration changed from economics to science during the nineteenth century. Early in the century, Thomas Jefferson (1743–1826) justified exploration for trade. By the 1890s, however, explorers like John Wesley Powell were gathering knowledge for knowledge's sake.

The land area of the United States doubled in size with the Louisiana Purchase, completed on 30 April 1803. Even before this deal with France, President Jefferson asked Congress to fund an expedition up the Missouri River, saying this journey, over soil that was ostensibly Spanish but secretly French, would bring great commercial gain from the fur trade and from agriculture.

The acquisition of well over 800,000 square miles, the Louisiana Territory, provided an impetus for an expedition. To head it, President Jefferson selected Meriwether Lewis (1774–1809), an army captain and private secretary to the president. Lewis chose his friend William Clark (1770–1838), a former artillery lieutenant, as co-commander. The "Corps of Discovery" consisted of about thirty-five men, one woman, one infant, and one dog. The woman was Sacagawea (1786?–1812?), a Shoshone Indian; the infant was her son, Jean Baptiste Charbonneau; and the dog was a Newfoundland dog named Seaman belonging to Lewis. On 14 May 1804 the corps started up the Missouri River from the St. Louis, Missouri, area. They returned there from the Pacific encampment, Fort Clatsop, on 23 September 1806.

In 1800 the United States had no grizzly bears, prairie dogs, cutthroat trout, pronghorn antelope, ponderosa pines, or sage grouse. That changed after 1803 and the Louisiana Purchase.

The explorers gave American names to the routes westward. Indigenous, continentwide transportation routes were used by American Indian traders, warriors, messengers, exploratory travelers, and visiting diplomats and delegates. The journey of Lewis and Clark followed long-used Indian water routes, such as the Missouri, Snake, Columbia, and Yellowstone Rivers, as well as mountain passes. It is not surprising that these constituted the major components of the Lewis and Clark route.

Lewis and Clark also used contemporary Indian transportation modes, including canoeing, walking, and riding horses. They innovatively navigated the rivers in boats propelled by long poles, sails, horses or humans pulling tow ropes from river banks, and oars. They employed a keelboat of twenty-two oars specially built for the expedition and designed by Lewis and Jefferson.

Sacagawea and Lewis and Clark

Sacagawea, romanticized as a heroine guide, lived in what is now North Dakota near the corps' first winter encampment, made in mid-November 1804, and she traveled along with the explorers through mid-August 1806. She guided the expedition through her native territory around Three Forks, Montana, and pointed out the Bozeman Pass through the Rocky Mountains on the return journey. In addition she showed the travelers how to gather edible wild plants. But her critical role was that of interpreter and culture broker among the tribes the explorers encountered. Her brother Cameahwait was, by August 1805, head of the Shoshone band to which Sacagawea belonged. In a meeting with Cameahwait in what now is Lemhi County, Idaho, Sacagawea negotiated for horses and guides to cross the Bitterroot Range of the Rockies through the country of the Salmon and Snake Rivers.

Sacagawea's formal status with the Corps of Discovery was as a wife of Toussaint Charbonneau, a French Canadian fur trapper hired by Lewis and Clark under the proviso that he accompany them from Fort Mandan (North Dakota) with one of his Shoshone wives, who would act as interpreter. Sacagawea was his choice. Her informal status was as a highly respected goodwill ambassador from the corps to various Indian groups, a fact noted by Clark in his journal on 13 October 1805. Sacagawea fared better than the equally competent York, Clark's African American slave. York effectively endured many hardships that could have meant sacrificing his life for Clark's. Yet, for economic reasons, Clark was unwilling to give up his slave property after the expedition to honor York's pleas for freedom.

Science and Lewis and Clark

Lewis and Clark traversed or bordered by river route the following present-day states: Missouri, Kansas, Nebraska, Iowa, South Dakota, North Dakota, Montana, Idaho, Oregon, and Washington. For economic reasons, President Jefferson was interested in finding a northwest passage to the western sea to link the new territory with the West. But Jefferson also asked the explorers to pay close scientific attention to all aspects of the nature of the land—to new plants and their growth cycles, to the animals characteristic of the countryside, and to the various indigenous peoples who inhabited the land.

Captain Lewis was an accomplished naturalist, and Co-captain Clark excelled in geography and cartography. Both men devoted much journal space to precise descriptions of the flora and fauna they observed. The ragged robin flower, *Clarkia pulchella*, an evening primrose, was named after Clark. He is further known for his 1810 map of western North America.

Zebulon Montgomery Pike

In 1805 and 1806, while Lewis and Clark were in the field, Zebulon Montgomery Pike (1779–1813) sought the headwaters of the Mississippi River in present-day Minnesota. In 1806 and 1807 his U.S. Army expedition searched for the headwaters of the Arkansas River in present-day Colorado. Pike, an army lieutenant who later became a brigadier general, never actually found the headwaters of the Mississippi. Nevertheless, in his journal map he produced the first genuine systematic depiction of the upper Mississippi.

Pike did find the source of the Arkansas River. Afterward he crossed the Sierra Sangre de Cristo and then the Rio Grande into Spanish territory, claiming he thought the latter was the Red River of the South. There Pike was arrested by a Spanish military unit and taken to Sante Fe. On 30 April 1807 Pike was returned from New Spain to the United States at Natchitoches, an old settlement in the newly acquired Louisiana Territory.

Pike published his journals in book form in 1810, three years before the Lewis and Clark journals appeared. Pike's book revealed some of the motivations for U.S. exploration in the early nineteenth century, especially to reconnoiter possible routes and areas that could be fortified for trade and military operations; to map river ways, including previously unidentified headwaters; and to identify and encourage greater communication with Native American peoples.

Pike is best known for attempting to climb a prominent peak in the Front Range of the Rocky Mountains, which he called Grand Peak in his journal. It was later renamed Pikes Peak. At 14,110 feet (4,301 meters), it is not the highest of the Rocky Mountain peaks, but it may well be the most famous.

Other Expeditions on the Southern Plains

Other American explorations of the Red River of the South involved John Sibley in 1803, Thomas Freeman in 1806, Thomas Sparks in 1806, and Stephen Harriman Long in 1820. Sibley, a physician at the army post at Natchitoches, Louisiana, is known for his 1807 geographic account of the Red River, which included notes on the Indians of the area.

Sibley, Freeman, Sparks, and Long, in search of the elusive headwaters, reconnoitered the Red River in separate expeditions. All four men were particularly interested in the river as a trade route with military implications, and they succeeded in establishing the headwaters incrementally. The Red River flows primarily from branching headwater streams in present-day northern Texas, but also from similar streams in present-day eastern New Mexico, and ultimately flows through present-day Louisiana, where it joins the Mississippi. Militarily, the Red River was

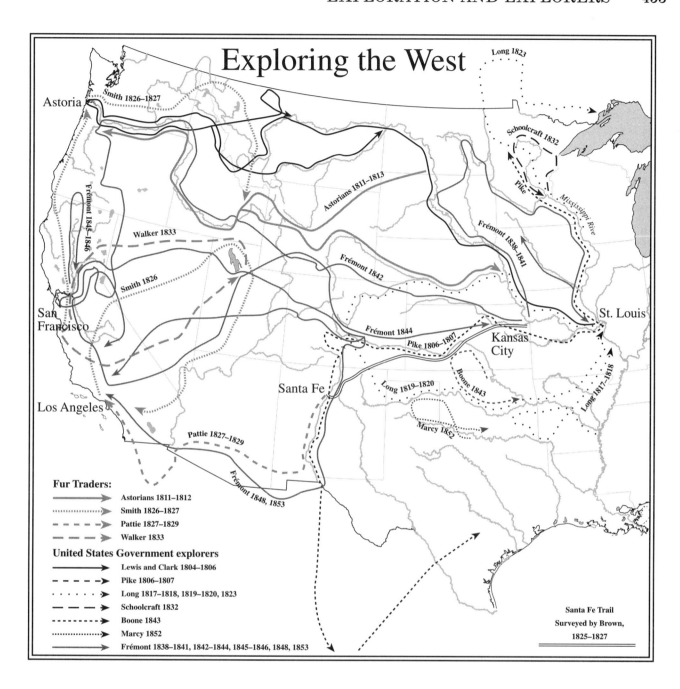

Exploring the West

Fur Traders:

➝	Astorians 1811–1812
┈➝	Smith 1826–1827
─ ─➝	Pattie 1827–1829
— —➝	Walker 1833

United States Government explorers

──➝	Lewis and Clark 1804–1806
─ ─ ─➝	Pike 1806–1807
· · · ·➝	Long 1817–1818, 1819–1820, 1823
— — —➝	Schoolcraft 1832
─ ─ ─ ─➝	Boone 1843
┈┈┈➝	Marcy 1852
──➝	Frémont 1838–1841, 1842–1844, 1845–1846, 1848, 1853

Santa Fe Trail
Surveyed by Brown,
1825–1827

(Map labels: Long 1823, Smith 1826–1827, Astoria, Schoolcraft 1832, Pike, Mississippi River, Frémont 1845–1846, Walker 1833, Frémont 1838–1841, Frémont 1842, Smith 1826, San Francisco, Frémont 1844, Pike 1806–1807, Kansas City, St. Louis, Santa Fe, Long 1819–1820, Boone 1843, Long 1817–1818, Los Angeles, Pattie 1827–1829, Marcy 1852, Frémont 1848, 1853)

important because a portion of it marked the southwestern boundary of the new U.S. territory.

Stephen Harriman Long

Stephen Harriman Long (1784–1864) led an expedition in 1820 into the Front Range of the Rocky Mountains. Long, whose map gave the name "the Great American Desert" to the Great Plains east of the Rockies, was an officer and a civil engineer serving in the Corps of Topographical Engineers of the U.S. Army. Edwin James (1797–1861), a physician and a member of Long's party, wrote the official report of the expedition, which reflects his scientific background. Two artists with the expedition, Titian Ramsay Peale (1799–1885) and Samuel Seymour (fl. 1797–1823), produced, respectively, the first European American images of Plains Indian life and the topography of the Rockies. With the discerning eyes of naturalists, they accurately reproduced, in paintings and drawings, plants, animals, landscapes and other geographic features, and scenes of Indian life, including the bison hunt.

Jedediah Strong Smith

Jedediah Strong Smith (1798–1831) began exploring as a member of William Henry Ashley's 1822 expedition up the Missouri River. Ashley (1778–1838) was a successful fur trader who later served a Missouri district in the U.S. House of Representatives.

After learning of its location from Crow Indians in the Rocky Mountains, Ashley's fur expedition crossed South Pass (Wyoming) in the spring of 1824. Smith, who led that expedition, realized the strategic importance of this passageway to the West. Ashley popularized South Pass, using it himself in 1825 and telling others about it. Robert Stuart (1785–1848) on the other hand told no one of the pass, perhaps to limit competition in the fur trade. Stuart was a fur trapper employed by John Jacob Astor (1763–1848), the New York fur merchant and financier. Stuart is credited with leading the first European American fur trappers across South Pass in October 1812 on his return from an expedition to the Pacific.

Smith led a group of fur trappers on a trek during 1826 and 1827. Searching for new routes to trapping grounds from the Great Salt Lake area, they traveled as far as southern California after crossing the Mojave Desert. Smith thus reportedly became the first European American to reach California via an overland route from the east. He did not tarry in what was then Mexican territory but went north and east again via the American River into and over the Sierra Nevada. In so doing Smith achieved two more American firsts. He was the first American to cross the Sierra Nevada and the first American to traverse the Great Basin. He found routes that physically linked northern, southern, western, and then eastern areas of the Great American West. A literate and compassionate man, Smith remains a symbol of the "can do" trait in the American character. He acquired and shared geographic knowledge crucial to nineteenth-century westward expansion.

John Charles Frémont

John Charles Frémont (1813–1890) was a presidential candidate, a territorial administrator on two separate occasions, a senator, and an army officer who, after a hiatus in service, retired as a major general. A path marker rather than a pathfinder, Frémont participated in or conducted seven expeditions, beginning in 1838 and 1839, when he was a member of Joseph Nicolas Nicollet's expedition of the U.S. Army Corps of Topographical Engineers. In two surveys Frémont and Nicollet mapped the vast prairie region between the upper Mississippi and Missouri Rivers. Joseph Nicolas Nicollet (1786–1843), a French citizen and scientist, arrived in the United States in 1832 and subsequently trained Frémont in cartography. Frémont's third expedition, in 1842, reached South Pass, then turned northwest into the Wind River Range of the Rockies. Congress printed his report and map.

During 1843 and 1844, Frémont surveyed the Oregon Trail to the mouth of the Columbia River. He entered California, crossed the Sierra Nevada in the winter, explored the northeastern area of the Great Salt Lake, and reached Bent's Fort trading post on the Arkansas River in present-day Colorado. On this fourth expedition Charles Preuss (1803–1854) and Kit Carson (1809–1868) accompanied Frémont as cartographer and guide, respectively. (Carson guided Frémont on three western expeditions—1842, 1843–1844, and 1845–1846.) Frémont's fifth expedition, in 1845, was to California via the Great Salt Lake. While in the Pacific West, Frémont supported the Bear Flag Rebellion of 1846 against Mexico by Californians who wanted to join the United States.

Frémont next led a privately financed expedition to California in 1848–1849 to find passes for a railroad to the Pacific. It was unsuccessful, and ten men died. Frémont's seventh and last expedition, in 1853–1854, was again motivated by the desire to discover east-west railroad passes. It proved successful in that he demonstrated the feasibility of a southern railway route to the coast.

Frémont had a sense of his work's importance to American society. His reports, which he mostly wrote with the assistance of his wife, Jessie Ann Hart Benton (1824–1902), were valuable to a range of readers. Widely circulated, his reports included maps and were used by the military, pioneers moving west, and railroad promoters. Perhaps because he was also a politician, Frémont is recognized more than other explorers for linking exploration and Manifest Destiny.

Charles Wilkes

As Frémont began his expeditionary career, Charles Wilkes (1798–1877), a navy lieutenant, embarked upon an around-the-world sea voyage, the U.S. Exploring Expedition. Wilkes's fleet departed from Norfolk, Virginia, in August 1838, and terminated in New York City in July 1842. Frémont subsequently compared his own map of the mouth of the Columbia with that of Wilkes. Much of the latter's work was highly detailed and accurate, especially his maritime charts of some of the Pacific islands. U.S. forces would draw upon them during World War II.

Gouverneur Kemble Warren

As an engineering graduate, second in his class of 1850 at the U.S. Military Academy at West Point, Gouverneur Kemble Warren (1830–1882) became a lieutenant colonel in the regular army and a brevet major general in the Union volunteer army. In 1855,

COL. FREMONT
PLANTING THE AMERICAN STANDARD ON THE ROCKY MOUNTAINS.

John C. Frémont (1813–1890). Campaign banner for John C. Frémont's presidential bid in 1856, capitalizing on his career and reputation as a great explorer in the West. LIBRARY OF CONGRESS: PRINTS AND PHOTOGRAPHS DIVISION

1856, and 1857 he conducted three separate expeditions to continue efforts to map river systems in the present-day states of Nebraska, Wyoming, South Dakota, North Dakota, and Montana. The rivers included the Platte, White, Missouri, Yellowstone, Cheyenne, and Niobrara.

During his topographical career Warren compiled different sources to draw a comprehensive map of the western United States that set the standard for all subsequent efforts. Like other explorers with a scientific bent, including Edwin James and John Wesley Powell, Warren maintained a keen interest in American Indian peoples and cultures.

John Wesley Powell

The career of John Wesley Powell (1834–1902) marks the ascendancy of science in American western exploration. Earlier explorers had produced positive contributions to scientific knowledge, but generally these were secondary considerations. The primary goal was discovering paths and sites for trade, military, and settlement purposes. Powell was a genuine scientist who successfully advocated the acceptance of science as an appropriate part of government.

As a Union artillery officer in the Civil War, Powell lost part of his right arm. He then taught science at Illinois Wesleyan College. In 1867 and 1868 Powell led geological expeditions of students and fellow scientists to Colorado and Utah, where he became intrigued with the Rocky Mountains. Congress authorized the 1868 expedition. With more government backing in 1869, Powell conducted a geological survey of the canyons of the Green and Colorado Rivers. This expedition, consisting of ten men in four boats, floated down the Colorado River through the Grand Canyon, for one thousand miles and a period of three months. Braving the unknown, they emerged successfully, despite churning rapids and other dangers. Powell took a second trip down the Colorado in 1871, and in 1874 and 1875 he led expeditions investigating the Uinta Mountains and their geology. Powell mapped the Colorado Plateau, and he prepared another chart in which he classified and identified the distribution of fifty-eight language families of the indigenous peoples of the United States and Canada. His 1891 language map was a significant contribution to cultural anthropology. Powell was an effective administrator as well as a field researcher. In 1879 he became the first director of the Bureau of American Ethnology, and from 1881 to 1892 he directed the U.S. Geological Survey.

Conclusion

Whether pathfinding or path marking, the pursuit of geographic knowledge to promote trade began and remained the dominant motivation to explore the American West through at least the first half of the nineteenth century. But motivations for exploration shifted during the course of the century—from including a component to gather all sorts of knowledge, to eventually emphasizing science for its own sake.

See also **Anthropology; Expansion; Frontier; Gadsden Purchase; Geography and Cartography; Geography and Ecology; Hunting and Trapping; Jeffersonian Era; Lewis and Clark Expedition; Louisiana Purchase; Manifest Destiny; Sciences, Physical; Trails to the West; Transportation,** *subentry on* **Railroads; West, The.**

Bibliography

Abel, Annie Heloise. "Introduction." In *A Report from Natchitoches in 1807*, by John Sibley. Indian Notes and Monographs Series, edited by Frederick W. Hodge. Woodville, Tex.: Dogwood Press, 1996. First published New York: Museum of the American Indian, Heye Foundation, 1922.

Ambrose, Stephen E. *Undaunted Courage: Meriwether Lewis, Thomas Jefferson, and the Opening of the American West.* 1996. Reprint, New York: Simon and Schuster, 1997.

Bartlett, Richard A. *Great Surveys of the American West.* 1962. Reprint, Norman: University of Oklahoma Press, 1966.

Cutright, Paul Russell. *Lewis and Clark: Pioneering Naturalists.* Urbana: University of Illinois Press, 1969. Reprint, Lincoln: University of Nebraska Press, 1989.

Dodds, Gordon B. "Smith, Jedediah Strong." In *The New Encyclopedia of the American West.* Edited by Howard R. Lamar. New Haven: Yale University Press, 1998.

Fisher, Ron. "Lewis and Clark: Naturalist-Explorers." *National Geographic*, October 1998, pp. 76–93.

Goetzmann, William H., and Glyndwr Williams. *The Atlas of North American Exploration: From the Norse Voyages to the Race to the Pole.* New York: Prentice Hall, 1992. Reprint, Norman: University of Oklahoma Press, 1998.

Hollon, W. Eugene. *The Lost Pathfinder: Zebulon Montgomery Pike.* 1949. Reprint, Norman: University of Oklahoma Press, 1969.

McBeth, Sally. "Sacagawea." In *Encyclopedia of North American Indians.* Edited by Frederick E. Hoxie. Boston: Houghton Mifflin, 1996.

Ronda, James P. *Lewis and Clark among the Indians.* 1984. Reprint, Lincoln: University of Nebraska Press, 1988.

Tanner, Helen Hornbeck. "Travel and Transportation Routes." In *Encyclopedia of North American Indians.* Edited by Frederick E. Hoxie. Boston: Houghton Mifflin, 1996.

Van Horn, Lawrence F. Review of *Little Chief's Gatherings: The Smithsonian Institution's G. K. Warren 1855–1856 Plains Indian Connection and the New York State Library's 1855–1857 Warren Expedition Journals*, by James A. Hanson. *South Dakota History* 27, no. 4 (winter 1997): 263–264.

Wheat, Carl I. *Mapping the Transmississippi West, 1540–1861.* 5 vols. San Francisco: Institute of Historical Cartography, 1957–1963.

Whitfield, Peter. *New Found Lands: Maps in the History of Exploration.* New York: Routledge, 1998.

LAWRENCE F. VAN HORN

EXPOSITIONS.   See **World's Fairs.**

F

FAMILY. See **Birth and Childbearing; Domestic Life; Life Cycle,** subentry on **Childhood and Adolescence; Marriage.**

FARMING. See **Agriculture.**

FEDERALISM. See **Politics,** subentry on **The First Party System.**

FEDERALIST PARTY The Federalist Party was created by Secretary of the Treasury Alexander Hamilton in the early 1790s to support the financial programs of the Washington administration. Hamilton wanted a strong nation with good credit and a program of economic modernization. The opposition Republicans, led by Thomas Jefferson and James Madison, included most of the Antifederalists who opposed ratification of the Constitution. The Republicans thought Hamilton was a monarchist who planned to impose the corrupt British system of government and a heavy national debt, thereby threatening individual liberties and states' rights. The French Revolution escalated tensions, with the Republicans backing the radical French.

Gradually the two factions became permanent parties. That evolution took a major step forward when the Federalists ratified Jay's Treaty of 1794 with Britain, over strenuous Republican opposition.

The Federalist versus Republican party system was fully evident in the election of 1796 when the Federalist candidate, John Adams, narrowly defeated the Republicans' Thomas Jefferson. George Washington had increasingly sided with Hamilton, and after his death in 1799 he became the icon of Federalist legitimacy. In his Farewell Address, Washington had warned against sectional polarization and the baneful influence of party, but to no avail. New England was the Federalist stronghold, along with commercial cities up and down the coast. The Republican base was the plantation South—the sort of idyllic rural society Jefferson feared would be in danger should the Federalists succeed in modernizing and urbanizing America.

The failure of diplomacy, as in the XYZ affair, led to an undeclared "quasi war" with France (1797–1800) as American and French ships attacked each other. Congress, controlled by the Federalists, made extensive war preparations. A new army, paid for by heavy new taxes and more borrowing, was raised, with Hamilton in charge. The Federalists tried to silence opposition, especially Republican newspaper editors, with the Alien and Sedition Acts (1798). Jefferson and Madison responded with the Kentucky and Virginia Resolutions, holding that the states could declare federal laws unconstitutional. In 1799 Adams stunned his party by breaking with Hamilton and negotiating peace with France.

The 1800 election was close, but Hamilton's refusal to support Adams made the latter's defeat certain. The Republicans were much better at mobilizing public opinion at the grass roots. The Federalists

457

tried to organize from the top down, but their visible disdain for the common man proved a fatal weakness.

Republican efforts to coerce Britain economically during the war between Britain and Napoleon's France (1808–1812) had a devastating negative impact on the nation's business community, leading to a Federalist resurgence. In 1812 the Republican Congress declared war on Britain, primarily to assert national honor. The war went poorly, as the Federalists refused to support it in any way. Their presidential candidate in 1812 was DeWitt Clinton, a dissident Republican; he narrowly lost to Madison. In late 1814 and early 1815 the Federalists assembled at the Hartford Convention reversed their previous position and called for states' rights and a weak central government. By this time the Republicans had adopted many Federalist ideas, including a national bank and a strong national government. Simultaneous news of a peace treaty and Andrew Jackson's great victory at New Orleans made the Hartford demands seem preposterous. The Federalists vanished except in Delaware and a few backwaters. However, Chief Justice John Marshall, the Federalists' top leader in the late 1790s, succeeded in creating a powerful judiciary that could act as a brake on democratic excesses.

See also **Jeffersonian Era; Supreme Court,** *subentry on* **The Marshall Court; War of 1812.**

Bibliography

Ben-Atar, Doron, and Barbara Oberg, eds. *Federalists Reconsidered.* Charlottesville: University Press of Virginia, 1998.

Elkins, Stanley M., and Eric L. McKitrick. *The Age of Federalism: The Early American Republic, 1788–1800.* New York: Oxford University Press, 1993.

Miller, John C. *The Federalist Era: 1789–1801.* New York: Harper, 1960.

RICHARD JENSEN

FEDERAL LAND POLICY   From the passage of the first American land act in 1785 the federal government controlled the sale of public lands. By moving past the haphazard system of land grants that characterized the colonial period, the government hoped to avoid multiple ownership and fraud. The Land Survey Ordinance of 1785, written by Thomas Jefferson, guaranteed systematic land surveys and sales. Jefferson incorporated the New England system of land division, townships of thirty-six square miles divided into 640-acre sections, into his vision of the American landscape consisting of small-scale family farms. This new measure sold land at a minimum purchase size and price. Beginning west of Pennsylvania and north of the Ohio River, the government conducted the first survey of land that became known as the Seven Ranges. The land was laid out in a grid system that identified each section or township to be sold and became part of the federal public domain. Land was sold at public auction at a minimum price of one dollar per acre, with 640 acres (one section) being the smallest lot purchased, with section 16 reserved for education. In addition, buyers were given three months to pay for their purchase.

However, at the time of the land ordinance, few small-scale farmers could afford to pay $640 for a section of land. Recognizing the speculative aspect of the first land legislation, the new country attempted to rectify that situation with the passage of additional legislation. In 1796 a policy change required a minimum purchase price of two dollars per acre and the purchase of 640 acres with a 10 percent discount for full payment at that time. This scheme resulted in a higher purchase price but easier terms: the government allowed 5 percent down, 50 percent within thirty days, and the remainder within one year. While the payment schedule still proved too challenging for the average farmer, speculators capitalized on these measures and acquired large tracts of land, reselling them to area newcomers.

To rectify the inequities in the system the federal government reduced the number of acres required for purchase and extended the schedule to four years at 13.5 percent interest in 1800. A homesteader's minimum purchase after 1800 was 320 acres at two dollars per acre. While through this amendment the federal government hoped to move away from the stigmatism of not establishing a land policy that supported the independent farmer, the policy's terms still made it difficult for anyone other than a speculator to purchase land.

Further recognizing the need to reduce the minimum purchase requirements, lawmakers passed the Land Act of 1820. In that measure the federal government reduced the price per acre to $1.25 and the number of acres for purchase to eighty, with the assumption that any pioneer or settler could find one hundred dollars to buy land. However, the panic of 1819 and subsequent depression made the collection of even a hundred dollars difficult for most potential pioneers. In addition, the government ended the practice of granting land sales on credit; after 1820 land was paid for in cash. With little currency in circulation and no credit system in place, most prospective buyers found themselves unable to purchase land, and many pioneers on the unsurveyed frontier resorted to the practice of "squatting." These settlers gambled that they would have the means to purchase when the federal government arrived to sell the land.

The presence of squatters on the public domain

"Where Land Is Cheap." New Mexican farmers play checkers on large squares of land. From *Puck's Library*, 1890. LIBRARY OF CONGRESS

was a problem from the first. Cash-poor families moved onto unclaimed land, made improvements, and waited for the federal survey to reach their land. Years of hard work might be challenged and lost if these settlers could not then meet the purchase price at public auction. Eventually, squatters formed claims clubs to protect their land interests during public auctions. The government, however, did not address squatting until 1830. The Preemption Act of 1830 gave those who had settled land in 1829 with the intention of farming first rights to buy their land, up to 160 acres. Still, it proved difficult for these farmers to pay the two hundred dollars necessary for purchase.

The Preemption Law of 1841 guaranteed squatters the opportunity to buy 160 acres at a minimum price of $1.25 per acre. To further open the frontier, the government initiated a new policy in 1854 that reduced the cost of unclaimed public domain land. The price of land that had remained in the public domain for thirty years or more was reduced to 12.5 cents per acre. This measure brought a land rush to the Great Plains and midwestern states. The number of acres sold at these minimal prices amounted to several million acres across the region.

In 1862 the federal government took the next logical step in this trend of successive liberalization, passing the Homestead Act. (A southern version of

the measure was passed in 1866.) The new law—a cornerstone of the Republican platform—guaranteed a settler 160 acres if the property was improved, lived on, and worked for five years. For a minimal filing fee, settlers could claim a quarter-section of the public domain to establish a homestead. In the years following passage of this act, homesteaders claimed land in the midwestern states, such as Minnesota, rather than those of the Great Plains. In western states, less land was claimed under the Homestead Act than land purchased from railroads, speculators, or settlers. In many cases the law drew settlers west, only to have them give up their claims or borrow against them for other land.

The Homestead Act, championed as the measure to rescue the farmer from his lack of cash and provide him the means for land, successfully eased the farmer's terms but could not address the land's conditions. The public domain available for settlement at that time proved difficult to cultivate and improve. While the Old Northwest had been suitable for traditional agriculture, the Great Plains would require considerable adjustment of traditional practices. The lack of rain and other resources were hindrances to agricultural settlement. Many failed to remain on homestead land for the required five years; instead they sold the land for profit or collateral or abandoned the claim for another. Over time, the federal government allowed homesteaders to purchase their title before the five years passed. Fraudulent claims by homesteaders also increased at a tremendous rate. Farmers and speculators filed claims for nonexisting family members in an effort to gain more than the allowed quarter-section.

In 1862 the federal government also passed a measure to provide land to railroads. Building on its long-time practice of granting railway companies land in exchange for laying track, the government passed the Pacific Railroad Act, which gave the Union Pacific Railroad free access across the nation for a transcontinental railroad. From Omaha to California the railroad received alternating sections of land on either side of the track that extended for ten miles on each side. They sold the land to raise revenue to lay track and cover other expenses. Within two years the railroad had been granted control of twenty-five miles of land on both sides of the track, representing a fifty-mile lane westward from Nebraska. Settlers paid high prices per acre to the railroad for transportation access, causing the federal government to assume erroneously that settlers would also purchase federal lands at railroad prices. Still, the railroad presence helped populate previously uninhabited areas. Eventually, five transcontinental railroads received millions of acres of land from the public domain.

In the 1870s several measures came before Congress to alter federal land policy. The Timber Culture Act of 1873 allowed western settlers to claim land on which they planted trees. These farmers discovered, however, that trees, like corn, did not grow in a region of limited rainfall. This measure, along with the Preemption Act, was repealed in 1891 after decades of disaster. The Desert Land Act of 1877 allowed settlers to purchase one section or 640 acres in western states for $1.25 per acre if the settler agreed to irrigate the land. Again, the speculator received greater claim benefits than the farmer or pioneer settler. In 1890 the government reduced each settler's commitment to 320 acres. The General Revision Act of 1891 also altered conditions of the Desert Land Act, along with the Homestead Act, by limiting the amount of land claimed by one individual. According to stipulations of the General Revision Act, only 80 of the 320 acres needed to be irrigated. While the Desert Land Act is considered to have been unsuccessful, it remained policy until it was repealed in 1976. One of the last land measures passed during the nineteenth century was the Carey Act of 1894. This law "provided relief for private irrigation companies in six arid states" (Opie, *The Law of the Land*, p. 106).

In addition to land policy, the federal government created a land commission in 1879 to examine the question of the public domain and how to administer that land. The Public Land Commission addressed contemporary issues, including the status of homesteaders who filed claims along the 100th meridian. Echoing ideas of the government scientist and explorer John Wesley Powell, the commission saw wisdom in classifying land according to use, to distinguish between agricultural and nonagricultural lands. In addition the commission suggested a prorated (by year) fee scale for land still in the public domain.

By the 1880s and 1890s the government had adjusted its thinking regarding the amount of land needed to be a successful farmer and saw the need in some cases to increase the size of western homestead claims. This recognition of issues would serve well in the twentieth century, when land use, farm size, and water rights became concerns.

See also **Agriculture; Frontier; Homesteading; Transportation,** *subentry on* **Railroads.**

Bibliography

Gates, Paul W. *History of Public Land Law Development.* Washington, D.C.: Public Land Law Commission, 1968.

Opie, John. *The Law of the Land: Two Hundred Years of American Farmland Policy.* Lincoln: University of Nebraska Press, 1987.

Rohrbough, Malcolm J. *The Land Office Business: The Settlement and Administration of American Public Lands, 1789–1837.* New York: Oxford University Press, 1968.

STEPHANIE ANN CARPENTER

FEDERAL-STATE RELATIONS

[This entry includes three overlapping subentries covering the periods 1800–1833, 1831–1865, and 1861–1900.]

1800 TO 1833

The nature of federal-state relations was the central constitutional issue in America between 1800 and 1833. It had its origins in the fact that the United States is governed under the Federalist system in which powers are distributed between central (national) and local (state) authorities. When the Constitution was adopted many Americans were hostile to a strong centralized authority, an attitude buttressed by the colonial experience and the American Revolution, which among other things was a revolt against a distant central government. It was natural that under the Articles of Confederation (1781) the balance of power was left in the hands of the states. The Constitution (1788) increased the strength of the central government at the expense of the states, which was the major source of Antifederalist opposition to its adoption.

Yet the Constitution was not clear on how conflicts between the national and state governments on points of constitutional interpretation were to be resolved. To ensure the supremacy of the national government, the more aggressive nationalists at the Constitutional Convention had tried to explicitly give the federal government the right to review and negate all state actions. But this provision was not included in the final draft of the Constitution. A clause in Article VI of the document provided that the Constitution, the laws of the federal government, and the treaties of the United States should be "the supreme law of the land," that state judges were bound by this, the "laws of any state to the contrary, notwithstanding," and that the state legislators were to be bound by an oath to support the Constitution. But this provision did not explicitly indicate what authority was to determine when a particular action was in violation of the Constitution. To remedy this the First Congress in Section 25 of the Judiciary Act of 1789 gave that power to the U.S. Supreme Court. This was the nationalist solution to the problem. Its theoretical justification was that the Constitution had been created and formally ratified by the people of the United States in a collective sense, and therefore could hold the states accountable.

Former Antifederalists and even many who had supported the adoption of the Constitution but were concerned that the central government might arrogate too much power to itself were unwilling to accept this way of implementing the supremacy clause, or the interpretation of the origins and nature of the federal government upon which it was based. They argued that the Supreme Court was a creature of the Constitution and therefore should not be its final interpreter. Moreover, the Justices received their salaries from the federal government and would, by increasing the authority of the federal government, add to their own powers. This point of view was formalized by the adoption of the Kentucky and Virginia resolutions in 1798 and 1799. Drafted by Thomas Jefferson (1743–1826) and James Madison (1751–1836) in response to the Alien and Sedition Acts (1798), they argued that the Constitution was a compact between the states with only limited powers delegated to the central government, and that if the federal government should overstep its constitutional bounds, the states had the right to declare a federal law unconstitutional. Besides being a statement of constitutional principles, the Kentucky and Virginia Resolutions were a political rallying cry that helped to overthrow the Federalists in the election of 1800. Although the Kentucky and Virginia Resolutions were never implemented, they are significant because they became the constitutional bible of orthodox Jeffersonians and their successors, the Jacksonians, who were the dominant political force until the Civil War crisis in 1861.

Of particular concern to these people were the nationalist decisions handed down by the U.S. Supreme Court under the leadership of John Marshall (1755–1835). Using Section 25 of the Judiciary Act of 1789, he reversed a number of state supreme court decisions. These included *Fletcher v. Peck* (Georgia) in 1810; *Martin v. Hunter's Lessee* (Virginia) in 1816; *Trustees of Dartmouth College v. Woodward* (New Hampshire) in 1819; *Sturges v. Crowninshield* (New York) in 1819; *McCulloch v. Maryland* in 1819; *Green v. Biddle* (Kentucky) in 1823; *Gibbons v. Ogden* (New York) in 1824; *Osborn v. Bank of the United States* (Ohio) in 1824; and *Worcester v. Georgia* in 1832. These controversial decisions outraged states' rights advocates, who unsuccessfully attempted to repeal Section 25, and sought to amend the Constitution so as to make the U.S. Senate the final arbiter of the conflicts between the states and the federal government. Moreover, a number of the Supreme Court's decisions proved to be unenforceable or were ignored.

This hostility to the Court contributed to Andrew Jackson's (1767–1845) election in 1828, and he proved to be an important and vigorous advocate of states' rights. He strongly believed that it was more efficient, safer, and easier to determine the will of the majority if power was decentralized and left in the hands of the states. As a result, under Jackson's leadership the country abandoned most of the nationalist economic program adopted after the War of 1812. And when Marshall died in 1835 Jackson appointed as chief justice Roger Brooke Taney (1777–1864), who with a number of other newly appointed Justices was much more supportive of the rights of the states.

It was in the midst of these developments that a different kind of states' rights thought emerged in South Carolina under the leadership of John C. Calhoun (1782–1850). Denouncing the protective tariffs of 1828 and 1832 as oppressive, unjust, and unconstitutional, it built upon the theory of the origins and nature of the federal union expressed in the Kentucky and Virginia Resolutions to argue that a single state, by calling a special constitutional convention, could declare a federal law unconstitutional and unenforceable within its boundaries. It also went beyond the Kentucky and Virginia Resolutions in writing that, should the federal government try to enforce these laws or legitimize the contested laws through the adoption of an amendment to the Constitution, the concerned state had a legal right to secede from the Union.

When in the fall of 1832 South Carolina actually implemented its doctrine of nullification, or state interposition as some called it, there ensued the most serious constitutional crisis in American history between the adoption of the Constitution and the Civil War. President Jackson denounced this as an illegitimate use of the states' rights argument, claiming that it endangered the continued existence of the Union and undermined the concept of majority rule. He threatened to use force if necessary to enforce the tariff. For its part, South Carolina indicated that it had no intention of backing down. With the country on the verge of civil war, Congress under Henry Clay's (1777–1852) leadership arranged a compromise whereby the tariff was lowered to South Carolina's satisfaction and the federal government's right to use force to enforce its laws was provided for by legislation. Both measures were approved by Jackson. South Carolina, however, proceeded to nullify what it called the Force Bill. Having gotten their way on the tariff, Calhoun and his allies proceeded to link the concepts of nullification and secession with the defense of slavery, and it became the dominant issue between 1830 and 1860.

The Compromise of 1833 did not resolve the theoretical question of where final authority in federal-state disputes stood. During the period from 1830 to 1860, first members of the Whig party and then Republicans argued that it belonged to the U.S. Supreme Court. This point of view was most clearly manifested in the famous debate in 1830 between Daniel Webster (1782–1852) and Robert Y. Hayne (1791–1839) over nullification. In the end the North's victory over the South in the Civil War settled the issue, ensuring the supremacy of the federal government and the Supreme Court in federal-state relations.

See also **Constitutional Law,** *subentry on* **Before the Civil War; Courts, State and Federal; Jacksonian Era; Jeffersonian Era; Law,** *subentries on* **Federal Law, State Law; States' Rights; Supreme Court,** *subentry on* **The Antebellum Court.**

Bibliography

Ames, Herman Vandenburg. *State Documents on Federal Relations: The States and the United States.* New York: Da Capo Press, 1970.

Bestor, Arthur. "State Sovereignty and Slavery: A Reinterpretation of Proslavery Constitutional Doctrine, 1840–1860." *Journal of the Illinois State Historical Society* 54 (Summer 1961).

Ellis, Richard E. *The Union at Risk: Jacksonian Democracy, States' Rights and the Nullification Crisis.* New York: Oxford University Press, 1987.

RICHARD E. ELLIS

1831–1865

The relationship between the states and the national government between 1831 and 1861 began and ended with the same issue on the table: the right of the states to nullify federal law and, if that failed, to leave the Union.

Decline of Traditional Causes of State-Federal Tensions

Before 1833 banking policy, internal improvements, and tariff policy had all led to state-federal conflicts. So, too, had the power of the Supreme Court to overrule state laws. By the end of President Andrew Jackson's administration these issues had all but disappeared as a flash point in state-federal relations. Banking and currency policies had become party issues, with Democrats and Whigs having different agendas. But with national policy weak in this area, no state had any reason to challenge the central government as Maryland had done in a statute leading to the landmark Supreme Court decision in *McCulloch v. Maryland* (1819). Internal improvements also were no longer a point of controversy. Andrew Jackson had ended federal development of roads and canals, and until after the Civil War internal improvements were generally left to the states. Like banking, tariff policy was a party issue, but never again led to a state-federal crisis. Even the power of the Supreme Court diminished as a point of controversy. Jackson virtually remade the Court in his own image, with his close colleague and ideological soul mate Roger B. Taney as chief justice. The Taney Court generally showed great deference to the states, developing such notions as "police powers" to sustain state legislation that the Marshall Court would probably have found unconstitutional.

In other areas, Jackson and his successors did the bidding of the states. For example, in violation of treaties, states moved against Native Americans throughout the Southeast, trying to seize their land and destroy their culture. Rather than support federal treaties and the U.S. Supreme Court decision in *Worcester v. Georgia* (1832), Jackson stepped up the removal of virtually all southeastern tribes. Unable to force the Seminoles west, the United States fought two wars (1817–1818, 1835–1842) against this tribe, in part to please state officials in Georgia.

The Legacy of Nullification

Between 1831 and 1833 South Carolina challenged the power of the national government to impose a high tariff on imported goods, ultimately declaring the tariff null and void within the state. Faced with the firm determination of President Andrew Jackson, a military hero who threatened to personally lead troops into the state to suppress what he considered treason, South Carolina backed down.

Although ostensibly about a tariff, the nullification crisis was in fact about state power, and the growing discomfort in the Deep South with the nature of the federal Union. Beginning with the Missouri Compromise debates (1819–1821), the political leaders in South Carolina and other slave states began to see themselves as oppressed members of a conscious minority. By 1860 this feeling would evolve into a siege mentality that would ultimately convince South Carolina and ten other states to attempt to leave the Union.

Indeed, throughout this period the central conflict between the states and the national government turned on slavery, in one way or another. Ironically, at each end of the period the slave states stood arrayed against the national government; but in the 1840s and 1850s the free states felt most threatened by the national government.

John C. Calhoun (1782–1850). In 1832 Calhoun supported the right of the states to nullify federal law and continued to advocate states' rights for the rest of his career. Photograph by Brady, New York. PRINTED WITH PERMISSION OF ROLF LANG

Northern Challenges to Federal Authority

Starting in the 1820s, a number of free states passed personal liberty laws designed to protect free blacks from being kidnapped as fugitive slaves. These laws also interfered with the return of fugitive slaves. In the 1830s judges in New York, New Jersey, and Pennsylvania challenged the power of Congress to legislate on fugitive slaves. In *Jack v. Martin* (New York, 1835) Chancellor Reuben Walworth of New York found the Fugitive Slave Act unconstitutional because Congress lacked the power to pass such a law. Walworth had

> looked in vain among the powers delegated to congress by the constitution, for any general authority to that body to legislate on this subject. It is certainly not contained in any express grant of power, and it does not appear to be embraced in the general grant of incidental powers contained in the last clause of the constitution relative to the powers of congress.

Walworth ordered the slave Jack returned to his master, under the theory that the states were obli-

gated to implement the Constitution's fugitive slave clause. Thus the Supreme Court did not have an opportunity to review Walworth's opinion.

In *Prigg v. Pennsylvania* (1842) the Supreme Court was able to review a decision challenging congressional power over fugitive slave cases. Speaking for an 8–1 majority, Justice Joseph Story ruled that all state personal liberty laws were unconstitutional because they interfered with Congress's power to regulate the return of fugitive slaves.

Prigg led to a rash of new personal liberty laws in which free states completely withdrew from the business of capturing fugitive slaves. By the 1850s some states had banned any lawyer practicing in the state, as well as any state official, from helping someone recover a fugitive slave.

Fugitive Slave Law of 1850

Until the passage of the 1850 fugitive slave law, the free states did not directly challenge the power of the national government. But this harsh law, with its draconian penalties, stimulated resistance by the citizens of the free states and by some public officials. In Syracuse, New York, for example, a local grand jury indicted a federal marshal for kidnapping after he had helped arrest a fugitive slave known as Jerry Henry (or Jerry McHenry). The marshal was acquitted after the trial judge charged the jury that, as a federal official, he could not be prosecuted by the state for carrying out a federal law. This result suggests that even in response to a hated law, many northern officials respected federal supremacy.

The most important challenges to the federal government came out of Wisconsin and Ohio. Following the arrest of Sherman Booth for helping a fugitive slave escape, the Wisconsin Supreme Court declared the 1850 law unconstitutional. The state court subsequently refused to forward the record of this case to the U.S. Supreme Court. In *Ableman v. Booth* (1859) the U.S. Supreme Court overturned the Wisconsin decision with a powerful decision rejecting the states' rights argument of the Wisconsin court. Later that year, in *Ex parte Bushnell and Langston*, the Ohio Supreme Court refused to support a writ of habeas corpus ordering a federal marshal to release prisoners arrested for violating the Fugitive Slave Law of 1850. Had the writ been issued, the governor of the state, Salmon P. Chase, was prepared to use state militia to enforce it.

Federal Support for Slavery in the South

While northern state legislatures and some courts challenged the national government over the fugitive slave laws, southern states looked to the federal government for protection. In the 1830s mobs in the South burned U.S. mail thought to contain abolitionist propaganda. The federal government did nothing to stop these attacks. Similarly, the national government refused to interfere when southern police officials arrested free black sailors from the North or foreign nations. Indeed, the Taney Court indicated in dicta that the slave states could act this way under their internal police powers. Similarly, the national government used its military force to suppress Nat Turner's rebellion (1831) and John Brown's attempt to start a war against slavery (1859).

Civil War

From 1829 until the election of Lincoln, southern politicians controlled the national government. Even northern presidents, like Millard Fillmore, Franklin Pierce, and James Buchanan, filled their cabinets with southern nationalists and northerners willing to accept slavery. Lincoln's election changed this. For the first time since the adoption of the Constitution,

the nation had a president both committed to stopping the expansion of slavery and personally hostile to it. Southern states saw this as a threat to their safety. The power of the national government would no longer be on the side of slavery. In December 1860, South Carolina left the Union. By May 1861 ten other states had followed.

The Civil War fundamentally altered state-federal relations. With a tiny standing army, the United States initially had to rely on state militias to prevent confederate seizure of Washington, D.C., and to help prevent Maryland from leaving the Union. Massachusetts troops under the command of General Benjamin Butler helped accomplish both of these goals in April and May 1861. Most troops during the war were recruited at the local level and served in state units. Thus, the states became key agents for preserving the national government. At the same time, expenditures by the national government brought vast sums into the economy, which generally helped the economic conditions of the states.

Theoretically Lincoln never accepted the legality or constitutionality of secession. He and other politicians contemplated what had happened. Had the states committed suicide? Had they become territories again? When back under control of the United States, would they be conquered provinces? None of these theories exactly fit the reality of the situation. Yet, however defined, the war fundamentally altered the relationship between the national government and the states. Furthermore, the war allowed for the final destruction of slavery, the root cause of most of the sectional and state-federal conflicts of the preceding four decades.

At the beginning of the war, constitutional limitations prevented the national government from touching slavery where it existed. Lincoln acknowledged this, as did all serious constitutional scholars and commentators. Nevertheless, the war set the stage for an end of slavery. Using his powers as commander in chief, Lincoln issued the Emancipation Proclamation, which freed slaves in those areas under rebel control. Cynics claimed that Lincoln freed the slaves only where he had no power to do so, in the Confederacy. But, in fact, the opposite was true. Lincoln could not emancipate slaves where there was no armed conflict. He could attack slavery only as a war measure, necessary to suppress the rebellion by taking from those in rebellion the slaves they were using to support their efforts to make war against the United States. Thus, as United States troops moved farther into the Confederacy, the slaves in those areas gained actual freedom, having already been emancipated by the commander in chief.

The Civil War finally settled the issues of state

nullification and state secession. Never again would any states presume to challenge the power and authority of the national government. Federal law would remain supreme, although the federal courts remained a powerful force in limiting the national government under the Constitution. The war also led to three constitutional amendments that forever altered the nature of state-federal relations by giving Congress the power to legislate on issues directly affecting the status and liberties of the citizens within the states, and by limiting the powers of the states to discriminate against their own citizens. Ironically, the ultimate cost of the war, for the South, was not only the destruction of slavery but also a constitutional revolution that strengthened the national government, weakened the states, and permanently tipped the balance of state-federal relations in favor of the federal government.

See also **American Indians,** *subentry on* **Indian Removal; Fugitive Slave Laws; Nullification; Sectionalism; Slavery,** *subentry on* **Defense of Slavery; States' Rights; Supreme Court,** *subentry on* **The Antebellum Court.**

Bibliography

Cover, Robert M. *Justice Accused: Antislavery and the Judicial Process.* New Haven, Conn.: Yale University Press, 1975.
Freehling, William H. *Prelude to Civil War: The Nullification Controversy in South Carolina, 1816–1836.* New York: Harper and Row, 1965.
————. *The Road to Disunion: Secessionists at Bay, 1776–1854.* New York: Oxford University Press, 1990.
Potter, David M. *The Impending Crisis, 1848–1861.* New York: Harper and Row, 1976.

PAUL FINKELMAN

1861–1900

During the last four decades of the nineteenth century, the issue of federal-state relations developed in the shadow of the Civil War. Amid the fighting, Abraham Lincoln contended that the states did not have an independent sovereignty relative to the Union. The victory of the North in 1865 meant that the older theories of nullification and secession had been discarded as possible alternatives within the political debate. Yet while the national government had gained power after the defeat of the Confederacy, the doctrine that substantial authority should remain with the individual states continued to command widespread support. Most Democrats, for example, believed in states' rights as a cornerstone of their political faith. In the South the idea of state sovereignty had gone underground after the Civil War as a way of maintaining white supremacy.

Divisions over federalism surfaced during the political battles of the Reconstruction era. Andrew Johnson argued that the Civil Rights Act of 1866, which he vetoed, was flawed because it concentrated power in Washington to advance the rights of the freed slaves. In reaction to Johnson's constricted view of federal power, the Republicans on Capitol Hill pushed the Fourteenth Amendment, as a way of limiting the capacity of southern states to infringe on the rights of black citizens. By reaffirming the concept of national citizenship, the amendment wrote the Republican view of federalism into the Constitution. The Democrats did not regard this outcome as a final decision on the issue.

Throughout the Gilded Age, Republican presidents stood by the concept of federalism. James A. Garfield contended that the result of the Civil War had been to make the Constitution the supreme law of the land. The states had their place in the federal union, but for Garfield and like-minded Republicans it was clearly a subordinate position. Republicans believed that the national government could protect voting rights in the individual states; regulate interstate commerce, including railroads, when the states could not do it; and promote national goals in education by sending federal monies to the states, as in the unsuccessful Blair bill of the 1880s. Introduced by Henry W. Blair of New Hampshire, the measure would have provided money to states for education on the basis of illiteracy. Although the funds were badly needed, southern states and their lawmakers resisted on the grounds that it would mean federal control of a state function. The bill passed the Senate four times, but always died in the House.

Federalism in the Cleveland Era

The return of the Democrats to the White House in 1885 under Grover Cleveland brought a resurgence of the doctrines of states' rights and localism. Cleveland often lectured the people against what he believed were the pernicious trends of intruding a federal presence into areas that the states could better handle. His most famous statement of the position came in 1887 after Congress passed a law appropriating ten thousand dollars to buy seed for drought-ravaged counties in Texas. The president said that it was wrong to have the national government try to relieve individual suffering when the larger issue of public service was not involved.

Federal-state issues have often brought about a change of ideological position in individuals when circumstances favor such a reversal. In Grover Cleveland's case, this change of heart occurred in 1894 when a railway workers' strike against the Pullman

Car Company immobilized railroads and threatened disruptions in Chicago and the Middle West. Faced with what he and his attorney general, Richard Olney, regarded as civil unrest, the president dismissed the states' rights objections of the governor of Illinois, John Peter Altgeld, to the introduction of federal troops into a labor dispute. The army went into Chicago to restore order.

Federalism and Race Relations

On the issue of race relations during the Gilded Age, the nationalistic view of federalism gave way to the prejudices of the time. Some Republicans, such as President Benjamin Harrison and Representative Henry Cabot Lodge of Massachusetts, believed that the broadening of federal power was justified in order to reform state election laws in the South that prevented blacks from voting. Their efforts to gain passage of a federal elections bill in 1890, however, failed in the face of unyielding opposition from southern Democrats and their northern allies. Thereafter, Presidents Grover Cleveland and William McKinley acted on the premise that chief executives lacked the power to wield the authority of the national government in preventing racial oppression in states, counties, and cities of the South. Federalism became a primary means of sustaining segregation at the end of the nineteenth century.

Other forces affected the balance of federal-state relations during the Gilded Age. The U.S. Supreme Court was more active in overturning state and federal laws that seemed to violate property rights on the basis of the due-process clause of the Fourteenth Amendment. While the justices upheld most of the state regulatory legislation that came before them, the sense that the Court offered an arena in which state laws might be challenged acted as a kind of implicit restraint on the exercise of state power within the federal system. Of course, in the case of *Plessy v. Ferguson* (1896), the Court upheld a state law providing for segregated railroad cars, and in the affirmation of state autonomy solidified the racial system in the South that kept African Americans in a second-class position.

The States Revitalized

By the mid-1890s the severe economic depression of the decade prompted individuals and interest groups in states such as Wisconsin, Massachusetts, Michigan, and California to press forward with efforts to curb corporate power through regulatory agencies and increased taxation. The rise of reform governors such as Robert M. La Follette of Wisconsin signaled that the states were becoming what Louis D. Brandeis would later call laboratories of democracy. The ferment on the state level led the proponents of change to seek more activism from Washington to achieve national solutions to problems such as the power of interstate railroads and holding companies. Opponents of reform in the business world saw the federal government as a refuge from diverse state laws. By 1900, the balance of power in the federal system shifted again toward the national government. This development was a testament to the political energy that was emanating from within the states as the nineteenth century ended.

See also **States' Rights.**

Bibliography

Brock, William R. *Investigation and Responsibility: Public Responsibility in the United States, 1865–1900.* Cambridge, U.K.: Cambridge University Press, 1984.

Campbell, Ballard. "Public Policy and State Government." In *The Gilded Age: Essays on the Origins of Modern America.* Edited by Charles W. Calhoun. Wilmington, Del.: Scholarly Resources, 1995.

Keller, Morton. *Affairs of State: Public Life in Late-Nineteenth-Century America.* Cambridge, Mass.: Belknap Press of Harvard University Press, 1977.

Kens, Paul. *Justice Stephen Field: Shaping Liberty from the Gold Rush to the Gilded Age.* Lawrence: University Press of Kansas, 1997.

LEWIS L. GOULD

FEMINISM.   See **Women,** subentry on **Women's Rights.**

FIFTEENTH AMENDMENT.   See **Constitutional Amendments,** subentry on the **Thirteenth, Fourteenth, and Fifteenth Amendments.**

FILIBUSTERS   Privately established and funded armed bands known as filibusters—intent on seizing territory by attacking small independent countries—were a small but dramatic example of the expansionistic urge that gripped the United States during the 1840s and 1850s, the height of Manifest Destiny. Individuals such as William Walker and Narciso López organized armed groups in the United States for attacks on Mexico, Cuba, and Central America. Their tangible accomplishments were few. The consternation and embarrassment they caused for U.S. diplomacy, and the heightened tensions they contributed to the domestic debate on slavery, were the most significant results of their activities.

Filibusters were driven by a number of factors. Romantic notions of conquest and wealth fueled some, while others believed they were carrying out the Manifest Destiny of domination of the western hemisphere that had been preordained for their Anglo-Saxon race. In addition, the thought of moving southward into Mexico, the Caribbean (particularly Cuba), and Central America had long appealed to many proslavery expansionists. The outcome of the Mexican War had indicated how divisive such expansion might be, as angry debates erupted between proslavery groups and those opposed to the expansion of the "peculiar institution." The activities of the filibusters, who were given moral support, and sometimes financial or material aid, by southerners, indicated that the proslavery expansionists had not entirely given up their goals.

The two most famous filibusters were Narciso López and William Walker. López, a Venezuelan national, had become involved in the independence movement in Cuba. Arriving in the United States in 1848, he immediately made plans to raise a military force and liberate the island. He was thwarted when the U.S. government seized his ships and supplies because he had violated a federal statute against such activities. For his second attempt López secured backing from southern expansionists, and he invaded Cuba in 1850. Despite initial success his small army was forced to withdraw. He was killed while making a third try in 1851, when his force was crushed by Spanish troops.

William Walker was a staunch expansionist with near legendary charisma and no little streak of megalomania. In 1853 he led a group of mercenaries into the Mexican territory of Lower California, which he seized. He proclaimed himself its president, but he was forced to withdraw the next year. In 1855 he turned his attention to Nicaragua, which was embroiled in a civil war. Enticed by promises of land and pay from members of the Liberal faction in that nation, fifty-seven men enlisted with Walker. Initial funds for the expedition were provided by U.S. businessmen looking to gain control of transit routes across Nicaragua. Working with Liberal forces in Nicaragua, Walker captured the city of Grenada in September 1855, and a coalition government was established, with Walker as commander of military forces. In mid-1856 Walker was "elected" president of the nation, but his power did not last long. He had become a romantic idol to many in the United States, but his repressive rule and his legalization of slavery quickly lost him much of that support. Other Central American nations declared war on Nicaragua, and disease and corruption weakened Walker's army. The American businessman Cornelius Vanderbilt, who had substantial interests in Nicaragua, also turned against Walker. In May 1857, his army wracked by internal dissension and disease, Walker fled Nicaragua. He made three additional attempts to reconquer Nicaragua, all unsuccessful. In 1860 he was captured in Honduras and executed.

The efforts of filibusters such as López and Walker had decidedly negative effects on U.S. foreign policy. López's attempts to seize Cuba soured U.S.-Spanish relations just when the United States was trying to purchase the island from Spain. Walker's exploits raised the fears and concerns of Central American governments, which believed that Walker was an agent of U.S. expansionism. Both men, but especially Walker, also widened the sectional divide in the United States in the 1840s and 1850s. They were portrayed as heroes by many southerners and as proslavery demons by antislavery advocates in the North. When Walker was arrested by U.S. military forces in 1857, while attempting to launch a second invasion of Nicaragua, an angry debate broke out in Congress. Southerners called for Walker's release, but many antislavery northerners praised the government's action.

With Walker's death in 1860, the age of filibustering effectively came to an end. Although the U.S. government officially denounced filibustering and many northerners decried what they perceived as attempts to spread slavery southward, U.S. interest in Cuba, Central America, and Mexico continued.

See also **Central America and the Caribbean; Cuba.**

Bibliography

Brown, Charles H. *Agents of Manifest Destiny: The Lives and Times of the Filibusters*. Chapel Hill: University of North Carolina Press, 1980.

Carr, Albert. *The World and William Walker*. Westport, Conn.: Greenwood, 1975.

Chaffin, Tom. *Fatal Glory: Narciso López and the First Clandestine U.S. War against Cuba*. Charlottesville: University Press of Virginia, 1996.

May, Robert E. *The Southern Dream of a Caribbean Empire, 1854–1861*. Baton Rouge: Louisiana State University Press, 1973.

Scroggs, William O. *Filibusters and Financiers: The Story of William Walker and His Associates*. New York: Macmillan, 1916.

MICHAEL L. KRENN

FINANCE.   See **Banking and Finance.**

FIREARMS   Until well into the nineteenth century, firearms were loaded at the muzzle and fired by a variety of devices designed to ignite the explosive charge that propelled the bullet. The flintlock dominated the eighteenth century. A flint is held between metal jaws that are part of a spring-loaded hammer. When released, the hammer and its flint fall quickly against a hinged, steel pan cover. The small pan is loaded with a fine grain of black powder, which is ignited by the spark generated by the flint striking the steel cover. This entire device is called the lock, leading to the expression "lock, stock, and barrel," which accurately described most firearms well into the nineteenth century. With a flintlock mechanism, the main charge that propels the bullet (or ball) is ignited by the flash in the firing pan, which enters the side of the rear of the barrel by a flash hole. The phrase "flash in the pan" indicated that the sparks from the flint and steel had failed to ignite the full load of powder in the barrel.

The major innovations of the nineteenth century were a firing system called percussion ignition and the rifled barrel. In percussion ignition, when the hammer is released from its cocked position by pressing the trigger, it falls forward against a steel nipple. This nipple is covered by a small, replaceable, copper "percussion cap" containing fulminate of mercury, an unstable compound that, when struck, creates a small intense fire that travels through the hollow nipple and into the main charge. Shooting reliability was increased substantially by this new firing system, as well as by rifling. By the early nineteenth century, all but shotguns were rifled, that is, grooves were cut in a spiral fashion inside the length of the barrel. Rifling is visible inside the barrel as "lands" (the high points in the metal that are not cut away) and "grooves" (the portion of the inside of the barrel that is cut away when the barrel is rifled). This design gave spin or rotation to the lead bullet while in flight toward its target, which dramatically increased the shot's accuracy. By the middle of the nineteenth century, all forms of firearms were both reliable and accurate by virtue of these major changes. The percussion cap lock remained the firearm of issue for the United States Army and many other armies in the world, even past the development of further innovations.

By the 1860s the paper- and cloth-patched lead balls and bullets of the muzzle-loading cap locks had been replaced by breech-loading metal cartridges. Along with breech loading came the ability to eject spent cartridge cases and to reload a fresh, loaded cartridge by manipulating a lever or hammer in the case of a handgun. Earlier ideas also were updated from previous technologies, and revolving-barrel repeating weapons, like the Gatling gun, were manufactured. The self-loading (semiautomatic) and the military machine gun (fully automatic) had been born.

The late nineteenth century and early twentieth century were marked by rapid innovations in firearms design. Although various "repeating," multibarrel, rotating cylinder (five- or six-shot), and lever-action reloaders date back to the early nineteenth century, their perfection was achieved in the twentieth century. Samuel Colt (1814–1862), John M. Browning (1855–1926), Smith and Wesson, Remington Arms, and Winchester Repeating Arms are part of a long list of inventors and manufacturers of the industrial revolution that enabled these rapid changes. This was also the period of the development of the bolt-action repeating rifle. Multiple fixed-cartridge ammunition rounds could be loaded into the rifle into a metal box called a magazine. The magazine was sometimes within the rifle stock, at the side of the breech, or detachable. As the bolt is pushed and rotated forward, a fresh round is stripped from the magazine and seated into the breech, ready for firing. These modern cartridges are ignited by an explosive cap inserted in the rear of the metal cartridge case. The cap is struck and ignited by a firing pin that is within the bolt. When the bolt is pulled to the rear, the spent cartridge is ejected and, as the bolt is pushed forward, a fresh round is seated. This innovation was illustrated by the Mauser-type action, which remained in military use into the 1940s.

Of the firearm types, shotguns have changed the least historically in terms of appearance. Modern single-shot and double-barreled guns look much like their earlier counterparts, but load at the breech. The major mechanical developments began in the late nineteenth century and resulted in the pump loader, semiautomatic loader, and a variety of military application shotguns.

At the end of the twentieth century, there were probably more guns than people in the United States. The firearm is a part of the country's history and culture. There are more nineteenth-century "six-gun" replicas built for black powder and modern smokeless powder than existed in that century.

See also **Military Technology.**

Bibliography

Browning, John, and Curt Gentry. *John M. Browning: American Gunmaker. An Illustrated Biography of the Man and his Guns.* Garden City, N.Y.: Doubleday, 1964.

Ezell, Edward Clinton, ed. *Small Arms of the World: A Basic Manual of Small Arms.* 11th ed. Harrisburg, Pa.: Stackpole Books, 1977.

Mueller, Chester, and John Olson. *Shooter's Bible Small Arms Lexicon and Concise Encyclopedia.* South Hackensack, N.J.: Shooters Bible, Inc., 1968.

RICHARD T. OAKES

FIRES AND FIREFIGHTING   During the nineteenth century, fire was perhaps the most severe environmental threat faced by Americans, especially in urban areas. Before the Civil War, hundreds of large fires destroyed property worth over 200 million dollars in the nation's principal cities. After 1865, conflagrations routinely destroyed large parts of cities such as Boston, Chicago, and Baltimore. Volunteer and professional firefighters were the first line of defense against this danger.

In Philadelphia in 1803, a group of young artisans used lengths of hose to connect fire engines to the city's newly built water supply. With this simple technological innovation, the Philadelphia Hose Company redefined the work of firefighting in the United States. Over the course of the nineteenth century, firefighters created more specialized organizational forms and work processes. They would eventually establish a new occupation with its own professional organizations and work identity, as reflected in the pages of Charles Hill's book *Fighting a Fire* (1897)—one of the earliest studies of the firefighting techniques of urban professional firemen.

During the first five decades of the nineteenth century, volunteer firefighters relied on physical labor and technical competence with tools. On hearing a fire alarm, typically rung by church bells, firefighters rushed to neighborhood engine houses. Their teams of horses pulled hose carriages or engines, which sometimes weighed as much as two tons, through crowded, narrow, and unpaved streets. Hose companies then located hydrants, used spanner wrenches to open them, and connected their engines to cities' burgeoning networks of water pipes. The firefighters then stroked levers attached to the sides of the hand-pumped engines to create enough pressure to spread water on the blaze. No firefighter could pump for longer than ten minutes, and company members rotated frequently, sometimes for hours.

Volunteers created a shared but competitive brotherhood that valued physical strength, technological acumen, and public service. Companies measured their effectiveness by the lengths of hose streams generated by pumping. During 1850, the Missouri Fire Company of St. Louis described the operation of its new engine in the company ledgerbook thus: "She threw one hundred and ninety four feet from the end of the nozzle one inch through a ten foot section of hose. My opinion of the engine is that she is a powerful engine, she throws well but she is a perfect mankiller to work, give her as much water as she can use and it would take a company of two hundred men to keep her working steady." Firefighters expressed their ritualized culture through balls, parades, and visits to fire departments in other cities,

all of which demonstrated the colorful array of differences between companies but also affirmed a shared mission as guardians of the social and economic order.

The brotherhood of firefighters was limited, and strengthened, by shared beliefs regarding gender, race, ethnicity, and class. Most obviously, volunteers defined firefighting as male work and responsibility. The ideal of brotherhood presupposed an all-male workforce, so women were not included in company membership. Race, too, mattered in much the same way, although its expression varied to some degree by geographical location. In western and eastern cities, as in northern and southern towns, firefighters systematically excluded African Americans, defining firefighting as the exclusive province of white men. Volunteer firefighters in Philadelphia threatened to strike in 1809 when African Americans sought to form a fire company. By contrast, in a few southern cities, such as Charleston and Savannah, black men fought fires shoulder to shoulder with whites. The service of African Americans was limited to physical labor, however; company leadership was maintained by white men.

Starting in the 1840s, and spurred by industrialization, urbanization, and immigration, cities and fire departments became ethnically diverse, a situation that threatened their unity. Groups with different ethnic, class, political, and/or religious convictions used the fire service to express those values, which existed in precarious balance with the ideal of brotherhood. Sometimes companies engaged in open conflict, but even when conflict was masked—at fires and in parades, for instance—significant differences were visible in costumes, rituals, and membership certificates.

To quell conflict and maintain singularity of purpose, departments formed specialized management associations. These organizations often allied with politicians seeking to expand municipal control over urban services, and both groups attempted to make department funding tied less to neighborhoods and more to citywide administration. Like their predecessors who used hose and engine technologies to make firefighting more efficient, the leaders of management associations used bureaucratic techniques to promote efficiency and commonality.

In the 1850s, the fire insurance industry experimented with new technologies to manage its business, including actuarial methods, standardization of practices, and mapping techniques. As the industry embraced rationalized business methods, it urged the rationalization of fire protection. Insurers advocated bureaucratic fire departments operated by expanding municipal governments, the use of steam engines to

Fire at Cripple Creek, Colorado, 1896. Fires were a common occurrence in cities and communities. By the end of the century firefighters had organized to create a profession in which they could expect to serve for twenty years in some cities. LIBRARY OF CONGRESS

make firefighting more efficient, and paying firemen wages.

Conflict between firefighters and insurers' recommendations spurred debate over the efficacy of volunteer firefighting in the 1850s. The terms and outcomes of those debates varied by locale, but they usually centered on the differences between steam engines and volunteers' muscle, which firemen sought to resolve by holding contests. The outcome differed from city to city, but usually firefighters' muscle won, as in Philadelphia in 1855. However, most volunteers agreed with the general sentiment that steam engines would eventually make firefighting more efficient. As a result, between 1850 and 1875 most large American cities replaced volunteers with steam engines operated by paid workers.

Volunteer firefighters in fact quite often led in the formation of professional fire departments, as was the case in St. Louis and Cincinnati, where the well-regarded former volunteer Miles Greenwood directed the formation of a new department in 1853. Other cities embraced the new order at different times and in a variety of ways. For instance, volunteer fire companies in New York rejected steam engines, and even after that city adopted a professional department in

1865, firefighters relied on a mixture of steam and hand-operated engines. By contrast, volunteer fire companies in Philadelphia used steam engines for over a decade, until they helped establish a professional department in 1871. Whatever the pace of change, professional firemen never completely replaced volunteers. As late as 1917, approximately 40 percent of American firemen in cities with populations between thirty thousand and three hundred thousand were volunteers. Nonetheless, as major American cities gradually adopted the new method of organizing fire departments, firefighting developed into a new occupation with national standards of work, training, and skill. This identity, like the new departments themselves, depended greatly on the labor and support of volunteer firefighters. In many cities the leaders of the new municipal fire departments came directly from the ranks of the volunteer fire departments, and as many as half the rank-and-file firefighters had once served as volunteer firemen.

The firefighters' occupational culture was expressed most strongly in images of heroic lifesaving, which appeared frequently in the popular press. This ideal developed from the work techniques and priorities of fire departments, especially as they strug-

Firemen at the World Columbian Exposition in Chicago, 1893. The National Association of Fire Engineers, founded in 1873, contributed to the professionalism of firefighters. LIBRARY OF CONGRESS

gled to maintain order in cities that grew taller, dense, and more flammable. In the context of ever-changing danger, firefighters devised new work strategies, such as skill with ladders and climbing techniques, that would allow them to rescue trapped civilians. In the 1880s, Christ Hoell of the St. Louis Fire Department spearheaded the formation of a climbing unit, and later toured the country, training other firemen to use the new techniques it required. Fire departments also purchased specialized tools to assist rescue and work efforts. Equipment such as ladder trucks was rare in the 1870s, but by the 1920s was nearly as common as engine trucks, depending on the size of the city.

Although firefighters engaged in a common occupation, their work varied greatly between cities and between firehouses within the same city. Few departments used the same terms for equipment, and one fireman reported that companies in Philadelphia used different nomenclature for tools and work maneuvers. Work conditions were dangerous and difficult. Firemen worked six or seven days per week, twenty-four hours per day, with only a few hours for family. Becoming a firefighter depended upon politics or neighborhood connections. In addition, some companies welcomed new recruits and trained them only if they shared a common ethnic, religious, or community background. Other groups hazed newcomers regardless of background, making them prove their mettle as "men" before welcoming them. Work rules were lax, drinking was common, and physical training was nonexistent.

The firefighters' claim to status as professionals was furthered by the National Association of Fire Engineers (NAFE), which was founded in 1873. As firefighting became a more visible occupation, NAFE advocated improved working conditions by publicizing the life-saving aspect of firemen's work. It demanded the dissemination of standard work techniques, shorter working hours, pensions, and control over employment conditions. As a result, firefighters found a common identity as men and as public servants, and created an occupation with great cohesion; indeed, firemen forged careers of unusual length. In 1885, over 36 percent of the nation's firefighters had been with their departments for longer than fifteen years. By the 1890s, the majority of men entering the departments in Philadelphia and St. Louis could expect careers longer than twenty years.

During the early twentieth century, firefighting began to become more standardized thanks in part to continued agitation by the National Association of Fire Engineers (NAFE). New training regimens, civil service, pensions, better pay, and shorter working hours helped to make firefighting more regularized. In addition, that firefighters continued to define their service as the purview of white men aided the further development of a common occupational identity. Women were excluded from departments, as were African Americans. However, some cities began to hire black firemen, but segregated them into separate companies, usually led by white officers. And although few first-generation immigrants appear to have joined departments, jobs as firefighters became increasingly desirable in working-class communities and among the children of immigrants.

See also **Disasters; Insurance; Steam Power; Working-class Culture.**

Bibliography

Dana, David. *The Fireman: The Fire Departments of the United States, with a Full Account of all Large Fires, Statistics of Losses and Expenses, Theatres Destroyed by Fire and Accidents, Anecdotes, and Incidents*. Boston: James French and Co., 1858. Reprint, Waterbury, Conn.: Brohan Press, 1999.

Greenberg, Amy S. *Cause For Alarm: The Volunteer Fire Department in the Nineteenth-Century City*. Princeton, N.J.: Princeton University Press, 1998.

Hazen, Margaret Hindle, and Robert M. Hazen. *Keepers of the Flame: The Role of Fire in American Culture, 1775–1925*. Princeton, N.J.: Princeton University Press, 1992.

Hill, Charles T. *Fighting a Fire*. New York: The Century Company, 1897.

Laurie, Bruce. "Fire Companies and Gangs in Southwark: The 1840s." In *The Peoples of Philadelphia*. Edited by Allen F. Davis and Mark Haller. Philadelphia: Temple University Press, 1973.

Pyne, Stephen J. *Fire in America: A Cultural History of Wildland and Rural Fire*. Princeton, N.J.: Princeton University Press, 1982.

Tebeau, Mark. *"Eating Smoke": The Problem of Fire in Urban America, 1800–1950*. Baltimore: Johns Hopkins University Press, 2001.

MARK TEBEAU

FIRST LADIES   The public role of the president's wife was gradually defined in the 1800s to include many of the elements that Americans expected of a first lady a century later. From a local figure who was little known outside the federal city, the spouse of the president became a national figure known by her first name across the continent. Beginning with a job that revolved around their family roles, the first ladies enlarged it to include other duties, such as overseeing the furnishing and running of the executive mansion, entertaining political and foreign guests, heading up causes, and serving as a model for American women. In addition the leeway given the chief executive to seek advice widely gave spouses the opportunity to exert considerable influence in personnel and policy. Addressed in the beginning as "lady" or "presidentress," the president's wife finally gained a title that stuck, "first lady." The transformation owes as much to changes in the nation generally as to the women who held the job.

Early Precedents

Abigail Smith Adams (1797–1801) initiated the new president's house in Washington in November 1800, but she had hardly unpacked before the voters retired John Adams to Massachusetts. Intelligent and politically astute, she enjoyed the confidence of her husband and felt free to express her opinions, a contrast to her predecessor, Martha Washington, who had kept clear of politics. The Washingtons, however, had set the precedent for the presidential family to combine its residence with the president's office. On New Year's Day 1801 Abigail Adams held "open house," initiating a custom that continued until the 1930s.

Substitutes

With the inauguration of Thomas Jefferson in March 1801, the nation had its first widower president. Jefferson turned to his married daughter and to Dolley Madison, the wife of Secretary of State James Madison, to help with entertaining at the executive mansion. Others accepted this solution, asking a substitute rather than using hired staff, whenever the president's wife could not assume a public role, and later widower presidents followed Jefferson's example. Andrew Jackson (1829–1837) relied on a niece and a daughter-in-law; Martin Van Buren (1837–1841) turned to his daughter-in-law, Angelica Singleton Van Buren, a distant relative of Dolley Madison; and Chester Arthur (1881–1885) called on his married sister.

Presidents whose wives were ill or unwilling to serve in a public role also turned to young substi-

Louisa Catherine Johnson Adams (1775–1852). The wife of John Quincy Adams, Louisa Adams was the niece of the governor of Maryland. LIBRARY OF CONGRESS

tutes. William Henry Harrison asked a daughter-in-law to accompany him to Washington in 1841, and his ailing wife, Anna Symmes Harrison, had not yet joined him when he died a month later. Letitia Christian Tyler, the wife of John Tyler (1841–1845), died in 1842, and President Tyler installed his popular daughter-in-law, the actress Priscilla Cooper Tyler, to help with presidential entertaining until he remarried in June 1844. His second wife, Julia Gardiner Tyler, who was twenty-four years old when they married, approached the job with gusto, even hiring an assistant to improve her public image. But her short tenure left her little time to make big changes. Margaret Mackall Smith Taylor, the wife of Zachary Taylor (1849–1850), kept to her room, and her married daughter Betty Bliss acted for her. Abigail Powers Fillmore, the wife of Millard Fillmore (1850–1853), relied on her teenaged daughter Mary Abigail Fillmore in the same way. When Andrew Johnson (1865–1869) assumed the presidency, his wife, Eliza McCardle Johnson, pleaded ill health, and their daughter Martha Patterson acted as hostess. While older women were often criticized for fashion flops or gastronomic gaffes, these youthful stand-ins became very popular, helping to propel the job of White House chatelaine to public attention.

President James Buchanan (1857–1861), a bachelor, invited his niece Harriet Lane, who was twenty-seven, to help host White House parties, and she became popular with Native Americans and artists, whose causes she supported. Songs honored her, people named their babies for her, and she was credited with bringing new attention to the role. When another bachelor, Grover Cleveland, entered the White House in 1885, his sister Rose Cleveland filled hostessing duties until June 1886, when he married Frances Folsom, who was twenty-one. Frances Cleveland's simplicity and youthful beauty made her one of the most popular presidential wives of all time. When advertisers began using her image to sell their products, one member of Congress introduced legislation banning such practices.

Strong Models

Several nineteenth-century first ladies played important roles in the development of the position. Dolley Payne Todd Madison (1809–1817) became a model that her successors imitated for generations. A charming complement to James Madison, who was as dour as he was brilliant, Dolley Madison tempered the elitist side of the presidency with a large dose of democracy. Her parties included guests from the wealthiest segment of Washington along with the more humble, and she insisted on calling on all the

Mary Todd Lincoln (1818–1882). Socially and politically well-connected, Mary Todd Lincoln was successfully wooed by the future president Abraham Lincoln. She was deeply affected by the war and the death of her son. LIBRARY OF CONGRESS

legislators' wives who came to the city. Eschewing the openly partisan stance of Abigail Adams, Madison entertained her husband's opponents during the 1812 campaign, and when the votes were counted, her efforts were credited with helping him to victory.

Madison's successor, Elizabeth Kortright Monroe (1817–1825), was less inclined to court the masses. A New Yorker who had lived in Paris, where she was praised as "la belle americaine," Monroe refused to devote hours to calling on Washington wives, who retaliated by boycotting the few parties Monroe gave. Louisa Johnson Adams (1825–1829), John Quincy Adams's first lady, worked out a truncated calling schedule, an arrangement her successors adopted, but she was unable to engineer a complete withdrawal from the very public role now expected of the president's wife.

Over the next forty years (1829–1869) only a handful of strong women lived in the executive mansion, and the job was eclipsed. Because very few magazines and newspapers circulated across the nation and travel was still relatively difficult, little was known about the president's wife outside of Washington, D.C. Yet two exceptional first ladies did leave marks in this four-decade span. Sarah Childress Polk

(1845–1849) took a strong interest in politics and accompanied her husband to Washington during the years he served in Congress. With an active intelligence and no children to claim her attention, she reportedly influenced her husband on important matters. One of his colleagues insisted that few men in Congress were as influenced by their wives as James K. Polk.

Also notable, Mary Todd Lincoln (1861–1865) became one of the most controversial first ladies for reasons partly beyond her control. Because some of her relatives fought for the Confederacy, she was suspected of treason, and her own personal insecurities fed these and other rumors. Although well educated for her time, she feared she did not measure up to Washingtonians' expectations, and she overspent on herself and the executive mansion to compensate. In a time of war, when many Americans lost loved ones, she continued to give lavish parties. Unable to resist requests for favors, she sometimes arranged appointments for people to see the president, thus initiating an access route that later became popular.

Julia Dent Grant (1869–1877) encountered new curiosity about the president's family. National magazines carried articles on her and her children, and one regular column on social news in the capital zeroed in on the first lady, describing her appearance and her parties. After leaving Washington, Grant wrote her autobiography, which was not published for nearly a century. Her memoirs marked the advent of what subsequently became a standard practice.

Lucy Webb Hayes (1877–1881) built upon the preceeding record. Her ban on alcohol at official receptions endeared her to temperance advocates, although opponents dubbed her "Lemonade Lucy." While Hayes's feelings on temperance have no doubt been exaggerated, later first ladies also associated with a cause. In 1881 Lucy Hayes traveled with her husband from the Atlantic to the Pacific, thus increasing her exposure and popularity, and newspapers began referring to her as the "first lady of the land."

Caroline Scott Harrison (1889–1893), the wife of Benjamin Harrison, transferred her own strongly patriotic views to the job of presidential spouse. Choosing American themes and workmanship for her own clothing and for the official china, she tried to extend those preferences to the executive mansion. Her plans for an enormous addition, including a museum and office space alongside the residence, were never implemented, but she underlined the responsibility of the president's wife for the mansion's appearance and maintenance.

Ida Saxton McKinley (1897–1901), too sickly to extend the job of first lady, nevertheless refused to take a backseat during her husband's presidency. By the time she left, the role had been set. The president's spouse would play a public role, taking responsibility for the upkeep of the White House and holding herself up as a model of American womanhood. Congress had quietly accepted such an interpretation in 1799, when it granted Martha Washington the franking privilege at the time of her husband's death. In the 1880s Congress extended the concept of the widow as a public servant by voting a pension to each one who applied.

During the twentieth century the first lady became an international figure and a more prominent leader. The foundation for those developments was laid before 1900.

See also **Gilded Age; Manners; Women,** *subentry on* **Woman as Image and Icon.**

Bibliography

Anthony, Carl Sferrazza. *First Ladies: The Saga of the Presidents' Wives and Their Power.* Vol. 2. New York: W. Morrow, 1990.

Caroli, Betty Boyd. *America's First Ladies.* Garden City, N.Y.: Doubleday Direct, 1996.

———. *First Ladies.* 1987. Reprint, New York: Oxford University Press, 1995.

Gould, Lewis L., ed. *American First Ladies: Their Lives and Their Legacy.* New York: Garland, 1996.

Holloway, Laura C. *The Ladies of the White House; or, In the Home of the Presidents.* Philadelphia: Bradley and Company, 1881.

BETTY BOYD CAROLI

FISHERIES   U.S. fisheries underwent dramatic changes in the nineteenth century. The introduction of new technologies and industry expansion changed how Americans viewed and worked in fisheries. However, the ethnic and racial diversity of American fishermen persisted throughout the century.

Many people—Indian, white, and black—harvested fish for subsistence and local markets in the early and antebellum United States. Along the eastern seaboard, they fished for salmon, shad, and herring in the rivers and near the shore. Subsistence and small-scale fishermen who worked the Atlantic coastal rivers faced challenges from other economic interests. Milldams limited the migration of anadromous fish, like shad and salmon, which spend their adult lives in oceans and spawn in fresh water. As spawning runs decreased, so did the importance of fishing to local subsistence economies.

Larger fishing operations along the shore also limited the spawning of anadromous fish by harvesting them with huge haul seines and more laborers. Along the North Carolina coast, the slave-labor system of the plantation was transferred to the fisheries. Under the direction of white overseers, crews of enslaved African Americans harvested fish for their subsistence and local markets. Some pickled herring was sold to Chesapeake merchants and then resold, along with pickled mackerel from New England, to Upper South and Caribbean plantations. Baltimore served as the center of much of the southern fish trade.

Commercial fishing in the United States was dominated by New England. There, the economies of many coastal communities depended on cod and mackerel fisheries and on the production of dried and salted or pickled fish. Oysters were another important commodity to New England crews, some of whom fished as far south as the Chesapeake Bay early in the century. In 1820 Maryland prohibited oystering by nonresidents. Northeastern canneries moved to the Chesapeake and started the expansion of commercial oyster fishing down the southern coast and into the Gulf of Mexico.

Commercial fishing was both helped and hindered by federal government policies. From 1789 until 1866, government bounties (grants) were given to vessels based on their tonnage, to be shared between the owner and the crew. In contrast, the Embargo Act of 1807 and retaliation by European countries were a major blow to New England's fish trade with Europe. The War of 1812 ended Europe's importance as a market for American fisheries. Treaties with Great Britain in 1818 and 1854 over fishing rights along the New England and Canadian coasts helped the industry rebound and grow until the Civil War. New markets emerged in the Spanish colonies of the Caribbean and also in the interior of the United States, thanks to better transportation.

Commercial fishing grew in other regions of the United States after the Civil War, challenging New England's supremacy. This growth coincided with technological advances and increased domestic demand for fresh fish. While the Civil War had ended slave labor in southern fisheries, they nevertheless were able to expand thanks to improved transportation, the introduction of ice, and the investment of northern capital. Many northern fishing enterprises moved south after the Civil War to exploit the abundant fisheries there. Southeastern fisheries grew to such an extent that by the end of the nineteenth century, Morehead City, North Carolina, was the second-leading fishing port on the Atlantic coast, behind only Gloucester, Massachusetts. The harvesting of many fish for food and menhaden for oil lured the industry south.

The western market for New England fisheries was challenged by the growth of the Great Lakes commercial fisheries and the salmon fisheries of the Pacific Northwest. Fishing in the Great Lakes first became significant in the 1830s, as the region's population grew. By the 1870s Great Lakes fish harvests, especially of lake herring, were beginning to compete with New England in midwestern and southern markets.

Into the nineteenth century, the economies of the Columbia River Indians revolved around salmon fishery. Trade in salmon increased in importance as commercial contacts grew between Indians and whites. As white settlements expanded, canneries were built from northern California, beginning in the Civil War, extending to Alaska in the 1880s. Salmon became a major competitor in the domestic marketplace.

Fisheries in all U.S. regions underwent business consolidation after the Civil War. Schooners became larger and were able to transport several dories—small boats that held one or two men and allowed crew members to broaden their fishing range. Schooners gradually were replaced by steam-powered vessels late in the century. Steam came into greater use to power winches for haul seines, and new and larger nets were introduced. All of these developments dramatically increased fishery harvests in the late nineteenth century. They also required more capital investment, which drove independent entrepreneurs and small-scale operations out of business or forced them to consolidate. In 1866 the entrepreneurs lost the payments from government bounties. Concurrently, crews began to be paid in wages instead of a lay, or share, of the catch. Crews resisted this change for a time by unionizing, but the wage system won out when owners began to hire cheaper labor, especially Canadians.

Ever-greater harvests and the depletion of some fishing beds led to calls for conservation and to the creation of the United States Commission of Fish and Fisheries in 1871. The commission studied the fisheries, established hatcheries, and attempted to replenish stocks. Consolidation was aided by changes in American tastes. By mid-century, Americans began wanting less dried and salted or pickled fish and more fresh fish. Ports like Boston, with the best inland transportation, were better suited to providing fresh fish, and, thus, businesses consolidated there. A growing American appetite for beef led to an overall decline in fish consumption and the importance of the fishing industry to the U.S. economy. But fisheries remained, as they always had, an important part of specific regional economies.

See also **Food; Foreign Trade and Tariffs; Maritime Technology; New England.**

Bibliography

Goode, George Brown, ed. *The Fisheries and Fishery Industries of the United States.* 7 vols. Washington, D.C.: Government Printing Office, 1884–1887.

O'Leary, Wayne M. *Maine Sea Fisheries: The Rise and Fall of a Native Industry, 1830–1890.* Boston: Northeastern University Press, 1996.

Taylor, Joseph E., III. *Making Salmon: An Environmental History of the Northwest Fisheries Crisis.* Seattle: University of Washington Press, 1999.

Taylor, Mark T. "Seiners and Tongers: North Carolina Fisheries in the Old and New South." *North Carolina Historical Review* 70 (1992): 1–36.

JOSEPH KEY

FITNESS.   See **Health Consciousness and Fitness.**

FLORIDA   Florida is a tropical region with sandy beaches, lakes, swampy marshes, and fertile hills. Juan Ponce de Léon, a Spanish explorer, became the first European to arrive in Florida when he landed in the vicinity of Saint Augustine in 1513. He named the area *Pascua Florida,* which means Feast of Flowers or Easter. In 1565 Pedro Menéndez de Avilés established Saint Augustine, the oldest continuous European settlement in North America.

The Adams-Onís Treaty, which was negotiated in 1819 and ratified by the U.S. Senate in 1821, transferred Florida from Spanish control to the United States. By 1821 Florida had twelve thousand residents. About half of the population was made up of Seminoles, Miccosukees, Calusas, and Creeks, new arrivals who lived in south and central Florida. Plantation owners, runaways, slaves, free blacks, traders, hunters, and adventurers, living mainly in north Florida, comprised the rest of the population. In 1824 the federal government hired John Bellamy to build a highway from Saint Augustine to Pensacola. Several towns developed along the Saint Augustine Road, which followed the old Spanish trail to Tallahassee, the midpoint.

After 1823 the federal government forced the Seminole Indians out of the swampy area that became Gainesville as Florida's white population increased to 34,730 by 1830. In 1835 the Seminole resistance to removal precipitated a vicious war that lasted until 1842 and cost the United States $40 million and more than fifteen hundred men. By 1850 most of the Indian tribes had been removed from Florida.

During the period 1830–1850 Florida experienced economic expansion along rivers in the Panhandle, where cotton, naval stores, and lumber were shipped to Georgia. On 3 March 1845 Florida joined the Union as the twenty-seventh state. In 1860 census

Silver Springs, Florida, c. 1886. This tourist center began in the late 1870s when rides in a glass-bottomed rowboat were offered to visitors. LIBRARY OF CONGRESS

takers counted 140,424 Florida residents, including 77,747 whites, 61,745 slaves, and 932 free people of color. One of the original states of the Confederacy, Florida seceded from the Union on 10 January 1861. With its small population and its great distance from most military action, the state was a minor player during the Civil War, supplying perhaps fifteen thousand soldiers to the Confederacy and a much smaller number to the Union. But the war brought enormous changes to Florida as slavery ended and black men gained the right to vote.

In the late nineteenth century Florida's population grew rapidly, accompanied by active economic development. For a time the Jacksonville area led the way in agriculture, trade, and tourism. From Jacksonville south along the east coast, citrus and sugar farming increased in significance. Many farmers fell on hard times, fueling the emergence of the Farmers' Alliance. A national convention of farmers' representatives met in Ocala in 1890 and issued the Ocala Demands for more favorable federal policies regarding banking, currency, and taxation. Several wealthy northerners, including Henry B. Plant, Henry M. Flagler, and William D. Chipley, invested in railroads that fostered development in central Florida, on the Gulf Coast, and in the Panhandle. These railroads connected Jacksonville with Tampa, Pensacola, and Miami. Flagler, a partner of John Rockefeller of Standard Oil Company, also built resort hotels in south and central Florida. In the 1890s soldiers fighting in the Spanish-American War embarked from Tampa on their way to fight in Cuba, encouraging Tampa's expansion. In the late 1890s Miami emerged as a city as Flagler opened luxury hotels there. By 1900 Florida had 528,542 residents.

See also **American Indians,** *subentry on* **Indian Removal; Miami; Seminole Wars.**

Bibliography

Burnett, Gene. *Florida's Past: People and Events That Shaped the State.* Englewood, Fla.: Pineapple, 1986.

Gannon, Michael, ed. *The New History of Florida.* Gainesville: University of Florida Press, 1996.

Patrick, Rembert W., and Allen Morris. *Florida under Five Flags.* Gainesville: University of Florida Press, 1967.

Smiley, Nixon. *Yesterday's Florida.* Miami: E. A. Seemann, 1974.

Tebeau, Charlton. *A History of Florida.* Rev. ed. Coral Gables, Fla.: University of Miami Press, 1980.

ABEL A. BARTLEY

FOLK ARTS   The folk artifacts and traditions of the nineteenth-century United States tended to be utilitarian—shaped by function, resources, and culture—but often possessed aesthetic qualities that transcended necessity; a scrimshaw crimper of 1850, for instance, took the delicate form of a bird (Whaling Museum, New Bedford, Mass.). These arts, the material expressions of a communal aesthetic transmitted from generation to generation, reflect folk artists' ethnicity, gender, economic status, occupation, religion, and environment. Nonfunctional arts, such as easel painting ("plain" portraits and landscapes in imitation of an academic tradition), still lifes and memorial watercolors, presentation pieces, *scherenschnitte* (decorative paper cutouts), pasties, tatting, and other crafts—macramé, for example—are properly described as popular arts, but are often classified as folk arts in the gallery and museum world.

Nineteenth-century folk arts are generally characterized as having been shaped by five phenomena in American culture: a general division of media by gender; ethnic influences resulting from the influx of imported slaves and immigrants from western and northern Europe; the creolization, or the confluence of two or more cultures and their traditions; geographic diffusion of culture by migration within the United States; and the beginnings of industrialization.

"Hard" and "Soft" Crafts

Men were traditionally the makers of "hard" crafts, those requiring strength and involving the use of "dangerous" tools, such as house-building, woodworking and carving, ceramics (dynastic potteries like that of the Brown family of Mossy Creek, Georgia, which was eight generations old, were thriving in the nineteenth century), metal work, traps, and heavy-duty basketry. Women's arts were the "soft" ones: sewing, weaving, cloth-making and dyeing, medicinal arts, foodways (the culinary expressions of a culture and the related cultivation, gathering, procuring, and preparation of food), small gardening, and finer basketry.

Quiltmaking is probably the most interesting of the women's folk arts because the form was not only highly functional, but allowed women to express themselves individually through the choosing of patterns, colors, and configurations that were pleasing to them. Sometimes quilts were made to commemorate community or family events, like the poignant Elizabeth Mitchell quilt made in Lewis County, Kentucky, in 1839, which represented a family graveyard. Quilting also served as an important function in women's lives by providing them an opportunity to come together and socialize with one another while they worked. The Baltimore album quilts, made between 1846 and 1852 by a group calling itself the Ladies of Baltimore, are good examples. While most expressions of women's work were of an ephemeral nature, such as cooking, housekeeping, and canning and preserving, a quilt was a tangible expression of care, resourcefulness, personal aesthetic, family, and sometimes community history or religious beliefs.

Folk arts also offered the opportunity for political expression. The decorative components of crafts sometimes included patriotic symbols such as the eagle, the flag, and the national capitol. Potholders made by abolitionist women carried the slogan "Any holder but a slaveholder" (in the Chicago Historical Society).

Settlement Influences

Burgeoning immigration in the nineteenth century affected all aspects of American culture. (Roughly 60,000 immigrants came to the United States between 1831 and 1840, and by 1860, 260,000 immigrants, mostly northern and western Europeans, were arriving annually.) Immigrants brought with them their craft traditions and aesthetics. For instance, beginning around 1840, Pennsylvania Germans brought their traditional brightly painted tulip, bird, and "hex" motifs, which they applied to barns and furniture in eastern Pennsylvania. In the Southwest, artists of Spanish ancestry carved traditional wooden figures of saints called *bultos*. Scandinavian settlers in the upper Midwest brought distinctive carpentry and building techniques. Moravian settlers brought fraktur writing and taufschein (birth or baptismal certificates) and *scherenschnitte*. Since the seventeenth century, African craft traditions and aesthetic ideals were remembered, transmitted, and kept alive by slaves. By the nineteenth century, many African folk arts adapted, combined, or reinterpreted European forms, creating creolized variations. African American quilts, for instance, rendered a basically European form in patterns, techniques, and color configurations that strongly recalled African traditions. Two very famous Bible quilts created in the 1880s by the former slave Harriet Powers (now in the Smithsonian and the Boston Museum of Fine Arts) show unmistakable similarities to the style and appliqué technique of textiles created for centuries by the Fon people of Dahomey (new Bénin). The banjo, which became a ubiquitous instrument of white mountain music, is a descendant of African gourd instruments, and the shotgun house (square rooms positioned one behind the other, with doors aligned from front to back) form has a lineage that can be traced from Yoruba huts to Haitian houses to the frame row houses built by free blacks in New Orleans around 1820. Over centuries Native Americans developed strong pottery and basketry traditions like the graceful, hand-coiled vessels of the Pueblo, Navaho, and Hopi and the intricately dyed twilled cone baskets of the Choctaw. Cherokee Indians in the southeast continued their old woodcarving traditions such as ceremonial "booger masks."

Migration diffused folk arts. In the East, folk culture spread in many directions from coastal "hearth" areas. African American carving traditions spread with the movement of slaves from the Georgia low country westward to Mississippi. Quintessential American folk housing types like shotgun and dogtrot houses (two square "pens" with an open passage between them, having a common roof) developed during the nineteenth century and were diffused along various migratory routes. Log cabins, a form imported from northern Europe, became a common feature of the eastern coast, as George Washington noted in his journals in 1791. By the nineteenth century, the cabin was a standard pioneer houseform and a ubiquitous feature of the western migration.

Industrialization

Folk arts in the nineteenth century were also influenced by the beginnings of the machine age. Mechanization and improvements in materials and technology certainly saved labor but also meant that the character of folk arts would be forever changed, particularly in textiles and vernacular architecture. Inventions like the sewing machine in the mid–nineteenth century and the power loom, which replaced the hand-looming of cotton by 1850, facilitated mass production and made "store bought" cloth and dry goods readily available. (The Harriet Powers quilts, made circa 1886 and 1898, show some machine stitching, which probably would have enhanced the maker's status and heightened the quilts' value.) The invention of power woodworking machines, such as the milling machine around 1825 and the hand saw in 1835, meant that houses and furniture could be much more easily constructed and accessible. Ancient Native American pottery traditions in the Southwest, like those of the Hopi, declined with the availability of mass-produced cookware introduced by traders. Still, many folk art traditions, like the handweaving of coverlets, the making of musical instruments, and dynastic potteries, continued into the twentieth century, partly because of the isolation and poverty of those who practiced them, but also because of the new tourist trade and craft revivals.

See also **Gender,** *subentry on* **Interpretations of Gender; Immigration and Immigrants,** *subentry on* **The Immi-**

grant Experience; Industrialization and the Market; Popular Culture.

Bibliography

Ames, Kenneth L. *Beyond Necessity: Art in the Folk Tradition.* Winterthur, Del.: Winterthur Museum, 1977.

Glassie, Henry. *Pattern in the Material Folk Culture of the Eastern United States.* Philadelphia: University of Pennsylvania Press, 1968.

Lipman, Jean, and Winchester, Alice. *The Flowering of American Folk Art: 1776–1876.* Philadelphia: Courage Books with the Whitney Museum of American Art, 1987.

Quimby, Ian M. G., and Scott T. Swank, eds. *Perspectives on American Folk Art.* New York: Norton, 1980.

Vlach, John Michael. *The Afro-American Tradition in Decorative Arts.* Athens: University of Georgia Press, 1990.

LISA HOWORTH

FOLKTALES AND TALL TALES　The term "folktale" is an umbrella category for a wide variety of prose narratives derived from oral tradition. Such tales include fairy tales, fables, magic tales, animal tales, jokes, and many others. Tall tales are a particular kind of folktale, known also as "lies" or occasionally as "windies." The tall tale genre refers to humorous, artful short stories that center on a single theme or incident and usually depict the landscape and feats of men and women in exaggerated detail. The degree of exaggeration varies greatly, and the structure varies from a full narrative to a simple one-line "whopper," not really a structured tale at all. Due to this plasticity, tall tales have been classified in many ways, including by content, form, and storytelling situation. One common characteristic, however, is style. Although tall tales can be either written or told, because they stem from a particular style of oral tradition they are narrated using informal language. Further, they are performed with deadpan seriousness in a dry, laconic manner. Only at the end of a tale will a narrator clue the audience in to the lie, and sometimes not even then. Another important stylistic element is that tall tales entail not only mere extravagance but also comic artistry, often involving concrete comparisons, non sequiturs, and understatements.

A final common element of tall tales is their ambivalent relation to truth. Although tall tales are mostly fictional, they are cast as true and contain a kernel of moral, emotional, or physical truth, which often serves as the underlying theme of the tale. The humor of the genre derives from the disjunction between the performed seriousness of the narrator, the absurdity of the tale, the fuzzy boundary between truth and fiction, and the potential ambivalence of the audience.

Tales and American Oral Tradition

The art of lying dates to ancient times, and tall tales are found throughout the world. The antecedents of the American nineteenth-century tall tale are the European "Münchausen" stories, lying tales attributed to the eighteenth-century German Baron Karl F. H. von Münchausen. Yet despite their geographic and cultural ubiquity, tall tales historically were characterized as a particularly "American" genre for a number of reasons. First, many scholars associated them with such frontiers as the Old Southwest and the Far West, which were distinctly American phenomena. Second, nineteenth-century Europeans who toured the United States and early national character scholars such as Constance Rourke purported that comic, artful exaggeration was a particularly American form of humor. Third, tall tales have been collected and studied by scholars more in the United States than in Europe and other places. These events helped fuel the notion that tall tales were somehow a quintessential American genre. In reality, however, tall tales were popular throughout the country as well as the world.

Samuel Clemens (1835–1910). Samuel Clemens, known more commonly by his pen name Mark Twain, insisted on sleeping at the foot of his bed so that he could view its elaborate headboard. LIBRARY OF CONGRESS

Nevertheless, tall tales became especially prevalent in the United States after the War of 1812, finding their way into print in almanacs and newspapers such as the *Spirit of the Times*. Amidst the plethora of tall tales and tall characters that circulated, a few figures became widely well-known for their antics or storytelling talents. According to Richard Dorson, among the most famous is Davy Crockett, a backwoods politician with a talent for storytelling and rhetoric whose colorful life and tales inspired a number of publications such as *Sketches and Eccentricities of Col. David Crockett of West Tennessee* (1833), *A Narrative of the Life of David Crockett of the State of Tennessee* (1834), a series of Crockett almanacs issued from 1835–1856, and James Kirke Paulding's 1831 comedy *The Lion of the West*. In Crockett's case, as with other tall figures, people connected his name with traditional stories, a strategy that fueled their popularity. Other famous tall figures include Mike Fink, a rough Mississippi keelboatman characterized as half-horse, half-alligator, and Sam Patch, a mill hand who jumped over Niagara Falls in 1829 and lived, but who died a few months later in an attempt to jump Genesee Falls near Rochester, New York.

Few female tall tale narrators—if any—are known. While there were some tall tales about women, these were neither told nor written by them. These tales portrayed the female characters as ugly—even physically deformed—unfashionable, and coarse; in general they embody the same qualities as their male counterparts. This has led most scholars to characterize the tall tale as something of a male genre. In his book, *America in Legend*, Richard M. Dorson stated that such characters embody a "backwoods" (p. 3) or "common man" mentality and style, and that a spirit of "shaggy egalitarianism" (p. 58) pervades this oral and printed literature. While he recognizes the European roots of tall tales, Dorson suggests that the manners and exploits of tall tale characters contrast dramatically with eastern gentility, evince disdain for European snobbery, and set Americans as a nation apart from European tradition.

One famous and controversial character intimately associated with tall tales is Paul Bunyan. In contrast to Crockett, Fink, and Patch, Bunyan was not an actual person and only a few oral stories related to him ever existed. Rather, he was largely the result of a successful advertising campaign for the Red River Lumber Company, initiated around 1914. An appealing figure, Bunyan prompted popular writers to invent a plethora of literary tales about him, portraying Bunyan as a hero of lumberjacks and claiming the stories came directly from oral tradition. Yet the few oral tales that did exist were off-color, or

Davy Crockett (1786–1836). The quintessential figure of the frontier. From a painting by J. G. Chapman. © BETT-MANN/CORBIS

portrayed Bunyan as a shrewd knave, while the literary Bunyan tales generally were romanticized stories written for children that emphasized his masculinity, ruggedness, and ability to tame nature as qualities that represented the American spirit. Thus, the claims of these writers that their tales represented actual oral lumberjack stories provoked much controversy and ire in tall tale scholarship during the first part of the twentieth century. These stories, however, propelled Bunyan to national fame by the 1920s, and Bunyan has remained an important part of American popular culture ever since.

Tall Tales and the American West

The newspapers of the Far West often perpetrated tall tales and hoaxes, especially the sensationalist newspapers that sprang up in the mining areas of Colorado and Nevada. When starved for "real news," for example, editors circulated hearsay, jokes, hoaxes, and outright lies. The humorist Mark Twain and his peers were particularly infamous in this respect. For example, Twain's editor at the *Daily Territorial En-*

terprise, William Wright (pseudonym Dan De Quille), invented such hoaxes as the "discovery" of four-inch Washoe "shoo-flies" (a black "bug" of the genus "hum"), stories of migrating stones, spring water that tasted like chicken soup if heated, and solar armor to protect the wearer from desert heat.

These stories and hoaxes had a more serious side as well. While they were invented for the entertainment of people living in harsh western conditions, the butts of tall tales were often naive newcomers or outsiders, particularly easterners, who seemed more than willing to believe the wild stories. Some scholars have interpreted the perpetration of these tales and hoaxes as westerners' subtle resistance to eastern domination and colonialism, using easterners' own fantasies about the western landscape against them. It was common practice, for example, to initiate newcomers to an area by telling them falsehoods. Mody C. Boatright identified this as "loading the greenhorn" (*Folk Laughter on the American Frontier,* p. 67), that is, filling a newcomer's ear with lies to make him or her appear foolish, and thereby drawing clear distinctions between insiders and outsiders. Twain rendered such tales into the literary tall tales that fill his books, such as *Roughing It* (1872), which features a serious narrator who conveys that he cannot be trusted.

Conclusion

Although scholars such as Dorson and Boatright view tall tales as resistance to eastern cultural arrogance or as asserting an independent, egalitarian, common-man identity, others point out that the peculiar qualities of tall tale tellers and characters embody the nativist, nationalist, and imperialist ideologies prevalent throughout the nineteenth century and that interpreting these tales as egalitarian perpetuates nationalist ideals. While ultimately the meaning and function of nineteenth-century tall tales depended on how they were used in specific situations, both the oral and literary tall tales flourished during a time of aggressive nationalism and imperialism, exemplified by the Louisiana Purchase, the forcible acquisition of territory from Mexico, the ideology of Manifest Destiny, the Monroe Doctrine, and the issue of slavery in the territories. For many women, blacks, Native Americans, Mexican Americans, and immigrants, this was decidedly not an egalitarian or democratic era. Furthermore the notion that such stories grew out of the peculiarities of an immense and unfamiliar frontier landscape reflects the nationalist idea that culture and democracy in the United States were shaped by an inherent relationship between humans and the landscape, an ideo-

logical and gendered fantasy. Whether or not the landscape played a literal role in the proliferation of stories, the fact that this perception continues reveals their importance to the construction of national myth.

See also **Humor; Interpretations of the Nineteenth Century,** *subentry on* **Popular Interpretations of the Frontier West; Popular Culture.**

Bibliography

Bauman, Richard. *Story, Performance, and Event: Contextual Studies of Oral Narrative.* Cambridge, U.K., and New York: Cambridge University Press, 1986.

Boatright, Mody C. *Folk Laughter on the American Frontier.* 1942. Reprint, New York: Collier, 1961.

Brown, Carolyn S. *The Tall Tale in American Folklore and Literature.* Knoxville: University of Tennessee Press, 1987.

Brunvand, Jan Harold. *The Study of American Folklore: An Introduction.* New York: Norton, 1968.

Dorson, Richard M. *America in Legend: Folklore from the Colonial Period to the Present.* New York: Pantheon, 1973.

Toelken, Barre. *The Dynamics of Folklore.* 1979. Rev. and expanded edition, Logan: Utah State University Press, 1996.

LISA GABBERT

FOOD   By the start of the nineteenth century, a distinctly American cuisine had emerged. In the East and North, the essentially English food culture had already undergone basic, and usually climatically required, shifts from old, preferred ingredients to North American ones, thereby creating a set of American dishes. A shift from peas to beans yielded baked beans; a shift from wheat to cornmeal created corn bread and rye-and-indian (brown) bread. From grain-based beer there was a shift to apple-based cider. In the Southwest, the influence of Spanish colonization characterized that region's cookery, but there, too, adjustments to the climate and borrowings from the native populations yielded distinctly regional dishes. Greater prosperity in the New World meant that Americans ate more meat, as often as three times a day. As national identity solidified, so did national cuisine.

By the early 1800s, Americans showed their proclivity for speed and efficiency in food preparation and in dining as well, especially in the Northeast and on the frontier. They early embraced chemical leavenings, at first pearl ash (potassium carbonate), which was named as an ingredient in the nation's first cookbook, *American Cookery* (1796), by Amelia Simmons. Many foreign visitors noted that Americans, especially the middle classes, ate quickly, as if more interested in the next thing to do. After the seventeenth century, few people ate communally with shared utensils. By the eighteenth century's end, most were accustomed to individual plates, drinking vessels, and knives and spoons. More elaborate and traditional cuisines, together with refined dining, thrived among the gentry in urban centers and the plantation South. The collective respect for speed and efficiency and low regard for flavor or elaboration meant ready acceptance of technological and commercial contributions to foodways.

While humankind had for centuries sought to preserve abundance for use in times of seasonal scarcity,

---

In his autobiography, the nineteenth-century humorist Samuel Clemens, whom we know as Mark Twain, described the food he remembered served at his uncle's farm in Missouri.

It was a heavenly place for a boy, that farm of my uncle John's. The house was a double log one, with a spacious floor (roofed in) connecting with the kitchen. In the summer the table was set in the middle of the shady and breezy floor, and the sumptuous meals—well, it makes me cry to think of them. Fried chicken, roast pig, wild and tame turkey, ducks and geese; venison just killed; squirrels, rabbits, pheasants, partridges, prairie chickens; biscuits; hot batter cakes, hot buckwheat cakes, hot "wheat bread," hot rolls, hot corn pone; fresh corn boiled on the ear, succotash, butter-beans, string beans, tomatoes, pease, Irish potatoes, sweet potatoes, buttermilk, sweet milk, "clabber"; watermelons, muskmelons, cantaloupes, all fresh from the garden—apple pie, peach pie, pumpkin pie, apple dumplings, peach cobbler—I can't remember the rest. The way that the things were cooked was perhaps the main splendor—particularly a certain few of the dishes. For instance, the corn bread, the hot biscuits and wheat bread and the fried chicken. These things have never been properly cooked in the North—in fact, no one there is able to learn the art, so far as my experience goes. The North thinks it knows how to make corn bread, but this is gross superstition. Perhaps no bread in the world is as good as Southern corn bread, and perhaps no bread in the world is as bad as the Northern imitation of it. The North seldom tries to fry chicken, and this is well; the art cannot be learned North of the line of Mason and Dixon, nor anywhere in Europe. This is not hearsay; it is experience that is speaking.

MARK TWAIN

Chapters from My Autobiography (New York: Oxford University Press, 1996), p. 452.

---

gentrification contributed to novelty and variety in diet. For example, icehouses made possible rare and out-of-season foods, such as melons in January, and coastwise trade brought wheat flour from south to north. From the start, America had a blend of ethnicities contributing to the national cuisine. To the earliest settlers, Spanish and English, were added Dutch, Scots-Irish, Germans, Africans, and French. In the Southwest, the Spanish elite retained its traditional cuisine filtered through Mexico while lower classes intermarried with native populations and created a new, blended foodway. Most new groups accepted Native American foods that most closely matched familiar foods and then prepared them in familiar ways. The newcomers did not usually adopt Native American cooking methods as dining habits. In the nineteenth century the agencies of refinement and reform—new ethnicities, science and technology, and commerce and industry—worked upon American foodways to create modern dishes and customs.

Refinement

Refinement in food habits, which began in the Renaissance, combined an impulse toward self-conscious elaboration and display with increased focus on the individual, a result of the Reformation. Refinement brought, at first to the aristocracy, finely crafted, ornamented, and specialized eating utensils used at tables in rooms designated for dining and entertainment. Individual place settings became the rule, and only unrefined middling or poorer sorts tolerated eating with fingers from shared containers. Changed codes of behavior at the table required etiquette books to guide those aspiring to gentility.

Elements of refined dining trickled down to the middle classes by the early 1800s, and as the century progressed, dining room furniture appeared in more homes, the tables set with mass-produced ceramics and flatware, including decorative and highly specialized dishes and serving pieces. By century's end, the minimum standard for proper middle-class dining included a matching set of knives, forks, teaspoons, soupspoons, and often salad forks as well as plates, soup bowls, cups and saucers, tumblers, and stemware. When possible, families also acquired matching service pieces—platters, tureens, sauceboats, and vegetable dishes. To this list the more genteel added specialized plates and flatware for other courses, such as fish forks and plates, custard cups, wineglasses, and even asparagus tongs, horseradish spoons, and pedestaled banana boats.

Food itself underwent refinement, especially as consumers were increasingly separated from the source of their food. Ungainly joints gave way to cuts

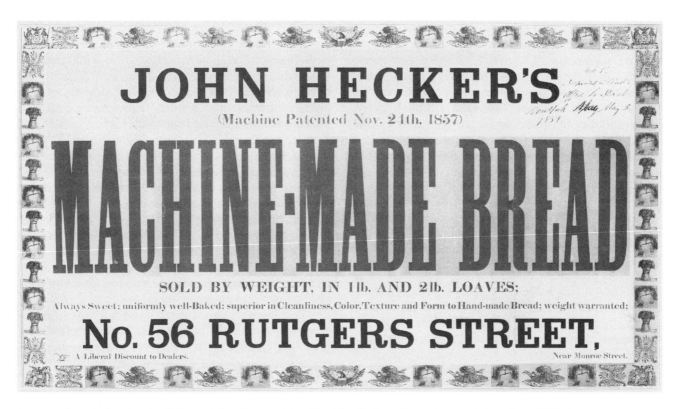

Industry Revolutionizes the Bakery. Advertisement lauding the glories of machine-made bread, c. 1858. LIBRARY OF CONGRESS: PRINTS AND PHOTOGRAPHS DIVISION

of meat easily and neatly carved at the table or even cutlets that diners cut apart on their plates. Foods not easily eaten with fork and knife fell out of favor. Except in rural America or among poorer classes, parts of meat that retained an animal's appearance gave way to dressed pieces scarcely resembling the original creature. For example, cooks removed necks of poultry and trussed legs and wings. Calves' or pigs' heads were served less often whole in preference to dishes like calf's head soup or head cheese. Even whole fish began to fall from favor by the 1890s in preference for fillets. Many formerly relished organ meats appeared less frequently on menus. Similarly, cooks carefully dressed and garnished vegetables, sometimes even molding them for presentation. Elaborate jellied desserts, ices, and ornamented cakes, formerly the perquisite of the wealthy, became, with the help of technology and industry, common on middle-class tables.

Reform

Of the reform movements that shook the nineteenth-century status quo, the temperance movement had a profound effect on food, drink, and even cookery. Per capita alcoholic beverage consumption peaked during the first fifty years of American nationhood. Its excesses attracted the attention of temperance re-

formers, headed primarily by Protestant clergy. The sense that a new millennium was impossible until society attained a certain perfection contributed to the growth of the movement, but expanding industry and commerce, where many more workers found employment, benefited from, and even required, a sober workforce and therefore supported temperance. As temperance grew, individual and family alcohol consumption declined. Small (low alcohol) beer and hard cider had been considered family beverages, even for young people; coffee, tea, and even water began to be preferred. At social functions, such temperance beverages as raspberry shrub and lemonade took the place of wine. By the end of the century, a wide range of soft drinks appeared that were the prototypes of many modern commercial ones.

Many early alcoholic beverages were homemade. Brewing beer went hand in hand with baking bread in the housewife's routine. Brewing both used and cultivated the yeast needed for raising bread. When home beermaking ceased under temperance pressure by the mid-1800s, home bakers turned to commercial bakers or brewers for a yeast supply or learned how to make and keep yeasts based on potatoes or grains. Another response, especially for zealots who wished to divorce bread from all forms of alcohol, was to turn to chemical leavenings. Over the century, chemical leavenings changed and improved in reliability and palatability and gained favor even among nontemperance adherents. The national taste for quick breads—biscuits, corn bread, breakfast breads, muffins—rested largely on chemical leavening's popularity. Sylvester W. Graham (1794–1851), a temperance leader and diet reformer, promoted the use of chemical leavening and, alarmed at the increased use of bolted white flour, brought the benefits of whole wheat flour to the nation's attention.

New Ethnicities

Beginning with the wave of Irish immigrants following the potato famine in Ireland during the late 1840s, America, particularly urban centers, absorbed succeeding groups of Europeans arriving on the East Coast and of Chinese on the West Coast. Most arrived voluntarily, seeking to escape poverty and/or aspiring to a better life. Another large group, African Americans, came involuntarily and were held in slavery until freed in 1865. To some extent all adopted

SCHOOLEY'S MEAT, PROVISION AND FRUIT PRESERVER,

In which is introduced his patent process of producing a *dry, cold current of air from ice*. The inside of this PRESERVER, intended for household purposes, is warranted to be dry—consequently free from moisture, mould, must, or impure flavor.

Pamphlets giving full description of the different applications of the process, and all information respecting the purchase of manufacturing rights, can be had by addressing   JOHN C. SCHOOLEY, *Patentee*.
    june 16   Cincinnati, Ohio.

The Precursor of the Modern Refrigerator. The preserver, intended for household use, kept food fresh by contact with a current of ice-cooled air. Advertisement, 1855. LIBRARY OF CONGRESS

the prevailing national foodway while simultaneously altering it and contributing to it over time.

Refinement and new immigrants often clashed. Irish women hired as cooks and maids, accustomed to open hearths and peat fires and to a peasant diet based on oats, fish, salt meat, and potatoes, seemed hopelessly ignorant and incapable when faced with cookstoves, fine china, and rarefied dishes in the prosperous urban households where they worked. The poverty of urban slums inhabited by Italian and Eastern European immigrants drew reform-minded social workers intent on mainstreaming their diets. Pungent flavoring, particularly the use of garlic, offended those with refined sensibilities, who often associated the strong odors with the newcomers' poverty and foreignness. Some ethnic groups continued to prefer beer and wine to other beverages and thus clashed with temperance reformers.

Many newcomers, intent upon becoming mainstream Americans, adopted new foodways while retaining traditional festival dishes. To this day, holidays like Easter and Passover, Christmas and Hanukkah, often feature ethnic foods, especially breads and pastries, steeped in associations with the past and the old country. As soon as they were prosperous enough, many newcomers ate meat more frequently than formerly, abandoning foods associated with poverty and hard times, including many legume- and grain-based dishes.

Where ethnic groups clustered together, traditional foodways endured, supported by markets catering to them (kosher butchers, Italian bakeries, Chinese produce and fish markets) and institutions (churches and temples) that fostered community life. In some instances, when preferred ingredients were in short supply, a group adapted American ingredients while maintaining the basic structure of their native dishes. Among German settlers in America, for example, apples were easier to grow than the preferred plums used in plum butter. They substituted apples to create apple butter. Enslaved African Americans, whose diet was largely controlled, adapted rationed food supplies, which in the nineteenth century included rice (familiar to Africans) and American cornmeal, and combined them with foods they grew, foraged, and otherwise appropriated to re-create the starch-with-vegetable sauce dishes common in Africa. The Spanish, with a long tradition of lentil or garbanzo stews, used the *bolita*, an ancestor of the pinto bean, or adapted hominy to the structure of the dish to create *posole*, or *pozole* (a stew-like dish combining dried corn and meat).

Some regions carried an ethnic identity from earlier times: Spanish and Mexican influence continued in the West and Southwest. In Louisiana, Creole cookery lent its particular flavor to that region. Part of the Creole tradition included French cookery, but even though there is plentiful evidence of French cuisine's influence on menus and particular dishes, it entered the mainstream via the gentry's self-conscious adoption of French style. Rather than being absorbed from French ethnic group members, it trickled down from the most prosperous classes, often via later nineteenth-century hotel fare and the phenomenon of cooking schools.

Gradually, ethnic dishes entered mainstream American cookery, often in proportion to the number of newcomers. In the nineteenth century, people of German ethnicity, either newly arrived or by descent, predominated in America, so by 1900 there were more dishes in mainstream cookbooks with German names than dishes of other groups. In some instances, German ethnic foods like sauerkraut, apple butter, scrapple, sausages, and some baked goods were common enough to be identified as regional foods where Germans were especially numerous.

Science and Technology

Humankind has long made the connection between food and health, over the centuries creating many systems to promote healthful eating. Early Americans were aware of the doctrine of humors, based on four bodily fluids, or humors, correlating to earth, fire, air, and water. By the nineteenth century, it had faded from use, replaced by the early outlines of a recognizably modern science of nutrition.

Until the mid–nineteenth century, much nutritional theory was based on the concept of digestibility that arose from the work of an American army surgeon, Dr. William Beaumont, who in the 1820s, observed and experimented with digestion. He watched the action of a young Canadian laborer's stomach via an opening left after a wound. The rates at which various foods were absorbed, together with their chemical analysis, helped early nutrition science identify carbon, recognized as a source of energy, and nitrogen, understood to build muscle, and recognize fiber's role in the diet. Domestic advice writers and diet reformers like Harriet Beecher Stowe and Catharine Beecher promoted some of these ideas.

Later in the century, cooking schools and nutritional science cooperated to reform the American diet, which, many recognized, relied too heavily on meat and refined products like white flour and sugar. Wilbur O. Atwater, a Wesleyan University chemistry professor, popularized the concept of the calorie in the 1890s with his work on the chemical composition of foods. His recommendations correlated an ideal diet to the level of energy exerted in one's activities. Still,

for many, especially the poor, good nutrition was defined simply as enough to eat.

Science and technology made understanding nutrition easier and also transformed the world of work supported by food. As the century progressed, more people, especially in urban and suburban places, lived lives requiring fewer calories. Factory work was tedious but not aerobic. The sedentary professional class increased. More homes had central heating. New modes of transportation diminished walking time. Those who labored at traditional jobs, such as farming, fishing, logging, mining, and crafts like carpentry and masonry, could continue to enjoy the standard diet of meat, potatoes, and pie as long as they could afford it, but new workers, especially the prosperous, encountered discomfort and disease as lower rates of metabolism no longer required the traditional diet.

Technology changed domestic foodways with the development of stove cookery, artificial refrigeration, and food preservation. Cookstoves benefited urbanites, whose fuel was more costly, by making possible more fuel-efficient food preparation. Over the century other fuels—coal and eventually kerosene—replaced wood. By century's end, gas stoves were available to some.

Stove cookery changed the shape of the American bread loaf from the round loaves baked on stone or brick oven floors, to rectangular loaves baked in pans placed on the racks of stoves, which lacked a floor for baking. Easily heated stoves made possible more frequent and convenient baking, including that of previously expensive and seldom made cakes and pastries. Making cookies moved down the social scale to middle-class kitchens equipped with stoves and easily heated ovens. Traditional roasting, which formerly relied upon open flame, gave way to baking meat (though the process was not renamed). Stovetop cookery tended to encourage stewing, frying, and boiling; grilling decreased.

Families living in cooler regions had long enjoyed winter's natural refrigeration, conducting much butchering in the fall, when the cold could be relied upon to chill carcasses and even freeze them for use later. The drive to overcome seasonality promoted the development of domestic refrigerators chilled by winter-harvested ice. Refrigerated train cars made possible a shift from meat produced in rural areas surrounding urban centers and driven on hoof to city markets for slaughter to centralized processing and distribution centers in the West. Cattle ranches in newly opened western areas raised beef driven to cities like Omaha and Chicago, where animals were slaughtered, partially butchered, and then shipped east. Families who had relied upon local butchers, or even intrafamily or community fresh meat exchange, came to rely on supplies brought from distant cities. Beef and pork production shaped the character of many western areas—the landscape, economy, and occupations.

Further technological development improved upon the 1809 advance by the Frenchman Nicolas Appert—hermetically sealed, vacuum-packed food in jars. Domestic canning in glass jars joined summer vegetables like beans, corn, and peas to the more traditional pickled and dried vegetables and fruits on the winter menu—and added another chore to the housewife's year.

Commerce and Industry

Industry seized upon Appert's developments and led the way in improvements on it, with both glass and tin containers, thus greatly expanding the variety of food canned. These essentially ready-to-use foods found a natural market with the military and seafarers and in lumber and mining camps—mostly male institutions. Domestic consumers readily accepted some fancy goods in cans—condensed milk and sardines, for example—but most nineteenth-century housewives needed convincing to abandon home preservation and cookery. The nascent advertising industry was called upon to encourage domestic consumption of commercially canned food. By the end of the century, canners produced a range of ready-to-eat dishes, including baked beans, succotash, fish cakes, sauces, and soups. But not until the twentieth century would housewives be free of a certain opprobrium attached to making dinner out of a can.

Industry and wider transportation brought other foods and ingredients more cheaply and plentifully into the marketplace. For instance, in the 1820s the Erie Canal brought wheat from New York State and beyond to New York City, and New Englanders quickly shifted back to wheat bread from the rye and cornmeal bread of the previous two centuries. Sugar refining improved so that those who had formerly relied on molasses and brown sugar found white sugar more affordable. By mid-century the grain industry prepared mixes for a variety of breads, and by century's end the breakfast cereal business, largely under the impulse of diet reform, created many ready-to-eat products. Commercial bakers, found in nearly all sizable cities and towns, were brought by a few major companies that created national brands of crackers, cookies, and bread. Chemical leavening companies became similarly nationalized.

Commerce and industry also supported and promoted the refinement of American dining by creating mass-market goods—ceramics, glass, flatware—and put more specialized cooking utensils into middle-class homes. Grinders, choppers, beaters, and molds replaced the labor of many hands, so even a home with a small domestic staff could aspire to gentry fare. These utensils, along with commercial preparations like gelatin, granulated sugar, ground spices, sifted flours, flavor extracts, and other items available to the middle class, required the gentry of the Gilded Age to ratchet up elaboration and refinement at the century's end.

The New Century

All these influences continued into the twentieth century, gaining momentum and joined by new impulses. At the turn of the twentieth century, a diet most of us would consider modern even today was firmly in place, about to undergo further refinements, adjustments, and additions.

See also **Alcoholic Beverages.**

Bibliography

Belden, Louise Conway. *The Festive Tradition: Table Decoration and Desserts in America, 1650–1900.* New York: Norton, 1983.

Bushman, Richard. *The Refinement of America: Persons, Houses, Cities.* New York: Vintage Books, 1993.

Carson, Barbara G. *Ambitious Appetites: Dining, Behavior and Patterns of Consumption in Federal Washington.* Washington, D.C.: American Institute of Architects Press and Octagon Museum, 1990.

Child, Mrs. Lydia Maria. *The American Frugal Housewife.* 1883. Reprint, Mineola, N.Y.: Dover, 1999.

DeVoe, Thomas F. *The Market Assistant, Containing a Brief Description of Every Article of Human Food Sold in the Public Markets of the Cities of New York, Boston, Philadelphia, and Brooklyn.* 1867. Reprint, Detroit: Gale, 1975.

Farmer, Fanny Merritt. *The Boston Cooking-School Cook Book.* Boston: Little, Brown, 1896.

Felker, Peter H. *The Grocer's Manual, Containing the Natural History and Process of Manufacture of All Grocers' Goods.* Claremont, N.H.: Claremont Manufacturing, 1878.

Hale, Sarah Josepha Buell. *Mrs. Hale's Receipts for the Million: Containing Four Thousand Five Hundred and Forty-five Receipts, Facts, Directions, etc.* Philadelphia: T. B. Peterson, c. 1857.

Harris, Jessica B. *Iron Pots and Wooden Spoons: Africa's Gifts to New World Cooking.* New York: Atheneum, 1989.

Hess, Karen. *The Carolina Rice Kitchen: The African Connection.* Columbia: University of South Carolina Press, 1992.

Rorabaugh, William J. *The Alcoholic Republic: An American Tradition.* New York: Oxford University Press, 1979.

Shapiro, Laura. *Perfection Salad: Women and Cooking at the Turn of the Century.* New York: Farrar, Straus, and Giroux, 1986.

Williams, Susan. *Savory Suppers and Fashionable Feasts: Dining in Victorian America.* New York: Pantheon–Strong Museum, 1985.

Wilson, David Scofield, and Angus Kress Gillespie, eds. *Rooted in America: Foodlore of Popular Fruits and Vegetables.* Knoxville: University of Tennessee Press, 1999.

SANDRA L. OLIVER

FOREIGN INVESTMENT

FOREIGN INVESTMENT   American industrialization in the nineteenth century was facilitated greatly by foreign investment. This grew from $70 million in 1803 to $3 billion by 1900, making the United States the most indebted nation the world has ever seen before or since. Foreign investment in the United States during the 1800s was, however, uniform neither in rate of growth nor in character. Three distinct phases coincided with different stages of economic development: these lasted roughly from 1800 to 1850, 1850 to 1875, and 1875 to 1900 and beyond.

Phase One: 1800–1850

The first half of the nineteenth century saw a continuation of earlier patterns of foreign investment. The principal U.S. borrower of funds from abroad was the government. The balance of indebtedness shifted between the federal and state governments, but approximately one-half to three-quarters of total foreign investment was in the form of government bonds. Foreign lending to the private sector remained in its infancy. The most notable change between 1800 and 1850 was the growth in state liabilities, which were taken on to fund local business development.

At the century's start, the states held no debt independent of obligations to cover the federal government's deficit. New York was the first state to float debt in the London market, in 1817. Then came Pennsylvania, Virginia, and Louisiana in 1824; Ohio in 1828; Maryland in 1830; Mississippi in 1831; Indiana and Alabama in 1833; and so on. State governments fronted for chosen private-sector initiatives. The stronger credit rating of sovereign states enabled them to issue bonds cheaply. The proceeds were funneled into banks in Philadelphia, canal projects in New York state, and railroad companies throughout the United States in exchange for the firms' stock. In the early days of industrial development, state governments essentially acted like venture capitalists, directing overseas funds into the U.S. economy.

The success of these financial arrangements depended on three factors: the profitability of the ventures supported by the states, the continued buoyancy of the world market, and the skill of merchant bankers responsible for floating the debt. At each stage, such credit-led economic development could go badly wrong. The first intimations of a credit crunch came in the late 1830s. By then, foreign investors had grown used to the profitability of such projects as the Erie Canal (opened in 1825). Naturally they were happy to lend to American ventures when the prospect of high returns seemed reasonable. However, the real profitability of each successive investment had begun to decline. Diminishing returns had set in, and some states could not meet the interest payments on their outstanding bonds. A concurrent downturn in the global economy hit both borrowers and lenders; U.S. industry was dependent on international trade in such commodities as tobacco and cotton, and international lenders needed to sell assets to cover declining profits. Several states defaulted on their loans. In the international market for government bonds, the London Baring and Rothschild banks dominated the credit rating and placement of loans. Without the cooperation of such powerful intermediaries, borrowers were fated to be disappointed. With the succession of defaults, the London banks turned their backs on U.S. loans and, as a result, American borrowers were blackballed through the 1840s. Several states tried to overcome the credit crunch by issuing their bonds below par (and so subsidizing lenders), but the lean years lasted through the 1850s.

Phase Two: 1850–1875

Foreign investment in the United States entered a new phase in the decades surrounding the Civil War. The European bourses continued to be suspicious of American ventures through the 1850s. However, by the end of the 1860s, inflows of foreign capital had reached a new peak. Foreign investment in 1869 represented nearly one-third of total investment in the U.S. economy, a remarkably high proportion. The reason was the railroad.

Government borrowing from London, Paris, and Amsterdam (the main European money markets) continued through the middle decades of the nineteenth century, primarily to fund the Union's military campaigns. But railroad securities became the main instrument of investment growth, increasing from near insignificance in 1850 to nearly one-third of the much larger total U.S. indebtedness by 1875.

The 1850s and 1860s saw the rapid diffusion of two great nineteenth-century technological advances: the steam engine and the telegraph. Transatlantic steamers reduced passage times from two or three weeks to six days. Their reliability and speed encouraged trade and unlocked natural treasures from within the American continent. The California gold rush prompted massive foreign speculation in the late 1840s. But the more mundane coal, iron ore, and other minerals attracted foreign investment in the 1850s and 1860s. The growth of the railroad made it possible—and profitable—to transport high-bulk, low-value commodities like coal to ports and industrial centers. The railroad grew quickly; between 1853 and 1860 nearly seventeen thousand miles of track were built, plus nearly forty thousand more between 1865 and 1874. Almost all were built with British money.

Economic historians long have debated the true impact of the railroad on U.S. economic development. Telegraph construction, market integration, and the emergence of the American corporation were related strongly to the huge amounts of money invested in railroad construction. The historical debate concerns the effectiveness of those investments. Based on historical knowledge at the end of the twentieth century, it appears that without such rapid railroad development, the process of U.S. economic integration would have been somewhat slower. Nineteenth-century Europeans were as aware as modern economic historians of the dangers of overinvesting.

There was a spate of defaults after the panic of 1873, but the response of European investors differed from that of the 1840s. Earlier European lenders simply had stayed away from U.S. securities. In the 1870s Europeans began to exercise an option that previously was impractical. With steamships, railroads, and the telegraph in place by the 1870s, it was possible to exercise long-distance managerial control over investments. As American borrowers defaulted, European lenders took more control over their investments. This heralded an important development: the emergence of significant amounts of direct foreign investment.

Phase Three: 1875–1900

From 1875 to 1900 foreign investment in the United States doubled in value, from $1.5 billion to $3 billion. The total value of all economic activity—the gross domestic product—more than trebled, so foreign investment had become less significant overall. However, this development masked important sectoral shifts.

It is useful to separate foreign investment into two categories. One is portfolio investment, where foreign investors simply buy a security for its return. Before 1875, foreign investment in the United States was overwhelmingly portfolio in nature and, after railroad bonds, remained the single most important source of foreign indebtedness. But increasingly foreign lenders were investing in the American market with methods that enabled them not only to own the operations but also to control them. Foreign ownership and managerial control marked these initiatives—direct investments—as distinct from the portfolio holdings.

Direct investment is more risky than portfolio investment. Yet the motive for European firms was simple. By the late nineteenth century, the U.S. domestic market was large, growing, and wealthier than anywhere else in the world. But for most European manufacturers the American market was increasingly off limits, hidden behind high tariff walls. Faced with a loss of important export revenues, many European firms chose to open a subsidiary business in the United States rather than lose out.

Direct foreign investments in mining, oil, chemicals, brewing and distilling, textiles, insurance, and many other sectors became important features of the American industrial landscape. Large European businesses such as J & P Coats (a Scottish cotton thread manufacturer), Bayer (a German chemicals producer), and Royal Dutch Shell (an Anglo-Dutch oil firm) introduced new and superior technologies into the U.S. market. These were among the largest firms in the world and, along with many other American and European giant multinational enterprises, were responsible for shaping the global markets that operated in the years before World War I.

During the nineteenth century, the United States absorbed capital from abroad as no nation either before or since. These funds came from many different European sources, though primarily from Britain. On occasions American commentators grew uneasy at the extent of foreign, especially British, ownership. On balance, however, the U.S. economy benefited. Foreign investment flowed into many industries, in both public and private sectors, acting as one of the fundamental catalysts of U.S. industrialization. The benefits of faster economic growth for American families were seen in the high wages earned. But the consequences of foreign investment went further, drawing the United States, through its ties to lenders, into the global economy, where international trade was seen as an essential component of world peace and civilization. Nineteenth-century foreign investment in the United States therefore did far more than simply speed up economic development. By cementing America's ties with the outside world, it fomented outward-looking attitudes and cultural values, which were critical to U.S. behavior and development in the twentieth century.

See also **Corporations and Big Business; Foreign Trade and Tariffs; Investment and Capital Formation; Panics and Depressions; Transportation,** *subentry on* **Railroads.**

Bibliography

Corley, Tony. "Britain's Overseas Investments in 1914 Revisited." *Business History* 36 (1994): 71–88.

Edelstein, Michael. "Foreign Investment and Accumulation, 1860–1914." In *The Economic History of Britain Since 1700.* Edited by Roderick Floud and Donald McCloskey. Vol. 2. Cambridge, U.K.: Cambridge University Press, 1994.

Ferguson, Niall. *The World's Banker: A History of the House of Rothschild.* London: Weidenfeld and Nicolson, 1998.

Wilkins, Mira. *The History of Foreign Investment in the United States to 1914.* Cambridge, Mass.: Harvard University Press, 1989.

ANDREW C. GODLEY

FOREIGN OBSERVERS

FOREIGN OBSERVERS The literature of travel in the United States in the nineteenth century is vast. Hundreds of individuals reported on their visits. Numerous bibliographies list these observers by country of origin and by topic. Extensive literature has been written on America by people who never set foot on the continent, with the shortcomings one would expect from secondhand, thirdhand, or fourth-hand information. Some accounts remain valuable as classic commentaries and sources of information on nineteenth-century America. Others continue to engage readers for their literary value. Some are of interest only to see what prejudices their authors confirmed by their visits.

Visitors came from around the world, but the vast majority came from Europe, primarily from western Europe. There are hundreds of English accounts and a significant number from French and German travelers. Only a few visitors came from the Russian or the Austrian Empires, in part because travel was severely restricted by those governments. Only a handful of East Asians left accounts. Both China and Japan restricted travel by their subjects as severely as they refused foreigners admission to their countries.

Observers came for many reasons. Some were sent by their governments on formal diplomatic missions or to look at American institutions. Some came mainly to observe and publish, either as newspaper reporters or as recognized authors whose observations would be sure of an audience. A few came on tours as musicians or actors, and some came as exiles from their home countries. Others came to settle and wrote to explain life in the United States for others contemplating immigration. The results of these observations were published in many forms, including dispatches to newspapers, private letters and diaries, memoirs, and more formal accounts. Volumes of observations continue to be published, as letters and diaries are discovered or are translated into English.

Observers arrived with much mental baggage, which influenced what they saw in the United States and how they interpreted their experiences. These factors included, besides gender and national origin, whether they were supporters or critics of the political regime at home, their social class, and the reading they had done. Each visitor had only a partial view of the country, limited by the length of the visit, the distance traveled, the people encountered, the economic circumstances observed, and the section or region visited. Most important, the United States changed greatly between 1800 and 1900, and the differences naturally were reflected in the responses of visitors.

Regardless of country of origin, visitors were overwhelmingly middle- or upper-class, and a great many restricted their experiences to visits with Americans to whom they had letters of introduction. Few tried to observe or speak with workers, miners, or ordinary farmers. Many women wrote of their visits to the United States, but they were often even more constricted in the scope of their observations than were their male counterparts.

What parts of the country visitors explored varied, but there were a few common itineraries. In the first half of the century, from arrival at an Atlantic port, most proceeded to visit the major cities of Washington, D.C., Philadelphia, New York, and Boston, and many ventured into the South. Then some headed west by carriage and boat, usually following the Ohio River to the Mississippi, which they sometimes took south as far as New Orleans. Or the loop could be made in reverse, traveling north from New Orleans and then east. After the development of the railroads travel was much easier, and much more of the continent was available to ordinary travelers. Still, few made the entire circuit of the continent.

The most commonly cited individual points of interest were Niagara Falls; the mills at Lowell, Massachusetts; and the monuments of Washington, D.C. Later travelers provided good descriptions of natural sites in the West. Some examples are Isabella Bird's 1873 exploration of Lake Tahoe and the Colorado Rockies, Rudyard Kipling's tour of Yellowstone National Park in 1889, and the Hungarian naturalist John Xántus's verbal and pencil sketches of the source of the Arkansas River in southern Colorado in 1856.

Most travelers reported excellent treatment by the Americans they met. They may have found the behavior of some of the Americans unpleasant, but they agreed that local people were generous with their hospitality and willing to put up with strangers. Louis Kossuth, exiled from Hungary after his leadership in the revolution of 1848, was greeted everywhere by cheering crowds as he toured the country by train to raise support for his national cause, and his soft felt, feathered hat became the fashion rage. Well-known visitors, such as Charles Dickens in 1842, found their

The Trollope Family. Frances Trollope *(seated with book)* traveled to Cincinnati with her son, the English novelist Anthony Trollope, where they resided from 1827 to 1830. Upon her return to England, Frances Trollope (1780–1863) wrote *Domestic Manners of the Americans,* which attracted widespread resentment in the United States. Sketch, 1829. Lithograph, Childs & Inman, Philadelphia. LIBRARY OF CONGRESS

privacy invaded by curious fans whenever they appeared in public.

Not everyone was welcomed everywhere. For one thing, people of color encountered Americans' distrust of black and Asian people. Others found doors closing after they published materials disliked by Americans. One example is the *Times* of London reporter William Howard Russell, who was given full access to government officials when he arrived in 1861. After his report on the First Battle of Bull Run as a rout of the Union forces, however, he was no longer welcome.

Observers looked at many aspects of American life. Some accounts read much like gossip and others are more analytical. In many cases travelers relied on secondhand or thirdhand reports, generalized from anecdotes, and editorialized extensively. Therefore most of these writings are more valuable for what they reveal of their authors' viewpoints than as reliable information about the country. In addition, most accounts owe a great deal to their predecessors. Original observations are hard to extract from the large amounts of derivative material.

Traditions in the Literature on America

Two major threads wind through nineteenth-century writing about America by Europeans. The older, more intellectual tradition goes back to the very earliest works on the New World, produced largely by Spanish and French writers. The second strain is more personal or literary. Both left clear tracks in the literature.

The intellectual tradition originated with sixteenth- and seventeenth-century attempts to understand the flora and fauna of the Western Hemisphere, especially in comparison with Old World life-forms. By the eighteenth century these accounts focused on how climate affects physical development. Cornelius De Pauw, a native of Amsterdam writing in Prussia in 1768, argued that the smaller and weaker forms of life found in America indicated that the climate of the New World would inevitably result in the degeneration of both native and introduced forms of life. Others, the most important being Georges-Louis Leclerc de Buffon, the French naturalist who influenced Darwin, argued the opposite viewpoint. In 1777 Buffon stated that American flora and fauna were smaller than those of Europe because the New World was immature, much younger than the Old. Unlike De Pauw, however, he believed that mankind could counter the effects of the environment and thrive in the New World.

Echoes of this debate, whether concerned with physical or cultural development, recurred in nineteenth-century works about the United States. Domingo Sarmiento from Argentina exclaimed in 1847: "European immigration is a barbaric element. Who would have believed it!" (*Travels in the United States in 1847*, p. 191). His surprise betrays his assumption that the Old World was superior to the New. James Burn, an English hatmaker and one of the very few working-class visitors who published comments, predicted in 1865 that the influence of the climate would cause Americans to degenerate. Evidence was already appearing, he asserted, in the paleness and thinness of Americans.

The second tradition of writing about America includes the writers who made no pretense at philosophical understanding but related their own personal experiences. Again, many repeated or reflected earlier comments. Perhaps writers edited themselves to fit the popular patterns.

Private letters and journals are among the exceptions to the rule that observers shaped their perceptions to fit the prevailing mode. Immigrant guides did not pretend to be literature but rather purely practical sources of information, and therefore they avoided some the pitfalls of the more literary works.

The pattern of borrowing is most clearly seen in the example of Frances Trollope. While her work, *Domestic Manners of the Americans* (1832), was not the first to denounce American behavior, it was the most widely read and the most notorious. Her influence is found throughout much of the literature that followed her book. Despite its title, which implies an almost anthropological approach to her subject, Trollope's responses were highly personal. She had experienced three years (1827–1830) in the United States, unlike some who made sweeping pronouncements on the basis of a few weeks' stay. Trollope spent most of her time in the United States in frontier Cincinnati, a burgeoning but unfinished town in 1830, and she did not limit herself to visits mediated through connections with well-known Americans. Her conclusions were notoriously splenetic, and they provoked an impassioned outcry from those she criticized.

Trollope's hostility probably arose from her lack of success in the United States. She had come hoping to make money but ended up bankrupt. Her book was an instant success, partly due to the fact that it appeared in England just as the first Reform Bill was being debated. The Tories opposed the bill, and Trollope's account of life in a democracy supported their view that "the people" were not capable of self-government. Trollope was certainly not objective. She exaggerated, generalized on the basis of anecdotes, and relied on dubious sources. For example, she quoted one Englishman to the effect that he had never observed a conversation between two Americans without the word "money" entering into it. Serious illness was much more common in America than in England, and she never saw such misery as that in an American "peasant cottage." She never saw a plump, smiling face like those so common among the English poor. Her account of an alligator attack (she called them "crocodiles") on a farm near the Mississippi River, in which a woman and five children were devoured, clearly seems to be a tall tale told to a gullible audience.

Nonetheless her book established a pattern subsequently adopted by a large number of writers. The practices of generalizing and describing similar American habits appear again and again. Whether these comments recur because later writers' reading of Trollope made these habits obvious to them, or because such stereotypes simplified the writers' need to describe the Americans they met, is not possible to determine. Out of the wide variety of subjects addressed by these travelers, a few stand out. These include American manners, women and family life, equality, American materialism, treatment of minorities, and American democracy.

American Manners

Trollope's discussion of manners is not only the most stringent, it also had the greatest impact on later writers. Her criticisms provoked much protest among Americans, although some Americans admitted that her comments had merit. According to Trollope, Americans ate terrible food in great quantity and with great rapidity. Dinner conversation was almost nonexistent. Diners drank little wine, but men indulged in large amounts of hard liquor. Many young couples lived in boarding houses or hotels instead of establishing their own households. A literary conversation consisted of denigrating the great English writers, including the "obscene" Shakespeare. The pursuit of money was all-consuming. To complete the ignominy, Americans boasted of their superior institutions, beautiful cities, and lofty morals.

Trollope's complaints were repeated by many later writers. A set piece was based on her description of the boor who put his feet on the table or mantlepiece and chewed tobacco, spewing the juice at random, thereby coating the floor and endangering women's skirts, all the while wearing his hat. Isabella Bird hired a horse in Truckee, California, in 1873 from a man she described as a typical westerner, who bowed

Alexis de Tocqueville (1805–1859). Alexis de Tocqueville came to America in 1831 and wrote his seminal work *Democracy in America* (1835) based upon his observations. Lithography by Chasseriau. LIBRARY OF CONGRESS

to her, "threw himself into a rocking-chair, drew a spittoon beside him, cut a fresh quid of tobacco, began to chew energetically, and put his feet, cased in miry high boots, into which his trousers were tucked, on the top of the stove" (*A Lady's Life in the Rocky Mountains*, p. 9).

Of these signature traits of the Americans, the use of rocking chairs hardly seems in the same class. Rocking chairs were virtually unknown outside of the United States at this time, but the frequent objections to them seem overblown. Whether they illustrated an excessively informal style or indicated the speed of life in America, where even sitting still was impossible, is not clear.

Women and Family Life

The consensus was that women were treated extremely well and were shielded from the harder aspects of life. In return they yielded any influence outside the home, and they often had little control there either.

Almost all writers agreed that a woman was perfectly safe traveling alone. Numerous anecdotes attest to the courtesy extended to them. One man gave up his place in an omnibus to his own housemaid simply because she was a woman. Two young men rode at great risk on the top of a carriage to allow a young woman to stretch out her legs inside the coach. Rosalie Roos from Sweden countered this generalization, however, by relating in 1854 that she could not take

a trip from South Carolina to Georgia by herself because her American hosts disapproved. Unchaperoned young women were everywhere. While girls and young women were expected to enjoy themselves and even to flirt, once married they settled into dowdiness. Women were educated for marriage alone and were not expected to have or to express independent opinions.

Some writers wondered if the practice of providing separate gathering places for women was what women really wanted and if they enjoyed their economic dependence, enforced by the limited number of occupations open to women. Even some of those writers who approved of women's position, such as Fredrika Bremer of Sweden, believed that American women were not using their potential to change their world. In 1853 she wrote that if women would address such an issue as slavery, they would be able to eliminate it. Instead, the English reformer Harriet Martineau complained in 1836 that Margaret Fuller and her circle spent their time gorgeously dressed, discussing astronomy, literature, and philosophy, and ignoring the social issues facing their country.

European visitors tended to take the independence of American women in stride, but Latin American visitors found U.S. behavior in great contrast to that of their countries, where women were kept virtually cloistered. Japanese visitors, also accustomed to secluded women, were surprised to find them everywhere, even in business offices. Dancing couples evoked disgust. Hopping around the floor seemed ugly and unnatural to Japanese visitors, while the deference given to women in the United States was compared to that given parents in Japan.

Children were seen as inappropriately independent. They shared the dinner table with their elders and felt free to speak out and even to disagree with their parents. While the consequent lack of shyness was hailed by some as the self-assertion everyone needed to compete in American society, several writers felt that it led to a lack of discipline and order.

American Materialism

Besides the boorishness of American manners, almost nothing excited as much comment as the American preoccupation with money, the pursuit of the "almighty dollar." For some observers this was a critical failure, while for others the prosperity of the United States was a good in and of itself. Wealth was considered the chief criterion by which men were measured. People said not "Mr. X has so much" but rather "he is worth so much" (Sienkiewicz, *Portrait of America*, p. 19).

The emphasis on prosperity affected all aspects of American life, according to visitors. Even clergymen had to contend with the attitude that only practical effects interested people, that the spiritual side of life was secondary. While many saw this as a grave defect, others believed that prosperity and the freedom Americans enjoyed were profoundly connected.

The fixation on money meant that the display of wealth substituted for the more subtle signs of aristocracy in Europe. For some this merely reinforced the impression of crudeness among the Americans, while for others it was an advantage. According to the Polish visitor Adam de Gurowski, Europeans were as greedy as Americans but disguised it under conventional behavior. While the European aristocracy might disdain the open pursuit of money, he noted in 1857, they made money by oppressing millions of people and living on the labor of others.

Some argued that, while Americans sought wealth, their striving was without rancor. The possibility of failure did exist, but a new beginning was always possible. Americans saw wealth as benefiting not just themselves and their families but also the whole of society. As the English observer Edward Dicey put it in 1862, "Money-making is the chief object of the nation; but they value the possession of the 'almighty dollar' rather as a proof of success in life than as an end of existence" (Commager, *America in Perspective*, p. 181).

Equality

Some observers noted that, while the obsessive pursuit of gain seemed a grievous fault, it was the natural outgrowth of a society just as obsessive about equality. Whether they approved or not, observers agreed that the lack of class distinctions was the most remarkable quality of American life.

Lack of social distinctions was the norm everywhere in the United States. First-, second-, or third-class carriages were not distinguished on the railroads. On steamships everyone appeared at the same tables for meals. An English gentleman might find himself next to a rudely dressed farmer. Household and farm help joined employers at the family dinner table, shocking as it was to visitors from abroad.

Many comments were made about the American habit of using such titles as general, captain, or esquire for even the least-impressive men. One story noted that a steamboat captain at a dinner table inquired, "General, a little fish?" and almost all of the men present answered.

On the other hand most visitors were struck by the accessibility of officials and dignitaries, even the president. At White House receptions, which were open to all regardless of rank, the president, wearing ordinary dress without uniform or decorations, mixed with the visitors. Emily Faithfull commented in 1884 on the contrast between an American democratic reception and the special dress, elaborate protocol, deep curtsies, and careful language required for an introduction to Queen Victoria. Trollope was shocked to see President Andrew Jackson walking unguarded through the crowds in Cincinnati, where even rude and stupid questions could be addressed to him.

Most English observers, especially in the first half of the century, found the degree of equality unsettling. They commented on the difficulty of finding servants and the need to treat the "help" with dignity rather than as the inferiors they would be at home. On the other hand, in 1837, Harriet Martineau, an English liberal, was pleased to note no poverty, ignorance, servility, or insolence.

Visitors from politically repressive countries, such as the Habsburg Empire, were impressed not only by the absence of aristocracy but also by the absence of secret police and internal passports. The Russian liberal Aleksander Lakier reported in 1857 that the only distinctions were between rich and poor, and those were only temporary. He gave the example of a coal miner from Germany, who said that while work in the mine was indeed menial, he would soon move west and find land and a fortune of his own. Lakier, like many others, may have confused mobility with lack of class distinctions.

Slavery and Race

The glaring exception to the prevalent equality was the treatment of blacks. Visitors before the Civil War almost universally condemned slavery. Many made a point of showing the hypocrisy of Americans who believed in equality but lived with the peculiar institution. Trollope made the case that Thomas Jefferson was a hypocrite who wrote of the inherent freedom of men while subjecting some men to the bonds of slavery on his own plantation. Many commented on the slave auctions held in the shadow of the national Capitol, which made an indelible and negative impression on all visitors who witnessed them.

Foreigners frequently commented on the contrast between slave and free territories. On the north side of the Ohio River and the Mason-Dixon line, farms were substantial and well kept, while on the other side dwellings were more like huts and fields were poor and overworked. Roads and bridges in the slave territories were in worse condition than those in the North. Some stated that the existence of slavery worked against that symbol of civilization, the town, as free commerce was not needed where the slave owners provided all the necessities to their people.

Many wrote more of slavery's baneful effect on the slave owners than its effect on slaves. On the other hand a few observers approved of the slave economy because it allowed for the development of a leisure class with the requisite good manners and elegant conversation. Often visitors commented that slaves were better off than free blacks because, as valuable commodities in a money economy, slaves commanded respect that members of an inferior race would not. But most deplored the effects that left slave owners with little respect for the value of work. The ability to command absolute obedience corrupted even the young men, who were free to exercise their tempers and their sexual urges at will. As for the effects on the wives of slave owners, these women were kept on pedestals even more than women in the North.

Despite these criticisms, very few writers apparently had firsthand knowledge of what life was like for slaves or for free people of color. In 1838–1839 Fanny Kemble, an English actress who married a South Carolina planter, commented on the helplessness of being only the wife of the owner, unable to mitigate his cruelty to his slaves. In 1857–1858 Barbara Leigh Smith Bodichon spent two months in New Orleans, where she came to know a wide variety of people and to understand the effect of the color line, which left well-educated and prosperous free people of color unable to enter white society.

Emancipation had its supporters and detractors among the visitors, but few believed that African Americans would ever become full citizens. Even the colonization efforts created to move freed slaves to Liberia were deplored by some as a useless attempt to allow an inferior race to try to live freely.

Edward Wilmot Blyden (1832–1919) saw the situation quite differently. A West Indian who was educated in the United States but emigrated to Liberia, he found the situation in America deplorable. His status as an official representative of Liberia did not free him from the restrictions under which blacks suffered. He needed an affidavit from a white man declaring that he was a free man, he was unable to find hotel accommodations, and he had to travel in the railroad cars reserved for blacks, which lacked seats. Even in Philadelphia, the Quaker city, blacks were excluded from public transportation, regardless of education or wealth.

American Indians were the subject of great curiosity, but visitors frequently were disappointed by the reality. Real Indians did not resemble the noble savage of literature. Some writers deplored the policies of Indian removal and annihilation, and others dismissed the Indians as uncivilized. Few visitors had enough direct contact to appreciate both the humanity and the limitations of the Indians. Among those who did was John Xántus, who accompanied U.S. Army expeditions through Kansas, Wyoming, and Colorado in 1856. He recorded details of Wichita and Comanche people's dress, houses, artifacts, and manners in his letters and drawings.

Asian visitors shared with blacks the condition of being racially distinct from the vast majority of Americans, and consequently their consciousness of racism was strong. From the Japanese who made up the official delegation in 1860 to a Chinese diplomat who objected to having his papers searched by customs officials in 1886, Asian visitors saw parallels between their own treatment and that of American blacks. However, some of the Japanese agreed with their white hosts that blacks were little better than savages.

The Experiment in Democracy

In one way or another virtually all observers commented on American democracy. Curiosity led men and women alike to visit the institutions of the state and federal governments and to examine American society for signs, good or bad, of the new form of government.

Reactions were as much due to the observer's origins as to what was observed. The innumerable British visitors tended to skepticism arising from complacency about their own situation. Few went to such extremes as Captain Basil Hall, who in 1829 considered the absence of primogeniture, by which all landed estates descended undivided to a single male heir, to be a fatal defect in American law. But even reformers such as Martineau and Dickens, aware of the negative effects of industrialization on the lower classes, did not believe that American governmental institutions were better than those at home.

At the other extreme, visitors from Asia did not write about issues of democracy at all. They were as impressed as any by the informality of American officials, but, probably because their own governments were so autocratic, they did not offer any points of comparison. Both China and Japan were just beginning to look to the West, including the United States, for possible keys to their own development. Neither had undergone anything like the social and political upheavals that Europe was undergoing during the century.

The visitors from continental Europe and Latin America tended to look to American models for support for their own efforts at institutional change. Many of these observers were exiles from their own countries, a factor that could only strengthen their desire for change at home. For example, three future leaders of France spent time in the United States to avoid difficulties at home. Louis-Philippe, who reigned as king from 1830 to 1848, was in the United States from 1796 to 1798; Louis-Napoléon Bonaparte, who reigned as Emperor Napoleon III from 1852 until 1870, was exiled by Louis-Philippe in 1836; and Georges Clemenceau, while not technically driven out of France, found that his opposition to Napoleon III made life in France too uncomfortable and spent the years from 1865 to 1870 in the United States.

The best known of the writers on American democracy was Alexis de Tocqueville, who visited the United States in 1831–1832 to study the country's emerging prison system. While his report on American prisons is useful, his two-volume *Democracy in America* (1835 and 1840) remains the most important analysis of American institutions and behavior. He emphasized the New England town meeting as a model of direct democracy and emphasized the lack of central control by the national government. In this he reflected his concerns about the centralized, bureaucratic system of administration in France, which defeated attempts to liberalize, either through repeated revolutions or through legislation. His fear that the majority in an egalitarian democracy could tyrannize the country continues to be relevant.

After Tocqueville, the Scot James Bryce was the second most important analyst of American democracy. Like his predecessor, his interest arose out of discussions at home on how to expand representational government while preventing loss of control as Great Britain debated what would become the Second Reform Act of 1867. Like Tocqueville's work, Bryce's was considered authoritative, and his *The American Commonwealth* (1888) was used as a textbook for students of American government. Bryce's massive work examined federal, state, and local governmental institutions and included discussions of political parties and issues of corruption. He was much influenced by friends and collaborators in the United States who shared his interest in reform. Of the political exiles who wrote about American democracy, most were enthusiastic. One of these was Charles Sealsfield from Bohemia, then part of the Austrian Empire. Sealsfield was in exile, not because of his political activities but because he had left a monastic order in Prague and was evading the Austrian secret police. In 1828, under the pen name of Karl Postl, he extolled the virtues of democracy in the United States although he did not believe that democracy would work in European countries, where people were accustomed to obey.

No such skepticism dampened the enthusiasm of Domingo Sarmiento for American democracy. After a long exile and two visits to the United States (1848

and 1865), he became president of his native Argentina in 1868. In that role he endeavored to introduce U.S.-inspired institutions, especially schools and libraries. Unstinting in his regard for American life, he observed that the availability of cheap land in the United States provided the basis of the equality so much a part of U.S. democracy, an obvious contrast to the large landholdings characteristic of Spanish colonies. In 1880–1881 the Norwegian Bjørnstjerne Bjørnson used his impressions of American democratic government, lack of class discrimination, healthy and clean workers' homes, and women's freedoms to advocate for democratic reforms at home.

Henry Sienkiewicz, who was awarded the Nobel Prize for literature for *Quo Vadis?* (1896), went to California in 1876 with a small group of Polish friends in an attempt to establish a utopian community. While not literally an exile, Sienkiewicz was depressed by the failure of the 1863 Polish uprising against Russian rule over Poland. He hoped that the New World would make a freer life possible. His little group, which included the actress Helena Modjeska and her husband, was totally unprepared to farm, and their experiment ended quickly. Sienkiewicz's charming letters to a Warsaw newspaper vividly describe the countryside he traveled through by rail from New York to California and the people he encountered. The people included gold seekers rushing into the Black Hills and Indians determined to resist that incursion, which violated their treaty rights. He also offered a fine analysis of American democratic style, which he found very different from the closed society at home, which was dominated by an autocratic, centralized government imposed by a foreign power.

The Cuban national hero José Martí (1853–1895) was another political refugee. After years in exile in Spain and Mexico, he came to New York in 1880. He returned to Cuba in 1895, where he was killed in an unsuccessful uprising against Spain. His essays, published in Latin American newspapers, showed his admiration of the freedom and material progress of the United States. Yet for Martí progress was not enough. He longed for the idealism of his Latin American homeland. Ultimately Martí denounced the soulless materialism of American life, the pursuit of fortune at the expense of love and art. He blamed the practical curriculum of the public schools for this lack of interest in what he called the priestly side of man. He also foresaw U.S. expansion, which made virtual colonies of Cuba and the Philippines after the Spanish-American War.

Of these many and diverse works, are any worth reading now? Some are, because of their literary merit. Others stand out for the nature of their descriptions rather than their literary style. Some of the guides to immigrants provide concrete information on conditions in the United States, and some are useful sources on life in the country.

Another group of writers is memorable because they demonstrate an understanding of why the United States attracted so much attention in the nineteenth century. Among them are the analysts Tocqueville and Bryce and the many political exiles who appreciated U.S. freedom mainly because it differed sharply from conditions in their own countries. For many visitors the sight of Americans, newcomers and native-born alike, standing straight and proud was the most impressive part of their visit. In that spirit Sarmiento wrote, "The American is a man . . . [who] is master of himself, with a spirit elevated by education and a sense of his own dignity" (Pachter and Wein, eds., *Abroad in America*, p. 105). In the words of Bjørnson, the United States had taken "all the human slag from the mines of monarchical Europe" (ibid., p. 201) and extracted the precious metals from it, transforming people into confident, frank, and unafraid citizens.

See also **Class, Social; Gender,** *subentry on* **Interpretations of Gender; Gilded Age; Manners; Popular Culture; Victorianism; Women,** *subentry on* **Woman as Image and Icon.**

Bibliography

Arkush, R. David, and Leo O. Lee, trans. and eds. *Land without Ghosts: Chinese Impressions of America from the Mid-Nineteenth Century to the Present*. Berkeley: University of California Press, 1989. Good introduction.

Berger, Max. *The British Traveller in America, 1836–1860*. New York: Columbia University Press, 1943. Excellent commentary, including numerous sources and an annotated bibliography.

Bird, Isabella L. *A Lady's Life in the Rocky Mountains*. Norman: University of Oklahoma Press, 1960.

Bodichon, Barbara Leigh Smith. *An American Diary, 1857–8*. Edited by Joseph W. Reed Jr. London: Routledge and Kegan Paul, 1972. Excellent introduction on English travelers.

Burn, James Dawson. *Three Years among the Working-classes in the United States during the War*. London: Smith, Elder, 1865.

Commager, Henry Steele. *America in Perspective: The United States through Foreign Eyes*. New York: Random House, 1947.

Dickens, Charles. *American Notes for General Circulation*. Edited and with an introduction by John S. Whitley and Arnold Goldman. Harmondsworth, U.K.: Penguin, 1972. Excellent introduction.

Downs, Robert B., comp. *Images of America: Travelers from Abroad in the New World*. Urbana: University of Illinois Press, 1987.

Echeverria, Durand. *Mirage in the West: A History of the French Image of American Society to 1815*. Princeton, N.J.: Princeton University Press, 1957.

Gerbi, Antonello. *The Dispute of the New World: The History of a Polemic, 1750–1900*. Translated by Jeremy Moyle. Pittsburgh, Pa.: University of Pittsburgh Press, 1973. An exhaustive study of the debate over the influence of climate in the Western Hemisphere.

Kipling, Rudyard. *American Notes: Rudyard Kipling's West*. Edited and with an introduction by Arrell Morgan Gibson. Norman: University of Oklahoma Press, 1981.

Lakier, Aleksandr Borisovich. *A Russian Looks at America: The Journey of Aleksandr Borisovich Lakier in 1857*. Translated and edited by Arnold Schrier and Joyce Story. Chicago: University of Chicago Press, 1979.

Mesick, Jane Louise. *The English Traveller in America, 1785–1835*. New York: Columbia University Press, 1922.

Miyoshi, Masao. *As We Saw Them: The First Japanese Embassy to the United States (1860)*. Berkeley: University of California Press, 1979. Excellent critical work.

Nevins, Allan, ed. *America through British Eyes*. New York: Oxford University Press, 1948.

Pachter, Marc, and Frances Wein, eds. *Abroad in America: Visitors to the New Nation, 1776–1914*. Reading, Mass.: Addison-Wesley for the National Portrait Gallery, Smithsonian Institution, 1976. Essays on a variety of visitors, including some whose works are not available in English.

Reiersen, Johan Reinert. *Pathfinder for Norwegian Emigrants*. Translated by Frank G. Nelson. Northfield, Minn.: Norwegian-American Historical Association, 1981.

Sarmiento, Domingo Faustino. *Travels in the United States in 1847*. Translated and introduced by Michael Aaron Rockland. Princeton, N.J.: Princeton University Press, 1970.

Sienkiewicz, Henry. *Portrait of America: Letters*. Edited and translated by Charles Morley. New York: Columbia University Press, 1959.

Teng, Ssu-Yü, and John K. Fairbank. *China's Response to the West: A Documentary Survey, 1839–1923*. Cambridge, Mass.: Harvard University Press, 1965.

Tinling, Marion, ed. *With Women's Eyes: Visitors to the New World, 1775–1918*. Hamden, Conn.: Archon, 1993.

Torrielli, Andrew J. *Italian Opinion on America as Revealed by Italian Travelers, 1850–1900*. Cambridge, Mass.: Harvard University Press, 1941.

Trollope, Frances Milton. *Domestic Manners of the Americans*. Edited by Donald Smalley. New York: Knopf, 1949. Excellent introductory material.

Tuckerman, Henry T. *America and Her Commentators. With a Critical Sketch of Travel in the United States*. New York: Scribners, 1864.

Xántus, John. *Letters from North America*. Translated and edited by Theodore Schoenman and Helen Benedek Schoenman. Detroit, Mich.: Wayne State University Press, 1975.

ELLEN HUPPERT

FOREIGN PARTS During most of the nineteenth century, the people of the United States viewed the rest of the world with a complex and sometimes contradictory mixture of emotions and perceptions. At once resentful, fearful, jealous, condescending, and arrogant, Americans could also be admiring, curious, open-minded, and genuinely concerned with other nations and peoples. To fully grasp the American view of "foreign parts," one must move beyond the realm of traditional diplomatic contacts and consider other forms of interaction arising from cultural and artistic exchanges, tourism, and the world of science.

In many ways, how Americans viewed the rest of the world was predicated on how they viewed themselves. As they defined what the United States was and what an American was, they also began to define what was not American. Having differentiated themselves and their nation from other peoples and other countries, they then ranked them. Inevitably, in almost any sort of comparison Americans used, the United States and its citizens emerged on top. Americans considered their nation the shining "city upon a hill," as first stated by John Winthrop in a sermon during his 1630 voyage to America, and a clear example to the rest of the world of the perfect revolution leading to the formation of the perfect form of government that ruled over a perfect nation inhabited by perfect people. The American Revolution had been a real revolution, designed to throw off the shackles of Old World monarchy and free Americans to chart their own destiny. Few Americans doubted that it was a glorious destiny indeed. For many, the Revolution and the United States had been divinely inspired or at least blessed, and the future of the country was assured. Peopled largely by a solid Anglo-Saxon stock, the United States was the latest and possibly the penultimate accomplishment of this hardy race.

Ethnicity

In comparison, the rest of the world was sadly lacking in the qualities so admired by Americans. Racially, much of the world was highly suspect. Even the British seemed to be the somewhat anemic progenitors of their more dynamic American relatives. Indeed, as the nineteenth century progressed, more and more Americans began to speak of a distinct Anglo-American race rather than the more inclusive Anglo-Saxon race. With the Anglo-Saxons just below the Anglo-Americans, the other peoples of the world took their decidedly inferior places in what the historian Michael Hunt has referred to as the "hierarchy of race." To give a scientific patina to such thinking, philosophers and intellectuals such as Benjamin Franklin took great pains to categorize and rank the inferior races. The various European groups, including the Latin (French, for example), the Mediterranean (Italian, Greek), the Germanic Nordic (German, Scandinavian), and the Slavic (eastern European), were grouped directly below the Anglo-Saxons. While each group had its good qualities, each also had a number of deficiencies that could not be overcome. The Germans were too clannish, the French too weak-willed, and the Italians too emotional. All Europeans suffered from living in societies dominated by Old World thinking, such as slavish devotion to outmoded customs and ideals, foolish adherence to corrupt and decadent monarchies, and in many cases blind faith in the Catholic Church, itself a nest of thieves and petty dictators. Americans admired the cultural achievements of Europe, but for most Americans the Old World was the world of the past, while the United States was the world of the future.

Latin Americans often ranked in the next group. Their European blood counted for something, although since most of that blood came from the Spanish and Portuguese, races given to violence, laziness, and abject devotion to popism, it was a mixed blessing. Moreover, the feeling was that most Latin Americans had become mongrelized through excessive race mixing with Native Americans and blacks. This "watering down" of the European blood produced the stereotypical Latino—hot-tempered, childlike, lazy, thieving, and licentious. What had been reproduced in Latin America, therefore, were the worst attributes of European culture. The Catholic Church dominated society, economics, and politics with deleterious effects. Corrupt and ignorant tyrants ruled most Latin American countries, and the ill-educated and enfeebled masses did nothing about it. The enervating tropical climate, which sapped the will and strength of even hardy Anglo-Saxons, only added to the region's backwardness. The only hope lay in a stronger and continuous infusion of European blood that perhaps would invigorate the stagnant nations of Latin America.

Asians were next on the racial ladder. Although usually divided into two or three subgroups—the more advanced Chinese and Japanese and the more primitive Filipinos, for example—they were almost always lumped into the same general "Oriental" category. Potentially dangerous because of their numbers and deviousness, their propensity for vices such as gambling and opium use made them relatively easy to dominate. Most Americans gave them little thought until the mid-1800s, when large numbers of Chinese laborers came to the United States looking for work constructing the railroad lines. Almost immediately Americans, most notably in California, cried for strict regulation of Asian immigration. Violence sometimes accompanied these demands, and in cities such as San Francisco anti-Chinese groups sprang up. Responding to anti-Chinese sentiments, Congress in 1882 passed the Chinese Exclusion Act.

Africans almost always occupied the bottom rung. Aside from the slave trade, most Americans had little knowledge of (or interest in) Africa during the nineteenth century. It was, quite literally, the "dark continent," inhabited by headhunters, cannibals, man-eating lions, poisonous snakes, and intrepid white explorers who risked life and limb to bring civilization and Christianity to the heathen savages. A notable exception, the establishment of Liberia in the early nineteenth century as a colony for the repatriation of freed blacks, spurred a tremendous amount of interest among African Americans concerning the possibilities of resettlement in Africa. With the end of slavery in the United States, however, even that limited interest in African affairs began to wane.

One mitigating factor determining how any particular American viewed the rest of the world was the ethnic identity of the observer. For example, Irish Americans naturally viewed the land of their heritage in a more favorable light than did British Americans. German Americans took umbrage at any notion of Anglo-Saxon superiority that excluded themselves. Polish Americans bristled at the idea that they were lumped together in the Slavic category with Russian Americans. African Americans, as noted, were some of the only Americans to take a more generous view of Africa and its peoples. In the main, however, the telescope through which most Americans saw the world was solidly constructed on, or distorted by, a strong racial foundation.

The ideas that Anglo-Americans formed a superior race that had built a superior nation and that other people and nations around the world were more or less inferior manifested itself in a number of ways. Using the American Revolution as a measuring stick, for example, many in the United States were apt to judge revolutions elsewhere as disappointments at best or dismal failures at worst. The French Revolution, the Latin American revolutions for independence, and the Cuban Revolution of the 1890s were all greeted with at least some degree of initial enthusiasm in the United States. After all, they were following the American example. Yet in the eyes of the majority of Americans, each revolution that followed the American Revolution was but a pale imitation. The French, emotional and given to demagoguery, let their revolt get out of hand and ended up ruled by a dictator. They had failed to shake off the shackles of the papacy and were little better off than before. The numerous anticolonial revolts in early-nineteenth-century Latin America had much the same result. Even with the example of the United States, Latin Americans ran revolutions no better than they ran their independent nations. Cruel, ignorant, and greedy rule by the Spanish had been replaced by cruel, ignorant, and greedy rule by mestizos and other half-breed rulers. Observers in the United States could only shake their heads. When Cuba revolted against Spanish rule in the 1890s, the reaction in the United States was mainly positive. The Cubans, who were referred to as "bronzed Europeans" in the American press, were heroic freedom fighters. Once the United States directly intervened in the struggle in 1898, however, the response quickly changed. American soldiers and officials were horrified to discover that many of the revolutionaries were black or of mixed blood. Americans quickly decided that, after the removal of the Spanish, a period of American "tutelage" would be necessary before the Cubans could adequately govern their own affairs.

American reactions to immigration were also conditioned by the dominant racial perceptions. Not surprisingly, Anglo-Saxon stock was preferred as far as immigrants were concerned. Throughout the nineteenth century various groups and organizations attempted to limit, or even eliminate, new immigration into the United States. Each new wave of immigrants raised anew fears of diluting America's bloodline. The Germans were sullen and solitary, and even Benjamin Franklin questioned their loyalty to their new country. The Irish, who frankly appalled many Americans, were usually portrayed as hard-drinking, penny-pinching papists. Scandinavians were considered dumb, and Chinese and Japanese immigrants were almost unanimously opposed by the Anglo-Saxon majority in the United States. In the late nineteenth century, when immigrants from eastern and southern Europe began to flow into the United States, Italians, Poles, Russians, eastern European Jews, and others got a taste of the xenophobia that had greeted each preceding generation of newcomers.

Literature

Although Americans had developed rather definite impressions about foreign places and peoples during the nineteenth century, they did so based upon limited information. Unlike in the twentieth-century with its "information highway," in the 1800s Americans had few sources of reliable data on the world outside their own. Newspapers devoted most of their space to domestic events. Much of the fiction read during the nineteenth century was set in exotic overseas locales, but a great deal of this material merely perpetuated the stereotypes already popular in the United States. Novels and short stories were replete with a stock cast of characters, such as drunken Irishmen, haughty and somewhat effeminate Frenchmen, evil Chinese, and man-eating Africans.

One very popular source of information about the world beyond American shores was the travel genre of literature. Magazines such as the *North American Review* often carried short pieces about travel abroad, and a number of travelers wrote longer pieces and even books detailing their adventures. Although tourism was limited mostly to the well-to-do, thousands of Americans left their country every year for trips to the rest of the world. Americans of every class, however, could vicariously experience foreign lands and peoples through the writings of fellow Americans traveling the globe. Europe attracted most of the American travelers, and London and Paris were the two most popular stops. Italy was another popular destination. Most Americans traveled to experience the art, architecture, music, and literature that seemed to them the only beneficial legacies of the Old World past. And, in the main, they were suitably impressed, contemplating with reverence the Louvre in Paris, the stunning art collections in the Vatican, and the architecture of Venice. Other aspects of European life, however, left Americans with decidedly less enthusiastic impressions. European morality, especially that of the French, scandalized many American travelers. The stuffy, class-based structure of European society frustrated Americans, who were committed, at least rhetorically, to a democratic society. Both European political and economic development seemed stagnant in comparison to the American dynamo.

Other areas that attracted American travelers included the Holy Land, Latin America, the Far East, and the Pacific Islands. In nearly every description, the beautiful landscapes and exotic lifestyles of these distant lands contrasted with the overall backwardness and lack of development. Latin America, in particular, attracted a wide range of visitors from the north. Geographical surveys conducted by the U.S. Navy that penetrated into virtually unknown nooks and crannies of South America and the Caribbean often included artists and scientists. Businesspeople and speculators invaded Latin America looking for opportunities. Aside from the official records of their visits, such as maps, government reports, and business transactions, these travelers left writings, drawings, paintings, and studies rich in personal observations. Even in describing the great natural beauty they found, however, most of these visitors could not refrain from commenting that it was a shame that such a rich area was still so backward.

Culture

Not all Americans were quintessential "ugly Americans" when they were abroad. Scientists, educators, scholars, writers, and artists were perhaps the most liberal in terms of learning about and accepting foreign lands and peoples. American scientists quickly saw the benefits of working with their colleagues abroad, and many went to study and work in the leading educational and research institutes in Europe. They established a two-way street of interchange, as European natural scientists came to study in the "living laboratory" of the North American continent. American archeologists worked throughout the Middle East, often acquiring in the process an appreciation for the language and culture of the people they met and collaborated with. American medical doctors traveled to Paris and London by the hundreds to acquire the newest skills and techniques.

Some of the greatest and most lasting interchanges took place in the arts. Culture was the one area in which many Americans felt a definite inferiority when dealing with their European cousins. Not surprisingly, therefore, many American artists—painters, architects, sculptors, and writers—spent periods in Europe ranging from a few months to many years. Indeed the leading American painters of the early eighteenth century, such as Benjamin West and John Singleton Copley, spent most of their productive careers studying in Italy and residing in England. The trend continued into the late 1800s, when artists such as James McNeill Whistler and Mary Cassatt left the United States for life abroad. Many American writers followed the same career path. Washington Irving spent nearly a quarter century living abroad, and James Fenimore Cooper worked in Europe for almost ten years. Henry James, considered by some the finest American novelist, left the United States in the 1870s, established permanent residency in England, and became a British citizen before his death. Some, like James, contended that the United States simply did not have the cultural depth to sustain the creative arts. Others were more pragmatic, complaining that the United States did not financially support artists. For many, sojourns to England, France, Italy, and elsewhere were searches for both the creative tradition and the newest styles.

Europe was not the only stop for American artists. Latin America, for example, was a magnet for dozens of painters during the nineteenth century. Such well-known figures as Frederic Church, Louis Mignot, George Catlin, Martin Heade, and Whistler all made trips to Latin America during the 1800s. All were stunned by the natural beauty and colors, and all felt their art was changed by the experience.

In all cases the work of American artists abroad brought foreign lands and peoples into sharper focus for the American public at large. While some of this work no doubt merely repeated the stereotypes and myths prevalent at that time, much of it bridged the gaps between cultures by synthesizing the American and foreign experiences into books, paintings, buildings, and sculptures.

During the nineteenth century the United States was never an island nor a fortress isolated and aloof from the rest of the world. Despite the lack of substantial evidence about the world outside the United States, Americans developed well-defined perceptions of the lands and peoples beyond their shores. Many of these perceptions were born of arrogance and notions of race. As the century progressed, however, Americans found a number of things to admire among foreign cultures, particularly in the fields of art and science. In economic, political, and cultural terms, U.S. participation in the interconnected and interdependent world of the twentieth century began during the nineteenth century.

See also **Class, Social; Foreign Observers; Grand Tour; Literature,** *subentry on* **The Influence of Foreign Literature; Race and Racial Thinking.**

Bibliography

Blumenthal, Henry. *American and French Culture, 1800–1900: Interchanges in Art, Science, Literature, and Society.* Baton Rouge: Louisiana State University Press, 1975.

DeConde, Alexander. *Ethnicity, Race, and American Foreign Policy: A History.* Boston: Northeastern University Press, 1992.

Earnest, Ernest. *Expatriates and Patriots: American Artists, Scholars, and Writers in Europe.* Durham, N.C.: Duke University Press, 1968.

Hunt, Michael H. *Ideology and U.S. Foreign Policy.* New Haven, Conn.: Yale University Press, 1987.

Manthorne, Katherine Emma. *Tropical Renaissance: North American Artists Exploring Latin America, 1839–1879.* Washington, D.C.: Smithsonian Institution Press, 1989.

MICHAEL L. KRENN

FOREIGN RELATIONS

[This entry includes an overview and three subentries on Foreign Relations during the periods 1789-1860, the Civil War, and 1865-1917.]

OVERVIEW

When the French politician and writer Alexis de Tocqueville visited the United States in the 1830s, he saw much to admire in the distinctive political system that was barely a half-century old. In *Democracy in America* he expressed concern, however, about the potential for disaster in the way foreign policy had been conducted in the new Republic:

> Foreign policies demand scarcely any of those qualities which a democracy possesses; and they require, on the contrary, the perfect use of almost all of those faculties in which it is deficient. . . . It cannot combine measures of secrecy, and it will not await their consequences with patience. . . . Democracies . . . obey the impulse of passion rather than the suggestions of prudence . . . and abandon a mature design for the gratification of a momentary caprice.

No democracies had existed in modern times to which Tocqueville could compare the United States. For him and most European observers, that odd nation across the Atlantic Ocean still appeared to be a shaky experiment, attempting to make its way in the world with a cumbersome political structure and some rather unconventional ideas about international relations.

Avoiding Entanglements

When the thirteen colonies revolted in the 1770s, they hoped to sever their ties not only to the British Empire but also to an international system dominated by monarchs who had used the New World as an auxiliary playing field in their lethal games against one another during the previous two centuries. In 1776 the Americans proclaimed their separateness in a "Model Treaty" that would be applied to all international relationships. This treaty foresaw a United States dropping out of the old system, maintaining a distant neutral posture toward European alliances and alignments, and establishing commercial relations with all nations, hopefully in a free-trading world.

The exigencies of the Revolution made it necessary for the Americans to forge an alliance with France in 1778. After the war, the alliance, an unwelcome connection to European broils, turned sour, dramatically affecting the domestic political system and ultimately leading to an undeclared naval war against France (1798–1800). No wonder President George Washington warned the nation against contracting alliances in his 1796 Farewell Address. In part because of that warning, the French alliance was the first and last alliance for the United States until 1942.

The Revolution also necessitated that U.S. untested "militia diplomats" involve themselves in international politics to help secure their nation's independence. This meant becoming involved in unsavory and amoral diplomatic intrigues with the

French, Spanish, British, and others on the way to achieving a decent peace treaty with Great Britain in 1783.

Once liberated, the thirteen colonies tried to retreat to their earlier posture, fearing diplomatic entanglements with Europeans that might be promoted by a strong executive. Under the Articles of Confederation system, John Jay played the role of secretary for foreign affairs, but he had virtually no power to compel the independent states to accept his diplomatic initiatives. Indeed, the incapacity of the new nation to conduct an effective foreign policy under the Articles, especially to negotiate commercial treaties, was one of the main reasons why American leaders realized they needed a new system.

The foreign policy system that the nation's founders built into the federal Constitution still did not resemble the systems prevalent in Europe at the time. Distrustful of a strong executive who might too easily involve the United States in foreign ventures, the delegates to the Constitutional Convention (1787) divided responsibility for foreign affairs between the executive and legislative branches of the new federal government. The president was the commander in chief of the armed forces, but Congress declared war. The president appointed diplomats, but the Senate had to confirm them. The president could negotiate treaties, but the Senate had to approve them by a two-thirds vote. These seemingly unwieldy arrangements concerned Tocqueville and would continue to concern America's diplomatic partners throughout U.S. history.

The European Challenge

Fortunately for the United States, its oceanic barriers and relatively modest power precluded it from becoming intimately involved with European power politics, even had it wanted to do so. Throughout much of the nineteenth century, the United States was a backwater as well as a pariah republican nation. As late as the 1880s, Turkey could close up its legation in the United States in an effort to economize since so little that mattered in the Eurocentric great-power system occurred in Washington. In fact, for more than one hundred years the European powers refused to exchange diplomats at the ambassadorial level with the United States and instead exchanged ministers, a lesser rank. To be sure, Americans contended that this did not bother them since the diplomatic code mandated that ambassadors be accredited by monarchs to the courts of other sovereigns. Yet in the 1890s, when the United States was finally "granted" membership in the great-power club and the Europeans began to exchange ambassadors with the country, few Americans complained.

While the literal and figurative distance of the United States from Europe through most of the nineteenth century meant that the Republic would have little impact on European affairs, those distances also played the major role in affording protection to a weak, unpopular, and even revolutionary nation from physical attack from its enemies. Time and time again, when it appeared that European powers, either alone or in concert, were prepared to crush the upstart United States once and for all, the logistical difficulties involved in sending an invasion and occupation force across the Atlantic proved insurmountable.

Thus it was that the British, fresh from a triumph over Napoleon Bonaparte's French forces in 1814, decided against launching a full-scale invasion of the United States in order to win the War of 1812. Similarly, in 1823 no European powers were willing to return militarily the rhetorical shot across their bows fired by President James Monroe in his famous pronouncement—the Monroe Doctrine—warning them to stay out of his hemisphere. Comparable logistical considerations weighed heavily on the British when they compromised over the Maine boundary dispute in the Webster-Ashburton Treaty (1842) and the Oregon dispute in 1846, and when they and the French refrained from intervening in the Mexican-American War and the American Civil War, even though they were sorely tempted to do so. By the time that the Spanish king Alfonso XIII asked his fellow European monarchs for support in his conflict with the United States over Cuba in 1898, Washington not only was an ocean away but had become a formidable power.

Controlling the seas, Great Britain was the only nation capable of mounting a serious threat to the United States in the nineteenth century. Fortunately for the United States, during much of the century its general international and political orientations often paralleled those of the British. Even so, most of Washington's major diplomatic crises in the nineteenth century involved London. Serious problems dealing with boundaries, fisheries, and economic relations were left over from the peace treaty of 1783. The last major Anglo-American boundary problem was not settled until 1903, while conflicts over fishing off the coast of British North America that sometimes erupted into miniature naval wars were not settled until later in the twentieth century. During those crises, however, except during the War of 1812, Americans were spared having to confront the world's only superpower because the British had to deal with more dangerous crises relating to the defense of their global empire.

When in 1895 the proud British decided to accept Secretary of State Richard Olney's rhetorical effrontery during the Venezuelan border dispute, they finally reached the conclusion that the United States was supreme in its hemisphere and that it was best to try to cooperate with Washington while dealing with the threats posed to British interests by the rise of Germany on the Continent. During the last twenty years before World War I, American and British elites constructed a "great rapprochement," which by 1914 made it unthinkable that the United States would become involved militarily on the side of London's enemies. Indicative of the new relationship was President Theodore Roosevelt's mediation during the Russo-Japanese War (1904–1905) and during the Moroccan crisis (1906), when he adopted positions favorable to the British.

Becoming a Great Power

By the time of the great rapprochement the United States had achieved great-power status and was recognized as potentially the strongest nation in the world. The United States had achieved this status in good measure through the economic and geopolitical power gained from its relentless territorial expansion. Between President Thomas Jefferson's Louisiana Purchase in 1803 and the acquisition in 1898 under President William McKinley of extracontinental empire after the Spanish-American War, the United States had filled out the continent and expanded politically and economically beyond its natural boundaries. Some of this expansion came through war, first in century-long conflicts with Native Americans, who sometimes refused to yield to American settlers moving west, and then in a war with the Mexicans (1846–1848) that secured California, Texas, and the Southwest. In addition, during the years between the Civil War and World War I, the United States bought Alaska (1867), acquired Guam and Puerto Rico (1898), annexed Hawaii (1898), crushed an independence movement in the Philippines (1898–1902), intervened in several Central American states to establish or maintain protectorates, and acquired the Virgin Islands (1916). It is interesting to note that historians generally consider John Quincy Adams (1817–1825), William Seward (1861–1869), and John Hay (1898–1905) the three greatest secretaries of state of the nineteenth century; all three were notable expansionists.

Much of American expansion involved an ugly imperialism, which some labeled "Manifest Destiny." The term, which had originated in the writings of the editor John L. O'Sullivan in the 1840s, suggested that the United States was on a divine mission to spread its democratic system throughout North America and perhaps beyond. Manifest Destiny was buttressed by a racist claim that Americans of European ancestry were superior to the original inhabitants who, if they did not submit peacefully, would have to be forcefully moved aside to make way for Christian civilization.

Behind rhetorical arguments about uplifting the heathen lay cold-blooded economic calculations. While the United States tried to maintain political isolation from the rest of the world, it was eager from the start of its independent existence to expand economically. Whether it involved control of California ports in the 1840s, the purchase of Alaska in 1867, or taking the Philippines in 1898, a good deal of American economic expansion revolved around Asia, especially the allegedly limitless China market. When Secretary of State John Hay announced his Open Door policy in 1899–1900, lobbing another rhetorical grenade like the Monroe Doctrine, he was merely making explicit a principle Americans had been promoting ever since they sent the *Empress of China* on a trade mission to the Orient in 1784. That the Open Door was more concerned with trade than with the Chinese themselves is reflected in the Chinese Exclusion Act (1882), which made citizens of China the only foreigners barred because of nationality from immigrating to the United States.

Throughout the entire world, Americans hoped to break down barriers to their ability to trade freely. The issue of foreign trade became central to American economic health after several recessions rocked the nation during the last quarter of the century, topped by the greatest depression of all in the period 1893–1895. American politicians, businesspeople, and opinion makers agreed that the economic crises had been caused by overproduction. The solution was to find new markets abroad, a solution that brought them into direct competition with Europeans, who controlled much of the world's raw materials and markets in their vast colonial empires.

Peace and War

Americans pursued an aggressive economic and diplomatic agenda without the force necessary to support their tough rhetoric. Suspicious of a professional military and penurious when it came to government expenditures, the United States tended to speak loudly but carry few sticks. Throughout the nineteenth century and into the twentieth century up to World War II, the United States in peacetime maintained a feeble professional military establishment, with the exception of the powerful new navy, the Great White Fleet, that it began building in the 1890s.

This lack of emphasis on military preparedness was, in part, a reflection of the nation's relative impregnability behind its oceanic barriers, but it also had to do with the success enjoyed by America's volunteer forces against the British professional militia during the Revolution. When the United States fought England to a standstill in 1814 (although had it been better prepared it could have occupied Canada) and then easily dispatched Mexico in 1848 and Spain in 1898, it demonstrated once again the effectiveness of its nondefense policy. Of course the United States had escaped defeat by Britain in the War of 1812 principally because the stronger British were involved in a world war against Napoleon at the time, and the Mexicans and Spanish, even with their professional cadres of well-trained soldiers, were not significant military powers.

Congress declared war in each of America's three major nineteenth-century wars and, in the case of the first two, did so only after rather contentious debates. However, the fact that Presidents James Knox Polk and William McKinley were commanders in chief of the armed forces who placed American soldiers and sailors in harm's way in 1846 and 1898 had a good deal to do with the reason Congress accepted their requests for war. One could also make the case that President Woodrow Wilson's neutrality policies during World War I compelled Germany to take actions that forced Congress to declare war in 1917. In addition, as commanders in chief, during the nineteenth century presidents sent military forces into action without formal consent from Congress on more than one hundred occasions, including the undeclared naval war with France, skirmishes with the Barbary States of North Africa during the same period, scores of "wars" with Native Americans, and interventions in Central America.

During the nation's diplomatic crises and wars, ethnic groups with ties to their homelands sometimes tried to intervene in the policy debate. Few other nations during the nineteenth century had to contend with the problem posed by a situation in which a large percentage of the population maintained emotional and even political ties to former homelands. The most prominent such group in the nineteenth century was the Irish Americans, who bore a strong resentment against the British. At times politicians twisted the British Lion's tail in an attempt to appeal to that growing political lobby in ways that were not necessarily in the national security interests of the nation as a whole. Irish American Fenians launched attacks on Canada on several occasions just after the Civil War in an attempt to start a British-American war to free Ireland, and Irish Americans affected the outcome of the election of 1888, when they voted for the Republicans because the British minister supported the Democrats. Not surprisingly, among the significant minority of Americans who opposed war against Germany in 1917 were German Americans, Irish Americans, and Scandinavian and Jewish Americans who bore an animus to Germany's foe Russia, which they perceived as their enemy.

Neither problems with the loyalties of ethnic minorities nor the nation's unique and often awkward diplomatic apparatus and processes dramatically affected U.S. ability to protect itself against enemies. After making it through a wide variety of crises and several wars throughout the nineteenth century with a solid record of diplomatic and military victories, with the exception of the standoff in the War of 1812, the United States stood poised to claim its self-perceived god-given position as the most powerful nation in the world, convinced of its destiny to lead others toward democracy and a free-market economic system.

See also **Diplomatic Corps; Europe, Foreign Relations with; Great Britain, Foreign Relations with; Mexican War; Monroe Doctrine; Overseas Possessions; South America, Foreign Relations with; Spanish-American War.**

Bibliography

Bourne, Kenneth. *Britain and the Balance of Power in North America.* Berkeley: University of California Press, 1967.

DeConde, Alexander. *Ethnicity, Race, and American Foreign Policy: A History.* Boston: Northeastern University Press, 1992.

Hunt, Michael H. *Ideology and U.S. Foreign Policy.* New Haven, Conn.: Yale University Press, 1987.

LaFeber, Walter. *The American Search for Opportunity, 1865–1913.* Volume 2 of *The Cambridge History of American Foreign Relations.* New York: Cambridge University Press, 1993.

Langley, Lester D. *America and the Americas.* Athens, Ga.: University of Georgia Press, 1989.

Perkins, Bradford. *The Creation of a Republican Empire, 1776–1865.* Volume 1 of *The Cambridge History of American Foreign Relations.* New York: Cambridge University Press, 1993.

Perkins, Dexter. *A History of the Monroe Doctrine.* Boston: Houghton Mifflin, 1963.

Small, Melvin. *Was War Necessary? National Security and U.S. Entry into War.* Beverly Hills, Calif.: Sage, 1980.

Sofaer, Abraham D. *War, Foreign Affairs, and Constitutional Power.* Cambridge, Mass.: Ballinger, 1976.

Williams, William A. *The Tragedy of American Diplomacy.* New York: Dell, 1972.

MELVIN SMALL

1789–1860

In 1789 the First Congress created the Department of State to oversee the foreign relations of the United States. That year President George Washington nominated his first ministers to the major powers.

After Independence

One of the initial problems the United States confronted centered on its treaty of alliance with France, which had originated in the American Revolution. The revolutionary French republic found itself at war with much of the rest of Europe and called upon its American ally to come to its assistance. President Washington responded with a proclamation of neutrality, effectively abrogating the treaty of alliance.

Concerns lingered regarding the peace treaty that ended the American Revolution—the Treaty of Paris (1783)—because of mutual violations by the United States and Great Britain and because of conflicts over the rights of neutrals. The latter concern was of growing importance as the Anglo-French struggles resumed at sea. Although much criticized, Jay's Treaty (1794) accomplished the British evacuation of the Northwest Territory, which had been ceded to the United States.

Meanwhile, the American envoy Thomas Pinckney pursued negotiations with the Spanish government concerning the borders of Florida and Louisiana and the right of deposit and transit for Americans in the port of New Orleans. These points were satisfactorily resolved by Pinckney's Treaty (1795). The last years of Federalist rule saw a serious deterioration in Franco-American relations. The XYZ affair, wherein representatives of France demanded a loan from the United States for France (actually a bribe to the French ministers) and an apology from President John Adams for some allegedly hostile references to France in a speech, produced a virulent reaction in the United States. From 1798 to 1800 the United States conducted a quasi war with France. This undeclared naval conflict, during which the United States captured ninety French vessels, opened the way for productive negotiations with the French. By a treaty in 1800 France recognized the abrogation of the treaty of alliance of 1778 and promised to respect neutrality rights and to reciprocally open its seaports to U.S. shipping.

By 1803 Franco-American relations had undergone serious changes. As part of his design to create a New World empire, Napoleon had attempted to suppress a Haitian slave revolt but failed. After the Spanish retrocession of Louisiana to France, the United States became urgently concerned with the possibility of a Napoleonic army on its land borders. Even the nor-mally Francophile president Thomas Jefferson, in a letter to Napoleon, threatened to enter into an alliance with Britain if French troops were placed in Louisiana. In 1803, discouraged by his failure to reconquer Saint Domingue (Haiti), Napoleon sold to the United States the massive Louisiana Territory for $15 million, an acquisition that effectively doubled the domain of the United States.

In 1810, with revolts in Spanish America against the Napoleonic usurpation of the Spanish throne spreading, the population of Western Florida declared independence and requested annexation by the United States. During 1810 and 1811, President James Madison authorized the U.S. governor of the Louisiana Territory, William C. C. Claiborne, to occupy West Florida from the Mississippi River to the Perdido River.

The War of 1812

A great acquisition of territory was contemplated by American statesmen as they declared war on Britain in 1812. The nominal cause of the war was the British practice of impressment of U.S. seamen and other interferences with the rights of neutrals. Of the numerous incidents of provocation, the most famous had occurred in 1807 with the firing upon and boarding of the USS *Chesapeake* in American waters. This led to President Jefferson's use of the Nonintercourse Act and his establishment of a general embargo on overseas shipping in an attempt to force Anglo-French respect for neutral rights. When Napoleon pretended to exempt U.S. ships from his Continental system, additional opprobrium attached to Britain, which refused to repeal its Orders in Council.

The drive for a declaration of war on Britain was fueled in large part by the desire to annex Canada (for the expansion of the northern states) and Florida (and possibly Texas, for the expansion of the southern states). The war did not ultimately go well for the United States. The Spanish Empire remained neutral, and the U.S. Army was driven from Canada. By sheer diplomatic skill John Quincy Adams, who headed the American deputation to the peace negotiations, obtained a status quo ante peace in the Treaty of Ghent (1814), restoring the prewar territorial conditions.

In the Rush-Bagot Agreement (1817) the United States and Britain agreed to the virtual naval disarmament of Lake Champlain and the Great Lakes, and in a boundary treaty in 1818 both nations agreed to a joint occupation of the Oregon Territory, which included the present-day states of Washington and Oregon and province of British Columbia. Also the specifics of the open fisheries rights that had been

The Birth of the Monroe Doctrine. President James Monroe *(standing)* and John Quincy Adams *(seated, at left)* are depicted in what is probably one of the Cabinet meetings in November 1823 when the policy was formulated. From a painting by Deland, 1912. © BETTMANN/CORBIS

promised to Americans in the Treaty of Paris were worked out to mutual satisfaction.

Spanish Florida presented continual problems for the United States. West Florida blocked the access by much of the United States to the Gulf of Mexico. Even though the United States occupied West Florida in 1810, the remainder of Spanish Florida was still vexing because pirates operated from its islands, fugitive slaves fled into the colony, and hostile American Indian tribes utilized it as a sanctuary from which to attack.

During the War of 1812, General Andrew Jackson led an expedition into Florida in pursuit of retreating Creek Indians. Secretary of State John Quincy Adams eventually issued an ultimatum to Spain, demanding that it either station sufficient forces within Florida to maintain order or cede the colony to the United States. In 1819 the Adams-Onís Treaty, often called the Transcontinental Treaty, settled a series of issues between Spain and the United States. Florida was ceded to the United States, and the United States agreed to pay the claims of its citizens against

the Spanish government, not to exceed $5 million. Spain relinquished its claims to the Pacific Northwest, as the United States did its claims on Texas. The borders between Spanish territory and the vast Louisiana Territory were finally delineated.

Monroe Doctrine

By 1823 the mainland Spanish colonies in the New World and Portuguese Brazil were in revolt, attempting to maintain their independence against reconquest. The United States had maintained a strict neutrality in this struggle, but a threatened pro-Spanish intervention by the Quadruple Alliance of Russia, Prussia, Austria, and France created anxiety. The United States was concerned about its trade and security, and Britain was worried about the potential loss of its Latin American markets, which had flourished in the absence of mercantilistic regulation. George Canning, the British foreign secretary, proposed to John Quincy Adams, then secretary of state, that the United States and Britain issue a joint declaration against the policy of the Quadruple Alliance.

Adams, partly motivated by nationalistic considerations and partly out of fear concerning British intentions toward Cuba, recommended to President James Monroe that he unilaterally issue a U.S. declaration. Despite the U.S. repudiation in the Monroe Doctrine of a virtual alliance with Britain, the willingness of Britain to use its naval power against the reconquest of Latin America solidified the doctrine.

Later, the no-colonization policy of the United States led to confrontations and contentions with various European powers. In the early 1840s Secretary of State Daniel Webster persuaded Britain not to confirm the protectorate over the Sandwich Islands (Hawaii) proposed by the British consul in the islands, and in 1851 the United States vigorously opposed French intervention in Hawaii. Under President Franklin Pierce, the United States negotiated a treaty of annexation with the royal Hawaiian government, but the U.S. Senate rejected the treaty, in part because of a section in the Hawaiian constitution forbidding slavery.

Interest in an interoceanic canal combined with the standard no-colonization position of U.S. foreign policy prompted the United States to seek an understanding with Britain over Central America. By the Clayton-Bulwer Treaty (1850) Britain gave up its claims to the Mosquito Coast of Nicaragua, and the United States and Britain agreed that any canal connecting the Atlantic and the Pacific would be a joint Anglo-American undertaking.

Dealings with Canada

Concerns with Canada quite naturally occupied much of U.S. foreign policy. Problems with the border led to a number of treaties, the most important of which was the Webster-Ashburton Treaty (1842), which ended the Aroostock War between competing Canadian and American lumberjacks in the disputed borderlands of New Brunswick and Maine.

More serious was the dispute over the Oregon Territory, which had originally been claimed by the United States, Britain, Russia, and Spain. By 1818 Britain and the United States had arranged an informal condominium. Increased population and commercial activity made the continuation of this arrangement untenable, however, and President James K. Polk campaigned for office in 1844 on a platform of asserting unqualified U.S. ownership of the entire territory. Once in office Polk found it prudent to settle for a division of the territory along the forty-ninth parallel.

During the Canadian rebellion of 1837–1838 serious difficulties developed in Anglo-American relations. Irish Americans set up camps along the Canadian border, where they armed and trained for intervention in that rebellion. Britain protested this activity to Washington, but before any U.S. action was undertaken, Canadian forces struck across the Niagara frontier into New York State, burning several of these camps in an international incident known as the *Caroline* affair. War was averted, but in 1842 Secretary of State Webster sent a note of protest that is held to be a model statement of the rights and duties of neutrals. An agreement in the Canadian Reciprocity Treaty (1854), which remained in effect until 1865, decided issues concerning the navigation of the St. Lawrence River and Lake Michigan and trade relations.

Relations with Mexico

Relations with Mexico also absorbed considerable U.S. diplomatic energy. Large numbers of Americans moved into Texas to ranch and farm under Mexican authority. Conflicts quickly arose, however, especially over slavery, which was illegal in Mexico but existed de facto in Texas. In addition the Americans bridled under the dictatorship of President Antonio López de Santa Anna and the increased centralization that was destroying the traditional self-government of the provinces. On 2 March 1836 the province of Texas declared its independence from the Republic of Mexico.

The sympathies of Americans were largely on the side of their countrymen in Texas, but the administration of President Andrew Jackson observed a strict neutrality. Nevertheless many Americans volunteered to aid the Texas rebels. At the Battle of San Jacinto in 1836, Santa Anna was captured and forced to agree to the independence of Texas. The United States moved at once to grant diplomatic recognition, but the U.S. government declined the Texas proposal for annexation. In the last days of his administration, President John Tyler invited Texas to become a state under a joint resolution of Congress, in part motivated by a fear of Texas seeking alliance with Britain or France.

Mexico had never officially recognized the independence of Texas, and to make matters worse, the boundaries of Texas were uncertain. President Polk, taking advantage of this ambiguity, sent U.S. troops into the region claimed by both nations, sparking a violent confrontation. On 13 May 1846 Congress declared war on Mexico. Military operations by U.S. forces captured all Mexican lands above the Rio Grande, including the territories of California and New Mexico. When Mexico failed to sue for peace, U.S. military forces were dispatched to capture Mexico City. In 1848 the Treaty of Guadalupe Hidalgo granted the United States all the lands above a line following the Rio Grande and the Gila River and the provincial border between Upper and Lower California. In addition the United States assumed the debt of claims owed by Mexico to U.S. citizens and paid $15 million to Mexico for the transfer of the territories. In 1853 the Gadsden Purchase completed the U.S. acquisition of contiguous territory. For $10 million the United States acquired a strip of land between the Rio Grande and the Colorado River to be used for a southern railroad route.

The Problem of Slavery

In 1854 the obsession of many Americans regarding Cuba revealed itself in the Ostend Manifesto, a secret report to the U.S. secretary of state from several of the most important U.S. diplomats in Europe that was made public. The manifesto claimed that the United States had a right to possess Cuba, which would also benefit from the transfer. If Spain refused to sell Cuba, the United States would be justified in seizing it if conditions on the island endangered the security of the Union. American concern with Cuba arose from several sources. Cuba offered an area for the expansion of slavery, and several of its harbors could offer a threat to the southern coasts of the United States, which lacked superior naval harbors, if the island passed into the possession of a significant naval power. No further serious efforts were pursued in acquiring Cuba during the antebellum period.

A recurring problem in foreign policy involved slavery and the slave trade. Fugitive slaves from the United States often sought refuge in Canada, where officials would refuse rendition. The United States outlawed the international slave trade in 1808, but the U.S. Navy lacked the resources to enforce effectively the ban. The Royal Navy was the chief instrument of the ban, but the United States refused to grant rights to Britain to visit ships of U.S. registry. Consequently many slavers illicitly flew the Stars and Stripes as a way around British antislaver patrols. After the abolition of slavery throughout the British Empire in 1833, problems arose when U.S. ships bearing slaves in the coastal trade were forced by storms into British ports in Bermuda, the Bahamas, and the British West Indies. British officials freed the slaves as contraband within British waters.

This source of tension in Anglo-American relations was exacerbated by the incident of the *Creole* in 1842, when slaves on that ship mutinied and the ship strayed into British waters. British authorities refused extradition or rendition of the mutineers and instead freed the slaves. In the Webster-Ashburton Treaty (1842), Britain pledged to avoid "officious" interference with U.S. slaves brought into British waters or ports by storm or violence. The United States, for its part, promised to keep a squadron off the Atlantic coast of Africa to help enforce the ban on the international slave trade.

In 1856 the U.S. Congress passed the unusual Guano Islands Act, which authorized the president to take possession of any uninhabited, unclaimed island rich in guano deposits. Guano was desperately needed, especially in the southern states, where the continual cultivation of cotton had exhausted the soil. Dozens of islands in the Caribbean, the Atlantic, and the Pacific were annexed under this law, including Baker and Jarvis Islands.

The Far East

China and Japan attracted the interest of the United States. As a beginning, the Anglo-Chinese Opium Wars opened China to Britain's commerce. In 1844 the Treaty of Wanghia opened five ports to U.S. merchant ships and granted extraterritoriality, the right to be tried by one's own courts, to U.S. citizens in China. The United States led efforts to open Japan to the world. American sailors were sometimes stranded in Japan by shipwreck, and they complained of maltreatment. Commodore Matthew Perry visited Japan in 1853 and 1854 and delivered a letter from President Millard Fillmore to the Japanese emperor. The government of the shogun, officially the head of the military but actually the de facto ruler of Japan, opened two ports to American ships for coaling and revictualing stations, promised humane treatment for shipwrecked American sailors, and granted most favored nation status to the United States, guaranteeing to Americans any rights subsequently granted to citizens of other powers.

In the Far East, the United States did not desire to acquire territory but was interested in commercial opportunities. U.S. policy opposed breaking China into European colonies or into spheres of influence in informal empire. U.S. policy in the case of China and Japan essentially fitted in with British policy, which, despite the acquisition of Hong Kong, opposed the partition of China and Japan. As early as the 1850s U.S. policy on China already anticipated what became known as the open door policy in the 1890s. The dream of seemingly limitless markets in the Orient stirred the imaginations of U.S. statesmen and helped forge practical policies that served American interests as the United States evolved into a world power.

See also **Canada; Cuba; Expansion; Florida; Foreign Trade and Tariffs,** *subentry on* **Trade and Tariffs; Gadsden Purchase; Louisiana Purchase; Mexican War; Monroe Doctrine; Oregon; Presidency,** *subentries on*

1801–1829, 1829–1849, 1849–1861; Slavery, *subentry on* African Slave Trade; War of 1812.

Bibliography

Hickey, Donald R. *The War of 1812: A Forgotten Conflict*. Urbana: University of Illinois Press, 1989.

Horsman, Reginald. *The Causes of the War of 1812*. Philadelphia: University of Pennsylvania Press, 1962.

Pratt, Julius W., Vincent P. DeSantis, and Joseph M. Siracusa. *A History of United States Foreign Policy*. 4th ed. Englewood Cliffs, N.J.: Prentice-Hall, 1980.

PATRICK M. O'NEIL

THE CIVIL WAR

When hostilities erupted between the United States and the Confederacy in April 1861, one of the most critical issues facing the leaders on both sides was the possible reaction of the European powers, especially Great Britain. Abraham Lincoln and his secretary of state, William H. Seward (1801–1872), understood that much as the bid for independence by the English colonies at the end of the eighteenth century had depended on the intervention of France, so too could the interference of Britain or France in the present conflict effect a permanent fracturing of the Union. While the specter of foreign engagement caused the Lincoln administration to devote itself to the characterization of the conflict as an internal struggle, its southern counterpart, the Confederate administration of Jefferson Davis (1808–1889), worked to draw the Europeans in, pressing London and Paris for diplomatic recognition. To achieve these disparate ends, the North relied on the threat of war against meddling Europeans, and the South depended on Europe's hunger for southern cotton. Conspicuously absent from the machinations of both sides was the root cause of the war, slavery. Neither appeared anxious to raise the issue and only belatedly applied it to their diplomatic efforts.

At the onset of war Lincoln and Seward defined the conflict as an insurrection and thus of domestic concern only. Its prosecution had nothing to do with slavery but rather with preserving the Union. Both of these assertions complicated the Northern goal of keeping the Europeans out. On 19 April 1861 Lincoln announced a naval blockade of the thirty-five-hundred-mile southern coastline. Under international law a blockade could be imposed only against a belligerent. This called into question the domestic nature of the conflict, elevated the Confederacy to a level beyond insurrection, and made it possible for other nations to consider recognition. When Britain declared neutrality, merely affirming the belligerent status of the South, tension rose between Washington and London that would continue for the better part of two years. Had Lincoln consulted with international law experts before issuing his proclamation, he likely would have used different terminology and thus avoided some diplomatic difficulties.

Lincoln's desire to keep the slave-holding border states in the Union and not liberation cost him the high road with Britain in particular. The Crown had abolished slavery by the 1830s and would have found it difficult to consider supporting an independence movement likely to guarantee its survival in North America. Lincoln removed this impediment and allowed British advocates of the South to press for acceptance of the Confederacy on the aseptic grounds of British interests.

When Davis dispatched commissioners to the European capitals, promising the uninterrupted flow of cotton, free trade, and a tacit invitation to the expansion of European power in the western hemisphere, they found a receptive audience. Unfortunately for the Confederacy, however, the lure of "King Cotton" was not as great as had been anticipated. A bumper crop just before the war had produced a glut in the warehouses of the textile districts of Britain: a slowdown at the beginning of the war would actually be a help rather than a hindrance to the industry. By the time the so-called cotton famine was felt in Europe, textile interests were cultivating alternative sources in Egypt and India, cotton confiscated by Union forces had been injected into the market, and the critical moment when the pressure might have won recognition had passed.

Meanwhile, the North nearly did for the South what its own diplomatic efforts had failed to do—produce British intervention. In October 1861 two southern diplomats, James Mason (1798–1871) and John Slidell (1793–1871) slipped through the Union blockade at Charleston on their way to London and Paris, respectively. In Havana the two transferred to the British steamer *Trent* for passage to Europe. When they left Cuba in early November, the *Trent* was stopped by the USS *San Jacinto*, boarded by a detachment of marines, and the two southern envoys were seized, all actions in clear violation of British rights. In Washington the public, hungry for something to cheer about after the chronic battlefield setbacks that had thus far characterized Union efforts, hailed Captain Charles Wilkes (1798–1877) a conquering hero. The British were appalled, talked of war, watched as the market plunged, and proceeded to deploy eleven thousand troops to Canada, pointedly boarding for the trip to the tune of "Dixie."

The able American minister to London, Charles Francis Adams (1807–1886), was equally stunned at

The Confederacy Woos Europe. A political cartoon depicts Jefferson Davis soliciting aid from France and England, 1861. Davis *(right)* offers bonds and cotton to Napoleon III, which the French ruler refuses to accept. Queen Victoria *(center)* brandishes her 13 May 1861 proclamation of neutrality. LIBRARY OF CONGRESS: PRINTS AND PHOTOGRAPHS DIVISION

the ramifications of a needless incident that jeopardized his best efforts to keep Britain clear of the American conflict. British Prime Minister Lord Palmerston's (1784–1865) cabinet, including the seasoned Lord John Russell (1792–1878) at the Foreign Office, recommended that Adams's counterpart in Washington, Lord Richard Lyons (1817–1887), demand reparations: the immediate release of Mason and Slidell, and a formal apology for the affront to British rights and honor. These demands carried an ultimatum of seven days. Fortunately for Anglo-American peace, the transatlantic cable connection was down, delaying the missive's transmission. This delay allowed passions to cool on both sides and provided an opening for the intercession of Queen Victoria's Consort, Prince Albert. From what soon became his death bed, Albert softened the ultimatum before it left England. Perhaps Wilkes had been mistaken, or had acted outside his authority. Rather than demand an apology, Lyons should merely seek an explanation. By the time Lyons delivered the revised communiqué to Seward, such influential Americans as Charles Sumner (1811–1874), chairman of the Senate Foreign Relations Committee, pushed on the American side for a remedy that closely resem-

bled Prince Albert's. Lincoln, pragmatically conceding the folly of tempting war with Britain, quietly released Mason and Slidell and sent them on their way. Seward could not resist, however, straining to portray the admission of error as an overdue acceptance by the British of longstanding American views on impressment and the rights of neutrals.

While the *Trent* affair escalated into a war crisis, Adams had watched with growing concern as British shipbuilders found profit in the construction of a Confederate navy. James Bulloch (1823–1901), head of the Confederate Secret Service in Europe, exploited a vagary in British law to contract with British shipbuilders. According to the letter of the law, ships intended to engage nations at peace with Britain could not be fitted out or armed within British jurisdiction. Bulloch simply had the ships fitted out after they had cleared port. The two most famous, the *Florida* and the *Alabama*, together took over one hundred prizes. Before the war ended many northern merchants could not stand the loss or afford the insurance to continue to engage in international commerce. Despite the objections of Adams, Bulloch continued to manipulate the system until 1863 when he was finally frustrated in his effort to launch steam-powered ironclad rams. By then the acerbic protests of Adams and the acquiescence by the Palmerston government to the likely failure of the South converged to prompt Lord Russell to seize the rams and secure them for British service.

As the war progressed from months to years and the rate of bloodshed rose to staggering dimensions, pressure mounted on the British government to end the carnage. Early in the war Napoleon III (1808–1873) of France had suggested joint mediation. But a bold commitment to the revival of France's former glory that involved a scheme to convert the frail Mexican Republic into a French satellite, an unwieldy political opposition at home to palliate, and Italians talking unification mitigated against any ac-

tion in the American contest that did not include Britain. Palmerston had adopted a posture of watchful waiting to determine whether the South was indeed capable of victory. In early 1862 Union battlefield successes seemed to confirm the prudence of this policy.

That fall, however, Confederate General Robert E. Lee's (1807–1870) Army of Northern Virginia crossed into Maryland, reviving talk among Palmerston's cabinet members of joining France to mediate a conclusion to the conflict. The cotton slowdown, made worse by the Confederacy's calculated destruction of thousands of bales, had finally taken a toll. Unemployed textile workers joined with southern sympathizers to push for relief. Virtually every in-

The Union Warns Off Europe. While plucking cotton, John Bull is collared by a Union soldier—Uncle Sam—who warns: "John, you lost your non-interfering principle. I'll lay it on your back again." Napoleon III is depicted as a rooster. African American faces are hidden in the cotton plants. Cartoon by E. Stauch, 1861. LIBRARY OF CONGRESS: PRINTS AND PHOTOGRAPHS DIVISION

terest of Britain, whether humane or commercial, urged some type of action. With Lee on the offensive, perhaps the time was right. But then, in early October 1862, word circulated through Europe that Lee's advance had been repelled at Antietam Creek. Palmerston reverted to continued waiting.

After Antietam, Lincoln determined to end any prospect of support for the South by announcing his intention to emancipate all slaves in the rebellious states on 1 January 1863. This, he believed, would channel the antislavery elements toward support for the noble crusade of the Union. Once again, however, Lincoln's means ran at cross purposes with his ends. Abolitionists on both sides of the Atlantic criticized the proclamation for its timidity, complaining that Lincoln had shrewdly avoided freeing the slaves in the border states and areas actually under his control. In Britain, supporters of the Confederacy decried the Emancipation Proclamation as an act of desperation by the Lincoln administration designed to incite a slave rebellion and race war. The British press echoed the charges, accusing Lincoln of stirring slaves to murder their masters' families. Contrary to Lincoln's hopes for ending talk of intervention, the Emancipation Proclamation had actually revived it.

Palmerston's cabinet deliberated the question of intervention through the remainder of 1862. Chancellor of the Exchequer William Gladstone (1809–1898) pressed for intervention. Secretary of War George Cornewall Lewis (1806–1863) joined with Palmerston to push for a temporary end to the fighting to allow for a mediated settlement. Lord Russell, bolstered by renewed efforts by Napoleon III, who suggested a halt in hostilities for a period of six months and a suspension of the blockade, argued for action. But in the end Lewis made the more compelling argument. Dismissing Napoleon's input with a reminder of France's grand designs in Mexico, he cautioned against the hazards inherent in determining the point at which a rebellious people had proved their nationhood and raised practical queries concerning the actual form and substance of any action that Britain might take.

One last gasp in Confederate diplomacy occurred late in the war as southern reverses on the battlefield mounted and Union victory appeared imminent. Ironically, it hinged on an effort by Davis to win European support through his own emancipation pledge. In 1864 Davis sent Duncan Kenner (1813–1887), a Louisiana politico who had advocated freeing the slaves earlier in the war, to Europe to instruct Mason and Slidell to offer emancipation of the slaves in exchange for British and French recognition. At this juncture neither Napoleon nor Palmerston exhibited interest in the proposal. In fact, Palmerston

intimated that the inability of the South to prove its independence remained the reason for nonrecognition, not slavery. Within a month the subject was moot with the surrender of Lee to Ulysses S. Grant (1822–1885) at Appomattox Court House.

Despite the appeal of cotton, the benefits likely to accrue to Britain from a divided and weakened United States, and the errant steps of the Lincoln administration, Britain and hence Europe had rejected intervention. When European leaders assessed the ledger, they found a pro-Union Russia opposed to intervention and distracted by problems with its Polish subjects; Napoleon III calling for mediation but diluting his likely contribution through adventures in both hemispheres; and Britain attached to Union wheat, goodwill, and, gradually, the hopes that real liberation might yet evolve from Lincoln's tepid move toward emancipation. These factors colluded with the failure of King Cotton on the diplomatic front and Lee's generals on the military front to stay intervention. Although the battlefield determined the ultimate outcome of the Civil War, there is little doubt that a different decision on the part of either France or Britain could have produced considerably different results.

See also **Civil War,** *subentries on* **Causes of the Civil War, Battles and Combatants; Confederate States of America; Emancipation; Europe, Foreign Relations with; Great Britain, Foreign Relations with; Slavery,** *subentry on* **Defense of Slavery.**

Bibliography

Adams, Ephraim Douglas. *Great Britain and the American Civil War.* 2 vols. New York: Longmans, Green and Co., 1925.

Case, Lynn M., and Warren F. Spencer. *The United States and France: Civil War Diplomacy.* Philadelphia: University of Pennsylvania Press, 1970.

Crook, David P. *Diplomacy during the American Civil War.* New York: John Wiley and Sons, 1975.

Ferris, Norman B. *Desperate Diplomacy: William H. Seward's Foreign Policy, 1861.* Knoxville: University of Tennessee Press, 1976.

Jenkins, Brian. *Britain and the War for the Union.* 2 vols. Montreal: McGill-Queens University Press, 1974, 1980.

Jones, Howard. *Union in Peril: The Crisis over British Intervention in the Civil War.* Chapel Hill: University of North Carolina Press, 1992.

Monaghan, Jay. *Diplomat in Carpet Slippers: Abraham Lincoln Deals with Foreign Affairs.* New York: Bobbs-Merrill Company, 1945.

Owsley, Frank Lawrence. *King Cotton Diplomacy: Foreign Relations of the Confederate States of America.* 2d ed., revised by Harriet Chappell Owsley. Chicago: University of Chicago Press, 1959. The original edition was published in 1931.

Warren, Gordon H. *Fountain of Discontent: The Trent Affair and Freedom of the Seas.* Boston: Northeastern University Press, 1981.

DONALD RAKESTRAW

1865–1917

From the end of the Civil War to the outbreak of World War I, American foreign policy moved from relative isolation to acceptance of the responsibilities attendant upon being a world power with overseas obligations. The process by which the United States evolved from its traditional aloofness in world affairs to playing a major role in international diplomacy began slowly in the late 1860s and into the 1870s, gathered momentum in the 1880s, and reached a climax during the war with Spain in 1898. Following the acquisition of an empire, the nation, under Presidents William McKinley and Theodore Roosevelt, found itself involved in some of the international crises that preceded World War I. The American people did not seek a greater involvement in world affairs; rather, their long-standing suspicion of European diplomacy and balance-of-power politics faced greater tests by 1914.

When the Civil War ended in a Union victory in April 1865, few problems existed in foreign affairs. The French presence in Mexico under Emperor Maximilian, an ill-starred intervention, collapsed in 1867. The British and Americans felt tensions left over from the war regarding the damages the Confederate raider *Alabama* had inflicted on Union shipping, but those problems yielded to negotiations in the *Alabama* claims talks of the early 1870s. Otherwise the nation remained interested only in the North American continent, as exemplified in the acquisition of Alaska in 1867. Efforts to acquire Santo Domingo (now the Dominican Republic) during the administration of Ulysses S. Grant were turned back by an unsympathetic Congress.

A Growing Interest in World Affairs

In the 1880s concern for the world beyond the Atlantic and the Pacific became greater as industrialism and big business transformed the American economy. The abundance of manufactured goods and the productivity explosion in the agricultural sector during the Gilded Age convinced many American entrepreneurs and farmers to look for overseas markets in which to sell their surpluses. While the nation's trade policy remained protectionist, an interest in foreign markets contributed to an atmosphere that encouraged policymakers to pursue expansionist goals. At the same time the example of major European powers

acquiring possessions in Asia and Africa instilled a sense that the United States should not be left behind in the race for world greatness. Some Americans believed the nation had a duty to spread its democratic ideals to countries where civilization and culture were less "developed" than in North America.

These sentiments drove a program of naval expansion throughout the 1880s. The United States had an obsolete navy at the start of the decade, so Presidents Chester Alan Arthur and Grover Cleveland persuaded Congress to upgrade the nation's maritime power with modern steel battleships and other vessels. The new Naval War College prepared officers for their growing responsibilities. The influential writings of Captain Alfred Thayer Mahan convinced his naval colleagues that the nation needed bases and coaling stations to sustain a worldwide presence on the oceans.

Beginnings of Expansionism

By the early 1890s these forces began to have an effect on the world role of the United States. Under President Benjamin Harrison and Secretary of State James G. Blaine, a Pan-American Congress was held in Washington in 1889–1890 to promote cooperation among the nations of the Western Hemisphere. Through the reciprocal trade provisions of the McKinley Tariff of 1890 and subsequent trade treaties, the Harrison administration sought to open up markets in South America. In the Pacific the long-standing goal of acquiring the Hawaiian Islands seemed close to fruition when a revolution there in 1893 toppled the native monarchy. As Harrison left office, the expansionist agenda had been set in motion.

During the second Grover Cleveland administration (1893–1897), however, the impetus for empire slowed as the president rejected the proposed treaty for Hawaiian annexation. In the case of Cuba, which began a revolution against Spanish rule in 1895, the White House followed a policy of allowing Madrid to try to subdue the uprising and resisted the popular clamor for intervention. Cleveland and Secretary of State Richard Olney did assert American dominance in the Western Hemisphere when Great Britain became involved in a boundary dispute with Venezuela in 1895. That incident was more a reaffirmation of the Monroe Doctrine and traditional American attitudes than an example of a more aggressive foreign policy.

During the depression of the 1890s, talk of overseas markets in Asia and Latin America as an answer to hard times mounted. The Cuban revolution affected American business interests in the island, and

Main Street, Unalaska, c. 1899. The oldest Russian settlement of the Aleutian Islands, Unalaska was established in the 1760s on the eastern end of Unalaska Island. LIBRARY OF CONGRESS: PRINTS AND PHOTOGRAPHS DIVISION

the island's fate attracted the attention of humanitarian groups concerned by Spain's brutal policy of relocating the population in urban concentration camps. The march of European imperialism fed American desires to keep up with what seemed to be the tide of history. Important segments of society remained unenthusiastic about expansionism, but the mood of the country was swinging toward a broader role in the world.

The Spanish-American War and Imperialism

The new administration of William McKinley brought a more assertive policy to world affairs in 1897. Aware of extensive Japanese immigration into Hawaii, the president sent an annexation treaty to Capitol Hill. Although the pact could not command a two-thirds majority by early 1898, it had strong support in Congress. At the same time the McKinley administration intensified the pressure on Spain to reach a settlement with the Cuban rebels that would include independence for the island's inhabitants. Spain resisted any abridgment of its sovereignty until the series of events involving an anti-American letter written by Enrique de Lôme, the Spanish minister to the United States, and the explosion of the USS *Maine* in February 1898. Exponents of empire, such as Theodore Roosevelt and Henry Cabot Lodge, clamored for tough action against Spain.

McKinley tried to persuade Spain to accept a negotiated agreement and leave Cuba, but Madrid, facing domestic opposition to relinquishing Cuba, rejected all such proposals. By April 1898 the most that Spain would agree to was a temporary suspension of hostilities on terms that favored its interests. In response, Congress authorized the president to intervene, and war began later in April. The three-month conflict, in which American forces were everywhere victorious, brought the United States an overseas empire and an expanded world role. Part of the war plan for defeating Spain involved an attack on the Philippine Islands. The smashing victory of Commodore George Dewey on 1 May 1898 opened up the possibility that the United States would acquire the islands in the peace settlement. During the spring and summer McKinley shaped events so he could insist on obtaining the Philippines if that course seemed prudent.

As events developed, the possibility of allowing the Filipinos independence receded because of the presence of Germany and Japan as rivals for the Philippines if the United States departed. By the fall of 1898 McKinley had decided that acquiring the Philippines was the only logical course for the United States to follow. In the Treaty of Paris (December 1898) the United States received Puerto Rico, Guam, and the Philippines. Spain received $20 million and withdrew from Cuba. The United States observed the provisions of the Teller Amendment, adopted when the United States entered the war, that disclaimed any attempt to acquire Cuba, and a military government oversaw Cuban affairs until 1901. When the island became independent, the United States endorsed the Platt Amendment (1901), which gave the United States the right to intervene in Cuba to maintain political stability and prevent outside interference. The United States also received a naval base at Guantánamo Bay as a result of the Platt Amendment.

The United States soon faced the consequences of its imperial path. Filipino nationalists rose up against the U.S. Army in 1899, and the ensuing bloody war lasted for three years. Although the U.S. Army defeated the insurgents in conventional combat, a guerrilla war proved more difficult to subdue. Brutal American tactics in the conflict and a strong anti-imperialist movement at home cooled popular ardor in the United States toward the policy of empire.

The New American Empire

As the fighting went on, President McKinley put in place the mechanisms of colonial government in the

"The White Man's Burden." Satire on imperialism showing Uncle Sam, the United Kingdom's John Bull, and Germany's Kaiser Wilhelm being carried on the shoulders of the subjugated races. Cartoon by William H. Walker. From *Life*, 16 March 1899. LIBRARY OF CONGRESS

form of a civilian administration for the Philippines under the leadership of William Howard Taft. Congress ratified these decisions in the Spooner Amendment (1901) and made provisions for Puerto Rico in the Foraker Act of 1900. The inhabitants of the new American possessions were subjects of the United States but did not receive full citizenship within the imperial framework because of racial discrimination and Anglo-Saxon bigotry.

With the acquisition of the Philippines, the United States looked to economic and political opportunities in Asia. In 1899 and 1900 Secretary of State John Hay issued the Open Door Notes, which asserted an American interest in the territorial integrity of China and the right to equal economic opportunity for American business interests on the Asian mainland. When the Chinese expressed their dislike of foreign presences in the Boxer Rebellion during the summer of 1900, President McKinley sent American troops into a nation with which the United States was not at war. His action was an indication of how much the power of the presidency had expanded to meet the needs of a world power.

The war with Spain had also demonstrated the need for a commanding American presence in the Caribbean to safeguard a potential canal across Central America. To that end the administration began talks with the British to abrogate the Clayton-Bulwer Treaty of 1850 and give the United States the right to construct the canal as it saw fit. These talks ended successfully in 1901, and the treaty was being readied for submission to Congress when McKinley was assassinated in September 1901. Under McKinley the United States had set out on a new departure in foreign policy that saw a strengthening of the presidential office, the expansion of the reach and power of the federal government, and enhanced military and diplomatic commitments around the world.

Roosevelt at the Helm of Foreign Policy

The accession of Theodore Roosevelt to the presidency in 1901 brought into the White House a vigorous exponent of the doctrine of world responsibility for the United States. During nearly eight years in office, Roosevelt built on McKinley's initiatives and tried to act as a full participant in world affairs. He carried forward the improving relationship with Great Britain, and in the Caribbean he pushed for the construction of the isthmian canal. When Colombia balked at a treaty that would have granted the United States the right to construct a waterway across Panama, Roosevelt encouraged the Panamanians to revolt against Colombian rule in 1903. The president imposed an agreement with the new government of Panama, the Hay–Bunau-Varilla Treaty, which gave the United States a very favorable arrangement for the canal. Over the next decade the Panama Canal became a reality.

In 1904 Roosevelt also issued what became known as the Roosevelt Corollary to the Monroe Doctrine. Under that principle the United States claimed a right to ensure that governments south of its borders did not engage in what Roosevelt called chronic wrongdoing that might invite European intervention. The corollary was part of a general assertion of American supremacy in the region that characterized foreign policy during the half-century.

Roosevelt also played a leading role in Asian affairs in pursuit of the national interest. In 1904, when war broke out between Russia and Japan, he helped arrange a peace conference that resulted in the Treaty of Portsmouth (1905). The president accepted Japanese dominance on the Asian mainland in return for assurances that American rule in the Philippines would not be jeopardized. In an area of the world where American power could be exerted only with difficulty and at high domestic political cost, Roosevelt limited the nation's commitments to what he deemed to be practical.

Still problems with Japan remained. The immigration of Japanese nationals into California led to the Gentlemen's Agreement of 1907, in which the two nations informally restricted further movement of Japanese into the United States. In 1907–1909 the Great White Fleet of the U.S. Navy circumnavigated the globe in a symbolic show of power in the Pacific.

As far as Europe was concerned, Roosevelt continued the improving relationship with the British that had begun under McKinley. Through forceful negotiations in 1903 he resolved the long-standing boundary dispute between Alaska and Canada in a manner favorable to the United States. Although no formal alliance emerged, the two countries had drawn much closer together as 1914 approached.

The first decade of the twentieth century saw increasing tensions over Germany's ambitions in Latin America, the erratic behavior of Kaiser William II, and the growing likelihood of a war in Europe. Participating in the Algeciras conference concerning Morocco in 1906, Roosevelt favored France rather than Germany. These actions established the context in which American neutrality would be tested once war broke out in 1914.

Taft and Wilson

Roosevelt left office in 1909 with the nation at peace, and the presidency of William Howard Taft did not disrupt that situation. Nonetheless, the new president did depart from Roosevelt's style. Taft and Secretary of State Philander Knox followed what became known as "dollar diplomacy," which sought to replace American military forces with economic investments in Asia and Latin America that would strengthen local governments against outside interference. In Asia the program encountered opposition from Chinese, Japanese, and Russian interests. The eventual outcome of dollar diplomacy disappointed its advocates. Taft also failed to achieve tariff reciprocity with Canada and arbitration treaties with other nations.

Taft's difficult presidency gave way to that of Woodrow Wilson in March 1913. Wilson continued the broad outlines of American foreign policy with a more moralistic tone. He repudiated dollar diplomacy and encouraged friendly governments in Latin America through a less intrusive U.S. presence. However, that approach encountered difficulties in revolutionary Mexico, where the Wilson administration became entangled in a complex and fluid situation. In other Latin American countries, such as Nicaragua and Haiti, Wilson ended up as interventionist as his Republican predecessors. Until the outbreak of war in Europe, however, the Wilson administration did not envision much interaction with Europe beyond the usual trade relations.

A half-century after the Civil War, the United States had become an imperial and world power. The country had a dominant role in Central America and military commitments in the Philippines that gave it a significant presence in Asia. Despite these developments, the American government and its citizens still believed that the United States could stay apart from European developments and remain in isolation from the world at large. The guns of August 1914 brought an end to those beliefs and moved the nation into the greater participation in the world that had been started during the period from 1865 to 1914.

See also **Asia, Foreign Relations with; Expansion; Navy; Overseas Possessions; Presidency,** *subentry on* **1877–1901; South America, Foreign Relations with; Spanish-American War.**

Bibliography

Beisner, Robert L. *From the Old Diplomacy to the New, 1865–1900.* Arlington Heights, Ill.: Harlan Davidson, 1986.

Campbell, Charles S. *The Transformation of American Foreign Relations, 1865–1900.* New York: Harper and Row, 1976.

Gould, Lewis L. *The Presidency of Theodore Roosevelt.* Lawrence: University Press of Kansas, 1991.

———. *The Presidency of William McKinley.* Lawrence: University Press of Kansas, 1980.

Healy, David. *U.S. Expansionism: The Imperialist Urge in the 1890s.* Madison: University of Wisconsin Press, 1970.

LaFeber, Walter. *The New Empire: An Interpretation of American Expansion, 1860–1898*. Ithaca, N.Y.: Cornell University Press, 1963.

May, Ernest R. *Imperial Democracy: The Emergence of America as a Great Power*. New York: Harper and Row, 1961.

Offner, John L. *An Unwanted War: The Diplomacy of the United States and Spain over Cuba, 1895–1898*. Chapel Hill: University of North Carolina Press, 1992.

Plesur, Milton. *America's Outward Thrust: Approaches to Foreign Affairs, 1865–1890*. DeKalb: Northern Illinois University Press, 1971.

Trask, David F. *The War with Spain in 1898*. New York: Macmillan, 1981.

LEWIS L. GOULD

FOREIGN TRADE AND TARIFFS

[This entry includes two subentries, **Trade and Tariffs** and **The Politics of Trade**.]

TRADE AND TARIFFS

The issue of trade and tariffs was one of the most divisive and persistent political questions that the United States faced throughout the nineteenth century. Since customs duties made up a significant proportion of the revenue of the federal government before the advent of the income tax, decisions about the rate and extent of tariffs on imported goods determined the size and scope of the national government itself. Duties might be based on the value (ad valorem) of an imported product, such as British tinplate, or based on a specific amount of a good, such as pounds of flax. Two broad positions emerged. One theory, associated with Alexander Hamilton, Henry Clay, and the Republican Party after 1854, regarded the tariff as a way to use the power of government to promote the expansion of the economy. Clay's American System tied revenues from tariff protection for internal improvements into an even broader nationalistic vision. High duties on foreign goods would protect American industries and provide jobs for working people. The alternative case argued that tariffs should be used only to raise the minimal revenues to support a small government. Since Americans were also consumers, the low-tariff position contended that imports from abroad kept down the price of goods that individuals had to buy.

This running debate began in the First Congress with the Tariff Law of 1789 and Hamilton's *Report on Manufactures* of 1791, which advanced the case for protectionism. The nation's tariff policy followed protectionist doctrine during the first three decades of the nineteenth century. By the 1820s, however,

signs of low-tariff sentiment appeared in the South, where high tariffs were seen as the North's attempt to increase its power over other sections of the country. The Tariff of Abominations of 1828 aroused southern ire because it protected agricultural products and raw materials to the disadvantage of the cotton South, which depended on exports.

A key confrontation over the tariff occurred in 1832 and 1833, when John C. Calhoun led a campaign to block enforcement of the 1828 and 1832 tariffs through the doctrine of nullification. The result was the 1833 Tariff Act, which began a general reduction in tariff rates that continued for two decades. With Democrats in control of the White House and Congress during the mid-1840s and throughout the 1850s, the concept of a tariff for revenue only was enacted into law in measures such as the Walker Tariff of 1846. The high point of Democratic ascendancy on the tariff question was the 1857 Tariff Act, which slashed rates by 20 percent. Advocates of this policy believed that lower rates favored consumers and the agrarian regions of the country, and the diminished revenues helped keep the national government smaller.

The Rise of Protectionism

The victory of the Republican Party in the 1860 presidential election and the outbreak of the Civil War enabled the Republicans to pass the Morrill Tariff Act of 1861, which returned to the policy of protecting American industries. The ascendancy of the Republicans and their adherence to protection made the tariff issue one of the key points of division between the two major parties for the remainder of the nineteenth century. The Republicans were strongest in the Northeast, where the protective tariff was popular. Midwestern industrial areas joined the Republican coalition, as did farmers in New York, Pennsylvania, Michigan, and Wisconsin, who were faced with competition from Canadian agricultural and timber products. The center of low-tariff sentiment was in the South, where staple crops such as tobacco and cotton did not have protection. Although pockets of Democratic support for the tariff existed, on the whole the Republicans were the high-tariff party of an active government that promoted economic growth that benefited all sections of society. The low-tariff stance of the Democrats reflected their faith in a smaller government that allowed individuals to function as autonomous consumers.

The even balance between the two major parties at the end of the nineteenth century complicated the task of shaping tariff policy. The process of tariff making became an elaborate ritual in which the ma-

William McKinley (1843–1901). As a member of the House of Representatives, McKinley was the architect of the 1890 tariff that bears his name. The notion of commerical reciprocity, central to this tariff, was to remain important in McKinley's policies. Photograph, 1898. LIBRARY OF CONGRESS

jority in the House held highly publicized, partisan hearings. Next, a bill emerged in the House that was then amended and passed. The Senate usually composed its own version. The real bill was often drafted in the House-Senate conference committee, as happened in 1890 and 1894. In the 1888 presidential election Grover Cleveland endeavored to make the tariff the primary issue, but the debate helped the Republicans put Benjamin Harrison in the White House. With their victory for protectionism, the Republicans enacted the McKinley Tariff of 1890, which raised duties. That measure protected industrial areas of the country and sought to encourage such domestic industries as tinplate. Rates on iron, steel, and wool went up. Duties on agricultural commodities such as cereals and meats rose to compensate domestic producers against competition from Canada and Mexico. The tariff bill became a way for the Republicans in this case to shape the economic future of society and to reward those economic interests who sustained protectionism. In the 1890 elections the Democrats won a sweeping victory, in part because of popular discontent with the McKinley law. The Democrats won the White House in 1892 by promising to lower the tariff.

The Tariff in the 1890s

The onset of the panic of 1893 and Democratic disunity on other issues frustrated their hopes for tariff reform. To get the Wilson-Gorman Tariff of 1894 through the Senate, the Democrats had to accept some upward revisions of duties. Consequently President Cleveland let the bill become law without his signature. Large-scale Democratic losses in the congressional election of 1894 emboldened the Republicans to resume protectionism, and the election of William McKinley as president in 1896 signaled a return to higher rates.

The Dingley Tariff of 1897 reflected the high-tariff views of the Republicans but also included some provisions for reciprocal trade agreements intended to lessen the effects of increased duties. Although McKinley worked hard for reciprocity, he did not achieve much before he was assassinated in 1901. McKinley's successor, Theodore Roosevelt, largely abandoned reciprocity and endorsed high tariffs during his first term.

The Tariff Issue. A Harrison "No Free Trade" parade clashes with a Cleveland "Reform" parade on Broadway in New York City. Protective tariffs were the focus of the presidential campaign of 1888: Harrison supported high tariffs and Cleveland, low tariffs. LIBRARY OF CONGRESS

By the end of the century, as prosperity returned to the United States and inflation became a problem, popular approval of protectionist policies cooled. Americans thought of themselves as consumers, so the higher prices that protectionism entailed became a liability for the Republicans. Debate over the issue contributed to the problems that led to a Republican split in 1912. When a Democratic administration enacted the income tax in the Underwood Tariff in 1913, tariffs lost their importance as a major source of government revenue. Nonetheless, the divisions established over the tariff issue in the nineteenth century continued to affect American politics. In a reversal of historic roles in the twentieth century, the Republican Party began to advocate free trade, and the Democratic Party became sympathetic to protectionist views. Largely discredited as an economic policy among trade experts, protectionism remained an attractive position when American manufacturers and farmers and their employees felt threatened by foreign competition. To that extent the nineteenth-century debates over the tariff, which spoke to the size and role of government in the economy, resonated a century later.

See also **Consumerism and Consumption; Democratic Party; Economic Theory; Monetary Policy; Republican Party; Sectionalism; Taxation and Public Finance.**

Bibliography

Pincus, John J. *Pressure Groups and Politics in Antebellum Tariffs.* New York: Columbia University Press, 1977.

Ratner, Sidney. *The Tariff in American History.* New York: D. Van Nostrand, 1972.

Reitano, Joanne. *The Tariff Question in the Gilded Age: The Great Debate of 1888.* University Park: Pennsylvania State University Press, 1994.

Stanwood, Edward. *American Tariff Controversies in the Nineteenth Century.* Boston and New York: Houghton Mifflin, 1903.

LEWIS L. GOULD

THE POLITICS OF TARIFFS

The issue of trade and tariffs was one of the most divisive and persistent political questions that the United States faced throughout the nineteenth century. Since customs duties made up a significant proportion of the revenue of the federal government before the advent of the income tax, decisions about the rate and extent of tariffs on imported goods determined the size and scope of the national government itself. Two broad positions emerged. One theory, associated with Alexander Hamilton, Henry Clay, and after 1854 the Republican Party, regarded the tariff as a way to use the power of government to promote the expansion of the economy. High duties on foreign goods would protect American industries and provide jobs for working people. The alternative position was that tariffs should be used only to raise minimal revenues to support a small government. Because Americans were also consumers, the low-tariff position contended that imports from abroad kept down the prices of goods that individuals had to buy.

This running debate began in the First Congress with the Tariff Law of 1789 and Hamilton's *Report on Manufactures* of 1791, which advanced the justification for protectionism. The nation's tariff policy followed protectionist doctrine during the first three decades of the nineteenth century. By the 1820s, however, signs of low-tariff sentiment appeared in the South, where high tariffs were seen as the North's attempt to increase its power over other sections of the country. The Tariff of Abominations of 1828 aroused southern ire because its higher rates were regarded as a threat to economic interests below the Mason-Dixon line.

In a key confrontation over the tariff in 1832–1833, John C. Calhoun led a campaign to block enforcement of the 1828 and 1832 tariffs through the doctrine of nullification. Consequently, Congress enacted the 1833 Tariff Act, which began a general reduction in tariff rates that continued for two decades. With the Democrats in control of the White House and Congress during the mid-1840s and throughout the 1850s, the concept of a tariff for revenue only was enacted into law in measures such as the Walker Tariff of 1846. The high point of Democratic ascendancy on the tariff question was the 1857 Tariff Act, which slashed rates by 20 percent.

The Rise of Protectionism

Following the victory of the Republican Party in the 1860 presidential election and the outbreak of the Civil War, Congress passed the Morrill Tariff Act of 1861, which returned to the policy of protecting American industries. The ascendancy of the Republicans and their adherence to protection made the tariff issue one of the key points of division between the two major parties for the remainder of the nineteenth century. The Republicans were strongest in the Northeast, where the protective tariff was popular. Industrializing areas in the Midwest joined the Republican coalition, as did farmers in New York, Pennsylvania, Michigan, and Wisconsin who faced competition from Canadian agricultural and timber products. The center of low-tariff sentiment was in the South, which manufactured little and thus could not benefit from high tariffs. A few Democrats supported the tariff, but on the whole the Republicans were the high-tariff party of an active government, while the Democrats endorsed lower duties and a tariff "for revenue only." Industrialists and entrepreneurs in developing businesses liked the Republican protective policy that insulated them from foreign competitors. The Democratic bent toward smaller government and fewer trade restrictions attracted merchants and those engaged in international commerce.

The even balance between the two major parties at the end of the nineteenth century complicated the task of shaping tariff policy. In the 1888 presidential election, Grover Cleveland endeavored to make the tariff the primary issue, but the debate on the subject helped the Republicans put Benjamin Harrison in the White House. After their victory for protection, the Republicans enacted the McKinley Tariff of 1890, which raised protective duties. In the 1890 elections the Democrats won a sweeping victory, in part because of popular discontent with the McKinley law. Promising to revise the tariff downward, the Democrats won the White House in 1892.

The Tariff in the 1890s

The onset of the panic of 1893 and party disunity on other issues frustrated Democrats' hopes for tariff reform. As a result Congress approved the Wilson-Gorman Tariff of 1894. In order to get the measure through the Senate, the Democrats had to accept some upward revisions of duties, and President Cleveland let the bill become law without his signature. Large-scale Democratic losses in the election of 1894 emboldened the Republicans to resume protectionism, and the election of William McKinley as president in 1896 signaled a return to higher rates.

The Dingley Tariff of 1897 reflected the high-tariff views of the Republicans, but it also included some provisions for reciprocal trade agreements that lessened the effects of increased duties. Although McKinley worked hard for reciprocity, he did not achieve much before he was assassinated in 1901. His successor, Theodore Roosevelt, largely abandoned reciprocity and endorsed high tariffs during his first term.

By the end of the century, as prosperity returned and inflation became a problem, popular support for protectionist policies declined. Americans increasingly thought of themselves as consumers, and the higher prices that protectionism entailed became a liability for the Republicans. Debate over the issue contributed to the Republican split in 1912. When the Democratic Congress enacted the income tax in the Underwood Tariff in 1913, tariffs lost their importance as a major source of government revenue.

Nonetheless, the divisions established over the tariff issue in the nineteenth century continued to affect U.S. politics. In an odd reversal of historic roles, the twentieth-century Republican Party advocated free trade and the Democratic Party became more sympathetic to protectionist views. While protectionism was largely discredited as an economic policy among trade experts, it remained an attractive position when American manufacturers and farmers, and their employees, felt threatened by foreign competition. To that extent the nineteenth-century debates over the tariff, which spoke to the size and role of government in the economy, resonated a century later.

See also **Democratic Party; Economic Regulation; Elections; Nullification; Panics and Depressions; Republican Party; Sectionalism.**

Bibliography

Pincus, Jonathan J. *Pressure Groups and Politics in Antebellum Tariffs.* New York: Columbia University Press, 1977.
Ratner, Sidney. *The Tariff in American History.* New York: Van Nostrand, 1972.
Reitano, Joanne. *The Tariff Question in the Gilded Age: The Great Debate of 1888.* University Park: Pennsylvania State University Press, 1994.
Stanwood, Edward. *American Tariff Controversies in the Nineteenth Century.* Boston: Houghton Mifflin, 1903.

LEWIS L. GOULD

FORTS. See **Military Technology.**

FOURTEENTH AMENDMENT. See **Constitutional Amendments,** subentry on the **Thirteenth, Fourteenth, and Fifteenth Amendments.**

FREEDOM OF THE PRESS. See **Newspapers and the Press.**

FREEMASONRY. See **Masons.**

FRONTIER The term "frontier," in its American context, is most commonly linked with the historian Frederick Jackson Turner, who first delivered his essay "The Significance of the Frontier in American History" in 1893. Turner defined the frontier variously as the "meeting point between savagery and civilization," "the place which 'lies at the hither edge of free land,' " and "the margin of that settlement which has a density of two or more to the square mile." The American frontier, Turner and numerous other American thinkers emphasized, was transitory. It was a line of settlement, a phase, a process, not a stationary natural or fortified barrier like the frontiers of Europe.

Frederick Jackson Turner's Frontier

Turner, writing at the end of the nineteenth century, viewed the frontier as the wellspring of American democracy, nationalism, and individualism and central to understanding American social and cultural mores. In Turner's words, "The existence of an area of free land, its continuous recession, and the advance of American settlement westward explain American development." To study the frontier, Turner proclaimed, "is to study the really American part of our history." The frontier, he believed, was the key shaping force of American national consciousness.

By the end of the nineteenth century Turner had popularized his ideas about the frontier in a series of essays in leading magazines. By the early twentieth century he had risen to academic superstardom, and in *The Frontier in American History* (1920) he further

broadened the audience for his ideas. None of this is surprising since the frontier thesis provided a young nation with a triumphant creation myth, a truly American story that emphasized pioneer struggle and conquest of a forbidding wilderness. Turner's account, of course, was riddled with irony. The free lands he spoke of were neither free nor unoccupied, and Native American populations were decimated during the course of the nineteenth century as white Americans "settled" the frontier. But the late nineteenth century was, in the minds of many Americans, the great age of progress, and the spread of white "civilization" from the Atlantic to the Pacific, the securing of America's Manifest Destiny, seemed an achievement of the highest order. And, if native peoples were brutally defeated in battle, placed on reservations, then forcibly assimilated into mainstream American culture, that was simply the price of progress, according to the social Darwinist mind-set of the time. White Americans could convince themselves that they were doing native peoples a favor by raising them up, through defeat and assimilation, to a supposed higher level of civilization.

Turner's thinking on such matters was quite complex. He certainly was not an unqualified supporter of America's imperial march across the continent, and

Leading the Way Through the Wilderness. In 1769, Daniel Boone and five explorers entered Kentucky through the Cumberland Gap on what would later be known as Wilderness Road. He escorted five families in 1773. Painting by George Caleb Bingham, 1851. Library of Congress

he was aware of some of the shortcomings of frontier society and the consequences of frontier expansion. The frontier thesis was not just a testament to a triumphant past. It was actually a symptom of a broader concern over the perceived closing of the frontier that emerged as a significant force in American intellectual life in the 1880s and 1890s. If the frontier had, as Turner and many others contended, been the chief source of American democracy and the key force for assimilating the nation's immigrants, then what would happen to American democracy and national unity in the wake of the frontier's passing? How would new immigrants from southern and eastern Europe be Americanized in a frontierless United States? Such fin de siècle concerns occupied a wide range of American intellectuals in the late nineteenth century, and Turner was far from unique in expressing them.

The Frontier in the Popular Imagination

Turner drew on a rich frontier legacy in American popular and intellectual thought. His frontier thesis was certainly original, but he used numerous building blocks to construct it. America's frontier heritage gradually formed during the course of the late eighteenth and the nineteenth centuries, and the symbols Turner drew on in forming the frontier thesis resonated strongly because they were familiar to his audience. As early as the 1780s Benjamin Franklin, Thomas Jefferson, and the French expatriate Hector St. John de Crèvecoeur commented on the role that western lands would play in developing an agrarian democracy. As the nineteenth century unfolded, sketches, paintings, lithographs, and dime novels created a distinctive frontier type in the American popular imagination.

Consider the scene at the World's Columbian Exposition in 1893, when Turner first delivered his famous paper. He spoke to a comparatively small audience of professional historians, and his ideas took two or three years to reach a broader audience. But across the street from the exposition's exhibits "Buffalo Bill" Cody was performing twice daily in an arena that held some eighteen thousand people. Cody reenacted famous scenes of frontier conflict, most notably "Custer's Last Stand." In doing so he managed to make the white conquerors of the Indian West appear as noble victims, heroic in defeat, to his largely white audiences. Inside the exhibit grounds tens of thousands of visitors walked past a small log cabin constructed by members of the Boone and Crockett Club, an organization founded by Theodore Roosevelt and Henry Cabot Lodge to remind Americans of the importance of their frontier past.

Cody had been presenting his Wild West extravaganza before outdoor crowds since 1882 and had performed in a simple play about frontier heroism, *Scouts of the Prairies*, as early as 1872. He was first immortalized in 1869 in the dime novel *Buffalo Bill, King of the Border Men*. By the time of his frontier drama at Chicago in 1893, Cody was a legend, and the consensus was that the last days of the wild frontier had long since passed.

The Frontier in Art and Literature

The American public was reminded of that frontier past in the work of "cowboy and Indian" artists such as Frederic Remington and Charles M. Russell in the late nineteenth and early twentieth centuries. In the 1870s Thomas Moran had served up grand, romantic frontier landscapes to an eager public, and in the 1860s Albert Bierstadt treated the public to huge canvases capturing the drama and grandeur of the far western frontier. In the mid-1850s the nation's Manifest Destiny in the West, unabashedly declared by William Gilpin in 1846, was depicted in Currier and Ives prints. Around the same time George Caleb Bingham depicted in his art both the wonders and the shortcomings of America's rugged frontier democracy. Indeed, the frontier theme can be traced to the 1830s in the work of Alfred Jacob Miller, Karl Bodmer, and George Catlin, who chronicled the indigenous peoples of the frontier in their art.

That frontier legacy can also be traced across the nineteenth century in American literature. The legend of the archetypal western frontiersman Daniel Boone was constructed as early as 1784 in John Filson's *The Discovery, Settlement, and Present State of Kentucke*. Boone, like Buffalo Bill, became a frontier legend in his own lifetime. Boone's nephew, Daniel Bryan, published *The Adventures of Daniel Boone* in 1813, and Timothy Flint's widely read biography, *The Biographical Memoir of Daniel Boone*, appeared in 1833. These works about Boone claimed to be factual accounts, but all strayed irretrievably into the realm of fiction.

The following year, 1834, Davy Crockett's autobiography, *A Narrative of the Life of David Crockett of the State of Tennessee*, appeared. Crockett, like Boone, had become a frontier legend in his own lifetime and his reputation would only be enhanced after his death at the Alamo on 6 March 1836. Crockett almanacs were published for every year from 1835 to 1856 in New York, Boston, and other cities. By the time Turner delivered his famous paper "The Significance of the Frontier in American History," a play entitled *Davy Crockett; Or, Be Sure You're Right, Then Go Ahead*, had been running for more than two decades in the United States and England and would continue its run until 1896. The Crockett legend was still very much alive in the twentieth century, boosted by the media of film and television. The year 1955 was the height of the Crockett craze, which saw massive sales of coonskin caps, toy guns, and other frontier and pioneer garb, and the purchase of seven million copies of a record, "The Ballad of Davy Crockett."

Contemporaneous with the emergence of Boone and Crockett as real-life frontier heroes, a fictional frontier hero was being popularized by the novelist James Fenimore Cooper in his Leatherstocking series, which included *The Pioneers* (1823), *The Last of the Mohicans* (1826), *The Prairie* (1827), *The Pathfinder* (1840), and *The Deerslayer* (1841). In the 1830s Washington Irving played a role in popularizing the frontier type in his western histories *Astoria* (1836) and *The Adventures of Captain Bonneville, U.S.A.* (1837). A decade later the historian Francis Parkman published his romantic account of the pioneer tradition, *The California and Oregon Trail* (1849; later editions appeared under the title *The Oregon Trail*). By the middle of the nineteenth century, while the western frontier was still being settled, a frontier tradition had already developed. In fact, the tradition was so firmly established that it had become the object of satire in Mark Twain's *Roughing It* (1872). Twain's travel narrative took a great deal of the romance and high adventure out of the frontier legend, but the legend clearly prevailed in the dime novels, Wild West shows, and artwork of the late nineteenth century. Frontier mythology was complex and malleable, capable of ascribing heroic status to outlaws such as Billy the Kid (Henry McCarty, alias William H. Bonney) and Jesse James, and of incorporating women, such as Annie Oakley (Phoebe Anne Moses [or Mosey]) and Calamity Jane (Martha Jane Cannary [or Canary or Connarray]), into an essentially male genre.

The Frontier Tradition in American Politics

During the nineteenth century the frontier had emerged as a theme in American popular culture and in art and literature. Meanwhile, the same theme was playing a vital role in the political arena. President Thomas Jefferson had extended the frontier and doubled the size of the nation with the Louisiana Purchase of 1803. From his victory over the British at the Battle of New Orleans in 1815, Andrew Jackson was being presented by the press as an archetypal hero of the American frontier. In the 1828 presidential campaign the public was given the choice of the former Harvard professor and Whig Party candidate John Quincy Adams and the frontier philosopher and Democratic Party candidate, Jackson. Adams was undoubtedly learned, Jackson's supporters readily admitted; but Jackson, they contended, possessed a deeper frontier wisdom. Jackson would be reelected in 1832, and succeeded by another Democratic candidate, Martin Van Buren. But in the famous 1840 campaign the Whig Party beat the Democrats at their own game, presenting their candidate, General William Henry Harrison, as a genuine hero of the frontier in what became known as the log-cabin campaign. Harrison defeated Van Buren, but, ironically, the great symbol of frontier hardihood died a mere month into his term. A generation later the office of the presidency would be occupied by Abraham Lincoln, a figure with a more substantive frontier legacy. Lincoln had been born in a Kentucky log cabin in 1809 and had spent the first twenty-one years of his life on the Kentucky-Indiana frontier.

The frontier theme did not disappear from American politics in the twentieth century. Theodore Roosevelt, who had spent a few years in the 1880s on a Dakota ranch, became the first "cowboy president" in 1901. During the Great Depression, his cousin, Franklin D. Roosevelt, and key New Dealers promoted their programs as a necessary corrective to the loss of opportunity stemming from the closing of the frontier. A youthful John F. Kennedy played up the theme of the New Frontier in the 1960 election campaign and during his abbreviated term in office. And a generation later, in 1980, the nation's second cowboy president, former Western movie actor Ronald Reagan, won the presidency and drew heavily on frontier mythology in his speeches.

In the proceedings of the first settler societies and pioneer societies that had been forming in the Midwest and the West since the middle of the nineteenth century, one finds a mountain of speeches devoted to the arduous process of frontier expansion and settlement and the distinctive pioneer type that those struggles helped create. Turner's frontier thesis had been delivered in embryo thousands of times by less scholarly Americans reminiscing about the frontier trials, tribulations, and glories of their youth. Depictions of frontier drama adorned the walls of taverns across the country. The vast bulk of Americans seeking a taste of the frontier at the World's Columbian Exposition in 1893 would have visited Buffalo Bill's Wild West extravaganza or the simple log cabin of the Boone and Crockett Club, not the annual meeting of the American Historical Association. Turner spoke to a relatively small audience of scholars about why the frontier was so central to understanding American thought and character. In doing so he gave academic respectability to ideas that had been circulating in popular culture for over a century, and his frontier thesis and the frontier's legacy have remained topics of debate.

See also **Manifest Destiny; West, The.**

Bibliography

Goetzmann, William H., and William N. Goetzmann. *The West of the Imagination.* New York: Norton, 1986.

Grossman, James R., ed. *The Frontier in American Culture: Essays by Richard White and Patricia Nelson Limerick.* Berkeley: University of California Press, 1994.

Klein, Kerwin Lee. *Frontiers of Historical Imagination: Narrating the European Conquest of Native America, 1890–1990.* Berkeley: University of California Press, 1997.

Limerick, Patricia Nelson. *The Legacy of Conquest: The Unbroken Past of the American West.* New York: Norton, 1987.

Smith, Henry Nash. *Virgin Land: The American West as Symbol and Myth.* Cambridge, Mass.: Harvard University Press, 1950, 1978.

Turner, Frederick Jackson. *The Frontier in American History.* New York: Henry Holt, 1920. Reprint, Tucson: University of Arizona Press, 1986, 1992.

Wrobel, David M. *The End of American Exceptionalism: Frontier Anxiety from the Old West to the New Deal.* Lawrence: University Press of Kansas, 1993.

DAVID M. WROBEL

FUGITIVE SLAVE LAWS   Article IV, Section 2 of the U.S. Constitution provided that "fugitives from labour"—whether slaves, apprentices, or indentured servants—could not become legally free by escaping to other states, but instead had to be returned "on demand" of the person to whom they owed "service or labour." The provision did not contain any indication of how it was to be enforced. In 1790 a controversy developed over the extradition of three Virginia men accused of kidnapping a free black in Pennsylvania. The Virginia governor claimed the man was a fugitive slave and refused to extradite the kidnappers. This controversy eventually led Congress, in 1793, to pass an act that regulated the return of both fugitives from justice and fugitive slaves.

The 1793 Act allowed a master or a master's agent to seize an alleged fugitive slave and bring that person before any state or federal judge or magistrate for a summary hearing to determine if the person seized was the runaway slave of the claimant. The judge was free to accept any evidence he found persuasive on the status of the alleged slave. The judge or magistrate would then issue a certificate of removal, allowing the claimant to take the slave back to his home state. The law introduced a $500 fine for anyone interfering with the return of a fugitive slave. In addition, a master could sue anyone abetting the fugitive for his costs plus the value of any slaves actually lost.

These lax rules, as well as blatant acts of kidnapping by some southerners, led to the passage of personal liberty acts in many northern states. These laws provided extra procedures to protect free blacks from kidnapping. Many northerners also argued that Congress had no power to pass the fugitive slave law. In *Jack v. Martin* (1835), New York chancellor Reuben Walworth declared the law unconstitutional. He held, however, that New York had an obligation to enforce the constitutional clause, and thus ordered that the slave Jack be turned over to his owner. In *State v. Sheriff of Burlington* (1836), Chief Justice Joseph Hornblower implied that the federal law was unconstitutional but freed the alleged slave Alexander Helmsley on procedural grounds.

The U.S. Supreme Court resolved these issues in *Prigg v. Pennsylvania* (1842). Speaking for an 8–1 majority, Justice Joseph Story of Massachusetts upheld the 1793 law and struck down all state laws that interfered with the return of a fugitive slave. Story also held that any slaveowner had a common law right of recaption to take his slave back to the South without any judicial hearing if this seizure could be accomplished without any breach of the peace. Finally, although he believed state jurists had a moral obligation to take jurisdiction in fugitive slave cases, he asserted that Congress could not constitutionally obligate them to do so.

Since *Prigg* prevented the free states from protecting their black residents, the states did the next best thing: they passed new personal liberty laws withdrawing state support for enforcement of the 1793 law. Without state aid, slaveowners had to rely on the tiny number of federal judges and marshals to aid them in their quest for runaway slaves. Meanwhile, in *Jones v. Van Zandt* (1847) the U.S. Supreme Court upheld a harsh interpretation of the 1793 law, which in effect applied to the North the southern legal presumption that all blacks were slaves until they could prove otherwise.

Without northern help, southerners found it almost impossible to capture runaways. As a result, they demanded a new, stronger law with federal enforcement, which they obtained with the Fugitive Slave Law of 1850. Technically an amendment of the 1793 law, the Fugitive Slave Law was in reality an entirely new approach to the problem. The 1850 law allowed for the appointment of federal commissioners throughout the nation. These commissioners would hear fugitive slave cases and were empowered to call out federal marshals, posses, or the military to aid slaveowners. Penalties for violating the law included $1,000 fines and six-month jail sentences. In addition,

Holy Bible.

Thou shalt not deliver unto the master his servant which has escaped from his master unto thee. He shall dwell with thee. Even among you in that place which he shall choose in one of thy gates where it liketh him best. Thou shalt not oppress him.

Deut XXIII 15-16

Effects of the Fugitive-Slave-Law.

Declaration of independence.

We hold that all men are created equal, that they are endowed by their Creator with certain unalienable rights, that among these are life, liberty and the pursuit of happiness.

Slave Owners Capture Free African Americans. This political cartoon cites readings from the Bible and an excerpt from the Declaration of Independence that oppose slavery and the return of escaped slaves to their former masters. Drawing, 1850. LIBRARY OF CONGRESS

anyone helping fugitive slaves could be subject to a $1,000 penalty to compensate the master for the loss of each slave, and any marshal who allowed a slave to escape from his custody could be sued for the slave's value.

The procedure of a hearing under these commissioners outraged the North for its lack of due process. No jury could hear the case of a fugitive slave, and no writ of habeas corpus could interfere with the process. The alleged slave could not testify at the hearing, and minimal evidence would be sufficient to remand a black to a claimant. A U.S. commissioner hearing such a case would get five dollars if he decided in favor of the alleged slave, but if he held for the master he would get ten dollars. This disparity was in theory designed to compensate commissioners for the extra work of filling out certificates of removal, but to most northerners it seemed a blatant attempt to bribe commissioners to help slaveowners.

The law led to riots, rescues, and resistance in a number of places. In 1851 a mob stormed a court-

room in Boston to free the slave Shadrack; in Syracuse a mob rescued the slave Jerry from a jail; and in Christiana, Pennsylvania, a master was killed in a shoot-out with fugitive slaves. In 1854 citizens in Milwaukee, led by the abolitionist editor Sherman Booth, freed the slave Joshua Glover from federal custody, and in 1858 most of the students and faculty of Oberlin College charged a courthouse and freed a slave arrested in Wellington, Ohio. All of these cases led to prosecutions under the 1850 law, but most were unsuccessful. With the exception of one man who died while on bail waiting an appeal, all of the Jerry rescue defendants were either acquitted or set free after hung juries. After the Christiana riot, the federal government conducted the largest treason trial in U.S. history, but gained no convictions. A few of the Oberlin-Wellington Rescuers paid small fines in a negotiated settlement with federal prosecutors. The Sherman Booth case proved to be the most important. The Wisconsin Supreme Court set Booth free, declaring the 1850 act unconstitutional, but in *Able-*

man v. Booth (1858) the U.S. Supreme Court upheld the 1850 law and asserted that states could not interfere with the federal courts.

In the long run the 1793 and 1850 slave laws did little to help masters recover runaway slaves, but did much to undermine the Union. Outrage over the 1850 law in the North helped create the constituency for the Republican Party, enabling the election of Abraham Lincoln. Meanwhile, in 1860–1861 a number of southern states cited failure to enforce the fugitive slave laws as one of their reasons for secession. In 1864 Congress, dominated by Republicans, repealed both fugitive slave laws. President Lincoln happily signed the bill into law.

See also **Abolition and Antislavery; African Americans,** *subentry on* **Free Blacks before the Civil War; Slavery, Overview** *and subentries on* **Runaway Slaves** *and* **Law of Slavery; Supreme Court,** *subentry on* **Slavery; Underground Railroad.**

Bibliography

Campbell, Stanley. *The Slave Catchers.* Chapel Hill, N.C.: University of North Carolina Press, 1968.

Finkelman, Paul. *Slavery in the Courtroom.* Washington, D.C.: Library of Congress, 1984.

Finkelman, Paul. "Story Telling on the Supreme Court: *Prigg v. Pennsylvania* and Justice Joseph Story's Judicial Nationalism." *Supreme Court Review 1994* (1995): 247–294.

Morris, Thomas D. *Free Men All: The Personal Liberty Laws of the North, 1780–1861.* Baltimore: Johns Hopkins University Press, 1974.

PAUL FINKELMAN

FUR TRADE   By 1800 the fur trade of North America was an old institution. The Hudson's Bay Company and the North West Company built a string of posts and established waterborne and overland express systems that delivered furs to central depots and managerial points. Following the American Revolution, Jay's Treaty with England in 1794 forced closure of British posts within U.S. territory but allowed foreign traders to operate in the Northwest Territory with American sponsorship. This new diplomatic atmosphere and treaties with American Indian tribes beyond the Appalachians led the German immigrant John Jacob Astor to form partnerships with North West Company personnel for tapping the Great Lakes region. By 1800 Astor had amassed $250,000 and had become the leading fur merchant in the United States. Astor formed the American Fur Company in 1808 in New York City and created two subsidiaries, the Southwest Company for the Great Lakes area, which absorbed the Canadian-owned Mackinaw Company, and in 1810 the Pacific Fur Company, intending to build posts from the Great Lakes to the Pacific Coast.

The Treaty of Ghent in 1814 and the Convention of 1818, which allowed joint occupancy of Oregon for ten years and which was renewed for another ten years in 1827, left American and British traders vying for furs in the Pacific Northwest. Astor organized a Western Department of the American Fur Company in 1822 and sent Ramsay Crooks, his operations manager, to St. Louis, Missouri. There Crooks established links with Bernard Pratte and Company and formed the Upper Missouri Outfit in 1827 with ambitions to expand into the Rocky Mountains. For the next four decades, through Pratte, Chouteau and Company, successor to Bernard Pratte and Company, the American Fur Company dominated trade on the upper Missouri. Absorbing or driving out smaller concerns, the American Fur Company used St. Louis as its collecting and distributing center. Chouteau built Fort Union in North Dakota in 1828 and Fort Pierre in South Dakota in 1831 and in 1835 acquired Fort Laramie in Wyoming to use as warehouses in Indian country.

In the Great Lakes region raccoon replaced beaver for hats, while in the West buffalo robes replaced beaver and other small furs as the major item of commerce. In 1835 Pratte, Chouteau and Company reported sales of 25,375 buffalo robes, which sold, on average, for four dollars per robe in St. Louis for a profit of one dollar or 25 percent. The American Fur Company marketed most of its prime smaller furs abroad through a London middleman. American Fur Company business in the Rocky Mountains was small, owing to intense competition from "free trappers" and independent trading companies, such as Manuel Lisa and the St. Louis Missouri Fur Company, founded in 1808 and dissolved in 1823.

In the Pacific Northwest, Nathaniel Wyeth in 1834 built Fort Hall in southern Idaho as a commercial venture designed to supply American trappers at rendezvous. The scheme failed, and the fort was sold to the Hudson's Bay Company in 1835. Other New England merchants, missionaries, and colonizers settled among and ministered to the region's native peoples. From 1818 through the mid-1840s the Hudson's Bay Company continued to dominate commerce and diplomacy with Indians of the Northwest, sending annual "brigades" of trappers into Idaho and Utah and as far as California that left behind "fur deserts" in many places. The thrust of American expansion by settlers bound for Oregon, Utah, and California disrupted migratory patterns of game animals, depleted wildlife, and precipitated diplomatic problems with resident Indians. In 1843 the Hudson's Bay

Company moved its headquarters from Fort Vancouver on the Columbia River to Fort Victoria on Vancouver Island. After the Oregon Treaty of 1846, the Hudson's Bay Company retained trading privileges on American soil. However, following the Canadian confederation in 1867, the company withdrew its operations completely in 1870.

During the 1850s and 1860s many fur trade posts in the American West were abandoned or sold to the U.S. Army. A bonanza in buffalo hides began in 1870, when European manufacturers converted production of leather goods from South American cattle to American bison. By 1885 only a few hundred buffalo remained from herds that had initially numbered in the millions, and consequently the subsistence patterns of native peoples were disrupted. In 1867 the United States purchased Alaska's Pribilof Islands from Russia, and a similar saga of waste subsequently occurred there. Up to 100,000 fur seals were killed annually for their pelts, leaving the species endangered by the end of the century. Throughout the United States, canids—wolves, foxes, and coyotes—as well as bears, cougars, and badgers continued to face hostile farmers, rangers, and townspeople eager to see their demise. Rabbits, raccoons, skunks, and muskrats continued to be in high demand for common furs, while minks and sables, primarily from Canada's Far North, supplied the demand for fancy furs in Europe and North America. As in the early days of the fur trade, native hunters continued trapping and hunting for themselves and for trade to the Hudson's Bay Company. That company's York Factory on the Hudson Bay, built in 1684, remained in business until 1957.

See also **Hunting and Trapping.**

Bibliography

Clayton, James L. "The Growth and Significance of the American Fur Trade, 1790–1890." In *Aspects of the Fur Trade: Selected Papers of the 1965 North American Fur Trade Conference.* St. Paul: Minnesota Historical Society, 1967.

Hafen, LeRoy R., ed. *The Mountain Men and the Fur Trade of the Far West.* 10 vols. Glendale, Calif.: Arthur H. Clark, 1965–1972.

Phillips, Paul C., with J. W. Smurr. *The Fur Trade.* 2 vols. Norman: University of Oklahoma Press, 1961.

Ray, Arthur J. "The Fur Trade in North America: An Overview from a Historical Geographical Perspective." In *Wild Furbearer Management and Conservation in North America.* Edited by Milan Novak et al. Toronto: Ministry of Natural Resources, 1987.

Rich, E. E. *Hudson's Bay Company, 1670–1870.* 3 vols. New York: Macmillan, 1960.

Swagerty, W. R. "Indian Trade of the Trans-Mississippi West to 1870." In *Handbook of North American Indians.* Edited by William C. Sturtevant. Volume 4: *History of Indian-White Relations,* edited by Wilcomb Washburn. Washington, D.C.: Smithsonian Institution, 1988.

Utley, Robert M. *A Life Wild and Perilous: Mountain Men and the Paths to the Pacific.* New York: Holt, 1997.

Van Kirk, Sylvia. *Many Tender Ties: Women in Fur Trade Society, 1670–1870.* Norman: University of Oklahoma Press, 1980.

Wishart, David J. *The Fur Trade of the American West, 1807–40: A Geographical Synthesis.* Lincoln: University of Nebraska Press, 1979.

WILLIAM R. SWAGERTY

G

GADSDEN PURCHASE The Gadsden Purchase of 1853–1854 arose out of the problematic border settlement between the United States and Mexico following the Mexican War. U.S. railroad promoters and expansionists desired control of the Mesilla Valley, which was thought to be a natural route for a southern transcontinental railroad. The valley was one of the areas left in dispute after the war, and both Mexican and American settlers flowed into the region.

In 1853 the U.S. minister to Mexico, James Gadsden, who was a railroad promoter and a strong supporter of a southern transcontinental railroad, was instructed to negotiate a purchase price for the Mesilla Valley area. In the negotiations that followed, Mexico pushed hard for the settlement of a host of other unresolved issues emanating from the war, but Gadsden remained fixed in his purpose. Frustrated by the Mexican demands and the slow pace of the negotiations, he eventually asked for a show of U.S. military force to expedite matters. Mexico, ruled at that time by America's old nemesis, the general Antonio López de Santa Anna, finally gave in and signed the Gadsden Treaty, which was finalized in 1854. The United States bought the Mesilla Valley territory for $10 million, a purchase that completed the outline of the contiguous United States.

The treaty was a catastrophe for Santa Anna. Opponents accused him of giving Mexican territory away, and they rose up in rebellion. The old dictator was driven from power in 1855.

See also **Expansion; Mexican War.**

Bibliography

Garber, Paul N. *The Gadsden Treaty.* Gloucester, Mass.: Peter Smith, 1959.

Vázquez, Josefina Zoraida, and Lorenzo Meyer. *The United States and Mexico.* Chicago: University of Chicago Press, 1985.

Michael L. Krenn

GAMES AND TOYS, CHILDREN'S Many nineteenth-century games and toys had existed for centuries. Ring-a-ring-a-rosie and how many miles to Miley Bright, popular throughout the nineteenth century, dated from medieval Europe, and children in early Rome had played with tops. Children's play, however, also reflects its particular time and place. That of the nineteenth-century United States mirrored American society's diverse conditions and profound transformations.

Traditional Games

Children have always played "rehearsal" games that mimic the roles they see awaiting them as adults. In agrarian America boys and girls created miniature fields and barnyards and made tiny wagons from matchboxes and spools, sometimes with beetles in harness. American Indian boys shot arrows at the pretended prey of bushes and rocks, and ranch children "branded" dead antelope with sticks. Town children constructed buildings from scrap wood, then acted the parent, shopkeeper, clergyman, or teacher. The century's central trauma, the Civil War, had barely begun when boys and girls on both sides formed mock militia companies and drilled with broomstick guns. Such imitative play allowed boys and girls to explore the dynamics of social relations and to gain a sense of control over frightening events and forces. After hearing evangelists threaten damnation, youngsters in frontier Kansas created the game of heaven and hell, with sinners tossed into an earthen cellar full of chaff and broomcorn. As James Marten relates in *The Children's Civil War* (1998), in wartime Virginia a mother wrote of her five-year-old son making play from an increasingly common sight: "He gets sticks and hobbles about, saying that he lost a leg at the Second Battle of Manassas" (p. 165).

Other games had structure and rules. At a time before sons and daughters had become the center of parents' concerns, games were devised by children themselves and were passed on through the generations. Some chanting games stressed verbal facility and mental reflexes, as with *¿cuántas naranjas?* (how many oranges?), during which Spanish-speaking youngsters subtracted and counted backward rapidly.

Most nineteenth-century games were highly physical and were played outdoors, fitting a rural life of generous spaces and considerable labor. Among the dozens of variations, some of the most popular were run, sheep, run; prisoner's base; blindman's bluff; fox and geese; and leapfrog. Typically they stressed individual achievement through speed and agility, and strategy counted more than strength. Many games involved chase and pursuit, either in teams or with an "it" player against the crowd. Any structure required was easily established with a few boundaries or bases, and equipment was limited to sticks, balls, or bits of cloth. Therefore play could be arranged instantly in fields, schoolyards, vacant lots, or camping spots along the overland trails. Simple and familiar rules brought young strangers into instant community, a useful social tool anytime but especially during the dislocations and unprecedented mobility of nineteenth-century America.

Girls to some degree favored less physical games, such as London Bridge and ring-a-ring-a-rosie, but, especially on the frontier, both sexes joined in. Everywhere the preferences of boys and girls tended to draw closer together during the century, a change one commentator explained by the "hardier education of the young ladies of the present day" (Grover, *Hard at Play*, p. 242).

The nation's many cultures developed their own variations of common patterns of play. Sioux boys formed teams that threw flaming torches at one another. African American children before the Civil War acted out slave auctions and emphasized whipping games like hide-the-switch. Before and after the Civil War, black children favored verbal contests with friendly exchanges of direct and indirect insults, "sounding" and "signifying," that encouraged quick thinking, self-discipline, and nonphysical aggression.

Evolution of Games

Children adjusted their play to the century's changes. When families moved to the city, a hydrant or lamppost became home base for I spy, and the two sides of a street became goals to race between in Black Tom. Hare and hound, a popular rural game in which a boy or girl ran several miles across fields while tossing scraps of paper as "scent" for pursuing players, became chalk chase in the city, where the "hare" showed his or her path with arrows drawn on the pavement. Games like marbles, well suited to a confined play space, flourished, and new games appeared. Boys pitched the picture cards sold with cigarettes, the winner being the one whose toss came closest to a building wall without touching it. Most significant was the rise of team sports, such as street hockey, or shinny, football, and above all baseball. Far and away the favorite boy's game by the end of the century, baseball acted out the tight integration of urban life. Success on the diamond, as in the city generally, came from rapid adjustment to changing circumstances and strategic maneuvers within many factors, personalities, and skills.

Baseball exemplified two other changes during the century. Especially in the expanding middle class, new games more often were shared by young and old, and children's play was more controlled by adults. Both were part of a broader development that brought children closer to the center of family and social life. Children in the countryside played football and baseball mostly on their own, and working-class boys and girls played stickball on city streets and in vacant lots, sometimes with rocks and broomsticks. But among middle-class families such sports were also organized and directed by grown-ups, sometimes within school curricula, as part of expanding parental efforts to instill proper values by controlling their youngsters' ordinary activities. Indoor games came under even closer adult supervision. Increasingly popular board games, played by parents and children, summed up Victorian virtues of competition, honor, patriotism, self-discipline, and the sanctity of the home. The Siege of Havana celebrated the Spanish-American War. In the Checkered Game of Life the winner reached happy old age by avoiding ruin through frugality and moral living, and in Mansion of Happiness players moved toward the goal of

Toys, 1886. An assortment of dolls and other toys from a pictorial catalog. LIBRARY OF CONGRESS

domestic bliss by avoiding spaces labeled "anger" and "dishonesty."

Toys

Toys followed much the same patterns as games. Traditionally toys were children's inventions that expressed their own interests and amusements. Boys and girls fashioned boats from bark and imagined branches into horses and rifles. Noisemakers were favorites. Bull roarers, made from plants, bellowed when swung around on a string, and whistles and flutes, whittled from willow, were blown loudly in concert. Household objects were borrowed for toys, such as using a knife to play mumble peg. The most universal toys, dolls, were bought and given by adults, but both girls and boys also made their own from corn shucks, grass, and discarded cloth. Like imitative play and traditional games, toys were the children's means of exploring creativity, testing skills, rehearsing the future, and converting the adult world to their own terms.

As with games, changes in toys during the century corresponded to national transformations. Industrialization brought hundreds of mechanical toys to the market. Especially popular were cast-iron locomotives, fire engines, carriages, and rearing or trotting horses. All had intricate moving parts and were either spring-powered or pulled along by a string. Even dolls felt the change. The first to say "mamma" with the help of a small bellows appeared in the 1830s. Shortly after 1900 children joined the urban industrial age with the first construction sets—collections of tiny winches, pulleys, cables, and hundreds of metal pieces youngsters bolted together to create buildings.

Unlike traditional toys, the new toys were not children's creations but were designed, manufactured, bought, and given by adults. Like many new games, they spoke of parents' desires to choreograph their sons' and daughters' lives and to implant what they considered essential values. Periodicals like *St. Nicholas* offered advice on the most instructive choices from a rapidly expanding toy industry. Increasingly elaborate dolls and dollhouses reinforced the duties of future mothers and the ethics of Victorian womanhood. An especially revealing example of toys as teachers were cast-iron mechanical banks, which enjoyed phenomenal popularity after first appearing in the 1870s. Each bank featured a familiar figure, such as an organ-grinder, policeman, or baseball pitcher, that would fling a coin into a container when activated by a trigger. While overtly reinforcing the virtues of frugality and saving, these banks also expressed admiration for some figures, such as a cigar-smoking General Ulysses S. Grant, and intolerance of others, like a drunken Irishman, a lazy Chinese man, and African American boys stealing watermelons.

In both toys and games, however, these trends were confined mostly to middle-class parents who had money to spend and time to direct children's days and nights. At the century's end, boys and girls of most frontier and rural families amused themselves much as others had early in the century. So did city working-class children, who also found fun in new urban enterprises far outside conventional standards of child rearing, such as burlesque houses, arcades, and amusement parks. As children had for centuries, American youngsters jealously guarded their play as a time of independence and of engaging life on their own terms.

See also **Life Cycle,** *subentry on* **Childhood and Adolescence; Recreation.**

Bibliography

Asakawa, Gil. *The Toy Book.* New York: Knopf, 1992.
Clement, Priscilla Ferguson. *Growing Pains: Children in the Industrial Age, 1850–1890.* New York: Twayne, 1997.
Grover, Kathryn, ed. *Hard at Play: Leisure in America, 1840–1940.* Amherst: University of Massachusetts Press, 1992.
Mergen, Bernard. *Play and Playthings: A Reference Guide.* Westport, Conn.: Greenwood, 1982.
Sutton-Smith, Brian. *The Folkgames of Children.* Austin: University of Texas Press, 1972.
———. *Toys as Culture.* New York: Gardner, 1986.
West, Elliott, and Paula Petrik, eds. *Small Worlds: Children and Adolescents in America, 1850–1950.* Lawrence: University Press of Kansas, 1992.

ELLIOTT WEST

GENDER

[This entry includes two subentries, **Interpretations of Gender** and **Gender and the Law.**]

INTERPRETATIONS OF GENDER

Throughout the nineteenth century, the topic of appropriate gender roles was much discussed, especially by white women and men of the middle and upper classes. The nineteenth century was one of cataclysmic change, ranging from the abolition of slavery to massive urbanization and industrialization. Women participated in these and other movements as leaders, reformers, and workers. As they recognized the limitations placed upon them as females, many women, and some men, called for the revision of prevailing gender theories.

Antebellum Concepts of Gender

At the beginning of the nineteenth century, the legal concept of "civil death" regulated women's actions. If a woman was unmarried, she was considered *feme sole* (single woman), meaning she could conduct business affairs, sign contracts, and manage her own money. Divorced women who asked for and received *feme sole* status in their divorce petitions and widows enjoyed the same rights. When a woman married, however, her standing changed to that of *feme covert*, or a woman covered. She was one with her husband, meaning that she could not conduct business affairs, sign contracts, or manage her own money.

The idea of civil death was softened by the realities of everyday life and by decisions of local equity courts. For example, if a husband went on a three-year whaling voyage, a wife could manage home and business affairs. She might even ask a court of equity to give her *feme sole* status. Or she might go to court to adjudicate a business contract and discover that the court considered her a valid representative of her husband's business.

As American society became more industrialized, however, men's workplaces increasingly moved away from the home, and the doctrine of "separate spheres" appeared. The domestic realm belonged to women, the public one to men. Women managed the home, oversaw the servants, and maintained, within that home, such moral values as kindness and honesty. Men left the home to conduct business, follow a profession, vote, and run for political office. Whatever contamination a man acquired from his daily dealings was washed away when he entered the door to his home, where his virtuous and domestic wife had preserved decency.

There were several variations on this theme. After the American Revolution, women were elevated to the stature of "republican women," who needed education as well as a heightened moral sense to raise republican children. Around the time of the War of 1812, a doctrine referred to as "true womanhood" or "domesticity" urged women to be quiet, domestic, virtuous, and spiritual. In the South, true womanhood translated to "southern womanhood," which stressed the need for women to show intense loyalty to their men and to southern culture. A true southern woman would not speak about politics or oppose slavery.

This kind of thinking applied primarily to women of the middle and upper classes, who had the education, leisure, and energy to explore the implications of separate spheres or women's imputed morality. Other groups, such as female factory workers, domestic servants, seamstresses, and thousands of other wage earners, were unable to follow the dictates of true womanhood. Although such women dreamed that someday they, too, would become "ladies," they were more concerned with obtaining higher wages, more reasonable hours, and better working conditions.

In the South, true womanhood was not considered applicable to black slave women, who were viewed more as laborers than as women. Ironically, some African American women turned the ideal of domesticity to their own advantage. By maintaining gender divisions of labor within their own homes and acting as moral guardians of their families, slave women mocked their owners, who treated them as pseudomen and beasts of burden rather than as wives and mothers.

On the southern and western frontiers, the philosophy of domesticity had different meanings for different women. Factors such as race, religion, and the demands of work shaped the lives of most frontier women. The toil and instability of frontier life offered little opportunity to develop domestic "virtues," act "feminine," or raise children in "proper" ways. White women and women of color took what they could from prevailing gender theories and ignored the rest.

Unfortunately, Indian women could not so easily dispose of "domesticity," for its assumptions were inconsistent with their traditional roles. For instance, government officials, especially the Bureau of Indian Affairs in Washington, D.C., who supported stereotypical standards of womanhood, issued orders that Indian women (from tribes such as the Sioux, Nez Percé, Omaha, Ute, Iroquois, Seneca, and Cheyenne) give up their customary, valued pursuit of agriculture and, like white women, learn to weave and sew. To their dismay, native men discovered they were to take over the women's agricultural tasks.

Eventually, tenets of domesticity began to lack appeal to some middle- and upper-class women in the North, who found them unduly restrictive. Such women discovered a way to use gender beliefs to widen their domestic sphere. For example, Sarah Josepha Hale (1788–1879), a widow who became editor of *Godey's Lady's Book* in 1836, maintained that her purpose was to make female readers better wives and mothers. But Hale subtly subverted the ideology of separate spheres, arguing that "moral" women should teach the impressionable young in regular schools and Sunday Schools. She also asserted that female authors should write the morally improving literature that women read, that women missionaries should carry their morality to the downtrodden, and that female reformers should clean up society much as they cleaned up at home.

As a result of such reasoning by Hale and others, many women came to believe that they had a moral mission to expand their domestic sphere to include secular and religious teaching, writing and publishing, missionary work, and social reform. This was especially true of elite white women in the North and educated free black women in such northern cities as Boston and Philadelphia. Beginning in the late 1820s and early 1830s, female reformers campaigned for improved education for women, prison reform, temperance, and, in the North, the abolition of slavery.

In addition, a number of women and men wanted more egalitarian marriages. Instead of a submissive wife and dominant husband, they advocated partnerships in which women and men gave each other romantic love and companionship. Other suggestions for marital reform came from the founders of utopian communities. In 1826, Nashoba, the community founded by the Scottish reformer Frances Wright (1795–1852), rejected the idea of legal marriage. In 1848, the Oneida community established by John Humphrey Noyes (1811–1886), practiced "complex" marriage, in which all male members were married to all the women, though not all members were married to each other, and cared for the children as a group. Noyes's goal was to free women from lifelong service to men. Other reformers took a different tack. In 1832, Robert Dale Owen and Mary Robinson and, in 1855, Lucy Stone and Henry Blackwell signed marriage "contracts" intended to free their marriage of gender inequalities.

Such reforms in marriage appeared strange and even uncivilized to many Americans. Critics branded such communities as Nashoba and Oneida as immoral, "free love" organizations. People like Owen and Stone were caricatured in the press. Apparently, the time was not right for Americans to reject separate spheres for women and men.

Female reformers faced problems in other areas as well. When they clashed with the male establishment, women became painfully aware of their lack of rights. How could women reform society, they asked, if they were discouraged or forbidden to speak in public, write tracts, vote, or hold office? Women in the temperance and abolitionist movements felt particularly stymied because their causes demanded politi-

The Women's Sphere. The notion of "separate spheres" for men and women is illustrated in this 1869 lithograph, which shows a domestic scene dominated by women and girls, who work and congregate at home. No men are in sight. LIBRARY OF CONGRESS: PRINTS AND PHOTOGRAPHS DIVISION

cal action, and many soon became advocates of women's rights. Although Elizabeth Cady Stanton (1815–1902) and Lucretia Mott (1793–1880) began their careers in the temperance and abolitionist movements, they organized the first women's rights convention at Seneca Falls, New York, in 1848. They argued that to use their inherent morality, women needed certain legal rights, including the right to own property, vote, and run for office.

The Civil War and After

When the Civil War erupted in 1861, female reformers put aside many of their causes except the abolition of slavery. Instead, women's organizations in the North and South sent much-needed supplies to the front, and individual women served as nurses, spies, saboteurs, and even soldiers. Americans appreciated women's war efforts, but when the war ended in 1865, women's rights advanced little. Black men won the right to vote, but black and white women did not. Even when the Wyoming Territory granted women the vote in 1869, it did so only to attract "moral" women settlers who would introduce law and order into Wyoming's rough, male-dominated society.

During the last three decades of the nineteenth century, traditional views of gender roles persisted. Women were expected to stay at home while men went to work. In reality, however, women of many social classes and racial backgrounds moved into wage work in huge numbers. Women toiled in factories and on farms. They also entered the professions, becoming teachers, nurses, doctors, and lawyers. Women even refused to remain physically inactive within the walls of their homes and gardens. Alongside the old model of the "true" woman developed a new image of the healthy American woman. She was the mountain climber, the camper and hiker, the clubwoman, the western woman, and the rodeo star.

The American woman was also a reformer and a suffragist who hoped to introduce the principle of equality into theories of gender. Most suffragists believed that the right to vote and hold office would promote equal employment opportunities, equal pay, liberalized divorce, and "voluntary motherhood," which would allow women to choose how many children they would bear. These platforms alarmed many men, and a significant number of women, who worried that such reforms would create chaos in American society.

Consequently, while some women and men promoted change, others opposed it. For instance, although many women worked outside their homes, usually at low pay and under poor conditions, few male labor unions accepted women members. In 1881, the Knights of Labor opened membership to women and in 1888, the American Federation of Labor began to recruit women members. But the majority of male workers adhered to the customary ideology of women as wives and mothers, in part because male workers feared that women's willingness to accept low wages would decrease men's earning power.

Fearful women and men fought other changes in gender roles. Because such groups as the American Medical Association and the Young Men's Christian Association believed that "voluntary motherhood" would cause a population decline and promote a decline of morality among women, they sought a federal law that would prevent birth control information from being sent through the mail. Similarly, in 1888, the New England Divorce League became the National Divorce Reform League, which hoped to repeal laws that allowed a growing number of women to divorce their husbands.

During the 1890s, however, calls for change became dominant. The Progressive movement sought reform in virtually every area of American life, including the family and women's roles. Such organizations as the Populist Party, founded in 1892, not only welcomed female members but also fought for women's issues. In 1890, the two wings of the woman's suffrage movement, the National Woman Suffrage Association and the American Woman Suffrage Association, united into the National American Woman Suffrage Association. And the Woman's Christian Temperance Union became the largest women's association in American history.

Clearly, the heated national debate over gender was far from settled. Granted, many aspects of civil death were themselves dead. In most states, married women could own property, seek a divorce, or work for a wage. But a huge range of gender issues remained unresolved and would spill over into the twentieth century.

See also **Civil War,** *subentry on* **Women on the Front; Contraception and Abortion; Divorce and Desertion; Domestic Life; Education,** *subentry on* **Education of Girls and Women; Law,** *subentry on* **Women and the Law; Magazines, Women's; Marriage; Voters and Voting,** *subentry on* **The Women's Vote; Women,** *subentries on* **Women's Rights, Women's Labor, Women in the Professions, Woman as Image and Icon.**

Bibliography

Córdova, Teresa, et al. *Chicana Voices: Intersections of Class, Race, and Gender.* Albuquerque: University of New Mexico Press, 1990.

Foster, Martha Harroun. "Of Baggage and Bondage: Gender and Status Among Hidatsa and Crow Women." *American Indian Culture and Research Journal* 17 (1993): 121–153.

Holland-Braund, Kathryn E. "Guardians of Tradition and Handmaidens to Change: Women's Roles in Creek Economic and Social Life During the Eighteenth Century." *American Indian Quarterly* 14 (1990): 311–344.

Kerber, Linda K., et al. "Beyond Roles, Beyond Spheres: Thinking about Gender in the Early Republic." *William and Mary Quarterly* 46 (July 1989): 565–585.

Lasser, Carol. "Gender, Ideology, and Class in the Early Republic." *Journal of the Early Republic* 10 (Fall 1990): 331–337.

Nash, Margaret A. "Rethinking Republican Motherhood: Benjamin Rush and the Young Ladies' Academy of Philadelphia." *Journal of the Early Republic* 17 (Summer 1997): 171–191.

Russett, Cynthia Eagle. *Sexual Science: The Victorian Construction of Womanhood.* Cambridge, Mass.: Harvard University Press, 1989.

White, Deborah Gray. "Female Slaves: Sex Roles and Status in the Antebellum Plantation South." In *Unequal Sisters: A Multicultural Reader in U.S. Women's History.* 2d ed. Edited by Ellen Carol DuBois and Vicki L. Ruiz. New York: Routledge, Chapman, & Hall, 1994.

GLENDA RILEY

GENDER AND THE LAW

During the revolutionary decades most Americans rejected the possibility of legal equality for men and women. Constitutional convention delegates considered free white adult women essentially as dependencies and excluded them from the electorate. Well into the nineteenth century legislators and judges retained the traditional unitary household head for purposes of family governance. In the political realm, sovereign citizens supposedly authorized governments to make laws for the benefit of the entire community, a line of reasoning that seemed to mandate universal suffrage; within the family, sovereignty resided in *barons* or *petit* kings, who "laid down the law" for household subordinates (for example, wives, children, apprentices, and, in slaveholding states, bonded laborers). The household head, whose sovereignty like a king's was presumed indivisible, functioned with explicit state permission as the family's representative in political and, with some exceptions, legal matters. State and federal constitutions embodied what has been called a "sexual contract," within which women assumed the responsibilities of republican motherhood or, when unmarried, mothers-in-waiting. These decisions, in turn, permitted the retention of premodern doctrines in property, contract, inheritance, and domestic relations laws.

Political practices vividly reflected Americans' conceptions of the "good" republican man and woman. As early as 1805–1807, lawmakers affirmed women's political invisibility and the subordination of wives to husbands. In New Jersey single women and widows could vote in the early nineteenth century. But this was exceptional, and they were disfranchised in 1807. Elsewhere customary bans against female involvement in politics were codified in the constitutions and election laws adopted after 1776. State courts formally blessed the reception of ancient constitutional and legal doctrines in rulings such as *Martin v. Massachusetts* (1805), in which the court decided, after explicit discussion of the implications of republicanism for gender relations, that married women did not possess a political will of their own. Judges in Connecticut and New Jersey ruled that revolutionary doctrine had not enfranchised women or augmented their ability to deal in property during marriage. Justice Joseph Story's decision to the contrary in *Shanks v. Dupont* (1830), which might have allowed public officials to distinguish between marital and political status, did not find its way into American law for more than a century.

Early national lawmakers also chose not to tamper with a received tradition in domestic relations law, which constructed married women as passive recipients of male protection and wealth, disabled by marriage and merged (under the doctrine of marital unity) into the legal personalities of their husbands. Marriage was not a species of slavery, except in the hands of vicious men, and then without legal sanction. Plantation masters legally owned slaves' bodies; the incidents of personal sovereignty were eradicated almost completely. Marriage, by contrast, imposed a subordinated status called "coverture" akin to perpetual servitude. Many writers called it the "marital indenture." To be sure household heads could inflict great harm without running afoul of the law. Throughout the century judges were more willing to intervene in disputes between black men and women than in analogous conflicts in white households, with dire consequences for black women's privacy and white women's personal security. But, as a rule, men could not maim or kill free women with impunity or force them to act "against nature," as masters could do with bondswomen.

By the early 1850s scholars thought of the marital indenture as a social institution conveying sex-specific, unequal bundles of rights and obligations to spouses. Husbands were bound to provide "necessaries," for example, food, clothing, and shelter; "pin money," a legal term; and protection. They also had responsibility for their wives' debts, even when couples were estranged, and for crimes short of treason and homicide. In return, men claimed exclusive rights to wives' company, conjugal (or sexual) services, and domestic labor. Delinquent or resistant women violated the marriage contract. A woman's assumption of her husband's surname signified the passage of rights in labor from father to husband. Because she no longer possessed a distinct legal personality, a wife could not serve as an agent or attorney, even for family enterprises.

Early in the century legislatures sometimes granted special trading licenses to married women, in effect transforming them into unmarried women for limited business purposes. In communities characterized by gender imbalances or rapid growth, Americans sometimes blinked at the letter of the law so women might contribute to development.

As more than one writer noted, the law of coverture was on a collision course with capitalism. But before the 1840s marriage typically eliminated female economic agency. Wives lost the ability to deal in most species of property, to retain earnings, or to make legally enforceable contracts. Only by making special arrangements before marriage could a married woman keep personal property away from a husband or his creditors. Wives retained title to inherited real estate, but with few exceptions they gave over management even of separate estates to court-appointed trustees, who could be husbands, at the moment of marriage. Men could sell or impound their wives' personal property without women's permission. A woman in a common law state could not prevent a man from squandering the marital estate. In the civil law jurisdictions, where many old French, Spanish, or Dutch rules prevailed, women were viewed as cotenants of the marital estate and could deal within limits in property and participate in estate transactions. But in common law states women were something less than coproprietors. Notwithstanding male generosity, which often mitigated black-letter law, men were the household rulers, and women were the ruled.

The long shadow of coverture followed women even after divorce. Until the 1840s, when law on the point began to change, judges typically assigned custody of minor children to husbands rather than wives on the ground that rights to their labor inhered in the family head. Except in cases of extreme abuse or husbandly neglect, a divorcing woman could hope only for judicial assignment of a relatively "soft" possessory right to a child's person, subject always to men's superior "natural" right (title) in the child's labor. And, despite a shift to maternal custody by century's end, judges often refused to transfer the property right itself to women, granting women only possession of the child's person rather than title, which they reserved for men. Decisions to grant custody to women, moreover, typically reflected notions of their "natural" maternalism, which reinforced the line between "public" and "private" spheres.

In sum, men and women did not occupy the same legal ground. Throughout the century scholars asserted both that women were citizens and that sex disabled the entire female class. Sex distinctions seeped into odd nooks and crannies of the law. After mid-century, for instance, prevailing views of ladylike deportment supported disparate standards of blameworthiness for the sexes in nuisance and negligence suits, so that, in a late-century Colorado case involving the injury of a woman at a train station, a judge could say that jurors need not "exact the same degree of care and diligence from a woman that we would from a man under the same circumstances" because women were "not accustomed" to train stations. Sex-specific doctrines emerged as well in cases involving, among other categories, felony and breach of promise. In the latter, judges developed rules by which the court might take account of a woman's "natural" timidity and a man's "natural" aggression.

By the 1850s, moreover, legislators began to respond to industrialization and the presence of women and children in the workforce with protective economic legislation. By the century's end these measures limited the hours that affected classes might work, the occupations they might choose (women, for instance, might be barred from mining or bartending), and the burden that employees bore for workplace accidents. Americans had come to associate male citizenship with the ability to command a "family wage," so that female incursions into the workplace literally threatened men's civic identities. For such reasons, by 1900–1910, state authority supported an increasingly complex, ostensibly progressive web of rules limiting female access to overtime, night work, and prestigious managerial posts; and state courts generally supported these innovations.

Victorian men and women had radically different experiences of freedom. Although the First Amendment was sex-neutral, custom effectively barred the female sex from speaking or assembling in public without male permission. When women tried to gain access to pulpits, university lecture halls, or reform conventions, many were ejected, heckled, or shamed into silence. Women sometimes asked men to read speeches for them, especially when audiences were mixed (or "promiscuous"). Nor did governments protect the personal security of men and women equally. Sex-specific violence (rape, street harassment, battering) continued unabated into the twentieth century. Because of their legal rights to women's labor and company, men could impound wives in attics,

prevent friends from visiting, or lock estranged women out of houses. If a woman fled, a man could ask the sheriff to retrieve her. Lawyers and reformers understood that a woman's right to move about freely and to what by the 1890s was called a "right of privacy" did not approach the male standard. Marital rape was literally inconceivable: to rape one's wife was to rape oneself. Bondswomen regularly endured sexual abuse at the hands of white men, who sometimes viewed black women's bodies as the white race's property. White working women, as well as any woman bold enough to take a walk without a male companion, fended off sexual slurs, since Americans associated physical labor or escape from the "marital buttons," as one woman put it, with loose morals. Criminal courts treated working-class and black women differently than their middle-class white counterparts. Masters demanded sexual services of housemaids; saloon patrons manhandled barmaids; after the Civil War, white southerners assaulted or killed numerous black women as punishment for freedmen's uppity behavior.

Beginning in the 1830s an organized woman's movement appeared, sometimes called the "first wave" of modern feminism. By mid-century reform had made its mark. When Louisiana, California, Texas, and other jurisdictions initially controlled by continental European powers came under British and American control, the relatively generous rules associated with civil law regimes were temporarily eclipsed by stringent common law rules. But, beginning in the late 1830s in Mississippi, reformers began to restore old principles, so that married women might deal in their own property, if not always in the marital estate. Also in the 1830s, Americans began to grant limited suffrage to women. In Kentucky, for instance, legislators in 1837 and 1838 extended school suffrage to unmarried, propertied women and widows alongside the guardians of propertied minors and the agents of banking houses. A handful of other states followed suit with partial suffrage in municipal or school elections.

Then, in the 1840s and 1850s, except in much of the Old South, legislators began to modify law codes, often by imitating the rules prevailing in civil law (sometimes called community property) jurisdictions. Notably but not exclusively in Texas, laws significantly augmented female agency by means of married women's property acts and related measures. The panic of 1837 triggered discussion in a number of states of the merits of liberalized property acts. Maryland acted in 1842–1843. Between 1844 and 1847 Alabama, Connecticut, Iowa, Massachusetts, Maine, Ohio, New Hampshire, Indiana, and Vermont joined the parade. In 1847–1848, after twenty years of debate, New York, borrowing heavily from Texas, finally passed its celebrated property act, followed over the next two decades by a series of lesser-known elaborations and retreats.

As of 1850, half of the states permitted wives to claim separate property during coverture beyond assets brought into marriage, and five decades later 89 percent had done so. While these statutes underscored the sex's separateness, they also permitted women to gain experience with property. By 1860, 24 percent of the legislatures had adopted earnings laws by which wives might retain their own wages during coverture; and by 1900, 61 percent had so moved. In 1850, about one-third of the states granted *feme sole* status to abandoned wives so that they might engage in economic self-defense; fifty years later, the portion was two-thirds. By the 1870s, lawmakers had begun to erode the old widow's dower (traditionally one-third of the estate, reserved for widows at husbands' death) in light of women's increased access to property. Within another decade, legislators in most states had adopted sex-neutral custody laws; Congress meanwhile included married women as potential land claimants in the Homestead Act, thereby encouraging both sexes to consider westward migration and settlement.

Typically, reform originated in a desire either to prevent male abuse of women's trusts or to allow women to contribute to economic recovery after major depressions. Yet lawmakers sometimes recognized the merits of liberalization after listening to women's rights lecturers or learning of progressive practices in other jurisdictions; and, whatever the impetus, the long-term effect of the legislation was to enhance women's power. Probate records show that, fifty years after adoption of the first married women's property acts, women's wealth had increased exponentially. By 1900 slogans like "no taxation without representation" had great resonance in suffrage campaigns. Wherever civilian principles held sway, moreover, women were cotenants of the marital estate and therefore co–household heads, which compelled legislators in Washington Territory to enfranchise women in 1882–1883. Wyoming officials had made much the same decision in 1869. A class contributing equally to economic development, they thought, surely had a right to participate as equals on election day.

On the downside, Victorian lawmakers steadily curtailed women's ability to control fertility. By the first decades of the twentieth century most states had declared a public interest in maternity to justify increased scrutiny of childbearing, abortion, contraception, and child care. The 1840s saw an upsurge in laws criminalizing abortion and commerce in contracep-

tives. During Reconstruction, Congress joined the fray with adoption of the Comstock Act, which among other provisions banned interstate movement of information, compounds, or devices associated with fertility control. States quickly adopted mini-Comstock measures. State legislators also lent support to the idea, pressed by medical professionals, that licensed physicians ought to replace "irregular" providers of health services, with dire consequences for poor women.

Many activists concluded in the wake of the Civil War that women's status had deteriorated since 1850. During the war years, Congress continued to exclude women from the polity. More alarming, for the first time in the nation's history, the word "male" appeared in constitutional texts. Despite fierce opposition from reformers, the Fourteenth and Fifteenth Amendments explicitly created a national political community composed entirely of men. The omission of the term "female" seemed to constitutionalize female inferiority as compared to all men, including aliens, who in some territories could vote. To make matters worse, Americans refused to allow women to share responsibility for jury duty, military service, and other obligations of citizenship.

Women's rights activists therefore turned increasingly to campaigns for political freedom, including the right to retain citizenship whenever men could retain it (for example, when marrying an alien). Fears were not groundless. In *Bradwell v. Illinois* (1873) the U.S. Supreme Court ruled that the Reconstruction Amendments did not prevent states from barring women from particular occupations, such as the practice of law. The same Court ruled against the attorney Belva Lockwood's demand for admission to the federal bar, which prompted Congress to pass a law forcing federal courts to admit women. Into the 1880s state courts decided that Lavinia Goodell, Lelia Robinson, and other would-be attorneys violated natural law when they entered courtrooms as agents rather than as supplicants. The Supreme Court ruled as well in *Minor v. Happersett* (1875) that the new amendments did not prevent state legislators from adopting sex-specific election laws.

As they tinkered with legal rules, nineteenth-century reformers and lawyers often aimed to protect disadvantaged classes, to improve the lot of women, or to force men to make good on their promises. Nevertheless, public policy tended to affirm the sex's ineluctable differences, women's second-class citizenship, and men's special claim to the public realm. Small wonder that thousands of late-century club women organized to exchange information, hone intellect, and gather skills necessary to citizenship.

Activists like Margaret Sanger mobilized to defend the sex's personal security in the birth control movement and elsewhere. Mary Church Terrell and other African Americans eloquently pointed to black women's peculiarly disadvantaged position in relation to every other class of citizens. Late-century women stormed technical schools and corporations, demanded equal pay for equal work, and struggled to reverse the galloping sex segregation of the workplace. Only after 1890, when suffragists formed the National American Woman Suffrage Association, did campaigns for universal balloting gain widespread popular support. Decades later, in 1920, state legislatures ratified the Nineteenth Amendment. A scant handful of first wave activists lived to see the day when, as novelist Mary Johnston put it in 1912, men and women finally could be "kings and queens—not kings with a queen-consort walking behind, but fellow sovereigns—Williams and Marys, Ferdinands and Isabellas!"

See also **Civil Rights; Clubs,** *subentry on* **Women's Clubs and Associations; Contraception and Abortion; Divorce and Desertion; Domestic Life; Law,** *subentry on* **Women and the Law; Marriage; Reform, Political; Reform, Social; Republican Motherhood; Voters and Voting,** *subentry on* **The Women's Vote; Women,** *subentries on* **Women's Rights, Women's Labor.**

Bibliography

Bardaglio, Peter W. *Reconstructing the Household: Families, Sex, and the Law in the Nineteenth-Century South.* Chapel Hill: University of North Carolina Press, 1995.

Basch, Norma. *In the Eyes of the Law.* Ithaca, N.Y.: Cornell University Press, 1982.

Boydston, Jeanne. *Home and Work: Housework, Wages, and the Ideology of Labor in the Early Republic.* New York: Oxford University Press, 1990.

Bredbenner, Candice Lewis. *A Nationality of Her Own: Women, Marriage, and the Law of Citizenship.* Berkeley: University of California Press, 1998.

Brodie, Janet Farrell. *Contraception and Abortion in Nineteenth-Century America.* Ithaca, N.Y.: Cornell University Press, 1994.

Clinton, Catherine. *The Other Civil War: American Women in the Nineteenth Century.* New York: Hill and Wang, 1984.

Cott, Nancy. "Marriage and Women's Citizenship in the United States, 1830-1934." *American Historical Review* (1998): 1440-1474.

DuBois, Ellen Carol. *Feminism and Suffrage: The Emergence of an Independent Women's Movement in America, 1848-1869.* Ithaca, N.Y.: Cornell University Press, 1978.

———. "Outgrowing the Compact of the Fathers: Equal Rights, Woman Suffrage, and the United States Constitution, 1820-1978." *Journal of American History* (1987): 836-862.

Edwards, Laura. *Gendered Strife and Confusion: The Political Culture of Reconstruction.* Urbana: University of Illinois Press, 1997.

Grossberg, Michael. *Governing the Hearth: Law and the Family in Nineteenth-Century America.* Chapel Hill: University of North Carolina Press, 1985.

Hoff, Joan. *Law, Gender, and Injustice: A Legal History of U.S. Women.* New York: New York University Press, 1991.

Isenberg, Nancy. *Sex and Citizenship in Antebellum America.* Chapel Hill: University of North Carolina Press, 1998.

Kerber, Linda K. *No Constitutional Right to Be Ladies: Women and the Obligations of Citizenship.* New York: Hill and Wang, 1998.

———. *Women of the Republic: Intellect and Ideology in Revolutionary America.* Chapel Hill: University of North Carolina Press, 1980.

———. "The Paradox of Women's Citizenship in the Early Republic: The Case of Martin vs. Massachusetts, 1805." *American Historical Review* (1992): 349-378.

Kessler-Harris, Alice. *A Woman's Wage: Historical Meanings and Social Consequences.* Lexington: University Press of Kentucky, 1990.

Lebsock, Suzanne. *Free Women of Petersburg: Status and Culture in a Southern Town, 1784-1860.* New York: Norton, 1984.

Matthews, Jean V. *Women's Struggle for Equality: The First Phase, 1828-1876.* Chicago: Ivan R. Dee, 1997.

Mohr, James C. *Abortion in America.* New York: Oxford University Press, 1978.

Myres, Sandra L. *Westering Women and the Frontier Experience, 1800-1915.* Albuquerque: University of New Mexico Press, 1982.

Nelson, Dana D. *National Manhood: Capitalist Citizenship and the Imagined Fraternity of White Men.* Durham, N.C.: Duke University Press, 1998.

Norton, Mary Beth. *Liberty's Daughters: The Revolutionary Experience of American Women, 1750-1800.* Boston: Little, Brown, 1980.

Pateman, Carole. *The Sexual Contract.* Stanford, Calif.: Stanford University Press, 1988.

Reagan, Leslie. *When Abortion Was a Crime: Women, Medicine, and Law in the U.S., 1867-1973.* Berkeley: University of California Press, 1997.

Rotundo, E. Anthony. *American Manhood: Transformations in Masculinity from the Revolution to the Modern Era.* New York: Basic Books, 1993.

Salmon, Marylynn. *Women and the Law of Property in Early America.* Chapel Hill: University of North Carolina Press, 1986.

Shammas, Carole. "Re-Assessing the Married Women's Property Acts." *Journal of Women's History* (Spring 1994): 9-30.

Siegel, Reva. "The Rule of Love: Wife Beating as Prerogative and Privacy." *Yale Law Journal* (1996): 2117-2207.

Stanley, Amy Dru. *From Bondage to Contract: Wage Labor, Marriage, and the Market in the Age of Slave Emancipation.* New York: Cambridge University Press, 1998.

VanBurkleo, Sandra F. *"Belonging to the World": Women's Rights and American Constitutional Culture.* New York: Oxford University Press, 2000.

White, Deborah. "Female Slaves: Sex Roles and Status in the Antebellum Plantation South." In J. William Harris, ed., *Society and Culture in the Slave South.* New York: Routledge, 1992.

SANDRA F. VANBURKLEO

GEOGRAPHY AND CARTOGRAPHY   The geography of the United States had a profound impact on the country's development in the nineteenth century, providing the nation with both daunting obstacles and unbounded benefits. Mapping the continent became increasingly important for strategic, political, and economic purposes.

The territory east of the continent's most significant feature, the Mississippi River, was fairly well understood at the beginning of the nineteenth century. Yet glaring lapses in geographical knowledge remained. The source of the Mississippi itself defied discovery for many years. The watershed of this great river provided a ready transportation network for exploiting the natural resources of the region and spurred westward expansion. Flatboats, keelboats, and steamboats plied the waters of the Ohio, Tennessee, and Cumberland Rivers and their tributaries, accessing once-remote corners of the continent and fueling an economic engine that became the envy of the world by the end of the century.

The United States military took the lead in exploration during this century. An understanding of geography and cartography were considered vital to national interests, and the United States Army trained students in these disciplines. Map drawing was a required course at the military academy at West Point. Top graduates of that institution joined the highly selective Army Corps of Topographical Engineers, and it was U.S. Army officers who led the way into the wilderness as Americans explored the continent.

After the Louisiana Purchase in 1803, American attention turned toward the Trans-Mississippi West. Understanding this region became a priority for the administration of President Thomas Jefferson, who dispatched several military and quasi-scientific expeditions like those of Meriwether Lewis and William Clark or Zebulon Pike to discover the sources and resources of such major water arteries as the Red, Missouri, and Arkansas Rivers. All of the explorers reported a landscape that differed greatly from the familiar forests of the East. They described much of the nation's new western domain as "the Great American Desert." Later in the century, once improved agricultural technology and techniques made settlement and exploitation of arid prairies possible, the gentler-sounding "Great Plains" came into more common use.

Further west the geography of the continent offered both doom and hope. Bordering the plains on the west, the Rocky Mountains—by far the most formidable natural obstacle to western travel—teemed with furbearing animals. Beyond the mountains the dusty lands of the Great Basin were bleak and discouraging. Just a few decades into the century, however, fur trappers, returning sailors, and fortune hunters reported that the lands of the Pacific Slope were a potential paradise. Boosters extolled the wonders of the West well in advance of cartographers' abilities to accurately describe it.

The West of the popular imagination had a great impact on the foreign policy of the United States in the nineteenth century. In the first two decades trappers working for U.S. and British firms penetrated the valleys of the western cordilleras as far as the Pacific, leading to disputed claims to the region described as the Oregon Territory. After 1821 U.S. settlers penetrated the frontier of the newly independent Mexico, and by 1823 regular commerce flowed between Chihuahua and St. Louis via the Santa Fe Trail. In the 1830s and early 1840s the pressure of American migration into Mexican territory led to war, first in Texas in 1835, then between the United States and Mexico in 1846. Coolheaded negotiation averted war between the United States and Great Britain over the Oregon question.

By 1848 most of the territory comprising the present-day United States had been annexed to the nation, but surveyors and cartographers required decades to decide the actual boundaries. The most accurate portrayal of the North American continent up to that point was the so-called Disturnell map created by John Disturnell. Its erroneous depiction of the American Southwest led to much diplomatic wrangling between the United States and Mexico. The 1854 acquisition of an additional slice of Mexican territory, including the town of Tucson, in the Gadsden Purchase solved many of these issues and established the present-day borders of the continental United States.

Americans were interested in their own country, as well as in the nations of the world, but more as a hobby than a serious field of inquiry. At the beginning of the 1800s, most Americans learned geography from Jedediah Morse's *The American Universal Geography*, first published in 1797 and widely popular. By mid-century, the public's interest in the world led to such works as R. C. Smith's *Atlas of Modern and Ancient Geography*, which appeared in many middle-class parlors. The War with Mexico and, later, the Civil War led to a spate of "seat of the war" maps affording the folks at home a glimpse at where their sons were fighting.

In the waning days of the century, American interest in the field became more profound. The government established the U.S. Geological Survey within the Department of the Interior under the leadership of the dauntless explorer John Wesley Powell. Its mission was to regulate and conduct the mapping of the nation. In 1888, American interest in places and people led to the founding of the National Geographical Society. Even so, geography remained an adjunct of history and geology classes, and was rarely taught as a discrete school subject. Clark University in Worcester, Massachusetts, would become the first institution of higher learning to offer graduate courses in geography, but not until 1920.

In the second half of the century the people of the United States explored and familiarized themselves with this great land and its resources. The army took the lead in scouting and mapping. Immigration agents sketched the land and made careful notes of prime territory. Seeking gold and silver deposits, miners swarmed into California in the 1850s, into Colorado, New Mexico, and Nevada in the 1860s, and into the Dakotas in the 1870s. The Homestead Act of 1862 moved farmers onto the Great Plains. Railroad companies hurried to keep up with the accelerating pace of western immigration, and their surveying crews made great strides in mapping the West. By 1900 technological advances, including rail transportation, barbed wire, and windmills, had overcome the geographical barriers of the West. This once-remote and unpromising region was fully integrated with the rest of the nation. Nevertheless, maps of the nation remained imperfect well into the twentieth century.

See also **Boosterism; Expansion; Exploration and Explorers; Federal Land Policy; Frontier; Gadsden Purchase; Geography and Ecology; Gold Rushes and Silver Strikes; Great Plains; Jeffersonian Era; Lewis and Clark Expedition; Louisiana Purchase; Mexican Cession; Natural Resources; Oregon; Population; Railroads; Trails to the West; Transportation; West, The.**

Bibliography

Goetzmann, William H. *Army Exploration in the American West, 1803–1863.* New Haven, Conn.: Yale University Press, 1959.

———. *Exploration and Empire: The Explorer and the Scientist in the Winning of the American West.* New York: Knopf, 1966.

Goetzmann, William H., and William N. Goetzmann. *The West of the Imagination.* New York: Norton, 1986.

Prucha, Francis Paul. *Broadax and Bayonet: The Role of the United States Army in the Development of the Northwest, 1815–1860.* Lincoln: University of Nebraska Press, 1967.

———. *The Sword of the Republic: The United States Army on the Frontier, 1783–1846.* New York: Macmillan, 1968.

DONALD S. FRAZIER

GEOGRAPHY AND ECOLOGY

During the nineteenth century, the American landscape, always subject to ecological processes and human agency, was transformed at an accelerated pace by unbridled economic development and mass settlement. In the East, expanding cities dominated the skylines. In the West, Americans of European, African, and Asian descent established settlements, while Native Americans were banished to reservations. Wildlife dwindled, forests disappeared, wheat fields took the place of grasslands, and the landscape was marked by railroad tracks, telegraph lines, and barbed wire as much as by rivers and mountain passes.

An Industrializing Northeast

The clearing of forests and the growth of farms during the colonial era lent the New England landscape a rural feel reminiscent of pastoral Europe. In the nineteenth century, the development of a manufacturing economy and the rise of great cities transformed the East into the nation's urban, mercantile, and industrial heartland. The Atlantic Ocean connected New England merchants with their European counterparts and rivers provided conduits of internal trade among farms, towns, and cities. Where natural watercourses failed to accommodate the flow of people and capital, engineers constructed canals. The linking of the Hudson River and Lake Erie by the Erie Canal in 1825 represented the high point of the canal-building era.

Water also powered American industry, but at a cost. The damming of rivers harnessed energy for early textile mills but threatened local fish populations. Mills and factories frequently transformed their settings into industrial satellites. The textile industry in Lowell, Massachusetts, established in 1823 along the Merrimack River, claimed to provide paternal care to a young female workforce in a rural setting. By 1840, however, Lowell resembled a wretched English factory town. Tired of long hours spent operating noisy machinery, employees longed for fresh air and green fields. Problems of water contamination and air pollution accompanied the development of iron and steel industries in places such as Pittsburgh and Cleveland.

Burgeoning cities meanwhile struggled to cope with a massive influx of European immigrants. Thousands of Germans and Irish fled the turmoil and famine of their homelands during the late 1840s, arriving in Boston and New York on overcrowded passenger ships. Only one in five or six stayed in New York, but the city's population still rose from just under eighty thousand in 1800 to almost 3.5 million by the end of the century. The urban poor lived in alleyways, cramped tenements, and shantytowns.

In the early 1800s, migrants from New York and New England populated the northern stretches of Indiana, Ohio, and Illinois, while Virginians and Pennsylvanians settled along the banks of the Ohio River. During the mid–nineteenth century, Yankee farmers joined European immigrants in penetrating the forests and tallgrass prairies of the Midwest. Scandinavians gravitated toward Wisconsin and Minnesota, to a climate and wooded environment similar to their homeland. Accustomed to abundant timber for housing, fencing, and fuel, pioneers found life on the prairie uninviting. Prairie farmers overcame their initial concerns by planting and improvisation, cultivating shade trees around homesteads and marking field boundaries with Osage orange hedges. The iron plow, featuring replaceable parts, assisted in tilling the heavy prairie sod. Midwestern farmers speedily transformed hills of wild rye and bluestem into wheat and corn fields. Their demand for timber was met by local merchants.

By the early nineteenth century, a commercial logging industry had emerged from the forests of New England, New York, and Pennsylvania to meet urban and industrial requirements for timber. Once eastern supplies were exhausted, the lumber industry migrated to the Great Lakes region in the 1850s. Aided by the new steam-powered circular saw, company loggers cut through the vast forests of Michigan and Wisconsin, and rivers carried the timber to awaiting vessels on the Mississippi River and Erie Canal. More than seventy mills were located in Saginaw, central Michigan. The speed with which the seemingly endless forests were cleared demonstrated the need for caution and conservation, but logging companies merely moved on to forests in the South.

Southern Agriculture

White slave owners in the antebellum South attempted to insulate themselves from the social and economic trends sweeping the North. Both distance and climate helped enforce a sense of isolation. Tales of whole towns swamped by malaria and yellow fever dissuaded many potential settlers from making the long journey south, fearful that warmer conditions fostered virulent and lethal diseases. In 1853, an outbreak of yellow fever in New Orleans claimed nine thousand lives. The scarcity of vibrant cities also reflected the dominance of the plantation in social and economic life. With the exception of cotton and tobacco products leaving for market, the majority of larger plantations were self-contained communities. The cash-crop economy centered on the controlled exploitation of African Americans and nature. Rich crops were produced at the expense of human lives and native soils. Endless rows of crops encouraged insect infestation, water pollution, and soil toxicity.

Crop rotation only partially offset the ecological damage.

The need for fresh land prompted southerners to move westward. Migrating farmers imposed their familiar agricultural blueprint on a diverse forest, prairie, and river ecology. Alabama (1819), Mississippi (1817), Louisiana (1812), and east Texas (1845) became part of the "Cotton Kingdom," a huge tract of land defined by its subtropical climate and rich soil. Favorable environmental conditions brought instant financial rewards.

Following the Civil War, sharecropping and tenant farming replaced the slave system. Parts of the southern landscape acquired a northern countenance. Prodigious steel production earned Birmingham, Alabama, the epithet "Pittsburgh of the South." The number of southern cotton mills, most in the Carolinas and Georgia, rose from 161 to 400 between 1880 and 1900. Lumber companies operated in the baldcypress swamps and pine forests of Georgia, Alabama, Louisiana, and Mississippi.

Transforming Western Lands

Reports of fur-bearing animals led American trapping parties westward in the early nineteenth century. Young men of American, French, Portuguese, Irish, and Canadian birth traveled to the Rocky Mountains and Great Plains. In the mountains, company agents and independent trappers hunted beaver for their valued pelts. "Mountain men" searched for beaver ponds in the Rockies during spring and fall. In late summer, trappers, traders, and Native American hunters met at rendezvous sites to exchange commodities and socialize. In contrast, the fur trade on the plains revolved around Missouri River trading posts. The American Fur Company, founded by John Jacob Astor, dominated commerce in the region from the late 1820s onward. Encouraged to swap bison robes for American and European commodities, local Indian tribes entered the global market economy. Native women processed skins and furs for trade, and those married to trappers became important cultural intermediaries.

During the heyday of the fur trade in the late 1820s and early 1830s, individual trappers proved capable of surviving even the harshest of winters and gained a reputation as hardy survivalists. Only the natural limits of beaver and bison reproduction, along with fluctuating market demand, constrained their activities. Mountain men such as Jedediah Smith and Jim Bridger covered huge stretches of territory in their search for fur-bearers. Their accumulated knowledge of western topography proved essential for early settlers making their way to California and Oregon in the 1840s and 1850s. Smith learned of the South Pass, a twenty-mile–wide plain used for crossing the Rockies, from Crow Indians in 1824. In the 1840s it became part of the Oregon Trail, which led settlers to the flowing rivers of the Willamette Valley.

Pioneers frequently underestimated the scale of the challenge awaiting them and saw only the land of riches to be found at the end of the journey. Guidebooks sold in eastern states misinformed citizens on what to take and when to travel. In 1846, the Donner party followed a guide's advice to leave the California Trail and was trapped by heavy snow in the high Sierras. Migrants discarded stoves, clothing, and even provisions along the trails. In 1850, one traveler saw two thousand abandoned wagons on a forty-mile stretch through the Nevada desert. The West simply posed too many physical challenges for some settlers, and most of the country seemed barren and unsuitable for settlement.

The comparative aridity of western lands shocked emigrants accustomed to abundant rain and rivers back East. The desert environment was particularly hard to endure. The explorer William Manly, on his treacherous crossing of Death Valley in 1849, chewed bullets to produce saliva and drank the blood of his

Henry Grinnell. Grinnell (1799–1874) was a merchant, sponsor of polar expeditions, and the first president of the American Geographical Society. LIBRARY OF CONGRESS: PRINTS AND PHOTOGRAPHS DIVISION

oxen. John C. Frémont, the expeditioner whose reports helped popularize the West as a land of opportunity, described the Great Basin region as a wasteland when he visited there in 1843.

By contrast, Brigham Young, leader of the Mormons, saw Zion in the saline waters and sandy shores of the Great Salt Lake. Young realized that in order to escape persecution, his people needed a land spurned by other Americans. The first Mormons arrived in the region in 1847. Their transformation of Salt Lake into a prosperous human settlement required substantial irrigation and collective responsibility. Few outsiders expected Mormon agriculture to succeed in an area with annual rainfall of between three and fifteen inches. Yet only three years after the first potatoes and beans had been planted near City Creek, the annual wheat crop exceeded a hundred thousand bushels. Later in the century, pioneers raised cattle in Arizona and practiced irrigation near Phoenix, but the Mormon settlement of the desert remained distinctive, marked by the convergence of alienated people and marginalized land.

The discovery of gold at John Sutter's mill, along the Coloma River, brought tens of thousands of Americans and foreigners to California in the hope of finding a land fantastically rich in mineral deposits. The arrival of Europeans, Australians, Chileans, Peruvians, Mexicans, and Chinese marked the 1849 Gold Rush as an event of global demographic significance. The non-Native population of California rose from approximately 14,000 in 1848 to 223,856 in 1852. Towns instantly arose around fresh finds and then were abandoned when miners discovered other strikes. Hasty mining settlements frequently lacked a decent water supply or easy access. Waste floated in nearby streams, garbage piled up, and a general lawlessness pervaded the streets. Few men considered mining towns their homes, and they freely despoiled local environments. In the quest to improve mineral extraction, mining technology became increasingly specialized. In the late 1860s, hydraulic mining, backed by large capital investment, destroyed entire hillsides as water jets stripped topsoil, grasses, and rocks in the search for gold and silver deposits. The ecological damage might have passed unnoticed had it not been for the toxic mine tailings flooding the farmland along the Sacramento River.

The discovery of silver in the Nevada desert (Cormstock Lode, 1859) and copper in the Rocky Mountains (Butte, 1882) thrust aside fears of settling in such remote and inhospitable environments. Mule teams traveled across the high Sierras to supply Virginia City, Nevada. Butte, Montana, home of the Anaconda Copper Mining Company, became known as "the richest hill on earth," although the mining produced slag heaps, vegetation loss, cave-ins, and toxic gases. Despite government promises to protect the land, miners defiled the Black Hills of South Dakota, a sacred Sioux homeland, beginning in the 1870s. The mining industry fueled the instant development of new cities in haphazard fashion, and mineral bonanzas helped push California, Montana, Colorado, and Arizona toward statehood.

The railroad dramatically transformed the West. Migration no longer required months of arduous, sometimes life-threatening travel. Resettling in western towns simply entailed loading belongings onto railcars and sitting on a train for a week. Where trailblazers once had succumbed to mountains and desert, the steam engine now transformed natural hazards into window scenery. Railroad companies actively encouraged the settlement process by selling land-exploration tickets. Having accumulated millions of acres of state land, the Northern Pacific, Union Pacific, and Burlington lines adopted sophisticated advertising tactics to offload their wares. Companies vied to sell the "best" land at the lowest prices. Where the railroad traveled, civilization appeared eminently practical.

The Great Plains

Reckless predation by casual and professional hunters caused the bison population to drop from as many as 40 million in 1830 to about a thousand in 1890. Goods wagons transported animal skins, tongues, and trophies to the East, but for each hide that reached market, between three and five bison lost their lives. What some Native Americans called the "spotted buffalo" replaced the bison. Cattle drives from Texas brought the Texas longhorn to the plains. The longhorn was a hardy creature, tolerant of cold winters. From the late 1860s to early 1880s, huge numbers of longhorns roamed the open range. Cowboys drove herds to hastily built cattle towns, such as Abilene and Dodge City, Kansas, for transport by rail to eastern markets. Some Native Americans as well as Mexicans and Mexican Americans joined cattle work crews, and in the 1870s about nine thousand of the thirty-five thousand cowboys were African Americans.

The work was difficult and often financially unrewarding. The rugged individualistic lifestyle, seemingly close to nature, was actually dependent upon demands and prices set by distant markets. The treatment of the plains as free pastureland encouraged ecological irresponsibility. Cowboys left their less hardy Herefords to fend for themselves during winters, and thousands of animals died before reaching the slaughterhouse. Watering holes were overused and native grasses depleted. Tumbleweed flourished to the extent that many believed it to be domestic rather than an exotic of Russian ancestry.

With the natural productivity of the plains overexploited, the cattle era quickly passed. The end of the open range was also brought about by the invention of barbed wire in 1873 and the advance of homesteading. Popular perceptions of the shortgrass prairies had changed considerably over the century. In the early 1820s, the expeditioner Stephen Harriman Long described the plains as the "Great American Desert," a place "almost wholly unfit for cultivation, and of course uninhabitable by a people depending upon agriculture for their subsistence." Long mistook the semiarid lands for desert, but an even greater error brought homesteaders to the region after 1860. Prominent land surveyor Ferdinand Hayden promoted the idea that "rain follows the plow," that the drier climate west of the 100th meridian could be improved by planting trees and crops. The transformation did not occur. Without access to timber, early settlers used sod for houses and buffalo chips for fuel. Tornadoes, prairie fires, drought, and locusts challenged pioneer resolve.

Despite these hardships, plains communities offered an escape from the industrialized and urbanized East. Agricultural towns often consisted of a simple main street with a railroad at one end. The closeted life allowed distinctive settlements to prosper. In Kansas, Neosha attracted vegetarians and Cheever drew prohibitionists. Thousands of African Americans migrated to Kansas during the 1870s and later to Oklahoma, where they created all-black towns to escape the humiliation and horror of the post-Reconstruction South. However, western life still depended upon eastern commodities, railroad transport, and market economies. Crops, cattle, and minerals usually traveled to Chicago or St. Louis for processing and shipment to the East. These two cities exercised significant influence both to the west and to the east. The growth of Salt Lake City and Denver on marginal lands meanwhile presaged an urbanized West that few had thought possible at the time of the Louisiana Purchase in 1803.

A Community Lost

As industries, cities, and farms marked the new landscape of the West, American citizens and politicians felt less and less obliged to accommodate the indigenous residents. Earlier in the century, Congress had set aside a tract of land as permanent Indian Territory, but the idea rested on a vulnerable concept of western land as worthless for white Americans. The fur trade, gold rush, and need for fresh land suggested otherwise. The colonization of the West by northerners, southerners, and European immigrants led to the forceful removal of most native tribes from their ancestral homes. Treaties were renegotiated and Indian Territory opened to white settlement.

The conquest of the Native American often entailed the simultaneous destruction of the land. Environmental despoliation became a valuable military strategy. In the early 1860s, Kit Carson, understanding the dependence of the Navajos upon their natural environment, burned orchards and crops and slaughtered animals. The killing of the plains bison was intertwined with the desire to force resistant bands of Native Americans onto reservations. Settlers, exercising their newfound property rights, then cleared the land of native flora and fauna. Homesteads, churches, ranches, and saloons displaced the beaver lodges, prairie dog towns, wolf dens, and teepee villages that predated them. The nineteenth-century story of settlement and economic development was also one of community loss and ecological sacrifice.

See also **Agricultural Technology; Agriculture; American Indians,** *subentry on* **Indian Removal; Boomtowns; Cities and Urbanization; Conservation; Exploration and Explorers; Frontier; Fur Trade; Gold Rushes and Silver Strikes; Great Plains; Homesteading; Hunting and Trapping; Lumber and Timber Industry; Mining and Extraction; Mormonism; Natural Resources; Nature; Northwest Territory; Ranching and Livestock Raising; Trails to the West; Transportation,** *subentry on* **Railroads; Waterpower; West, The.**

Bibliography

Bartlett, Richard A. *The New Country: A Social History of the American Frontier, 1776–1890.* New York: Oxford University Press, 1974.

Conzen, Michael P., ed. *The Making of the American Landscape.* Boston: Unwin Hyman, 1990.

Cowdrey, Albert E. *This Land, This South: An Environmental History.* Lexington: University Press of Kentucky, 1983.

Cronon, William. *Nature's Metropolis: Chicago and the Great West.* New York: Norton, 1991.

Merchant, Carolyn. *Ecological Revolutions: Nature, Gender, and Science in New England.* Chapel Hill: University of North Carolina Press, 1989.

Opie, John. *Nature's Nation: An Environmental History of the United States.* Fort Worth, Texas: Harcourt Brace, 1998.

Whitney, Gordon G. *From Coastal Wilderness to Fruited Plain: A History of Environmental Change in Temperate North America, 1500 to the Present.* Cambridge, U.K.: Cambridge University Press, 1994.

Wishart, David J. *The Fur Trade of the American West, 1807–1840: A Geographical Synthesis.* Lincoln: University of Nebraska Press, 1979.

Worster, Donald. *An Unsettled Country: Changing Landscapes of the American West.* Albuquerque: University of New Mexico Press, 1994.

———. *Under Western Skies: Nature and History in the American West.* New York: Oxford University Press, 1992.

JOHN WILLS

GEORGIA   At the beginning of the nineteenth century, Georgia was a virtual empire, stretching from the Savannah River in the east to the Mississippi in the west. The possibilities offered by western land intrigued Georgians. In 1795 the state legislature enacted the infamous Yazoo Act, granting most of the future states of Alabama and Mississippi to four companies for $500,000. The voting public became irate when they discovered that members of the legislature also were stockholders in the companies involved in the scheme. James Jackson (1757–1806) resigned his U.S. Senate seat to lead a reform movement, and a new legislature nullified the giveaway. However, the stockholders brought suit against the state, and the issue finally was decided in 1810 by the U.S. Supreme Court in the case of *Fletcher v. Peck.* The Court decided that, fraudulent or not, the Yazoo Act was valid and restitution had to be made to the stockholders. Foreseeing such a possibility, Georgia had turned over her western lands to the federal government for $1.25 million and a pledge by the government to remove the Indians from the state boundaries. In a reaction against the elitism of the Yazoo affair, the legislature decided in 1803 to give away all future Indian cessions by lottery. This forthrightly democratic policy meant that the state disposed of its capital asset and had no nontax means of paying for internal improvements or anything else.

In 1802 and 1804 the federal government obliged Georgia by securing territory between the Oconee and Ocmulgee Rivers. The state capital followed the western movement, from Augusta (1786–1795), to Louisville on the Ogeechee (1796–1807), to Milledgeville on the Oconee (1807–1867). Although the Lower Creeks of Georgia refused to join their fellow tribesmen in Alabama who followed the great Tecumseh (1768–1813), they had to relinquish a wide swath of territory adjoining the Florida border in 1814 as part of the peace settlement. Another huge tract was ceded by a minority headed by Chief William McIntosh (c. 1775–1825) in 1821, extending Georgia's available lands to the Flint River. Despite the warnings of the Creek Council, McIntosh signed away the remainder of the Creek lands in Georgia in 1825 and as a result was killed by his own people. President John Quincy Adams (1767–1848) removed the 1825 treaty from consideration by the Senate, but in the face of fierce opposition from Georgia, he concluded another removal treaty with the Creek Nation in 1826.

The expulsion of the Creeks left the Cherokees as the only aboriginal inhabitants of Georgia. In an effort to avoid removal, the Cherokee people adopted the trappings of white civilization, including a written language (developed by Sequoya [c. 1770–1843]) and the formation of the Cherokee Republic in 1827. Unfortunately for the Cherokees, gold was discovered in the Georgia mountains in 1829, and thousands of prospectors rushed into Cherokee territory. The missionary Samuel A. Worcester (1798–1859) challenged Georgia's legal right to extend its jurisdiction into the Cherokee country, and the U.S. Supreme Court agreed with him in an 1832 decision. Nevertheless, President Andrew Jackson (1767–1845) sided with Georgia, and in 1838 thousands of Cherokees were removed forcibly to Oklahoma, many dying on the tragic Trail of Tears.

Aided by the lottery system, settlers rapidly moved across the region vacated by the Native Americans. Parallel railroads were built westward from Savannah and Augusta in 1833 and converged at a junction later named Atlanta, where a state-owned line connected them with Tennessee railroads. Factories were built at the fall-line cities of Augusta, Macon, and Columbus and at the shoals of the Oconee at Athens, but the dominant institution in antebellum Georgia was the plantation. The cotton gin made cotton production profitable and fixed plantation slavery upon the Deep South. The number of blacks grew from 60,425 in a total population of 162,686 in 1800, to 465,698 in a total population of 1,057,286 in 1860. Georgia's cotton production increased from 90,000 bales in 1821 to 701,840 bales in 1860. The issue of slavery in the Mexican Cession territory created a crisis. Led by Alexander Stephens (1812–1883), Robert Toombs (1810–1885), and Howell Cobb (1815–1868), Georgians opted for Henry Clay's (1777–1852) Compromise of 1850 rather than John C. Calhoun's (1782–1850) call for secession. The 1860 election of Abraham Lincoln (1809–1865) on a platform supporting the exclusion of slavery from western territories nonetheless precipitated the secession of the seven southernmost slave states. By a margin of 208 to 89, the Georgia delegates, meeting in convention at Milledgeville, voted to secede on 19 January 1861. Georgia's Alexander Stephens was elected as vice president of the Confederate States of America organized in the following month at Montgomery, Alabama. The Confederate Constitution largely was written by another Georgian—Thomas R. R. Cobb (1823–1862), a proslavery legal theorist.

Besides the 120,000 Georgians who fought for the Confederacy, Georgia contributed a statewide rail system that linked the eastern and western theaters of war and a powder works at Augusta that furnished the Confederate armies with munitions. Union forces occupied Georgia's coastal islands in 1861 and battered down Fort Pulaski on 11 April 1862. However, the successful invasion of Georgia came from the northern mountains, not the sea. General Braxton Bragg turned back the first Union penetration of Georgia at Chickamauga on 19 September 1863, but a determined General William T. Sherman (1820–1891) broke through the mountain barrier in May 1864 and, in a series of flanking movements, laid siege to Atlanta, forcing the evacuation of that city in 1 September 1864. Sherman then gathered 60,000 of his best troops for his devastating march to the sea. He presented Savannah to President Lincoln in December.

White Georgians long believed that "Negro rule" caused corruption during Reconstruction. Actually, only twenty-eight members of the assembly's 216 members were classed as black, and they were expelled by the Democratic majority. A campaign of terror by the Ku Klux Klan prevented blacks from exercising their voting rights in 1868. A Freedman's Bureau report listed 262 instances of "outrage" between 1 January and 1 November 1868, including 31 killings, 42 shootings, 5 stabbings, 55 beatings, and 8 severe whippings. The federal military restored the expelled members of the assembly in January 1870, but they were displaced again by elections later in the year. Rufus Bullock (1834–1907), the only Republican governor of Georgia in the nineteenth and twentieth centuries, was acquitted of corruption charges when he was tried in 1876. The most lasting achievement of his abbreviated administration was the launching of Georgia's public school system.

From 1870 to 1890 a conservative Democratic Party, headed by the triumvirate of Joseph E. Brown (1821–1894), John B. Gordon (1832–1904), and Alfred Colquitt (1824–1894), ruled Georgia. The journalist Henry Grady (1850–1889) set the tone by promoting industrial growth in the "New South." Atlanta rose from the ashes of Sherman's fires as a symbol of postwar progress; the city became the temporary state capital in 1868 and the permanent capital beginning in 1887. The Atlanta expositions of the 1880s and 1890s proclaimed Georgia's importance to the New South. Booker T. Washington's (1856–1915) "Atlanta Compromise" speech at the 1895 exposition, endorsing racial separation, attracted national attention.

Farmers did not share in the state's new prosperity and joined the Populist Party under the leadership of Thomas E. Watson (1856–1922) in the 1890s. The defeat of the Populist candidates during that decade coincided with deteriorating race relations. Home to more blacks than any other state, Georgia adopted the white primary in 1900.

See also **American Indians,** *subentry on* **Indian Removal; Confederate States of America; Cotton; Reconstruction,** *subentry on* **The South; South, The.**

Bibliography

Coleman, Kenneth, et al. *A History of Georgia.* 2d ed. Athens: University of Georgia Press, 1991.

Dyer, Thomas G., et al. *The New Georgia Guide.* Athens: University of Georgia Press, 1996.

Wallenstein, Peter. *From Slave South to New South: Public Policy in Nineteenth-Century Georgia.* Chapel Hill: University of North Carolina Press, 1987.

Woodward, C. Vann. *Tom Watson, Agrarian Rebel.* New York: Macmillan, 1938. 2d ed. Savannah, Ga.: Beehive, 1973.

EDWARD J. CASHIN

GILDED AGE   The term "Gilded Age" refers roughly to the last three decades of the nineteenth century. Unlike such expressions as "early national period" and "Jacksonian era," "Gilded Age" is virtually unique as a period label in the sense of aspersion it carries, evoking notions of crassness, superficiality, pretense, and fraud. The term's connotation of sham is unfortunate, for through the years it has masked the period's enormous complexity and significance, and it has led to a facile dismissal of the era as unworthy of serious study. In truth, the United States experienced a profound transformation in the last third of the nineteenth century, with lasting historical implications.

The Book and Its Impact

The label derives from the title of the 1873 book *The Gilded Age: A Tale of Today* by Mark Twain and Charles Dudley Warner, Twain's first novel. According to Twain's biographer Albert Bigelow Paine, the idea to write the book arose when the two journalists scoffed at the popular fiction their wives had been reading and the women dared them to write something better. Twain and Warner accepted the challenge, each author penning several chapters more or less by himself and then reviewing the other's work. The result was hardly great literature, but the book was immensely popular, selling forty thousand copies in its first eight weeks in print. Its tangle of plots and subplots offered up a motley cast of characters headed by the irrepressibly optimistic and generally ridiculous speculator Beriah Sellers, best known for his trademark cry, "There's millions in it." As Twain later noted, the authors' aim was to satirize the greed pervading the capitalist system and the corruption worming its way into politics. Within a year, a dramatization of the book became an instant and enduring theater hit.

In part *The Gilded Age* was a roman à clef. Twain modeled Sellers and other characters on family members and other individuals he knew. More important for the political satire, just at the time the authors were writing the book, in early 1873, Washington and the nation witnessed several allegations of wrongdoing that shook Americans' already wavering confidence in the integrity of their political leaders. The alleged attempt to purchase reelection by a U.S. senator from Kansas, the so-called salary grab pay raise voted by Congress, and the Crédit Mobilier bribery scandal occurred or were under investigation during these months, and each incident found its satiric caricature in Twain and Warner's fable.

The burlesque of these relatively few but easily identifiable incidents whetted the suspicion, rarely much below the surface in American consciousness, that corruption suffused every aspect of the government and the community of politicians. Some observers readily recognized the book's broad exaggerations. The authors had, said the *Independent* (1 January 1874), selected "from real life what is worst and most repulsive." James A. Garfield, on 30 December 1874, found the play so "full of malignant insinuations . . . [as to] lead the hearer to believe that there is no virtue in the world, in public or in private life" (Harry James Brown and Frederick D. Williams, eds., *The Diary of James A. Garfield*, volume 2, 1967–1981, p. 412). But as early as 1875 a French literary critic adopted the book's title as a depiction of the nation at large in a review entitled "The Gilded Age in America," which appeared in *Revue des Deux Mondes*. Likewise, many other contemporaries and later historians took the lampoon more or less at face value. Thus, unfortunately for the development of a balanced and accurate understanding of the period, what began as a perhaps well-deserved gibe at some egregious tricksters and charlatans quickly metamorphosed into a portrait of an era.

Other contemporary works reinforced the negative impressions sparked by *The Gilded Age.* In 1880 Henry Adams anonymously published *Democracy: An American Novel*, which also satirized corruption in Washington; its ironic title reflected Adams's sense of the degeneration of the American democratic experiment. Eager for political influence in the postwar years, the elitist Adams soon found himself shoved aside by more capable and truly democratic politicians, and he spent the rest of his life carping at these politicians from his Olympian perch. Later, in *The*

Education of Henry Adams (1907), he offered the following withering observation: "One might search the whole list of Congress, Judiciary, and Executive during the twenty-five years 1870 to 1895, and find little but damaged reputation" (p. 294). The contemporary English observer James Bryce lent an air of scholarly authenticity to the image of American politics as a vacuous enterprise. His massive work, *The American Commonwealth*, published in 1888, asserted that the two major parties offered voters no distinguishing principles or beliefs but simply fought each other for the spoils of office.

Twentieth-Century Views

Through much of the twentieth century, historians carried forward this jaundiced view of the late nineteenth century. Among the earliest scholars to echo Twain and Warner were Charles A. Beard and Mary R. Beard, whose book *The Rise of American Civilization* (1927) included a chapter entitled "The Gilded Age." Like Twain and Warner, the Beards condemned "the new plutocrats, ignorant in mind and vulgar of tongue" and the "corrupt politicians, . . . given to high sounding verbalism and low pillage" (vol. 2, p. 437). Other scholars offered accounts under alternative titles that conveyed the same condemnation: "The Great Barbecue," in *The Beginnings of Critical Realism in America* (1930) by Vernon L. Parrington, "An Age of Cynicism," in *The American Political Tradition* (1948) by Richard Hofstadter, and *Age of Excess* (1965) by Ray Ginger. During the depression of the 1930s, when Americans' doubts about the fairness of their political and social systems ran particularly high, Matthew Josephson published *The Robber Barons* (1934) and *The Politicos* (1938), both stridently critical of Gilded Age politicians and businessmen who had reveled in a "saturnalia of plunder" (*Politicos*, p. 101). In the 1950s the historian Philip Foner, in *Mark Twain: Social Critic* (1958), concluded that *The Gilded Age* had made "clear the deep moral decay in the nation caused by the coarseness, hypocrisy, greed and lustfulness of the rich and their lackeys in government" (p. 84). In the next decade Bryant Morey French, in *Mark Twain and The Gilded Age: The Book That Named an Era* (1965), likewise argued that it was the book's essential verisimilitude that "made the novel so valuable a social document to historians" (p. 208).

In some quarters this pejorative view of the Gilded Age has persisted, but beginning in the 1960s a new generation of scholars began to offer a more balanced account of the era. These writers did not deny the Gilded Age's seamier elements, but they emphasized the need to assess the period as a whole, on its own

terms. They tended to cast the evolving society and economy in the broader analytic context of the prolonged and erratic process of modernization. As John A. Garraty argued in *The New Commonwealth* (1968), "Twain and Warner caught certain aspects of the times, yet their view was restricted and myopic, as must be any simplistic evaluation of a whole nation in a period of rapid change and growth" (p. 2).

On the political front, H. Wayne Morgan pointed the way to a reinterpretation of parties and political leaders that disputed Bryce's notion of empty spoils battles. Later studies focused on the fundamental differences that separated the two major parties and on the issues that inspired the rise of third parties. On the question of corruption, an increasing number of scholars began to regard actual wrongdoing in the Gilded Age as less significant than the allegations of wrongdoing that exacerbated partisanship and polluted public discourse. In addition to reevaluations of political leadership, studies of voting behavior theorized that, beyond economic considerations, ethnicity and religion exercised powerful influences over Americans' party affiliations and electoral choices.

Some twentieth-century historians abandoned altogether the term "Gilded Age," laden as it is with negative assumptions, in speaking of the late nineteenth century. Most scholars, however, continued to employ the nomenclature simply because its longstanding use makes it convenient to designate a well-defined chronological period if not to symbolize the nature of American society at that time. Moreover, many scholars recognized the continuities that existed between the late nineteenth century and the early twentieth century and found in the Gilded Age the origins of much that marked the political, social, and economic life of the twentieth-century United States. In the late 1980s historians specializing in this decades-long era of transformation and reform created their own professional organization, called the Society for Historians of the Gilded Age and Progressive Era.

An Age of Transformation

The late nineteenth century witnessed enormous changes in virtually every aspect of American life. Between Appomattox and the turn of the century, the nation's population not only doubled in size but also underwent fundamental changes in its makeup, distribution, and way of life. Immigrants, principally from Europe but also from East Asia, poured into the country in numbers so great that from 1870 to 1900 the number of foreign-born persons in the population grew by 86 percent. Americans, both old and new, continued to head west, and eight new states entered the Union in these years. Americans also streamed into the burgeoning cities. By 1900, 40 percent lived in urban places, and the country boasted thirty-eight cities of 100,000 or more in population.

Although urban growth reflected the arrival of immigrants, it also represented movement from the nation's countryside. Changes in American agricultural practice lessened the need for field hands and farmers. Hence, rural folk moved to cities, joining immigrants in manning the new factories. With the exploitation of natural resources, such as iron and coal, and with the application of new industrial processes, the economy experienced enormous expansion. In the last three decades of the century, railroad mileage more than quadrupled, annual steel output rose from 77,000 tons to 11.2 million tons, and the manufacturing sector grew by 480 percent. Industrialization profoundly transformed the lives of workers. The typical American no longer labored as an independent farmer, small entrepreneur, or artisan. Instead, by the end of the century, wage labor predominated and increasing numbers of Americans worked in ever larger impersonal enterprises. Moreover, as a powerhouse of productivity, the United States became a net exporter of goods and played an expanding role in the world economy and international relations.

Economic transformation reinforced a continuing evolution in the nation's political order. During the Gilded Age, the Civil War party system, dominated by issues of sectionalism and race, gave way to a new, often strident contention over economic questions, especially how large a role the federal government should play in the nation's economy. Although some issues cut across party lines, Republicans generally favored government activism in the form of tariff protection, subsidies, and "sound" money policy to encourage industrialization and foster growth. The Democrats, dominated by their preindustrial Southern wing, clung to notions of small government and states' rights, and they criticized Republicans' activism as favoring special interests. Some Americans revolted against the two dominant parties. Most notably, agrarian parties, such as the Greenbackers and the Populists, saw the solution to farmers' troubles in an inflated currency and greater regulation of banks, railroads, and industrial "monopolies." Nonetheless, throughout the Gilded Age the vast majority of voters stuck with the two major parties.

Although parties remained state-based organizations, the rail system and communication innovations, such as the telegraph, telephone, and inexpensive printing, fostered the nationalization of politics and culture. Improved transportation allowed more Americans to journey to expositions, museums, and theaters in urban centers, and it also permitted traveling exhibits and touring companies to fan out to the hinterland. Magazine circulation and book publication grew exponentially. In addition, one of the byproducts of capitalist enterprise was the willingness of captains of industry such as Andrew Carnegie to fund museums, libraries, universities, and other nurseries of culture, not only on the eastern seaboard but in towns and cities across the land.

By the end of the nineteenth century, the isolation of Americans in localized communities was diminishing. Increasing numbers of people defined themselves less by their rootedness in a particular geographic place and more by association with those who did the same sort of work or shared participation in similar political, social, or cultural endeavors. Thus the Gilded Age witnessed profound changes in American life. These changes formed part of a longer-term transformation from a largely agricultural, rural, isolated, localized, and traditional society to one that was industrialized, urban, integrated, national, and modern.

See also **Class, Social; Literature,** *subentry on* **Fiction; Politics,** *subentry on* **Corruption and Scandals; Populism; Reform, Political; Reform, Social; Third Parties.**

Bibliography

Adams, Henry. *The Education of Henry Adams.* Boston: Houghton Mifflin, 1918. Reprint, 1961.

Beard, Charles A., and Mary R. Beard. *The Rise of American Civilization.* 2 vols. New York: Macmillan, 1927, 1930.

Calhoun, Charles W., ed. *The Gilded Age: Essays on the Origins of Modern America.* Wilmington, Del.: Scholarly Resources, 1996.

Foner, Philip S. *Mark Twain: Social Critic.* New York: International, 1958.

French, Bryant Morey. *Mark Twain and The Gilded Age: The Book That Named an Era.* Dallas, Tex.: Southern Methodist University Press, 1965.

Garraty, John A. *The New Commonwealth, 1877–1890.* New York: Harper and Row, 1968.

Josephson, Matthew. *The Robber Barons: The Great American Capitalists, 1861–1901.* New York: Harcourt, Brace, 1934.

———. *The Politicos, 1865–1896.* New York: Harcourt, Brace, 1938.

Morgan, H. Wayne, ed. *The Gilded Age.* Rev. ed. Syracuse, N.Y.: Syracuse University Press, 1970.

Summers, Mark Wahlgren. *The Gilded Age; or, The Hazard of New Functions.* Upper Saddle River, N.J.: Prentice Hall, 1997.

Twain, Mark, and Charles Dudley Warner. *The Gilded Age: A Tale of Today.* Hartford, Conn.: American Publishing, 1873.

Wiebe, Robert H. *The Search for Order, 1877–1920.* New York: Hill and Wang, 1967.

CHARLES W. CALHOUN

GLASS In terms of production, product, and labor, the glass industry underwent greater change in the nineteenth century than it had in the preceding two thousand years. Nowhere was this change more profound than in the United States.

At the beginning of the century glass production methods were much like those of the colonial period. Glasshouses or glassworks manufactured and sold glass products. These glasshouses made either free-blown or mold-blown utilitarian pieces that were expensive because of the labor and resources required. Glassblowers created bottles, drinking glasses, and windowpanes without the aid of templates, though molds, metal templates used to add design to an individual piece, were becoming popular. Mold-pressed and lacy glass, characterized by a stippled, lacelike surface, were the two most favored types of mold-blown glassware, but they were reaching their height of fashionability in the 1830s. Cup plates, glass plates on which teacups were placed, and salts, small salt containers for the table, were the most common examples of lacy and mold-pressed glass. Because the Boston Sandwich Glass Company, which operated from 1825 to 1888, was the main manufacturer of pressed glass, that style was frequently called Sandwich glass. These pressed pieces often featured likenesses of famous political figures or objects, especially Henry Clay, William Henry Harrison, the steamboat *Ben Franklin,* and Fort Meigs. The Pittsburgh Flint Glass Manufactory produced notable pressed glass from 1808 to 1882.

By the end of the century the traditional glasshouses had disappeared, replaced by glass factories that predominantly used machines in production. For example, mechanical bellows blew air into glass placed in molds, thereby increasing production exponentially. Bottles were the most common mechanically produced items. Glass producers no longer marketed and sold their wares directly to customers but instead to retailers. Mass production made their pieces more uniform and less expensive. Among the best-known styles at the close of the century was the brilliant cut glass pioneered by the Libbey Glass Company of Toledo, Ohio. In this process an artisan using stone wheels cut intricate patterns into an annealed glass object.

Glassblowers of the nineteenth century were highly skilled craftspeople who spent years in apprenticeships. Each glassblower usually performed one task repeatedly. Thus if a glasshouse were making pitchers, one blower would make handles, another would make the main vessel, and a third would make the base. Sizeable support crews, usually apprentices, acted as fuel gatherers, furnace makers, and fire stokers. Mechanization of the glass-making process in the closing years of the century reduced the demand for skilled glassblowers because machines could blow glass into a mold more quickly and more cheaply.

During the first half of the nineteenth century furnaces burned wood to melt the batch of glass ingredients: silica sand, lime, potash, and metal. Since regulating the necessary glassblowing temperature—

Glassmaking in New Jersey. The town of Clayton, in Gloucester County, New Jersey, contained two glassworks facilities: Clevengor Brothers Glass Works and Moore Brothers Clayton Glass Works, pictured above. LIBRARY OF CONGRESS

1500° Fahrenheit—was difficult, some pieces contained unsightly seeding or blistering, air bubbles caught within the glass. Later glass furnaces burned coal and eventually natural gas. The latter was consistent and easily adjustable, so glass pieces could be properly heated and annealed. Consequently quality of glass production increased considerably.

Resources and demand dictated the location of glasshouses. The availability of fuel and sand were major concerns. The United States had an abundance of these raw materials, making it an ideal place for glass production. Early glassworks in Kensington and Rockville, Pennsylvania; Columbia, New Jersey; and Coventry, Connecticut, prospered near sand deposits, heavily wooded areas, and large markets in Philadelphia and New York. By the 1870s owners looked for natural gas deposits, and the Midwest, notably Indiana and the northwest section of Ohio, became a center of the glass industry. The leading producer at the end of the century was the Libbey Glass Company.

See also **Natural Resources; Work,** *subentry on* **Artisans and Craftsworkers.**

Bibliography

Barber, Edwin Atlee. *American Glassware, Old and New.* Philadelphia: Press of Paterson and White, 1900.

Lee, Ruth Webb. *Early American Pressed Glass.* Rutland, Vt: C. E. Tuttle, 1985.

Mehlman, Felice. *Phaidon Guide to Glass.* Englewood Cliffs, N.J.: Prentice-Hall, 1983.

DAVID RUSSELL HAUS JR.

GOLD RUSHES AND SILVER STRIKES

The second half of the nineteenth century was the heyday of gold rushes and silver strikes in the United States. Two of the world's most precious metals, gold and silver were in great demand as universal forms of currency, and anyone who could obtain a decent amount would thereby achieve significant status and wealth. Between 1848, when gold was discovered in abundance in California, and 1900, when the last Alaskan gold rush played out, tens of thousands of men and women from all over the world flocked to the western United States seeking to get rich quick, experience the adventure of a lifetime, or both. This massive influx of like-minded people contributed significantly to the development of the West and helped give that region its own distinctive personality. The tremendous amount of gold and silver produced during this time also played a major role in the national political debate during the century's last three decades.

Gold Rushes

The first and most important gold rush of the nineteenth century began in 1848, when gold nuggets were discovered in the American River at Sutter's Mill in California's Sierra Nevada. Word of the find spread quickly, and by the end of the year, four thousand prospectors were panning the river for gold. In 1849 another eighty thousand prospectors, known as forty-niners, descended upon California from the eastern United States. By 1852 approximately 200,000 adventurous souls from the eastern United States, Europe, Asia, and South America had streamed into Mother Lode country, a narrow, 150-mile belt of rich gold deposits in the Sierra Nevada's western foothills centered just east of Sacramento. After 1852 the rush to find gold subsided somewhat, and it ended by 1874. But before that happened, prospectors extracted from the mother lode almost a billion dollars worth of gold.

Several minor gold rushes took place in the four decades following the beginning of the California gold rush. In 1859 gold was discovered just north of Pikes Peak in north-central Colorado Territory. During the 1860s local residents called Central City, so named because of its location in the goldfields, "the richest square mile on earth." The Colorado gold rush began to subside around 1870, and by 1890 it had come to a complete halt. In 1860 gold was discovered in northern Idaho Territory and two years later in the central and southwestern part of that territory. After a large influx of prospectors, many of whom had failed to strike it rich in California, the rush wound down toward the end of the decade, and by 1870 it had virtually ended. Between 1862 and 1864 gold was discovered in Montana Territory, where the most important find was centered around Alder Gulch in the southwest. In 1874 a U.S. Army expedition discovered gold in Deadwood Gulch in the Black Hills region of western Dakota Territory on land that had been set aside as a Sioux Indian reservation. Two years later over twenty-five thousand prospectors were prowling the reservation illegally. Shortly thereafter the rush faded away, although the Homestake Mine in Lead, South Dakota, remained one of the largest gold mines in the Western Hemisphere for over a century.

During the last four decades of the century Alaska was either the site of or the gateway to several important gold rushes. In the early 1860s Wrangell was the major entrepôt to a minor strike on the Stikine River in British Columbia, Canada. Another minor rush occurred in 1880 around Juneau. Fortymile Creek, which traverses the border between Canada's Yukon Territory and Alaska, was the site of a major

Goldfield, Nevada. Goldfield, in southwest Nevada, was typical of many towns that sprung up after discoveries of nearby gold, then declined after peak production some years later. Goldfield quickly expanded after gold was found in the region toward the turn of the century, and shrunk around 1910. LIBRARY OF CONGRESS

find in 1886. Centered on the western portion of the Yukon River in Canada, in an area known as the Klondike, the strike spilled over into Alaska's eastern reaches. Tens of thousands of prospectors, known as "cheechakos," a Chinook Indian word for "tenderfeet," made their way to the goldfields by crossing the mountains in Canada on foot at Skagway and Dyea on the peninsula or by sailing up Alaska's stretch of the Yukon. By 1900 the rush had ended. In 1898 gold was discovered along Anvil Creek near Nome on the west coast, and within two years twenty thousand miners were panning for gold.

The same basic pattern played itself out in every gold rush. First someone discovered gold nuggets lining the bed of an isolated creek, but these usually disappeared before word of the discovery got out. The earliest arrivals staked out claims along the creeks and began either panning or placer mining. Panning involves scooping up gravel, dirt, and water from the creek bed with a pan that resembles an oversize pie tin; swishing the mixture around and around to separate from the gravel tiny specks of gold, which, being heavier than gravel and dirt, sink to the bottom of the pan; and then sloshing everything in the pan but the gold back into the creek. Placer mining employs either a cradle-like box called a rocker or a Long Tom, a long sluice with riffles in the bottom.

In both cases gravel and water are dumped into the box. The rocker is shaken from side to side, thus separating gold from gravel as in panning. The riffles in the Long Tom catch the gold and let the gravel and water wash out. Prospectors who arrived after the creek beds had been worked headed for the hills to begin the arduous process of finding a central vein and digging out the gold with pick and shovel.

The gold rushes ended when these primitive methods no longer produced a sufficient quantity of gold. However, in most cases much gold remained. As the prospectors moved on to other gold rushes or to less-adventurous occupations, they were replaced by heavily capitalized, efficiently managed mining companies that found and extracted gold scientifically. In some cases these companies used powerful hydraulic nozzles to blast away shallow layers of dirt and gravel and on occasion entire hills to expose gold deposits. In other cases deep mines were drilled, blasted, dug out, and worked by former prospectors in conditions that made commercial mining the most dangerous occupation in the United States.

Silver Strikes

Silver was often found in conjunction with gold during the rushes. Silver, however, commanded only one-

Prospectors. Prospectors with gold mining equipment on a trail in Alaska, c. 1897. LIBRARY OF CONGRESS

tenth the price of gold, it could rarely be found by panning or placer mining, and it was difficult to identify because it often took on the color of the minerals with which it was mixed. Consequently, silver mining was neglected until the gold veins began to play out. Such was the case in the century's biggest silver strike, the discovery in 1859 of the Comstock Lode, running for over two hundred miles through the eastern foothills of the Sierra Nevada range in western Nevada's Gold Canyon. During the 1870s prospectors worked approximately twenty-five thousand different claims in the Comstock, most of them little more than big pits in the ground. By the late 1880s, when the boom ended, silver and gold worth over $400 million had been extracted from the Comstock. Other major silver strikes occurred in 1862 along the southern border between Oregon and Idaho, in 1870 in central and southwestern Colorado around Leadville and Telluride, in 1874 in southeastern Arizona

around Tombstone, and in 1883 in northern Idaho around Coeur d'Alene.

Miners, Merchants, and Suppliers

A majority of the prospectors came from the eastern United States and included a large contingent of former Confederates, who played a major role in the Idaho gold rushes. Virginians were particularly prominent, as evidenced by the fact that two boomtowns, in Montana and Nevada, were named Virginia City. However, a significant number of South Americans, Europeans, Asians, and Australians took part in the gold rushes and silver strikes as well. Almost all of the prospectors were single, and men outnumbered women ten to one. Mining camps were universally shabby, dirty, and dangerous. Prospectors spent every possible waking moment looking for precious metal and devoted so little attention to either the appearance or hygiene of their surroundings that many suffered from depression, disease, and malnutrition. Broken bones proliferated, particularly in the hillside mines, as did knife and gunshot wounds, the natural result of widespread claim jumping and thievery.

Even though most miners worked isolated stakes, they still required towns in which to file their claims, sell their gold and silver, and buy provisions and tools. In response to this demand, boomtowns sprang up near the center of each outbreak of mining frenzy. Virginia City, Montana; Virginia City, Nevada; Idaho City, Idaho; Deadwood, South Dakota; Central City, Colorado; Nome, Alaska; and several towns in California each had populations of over twenty thousand during their heyday, and several served as territorial capitals. In addition to offering food and supplies, these towns provided miners with such services as bakeries, laundries, barbershops, medical clinics, saloons, and brothels. Some boomtowns, but not all, even had a church or two. Although local merchants attempted to maintain law and order, boomtowns were wild and woolly places. The most notorious was Skagway, Alaska, which became the personal plaything of Soapy Smith and his gang of cutthroats and con artists, who had perfected their talent for bilking cheechakos in the boomtowns of

Women Prospectors. Women prospectors on the way to Klondike, while throngs of men congregate down the street. LIBRARY OF CONGRESS

Colorado. These enterprises, legal and otherwise, were hugely profitable owing to the scarcity of goods and services and the abundance of gold. It sometimes seems as if everyone but the prospectors made money during a gold rush or silver strike.

Ecological and Social Effects

Rushes and strikes in the continental United States had an ecological impact on the land. Panning and placer mining disturbed creek beds, but this damage was easily repaired by nature. The pits and mines dug by prospectors caused more permanent damage, although primitive methods and tools prevented most from descending very far underground. Ecological damage was more serious in Alaska, where the frozen ground had to be thawed using fires before it could be shoveled into rockers or Long Toms. Perhaps the most serious ecological disruption took place around the mining camps. The cleaner shantytowns bred trash dumps filled with tin cans, broken tools, discarded furnishings, and human waste, while in the dirtier ones such refuse was strewn about willy-nilly.

The social effects of rushes and strikes were profound. Proprietors of land on which gold was discovered, such as John Augustus Sutter in California, or owners of land through which prospectors traveled in droves, such as Skagway's principal landowner, an old sea captain named Moore, suffered great financial loss owing to the depredation of their personal holdings. Even more disturbing was the effect on Native Americans who had the misfortune to live in the goldfields. In California, "Indian hunters" helped reduce the American Indian population from 150,000 in 1850 to 30,000 twenty years later, while a number of indigent Indians were forced to work as indentured laborers under conditions that approximated slavery. In 1877 the Teton Sioux were forced to cede and vacate that portion of their reservation in the Black Hills on which gold had been discovered.

The influx of thousands of prospectors and those who "served" them into the territories of California, Colorado, Dakota, Idaho, Montana, and Nevada increased the population to the point that statehood generally followed within a few years. These early settlers, many of whom were imbued with a fierce spirit of independence, a fondness for adventure, a nonchalant attitude toward the environment, and a burning desire to get rich quick, contributed to the development of a western personality significantly different from other regions of the country. Because these newcomers came from virtually every corner of the world, they also helped to give the West a more heterogenous population than existed in either the North or the South.

See also **Boomtowns; Frontier; Gunfighters; Mining and Extraction; Outlaws; West, The.**

Bibliography

Dorset, Phyllis Flanders. *The New Eldorado: The Story of Colorado's Gold and Silver Rushes.* New York: Macmillan, 1970.

Goldman, Marion S. *Gold Diggers and Silver Miners: Prostitution and Social Life on the Comstock Lode.* Ann Arbor: University of Michigan Press, 1981.

Limerick, Patricia Nelson. *The Legacy of Conquest: The Unbroken Past of the American West.* New York: Norton, 1987.

Rohrbough, Malcolm J. *Days of Gold: The California Gold Rush and the American Nation.* Berkeley: University of California Press, 1997.

Smith, Duane A. *Mining America: The Industry and the Environment, 1880–1980.* Lawrence: University Press of Kansas, 1987.

Time-Life Books. *The Miners.* Text by Robert Wallace. New York: Time-Life, 1976.

Charles W. Carey Jr.

GOVERNMENT Government in the nineteenth century exhibited several paradoxes. American ideology prescribed explicit limits on civic authority, yet government intervened widely in commercial and social activities, using its powers with significant effects. Citizens held the protection of individual rights as a foremost obligation of government, but many persons were denied liberty. Theory instructed officials to serve the public interest, but certain groups received favored treatment. Some of these contradictions resulted from changes in the scale and direction of governance during the 1800s. Yet these paradoxes also reflected the tension between theory and practice inherent in American politics.

The American Revolution magnified the conflict between power and liberty in political thinking and conditioned citizens to view government with apprehension. This outlook held that the power of government tempted officeholders to abuse authority and thereby deprive citizens of their rights, including the enjoyment of private property. Civic norms dictated constant vigilance of power holders and faithful observance of constitutions as safeguards for liberty. Influenced by these strictures, the authors of the Constitution formed a national government with three separate branches and subdivided the legislature into a House of Representatives and a Senate. The body of the Constitution contained explicit limits on uses of power, as did the Bill of Rights (the first ten amendments). Finally, the Constitution distributed power between the central government and the states.

Early Americans envisioned the legislature as the dominant branch of government, an outlook that congressmen jealously guarded. Nineteenth-century legislators rarely served more than two terms, which made Congress a part-time and somewhat amateurish institution. But its size and workload grew during the period. The House expanded from 105 seats in the Sixth Congress (1799–1801) to 357 seats in the Fifty-sixth Congress (1899–1901). The Senate increased from 32 to 90 seats, and a small permanent staff was hired. The lawmakers turned to specialized organizations, such as permanent (standing) committees and explicit leadership positions, to manage the flow of legislation. The House led in these innovations, endowing the speaker, its chief officer, with considerable authority. Henry Clay, James G. Blaine, and Thomas Reed were famous occupants of the post. Beginning in the 1840s political parties influenced internal procedures in Congress, with partisanship reaching its apex toward the century's end. To overcome the dilatory tactics of the minority party, Speaker Reed imposed new rules in 1890 to expedite business. Partisan squabbling fed the public distrust of legislatures during the Gilded Age.

Presidents tended to be subordinate to Congress during the nineteenth century. Chief executives did not formulate comprehensive programs and had imperfect control over administrative operations, small as they were. Congress did not grant the president a permanent secretary until 1857, and it kept the White House staff minuscule during the remainder of the century. Yet some presidents acted decisively on occasion, as Andrew Jackson did in removing the government's deposits from the Bank of the United States in 1833. Analogous instances include Thomas Jefferson's imposition of a shipping embargo in 1807, Abraham Lincoln's rejection of secession in 1861, and Grover Cleveland's suppression of the Pullman strike in 1894.

A skeleton crew staffed the federal executive establishment when the century opened. Thomas Jefferson appointed secretaries to four cabinet departments (Treasury, State, War, and Navy) during his administration (1801–1809). Congress later added four more: Post Office (1829), Interior (1849), Justice (1870), and Agriculture (1889). From a mere 2,800 employees in 1802, the federal civilian workforce grew to 26,000 by mid-century and 239,000 by 1901. The largest category of workers was fourth-class postmasters, who were compensated by fees. Customs offices in the 152 ports of entry in 1858 provided numerous other positions.

Because tariff duties provided the national government with its principal revenues, customs officers oversaw an important function. Federal expenditures, however, were very low in comparison with those of the twentieth century. National spending averaged two dollars per person in 1800 and declined by mid-century. Outlays mushroomed during the Civil War and then receded, but not to their pre-1860 level. Economic depressions (such as those of 1837–1843/44 and 1893–1897) lowered revenue collections, causing Congress to retrench on expenditures. The lack of centralized budgeting hampered financial coordination and contributed to the disorganized condition of public administration. Yet some federal officials, especially judges, possessed specialized skills. The seven justices (later expanded to nine) on the Supreme Court in 1807, as well as appointees on district and circuit courts, were usually erudite individuals who often stayed on the bench for decades.

The great majority of judges and other public officials served state and local governments. The Constitution provided for a federal arrangement whereby authority was apportioned between the central government and the states. Congress possessed certain enumerated powers, while power over most residual matters remained with the states. The division of these powers produced repeated debate, beginning with the exchange between Alexander Hamilton and Thomas Jefferson over the constitutionality of a national bank. Jefferson claimed that Congress could not create the institution and held that the national government was restricted to its explicitly enumerated powers. Hamilton took the position that the Constitution conveyed flexible authorities. Under this broad interpretation, he saw a bank as a logical extension of Congress's fiscal and monetary powers. The federal courts arbitrated disputes over the constitutionality of national and state laws throughout the century and gradually defined the boundaries of authority within the federal system. Some of the sharpest disputes over federalism were political rather than legal, as in South Carolina's "nullification" of the tariffs of 1828 and 1832. President Andrew Jackson's forceful repudiation of this challenge and a compromise in Congress defused the crisis. Normally both levels of government coexisted harmoniously within a pattern of "dual federalism," in which the states and the nation supervised separate functions. Washington enacted tariffs and governed the territories, for example, while the states legislated on education, police, and health issues. Dual federalism ensured a noncentralized approach to civic affairs in nineteenth-century America. Presidents regularly saluted the system as a safeguard of liberty.

Constitutional tenets and political practice limited the scope of the powers of the national government, but it was hardly impotent. The central government recorded substantial achievements during the nineteenth century, with most of this activity in three fields: the organization of government, national security, and economic assistance and services.

Within two generations policymakers pushed the sovereignty of the nation across the North American continent. Territorial acquisitions included the Louisiana Purchase (1803), the Spanish cession of Florida (1819), the annexation of Texas (1845), division of the Northwest Territory with Britain (1846), and Mexico's cession of the Southwest (1848). The United States purchased Alaska in 1867 and annexed Hawaii and Puerto Rico in 1898. The U.S. Army and state militias pacified Native Americans residing in the interior and moved them to reservations. Congress accommodated incoming settlers by creating territories, establishing territorial governments, and admitting new states to the union. Except for the War of 1812 and the Mexican War (1846–1848), the primary role of the nation's small army was putting down Native American resistance to the movement of white Americans westward.

Despite its limited powers the central government assisted economic development. Congress created a national bank with a twenty-year charter in 1791 and in 1816 authorized a second bank, which opened branches in twenty-nine cities by 1830. The bank attracted capital that was loaned for entrepreneurial ventures and regulated state-chartered banks. The national bank issued loan "notes" that circulated as currency, which supplemented coins manufactured at the mint. It held deposits of federal funds, a function assumed by the Independent Treasury in 1840. Besides their tax function, tariffs were used to protect American products from foreign competition, beginning with the act of 1816.

Territorial acquisitions made the United States the custodian of a huge "public domain," which Congress distributed to citizens, corporations, and state and local governments by grants and sales. Beginning with the admission of Ohio in 1803, each new state received acreage for the support of education and transportation. These grants were one way that Congress promoted internal and oceanic transportation. Development of the postal service and court rulings concerning business activities (such as contracts) and the protection of property, including slavery, constituted two important federal economic functions. National sponsorship of explorations and geographic surveys, beginning with the Lewis and Clark expedition to the Pacific coast (1804–1806) aided economic and scientific objectives.

After 1830 American politics shifted from the concept of government as an organic part of the community to a conviction that the public and private spheres should exist separately. The practice of granting monopolies to private citizens and the predominance of elites in government declined, and a more egalitarian regime that emphasized laws of general applicability and more democratic officeholding emerged. At the national level the lines of dual federalism became accentuated, federal spending decreased, and laissez-faire approaches to governance gained popularity. Democrats, who held a numerical edge over the Whigs after political parties appeared in the mid-1830s, took the lead in calling for restraints on government. The spread of male suffrage, denunciation of official privilege, commercial development, and the depression following the panic of 1837 spurred this policy realignment.

The Civil War reoriented the federal government toward unprecedented activism. Refusing to accede to secession, President Abraham Lincoln called for volunteers to "suppress insurrections" in the Confederate states. At their peak the Union army and navy numbered more than a million men. Most enlistees volunteered for a state regiment or the Union army, although Congress authorized a draft. Organizing, training, provisioning, and deploying these forces constituted an enormous undertaking whose costs dwarfed past outlays. Federal expenditures rose to $53 per person in 1865. Higher tariffs and new internal taxes paid some of the bill, but loans covered most war expenses. Congress authorized the creation of national banks in 1863 to accommodate this massive borrowing and imposed a tax on state banks to force participation. The Treasury also issued paper currency called greenbacks.

With Southerners absent, Republican congressmen legislated an economic development program that included the National Banking Act of 1863 (and amendments), higher tariffs, subsidies for transcontinental railroads, land grants to support agricultural colleges in each state, and the Homestead Act (1862), which offered 160 acres of virtually free land to settlers. Their most momentous action was the adoption of the Thirteenth Amendment to the Constitution (1865), which eliminated $2 billion of Southern property by granting freedom to slaves. Congress adopted the Fourteenth Amendment (1868) as protection for the civil liberties of the former slaves, and the Fifteenth Amendment (1870), which prohibited states from denying suffrage on account of race or color. Congress established rigorous conditions for the readmission of the seceded states during Reconstruction, when Union forces occupied the South. Northern military power had settled a fundamental question about federalism in favor of an indestructible union of states, but the war had even broader ramifications. Fanning the flames of nationalism, Lincoln's triumph can be seen as a step toward building a unified nation. As a state-building event, the impact of the Civil War was analogous to developments in Italy, Germany, and Japan during the nineteenth century.

The pace of federal activity subsided after the war, although the national government did not return to its prewar regime. Congress cautiously trailed the states and cities in widening its agenda. This transition toward a more instrumental style of governance, in which officials legislated innovations for various problems, was apparent by the 1880s. State governments, for example, allowed standardized procedures for the incorporation of businesses, enacted commercial regulations, mandated free common schools and sewer installations, enabled the construction of public water supplies, created uniformed police, and adopted rules regarding working conditions. The rate of public expenditure and borrowing increased substantially. At the federal level, per capita expenditures were three times greater in 1900 than in 1860, although the cities together with the states outspent Washington. National lawmakers expanded traditional areas of policy and entered new ones, notably commercial regulation, income assistance, and expansion into the Caribbean and Pacific. The growth of federal employment and administrative bureaus reflected this increased pace of activity. The number of federal workers expanded fivefold between 1870 and 1900, and some were integrated into a civil-service system as a result of the Pendleton Act (1883). The character of public administration has generated debate among scholars, some of whom claim that a conception of a "state" in the European sense did not take hold in nineteenth-century America. Yet federal service attracted some talented individuals, many of whom remained in their jobs for decades. Arguably, the combination of a broadly based democracy, the noncentralization of power under federalism, and ideological emphasis on individual rights constituted the American counterpart of the European state.

Federal officials pursued several economic policies during the Gilded Age. Congress adopted numerous laws concerning money and banking, subjects that gained importance as the rise of commerce proceeded and as panics strained the nation's financial system. Lawmakers modified land policies to fit the arid West and inaugurated the conservation of national resources, symbolized by the approval of Yellowstone Park (1872). Farmers benefited from the creation of the Agriculture Department (1862; cabinet status in 1889) and funding for scientific research, such as the Hatch Act (1887), which granted subsidies to agricultural laboratories ("experiment stations") in each state. The Post Office, a key federal service, began deliveries in cities in 1863 and in rural areas in 1896. The establishment of the Bureau of Labor Statistics in 1884 suggests the acknowledgment of workers' problems, but federal policy tended to favor employers.

The Interstate Commerce Act (1887) inaugurated national regulation of private enterprise. This act established the Interstate Commerce Commission with jurisdiction over railroads. Laws that disallowed monopoly, provided for the inspection of imported meat and the regulation of immigration, and set bankruptcy rules followed in the 1890s. The federal courts became more active in reviewing governmental intervention in the economy and disallowed some regulations. The justices stripped the Interstate Commerce Commission of power to fix rates, blocked antitrust actions against manufacturing ventures, and overturned a national income tax passed in 1894. The Supreme Court struck down many state regulations, including laws affecting railroad rates, in rulings that promoted the formation of national markets. Yet the great bulk of state and national commercial legislation survived legal challenge.

Social policy and the military-diplomatic establishment represented areas of federal growth. Congress created a pension system for Civil War veterans and their dependents, a program that consumed almost half of all federal expenditures in the early 1890s. Lawmakers began the modernization of the navy in 1883. This program paid dividends in 1898, when the enlarged U.S. Navy triumphed over Spanish fleets in a two-ocean war. Congress experimented with a few social regulations, such as the Comstock laws (1873), prohibiting the sending of obscene materials through the mail. Yet Washington did not use its power to combat racial segregation and violence toward African Americans.

Industrial and technological change was a primary stimulus of this growth, but other factors, such as the proliferation of interest organizations and the impact of unanticipated events (such as the depressions of the 1870s and 1890s), contributed to the expansion. State and municipal innovations offered models for national policymakers. The divided control of the Congress and the presidency between Democrats and Republicans, combined with strong partisan loyalty, blocked some legislation. Many policy innovations received bipartisan support. Yet even conservatives expanded federal power, as in the cases of President Grover Cleveland's intervention into the Pullman strike and President William McKinley's support of the war against Spain. This last action led to the occupation of the Philippines and increased U.S. influence in the Caribbean.

See also **Constitutional Amendments,** *subentry on* **Thirteenth, Fourteenth, and Fifteenth Amendments; Expansion; Federal Land Policy; Federal-State Relations; Foreign Trade and Tariffs,** *subentry on* **Trade and Tariffs; Monetary Policy.**

Bibliography

Leonard D. White's *The Jeffersonians* (New York: Macmillan, 1951), *The Jacksonians* (New York: Macmillan, 1954), and *The Republican Era, 1869–1901* (New York: Macmillan, 1958) survey administrative history. The chapters by Norman K. Risjord, "Congress in the Federalist-Republican Era, 1789–1828," pp. 89–106; Allan G. Bogue, "The U.S. Congress: The Era of Party Patronage and Sectional Stress, 1829–1881," pp. 107–129; and Garrison Nelson, "The Modernizing Congress, 1870–1930," pp. 131–156, in Joel H. Silbey, ed., *Encyclopedia of the American Legislative System* (New York: Scribner's, 1994), vol. 1, trace developments in Congress. Stephen Skowronek, *The Politics Presidents Make* (Cambridge, Mass.: Belknap Press of Harvard University Press, 1993), discusses styles of executive leadership. Paul Studenski and Herman E. Krooss, *Financial History of the United States* (New York: McGraw-Hill, 1963), review finances. Alfred H. Kelly, Winfred A. Harbison, and Herman Belz, *The American Constitution* (New York: Norton, 1983), cover legal issues. James Sterling Young, *The Washington Community, 1800–1828* (New York: Columbia University Press, 1966), profiles the early federal establishment. George Rogers Taylor, *The Transportation Revolution, 1815–1860* (Armonk, N.Y.: M. E. Sharpe, 1951), provides an overview of antebellum economic policy. Morton Keller's *Affairs of State: Public Life in Late Nineteenth Century America* (Cambridge, Mass.: Belknap Press of Harvard University Press, 1977) is a wide-ranging study of the late 1800s. Paul W. Gates, *History of Public Land Law Development* (Washington, D.C.: U.S. Government Printing Office, 1968); Allan R. Millett and Peter Maslowski, *For the Common Defense: The Military History of the United States* (New York: Free Press, 1984); and A. Hunter Dupree, *Science in the Federal Government* (Cambridge, Mass.: Belknap Press of Harvard University Press, 1957), examine particular functions.

BALLARD C. CAMPBELL